MONTVILLE TWP. PUBLIC LIBRARY
90 Horseneck Road
Montville, N.J. 07045

D1499459

ON LINE

REF
809.1
Poetr
Poetry criticism :
excerpts from criticism
27

For Reference

Not to be taken

from this library

Poetry Criticism

Guide to Gale Literary Criticism Series

For criticism on	Consult these Gale series
Authors now living or who died after December 31, 1959	*CONTEMPORARY LITERARY CRITICISM (CLC)*
Authors who died between 1900 and 1959	*TWENTIETH-CENTURY LITERARY CRITICISM (TCLC)*
Authors who died between 1800 and 1899	*NINETEENTH-CENTURY LITERATURE CRITICISM (NCLC)*
Authors who died between 1400 and 1799	*LITERATURE CRITICISM FROM 1400 TO 1800 (LC)* *SHAKESPEAREAN CRITICISM (SC)*
Authors who died before 1400	*CLASSICAL AND MEDIEVAL LITERATURE CRITICISM (CMLC)*
Authors of books for children and young adults	*CHILDREN'S LITERATURE REVIEW (CLR)*
Dramatists	*DRAMA CRITICISM (DC)*
Poets	*POETRY CRITICISM (PC)*
Short story writers	*SHORT STORY CRITICISM (SSC)*
Black writers of the past two hundred years	*BLACK LITERATURE CRITICISM (BLC)* *BLACK LITERATURE CRITICISM SUPPLEMENT (BLCS)*
Hispanic writers of the late nineteenth and twentieth centuries	*HISPANIC LITERATURE CRITICISM (HLC)* *HISPANIC LITERATURE CRITICISM SUPPLEMENT (HLCS)*
Native North American writers and orators of the eighteenth, nineteenth, and twentieth centuries	*NATIVE NORTH AMERICAN LITERATURE (NNAL)*
Major authors from the Renaissance to the present	*WORLD LITERATURE CRITICISM, 1500 TO THE PRESENT (WLC)*

ISSN 1052-4851

Poetry Criticism

*Excerpts from Criticism of the Works
of the Most Significant and Widely
Studied Poets of World Literature*

VOLUME 27

*Susan Salas and
Laura A. Wisner-Broyles*
Editor

GALE GROUP

Detroit
San Francisco
London
Boston
Woodbridge, CT

STAFF

Susan Salas and Laura Wisner-Broyles, *Editor*

Anna Nesbitt, *Associate Editor*
Jenny Cromie, Justin Karr, Linda Pavlovski, Debra A. Wells, *Assistant Editors*

Maria L. Franklin, *Permissions Manager*
Kimberly F. Smilay, *Permissions Specialist*
Sandy Gore, *Permissions Associate*
Erin Bealmear, *Permissions Assistants*

Victoria B. Cariappa, *Research Manager*

Michele P. LaMeau, *Research Specialist*
Julie C. Daniel, Tamara C. Nott, Tracie A. Richardson,
Norma Sawaya, Cheryl L. Warnock,
Research Associates

Mary Beth Trimper, *Production Director*
Deborah Milliken, *Production Assistant*

C. J. Jonik, *Desktop Publisher*
Randy Bassett, *Image Database Supervisor*
Michael Ansari, Robert Duncan, *Scanner Operator*
Pamela Reed, *Photography Coordinator*

Since this page cannot legibly accommodate all copyright notices, the acknowledgments constitute and extension of the copyright notice.

While every effort has been made to ensure the reliability of the information presented in this publication, Gale Research, Inc. neither guarantees the accuracy of the data contained herein nor assumes any responsibility for errors, omissions, or discrepancies. Gale accepts no payment for listing, and inclusion in the publication or any organization, agency, institution, publication, service, or individual does not imply endorsement of the editors or publisher. Errors brought to the attention of the publisher and verified to the satisfaction of the publisher will be corrected in future editions.

The paper used in this publication meets the minimum requirements of American National Standard for Information Sciences—Permanence Paper for Printed Library Materials, ANSI Z39.48-1984.

This publication is a creative work fully protected by all applicable copyright laws, as well as by misappropriation, trade secret, unfair competition, and other applicable laws. The authors and editors of this work have added value to the underlying factual material herein through one or more of the following: unique and original selection, coordination, expression, arrangement, and classification of the information.

All rights to this publication will be vigorously defended.

Copyright © 2000
Gale Group
27500 Drake Rd.
Farmington Hills, MI 48331-3535

All rights reserved, including the right of reproduction in whole or in part in any form.

Library of Congress Catalog Card Number 91-118494
ISBN 0-7876-3075-6
ISSN 1052-4851

Printed in the United States of America

10 9 8 7 6 5 4 3 2 1

0 1021 0126834 4

Contents

Preface

A Comprehensive Information Source on World Poetry

Poetry Criticism (PC) provides substantial critical excerpts and biographical information on poets throughout the world who are most frequently studied in high school and undergraduate college courses. Each *PC* entry is supplemented by biographical and bibliographical material to help guide the user to a fuller understanding of the genre and its creators. Although major poets and literary movements are covered in such Gale Literary Criticism Series as *Contemporary Literary Criticism (CLC), Twentieth-Century Literary Criticism (TCLC), Nineteenth-Century Literature Criticism (NCLC), Literature Criticism from 1400 to 1800 (LC),* and *Classical and Medieval Literature Criticism (CMLC), PC* offers more focused attention on poetry than is possible in the broader, survey-oriented entries on writers in these Gale series. Students, teachers, librarians, and researchers will find that the generous excerpts and supplementary material provided by *PC* supply them with the vital information needed to write a term paper on poetic technique, to examine a poet's most prominent themes, or to lead a poetry discussion group.

Coverage

In order to reflect the influence of tradition as well as innovation, poets of various nationalities, eras, and movements are represented in every volume of *PC*. Each author entry presents a historical survey of the critical response to that author's work; the length of an entry reflects the amount of critical attention that the author has received from critics writing in English and from foreign critics in translation. Since many poets have inspired a prodigious amount of critical explication, *PC* is necessarily selective, and the editors have chosen the most significant published criticism to aid readers and students in their research. In order to provide these important critical pieces, the editors will sometimes reprint essays that have appeared in previous volumes of Gale's Literary Criticism Series. Such duplication, however, never exceeds fifteen percent of a *PC* volume.

Organization

Each *PC* author entry consists of the following components:

- **Author Heading:** the name under which the author wrote appears at the beginning of the entry, followed by birth and death dates. If the author wrote consistently under a pseudonym, the pseudonym will be listed in the author heading and his or her legal name given in parentheses in the lines immediately preceding the Introduction. Uncertainty as to birth or death dates is indicated by question marks.

- **Introduction:** a biographical and critical essay introduces readers to the author and the critical discussions surrounding his or her work.

- **Author Portrait:** a photograph or illustration of the author is included when available.

- **Principal Works:** the author's most important works are identified in a list ordered chronologically by first publication dates. The first section comprises poetry collections and book-length poems. The second section gives information on other major works by the author. For foreign authors, original foreign-language publication information is provided, as well as the best and most complete English-language editions of their works.

- **Criticism:** critical excerpts chronologically arranged in each author entry provide perspective on changes in critical evaluation over the years. All individual titles of poems and poetry collections by the author featured in the entry are printed in boldface type to enable a reader to ascertain without difficulty the works under discussion. For purposes of easy identification, the critic's name and the publication date of the essay are given at the beginning of each piece of criticism. Unsigned criticism is preceded by the title of the journal in which it originally appeared. Publication information (such as publisher names and book prices) and parenthetical numerical references (such as footnotes or page and line references to specific editions of a work) have been deleted at the editor's discretion to enable smoother reading of the text.

- **Explanatory Notes:** introductory comments preface each critical excerpt, providing several types of useful information, including: the reputation of a critic, the importance of a work of criticism, and the specific type of criticism (biographical, psychoanalytic, historical, etc.).

- **Author Commentary:** insightful comments from the authors themselves and excerpts from author interviews are included when available.

- **Bibliographical Citations:** information preceding each piece of criticism guides the interested reader to the original essay or book.

- **Further Reading:** bibliographic references accompanied by descriptive notes at the end of each entry suggest additional materials for study of the author. Boxed material following the Further Reading provides references to other biographical and critical series published by Gale.

Other Features

- **Cumulative Author Index:** comprises all authors who have appeared in Gale's Literary Criticism Series, along with cross-references to such Gale biographical series as *Contemporary Authors* and *Dictionary of Literary Biography*. This cumulated index enables the user to locate an author within the various series.

- **Cumulative Nationality Index:** includes all authors featured in *PC,* arranged alphabetically under their respective nationalities.

- **Cumulative Title Index:** lists in alphabetical order all individual poems, book-length poems, and collection titles contained in the *PC* series. Titles of poetry collections and separately published poems are printed in italics, while titles of individual poems are printed in roman type with quotation marks. Each title is followed by the author's name and the volume and page number corresponding to the location of commentary on specific works. English-language translations of original foreign-language titles are cross-referenced to the foreign titles so that all references to discussion of a work are combined in one listing.

Citing *Poetry Criticism*

When writing papers, students who quote directly from any volume in the Literary Criticism Series may use the following general formats to footnote reprinted criticism. The first example pertains to material drawn from periodicals, the second to material reprinted from books:

[1]David Daiches, "W. H. Auden: The Search for a Public," *Poetry* LIV (June 1939), 148-56; excerpted and reprinted in *Poetry Criticism*, Vol. 1, ed. Robyn V. Young (Detroit: Gale Research, 1990), pp. 7-9.

[2]Pamela J. Annas, *A Disturbance in Mirrors: The Poetry of Sylvia Plath* (Greenwood Press, 1988); excerpted and reprinted in *Poetry Criticism*, Vol. 1, ed. Robyn V. Young (Detroit: Gale Research, 1990), pp. 410-14.

Comments Are Welcome

Readers who wish to suggest authors to appear in future volumes, or who have other suggestions, are cordially invited to contact the editors.

Acknowledgments

The editors wish to thank the copyright holders of the excerpted criticism included in this volume and the permissions managers of many book and magazine publishing companies for assisting us in securing reproduction rights. We are also grateful to the staffs of the Detroit Public Library, the Library of Congress, the University of Detroit Mercy Library, Wayne State University Purdy/Kresge Library Complex, and the University of Michigan Libraries for making their resources available to us. Following is a list of the copyright holders who have granted us permission to reproduce material in this volume of *PC*. Every effort has been made to trace copyright, but if omissions have been made, please let us know.

COPYRIGHTED EXCERPTS IN *PC*, VOLUME 26, WERE REPRODUCED FROM THE FOLLOWING PERIODICALS:

Agni, 1992. Reproduced by permission.—*The American Indian Quarterly*, v. 19, Winter, 1995. Copyright © 1995 University of Nebraska Press. Reprinted by permission of the publisher.—*The American Poetry Review*, v. 9, September-October, 1980. Copyright © 1980 by World Poetry, Inc./ v. XVIII, March/April, 1989 for "Listening to Wyatt" by W.S. Merwin. Copyright © 1989 by World Poetry, Inc. Reproduced by permission of the author.—*Anales de la literatura espanola contemporanea*, v. 12, 1987 for "Gloria Fuertes and the Poetic of Solitude" by Sylvia R. Sherno. © Luis Gonzalez-del-Nalle. Reprinted by permission of the author.—*The Antioch Review*, v. 48, Summer, 1990. Copyright © 1990 by the Antioch Review Inc. Reproduced by permission of the Editors.—*Chicago Review*, v. 32, Autumn, 1980; v. 33, Summer, 1981. Copyright © 1980, 1981 by *Chicago Review*. Both reproduced by permission.—*College Literature*, v. XI, 1984. Copyright © 1984 by West Chester University. Reproduced by permission.— *Critical Inquiry*, v. 13, Spring, 1987 for "Responsibilities of the Poet" by Robert Pinsky. Copyright © 1987 by The University of Chicago. Reproduced by permission of the publisher and the author.—*The Critical Review*, Melbourne, n. 20, 1978. Reproduced by permission.—*Criticism*, v. XX, Fall, 1978. Copyright, 1978, Wayne State University Press. Reproduced by permission of the publisher.—*Cross Currents*, Dobbs Ferry, Summer, 1991. Copyright 1991 by Cross Currents Inc. Reproduced by permission. —*Dada/Surrealism*, n. 4, 1974. 1974 © Association for the Study of Dada and Surrealism. Both reprinted by permission of the publisher.—*Éire-Ireland*, Fall/Winter, 1996. Copyright © 1996 by the Irish American Cultural Institute. Both reproduced by permission of the publisher.—*English Literary Renaissance*, v. XII, Autumn, 1982. Copyright © 1982 by *English Literary Renaissance*. Reproduced by permission of the editors.—*Essays in Criticism*, v. XVI, October, 1976 for "The 'Thing' in Wyatt's Mind" by Donald Friedman. Reproduced by permission of the Editors of *Essays in Criticism* and the author.—*The French Review*, v. XLII, Winter, 1970. Copyright 1970 by the American Association of Teachers of French. Reproduced by permission.—*The Hudson Review*, v. LI, Autumn, 1998; v. XL, Winter, 1988. Copyright © 1998 by The Hudson Review, Inc. Both reproduced by permission.—*The Huntington Library Quarterly*, v. 41, November, 1977. Reproduced with the permission of the Henry E. Huntington Library.—*The Journal of Medieval and Renaissance Studies*, v. XXIII, Winter, 1993. Copyright © 1993 by Duke University Press, Durham, NC. Reproduced by permission.—*Letras Femeninas*, v. XVI, 1990. Reproduced by permission.—*Los Angeles Times Book Review*, February, 1998. Copyright, 1998, *Los Angeles Times*. Reproduced by permission.—*The Massachusetts Review*, v. IX, Summer, 1968. © 1968. Reprinted from *The Massachusetts Review*, The Massachusetts Review, Inc. by permission. —*MELUS: Society for the Study of the Multi-Ethnic Literature of the United States*, v. 18, Fall, 1993. Copyright, *MELUS: The Society for the Study of Multi-Ethnic Literature of the United States*, 1993. Reproduced by permission.—*Mester*, v. XX, Fall, 1991. Copyright © 1991 by The Regents of the University of California. Reproduced by permission.—*Michigan Quarterly Review*, v. XXXII, Winter, 1993 for "An interview with Medbh McGuckian" by Susan Shaw Sailer. Copyright © The University of Michigan, 1993. All rights reserved. Reproduced by permission of the author. —*Modern Language Notes*, v. 104, March, 1989. Copyright © 1989 by The Johns Hopkins University Press. Reproduced by permission of The Johns Hopkins University Press.—*Modern Language Quarterly*, v. XXIX, June, 1968. © 1970 University of Washington. Reproduced by permission of Duke University Press.—*The Nation*, New York, v. 262, April, 1996. © 1996 *The Nation* magazine/ The Nation Company, Inc. Reproduced by permission.—*The National Review*, v. XL, February, 1988. Copyright © 1988 by National Review, Inc, 215 Lexington Avenue. New York, NY 10016. Reproduced by permission.—*The New Leader*, v. LXX, August, 1987; v. LXXXI, August, 1998. © 1987, 1998 by The American Labor Conference on International Affairs, Inc. Both reproduced by permission.—*The New Republic*, v. 194, January, 1986; v. 208, January, 1993; v. 218, March, 1998. © 1986, 1993, 1998 The New Republic, Inc. All reproduced by permission of *The New Republic*.—*The New York Times Book Review*, August, 1925; November, 1948; October, 1953; February, 1986; August, 1996. Copyright 1925, 1948, 1953, © 1986 by The New York Times Company. All reproduced by permission.—*The Ohio Review*, v. 48, 1992. Copyright © 1992 by the Editors of *The Ohio Review*. Reproduced by permission.—*Parnassus: Poetry in Review*, v. 18, 1993 for "Gurus and Gadflies" by

Bill Marx; v. 12, Spring, 1995 for a review of "Venus and the Rain" by Christopher Benfey; v. 21, 1996 for "Lasting Words" by David Kirby. Copyright © 1993, 1995, 1996 Poetry in Review Foundation, NY. All reproduced by permission of the respective authors.—*Partisan Review*, January-February, 1953 for "Macleish and Viereck" by Howard Nemerov; v. 61, Fall, 1994, for a review of "Canvas" by Charles Simic. Copyright © 1953, 1994 by *Partisan Review*. Both reproduced by permission of the respective authors.—*Perspectives on Contemporary Literature*, v. 7, 1981. Copyright © 1981 by The University Press of Kentucky. Reprinted by permission of the publisher.—*Poetry*, v. 73, February, 1949 for "Tall Ideas Dancing," by Paul Goodman; v. 89, February, 1957 for "Some New Poems by Peter Viereck," by Hayden Carruth; v. 100, September, 1962 for "A Poetry Chronicle" by John Woods; v. 112, August, 1968 for "A Poetry Chronicle" by Laurence Lieberman; v. CLVII, July, 1991 for a review of "On Ballycastle Beach" by Stephen Yenser. Copyright 1949, © 1957, 1962, 1968, 1991 by the Modern Poetry Association. All reproduced by permission of the editor of *Poetry* and the respective authors.—*Poets & Writers Magazine*, v. 23, July-August 1995. Reproduced by permission.—*Revista Hispanica Moderna*, v. XLI, December, 1988. Reproduced by permission.—*Revista/Review Interamericana*, v. XII, Spring, 1982. Copyright © 1983, Inter American University of Puerto Rico. Reproduced by permission.—*Salmagundi*, v. 80, Fall, 1988; Summer, 1994. Copyright © 1988, 1994 by Skidmore College. Both reproduced by permission.—*Saturday Review of Literature*, v. XXXI, October, 1948; v. XL, August, 1957. © 1948, 1957 Saturday Review magazine. Both reproduced by permission of Saturday Review Publications, Ltd.—*The Southern Review*, Louisiana State University, v. 31, July, 1995 for "How things begin to happen" by Peter Sirr. Copyright, 1995, by Peter Sirr. Reproduced by permission of the author.—*Studies in English Literature*, v. XXI, Winter, 1981. © 1981 William Marsh Rice University. Reproduced by permission of The Johns Hopkins University Press.—*Studies in the Literary Imagination*, v. XI, Spring, 1978. Copyright 1978 Department of English, Georgia State University. Reproduced by permission.—*The Times Literary Supplement*, February, 1970; March, 1987. © The Times Supplements Limited 1970, 1987. Both reproduced from The Times Literary Supplement by permission.—*TriQuarterly*, Winter, 1994-1995 for "A Conversation with Robert Pinsky" by *TriQuarterly*. © 1994-95 by *TriQuarterly*, Northwestern University. Reproduced by of the author.—*UNISA English Studies*, v. IX, December, 1971. Reproduced by permission.—*World Literature Today*, v. 66, Autumn, 1992. Copyright © 1992 by the University of Oklahoma Press. Reproduced by permission.—*Yale Review*, v. 40, Winter, 1951. Copyright 1951, by Yale University.

COPYRIGHTED MATERIAL IN *PC*, VOLUME 27, WERE REPRODUCED FROM THE FOLLOWING BOOKS:

Baranczak, Stanislaw. From the introduction to *Polish Poetry of the Last Two Decades of Communist Rule: Spoiling Cannibal's Fun*. Edited and with Translations by Stanislaw Baranczak with Clare Cavanagh. Northwestern University Press, 1991. Copyright © 1991 by Northwestern University Press. All rights reserved. Reproduced by permission.—Beitchman, Philip. From *I Am a Process with No Subject*. University of Florida Press, 1988. Copyright © 1988 by Philip Beitchman. All rights reserved. Reproduced with the permission of the University Press of Florida.—Birkerts, Sven. From *The Electric Life: Essays on Modern Poetry*. William Morrow and Company, 1989. Copyright © 1989 by Sven Birkerts. Reproduced by permission.—Bruchac, Joseph. From *Survival This Way: Interviews with American Indian Poets*. Sun Tracks and The University of Arizona Press, 1987. Copyright © 1987 The Arizona Board of Regents. All rights reserved. Reproduced by permission.—Corn, Alfred. From *The Metamorphoses of Metaphor: Essays in Poetry and Fiction*. Elisabeth Sifton Books, 1987. Copyright © Alfred Corn, 1987. All rights reserved. Reproduced by permission of the author.—Debicki, Andrew P. From *Poetry of Discovery: The Spanish Generation of 1956-1971*. The University Press of Kentucky, 1982. Copyright © 1982 by the University Press of Kentucky. Reproduced by permission.—Eddy, Gary. From "Earning the Language: The Writing of Lucien Stryk" in *Zen, Poetry, the Art of Lucien Stryk*. Edited by Susan Porterfield. Swallow Press, 1993. © Copyright 1993 by Swallow Press. All rights reserved. Reproduced by permission.—Gray, Cecile. From "Medbh McGuckian: Imagery Wrought to Its Uttermost" in *Learning the Trade: Essays on W.B. Yeats and Contemporary Poetry*. Edited by Deborah Fleming. Locust Hill Press, 1993. © 1993 Deborah Fleming. All rights reserved. Reproduced by permission.—Guillory, Daniel. From "The Oriental Connection: Zen and Representations of the Midwest in the Collected Poems of Lucien Stryk" in *Midamerica XIII*. Edited by David D. Anderson. The Midwestern Press, 1986. Copyright 1986 by the Society for the Study of Midwestern Literature. All rights reserved. Reproduced by permission.—Melander, Ingrid. From "Two Poems by Medbh McGuckian Symbol and Interpretation" in *Anglo-Irish and Irish Literature Aspects of Language and Culture*. Edited by Birgit Bramsback and Martin Croghan. UPPSALA Universitet, 1988.—Mills, Ralph J. Jr. From "Lucien Stryk's Poetry" in *Zen, Poetry, the Art of Lucien Stryk*. Edited by Susan Porterfield. Swallow Press, 1993. © Copyright 1993 by Swallow Press. All rights reserved. Reproduced by permission.—Porterfield, Susan. From "Portrait of a Poet as a Young Man: Lucien Stryk" in *Midwestern Miscellany XXII*. Edited by David D. Anderson. The Midwestern Press, 1994. Copyright 1994 by the Society for the Study of Midwestern Literature. All rights reserved. Reproduced by permission.—Stryk, Lucien. From "Making Poems" in *American Poets in 1976*. Edited by William Heyen. From The Bobbs-Merrill Company, Inc., 1976. Copyright © 1976 by the Bobbs-Merrill Company, Inc. Reproduced by permission of the author.

PHOTOGRAPHS AND ILLUSTRATIONS APPEARING IN *PC*, VOLUME 27, WERE RECEIVED FROM THE FOLLOWING SOURCES:

Harjo, Joy, photograph. Reproduced by permission of Joy Harjo.— McGuckian, Medbh (head and shoulders), photograph. BC Research.—Noyes, Alfred, photograph. The Library of Congress.—Pinsky, Robert, photograph by Sigrid Estrada. Reproduced by permission.—Stryk, Lucien, Photo by Barry Stark. Northern Illinois University. Reproduced by permission.—Tzara, Tristan, photograph. UPI/Bettman. Reproduced by permission.—Viereck, Peter, Photo by Clemens Kalischer. Mount Holyoke College. Reproduced by permission.—Wyatt, Thomas. Archive Photos. Reproduced by permission.—Zagajewski, Adam. University of Houston. Reproduced by permission of Adam Zagajewski.

Gloria Fuertes
1918–

Spanish poet and children's writer.

INTRODUCTION

One of the poets that emerged in post-Civil War Spain, Fuertes has made a valuable contribution to twentieth-century Spanish poetry. Through her highly personal verse as well as her popular children's poetry, she has become an appreciated figure in Spanish culture. She has garnered attention for her unwavering commitment to social issues, and the promotion of peace, world harmony, and human understanding are considered defining characteristics of her work.

Biographical Information

Born in 1918 in Madrid, Spain, Fuertes was born to working-class parents and educated at a trade school for women. A teenager during the Spanish Civil War, her wartime experiences imbued her with an appreciation for peace, a recurring theme in her work. In 1939 she was hired as an editor by a publishing house and became a contributing writer for the children's magazines *Pelayo* and *Maravilla*. She also began to write poetry during this time, and published her first collection of verse, *Isla ignorada*, in 1950. She wrote both children's verse and poetry in subsequent years. In 1955 she began to study library science, and five years later started her career as a librarian. The publication of *Que estás en la tierra*—an anthology of her previously published poetry—garnered critical and commercial attention. In 1961 she received a Fulbright Fellowship to teach Spanish at Bucknell University in Pennsylvania. She has been a popular figure in her homeland because of her frequent appearances on children's television and her successful poetry readings.

Major Works

Fuertes's first collection of verse, *Isla ignorada*, draws from nature imagery and contains highly personal material. Both *Antología y poemas del suburbio* and *Todo asusta* evince characteristics of Fuertes's later work: autobiographical subject matter, use of free verse and conversational language, and the incorporation of themes such as social justice, religion, family, and human suffering. Death and life are the major concerns of *Aconsejo beber hilo*, and the collection explores Fuertes's existential philosophy. Her humor and imagination are displayed in *Poeta de guardia*, and the poems touch on topical themes of the time, including the Vietnam War and other world events. Her best-known collection, *Historia de Gloria*, consists of poems taken from her own personal diary. Reflecting on her childhood and her adult life, Fuertes once again celebrates life, love, peace, and the power of poetry to address social injustice.

Critical Reception

Fuertes's verse has been viewed by critics as testimonial poetry, characterized by its personal subject matter and confessional approach. Stylistically, commentators deem her use of colloquial language and a humorous tone as effective devices to explore the absurdity of human existence. Her poems often investigate death, alienation, human suffering, and suicide. Injustice and war are a special concern for her, and commentators assert that her sensitivity to the poor, women, and the exploited are defining characteristics of her work. In fact, critics praise her devotion to social issues and attempt to place her within the context of the social poetry that emerged from post-Civil War Spain.

PRINCIPAL WORKS

Poetry

Isla ignorada 1950
Antología y poemas del suburbio 1954
Todo asusta 1958
Que estás en la tierra 1962
Ni tiro, ni veneno, ni navaja 1966
Poeta de guardia 1966
Cómo atar los bigotes al tigre 1969
Antología poètica (1950–1969) 1970
Cuando amas aprendes geografía 1973
Sola en la sala 1973
Obras incompletas 1975
Historia de Gloria 1980
Off the Map: Selected Poems 1984
Mujer de verso en pecho 1995
Pecábamos como ángeles: gloripoemas de amor 1997

Other Major Works

Canguara para todo (juvenile) 1967

CRITICISM

Timothy J. Rogers (essay date 1981)

SOURCE: "The Comic Spirit in the Poetry of Gloria Fuertes," in *Perspectives on Contemporary Literature,* Vol. 7, 1981, pp. 88-97.

[*Rogers discusses ways in which Fuertes deals with social issues in her work through the use of comedic elements.*]

If there is a tenor which seems to run as a pervasive undercurrent to contemporary Spanish poetry, especially since the Civil War, it probably can be summarized as man's existential dilemma *vis-à-vis* what Camus hailed as the absurdity of life.[1] Indeed, perhaps instead of calling modern man's plight the "tragic sense of life" one might rightfully proclaim it as the "comic sense of life." Wylie Sypher in his essay, "The Meanings of Comedy," observes:

> . . . since ours is a century of disorder and irrationalism, is it any wonder that along with our wars, our machines and our neuroses we should find new meaning in comedy or that comedy should represent our plight better than tragedy? For tragedy needs the "noble" and nowadays we seldom can assign any usable meaning to "nobility." The comic now is more relevant, or at least more accessible than the tragic.[2]

In light of Sypher's cogent statement, I would like to draw our attention to one of Spain's contemporary though lesser known poets, Gloria Fuertes (1918-),[3] and examine in an overview just how her poetry may well serve as a reflection of this "comic" spirit, not only for the humor that one may perceive in it from time to time, but also as a statement of the poet's attempt to confront and in some way diminish the seeming disparity, improbability, and absurdity of life. The comic voice of Gloria Fuertes, as we shall note, at times derives from this basic underlying spirit, and more often than not, becomes its very poetic expression. While it may serve to mask the absurdities of the human condition, it does at the same time become one of the effective techniques by which the poet manages to cope with her own sense of the comic.

It has been well noted by a number of critics that the poetry of Gloria Fuertes is, by and large, steeped in social consciousness and that her verses echo the concerns relative to the human condition similarly raised by her contemporaries of "la poesía comprometida." As Joaquín González Muela has observed, Gloria Fuertes' poetry may very well be summarized as "Soledad, sufrimiento, tristeza, incomprensión, contradicción . . . éstas son las tintas filosóficas con que escribe este poeta 'jocoso.'"[4] Her poetic language, at the same time, is direct, blunt, unobtrusive, unrhetorical, for the most part, and as José Luis Cano has noted, patently prosaic.[5] Nonetheless, as pertinent as these observations may be, it is in my opinion the manner in which Fuertes expresses those "tintas filosóficas," i.e., how her technique involves us as readers in her comic sense of life, which, in the end, gives her poetry its singular hallmark. Antithesis, ironic twists, unexpected and startling irrational resolutions which border on the absurd abound through a good number of her poems and thoroughly permeate them.

I believe we can see this poetic technique quite readily in her poem **"Aviso a los gobernantes del mundo"**:

> Me dirijo a Vuestras Ilustrísimas
> para deciros que en mi barrio hay peste,
> que se han venido todos los mendigos
> a refugiarse bejo el puente roto,
> —cuando venga el calor no habrá quien pare—.
> Parece ser que quieren armar una
> contra el Alcalde que no les da una casa,
> están enfermos y viven en las cuevas
> y les caen montocitos cuando duermen.
> Dicen que van a ir en una noche
> a vuestra tumba a colocaros . . . flores
> y yo lo aviso a Vuestras Ilustrísimas
> porque soy pacifista y no me atrevo
> a silenciarlo aunque lo creo justo.
>   Os aviso Ilustrísimas peligro corréis
> porque esta gente está borracha.
> De nada vale el bando recién dado,
> de nada no dar vino en las tabernas,
> de nada que haya pan en el comercio,
> de nada que prohiban los desfiles,
> de nada que recojan la verbena,
> es mejor que suspendan los mendigos.[6]

What intrigues us from the very opening verses of the poem is the pretentious but welcome naive poetic voice calling attention to the world leaders of a local problem—the *peste*—now somewhat rampant in its barrio. The very image of the *peste* suggests plague, a pestilence, and calls to mind what Wheelwright has identified as "tensive language"[7] whereby through the literal interpretation of the sign we are caught envisioning a physical disease while in the following verse we discover that it is in fact a social, economic, and political disease. The beggars in the ensuing verses seek only refuge, warmth, and the fulfillment of their needs, not the least of which is the attainment of human understanding. Rejected by the local alcalde they are ready to rise up not only against him but also against all authority. The curious allusion to the "tumba" of the world leaders causes a shifting in our expectations, for now we discover that they are dead and hence we are left with a conceptual interplay of words and ideas. On the rational level we expected an exhortative address to living leaders but in fact we must now entertain the "irrational conceit" (as Carlos Bousoño would suggest) insofar as the moribund state of the leaders is concerned. This conceit, undoubtedly fully intended by the poet, accures a sense of irony since the concept of dead world leaders certainly plays off the idea of contemporary leaders as being quite "dead" to the needs and the plight of the beggars, and on a larger scale to all the destitute and the unwanted.

Irony is carried even further when the poetic voice asserts that the beggars driven by the circumstances of their situation are indeed going to rise up and visit the leaders' tomb but surprisingly and unexpectedly not to raise havoc but to place "flores." This tongue-in-cheek humor unsettles us because the paradoxical nature of a revolution borne by flower-bearing militant beggars is, at least at first glance, the last thing we would have expected. Fuertes further sustains the parodic humor of the image by the intrusion of the poetic voice as a self-proclaimed "pacifista." The mock seriousness is embellished and enhanced by the voice's declared sense of moral responsibility to forewarn the "Ilustrísimas" of such dire and audacious action on the part of the *peste* even though the voice is fully in accord with the justice of its cause, and slyly forces us again to recognize the pseudo-gravity of the action, i.e., the placing of flowers on their tomb.

In the second strophe, the poetic voice reiterating the urgency of the situation calls the leaders' attention through the ensuing series of anaphoral enjoinders to the fact that all the rules, regulations, prohibitions, and bans against the beggars really have no fruitful value. Indeed, the resolution is quite simple if one were to consider it with reasonable cogency. Rather than promulgate unnecessary and perhaps unenforceable laws, why not simply exterminate the root and cause of the problem? Why not simply eradicate the beggars? "es mejor que suspendan los mendigos." The absurdity of the resolution of the social problem is, of course, what makes us susceptible to the wry smile that crosses our face. It's only a joke and we are relieved—but only momentarily. The absurdity forces us to reflect upon the poem for its more serious tone and inescapable theme. And in doing so, we are stripped of our self-assured smugness and we are thrust into the sensation of what Pirandello has called the "feeling or sensing of the opposite"[8] in the seriousness and the pathos of the apparent comic situation.

Certainly, the horror of Spain's destitute as reflected in Gloria Fuertes' sensitivity toward poverty, solitude, and injustice rings out clearly in the brief poem **"Ficha Ingreso Hospital General"** wherein she at first disorients us as she constructs the poem in the manner of a three-by-five notecard and in clinically precise but insouciant statements describes the pathos of human life:

> Nombre: Antonio Martín Cruz.
> Domicilio: Vivía en una alcantarilla.
> Profesión: Obrero sin trabajo.
> OBSERVACIONES: Le encontraron moribundo.
> Padecía: Hambre.
>
> *(OI*, 135)

The poem surprises us since at first glance it appears to be a humorous and disinterested anecdote, but actually turns out to be a very serious indictment against social injustice on the one hand, and on the other, a restatement of the pathetic plight of man's existentialist displacement. The sum total of a man's life is reduced to the dehumanization of a cryptic notation on a hospital file card. One is not very far removed from the plaintive cries

of Fuertes' contemporary, Blas de Otero, who vented his anger against social injustices by shouting out against God and country while inwardly he wept for the barefoot impoverished child (as Gabriela Mistral had done in Chile) and moaned the haplessness of the peasant servant girls forever destined to poverty and petrified in their "sayitas deshilachadas."

At other times the comic spirit of Gloria Fuertes, seen through the intermixing of the absurd with the rational, startles us even more when the poetic voice purports to proffer sentiments of metaphysical proportions. The poet hides behind the mask of dissimulation whereby the comic spirit is again steeped in pathos and we as readers are once more required to respond to a higher meaning of her poetry. In the poem, **"A veces me sucede,"** a poignant statement of the loneliness of man confronted by the reality of his essence is enmeshed in the almost imponderable depths of spiritual malaise:

> A veces me sucede que no me pasa nada,
> ni sangre ni saliva se mueve en mis canutos;
> la mente se me para y el beso se me enquista
> y a siglos con pelusa me saben los minutos.
> El río es un idiota, un terrible obediente,
> el mar sigue llamándole como a can hechizado
> el mal esclavo húmedo, se arrastra por los suelos;
> —ya se me están quedando los pies fríos—
> ¡Qué voz triste el trapero! ¿qué tiene por su saco?
> El día se despeina, la Rufa está preñada,
> la vaca de Pedrito me sigue haciendo señas,
> a veces me sucede que no pasa nada . . .
>
> *(OI*, 93)

The opening four lines set the tone and theme of the poem. Life, spiritual and physical, has momentarily come to a halt. Neither blood nor saliva flow through the speaker's veins. The juxtaposing of "saliva" with the "canutos" is again a tensive image insofar as we don't expect the irrational mixing of saliva and veins unless we can carry the potential symbolism to the following verse and associate it with the "beso." The kiss itself, in turn, reinforces the listless state ("la mente se me para") of the speaker insofar as it is encased in a cyst and thus sustains the idea that again the poetic voice is out of touch with its reality and its own humanity; not even love, human or spiritual, is within its grasp. Time becomes an implied enemy as even the minutes seem to crawl like centuries laden with hoary down and surely the image underscores the psychic pessimism and potential despair of the poetic voice.

In the following three lines the voice shifts from the ego-centered focus to the more metaphysical pretensions perceived in the allusions to the inevitable passage of time and to the inexorable realization of death as it ponders the river forever terribly and idiotically obedient to its interminable destiny, the sea. It is certainly reminiscent of Jorge Manrique's famous and oftrepeated metaphor and through it the poetic voice is drawn to a recognition of its own destiny and by analogy is dragged along the path of life like a sad and wet slave, "como a can hechizado." To this point the poetic voice challenges us as readers to potential universal concepts that whet our intellectual appetites and entice us to anticipatory expectations, expectations of philosophical portent. We are involved in the potentiality of the speaker's either resolving the impasse by offering a reasonable resolution or, at the very least, offering rhetorical questions which while they have no resolute answers at least allow us as readers to inwardly perceive our own. The abrupt break set off by the verse "—ya se me están quedando los pies fríos—" merely supports once again the speaker's self-recognition of its reality and its inability to take the first step forward. This we can accept but when the voice suddenly shifts, as it does in the final four lines of the poem, we are caught in the unexpected, the comical. The expectant lofty sentiments offered in the earlier verses are now counterposed by the rather banal and even trivial reference to the ragman and his bag. Our own ascending feelings are suddenly and unceremoniously dispelled, and we are reminded once again that life is indeed the sum total of everyday commonplaces. The reference to the sad voice of the ragman shifts the focus and unconsciously we wonder, with the poet, what indeed does his bag contain. And, for that matter, the notion that "el día se despeina" should indeed lead us to wonder if days aren't likely to be a disarray of the unexpected since who among us has that unassailable premium of patterning daily experiences as we would wish to devise them? Further, to our surprise we are now informed that "la Rufa" is pregnant. The allusion is certainly startling, given that we were hardly expecting to consider "la Rufa," let alone her pregnancy. Yet, does not daily life consist of the unforeseen, the unsuspected? If we are not persuaded by now of the poet's penchant for the juxtaposing of the paradoxical, the rational with the irrational, and the antithetical, surely the idea of Pedrito's cow making eyes at the speaker must at least moderately bemuse us by the very absurdity of the situation with its overtures of chaplinesque and anti-heroic stature. It is an image at which Nicanor Parra, emboldened by his own anti-poetic sentiment, would have smiled. If we are amused by these curious images we are so because we perceive our own susceptibility at being caught in an anticipation for some potential platonic idealism suggested, or thought to be suggested, in the opening lines and then being brought back to earth with a thud as it were. Yet, the final verse is deceiving in itself. For has nothing really happened to the poet and to us for having followed her in this seemingly nonesthetic poem? Are not the allusions to the cold feet, the ragman and his bag, "la Rufa" and her pregnancy, Pedrito's cow (menial images as they may appear to be) realities that indeed equate to life itself and, in the end, to that dishevelled banality of everyday existence?

The positing of antithetical relationships of ideas, human sentiments, and aspirations surfaces as a constant in many of Fuertes' poems and more than once she utilizes self-parody as the vehicle to remind us of our own human nature entangled in the paradox of our realities. In **"Tengo que deciros"** Fuertes toys with the idea of the illusion and the reality of the poetic process:

Tengo que deciros . . .
que eso del ruiseñor
es mentira.
Que el amor que sintió
era deseo.
Que la espiga no danza,
se mueve,
porque el aire la empuja.
Que estoy sola,
aunque me estáis oyendo.
Cómo duelen, me duelen, duelen mucho
las abejas que salen de mi cuerpo.
Que la luna se enciende,
no es verdad.
El pianista envenenaba a sus hermanos,
y los poetas guisan y comen y hasta odian.
Tenía que deciros . . .
hoy tengo algarabía.
Cuando piso el paisaje que quiero
se me llena el talle de avispas
que tengo fuerzas en los senos y en las piernas.
¡Voy a curarme!
¡La vida me sonría como tonta!
. . . Todo es falso . . .
La verdad,
que estoy sola esperando el coche de línea.

(*OI*, 80)

Again, we succumb to anticipatory expectations in the early lines of the poem. "I am going to tell you," the poetic voice informs us as it draws us to it, "that that business of the nightingale [obvious allusion to the classical or at least romantic symbol of love] is phony, that the idea of love itself is only a cover for sexual desire, that the spikenard doesn't dance but rather is moved only by the wind, and that the notion that the moon lights up is fiction." Grave thoughts are these which would purport to make a sham of perhaps some of our more cherished myths. We expect then to be told why they are false, but again such is not the case. The poetic voice's implied sense of inspiration (the allusion to Antonio Machado's well-remembered symbol of the *abejas*) would lead us to anticipate positive sentiments. However, the *abejas* here cause pain and no lofty sentiments burst forth from the speaker. Moreover, if nothing else, the poetic voice confesses its utter futility: "hoy tengo algarabía." And even the source of inspiration and creativity normally found in the countryside where the *avispas* (another metaphorical allusion to Machado?) fill the speaker's body with poetic potential does not bode well as the poetic voice proclaims—"Voy a curarme." Of what is the voice going to cure itself? Of illusions, of prophetic pronouncements? The shift in tone, especially in the last lines of the poem surely attests, once again, to the opposition of the ideal and the real. Indeed, creativity cannot always be inspiring since after all, artists, poets, are quite human. Pianists do indeed poison their brothers, and poets cook, eat, and even hate. Thus, the direct and unequivocating statement emphasizes even more the fact that we are all caught in the irrational complexities of our human condition. Indeed, if in the final verses we expected some reasonable and perhaps even inspirational statement on the part of the speaker as to the *why* of its present state, we are quickly undeceived as the speaker unobtrusively declares that if the truth must be known, it is this, "I am simply waiting for a street car." Thus, we are reminded once again that any notion of idealism must perforce carry with it its own paradoxical counterpart, the trivial.

As such, in this poem as well as others of a similar vein, while Gloria Fuertes constantly poses universal concepts relative to one's being and one's reality, she rarely loses sight of the comic sense of life found in man's nature and in his world. She reminds us that we too, similar to Blas de Otero's "ángel encadenado," are still chained to the imponderables of our own existential dilemma. The frustrations, the anxieties, the pain, and the solitude can at least be mitigated if only through an awareness of our paradoxical and all too human essence and if nothing else perhaps they can at least be softened by a smile or laughter at one's own absurdities and those of life.

And it is on this note that we find ourselves ensnared, happily I trust, in poems that are underscored with satirical, humorous, and witty criticisms of human institutions as well as the taunting and teasing of cultural, social, and religious customs and beliefs. "Cartas" (a favorite poetic form of Fuertes) are written to God pleading for the relief of the underprivileged, "cartas" are sent to her "queridos pobres" informing them that in spite of their situation they are not abandoned—"aquí un poeta os canta" and perhaps later "vendrán más." "Cartas de auto-nominación" (as José Luis Cano calls them)[9] are written to remind herself of her absurd situation and to chide herself for "not being happy."

Religious icons and relics find little escape from her humorous, albeit critical pen. The plastic Virgin seen in a Harlem five and dime store, tawdry of dress in its cheap molded plastic and sold in "tres colores," can only manage to strike a pathetic note in the poet's sensitivity. To the Virgin she must confess: "se me quitó la gana/de pedirte un milagro (*OI*, 284). In **"El guía de la abadía"** she pokes fun at the cloistered monk who as the official tourist guide and custodian of the patron Saint's relics points out with unreserved pride:

las tres calaveras
del Santo Patrón,
calavera de San Palemón niño
calavera de San Palemón adolescente
y aquí, la calavera de San Palemón ya anciano en el
    martirio.

(*OI*, 237)

In mock serious tones, she petitions a pseudo-bureaucratic commission, the "Sociedad de Amigos y Protectores de Espectros, Fantasmas y Trasgos," that they come and retrieve a certain goblin which has taken over her modest "pisito," insists on speaking "polaco," and claims to be not only "dos muertos de edad," but also the spirit of Genghis Khan:

Ruego a ustedes manden lo que tengan que mandar
y se llevan de mi honesto pisito
a dicho ente,
antes de que le coja cariño.

(*OI*, 145)

If we smile at the combined irony and pathos of the final line of the poem, it may be that we do so because of the cathartic relief that we as readers gain from the foibles and incongruities which surround us and which we ourselves may have experienced and for a moment, however brief, we are permitted a sense of superiority since, after all, it is the poetic speaker who is caught in the web of human pathos.

And, if we smile then at the above poems as well as the many other humorously couched poems of Gloria Fuertes, it is undoubtedly because she brings to us a sense of the comic, a sense of release from the tensions of quotidian existence with its attendant irrational and incomprehensible perplexities. The comic-seriousness, that polarity between reality and ideality, founded on the antithetical relationships of the imagery and poetic language, the ironic and unexpected resolutions tinged with wry humor, is the thread that knits the fabric of Fuertes' poetry.

While her poetry does abound in social consciousness with its underlying themes of man's aloneness enmeshed in the inexorable vicissitudes of life and death, one cannot help but note the manner in which the poet adapts a posture and style that is disarming and, perhaps in a curious fashion, refreshing. Notwithstanding the gravity of the content and themes of her poetry, she never takes herself seriously. As she more than once informs us, the role (at least the self-professed role) that she seeks is that of a "payaso." In the poem, **"Oración,"** she unequivocally cries out to God:

Haz que me acostumbre a las cosas de abajo.
Dame la salvadora indiferencia,
haz un milagro más,
dame la risa,
¡hazme payaso, Dios, hazme payaso!

(*OI*, 128)

This fusion then of the seriousness of the theme with the comic and the ironic brings to mind Pirandello's observation that "irony reduces the artistic matter to a perpetual parody in which the author never loses, even in those moments of pathos, his awareness of the unreality of his own creation."[10] The jocular tone which vibrates like a resonant leit-motiv is what draws us to her voice and in the absurdities of the experiences which it offers to us, we can either find the humor and smile or we can despair. Gloria Fuertes, I believe, would prefer that we smile.

NOTES

[1] I use the term "absurdity of life" in the sense that Jean-Paul Sartre uses it in his essay "An Explication of *The Stranger*" in *Camus: Collection*

of Critical Essays (Englewood Cliffs, N.J.: Prentice-Hall, 1962), p. 109. The absurd in life Sartre explains is "the cleavage between man's aspirations to unity and the insurmountable dualism of mind and nature, between man's drive toward the eternal and the *finite* character of his existence, and the efforts of his efforts. Chance, death, the irreducible pluralism of life and of truth, the unintelligibility of the real—all these are extremes of the absurd."

[2] Wylie Sypher, "The Meanings of Comedy," in *Comedy: Meaning and Form,* ed. and introd. Robert W. Corrigan (San Francisco: Chandler Publishing Co., 1965), pp. 23-24.

[3] Gloria Fuertes was born in Madrid in 1918 and has written extensively, not only poetry but also dramatic works, as well as children's books. In 1950 she published her first volume of poetry, *Isla ignorada.* Subsequent volumes include *Aconsejo beber hilo* (1954), *Todo asusta* (1958), *Ni tiro, ni veneno, ni navajo* (1965), *Poeta de guardia* (1968), *Sola en la sala* (1973).

[4] Joaquín González Muela, *La nueva poesía española* (Madrid: Ediciones Alcalá, 1973), p. 18.

[5] José Luis Cano, *Poesía española contemporánea. Las generaciones de posguerra* (Madrid: Guadarrama, 1974), p. 174.

[6] Gloria Fuertes, *Obras incompletas* (Madrid: Ediciones Cátedra, 1977), p. 134. Subsequent references to poems cited in this study shall be referred to as *OI* accompanied by the specific page number.

[7] For an in-depth study of poetic language as tensive language (e.g., the function of image, metaphor, symbol, plurisignation, paradox, etc.), see Philip Wheelwright, *Metaphor and Reality* (Bloomington: Indiana Univ. Press, 1962), pp. 45-69.

[8] Luigi Pirandello, *On Humor,* introd., trans., and annotated Antonio Illiano and Daniel P. Testa (Chapel Hill: Univ. of North Carolina Press, 1974), pp. 113-14.

[9] Cano, p. 177.

[10] Pirandello, *On Humor,* p. x.

Margaret H. Persin (essay date 1982)

SOURCE: "Gloria Fuertes and (Her) Feminist Reader," in *Revista/Review Interamericana,* Vol. XII, No. 1, Spring, 1982, pp. 125-32.

[*Persin assesses ways in which Fuertes develops her ideas about the burden—and resulting isolation—imposed upon women by contemporary attitudes toward behavior, relationships, distribution of wealth, and conformity.*]

Critics have just begun to recognize the value of the post-Civil War poets who became active in Spain in the late 1950s and 1960s.[1] Gloria Fuertes's poetry is linked to that of her contemporaries not so much by a given theme or style as a common attitude: all of these poets stress the value of poetry as cognition and communica-

tion of our modern reality. In keeping with their aim to present everyday reality, they generally utilize colloquial language, slang, humor, and scenes from daily existence.[2]

The work of these poets is also unified by the subtle effects that it produces in the reader.[3] For example, Gloria Fuertes utilizes the language of common everyday experience but manipulates this language in order to achieve an artistic effect. The speaker in these poetic texts does not rely upon traditional literary devices and rethoric, but rather invites the reader to collaborate in creating the poetic experience within the text. The reader constantly must reevaluate more traditionally held views on themes, language level, poetic personae, and artistic perspective. Fuertes requires that the reader accept a new and updated definition of poetic creation. Indeed, in this poetry, the reader's role is redefined: the reader is no longer a passive receptor of the text, but rather an active participant.

Gloria Fuertes also attempts in her poetic texts to convince her reader of the need to examine and perhaps reorder the priorities of twentieth-century life. She puts forward a more humane point of view on life, a view that is oftentimes labelled as feminine, or even more radical yet, feminist. It is obvious that this feminist view is many times at odds with the prevailing social mood. Moreover, her innovative use of language, which also reflects the feminine point of view, once again makes demands on the reader as a recipient of the poetic text. But because of her conciliatory rather than strident tone, Fuertes is able to win over her reader to her feminist stance, and her feminist use of language.

In the first text that I wish to consider, Fuertes uses linguistic word play in order to set the tone of the text:[4]

> Yo,
>
> remera de barcas
>
> ramera de hombres
>
> romera de almas
> rimera de versos
> Ramona,
>   pa' servirles.

By stating her point of view from a feminine perspective, Fuertes affirms her belief that the female poet can indeed interpret the hopes, dreams and aspirations of the community as well as her male counterpart. By placing herself, the "rimer of verses", next to the other works in mundane tasks, Fuertes succeeds in removing some of the mystery from poetry. She brings it out onto the street. It is a commodity that is or should be available to all. The speaker describes herself with only a given name in the penultimate verse, and offers a standard statement connoting servitude, "pa'servirles," in its colloquial pronunciation. This mode of presentation, combined with the word play on the various female occupations or vocations allows Fuertes

not only to set a playful mood, but also to make a statement about her beliefs concerning the role of the female
poet. She is a worker, a servant to those around her, it is
her duty to sing the song of the community. Through the
juxtaposition of the various female occupations, she invites the reader to see a second level of meaning which is
more profound, i.e., that the female poet must be the bard
of the cultured as well as the working class.[5]

This point of view is echoed in virtually all of Fuertes'
poetry. Take for example the poem **"Soy sólo una mujer"**:

> Soy sólo una mujer y ya es bastante,
> con tener una chiva, una tartana
> un "bendito sea Dios" por la mañana
> y un mico en el pescante.
>
> Yo quisiera haber sido delineante,
> o delirante Safo sensitiva
> y heme,
> aquí
> que soy una perdida
> entre tanto mangante.
> Lo digo para todo el que me lea,
> quise ser captán, sin arma alguna,
> depositar mis versos en la luna
> y un astronauta me pisó la idea.
>
> De PAZ por esos mundos quise ser traficante
> —me detuvieron por la carretera—
> soy sólo una mujer, de cuerda entera,
> soy sólo una mujer, y ya es bastante.
>
> (p. 256)

In the first stanza she signals characteristics of her existence, which serve to identify as well as define her role in
life: to be the owner of possessions rather than the achiev-
er of goals. In the second stanza she states what she would
have been, had not others beat her to the punch. But this
sense of frustration evolves into one of acceptance: "soy
sólo una mujer, de cuerda entera, / soy sólo una mujer y
ya es bastante." It is not in this text but in others that the
reader finds the clue to this sense of satisfaction. For
Fuertes sees the female poet as one who fulfills not only
an artistic role but also a nurturing and caring one. Fuertes is willing to seek out the poetic experience in any
quarter, and asks that the reader follow her in her artistic
search. In the poem **"Madrugada"** she asks that the reader
accept the view that poetry is not strictly a bourgeois
production and preoccupation:

> Amiga de serenos y de ex-presos
> —igual que un operario de la Renfe—
> conozco los caminos de la noche,
> los caminos del clown que ríe inútilmente,
> y los torcidos pasos del que bebe derecho
> —derecho tiene a su vida beberse—.
> Conozco los retratos de los hijos de pobre prostituta
> que con toda ternura sus madres tienen,
> y los enseñan—igual que todo—
> en un rincón del bar antes de recogerse.
>
> (p. 250)

The speaker in this text implies that the more traditional
poets, who speak of unrequited love, the beauty of the
universe, and conventional feminine beauty, present the
reader with a bourgeois and thus limited view of life.
Fuertes, on the other hand, through her unprejudiced perspective, finds beauty and poetic inspiration in the common people of the workaday world, the down-and-out,
and the love of prostitutes for their children. With the
expression *igual que todo*, Fuertes asserts that human
value is defined not by environment, social class or occupation, but rather by the universal qualities of love,
devotion and friendship.

Fuertes also employs a feminist perspective in order to
deal with such private topics as her relationship with God,
the effects of war, and her own state of mind. By viewing
the speaker's world in this light, it is impossible for the
reader to be threatened by it. Fuertes uses the technique
of a feminist perspective to emphasize the similarities
between her world and that of her reader. In "Sola con
esperanza" Fuertes first establishes the subject of her
poetic inspiration by denouncing society's encumber-
ments:

> Sola moro
> moro sólo
> sola moro.
>
> Muchas veces se está solo
> pero mejor con decoro
> ¡A la mierda el oro
> y a la mierda el coro!
> ¡Sola!
> *Sola-solo.*
> (Fuertes' italics)
>
> (p. 186)

She denounces very strongly the shackles of a twentieth-
century society gone awry—those values of proper behavior, money, matrimony, and being just like everyone
else. These values are especially burdensome to the female half of the population, since women are the ones
who are most often expected to keep up appearances, to
not talk back, and to know their proper place in society,
i.e., to be seen and not heard, to be a helpmate to male
success.

She then introduces her particular "Soleá", pronounced in
the Andalusian dialect, and surrounded with the ambience
of that region's *cante jondo*:

> Entonces la soleá
> se puebla de luz y canto
> y la niebla va y se va.

Fuertes' personified "aloneness" here takes a positive
value rather than a negative one, and becomes identified
with her poetic voice. The comings and goings of poetic
inspiration are ephemeral and fickle. Fuertes then, as the
speaker, personifies her solitude in the body of a flashy
street whore attired in a green dress, who beckons the
speaker and the reader to join her:

Semivestida de verde
me excita la Soledad
esta noche va y me dice:
—me dice y luego se va—,
que me merezco otra cosa
—que vendrá—".

By embracing openly this tabooed poetic persona, that of the prostitute, Fuertes accomplishes two things. First, she thumbs her nose at the values of proper society, and second she underscores the idea that women are too often used as objects instead of accepted as equals to men. Women have long been the subjects of poetry, but not its creators. In this poetic text, Fuertes skillfully combines these two roles. As she says, "que me merezco otra cosa,—que vendrá".

In the final lines of verse, she accepts her pain, her solitude, and the rewards that they are able to bring to her:

¡Qué divina está esta noche
la zorra la Soledad!

Her solitude has given her life, and Fuertes has given life to her solitude. She has become the creator instead of the object of her poetry. The tabooed role of woman as the whore is now the personification of creative power. Thus, the speaker's private bout with loneliness has become a model for the feminist view of loneliness and its positive value in regard to poetic creation. The reader of the text is drawn into the poetic experience by the invitation of the speaker, whose presentation of solitude as a street walker catches the reader's attention and encourages a communal response to a private topic.

While in the poetic text of **"Sola con esperanza"** Fuertes reflects a very serious view on the female poetic voice, in **"Enfermera de pulpos"** she adopts a more playful tone. The pun on the word *tinta* facilitates a far-fetched comparison between the octopus and the poet:

Ellos viven en la mar
sin pecado terrenal
—sin mancharse con trilita—,
ellos viven como tú y como yo
de la tinta.
Los envidio por los brazos,
pues pueden al mismo tiempo
tres abrazos. Los pulpos
para el amor son siniestros
según un sabio de Harvard.
. . . . .

Las pulpas,
tocan el arpa
por la trade.

(p. 286)

The title of the text, **"Enfermera de pulpos"**, gives the impression that the speaker will focus on the role of the female as helper, soother, and recuperative muse in the life of the octopus/poet. But in the first stanza, the speaker's focus is on the male. It should be noticed that the first word of the text is *ellos,* a masculine pronoun. This switch perhaps may cause the bemused reader to ponder the double standard in society: the men get so much of the glory, while the women do so much of the work.

In the text, Fuertes introduces a novel juxtaposition, based on the ink expended by both poet and octopus. She also draws the reader into the text in the expression *como tú y como yo.* Our use of ink may not be as lofty as that of the poet. But ironically, that which seems cold, calculating and farthest removed from the poetic sphere is the impersonality of the expression *según un sabio de Harvard,* which refers to the human and specifically masculine sector. The female aspect enters only in the final two lines of verse of the text. The poem ends with the image of the female octopus, harp and music, an image which remains with the reader as a lasting reminder of the romantic beauty and poetic quality of this animal. The female octopus has been turned into the true siren of the sea, beckoning the reader to join her and her music, just as Fuertes, the poet does with her verse. Thus, in spite of the fact that the female focus dominates in only two lines of verse, Fuertes succeeds in winning her reader over a feminist view of poetry. According to this view, poetry written by men has become too cold, too official, too removed from daily experience. On the other hand, the feminine voice remains true to the eternal poetic ideal.

The final poem to be considered here is **"El camello"**, which carries the subtitle of "Auto de los Reyes Magos". This text casts a disparaging glance on bourgeois values, but in a refreshing way. Briefly, the poem tells the story of the arrival of the Magi at Bethlehem. The Three Kings complain bitterly that the camel is a lemon, they become lost on the way, and they argue among themselves about the best way to get to their destination. The speaker demonstrates obvious sympathy for the lowly camel, who along the way goes lame, is blamed for the tardiness of the arrival, and as an ultimate insult to his dignity, suffers an attack of hiccups. The speaker inserts very purposefully an anachronistic note by stating that Melchior, the resident mechanic, frets about their late arrival upon consulting his Longine watch. He complains that the camel has thrown them hopelessly off schedule. But finally the journey is complete, they have arrived at the manger, the prophecy has been fulfilled:

Y a las tantas ya del alba
—ya cantaban pajarillos—
los tres reyes se quedaron
boquiabiertos e indecisos,
oyendo hablar como a un Hombre
a un Niño recién nacido.
—No quiero oro ni incienso
ni esos tesoros tan fríos,
quiero al camello, le quiero.
Le quiero—repitió el Niño.
A pie vuelven los tres reyes

cabizbajos y afligidos.
Mientras el camello echado
le hace cosquillas al Niño.

(pag. 241)

The final vindication of the camel teaches a lesson of which the reader must become aware. Bourgeois existence has become too complacent and smug, too much a slave to the demands of the clock. There must be a balance between the traditional male view of commerce, punctuality, machines and chains of command, and the traditionally held feminine ones of love, tenderness, and familiar devotion. In this text, Fuertes campaigns for an examination of priorities on both a professional and personal level. There must be balance and harmony, if existence is to be worthwhile. We must respond to our own emotional needs and to those of our neighbor, even if schedules, social appearances and conventions may suffer. Perhaps the reader would reject this message if it were presented in a straightforward, didactic and pedantic manner. But through a feminist approach, in which the speaker emphasizes intimate rather than pragmatic values, Fuertes wins the attention and approval of the reader, and thus gains easy support for her more humane point of view on what our priorities ought to be. These priorities have become acceptable through this simple anecdote of the Christ Child and the camel. Now we can examine them in a new light and not be threatened or put off by the speaker's point of view.

Although Gloria Fuertes has stated that she is a poet independent of any particular literary affiliation, her work in truth reflects both the social and psychological environment which produced it. In her poetry the reader finds the main concerns of the twentieth century: alienation, distancing, the devalorization of human existence, and the loss of a sense of community. But through the feminist stance that Fuertes adopts, and encourages the reader to adopt, this Twentieth-century bard of the working class attempts to stem the tide of indifference, spiritual nullity and existential anguish. But this feminist perspective serves more than a social end. Through it, Gloria Fuertes also encourages the reader to focus on the poetic process, the act of artistic creation. This focus also binds her to her contemporaries. In her poetic texts, the speaker demands the reader's collaboration and participation in the creation of a poetic experience. This poetic experience is shown to be one that can include a more holistic and feminine view of modern reality and modern existence. Gloria Fuertes sings the song of the community, and through her verse, proves that the female voice is just as capable of expressing the poetic song of twentieth-century life. Her range is unique, but still remains true to the eternal poetic ideal.

NOTES

¹ Gloria Fuertes has published the following books of poetry: *Isla ignorada* (Madrid: Musa Nueva, 1950); *Antología y poemas del suburbio* (Caracas: Lírica Hispana, 1954); *Aconsejo beber hilo* (Madrid: Arquero, 1954: *Todo asusta* (Caracas: Lírica Hispana, 1958); *Que estás en la tierra* (Barcelona: Seix Barral, 1962); *Ni tiro, ni veneno, ni navaja* (Barcelona: El Bardo, 1965); *Poeta de guardia* (Barcelona: El Bardo, 1969); *Antología poética 1950-1969* (Barcelona: Plaza y Janés, 1971), 2nd ed., 1973, 3rd ed., 1975; *Sola en la sala* (Zaragoza: Javalambre, 1973); *Cuando amas aprendes geografía* (Málaga: Curso Superior de Filología, 1973).

² My article on the use of humor in Fuertes' poetry, entitled "Humor as Semiosis in the poetry of Gloria Fuertes" has been accepted for publication in *Revista Hispánica Moderna*.

³ In recent literary criticism, importance has been granted to the relationship between the reader and the text. See for example Jonathan Culler, "Stanley Fish and the Righting of the Reader," *Diacritics*, (Spring, 1975), 26-31; Paul de Man, *Blindness and Insight: Essays in the Rhetoric of Contemporary Criticism*, (New York: Oxford University Press, 1971); Umberto Eco, *The Role of the Reader* (Bloomington, Indiana: Indiana University Press, 1979); Stanley Fish, "Literature in the Reader: Affective Stylistics," *New Literary History* 2 (1970), 123-163; Wolfgang Iser, *The Act of Reading: A Theory of Aesthetic Response* (Baltimore: The Johns Hopkins University Press, 1978); Wolfgang Iser, *The Implied Reader* (Baltimore: The Johns Hopkins University Press, 1974); Michael Riffaterre, *Semiotics of Poetry* (Bloomington, Indiana: Indiana University Press, 1978).

⁴ "Yo", p. 223. In the preparation of this manuscript I used Gloria Fuertes' *Obras incompletas* (Madrid: Ediciones Cátedra, 1978). From this point forward, all page numbers will be included in the body of the text.

⁵ Fuertes' poem entitled "Cabra sola" (p. 212) offers a more personalized view of her role as a (female) poet:

Hay quien dice que estoy como una cabra;
lo dicen, lo repiten, ya lo creo;
pero soy una cabra muy extraña
que lleva una medalla y siete cuernos.
¡Cabra! En vez de mala leche yo doy llanto.
¡Cabra! Por lo más peligroso me paseo
¡Cabra! Me llevo bien con alimañas todas.
¡Cabra! Y escribo en los tebeos.
Vivo sola, cabra sola
—que no quise cabrito en compañía
cuando subo a lo alto de este valle,
siempre encuentro un lirio de alegría.
Y vivo por mi cuenta, cabra sola;
que yo a ningún rebaño pertenezco.
Si sufrir es estar como una cabra,
entonces sí lo estoy, no dudar de ello.

Andrew P. Debicki (essay date 1982)

SOURCE: "Gloria Fuertes, Intertextuality and Reversal of Expectations," in *Poetry of Discovery*, 1982, pp. 80-101, 222-23.

[*Debicki assesses Fuertes' use of various devices in her poetry to unify disparate elements into fresh presentations of her ideas.*]

The poetry of Gloria Fuertes is marked by its colloquial tone and its resemblance to conversational address. Her works are filled with references to everyday objects and events: buses, storefronts, newspaper advertisements; any more significant themes emerge from these. Almost all her poems are written in free verse, a verse that seems to deliberately avoid rhythmic regularity and consistently break the conventions of the traditional lyric. These qualities are so patent as to suggest that the author is constructing a very special kind of poetic expression.

Noting the presence of social concerns in much of Fuertes's poetry, one is tempted to situate her in the current of social poetry that emerged in Spain after the Civil War. Yet such a view needs to be qualified: an attitude of rebellion against the injustices of the social system certainly underlies Fuertes's poetry, and one can find many negative references to war, to lack of love, to the problems of a modern industrial city. But the main impact of her poems is never didactic: rather than argue a certain stance, they make one witness and share a wide variety of human experiences which emerge from the problematic and often cruel world of a modern, industrial Spanish society.[1] Social issues are intertwined with personal ones: many of her poems deal with love, with loneliness, with attempts to define a rather unusual God. The speaker never mythifies herself as a visionary prophet or social leader, but speaks from a much more individual perspective. All of this differentiates Fuertes's work from much of the social poetry written in Spain in the early 1950s, and gives it a character all its own.

Fuertes makes effective use of common language to communicate these individual experiences that arise out of her poetry. References to objects of daily life and the use of specific tones of spoken language serve to take the poem beyond generalized didacticism, to give it its unique expressiveness. The frequent use of humor and word play, as Margaret Persin has aptly noted, involve the reader in a different vision of the world. And for all its apparently prosaic nature, Fuertes's poetry makes use of precise linguistic techniques (paronomasias, alliterations, other word plays).[2] Seen this way, her poetry fits well with that of the other writers who became prominent in Spain in the late 1950s. Like Rodríguez, Brines, and González, Gloria Fuertes has found her own way of making artistic use of seemingly ordinary materials and thus verbally creating and conveying significant visions and experiences.

Fuertes's poetry seems even more colloquial than that of these other writers. While Brines and Rodríguez use everyday language and make poetry out of ordinary scenes, their works are not so full of slang expressions and idiomatic language as those of Fuertes. This profusion of everyday elements could lead us to consider her work less creative, less significant; if we examine it with some care, however, we will see that in its colloquialism lie the seeds of its originality and its value.

Again and again, a poem that deals with a significant theme of human life or with a conventionally poetic subject will jar us by using seemingly inappropriate language (which may include slang, advertising slogans, references to trivial events). In each case, this inappropriate language intro-duces, as it were, a new and different "text," at odds with the one we have come to expect in light of the poem's subject.[3] The meaning of the work emerges from the confrontation and the weaving together of the two texts. This may occur explicitly (when two easily identifiable modes of expression clash in the poem) or implicitly (when the language merely suggests a conflicting convention or form of expression). In either case the poem deliberately disorients its implied reader. The latter finds that the attitude which she expected to take toward the serious subject of the poem has been undermined by the presence of the second text; she must then grope for some new way of organizing and resolving the materials of the poem.[4] In some cases, she will be left with an apprehension of the problems and discords of modern life. In all cases, however, she will have become involved in a complex play of perspectives between the two texts and will have obtained, as a result, a whole new vision. The process parallels and yet differs from that observed in Angel González's work: where in González's poems we saw the gradual restructuring of previous conventions, in Fuertes's we will witness drastic irruptions which destroy traditional visions and produce new perspectives.

As we examine various cases of textual irruptions in Fuertes's poetry, we will see that they take different forms; in some cases the second text appears as a symbol which the poet applies to the poem's literal level, in others as a specific literary allusion, in others as a single word that brings in a different form of expression, in yet others as a whole system (or code) of words and expressions that evoke a different reality.[5] The concept of intertextuality will allow us to see how all these function in similar fashion—how they serve, in the final analysis, to undermine the initial text, to modify the expectations of the implied reader, and to produce significant meanings in a novel way.

This process is present, if not dominant, in Fuertes's early works. Her first book, **Isla ignorada**, has practically vanished; the few poems that are available and the comments of critics indicate that it contained traditional nature descriptions with *modernista* echoes, and did not show the characteristics of her later work. But in **Antología y poemas del suburbio**, **Aconsejo beber hilo**, and **Todo asusta**, such intertextual irruptions already appear, if not as blatantly as they do later on. Nevertheless, they are significant in determining the meaning of many poems. A good example is "El vendedor de papeles o el poeta sin suerte" from **Antología y poemas**, which uses the language of commercial advertisements:

> Vendo versos,
> liquido poesía,
> —se reciben encargos
> para bodas, bautizos
> peticiones de mano—,
> ¡aleluyas a diez!
> No se vaya,
> regalo poesía,
> llévese este cuarteto
> que aún no me estrené!

[p. 52]

The implied reader comes to this poem with a preconceived, traditional vision of poetry as a serious and dignified occupation, removed from the triviality of everyday life. Fuertes plays against this vision and this conventional text in developing her poem. By presenting poetry as something which can be marked down and sold cheap, or produced for practical reasons, and in adopting the specific language of commercial exchange ("liquido," "se reciben encargos," "no me estrené"), she sets up an opposing text—a colloquial poem. This destroys our premise that poetry and everyday life stand well apart from each other. The reversal of expectations, especially when seen in context of the whole book from which this poem comes, makes us attentive to the meanings that the poet can find in seemingly ordinary circumstances and to the possibility that poetic insights can arise from daily life.

Another weaving together of two texts occurs in **"Oración,"** from *Antología y poemas*. Here the original language of the "Our Father" and our traditional views of God as a transcendent being and of prayer as a solemn activity are undercut by the tone and attitude of the speaker:

> Que estás en la tierra Padre nuestro,
> que te siento en la púa del pino,
> el el torso azul del obrero,
> en la niña que borda curvada
> la espalda mezclando el hilo en el dedo.
> Padre nuestro que estás in la tierra,
> en el surco,
> en el huerto,
> en el mina,
> en el puerto,
> en el cine,
> en el vino,
> en la casa del médico.
> Padre nuestro que estás en la tierra,
> donde tienes tu gloria y tu infierno
> y tu limbo que está en los cafés
> donde los burgueses beben su refresco.
>
> . . . . .
>
> Padre que habitas en cualquier sitio.
> Dios que penetras en cualquier hueco,
> tú que quitas la angustia, que estás en la tierra,
> Padre nuestro que sí que te vemos,
> los que luego te hemos de ver,
> donde sea, o ahí en el cielo.
>
> [pp. 47-48]

By taking the first phrase of the "Our Father," altering the word order, and substituting *la tierra* for *los cielos,* the speaker reveals her break with the view of a superior and remote God. She continues repeating and modifying her version of that phrase to stress God's worldliness and earthly presence, and finally to suggest that our ultimate union with God may not be the grandiose rising to Heaven traditionally anticipated. The colloquialism of the last line ("donde sea, o ahí en el cielo") eliminates any grandiloquent vision of such a heaven, while the mention of specific places of our world stresses that it is in them that God and religion must be found.

Just as **"El vendedor de papeles"** related poetry to everyday life, **"Oración"** suggests that religion and our relationship with God emerge from the circumstances of daily existence. The poet's tactic of setting her text against the conventional one of the "Our Father," destroying the implied reader's expectations regarding prayer, and presenting her with a colloquial address and a commonplace God makes the vision emerge gradually and vividly from the poem.

In **"Me crucé con un entierro"** from *Aconsejo beber hilo,* a contrast to our ordinary way of seeing deaths and funerals is used to communicate an experience of despair (although that only becomes clear at the end of the poem):

> Me crucé con un entierro
> —el de la caja iba muerto—
> —¿A dónde vas?—me decía—.
> —Adonde tú—respondiendo—.
> Se marchaba muy tranquilo,
> me quedaba sonriendo.
> ¿Quién va más muerto que vivo,
> quién va por mejor sendero,
> el de la caja o yo misma,
> que todavía te quiero?
>
> [pp. 90-91]

This poem again sets itself against the reader's "horizon of expectations," which dictates that the subject of death and funerals be approached with reverence. The colloquial way of describing the dead man ("el de la caja iba muerto") indicates a flip irreverence that clashes with the serious tone normally used on such occasions. The conversation with the corpse not only contradicts the rules of reality but also takes on a casual tone that contrasts with the solemnity with which the dead are usually approached in our culture. The denouement of the scene, with its calm parting of the protagonists, adds to the sense of an ill-fitting improbability. All of this makes the poem the opposite of any traditional poem about the dead. The implied reader must notice how this text sets itself against others with which she is familiar—a serious report, a lament on someone's death, perhaps even a poem addressed to the dead. Until the last four lines of the poem, the reader is left wondering where this intertextuality is going to take her.

In these last lines the speaker finally reveals her theme, suggesting that her continued love for a "tú" (who presumably scorns her) makes her more dead than the corpse. This hyperbole, which would probably seem unacceptable were it to stand alone, is much easier to accept in the context of the whole poem. We do not, for one, have to see it as grimly serious: the speaker of the poem has already revealed a colloquial tone and a critical posture with respect to traditional texts, which suggest that she can see her own predicament in matter-of-fact fashion. In addition, the way in which the first part sets itself against conventional writing suggests that the whole poem may be a parody of another conventional text, a romantic lament for a love lost.

This becomes clear when we recall the characteristics of such romantic poems, in which images of death, graveside laments, and hyperbolic complaints abound. Fuertes undercuts these stock images of an abandoned lover's lament and the stock setting of a funeral procession by turning them into an abrupt street scene. (The dialogue in lines 3-5, for example, seems more fitting to a casual encounter between neighbors running errands.) Even the form of the poem may contribute to this sense of parody. It is a *romance* in e-o, a form employed to recount heroic deeds in the traditional *Romancero* and often used later on by romantic poets; here it is utilized by a contemporary poet (who normally writes in free verse) to give a very colloquial twist to a traditional theme.

It is hard to define with certainty the final experience produced by this poem: should one read it as a broad parody of a romantic lament, or as a modern and somewhat ironic, yet partly serious, restatement of such a lament? The latter reading seems more convincing to me: the last line suggests real suffering, though one tempered by a very modern awareness or the world around us. By setting her text against others—conventional reports of death, romantic poems—Fuertes has woven within her reader's mind and experience a new and complex vision, a product of the interplay between all these texts.

A similar undercutting of conventional texts and attitudes occurs in two other poems which refer to the dead, **"Los muertos"** from *Aconsejo beber hilo* and **"Mis queridos difuntos"** from *Todo asusta.* Both present the dead as much happier and better adjusted than the living. In the first work, (pp. 99-100) they go about daily activities in the cemetery in matter-of-fact fashion; in the second (p. 123) the speaker expresses regret at having to leave the harmonious world of the dead and return to the discord of the living, cautioning the dead not to be resurrected. Fuertes does not describe the dead as being in Heaven or in a glorified afterlife: they are happier simply because they are away from the world. This denial of life as worthwhile highlights one theme of Fuertes's poetry, the limitations of our world and our society.

A somewhat different kind of intertextuality is engendered by **"Guía comercial"** (p. 115), a work made up entirely of sentences that imitate typical advertisements. By thus introducing previous texts which we normally consider highly antipoetic, Fuertes contradicts our expectations of what is proper to poetry and what is proper to everyday life. This not only satirizes and denigrates the prosaic world which the poet is confronting but also reopens the question of the relationship of poetry to the everyday forms of expression of this world. A similar effect is produced by **"De los periódicos,"** (p. 127), which lists a number of haphazard objects supposedly found in an ostrich's stomach, as reported by a newspaper. Neither of these poems is a simple message regarding the relationship of poetry to popular culture and forms

of expression; both refer to the texts of this culture to raise the issue of this relationship and to invite us to reexamine its implications in new ways.

In all of the poems we have seen so far, Fuertes has constructed internally consistent pictures or stories which nevertheless oppose previous texts which they evoke, and consequently alter the implied reader's preconceived attitudes. In most cases this serves to destroy conventional notions regarding the value of human life and of social order, the independence of poetry, or the grandiloquence of religion. All of these poems depend on the reader's "horizon of expectations" to furnish these conventional notions, making the reader anticipate attitudes which are then dramatically undercut within the text.[6] This procedure ultimately engenders an irreverent view of our world, based on the problems of the reality surrounding us. By making that view emerge within the implied reader as she gropes with the contradictions between her expectations and the text she is reading, Fuertes has made a vivid poetic experience out of what could have been otherwise no more than a didactic message.

These poems also demonstrate how, in order to convey the problems of the modern world, Fuertes creates intertextual weavings which engender a variety of tensions, destroy conventional visions, and produce a new form of expression. Fuertes actually states this as a conscious goal of her work on several occasions.[7] It also emerges from the way in which she draws the *persona* of her speaker. In **"Es obligatorio,"** the speaker pictures herself as rebelling against the hypocritical niceties of society and polite language in order to achieve real communication:

> Es obligatorio tener mitos
> y yo gustosa desobedezco,
> gustosa me plancho las blusas,
> cuando tengo tiempo,
> porque antes es hablar con los amigos.
>
> [p. 136]

The colloquial expressions and the clash with previous texts present in Fuertes's early work, far from indicating expressive inadequacies, convey the poetry's subjects in a new and effective fashion.

Three books of poetry published by Gloria Fuertes in the 1960s, *Ni tiro, ni veneno, ni navaja, Poeta de guardia,* and *Cómo atar los bigotes al figre,* reveal an even more creative use of everyday language and commonplace materials. As Francisco Ynduráin has noted, individual episodes and personal themes now point even more clearly to larger questions of the value of human life, of basic emotions and feelings, of the role of God, of poetry.[8] Fuertes exploits colloquial expressions, Madrid slang, and specific allusions to create unique perceptions and to embody her themes in novel ways. Her humor jars the reader, recreating within her a new vision of the poem's subject. As she does all this, Fuertes makes even greater use of intertextual correspondences and contrasts to create rich experiences. Frequently the other texts alluded to are now more specific; where in the earlier poems we could discern general echoes of advertisements or romantic laments, we now see detailed evocations of an automobile accident, a Madrid store, or a poem by Saint John of the Cross. This produces works which are on the one hand more complex and more jarring to our expectations; it leads on the other to more frequent and more elaborate relationships between the specific subject of a poem and some larger theme. The intertextual relationships make the reader see these themes in unusual and compelling ways.

All this is perhaps most apparent in **Poeta de guardia**, published in 1968. As Ynduráin has noted, this book is not only one of the most extensive written by Fuertes, but also perhaps the most significant.[9] The title and several poems in the work assert the author's role as viewer of and commentator on reality. The book deals with a wide range of themes, encompassing universal issues such as social injustice, the meaning of life, and the impact of death, and more personal subjects such as love, the monotony of daily life, the problems of a writer. None of them are in themselves novel or unusual. What makes their treatment unique, however, is the way in which Fuertes uses intertextuality to set these themes in the modern context and give them new dimensions. We can see how this occurs in **"Galerías Preciadas"**:

Todo te viene pequeño
—o demasiado grande—,
ni siquiera lo que escoges te va,
todo te viene pequeño.
Con el alma desnuda por una cosa u otra
                    imploramos el Tendero.

Y si llegas a encontrar . . .
quien bien te quiere te hará llorar . . .
                    —¡Vaya consuelo¡
(¡Qué suerte ser eremita o farero!)

                                        [p. 192]

The title contains a pun, immediately perceived by any resident of Madrid. In titling the poem with a modified version of the name of Madrid's best known middle-class department store (Galerías Preciados), Fuertes calls to mind a very specific second text, which we immediately associate with prosaic shopping trips, with bargain hunting, and perhaps with shoddy merchandise. All these associations clash with the poem's theme, the larger question of what is valuable in life. ("Preciadas" is obviously rooted in "preciado"—that which is valued or esteemed.) This clash is continued in the body of the poem, in which the common happening of not finding an article of clothing that fits is linked to and contrasted with the question of finding something meaningful in one's existence. The first four lines stress the anecdotal event; the next two, in contrast, point to the wider question. By referring to the soul and capitalizing "Tendero," Fuertes obviously creates an allusion to man's questioning of God.

In a conventional reading, we might say that Fuertes has done no more than construct a symbol, making the search

for clothing stand for a quest for some deeper meaning. This is of course technically true; but the effect of this "symbolism" depends almost entirely on its surface inappropriateness, on the conflict between texts, and on the jarring effect it produces. The activity of hunting for clothes that fit in an inexpensive store turns the larger quest for something meaningful into a pedestrian activity. We are tempted to stand back with the speaker and mock this quest a little, or at least to realize that we live in a world in which grand searches get mixed in with very trivial activities, and in which it is hard to be uniformly significant and heroic.

It might be best to see this poem as a combination of two different codes, in the sense attributed to that term by Roland Barthes. Fuertes has violently joined a representational code referring to a shopping expedition (a code formed by the colloquial expressions "te viene pequeño," "[te viene] grande," "te va") to another symbolic one referring to a deeper, seemingly religious quest (a code formed by "alma" and the capitalization of "Tendero"). In line 5, both codes appear almost simultaneously, as a reference to the soul is followed by the colloquial "una cosa u otra," and as the storekeeper and God become fused in "Tendero." All in all, the two codes interfere with each other and thus jar the reader into feeling the inappropriateness of their conjunction. This leads, in the final analysis, to a paradoxical vision of our world in which larger questions emerge in trivial ways, and yet in which daily happenings also become tied to deeper issues.

The second stanza defines the large quest more specifically: it becomes the search for someone, presumably a beloved. By indicating that this search would only lead to suffering even if it were to succeed, the speaker adds another dimension to the earlier pessimism. The wish to be a lonely hermit or lighthouse keeper dramatizes her final hopelessness of finding meaningful union or communication.

It is important to note that the allusions to the second text (the store) and the resultant conflict of codes are not continued in this second stanza. Once the poem defines its particular quest, it no longer maintains the tension between perspectives which it set up at the beginning. That tension nevertheless affects our evaluation of the second stanza. Aware that for the speaker of the poem larger questions are mixed with, and seen in the terms of, the most prosaic reality, we will not read her final lament as a repetition of romantic clichés but as the complaint of someone who realizes the tensive mixture of the serious and the petty, the grand and the trivial, in the world in which we live.

In the light of this, we can see a new intertextual play taking place in the second stanza. In evoking hermits, lighthouse keepers, and a love doomed to suffering, the speaker calls to mind the tragedies and conventions of sentimental fiction. That intertextuality, however, serves mostly to underline a contrast: unlike the heroines of such fiction, this poem's speaker has taken everyday reality into account and has not fallen into conventional lamentations. In this sense, the intertextuality of the first stanza has played a crucial function: it has set up a perspective which now lets the speaker present a romantic complaint without seeming trite or naive. In a larger sense, it has allowed Fuertes to treat the old theme of the hopelessness of finding love in a new and acceptable way.

Another poem in the same book is titled **"Extraño accidente"**:

> En aquella primavera se le aflojaron los tornillos;
> en unas curvas peligrosas
> se le rompió la dirección.
> Los testigos afirmaron que se lanzó al bello,
>   precipicio
> —como a sabiendas—.
> Murió de corazón roto
> a tantos de tantos, como tantos,
> aunque continúa yendo a la oficina.
>
>   [p. 195]

Here the words and images suggest and juxtapose two distinct realities and two texts. The description of the first four lines, as well as the specific references to "tornillos," "curvas peligrosas," "precipicio," and the loss of direction, evoke an automobile accident. Less evident at the beginning, yet nonetheless present, is the suggestion of a disorienting romance. "Aflojarse los tornillos," is of course an idiomatic phrase for losing one's senses, and may recall the phrase "aflojarse(le) las rodillas," a cliché reference to the timidity of a lover. "Curvas peligrosas" covertly alludes to the figure of a woman, and the adjective "bello" in line 4 suggests that the precipice is a metaphor for a dangerous woman rather than a literal chasm. This second reality or second text of the poem becomes explicit in line 6, which makes the reader go back and see more clearly what she probably only felt or suspected when she first read the poem's beginning. Fuertes has offered us a very evident text and code which allude to an accident, and initially less evident ones which suggest a romance and gain importance in the poem's ending.

In one sense, this process makes the poem function like **"Galerías Preciadas"**: it lets Fuertes present an old subject in a novel way, avoiding the dangers of conventionalism and sentimentality. (The last three lines of the poem, were they to stand alone, would give a grim and almost moralistic vision.) In addition, its way of setting up two simultaneous texts and codes, playing with the meaning of words, and thus producing a lighter tone, suggests that the catastrophes of modern life, while serious, are also somewhat petty and comical. The scorned lover is not a noble figure but a miserable middle-class victim of something resembling a foolish automobile accident. The presence of the "accident text" imparts an air of mechanization to the love affair. In this fashion, the intertextual play suggests a second tragedy, in some ways larger than that of the protagonist; our world offers but a limited and mechanized version of archetypal catastrophes. At the end, the protagonist who keeps going to the office but is a mere shell of himself seems (some-

what like T.S. Eliot's Prufrock) a bureaucratic parody of a romantic hero. Fuertes has again woven together two texts to portray a limited tragedy of the modern world.

Whether we talk of the interplay of codes or of the presence of two texts in discussing **"Galerías Preciadas"** and **"Extraño accidente,"** we end up stressing the same effect.[10] By setting up two frames of reference and pointing in two directions at once, Fuertes has modified our normal expectations and ways of seeing old subjects (the hopelessness of finding love, a lover's catastrophe). By creating an interplay between a text and a code focused on modern reality and another focused on love, she has conveyed to us her sense of a world in which perennial human problems occur, but in ways that are peculiarly down-to-earth, comical, and fitted to the characteristics and limitations of our everyday lives.

In **"Mi suerte,"** Fuertes creates an intertextual conflict that goes in the opposite direction from the ones we have just seen. The poem begins by focusing on the universal questions of one's fate in life; then suddenly it shifts to the petty "fate" of winning a saucepan in a lottery. In this fashion it undercuts and modifies its basic philosophic text by inserting into it the everyday text of petty chance (rather than Fate):

> En la vida
> ya he hecho un poco,
> pero me queda mucho.
> En el amor,
> ya he hecho mucho,
> pero me queda un pozo.
> En la Rifa,
> todo lo perdí . . .
> —pero me tocó un cueceleches.
>
>   [p. 177]

The focus on the universal (as well as the capitalization of "Rifa" and the sweeping statement "todo lo perdí") makes us see the lottery as a cosmic metaphor for life, and tempts us to read the whole poem as a grand pronouncement.[11] When Fuertes then shocks us by the petty, everyday image of the "cueceleches," we again sense that larger questions come to the speaker (and to us) in the context of our immediate lives. This in no way destroys the symbolic level of the poem: the "cueceleches" is, in fact, a good image for the limited successes that life offers. But it functions in a dramatic and earthbound way, not in the grandiose manner we had been anticipating. A similar break in expectations occurs in " . . . Y me tengo todavía," in which a serious presentation of the monotony of life is undercut by another text—by a petty self-portrayal of the speaker: "bebo, fumo, escribo cartas / y meo una siempreviva" [p. 222].

"A San Juan de la Cruz" creates a different kind of intertextuality, setting the language and tone of the poem against those of the poetry of Saint John of the Cross:

> Querido Juanito:
> No,

si poseer poseo
el entendimiento del amor;
lo que no alcanzo
ni con amor ni con oración ni con bondad ni con
    poesía,
es ser por el amado correspondida.
Está mi alma cautiva
y al paso está cautivada
por una esquiva, mirada,
que ni miro ni me mira.
Y si salgo de vuelo
o me voy por las ramas,
sólo es para dar a la Caza caza,
me remonto y bajo rauda,
porque aún es la tierra mi sitio,
mientras que me quede un ala.

[pp. 220-21]

The colloquial tone stands, of course, in stark contrast to the elevated one of Saint John's verse. This contrast corresponds to a thematic and attitudinal one: where Saint John speaks of an idealized love, the speaker here deals with a much more ordinary one; where Saint John paints a picture of elevated lovers in perfect communion, the speaker expresses her annoyance at not being loved in return. All of this not only lets us see the difference in kinds of love and attitudes to them, but makes us feel very strongly the conflict between the whole vision of reality that underlies Saint John's work and that which is present in this poem (and, by extension, in our own everyday world).

That conflict is heightened by the use of specific words and images that echo Saint John's work but that here carry quite different meanings and implications. The references to the speaker's captive soul allude to an infatuation rather than a transcendent love; the word "esquiva" (which appears in Saint John's "Llama de amor viva") here describes a scornful lover; the image of the hunt (the main metaphor of Saint John's "Tras de un amoroso lance") seems to refer to a very earthly love chase. "Salgo de vuelo" echoes specifically the phrase "voy de vuelo" used by the Amada in Saint John's "Cántico espiritual," but it is undercut by the prosaic "me voy por las ramas," which evokes a literal picture of a bird, and at the same time is a colloquial idiom for disorientation. Other prosaic lines also help undercut any mystic echoes: the long list of efforts to move the lover in line 5 makes the quest desperate rather than significant, and the speaker's view of herself in line 15 ["me remonto y bajo rauda"] is jarringly physical.

The final effect of this textual interplay and apparent parody may be harder to define. The poem does make us feel that in this earthly reality love is very different from that described by Saint John. Yet the speaker is cognizant of the latter's transcendence, and may be expressing some desire for elevation, especially in the last line—even as she realizes that in the world in which she lives any idealism is quickly undercut. Like many other poems in *Poeta de guardia*, this one engenders a conflict which offers a complex and unusual view of a larger theme, the quest

for love, set in modern prosaic circumstances. (A similar conflict occurs in **"Empeoro y mejoro"** [pp. 181-182], where the speaker's seemingly private striving for serenity is suddenly rendered in a quotation from Fray Luis de León.)

In **"El camello (auto de los Reyes Magos)"** (pp. 240-41), Fuertes takes the biblical scene of the adoration of the Magi and gives it an entirely new focus. The poem dwells on the plight of the kings' camel, ignored and scorned by the Magi and yet finally treasured by the child Jesus, who rejects the cold gifts of gold and incense and starts playing with the camel. Fuertes here evokes a second text, the original story of the Magi in the New Testament, and uses it to create a contrast as well as a parallel. Unlike the Christ in the Bible, her child Jesus scorns the rich gifts and turns to the lowly camel—suggesting a critique of earthly values in religion. On another level, however, Fuertes's version of the story conveys in a new way what is essentially a traditional vision of Christ as interested in love rather than material possessions.

In **"El lo sabe,"** a religious subject is handled by another textual interplay. God's control over our lives is presented as if it were a petty accountant's keeping track of statistics. This not only reduces any notion of God's grandeur (fitting the book's general view of God as a very human being with whom the poet is engaged in a debate), but also captures the tedium and the lack of transcendence of our lives. Events which we normally judge individual and central become mere statistics in a file controlled by an impersonal statistician:

Porque Él lo sabe todo de antemano,
Él o ELLA, quien sea, se lo sabe.

Hay Alguien que recita de noche tu futuro,
que escribió antes del parto tu estadística . . .

Fecha de muerte tal, fecha de nacimiento . . .
Balance de besos dados . . . recibidos . . .
Total que faltan . . .
Número de amores . . .
Litros de llanto . . .
        . . . . .

En infinito archivo están nuestros "papeles";
en carpetas de hule nuestro expediente escrito;
marionetas somos,
        . . . . .

Y ni Dios con ser Dios puede rectificarse,
desdecirse,
borrar, tachar,

[pp. 207-08]

An additional complexity is introduced into the poem at the end, when the speaker wonders if this is reality or simply a perspective adopted "para calmarme." The main effect of the poem, nevertheless, lies in its dramatization of a skeptical view of reality and religious meaning.

Ni tiro, ni veneno, ni navaja is much shorter than *Poeta de guardia*, containing only thirty-two brief poems. Many deal with the theme of death and the subject of God, although the task of the poet, the issue of love, and the sterility of modern life are also touched on. The irruptions of other texts are often brief and result from the appearance of an unexpected detail, rather than from the more sustained interplays of texts or codes which we saw in *Poeta de guardia*. In **"Zoo de verbena,"** for example, a list of unusual animals in a zoo of freaks suddenly takes an unexpected turn: "En la jaula se exhibe lo nunca visto, / fue muy difícil atraparlo . . . / ¡A peseta le entrada vea al *hombre feliz!*" (p. 163). The appearance of the "happy man" brings in a whole new level and text: what seemed to be a descriptive poem turns into a philosophic statement on the impossibility of human happiness.

"La vida a veces es un río frío y seco . . ." exemplifies another kind of intertextuality. Here Fuertes evokes the traditional *carpe diem* image of life as grapes, only to give it a different value from the one normally attributed to it:

> Robemos los racimos,
> los han puesto al alcance de la mano
> —y la Esperanza tiene más alcohol que la uva—.
>
> Para pasar el río frío y seco
>   "¡Venga alegría
> señores venga alegría . . . !"
> ¡Emborrachémonos
> para la travesía!
>
> [p. 149]

By turning a traditionally serious and positive image into an invitation to drunkenness as a solution to the problems of life, the poem undercuts not only the value of this solution but that of the whole *carpe diem* vision of joyous affirmation of life. By alluding to, and turning upside down, an old image and text, it dramatizes a pessimistic rejection of a traditional and easy optimism.

Several poems in this book contain a type of intertextuality that we have not yet seen in Fuertes's poetry. They are cast in the form of other kinds of writing—telegrams, letters, file cards, examination questions. The reader is obligated to take into account her view of the kind of writing involved and somehow relate it to her view of poetry; in every case this produces disorientation, since the other writings evoked differ radically from conventional poetry in their goals and language. In most cases, this kind of intertextuality makes us feel that a superficially "anti-poetic" form can in fact best fulfill the communicative goals of some poetry.

"Telegramas de urgencia escribo" offers a good example of this kind of textual interference:

> Escribo, más que cantar cuento cosas:
> Destino: La Humanidad.
> Ingredientes: Mucha pena
>   mucha rabia
>   algo de sal.

> Forma: ya nace con ella.
> Fondo: que consiga emocionar.
> Música: la que el verso toca
>   —según lo que va a bailar—
> Técnica: (¡Qué aburrimiento!)
>
>   . . . . .
>
>   Y nace sólo el poema . . .
>   Y luego la habilidad
>   de poner aquello en claro
>   si nace sin claridad.
>
> [p. 141]

This is the first poem in *Ni tiro, ni veneno*. Like the title poem of *Poeta de guardia*, it constitutes a kind of poetics, stressing the poet's attempt to convey significant meanings rather than to follow certain formal rules or to produce decorative writing. The evocation of another kind of text, the telegram, supports its meaning perfectly. The very notion of a telegram of course contradicts the notion of an idle, profusely decorative work. In addition, the features of this particular work—its condensation, its brief disconnected sentences and phrases, its outline form—all contradict the view of poetry as a rich verbal exercise. The reader who holds this view sees her expectations reversed and is led to the poem's message. The starkness of the work and the reference to the telegram text embody and convey Fuertes's defense of a nondecorative, nondiscursive, yet profoundly meaningful poetry.

Another poem in this book, **"Sociedad de amigos y protectores"** (p. 145), is cast in the form of a public address to a society of friends of ghosts, asking them to take care of a phantom that disturbs the speaker's equilibrium. The cliché form of a speech clashes with the rather poetic image of one's problems and anxieties as a ghost; the poem also seems to allude to the view of society as a menacing protector during the Franco regime. All of this engenders a tensive view of safety and order.

Similar uses of other kinds of texts to give form to her poems can also be found in Fuertes's other books: even as early as *Todo asusta* the tragedy of a worker is evoked in a poem written as a file card in a hospital admissions office:

Ficha ingreso Hospital General

> Nombre: Antonio Martín Cruz.
> Domicilio: Vivía en una alcantarilla.
> Profesión: Obrero sin trabajo.
> OBSERVACIONES: Le encontraron moribundo.
> Padecía: Hambre
>
> [p. 135]

Apart from any intertextual effects, the stark and apparently prosaic form of the file card captures summarily the impact of the man's tragic life, making it emerge right from the work and without any didactic commentary which would weaken its effect. The reference to another kind of text, the file card, makes us explicitly conscious of the fact that this sparse writing may capture modern tragedies better than a conventional lyric poem. As in the poems that evoke or imitate other kinds of texts, Fuertes here draws on an unexpected and seemingly antipoetic form of writing to give impact to her subject and to suggest the need for new forms of poetry.

Cómo atar los bigotes de tigre does not differ radically from *Poeta de guardia* and *Ni tiro*. The social implications of many poems are more evident, and personal happenings and themes acquire, as Ynduráin has noted, more collective implications—the speaker's dilemma echoes or presages those of others.[12] Fuertes uses humor even more frequently than before, and makes more allusions to everyday scenes, events, and phrases. The juxtapositions in this book are more often formed by brief vignettes, images, and verbal twists than by the more sustained interpolations of different planes of *Poeta de guardia*, although we can find some examples of the latter. Fuertes seems to be expressing a vision similar to that of her previous book in a slightly more terse and playful way.

One poem is presented as a letter to God, filled with the prosaic clichés of middle-class letter writing and cast in a conventionally respectful tone. The insertion of this highly antipoetic text, when combined with the religious allusions, produces a parody of traditional religious images:

> Muy Señor mío:
> Hace mucho tiempo que debía haberle escrito,
> espero que sabrá perdonar y comprender mi tardanza
> cuyo motivo,
>   Usted bien sabe.
> Deseo que al recibo de estas líneas
> se encuentre bien en compañía de su Sagrada Familia
> y demás Santos de la Corte Celestial.
>
>   [pp. 287-88]

Fuertes has used the letter-writing form to shock the reader out of conventional postures taken to religion and to evoke the picture of a worldly and bourgeois divinity, fitted to our modern society and caught in the same daily dilemma as "his" people.

In "La excursión" we find another kind of intertextuality, somewhat similar to ones we have seen in earlier books. Here a text referring to the coming of death is inserted into another which apparently describes the preparations for a very ordinary trip:

> Habrá que madrugar, eso sí.
> Sin saber
>   a qué hora
>   poner
>   el despertador.
> Preparar la tartera, el bocadillo,
> las botas o el termo de café;
> y abrigarse,
>   hará frío,
> —cuatro tablas de pino no calientan—.
> Es mejor hacer una fogata con el ataúd,

> iluminar la Excursión con la Esperanza
> o quedarme durmiendo hasta la cita.
>
>   [p. 255]

The poem unfolds very slowly, using a profusion of details to describe the preparations needed for the early start of an expedition. This immerses the reader in a seemingly common happening (although she may wonder why one doesn't know what time to set the alarm for). In this fashion, the indication that the planned trip is in fact death causes a shocking break in expectations, accentuated by the indirect nature of the revelation (there is no heat in a coffin).

By forcing us to approach death as though it were a petty trip, Fuertes jars us out of our conventional solemnity in dealing with the subject. She also takes the traditional metaphor of life as a trip and gives it a completely new "realistic" dimension. Far from weakening the effect of the poem's subject, this procedure intensifies it: the coming of death is no longer an old subject, as seen in many poems we have read, but a shockingly real experience, akin to things that happen to us in our own lives. The jarring effect of this poem leads us right into the last stanza, making more credible the speaker's decision either to take an attitude of violent rebellion or to ignore and block out the coming event. This poem stands as another excellent example of how Fuertes makes intertextualities embody basic themes in new and expressive ways.

In *Sola en la sala*, Fuertes continues to deal with a variety of themes in colloquial language. She continues noting her vocation for poetry and the way in which her poems emerge from daily life ("**Carta explicatoria de Gloria**," pp. 293-94), but she places greater stress than before on the spontaneity of the process and on the variety of the resulting works ("**Este libro**," p. 294). This stance corresponds to the nature of the book itself: it contains many brief poems and tends to aphorisms and epigrams. Even more than Fuertes's earlier work, it is filled with references to modern subjects and events that range from boxing and bullfights to man's landing on the moon. Quick but penetrating psychological perceptions alternate with unusual visual images and with metaphors that capture emotional states. The intertextualities that we find in the work fit very well its epigrammatic nature, and are in almost all cases brief and unusual metaphors or unexpected combinations of image and idea. Most often they are used to describe states of emotion, as in "**Nunca se sabe**":

> Si no tuviera esperanza,
> me tiraría por la ventana;
> pero . . .
>
> ¿dónde está la esperanza y la ventana,
> si vivo en un sótano?
>
>   [p. 347]

The first stanza sets up a stock image and makes us think that we will have a traditional (maybe trite) poem about hope, presumably one with a positive ending. When the speaker switches to a more literal perspective and brings in a very different kind of text, a matter-of-fact statement that she cannot jump because she lives in a basement, she forces us to witness the undercutting of both our expectations and a poetic image and convention. All this helps highlight the poem's theme—the real frustration of a modern person who is set in such a petty world that she cannot even act with romantic desperation.

In another brief poem, Fuertes inserts a second text—an old propaganda slogan of the Franco regime—, remaking it to assert Spain's need to rise above its limitations: "Para conseguirlo, / pagarás la cuota de veinticinco o cincuenta / años de paz y riñones" (p. 355). Undeniably, however, intertextualities do not have as significant a function in this book as they did in several of Fuertes's previous ones. The more elaborate relationships between texts and the more complex visions that we found in *Poeta de guardia* are simply not a feature of *Sola en la sala*.

As Yndurán has indicated, Gloria Fuertes is very conscious of her poetic stance and goals. In every book we find some poems that deal with her poetics, and she has not hesitated to make prose statements about her work.[13] She talks about the need to write clearly, to make one's poetry deal with the main issues of life, to use it in order to convey one's emotional insights and also to help others gain such insights. Apart from any value they may have in defining poetry in general, such statements make clear the author's devotion to her art and her consciousness of her goal of creating a new and significant kind of expression. Keeping them in mind, we can see her novel use of the everyday and her way of juggling texts and producing reversals in reader expectations as a way of reaching this goal.

This becomes even clearer when we observe how Fuertes's statements about poetry and the poet give increasingly greater importance to the creative use of everyday language in poetry. "Nota Biográfica" from *Antología y poemas del suburbio,* for example, stresses the speaker's ordinary life and occupations: poetry is part of that life as well as an effort to express oneself in ordinary settings ("he publicado versos en todos los calendarios"). In the title poem of *Poeta de guardia* (p. 167), the speaker's role as poet has acquired greater transcendence: she is now the observer of and commentator on life. This vision culminates in Fuertes's view of poetry as underlying life and of her task as unearthing it, expressed in a poem from *Cómo atar los bigotes del tigre* (p. 283): "No te tapes Poesía / te reconozco en las cosas pequeñas / y en las casas grandes, / allí donde estés, daré contigo." At the same time, Fuertes stresses her need to avoid hollow forms: "no me tientes a retóricos sonetos, / vamos a hablar como siempre, / ¡o te mando de paseo!"

At about the same time, Fuertes ascribed a very high function to the writing of poetry. Answering José Batll 's 1968 questionnaire, she wrote: "Hoy mas que nunca el poeta debe escribir claro, para todo el mundo, que se le entienda, y si no le sale, que lo rompa y vuelva a la carga—de paz. Necesitamos un estado poético en el corazón

y en los países."[14] This lets us see that Fuertes's decision to use colloquial language and everyday events in her verse is no accident, but rather the result of a conscious and growing impulse to exploit such language and such events in poems both significant and accessible to all readers. The intertextualities and modifications of reader expectations are key elements in the creation of such poems. Through these techniques, Gloria Fuertes has made original and artistic use of seemingly trivial materials, and opened new directions for contemporary Spanish poetry.[15]

NOTES

[1] On the way in which social issues are handled creatively in Fuertes's poetry, see J. P. González Martín, *Poesía hispánica 1939-1969* (Barcelona: El Bardo, 1970), p. 97; Cano, *Poesía española contemporánea,* pp. 174-76; and Francisco Ynduráin "Prólogo," in Fuertes, *Antología poética 1950-1969,* pp. 26-28, 30-31.

[2] See Margaret H. Persin, "Humor as Semiosis in the Poetry of Gloria Fuertes," *Revista Hispánica Moderna,* in press; and Ynduráin, "Prólogo," p. 20.

[3] I am using "text" in its broad sense: a text is not only or necessarily a specific literary work, but any reality, recalled or read, that the reader has at her disposal and which affects her attitude to other texts that she confronts. As Jonathan Culler indicates: "A work can only be read in connection with or against other texts, which provide a grid through which it is read and structured by establishing expectations which enable one to pick out salient features and give them a structure." (*Structuralist Poetics* [Ithaca: Cornell Univ. Press, 1975] p. 139.) In the case of Fuertes's poetry, we will see how the deliberate infusion of other and conflicting texts produces intertextuality, a weaving together of texts that leads to the final meaning and experience of the work.

This broader view of intertextuality is very well defined by Culler in his more recent book, *The Pursuit of Signs,* pp. 37-39, 100-108; as well as by Roland Barthes in "From Work to Text," in *Textual Strategies,* ed. Josué V. Harari, pp. 73-81. It is especially useful in helping us to see a work as less static and more dynamic, in stressing ways in which the meanings derived by a reader emerge from a confrontation between the text at hand and previous texts. Fuertes's poems achieve their effects by denying or modifying the presuppositions of those previous texts. (On the notion of presupposition, see Culler, *Pursuit of Signs,* pp. 112-18).

[4] Fuertes's poems often depend on the reader to have a certain attitude to their subject, and then undercut that attitude to produce their effect. Following Hans Robert Jauss's formulation, we might say that these poems assume the "horizon of expectations" of a typical modern city dweller and then twist or frustrate that set of expectations. This does raise questions on the reception of these poems by readers of other times and cultures. On this topic see Jauss, "Literary History as a Challenge to Literary Theory," *New Literary History* 2 (1970): 7-37.

[5] Some of the cases of intertextuality we will see also fit the narrower definition espoused by Gustavo Pérez Firmat in "Apuntes para un modelo de la intertextualidad en la literatura," *Romanic Review* 69 (1978): 1-14. Pérez Firmat limits intertextual correspondences to those established with specific literary works, explicitly cited by the text at hand. He suggests that in these cases the reader in fact experiences a "new" text,

a product of the interplay within her consciousness of the one being read with the previous ones being evoked.

[6] On this issue see Jauss, "Literary History," pp. 7-37; and note 4 above.

[7] See "Poema," p. 55, and "Hago versos, señores!" p. 137.

[8] Ynduráin, "Prólogo," pp. 34-36.

[9] Ibid., pp. 31-33; see also Cano, *Poesía española contemporánea*, pp. 176-77.

[10] I nonetheless feel that the concept of intertexuality is the most helpful one in explaining this aspect of Fuertes's poetry. Not only does it allow us to discuss poems which suggest another text that might not have an easily definable code ("Me crucé con un entierro"); it also places appropriate stress on the way in which these poems counterpose different works and different traditions in order to produce new visions. The counterpositions we have seen in these last two poems are somewhat akin to what Carlos Bousoño has called "superposiciones" and "ruptura del sistema," since they point in two directions at once and set up two simultaneous frames of reference. (Other examples of intertexuality in Fuertes's work, however, do not fit these concepts.) See Bousoño, *Teoría de la expresión poética*, 4th ed. (Madrid: Gredos, 1966), pp. 231-34, 270-73.

[11] Persin has commented perceptively on the effect of the last line of this poem, and on the humor and meaning produced by it ("Humor as Semiosis").

[12] Ynduráin, "Prologo," pp. 36-37.

[13] Ibid., pp. 38-42; see also Fuertes's statements on her poetry in Batlló, *Antología*, pp. 337-38.

[14] Batlló, *Antología*, p. 338.

[15] As Ynduráin has noted ("Prologo," p. 42), Gloria Fuertes frequently recites and records her poetry and is very conscious of her effect on the listener. The intertextual plays and denials of reader expectations which we have seen undoubtedly contribute to this effect.

Sylvia R. Sherno (essay date 1987)

SOURCE: "Gloria Fuertes and the Poetics of Solitude," in *Anales de la literatura espanola contemporanea / Annals of Contemporary Spanish Literature*, Vol. 12, No., 1987, pp. 11-26.

[*Sherno examines the individual design of Fuertes' poetry, in which the key element of solitude, grounded in individual, personal experiences, is presented for the reader to perceive and participate in with the author.*]

From the outset of her literary career, Gloria Fuertes has distinguished herself as a poet resistant to categorization.[1] Born in 1918, Fuertes is approximately contemporaneous with Gabriel Celaya, José Hierro, Blas de Otero, and José Luis Hidalgo, poets who rose to prominence after 1944, the year of Dámaso Alonso's *Hijos de la ira*. Fuertes shares with those poets the mark of that pivotal work, apparent in expressions of an anguish both personal and communal, in the rejection of an elitist esthetic in favor of accents decidedly colloquial, conversational, prosaic, even grotesque. Still, by virtue of her very personal vision of the world and by her equally idiosyncratic way of conveying that vision, Gloria Fuertes diverges from her chronological contemporaries and has been linked to younger poets like Claudio Rodríguez, Ángel González, Francisco Brines and others who comprise what has been called the "generation of 1956-1971."[2]

Fuertes is the first to recognize her own eclecticism and uniqueness: "Fui surrealista, sin haber leído a ningún surrealista; después, aposta, 'postista'—la única mujer que pertenecía al efímero grupo de Carlos Edmundo de Ory, Chicharro y Sernesi."[3] She has called herself "antipoeta," and while the repetition in her work of mundane preoccupations, of vulgarities, and of an antirhetorical stance is on occasion reminiscent of antipoetry, her generous spirit is not given to ridicule and lacks the fundamental nihilism of antipoetry.[4] Further, whereas antipoetry represents the dissolution of the traditional lyric voice, "que de una caracterización definida y personal pasa al anonimato, la imprecisión y la ambigüedad,"[5] it is clear just from the innumerable "autobiografías" which figure so often in the body of her work and from the frequency with which she playfully injects her own name into her verses that her voice is far from anonymous, imprecise, or ambiguous.

In a poem written at the precocious age of seventeen and which later came to lend its title to her first published work, *Isla ignorada* (1950), Fuertes declared her identification with that island, "en el centro de un mar / que no me entiende, / rodeada de nada, /—sola sólo" (*OI*, 21). These early words prefigure the poet's reiterated theme of solitude and her insistence on self-definition. Fuertes is aware of what is perhaps the most salient feature of her poetry: "Reconozco que soy muy 'yoísta,'" she has allowed, "que soy muy 'glorista'" (*OI*, 22). In spite of her sincere and continuous social concerns, almost all of her poetry is self-referential since, in her view, "Lo que a mí me sucedió, sucede o sucederá, es lo que ha sucedido al pueblo, es lo que ha ocurrido a todos" (*OI*, 22). The persistent presence of her original and unique poetic voice is the unifying thread that runs through all of her work, and the imposition of her voice is, in fact, the manner in which she seeks to confront the solitude which lies at the core of even her earliest verses. It is the very reassertion and recreation of herself as a figure "rodeada de nada" that constitutes her poetry's most constant theme.

Through her verses Gloria Fuertes arrives at a kind of poetics of her own individualistic design: the title "Poética" occurs almost as frequently as does "Autobío." She knows precisely what poetry should do and be: it must thrill, disconcert, and amuse, be a warning against injustices and "una aspirina inmensa" to relieve pain. Poetry must, above all, "poblarnos la soledad." The poet assumes roles to invite our participation in this enterprise. She becomes variously a temptress to lure us, a clown to make us laugh (and cry), a terrorist to coerce us. Whatever the mask, Fuertes' supreme purpose is to confront *la nada* by the vehicle of her poetry. For this purpose she opens her ample embrace to include her readers as active participants in her poetry, thus joining with them to inhabit, communally, the void.

The solitude which Fuertes so poignantly depicts derives from the failure of personal love, the rejection by others of her affection, and her own inability to return love once proffered. It also springs from the poet's very real sense of herself as an anomalous figure who leads "una vida extraña," a "fabuloso desastre," a "tierna amazona," an outlandish creature isolated from others by nature and by design:

> Vivo sola, cabra sola
> —que no quise cabrito en compañía—,
> cuando subo a lo alto de este valle,
> siempre encuentro un lirio de alegría.
> Y vivo por mi cuenta, cabra sola;
> que yo a ningún rebaño pertenezco.
> Si sufrir es estar como una cabra,
> entonces sí lo estoy, no dudar de ello.
>
> (*OI*, 212)

Much as she views herself, Gloria Fuertes envisions solitude as a bizarre personage upon whom she confers some of the aura of a character in an allegory. Intriguingly evocative of the Arcipreste de Hita's Trotaconventos, this personified Solitude challenges conventional ideas of morality, respectability, even femininity, just as the poet herself demands that the reader likewise weigh preconceived notions about what is the proper scope of poetry:[6]

> La Soledad que yo tengo
> es una mujer fatal,
> buena—como buena puta—
> me lo dice y va y se va.

Like a gypsy, this phantasmagorical *belle dame sans merci* is not devoid of her own crafty charms which invite the poet to join in her *soleá*, her dance of melancholy and of hope:

> Semivestida de verde
> me excita la soledad
> esta noche va y me dice:
> —me dice y luego se va—,
> "que me merezco otra cosa
>   —que vendrá—"
>
> ¡Qué divina está esta noche
> la zorra la Soledad!
>
> (*OI*, 186)

Fuertes' solitude coincides as well with an acutely-felt sense of nothingness which assumes such various shapes in her work as the spaces representing missed connections between the poet and those around her, the hollow which she equates with death and with God. It is an oblivion, alternately longed for and dreaded, "en el fondo del fondo de la botella" (*OI*, 312). It is the emptiness of a gnawing spiritual hunger: the poet declares herself "asténica y anoréxica," conditions infinitely less tolerable to her than "estar en la India, / pasando un hambre distinta"

(*OI*, 302). Fuertes imagines her loneliness as "la tristeza del átomo solo / sin su molécula" (*OI*, 355) and as the stab of pain to the heart—"no le claves ya más alfileres," she pleads—which is very like the minute but no less intense wound which a pin inflicts upon entering a pincushion. She feels herself open, like "un ojal inmenso, / que no encuentra botón / donde abrocharse para siempre" (*HG*, 198). The images, whether that of an empty refrigerator, a buttonhole, or a pincushion, are concrete and homely, even banal. They are therefore easily accessible to the reader, who might expect, and indeed first experience, a momentary comfort upon meeting such everyday objects. Yet their very plainness and accessibility make more identifiable and in this way less avoidable, the association with the emotional and spiritual void which the poet intends. The ultimate effect is unexpected and disconcerting: the poet, herself like "una mujer fatal," does what "la zorra Soledad" does to her, luring us, her unwitting but not unwilling readers, into the void, and thus accompanied, she equips herself and us to confront it.

In this poem which is an extended and complex play on words, Fuertes likens her solitary state to that of a choking singer or a drowning swimmer:

> Es mejor no tener nada que Nada.
>
> ¡Nada que te ahogas cacho cabrón!
>
> ¡Respira y canta que sigue el orfeón,
> te pagan por cantar!
> Y a nadie importa nadie
> y menos tu naufragio . . .
>
> ¡Nada!
>
> Todos los santos tienen octava
> y Beethoven novena.
>
> (*OI*, 307)

The poem evokes the helplessness of a lone swimmer immersed in the silent world of surrounding waters; of a singer deafened, perhaps like Beethoven, amid the muffled sounds of a chorus. The entire piece is an excellent example of what Andrew Debicki calls "reversal of expectations" resulting from the interrelationship or superimposition of various, often disparate texts.[7] Beginning with the title, repeated in the first line of the poem, Fuertes cues the reader (or at least appears to do so) that the poem will deal with two not notably contradictory but still somewhat divergent concepts: "no tener nada," a reference to lack of possessions, and "Nada," nothingness, the void, suitably capitalized to suggest the more transcendental state of spiritual isolation. The poet opines that material poverty is preferable to the abstraction of a more overwhelming and all-encompassing nothingness. This observation might at first seem in danger of collapsing from lack of inspiration, or under the weight of its own unoriginality.[8] But the reader is forced to attention by the following exclamation: "¡Nada que te ahogas cacho cabrón!" Fuertes now introduces a third meaning to the word "nada," this time alluding to the verb "nadar," and in so doing deliberately upsets the reader's expectations of further philosophical musings, hurling at him instead not only insulting vulgarities but the bewildering command to swim because he is drowning. The implicit humor of the word play collides with the sobriety of tone already established, and disorients the reader, just as a drowning swimmer is disoriented.[9]

Having set up this disturbing interplay of meanings, the poet heartlessly proceeds to confound her reader still further with a second command: "¡Respira y canta que sigue el orfeón, / te pagan por cantar!" The notion of breathing would seem a logical extension of the act of swimming, but the order to sing is indeed a new twist and the cause of further befuddlement. By the time he arrives at the final exclamation, "¡Nada!", the reader, unlikely to know which of the meanings to attach to the word, is now quite literally at sea.

Nevertheless, the closing lines of the poem provide a clue. By reversing the logical associations of a musical term, "octava," with Beethoven, and of a religious term, "novena," with the saints, the final words point out the chasm that lies between extraordinary souls who have achieved exalted status, and the poet, an ordinary being who possesses nothing and matters to no one. To understand the relationship between these closing words (an apparently flippant and disconnected comment about Beethoven and the saints) and the rest of the poem, we are obliged to retrace our steps. By rereading, we can hear once again the voice of the poet calling attention by devious means to what is her fundamental concern: the threat of nothingness. The final verses, it becomes clear, are an anxious comment by a poet (not, after all, wholly unlike a singer) who fears being lost to oblivion, not to material poverty or to capricious rejection by those who "pagan por cantar" and who in any case are indifferent to her fate. "Nada" is a command directed towards herself, a mandate for the poet to write poetry and thereby to save herself from drowning in a sea of nothingness. The end of the poem thus underscores the maze-like confusion of codes which characterizes both the literal meaning of the poem and the underlying message which must be read between the lines.[10] Fuertes stops us at every turn, and deliberately causes us to lose our bearings. Subtly, uncannily, even subversively,—she forces us to experience what she herself most fears—the encroaching blackness of solitude and the silence of the void.

This silence best expresses the nothingness against which Fuertes' poetic voice struggles to be heard. Indeed, all of her poetry might accurately be described as a counterpoint of silence and sound, or as an alternation between the presence and absence of voice. The poet perceives her verses as growing out of silence: "Al calor del silencio se maduran mis versos" (*OI*, 308), she announces in a poem composed of this single statement. Fuertes, of course, writes many such "poems" which consist of one or two verses, usually pithy observations on the human condition, or flashes of insight and discovery, as in this instance of self-revelation: "El poeta al sentir / descubre todo lo que no le han enseñado" (*OI*, 300). Many of

these short poems are similarly aphoristic in nature, reminiscent of Moratín or of the eighteenth-century fabulists, or resemble Japanese *haiku,* in which poetic expression is very much compressed to demonstrate a similar interplay of silence and sound, and to oblige as well the reader's involvement in the act of poetic creation.[11] Fuertes' affinity for these short poetic forms is evident from her earliest work, when in *Isla ignorada* she designated them "Momentos." *Poeta de guardia* (1968), the collection that assured her serious critical regard,[12] includes an entire section of verses called "Mini-poemas," although these are significantly longer than the epigrammatic verses which comprise much of *Sola en la sala* (1973) and *Historia de Gloria* (1980).[13] Many are in fact mere repetitions of the titles, as if to indicate the conscious suppression of the poetic process, or to suggest that the instantaneous bolt of inspiration, emotion, or awareness is alone emblematic of that process. José Luis Cano observes that Fuertes

> suele huir tanto de la retórica como del
> subjectivismo divagatorio. Su técnica es
> la vieja técnica popular de ir al grano,
> de contar en pocas palabras lo que pasa
> en el mundo y lo que les pasa a sus amigos
> —reales o fantasmas—y a ella misma.[14]

In one of her many "Poéticas," Fuertes questions the need for an excess of words, "si ya está todo dicho" (*OI*, 190), and even more directly she affirms:

> Hay que decir lo que hay que decir pronto,
> de pronto,
> visceral
> del tronco;
> con las menos palabras posibles
> que sean posibles los imposibles.
>
> (*HG*, 120)

Gloria Fuertes uses "the least words possible" to approximate the silence which for her is another name for *la nada*. Significantly, many of these one- or two-line verses do not conform to conventional definitions of poetic expression: more than once the poet herself intimates that her verses are not, in fact, poetry. When Fuertes writes, for example, "Estoy mejor que ayer, / hoy lloré menos" (*HG*, 76), or when she observes that "El pobre no tiene la culpa de ser pobre, el rico, sí" (*HG*, 90), she has pruned the lines of rhetoric and distilled the message to such a point that it seems utterly lacking in depth, mystery, or in any meaning beyond the surface. To look beneath this surface is to discover the vast emptiness, the nothingness, which is for Gloria Fuertes the inescapable fact of human existence.

To the extent that Fuertes effectively absorbs the silence of *la nada* into these very brief poems, and to the extent that she finds recourse as well in presumably extrapoetic forms, she oversteps the bounds of the conventional and flirts with antipoetry. But unlike the antipoet, she does not parody traditional poetry in an effort to destroy what the antipoet deems artificial and hermetic.[15] Hers is not a destructive art; rather, Fuertes attempts to erect in her poetry bridges of communication. To that end, she selects forms that are odd, most certainly, but also endearing, clearly designed to narrow the gaps in communication and to extend herself to her fellow man. She writes, for example, letters, both to herself and others; telegrams, radio messages, commercial announcements, recipes, menus, even reprimands. The sound of the telephone is important to Fuertes: "el teléfono que no cesa," she describes it by way of gentle tribute to Miguel Hernández' *El rayo que no cesa*. So too are doorbells and stairways, signs of connection which she perceives as means of breaking through the isolation and the silence.

Those extrapoetic verses, marked by brevity of mode and urgency of message, are destined to communicate over the silence. The one- and two-line poems, characterized by a lack of artifice and a virtual suppression of message, are meant to echo the silence of the void. Balanced against these minimalist verses of self-imposed authorial restraint is another whole body of poems—longer, verbose, often repetitious and enumerative—in which the poetic voice serves not to imitate but to counter and fill the void. These longer poems take the form, for example, of litanies, as in "Letanía de los montes de la vida," a poetic transcription of the Beatitudes. Here the poet casts a typically benign and humorous glance at humanity in high and low stations, including poets and thieves, virgins and cynics. In a far different vein is "A la muerte," a veritable catalogue of insults aimed at the arch-foe death, in the same vituperative spirit that the Arcipreste de Talavera directed against women.[16] Among these longer verses figures also a group of poems dedicated simply to the repetition of sounds, from which the following brief selections will serve as examples:

Manolo mío:
    Mi madrileño marchoso,
maduro melocotón maleable,
macedonia mascaré mañana,
mortadela moscatel mío

(*HG*, 80)

Todo tiene eñe en España,
¡hasta España!

Eñe el coño o la cigüeña que nos trae,
eñe la cizaña o la guadaña que nos lleva,
eñe la niña que nos enfría, . . .
o eñe de niño, que somos todos,
los que aún latimos con un poema.

(*HG*, 115)

Fea, fascista y fulana,
formidable era de cuerpo
(frío me dejó en el alma);
flato, flojera y más efes
tenía por la mañana

(*HG*, 124)

De este molesto caparazón
la única salida de mi prisión
cuando me encierra tu despreocupación,

es el escape de mi inspiración,
es la escalera de mi creación,
es hacer poesía con lo que vomita mi corazón.

(*HG*, 125)

To be sure, these protracted verses, at first glance absurd and incoherent, diverge sharply from more conventional definitions of poetry. But the oddly naive repetitions, which the reader might at first dismiss as the failed efforts of an unschooled artist, contain their own veiled meaning. If we listen carefully to the sounds of the hammering alliterations, we hear the letterwriter sending her urgent, passionate message; the rejected lover, desperately finding excuses to reject in turn; the child conjuring up visions of birth, death, Spain. We hear at last the poet, whose poetry provides her the only escape from the prison of her own solitude. When later, in the epigraph to **"Lo, lo lógico,"** Fuertes says "hasta tartamudeo por lo que voy a decir" (*HG*, 183), it becomes clear that the significance of these "poems" resides in the transmitting, however faltering, of sound waves across the silence, and that that sound is the voice of the poet.

The distinctive sound of Fuertes' voice is finally what we come to identify unquestionably with the conception she has of her own poetry. The inherent kindliness of her voice is conveyed most transparently in her portrayal of the street hawker in **"Puesto del Rastro"**:

—Hornillos eléctricos brocados bombillas
discos de Beethoven sifones de selt
tengo lamparitas de todos los precios,
ropa usada vendo en buen uso ropa
trajes de torero objetos de nácar,
miniaturas pieles libros y abanicos.
Braseros, navajas, morteros, pinturas.
Pienso para pájaros, huevos de avestruz.
Incunables tengo gusanos de seda
hay cunas de niño y gafas de sol.
Esta bicicleta aunque está oxidada es de buena
    marca.
Muchas tijeritas, cintas bastidor.
Entren a la tienda vean los armarios,
tresillos visillos mudas interiores,
hay camas cameras casi sin usar.
Artesas de pino forradas de estaño.
Güitos en conserva,
óleos de un discípulo que fue de Madrazo.
Corbatas muletas botas de montar.
Maniquíes tazones cables y tachuelas.
Zapatos en buen uso, santitos a elegir,
tengo santas Teresas, San Cosmes y un San Bruno,
palanganas alfombras relojes de pared.
Pitilleras gramófonos azulejos y estufas.
Monos amaestrados, puntillas y quinqués.
Y vean la sección de libros y novelas,
la revista francesa con tomos de Verlaine,
con figuras posturas y paisajes humanos.
Cervantes Calderón el Oscar y Papini
son muy buenos autores a duro nada más.
Estatuas de Cupido en todos los tamaños
y este velazqueño tapiz de salón,

vea qué espejito, mantas casi nuevas,
sellos importantes, joyas . . .

(*OI*, 66-67)

The poet-vendor exalts her merchandise, objects of dubious value commonly disdained by those of higher social status. She is properly proud of her wares—the ostrich eggs, the almost-new beds, the figurines and rusted bicycles—is genuinely fond of their modest virtues, as she is fond of those who would buy them. She invests these objects with their own poignant dignity despite, or because of, their value to souls of less refined sensibilities and tastes. Moreover, Fuertes expands her readers' sights to adjust to her own generous notions regarding the proper domain of poetry. She is less interested in the finely-turned phrase—"no me tientes a retóricos sonetos"—than in poetry which she recognizes "en las cosas pequeñas." For her, it is perfectly suitable for poetry to be banal, eccentric, vulgar to the point of kitsch. Included among her titles, after all, are **"Camp," "Minicursi," "Almas de Duralex,"** and **"Virgen de plástico,"** and it is true that like "the connoisseur of Camp," Gloria Fuertes manifestly delights in the "commonest pleasures, in the arts of the masses."[17]

Beyond the enumeration of objects, among which poetry must be counted as yet another commodity, what we most remember from "Puesto del Rastro" is the pervasive voice of Gloria Fuertes.[18] The voice that carries through all of her poetry is many-faceted. For example, she characterizes herself with Franciscan humility as an all-seeing eye:[19]

Porque yo, tan mínima, sé tantas cosas,
y mi cuerpo es un ojo sin fin
con el que para mi desventura veo todo.

(*OI*, 76)

She is ever vigilant, waiting in silent expectation, a "poeta de guardia," "sola en la sala." That is why we see her, again and again, in a characteristically contemplative pose, "esperando el coche de línea," "sentada en una silla dibujando," "yo misma sobre las baldosas," "aquí estoy, clavada a la silla." Poetry and life are for her the same private experience, a silent and mysterious process by which she arrives at a state of inner awareness.

In **"Prologuillo"** (*HG*, 57), the initial poem of Fuertes' most recent collection, *Historia de Gloria*, the diminutive of the title reflects the simplicity and unpretentiousness of its author. Yet these qualities are not without a concomitant sureness of self. Even as she questions the nature of her efforts—"Los poemas (¿son poemas?)"— she is quick to assure us that the book we are beginning has been written with the utmost sincerity and love. Paraphrasing Walt Whitman, she avers, "Esto no es un libro, es una mujer."[20] This declaration unlocks a series of interconnected texts or realities. It recalls Whitman's literal use of the word "man" in the original quotation to mean himself specifically, as well as the openheartedness with which he extended the word to all of humanity. Fuertes amplifies our understanding of humanity by insisting on her own womanhood as representative of humankind's feminine component. Her vision embraces all of these meanings since her book, she tells us, is not a book, but rather the fullest expression of its author's personal integrity.

That integrity is manifold and complex. Juxtaposed against the picture of a silent, solitary figure is a converse image: not Gloria Fuertes, humble and self-effacing, but Gloria Fuertes, bold, even larger-than-life; not the meditative, seated spectator but the aggressive participant. Here is the poet in **"Autoprólogo,"** presenting herself to the readers of *Historia de Gloria*:

Un barco atraca en un puerto.
Un terrorista atraca en un Banco.
Yo os atraco con una ternura de cañones recortados
para que me entreguéis vuestra atención.

—Esto es un atraco,
¡Manos unidas!
A punto de poema vengo a asaltar
corazones cerrados,
a robaros la indiferencia.
Si al salir por esta puerta (libro)
os dejo "tocados,"
Perdón (serán rasguños de amor sin importancia).

(*HG*, 57)

Once again, the poet intermingles strikingly different texts, disparate levels of reality which turn on the various senses of the verb "atracar." The poem begins with the relatively peaceful image of a ship pulling into harbor, an image which does nothing to dislodge our anticipation at beginning the book. But the serenity of the scene is instantly disrupted by the intrusion of a terrorist robbing a bank. The unexpectedness of this new image provides exactly the jolt that Fuertes wishes us to experience. The lines are meant to shock us out of our indifference, and to dispel any prior thoughts we may have about the tranquil and dignified nature of poetry. The poet takes on the role not of the gentle guide and companion, but of the terrorist who commandeers her unsuspecting readers' attention. Fuertes will not be eluded, even if it means assaulting us "con una ternura de cañones recortados." Even so, poetry is a tender subversion. "¡Manos unidas!," Fuertes exclaims, slyly compelling us to accept the comradeship which is one of the aims of her poetry. We are forced to see poetry not as mere passive introspection, but as a confrontation and an attack on closed minds and hearts. It will not leave us unscathed, even though the poet reverts, at the close of the poem, to her more recognizable attitude of humility by begging her hostages' forgiveness for wounds inflicted in the name of love.

Central too to our grasp of the poem is the unavoidable realization that the enforced, though tender, relationship established between poet and readers implies that poetry is not just a solitary activity but a public one as well. When Fuertes portrays herself "sola en la sala," she absorbs and internalizes her solitude. By confronting us now, "a punto de poema," she obliges us to join with her in externalizing the inner drama of solitude.

The curious and paradoxical commingling of inner awareness and outer experience summarizes Fuertes' conception of her poetry and the sense of nothingness which informs it. "Aquí estoy expuesta como todos," she says later, confirming her isolation but recognizing it as a communal experience. Gloria Fuertes is willing to expose herself, much as an actor does on the stage. In fact, when she says of existence, "Esto, es Teatro," she makes of it a public spectacle raised to the level of ritual and therefore possessed of an aura of timelessness. She perceives life as "la gran Función," an immense game of risk whose stakes are mystery and silence. Rather than succumbing to the impossibility of *la nada,* she openly and publicly embraces the impossible and, in the titles of her poetry, she would have us do the same: she advises us to "beber hilo," like madmen; to fear "ni tiro, ni veneno, ni navaja"; she tells us how to "atar los bigotes al tigre." To accomplish these harrowing feats—to defy, in short, the impossible—the poet assumes a series of guises which instill her with daring. She calls herself "atleta-poeta," appearing now as a boxer, now a surfer. She is often a bullfighter—since in that capacity she is most like God, "Torero nuestro de cada día," staving off the void which is God's inverse form. She clothes herself as an astronaut, surrounded by a crushing infinity, and as a dancer of tangos, that very dramatic, even ritualized dance of seduction. Not surprisingly, among the faces Gloria Fuertes presents are those of the circus clown, whose "místico . . . es reír." This incarnation is peculiarly suited to her, since it blends the qualities of humor and pathos which so often co-exist in her work. In another metamorphosis Fuertes is a magician who finds doves under her petticoat, and makes poetry appear or disappear. She transforms herself into a mime, gesticulating at the silence, and into a wild animal trainer, whose purpose is to "domesticar al destino. / Amaestrar el deseo" (*HG,* 247). She becomes a tightrope artist, "crucificado en el aire," suspended over the vast hollow below.

The tango, the bullring, the circus, infinite space: the poet enters realms of confrontation which nonetheless house a center of stillness and mystery. By means of her various roles, she becomes a monumentalized figure and her voice a hyperbolic "ay atroz" resounding in the silence. Through her poetry, Fuertes achieves a singular luminescence of character which is itself a kind of apotheosis:

> Yo,
> remera de barcas
> ramera de hombres
> romera de almas
> rimera de versos,
> Ramona,
>   pa' servirles.

(OI, 223)

Gloria Fuertes is ever willing to dare the impossible—to become everything—to fill *la nada.* This is, finally, the way she envisions her poetry: as a perpetual unfolding of herself and a continual challenge—a laughing defiance, a taming, a seduction—of solitude.

NOTES

[1] Among the works consulted for the present study are the following: Andrew P. Debicki, *Poetry of Discovery: The Spanish Generation of 1956-1971* (Lexington: The University Press of Kentucky, 1982); Pablo González Roads, "Introducción," in Gloria Fuertes' *Historia de Gloria* (Madrid: Cátedra, 1980); Francisco Ynduráin, "Prólogo," in Gloria Fuertes' *Antología poética 1950-1969* (Barcelona: Plaza y Janés, 1970).

[2] Debicki (p. 18) ties Gloria Fuertes to this generation for the "intertextuality and the way of conveying meaning" exemplified by her poetry.

[3] Gloria Fuertes, *Obras incompletas* (Madrid: Cátedra, 1977), p. 22. I have used this text and also *Historia de Gloria* (Madrid: Cátedra, 1980). The former collection is a compilation of *Isla ignorada* (Madrid: Musa Nueva, 1950); *Aconsejo beber hilo* (Madrid: Arquero, 1954); *Todo asusta* (Caracas: Lírica Hispana, 1958); *Ni tiro, ni veneno, ni navaja* (Barcelona: El Bardo, 1955); *Poeta de guardia* (Barcelona: El Bardo, 1968); *Cómo atar los bigotes al tigre* (Barcelona: El Bardo, 1969); and *Sola en la sala* (Zaragoza: Javalambre, 1973). Subsequent parenthetical references are to *Obras incompletas* (*OI*) or *Historia de Gloria* (*HG*).

Pablo González Rodas cites Félix Grande's definition of *postismo* as "un movimiento estético cuya audacia y frescura expresivas significaron, aparte de la aventura de lenguaje más joven y rigurosa, el único vínculo profundo con el surrealismo desde nuestro país" ("Introducción" to *Historia de Gloria,* p. 30).

[4] See Paul W. Borgeson, Jr., "Lenguaje hablado / lenguaje poético: Parra, Cardenal y la antipoesía," *Revista iberoamericana* (Jan.-June 1982) 48 (118-119), pp. 383-89; and Iván M. Carrasco, "La antipoesía: escritura de la impotencia expresiva," *Estudios filológicos* 17 (1982), pp. 67-76.

[5] Carrasco, p. 76.

[6] Margaret H. Persin has made illuminating comments about this poem, "Sola con Esperanza," in "Humor as Semiosis in the Poetry of Gloria Fuertes," *Recent Spanish Poetry and the Role of the Reader* (Lewisburg: Bucknell University Press, 1987). See especially pp. 128-29.

[7] Debicki, in *Poetry of Discovery,* dedicates a chapter to Fuertes entitled "Intertexuality and Reversal of Expectations."

On the complex problem of intertextuality, see Julia Kristeva, *Semiotikè: Recherches pour une sémanalyse* (Paris: Seuil, 1969); Michael Riffaterre, *Semiotics of Poetry* (Bloomington: Indiana University Press, 1978); Gérard Genette, *Palimpsestes: La littérature au second degré* (Paris: Seuil, 1982).

Regarding the concept of "superposiciones," the reader should consult Carlos Bousoño, *Teoría de la expresión poética,* 5th ed. (Madrid: Gredos, 1970), pp. 303-36.

[8] Nancy Mandlove discusses the recycling of cliches in "Used Poetry: The Trans-parent Language of Gloria Fuertes and Ángel González," *Revista canadiense de estudios hispánicos,* Vol. vii, No. 2 (invierno 1983), pp. 301-06.

[9] On the subject of humor in Gloria Fuertes, see José Luis Cano, "Humor y ternura en la poesía de Gloria Fuertes," *Poesía española contemporánea: Las generaciones de posguerra* (Madrid: Guadarrama, 1974), pp. 174-80; and Timothy J. Rogers, "The Comic Spirit in the Poetry of

Gloria Fuertes," *Perspectives on Contemporary Literature,* Vol. 7 (1981), pp. 88-97. See too Margaret H. Persin's "Humor as Semiosis in the Poetry of Gloria Fuertes."

[10] Mandlove (p. 301) uses the term "trans-parent language" to refer to "those poems in which the reader must see through the apparent message, must read between the lines to perceive the silence, *la nada,* behind the poem."

[11] Joaquín González Muela associates Fuertes with the tradition of Moratín, the eighteenth-century *fabulistas,* and the *sainete* of Ramón de la Cruz. "Gloria Fuertes, 'poeta de guardia,'" in *La nueva poesía española* (Madrid: Alcalá, 1973), pp. 13-29.

[12] See González Muela in the work cited.

[13] Gloria Fuertes states in her prologue to *Obras incompletas* (p. 31): "Cuando escribí *Sola en la sala* yo estaba por primera vez enferma, tenía mucha prisa, y decía lo que tenía que decir con la rapidez de un dardo, un navajazo, una caricia." In her own prologue to *Obras incompletas,* p. 31.

[14] Cano, "Humor y ternura . . . ," p. 176.

[15] See Borgeson, pp. 385-86 and Carrasco, p. 69.

[16] Rubén Benítez links this poem to the medieval "danza de la muerte" as well as "los versos de escarnio y de maldecir" ("El maravilloso retablo popular de Gloria Fuertes," *Mester,* Vol. 9 [enero 1980], pp. 29-30).

[17] Susan Sontag, "Notes on 'Camp,'" in *A Susan Sontag Reader* (New York: Vintage, 1983), p. 116.

[18] Debicki (p. 83) discusses a similar poem, "El vendedor de papeles o el poeta sin suerte," in the light of opposing texts which break down the barriers between poetry and everyday life.

[19] Benítez, p. 25.

[20] The original words of Walt Whitman are as follows: "Camerado this is no book, / Who touches this touches a man." "So long!" in *Leaves of Grass,* ed. Sculley Bradley and Harold W. Blodgett (New York: Norton, 1973), pp. 503-06, l. 53-54.

Margaret Persin (essay date 1988)

SOURCE: "Humor as Semiosis in the Poetry of Gloria Fuertes," in *Revista Hispanica Moderna,* Vol. XLI, No. 2, December, 1988, pp. 143-57.

[Persin discusses Fuertes' manipulation of humor—linguistic and semiotic—to expand her readers' awareness of the various levels of meaning in her work.]

Gloria Fuertes forms part of a group of poets who became active in Spain in the 1950s and 1960s.[1] Similar to that of Dámaso Alonso, with its iconoclastic tone, her poetry generally is devoid of traditional poetic diction and tropes; her texts are written in the everyday language of ordinary existence, with its disposition toward slang, ellipsis, and most importantly, humor. Although humor is present in all of the poetry of Gloria Fuertes, her ability

to elicit and control in a masterly fashion the particular reader response of laughter and make it a part of the aesthetic experience is most evident in her later books of verse, most especially in *Poeta de guardia* (1968) and *Cómo atar los bigotes al tigre* (1969).[2] Indeed Fuertes herself acknowledges the importance of humor in her poetry, since one of her most recent works contains a reference to this very human perspective in its title, *Historia de Gloria* (*Amor, humor y desamor*) (1980).[3]

The humor in Gloria Fuertes' poetry functions on two levels. On the first level, the language of humor refers only to itself: the reader laughs at the poet's tricks, changes, and foolery on the linguistic plane. This brand of humor may include puns, double-entendres, intertextual incongruities, and changes in language level. On the second or semiotic level, Fuertes' humor goes beyond the text and encourages the reader to see not only her poetry but also the reality that it wishes to communicate in a new light. Through humor, whether linguistic or semiotic, Fuertes is able to broaden the reader's experience by allowing an intellectual distancing to take place. From the vantage point of such distance the reader is able to become detached enough from the scene or event presented to make an intellectual judgment, and also to see a higher level of meaning.[4]

Of the two types of humor that function within the poetry of Gloria Fuertes, the first is on the linguistic level and is usually self-referential in nature.[5] One can see examples of this type of humor in Fuertes' play on words, her intentional verbal slips, and her irrational combinations of words in the surrealist mode.[6] The purpose of this first type of humor, which usually is presented in quick and efficient doses, is to surprise and catch the attention of the reader. As Fuertes states in her introduction to *Obras incompletas*, "Es necesario obtener comunión-comunicación con el lector u oyente para conseguir conmover y sorprender." (30) The response of a smile, a chuckle, or a laugh is spontaneous. Fuertes appeals to the ligher side of human nature in order to manipulate the reader into an accepting stance when confronted with her poetry.

Examples of this first type of humor abound in Fuertes' work. In *Poeta de guardia*, her opening poems deal with the poet's function. In **"Aquí estoy expuesta como todos"** (169) she begins:

> Aquí estoy expuesta como todos,
> con una mano ya en el otro mundo,
> con una suave cuerda en la garganta
> que me da música y me quita sangre.
>
> (ll. 1-4)

The use of the word *cuerda* juxtaposes the image of both murder and music. The incongruity of these two images puts the reader off balance. Can the speaker be taken seriously? But it is precisely this imbalance that the poet wishes to emphasize, for in the remainder of the poem she points to the incongruities of her own existence.

> Nos desprecian los jefes, se nos ríen
> detrás los empleados,

y los perros nos siguen por las calles.
Que yo tengo de santo y de mendigo
esto de amar a un ser sobre las cosas
esto de no tener nunca zapatos
y esto de que Dios baje por peinarme.

(ll. 14-20)

Through this linguistic word play, the speaker sets the tone of the text. And the use of tone is integral to the whole of Fuertes' artistic intention.[7] Also concerning the poet's function is the poem **"Yo"** (223) of the same collection:

Yo,
remera de barcas
ramera de hombres
romera de almas
rimera de versos,
Ramona,
        pa' servirles.

The speaker describes herself with only a given name in the penultimate line of verse, and offers a standard statement connoting servitude, "pa' servirles," in its colloquial pronunciation. This mode of presentation, combined with the clever linguistic word play on the various occupations, allows Fuertes not only to set a playful mood, but also to make a statement about her beliefs. The poet is a worker, a servant to those around her. It is her duty to sing the song of the community. By casting the speaker into an inferior position, Fuertes increases the distance between the reader and the text, and thus also increases the probability that the reader will be able to see a second level of meaning which is more profound: the poet must be the bard of the cultured as well as the working class. Moreover, the female poet must take her rightful place as the representative voice of a given social context and milieu. Fuertes here sets in motion the mechanism of intertextuality. Her stance, that of an unconventional poet, encourages the reader to judge her poetry in a much broader cultural context. On one level, her work may indeed be read and appreciated by the uneducated. But on another level, the more sophisticated reader cannot but recognize and appreciate in it the resonances of traditional Spanish popular poetry, which has its origins in the early Middle Ages.

In *Cómo atar los bigotes al tigre* Fuertes continues to make use of puns as well as verbal slips in order to attract and then retain the reader's attention. In the brief poem **"Advertencia"** (266) the finality of death is contrasted with the continuity of a very real urban existence. But this contrast is made only after the speaker has set the tone through a humorous detailing of the physical effects of death:

Cuando estés recién muerto,
aún con la tibia tibia,
aún con las uñas cortas,
querrás hacer algo
—lo que podías hacer ahora—,
y ya habrán cerrado las tiendas y portales

y ya será muy tarde para llegar a tiempo
a los que hoy te aman.

Because of the comic note that is struck, the speaker makes it easier for the reader to contemplate a message which is quite didactic in nature. The distance effect of humor allows Fuertes to moralize without threatening the reader. One must laugh at the vivid description of death and its effects upon corporal existence, but also take heed of the advice which accompanies the speaker's gallows humor. The juxtaposing of comic elements with more serious ones lessens the terror of death's approach and allows the speaker to emphasize earthly duties before it is too late.

In the poem **"Enfermera de pulpos"** (286), the speaker adopts a playful tone. The title gives the impression that the speaker will focus on the role of the female as helper, soother, and recuperative muse in the life of the male octopus/poet. Through humor, Fuertes introduces a novel, simultaneous juxtaposition *and* inversion, based on the ink expended by both poet and octopus:

Ellos viven en la mar
sin pecado terrenal
—sin mancharse con trilita—,
ellos viven como tú y como yo
de la tinta.
Los envidio por los brazos,
pues pueden al mismo tiempo
tres abrazos. Los pulpos
para el amor son siniestros
según un sabio de Harvard.

     . . . . .

Las pulpas,
        tocan el arpa
        por la tarde.

It should be noted that in this very unlikely comparison between octopus and poet, the speaker makes a very clear distinction between the masculine and the feminine. The former is identified with the libidinous and potentially lethal aspects of physical love ("Los pulpos / para el amor son siniestros") [ll. 8-9], as well as the coldly calculating, scientific aloofness of academia ("según un sabio de Harvard") [l. 10]. She sets apart the feminine component typographically on the page by means of ellipsis, signalling perhaps the separation and lack of societal acceptance of the female bard. But this separation may also serve a higher purpose: it could indeed indicate that the female poet is more in tune with her being and creative animus, and now both prepared and willing to go against the traditional (patriarchal) model of woman as object rather than creator of art. She is neither swayed nor sullied by the sophomoric urges of sexuality or the fleeting adulation of sycophantic admirers, and is thus more capable of personifying both the lyric muse *and* the poet who receives that inspiration. Poetry written by men has become too cold, too official, too removed from daily experience. The feminine voice on the other hand, remains true to the eternal poetic ideal. The poem ends enigmatically with the image of the female octopus, harp and music, suggesting to the reader that there remains other music to be heard, other poems to be conceived. It is an image that remains with the reader as a lasting reminder of the unsuspected beauty of this marine animal. And on a higher level, it represents the unheralded and usually unappreciated female poet in a male-dominated society. Through gentle humor, the female octopus has been turned into the true siren of the sea, backoning the reader to join her and her music, just as Fuertes, the female poet, does with her verse.

Another of Fuertes' techniques on this same level is what Carlos Bousoño calls "una ruptura del sistema".[8] In this case the speaker without warning switches away from what is expected. The reader's expectations may be based on a set phrase, an expression from colloquial language, a stance or style from a previous text, literary or otherwise, or even a system present in previous works by the same author. Fuertes employs this technique with individual words or lines of verse, as well as with total context. She leads the reader to expect a certain outcome, then changes direction, which produces a comic effect. This surprises the reader into becoming aware of new combinations of elements.

Numerous examples of this technique can be found in both *Poeta de guardia* and *Cómo atar los bigotes al tigre*. From the first collection comes the poem **"Mi suerte"** (177), where "suerte" in the first part of the text refers to the speaker's lot in life. But in the last three lines of the poem, "suerte" comes to mean luck or good fortune in a raffle. As she states:

    En la vida
    ya he hecho poco,
    pero me queda mucho.

    En el amor,
    ya he hecho mucho,
    pero me queda un pozo.
    En la Rifa,
    todo lo perdí . . .
    pero me tocó un cueceleches.

Previous to the final line the reader has the option of interpreting this text on a universal plane, namely, that the speaker's fortune in the grand raffle of life has not led to good results. But the break in the system of the last line of verse, the juxtaposition of the game of life with the winning of a lowly saucepan, causes one to laugh both at the initial seriousness and at the tawdry, carnivalesque image then presented by the speaker.

Fuertes also applies the "ruptura del sistema" to a total context. In the poem **"Extraño accidente"** (195) of *Poeta de guardia* the reader expects that the accident referred to in the title concerns automobiles and some dangerous highway curves:

    En aquella primavera se le aflojaron los tornillos;
    en unas curvas peligrosas
    se le rompió la dirección.
    Los testigos afirmaron que se lanzó al bello precipicio

    —como a sabiendas—.
    Murió de corazón roto
    a tantos de tantos, como tantos,
    aunque continúa yendo a la oficina.

It is only after reading the final line that one realizes that the loose screws can also refer to the victim's being smitten by a woman with a beautiful figure, who played with the suitor's heart, then broke it and finally discarded it. As a result, the reader is encouraged to read the poem once again, the second time appreciating fully the humorous effect produced by interpreting the various words and phrases as pertaining to *both* a highway accident and an unfortunate love affair: "se le aflojaron los tornillos," "unas curvas peligrosas," "se le rompió la dirección," "se lanzó al bello precipicio," and "murió de corazón roto." This text in subtle fashion refers to not only its surface message—a humorous look at love and its similarity to traffic accidents—but also to the process of signification. By encouraging the reader, through humor, to read the poem for a second time, Fuertes calls attention to the reader's role in the creative process, the function of ambiguity, and the poet's own view of what is to be considered poetic.

In another poem of *Cómo atar*, **"Desajuste en el desgaste"** (247), one again must wait until the final line to decipher the code: the punch line forces the reader to reread, to reconsider, and then to laugh. For the speaker states that the eyes are the first to go, followed by hearing in the left foot. Then one gets bald, fat and sloppy, and begins to miss important moves in dominoes. Desire begins to wane, and teeth begin to loosen in the gums. The not-so-gentle approach of old age and senility? The arrival of the courier of death? No, for the final line of the poem is "cuando sabes amar esto te pasa."

In sum then, this first level of humor in Gloria Fuertes' poetry is superficial only in a certain sense, because it deals with the surface level of language. Fuertes encourages the reader to take a closer look at how language can be self-referential in a comic way. But this type of humor is not superficial if one considers the poet's artistry, because humor is an integral part of Gloria Fuertes' style. The play on words, the puns, the juxtaposition of diverse elements and the switching of semantic focus all serve to attract and then retain the interest of the reader, who is drawn into the text and must react to the comic situations presented by a wide variety of poetic personae. And more importantly, this first level of humor also aids the reader in becoming aware of the linguistic subtleties that are a trademark of Fuertes' texts. With humor, the poet establishes a familiar line of communication with the reader, and also widens the scope of themes and poetic voices to include those that originate in typical if clichéd twentieth-century experience.

Gloria Fuertes' humor often goes beyond this merely superficial and self-referential level of language. A second type of humor leads the reader in a new direction or suggests different interpretive dimensions to be considered. The poet's humor means one thing and induces laughter, but at the same time points to another and encourages viewing timeworn topics from a different perspective. In other words, the speaker may at times literally and figuratively make a fool of herself, but her antics will also provide the reader with much food for thought. That reader reacts spontaneously on the intellectual level but also must consider the ramifications of the immediate response. By inducing a jovial reaction, the speaker prompts the reader to explore new areas of meaning, while maintaining a psychologically safe distance from potentially unsettling scenarios. One therefore could call this second type of humor semiotic in nature, since it is able to convey a level of meaning above and beyond that which is communicated through the syllables on the printed page. Whereas the first level of Fuertes' humor is self-contained and self-referential, the semiotic level has wider implications. The humor of an entire situation or context may be the stimulus which induces the reader to attain a new level of awareness. Through this semiotic level of humor, just as through other processes of verbal creativity, the reader is able to discover new meanings and gain new insights that perhaps would not have surfaced but for the use of humor. Although puns and plays on words can and do stand their own ground in Fuertes' poetry, more often than not they also point to another level of significance. Therefore in many of Fuertes' poems both types of humor are at work. The reader laughs at her abrupt switching of codes on the linguistic level of the text, but this code switching may also lead in a new direction.

This second function of humor, the semiotic, first may be considered from the speaker's point of view. Through humor, the speaker has access to a broad range of possibilities for contact with the reader. Secondly, this type of humor also allows the speaker to manipulate the reader's response in a specific way, to lead the reader in a certain direction. By controlling the tone of the text, the speaker also controls the psychological distance of the reader.[9] To begin, humor on the semiotic level allows Fuertes more flexibility in the poetic voice that she wishes to adopt. In two poems from ***Poeta de guardia***, God is the speaker. The first, **"Dios llama al fontanero"** (235), deals with God's problems with plumbing. As would be expected, Fuertes utilizes the vocabulary of that trade in order to create a rather comical image of God's need of a plumber. But on a higher level, it represents divinity's helplessness in light of humanity's suffering. God pours out his heart to the lowly plumber, and the poem ends with "Usted me inspira confianza, Señor Fontanero." The incongruity of the conflicting codes—the world of plumbing and the supposedly divine recipient of the plumber's professional and spiritual ministrations—points to another level of meaning.[10] The humorous aspect of this poem, that God himself has need of assistance now and then, and the conversational style of its presentation, belies a much more serious message: God continues to suffer, not out of love, but out of his inability to do anything about humanity's woeful existence. The reader laughs at the superficial image of a divine being so portrayed, but this laughter is thought-provoking. Fuertes has pointed to the doubt and skepticism of twentieth-century existence when confronted with traditional theology's inability to give convincing answers to life's basic and ineluctable difficulties.

The second poem, **"Ahora habla Dios"** (253), juxtaposes the needs of God and those of humankind. Who must be the object of love and devotion? Who must be the one to forgive?

> Ya no . . .
> Ya no crees tanto en mí, hijo,
> por culpa de mis fallos . . .
> Ya no crees en mí, hombre
> -por culpa de tus hermanos-
> que me salieron mal
> —a veces pasa—.
> ¿Qué te habré hecho yo
> sin darme cuenta hijo,
> que tan mal te sentó que no perdonas?
> . . . . .
>
> (ll. 1-10)

God as the speaker shows traits of insecurity, guilt, and unwillingness to accept responsibility, all classic neurotic symtoms of the twentieth-century personality gone awry. The reader's reaction is first one of rueful laughter, and then seriousness. If God expresses such a deep-seated insecurity, with supposedly infallible and absolute powers, how much worse is our existence, with far fewer options of choice. By projecting humanity's comical yet pitiful foibles onto God, the reader is granted an objectifying if sobering distance, to view human weakness, and to opt for change.

Humor also allows the speaker to adopt an official point of view at the start of the text, only to break the rules - and the reader's expectations—in order to bring about a comic effect and also, more importantly, to divulge a new facet of meaning. In the poem entitled **"Temas candentes. Agricultura"** (234-235), of *Poeta de guardia,* the speaker opens the poem with:

> La mosca mediterránea
> (ceratitis capitata)
> procrea en el naranjal.
>
> (ll. 1-3)

This language, reminiscent of that of Dámaso Alonso in his *Hijos de la ira* could have been taken from a scientific text or journal.[11] The poem continues in this same mode with

> (Se comprueba la existencia de "Tristeza"
> en algunos huertos y huertas de Alcira).
>
> (ll. 4-5)

The speaker has removed sadness from the emotional sphere and placed it within the realm of scientific investigation and classification; it now resembles more the contagion spread by the Mediterranean fruit fly, the typical and repugnant carrier of tropical disease. The juxtaposition of the two codes, scientific jargon and an emotional state, causes one to laugh, which the speaker—tongue in cheek—has wholly anticipated:

En Alcira y en Angola,
y en ese señor que cruza
y en aquella damisola,
en usted que ahora sonríe,
y aquí en una servidora,
bien se puede comprobar
la existencia de "Tristeza" virocal
que amenaza el litoral
de la huerta comunal.

(ll. 6-14)

In the final lines of the text the speaker has returned the reader to the system established in the first three, but always has maintained a proper scientific distance from the subject under consideration. The use of "usted" and its corresponding verb form underlines the formality of the speaker's stance. Moreover, the singsong type of rhythm and the forceful endline rhyme of the closing lines of verse emphasize the speaker's supposed ignorance of the nuances and niceties of poetry, and once again draw attention to the objective scientism of their content. The speaker also has caused the reader first to respond with laughter, and then become aware of a new point of view on sadness: that it, like the fly, can be the source of humanity's contagion with the dreaded diseasess of depression, loneliness, and pain. In effecting this novel juxtaposition, the characteristics common to contagious disease are now also attributable to the emotional state of sadness. Concomitantly, if physical ills can be cured by quick, logical, and scientific intervention, then so must those of the emotional state of sadness. Ironically, the speaker motivates the reader to see sadness in a humorous light. Again in this case, humor serves as a pointer. It indicates a level of meaning perhaps impossible from any other vantage point.

Fuertes also employs humor in order to deal with such private topics as her relationship with God, the effect of war, or her own state of mind. By viewing the speaker's world in a comic light, it is impossible for the reader to be threatened by it. Fuertes uses humor in this way to emphasize the similarities between her world an that of the reader. By evoking a sympathetic response from her readers, the poet brings those readers closer to her point of view.

In **"Sola con esperanza"** (186) of ***Poeta de guardia***, Fuertes first establishes the subject of her poetic inspiration by denouncing (male) society's encumbrances and expectations:

Muchas veces se está solo
pero mejor con decoro
¡A la mierda el oro
y a la mierda el coro!
¡Sola!
Sola-solo
[Fuertes' italics]

(ll. 4-9)

She condemns the bonds of conventional twentieth-century society: those values of proper behavior, money, mat-

rimony, and being just like everyone else. These values are especially burdensome to the female portion of the population, since women are most expected to keep up appearances, to not talk back, and to know their proper place in society: to be seen and not heard, to be a help-mate to male success.

Next, she introduces her particular "Soleá," pronounced in the Andalusian dialect, and surrounded with the ambience of that region's *cante jondo*:

Entonces la soleá
se puebla de luz y canto
y la niebla va y se va.

(ll. 20-12)

It is only then that Fuertes as the speaker personifies her solitude in the body of a flashy street whore, attired in a seductive green dress, who beckons the speaker, and the reader, to join her. This particular persona is significant in that the prostitute represents at once the female flouting of male society's values of proper female decorum and the meaner aspect of women's exploitation by men. But here Fuertes bestows upon her harlot a totally positive value. She represents Fuertes' cry for freedom from both societal and artistic shackles. She is the unfettered female creative animus who desires to be mistress of her own existence, her own destiny, and her own voice. Thus, the poem takes on a distinctively metapoetic dimension with the evaluative inversion of the harlot's image:

Semivestida de verde
me excita la Soledad
esta noche va y me dice:
—me dice y luego se va—,
"que me merezco otra cosa
                    —que vendrá—"

(ll. 17-21)

With beating heart, the speaker enters into dialogue with the female animus ("me excita la Soledad / esta noche va y me dice"), but finds, as all poets do, that inspiration is not to be inalienably possessed ("me dice y luego se va".) "Soledad" thus personifies the poet's particular and female bout with societal expectation on one level, and lyrical creativity on another. By embracing openly the tabooed persona of the prostitute, Fuertes accomplishes two things. First, she rejects the standards set by society for women, and second, she underscores the idea that women are too often used as objects instead of accepted as equals to men, both in the social and the artistic sphere. Women have long been the subject(s) of poetry and visual art, but not their creators. In this poetic text, Fuertes skillfully combines the two roles. As she says, "que me merezco otra cosa, /—que vendrá." The alluring prostitute is very effective, since she evokes the independence of spirit necessary to combat both sexism and those moments of darkness in the search for poetic expression. The speaker's presentation of solitude as a female street-walker catches the reader's attention and perhaps even encourages the reader, male and female alike, to view societal pressures and poetic creativity from a feminist perspective. In the final lines of verse, the speaker accepts her solitude, and the rewards that it is able to bring her: "¡Qué divina está esta noche / la zorra la Soledad!" Fuertes' solitude has given the poet her voice, and Fuertes has given voice to her solitude. She has become both the creator and the object of her own poetry. The tabooed role of woman as whore is now the personification of creative power.[12]

Fuertes' relationship with God is also offered up for scrutiny and consideration of the reader.[13] While in poems like "Dios llama al fontanero" the reader laughs at the incongruities built into the God/humanity relationship by the speaker, in other cases Fuertes presents modern nihilistic antitheology in humorous terms. In **"La pica"** (210) of *Poeta de guardia,* as in **"Oración"** (266) and **"Exageraciones divinas"** (275) of *Cómo atar,* she examines the relationship not of Superior Being with an inferior one, but rather of two beings who each must fight for self-realization and justification. God is not the all-powerful controller of humankind's destiny, but rather only one element among many which complicate human existence. In **"La pica"** Fuertes addresses herself in letter to God, the "Torero Supremo," who is waiting to do in the human race. By her intentional slips of phrasing—"llegan medio vivos a la muerte," "picador/pecador," "el Dolor nos mate antes que Vos"—the speaker exposes the true state of affairs. The human species must fight God to the death in a situation where the former is bound to lose. The cards are stacked against humanity, or, as in the metaphor of the poem, the final sword thrust must be executed. In spite of his professed love, God too is waiting to defeat the human sector, not out of sadism, but in an act of self-preservation, much as the lonely bullfighter. The speaker, through the use of the all-inclusive Nosotros, bids the reader to join her in this fight to the death. The outcome is already predetermined, as in the bull ring; only the manner of losing—through sorrow or God's direct intervention—is yet to be decided. This humor again belies a more serious point of view. The nihilism of twentieth-century existence has put God to death. But in this text, the metaphor is reversed. He must do humanity in first, so that He can go on living, if only as a dreamed-of reality. Through humor, Fuertes neutralizes this sobering perspective; the reader may accept or reject the poet's conclusions.

Fuertes' humor on this semiotic level also allows for fresh insights into the commonplace. Through defamiliarization of the prosaic, the poet forces the reader to take note of objects, perspectives and people which may not be middle-class.[14] She defamiliarizes in the sense that she compels the reader to see our everyday environment without prejudice, much like what occurs at a first encounter. The poet's intention is to reverse the numbing process that has occurred on our senses and sensibilities. At times she also pokes gentle fun at the bourgeois existence through this defamiliarization. Those who read her poetry must become aware of a not so elegant side of life that, according to Fuertes, is also entirely worthy of comment in poetic form. These fresh insights produce in the reader unexpected reactions, and in turn cause the

reader to see, if not accept, Fuertes' point of view.

Like **"Virgen de plástico"** (283) of *Cómo atar,* the poem **"El guía de la abadía"** (237) of *Poeta de guardia* pokes fun at religious beliefs, and the blatant materialism that frequently intrudes upon that sphere. Religious experience is merely a commodity upon which a profit can be turned. The speaker makes no comment about the beliefs, but rather only presents the situation as it is and allows the reader to draw private conclusions:

> —Y ahora, pasen al salón
> vean las tres reliquias
> de San Palemón;
> aquí en el Sacristorio
> se conservan
> limpias de polvo y paja
> —niño abre la caja—;
> vean las tres calaveras
> del Santo Patrón,
> calavera de San Palemón niño
> calavera de San Palemón adolescentre
> y aquí, la calavera de San Palemón ya anciano en el
>   martirio
> —niño sujeta el cirio—.
> (Las estampitas benditas
> y pasadas por sus cuencas
> valen a treinta.)

However comically outrageous the situation may be, however spontaneously laughter may come forth, the message still remains the same. Religion has become an opportunity for economic advancement. The friar appears not in his capacity as a saver of souls, but rather as a trafficker in goods and services. The defamiliarization of that person's function jars the reader into a new point of view.

"El mendigo que entregaba un papel," (229) also of *Poeta de guardia*, deals with the seamier side of human existence. By presenting this character in a positive light, Fuertes invites the reader to examine an alien life-style, one distanced from the comfortable perspective of the middle class, and perhaps gain something from it. She desires that the reader not turn away uncaring eyes, as one so often does on the street. In "El mendigo," written in the first person, the beggar hands the passerby a sheet of paper upon which is outlined his life story. Fuertes here compares implicitly the beggar to the poet, who in humility hands the reader her poem, in the hope that it will be read through to the end. The poem comes to a close with a simple request, which underscores all the more poignantly the poverty of the speaker: ("Devuélvame el papel no tengo copia".) In this way the poet aligns herself with the beggar who pleads for recognition and perhaps the sympathy of those who are encountered on the street. As in the previous example, a poetic voice does not interject any comment. The reader must accept or reject the perspective thus presented on its own merits. But the obvious leanings of the speaker lead one to ponder if not accept the point of view presented.

The poem **"Cielo de tercera,"** (231) also of the same collection, again deals with a perspective decidedly not middle-class. The speaker demonstrates a definite sympathy toward the subject, the ambience on a third-class train. Although the mixture of elements is chaotic, from "flores de plástico" to "racistas arrepentidos" to "putas baratas" to "estrellas flacas," this sympathy does pervade the scene. Beauty is in the eye of the beholder. The reader also must consciously see a face of beauty that previously and carelessly had escaped notice. The speaker, through a light touch of humor, invites an examination of the scene by defamiliarizing the prosaic, sordid side of life.

The final poem of **Poeta de guardia**, **"El camello,"** (240-241) which carries the subtitle of "Auto de los Reyes Magos," also casts a disparaging glance on bourgeois values, but in a refreshing way. Briefly, the poem tells the story of the arrival of the Magi at Bethlehem. The speaker demonstrates obvious sympathy for the lowly camel, who along the way goes lame, is blamed for the tardiness of the arrival, and as an ultimate insult to his dignity, suffers an attack of hiccups. The speaker also inserts very purposefully an anachronistic note by stating that Melchior, the resident mechanic, frets about their late arrival upon consulting his Longines watch. He complains that the camel has thrown them hopelessly off schedule. But finally the journey is complete, they have arrived at the manger, the prophecy has been fulfilled:

> Y a las tantas ya del alba
> —ya cantaban pajarillos—
> los tres reyes se quedaron
> boquiabiertos e indecisos,
> oyendo hablar como a un Hombre
> a un Niño recién nacido.
> —No quiero oro ni incienso
> ni esos tesoros tan fríos,
> quiero al camello, le quiero,
> le quiero—repitió el niño.
> A pie vuelven los tres reyes
> cabizbajos y afligidos.
> Mientras el camello echado
> le hace cosquillas al Niño.
>
> (ll. 32-45)

The final vindication of the camel teaches a lesson of which the reader must become aware. Bourgeois existence has become too complacent and smug, too materialistic, too much a slave to the demands of the clock. There must be a balance struck between the traditional male views on commerce, punctuality, machines, and chains of command, and the traditionally female ones of love, tenderness, and familial devotion. The speaker implicitly demands that the reader respond to emotional rather than materialistic needs, even if schedules, social appearances, and conventions may suffer. Perhaps the reader would reject this message if it were presented in a straightforward, didactic, and pedantic manner. But through gentle humor Fuertes wins the attention and approval of the reader and thus gains easy support for her

more humane point of view on what priorities ought to be essential, namely, intimate rather than pragmatic values. These priorities have become defamiliarized enough so that now the reader can examine them from a different perspective and not be threatened or put off by the speaker's point of view.

Although Fuertes has stated that she is a poet independent of any particular literary affiliation, her poetry in truth reflects the concerns and artistic perspective common to her contemporaries.[15] Her consciousness of the artfulness of her work, as both communication and creation of a poetic reality, puts her in the mainstream of the second generation of post-Civil War poets. Her themes also reflect that same social milieu: alienation, distancing, the devaluation of human existence, and the loss of a sense of community. Her poetry is social in that the thrust of some of her humorous poems ties her in part to the tradition of not only Dámaso Alonso, Blas de Otero, and José Hierro, but also that of Ángel González and José Ángel Valente. In addition, she involves the reader socially as well as artistically in the text, and compels that reader into a stance that may at times be at odds with the comfortable bourgeois perspective. Humor is one of the means through which she not only communicates the reality around her, but also creates a new one inside her poetic texts, and attempts to stem the tide of indifference to the suffering of others, spiritual bankruptcy, and existential anguish.

It has been shown that Fuertes' humor has two functions, both of which contribute to her poetry's unique tenor. First, it encourages the reader into becoming aware of the surface level of language and the artistic process operant at that level. And second, it also induces the reader to go beyond the text at hand: that which is presented in the text must be related to the reader's own world. Humor fulfills this second function by pointing to the present human condition, and what can be done to improve it. Fuertes' poetry conveys a message that goes beyond the confines of the text, and reaches out to the community at large. Through humor, humanity can face common problems and defeat them, or at least defeat the terror that they have come to represent. Thus, through her verse Fuertes gives her readers some insights on *Cómo atar los bigotes al tigre*.

It has been said that tragedy is universal because of its ability to transverse time and culture. But humor is the common bond that cements the community's purpose and the poet to the community. Through humor, Fuertes is able to make us laugh at ourselves and ourt weaknesses, and to see the bonds which unite us all. Her use of humor is an element that grants her work singularity but, through its artfulness and dual function, also gives her poetry beauty and transcendence. She sings the song of the community and through her verse, proves that the female voice is capable of expressing the poetic song of twentieth-century life. Her range is unique, but her art still remains true to the eternal poetic ideal.[16]

NOTES

[1] Although her poetry is usually included in post-Civil War antholo-gies, little critical work has been published on her verse. Major critical studies include: José Batlló, *Antología de la nueva poesía española* (Madrid: El Bardo, 1968): 337-38; Catherine B. Bellver, "Gloria Fuertes, Poet of Social Consciousness." *Letras Femeninas,* 4, no. 1 (1978): 27-38; Rubén Benítez, "El maravilloso retablo popular de Gloria Fuertes." *Mester* 9 (Jan., 1980): 21-33; José Luis Cano, *Poesía española contem-poránea: las generaciones de posguerra* (Madrid: Guadarrama, 1973): 174-80; Andrew P. Debicki, *Poetry of Discovery* (Lexington: University Press of Kentucky, 1982): 81-101; Joaquín González Muela, *La nueva poesía española* (Madrid: Alcalá, 1973): 13-29; Pablo González Rodas, introduction to Fuertes' *Historia de Gloria (Amor, humor, y desamor)*, 25-50; Nancy B. Mandlove, "Used Poetry: the Trans-parent Language of Gloria Fuertes and Ángel González." *Revista Canadiense de Estu-dios Hispánicos* 7 (Winter, 1983): 301-6; Timothy J. Rogers, "The Comic Spirit in the Poetry of Gloria Fuertes, *Perspectives on Contemporary Literature* 7 (1981): 88-97; Francisco Ynduráin, introduction to Fuertes' *Antología poética (1950-1969)*, 9-45.

[2] In the preparation of this study I used Gloria Fuertes' *Poeta de guardia* (1968) and *Cómo atar los bigotes al tigre* (1969), both of which are contained in her *Obras incompletas,* 4th edition (Madrid: Cátedra, 1978). From this point forward, all page references will be given in parentheses in the text, and refer to this 4th edition.

Fuertes herself considers her later works to be more important as well-rounded statements of her poetic intention. In the introduction to *Obras incompletas,* she states: "Tener la suerte y el valor de reeditar hasta mis antiguos versos (los primeros libros casi nunca son buenos), gracias a este volumen, me responsabiliza de una manera atroz". (33)

[3] Humor, as the title would suggest, is indeed a salient feature of this latest addition to Fuertes' poetic work. In the vast majority of cases, the poems from the latest collection are very short. Therefore, I have chosen to exclude them from this study, since their brevity does not allow for as much development of humor's effect as those in *Poeta de guardia* and *Cómo atar.* But both levels of humor, the self-referential and the semiotic, are present in *Historia de Gloria.*

[4] In his thesis contained in *Comedy,* ed. Wylie Sypher (Garden City, N. Y.: Doubleday & Co., 1956), Henri Bergson states that comedy always distances the reader or observer. According to Bergson, laughter is an intellectual response rather than an emotional one. In this study I adhere to Bergson's theories on comedy and laughter.

[5] For a fine discussion of humor in modern poetry see Michael Riffaterre, *Semiotics of Poetry* (Bloomington: Indiana University Press, 1978), espe-cially 124-34 and 137-38. Other studies that consider comedy and culture in general are Norman N. Holland, *Laughing: A Psychology of Humor* (Ithaca: Cornell University Press, 1982); Edith Hern, *The Absolute Comic* (New York: Columbia University Press, 1980); Harry Levin, ed., *Veins of Humor* (Cambridge: Harvard University Press, 1972); George McFadden, *Discovering the Comic* (Princeton: Princeton University Press, 1982); and Neil Schaeffer, *The Art of Laughter* (New York: Columbia University Press, 1981).

[6] Fuertes' possible relationship with surrealism will not be dealt with here. Others—including Fuertes herself—see her work as a successor to the "postismo" movement. See for example, Fuertes' introduction to her *Obras incompletas,* 27-28; Félix Grande, "1939 Poesía en castellano 1969," *Cuadernos para el diálogo* (número extraordinario) 14 (May, 1969): 43-

61; José Manuel Polo de Bernabé, "El postismo como aventura del lenguaje en la poesía de posguerra en España," contained in Alan M. Gordon and Evelyn Rugg, eds., *Actas del sexto congreso internacional de hispanistas, celebrado en Toronto del 22 al 26 de agosto de 1977* (Toronto: Dept. of Spanish & Portuguese, University of Toronto, 1980): 579-82. For a general source on "postismo," see Jaume Pont, *El postismo* (Barcelona: Edicions del Mall, 1987).

[7] See Cleanth Brooks and Robert Penn Warren, *Understanding Poetry,* 4th edition (New York: Holt, Rinehart and Winston, 1976): 112-15, where they discuss a poem's tone and the relationship of speaker and reader.

[8] Carlos Bousoño deals with the idea of "ruptura del sistema" in his *Teoría de la expresión poética,* 5th edition (Madrid: Gredos, 1970), vol. I, Chap-ters 15 and 16. He also treats the subject in his "Un ensayo de estilística explicativa (Ruptura de un sistema formado por una frase hecha)," con-tained in *Homenaje universitario a Dámaso Alonso.* Reunido por los estudiantes de Filología Románica, curso 1968-9 (Madrid: Gredos, 1970): 69-84. See also Andrew P. Debicki, *Poetry of Discovery,* 81-101.

[9] The concept of psychological distance is discussed in an article by Edward Bullough, "'Psychological Distance' as a Factor in Art and an Esthetic Principle," reprinted in *A Modern Book of Esthetics,* ed. Melvin Rader, 2nd edition (New York: Henry Holt and Co., 1952): 401-28. Briefly, Bullough states that the manipulation of psychological distance is a poetic device utilized by the poet in order to win or reject the reader's assent to the speaker's point of view.

[10] Roland Barthes, in his essay *S/Z,* trans. Richard Miller (New York: Hill and Wang, 1974), explains the concept of linguistic codes. According to Barthes, a code is a series of elements (signifiers) which when combined, produce a certain level of meaning in a given text. Thus, Barthes sug-gests that the text's meaning is not such that it can be captured in a linear statement. Rather, interpretation on the part of the reader is a result of the juxtaposition and interplay of several codes. It is through the plurality of the codes and their effect upon one another as well as on the reader that the text finally communicates its meaning.

[11] His poem entitled "Insomnio" begins with "Madrid es una ciudad de más de un millón de cadáveres / (según las últimas estadísticas)."

[12] In his introductory essay to *Historia de Gloria,* Pablo González Rodas states that "empezará a dialogar con su soledad, a acostumbrarse a ella y a su sombra, a burlarse de ella para, finalmente, aceptarla como fiel compañera, inspiradora de sus versos". (37)

[13] González Rodas does a quick survey of "Dios en la poesía de Gloria Fuertes" in his introduction to *Historia de Gloria,* 42-45. See also Luz María Umpierre, "Inversión de valores y efectos en el lector en 'Oración' de Gloria Fuertes", *Plaza* 5-6 (1981-82): 132-44.

[14] See Victor Shklovsky, "Art as Technique," in *Russian Formalist Crit-icism,* trans. with an introduction by T. Lemon and Marion J. Reis (Lincoln: University of Nebraska Press, 1965), 3-24.

[15] In "Cabra sola" (212) of *Poeta de guardia,* Fuertes states in part:

> Vivo sola
> —que no quise cabrito en compañía-
> cuando subo a lo alto de este valle,
> siempre encuentro un lirio de alegría.
> Y vivo por mi cuenta, cabra sola;

que yo a ningún rebaño pertenezco.
Si sufrir es estar como una cabra,
entonces sí lo estoy, no dudar de ello.

(ll. 9-16)

[16] A shorter version of this article appeared in my *Recent Spanish Poetry and the Role of the Reader* (Lewisburg: Bucknell University Press, 1987), 119-36.

Sylvia Sherno (essay date 1989)

SOURCE: "Carnival: Death and Renewal in the Poetry of Gloria Fuertes," in *Modern Language Notes,* Vol. 104, No. 2, March, 1989, pp. 370-92.

[*Sherno examines the celebratory nature of Fuertes' verse.*]

The word "carnival," as used by Mikhail Bakhtin, refers to the culture of the marketplace and the forms of folk humor which arose in the Middle Ages and Renaissance. The manifestations of this popular culture included comic festivities and ritual activities, memorialized in the oral and written parodies from which an entire body of recreational literature was born. Among the most salient traits of carnivalesque compositions are licentiousness, irreverence, and an exaggerated fascination with the human body and with its appetites and instincts, both noble and base. The ambivalence inherent in the portrayal of bodily impulses is central to the grotesque realism that Bakhtin attributes to Rbelais in particular and to carnival expression in general. For Bakhtin, the grotesque character of popular parodical literature is perhaps carnival's greatest triumph, for the very ambivalence of praise and degradation echoes the eternally "unfinished metamorphosis, of death and birth, growth and becoming" (Bakhtin, 24). The grotesque, in short, signals the cosmic triumph of regeneration over death.[1]

The world of carnival, according to Bakhtin, traditionally stands outside of an "official" culture marked by sobriety and asceticism, intolerance and repression.[2] These elements conspire to produce the solemn tone deemed appropriate to the expression of "the true, the good, and all that [is] essential and meaningful." (Bakhtin, 73). In the Middle Ages, such values were determined and enforced by the dogmatic and stringently absolutist canons of the feudal and theocratic orders. Yet the gray solemnity and "icy petrified seriousness" described by Bakhtin are not exclusive to the official medieval world. In Spain these qualities are as ascribable to the forty years of Franco's dictatorship as to the centuries of Inquisitorial domination. Even a cursory glance at the Spanish architectural landscape, configured by monuments like El Escorial and the Valle de los Caídos, reveals a history of grim authoritarianism and inflexible dogmatism.

Such a history has provided rich and fertile ground for the rebellious inversion of the official order which is the primary activity of the grotesque imagination. Indeed, the grotesque tradition has thrived in Spain, from the ingen-

uous piety of Berceo to the hyperbolic aggressiveness of Quevedo; from the eccentricities of Gómez de la Serna's "greguerías" to the tragicomedy of Valle Inclán's "esperpentos"; from the satirical wedding of human and animal domains by the eighteenth-century fabulists to the sordid metaphors of Dámaso Alonso.

Among the poets of post-Civil War Spain, Gloria Fuertes is a beneficiary of the Spanish grotesque tradition. Gloria Fuertes shares with the first generation of postwar poets her view of poetry as an instrument for righting the social injustices born of the Civil War and its aftermath. Like those of the second generation, Fuertes has committed herself to the distinctively personal creative vision only made possible by the breakdown of the earlier repressive system (Debicki, 14). Fuertes' poetry, however, diverges from the poetic generations of postwar Spain because of the exultant, celebratory quality that marks her as a direct descendent of the ancient carnival spirit. As in the carnival tradition, laughter and revelry are central to her world view and thus to her conception of poetry as a means to counteract the ills—social, artistic, and sexual—of official society. The clowns, trapeze artists, vendors and street figures who people Fuertes' verses evidence her affinity for popular, "unofficial," culture. So too do the double entendres, colloquialisms, and vulgar expressions with which she spices her language. Her poetry mirrors the ancient dichotomies of reverence and subversion, manifested on the one hand by prayers, litanies, and verses in a contemplative vein; on the other hand, by diatribes, reprimands, and billingsgate. The coexistence of such contradictory forms is concordant with the carnival spirit, especially in its preference for the grotesque. Allusions to food and drink, to the human body and its natural impulses, abound in her work. Disease and health, both physical and emotional, are of equal poetic import: in Gloria Fuertes' vision, life is an open-ended cycle of death and rebirth, just as poetry itself is the continuing process by which she denounces official culture and reaffirms her faith in popular renewal.

What is more, Gloria Fuertes stands apart from her poetic compatriots by virtue of her gender. For this reason she maintains a unique position in relation to an official culture historically molded by and destined for men. Fuertes unabashedly confesses that her work "en general, es muy autobiográfica, . . . muy 'yoista,' . . . muy 'glorista,'" and it is clear that she insistently employs poetry as a way of creating her own personal and artistic identity.[3] Yet her work transcends the private issues of her "autobiografismo irremediable" (*OI*, 25), for it is by means of her poetry that Fuertes confronts the male-ordained codes by which women have historically been constrained, the male-sanctioned hierarchies from which women have traditionally been excluded. Armed, therefore, with the forms and rhetoric of carnival, Fuertes assumes the "negative function" within the existing official structure that obliges women to "reject everything finite, definite, structured, loaded with meaning. . . . [and which] places women on the side of the explosion of social codes: with revolutionary moments" (Kristeva, 166).

Fuertes has lightheartedly alluded to the "mosqueantes aficiones" to which, as a young Spanish girl of the working class, she was denied access: " . . . en aquellos tiempos, antes de la garra de la guerra, pocas muchachas practicaban hockey, baloncesto y menos, poesía" (*OI*, 27). Social historians have noted how restrictions imposed by patriarchal socialization on the free expression of a woman's individuality and artistic integrity often result in diseases of maladjustment, in madness, and even in death (Gilbert and Gubar, 45-92). These ills find expression in a kind of discourse of impossibility commonly created in women's writings. In the poetry of Gloria Fuertes, for example, negation and silence figure among the stratagems by which she resists the impossible codes and conventions of established culture and language.[4] Expressions of inversion further demonstrate the poet's sense of marginality: she views herself repeatedly as "al borde" (*OI*, 42, 228) and describes her soul "desde siempre . . . cabalgando al rev s" (*OI*, 74).[5] Within the context of popular imagery, negation and inversion represent the carnivalesque displacement and destruction of hierarchies. Rabelais, avers Bakhtin, "intentionally mixed the hierarchical levels in order to discover the core of the object's concrete reality, to free it from its shell and to show its material bodily aspect—the real being outside all hierarchical norms and values" (Bakhtin, 403). In similar fashion, Gloria Fuertes registers her nonconformity with the accepted order and, in so doing, engages in precisely the activity that Julia Kristeva envisions for women in the revolutionary dismantling of official society.

The discourse of impossibility reflected rhetorically by negation and inversion is thematically represented by the innumerable allusions in Fuertes' verses to sickness, madness, and various other physical pathologies and psychic ailments. Pain, for example, is everywhere present and heightens, somehow, her perception of the tenuousness of life: "¡Qué viva estoy porque me duele todo! . . ." (*OI*, 262). "Todos estáis perdidos," she cautions, "picados por pecados, / los altos y los bajos tenéis algo en la voz. / / Inicio cura urgente" (*OI*, 59). She announces to her lover that "aunque me dueles ya menos cada día, / la enfermedad va peor" (*HG*, 103). During the war, she remembers, "el hombre y el hambre / me dolían todos los días" (*HG*, 103). And when she is asked, "¿Dónde te duele, Gloria?", she can only reply: "Ahí me duele, / en la mismísima vida" (*HG*, 102).

Sicknesses of all kinds, prominent in Fuertes' poetry, not only exemplify the grotesque fascination with bodily functions but also ally the poet with life's unfortunates. A small bird imprisoned in a balcony "pidiendo a gritos la revolución" (*OI*, 104) suffers from the same claustrophobia and acrophobia that envelop the poet herself (*OI*, 155-56). "Yo soy asténica / y anoréxica" (*OI*, 313), she informs us, and in fact overly thin women and skinny children are haunting reminders of a gnawing hunger (Gilbert and Gubar, 53-59; Michie, 12-29). Like the beggars to whom she extends her compassion and love, she begs, "¡Un poquito de pez, / que tengo hambre. . . . !" (*OI*, 106) and, opening her empty refrigerator, she ob-

serves, "Me gustaría estar en la India / pasando un hambre distinta" (*OI*, 302). Tellingly, she shares with the circus elephants and walruses an arrhythmic heartbeat caused by "la vergüenza de haber llegado a ser mansos domesticados" (*OI*, 360) (Bakhtin, 229-30). In Fuertes' poetry, people sweat and cough (*OI*, 298), scratch and are allergic (*OI*, 272-73); they are visited by such indignities as "múltiples granulosis en su sexo" (*OI*, 303), "álgidas neuralgias" (*HG*, 345), and "jaqueca y congoja" (*HG*, 264). She writes a lullaby to ease her sleeping foot out of its cramp (*HG*, 122-23) and consults a physician because "Penitis tengo doctora, /—pena inflamada—, / amar y no ser amada" (*HG*, 312).

The fact that illness so occupies the poet's attention recalls, of course, the prevalence of disease in the writings of many eighteenth- and nineteenth-century women writers, if not more contemporary ones. As Gilbert and Gubar explain this phenomenon, women writers of earlier times "struggled in isolation that felt like illness, alienation that felt like madness, obscurity that felt like paralysis to overcome the anxiety of authorship that was endemic to their literary subculture" (51). The emotional and psychological distress that appears as a recurring motif in Gloria Fuertes' poetry serves as a reminder, then, of the debilitating effects of social and political marginality on women's lives and works. Nonetheless, emotional disturbances merit Fuertes' compassion, not her bitterness. Confessing her clandestine activism in the cause of peace, she refuses to believe that people are bad; rather,

> ¡La gente es enferma!
> El opresor sufre regresión,
> el agresor frustración,
> el terrorista ya no pueda más
> (a su modo se la juega por los demás).
> El ladrón padece cleptomanía,
> el criminal sicopaía,
> el delincuente infantil,
> locura senil.
>
> (*HG*, 86)

Humankind is afflicted with a collective "náusea psíquica seca / . . . peor que arcada y vomitona" (*HG*, 89). Gloria Fuertes is herself preoccupied with madness, a condition evidenced by the ghosts, phantasmagoria, and magical events that are attended in her verses by shadows and moonlight. (These phenomena are proper, incidentally, to the "lunacy" and emotionally charged atmosphere of Gothic romances, so cultivated by women writers).[6] The convalescent poet is aware in herself of a lingering "alma dislocada" (*HG*, 156) and knows that "la anguistia, / el aburrimiento, / la mala leche y la tristeza, / se contagian tanto como la lepra" (*HG*, 263).

Witness to these spiritual maladies are the myriad references to alcohol and drink. At times the poet's proclaimed fondness for drink is part of her celebratory spirit: "Cuando el sol se apague . . . / ¡Comienza a beber!" (*OI*, 85). On these occasions she is moved to raise her glass in a toast to peace and joy on the planet; in a humbler tone, she toasts rice and lentils, emblems of a smaller happiness (*HG*, 98). Such lusty references to drink hearken back to images of victorious abundance, fertility, and liberation which in ancient recreational literature signified defeat of the official world (Bakhtin, 294-302). At other times, however, drink is merely symptomatic of perceived dysfunctions or lacks and hence recalls the female deprivation or hunger that "is inextricably linked to rebellion and rage" (Gilbert and Gubar, 373):

> Bebo porque la gente no me gusta,
> porque a la gente la quiero demasiado . . .
>
> (*OI*, 217)

> Cuando me aprieta todo
> yo bebo, bebo siempre . . .
>
> (*OI*, 86)

> conozco los caminos de la noche,
> los caminos del clown que ríe inútilmente,
> y los torcidos pasos del que bebe derecho
> —derecho tiene a su vida beberse—.
>
> (*OI*, 250)

Drink affords the poet a singular acuity and insight: "Se bebe para olvidar una cosa / y se olvida todo menos esa cosa" (*OI*, 299). At the same time, it provokes bizarre hallucinatory visions. In "Mariposa muerta en el sofá," she hallucinates her house into a terrifying still-life with herself the dead butterfly of the poem's title. From the distorted perspective of the upended bottle, she does not look at her past; on the contrary, her past looks at her and converts "las niñas de mis ojos" into "las niñas" of her lost girlhood. She glimpses the transformation of drink into tears and of herself into a Kafkaesque insect-lover, "una amante religiosa." "Todo esto," she concludes, "acabo de verlo / en el fondo del fondo / de la botella" (*OI*, 312).

Similarly disquieting are the numerous references to suicide. Human beings are moved by invisible forces; suicide alone permits the exercise of free choice (*OI*, 178). Fuertes herself contemplates taking gas or chloroform and allows that "todas las noches me suicido un poco" (*OI*, 178, 215). "Creo en los suicidas" (*HG*, 122), confides the poet, and declares that she would be tempted to throw herself out of a window, if only she did not live in a basement (and if only she did not have hope) (*OI*, 347). Among the wares she advertises in her "Guía comercial" the poet numbers neckties for potential suicides (*OI*, 116). She warns against excess of all kinds: too much of a good thing can turn sour, just as knowing too much can inspire thoughts of suicide (*OI*, 162). Trees, vineyards, even raccoons are capable of taking their own lives (*OI*, 199, 202, 336). Not seeing her lover is tantamount to a death-wish (*OI*, 318) while "Autoeutanasia sentimental" is another kind of suicide occasioned by an enforced docility, a desire "por no estorbar, / por no gritar / más versos quejumbrosos" (*HG*, 347)—in short, a wish both to suppress artistic expression and to quell personal identity. The repeated insistence on suicide paradoxically suggests feelings of impotence and imaginatively signals death to what the poet perceives as the conventions of

prescribed female behavior. Thus, the duality inherent in the allusions to suicide provides a potent figure for what Adrienne Rich has described as a "counterpull between female self-immolation—the temptation of passive suicide—and the will and courage which are [woman's] survival tools" (103).

Nonetheless, as occurs in the carnival tradition of the grotesque, the presence of death and disease is paradoxically contradicted by and unified with manifestations of vitality. Indeed, in the ambivalence of the carnivalesque conception, death and life are the two faces of Janus, together evidence of what Bakhtin views as "the drama of laughter presenting at the same time the death of the old and the birth of the new world. Each image is subject to the meaning of the whole; each reflects a single concept of a contradictory world of becoming" (149). Gloria Fuertes believes that we are made for a life on earth and, although she questions the notion of life under the earth, the meaning she attaches to existence is ultimately a larger one: "morir pariendo como las olas / para que el mar perdure" (*OI*, 176). Sometimes the pain of love and solitude renders life another form of death (*HG*, 77, 157-58); likewise, unquenchable hatred "nos amomia" (*OI*, 153). Over and over in Fuertes' verses death and birth appear side by side, natural companions in the continuum of human existence.[7] In a single night, for example, "se puede parir o desnacer" (*OI*, 253). Her own birth, we read in "Nota biográfica," was so difficult a delivery that her mother "si se descuida muere por vivirme" (*OI*, 41) (Bakhtin, 151).

Fuertes rejoices in each stage of human existence, accepting old age and infancy with equanimity. The faltering steps of the old man, in her estimation, are merely a wistful reminder of the hesitant steps of the small child (*OI*, 92). She sees God both "en el viejo que pasa [y] / en la madre que pare" (*OI*, 43). In this same spirit of equanimity Gloria Fuertes neither denigrates nor glorifies the human body but rather makes unabashed poetry out of all of its natural functions. In **"El sacamuelas,"** for example, the poet offers her young female customers bargain prices on special pills "para los días duros" (*OI*, 240). Bodily functions not commonly a part of polite discourse (urination, defecation, masturbation) are granted humorous welcome within Fuertes' verses (*OI*, 222, 270, 272, 293, 346-47, 353; *HG*, 170) since such functions quite literally embody the cosmic forces of creation and destruction, life and death (Bakhtin, 335).

Not surprisingly, eating is another cause for merriment and the appearance in her verses of soups, fried eggs, lentils and stews provides convincing evidence of the poet's own "apetito envidiable" (*OI*, 71). To have a little of everything is her philosophy, as the following lines attest:

> Tener de todo un poco—como el pato—
> que nada, vuela y anda y pone huevos,
> tener de tierra y mar de niña y niño
> tener de bien y mal
> eso tenemos.

No ser tan sólo hombres o mujeres
no ser tan sólo alma o sólo cuerpo,
no ser tan criminales como somos,
no ser tan fantasmal como seremos.
Tener de todo un poco,

trigo, avena, y dejar un rincón para el centeno.

(OI, 180)

While for lack of food she might propose, "esta noche cenamos Poesía" (*OI*, 116), hers is a world of abundance, a "banquet for all the world" (Bakhtin, 19). Eating signals communal solidarity in "the process of labor and struggle . . . against the world":

> The popular images of food and drink are active and triumphant,. . . . They express the people as a whole because they are based on the inexhaustible, ever-growing abundance of the material principle. They are universal and organically combined with the concept of the free and sober truth, ignoring fear and piousness and therefore linked with wise speech. Finally, they are infused with gay time, moving toward a better future that changes and renews everything in its path

(Bakhtin, 302).

With typically carnivalesque glee, Fuertes concocts a "menú de guerra" complete with a donkey's tail, garbanzos and the odd weevil, and serves it as a reminder of the fine line between life and death in times of war and peace alike (*HG*, 113). Elsewhere, she prepares a witch's brew composed of splinters, a relative's tooth, a mammoth's foot, a rock from an avalanche—an odd confection meant to invite good luck (*HG*, 271-72). Indeed, Fuertes quite regularly employs the language of recipes to make of woman's experience woman's art and, in so doing, fashions her own definition of poetry in defiance of the expected and the conventional.

Gloria Fuertes possesses a festive spirit which laughingly embraces both poles of human existence. Laughter, one of the primary ingredients of carnival relativity, is for Fuertes the distinguishing badge of the human species. "El niño," she says, "es el único cachorro / que ríe" (*HG*, 286) whereas, before being born into a new life, the dead "se mean de risa" (*OI*, 347). Laughter accounts for the festive merriment evident in allusions to popular celebrations. New Year's Day, signalling the death of the old and the birth of the new, elicits the poet's solemn promise to open "de par en par sonrisa y puerta" (*OI*, 164). Fuertes remembers as well Holy Thursday, although the eucharistic rituals of that day are rendered decidedly secular by the poet-lover: "Dame el pan de tu cuerpo en una carta, / bébete mis palabras con el mío" (*OI*, 325). The fifteenth of May occasions this salty plea for special blessings from Isidro Labrador, farmer and saint: "Toma, planta mi bolígrafo, / a ver qué coño nos sale" (*OI*, 338). Beneath these inversions of the sacred to the profane is the sound of carnivalesque laughter (Bakhtin, 218).

What is more, laughter permits the freedom of both fearlessness and revelry. That is why Fuertes is so drawn to the circus, the bullring, and sports. All are domains linked to the games, riddles, and other forms of play which Bakhtin views as an integral part of carnivalesque parodies of such cosmic questions as time, destiny and political power (231-39). They represent the enactment of communal spectacles which sustain their own rules while momentarily suspending those of the official social structure. The world of the circus, for example, although honored by popular approval, has traditionally been relegated to the margins of esthetics and its inhabitants, consigned to the outskirts of social legitimacy. Gloria Fuertes expresses affinity for circus performers like the mime, the trapeze artist, and the wild animal tamer (*OI*, 258, 259; *HG*, 247). Most especially, she favors the clown, the circus' central player and the one in whom laughter and pathos, delight and defiance are conjoined. The role of the clown is not unlike her own: for her, "todo es cuestión, / de saber sacar / la lengua a la Zorra de la Seriedad" (*OI*, 238).

The bullfight, analogous to the circus as spectacle and ceremony, presents another arena in which to exercise rebellion. Fuertes evinces a special fondness for the bullfighter, another popular icon of daring and valor. With the bullfighter, she shares a taste for adventure and revelry ("la brega" and "la fiesta"), and hence is rewarded by popular acceptance:

> Toro a verso verso a toro
> —la gente entusiasmada—
> y yo poeta de brega,
> quiero que no noten nada.
>
> (Tengo cariño a la fiesta.)

(HG, 242)

Barred by her gender from youthful participation in sports and games, Fuertes invades these male preserves by means of her poetry. In the guise of "atleta-poeta," she sets for herself the rigorous challenge to "hacer posible lo inalcanzable" (*HG*, 157):

> Toreo-miedo.
> Boxeo-miedo.
> "Surf"-miedo.
> —Deporte es droga—.
> Toreo-desafiar a un animal.
> Boxeo-desafiar a un ser.
> "Surf"-desafiar al mar.
>
> (Hay locos que ya no tienen miedo).

(OI, 306-07)

Poetry, like the circus, the bullfights, and sports, provides an arena of conflict and defiance, diversion and triumph. The ability to laugh in the face of danger is, of course, at the heart of all of these activities, just as playfulness and the will to risk constitute Fuertes' fundamental posture as a poet: "Juego con fuego / pero juego" (*OI*, 133). All of life is an immense game of chance, one to which she commits herself unflinchingly ("si pierdo en la Rifa, / será porque he jugado") (*OI*, 164) and whose stakes she willingly gambles since, "en este juego a cartas que es la vida / gana el que más sonrisas ponga sobre el tapete" (*OI*, 170).

Laughter, then, serves as a catalyst for the poet's defiance, and enables her to overturn the structures and dogmas of official culture. In her view, official society is worthy if not of her disdain then most certainly of her ridicule, since the sanctions and prohibitions enforced by that society are hopelessly muddled: "Es obligatorio tener mitos / . . . / Es obligatorio presentarse con buenas ropas, / con buenas obras—no interesa tanto— . . ." (*OI*, 136). Why, she suggests, forbid eating animals when innocent children are cannibalized by wars? In a consumer society in which dolls are better dressed than children, in which opium can be openly bought and young people sold, lofty sentiments are worth nothing; "hay que tener arranque y ganas de gritar" (*OI*, 56-57). The poet's task is to bear witness to what she sees and to do so heedless of accepted codes and conventions.

Poetry is essentially a subversive art; yet even poetry and language are not immune to the poet's barbs. Fuertes turns her sights on the language of established poetic canons in poems such as **"Carta de la eme," "Poema a la eñe," "'Todas les efes tenía la novia que yo quería,'"** and **"Poema en ón"**:

Manolo mío:
  Mi madrileño marchoso,
maduro melocotón maleable,
macedonia mascaré mañana, . . .

                                        (*HG*, 80)

Todo tiene eñe en España,
¡hasta España!

Eñe de coño o la cigüeña que nos trae,
eñe la cizaña o la guadaña que nos lleve, . . .

                                        (*HG*, 115)

Fea, fascista y fulana,
formidable era de cuerpo
(frío me dejó en el alma); . . .

                                        (*HG*, 124)

De este molesto caparazón
la única salida de mi prisión
cuando me encierra tu despreocupación,
es el escape de mi inspiración, . . .

                                        (*HG*, 125)

The stammering rhythms, wordplays, alliterations, and rhyme schemes are reminiscent both of children's verses and of the ancient forms of popular comic speech known as *coq-à-l'âne* (Bakhtin, 422-26). Such verbal disruptions display an infantilism akin to the aphasia that Gilbert and Gubar see as a parody of "the sort of intellectual incapacity patriarchal culture has traditionally required of women" (58). Moreover, these distinctive features not only provide the poems their phonetic underpinning and thematic fuel, but reveal as well the disintegration of words into sounds, the collapse of romantic clichés into

linguistic absurdities. As in the forms of carnivalesque expression, Fuertes' use of language in unusual, deliberately absurd ways evinces "victory over linguistic dogmatism" (Bakhtin, 473) and therefore a sense that "poetry is, among other things, a criticism of language. In setting words together in new configurations, . . . in the relationships between words created through echo, repetition, rhythm, rhyme, it lets us hear and see our words in a new dimension" (Rich, 248).

Fuertes refuses to conform to any a priori expectations about the nature of her art. She modestly questions whether the products of her pen are really poems ("Los poemas (¿son poemas?)") (*HG*, 57), yet boldly asserts, "escribo como me da la gana" (*OI*, 32). In the cause of freedom and fearlessness, Fuertes avails herself of extrapoetic modes of discourse: her verses take the shape of recipes, letters, telegrams, news announcements, hospital registration cards, surveys, and other forms not usually a part of the poetic domain (Debicki, 82). She removes poetry from the academy and the salon (although *Sola en la sala* figures among her titles); the proper venues of poetry are for her popular meeting-grounds like the street and the marketplace. Like Antonio Machado "soñando caminos de la tarde," Gloria Fuertes "[va] haciendo versos por la calle" (*OI*, 89). She travels on the Metro, frequents book fairs, and

me meto en las tabernas,
también en los tranvías,
me cuelo en los teatros
y en los saldos me visto.
Hago una vida extraña.

                                        (*OI*, 73)

In short, Fuertes knows about herself that "Mi sitio es estar en medio del pueblo / y ser un medio del pueblo / para servir sólo al pueblo" (*HG*, 107).

In her outspoken allegiance to the people, Gloria Fuertes is a modern-day recipient of the carnival legacy. She is almost certainly familiar with the ancient comic tradition, from which she inherits many forms and images. Like many practitioners of medieval recreational literature, Fuertes hides behind a facade of naïveté, using humor and hyperbole to conceal a high degree of erudition as well as an attitude of incredulity and skepticism regarding the myths of official culture.[8] She advises her readers, for example, "no creer todo lo que os digan, / el lobo no es tan malo como Caperucita" (*HG*, 65). Even as a child, we are assured, she herself never ascribed to oft-told stories like "lo del clero" or "lo de la cigüeña" (*HG*, 61).

Carnivalesque literature of the Middle Ages, furthermore, contains a wealth of parodical treatments of dialogues, debates, treatises, and grammars. Such comic compositions, representing an unofficial mockery of official thought and ritual, figure importantly in Fuertes' work (Bakhtin, 13-15). "Oraciones gramaticales" imitates the straightforward phraseology and sentence structure proper to a child's grammar lesson:

Yo tengo esperanza.
El perro tiene hambre.
El banco del jardín respira mal.
La niña se peina.
Le vaca se lame.
Las cosas me miran,
es peor si me hablan.
En el suburbio hay flores maleantes.
Las macetas son botes,
los hombres son tigres,
los niños son viejos,
los gatos se comen,
las mondas también.
Los huérfanos huelen a madre.
Los pobres a humo.
Los ricos a brea.

(*OI*, 61)

The verses reveal the whimsy beneath Fuertes' poetic vision. Objects capable of speech, tiger-men, cats that eat each other (if not themselves), exemplify the magical metamorphoses and inversions that are commonplace in Fuertes' world.[9] The very simplicity of the verses, however, belies the harshness of social realities like the distinctions between rich and poor.[10] "Examen de preunice-mentario" combines a parody of bureaucratic language with a similarly mordant black humor:

1.°—¿Hasta cuánto y hasta cuándo puede durar
        un sufrimiento?
2.°—¿Qué largura de meses años siglos puede
        tener un dolor?
3.°—¿Cuántos grados bajo cero de desamor aguanta
        un ser humano?
4.°—¿Si usted es amorlófilo, explique cómo
        reaccionaría ante el desvío de quien ama.
5.°—El quinto es no matar. ¿Qué haría usted
        con usted en la anterior circunstancia?

(*OI*, 274)

Parodying the language of official documents or of university examinations, Fuertes creates a feeling of tension in her readers.[11] Her demanding tone requires specific answers to precisely-worded questions ("¿Hasta cuánto y hasta cuándo . . . ?", "¿Cuántos grados bajo cero . . . ?", etc.) and commands ("explique cómo"). The pompous vocabulary ("preunicementario," "amorlófilo") and peremptory tone are those commonly discerned in "offi-alese" to reinforce the distinctions between the powerful and the powerless. Yet the seeming rationality of the inquiries, together with an inquisitorial undercurrent, is deflated by absurdity and exaggeration. Suffering, after all, cannot be calculated. Pain can last as little as a month, as long as centuries. The loss of love is surely not measurable by any known barometer. The poet thus challenges us to ponder questions of a very serious nature, but questions that are ultimately unanswerable. This realization leaves us ill at ease, perhaps with a momentary sense of helplessness in the face of an inexplicable human destiny. At the same time, the very futility of the exercise contains a double-edged irony: pain, failed love, even death await the powerful and the powerless alike—those in

command of the hierarchy as well as those who are at its mercy. Like the medieval parodist, Gloria Fuertes sees the world in all its relativity, and employs laughter for all its paradoxical but democratic effects, its "gay, triumphant, . . . mocking, deriding" aspects (Bakhtin, 11-12).

"Este libro" is another carnivalesque parody of the kind of official mentality that defines the world according to inflexible criteria and cements its inhabitants into rigid categories. In this poem, the second piece in *Sola en la sala*, Fuertes adopts both the tone and the hyperbolic language of medieval street cries:

Este libro
es el más serio
más alegre
más triste
más acertado
más despiste
más raro
más normal
más directo
más indirecto
más clásico
más futurista
más oscuro
más realista
más cuerdo
más demente
más libro
más conveniente
de todo el siglo XX

(*OI*, 294)

Hyperbole and enumeration are tools for poking fun at absolutist ways of thinking. The contradictory nature of the list suggests the impossibility of formulating satisfactory definitions of Fuertes' book and, by extension, the fruitlessness of encapsulating reality within restrictive labels. The reality embodied in Fuertes' book is not static; rather, it is continually changing and growing, because the world it represents is the carnival world of becoming (Bakhtin, 181-82).

In her role of street hawker, Gloria Fuertes is faithful to the popular-festive tradition of uniting the dualities of praise and abuse (Bakhtin, 160-66). Her book, she boasts, is an exemplar of virtues, a compendium of imperfections. Offering her book as a saleable commodity reduces poetry to the level of the base and the crass; paradoxically, though, the superlatives glorify and raise poetry to the status of Platonic ideal: "Este libro / es el . . . / más libro / . . de todo el siglo XX" (Debicki, 83).

The popular dichotomies of reverence and subversion, apparent in **"Este libro,"** occur repeatedly throughout Fuertes' work. Prayers represent the poet's reverence for and trust in God, **"Poderoso Quienseas"** (*OI*, 266), **"Torero nuestro de cada día"** (*OI*, 210). Hers is a distinctly human God who doubts, is lonely, and suffers; unlike Unamuno's, however, Fuertes's God "no es problema" (*OI*, 220). She cannot help but question the elusiveness of her God: "La Alegría estudié por entenderte / e inventas otro idioma / de repente" (*OI*, 209), but never His (or Her) wisdom: "Porque El lo sabe todo de antemano, / El o ELLA, quien sea, se lo sabe" (*OI*, 207). In her own delightful turn on the Lord's Prayer (Debicki, 84-5), Fuertes contemplates the presence of God in even the humblest of quarters:

Que estás en la tierra Padre nuestro,
que te siento en la púa del pino,
en el torso azul del obrero,
en la niña que borda curvada
la espalda mezclando el hilo en el dedo.
Padre nuestro que estás en la tierra,
en el surco,
en el huerto,
en la mina,
en el puerto,
en el cine,
en el vino,
en la casa del médico.

    . . . . .

Padre nuestro que sí que te vemos,
los que luego te hemos de ver,
donde sea, o ahí en el cielo.

                            (*OI*, 47-48)

Poetry itself is, for Gloria Fuertes, a form of prayer; alternately, prayers inspire Fuertes to poetry. Among her prayers are numbered hymns of praise: "¡Bendito tú, / ser luciente, / . . . / ¡Bendecido sea quien deja lo que ama por iluminar" (*OI*, 183-84). She praises the name of God for bestowing upon her "tantos zarpazos como besos" (*HG*, 94). Even her **"Brindis cotidiano"** becomes a kind of laud not only to universal peace and joy but to rice and lentils on the tables of all human beings (*HG*, 98). **"Angelus"** represents a secularized renewal of the midday prayer in which the poet recites "medio rosario / de poesía y pavor" to be delivered from the weariness of the workaday world (*HG*, 358). In **"Oración para altas horas de la madrugada,"** Fuertes adopts a typically Franciscan tone of humility to express oneness with lowly objects but also harmony with the divine. She implores her broom, "Fray Escoba," to sweep away the bad and leave her with the good and at the same time recognizes Christ as a fellow poet: "junta nuestras manos / así como tú y yo / juntamos nuestros versos" (*HG*, 142-43). **"Letanía de los montes de la vida,"** Gloria Fuertes' version of the Sermon on the Mount, celebrates the paradoxical richness of life and beatifies all those to whom she would extend her ample embrace:

Dichosos los blancos,
porque ellos son reyes de la sonrisa.
Dichosos los negros,
porque ellos tocarán la concertina.
Dichosos los niños,
semillas inocentes.
Dichosos los locos,
porque ellos beben hilo.

                            (*OI*, 73)

Letters, a medium historically favored by women writers, afford the poet a way to approach familiarly her heavenly intercessors. Parodying the formulas that are part of the language of letters, she writes this message:

Muy Señor mío:

    . . .

Deseo que al recibo de estas líneas
se encuentre bien en compañía de su Sagrada Familia
y demás Santos de la Corte Celestial.
Servidora está bien,
        como Usted bien sabe . . .

                            (*OI*, 287-8)

Fuertes employs the prosaic conventions of commercial correspondence in an ironic way, in order to transform empty language into newly meaningful expression (Mandlove, 12-13). In like fashion, another missive posted to "Querido Juanito" echoes the poetry of San Juan de la Cruz, but confers upon the language of mysticism unequivocally earthly dimensions:

Y si salgo de vuelo
o me voy por las ramas,
sólo es para dar a la Caza caza,
me remonto y bajo rauda,
porque aún es la tierra mi sitio,
mientras que me quede un ala.

                            (*OI*, 221)

The Virgin Mary, "Neustra señora de la mayor soledad," is the object of Fuertes' most profound compassion because "vuestro Hijo / me caía bien" (*OI*, 361). She impatiently (and irreverently) invokes the names of lesser-known saints (Santa Paulina, San Filemón, San Florilipo) to beg deliverance from the promises and hopes of an elusive tomorrow—"Mañana mañana /—ipor algo se escribe con eñe de coño!—" (*OI*, 234). Typically, her prayerful wish is enlivened by the language of irreverence.

In echo of the carnivalesque tradition, Fuertes counterposes these prayers, litanies, and other contemplative verses against poems written in a subversive mode. Indeed, it is when her voice is most vehemently abusive that her laughing presence is most striking because it is then that she is at her most liberated. Poems like **"A la muerte"** and **"Bomba,"** diatribes reminiscent of popular parodical forms, summon all the recourses of the ancient grotesque esthetic:

Muerte: idioma inédito,
    absurdo, intraducible,
    palo en la cresta
    diplodocus, graja,
    quitameriendas,
    turmis,
    chupa sangre,
    come colores,
    lava.
    Ubre de palidez,
    leche de cara,
    solapada sin sol,

ihipocritilla!
—sabes lo de después
y no lo dices—,
haces más daño al vivo que al que matas,
llevándote los vivos de los muertos. . . .

(*OI*, 143)

Bomba,
estertor,
vergüenza;
monstruo de medusa cruzada con sabio,
parida de un hombre
sin pecho, anormal.
Fotógrafa fofa,
la Muerte en cadena "retrata" al minuto,
de cuerpo presente
saca el primer plano.

. . . . .

Colif lor venenosa
calcinado de cólera,
flatulenta de cal,
garrafa del diablo,
corcho, de una fétida
botella de champán.
Pareces un cerebro
con una sola idea
que radia desde arriba.
"ODIAR ODIAR ODIAR"
Nuevo aguijón que flota
y clava desde el aire.

. . . . .

¡Maldita sí maldita bomba de nuevo tipo
y por siempre maldita tu raza y tu historial!

(*OI*, 268-69)

Both poems revive the medieval tradition of oaths and curses, in a hyperventilated tone based on exaggeration, exclamation, and enumeration. The poet's voice resonates with venom against the horrors inflicted by Death and the bomb. Still, the poems are not devoid of humor, humor that stems from the deliberately offensive nature of some of the images and from the anachronistic collision of dinosaurs and the so-called advances of the nuclear age. Both poems borrow from the medieval arsenal: death is envisioned as an allegorical personage; plant and animal kingdoms are invaded to ground the poems in the natural world and thus to remind us of nature's cycle of death and regeneration.

Gloria Fuertes is drawn to expressions of abuse and subversion, is partial to the language of irreverence and impropriety outlawed by poetic canons. In one short poem, for example, she recounts the misadventures of a blind goat, encumbered by grotesquely-proportioned udders, that eats paper and "veía con el ojo del ano" (*HG*, 95). Elsewhere, she admits to an allergic reaction to prudes with delicate handwriting "como dos cagadas de mosca en el 'te amo'" (*OI*, 272). She laments that her verses "hayan salido a su puta madre" (*OI*, 293). And a sense of futility and defeat informs this shock of recognition: "Es una mierda / volver a tener luz y ver tan claro, / que soy

un nombre más, / en el amado" (*HG*, 158). This is the way she justifies her indecorous language:

. . . Si a veces hablo mal,
es porque me dejan
como un mueble,
como una mesa cojitranca me dejan,
sin equilibrio
me tambaleo,
y me tengo que calzar con un taco
¡Coño!
Aunque se horroricen los eruditos
¡Leche!

(*HG*, 147-8)

Such "unpoetic" language is meant to shock, most certainly; it also captures the colors of popular speech so prized by the poet. Like a child tasting forbidden pleasures, Gloria Fuertes delights in forbidden language as a way both of transgressing the barriers imposed on women's discourse and of vaulting the limits of poetic reality. Again, as in medieval and Renaissance grotesque literature, vulgarisms and profanities enable the poet to undermine conventional thinking, to liberate language from the strictures of dogma, and to do so in a laughing spirit (Bakhtin, 27-8).

Finally, Gloria Fuertes avails herself of the curative aspects of laughter and poetry to mediate between the forces of life and death. Poetry, after all, "es un milagro . . . es un misterio" (*OI*, 53) that heals souls wounded by the pain of lovelessness and staves off the inevitable approach of death. "Y canto y canto y me canto / . . . / Y ya no tenéis congoja, / y ya no tenéis jaqueca" (*HG*, 264). The poet's task is to "vendar corazones y escribir el poema / que a todos nos contagie" (*OI*, 45). To the emotional scrapes incurred in the name of love, she tenderly applies "la pomada necesaria o inútil / de mi poema" (*HG*, 362). She has spent half a lifetime, she notes, "destristeando a este hospital de locos" and not without signs of contagion (*HG*, 263). Her poetry beckons us to relieve our hunger: "toma el pecho, / el mío, que te doy para que vivas" (*OI*, 325). In **"Penúltima canción de Don Simón,"** a play of words revolving around the meanings of "coma" juxtaposes physical suffering and the tools of the writer's trade. The poet thus not only draws attention to the notion of illness as an inspiration for woman's art but plies her readers with the nutritive qualities of poetry:

Ahora que estoy a punto
antes de entrar en coma,
coma
estos boquerones que he frito,
entre dolor y dolor,
lea estos papeles que he escrito,
entre dolor y dolor.
Ahora que estoy a punto
antes de entrar en coma,
diga que me perdona
(como perdono yo
a toda la persona
que a mí me apaleó).

Ahora que estoy a punto

antes de estar en coma.

(*HG*, 251)

Above all, Gloria Fuertes aspires to be "una aspirina inmensa / —que quien me cate se cure—" (*OI*, 270). She perceives of her chosen profession as one of the healing arts and, in fact, its restorative qualities endow poetry with a singular grace:

Mi verso tiene vocación de curandero,
ponle donde te duela,
si te mejora,
será poesía de verdad.

(*HG*, 228)

The ancient carnival tradition is Gloria Fuertes' happy inheritance. As such, her work bears the joyous stamp of much of popular recreational literature, which she reinvents with her own womanly imagination. Laden with disease, loneliness, and other forms of human suffering, her verses are also rich with celebratory rituals and festive activities. Poetry is, for her, a way of marking each phase in the cycle of life and death. She enters the merriment with a laughing heart to free her verses from fear and constraint, to restore her world from pain and death.[12]

NOTES

[1] The ideas suggested above are elaborated throughout *Rabelais and His World*.

[2] Umberto Eco's view of carnival (p. 6) differs from that of Bakhtin. According to Eco, "Carnival can exist only as an *authorized* transgression . . . [comedy and carnival] represent paramount examples of law enforcement. They remind us of the existence of the rule."

[3] Gloria Fuertes, *Obras incompletas* (Madrid: Cátedra, 1983), p. 22. I have used two texts for this study, *Obras incompletas* and *Historia de Gloria* (Madrid: Cátedra, 1983), subsequently referred to as *OI* and *HG*. *OI* compiles the following titles: *Isla ignorada* (Madrid: Musa Nueva, 1950); *Aconsejo beber hilo* (Madrid: Arquero, 1954); *Todo asusta* (Caracas: Lírica Hispana, 1958); *Ni tiro, ni veneno, ni navaja* (Barcelona: El Bardo, 1955); *Poeta de quardia* (Barcelona: El Bardo, 1968); *Cómo atar los bigotes al tigre* (Barcelona: El Bardo, 1969); and *Sola en la sala* (Zaragoza: Javalambre, 1973).

On the question of Gloria Fuertes' self-referentiality, I refer the reader to my articles, "Gloria Fuertes and the Poetics of Solitude" and "The Poetry of Gloria Fuertes: Textuality and Sexuality."

[4] In my unpublished essay, "The Poetry of Gloria Fuertes: Textuality and Sexuality," I study the use of negation and silence as expressions of impotence and as a kind of prelude to creativity.

[5] Regarding the esthetics of marginality, see Rosette C. Lamont, "The Off-Center Spaciality of Women's Discourse."

[6] Gubar and Gilbert explore the theme of madness, as does Yalom. Regarding the many "magical" metamorphoses that transpire in Fuertes' verses, please see my article, "Weaving the World . . ."

[7] The theme of poetry as an analogue of physical birth is treated in "The Poetry of Gloria Fuertes: Textuality and Sexuality." Yalom pursues the issue of maternity as a literary theme in her excellent study.

[8] Benítez interprets Fuertes' work as that of a primitive or naif.

[9] Benitez sees the bestiary in Fuertes' poetry as a modern-day counterpart of traditional altarpieces. In "Weaving the World . . . ," I study the presence of animals, machines, and other objects.

[10] Rogers is concerned with the relationship between Fuertes' "comic spirit" and her social consciousness. Persin also sees humor as the way Fuertes awakens the readers to deeper levels of meaning.

[11] Hutcheon provides an illuminating discussion of parody as a modern art form.

[12] The idea for a study of Gloria Fuertes' poetry in light of the work of Mikhail Bakhtin was suggested by Professor Mary Lee Bretz of Rutgers University. I gratefully acknowledge that suggestion.

WORKS CITED

Bakhtin, Mikhail. *Rabelais and His World*. Trans. Hèléne Iswolsky. Bloomington: Indiana University Press, 1984.

Benítez, Rubén A. "El maravilloso retablo de Gloria Fuertes." *Mester*. Vol. 9 (Jan. 1980): 21-33.

Debicki, Andrew P. *Poetry of Discovery: The Spanish Generation of 1956-1971*. Lexington: The University Press of Kentucky, 1982.

Eco, Umberto. "The Frames of Comic 'Freedom.'" *Carnival!* Ed. Thomas A. Sebeok. Berlin: Mouton, 1984. 1-9.

Fuertes, Gloria. *Historia de Gloria*. Madrid: Cátedra, 1983.

———. *Obras incompletas*. Madrid: Cátedra, 1983.

Gilbert, Sandra M. and Susan Gubar. *The Madwoman in the Attic*. New Haven: Yale University Press, 1979.

Hutcheon, Linda. *A Theory of Parody: The Teachings of Twentieth-Century Art Forms*. New York: Methuen, 1985.

Kristeva, Julia. "Oscillation du 'pouvoir' au 'refus,'" Interview by Xavière Gauthier in *Tel quel* (Summer 1974). Trans. Marilyn A. August. Marks and de Courtivron 165-67.

Lamont, Rosette C. "The Off-Center Spaciality of Women's Discourse." *Theory and Practice of Feminist Literary Criticism*. Ed. Gabriela Mora and Karen S. Van Hooft. Ypsilanti: Bilingual Press / Editorial Bilingüe, 1982. 138-55.

Mandlove, Nancy. "Oral Texts: The Play of Orality and Literacy in the Poetry of Gloria Fuertes." *Siglo XX / 20th Century*. Vol. 5, Nos. 1-2 (1987-88): 11-16.

Marks, Elaine and Isabelle de Courtivron, ed. *New French Feminisms: An Anthology*. Amherst: University of Massachusetts Press, 1980.

Michie, Helena. *The Flesh Made Word: Female Figures and Women's Bodies.* New York: Oxford University Press, 1987.

Persin, Margaret H. *Recent Spanish Poetry and the Role of the Reader.* London and Toronto: Bucknell University Press, 1987.

Rich, Adrienne. *On Lies, Secrets, and Silence: Selected Prose 1966-1978.* New York and London: W. W. Norton and Company, 1979.

Rogers, Timothy J. "The Comic Spirit in the Poetry of Gloria Fuertes." *Perspectives on Contemporary Literature.* Vol. 7 (1981):88-97.

Sherno, Sylvia R. "Gloria Fuertes and the Poetics of Solitude." *Anales de la literatura española contemporánea* (forthcoming).

———. "The Poetry of Gloria Fuertes: Textuality and Sexuality" (unpublished).

———. "Weaving the World: The Poetry of Gloria Fuertes." *Hispania* (forthcoming).

Yalom, Marilyn. *Maternity, Mortality, and the Literature of Madness.* University Park: The Pennsylvania State University Press, 1985.

Silvia R. Sherno (essay date 1990)

SOURCE: "Gloria Fuertes' Room of Her Own," in *Letras Femeninas,* Vol. XVI, Nos. 1-2, 1990, pp. 85-99.

[*Sherno examines the roles of both nature and civilization in defining Fuertes' personal space.*]

If the somber hues of the Castillian countryside have been most memorably painted by Antonio Machado; if the brilliant colors of Andalucía have been captured by any number of poets, including Lorca and Alberti; then the favored landscape of Gloria Fuertes is undoubtedly the city of Madrid. The colloquial character and the insouciant tones of Fuertes' language lovingly duplicate the flavorful rhythms and patterns overheard in any street corner conversation in Madrid. Busses, trains, and cars traverse the streets and barrios of her native city, cited along with other place names like the Rastro and the department store, Galerías Preciados. The title of one of her early collections of poetry, *Antología y poemas del suburbio* (1954), attests to the poet's very urban sensibility, as does the presence in her verses of telephones and doorbells, typewriters and telegraphs, robots and, in a more sinister vein, the atomic bomb. Her most common themes are those of everyday life: the joys and disappointments that accompany love and the loss of love, alienation and the desire for human connection, the injustices suffered by those at the lower reaches of society. In short, Fuertes' voice is that of the ordinary inhabitants of Madrid or perhaps of any other modern metropolis. In her own words, "en la ciudad me dirijo a todo ser que sufre o goza sobre el asfalto" (*OI*, 32).

Despite these myriad manifestations of modern urban life, it is clear that nature is an equally felt presence in her work. While Fuertes acknowledges that "no soy demasiado descriptora de exteriores. No soy paisajista" (*OI*, 32), she gives ample evidence of an active, even symbiotic relationship with nature in the form of sky, moon, trees, and animals. It is in the natural world that Fuertes experiences a rebirth from the nothingness that for Carol Christ is "a spiritual experience, a stripping away of the facade of conventional reality" (Christ, xviii). In nature Fuertes emerges into a new light of heightened consciousness. Merging with nature, less an objective reality than an expression of metamorphosis, she undergoes the transformations that allow her to create her authentic selfhood. Nature becomes a new space where she retrieves a lost paradise of harmony and freedom.

Ultimately, whether in the midst of the natural world or in the center of Madrid, Gloria Fuertes creates a room of her own, a space to conform to what she calls her own "geografía humana," what Gaston Bachelard has designated the "topography of . . . intimate being" (xxxii). Fuertes' verses are filled with references to rooms, cells, and attics on the one hand; on the other hand, to the open, empty spaces of islands and windows. Employing her own body as a point of spatial reference, Gloria Fuertes draws upon images of miniature and immensity, inside and outside, to mirror the expansion and compression of her own voice, to suggest the enclosure and freedom of her intimate self, and in turn, to explore issues of being and non-being.

Two paradigms provide valuable tools for reading Fuertes' poetry in a new way and for understanding its deeper implications. Annis Pratt's *Archetypal Patterns in Women's Fiction* proposes that the female hero quests for a lost "green world" of matrilineal roots. This search is followed by transformation and subsequent re-entry into patriarchal society (135-143). Carol P. Christ studies women writers' spiritual quests in terms of a new mysticism enacted within a spiral of nothingness, awakening, insight, and naming. Whether we read Fuertes' work as an archetypal rebirth story or as a spiritual quest, we can see her verses as steps in an ever-spiraling journey inward.

The image of the spiral, of course, suitably describes the journey of Gloria Fuertes, author of *Obras incompletas*. With that felicitous title, Fuertes has intuited that the unending process of self-discovery occurs in a time zone peculiar to female consciousness, attuned as it is to the endlessly recurring seasons and cycles of nature (Christ, 14; *APWF*, 169). The unfolding of female authenticity, Mary Day explains, coincides with "women's *own* time. It is our *life-time*" (43). Not surprisingly, Gloria Fuertes is conscious that "la vida es un maldito sube y baja, / un baja y sube . . ." (*OI*, 146) and that "todo . . . que es, / termina para volver a empezar" (*HG*, 145). She allows that life is an endless "empeoro y mejoro" and that, not unlike Sisyphus, "subiré y subiré donde la pena" (*OI*, 182). Yet she knows too that "lo mejor del recorrido / no es la meta, es el paisaje" (*OI*, 173).

Gloria Fuertes tells us that her mother died when the young poet was fifteen years old (*OI*, 41). Two years later, Fuertes published her first autobiographical poem,

"Isla ignorada." Although later dismissed by the author for its "lógica inmadurez" (*OI*, 21), the poem proves surprisingly prescient because it depicts a natural world that is clearly inseparable from issues of creativity and selfhood that have repeatedly occupied Fuertes' imagination.

> Soy como esa isla que ignorada,
> late acunada por árboles jugosos,
> en el centro de un mar
> que no me entiende,
> rodeada de nada,
> —sola sólo.
> Hay aves en mi isla relucientes,
> y pintadas por ángeles pintores,
> hay fieras que me miran dulcemente,
> y venenosas flores.
> Hay arroyos poetas
> y voces interiores
> de volcanes dormidos.
>
> Quizá haya algún tesoro
> muy dentro de mi entraña.
>   . . . . .
>
> Los árboles del bosque de mi isla,
> sois vosotros mis versos.
> ¡Qué bien sonáis a veces
> si el gran músico viento
> os toca cuando viene el mar que me rodea!
>   . . . . .
>
> Para mí es un placer ser ignorada,
> isla ignorada del océano eterno.
>
> En el centro del mundo sin un libro
> sé todo, porque vino un mensajero
> y me dejó una cruz para la vida
> —para la muerte me dejó un misterio—.
>
>   (*OI*, 21-22)

Curiously evocative of Henri Rousseau's primitive landscapes and mysterious creatures, "Isla ignorada" exemplifies Annis Pratt's analysis of the young female protagonist's retreat from the normative restrictions of patriarchy. This retreat imitates the story of how Daphne escapes being ravished by Apollo by magically changing into a laurel tree. Pratt associates the "green world" of childhood innocence and freedom with matrilineal values (*APWF*, 16-29). Clearly, the lush vegetation and animal life of Gloria Fuertes' utopian island suggest fertility and abundance and are therefore closely allied with the inner voices of imagination and creativity: birds are painters and brooks, poets; winds make music, trees are verses. Even potentially lethal elements of nature ("fieras," "venenosas flores," "volcanes dormidos") accompany her in her artistry. Significantly, the speaker feels herself cradled ("acunada") by the world of nature. She absorbs the natural world into herself, becoming the island ("esta isla que soy") she blissfully inhabits. She transmutes herself into a kind of mother earth ("y soy tierra feliz") and, in so doing, at once figuratively recovers her lost mother and unites with a cosmic maternal figure.

Annis Pratt views the young female protagonist setting out on her archetypal journey as standing at the interstices of past, present, and future: the green world is swiftly receding into the past as the young woman faces initiation into experience and enclosure within the dominant male society (*APWF*, 122). **"Isla ignorada"** is a particularly affecting adolescent fantasy of a natural world of serenity and beauty, with the poet herself "en el centro del mundo sin un libro." She senses her precarious position at the juncture of childhood and maturity, of her own intuitive knowledge and the kinds of institutionalized thinking of which the book is a figurative artifact. Still, she divines within herself a personal power and authenticity of self ("quizá haya algún tesoro / muy dentro de mi entraña"). This understanding of herself, both as woman and as poet, enables her to recreate within herself her lost green world, to find her own centeredness as she inevitably faces encroachments from the outside world.

With **"Isla ignorada,"** Gloria Fuertes embarks on her peregrination towards selfhood and beyond. Like that of many other women writers, Fuertes' art is not only a vehicle for self-discovery and a quest for transcendence but also a way of disencumbering herself of patriarchal authority. As a woman in a patriarchal culture, and as a writer as well, Fuertes has endured constraints on her artistic and personal integrity. She traces the alienation brought about by her ancillary status as a female to the time of her birth, when "mi madre pensaba en un muchacho" (*OI*, 58), an admission that sheds an especially poignant light on Fuertes' artistic search for her mother. The dismay at bearing a girl child, communicated to her by her mother ("señora la cual no se hizo querer por servidora en vida") (*OI*, 356), was no doubt rendered more excruciating for being part of a general bewilderment regarding this girl child's propensity for "mosqueantes aficiones, impropias de la hija de un obrero—tales como atletismo, deportes y poesía" (*OI*, 27). "Cuando yo era pequeña," the poet informs us, "nadie me comprendía" (*OI*, 59). Still less, to be sure, because "en mi pueblo / no dejan escribir a las mujeres" (*OI*, 72).

The emptiness provoked by this early incomprehension and failure of love is endlessly relived in Fuertes' poetry through expressions of solitude as well as of illness, self-loathing, madness, and suicide. Her solitude, for example, takes the shape of mysterious beings "que abren y cierran puertas y ventanas / mueven papeles y alzan los visillos / y hay un muerto de miedo sobre mi cama. / Y hay algo que no hay entre las patas de mi silla" (*OI*, 206). At times, the poet is merely visited by a nettlesome sense of malaise. In "Una de la madrugada en Madrid," she suffers nocturnal fears of drowning, "y no hay dónde llamar," and finds small consolation in the strait-jacket of the morning routine: " . . . Por la mañana azul ya es otra cosa, / te afeitas o te pegas maquillaje, / te pones el vestido o tú el traje, / coges el autobús y eres un muerto" (*OI*, 221). At other times this malaise is induced by disembodied voices that invade her solitude and echo dubious axioms of conventional authority and wisdom, truisms like "/ Por favor, no beba líquido antes de comer!" or more pointedly, "La que no se casa es porque no puede

/ el que no es feliz es porque no quiere . . ." (*OI*, 310). She feels asphyxiated by the certainty that "Todo el mundo tiene rejas. / Esta vida es una cárcel, / una jaula, una cisterna / y te ahogas cuando sales" (*OI*, 197) (*APWF*, 29). Repeated images of claustrophobia, drowning, and suffocation, frequent in women's writings, express the poet's feelings of "social confinement and . . . yearning for spiritual escape" (*OI*, 155-56, 255, 307) (Gilbert and Gubar, 86).

Almost always, phantasmagorical creatures appear in the darkness and fearsome events occur at night. "Todas las noches," she announces, "me suicido un poco" (*OI*, 215). As it is for the mystic poets before her, the dark night is the scene of her deepest despair. A poem entitled "**A la Ausencia**" draws upon the mystic and courtly traditions to foreground the emptiness produced by her lover's absence, amidst a landscape that is the absolute inversion of her lost green world:

> La Ausencia es una tierra que da espinos,
> espinas y serpientes, caracolas
> con arañas gigantes, con ortigas,
> La Ausencia es mar de cieno, precipicio,
> es pozo y alacrán, volcán y rayo.
> No es buena para nada, te destruye.
> Conmigo no vale. Es una ola,
> nado contra corriente, ¡pero nado!
> . . . En la Ausencia se quiere más al otro,
> ¡pero también se duda y se estremece!,
> el esqueleto suena a "no me acuerdo,
> "¿cómo era su rostro, Dios, cómo era?".
> Se vive sin vivir, flotando siempre,
> de sin voz sin querer se olvida uno
> y por la noche no nos nace sueño.
>   · · · · ·
>
> Ausencia, grito en flor y llama viva,
> enfermedad mayor de los amantes,
> epidemia de cínifes y grajos,
> muerte que se nos mete y no nos mata.
>   · · · · ·
>
> la cueva de la Ausencia está infectada;
> ¡que se rompe la vena de la tarde!
> ¡Que ya sangra la noche su tristeza!
> ¡Que te punzan los ganchos de las horas!
> ¡Que te queman las brasas de las brisas!
> Que la gente es odiosa y es veneno
> todo lo que no sea su mirada.
> Su presencia en la ausencia la evocamos,
> la soledad se mete por las uñas,
> un diablo rojo baila de contento
> mientras dos en silencio se deslágriman.
>   (*QEELT*, 80-81)

Employing the paradoxical language of Santa Teresa ("llama viva, se vive sin vivir," "muerte que no nos mata"), Fuertes recapitulates the theme of alienation, a condition described in upper case to grant the earthly lover's absence an almost allegorical status. Fuertes borrows too from the vocabulary of the courtly poets both to convey the physical effects wrought by the lover's abandonment ("enfermedad mayor de los amantes," "epidemia de cínifes y grajos," "la cueva de la Ausencia está infectada") and to protest against the disease of love ("¡que se rompe la vena de la tarde / ¡Que ya sangra la noche su tristeza! / ¡Que te punzan los ganchos de las horas! / Que te queman las brasas de las brisas!").

"**En la Ausencia**" depicts a menacing nocturnal wasteland, a surreal scene reminiscent of Bosch. This infernal nature of cliff and chasm, inhabited by giant crawling insects, represents the poet's plunge into spiritual nothingness and her consequent apotheosis as hero. The poet's determination to swim against the current ("Es una ola, / Nado contra corriente, ¡pero nado!") marks her induction into a heroic enterprise whereby she rejects the convention of alienating love. Tellingly, the sea stands as the site both of spiritual death and the poet hero's rebirth (*APWF*, 142; Christ, 16). Moreover, the end of the poem, with its lighthearted image of a dancing red demon, calls for an end to alienating love ("su presencia en la ausencia la evocamos") and thus offers a tantalizing preview of a new space "experienced, both as power of presence and power of absence . . . a flow of healing energy which is participation in the power of being" (Daly, 41).

Much as the mystic dark night anticipates an experience of illumination, Gloria Fuertes crosses "the cratered night of female memory" (Rich, 228) and awakens to a newly enlightened reality. However, unlike the mystic's passive surrender of self and annulment of the outside world, Fuertes' reborn state is one of active watchfulness, "a coming to self" through which she re-defines her consciousness of being and power and reestablishes her relationship with the world (Christ, 19). In her capacity as *Poeta de guardia* (the title of her 1968 collection), she generously offers herself to others as a kind of optical aide: "El poeta sirve como unas gafas, / para que *veas*, hijo mío, para que *veas*" (*HG*, 274). "Quisiera convertirme en tu linterna," she says, "y serte útil cuando no ves claro" (*HG*, 336).

Light, both from within and from without, is a necessary condition for life; otherwise, "es insoportable a oscuras" (*HG*, 294). Windows, with their implications of presence and absence, freedom and enclosure, image the poet's acuity of insight into the nature of being and nonbeing (Bachelard, 211-31). When she remembers painfully her childhood home, with its two real windows and its two painted ones, she revives a desire to open a window to the truth, "para ver lo que se veía / desde aquellas ventanas que no existieron" (*OI*, 26). Now, we are told, "mi ventana es un cine. ¡Hay que ver lo que veo!" (*OI*, 84). Gloria Fuertes fashions for herself a new poetic mission: "Voy por la noche, sabes, / haciendo versos; / . . . / ¡Cállate, si te gusto, / estoy alumbrando!" (*OI*, 89). She herself possesses newly-acquired powers of lucidity and clairvoyance, a gift of nature "que me hace saber / de antemano" (*HG*, 300). "Sospecho lo sospechable, / intuyo lo que pulula en la oscuridad" (*HG*, 284). She intuitively knows and feels "todo lo que hacéis y lo que os pasa" (*OI*, 113), is surrounded by other clairvoyant beings (*OI*, 120), and recites a witch's incantation to exorcise the spirits of darkness and death (*OI*, 236). She converts her often recounted madness into a new kind of witchcraft that upends conventional ways of thinking. She deems so-called normality, for example, as nothing more than "una locura controlada" (*HG*, 291). Indeed, she participates in the historically reviled sorority originally designated the "craft of the wise" and inherits her sisters' gifts of fertility, healing, and female strength that in ancient times expressed "that cluster of values constituting totality of self" (*APWF*, 176).

Above all, Fuertes' awakening assures a new way of envisioning herself: "porque yo, tan mínima, sé tantas cosas, / y mi cuerpo es un ojo sin fin / con el que para mi desventura veo todo" (*OI*, 76). The poet counterposes paradoxical terms of miniature and immensity to affirm self-awareness and knowledge of the world. Diminishing herself in size ("yo, tan mínima"), Fuertes nonetheless conceives of herself as an eye that grotesquely occupies the entire dimensions of her body ("mi cuerpo es un ojo sin fin"). Of course, all of Fuertes' work reveals the twin impulses towards miniaturization and immensity. Miniaturization is apparent in the use of diminutives ("prologuillo," "librito," and "minipoemas" to refer to her writings; "mi vasito de leche," to toast her readers). These diminutives both echo and parody the self-effacement and infantilization traditionally demanded of women in general and the anxieties of authorship suffered by female artists in particular (Gilbert and Gubar, 108). Miniaturization is present in the minutiae of domestic activities, typically dismissed as "woman's work" but which Fuertes dignifies with poetic status; and in the abundance of epigrammatic verses in which her voice virtually fades into silence (Gubar, "Blank Page"; Sherno, "Solitude," 316-17). Fuertes' own body is the object of this process of diminution. She metaphorically reduces her heart to the size of a pincusion and by extension, diminishes her anguish: "no le claves ya más alfileres," she cautions (*OI*, 298). With advancing age she notes that "empiezo a encogerme," but her smallness makes her like an infant in the arms of "esta madre que es la muerte" (*OI*, 64). These instances of self-minimalization evidence the same fascination with the world of childhood as that exhibited in "Nana para adultos" and other lullabies, and in various poems that mimic the rhymes and nonsense patterns of children's verses (*HG*, 80-81, 115, 124, 125). Imitating a child's perspective of herself in relation to the exterior world thus expresses nostalgia for her distant childhood.

Whereas miniaturization draws the poet further into the intimacy of being, the counter-pull of gigantism thrusts her upon the world. Her magnified perspective creates a sense of spectacle that informs her perception of self, as when she allows "aquí estoy expuesta como todos" (*OI*, 169). This sense of a public self accounts in part for the presence in Fuertes' verses of bullfighters, athletes, and circus performers, especially clowns, with whom she shares the "mysticism of laughter" (*OI*, 55) (Sherno, "Carnival"). She conceives of existence as a spectacle and of

herself, as an at times beleaguered participant:

> Esto, es Teatro.
> Vivir como espectador
> es apasionante e interesante,
> como protagonista
> ¡es acojonante!
>
> ¡Ay que lucha, digo qué leche!
>
>   (*HG*, 121)

Expressions of immensity underpin Fuertes' depiction of herself as powerful. Ever mindful of her womanliness, she calls herself "la mujer fuerte que se viste / y medita mirando a calendario" (*OI*, 98). She is a self-confessed "fabuloso desastre" (*OI*, 294), a "tierna amazona," at once vulnerable to pain and as strong as her name implies (*HG*, 144-45). Like a modern-day dragon-slayer, Gloria Fuertes is capable of single-handedly defending the cause of peace: her duty, after all, is to "arreglar el mundo" (*OI*, 59). Gloria Fuertes dares to vaunt her own assets, as when she boasts, "Soy una de las mejores personas / que he conocido" (*HG*, 213). Indeed, contrary to expectations regarding female docility and inconspicuousness, she exclaims in a burst of braggadocio, "¡ . . . montaña soy yo! / . . . / Cuando se dinamita algo / es porque significaba algo" (*HG*, 59).

Many of Fuertes' poems, like **"A la muerte" "Puesto del Rastro,"** and **"Bomba,"** are characterized by enumeration and exaggeration. These and numerous other lists, litanies, and diatribes incorporate the perspectives of both the miniature and the gigantic since they supply a multiplicity of detail while miming "the process whereby space becomes significance, whereby everything is made to 'count'" (Stewart, 47). In these poetic curiosities, Fuertes' voice amplifies and extends itself, and assumes a kind of grandiosity of its own. This is her way of protesting against the rule of silence historically imposed upon women, of demanding entrance into the outside world.

In fact, the processes of miniaturization and gigantism alike constitute spacial exaggerations which transcend and distort perspectives, proportions and boundaries. The miniature retracts into itself, distances and democratizes the world, and becomes its microcosm. The miniature inhabits "the center of decision" (Bachelard, 165). The gigantic, on the other hand, not only overshadows the world but makes the world a microcosm of itself. Both points of view are articulated from positions of power and therefore mock the hierarchies implicit in conventional values and modes of thought (Bachelard 148-210; Stewart, 37-103). Both perspectives, moreover, offer the poet a transcendent vision of herself in relation to the world.

Ultimately, it is her own body that provides Fuertes with a measure of the world as well as a point of reference by which to gauge her own place in it. Instructing her readers in a lesson of "human geography," she transforms her body into a mirror of the universe:

Mirad mi continente conteniendo
brazos, piernas y tronco inmesurado,
pequeños son mis pies, chicas mis manos,
hondos mis ojos, bastante bien mis senos.
Tengo un lago debajo de la frente,
a veces se desborda y por las cuencas,
donde se bañan las niñas de mis ojos,
cuando el llanto me llega hasta las piernas
y mis volcanes tiemblan en la danza.

. . . . .

Dentro del continente hay contenido,
los estados unidos de mi cuerpo,
el estado de pena por la noche,
el estado de risa por el alma
—estado de soltera todo el diá—

. . . . .

el caso es que mi caso es ser la isla
llamada a sumergirse o sumergerse
en las aguas del océano humano
conocido por vulgo vulgarmente.

(*OI*, 245-46)

The poet replicates in her body's terrain the topography of intimate being which in turn describes a dialectic between inside and outside. Tears become lakes, and feelings, convulsing volcanoes. Her body contains her, yet she is herself encased within nature. She acknowledges the harmony contained by her body ("los estados unidos de mi cuerpo") and views pain and laughter with the same equanimity as she does her unmarried state ("estado de soltera todo el día"). Imagining herself once again the island of her youthful fantasies, she can no longer ignore nor be ignored by "el océano humano." She becomes, in Annis Pratt's words, "a hero representing the possibilities of growth and survival" (127).

Within nature Gloria Fuertes comes most profoundly into authentic selfhood, completing the quest for fulfillment begun in her youth. In nature she experiences the transformations that attune her to the powers residing in the universe and in turn within herself. Among the numerous metamorphoses she undergoes, Fuertes masks herself as an eagle, an ostrich, and a dove (*HG*, 81, 99, 151). She is fond of the elephant and the walrus, awkward beasts that like her, "padece[n] del corazón" (*OI*, 360). She envies the fish in the sea, capable of reproducing "sin 'hacerlo'" (*HG*, 326). A rock'n'roll centipede is the object of her admiration (*OI*, 285), as is the platypus (*OI*, 286). She sees herself as a sweet-natured hedgehog but also as a "cabra sola" (*OI*, 286, 212), a lamb but also a lion (*HG*, 234). Bees and wasps swarm in her body (*OI*, 80). "¿Tú sabes que vienes de las algas?," she demands—because this knowledge preserves in her a necessary humility and reminds her of the cyclical nature of human existence (*OI*, 171). That is why she exhorts us in turn to learn the lessons of nature: "aprendamos por fin de las bestias, / imitemos las formas de las flores, / de los insectos aprendamos vida / y de la hierba danza" (*OI*, 62) (Benitez, 23-25).

Most importantly, Fuertes imagines herself again and again as a tree, the all-encompassing symbol of "the whole of manifestation": life and immortality, knowledge and power, femininity and androgyny, the bridge between earth and the rest of the universe (Cooper, 176-79). " . . . Y por Castilla veo un árbol / y parece que veo alquien de mi familia": the tree affords her not only a patriotic connection but also a spiritual oneness with nature (*OI*, 295). She laments the advances of the modern industrial society, triumphs produced at the expense of the natural world: "Cuando nace un cueceleches de aluminio / muere un árbol" (*OI*, 336). Though she has not "planted" any children, she concedes: "He plantado muchos árboles, / he plantado muchos libros/ y he plantado a muchos tíos" (*HG*, 228). She is herself a kind of "noble roble" (*HG*, 242) and "en el árbol de mi pecho" she shelters a small bird (*OI*, 95). In a poem entitled "Los pájaros anidan," Fuertes transforms herself into a tree and, what is more, into a force of nature:

Los pájaros anidan en mis brazos,
en mis hombros, detrás de mis rodillas,
entre los senos tengo codornices,
los pájaros se creen que soy un árbol.
Una fuente se creen que soy los cisnes,
bajan y beben todos cuando hablo.
Las ovejas me pisan cuando pasan
y comen en mis dedos los gorriones,
se creen que yo soy tierra las hormigas
y los hombres se creen que no soy nada.

(*OI*, 49)

The poem completes Gloria Fuertes' perception of herself in solidarity with the natural world. Hearkening back to the archetypes of the Lady of the Beasts and of the wise old maid she provides a nurturing presence to bird and beast (*APWF*, 126-27). All the creatures in this utopian nature sense in her a sympathetic soul; men alone reject her very existence. Still, Fuertes finds in nature the source of her own womanly power. By means of the tree motif, she revives the ancient prepatriarchal iconography of goddesses and other powerful female figures (Pratt, "Aunt Jennifer's Tigers," 175). Through her incarnation as a fountain, she suggests immortality and paradise while, as earth, she summons the archetype of the Great Mother (Cooper, 71-72, 59). She embodies here the favorable associations surrounding women long-ago supplanted by patriarchially inspired biases. In the same proportion as she is energized by the natural elements, Gloria Fuertes, self-proclaimed poet of the suburbs, delights in and is empowered by objects. The simple enumeration of used and rusted wares, in **"Puesto del Rastro"** (*OI*, 66-67), sanctifies both the street-hawker and her inventory (Debicki, 83). She voices admiration for the independence of objects like records and telephones (*HG*, 170) and expresses a desire to become one day a motor, "sí, motor. / ¡Que os mueva al amor!" (*HG*, 179). Objects are possessed of a singular and enviable humanity, like the typewriters that transform their sinister office by writing each other love letters (*HG*, 78). Among the things that she likes, she tells us in a poem that bears that title, she includes the following:

Me gusta,
divertir a la gente haciéndola pensar.
Desayunar un poco de harina de amapola,
irme lejos y sola a buscar hormigueros,
santiguarme si pasa un mendigo cantando,
ir por agua,
cazar cínifes,
escribir a mi rey a la luz de la una,
a la luz de las dos,
meterme en mi pijama
a la luz de las tres,
caer como dormida
y soñar que soy algo
que casi, casi vuela.

(*OI*, 78)

The poet assumes the tone of a witch's incantation and in fact invests her list of eccentricities with a magical aura. Intoning the hours ("a la luz de la una, / a la luz de las dos, / . . . / a la luz de las tres"), she conjures forth the mysterious powers of the moon (long a female symbol) to intercede in her dreams of flight. Similarly, she recognizes the interdependence of people and objects which she endows with vitality and feelings: "Las cosas, nuestras cosas, / les gusta que las quieran; / . . . / "¿Qué será de las cosas cuando el hombre se acabe? / Como perros las cosas no existen sin el amo" (*OI*, 215-16). In sum, Fuertes' understanding of the magic, even the spirituality, inherent in things "is a key to revelations that enable her to contact the source of her power" (Christ, 43; Sherno, "Weaving").

By naming the source of her womanly power in the world of nature and in the nature of things, Gloria Fuertes completes her poetic quest for authentic selfhood. For Fuertes, integrity of being is manifested in the harmonious convergence of male and female and, indeed, in the transcendence of gender.[1] That is why androgynous characters figure prominently in her work. The phantom artist with whom she paints pictures, for example, "a veces . . . parecía hombre y a veces mujer" (*OI*, 214). She tells about the fish with a woman's name and a man's gills (*OI*, 87) and about the hen that laid golden eggs and then "se convirtió en gallo" (*HG*, 167). The merman, born of a mermaid, has no legs and is secretly asexual (*OI*, 230-31). An equally magical figure, shepherd of cats and expert in the night, is in fact a transvestite, "un sabio vestido de princesa" (*OI*, 91-92). Transvestites earn her unqualified affection—she calls them "mis amigas los hombres"—and assures them that "no soy un hombre, / pero bueno sí, / es igual" (*HG*, 355). All are fantastic creatures, endowed with special powers and virtues, who overleap the bounds of logic and the expectations created by more conventional minds. Most tellingly for her concept of spirituality, Fuertes envisions God as the ultimate androgyne ("Porque El lo sabe todo de antemano, EL o ELLA, quien sea, se lo sabe") who controls human destiny and in so doing, offers the poet a strange consolation (*OI*, 207-08).

Annis Pratt tells us that for many female heroes who have experienced rebirth, "gender becomes one among other elements in the crucible of transformation" (*APWF*, 10). Gloria Fuertes' affinity for fantastic, androgynous beings is in fact the way she images her own fully realized identity. Much as the spinsters of old wove a dynamic world of nature into their tapestries, Fuertes fashions a utopian space—a kind of "womanspace"—where she experiences "a wave of union with the whole universe" (*APWF*, 129). By virtue of what Carol P. Christ calls her "grounding in nature," Fuertes returns to her longed-for green world, a world that she encounters "dentro dentro, no fuera, dentro" (*OI*, 144). In imagined rooms and houses she recaptures the independence and freedom predicted in the adolescent reveries of "Isla ignorada" (Bachelard, 3-73). Hers is a "casa sin amo" (*OI*, 83), a convent without walls (*OI*, 89), a utopian island "que no viene en el mapa" (*OI*, 219). In this intimate space she finds not the embittered loneliness of the "solterona" but the unbound state of "la perfecta soltera, / una dulce pera, / perita en dulce, / su amor sin papeleos / ¡Qué bien la luce!" (*HG*, 285). In the "room of her own" so eloquently described by Virginia Woolf, she creates the site of her own womanly integrity and authentic being. This is, finally, the lesson her verses deliver:

Me siento sola y una
como una sola luna
—por ser igual a todas las mujeres
y no parecerme a ninguna—,
me siento sola y una
en mi vacía cuna.

(*HG*, 198)

NOTES

[1] Although critical of Jung's stereotyping of gender qualities, Pratt suggests that "Jung's most important contribution to psychology is his recognition that a fully developed individual personality must transcend gender. His recognition of the destructive effects of excessive masculinity and femininity goes beyond the psychological to the social realm, where he attributes our century of total war to the disjunctions in the repressed personality." (*APWF* 10).

Virginia Woolf cites Coleridge's view of the androgynous mind as "resonant and porous; . . . it transmits emotion without impediment; . . . it is naturally creative, incandescent and undivided" (102).

WORKS CITED

Bachelard, Gaston. *The Poetics of Space*. Boston: Beacon, 1969.

Benítez, Rubén A. "El maravilloso retablo popular de Gloria Fuertes." *Mester*, Vol. 9 (Jan. 1980), 21-33.

Christ, Carol P. *Diving Deep and Surfacing: Women Writers on Spiritual Quest*, 2nd ed. Boston: Beacon, 1986.

Cooper, J. C. *An Illustrated Encyclopedia of Traditional Symbols*. London: Thames and Hudson, 1978.

Day, Mary. *Beyond God the Father: Towards a Philosophy of Women's Liberation*. Boston: Beacon, 1985.

Debicki, Andrew. "Gloria Fuertes: Intertextuality and Reversal of Expectations." *Poetry of Discovery: The Spanish Generation of 1956-1971.* Lexington: The University Press of Kentucky, 1982. 81-101.

Fuertes, Gloria. *Historia de Gloria.* Madrid: Cátedra, 1983.

———. *Obras incompletas.* Madrid: Cátedra, 1983.

———. *Que estás en la tierra . . .* Barcelona: Seix y Barral, 1962.

Gilbert, Sandra M. and Susan Gubar. *The Madwoman in the Attic: The Woman Writer and the Nineteenth-Century Literary Imagination.* New Haven: Yale UP, 1979.

Gubar, Susan. "'The Blank Page' and the Issues of Female Creativity." Showalter 292-313.

Pratt, Annis. *Archetypal Patterns in Women's Fiction.* Bloomington: Indiana UP, 1981.

———. "Aunt Jennifer's Tigers: Notes Toward a Preliterary History of Women's Archetypes." *Feminist Studies,* Vol. 4, No. 1 (Feb. 1978): 163-93.

Rich, Adrienne. *Of Woman Born: Motherhood as Experience and Institution.* 1976. Toronto: Bantam, 1977.

Sherno, Sylvia R. "Carnival: Death and Renewal in the Poetry of Gloria Fuertes." *Modern Language Notes* (forthcoming).

———. "Gloria Fuertes and the Poetics of Solitude." *Anales de la literatura española* Vol. 12, No. 3 (1987): 311-26.

———. "The Poetry of Gloria Fuertes: Textuality and Sexuality." *Siglo XX/20th Century* (forthcoming).

———. "Weaving the World: The Poetry of Gloria Fuertes." *Hispania* (forthcoming).

Showalter, Elaine, ed. *The New Feminist Criticism: Essays on Women. Literature and Theory.* New York: Pantheon Books, 1985.

Stewart, Susan. *On Longing: Narratives of the Miniature, the Gigantic, the Souvenir, the Collection.* Baltimore: Johns Hopkins UP, 1984.

Woolf, Virginia. *A Room of One's Own.* New York: Harcourt, Brace and World, 1929.

C. Brian Morris (essay date 1991)

SOURCE: "Strategies of Self-Effacement in Three Poems by Gloria Fuertes," in *Mester,* Vol. XX, No. 2, Fall, 1991, pp. 67-76.

[*Morris uses three of Fuertes' poems as examples of the author's use of self-deprecation as a strategy to emphasize the strength and power of women.*]

Although poems about poetry are not peculiar to the twentieth century, its poets have brought to the theme an anxiety and an insecurity exemplified by T. S. Eliot's mor-

dant yet eloquent definition of language in *Four Quartets* as "shabby equipment always deteriorating / In the general mess of imprecision of feeling" (128). "Shall I say . . . ?" asked Eliot through the persona of J. Alfred Prufrock in an early poem that, as he draws attention to the dilemma of finding the right words, questions the purpose and the texture of a poem in the act of penning it. In poems from *Espadas como labios* and *Un río, un amor,* Aleixandre and Cernuda share Eliot's malaise as they target the word *palabras* for contemptuous repetition. Yet, however unsatisfactory the language they are obliged to use, the compulsion to use it is—has to be—constantly advertised, so that the product we are reading—the poem—is often a commentary on the person who produced it, on the means by which it was produced, and even offers in its title a classification that helps us to understand it. In the same way as Eliot wonders "Shall I say . . . ?" before going on to say it, Gloria Fuertes asks **"¿Antipoema?"** (273) before writing a poem whose status as a poem she has already questioned. Other titles categorize her poems as **"Nota biográfica"** (41-42), **"Escrito"** (77), "Ejercicio" (359), "Oraciones gramaticales" (61), and as a "Carta explicatoria de Gloria" (293-94). "Voy haciendo versos por la calle" (89), she announces in another title, and in others defines herself as a "Poeta de guardia" (167), confesses "Nací para poeta o para muerto" (160), and counsels sagely "Sale caro ser poeta" (168-69). Another title—"Telegramas de urgencia escribo" (141)—stresses through inversion the verb that documents a fundamental activity recorded in such lines as "Escribo por las noches / y voy al campo mucho" (**"Nota biográfica,"** 41-42), "Escribo en las paredes y lloro en los armarios" (**"Escrito,"** 77), and commemorated—in **"Carta explicatoria de Gloria"**—in a litany that transforms poetic vocation into an obsession, or an incurable disease:

> Me pagan y escribo,
> me pegan y escribo,
> me dejan de mirar y escribo,
> veo a la persona que más quiero con otra y escribo,
> sola en la sala, llevo siglos, y escribo,
> hago reír y escribo.
> De pronto me quiere alguien y escribo.
> Me viene la indiferencia y escribo.
> Lo mismo me da todo y escribo.
> No me escriben y escribo.
> Parece que me voy a morir y escribo
>
> (293-94).

The rhyme in "explicatoria/Gloria," the minimal variations in "Me pagan . . . me pegan," the alliteration of "sola en la sala": these are simple but effective signs that her tenacity in writing does not suppress the pleasure she feels in manipulating words, in transposing vowels and consonants. Her declarations "Nací para puta o payaso" (160), "Caí caí Caín" (161), "Remata la mata" (359), and "Pobres probetas si no podéis más que los poetas" (332) are part of her defense against ordinariness, are one feature of her individuality, which she advertises in a series of poems whose titles are explicitly autobiographic:

"Nota biográfica," in which she shifts quickly from "Gloria Fuertes" to "Yo"; **"Naci en una buhardilla"** (58-59), **"Autobiografía"** (71), **"Carta explicatoria de Gloria," "Nací para poeta o para muerto"** (160), and one that I shall soon turn to, **"Yo."** If we are familiar with the self-portraits that artists and other poets have executed, we should use caution in reading those of Fuertes, whose purpose may be to intrigue as much as to inform, to confuse as much as to communicate. There are, of course, many self-portraits that demand to be taken seriously, on their own terms. Velázquez reminds us in *Las meninas* that, were he not doing what he is doing in the painting, were he not an artist in control of his medium, there would be no painting and we would be staring at a blank canvas, in the same way as we would be staring at a series of blank pages were it not for the poets who filled them. Yet are other self-portraits less self-portraits for including elements that contribute nothing to the depiction but a great deal to its interpretation? Why, for example, did Edvard Munch paint his *Self-Portrait with Skeleton Arm* (1895)? Does the arm answer Velázquez's confident grasp of his brush? Does it remind Munch—and us—of his own mortality in contrast to the painting that will outlive him? Was Lovis Corinth motivated by the same reason to paint his *Self-Portrait with Skeleton?* Clearly, the self-portrait is a much more subtle and resourceful genre than it may at first promise, and we may fruitfully repeat Pascal Bonafoux's questions: "What is selfportrayal? Is the self-portrait the portrait of a mirror? Which mirror is it that poses for the portrait?" (8)

The act of writing to which Gloria Fuertes so compulsively alludes is the mirror-image of her destiny, whose difficulty—self-expression—is compounded by her sex. Her conviction—"Nací para poeta o para muerto" (160)—is threatened by those pressures that lead her to declare in **"Hago versos, señores"**—a poem she addresses ironically to men—that "no me gusta que me llamen poetisa" and to state in **"No dejan escribir"**:

Sé escribir, pero en mi pueblo,
no dejan escribir a las mujeres.

(72)

What the poems of Fuertes demonstrate time and time again is that what she does is inseparable from what she is. The need to express herself is the need to affirm herself, yet the pressures she documents enter into her poetry in such a way that the reader has to decide whether her self-projection is self-effacement or whether her self-effacement is self-projection. Patently, the poet who is bold enough to entitle a poem **"Poemo"** does not bow down her head before conformity, and her statement "Soy sólo una mujer y ya es bastante" (256), which is an apparent avowal of submission, recoils on those who have defined and enforced her function and destiny as a woman.

Fuertes retaliates in the way she was born to do: through poetry; and the shorter her poems, the more trenchant and pithy are her comments on her life and on those who

shape it, especially when she imposes on her poems the structural disciplines of parallelism, declension, definition, or record card. I know of few twentieth-century poets who can use tight, taut structures so productively; even Louis Aragon, that most sardonic and laconic of the French Surrealists, needed more space than Fuertes to spin his comments on language and friendship and love. Within a few lines Fuertes can take us back in time to show us woman through the ages and can lead us into the minds of men to show us how little that heritage means to them. With a few words she can underline the narrow line between life and death and the loneliness of being a woman. The title **"En pocas palabras"**—from *Cómo atar los bigotes del tigre* (1969)—announces the need to summarize, to encapsulate experience; the definitions that comprise it exemplify the need to order it:

DEPORTE: un hombre
            una tabla
            una ola.
MUERTE: un hombre
            unas tablas
            una ola.
AMOR: un nombre
            una cama
         y una
            —sola—.

(279)

While the words that are being defined—"deporte," "muerte," "amor"—are very different, the definitions force them into line, induce a similarity that blurs the distinctions between "tabla" and "tablas," "hombre" and "nombre," "ola" and "sola." The typographical space that "sola" occupies as the last word, barricaded or quarantined by dashes specifying a pause as in a musical score, postulates loneliness as the only consequence—phonic as well as personal—of living; the sequence "ola—ola—sola" is the truth of her experience, which denies and reverses the festive, zestful message explicit in the popular song sung on the beaches of Spain in the 1960s when the singer supposedly turned to the sea and intoned: "Ola, ola, ola, no vengas sola . . ." Sport and death, life and death, are so close that the letter "s" can transform the vision of a surfboard riding a wave to the boards—the "fine white boards" echoing in Synge's *Riders to the Sea*—out of which will be fashioned a coffin that will be carried away on the sea of death.

The "cama" that belongs to Fuertes's definition of love offers no more hope or warmth than the "tablas": if the latter signifies the death of the body, the former represents the coldness of human relationships, which in the poem permits no phonic distinction between life, death, and love, all of which are represented by "un hombre." In forcing "un hombre" and "un nombre" into homophonous compliance, Fuertes desexes the male, who becomes one more name in a diary, the sign of a casual liaison that causes more solitude than it remedies. If man is the lead factor in each definition, the fate that he represents is shared by woman, and it is this woman's sensibility that records man's insensitivity and this woman poet's skill that translates communication into codification.

Articulation through formulation is seen at its most pithy and concise in the poem **"Yo"**—from *Poeta de guardia* (1968)—whose title promises a display of subjectivity that necessarily puts us in mind of the forceful egos of Romantic writing:

"Yo"

Yo,
remera de barcas
ramera de hombres
romera de almas
rimera de versos,
Ramona,
    pa' servirles.

(223)

Although this is clearly a poem about herself, it is not egocentric, for the woman has no center to control, no individuality, no independence; the repetition of "Yo," rather than affirming independence, denies and impedes it as the image of a wooden ball being jerked on a string— a yoyo—represents her destiny and announces the pattern and pacing of the poem. "Remera," "ramera," "romera," "rimera" create a web, trap Fuertes between two consonants; the variations of vowel allow no escape but merely designate one more role in a series of roles, two of which—"ramera" and "romera"—document and perpetuate the old Christian duality between good and bad discussed by Willi Moll, who outlines the distinctions between woman as the gate to heaven (as perceived by the Provençal poets) and woman as the gate to hell (as represented by Tertullian), the great whore of the twelfth chapter of the Apocalypse (41).

The roles that Fuertes knows have been assigned to woman and that she now assigns to herself are compacted into layers, forced into sameness by words that both rhyme and alliterate not at the end of the lines but at the beginning. As these echoing and self-supporting words eliminate differences, they also banish time. Simultaneity replaces sequence; the lack of punctuation and conjunctions from lines 2 through 5 gives Fuertes no time or space to adjust to one role or another. Asyndeton can generate a litany; the suppression of commas in these lines makes asyndeton into a rhetorical strategy that accelerates the recital of each role and narrows the difference between them, thus creating a reprise without reprieve, variations without variety. There is an intriguing similarity between this poem and the six words chosen by August Strindberg in 1896 to interpret Edvard Munch's painting *Woman in Three Stages* (1894); under the title "Trimurti de la femme," Strindberg places at the vertices of one triangle the words "Hommesse," "Maîtresse," "Pecheresse"; at the vertices of another he puts "Peinte," "Sainte," "Enceinte." Detached from their triangles, these words generate the simultaneity that marks Fuertes's poem; artistic convention has conditioned us to expect chronological progression in the topic of the ages of man, who is invariably woman, seen, for example, in the painting by Hans Baldung that hangs in the Museo del Prado. Not even in the twentieth cen-

tury can woman escape the gruesome responsibility of bearing witness to the ravages of time. A cartoon by Xaudaró published in *Blanco y Negro* in 1929 may use a bright new title popularized by women's magazines, "El arte de sonreír," but his pattern is traditional and his target is familiar as he matches cruel images with no less cruel captions:

1. A los quince años, la duquesita sonreía mostrando su espléndida dentadura.

2. A los veinticinco, las perlas de sus dientes iluminaban su dulce sonrisa.

3. A los cuarenta, aún prestaban sus dientes indecibles encantos a su sonrisa.

4. Hoy, cuando la duquesa quiere sonreír, se acerca a su "secretaire," lo abre . . .
5. Saca una cajita de plata delicadamente cincelada, obra de artífices venecianos . . .

6. Y muestra todos sus dientes, como en los buenos tiempos de sus quince años.

At this point Xaudaró could have added as a *moraleja* Quevedo's conclusion to his sonnet to the "vieja desdentada":

no llames sacamuelas: ve buscando,
si le puedes hallar, un sacaabuelas.

(571)

Munch modified this topic by substituting coincidence for chronology, by replacing development with a multiplicity of roles symbolized by the sphinx. In another painting entitled simply *Woman* (1895), we can look from left to right; in *Three Stages of Woman (The Sphinx)*, painted in 1899, we can look from right to left and receive the same message: that woman, according to Munch's own words quoted by Sarah G. Epstein, "suddenly becomes saint, whore, and an unhappy self-sacrificing victim" (11). It is irrelevant where Munch derived the idea of three women standing side by side; it could owe as much to paintings of the Three Graces as to those of the Judgment of Paris, postulated by Reinhold Heller (78). What is more important is that he tried to configurate and dramatize the complexity of woman's roles, to depart from a simple pattern imposed by linear time and a single, exclusive interpretation to a series of simultaneous images, all of which are valid.

Munch's paintings show woman through the eyes of a man; Fuertes's poem is a woman's recreation of how men perceive her, an interpretation that evinces an enforced subservience, which she makes recoil on those who expect it in her display of servility: "Ramona, pa' servirles." Even the identity designated by Ramona is suspect, ambivalent; at one extreme, it conjures up associations of the saccharine story still commemorated in Hemet, California by the Ramona Pageant and of the sentimental song that was written to exploit the second silent film version in 1927; at the other extreme, it could put us in mind of the resourceful if immoral Doña Ramona Braga-do, "una vieja teñida pero muy chistosa," according to Cela in *La colmena,* who presides over her *lechería* in the Calle de Fuencarral, which she had bought with money left to her by her longtime lover, the Marqués de Casa Peña Zurana. Whatever associations it permits beyond the poem, within the poem the name of Ramona is constricted by its phonic proximity to "ramera," so that the only part of the word that is repeated—"ram"—assigns a particular meaning to service. One woman, who has to play four roles and discharge four functions, is at the service of unnumbered, unidentified men. Yet that service is not rendered without a fight; the simulated humility of her formula—reminiscent of Micawber's "Your 'umble servant"—is given the hard edge of a retaliatory blow with the apocopation of *para* to *pa',* which, to quote Werner Beinhauer's comment on the expression "¡Toma, pa que te enteres!," is like "una manifestación tajante en forma de bofetada" (56). Other grammarians—John Butt and Carmen Benjamin—rule that "The form *pa* is substandard for *para* and should be avoided" (363). This stricture has never inhibited those anonymous Andalusian poets who use the form frequently and defiantly, as in this *solear* collected by Fernández Bañuls and Pérez Orozco (188):

> Quisiera ser como el aire
> "pa" yo tenerte a mi vera
> sin que lo notara naide.

Fuertes's consciousness of the diverse roles of women and her ability to articulate that diversity stand out against the silence and the implied insensitivity of men, who are classified and herded into the anonymous pronoun with which she ends the poem; with "servirles" she demonstrates the unequal battle between the dominant and unthinking group and the individual, victimized, yet analytical woman.

Men as an unthinking group are given a decisive role in the last line of **"Los pájaros anidan"**—from *Antología. Poemas del suburbio* (1954)—which denies the poem a triumphant climax as male arrogance nullifies the heritage of centuries, dismantles the poem, crushes with "no soy nada" every exultant first-person statement or proud first-person pronoun:

> **"Los Pájaros Anidan"**
> Los pájaros anidan en mis brazos,
> en mis hombros, detrás de mis rodillas,
> entre los senos tengo codornices,
> los pájaros se creen que soy un árbol.
> Una fuente se creen que soy los cisnes,
> bajan y beben todos cuando hablo.
> Las ovejas me pisan cuando pasan
> y comen en mis dedos los gorriones,
> se creen que yo soy tierra las hormigas
> y los hombres se creen que no soy nada.
>
>   (49)

When we highlight the first-person statements—"entre

los senos tengo codornices," "soy un árbol," "Una fuente . . . soy," and "yo soy tierra"—Fuertes emerges before us, if we put our trust in the natural homing instincts of birds, swans, and ants, as the Earth, the goddess who as Gaea was revered by early Greeks as the universal mother whose soil nourishes all living things, nurtures the flowers and fruit that Arcimboldo used to construct his image of *Spring.* Frida Kahlo's *Self-Portrait* (1940) derives from the same tradition, even though some of its elements—such as a bird hanging by wire from tendrils meshed around her neck—are dissonant and speak to us in different ways. The same awareness of a traditional pose informs Kahlo's *Roots* (1943), where the recumbent nude duplicates the pose of the reclining water nymph painted so often by Lucas Cranach but underscores the latter's harmony with nature by making her grow out of it. To find in Whitney Chadwick's book *Women Artists and the Surrealist Movement* (1985) a chapter entitled "The Female Earth: Nature and the Imagination" is to find more corroboration of a fundamental—and highly creative—paradox in Surrealist writers and artists: that a movement that strove to break new ground trod old ground time and time again. In one of his drawings, André Masson exploited the shock-tactics essential to Surrealism in order to change the posture of the reclining nude: in a raw display of frankness, he opened her legs and entitled his drawing, which is automatic in name only, *The Earth.*

Essential to Fuertes's depiction of herself in **"Los pá-jaros anidan"** are the traditional and complementary views of woman as nourishment and habitat. The quail nestling between her breasts, the swans that drink from her as if she were a fountain, identify Fuertes as a descendant of the *virgo lactans,* whom Lucas Cranach designated as *Charity.* Seated under a fruit tree with birds feeding from the ground, Cranach's Charity is as close to nature as the reclining water nymph, who also has trees behind her. The Surrealists closed the gap between woman and tree, fusing them so closely that, in order to take a woman in his arms, Vicente Aleixandre has to embrace vegetation as well, according to *La destrucción o el amor,* where, in the poem "Triunfo del amor," he intones:

> ¡Ah maravilla lúcida de estrechar en los brazos
> un desnudo fragante, ceñido de los bosques!
>
>   (386)

Elsewhere I have used these lines as a caption to Masson's drawing *La Forêt,* in which the woman's body is intertwined with the natural world. In the light of this artistic tradition, it is perfectly natural for Fuertes to affirm in this poem "Los pájaros anidan en mis brazos" and "los pájaros se creen que soy un árbol," and for her to declare in another "En el árbol de mi pecho / hay un pájaro encarnado" (95). If nature is the broad setting for the poem and the justification of her existence, naturalness marks her narration of it. Each line of this poem, which nods in the direction of the traditional *décima,* makes a statement with an unhurried ease and with a candor that is reinforced by the repetition of "se creen." The alliterations of "bajan y be-ben" and "me pisan cuando pasan" and the repetition of "se creen que soy" record a world of order and harmony in which woman's value is recognized and utilized by creatures—but not by man.

Man's dismissal of woman as "nada" assigns to "se creen" a special function: the birds "se creen que soy un árbol," the swans "Una fuente se creen que soy," the ants "se creen que yo soy tierra" because they have no mind and therefore no prejudices or inhibitions: they have instincts to guide them. When men "se creen que no soy nada," they respond in the same way as animals—only to conclude that she is nothing; while mindlessness is understandable in an animal, it is unforgivable in men, who dominate the end of the poem, powerful but ignorant. One line, phrased in a way that is damagingly familiar, brings down the cumulative evidence of the preceding nine lines as if they were a house of cards. The relaxed tempo, the terraced structure, were an illusion, for man's power is out of all proportion to his sensitivity and to his knowledge.

In the three poems I have considered men are essential protagonists: they cause solitude, demand service and servitude, and devalue woman. If Gloria Fuertes effaces and demeans herself in her poems, she does so in a way that underlines her own resilience, her own sensitivity, and her verbal power, for poetry in her hands is not a retreat but a retaliation. Self-effacement, therefore, is not the acceptance of defeat but a strategy that demonstrates subtly yet convincingly that, if she is

small in the minds of men, it is because men are small-minded.

FURTHER READING

Agosin, M. A review of *Off the Map. Choice,* Vol. 22, No. 3 (November 1984): 30.
    Short description of contents.

Cain, Joan. A review of *Obras completas. World Literature Today,* Vol. 51, No. 3 (Summer 1977): 18.
    Brief description of the style and themes of the poems.

Carmell, Pamela. "Gloria Fuertes: An Interview by Pamela Carmell." *American Poetry Review,* Vol. 20, No. 2 (March/April 1991):5-6.
    Fuertes discusses poetry, hers and other Spanish writers.

De Aguilar, Helene J.F. "Distressing Landscapes." *Parnassus,* Vol. 12, No. 2/Vol. 13, No. 1 (Spring/Summer, Fall/Winter 1985): 369-85.
    Discusses Claribel Alegria's *Flowers from the Volcano* and Gloria Fuertes' *Off the Map.*

Prado, Holly. A review of *Off the Map. Los Angeles Times Book Review* (3 June 1984):13.
    Brief mention of style and themes of poems in *Off the Map.*

Additional coverage of Fuertes's life and career is contained in the following sources published by the Gale Group: *Dictionary of Literary Biography,* Vol. 108; *Hispanic Writers.*

Joy Harjo
1951–

American poet, screenwriter, short story writer, and editor.

INTRODUCTION

Strongly influenced by her Muscogee Creek heritage, feminist and social concerns, and her background in the arts, Harjo frequently incorporates Native American myths, symbols, and values into her writing. Her poetry emphasizes the Southwest landscape and the need for remembrance and transcendence. She is also praised for her powerful poetic voice and clear vision.

Biographical Information

Harjo is a registered member of the Muscogee Creek tribe. Her father was Creek and her mother part French and part Cherokee. She is also a distant cousin of Native American poet Alexander Posey. Born and raised in Oklahoma, she graduated from the Institute of American Indian Arts, a boarding school in Santa Fe, New Mexico. After graduation she joined a Native American dance troupe and worked a series of odd jobs before pursuing a college education. As a student at the University of New Mexico, she began writing poetry after hearing American poet Galway Kinnell and Native American writers Simon Ortiz and Leslie Marmon Silko read from their works. She eventually graduated with a B.A. in poetry in 1976. Attending the University of Iowa Writers' Workshop, she took classes under the direction of Silko, earning a M.F.A. in 1978. In addition to teaching at various institutions, Harjo has worked for the National Association for Third World Writers, the National Endowment for the Arts, and the National American Public Broadcasting Consortium. She has received many honors, such as the American Book Award from the Before Columbus Foundation, the Delmore Schwartz Memorial Poetry Award, the American Indian Distinguished Achievement Award, and a NEA fellowship.

Major Works

Harjo's work is largely autobiographical, informed by her love of the natural world and preoccupation with transcendence, survival, and the limitations of language. The search for freedom and self-actualization are considered central to her volume *She Had Some Horses*, which incorporates prayer-chants and animal imagery. Nature is also a prominent theme of her prose poetry collection, *Secrets from the Center of the World*, in which each poem is accompanied by a photograph of the American Southwest. Each poem and picture underscore the impor-

tance of landscape and story within the Native American world view. *In Mad Love and War* focuses on politics, tradition, remembrance, and the transformational aspects of poetry. The first section relates various acts of violence, including attempts to deny Harjo her heritage, the murder of an Indian leader, the actions of the Ku Klux Klan, and events in war-torn Nicaragua. The second half of the book frequently emphasizes personal relationships and change. Her recent collection, *The Woman Who Fell from the Sky,* is named for an Iroquois myth about a female creator. The poems are concerned with the vying forces of creation and destruction in contemporary society, and utilize images ranging from wolves to northern lights and subjects such as the devastation of alcoholism and the Vietnam War.

Critical Reception

Harjo is considered an important figure in contemporary American poetry. Scholars note that while Harjo's work is often set in the Southwest, emphasizes the plight of the individual, and reflects Creek values, myths, and beliefs, her oeuvre also has universal relevance. She is often criticized for being too political in her work. Yet some critics see her concern over injustice as an integral part of being a Native American woman living in the twentieth century. Some commentators analyze the recurring image of the American urban landscape in her poetry, asserting that Harjo often juxtaposes the modern city with traditional Native American culture in order to underscore the alienation of native peoples in modern American society. Many critics trace her maturation as a poet, maintaining that as the body of her work unfolds, she expresses herself with increasing confidence and a stronger poetic voice.

PRINCIPAL WORKS

Poetry

The Last Song 1975
What Moon Drove Me to This? 1979
She Had Some Horses 1983
Secrets from the Center of the World [with Stephen Strom] 1989
In Mad Love and War 1990
The Woman Who Fell from the Sky 1996
The Good Luck Cat [with Paul Lee] 2000
A Map to the Next World: Poetry and Tales (poetry and short stories) 2000

Other Major Works

Origin of Apache Crown Dance (screenplay) 1985
The Spiral of Memory (interviews) [edited by Laura Coltelli] 1996

CRITICISM

John F. Crawford (essay date 1987)

SOURCE: "Notes towards a New Multicultural Criticism." *A Gift of Tongues*, Marie Harris and Kathleen AGuero, eds., Athens: University of Georgia Press, 1987, pp. 155-95.

[*In the following essay, Crawford provides a stylistic and thematic overview of Harjo's* She Had Some Horses.]

In her early writing, Joy Harjo already addressed themes of land and people, fear and healing. Speaking of her native landscape, she remarked:

> What is breathing here is some sort of dangerous anger that rises up out of the Oklahoma landscape. The earth is alive with emotions, and will take action on what is

being felt. This way of seeing is characteristic of most native poets and writers of Oklahoma. That which has happened to the earth, has happened to all of us as part of the earth. . . .

> What Oklahoma becomes, in a sense, is a dream, an alive and real dream that takes place inside and outside of the writer. . . . Our words begin inside of the dream and become a way of revealing ourselves within this landscape that is called Oklahoma. Language becomes all of the people that we are. Living voices surround us and speak from the diverse and many histories we have been, the ones we have become, and most of all, how we will continue. There are those voices among us who will assume the cadence of an ancient and living chant.[15]

Nothing in Harjo's early work quite prepares the reader for the overall arrangement—a plot structure operating on several levels—of *She Had Some Horses*, her third book, published in 1983.[16] The book begins by confessing the poet's fear. It then describes the fate of other "survivors" like herself who have had to deal with such fear. It introduces intermediary figures—human and symbolic—who negotiate between the poet and her fear. It tells a story of the breakup of the poet's relationship with a man and her discovery of the love of a woman. It ends with the freeing of the horses, who are the symbols of her frightened spirit, and the freeing of the poet from old, repressive images to live her own life. The end is a ritual prayer, closing off the matter begun with the first poem.

The first poem, **"Call It Fear,"** introduces most of the thematic material in the book.

> There is this edge where shadows
> and bones of some of us walk
>   backwards.
> Talk backwards. There is this edge
> call it an ocean of fear of the dark. Or
> name it with other songs. Under our ribs
> our hearts are bloody stars. Shine on
> shine on, and horses in their galloping flight
> strike the curve of ribs.
>
>   . . . . .
>
> There is this edge within me
>   I saw it once
> an August Sunday morning when the heat hadn't
> left this earth. And Goodluck
> sat sleeping next to me in the truck.
> We had never broken through the edge of the
> singing at four a.m.
>
>   . . . . .
>
>   And there was this edge—
> not the drop of sandy rock cliff
> bones of volcanic earth into
>   Albuquerque.
> Not that,
>   but a string of shadow horses kicking

and pulling me out of my belly,
        not into the Rio Grande but into the music
barely coming through
             Sunday church singing
from the radio. Battery worn-down but the voices
talking backwards.

The "edge" of fear is the subject of the book. The fear is protean, taking many shapes: notably the backwards-talking Holy Rollers on the radio and the nightmare of the horses pulling the poet's entrails out of her belly ("Or name it with other songs"). The people of Harjo's acquaintance sit by the volcanic cliffs outside Albuquerque trying to propitiate this fear ritually by talking and singing and "walking backwards." Still it persists ("Under our ribs / our hearts are bloody stars"). Someone who might stand as an intermediary between the poet and her fear, Goodluck, her friend and a symbolic figure, has been unable like her to "[break] through the edge of the singing at four a.m."

Succeeding poems speak of those who survive even in a hostile environment. The poet quickly establishes her sense of identity with people of color in America in her poem to Audre Lorde, **"Anchorage"**:

And I think of the 6th Avenue jail, of mostly Native
and Black men, where Henry told about being shot at
eight times outside a liquor store in L.A., but when
the car sped away he was surprised he was alive,
no bullet holes, man, and eight cartridges strewn
on the sidewalk
          all around him.

Everyone laughed at the impossibility of it,
but also the truth. Because who would believe
the fantastic and terrible story of all of our survival
those who were never meant
             to survive?

The survivors take many forms, but perhaps the most stirring image in these poems is the relationship of women to the earth. It begins in the poem **"For Alva Benson, and for Those Who Have Learned to Speak"**:

And the ground spoke when she was born.
Her mother heard it. In Navajo she answered
as she squatted down against the earth
to give birth. It was now when it happened,
now giving birth to itself again and again
between the legs of women.

The image is heightened in a later stanza, the action of which makes a completed circle, with Mt. St. Helens the governing symbol:

The child now hears names in her sleep.
They change into other names, and into others.
It is the ground murmuring, and Mt. St. Helens
erupts as the harmonic motion of a child turning
inside her mother's belly waiting to be born
to begin another time.

Contrasting to this woman-image of cyclic restoration is the tragic image of the man, drinking and out of control, which repeats itself in several poems. In **"Night Out"** it is a man in a barroom on New Year's Eve:

        Your voice screamed out from somewhere in
  the
darkness
        another shot, anything to celebrate this
  deadly
  thing called living. And Joe John called out to
bring
another round, to have another smoke, to dance
  dance it good
because tomorrow night is another year—
               in your voice.
      I have heard you in my ownself.
      And have seen you in my own past
  vision.

The poet takes pains to universalize and understand the figure:

It doesn't end
For you are multiplied by drinkers, by tables, by
    jukeboxes
        by bars.
You fight to get out of the sharpest valleys cut down
    into
the history of living bone.
        And you fight to get in.
You are the circle of lost ones
             our relatives.
You have paid the cover charge thousands of times
    over
with your lives
        and now you are afraid

              you can never get out.

These poems show separate ways of knowing: a man's way, harsh and fatalistic, of meaningless rebellion, or a woman's way, embracing the history of the whole earth of which one is a part. It is the second way the poet will choose to follow as the book develops.

The figure of Noni Daylight appears in three poems near the end of the first section. Old and shrunken, the mother of many children by as many fathers, she is first cited as the woman who stayed where she was to raise her family:

      Because she knew
that each star rang with separate
colored hue, as bands of horses
and wild
    like the spirit in her
that flew, at each train whistle.

                ("Kansas City")

In the next poem where she is mentioned, Noni is afraid of familiar voices.

She talks softly
softly
To the voice on the radio. All night she
drives.
Finally she perceives how she will free herself.

It is not the moon, or the pistol in her lap
but a fierce anger
that will free her.
                                                    (**"Heartbeat"**)

In the third poem in which she appears, Noni reveals her
true character to the poet and proposes the key to the
poet's rescue.

"We are closer than
blood," Noni Daylight
tells her. "It isn't
Oklahoma or the tribal
blood but something more
that we speak."

She speaks directly to the poet of her "cure" and reveals
herself as a spiritual intermediary.

"Should I dream you afraid
so that you are forced to save
yourself?

Or should you ride colored horses
into the cutting edge of the sky
to know

that we're alive
we are alive."
                            (**"She Remembers the Future"**)

The poet must now seize the initiative.

The second section, **"What I Should Have Said,"** focuses on the poet's changing of her relationship from a man
to a woman lover and the confusion, disruption, and difficulty she has in "commuting" (literally from Albuquerque to Santa Fe and back again) to teach, care for her
children, and be with her new lover. The moon becomes
the symbol of her new consciousness, but also her new
fate:

She is moon.
Her eyes slit and yellow she is the last
one out of a dingy bar in Albuquerque—
Fourth Street, or from similar avenues
in Hong Kong. Where someone else has also
awakened, the night thrown back and asked,
"Where is the moon, my lover?"
And from here I always answer in my dreaming,
"The last time I saw her was in the arms
of another sky."
                                                    (**"Moonlight"**)

In her acceptance of the promiscuity of the moon, the
poet affirms a new existence, one which Noni Daylight

unlocked when she told her she must "know / that we're
alive / we are alive." In a new poem, written while driving
between her lover and home, the poet begins to explore
the meaning of this.

Alive. This music rocks
me. I drive the interstate,
watch faces come and go on either
side. I am free to be sung to;
I am free to sing. This woman
can cross any line.
                                                    (**"Alive"**)

The horses which figured in the first poem in the book
return in the third section, bursting forth in a terrible and
wonderful emergence.

The title poem of the section **"She Had Some Horses"**
is an extended catalog of "horses"—personal traits, poetic images, manifestations of fear and anxiety or danger
from external forces—known to the poet. She writes it
with bare logical connection, in the manner of Christopher Smart's "For I Will Consider My Cat Jeffrey." The
ending of the poem gives some of its most important
elements, threats from within and without and what they
actually have amounted to.

She had horses who whispered in the dark, who
    were afraid to speak.
She had horses who screamed out of fear of the
    silence, who
carried knives to protect themselves from ghosts.
She had horses who waited for destruction.
She had horses who waited for resurrection.

She had some horses.

She had horses who got down on their knees for any
    saviour.
She had horses who thought their high price had
    saved them.
She had horses who tried to save her, who climbed
    in her
bed at night and prayed as they raped her.

She had some horses.

She had some horses she loved.
She had some horses she hated.

These were the same horses.

Several more poems treat horses in their different aspects. In the fifth poem, the remarkable **"Explosion,"** all
the horses are set free—those belonging to others and to
the poet herself.

The explosion—on a highway—takes place in the poet's
home country. (We may recall what Harjo saw elsewhere
as "some sort of dangerous anger that rises up out of the
Oklahoma landscape.") She first tries to associate it with
an apocalyptic future event of significance to her people.

Finally she sees what has happened.

> But maybe the explosion was horses,
>   bursting out of the
>   crazy earth
> near Okemah. They were a violent birth,
> flew from the ground into trees
>   to wait for evening
> night
> mares to come after them . . .
>   . . . . .

> Some will not see them.

> But some will see the horses with their hearts of
>   sleeping
>   volcanoes
> and will be rocked awake
>   past their bodies
>
>   to see who they have
> become.

It is important to view the horse poems not as simply a hodgepodge of loosely related material but as ceremonial shapes, from the naming of the horses to their freeing, which make it possible for the poet and others who believe her to look to the future with hope and to "see who they have become" (the "they" of the last line is, I believe, purposely ambiguous). This freeing is the climax of the book, leading to the concluding poem, which echoes the beginning.

"I Give You Back" works at many levels. The first level is the ritual release of the fear that was expressed in the beginning.

> I release you, my beautiful and terrible
> fear. I release you. You were my beloved
> and hated twin, but now, I don't know you
> as myself. . . .

> You are not my blood anymore.

Also released are paralyzing memories of genocide and the poet's susceptibility to future harm at the hands of the oppressor.

> I give you back to the white soldiers
> who burned down my home, beheaded my children,
> raped and sodomized my brothers and sisters.
>   . . . . .

> I release you, fear, so that you can no longer
> keep me naked and frozen in the winter,
> or smothered under blankets in the summer.

There follows a sequence in ritual repetition, first declaring simply, "I release you" and then itemizing what the poet is "not afraid to be." Then the poet admits her own past complicity in her fear:

> Oh, you have choked me, but I gave you the leash.

> You have gutted me but I gave you the knife.
> You have devoured me, but I laid myself across the
>   fire.
> You held my mother down and raped her,
>   but I gave you the
>   heated thing.

After another sequence announcing her separation from her fear, the poet ends with a passionate inversion, showing the formerly weak element to now be the strong and the strong the weak. It is a note of triumph and even of compassion for the enemy.

> But come here, fear
> I am alive and you are so afraid
>   of dying.

Harjo's indebtedness to traditional storytelling devices, such as her use of ceremonial elements at the beginning and end of the poem, her use of symbols like the horses, the moon, and the spiritual guide Noni Daylight, and her use of multilevel narrative are integral to the structure of the poem: they establish the naming of the fear at the beginning, the intervention of Noni Daylight in the middle, and the freeing of the horses at the end. Two levels of the narrative are literal: the story of the author's changes in lovers and the historical thread running through the book, reminding the reader of the history of white oppression. In both these cases it is important to notice the author's point of view. When she says, "You have gutted me but I gave you the knife," she is making a point both personal and political. Both she and her people, as she has come to understand them, are learning not to be victims.

Optimism is conveyed at the end of *She Had Some Horses* through the notion brought first by Noni Daylight, **"We are alive."** The poet pronounces this for herself in the course of the discovery of her new love while driving between Alburquerque and Santa Fe one day. Armed with the knowledge, she banishes fear: "I am alive and you are so afraid / of dying." We should recall again what Paula Gunn Allen describes as the "magic" involved in the enactment of ceremony. "Since all that exists is alive and since all that is alive must grow and change, all existence can be manipulated . . . according to certain laws." We may conclude that the method and content of Harjo's book are the same.

Joseph Bruchac with Joy Harjo (interview date 1987)

SOURCE: "The Story of All Our Survival: An Interview with Joy Harjo," in *Survival This Way: Interviews with American Indian Poets,* Tucson: The University of Arizona Press and Sun Tracks, 1987, pp. 87-103.

[*In the following interview, Harjo discusses the role of memory and storytelling in her poetry as well as the major themes and images found in* She Had Some Horses.]

This interview took place on December 2, 1982, in Santa Fe, New Mexico, where Joy Harjo was living while a student in a post-graduate film-making program at the College of Santa Fe. Although the interview was done before the publication of her new book of poems, *She Had Some Horses* (Thunder's Mouth Press), a proof copy of the book had just arrived in the mail and we made reference to it during the interview.

The living room of the rented house in which we talked was one of those open "modern" living rooms typical of contemporary southwestern architecture. It was dominated by a painting on the wall of a group of horses—the same painting which became the cover design for her book—and a large stereo with reggae tapes piled on top of it.

I began by asking Joy if there was a poem she would like to start off with. The one she chose came out of her recent experience of teaching a workshop in an Alaskan prison.

"Anchorage"

This city is made of stone, of blood, and fish,
There are Chugatch Mountains to the east
and whale and seal to the west.
It hasn't always been this way, because glaciers
who are ice ghosts create oceans, carve earth
and shape this city here, by the sound.
They swim backwards in time.

Once a storm of boiling earth cracked open
the streets, threw open the town.
It's quiet now, but underneath the concrete
is the cooking earth,
                    and above that, air
which is another ocean, where spirits we can't see
are dancing   joking   getting full
on roasted caribou, and the praying
goes on, extends out.

Nora and I go walking down 4th Avenue
and know it is all happening.
On a park bench we see someone's Athabascan
grandmother, folded up, smelling like 200 years
of blood and piss, her eyes closed against some
unimagined darkness, where she is buried in an ache
in which nothing makes
                    sense.

We keep on breathing, walking, but softer now,
the clouds whirling in the air above us.
What can we say that would make us understand
better than we do already?
Except to speak of her home and claim her
as our own history, and know that our dreams
don't end here, two blocks away from the ocean
where our hearts still batter away at the muddy shore.
And I think of the 6th Avenue jail, of mostly Native
and Black men, where Henry told about being shot at
eight times outside a liquor store in L.A., but when

the car sped away he was surprised he was alive,
no bullet holes, man, and eight cartridges strewn
on the sidewalk
                    all around him.
Everyone laughed at the impossibility of it,
but also the truth. Because who would believe
the fantastic and terrible story of all of our survival
those who were never meant
                    to survive?

[BRUCHAC]: I'm glad you started with that poem, Joy. Those last few lines, the "story of all of our survival, / those who were never meant to survive," are pretty much the theme I see as central in contemporary American Indian poetry: the idea of survival. What are you saying in this poem about survival?

[HARJO]: *I see it almost like a joke, the story about Henry in the poem I just read. You know, he was real dry when he was talking about standing out there and all those bullet holes and he's lying on the ground and he thought for sure he'd been killed but he was alive and telling the story and everybody laughed because they thought he was bullshitting. And it's like a big joke that any of us are here because they tried so hard to make sure we weren't, you know, either kill our spirits, move us from one place to another, try to take our minds and to take our hearts.*

That poem has many stories tied into it, stories of people that you know, stories of women, stories of things that you remember. Storytelling seems to run through and even structure much of the work by American Indian poets. Is that true for you?

I rely mostly on contemporary stories. Even though the older ones are like shadows or are there dancing right behind them, I know that the contemporary stories, what goes on now, will be those incorporated into those older stories or become a part of that. It's all still happening. A lot of contemporary American native writers consciously go back into the very old traditions, and I think I do a lot unconsciously. I don't think I'm that good of a storyteller in that sense, but it's something that I'm learning. I love to hear them and use them in my own ways.

If there's an image of the American Indian writer that many people, who are not very knowledgeable about what an American Indian writer is, have, it is of what I call jokingly the Beads and Feathers School, nineteenth-century "noble savages." The poetry in this new book of yours is not Beads and Feathers, yet to me it's very recognizably from an American Indian consciousness. What is that consciousness?

I suppose it has to do with a way of believing or sensing things. The world is not disconnected or separate but whole. All persons are still their own entity but not separate from everything else—something that I don't think is necessarily just Native American, on this particular continent, or only on this planet. All people are originally tribal, but Europeans seem to feel separated from that, or they've forgotten it. If European people look into their own history, their own people were tribal societies to begin with and they got away from it. That's called "civilization."

Leslie Silko and Geary Hobson have both attacked the phenomenon of "The White Shaman," the Anglo poet who writes versions of American Indian poems. What are your thoughts on that?

I agree with them. It's a matter of respect to say, "I'm borrowing this from this place," or "I'm stealing this from here," or "I'm making my own poem out of this," but the white shamans don't do that. They take something and say it's theirs or they take the consciousness and say it's theirs, or try to steal the spirit. On one hand, anybody can do what they want but they pay the consequences. You do have to have that certain respect, and you do have to regard where things come from and to whom they belong.

Origins are very important in your work. Where things came from, where you came from. The title of your first book is **The Last Song**, and you ended it with "oklahoma will be the last song / I'll ever sing." Is it not true that you have in your work a very strong sense of yourself as a person from a place which informs you as a writer?

I suppose. But the older I get the more I realize it's caused a great deal of polarity within myself. I recognized my roots, but at the same time there's a lot of pain involved with going back. I've thought about it many times, like why I travel, why I'm always the wanderer in my family. One of the most beloved members of my family died just recently, my aunt Lois Harjo. She always stayed in Oklahoma, and I've jokingly said the reason I'm always traveling is so that Andrew Jackson's troops don't find me. You know, they moved my particular family from Alabama to Oklahoma, and so I always figure I stay one step ahead so they can't find me.

Some American Indian writers—you and Barney Bush, for example—are the epitome, for me, of the poets who are always on the move, going from one place to another. Yet I still find a very strong sense in your work and in Barney's that you are centered in place. You are not nomads. There's a difference between your moving around and the way people in Anglo society are continually moving, always leaving something behind.

Oh, it's because in their sense they're always moving to get away from their mothers. They don't want to be from here or there. It's a rootlessness. But there will always be place and family and roots.

Those are things which you come back to in your work: those connections to family, to memory. A poem of yours is called **"Remember."** I think that's very important. The idea of remembering is central, isn't it, in the work of many, many American Indian writers?

The way I see remembering, just the nature of the word, has to do with going back. But I see it in another way, too. I see it as occurring, not just going back, but occurring right now, and also future occurrence so that you can remember things in a way that makes what occurs now beautiful. I don't see it as going back and dredging up all kinds of crap or all kinds of past romance. People are people, whatever era, whoever they are, they're people.

In other words, memory is alive for you. You're not just engaged in a reverie—like the old man sitting by the fire and going back over those things in the past. Memory is a living and strong force which affects the future.

Sure. People often forget that everything they say, everything they do, think, feel, dream, has effect, which to me is being Indian, knowing that. That's part of what I call "being Indian" or "tribal consciousness."

You also talk in your poems about the importance of saying things, *speaking*. What is *speaking* for you? What I'm asking, really, is for you to define words I see being used by American Indian writers very differently than most people use them. *Song* is one of those words. *Memory* is one of those words. *Speaking* is one of those words.

It comes out of the sense of not being able to speak. I still have a sense of not being able to say things well. I think much of the problem is with the English language; it's a very materialistic and a very subject-oriented language. I don't know Creek, but I know a few words and I am familiar with other tribal languages more so than I am my own. What I've noticed is that the center of tribal languages often has nothing to do with things, objects, but contains a more spiritual sense of the world. Maybe that's why I write poetry, because it's one way I can speak. Writing poetry enables me to speak of things that are more difficult to speak of in "normal" conversations.

I have a feeling that what many American Indian writers are attempting is to bring a new dimension, a new depth to English by returning a spiritual sense to something which has become, as you said, very materialistic and very scientific. German used to be described as the language of science. Today, English is the language of science throughout the world.

I've often wondered why we were all born into this time and this place and why certain things happen the way they do, and sometimes I have to believe it's for those reasons, to learn new ways of looking at things . . . not necessarily new, none of this is really new.

Even without the old language to say some of the things that were there in that old language?

Which is always right there beneath the surface, especially right here in North America, which is an Indian continent.

That ties into something I wanted to ask you, related to the whole question of the half-breed, the person who is of mixed blood. So many contemporary American Indian writers are people who have come from a mixed parentage. Does that mean a separation or isolation or something else?

Well, it means trouble. I've gone through stages with it. I've gone through the stage where I hated everybody who wasn't Indian, which meant part of myself. I went through a really violent kind of stage with that. And then I've gone through in-between stages and I've come to a point where I realize that we are who we are, and I realize in a way that you have to believe that you're special to be born like that because why would anybody give you such a hard burden like that unless they knew you could come through with it, unless with it came some special kind of vision to help you get through it all and to help others through it because in a way you do see two sides but you also see there are more than two sides. It's like this, living is like a diamond or how they cut really fine stones. There are not just two sides but there are so many and they all make up a whole. No, I've gone through a lot with it. I've talked to Linda Hogan, Lajuana, Leslie, a lot of other people about it, and everybody's probably been through similar stages with it.

Then there is that point where you come to realize that this is still Indian land, despite people who say, "Well, if you're only half-breed, why do you identify so strongly with Indian ancestry?"

Well, you can't not. I'm sure everybody's thought about it. I've thought about saying, "Hell, no, I don't have a drop of Indian blood in me. I'm not Indian, don't talk to me." Yeah, I've thought of doing that. But then I would be harassed even more. Everybody would come up to me and ask me why am I ashamed. But you just can't do it. And it also means that you have a responsibility being born into that, and I think some of us realize it much more than others. It's given to you, this responsibility, and you can't shake it off, you can't deny it. Otherwise you live in misery.

Barney Bush has spoken about the idea of being tested.

Sure.

Being tested from all kinds of directions at the same time. I especially feel that testing in some of your poems. A tension exists there. It seems to reach a point where it ought to break into violence and yet it doesn't. Why don't they go into violence as some of the poems of the Black American writers do? For example, Amiri Baraka's?

I don't know. I see where they could. There're always effective ways to deal with violence. There are ways to temper it. I just read this really neat quote by Gandhi. He's talking about anger and he says, "I have learned through bitter experience the one supreme lesson to

conserve my anger, and as heat conserved is transmitted into energy, even so our anger, controlled, can be transmitted into power which can move the world." It seems that the Native American experience has often been bitter. Horrible things have happened over and over. I like to think that bitter experience can be used to move the world, and if we can see that and work toward that instead of killing each other and hurting each other through all the ways that we have done it . . .

The world, not just Indian people, but the world.

Sure, because we're not separate. We're all in this together. It's a realization I came to after dealing with the whole half-breed question. I realized that I'm not separate from myself either, and neither are Indian people separate from the rest of the world. I've talked with James Welch and other writers about being categorized as Indian writers. We're writers, artists. We're human beings and ultimately, when it's all together, there won't be these categories. There won't be these categories of male/female and ultimately we will be accepted for what we are and not divided.

To connect, to celebrate, and also to understand. I think that there's a process of understanding that's going on right now in the United States and throughout the world. In fact, sometimes I think people in Europe are further ahead of many of the people in the United States in terms of listening to what writers such as the American Indian writers are saying and understanding what their messages can mean.

I suppose. I was in Holland a few years ago reading. I remember riding on a train and talking with a woman from Indonesia, and she told about how Indonesians are treated in Holland. I knew they were welcoming the American Indians and tribal people from all over, but they didn't realize that these Indonesians are tribal, too, you know. It's like during the Longest Walk when everybody was in D.C. And Carter wouldn't see the people, he said, because he had been out on some human rights mission involving the rest of the world.

Joy, I'd like to ask some questions that deal very specifically with your newest book of poetry, the one that's just about to be published, **She Had Some Horses**. Horses occur again and again in your writing. Why?

I see them as very sensitive and finely tuned spirits of the psyche. There's this strength running through them.

The idea of strength also seems to fit your images of women. Women in your poems are not like the women I've seen in poems by quite a few Anglo writers. They seem to be different.

I think they're different. I think they reach an androgynous kind of spirit where they are very strong people. They're very strong people, and yet to be strong does not mean to be male, to be strong does not mean to lose femininity, which is what the dominant culture has taught. They're human beings.

I like that. A woman or a man simply being a human being in a poem has not been very possible in the United States in poetry. Instead, the sexes are divided into stereotypes.

It's time to break all the stereotypes. The major principle of this universe, this earth, is polarity. Sometimes I think that it doesn't have to be, but the level that earth is, it is. You have to deal with it. I'm not saying it has to be that way—but this x-rated video game where Custer rapes an Indian woman—and then you have all these wonderful things going on in terms of consciousness. Such a split.

Ironic. It's like the old maxim that there wouldn't be angels without devils.

Or, again, like Gandhi's saying that bitter experiences can turn into a power that can move the world.

You're saying that things which are not properly used have destructive potential but then when they're used in the right way they become creative. Even those things which seem to be curses we can turn into blessings.

You always have to believe you can do that.

Another question about your images or themes . . . Noni Daylight. I've gotten to know and like her in your poems. Who is Noni Daylight, and how did she come to your poems?

In the beginning she became another way for me to speak. She left me and went into one of Barney's poems. I haven't seen her since. (laughter) Which poem was it? It was in his latest book. I remember when Barney showed me that poem, he was staying with me one Christmas and I looked at it and said, "Oh, there she is." She left and I really haven't written any poems about her since. It's like she was a good friend who was there at a time in my life and she's gone on.

When did you start writing poetry?

When I was at the University of New Mexico. Probably right around the time Rainy was born.

So you started relatively late in life—compared to some people.

Yeah, I never had a burning desire to write until rather recently. I always wanted to be an artist. When I was a little kid I was always drawing, and many of my relatives were pretty good artists. My favorite aunt, the one I spoke of earlier, was a very good artist. That's what I always did and it wasn't until much later that I got started, even interested, in writing.

What do you think created that interest?

Reading poetry and hearing that there was such a thing as Indians writing and hearing people read and talk, then writing down my own things.

Who were the people who were your influences at that time?

Simon Ortiz, Leslie Silko, Flannery O'Connor. The Black writers have always influenced me, also African writers, 'cause here was another way of seeing language and another way of using it that wasn't white European male.

Seeing that freedom of expression?

Sure. And I always loved James Wright. He was always one of my favorite poets. He has a beautiful sense of America. Pablo Neruda is also someone whose work I appreciate, learned from. . . .

Neruda speaks about writing a poetry of the impurity of the body, rather than a "pure" poetry. A poetry as broad as the earth is broad, bringing all things into it. I can see that feeling in your work.

Yeah, for sure.

What's the landscape of your poems?

The landscape of them? It's between a woman and all the places I've ever been. It's like the core of Oklahoma and New Mexico.

Traveling seems to be a really major force in your writing. Movement, continual movement. I think I see a sort of motion through your new book. Is there a structure you had in mind when you put it together?

*I had a hard time with this book for a long time. I could not put it together right. So a friend of mine, Brenda Peterson, who is a fine novelist and a very good editor, volunteered. She did an excellent job, and what I like about it is that the first poem in the first section is called **"Call it Fear."** It was an older poem. And the last section which is only one poem is called **"I Give You Back,"** which has to do with giving back that fear.*

The way it's arranged makes the book almost like an exorcism, too.

It is . . .

So it's not just another one of these cases where "poetry makes nothing happen."

No, I don't believe that or I wouldn't do it. I know that it does have effect and it does make things happen.

What does poetry do?

I've had all kinds of experiences that verify how things happen and how certain words or certain things make particular events happen. There's a poem that's in the new manuscript about an eagle who circled over us four times at Salt River Reservation. I went home and wrote an eagle poem for that eagle and took it back and gave it to the people who were there and one of the women took it outside the next morning to read it, and the eagle came back. You know, that kind of thing that happens. So I realize writing can help change the world. I'm aware of the power of language which isn't meaningless words . . . Sound is an extension of all, and sound is spirit, motion.

Yes, sound is spirit.

And realizing that everything also does, not just me, but anything that anybody says, it does go out at a certain level that it's put out and does make change in the world.

What about political poetry? Or do you think of your poetry as nonpolitical?

No, I think it's very political. But, yeah, I look at a lot of other people's poems, like June Jordan, Carolyn Forché, Audre Lorde—I love their work. It's very political. Political means great movers. To me, you can define political in a number of ways. But I would hope it was in the sense that it does help move and change consciousness in terms of how different peoples and cultures are seen, evolve.

That's great. Who do you like right now among contemporary writers? I'm not just thinking in terms of the American Indian writers, although maybe we could start with them. Who do you feel are the important people among Native American writers?

Well, I think everybody is. I don't want to mention certain people so that other people aren't mentioned.

That makes me think of what someone said to me at the American Writer's Congress. You remember that panel discussion?

Yeah, I remember that panel.

There were more of us than there were in the audience.

We had a good time.

It was great. But one person came up to me afterwards and said they couldn't understand why we all seemed to know each other and like each other.

That's because everybody else is busy hating each other, I guess. Trying to do each other in . . . That doesn't mean, however, that there's none of that going on in our community!

Why is there such a sense of community? Even when people get angry at each other or gossip about each other, there's a lot of that.

Oh, I know, I was gonna ask you what you heard.

Yet there does seem to be a sense of community among the people who are Indian writers today.

I suppose because the struggles are very familiar, places we've all been. It's very familiar and we feel closer. But at the same time I really can't help but think that at some point it will all be this way, the community will be a world community, and not just here.

Do you notice that tendency in contemporary American writing?

Yes, I do. I do more listening than I do reading about what's going on . . . I call it feeling from the air, like air waves. I see other people opening and turning to more communal things, especially among women.

That's a good point. Could you say a few words about that?

The strongest writing that's going on in the United States today is women's writing. It's like they're tunneling into themselves, into histories and roots. And again, I think maybe that has to do with the polarity of earth. In order to get to those roots, in order to have that vision, you keep going outward to see you have to have that, to be able to go back the other way. You have to have those roots. And it seems like they're recognizing that, whereas other writing doesn't often feel it has a center to work from.

I like the fact that you dedicated your book, partially, to Meridel Le Sueur.

She does recognize who she is, what she is from, and there is no separation. You know, she's been going at it a long time, has faced much opposition, and has kept on talking and speaking in such a beautiful and lyrical voice.

Scott Fitzgerald said there are no second acts in American lives. But Le Sueur's life and writing seem to prove Fitzgerald wrong.

She's really had a lot of influence on me in terms of being a woman who speaks as a woman and has been often criticized for it, and in the past she could not get her books published because she kept to her particular viewpoint and was sympathetic to certain unpopular viewpoints.

And has influenced a lot of other women, too.

Definitely.

To begin writing at a point when most people would say your career is all set. You're a housewife, you're this, you're that, you're something else, you're not a writer. To begin to write at an age when most men have already been writing for ten or fifteen years . . .

Well, I always knew I wanted to do something. When I was a kid I always used to draw, paint. I even had pieces at Philbrook Art Center, in a children's art show. I always knew I wanted to be some kind of artist . . . and here I am, writing.

One last question. Your Native American ancestry is Creek. How do you deal with that particular ancestry in your poetry? Does that affect you as it has some other Indian writers?

From the time I was a kid I knew I was Creek. But I was raised in an urban setting and in a broken family . . . It all influenced me. I was born into it and since then I've gone back and I'm very connected to the place, to relatives, and to those stories. They always recognize me. My father who was not always there but his presence always was—certainly the stories about him were!

But you're not artificially going back and, say, pulling Creek words out of a dictionary?

No, I mean that's who I've always been.

Yeah, you don't have to do that. There's no need to *prove* that ancestry.

No, they know who I am. They know my aunt Lois. You could sit down and talk with her, she knew who everybody was and who's related to who, you know, all of them, and they all know who everybody is. They'll say, "Oh, so you're so 'n' so's daughter." And they watch you real close, especially if you have white blood in you. Bad. (laughter) So in a way, I suppose, the whole half-breed thing gives you this incredible responsibility but it also gives you a little bit more freedom than anyone because you have an excuse for your craziness.

That's nice.

Of course, you realize it is because, oh, you're an Indian like Linda says, but it's the white blood that makes you that way. (laughter)

I like that.

And you also always have to have a sense of humor about it all.

Yes, a sense of humor is right. We didn't talk about that, did we?

I mean it's like that poem, **"Anchorage,"** *I remember that one jail. I went in there three times and the place would get more and more packed each time I came in because we would sit around and tell stories and—it was all men—and talk and laugh and they didn't want me to go because nobody allowed them to speak. We would all be crying at the end, and I remember when Henry told the story, yeah, you know, we were just laughing at him and saying, you know, you're full of crap, yet the story was really true. We all knew it was absolutely true and it was so sad that it had to be so funny.*

Nancy Lang (essay date 1993)

SOURCE: "'Twin Gods Bending Over': Joy Harjo and Poetic Memory," in *MELUS*, Vol. 18, No. 3, Fall, 1993, pp. 41-9.

[*In the following essay, Lang emphasizes the importance of memory in Harjo's poetry by examining her depiction of various urban American landscapes.*]

Contemporary Native American poet Joy Harjo expresses and reflects patterns of ongoing, multilayered and multivocal memories within the narratives of her poems. These memories flow and interweave on a continuum within a metaphysical world that begins deep within her personal psyche and simultaneously moves back into past memories of her Creek (Muskogee) heritage, as well as forward into current pan-tribal experiences and the assimilationist, Anglo-dominated world of much contemporary Native American life. Harjo's poetic memories may be personal stories, family and tribal histories, myths, recent pan-tribal experiences, or spiritual icons of an ancient culture and history. And, while Harjo writes using both an "alien" language, English, and within expected structural and narrative formats of contemporary poetry, her poems also frequently resonate with the distinctive chanting rhythms and pause breaks associated with traditional Native American oralities. As with other contemporary Native American women poets such as Paula Gunn Allen (Laguna Pueblo/Sioux), Linda Hogan (Chickasaw), and Wendy Rose (Hopi/Chowchilla Miwok), Harjo's past memories and present experiences seamlessly fuse together within individual poems; and when read together as a group, her poems construct in the reader's mind a single consistent, cohesive, and unified poetic utterance.

The importance of memory to Harjo's poetry best reveals itself through a survey and examination of one of her most important ongoing tropes, the contemporary American city. Within her varied urban landscapes, Harjo's poetry most clearly illustrates the multivoiced nature of any marginalized poetry, and of Native American women's poetry in particular. On the one hand, after a first reading Harjo may seem to be writing out of the city-as-subject tradition of American poets like Walt Whitman, Carl Sandburg, Hart Crane, and William Carlos Williams. On the other hand, her city landscapes do not reflect promise and optimistic excitement, as do many urban settings of earlier white male American poets. Rather, Harjo's cities resonate with Native American memories of an endless and ongoing history of Eurocentric and genocidal social and political policies: war, forced removal, imposed education, racism, and assimilationism.

While Allen, Hogan, and Rose often use the contemporary city as negative physical setting in a variety of ways, Harjo especially foregrounds the psychological and spiritual impacts, and the resulting personal chaos, of urban life on the Native American survivor. As Patricia Clark Smith and Paula Gunn Allen note, Harjo's "particular poetic turf is cities" (193), perhaps because she grew up in Tulsa, Oklahoma, and has spent much of her adult life in cities. In any case, the speakers within her urban narratives roam freely throughout the United States on a life's journey reflecting simultaneously Harjo's own current travels on the urban/academic lecture-powwow-poetry reading circuit, as well as the age-old, traditional wanderings of her Creek ancestors.

What sustains Harjo's contemporary speakers in such an alien environment are memories—memories of ancestral lands, family and tribal life, traditional spirituality, and a pan-tribal heritage. In Harjo's poems the multi-voiced city experiences of Native Americans living within indifferent and often hostile urban landscapes offer a strikingly different reading from contemporary Anglo experience of the American city, and thus they make an important statement about current American societies. Moreover, we can also trace a distinct growth in the richness, complexity, and tone of Harjo's city trope from her earliest to her most recent poetic texts.

Even in her first chapbook collection, **The Last Song** (1975), Harjo begins to develop a clear but subtle city-as-negative motif, as her speaker wistfully looks out from the streets of Albuquerque, off toward the distant natural world. In **"Watching Crow, Looking South Towards the Manzano Mountains,"** the speaker yearns for the freedom of a crow "dancing" with a New Mexico winter wind; and in **"3AM,"** she seeks both a physical and a spiritual escape from Albuquerque's airport, back to the Hopis' Third Mesa. This pattern of wanting to leave cities continues in **What Moon Drove Me To This?** (1979), where Chicago, Kansas City, Gallup, Albuquerque, and nameless bars in Oklahoma towns serve as meeting grounds for often negative and superficial social encounters between men and women. Here also, in **"The First Noni Daylight,"** appears the first statement of Harjo's early poetic "otherself," Noni Daylight, a beautiful young Native American urban woman caught in the assimilationist trap of contemporary life, while trying to hold on to her man by faking a suicide and thus tying him to her by guilt.

In his article "Nightriding with Noni Daylight: The Many Horse Songs of Joy Harjo," Andrew Wiget focuses on the specific "otherself" persona of Noni Daylight as an important clue into understanding Harjo's early poetry. Concentrating as he does on the growth in Harjo's poetic voice from **What Moon Drove Me To This?** (1979) to **She Had Some Horses** (1983), Wiget examines the developing complexities of Harjo's poetic voice by looking at several of her characteristic images. Noting that the otherself motif grows out of early descriptions of social and psychological alienation, especially of bar life and of troubled love relationships in **What Moon Drove Me To This?,** Wiget sees Harjo's more complex **She Had Some Horses** as developing a self/otherself dialogue that begins to build a "cyclic quest of a voice looking for a home" (186). While he foregrounds the importance of Harjo's using natural landscapes and the moon as recurring identifications with the earth and sky, Wiget also sees Noni Daylight as an early Harjo expression of the suffering individual who longs for the total ecstasy that might be found in a past of eternal comfort, "the womb-worn memory of her mother's heartbeat" (188).

Wiget's ideas help to give clarity to much of Noni Daylight's seemingly erratic behavior. For example, because of the psychological and spiritual hopelessness of her life, Noni Daylight often turns at night to high-speed interstate driving, which for her becomes a perfect form of escape into a soothing, rhythmic mindlessness. In **What Moon Drove Me To This?** **"Origin"** describes her driving west, toward Flagstaff, into a mysterious darkness, "where stars have come down into rocks" (33) and into memories of old Native American stories that tell of mythic origins as Noni tries to construct a pan-tribal map leading back into an understanding of herself and her mixed-blood heritage. But her efforts bring her no answers, and Noni's unnamed and unstated fears increase as she continues the journey of her life. In "heartbeat" she drives through a silent nighttime city, obediently waiting for red lights to change at empty intersections, and toying with the trigger of the pistol cradled in her lap. In the **"Evidence"** of She Had Some Horses, her nighttime flirting with the highway's yellow line becomes more than just a veiled hint pointing toward Noni's dimly-formulated thoughts of suicide. Still, while the lure of complete oblivion tempts her, Noni Daylight also "needs / the feel of danger, / for life" (46). Unlike the bilingual little girl of **"For Alva Benson, and For Those Who Have Learned to Speak,"** Noni Daylight freezes into an inarticulation far surpassing that of words and language.

Wiget sees Harjo's ongoing and often contradictory dialogues of and with the poetic self as best reflected in the more mature, seemingly paradoxical language and imagery of **"She Had Some Horses,"** one of Harjo's most powerful poems, and also a poem that illustrates Wiget's idea of "crossing over to apocalypse" (192). Through its often paradoxical juxtapositions, **"She Had Some Horses"** also foregrounds the important truths of borders and living on the borders, or what Gloria Anzaldúa in her "Preface" to *Borderlands: La Frontera* defines as that place where "two or more cultures edge each other, where people of different races occupy the same territory, where under, lower, middle and upper classes touch" (np). The interwoven and often violently clashing images in **"She Had Some Horses"**—"She had horses who threw rocks at glass houses. / She had horses who licked razor blades." (63)—also offer a broader, more all-encompassing statement of those fears and silences which so wracked Noni Daylight's unhappy, cramped life.

It is with the poems of **She Had Some Horses**, and especially with one of her most powerful poems, **"The Woman Hanging From the Thirteenth Floor,"** that Harjo fully articulates the interlocked problems of unnamed fears and the resulting speechlessness of an oppressed and dispossessed woman. Told in the flat, seemingly unemotional voice of a dispassionate observer, this highly rhythmic prose poem tells the story of a young Native American mother caught in the trap of her life and trying to find some way, any way, out of her nightmare. Memories of her own traditionally-oriented childhood, her family, her children, and her lovers no longer sustain her, as "her mind chatters like neon and northside bars" (23). Hanging in space, thirteen floors up from the city streets of an East Chicago ghetto, she hears some people scream-ing that she should jump, while others try to help her with their prayers. At the end of the poem "she would speak" (23), but *will* she take charge of her own life? Or, is she doomed to death and oblivion?

In an interview with Laura Coltelli, Harjo tells the story of how **"The Woman Hanging From the Thirteenth Floor"** came to be written. Growing out of a private experience she had at the Chicago Indian Center, the poem reflects Harjo's invented persona and voice, yet people continue to come up to her at readings and say they know a woman like that; or they have read such a story in the newspaper, but the incident occurred somewhere else (62). Whether by accident or by design, Harjo has con-structed a folkloric, urban Native American example of every woman's ultimate fear, the fear of being totally and absolutely frozen and helpless, without the power to speak, unable to function, and therefore not able to choose ei-ther life or death for herself.

Harjo writes a deliberately incomplete ending to the un-named woman's story, because the woman considers let-ting go and falling, as well as trying again by climbing back through her apartment window. In this way, Harjo gives her readers the freedom to become writers, since the unnamed woman's story has the potential to become every woman's multi-voiced yet muted struggle against fear, depression, death, and oblivion.

These same urban stresses and fears also echo in Harjo's final development of Noni Daylight's ongoing life story. In **"Kansas City,"** now a much older and no longer beau-tiful woman with many children by many fathers, Noni watches the trains roll by, remembers her past life, and vows that she still would choose to live her life as she always has. Yet her bravado seems hollow and pathetic, since she, too, is still spiritually and psychologically in-articulate, trapped in unnamed and unresolved fears, and still watching the trains roll out of a city where she is destined to live out her life.

In **"Anchorage,"** a poem dedicated to Audre Lorde, Harjo's speaker, now seemingly free from fear, strides purposefully through this Alaska city "of stone, of blood, and fish" (14). Speaking in a powerfully artic-ulate voice, and sustained by memories of a once-strong, now lost and buried Native American heritage echoing along the streets and lying under the earth, Harjo's central figure also knows that the spirit world still lives. While on the surface the Anchorage of Harjo's poem appears to be a city of mountains, an-cestral Athabascan voices, and creatures of the air and ocean, the speaker also knows that lying "underneath the concrete / is the cooking earth" (14), or the earth of suppressed volcanic forces barely held in check by the thin concrete skin of the modern city. Like the unarticulated stories of "someone's Athabascan / grand-mother" (14), the smothered earth and native peoples of Alaska are muted for now. Yet even so, sometimes a story breaks through, and someone pays homage to life. Within the 6th Avenue jail a man named Henry

tells his story of surviving eight shots aimed at him outside an L. A. liquor store, and the other inmates laugh at the impossible truths in his tale. Like the earth itself, Anchorage's poor and oppressed native people somehow continue to survive by creating bridges of ongoing dialogue with each other and the land.

In the same vein, but now within the radically different Deep South world of New Orleans, Harjo continues her travels. Unlike Hopi poet Wendy Rose's "Searching for Indians in New Orleans," a poem that comments on the unfamiliar "silence of petroglyphs, / stiff birds and stick women" (*What Happened When the Hopi Hit New York* 21), Harjo's poem returns to its spiritual Creek home through memory. Moving through an ancestrally familiar landscape, her memory "swims deep in blood, / a delta in the skin" (42), as the speaker moves from Oklahoma into the French Quarter, looking for Creek voices echoing along the streets of the present-day city. As she searches for historical or spiritual echoes of her Creek ancestors, she discovers a Spanish horse, frozen speechless as a statue, juxtaposed against a man in a rock shop selling magic stones and unaware of their power. Over and over again, Harjo refers to careless Anglo supremacist behav-ior, like the contemporary rock shop salesman and the historic Spanish explorer DeSoto, both of whom exert a strong but superficial power over deeper, more private native Creek and natural world powers. And always lying just under the surface of Harjo's New Orleans are those ancestral Creek "stories here made of memory" (43), waiting once again to be told.

Especially in **"She Had Some Horses," "Anchorage,"** and **"New Orleans,"** Harjo's ongoing circularities of memory, story, history, and ancestral voices all work to-gether to create and explain natural cycles underlying human existence, and thus to define the interconnected-ness of life itself. Out of the earth and ancestral lands and peoples comes memory, out of memory comes the present, and the resulting interplay of tensions fuses to-gether into story and life. Throughout the poems of *She Had Some Horses*, landscape and story often merge into an individual voice tied simultaneously to memories of a traditional past, as well as to the life of the present; and it is this voice that helps one to survive in the city.

While one may survive in the city, Harjo believes that one truly lives only on the land, or within memories of the land. In *Secrets from the Center of the World* (1989), she and photographer Stephen Strom together create an interlocked picture celebrating the fundamental impor-tance of landscape and story within the Native American world view. Harjo begins her prose poem by remarking that while New York, Paris, or Tokyo may operate as the center of the earth for some people, for her "my house is the red earth; it could be the center of the world"; and even more important, "words cannot construct it, for there are some sounds left to sacred wordless form" (2). This inherent spirituality of place, this cosmic spiritual link with a sentient being that is greater and more powerful than humanity (and indeed *is* the source of all humanity), serves to explain Harjo's deep reverence for specific landscapes in the Navajo Nation. While signs of an alien and dominating Anglo world may intrude—telephone and electricity poles, power plant smoke, and concrete highways—nonetheless "the land-scape forms the mind" (22), and "stories are our wealth" (24). Thus, Harjo's memory fuses together dinosaur tracks, an individual lifespan, and linear time into an ongoing spiritual dance of life.

With her most recent book, *In Mad Love and War* (1990), Harjo leaves her home once again and returns to the city as significant setting; and the sheer mass of those urban centers that she names underscores her vision of herself as wanderer in an alien Anglo land. From **"Climbing the Streets of Worcester, Mass."** to New York City, Denver, Anchorage, New Orleans, and especially Albuquerque and Santa Fe, Harjo is constantly moving through cities and almost never settling into them, but always aware of where the earth is, how the people are feeling, and what the spirit world is doing.

In **"We Encounter Nat King Cole as We Invent the Future"** Harjo speaks of an old friend, Camme, and the experiences they share of music, love, and old times. Within these seemingly rather ordinary shared memories, Harjo suddenly juxtaposes a dramatically heart-lifting, precisely described personal vision:

> Yesterday I turned north on Greasewood
> the long way home and was shocked to see a double
>   rainbow
> two-stepping across the valley. Suddenly
> there were twin gods bending over to plant something
>   like
> themselves in the wet earth, a song
> larger than all our cheap hopes, our small-town
>   radios,
> whipping everything back
> into the geometry of dreams . . .
>
>   (51)

What to non-Native Americans might be just a beautiful sight here speaks in a multi-voiced, spiritual discourse to Harjo. As she sees the double-arched rainbow dancing across the sky, the speaker simultaneously remembers stories describing the eternal Navajo *yei* bending down to the earth in rainbow curves, planting themselves as seeds and thereby fulfilling the sacred promise of life and renewal. Much the same sudden flash of spiritual insight also appears in **"Fury Of Rain,"** where in an unnamed city thunder-as-gods, "naked to their electric skeletons" (16), dance in the streets and shake their rattles of memory during a violent summer rainstorm.

Experiencing such sights and memories as these through a pantribal vision often leads, in turn, to Harjo's increasing awareness of time and space, as well as to ongoing dialogic patterns of latent and shared strength among oppressed peoples. In **"Hieroglyphic,"** a poem addressed to African American poet and activist June Jordan, Harjo describes a flash of personal insight that she experienced within the Egyptian Room of New York's Metropolitan Museum. As her memory connects stories of ancient

Egypt, her own childhood in Oklahoma, and her present life, she recognizes the ironic surrealism of an interlocking human pattern—while *who* holds power over others may change, oppression remains. Sometimes the clownish humor of **"Anchorage's"** Henry may temporarily relieve this surreal tension, but such humor is not the Eurocentric, Bakhtinian-related carnivalization of explosive laughter leading to release and relaxation. Rather, Native American clownish humor may often deliberately play the Fool in order to mask and subvert rising hysteria. For example, in **"The Book of Myths,"** the speaker sees the traditional Creek Trickster "Rabbit sobbing and laughing / as he shook his dangerous bag of tricks / into the mutiny world on that street outside Hunter [College]" (55). Trapped on the "stolen island of Manhattan" (55), both the speaker and Rabbit struggle to stay alive and hang on to their self-control in a dangerous place; and foolish behavior and stories help to keep terror at bay.

This postmodern humor of Harjo's **"Anchorage"** and **"The Book of Myths"** varies from Rose's angry, sardonic humor in "Stopover in Denver." Here Rose's speaker, embarking from a plane flight, sees herself caught in the tacky world of Plastic Kachina. Running the gauntlet of tourists, who "scrape my skin with / a camera lens" (*What Happened When the Hopi Hit New York* 10), she remembers childhood tricks of making and selling fake prayersticks, as the pain of ongoing cultural exploitation and personal alienation continues unabated in her life. Like Harjo's clownish Fool, Rose's sardonic poetic voice chooses the release of active laughter rather than passive tears.

When underlying and often unstated personal anger and fears link up with the shocks of urban socio-cultural experience, a highly distinctive, intensely personal poetic statement often results. The rich complexities of Harjo's most recent postmodernist voice are particularly evident in **"Santa Fe,"** a surreal and sensuous prose poem juxtaposing memories of lilacs, Saint Francis Cathedral, the De Vargas Hotel, a cocaine-addicted fox-woman, and a man riding a Harley-Davidson, all swirling in and out of a spiral dance through the speaker's memory, as time "is here . . .is there," and "space curves, walks over and taps me on the shoulder" (*In Mad* 42). Whereas Harjo's early city poems are usually set physically in bars, apartments, or automobiles and often describe aimless and alienated drifting, her later poems tend to be set in the mind and its memories of an urban experience, and to describe both a clear-eyed acceptance of life as it is and a quiet but fiercely unwavering commitment to the Native American belief in the inherent spirituality within all life forms.

Thus memory, what Paula Gunn Allen refers to as "that undying arabesque" (*Shadow Country*, 9), underlies all of Harjo's poetry. While all Native American cultures value the powers of memory, the contemporary urban pulse-beats and incidents recorded in Joy Harjo's poems bring memory most fully and dramatically into the non-Native American reader's awareness and understanding. When she juxtaposes her Native American memories of the earth against present-day urban life experiences, Harjo creates a uniquely surreal, yet frighteningly accurate and familiar picture of modern American cities and their alienated citizenry. As Harjo explains memory, one has no authentic voice without memory; and without an authentic voice, one is speechless, hardly human, and unable to survive for very long. Thus, Harjo's braided strands of multilayered memory and poetic voice intertwine into the very warp and woof of her poetic creation.

WORKS CITED

Allen, Paula Gunn. *Shadow Country*. Los Angeles: U of California American Indian Studies Center, 1982.

Anzaldúa, Gloria. *Borderlands/La Frontera*. San Francisco: Spinsters/ Aunt Lute, 1987.

Coltelli, Laura. "Joy Harjo." *Winged Words: American Indian Writers Speak*. Lincoln: U of Nebraska P, 1990. 55-68.

————, ed. *Native American Literatures*. Pisa: Servisio Editoriale Universitario, 1989.

Harjo, Joy. *Furious Light*. Cassette tape. Watershed C-192, 1985.

————. *In Mad Love and War*. Middletown, CT: Wesleyan U P, 1990.

————. *The Last Song*. Las Cruces, NM: Puerto del Sol, 1975.

————. "Ordinary Spirit." *I Tell You Now: Autobiographical Essays By Native American Writers*. Lincoln: U of Nebraska P, 1987. 263-70.

————. *She Had Some Horses*. New York: Thunder's Mouth, 1983.

————. *What Moon Drove Me To This?* New York: I. Reed, 1979.

————, and Stephen Strom. *Secrets From the Center Of the World*. Tucson: U of Arizona P, 1989.

Hogan, Linda. *Savings*. Minneapolis: Coffee House, 1988.

Jaskoski, Helen. "A MELUS Interview: Joy Harjo." *MELUS* 16.1 (1989-90): 5-13.

Norwood, Vera, and Janice Monk, ed. *The Desert Is No Lady: Southwestern Landscapes In Women's Writing and Art*. New Haven: Yale U P, 1987.

Rose, Wendy. *What Happened When the Hopi Hit New York*. New York: Contact II, 1982.

Scarry, John. "Representing Real Worlds: The Evolving Poetry of Joy Harjo." *World Literature Today* 66.2 (1992): 286-91.

Smith, Patricia Clark, with Paula Gunn Allen. "Earthy Relations, Carnal Knowledge: Southwestern American Indian Women Writers and Landscape." *The Desert Is No Lady: Southwestern Landscapes In Women's Writing and Art*. Ed. Vera Norwood and Janice Monk. New Haven: Yale U P, 1987. 174-96.

Wiget, Andrew. "Nightriding With Noni Daylight: The Many Horse Songs Of Joy Harjo." *Native American Literatures*. Ed. Laura Coltelli. Pisa: Servisio Editoriale Universitario, 1989. 185-96.

Mary Leen (essay date 1995)

SOURCE: "An Art of Saying: Joy Harjo's Poetry and the Survival of Storytelling," in *American Indian Quarterly*, Vol. 19, No. 1, Winter, 1995, pp. 1-3, 5-15.

[*In the following excerpt, Leen explores the function of storytelling in Harjo's poetry.*]

In her poem titled, **"The Book of Myths,"** Joy Harjo (1990:55-56) introduces "stories / that unglue the talking spirit from the pages" (lines 33-34). Stories have the power to take action, to unglue a spirit, to revise words on a page, to cross sacred boundaries to revisionist mythmaking. Another Native American writer addresses storytelling and crossing boundaries in his short story, "Four Skin." Gerald Vizenor (199:91) crosses the boundaries between science (computers and research) and art (storytelling), between nature (the night) and academia (graduate school): "The truth is that this computer time was given to me to do research, but research is too slow to hold the night, so I have been telling stories to this machine about being a crossblood skin and graduate student." This quote also crosses the vague oral (crossblood skin as noble/howling savage) and literate (graduate student) boundaries that many Native Americans—as do most oppressed minorities—consistently maneuver.

In oral cultures, storytelling maintains and preserves traditions. It takes listeners on a journey toward a renewal of life, a common survival theme in Native rituals and ceremonies. Older generations pass on stories told when they were young. Thus, storytelling knits a new generation into the fabric of generations gone. This act serves as a "gentle survival" tactic—a productive way to fight extinction. The poet Leslie Ullman (1991:180) has written of the active role of storyteller in Harjo's **In Mad Love and War**:

> [H]er stance is not so much that of a representative of a culture as it is the more generative one of a storyteller whose stories resurrect memory, myth, and private struggles that have been overlooked, and who thus restores vitality to the culture at large. As a storyteller, Harjo steps into herself as a passionate individual living on the edge.

As a storyteller in her poetry, Harjo promotes survival in the resurrection of memory, myth, and struggles. This act of storytelling is vital and generative.

For Native American cultures, storytelling has served as entertainment, as well as to answer questions from curious children about the origins of natural sights and phenomena. In her poem titled **"Eagle Poem,"** Harjo (1990: 65) names a site of human origin:

> We are truly blessed because we
> Were born, and die soon within a
> True circle of motion,
> Like eagle rounding out the morning
> Inside us
>
> (lines 19-23)

The story of the eagle's "sacred wings" that "swept our hearts clean" is a place of origin, an explanation of how people arrived on the land. In their book of Native American myths, Simon Ortiz and Richard Erdoes (1984: xiv) remind us that "[a]ll tribes have spun narratives . . . for the features of their landscape: how this river came to be, when these mountains were formed, how our coastline was carved." Sacred stories were considered factual, and the idea of history, of past and present and future for indigenous peoples before contact, was quite different from the linear, chronological way events are organized in the Western world. In a collection of interviews titled *Winged Words* Harjo spoke of time as nonlinear: "I also see memory as not just associated with past history, past events, past stories, but nonlinear, as in future and ongoing history, events, and stories" (Coltelli 1990: 57). The juxtaposition and incorporation of past and present, history and future, survive in contemporary stories within Harjo's poetry.

In relation to Native American myths, Erdoes and Ortiz (1984: xii) write: "Plots seem to travel at their own speed, defying convention and at times doing away completely with recognizable beginnings and endings." The boundaries of the chronological order of beginning and ending are vague and shifting—and not respected. Therefore, stories often seem to bridge the everyday and the supernatural, or the past and the present. In her prose poem titled **"Original Memory"** Harjo (1990: 47) presents notions of the past and future: "When I am inside the Muscogee world, which is not a flip side of the Western time chain but a form of music staggered in the ongoing event of earth calisthenics, the past and the future are the same tug-of-war." Rather than being another form of time, the Muscogee world is music and motion in calisthenics. In the Muscogee world the past and the future are the same struggle. Both are outside the present. Both pull at a member of marginal worlds by shouting to be remembered and begging to survive for the future. Traditional myths remind us that the "[N]ative American, following the pace of 'Indian time,' still lives connected to the nurturing womb of mythology" (Erdoes and Ortiz 1984: xi). As an example of a different perspective of time, consider that Native American ceremonies often lasted five to ten days. Candidates in rites of passage often fasted and sang for three or four days at a time with no sleep. Boundaries are crossed in the act of narrative: lengths of time, realities, histories, cultures, past/present.

In reference to diverse and multiple knowledges and subject-positions: boundaries to be crossed, or ignored, or acknowledged as imposed—a network of intertexts intersects and affects familiar and unfamiliar stories and subject-positions and knowledges. Many images in Harjo's (1990: 57-58) poem, **"Death Is a Woman,"** intersect to communicate among various worlds. The speaker walks "these night hours between the dead and the living" (line 1); she names this a "spiral of tangential stories" (line 5); she can see her own death trying on her shoes (line 6). The stories may be separate, but they connect by a thread, dialogue with each other, and they translate knowledge between the worlds of the dead and the living.

In her prose poem **"Deer Dancer,"** Harjo (1990: 5-6) tells the story of Indians and a woman dancer in a bar on the coldest night of the winter: "We were Indian ruins. She was the end of beauty" (page 5). The Indian patrons at the bar are described as "hardcore," "Indian ruins," Henry Jack's "head by the toilet," "broken survivors," and "children without shoes" (pages 5-6). As she tells the stories of Indian lives, she also refers to the story: "The music ended. And so does the story. I wasn't there" (page 6). The storyteller didn't experience the event she tells; she may not have invented the story, but she does invent her listeners—she *makes* a reader who listens to the story (that may not have happened), creates a listener out of any given reader.

$$\cdots\cdots$$

Several notions of narrative and storytelling operate in Harjo's poetry. Several types of borders are crossed. Storytelling proclaims different functions. In his essay, "Native American Oral Narratives: Context and Continuity," Kenneth Roemer (1983:45-46) describes a storyteller: "A good storyteller uses his body and his voice. . . . Old Cheyenne storytellers began their sacred narratives by smoothing the ground and going through a brief ritual of marking the dirt and touching their bodies." This act of smoothing the earth signified that the Creator made humans and the earth, and that the Creator was now witnessing this story. The storyteller ceremonially crosses the boundaries between the earth and humans by touching the soil of the earth to her body, for the Creator to see her tell the story. Such accounts of Native storytellers validate the idea that storytelling is a performance, that there are actions and consequences to consider. In an interview Harjo discussed energy, power, and action of stories: "We all felt the energy—after the trading of stories, and hearing the stories—the power of those stories. Many of them included torture, destruction, torture, destruction, over and over. And stories of survival." (Jaskoski 1989:9) The act of torture results in destruction, but the people survive as long as the stories are told, acted, performed.

Storytellers learn their stories from other storytellers and from experience. Their stories change with the speaker and with time and with circumstance. Each story is told from a subject-position which affects the telling of the story. In Harjo's book, *Secrets from the Center of the World*, co-authored with Stephen Strom, she writes of the "earth spirit" as the storyteller (Harjo and Strom 1989:54):

> Don't bother the earth spirit who lives here. She is working on a story. It is the oldest story in the world and it is delicate, changing. If she sees you watching she will invite you in for coffee, give you warm bread, and you will be obligated to stay and listen. But this is no ordinary story. You will have to endure earthquakes, lightning, the deaths of all those you love, the most blinding beauty. It's a story so compelling you may never want to leave; this is how she traps you.

Here the subject-position from which this story is being-told is that of the arth spirit. The story she tells is delicate and changing, so the speaker and the listener are both operating tactically, in a shifting environment. When the earth spirit invites you in for coffee, she takes the listener into her home—includes him/her in the "homeplace" bell hooks speaks of. And if her story makes you never want to leave, perhaps that effect is the function of the earth spirit's narrative.

In another excerpt from the same book, Harjo's speaker describes stories as a storage site, a place with boundaries in which wealth can accumulate:

> Stories are our wealth. Winter nights we tell them over and over. Once a star fell from the sky, but it wasn't just any star, just as this isn't just any ordinary place. That cedar tree marks the event and the land remembers the flash of its death flight. To describe anything in winter whether it occurs in the past or the future requires a denser language, one thick with the promise of new lambs, heavy with the weight of corn milk.

(Harjo and Strom 1989: 24)

While such a site for accumulation of wealth would imply definite boundaries, and thus strategic operations, the notion that a language can be "thick with the promise of new lambs" and "heavy with the weight of corn milk," implies a disregard for boundaries between language and nature, or text and nature. Thus, such a disregard for boundaries would point toward tactical operations. Additionally, the reference to the "we" that tells stories over and over, implies a multiple subject-position. And the idea that this "isn't just any ordinary place," suggests another viewpoint for hook's "homeplace" (a place to grow and develop and nurture our spirits) and de Certeau's "everyday" (a place where subjects operate tactically to invent themselves).

In "Four Skin," Gerald Vizenor (1991:92) presents Native American as inventions, not "just any ordinary" stories that have been narrated by whites:

> [W]e were invented by missionaries and theologians and social scientists subsidized by the federal government, and now, in the cities, we are rewarded, praised and programmed, for validating the invention of the Indian. In that dialectic we are impressed to assume ownership of strange experiences: imitate data, live out theories, pretend our lives in beads and feathers, hold their mirrors for portraits and photographs, and serve as models, wilderness brothers and sisters to campers and hunters and ecologists. We have even been taught to resist questions about ourselves, about the Indian invention, because the white world has invested too much in the invention.

Vizenor crosses many boundaries in this small excerpt from his narrative. He produces life imitating data, rather than data reflecting life. Theories become practice and are lived out. Functioning human beings are holding up mirrors, as well as serving as models. The type of narrative Vizenor describes here does not respect boundaries. Furthermore, for whites to be constructing Native identity is certainly traveling tactically in unfamiliar territory. The Indian-weknow is the invention of white men.

Their white subject-position is part of our definition of the American Indian.

The story referred to in the following excerpt lives, in part, because of the subject-position of the man in Harjo's poem (and the story within). The subject-position of the "he" in the following lines from Harjo's (1979: 5) poem **"Round Dance Somewhere Around Oklahoma City/November Night"** is presented in the poem as a "tall Creek man / who wanted to show me everything / in one night" (lines 11-14).

> he had almost the same story
> of last Oklahoma November
> that I did
> Indians surrounded by Indians
> surrounded by tall steel creatures
> of downtown Oklahoma City

(lines 1-6)

While the subject-position of the storyteller above may be other than the speaker or the poet, he has "almost the same story" the speaker of the poem does. Their common stories function as an act of solidarity. To be the "other" there must be boundaries between speaker of poem and the male storyteller. However, if they are telling almost the same stories, the boundaries get blurred or become less clear.

In the following quote from Harjo's (1979: 21) poem **"There Was A Dance, Sweetheart,"** the origin of the story or the storyteller's subject-position is unclear:

> And the next time was either a story
> in one of his poems or what she had heard from
>   crows
> gathered before the snow caught
> in wheels of traffic silent
> up and down Central Avenue.

(lines 11-15)

The speaker of the poem, who is also the one who heard the story, doesn't know whether the story was in a poem or in a crow's caw. Those are two very different sources, yet the boundaries around each that might separate them from each other are blurred because either the poem or the crow could be the source of the story. This possibility that a crow or a poem could be the storyteller almost makes them interchangeable—a poem is a crow's caw, and a crow's caw is a poem. The "he" who wrote the poem (within the Harjo poem), the subject-position of the storyteller (if the story was in the poem he wrote), is a man who "talked to the moon to stars and to / other voices riding in the backseat / that she and Carmen didn't hear" (lines 11-15). The function of storytelling in this poem might be to interact with the unknown, as does the male storyteller in the poem (within Harjo's poem). Or the function of the story in Harjo's poem might be to speak from the unknown, as the crow speaks from the sky. In either case, the unknown would point toward tactical operation. However, the moon and stars and the crow may not be viewed as the unknown in some Native American circles. In that case, the borders between nature and human are nonexistent; nature is not the other. There would be no boundaries around what humanity is, and so we humans could not retreat within those boundaries to think, work, rest, and accumulate things separate from nature.

In his essay, "Dreaming the Tribal Past into Tradition," Joseph Bruchac, a writer of Abenaki Indian and Slovak descent, writes of the "unsteadiness of the world" and that the world is "a tricky place" (1987:14). A tricky place might be one where boundaries are shifting or vague. A tricky place might be unfamiliar. Such sites require a tactical approach of operation. For many minority peoples, our dominant culture is that very site. And there is little respite or relief from tactical operations on a daily basis. Likewise, as a mainstreamed white woman operating within Indian literature, I am faced with shifting perimenters, changing narratives from different subject-positions. Roemer (1983:39) writes that

> [T]he popular written and mass media forms of transmitting information about Native American oral narratives often strip away the cultural and literary contexts of the stories. Furthermore, the narratives are usually associated with the dead past of the Vanishing American.

The contexts that are stripped away are part of the subject-position from which Native American myths are told. The dead past of the vanishing American is part of a new context, a new subject-position that is artificially imposed on Native American literature. Therefore, the matrix or womb in which Native myths lived, with indefinite and shifting boundaries, has been erased, and the definite border of a dead past of the Vanishing American has been drawn boldly around the stories by popular mass media. Any writer operating outside these indefinite and shifting boundaries is operating tactically.

In Harjo's (1990: 57-58) poem, **"Death Is A Woman,"** her storyteller's subject-position is that of a daughter remembering her dead father: "Instead I'll make up another story about who I think you really were / with the words left in the mouth of a cardinal" (lines 16-17). The abandoned daughter is telling a story with "words left in the mouth of a cardinal." Here, again, borders between language and nature, between words and cardinals, seem to vanish. The function of the story named in this poem seems to be to create the father she never had. This creation is an active process, a changing and growing event— a performance. The notion of invention (and reinvention) is strong in several poems from Harjo's book, *In Mad Love and War*. In a prose poem, **"If I Think About You Again It Will Be the Fifty-Third Monday of Next Year,"** the speaker in the poem is erasing someone's story and writing it again without the someone in it (Harjo 1990: 49): "Or, better yet, erase it, your whole story a sterile page, and I would rewrite it without you in it." The idea that erasing someone's story can erase the person crosses boundaries between narrative and human. The human seems defined and constructed by his/her story.

This act certainly would make narrative a performance, an act or process that produces effect, not description. Another prose poem, **"Santa Fe,"** echoes the notion of invention: "for that story hasn't yet been invented. . . . space is as solid as the bronze statue of St. Francis, the fox breaking through the lilacs, my invention of this story, the wind blowing" (Harjo 1990: 42). This quote reflects the importance of place in de Certeau's "tactic" and "strategy." One would think of the term "strategy" as having a solid space, a familiar and sound place in which to operate. However, the "solid" space Harjo offers is not only fixed and familiar (the statue), but it is also the motion of the fox through the lilacs, the process of the invention of a story, and the invisibility of the wind blowing. Therefore, the solid space is also in motion, in process, and invisible—which describes a place of de Certeau's tactical operation.

In her poem, **"Healing Animal,"** Harjo's (1990:38-39) storytelling functions as, not merely invention, but perfection: "from the somewhere there is the perfect sound / called up from the best-told stories / of benevolent gods, / who have nothing better to do" (lines 8-10). Here, invention is not the "end of the story." In fact, the stories do not end. They are the best-told stories, which have been told and keep being told. This is an ongoing, ever-changing process, not a fixed description that is offered as a finished product. The subject-position of the storyteller involves a place called "the somewhere." Again, this somewhere is probably not unknown to many Native Americans. What Western civilization knows as "God," can often be seen labeled as "the Great Mystery" in Native American literature. Mystery and the unknown and the unfamiliar do not seem to be problematic. Or perhaps the boundaries between humanity and the "Great Mystery" are culturally imposed and some individuals do not acknowledge those boundaries.

In her poem titled, **"The Real Revolution Is Love,"** Harjo (1990: 24-25) creates a speaker who awakens in a story being told from the subject-position of her ancestors: "[I] awake in a story told by my ancestors / when they spoke a version of the very beginning" (lines 45-46). The speaker's ancestors told a story, but they spoke "a version," not a Western notion of factual truth. This tendency toward a changing story and subjective, personalized versions characterizes a tactical operation in which definitions constantly shift. The storytellers' ancestral subject-positions exist within a poem that revolves around many subject-positions telling their stories, in one way or another. The poem is a story of several people spending an afternoon philosophizing and drinking around a table on a patio in Managua, the capital of Nicaragua on Lake Managua. There are banana trees and samba breezes, palm trees and rum. People's names hint at different subject-positions: Roberto, Pedro, Diane, Alonzo, Allen. These people are referred to as American, Anishnabe, Puerto Rican, Creek. They speak of revolution and love. In the midst of many subject-positions and many boundaries, which are probably not clear or fixed for anyone in the poem, the speaker says, "I do what I want, and take my revolution to bed with / me, alone" (lines 44-45). In bed with her revolution is where she wakes in the story told by her ancestors. The proximity of revolution and storytelling here might suggest the effect that narration and articulation can evoke: Storytelling is a performance which functions here to inspire revolution.

In the reverse, Harjo's (1990:19) poem, **"Legacy"** seems to provide a story that is inspired by and birthed from revolution:

> In Wheeling, West Virginia, inmates riot.
> Two cut out the heart of a child rapist
> and hold it steaming in a guard's face
> because he will live
> to tell the story
>
> (lines 1-5)

Here, the subject-position will be of the guard who is terrorized by the prisoners. That story will also be influenced by the subject-position of the inmates. And the function of this story and its performance is survival—survival of the story. The inmates know they will not survive, but the story can. Harjo doesn't say that the *inmates'* story will be told, but *the* story." If the guard is to tell the story, it won't be the inmates' story, though they will have contributed significantly to the content. In the content, the topic of this poem, I see de Certeau's "tactic" in operation: riots, rapists, steaming organs cut out of bodies. This is not an environment with proper places for the characters involved. However, the institution of the prison on a "usual" day probably functions as a place with familiar rules, a fixed structure, and something near autonomy.

In her prose poem, **"Autobiography,"** Harjo (1990: 14) compares the lack of stories to starvation: "Translating them [dreams] was to understand the death count from Alabama, the destruction of grandchildren, famine of stories." By comparing a "famine of stories" to the "Trail of Tears" from Georgia to Oklahoma in 1838, and to the cultural and racial genocide of her people, the speaker in the poem offers an abundance of stories as a source for survival. If the lack of stories is a famine and can starve many, then an abundance of stories can feed and sustain many. In the same way that stories can be sustenance and thus can interact with our bodies, Harjo's (1990:11-12) prose poem **"Strange Fruit,"** the title based on a Billie Holiday song, also presents stories in contact with human bodies: "Shush, we have too many stories to carry on our backs like houses" (page 11). Here, stories are a burden, perhaps like fat on the human body. And too many of them can weigh a body down, so the speaker's lover tells her to stop listening to the stories. The speaker in this poem (written for a civil rights activist named Jacqueline Peters who was lynched in Lafayette, California, in 1986) is performing for the reader, stories of "hooded sheets riding up in the not yet darkness," "crosses burning in my dreams," a black cat that stood in the middle of the road, the "scar under my arm." The speaker is the fruit of her mother, the fruits of her labor, fruit to be plucked by "hooded ghosts from hell on earth." In a time and place where stories weigh her down while she oper-

ates tactically, trying to escape the dominating forces, the speaker sheds the heavy stories and begins to perform the stories that will help her survive. She says, "I want to squeeze my baby's legs, see her turn into a woman just like me. I want to dance under the full moon, or in the early morning on my lover's lap. . . . I want only heaven" (*ibid*). She seems to be using narration to speak away the heavy stories that threaten her survival and, with enunciation, perform stories that will sustain her. Harjo spoke of this poem in relation to stories: "People don't know about Jacqueline Peters, unless someone tells her story. I feel that part of what I do as a writer, part of my responsibility, is to be one of those who help people remember. I feel I have a responsibility to keep these stories alive" (Jaskoski 1989:12). Harjo performs stories to sustain the lives of real, physical, earthly people, giving them the supernatural, spiritual power of immortality.

In **"Deer Dancer,"** a prose poem of significant length, Harjo (1990:5-6) tells the story of a magical woman who enters a bar, charms the patrons with her beauty, seems to become a sacred deer, and eventually strips naked as she dances for the silent crowd. However, in the last stanza of this long poem Harjo's speaker says, "The music ended. And so does the story. I wasn't there" (page 6). How much of the story are listeners to accept, if the storyteller wasn't even there for the experience she is relating? Her possibility for inaccuracy doesn't seem to be a problem for the speaker. She admits, "I imagined her like this . . . the deer who entered our dream in white dawn, breathed mist into pine trees" (page 6). If the Deer Dancer has entered dreams and has the power to breathe mist into trees, the story does not end. The protagonist—of the story told by the speaker of a poem written by Joy Harjo and read by this writer who offers this discussion (the many subject-positions through which my reader must hear the story)-is not a product, fixed and offered for consumption to a reader, but a force that lives actively in dreams and mist. And the boundaries between humans and nature are vague if the Deer Dancer can enter and affect both. She can move easily across boundaries that she might not even see, but that we cannot perceive ever crossing.

In her poem titled, **"For Anna Mae Pictou Aquash, Whose Spirit Is Present Here and in the Dappled Stars (for we remember the story and must tell it again so we may all live),"** Harjo (1990:7-8) again refers to storytelling as a way to survive. Anna Mae was a Micmac Indian and a member of the American Indian Movement, an active and radical organization still operating today in the United States. She was found killed on the Pine Ridge Reservation in South Dakota. Authorities cut her hands off and sent them to Washington for fingerprints when she was declared dead by exposure. When her family found her missing, they reported it and an investigation followed. Later it was discovered that Anna Mae was killed by a bullet fired at close range to the back of her head. Harjo's title states openly that the telling of this story will help keep us all alive. But Harjo's poem also tells other stories of Anna Mae. Though these stories seem contradictory, they are all true. Though the mutilation and murder are true, so is the beauty of the young woman described in the poem: "You are the shimmering young woman / who found her voice, / when you were warned to be silent, or have your body cut away / from you like an elegant weed" (15-18). Here "truth" can be seen as an entity with shifting boundaries, with multiple forms seen and described and invented from multiple subject-positions (Anna Mae's family, the federal government, Harjo as poet).

In her poem, **"Kansas City,"** Harjo (1983:33-34) tells one of many stories of Noni Daylight. In this poem she is "standing near the tracks / waving / at the last train to leave / Kansas City" (lines 43-46). The poem's speaker is Noni Daylight, and she tells of her relationships with the different men who fathered her children. Noni Daylight speaks of one man: "the one whose eyes tipped up / like swallows wings / (whose ancestors laid this track, / with hers), / all of them, their stories in the flatland belly / giving birth to children / and to other stories" (lines 36-42). These men's stories gave birth to human children and to more stories. Here, stories function as performances that result in effects, in procreation, in survival. Again, boundaries between humans and text are blurred. If stories can be the mother of both, that makes children and stories siblings.

The performance of the story can be seen in the musical details of Harjo's poetry. Pre-Columbian North American Native literature known today is based on songs and chants in religious ceremonies. This element of music is a commonality among the many nations indigenous to this continent. Music often appears as a topic, as well as in the language of Harjo's stories. A storyteller should tailor her stories for her audience. She should know her people and her story. Harjo includes familiar images in her stories to make her listeners comfortable and to give them a direct connection to the stories she tells. She offers a poem with music, and jazz musician Charlie Parker, as the topic of the story. Harjo's (1990:21) poem titled **"Bird,"** presents cultural images in the bird as identifiable object and the motion of its flight (line 2), the moon as object, its shape, its light, its motion (line 1), the act of hijacking a plane, news clips of actual hijacks, and films (line 13), and high heels as object, their sexual connotations, gender associations, their sound on a hard floor, the pain of wearing them for hours (line 16). Series or enigmas appear in such irreconcilable images as "the shoulder of the dark universe" (line 1), "the infinite glitter of chance" (line 2), "nerve endings longer than our bodies" (line 4), "the final uselessness of words" (line 8), and "the dimension a god lives" (line 19). Diversions leading to mystery might be located in phrases that readers know and recognize, but they may not have had enough experience with to escape the mystery. Such diversions might include the moon playing a horn (line 1), "the stairway of forgetfulness" (line 6), "a woman who is always beautiful to strangers" (line 7), "a leap into madness" (line 17), "the fingers of / saints" (lines 17-18), and "some poem / attempting flight home" (lines 22-23). Familiar words and images can be found in the familiar sounds and experiences in such phrases as "[t]onight I watched" (line 2), "I've always had a theory" (line 3), "all poets / understand" (lines 7-8), "if we're lucky" (line 9), "when I come out of the theater" (line 10), and "I want to see it" (line 20). Thus, Harjo tells a story that has familiar sounds, but can sometimes mystify or divert her listener. In another poem that uses music and a musician, here Nat King Cole, Harjo uses words and images to construct the framework of her story. In **"We Encounter Nat King Cole As We Invent the Future,"** the meanings in her words and images are contingent upon the reader's experiences and memories, as well as the time and place and circumstance of the storytelling (Harjo 1990: 51). This poem recalls individual and perhaps many-layered images and sensations for each reader, but the act of recognition and association of those familiar images is shared communally. Most of her women readers over thirty will identify with a few of the following sensations and images: "some well-slicked man" (line 2), "eat fried chicken, / drink cokes" (line 5-6), "tattoo of roses" (line 14), "white suede / shoes" and "spice hair creme" (lines 21-22), "small-town radios" (line 29). One can almost taste the chicken and Coke, and smell the hair creme. And these sensations recall further associations a reader brings to the story—or does that story bring the associations to the listener? In either event, our cultural system and its ideologies have built a foundation from which we, as readers and listeners, are able to come to this poem through the same process of recognition and expectation and yet leave the story with individual interpretations.

As a musical element, rhythm contributes dramatically to the performance of a story. Harjo's (1990:57-58) poem, **"Death Is a Woman,"** demonstrates complex rhythms of irregular duration, rapid unaccented beats that move independently of the melody in the pitches of the language as well as in the content of the story. While it is true that anytime a poem is scanned, the results are subjective and debatable, the possible ambiguities in the rhythm of the language in **"Death Is a Woman"** are marked and open wide alternative rhythms, as well as meanings for the story. The first ten lines (of a total of 42) are overflowing with rhythmic possibilities that could also influence different meanings for those lines. Line one might be scanned rhythmically as "I walk these **night'** hours" and "**see'** you," or "I **walk'** these night hours" and "see **you',**" or "I walk **these'** night hours" and "see you," which could be interpreted as "the time I walk is at night and what I do to you is see you," or "what I do is walk and what I see is you," or "the night hours I walk are these."

Line five could be scanned as "Four **years'** isn't long," or "Four years **isn't'** long," or "**Four'** years isn't long," which could be interpreted as "the amount of time this takes isn't too much," or "this particular amount of years isn't bad," or "four of these particular time increments are not bad."

Line six could be scanned as "I can **already'** see my own death," or "**I'** can already see my own death," or "I can already **see'** my own death," which can be interpreted as "at this time, I can already see my death," or "I am the one who can see my death," or "I have the ability to see my death approaching."

Line ten can be scanned as "**you'** would never be satisfied," or "you would **never'** be satisfied," which could be interpreted as "even back then I knew you, of all people, were the one who would never be satisfied," or "what I knew was that there would never be a time that you would be satisfied." These lines, and more, exemplify the many possibilities in the telling of this story.

In addition to rhythm, melody functions in the performance of storytelling. The tones in lines 12-14 in **"Death Is a Woman,"** plunge from the high pitches of "tonight" and "I" and "see" down to "sun" and "fold" and back up to "geese," "disappear," and "teeth." The tone that the melody seems to return to, the "tonic," is the /ee / sound, to which the plunges in these three lines consistently return. However, the following line (15) levels out at pitches that mediate between those highs and lows: "am ready to run." These vowel sounds are neither high nor low, but hover between. In contrast to lines 12-14, lines 19-27 contain comparatively few high pitches. In 96 words, only "I see," "side," "whirling," "my," "Tiger people," "whiskey," "bleached," "my Cherokee," "Pottowatamie," "dying," "money," and "spitting" (15 words) contain high sounds. This count results in 16 percent of the words in lines 19-27 sounding high, intense, and sharp, as opposed to lines 12-14 (25 words) in which 36 percent (9 words) of the words are high-pitched and intense. Comparisons of the round, solemn, gloomy sounds could highlight significant places in the story, emphasizing the seriousness and depth of events and topics. Not only do these melodic pitch patterns mark off sections of a song, they emphasize specific words and so affect the meanings of lessons and explanations within stories. Although the reader may not consciously say, "Oh look, Tiger people and whiskey and money and spitting are prominent images in this story," the listener's mind processes this information and organizes it somehow. As for the rhyme in **"Death Is a Woman,"** the internal rhymes result in most of the rhyme in the poem: "tracks" (line 13) and "black" (line 30), "night" (line 1), "high" (line 8) and l'[s]trikes" (line 29), and "street" (line 8), "sweet" (line 9), "geese" (line 13), "teeth" (line 13), and "bleached" (line 23). Assonance, consonance, and alliteration also serve as rhyming elements in the poem: "slick and black" (line 30), "reeking" (line 29) and "feeling" (line 30), and "same side" (line 32). The lack of structured rhyme creates a conversational effect for the storytelling, bringing the storyteller and the listener into the same room.

The storyteller and listener together present an image of closeness, of conversation in a personal space. The notions of everyday conversation and personal homeplace might be thought of in terms of gender, as female, small, private, domestic, and behind closed doors. Perhaps this kind of categorization is just another way of trying to find discreet and autonomous boxes into which we, as Western civilization, can neatly put away such dangerous notions: a place for everything and everything in its place. Imposing such boundaries is a strategic act. The act of writing and reading written texts encourages us to organize and present a product, which is visually fixed and finished in time and space. Oral narration, however, does not provide a time and space in which to build a product, but provides spaces that grow and change, spaces that are unfamiliar and require improvisation and spontaneity to survive.

FURTHER READING

Goodman, Jenny. "Politics and the Personal Lyric in the Poetry of Joy Harjo and C. D. Wright." *MELUS* 19, No. 2 (Summer 1994): 35-56.

Examines recent poetry by Harjo and Wright, contending that the two authors "work consciously at the borders of aesthetics and politics, reshaping the available language for both."

Harjo, Joy. "Writing with the Sun." In *Where We Stand: Women Poets on Literary Tradition*, edited by Sharon Bryan, pp. 70-4. New York: W. W. Norton, 1993.

Traces Harjo's interest in poetry and assesses the impact of her Native American background on her maturation as a writer.

———, John Crawford, and Patricia Clark Smith. "Joy Harjo." In *This Is About Vision: Interviews with Southwestern Writers*, edited by William Balassi, John F. Crawford, and Annie O. Eysturoy, pp. 171-79. Albuquerque: University of New Mexico Press, 1990.

Harjo discusses her theory of communication and her interest in music.

Holmes, Kristine. "'This Woman Can Cross Any Line': Feminist Tricksters in the Works of Nora Naranjo-Morse and Joy Harjo." *SAIL: Studies in American Indian Literatures* 7, No. 1 (Spring 1995): 45-63.

Compares the recurring female characters in Naranjo-Morse's and Harjo's work, asserting that the poets "challenge their readers' assumptions about feminists and tricksters as they bring trickster-like figures that originate in oral traditions into a tribal feminist context."

Jaskoski, Helen. "A MELUS Interview: Joy Harjo." *MELUS* 16, No. 1 (Spring 1989-1990): 5-13.

Discusses the origins of a few of her poems, as well as some of her literary influences.

Ruwe, Donelle R. "Weaving Stories For Food: An Interview with Joy Harjo." *Religion and Literature* 26, No. 1 (Spring 1994): 57-64.

Harjo explores the role of religion and myth in her work.

Additional coverage of Harjo's life and career is contained in the following sources published by the Gale Group: *Contemporary Authors*, Vol. 114; *Contemporary Authors New Revision Series*, Vols. 35, 67; *Contemporary Literature Criticism*, Vol. 83; *DISCovering Multicultural America*; *Dictionary of Literary Biography*, Vols. 120, 175; *Major Twentieth Century Writers*; *Native North American Writers*.

Medbh McGuckian
1950–

Irish poet.

INTRODUCTION

In her imaginative verse, Medbh McGuckian explores themes related to femininity while infusing her language with dense rhythms and erotic images. She often juxtaposes the concrete, everyday experiences of domestic life with evocative, dream-like imagery to create esoteric, sensual, and highly symbolic poetry. Her work has been compared to that of Emily Dickinson, Marianne Moore, and Elizabeth Bishop.

Biographical Information

McGuckian was born into a large Catholic family in Belfast, Northern Ireland. She attended school at a Dominican convent from 1961 to 1968, and before enrolling at Queen's University, Belfast, to study English. As a student, she was influenced by her instructor Seamus Heaney, a widely recognized poet. Her classmates at Queen's University included such promising young poets Paul Muldoon and Frank Ormsby. After graduation, McGuckian's verse was published in several local periodicals and newspapers. In 1979, she won the National Poetry Competition award for her poem "The Flitting," and the next year published her first chapbooks, *Single Ladies: Sixteen Poems*, and *Portrait of Joanna*. She continues to live and work in Belfast.

Major Works

Thematically McGuckian's poetry often concerns domestic matters such as the cultivation of gardens; everyday family activity; the simple beauty of furniture, windows, and doors; and the complex relations between mothers and daughters. An early poem, "The Flitting," chronicles her complicated feelings on moving to a new house. Her early chapbooks, *Single Ladies* and *Portrait of Joanna*, were praised for utilizing inventive figures of speech and sensual evocations. The accolades were tempered, however, by reservations that McGuckian's reliance on tropes often results in obscurity. In *The Flower Master* and *Venus and the Rain*, she employs the dramatic monologues of an indeterminate persona to focus on love, sex, and the relationship between females of different generations. *On Ballycastle Beach* draws not only from themes such as domesticity, fertility, and eroticism, but also on Irish legend and mythology. She explores separation and loss in *Captain Lavender*, including several elegies for her father. Some reviewers assert that verses in this collection that focus on personal relationships can be viewed as metaphors for the political and historical situations in Northern Ireland.

Critical Reception

Some critics link McGuckian with Paul Muldoon, Frank Ormsby, and other poets she met while attending Queen's University in the late 1960s and early 1970s. Although these poets do not rigidly adhere to particular topics or styles, their work displays painstaking craftsmanship in rendering a distinct poetic consciousness. Many commentators assert that McGuckian purposely avoids themes related to the political troubles in Ireland, instead transforming elements of everyday experience into metaphoric representations of the female psyche. Critical commentary focuses on the imaginative and lyrical qualities of her poetry; however, several critics consider the hermetic nature of her language as problematic for many readers.

PRINCIPAL WORKS

Poetry

Portrait of Joanna 1980
Single Ladies: Sixteen Poems 1980

CRITICISM

Christopher Benfey (essay date 1985)

SOURCE: "A Venusian Sends a Postcard Home," in *Parnassus: Poetry in Review*, Vol. 12, No. 2 & Vol. 13, No. 1, Spring-Summer and Fall-Winter, 1985, pp. 500-12.

[*In the following excerpt, Benfey surveys the major themes of McGuckian's verse.*]

Venus is speaking in the title poem of Medbh McGuckian's new book. "I am the sun's toy—"Venus says in another poem, "because I go against / The grain I feel the brush of my authority." With such oddly precise astronomical observations—Venus' orbit is the reverse of the orbits of the other planets—McGuckian creates her metaphorical atmosphere. Her poems are as lush and comfortable with astral themes as Elizabethan poetry. If Sidney's lonely moon can be in love, so can her planets. It is, I assume, the rain (or is it the earth?) that speaks in the following quatrain:

> My sister planet has no moon, she travels all alone
> Around the sun, while I am the paperstainer.
> A day with her is longer than a year—her heavy
>   gas
> Rewinds her as I tumble out the blue tent of our
>   bedchamber.
>
> ("A Day With Her")

The internal near-rhymes, "moon" and "alone" and "sun," at the caesurae, are subtle but compelling, as though this is a quiet litany that the rain repeats; the suggestion of a rhyme on "paperstainer" and "bedchamber" enhances this effect. The weather of Molly Peacock's poems, despite the rawness of heaven, is usually clear and fair: she gets her themes and arguments across. But what McGuckian wants from Venus is a thick cloud cover—"a cloud that never rains"—in which she can couch her favorite subject; for

> the inhabitants of Venus
> Are constantly in love, and always writing verses.

The astral logic of the poems suggests that the lover should be from Mars, and Venus says "with any choice / I'd double-back to the dullest blue of Mars." This at-traction accounts for a certain violence in the lovemaking, a martial strain:

> While he lay sleeping
> Like an air-force, she made parallels until
> She was the limb of the moon, or that Endymion
> Who captured her, inducing rain like fallout.
>
> Upwind and downwind, further from the earth,
> Mars' two moons, like the folded ears of a cat
> Made instant clearings in her head . . .
>
> ("Daisy Cutters")

McGuckian's poetry, which is often described as hermetic and mysterious, can be startlingly concrete in its images: the air-force, the rain like fallout, and the folded ears of the cat. The clouds of Venus clear unexpectedly.

But McGuckian is also an inhabitant of Belfast. She was a classmate of Paul Muldoon and she is often numbered among the "second generation of Ulster poets." There was an occasional reference to Ireland in her first book of poems, *The Flower Master* ("Ireland / So like Italy Italians came to film it"), but in these new poems McGuckian is first a Venusian and second—a distant second—an Ulsterwoman. She hasn't followed Seamus Heaney in searching for ways to be true to one's own private experience while registering the public strains of the North, nor has she found, like Derek Mahon, analogues in other artists in other times for her own ambiguous place in society. To scan her poems for allusions to sectarian violence would be as fruitless and naive as to sift Emily Dickinson's poems for references to the Civil War. Of course the reader will find things in both cases, but the reticence is as significant as the revelation. A poet must be faithful to her own imaginative urges; one feels in the poems of McGuckian (and of Dickinson) a powerful inner censor holding the poet to the sources of her own imaginative power. When a Venusian sends a postcard home (to modify Craig Raine's famous title) she writes about love.

There is nothing "raw" about McGuckian's treatment of love. It is as though all the conventional discourses of love had been forbidden, declared taboo, so that she must take whatever is at hand—clothes, furniture, flowers, colors, the weather—and fashion love poems out of these. Since this process resembles the machinery of dreams, her poetry is often dreamlike. Love becomes in her poems less taboo than tropical, a topic that can only be approached obliquely, by way of tropes. These tropes provide what she calls "a sort of hotel / In her voice," which is as much a refuge for her as Rilke's "temple in the hearing" was for him.

> I would bestow on her a name
> With a hundred meanings, all of them
> Secret, going their own way, as surely
> As the silvery mosaic of the previous
> Week, building itself a sort of hotel
> In her voice, to be used whenever
> The tale was ruthlessly retold.
>
> ("Hotel")

Such hermeticism would be merely annoying if it did not have a recognizable (if not easily describable) authority, and if McGuckian failed to convince us that, as she says in an uncharacteristic disclaimer, "This oblique trance is my natural / Way of speaking."

Usually she is as blunt and unapologetic about her obliquity as Emily Dickinson, whose advice was to "Tell all the Truth but tell it slant." A McGuckian poem will often assemble around the sound and connotations of a single word, "culprits," for example. A poem of that title ends with an extraordinary line: "My curtains skein the cold like culprits of light." Sometimes McGuckian confines her slantness to a modest device, for example the coupling of an ordinary adjective with an odd one: "this gray / And *paunchy* house," "this my / Brownest, *tethered* room," "that smart and / *Cheerful* rain." It is a device that Auden explored as well. But obliquity can invade an entire poem.

> Being stored inside like someone's suffering,
> Each piece of furniture now begins
> To interpret every eye as sunlight:
> And that smallness in me which does not vibrate
> Is moving none the less towards
> The white and unworked wool of the corded bed.

A poem about furniture? About suffering? About erotic love? Furniture is compared to suffering, but surely the metaphor moves the other way too. Odd that the eyes are being interpreted, rather than doing the interpreting. And what is the "now" of the poem—"*Being* stored inside . . . *now* begins . . . *Is* moving . . ."? Is "Being" a substantive, like "suffering"? The rest of the poem compounds the enigmas rather than resolving them:

> The old year in his mimic death
> Is my husband like a child unlooked for
> Moistening the wrong turnings I make
> Myself take, till the path into my body
> And out of it again is a sea-place
> Opening where you least expect.
>
> As from an irresponsible
> Brood of ten, my love of twenty years
> Might oversweetly part your fingers
> To count the points, telling why you ravish her.

Our eyes may interpret everything here as darkness, especially when we try to avoid making "wrong turnings" with double tropes such as "The old year . . . Is my husband like a child." Is McGuckian devising a fertility myth here, as when in another poem she muses: "I think the detectable difference / Between winter and summer is a damsel / Who requires saving"? (Of course the title of the book, *Venus and the Rain*, suggests such a fertility myth.) Or does the poem nest, finally, in the Venusian eroticism of "the path into my body"? This poem resembles certain "symbolist" poems in the way it offers a title as a possible key for decoding. The reader may well end up brooding on **"The Return of Helen"**: ten years in Troy, the journey to Egypt and the long way home, the Ledean body . . .

The furniture of the first few lines is in fact characteristic of McGuckian. Christopher Ricks has traced what he calls the reflexive image, or self-infolded image, through the poems of Marvell and the male poets of modern Ulster. In Seamus Heaney's waterfall, "The burn drowns steadily in its own downpour," or, in Marvell's description of a woman crying, "She courts herself in am'rous Rain; Her self both *Danae* and the Showr." Ricks suggests that this kind of metaphor may be tied to the experience of civil war, where identity and division of self are constantly in question. But the metaphors McGuckian's poems show off are self-infolded in a different way. Her moods find fit accommodation in the metaphors and similes of houses and furniture. In her first book, *The Flower Master*, McGuckian seemed pleased with the mechanical ease with which the device could bestow the illusion of concreteness on reported moods:

>   my mind was savagely made up,
> Like a serious sofa moved
> Under a north window.
>
> Even my frowns were beautiful, my tenable
> Emotions largely playing with themselves,
> To be laid like a table set for breakfast.

In *Venus and the Rain* the still ubiquitous furniture is more mysterious. McGuckian writes of "a lap-child's sense of chairs" and of "the overexcitement of mirrors." Her groping with chairs and tables and drapery reminds me at times of how victims of adult perversion are sometimes asked to rehearse, with dolls and blocks, what has been inflicted on them. Her poems resemble "play therapy" in the ways they fuse eroticism and the furnishings of houses:

> Yet some exactness about the posture
> Of the chairs would make me foam
> Against the beautiful moist heat that could
> Bring peaches to perfection on its own . . .

McGuckian's rooms and houses are filled with the decor of Victorian sitting-rooms: flowers carefully arranged, letters read and unread, embroidery, lace, silk kimonos. She seems unapologetic about her pleasure in these things. Her procedure in many poems is to rehearse the traditional metiers and meters of women—clothes, men and courtship, sex, child-rearing, and such domestic activities as knitting, sketching, arranging furniture—but to look at them so searchingly that they become strange. Her first book began with these lines:

> That year it was something to do with your hands:
> To play about with rings, to harness rhythm
> In staging bleach or henna on the hair,
> Or shackling, unshackling the breasts.

The evocation of the first rites of female adolescence remains oblique, but in certain poems McGuckian resolved the strangeness into something almost programmatic. A poem about composing a seed-picture—"the clairvoyance of seed-work has opened up / New spectrums of activity"—concludes:

The eyelids oatmeal, the irises
Of Dutch blue maw, black rape
For the pupils, millet
For the vicious beige circles underneath.
The single pearl barley
That sleeps around her dullness
Till it catches light, makes women
Feel their age, and sigh for liberation.

The censor has relaxed here, inviting rash remarks about
how, for McGuckian, the real stresses are not sectarian
but sexual, pitting men not against men but against wom-
en. "Some women save their lives with needles," she writes.
"I complicate my life with . . . a little ladylike sketching."
Here the first line seems indignant, almost angry, but the
second line undoes its vehemence.

Her poetry, while often courting this feminist interpretation,
seems more at home in an almost Japanese reticence and
reclusiveness. In her first book McGuckian found in the
Japanese tea ceremony the model for the mood she wanted
in her poetry. She developed, across several poems, her
fascination with such "ladylike" activities as flower arranging, the tea ceremony, and moon-viewing:

We do
Sea-fans with sea-lavender, moon-arrangements
Roughly for the festival of moon-viewing.

This black container calls for sloes, sweet
Sultan, dainty nipplewort, in honour
Of a special guest, who summoned to the
Tea ceremony, must stoop to our low doorway,
Our fontanelle, the trout's dimpled feet.
                                        ("The Flower Master")

Venus and the Rain remains, for the most part, in the
trancelike mood of the tea ceremony, but the language is
denser, weightier, more reclusive. Among American poets
Louise Glück probably resembles her most, but McGuckian's richer diction seems to draw from fin-de-siècle sources, the mood of *Pelléas et Mélisande* or of Yeats's brief
essay, "The Autumn of the Body."

There in the crimson, over-furnished drawing-room
You meet your match—a dayboy revisiting
The devastating banishment the summer
You're eleven, its transparency so often since
Misunderstood, abused: and do not argue
When I open presents provocatively
In front of you, resist the moon-watered
Tea I offer with one hand only,
Called improbably 'eyelashes of the swan.'
                                        ("Sky-House")

McGuckian's poetry may sometimes seem overfurnished.
The Zen sound of "with one hand only" suggests that she
is nonetheless withholding something, and yet it's hard to
imagine her poetry in a more straight-forward mode. The
lush modifiers—crimson, overfurnished, devastating,
moon-watered—would, in another poet, specify the set-

ting of the poem. In McGuckian they compound the enigma. She claims to offer us transparency and tea, but she
knows we may well misunderstand the transparency and
resist the tea. She seems to me to have written poems
that are odd and fascinating and finally convincing. Her
hotel in the voice is secure.

Ingrid Melander   (essay date 1988)

SOURCE: "Two Poems by Medbh McGuckian: Symbol and
Interpretation," in *Ango-Irish and Irish Literature: Aspects
of Language and Culture,* Vol. 2, Fall, 1988, pp. 237-41.

[*In the following essay, Melander analyzes the symbolism in two of McGuckian poems, "The Seed-Picture" and
"Tulips."*]

Medbh McGuckian has published two full-length collections of poems, *The Flower Master* (1982) and *Venus
and the Rain* (1984). Her poetry has also appeared in
various periodicals, in pamphlets and anthologies. In 1979
she won the annual Poetry Society competition for a poem
called **"The Flitting"** later included in *The Flower
Master*. She has received several other literary prizes
and recently became writer-in-residence at Queen's University, Belfast. She is the first woman to receive that
honour.

Critics unanimously praise McGuckian's attractive, sensuous style but also complain that her poems have a "mysterious" flavour which makes interpretation difficult. The
poet herself does not accept the view that her poems are
"mysteries" *per se,* only in so far as they attempt to chart
in complicated images the patterns of emotion most wom-
en experience—depression, anxiety, resentment, wistful-
ness, frustration, longing, desire, passion, fulfilment, maternity—all our hopes and fears.[1]

McGuckian's description of her poetry illustrates her poetic ambition as regards both form and content. Evidently,
one of her main techniques to express the emotional patterns of women is by way of imagery. It cannot be concluded from her statement what kind of images she is
referring to, only that they are "complicated". A closer
look at her poetry reveals, however, that many of them
function as symbols. It is my contention that symbol even
provides one of the best keys to the interpretation of a
large number of McGuckian's poems.

Definitions of *symbol* and *symbolism* abound in critical
guides and dictionaries. Many seem too precise for the
analysis of McGuckian's elusive poetry and may distort
the interpretive process right from the beginning. The
following offered by Patrick Murray is broad enough to
suit McGuckian's use of symbol very well:

Symbolism may be described as the art of expressing
emotions not by describing them directly, nor by defining
them through overt comparisons with concrete images,
but by *suggesting* what these ideas and emotions are
by re-creating them in the mind of the reader through
the use of unexplained symbols. These symbols help to

convey a mood to the subconscious mind rather than an appeal to the rational faculties.[2]

It should be added that the symbol is generally a fairly stable and repeatable phenomenon. There is a clear distinction between the *traditional symbol,* which "goes beyond the individual to the universal and is innate in the life of the spirit",[3] and the *personal* symbol, which has special significance for the individual poet when creating a particular poem. We find both categories in McGuckian's poetry, frequently mixed in the same poem and influencing each other.

The two poems, **"The Seed-Picture"** and **"Tulips"**, which will be analysed below, have been selected from *The Flower Master*, McGuckian's first full-length collection of verse.

"THE SEED-PICTURE"

"The Seed-Picture" is one of the most imaginative poems in *The Flower Master*. The title itself and the first six lines introduce the subject with intriguing ambiguity:

> This is my portrait of Joanna—since the split
> The children come to me like a dumb-waiter,
> And I wonder where to put them, beautiful seeds
> With no immediate application . . . the clairvoyance
> Of seed-work has opened up
> New spectrums of activity, beyond a second home.

As will be seen later in the poem, the old technique of seed-embroidery has been adopted to make a portrait of Joanna, probably one of the children mentioned in lines 2—3 and referred to as "beautiful seeds". The seed image is used here to suggest the elements of growth and vitality in the children and may thus carry a specific symbolic value.

In line 5 "seed" is repeated in the compound "seed-work". It seems to retain its basic sense of *semen,* but a shift of meaning is taking place within the poetic context, so that "seed-work" also refers to the very special form of embroidery described in the poem. As is evident in the following lines, this concept is enlarged to denote still another activity, that of writing:

> The seeds dictate their own vocabulary,
> Their dusty colours capture
> More than we plan,
>   . . . . .
> I only guide them not by guesswork
> In their necessary numbers,
> And attach them by the spine to a perfect bedding.

The seeds chosen by the protagonist for the seed-picture presumably also refer to the very words used in writing the poem. Two different artifacts are thus composed simultaneously, as it were, in different media.

Thus the portrait of Joanna is completed slowly and carefully. The seeds of vegetables and fruits, berries and flow-

ers selected for their colours and probably also for their magic power are attached to the background. Finally the last seed is put in its proper place in the portrait:

> The single pearl barley
> That sleeps around her dullness
> Till it catches light, makes women
> Feel their age, and sigh for liberation.

By the addition of the colourful seeds one after the other the protagonist of the poem *and* the poet create, step by step, the beautiful portrait of Joanna. The structure itself thus conveys a most vivid impression of the girl's development from a child's unconsciousness of life into women's awareness of their possibilities and their longing for freedom.

As has been shown above, the poet's use of the seed image undergoes a gradual change during the poetic movement: to begin with it is a metaphor for the children in the poem, a metaphor charged with symbolic meaning; in "seed-work" it is beginning to take on a more abstract nuance and, as the thematic movement proceeds, the seeds are experienced more and more as symbols of a young girl's spiritual development. This employment of the symbol is in harmony with tradition, which has it that *seed* signifies "potentiality, latent power". It thus suits the poetic context well, because it embodies the very principle of growth and evolution.

"TULIPS"

In **"Tulips"** the I of the poem hides behind the striking image of the tulips. She identifies herself with them, but at the same time she watches them from a distance (stanza 1, lines 1—2). The first stanza contains a characterization of the tulips which may also refer to the I of the poem. Two qualities, defensiveness and present-mindedness, are described by way of bold and elaborate imagery:

> —such
> Defensive mechanisms to frustrate the rain
> That shakes into the sherry-glass
> Of the daffodil, though scarcely
> Love's young dream; such present-mindedness
> To double-lock in tiers as whistle-tight,
> Or catch up on sleep with cantilevered
> Palms cupping elbows.

Defensiveness and present-mindedness are complementary traits of character, which help the tulips protect themselves against the rain or other disturbances. The young girl in the poem also needs protection: her shyness and the "defensive mechanisms" of the tulips probably coincide. The conclusion of the first stanza adds still another striking feature to those already presented:

> It's their independence
> Tempts them to this grocery of soul.

Admittedly, this statement is confusing, since it seems to contradict what has been said before about the tulips and their habit of withdrawing from what threatens them. This very tendency may, however, be a sign of independence, which can also, according to the last line, lead to betrayal of one's self ("this grocery of soul").

In the second stanza the tulips are seen from a totally different side:

> Except, like all governesses, easily
> Carried away, in sunny
> Absence of mirrors they exalt themselves
> To ballets of revenge, a kind
> Of twinness, an olympic way of earning,
> And are sacrificed to plot, their faces
> Lifted many times to the artistry of light—

This description of the tulips complicates the image of them in stanza 1. It reveals a split, "a kind / Of twinness", in their nature, which is captured brilliantly by the long simile of governesses. Governesses are usually dependent on others, are self-effacing and ambitious at the same time. They aspire to gain a more dignified position in life than they have as humble servants. Therefore they "exalt themselves / To ballets of revenge"; indeed, they even conspire against their superiors (" . . . are sacrificed to plot"). In doing so, they often lift their faces "to the artistry of light".

Light is a traditional symbol of the universal intellect, *gnosis,* truth. In the last three lines of the poem *light* is contrasted sharply to emotion as represented by the hearts of tulips—

> Its lovelessness a deeper sort
> Of illness than the womanliness
> Of tulips with their bee-dark hearts.

The "bee-dark hearts" of tulips probably refer to the black pattern of stamens and pistils visited by bees and used here as a metaphor for sexuality. Ultimately, **"Tulips"** is thus a poem on "Love's young dream" (stanza 1, line 6), in which love constitutes the very essence of life, whereas the "lovelessness" of the intellect is "a deeper sort / Of illness than the womanliness / Of tulips".

The symbolism of **"Tulips"** creates a sense of harmony and completeness, because the unifying image of the poem is charged with powerful symbolic overtones. Nature and human life form a whole which cannot be separated, because the tulips of the poem comprise both. This becomes even clearer when we learn that *tulip* is the Persian symbol of perfect love.

NOTES

[1] Quoted from a private letter written in April 1982.

[2] Patrick Murray, *Literary Criticism. A Glossary of Major Terms* (London: Longman, 1978), p. 157.

[3] J. C. Cooper, *An Illustrated Encyclopaedia of Traditional Symbols* (London: Thames and Hudson, 1978), p. 7.

Molly Bendall (essay date 1990)

SOURCE: "Flower Logic: The Poems of Medbh McGuckian," in *The Antioch Review*, Summer, 1990, 367-71.

[*In the following essay, Bendall investigates McGuckian's unique stylistic approach to her poetry.*]

In casual discussions of the Irish poet Medbh (pronounced like Queen Maeve) McGuckian's work, I've often heard the responses "flowery," "irrational," or "strange" used. Yet I think "sensual" and "intricate" are far better words to describe this poet's compellingly original poems. McGuckian's imagination does more than enhance a realistic sequence of events in the rendering of a poem. Her characteristic play with unexpected usages, quirky syntax, synesthesia, and even dazzling pathetic fallacies constantly confronts then abandons common narrative equations and structures.

This is true not only of the poems in *On Ballycastle Beach* (Wake Forest, 1988), McGuckian's most recent collection, but also of the poems of her previous volumes, *The Flower Master* (1982) and *Venus and the Rain* (1984, both published by Oxford University Press). While the poems appear (on the page) to be constructed in a fairly tight, lyric mode, the words and syntactical gestures create their own sphere of reality—and not necessarily a metaphorical sphere. For instance, these phrases seem to perform as image: "where all is leaf," "her madonna parting," "her milk-fed hands," "The tray / Clinks silver in the stage before coldness," "she smooths out her girlhood / Into a shadow of body-colour," but they defy any expected metaphorical correspondence with our orderly and named reality. The phrases should be understood instead as gestures contained in a fluid choreography that is the presence (the imagistic performance) of a McGuckian poem. Here is **"Minus 18 Street"** from the new collection:

> I never loved you more
> Than when I let you sleep another hour,
> As if you intended to make such a gate of time
> Your home. Speechless as night animals,
> The breeze and I breakfasted
> With the pure desire of speech; but let
> Each petal of your dream have its chance,
> The many little shawls that covered you:
> I never envied your child's face
> Its motherless cheekbones, or sensed in them
> The approach of illness—how you were being
> Half-killed on a sea-shore, or falling
> From a ladder where you knelt to watch
> The quartering of the moon. (You would never
> Swim to the top of the rain that bathed
> The mute world of her body.)
>
> Sleep for you is a trick
> Of the frost, a light green room in a French house,
> Giving no trouble till spring.
> The wedding-boots of the wind
> Blow footsteps behind me,

I count each season for the sign
Of wasted children.

Sky of blue water, blue-water sky,
I sleep with the dubious kiss
Of my sky-blue portfolio.
Under or over the wind,
In soft and independent clothes,
I begin each dawn-coloured picture
Deep in your snow.

Certainly there is an emotional reality to this poem but, as McGuckian explains in an interview with critic Kathleen McCracken, "the environment is an inner one, the sea and sky are mental attributes." She goes on to say, "I suppose it is the old microcosm thing. I do tend to explore the delicate balance of the human or female organism, which can so easily soar or drop from productivity to sterility." McGuckian also claims her poems are not following an "antilogic." What *is* working in the poems is a struggle to subvert what some feminist theorists have named as characteristics of phallocentric literature: a strict linearity and an affirmation of authority (which includes a faithful allegiance to only "literal" dictionary renderings of language). Much of the vocabulary in her poems is drenched with associations that evoke response in the feminine consciousness, especially in the realms of domesticity, fertility, and eroticism. Yet, even with these traditional resonances, the usage of that vocabulary is utterly surprising and new. Here is *"Aviary"* from *Venus and the Rain*:

Well may you question the degree of falsehood
In my round-the-house men's clothes, when I seem
Cloaked for a journey, after just relearning to walk,
Or turning a swarthy aspect like a cache-
Enfant against all men. Some patterns have
A very long repeat, and this includes a rose
Which has much in common with the rose
In your drawing, where you somehow put the garden
To rights. You call me aspen, tree of the woman's
Tongue, but if my longer and longer sentences
Prove me wholly female, I'd be persimmon,
And good kindling, to us both.

Remember
The overexcitement of mirrors, with their archways
Lending depth, until my compact selvedge
Frisks into a picot-edged valance, some
Swiss-fronted little shop? All this is as it
Should be, the disguise until those clear red
Bands of summerwood accommodate next
Winter's tardy ghost, your difficult daughter.

I can hear already in my chambered pith
The hammers of pianos, their fastigiate notes
Arranging a fine sight-screen for my nectary,
My trustful mop. And if you feel uncertain
Whether pendent foliage mitigates the damage
Done by snow, yet any wild bird would envy you
This aviary, whenever you free all the birds in me.

As the poem invokes its intimate, seductive imagery, the speaker asks to be heard in her *own* language, one that both commands the poems and generates their landscapes, not those landscapes that have been pruned and regulated, but rather those that have been "let go," allowing an organic logic to take over, one that brings with it all the mysteries and unpredictable qualities of nature. McGuckian says "I hope my poems will draw the reader into the particular mesh of thoughts and nexus of feelings, but I hope in the end to have spelled something out clearly. If the poem is swallowed whole it won't be digested. I want it to become part of the person. . . ."

J. Hillis Miller has said, "Language is at once the expression of a style of life and the embodiment of a local weather and geography." In McGuckian's work one may certainly detect the evidence of Irish literature, the Irish language itself, Catholicism, and the crisis in Northern Ireland. However, these remain elements that simply inform and transform the speaker's consciousness, and they cannot be pointed out as overt subject matter for any of the poems. Concerning the struggle in Northern Ireland, McGuckian, who was born and lives in Belfast, states, "I have touched on the subject implicitly . . . in a poem like **"The Blue She Brings with Her"** for a mother whose son was destroyed, but one could argue that I do not deal with or solve anything. I just suggest an attitude of compassion in what is part of a universal tragedy." Dedicated "for Teresa," here is that poem:

November—like a man taking all
His shirts, and all his ties, little by little—
Enters a million leaves, and that
Lion-coloured house-number, the sun,
Into his diary; with a rounded symbol—
NOTHING—to remind himself of callow apples,
Dropping with a sense of rehearsal in June
As if their thought were being done by others.

The mirror bites into me as cloud into
The river-lip of a three-cornered lake
That when the moon is new is shaped
Like the moon. With a sudden crash
My log falls to ashes, a wood of winter
Colours I have never seen—blood-kissed
The gold-patterned dishes
Show themselves for a moment like wild creatures.

While any smoke that might be going
Loose, the hot room gathers like a mountain
Putting out a mist, and not the kind that clears.
Something you add about mountains makes
My mouth water like a half-lifted cloud
I would choose, if I could, to restrain
As a stone keeps its memories.

Your eyes change colour as you move
And will not go into words. Their swanless
Sky-curve holds like a conscious star
A promise from the wind about the blue
She brings with her. If beauty lives

By escaping and leaves a mark, your wrist
Will have the mark of my fingers in the morning.

Reading this powerful elegiac poem, one feels over-
whelmed, yet at the same time poised on its stage of
grief. The suggestions of a domestic life and its untimely
winter illustrate the risky and unsolvable nature of her
work. The beauty and genius of these poems continually
redefine our notions of poetry. Medbh McGuckian offers us a poetic voice that is radically different from the
majority of her contemporaries; to appreciate it fully we,
as readers, must often forfeit many of our more conventional expectations.

Stephen Yenser (essay date 1991)

SOURCE: A review of *On Ballycastle Beach*, in *Poetry*,
Summer 1991, pp. 228-33.

[*In the following review, Yenser provides a laudatory
assessment of the poems comprising* On Ballycastle
Beach.]

Devastating as the impact of her language is on the famil-
siar and the quotidian, Medbh McGuckian's new poems
are distinctly homely in their settings and their details,
from their bowls to their china, their vases to their afternoon visits, their fireplaces to their fabrics. Houses appear explicitly in a remarkable number of the poems, and
everywhere there is a compelling carefulness, a feeling
for fragile things that we might connect with Elizabeth
Spires's work if not necessarily with the cozily domestic. Sometimes this quality is thematized, as in **"First
Letters from a Steamer"**:

> A broken vase I loved
> Had four small pieces out of the rim
> And three were saved—I covered it
> With clear cement and painted a half-inch
> Carnation over the seams.

And sometimes it is implicit in her own scrupulous images, as in **"Blue Sky Rain"**: "we lived then in a pink and
white / Seaside house with green shutters (really / A kind
of church, built out of old ships)." But neither of these
passages reveals how singular McGuckian's language usually is. Like Dickinson, whose own deceptively tidy stanzas McGuckian's rather recall, and who "tasted life" when
the "vast morsel" of a circus passed her window and days
later could still "feel the red in [her] mind," McGuckian
experiences the usual as unusual, the unusual as exotic
and perilous.

McGuckian's poems are discontinuous, eagerly digressive,
open-ended, riddled with enigma, fluid as dreams. They
evade the expectations they delicately arouse at nearly every
turn. If "All poetry is experimental poetry," some poetry is
still more steadfastly provisional than other poetry.
Stevens's own work is a case in point—as is the work, to
trace his lineage backwards and forwards, of Gertrude Stein
and John Ashbery. McGuckian, who is Irish, would seem

to have been inspired by this strain in American poetry. If
indeed it is American. English and French are a single
language, according to Stevens, and in different ways the
work of Stein and Ashbery testify to the cogency of the
coupling. McGuckian, for her part, relishes French terms,
and there is about her poems the air of Baudelaire's "Cor-
respondances," with its "parfums . . . Doux comme les
hautbois, verts comme les prairies," and Verlaine's "Art
poètique," with its "vers . . . Éparse au vent crispé du matin
/ Qui va fleurant la menthe et la thym." In **"Four O'Clock
Summer Street"** McGuckian says of a girl passing her
house that "I knew she was drinking blue and it had dried
/ In her," and here is a passage from **"Balakhana"**: "The
door I found / So difficult to close let in my first / European feeling which now blows about, / A cream-colored
blossom, with a blue vigor."

The door remains open, the air fresh throughout these
poems. Living from moment to moment, flouting logical
sequence and mimesis, they constitute a poetry of motion and transformation. A "blue vigor" precisely. The
cover illustration on the first edition is a painting by Jack
B. Yeats, a delicious swirl of blues and yellows, a sea-
scape with a lone figure, barely discernible. It is a paint-
erly canvas, its scumbling and turbulent brushstrokes
threatening to annihilate boundaries between land and sea,
sea and sky, medium and scene, and it is a fine choice for
this volume, in which all seems blue flux and flecked
blow, spindrift and rough draft, mystery overriding mere
mastery. McGuckian points to a principle in or rather
condition of her work in the opening quatrain of **"The
Time before You"**:

> The secret of movement
> Is not the secret itself
> But the movement
> Of there being a secret.

"A town will never draw your mind to it / Like a place
where you have camped," is one way that she puts her bias
toward the cryptic and the transitive. Time and again her
poems touch on the inextricability of the beautiful and the
elusive. In **"The Blue She Brings with Her,"** where the
poet suspects that "beauty lives / By escaping and leaves a
mark," she tells the inspiring figure that "Your eyes change
color as you move / And will not go into words."

"Grainne's Sleep Song" could be thought of both as a
parable of McGuckian's escape into a new language and
as a prime instance of it. The poem proceeds by means of
a radical slippage of terms that belies the conservative
pentameter norm:

> The day that I got up to was not right.
> It was hostile, it wanted to be alone
> Like a novel rough to the touch. The house
> Hadn't had enough sleep either, and
> In drudgery still heard the sound of kisses
> Pursuing her.

The setting, the hypothetical novel, the house, and the
speaker dissolve wonderfully into each other. There is no

background or foreground here, no "scene" *in* which "action" takes place. Instead, the elements in the complex make up together the poem's subject. So too the poem's subject, the novel's, and a legend's are stitched together. In the pertinent legend, Grainne, who is the Irish original of Iseult, married to an aging Finn, falls in love and elopes with his nephew Diarmait. One night, in the course of their escape from Finn, whose outraged pursuit has kept awake the natural world from stag to curlew, Grainne sings her lover to sleep with a song—the same song that (in the first English version) was to inspire W. B. Yeats's "Lullaby." Deprived of its title, McGuckian's poem could never be connected with Grainne's berceuse. Given the allusion, however, the reader sees lines like the following in a special light:

> Like a porch in winter,
> Blue, cold and affectionate, I stepped
> With you for a moment out of my
> Uncompleted story, something sterile
> I contracted fourteen years ago on the beach,
> Entitled "Wild Without Love." And stopping
> In the entrance of strange houses, sudden
> Downpours, I began to read, instead of
> Letters never answered, well, salads
> And love-walks.

In her funky "pre-war squirrel / Jacket," the wayward speaker is a free spirit, and she seems to have found her style in these refractory and mercurial lines. They turn in part on the queer puns, including "contracted," which involves the marriage license as well as the disease that the marriage introduced and which is all the stranger for the oxymoronic connection with "sterile," which might mean "barren," and certainly means "unsatisfying," but has ironic overtones in this context of "antiseptic." These lines' peculiarity is also a matter of extreme ellipticism, as in the clause beginning "I began to read," which implies the woman's exchange of a bitter, self-imposed sequestration for a freer life, *al fresco.* If the "salads," especially when "read," quirkily suggest dining out, the first associations are with hunger and, in proximity to "love-walks," wildness. That same untrammeled quality, in the area of imagination, represents this new carving, with "a stone from the crop"of her "writing / Pad," "some verses . . . from / 'Where Claribel low lieth' and, beneath, / Both our initials in full." Can that be a real poem? But then what is a "real poem"? Is **"Wild Without Love"** a real story? Probably not—yet evidently, since it can after all be escaped from. And in fact **"Claribel: A Melody"** is an early dirge by Tennyson. With its lugubrious repetitiveness, it is at once a sign of the death-in-life that the speaker remembers escaping (and the poet might have found her own name secretly inscribed in Tennyson's effort, where "The clear-voiced mavis dwelleth," since these days Medbh is pronounced just like the first syllable of that word for the songbird) and a foil for her own song of liberation, with its volatile language. Though we should remember, when musing on this language, that she says in another poem that "none of my removals / Was in any sense a flight—// More the invention of a new caress."

These poems want to keep moving—to change, to disseminate, to surprise. In a colorful lyric entitled **"Ylang-Ylang,"** a characteristically unlikely source voices the feeling that McGuckian goes in fear of: "My life, sighed the grass-coloured, / Brandy-inspired carafe, is like a rug / That used to be a leopard, beckoning / To something pink." Can even such a passage, new at every comma and line break, grow stale with familiarity? McGuckian, as alert as Stevens himself to the paradoxes of the poet committed to flux, knows that they must. In **"Through the Round Window"** she writes resignedly that "Each poem in my alchemist's cupboard / That was an act of astonishment has a life / Of roughly six weeks, less than half a winter / Even in the child's sense of a week." A daedal passage in **"The Dream-Language of Fergus"** obliquely describes her own ambitions in terms of a river that "Becomes a leaping, glistening, splashed / And scattered alphabet / Jutting out from the voice," as though this fluency were also its fish and rocks, but then as she continues her language envisions its rigor mortis, for "what began as a dog's bark / Ends with bronze, what began / With honey ends with ice." Yet the poem goes on in its protean fashion to conclude with this credo:

> And if I am a threader
> Of double-stranded words, whose
> Quando has grown into now,
> No text can return the honey
> In its path of light from a jar,
> Only a seed-fund, a pendulum,
> Pressing out the diasporic snow.

An isolated Latin term, "Quando" is clearly doubly stranded, but then so are all her words here, thrust out from her now and strung up with the others like pearls. Yet less pearls than seeds, or spores—seed-pearls, let's say, scattered on the page, in the copies of her book, both dispersing and recovering the honey or light of the motivating experience.

In such heterogeneous, lovely, puzzling passages McGuckian's poetry fulfills the longing set down in **"Blue Vase,"** another poem concerned with "dream-speech," "To be the insouciance of the room, / Interrupted, re-created—to be the innocence / You have just learned to say." Mulling these lines over with as much impatience as pleasure, I was glad to be reminded of Stein's caveat. "The characteristic quality of a classic is that it is beautiful," she says, but she goes on to remark that usually "first all beauty in it is denied" and that we are too indolent to "realise that beauty is beauty even when it is irritating and stimulating not only when it is accepted and classic." A classic in the making, *On Ballycastle Beach* will trouble many of us for some time to come.

Susan Shaw Seiler with Medbh McGuckian (interview date 1993)

SOURCE: "An Interview with Medbh McGuckian," in *Michigan Quarterly Review,* Winter, 1993, pp. 111-27.

[*In the following interview, McGuckian discusses the influence of Tess Gallagher on her work, autobiographical aspects of her poetry, and her philosophy of language.*]

Born in Belfast and having lived there all her life, Medbh McGuckian speaks of herself as a poet "from the North." Now forty-six, she has accomplished a great deal. In addition to several early chapbooks, she has brought out three collections of poems, all published by Oxford University Press. Her first, **The Flower Master**, won the Rooney Prize and Alice Hunt Barlett Award in 1982. **Venus and the Rain** (1984) and **On Ballycastle Beach** (1988) were acclaimed in *TLS* [Times Literary Supplement] and *The New Statesman*. Wake Forest University Press has just published a fourth volume, **Marconi's Cottage**. McGuckian was the first woman to be named writer-in-residence at Queen's University, a position she held from 1986 to 1988.

On June 25, 1990, I spoke with Medbh McGuckian about her writing, that of other poets, the role of poets, and life in Northern Ireland. We sat outdoors in the back yard of her home in Belfast, while her ten-month-old baby daughter Emer napped in the house and her three young sons attended their final week of school for the academic year. A well-used swing set, a soccer ball lying in a flower bed, and grass that functioned as a mat for her sons' play attested to the centrality of her children in McGuckian's life.

Although I had prepared questions, after speaking with McGuckian for a few minutes I decided that what came spontaneously from her would offer more insight into how she thinks and works than would her answers to my questions. So I abandoned the format of a question-and-answer interview and instead assumed the role of listener.

And McGuckian's talk surprised me. Although her poetry tends to be abstract in that it is often difficult to say what her poems are "about" and to make connections between contiguous passages, her conversation is concrete, dealing with the events of her daily life and how these interact with what becomes her poetry. Her speaking voice is simultaneously exploratory, tentative, wistful, and determined.

[Sailer]: *Something in your poetry reminds me of* Finnegans Wake, *not in the sense that you write like Joyce but in the way you make associations. I also see similarities in your poetry to that of John Ashbery and, to some extent, with surrealism.*

[McGuckian]: People say that. I did just an ordinary degree and I haven't done research. I haven't had time to read a book for the last ten years, really, with four kids, and my poetry has been written during those years. I did quite a lot of studying till my mid-twenties, so there could be a residue from that, but what I think is that there's an indirect influence from other poets I have read and assimilated. So possibly what other poets have derived from Joyce or Ashbery, maybe I have through them.

But I haven't directly read Ashbery or *Finnegans Wake*. I've read *Ulysses,* and I know about *Finnegans Wake*, but I just avoid it, because I know I couldn't read it at the minute.

I guess I do work through association, but I think it's so very female that it doesn't help to talk too much about male predecessors. Tess Gallagher, the American writer, may be influenced by both, and I have been influenced by her, so that might be a kind of solution.

And yet, your poetry seems very different from hers, in the way that your images link. It strikes me that Tess Gallagher has much more narrative connectedness.

She has, yes. Tess was here last week and we were talking about poetry. I showed her a poem I'd written, just an ordinary poem, and she said, "Oh, what is it about?" And I said it was about going to see these stones in Sweden. She said, "Well, why don't you mention the stones?" Because, you see, that's what she would do, she would tell the story. Her interest is in stories, or the narrative content, whereas I wouldn't want to say what it was like directly. I just wanted to get the experience, or the meaning of the experience, not the experience itself, because the experience itself was nothing. I had a baby with me and I didn't even see the stones, so from her point of view, maybe because she's a single person, things do happen to her. But for me they're all future things: I might come back again. So I think it's my lifestyle dictates the way I write.

And yet, for you to have a sense of the meaning, there must be some experience behind it, even though it would be very different from what Tess might experience.

Well, the experience was going there *with* my child. I was going there as an ordinary woman. You see, I think what I try to do is different than Tess whereas Tess is the professional traveling poet. Her main relationship is with her mother and dead husband.[1] And that's where she gains her strength at the minute from, from his memory. He's with her and sustaining her and those are her relationships whereas mine are the very basic, ordinary ones that all women have maybe had forced on them almost—like a child every year. I didn't have that forced on me, though, I wanted that. I had three sons and I really wanted a daughter. I wouldn't have cared if I ever wrote another line, to get her. But this is all not really helping very much.

Oh, no. I don't agree at all. It helps me to get a sense of you, and through that, I can approach your work.

Well, you see, my work is almost totally autobiographic. I am putting together a new book at the minute; I started it last night. I'm going to bring it out, hopefully, next year. All it deals with is 1988, '89 and '90. And there might be a little bit of '91 in it, but it just is about what has happened to me in that time. I don't write about anything beyond that. If I go to a place, I will write a poem about it but it may not be what other people would write. Nobody would know from the poem that that was where

I had been. I mean when I pick up the poem I know who it was for; each poem is associated with a person or a place or an event or a time. It's a very specific occasion but only for me. If the poem said what this is, I just feel that it wouldn't mean enough to other people if I kept saying "this is so very specific." But obviously the new book will be about Emer's birth. The pregnancy will be the central event, that last pregnancy. Every time I do poetry readings I stand up and I say, "This is a poem about early pregnancy," and "That is a poem about late pregnancy." And all these men are sitting there and the women are bored and the men I think are not too excited either, you know. But I think it probably has been for me a very fecund period till now, though it's not easy to reconcile the two forms of creativity.

Would you say that's frequently a theme in your work, the parallel between the fecundity of the body and the fecundity of words?

Yes, yes. Certainly when I'm expecting a child I'm really stable and really happy. I think a lot of women feel very much tied up with gestation itself and almost god-like. In their maternal state, they just feel very close to the riddle of the universe. They feel as if they have all the answers, and it is wonderful; I mean it's amazing. But at the same time there is an annihilation of the self, that leaves you bare afterwards, bereft, almost like a death has happened, that a self has died or you've left something. And certainly now at my age, not so much with the first baby as with the last one, I felt almost exhausted by it. And then that is definitely the last baby so it won't ever happen again, and you feel sad.

So that mutual fructifying of a physical baby and the literal, literary baby won't happen again?

No, no, not in that way anyway. No, that couldn't, couldn't happen again! I hope it doesn't happen again, I don't want it, couldn't face it. So when you were saying about my images that I tie them together differently than Tess, I'm not sure. Well, certainly I'd love to be able to write like her, I think she writes so clearly, but I have a different way of seeing things.

Like when she wrote a poem called "Valentine Delivered by a Raven"[2] I was thinking a lot about "Valentine." What does she mean, valentine. And all she meant was the card, the valentine *card.* But I was thinking of valentine as a name of someone or as this figure, so for me that would be a very obscure title and the raven wouldn't even be a literal bird or a bird of death. There would be an awful lot more invested. For her it's simply that.

Yes, for her there's always a literal base that things begin from. As far as I can tell from **The Flower Master** *and* **On Ballycastle Beach**, *I don't sense the literal base of experience in your poems.*

No, no. Well, there *is* a literal base but you're not really meant to sense it. Tess has this sense of herself being very, very special, and she is, and for her, experience is

on a height. It's the love she has for Ray. Whereas this is something I probably won't have, you know, this tremendous romantic and total love for another human being. I don't expect that, I don't think I could cope with that with the children. I mean, my relationship with my husband is settled, ordinary. It's like anybody else's marriage. It's not food for poetry. I think the death of my husband would devastate me so, so much even as regards how I would cope, that I couldn't write about it. It wouldn't feed my poetry, it would almost wreck it!

How would I just live? I couldn't live, basically, never mind write poetry, where she seems to have recovered from that and to have drawn from that. I don't know, I guess I'm talking about this because Tess has been here so recently.

But the **Ballycastle Beach** book: again I don't write in books, I just write a continual, continuing diary.

But you must have some way whereby these poems became this book and not some others.

Well, certainly it's a great way of organizing your pile, and I feel grateful now that, ok, I can get all that sorted. That's that part of my life in a book. It's so very blessed a thing, it's so very satisfying and ego-boosting, to have that. You need it. But I just hope that other women could reach into it and feel that their own life somehow was ordinary enough to be reflected there rather than feel they had to be a free spirit.

People have always felt that poets had to be free spirits. People keep saying to me, "Oh, you're a free spirit, you don't have to obey laws." I don't know, I feel very tied by laws and very bound. Once you have children you opt for law. You opt for a settled existence and you have to forego that freedom. I think Seamus Heaney talks about it a lot, you know, freedom of the imagination and the obligations of the social, domestic, political, on and on. I think he understands it because his poetry is full of tension and responsibility and right up against whatever. Heaney tries to give good examples and not let anybody down, and keep everybody happy, and that's the way I am too. I must not let my mother down or let my children down or do anything because a poet is, a poet's life *can* be very bohemian, they *do* every so often, they divorce somebody and go wild and end up in alcoholic ways or something and it just seems that when the poet does it it's so very destructive.

I have felt that, too. I was devastated during the 1960s and '70's by how many American poets committed suicide. I felt it as a personal threat: if they can't live, how can I possibly live.

Sure, I mean that's it, it's openness. The poet is kind of the standard bearer, or is trying to be, and yet they're all very weak. I know I am.

But no more so than anyone else, do you think? It's just that one is so aware of it.

Well, the poet has certain strengths—in his words and in his views and in his life, but they very much need a rock to lean on. The person they're married to or the person they're living with has to be, I think, almost like a saint. In his poem called "The Harvest Bow," I think Heaney very much puts his wife in that spot. There are so many other people involved that help, but basically this is the core relationship that poets have to have, this very sensible rock that shields them. Look at how Robert Lowell depended so much on Elizabeth Hardwick and went back to her so many times. Poets need to be absolutely loved, and not for their poetry, somehow. They need to feel the person loves them almost despite the poetry.

I do think the role of the poet in the modern world is very difficult and also very changing at the minute, changing a lot at the minute.

Could you get at that from what, to what?

Well, because we're in the '90's and we're going into a new century, we're trying to leave behind the terrible things. It was such a bad century, basically, and the first half of it was a mess. Everyone feels almost everything was lost. Almost all dignity. You know, we almost committed suicide as a race and, possibly, maybe spiritually, we have. I feel I am at the end of the worst. I was born in 1951, when the worst was over. Obviously bad things have been going on, but there hasn't been that full-scale, global violence that my parents lived through, and I live here in this extremely explosive place. But I do feel that what I have to do is kind of garner or trail or find out of all that, the positives, and reinvest language with meaning. There was a Polish poet over here recently, Piotr Sommer, and he is still reading poems about the Second World War, poems where poets in the fifties were still full of despair and full of accusation and full of division. The poems were extremely powerful but very, very negative and empty. Those poets were still in a world of terrible cruelty and terrible injustice and couldn't see their way out of it. One poem that struck me most was "they've taken away my stove but I have still got the hole or the place where the stove was." I don't want to hear that. I just want to begin again and have a new romanticist view, the friends of the earth and all that. Ok, that's phony, but it's so very important, the conservation thing.

So it's lovely when people say to you, "Send me a poem about a tree or write me a poem about a mountain." Into that mountain I will put the female, me, but I do also feel that it is important for women poets to redeem the feminine ideas of love, ideas of fidelity, ideas of nurturing. After all that, we still have to defend things and fight. What I say sounds pedantic, I know, as if I were some kind of Christ figure, but otherwise poetry is just going to complain about things.

Do you think it was important for poetry to be able to "complain" for a while after these atrocities and horrors?

Well, yes.

And so maybe that cycle is coming to an end with the turn of the century?

We were on the edge of it, here in Ireland. We were on the edge of everything. So our poetry—I mean Yeats hardly even referred to the first world war, and only a little bit to the second world war coming. And none of our poets were touched by it all that much. Therefore I feel that it was up to the Russians and the European poets and even the Americans to go to those places, to write about those things. But certainly here when the troubles were at their height, it was important for us to protest. Maybe people like Yevtushenko should write about the Jews being slaughtered.[3] But then to martyrize violence, I always felt, would be feeding into the conflict. If you write a poem celebrating someone as a martyr, you are just adding to it, or fueling it. I think when it's over maybe you can comment. But our violence was such an inbred thing, and so ongoing, it wasn't like a war. For years, the bloodshed was chaotic. Here it was like a person killed every night, like just a drip. I've never been able to write about it; I'm very squeamish about it.

So, at a number of levels you choose not to deal with the Irish Troubles or with war?

Oh God no. Oh, no, I couldn't. I mean, how could I? I can't even sit through the films of that. This is why these poets committed suicide, because they did try. I mean they definitely did try to confront it, and I think it's extremely dangerous. For me, it just would not work.

It sounds as though it would be contrary to what you perceive as the feminine principle in you, which is that of the bearer of life, the creator of life, but also the nurturer of life.

If you address yourself to evil, you are giving it a status, and it's got enough status. All it has to do is go on television and everyone will be shocked. But I feel that in my poetry I have to do something else. I just don't know what I do with this evil, probably ignore it and hope that it will go away, but I know it won't. I think I have to try and be very old-fashioned, and yet I'm very new, in a way.

Yes, you are. I remember when I was trying to read about you and your writing, I went to Contemporary Literary Criticism, but I was puzzled by some of the comments made about you. For instance, a critic—I can't remember who—wrote about your reaching backwards toward Victorian values and a kind of nostalgia for that world. That puzzled me because I didn't think that you were reaching backwards.

Well, I think I'm reaching backwards, but not nostalgically. You see, it's probably the Englishness. Living here in an English colony, you're not Irish, and there's no sense pretending you are. You're not, I mean I'm not Irish, I'm probably more English than the English. And so what we want all the time here is Laura Ashley floral little cottages. That's all we want here, because that's what we're being presented with.

But I've been brought up very securely, despite everything. I think I'm going through a funny phase right now, but I'm beginning to understand that what I'm reaching for is maybe even further back: all the things that people like Tolstoy sought, a universal understanding of the human condition. I mean, the modern century with its technology and with its fast-paced life: we've lost the whole thing. The material comfort and standard of life, and whatever else we're supposed to be placated with, does not make up for what it takes away, which is our sense that that cloud might not be there the next time we look. Our whole sky is just invaded in a way that other centuries didn't have to face.

Are you talking about the nuclear threat?

Well, not just the nuclear. You can't even step in the door but you've been barraged with false images of satisfaction, with the advertisements and the television. It's all "pleasure, pleasure, pleasure." Pleasure, selfishness, and "if you have this, then you will be happy" and "if you buy this," and "if you can afford this." And then you're neurotic because you haven't got the things that are there to be got. And even if you did have them, you've got all the time to compromise. The words: the words then are a battle, always a battle against those forces. I'm not saying technology is a bad thing. Obviously if people can be healed, or if somebody can be got to the hospital quick enough to save his life, that's great. But maybe there's too much emphasis on technology. I just feel I have to quietly battle against those things.

You're doing battle, in a sense, using the medium that the adversary is using. I mean, advertising has just . . .

. . . become so poetic. They will actually quote a poem, almost. They will ask you. Even Van Morrison is doing it. An LP with poets on it, in a sense commercial. We are being commercially exploited. I'm sure I will be and have been and ought to be maybe. The other day I went to Dublin and did a tape for an American who's completely soulless, as far as I could see. His only object was to have something that would sell. I don't know, maybe he did have a genuine concern for education. But then even for poetry to be so much involved with education is also, in a sense, not what it's for.

I understand. It's partly what I see in the States, the danger for writers having become poets-in-residence, novelists-in-residence, at universities. Somehow I think that's a threat to what they do, although it needn't be, but it seems to be.

Well, it's great in that you don't have to work, you don't have to starve, you don't have to have a grinding, decanting kind of job. See, I'm in a good position because I do work. I'm lucky in that I *have* to be very rooted in my family. So this keeps you from that danger, the poet as a lonely person. You need time. I was so jealous of previous poets because although they didn't have all of the relics—they weren't aristocrats—at least they had time.

But they didn't fare too well, did they?

They didn't fare too well, no. What they got, they got nowhere. But at least they had time. At least their poetry is enriched by its growth as a natural thing. You know, John Clare in his little world. There it is, there's emotion really grown, *now* we look at it. It must have been very frustrating for them, though, to know nobody knew who they were, or cared. I do relish having been allowed to speak and people listening. I love going to read places, but I'm always very glad to protect myself. I was in Sweden and my friend was a writer there, a writer-in-residence—she's a novelist—and she thought she couldn't get her own work done because students were in and out and she actually couldn't write *anything*.

I understand that. I teach at West Virginia University, and I know a couple of writers, very good ones, who experience the same thing.

It doesn't foster you because it is very artificial. I was at Queen's University, which is just across the road, and I went in two days a week. But the times I wrote were not there. I couldn't write. And I know Seamus Heaney never writes at Harvard, he writes here, in Ireland. But anyway I think that positions for writers-in-residence are useful economically to give the writer a break from his writing.

Have you ever been tempted to leave Northern Ireland?

Oh, yes. Yes.

What holds you here? Family connections?

Well, really, the only connections: roots and a sense of belonging and a sense of having spent forty years of your life—well, the first few years not voluntarily: you were here and that was it—but having voluntarily submitted to the worst twenty years in this country's history, probably, and lived through the worst of it. Then to get up and go when you've suffered so much—not you but the culture—it would be silly to leave when things are maybe on the upturn, when things are maybe over the next ten years going to get better. My children have already got a sense of identity here. They're doing all right. They're not suffering as much as we did. They're not as isolated from an event because it's even on the television.

Whereas when we were growing up, I didn't speak to a Protestant until I was twenty-two. It was just the way it was, you just didn't. There weren't any bridges, they weren't even spoken of. And now everything's quite open. But it's a very good place to be in some ways, because we've been so divided. I think the effort to harmonize is strong. Even on a bus, you'll know someone is different from you, you know they're from a different culture and would be extremely polite. But I think it's true in almost all of the countries around the world, people respect the children.

Does that mean there are greater efforts to avoid violence? Or are these efforts pretty much on the parts of people who are outside the violence?

Well, I think that when violence happens there's a greater reaction to it here. There's more of a sense of horror. Whereas in other places somehow—when I was in Boston, all I could feel was people being murdered.

In Boston?

Well, any of those cities, in downtown New York. It's so big and it's as if it didn't matter, it's as if nobody cares. There's no reason to it; here you feel like maybe that's the last one, maybe it'll end now. There is this feeling that it's going to stop. But anyway, I'm still here and have been tempted to go many times.

Going back to how you see yourself, is feminist a word you would apply to your position as a writer? You speak for women through a woman's perspective, but I'm not sure what connotations "feminist" has here.

Well, here we don't have abortion, and I'm almost very delighted that we don't have abortion, but I'm very torn by those issues. I'm certainly very, very much for women being equal, very much for—*totally* for—women being developed and for women being given every opportunity. But I also feel that—like this technological thing—that what might be lost would be those very values that we think of as most feminine. You know, if you're *too* demanding for your freedom then you are going to destroy your home.

I'm for feminism as long as it doesn't destroy in the woman what is the most precious to her, which is her ability to relate and soften and make a loving environment for others as well as herself. I just don't think people can live a very lonely life. Sometimes there is something in feminism that demands you to be almost masculine and that's what frightens me a bit about it, or to sort of repudiate reproduction. You know, I have friends who have gone through hard times desperately trying to avoid getting pregnant. And that must be such a *difficult* thing. I know I have this problem too, but at least my nature was—you know—in between all that.

Certainly you wouldn't want to have a child just for the sake of having a child. You'd almost want to have a child to be a friend or a companion for another child that you had or so many different reasons. I find feminism attractive in theory but in practice I think it ends up influenced by lesbians and—very lonely and embittered and stressed and full of hatred.

But me again, I've been lucky that I didn't have to fight. I managed to get certain things that I thought I wanted anyway and to be a poet. I mean I *did* want marriage, I *did* want children. And it's very, very, very, very difficult.

Almost impossible—yeah, it is. And then when I look at Tess and me, I see what she has done and what she has sacrificed for it. You know we'll have those problems, apart from all the sufferings of bringing children up, but you will still have them, coming in hopefully when they're grown up; and you'll feel you've done something else.

Whereas if writing poetry was all I had done, I would think it was not much to have done with my life. And certainly they've created something. They're all of them, all in there somehow. And the book wouldn't be there without them.

But I think that's the thing for Tess, too. You know, she would have loved a child, maybe just because you could write to it, or for it, or about it or out of it—but it *does* things to you.

So, therefore it changes you and therefore your imagery—our imagery—is different. Like I'll use the word "womb" where she would be terrified to use that word, you see. She would *recoil* from it because her womb never answered her, never lived for her, whereas for me my womb is almost my *brain*. For the other women in Ireland, their wombs are not their brains, but I think with Nuala Ni Dhomhnaill it is.[4]

I'm not familiar with her poetry.

She is like me in that way. She is the closest to me in that her womb is her center, her poetic center. And with Eavan Boland[5] she is that wee bit older and wee bit more academic, whereas we were '60's girls, you know.

Right, right. I was with the upper end of the '60's, but I know what you mean when you say that. If your womb is your brain, or very close to your brain, can a man understand what you write?

Yeah, yeah, they can. They do. I'm sure they do; and if they don't, they're very willing to be shown. Some of them get the wrong end of the stick, but maybe they do so deliberately.

I would assume so. I was thinking of John Lucas, who had said that your transitions are so obscure as to be self-defeating,[6] and it occurred to me that I thought the notion of transitions in your poetry was not all that helpful. I don't think it's a significant way to talk about what you do.

Well, I know that I make steps. I seem to step from one thing to another, in some kind of logical flow, but the flow is almost like a—almost even like part of a machine. When Tess writes a poem she will use the same word from one end of the poem to the other and her transitions are, as you said, part of the story. I'm trying to stay true to a certain pattern. You can't expect the poem to look like a machine just because it's written in a machine age. I mean, have you said what transitions were? Well, you'd really need to look at examples.

One of the things I was hoping you might do would be to look at a poem.

THE DREAM LANGUAGE OF FERGUS

i

Your tongue has spent the night
In its dim sack as the shape of your foot

In its cave. Not the rudiment
Of half a vanquished sound,
The excommunicated shadow of a name,
Has rumpled the sheets of your mouth.

ii
So Latin sleeps, they say, in Russian speech,
So one river inserted into another
Becomes a leaping, glistening, splashed
And scattered alphabet
Jutting out from the voice,
Till what began as a dog's bark
Ends with bronze, what began
With honey ends with ice;
As if an aeroplane in full flight
Launched a second plane,
The sky is stabbed by their exits
And the mistaken meaning of each.

iii
Conversation is as necessary
Among these familiar campus trees
As the apartness of torches;
And if I am a threader
Of double-stranded words, whose
Quando has grown into now,
No text can return the honey
In its path of light from a jar,
Only a seed-fund, a pendulum,
Pressing out the diasporic snow.

In **"The Dream Language of Fergus,"** *how is Fergus functioning? I really wasn't sure. This is the Fergus of mythology, yes?*

Yes, Fergus is also my mother's maiden name. My second book is dedicated to my mother. And Fergus is my son's name. My third son is called Fergus. And it's also the Fergus of the druids, and Fergus of the king of Ireland, and Yeats's Fergus, "Who Goes with Fergus?"

I love the word, but it was also about my child, Fergie. He was about a year and a half when I wrote this one, and was just beginning to speak, like the little one now. She's at that stage. She's beginning to make little noises and say "look." So the poem is really about him learning to speak English, and me regretting that he's speaking English instead of Irish, which is the real language of the Irish.

That helps a great deal. I had realized there's a progression in the poem from unvoiced speech, the potentiality of speech, to speech.

Well, this is about as political as I would get. You see, I would be political in a very homely way. I would say, my son is growing up speaking English, whereas his soul is Irish, so that's a pity. It's a pity that our language has been stolen, but there you are.

Do you think the Irish language is going to make a comeback?

No. Irish is not anywhere as culturally rich as the nation is, just not a language. What Nuala can write is so limited.

And she does write in Gaelic?

Yes, she writes beautifully in Gaelic, but when you put it into English, you have to do all sorts of things to it. The Irish language isn't strong enough to *hold* what I would want to say, or what a lot of people want to say. It hasn't evolved. It's a dead language. It's stopped. It doesn't have words for a lot of things. Really, in a way it's the language I *should* be using if I want to go back. But I don't want to go back to those times. I think you want to incorporate things like the complicated experience of living in the twentieth century. You can't forget it. You can't just say, "I'm going back to time before." Well anyway, I don't know enough about it. All I know is that people say it's very thin, and you have to say things in a very convoluted way. And it's an awkward language. I think it's good to have it there, but there's no point in crying over spilt milk.

I mean there's no way my first tongue was ever going to be Irish, or my children's. Basically what a lot of people are giving their kids is a lot of problems, trying to speak to them only in Irish. And then when they go, they just can't deal with things. The fact, the reality, is otherwise.

So at any rate, **"The Dream Language of Fergus"** is just in three parts. The first part talks to the child, then the second tries to discuss what is lost and what's gained. I thought this one was very logical in a way. It's not about me. Yeah, it is about me in the end, where I write "if I am a threader / Of double-stranded words." It is very *complicated*, my anguish at losing him.
To language?

No. My anguish at losing the baby. You see, his learning to talk is a kind of weaning, so the pain of the poem is not so much—well, it is my sense of having lost my language and him having lost his, his heritage in some way. But the pain of it is the fact that the child's growing away from me, and I'm losing him. So always the image is what began as being part of me—the child at the knee, playing—taking off on its own, the river as the tributary leaping away off elsewhere. And so what has she left? I can't get the child back into me, I wouldn't want that. "No text can return the honey / In its path of light." The child has to grow. There's nothing I can do. No poem can return the child into a seed. I wouldn't want that.

"No text can return the honey / In its path of light from a jar, / Only a seed-fund, a pendulum, / Pressing out the diasporic snow."—Again, this is sort of a weak ending, I think—All my poetry is like a seed fund, it's like your husband's sperm. Even though you're not always producing children, you still have this sense of vitality in the relationship. And a pendulum: you have a measure for time through the poems, a measure of time. And therefore, snow that has dissipated and spread out, is pressed into the earth, sort of like water, to bring something new up. And you know, the diaspora is races scattered all around the world. You feel that your children are leaving, but that something of the waters will come back to you somehow.

At the same time, you know, "what began / With honey ends with ice." This was so very sad for me. We were so very close and then it's like we're very far away from each other.

In the child's own life, the child is sleeping. Its little foot has no shoe on it.

Those are such wonderful images.

Well, they're very real, you know. "Your tongue has spent the night / In its dim sack": it's all very like the womb again. It's a very womby poem. Like the jar is the womb, the sack is the womb. You want a child to be free, you want the child to develop and have flight. But the sky is stabbed, the woman is stabbed by the leaving. And we're both leaving, but then you have to keep talking. I have to talk. English conversation is necessary. Though no matter "if I am a threader / Of double-stranded words." Women traditionally did sew, but I'm not sewing. Or rather, I'm sewing words.

And they are double-stranded words?

Yeah, they're double-stranded because there's an Irish and an English strain in them and they can live together. What I'm saying is really that would be a dream. The poem that goes with this is **"A Dream in Three Colors"** [*On Ballycastle Beach*]. Fergie was born in the spring, and I'm saying, "Look, you can be Irish or English [McGuckian at this point begins to discuss **"Dream in Three Colors"**]. These are the English colors: blue, white and red; red, white and blue. And the dream is that we could be, all English and all Irish and all European—or something [laughing].

You know, like Latin and Russian. The thing I used those to say was, "Look, why do we worry about losing a language, because look how Latin sleeps in Russian speech."

[McGuckian returns to discussing **"The Dream Language of Fergus."**] "Excommunicate" is an awfully difficult word, isn't it? "Excommunicate" means that you've committed some dreadful crime, and they've put you out of the church. And this child's being banished, you know? And then talking here about the diasporic snow, the Irish were exiled. But the child is sleeping peacefully, and it's very much like Yeats's poem, Yeats looking at his daughter in the cradle. "A Prayer for My Daughter" was Yeats's title.

That's very helpful, because I hadn't realized that Fergus was to be taken on other than a mythological level.[7] Something I had always wanted to ask you about: certain images appear over and over again. I'm thinking of the moon and the color blue, and then many, many others. They seem often to have very different ways of working in the different poems, but they're the same words.

Well, they're the same words except if you use a word that's, like, too dark, it darkens. If you use a word with two light words beside it, or a light one and a dark one, it darkens and lightens. So though they're the same words you can play with them. But see, there're some words I would maybe only ever use once in a lifetime, like "excommunicated." I will never use that again.

How do titles occur to you?

They come always afterwards. Always afterwards. I never have a title before. Sometimes I get a title by accident or just from a twist. Sometimes I would deliberately want to write a poem for a special thing and the title would come to mind. But sometimes I like the title to be a little poem itself, so I try to make it catchy, like . . .

*. . . like **"Harem Trousers"**?*

Yeah, I would try making two very funny words together, like a joke. But some of the titles I wouldn't use again now, like **"Four O'Clock, Summer Street"** [*OBB*]. That was a time and place title. And **"Death of a Ceiling"** [*OBB*] was referring to "Death of a Naturalist" [Heaney's poem in the volume so titled]. Not: I used to do a lot of "nots," you know: on *not* being your lover, on *not* pleasing. [McGuckian locates several such poems in *On Ballycastle Beach*.] **"On Not Being Listened To."** I am speaking *for* that, you see, it's *good* not to be listened to. Because someone won't . . . if you're not listened to, then that gives the person who *is* listening more of a chance to hear.

I think that's what I mean anyway. "One / Quarter of the staircase asks to know / What you have written." So I say "Look, don't worry." I think I wrote this after a long period of nobody listening to me. [Laughing]

NOTES

[1] American short story writer and poet Raymond Carver (1939-1988), whose stories are collected in four volumes: *Will You Please Be Quiet, Please* (1978), *What We Talk About When We Talk About Love* (1981), *Cathedral* (1983), and *Where I'm Calling From* (1988).

[2] This poem appears in Gallagher's volume, *Moon Crossing Bridge*.

[3] McGuckian refers here to Yevgeny Yevtushenko's poem "Babi Yar," which commemorates the slaughter in the U.S.S.R. during World War II of hundreds of Jews and other innocent victims.

[4] Nuala Ni Dhomhnaill is an Irish poet who lives in Dublin and writes in Gaelic. Though few of her books have been translated into English, *Pharaoh's Daughter* (County Meath, Ireland: The Gallery Press, 1990) contains poems translated by Irish poets, including McGuckian and Heaney.

[5] Eavan Boland, born in Dublin in 1944, has published six volumes of poetry, the most recent of which is *Outside History: Selected Poems 1980-1990* (1990). She lectures at the School of Irish Studies, Dublin.

[6] John Lucas writes that McGuckian's "transitions are so abrupt, opaque and inconsequential as to be self-defeating," *Contemporary Literary Criticism*, vol. 48, p. 275.

[7] Compare McGuckian's reading of "The Dream Language of Fergus" with that of Calvin Bedient in his review of *On Ballycastle Beach* and the works of other recent Northern Irish writers in "The Crabbed Genius of Belfast," *Parnassus*, Vol. 16, No. 1, 1990, pp. 195-216. See especially pages 201-202.

Cecile Gray   (essay date 1993)

SOURCE: "Medbh McGuckian: Imagery Wrought to Its Uttermost," in *Learning the Trade: Essays on W.B. Yeats and Contemporary Poetry*, 1993, pp. 165-77.

[*In the following essay, Gray explores the hermetic and obscure nature of McGuckian's verse.*]

On November 6 and 7, 1991, the Poetry Society of America and the Program in Hellenic Studies at Columbia University presented a program called "At the Edges of Europe: A Festival of Contemporary Greek and Irish Women's Poetry." It featured Eavan Boland, Medbh McGuckian and Katerina Angelaki-Rooke. During a panel discussion, Boland expressed her frustration with critics whose writing is so highly codified that the poets cannot understand what has been said about their own poems. Because poetry is "a language from the heart to the heart," she said, critics whose work lacks a concern for the poet's intention can in fact be hostile to her. The critical elite writing in this way places the poetic text itself in a position secondary to linguistic experimentation.

Yet poetry, especially as created by a personal and mystical writer like Medbh McGuckian, is highly codified as well. Some readers have been frustrated by what seems to be obscurity and impenetrability in McGuckian's work. Ironically, some of the best "sense" has been made of her poems by the sort of post-modernist critics that Boland found frustrating, including Susan Porter (*Canadian Journal of Irish Studies* 1989) and Clair Wills of the University of Essex, who presented one of the papers at the Festival. Both of these critics find a post-modern aesthetic at work in McGuckian. Even as I admired Wills's paper, however, I agreed with Boland that the poet's intention matters for interpretation and that criticism needs clarity.

Medbh McGuckian was much gentler than Boland toward her critics. In an interview at the end of the Festival, she expressed an awed gratitude toward her readers: "I have been so generously treated; I've had so much feedback. All I've written has been in between my children, in the time left over from the process of living and having children and trying to be a person. But the attention I've been given has been amazing. I couldn't say that anyone has been less understanding than they should have been." Still, she said, "I get mad when (the critical piece) actually is a cold one and has a chilling effect. I don't care what words they use as long as they use them with sensitivity.

. . . Maybe this is where a love for the actual text is missing. When they say they admire the text, maybe they don't, really." She also insisted that the critic's task may well be to protect the poem and the poet who places herself in an extremely delicate and vulnerable position. For this reason, McGuckian's critics need to try to write with as great sensitivity as possible, and to try to emulate the poet's own humility.

Far from reveling in obscurity, McGuckian wants people to understand her poetry. She read from her new book, *Marconi's Cottage*, which has the same absolute "rightness" of language that characterizes her previous books. Yet upon first encounter it seemed to be more readily accessible than her others. Most helpful during the Festival, perhaps, were what McGuckian called "information packets" or "notes" which she supplied as she read each poem. The new book includes a poem called **"Candles at 3:30."** She introduced the poem by explaining that she composed it in her cottage at Ballycastle Beach, which lacks both water and electricity. She wrote this poem at the change to Daylight Savings Time, "when everything suddenly is later or earlier." In this poem, she further explained, the sea gull is her mother and the sea is death. She had been told that her mother had six months to live, although she insisted: "My mother will live forever—physically, mentally, spiritually, everything else." She told us that the same theme occurs in **"Story Between Two Notes."** After giving this poem its title, she said that she learned a curious fact about the cry of the Banshee "which is what people hear when people are going to die." Someone who had heard it told her that the sound is "kind of between one and two notes."

The reference to the Banshee brings to mind, of course, W. B. Yeats's wonderful poem, "The Hosting of the Sidhe," and the question of McGuckian's relationship to him and to her Irish legacy, as well as the nature of her own private mysticism. I asked her about her relationship to Yeats by saying, "Four images—the moon, the apple, the house, the garden—are all images that I've seen again and again in Yeats. A lot of your critics have said that these are the images of a *female* poet, especially the house and the garden. But I see you and Yeats sometimes using these in images in much the same way. In the interview with you in *The Irish Literary Supplement* (Fall 1990), you said you saw yourself as existing 'somewhere on the Tree of Poetry on the same limb as Blake and Yeats, but many phone calls below them.' Did you intend just the mystical element, or also the house and garden as common ground with Yeats?"

She responded, "I would love to feel that Yeats and I have some connection. Wherever Yeats is, if he's aware of me at all, I would hope that he wouldn't be ashamed of me. I find him a difficult figure to relate to because he's so intimidating. I mean, his poems are *perfect*. He was overwhelmingly magical and again, if he hadn't been there, Heaney wouldn't be, and if Heaney hadn't been there, I wouldn't be. I feel that there is a continuum between Yeats and me through Heaney. But the house and garden I feel—his relationship with houses was of his time. And the house to him was a protected and threatened Big House. It was the house of English plantation, and when I think of Coole Park not being there (and the house is not there, this beautiful big one)—I feel it's a terrible indictment of the state of things, that this beautiful place where *he* wandered isn't there any more. But I was in Lissadell, in a room where he had slept. And it was a tremendously satisfying thing, although he was just a lodger. I mean, he was always a lodger, Yeats, and that's what I feel—the loneliness of Yeats. And for so much of his life he had no home, and it was only when he got to be fifty that he had even a home. If I touch upon houses and gardens due to him, as I've previously used them, I hope he doesn't feel I'm encroaching. What one poet owes to another is immeasurable—I mean it's indescribable." She continued on the topic of houses, "Yes, it's the loss of the farm. Heaney hasn't got houses and gardens because he has a farm. Maybe Yeats and I are deprived of something that he has."

The Catholic background which McGuckian shares with Heaney, certainly, sets both of them apart from Yeats. In the year that Heaney was fifty years old, McGuckian told me, she had a "huge emotional need to write a poem to Seamus, because he's Catholic, and because he is always a marvel, and because he's just a warm and tremendous personality." She had alluded to the significance of her being a Catholic poet in the interview with *The Irish Literary Supplement*, but although the mysticism in her poetry is one of its most pronounced features, I wanted to know more about the way it could be understood as specifically Catholic. She had provided a hint when she spoke about her frustrated desire to be a priest in that interview. In the reading, too, she shared a poem called **"Almond,"** which was about a priest friend of hers and quipped, "I've always wanted to be a priest, and actually some day I will be." It was hardly surprising, then, that when I asked her about the Catholic nature of her poetry, she described the priesthood of the poet.

She said, "I thought that I wanted to do something that would give people who couldn't relate to the Church something that would still give them a sort of consolation, and so I very much see that when I write a poem, that it is a spiritual—not adventure but—I feel that I am not even writing the poem. I sometimes feel that—I shouldn't use the word 'God,' but that some creative force is writing the poems through me. That is why all this talk about my 'importance' really makes me sick, because I feel all I am is a vehicle for the 'Importance' itself, with a capital 'I.' And so, if there is a priest-like function, it's one of just being a window, and you are nothing—you yourself are something that is seen through. I don't talk about myself, or I erase my experience. I mean, why should anyone be interested in me at all? I have nothing to give them but a way of entering this 'beyond' that speaks through me. But, again, even that is arrogant, even to say that is too much. All you are hoping for is that you might in some vague way aspire to that, you know? To be a medium for the Truth, or for whatever the priest is doing." That is to say, McGuckian sees the act of making a poem as sacramental.

As well as knowing that the poet's spirituality has its origin in Catholicism, the question remains: are there specifically Catholic themes and images in her poems? I lack an "information packet" to validate this observation, but I do see a Catholic basis for some of McGuckian's imagery about birth and maternity. I am speaking about mysticism rather than doctrine and about a sub- (or super-) conscious narrative behind certain poems which appears to be Marian. One such poem is **"Girls in the Plural"** from *On Ballycastle Beach*. In this poem a woman's voice speaks in traditional images about love, poetry and birth. In the first stanza she compares the summer roses to a woman. Summer's end fits "over the shoulders / And breasts of separating roses. . . ." The comparison of roses and breasts is traditional; but to say that roses *have* breasts and shoulders is startling. That "no one / Was passing the window" implies that the vision to follow is intimate and secret. Inside the window, a woman lets a letter lie for a whole year, and she compares herself to "one who had never given herself to him, / But found herself with child. . . ." This child is a spiritual being, a "thoughtless wind that grew in her / like some deflowered ghost." She "frittered / Away" the experience; in the next stanza she has "Lost days" as the child grows, as "far away / Cells were ordered otherwise." Then the woman in the poem becomes a poet who makes up "That simile about his eyes awakening," which seems to refer both to the child and his father. She has "ransacked the world" for an angelic presence, "for stained / Wings of the same possessive fabric. . . ." The angel and the mystical child together suggest Mary and Jesus, as the following line with its imagery of "flight" recalls their flight into Egypt. The woman in the poem insists, however, upon her difference and expresses a political and Irish sentiment, refusing the notion that any of her "removals / Was in any sense a flight—." She describes the birth of her son as "a new caress / . . . unmixed / with the round poems, the edged tools, / Pressing like a damaged cloud against the doors." Finally, her son or lover—or both—are separated from her, "Elsewhere," and she experiences a loss of what is rightfully hers in the separation: "he / Breathed in the air that belonged to me." The poem is not about the Virgin Mary, but her story provides a frame of reference for it.

At the time that she wrote *On Ballycastle Beach*, McGuckian had three sons, and yet she greatly desired a daughter. The poems in *Marconi's Cottage* include some about both her new daughter, Emer, and her mother. When I talked with her she said, "Having Emer was the best thing that has ever happened to me. When she was born, I felt that I would not die now. I guess that's very simplistic, because I had three sons, and my God they are adorable and beautiful and wonderful. But I just felt it was so much a gift. I had her very late when I had lost all hope I would ever have a daughter. All my poems before I had her, and even when I was expecting the little boys, right through from becoming pregnant the first time—had this deep, deep, deep, DEEP sense of wanting a daughter. Maybe because my relationship with my own mother was so unphysical, and I wanted a daughter so that I could give her this total love. I know my mother loves me, but she had so many, and she had such a harsh physical life herself, that the physical side of things was not intense. I phoned there a few hours ago, and my husband said, 'Here's Emer.' I said, 'Oh, let me talk to her.' He said she was kissing the phone. I thought, 'Well! to have a little creature of my own that is kissing the phone!' I just love that. It has expanded me and given me insight, and it's made me look at my own mother in a healthier way. I feel I am now equal to my mother in a way. I feel so enriched by having Emer that it's hard to even talk about." Certainly her passion to have a daughter for the sake of her own wholeness couldn't be further removed from Yeats's attitude in "Pardon, Old Fathers" toward his own lack of a son: he wanted a boy primarily to fulfill a duty owed his male ancestors.

I commented to McGuckian that her new poems have a fresh clarity as well as the new mother-daughter themes. The titles of the poems are no less daunting, though; when she told the audience that the title of her priest-poem was **"Almond,"** everyone laughed knowingly. I asked her about **"Balakhana"** from *On Ballycastle Beach* as an example. She explained: "Sometimes the title is like a label for me, but **"Balakhana"** was a record of a visit to Yugoslavia. So each poem is a record, and each poem is labeled according to the event. I will probably go home and write a poem about being in Columbia, but it won't be called 'Being in Columbia.' It will be called—I don't know yet. It will probably have some title that will not be in any way related to the real thing. But the 'Balakhana' was." She said that one Russian poet "was in exile and for a short time in Turkey, so I just used the word to sort-of link up with her. The title is a place where I can be really powerful and isolate and bring two, three or four things together in a single word. Maybe that's what makes them very difficult, because they're trying to contain a whole wealth of references."

The titles, of course, are not the only difficult places in McGuckian's work. I told her, "Usually, I will read the first stanza of any one of your poems and find it clear. After that, it's as if you take the image and push it to its uttermost. It's as if, maybe, the image goes beyond the initial experience and begins to weave itself out in more than one direction at once, and maybe it will have three or four different—"

She said, "Like a potter's vase."

"Or," I asked, "like a tree sprout that comes up from the trunk, and then all of a sudden has different limbs going different ways. Is that accurate?"

She said, "That's perfect. Because the poem has its own life. It starts as a seed with one word, two words together. And they bring four words, and then the four words bring eight words, and it is like a mathematical progression. It does go out of control, I know."

The **"Balakhana"** poem is a case in point. The first stanza clearly draws the speaker's memory of a place where she has camped, an image of a circle of caravans, and

compares remembering that to remembering a town. The first stanza links with the second in two ways. The rhyme of "town" and "sound" in the first lines of the two stanzas is reinforced by the contrast between the single word cried out in the caravan scene and the "metallic" noises of the town, or really city by this point: "elevators at night," "a car / Stopping outside, a plane throwing herself / Forward into space." Then the speaker who is the poet or very nearly the poet tells how the experience of the journey, or of "The door I found / So difficult to close" opened her to her first experience of Europe which "now blows about, / A cream-colored blossom, with a blue vigor." Colors and blossoms appear, which are symbols in her private mythology. Blossoms are erotic expressions of beginnings and possibility; the "blue vigor" recalls the **"Blue Sky Rain"** of the *Venus and the Rain* poems. And sure enough, in the next stanza, "rains," "the burning hours of the day" and a "giant upright cloud" all appear. The rain, clouds, sun and clothing are all familiar images of fertility in McGuckian's poetry, and the next stanza is tied to this one both by speaking directly of the sun and of women in labor. The stanza also goes back to the Yugoslavian landscape. "That flap of earth," which appears to be a mountain range, "leaned against the sun / As women lean their faces to the wall / Giving birth." The wild landscape, fertility and its conclusion, and the wall of a building are all united in these complex lines. The image of mountains dominates this stanza, with their smells and powerful shapes. Finally the image becomes mythic as mountain heights strike "sphere after sphere of sparks." The sparks have political significance as well, referring to war and violence.

McGuckian said that this poem was written to a male Cypriot poet whom she met in Yugoslavia. It is about coming together with European culture, but it is also about him, "how in Cyprus he'd lost his family house and the Turks had taken over his land, and so he'd had that kind of colonization. There is anger in his work, but he was such a soft and unangry person." Then the next stanza of the poem returns to personal images of domestic life in Ireland, "tea with smoked milk" and of mother-hood, "the stone / In the fruit, the meaning, the child / That left me no ground." In this sharp-edged picture of maternity, the child takes her ground as the child/lover breathes her air in **"Girls in the Plural."** From a window, she sees the sky again, but this time it becomes "a sword half / Out of its scabbard, and suddenly / Filled like a glass with wine." The evocative image of the wine represents a transformation of what all three of them—the male and female poets and the sword—have "drunk in" from their mountainsides: "More than one stormy sunset, and more / Than blood."

The final stanza of the poem branches out in yet another direction with the speaker's prayer that "the moon, / Meant only for the moment, / Would have it in him / To go on as beautifully as he had begun." This re-visioning of mythology reveals the poet's generosity as well as her expansive imagination. In the interview she said, "That is a tribute to the masculinity of the poet. It was like saying, 'Go on, write your poetry,' to him, and 'You have as much right to be the moon as I have,' in that he was in touch with feminine cycles. And I felt that there was a European dimension that did respect the female, that did respect nature in a way that I hadn't known before, so it was just a way of saying that." Thus in the final stanza the poet expresses her new experience of Europe again in an increasingly mythic way. She has taken up the traditional image of the moon, which Yeats used so powerfully in his later poems and in *A Vision*, and stretched the image beyond any previous imagining of it. Image branches into image in his poetic granddaughter's poem, and she finally even transforms a symbol of female creativity—and coldness—into one of masculine creativity and warmth.

Another poem that we discussed in terms of its symbolism was **"The Bird Auction."** She began with the title. "The word 'auction' is an old-fashioned word for me. My mother lived in the markets area of Belfast, and her mother was always going to auctions. So the word 'auction' is part of my childhood. But I wanted to imply in **'The Bird Auction'** a reference to Russian lifestyle. One of the Russian poets talked about going to a bird auction, and it reminds me of that. There are always these associations for me. My husband loves parrots, and he buys budgies and canaries. And I hate it; I hate the little things in cages. There's always that kind of dilemma in trapping beauty. When he comes in with this little thing in a cage, the last one having died or been eaten, it seems to me that it is a symbol of poetry, because you've captured something, but by capturing it you've tied it down, and it's not free. So **'The Bird Auction'** as an idea was tragic—as if I am a poet selling beauty at auction. And the thing with Ireland being up for grabs. So it is a very political poem, that one."

This poem, like **"Girls in the Plural,"** begins with an image of nature reimagined as a woman, but the image is harsher—dark trees "give a black kiss" with "lips well-reddened." Then the poet sketches an indoor scene, "the women's side of the chapel, "where the women are set apart under "blood-coloured glass." Here is, of course, another glimpse into the way that McGuckian's Catholic identity influences a poem. The next two stanzas show a woman opening a bright yellow and green umbrella before the fire, "Like a girl in a satin dinner dress." These are prettier images, apparently unrelated to the reddened lips of the treewomen or the bloody light of the chapel, although even the bright umbrella is a little bleak, since "the sun never got into" it. A new scene opens in the middle of the fourth stanza. In an outdoor but still-contained patio, "They are hanging sheets over doorways, / Keeping them wet with chloride of lime." This is a portrait of plague and sickness; now the reader knows why the women were in the chapel, where "Each stain reaches the eye / Unweathertight." They are praying for divine help against an invisible and terribly powerful foe. Then the poems turns to two men and significant places in their lives. The first is O'Neill, a political exile, and the castle where he "slept / His last night in Ireland. . . ." The Earl of Tyrone, Hugh O'Neill, was one of the earls of Ulster who went into voluntary exile in 1607, having signed the Treaty of Mellifont with the English in 1603. The English domination of Ulster had begun, and the ter-

rible Articles of Plantation would be published just two years later. A person on the brink of exile appears frequently in Irish poetry, and the poignancy of the image in this poem is enhanced by its juxtaposition with "the view at which Byron / Never tired of gazing." Yet Byron's good fortune in being able to look time and again at his beloved view ends in pathos as well. His valuables are being sold at auction, even "His too rich words. . . ." The words of the poet are as vulnerable as the lands of the patriot or the lives of women and those they love.

I asked McGuckian about the ending of the poem, a one-line stanza, "As I sat forgetting it." She responded, "It's about the news reels and my feeling of guilt that I am a part of all this, I am implicated in all this violence. And yet I sit there and I don't attend to it. I make sure that I survive. I don't go out. I don't stand in the streets and bewail and protect. I make sure that I survive—I guess because of the instinct to survive. Just this fear that I am feeding off and making a beauty out of something that is suffering. And 'so many / Fragrant and delicious souvenirs'—that is a terrible irony, a reference to disease and cholera and epidemics. There is a lot about my grandmother in the poem, and a lot about death. It's a poem that frightens me. As if life was a burden. As if we're all given these little souls in these little bodies, and the cage is the body; and yet when the cage is gone, is the bird totally unprotected then? Or is the whole point having the cage? I don't know."

McGuckian's poetry is intensely passionate, full of longings, fears, sufferings and—most of all—love. I told her that the poems in **On Ballycastle Beach** often seem to me to be love poems, but that I have a hard time discerning the identity of the beloved person. She replied, "I often have one individual in mind, that I loved absolutely for the space of that poem. And I have a lot of problems worrying about whether that is a betrayal. You know, because in the space of it I loved the person so totally when I wrote it, then as soon as the poem is finished, that love goes. And there are all the different kinds of love. With my immediate family—I always feel that if I am writing about my mother or my father, or my husband or children, nobody can quarrel with me, that I am allowed to love this person and I am *allowed* to write this poem. But it is so difficult. . . . There are a great number of people." **"The Rose Trellis,"** a poem from **Marconi's Cottage** that she read the evening before, had been written to someone with whom she had been discussing poetry on the phone. She said, "I wrote the poem thinking about what he had said, and the poem was a conversation with him. But not a love poem, although I felt it was important to say in this poem that he inspired it. So when I finished the poem, my first reaction was to send it to him. So I did, and I said, 'I wrote this poem after we were on the phone and because of what you were saying. And you are really a very sound person. I wanted you to have this poem.' It's very often right to other poets. . . . What I find peculiar is, why don't I write more poems to more people? Why do I choose one person rather than another? I think that if I could open myself to all the different people and poets, then that would be something I would really want."

This desire for a poetry that is ever-widening in its love and openness to people in general and poets in particular has to do with her "cosmology" of the poetic phenomenon. She said, "I think it's only one poet, you see. One poet may be as bright as a star in this constellation of whatever we are doing—no, we're not even doing—this configuration of—it's like Hopkins' 'look at the stars, look, look and see the diamond cylindars,' and all that." I asked her about Venus, the planet she appropriated in her second book. She said, "Venus—if I've found Venus as a ground—just for a while—maybe Venus is my star. Influences and relationships and effects—it's just going on all the time. Even as you're experiencing it, you don't want to express it; it's so delicate you would break it to speak about it, you know?"

McGuckian now has four significant collections—*The Flower Master*, *Venus and the Rain*, *On Ballycastle Beach*, and *Marconi's Cottage*—and several chapbooks. As well as her three most recent books, we discussed *Two Women, Two Shores* (1989), which contains poems by McGuckian and Nuala Archer. McGuckian's part, **"Blue Farm,"** is a group of poems that she calls "rejects," but, she continues, "they were still poems that I believed in. They are not in any particular order, but I do think they have a validity in that book. I love that wee book. I love that more than maybe the others." It contains her first poem which she kept, called **"Aunts,"** a delightful and simple piece which nevertheless suggests the direction her writing will take as she matures. The poem ends evocatively, "I caught them dancing on the bed, / With their undergrowth of hazel, / And their make-up sweated through." As she goes on, she hopes that people will see: "My first book is about flowers, a very innocent book, which kind of talks about sex and flowers—and the second talks about birth, with having experienced birth. The first one is about sex, the second one is about birth. To use metaphors like animal, vegetable, mineral—progression, or the Chain of Being as the medieval talk about it—I hope I'm going up a ladder from vegetable and mineral and animal. I don't talk about animals; I think that's the one thing that distresses me. Why have I no animals? And no one ever says to me, 'But you have no animals!' I don't have animals, and that's my big loss. But I can't have everything; my babies are my animals, I guess." We laughed, and I said, "And birds." She agreed, "And birds. I love birds, but I'm not too good on them either."

"But then I feel I'm going animal, vegetable, mineral through *Ballycastle Beach*; Ballycastle Beach is the name of a town and still on that level of naming things. The new one I see has a house in it, which is a human place, a human thing, and a man's name which is a human name and conjures up all Europe and all his achievement, his discovery and his fantastic inventiveness. So when we're going up the ladder—the next stage from that—I think I'll stay on the human level for a little while, then go on up to angels and devils and stuff." We laughed again. Then she said, "I worry that if I die young—I don't mean young, but if I die before Yeats's great age of wisdom—that people won't judge me saying, 'Well, she didn't get up there.' I should have got up there by thirty-three, you

know. You're supposed to get up there by thirty-three, aren't you?"

I said to her, "Yeats really 'got there' in his last poems, including 'The Black Tower,' which of course he wrote while he was dying." McGuckian replied, "Well, that frightens me, too; you feel that when you're dying you shouldn't sort of be holding onto these lesser things. . . . What I'm concerned about is, I know during these next ten years that I'll have a lot of testing things. I've had such a lovely life up to this. And I like to feel I could with courage record or live through the way Heaney has done, the way Heaney has assimilated the death of his parents and all. He has not flinched, he has not collapsed, he has not depressed us. He has taken those deaths and made life out of them. I feel this will be a great test of my integrity, which I'm not sure I'm going to be able to pass. . . . But this is the consolation: to write a poem, and feel I'm not writing the poem, that a creative force is writing the poem through me as a vehicle, the priest-like function of entering this beyond, though even saying *that* is arrogant."

WORKS CITED

McGuckian, Medbh. *On Ballycastle Beach*, Oxford UP, 1988.

————. *Venus and the Rain.* Oxford UP, 1984.

Steven Matthews (essay date 1994)

SOURCE: A review of *The Flower Master and Other Poems*, in *TLS*, April 15, 1994, p. 26.

[*In the following review, praises the revised poems comprising this edition of McGuckian's* The Flower Master.]

Medbh McGuckian's poetry studiously and notoriously resists paraphrase. It is protective towards its influences and origins, being concerned to present the essence of experience rather than its surface events. This is poetry full of the weather, flowers, the seasons, trees, earth, water, the sun, the moon, shifting light. Images of the familial, of nurture and fructification predominate.

Our experience of reading the poems is of witnessing a phrase or image exfoliate from the previous one. We are shown "Tricks [we] might guess from this unfastened button, / A pen mislaid, a word misread", and are left guessing, as the poem continues to hold the hiding-places of its fertility to itself. From line to line, from poem to poem, from collection to collection, McGuckian plays complex variations around and through her essential themes in an ever-open, playful, continuing exploration of nuance and possibility. The slightly hallucinatory quality of the writing; the sense of wandering from image to image, almost from sentence to sentence; the sense of slippage between images and sentences: all leave the relation between poem and world suggestively tenuous yet full of potential.

The revisions in this new edition of her first collection, **The Flower Master** (1982), confirm the intensity and coherence of McGuckian's poetic preoccupations and method throughout the past twelve years. Not only are there poems here which did not appear in the original edition, but twelve of the poems which appeared there have now been dropped. In the process, **The Flower Master** has become a much tighter, more concentrated book; nearly all of the poems now engage with floral imagery, either as generating idea, or metaphorical resource. The repositioning of poems which originally stood on their own as part of mini-sequences in this new version only furthers the sense of accumulation and concentration among and between the various parts of the book. McGuckian's are poems which always work through dialogue, the one with the other, and the addition of seventeen poems which did not appear in the first version of the collection sharpens the book's range of tones and adds a welcome note of scepticism towards its presiding theme.

The book's revised dedication, "for my mother without my father", indicates the centre of **The Flower Master**'s concerns, a concentration on the female and the poet's own move through a sense of adolescent potential and exuberance to the attainment of adult love. But even this narrative remains subliminal, oblique. The idea of the flower master that oversees the collection establishes its language of flowers as the language of both the poet's and the poetry's sources. As the title poem has it, here, "We learn the coolness of straight edges, how / To stroke gently the necks of daffodils / And make them throw their heads back to the sun."

There could be something complaisant about the way such descriptions can always be made to stand as metaphors for the manner and method of the poetry, however, and it is virtue of some of the new poems that they bring a heightened level of self-consciousness, which allows such slippages around notions of organicism to be questioned. In **Gladiolus"**, we are told that this flower's "only aim" is "the art / of making oneself loved"; in **"Spring"**, a poem which lends weight to the uneasy, frustrated adolescence in the book's early poems, the narrator rises from bed "To stare at the February moon. // . . . My breathing marbled the pane: / There was my face in the window, / Frosted, so hard to see through." This is an opaqueness which is alert to the dangers of self-regard in any mastery of image and form, and it enlivens the note of protectiveness which continues in other of the additional poems. "No one knows what goes on inside a clock", the last line of **"My Mother"** tells us; it is the achievement of this new edition of **The Flower Master** that it manages to make McGuckian's continued sense of the untranslatability of the sources of nurture more concentrated, but also more various and more questionable than it was in the book's original form.

Peter Sirr   (essay date 1995)

SOURCE: "How Things Begin to Happen," in the *Southern Review*, Vol. 31, Issue 3, July 1995, pp. 450-67.

[*In the following excerpt, Sirr examines the defining characteristics of McGuckian's poetry.*]

Medbh McGuckian is a much more problematic figure [than Eiléan N Chuilleanáin]. Her work resolutely refuses most of the norms readers have come to take for granted: an identifiable lyric centre, an underlying controlling voice speaking the lines and reining the images into an articulate shape, a narrative discipline. Here's a poet altogether looser, more perplexing, and it's probably fair to say that no contemporary Irish poet is as cautiously celebrated as McGuckian, as readers struggle to accommodate her lush and elusive rhetoric to their notions of where poems should properly go. It's not so much that she is obscure as that her reference points are usually out of sight, and the compass that could guide us through a thousand lyrics spins uselessly here.

The question of "obscurity" in poetry is naturally a fraught one. One reader's obscurity is another's clarity, after all. But it also raises the issue of the nature of the expectations a reader brings to bear upon a poem. These will depend among other things on his or her experience of reading: a reader immersed in Eliot, Stevens, Dickinson, Hopkins, Yeats, Kinsella, Muldoon, or Ashbery will have a great deal less trouble coping with McGuckian than someone who has never strayed from the rationalist-discursive tradition.

Nonetheless, it's true that all discussion of McGuckian begins with her difficulty: it is not a task for the faint-hearted to decipher or paraphrase a McGuckian poem. One view would explain her "dreaminess" as somehow female; i.e., female poets are less rational than male ones, more receptive to powerful (if vague) currents of energy. This is a patronising view of McGuckian's art, and of women: that her poetry represents a female way of being in the world—disorderly, diffuse, eroticised. It's also a categorisation McGuckian is at pains to reject and that poem after poem actively confronts. Critics who reach, desperately, for "womanliness" forget that her approach is as remarkable within the tradition of poetry produced by women as by men. To look at poetry by women here is to be reminded how much it shares with that by men: only in terms of subject-matter can it be said to differ, and that is never the crucially determining factor in the success of a poem. Think for example of Eavan Boland: what is most immediately striking about her work is the dominating authority of the voice, the controlled articulation of it. Her poetry and McGuckian's lie at opposite poles: one clear and commanding, the other abjuring precisely that kind of lyric clarity and control.

So how does McGuckian work? The poems are characterised by an unexpected connectedness between images as the imagination seems to cede control to mood-logic. They often proceed by unlikely analogy, so that, for instance, the two ends of a typical simile are like lengths of a cut rope, the comparative bit drifting down into a cloudy stream of succeeding, and seceding, conceits. She can have windows swing "Like the sickled gladiolus, swell your house / As Ireland's tiny mountains load her breast /

Like a necklace," elephants hold their tusks "like champagne," or a house have "perfect teeth," the "running water of its lovemaking / . . . pickled in silence." By the time one gets to the end of the chain the original referent no longer matters as much as it might in other poets. A different purpose is being served: the images are not there to elucidate but to detonate and resonate in all their weird energy. It's a mesmerisingly fluid poetry, its edges blurred, its voices half-inviting, half-challenging us to enter their paradigms of power and desire. If the poetry seems drenched in the observable natural world—and McGuckian constantly names and particularises—it's a world held together by a commanding rhetoric and an endlessly metamorphosing imagination.

The Flower Master is her most accessible book (any reader daunted by McGuckian's reputation might begin with **"Aunts," "The Seed-Picture," "The Soil-Map," "The Flitting,"** (the title poem), and the recently published new edition offers several poems omitted from the original and some alterations to others. The new or restored poems form a useful bridge into the familiar work and also throw light on the way this poet's imagination is shaped. **"Smoke,"** the opening poem, is concerned with control, as can be seen in its image of burning whins: "They seem so sure what they can do. / I am unable even / To contain myself, I run / Till the fawn smoke settles on the earth." That sense of being unable to contain herself informs the poetry throughout, and gives it its distinctive expansiveness. **"Slips"** is about the kinds of slippages and blurrings that cause things to tumble into each other, one word to slide into another, about the kind of compulsive imaginative fluidity that makes the poet "forget names, remembering them wrongly/ Where they touch upon another name, / A town in France like a woman's Christian name." The poem, with its blurrings and imagistic quirks and "tricks," can be read as an apologia for a poetry that is both sharply specific and strangely undefined, and whose dynamic is insistently sexual:

> I see my grandmother's death as a piece of ice,
> My mother's slimness restored to her,
> My own key slotted in your door—
> Tricks you might guess from this unfastened button,
> A pen mislaid, a word misread,
> My hair coming down in the middle of a
>   conversation.

From her grandmother's death to the unfastened button and cascading hair is a typical McGuckian trip. It's not just that the poems are charged with erotic imagery, but that her imagination beats with a sexual pulse. It's an imagination that fastens on tulips as an image of cold sexual restraint, displaying a "grocery of soul," though still susceptible, "like all governesses," to sudden release:

>   . . . their absent faces
> Lifted many times to the artistry of light—
> Its lovelessness a deeper sort
> Of illness than the womanliness
> Of tulips with their bee-dark hearts.

The natural world is always sexual, but its sexuality is curiously genderless: sex in McGuckian is always also metaphor for a benign, neutral imaginative space. In **"The Orchid House,"** McGuckian moves among her flowers, half-mistress, half-slave, as she secures them in the grip of her dreamy attention.

> A flower's fragrance is a woman's virtue;
> So I tell them underground in pairs,
> Or in their fleshy white sleeves, how
> Desirable their shapes . . .
>
>   . . . . .
>
> In my alpine house, the slavery I pay
> My wilful gentians, exploring all their pleats
> And tucks as though they had something precious
> Deep inside, that beard of camel-hair
> In the throat.

Or, again,

> The begonia's soil is rich and wet.
> I tuck it in around her
> As I would pat my hair,
> Straightening her tubered root.
> We keep our sources secret-she
> Swells with lymph and electricity,
> Her fibres transparently taped up, and I
> Sprout willowy as any sweet begonia.

One notices immediately that these flowers embody both male and female characteristics. The poet may seem to serve her "wilful gentians" passively, yet they quickly assume a more submissive demeanour, and the poet's actions are like those of a male lover. Similarly, the poet moves from the control-drama in which she seems again to assume a male role, firming the begonia's soil and so on, to the final sisterly alignment of her sexual desire with the flower's. The poems often plot a conflict between control and release, usually visualised in erotic terms, which the language incessantly acts out. The flower master in the poem of that title husbands a prettily enclosed world:

> Like foxgloves in the school of the grass moon
> We come to terms with shade, with the principle
> Of enfolding space. Our scissors in brocade,
> We learn the coolness of straight edges, how
> To stroke gently the necks of daffodils
> And make them throw their heads back to the sun.

As the poem develops, its images of sweet control lead to an allegory of sexual expectation:

> This black container calls for sloes, sweet
> Sultan, dainty nipplewort, in honour
> Of a special guest, who summoned to the
> Tea ceremony, must stoop to our low doorway,
> Our fontanelle, the trout's dimpled feet.

In **"Venus and the Sun,"** the speaker appears as a figure both controlling and controlled, thrown by "[t]he scented flames of the sun" that instruct her "how to move," but at the same time issuing orders: "I tell them / How to bend the light of shifting stars: / I order their curved wash so the moon / Will not escape. . . ."

One of the surprising aspects of McGuckian's work, given its density and its habitual state of cool reverie, is the directness of the poems' address. Again and again they engage a "you" whose identity is never clarified, but whose presence impels the poem. Sometimes reading McGuckian's poems there is a sense that they were at some stage in composition straightforwardly personal, but the confessional circumstances have been removed. Hers is a poetry of occasion whose occasions are meticulously withheld. The presence of an addressee certainly adds to the drama of the poem, even if it is an occluded drama:

> Since I was child enough to forget
> That you loathe poetry, you ask for some—

About nature, greenery, insects, and, of course,

> The sun—surely that would be to open
> An already open window? To celebrate
> The impudence of flowers? If I could
> Interest you instead in his large, gentle stares,
> How his shirt is the inside of pleasure
> To me . . .

This is from "The Sofa," and we can see how the poem's urgency depends on its mysterious and intimate dramatic context, the three people involved. We notice also how McGuckian is using the sexual context of the poem to define her poetics. She doesn't want to open any open windows; she mocks the kind of twee lyrics the addressee clearly wants. The added irony is of course that her poetry is saturated with the things she is refusing, with nature, greenery, insects, the sun, but not in a way that would be much use to the addressee. Mysteriousness is a longestablished part of the equipment of love poetry, and McGuckian's work is almost always, on some level, love poetry. Sometimes these "you" poems are also those in which the poet confronts her poetics (an insistent need in McGuckian) as well as the real or fictive addressee. This again has antecedents in the essentially male tradition that conflates love and Muse poetry. "Aviary" is one of those poems in which McGuckian examines her art with teasing lushness, and comes to no certain conclusions:

> Well may you question the degree of falsehood
> In my round-the-house men's clothes, when I seem
> Cloaked for a journey, after just relearning to walk,
> Or turning a swarthy aspect like a cache-
> Enfant against all men.

This seems to locate the drive of the poetry in a sexually indeterminate region and to link it with a childlike polymorphism. The addressee is a painter (identified in the companion piece, "Painter and Poet," as a man), and the poet defines herself in the light of his version both of the garden being "put . . . / To rights" and of her own nature:

"You call me aspen, tree of the woman's / Tongue, but if my longer and longer sentences / Prove me wholly female, I'd be persimmon, / And good kindling, to us both." She rejects the addressee's notion of a special female sensibility and instead moves towards an evocation of sexual fulfilment in which male and female are equal participants. The "both" at the end of that sentence specifically counters "woman's" three lines above. The poem that most explicitly blurs gender is "From the Dressing-Room," and since the strategies McGuckian employs here are those of the work as a whole, the poem will repay considerable attention:

> Left to itself, they say, every foetus
> Would turn female, staving in, nature
> Siding then with the enemy that
> Delicately mixes up genders. This
> Is an absence I have passionately sought,
> Brightening nevertheless my poet's attic
> With my steady hands, calling him my blue
> Lizard till his moans might be heard
> At the far end of the garden.

The difficulties here are familiar: the unclear nature of the addressee, the idiosyncrasies that belie the confidently declarative grammar. That "nevertheless," for example, implies a clarity of argumentative procedure that the poem has not really provided. The initial concept is clear enough: the femaleness of nature that would produce undifferentiated gender, and the poem's longing for that indeterminate state. The desire is no sooner articulated than modified radically, and the poet's hands enter the poem as a controlling force, giving pleasure but remaining "steady," as does the poem. The eroticism is notably temperate: the lover (if lover it is) might moan, but the poem moves coolly. The lines that follow record the poet's affection in a studiedly neutral manner: "For I like / His ways, he's light on his feet and does / Not break anything, puts his entire soul / Into bringing me a glass of water." She could be talking of a child here, the child who is careful not to break anything and can invest "his entire soul" into bringing her water. It is not, I should say, clear that we are talking about a lover. The tone suggests it, but McGuckian has gone to some pains to cloud his identity. We notice how abruptly he enters the poem: "calling him my blue / Lizard . . ." when he has not been referred to before. We notice that he is referred to with a kind of neutral eroticism; the figure is child and brother as well as, possibly, lover:

> I can take anything now, even his being
> Away, for it always seems to me his
> Writing is for me, as I walk springless
> From the dressing-room in a sisterly
> Length of flesh-coloured silk.

It's interesting how important to the poem is the devoted wholeness of attention afforded by the mystery man, or at least her perception that this is the case: it *seems* that he writes for her only. The poem is further complicated towards the end by the speaker's rhetorical address to (presumably) herself.

Oh there
Are moments when you think you can
Give notice in a jolly, wifely tone,
Tossing off a very last and sunsetty
Letter of farewell, with strict injunctions
To be careful to procure his own lodgings,
That my good little room is lockable,
But shivery, I recover at the mere
Sight of him propping up my pillow.

It's hard to determine what is happening here: the poem moves with a degree of sureness that might be in inverse proportion to its interpretability. It's often difficult to gauge the extent to which a McGuckian poem can be said to have developed or progressed: the poems are so resolutely non-linear that their constituent parts can seem interchangeable. What she creates in the reader is not a clear outline of a definable set of actions or emotions, but a state of associative fluidity: of very rich sense impressions conveyed with authoritative rhetoric in a framework of self-conscious artistry. McGuckian's poems get more complex as her career goes on. The demands she makes on the reader's willingness to yield to the peculiar processes of her imagination are greater in *On Ballycastle Beach* and *Marconi's Cottage*. I don't like everything she does, and there's a sense too that after protracted exposure to the work it sometimes becomes hard to tell one poem from another. This, though, is part of the risk she takes; her style is so distinctive, so recognisably her own, and so intricately linked with what she has to say to us that a certain amount of sameness is the price we pay. What we get in McGuckian's best work is an extraordinarily suggestive imagination operating on the language in ways that extend our notion of what a poem can do.

Mary O'Connor (essay date 1996)

SOURCE: "'Rising Out: Medbh McGuckian's Destabilizing Poetics," in *Eire-Ireland*, Winter, 1996, pp. 154-72.

[*In the following essay, O'Connor determines the manner in which the politics, history, and unique pressures of living in Northern Ireland influence McGuckian's poetry.*]

There are, indeed, clues in her poetry that Medbh McGuckian is an Irish woman, even a Belfast woman. One gathers them as the children in the Brothers Grimm folktale must have gathered the crumbs that guided them back home through the forest, for want of a clearly delineated path. We find Irish idiomatic expressions: "she gave it out that—"; "Live in the shelter of each other," a direct translation of the Gaelic saying *fé scáth a chéile a mhaireann na daoine*; "flitting," or vacating a flat without having paid the overdue rent. From history and mythology appear the poets of the bardic schools who "lie in the dark to compose / Verses as were taught"; Patrick, who comes to bless the house; Fergus, presumably the royal rival in the Queen Maeve story; Hugh O'Neill leading the

Flight of the Earls in 1609 after an almost successful rebellion; the 1916 Easter Rising; and, closer to home, appear the Belfast phenomena of checkpoints; of having soldiers occupy your house, of being frisked, of being conscious of "apartness." All these find their way into the poet's house of metaphor.

Other passing references to, for example, sickly weather, tiny mountains, "blue sky rain," "banding in volcanoes like potatoes," "the women's side of the chapel," bespeak the mental furniture, the particular lived experience which the Irish share. But it is not a physical country to which McGuckian gives her allegiance, or which is most deeply imprinted on her for her native town land is the territory of the unconscious, especially as it emerges into the subconscious in dreams. Like Seamus Heaney's "pioneers," she will strike "inward, downward,"[1] though not in their effortful, stalwart way, unearthing the makings of an identity from the prehistoric bogs. Rather, she will dissolve consciousness, volatilize the laws of logic—even as they apply to the ordering of a normal sentence—and let her poems "weather into meaning" as they will.

How may this Northern Irish writer, who is both a British subject and a Roman Catholic—and therefore, if she follows the stereotype, a Republican—situate herself in either conflicting tradition? McGuckian's choice has been to elide that question, to ignore the very obvious borders in her life, psychosocial and sociopolitical, breaking the rules in ways the establishment cannot punish her for. Her solution to the intense pressures of living in Northern Ireland has been a flight to the semiotic. Refusing questions of nationalism, McGuckian stakes her claims, in complex ways, to language, and to the encompassing power of the maternal body as paradigm for acts of inclusion.

Liam O'Dowd's account of his experiences as a lecturer in Queen's University, Belfast, throws light on the situation of Northern Irish writers, most of whom are graduates of Queen's, some of whom have taught there:

> [M]ost of my immediate colleagues at the University were English. While I saw the conflict against a backdrop of historical colonial conflict in Ireland, they knew little of that history and were seldom interested in it. . . . Our students, from both [Catholic and Protestant] communities, had suffered a type of enforced intellectual marginality. The conflict in which their families were embroiled was being represented to them by the media as irrational and incomprehensible, as a struggle between secular humanism and religious fanaticism, between peace and violence, even between good and evil. They had experienced an education system which, if it taught them any history, generally denied them their own. . . . The marginal role of moderates and intellectuals encourage them . . . to claim high ground "above" the conflict.[2]

It is clear that this syndrome has operated to different extents in the lives of Northern Irish poets, or even within the working career of the individual poet, and their responses have ranged from savage indignation to physical flight, from cautious interrogation to a retreat to the purely pastoral.

McGuckian's response is perhaps the least overt, the most subversive of any "politics of identity," to borrow David Lloyd's phrase. Could it be her feeling of powerlessness which mutes her response, an extension of the powerlessness she experiences in her life as a woman? She herself refuses such a deconstructive-feminist reading, saying, "I just don't think it makes good poetry, just condemning the things around you. So I try not to condemn in my poems." She also feels that "transitory" references would diminish the poem's long-term effect.[3] There are reasons to think, as I shall show, that McGuckian does indeed wish to be read as reconciling, forgiving—as containing those angry and disparate Northern energies within the maternal body of her unconscious, and, thence, of her poems. War, in this case, may remain the property of men.[4] But McGuckian's written response is so utterly different from that of her male colleagues because of her undermining of the authority of the Word. The problem, as Gilles Deleuze and Félix Guattari see it, is "how to tear a minor literature away from its own language, allowing it to challenge the language and making it follow a sober revolutionary path."[5] Medbh McGuckian has separated herself most naturally along the lines the poststructuralists describe. McGuckian manufactures a dream state by means of a dream language, heavily weighted with symbolic meaning, yet always at the threshold of logical discourse; she does this by inserting one thought or language pattern into another in order to disrupt structures of meaning. Though she works with almost stereotyped assumptions about masculine and feminine qualities, the overall effect of her poems eventually disturbs these conventional polarities. Her declared intention is to fragment the linguistic order, to disseminate dreams in a world of logic, to jilt "foursquare houses," to prise set notions "ever so gently apart."

Medbh McGuckian's poetry is not unapproachable, but it is necessary to sidle up to it with some humility and discretion. One of my own early avenues of approach was the painstaking charting of, for example, her use of the word "blue," or "light," or "house," and of its shifting meanings through succeeding collections; of the incidence of poems which had poetry as their subject, and those which spoke of the work of the poet through displacement or metaphor; and so on. I was patently the wrong kind of reader for anything even a touch avant-garde, but seeing patterns soothed my left-brain anxiety for order; and as I relaxed and let the music of McGuckian's ambiguous metonymy play independently of my constructions—or as independently as I could consciously allow—I learned to feast on textuality rather than "plot." My palate grew refined, I tasted subtle meanings, but practiced self-denial about asking what they meant in the ordinary scheme of things, and I was sometimes moved by engagement with non-narratives, for reasons I could not even explain to myself.

Taking my clues from the poems themselves, I started to speculate about what McGuckian believed she was doing

when she was writing poetry. Why, I asked, does the poet upturn syntactic conventions? It is clear that she is deliberately obfuscating: the speaker in **"The Return of Helen"** (*VR* 44) alerts us to

> the wrong turnings I make
> Myself take, till the path into my body
> And out of it again is a sea place
> Opening where you least expect.

The poet's project is similarly expressed in **"Hostel"** (*VR* 36), where the speaker wants a word to have "a hundred meanings, all of them / Secret." The poet, surely with a smile to the reader, goes so far as to have this voice declare that "[t]his oblique trance is my natural / Way of speaking" (*VR* 29).

Could it be that McGuckian renounces strict intelligibility in an effort to progress, in her own poet's way, beyond the limits set by a series of repressive colonizers of the mind? I refer to the closed Northern Irish society, the tribal demands of her church, the strictures of her excellent education within the patriarchy, the standards set by the university for its graduate students and teachers. The following passage from Julia Kristeva's essay on the semiotic and the symbolic makes clear the revolutionary effort involved. I have highlighted the guerrilla activity of Kristeva's verbs: "[A]rt specifies the means— the only means—that jouissance harbors for *infiltrating* [the social and symbolic] order . . . *cracking* the socio-symbolic order, *splitting* it open, *changing* vocabulary, syntax, the word itself, and *releasing* from beneath them the drives borne by vocalic or kinetic differences. . . . "[6] For all their quiet moods and gentle "diasporic" effects, it seems clear that McGuckian's poems are engaged in revolutionary action. But "I rock the boat in such a subtle way, they just sense it but they're not quite sure how to pin me down," she told me in a July, 1990, interview. She has in fact been rewarded many times—with prizes, with an appointment to be Queen's University's first female poet-in-residence—by the very establishment she wants to undermine with her subtle boat-rocking. Notably, McGuckian's audiences hardly ever react with outrage, anger, or complete bewilderment. In McGuckian's hands, each poem is "an act of astonishment."[7] And even in her most resistant, enigmatic pieces, as she says in **"Girls in the Plural,"** " . . . none of my removals / Was in any sense a flight—/ More the invention of a new caress" (*BB* 42).

And all is not chaos: the symbolic order holds the poetry together in carefully selected ways. McGuckian "breaks the rules" within the visual, and sometimes auditory, confines of ordered verse. Lines arrange themselves neatly against a left margin, solemn capitals at their head, into groups of eight, or six, or five. Though the rhythms may be loose, they are just, and do not stumble; one gets the feeling that McGuckian could do anything she wanted to do with her chosen instrument: from the smartass regularity of " . . . never / As compatible as Browning's troubled / Trochees to the house of salutation" in **"Another Son"** (*VR* 43) to the felicity of these lines from **"Har-**

vest," where assonance and rhythm work in blissful union to produce a *diminuendo* perfectly in tune with the subject: the ending of the day and its metaphorical extensions as falling, tapering rind and shredded poem, or vanishing foam—that part of the "sea" in "sea-poem" recalled by the whiteness of paper, and the position of foam as the sea's ecstatic articulation.

> I am the sky of a long day, working
> Out its twilight—how to make that steadily
> Impulsive blue taper off its solemn
> Rind, to fall like a sea-poem in shreds
> Between your fingers

It is true, too, that if her syntax does lead readers astray, there yet is much McGuckian seems to want them to understand. Certain key words accumulate meanings through McGuckian's four collections to form what appears to be developing as the poet's own system of signification. We shall pay special attention to the image of darkness, already by the second poem in *The Flower Master* particularized in its usage to describe the feminine, especially when joined to references to things South, under, below. This would seem to follow a mainline Freudian polarity criticized by feminists, except that this dark underneath place is not fearsome, blank, unknown, but rather sought, desired. And why? McGuckian implies an answer in many of her poems about poetry: the dark "room below" (*VR* 33) partakes of the characteristics of what Kristeva calls the "chora," from the Greek word for enclosed space or womb. As developed by Julia Kristeva from Plato's initial definition in *Timaeus,* this "nourishing, maternal" receptacle becomes a "dynamic charge," a "rhythmic space" which is presymbolic: it comes before, but is "always already" in relation to the symbolic. Kristeva describes this semiotic chora as "a wholly provisional articulation that is essentially mobile and constituted of movements and their ephemeral stases . . . it underlies figuration and . . . specularization, and . . . admits analogy with vocal or kinetic rhythm" (*RPL* 25, 26). The effect of this on poetry is that it "produces in poetic language 'musical' but also nonsense effects that destroy not only accepted beliefs and significations, but, in radical experiments, syntax itself."[8] Well, now, no wonder McGuckian would feel at home there.

But for Medbh McGuckian the maternal space is expressed in two ways, the second of which falls outside the parameters of Kristeva's theorizing. When she presents her female speaker as the womb, the house, the enclosed space, then the reader must consider what precious thing is carried, nurtured. Self? The dream? Identity? In the least metonymic reading, the child, in the ordinary way as "my fair copy" in **"Confinement"** (*VR* 42), or in more oppositional roles, as the split self, most often represented by speaker and sister, speaker and dream sister, speaker and artist's model.[9] Lastly, the speaker will contain her own bodily integrity, as seen in the speaker's resistance to the controlling, sculpting male hand in **"Head of a Woman"** (*OBB* 56) and in the pattern of references to shutting or locking the door to one's room. She is fully aware of sacrifices and selfabnegation of

such "pregnancies" and willing to bear and to repeat, for the seeds of the dream they nourish. Like "a cloud that never rains," McGuckian's speaker often becomes a model of the poet's work, maternally "not defecting," though occasionally "wanting to be rescued" (*VR* 39) from the burden of her commitment.

Despite her escape from the orthodoxies of the lyric, McGuckian's spiritual fathers, by her own admission and according to a variety of signs in her own work, are the English Romantics.[10] In his article on McGuckian and Paul Muldoon, "The Crabbed Genius of Belfast," Calvin Bedient says unhesitatingly that McGuckian "is the heir, however captious, of the Romantics."[11] He proves the point, in passing, by noticing her use of everyday diction and her references to some of their favorite subjects. She is also, like the Romantics, interested in formal experiment, though hers will appear in the breakdown of syntax rather than in the overthrowing of strict literary conventions. The Romantics crop up in other ways, too: the male speaker of **"Sabbath Park"**—McGuckian sometimes seems possessed by a Romantic animus—courts a Louisa with sonnets and wears a "fine lawn shirt" (*VR* 54). Sometimes she seems to be doing Pre-Raphaelite portraits of Romantic figures: the sleeping superman of **"Mazurka"** (*OBB* 22); the half-sister of **"The Sitting"** (*VR* 15) is superficially like the story of Margaret; it's what Wordsworth might have one of his women say.

"Coleridge" is an almost straightforward account of her debt to the poets of the Romantic Movement, and a tale of maturing responsibility to one's own voice. The poet describes the education of a poet by the masters:

> Very tightly,
> Like a seam, she nursed the gradients
> Of his poetry in her head,
> She got used to its movements like
> A glass bell being struck
> With a padded hammer.
>
>   (*OBB* 54)

Against that beat, the poet found her voice: "It was her own fogs and fragrances / That crawled into the verse." Not that she leaves Colelridge behind: the "master" poet is present like a husband, and between them they conceive something new which seems to be, if I am reading this properly, a loosing of her own creative energy, her expressiveness: in their intimacy, her "cold braids" find "Radiant escape,"

> as if each stanza
> Were a lamp that burned between
> Their beds, or they were writing
> The poems in a place of birth together.
>
>   (*OBB* 34)

A second step in the growth process can be catalyzed by the realization that one's idol has clay feet. Possibly the phrase "Quietened by drought" refers directly to Coleridge's own difficult later years: his last major poem,

"Dejection: An Ode," was written in 1802, and he died thirty-two years later, after long struggle with addiction and projects unstartable or unfinishable. But this change in the perception of the husband, mentor figure is introduced without anger or sadness, and even with a sort of protective kindness on the part of the speaker.

And so the woman poet finally leaves this place of birth, "easy / Easy," so as not to disturb the sleeping husband, and we—prepared by the rare, for McGuckian, use of "bloom" for flower in line three—hear Molly Bloom's five-times-repeated caution to herself as she leaves the bed in the final section of *Ulysses*. At this point in the novel, as we remember, Molly Bloom's particular concern is "not wake him have him at it again slobbering after washing every bit of myself back belly and sides."[12] If Molly Bloom is not there on purpose, at least she is echoing in McGuckian's head. Why does the poet recall her? Joyce's most successfully fleshed-out female creation never breaks free, for all the excursions she takes, from a somewhat unsatisfactory marriage. At the end of his wanderings, Bloom can come home to her, though she is not the purest version of Penelope. In fact, she is the sort of utterly ambiguous sign that most excited Joyce—a wife who breaks the rules. Nora Barnacle was faithful, by all accounts, but in the heady days of their courtship, Joyce was excited by her as an iconoclast of Victorian standards of propriety, when she would write scatalogical and erotic letters at his request. McGuckian may also see that breaking the rules of the patriarchy while still remaining in the marriage—agreeing to the use of the symbolic—is an effective compromise.

McGuckian's conclusion, her take on the poet's progress, has its own sweetness and warmth, not least that brought to the reader's senses by the poet's summoning up of the smell of fermented apples and the heat of the autumnal sun. Here are the last few lines of "Coleridge":

> If she stood up, easy,
> Easy, it was the warmth that finally
> Leaves the gold pippin for the
> Cider, or the sunshine of fallen trees.
>
>   (*OBB* 34)

On a second reading, we discover the verb "leaves," and the adjective "fallen," and understand the serious import of the images: independent thought, new life, requires a death, perhaps even the letting go of that perfect relationship between master and pupil. Might this conclusion work against the thesis that "containment" is also, for McGuckian, an essential part of her work as poet? On the contrary, the poem's mildly asserted thesis works well: accepting death is the work of encompassing, bearing, containing—and an act of the strong. True, something is lost or let go, but it is not forgotten or denied, and the living person continues to grow by actively taking in an uncomfortable, difficult factor of the human condition.

In *The Cloud of Unknowing,* the fourteenth-century mystic advises: "Reconcile yourself to wait in the darkness as long as necessary." Darkness, an essential component

of the creative life, is another key image in McGuckian's poems. Underlying and undercutting the rationality of patriarchal light is a place of darkness known to such mystics as John of the Cross, in whose system the Dark Night may be a prelude to union with God; and so, despite its latent terrors it is paradoxically just such a "place of birth" as we have been looking at in the last poem. The poet says "Black is my continuum" (*VR* 49) in **"Lime Trees in Winter, Retouched,"** which starts from a position in what one imagines as the inside of a womb, the heart of the chora, the depths of the unconscious,[13] in a blackness which runs the gamut "from peach black, vine black, to the resins of darkness." Paradoxically, for neither the chora nor the unconscious can be "chosen" except by descent into psychosis, this is very much a chosen position, accompanied by feelings of rightness and admonition: "That is how good a picture / Should be, oil abetting, light disturbing." The light, signifying logic, lucidity, the patriarchal order, must be disturbed by this oily dark. That is the work of the poet, the artist—not passively enduring the darkness, but actively resisting the light. Deeply ambivalent about light, McGuckian reserves her greatest suspicion for window light: the images of window, glass, and mirror collapse into each other as images of patriarchal control. In **"Tulip,"** "the artistry of light" is described as an "illness."[14] In **"A Day With Her,"** the speaker opens with the agitated line, "No, that mirror couldn't possibly have seen us" (*VR* 48) and the reader feels the spying menace the metonymic mirror holds for the two women of the poem. The **"Woman With the Blue-Ringed Bowl,"** who is said to have "that quality of night I most care for," agrees to be held in the light, but "Not the light controlled by a window" (*OBB* 58). Now, in **"Lime Trees"** the artist, like a Samson among the Philistines, hoists the dark power of her art "between two windows," pillars of the Temple of Logic, "constantly straightening against them."

In the poem's second and shorter stanza—the poems looks at first glance like a sonnet, leading us to expect a sextet with a lesson, and a lesson is in fact what we get— McGuckian posits, as she has done in **"The Rising Out,"** yet another component of the necessary ground of that art which can do the work of Samson. This time, alarmingly, it turns out to be the abject. The poet-artist finds herself "agitated" by "moisture trapped like a stain or white secretion." Whether one imagines semen, pus, smegma, or menses, the abject is clearly signaled. Here is that second stanza in full:

> But I am agitated less by glass or apertures,
> Then moisture trapped like a stain or white
> Secretion, an old swab I was confident
> Had broken down to paste, or was ingrained
> In the next meconium, my intent and cherished
>   waste.

It is not lack of cleanliness or health that causes abjection," Kristeva tells us, "but what disturbs identity, system, order."[15] By this definition, the chora is also contained by the abject, which makes the poem's internal logic all the tighter. In this stanza, McGuckian wants us to look directly at decay, to imagine the body's wastes, secreted rather than rejected, with some things, such as the swab, broken down and recycled into the next meconium. Of course, "glass" and "apertures" both refer to the windows of the first stanza, while introducing a new association—that of the vulnerable female body, which can be violated by the controlling order.

If the abject "is something recycled from which one does not part, from which one does not protect oneself as from an object,"[16] McGuckian strengthens the lesson: it is dangerous to expel meconium, the fecal matter of an unborn child, before its time, for if the meconium is accidentally expelled, during labor for example, the infant may ingest it. All the examples of abjection, thus, are given the cumulative importance of that-which-must-be-retained, and are made to equal meconium, "my intent and cherished waste." Kristeva notes that "it is the Word that discloses the abject . . . purifies from the abject . . . constitutes full powers against abjection."[17] But look at "cherished." Here McGuckian reveals a psychology willing to go a step further than stereotyped Freudian reactions: for the sake of her art, her child, she will cherish the waste matter; not reject it even mentally, but love it, if love is of the will. This constitutes intentional containment which Kristeva can not envisage.[18]

"Lime Trees in Winter, Retouched" has no plot in any exact, discursive sense: the bonding agent of the reader's own conscious and unconscious experience puts all the elements—images, rhythms, connotations, juxtapositions—together. McGuckian, by intent, remains riskily near the edge of that shattering of language proclaimed by the feminist critics to be the proper—*propre*—contribution of the feminine. But the poem is closely woven of chiming sounds and assonances, down to the last internal rhyme of "paste" with "waste." This penultimate, mid-line, full rhyme with the last word of the poem is something the poet likes to do now and then—in **"Daisy-Cutter," "Isba Song," "To a Cuckoo at Coolanlough,"** for example. Here, the purpose seems to be to emphasize further the "waste" which is the point of **"Lime Trees in Winter, Retouched."**

The word "retouched" of McGuckian's title obviously refers to the work of an oil painter, who, with the gardener and mother, is a frequent stand-in for the poet in McGuckian's discourse. This poet's work involves the slow building of layer upon layer. One is reminded of Rembrandt's thick impasto, of his backgrounds, "from peach black, vine black, to the resins of darkness," thickly laid on, shadow on shadow, or of his many *pentimenti,* worked until he got what he was satisfied with. On the surface, McGuckian's poems do not give the impression of being heavily worked over, but such reworking is probably the reason they remain fruitful rereading after rereading. Is the poet foregrounding and defending this "retouching" aspect of her work in the defiantly triumphant ending of **"Pain Tells You What to Wear"**?

> Fear of retouching is the very last
> Quality suggested by the flag-red,

> Flag-gold, storming flowers, that
> . . . reach out through winged
> Garments to the priceless vertebrae of the stars.

>   (*VR* 40)

A final element in McGuckian's poetics may be observed in action in a poem that also describes it. **"The Rising Out"** introduces a speaker within a paradigm of being central to Irish self-definition: the Easter Rising. The historical stage is indicated by the title and the first two lines, "My dream sister has gone into my blood / To kill the poet in me before Easter . . ." (*VR* 35). But this scenario is abandoned—an example of McGuckian's very glancing suggestion of Irish identity—almost as soon as it has been set, and the actors seem to be just two: a poet and her "dream sister." The Easter Rising was most famously responded to in Yeats's "Easter 1916," in which he demonstrates that "Too long a sacrifice / Can make a stone of the heart," and fears that the mythical beauty he has celebrated is, in such an unromantic economy of action, "terrible." But the "stone in the midst of all" may still make music, as a stone "sings" in a brook when water rushes over it. In McGuckian's feminized and personalized version of it, the struggle becomes a resistance—a refusal to fight to the death, a stern ability to hold on—rather than a revolution, and a resistance in which the conflict is hardly resolved within the space of the poem. Moreover, McGuckian's attitude is surprisingly affirming: the conflictual relationship itself may be fruitful. The poet describes her dream sister's presence:

> Such
> A tender visit, when I move my palaces,
> The roots of my shadow almost split in two,
> Like the heartbeat of my own child, a little
> Blue crocus in the middle of a brook, or the hesitant
> Beginning of a song I knew, a stone-song
> Too small for me, awaiting a drier music.

>   (*VR* 35)

A seductively gentle antagonist, the sister brings out defensive feelings in the speaker, clued for the reader by the images of a child's heartbeat, a pressed blue flower, "the hesitant beginnings of a song"—things too easily crushed. The temptress works, it seems, to push her poet sister towards the banal, the daily cliché, creating a lulling atmosphere of conventional or ironic commentary about the weather. Though the speaker continues on through the clatter, working on an "arm-long" poem which will perhaps keep her sister at arm's length, her subject, **"Venus Tying the Wings of Love,"** runs strangely contrary to any impulse toward "rising." And the artist fails to advert to this. Her only hope is that her dream sister will "recede like all my heroes." Simply waiting it out has made this speaker independent, perhaps by default, of romantic or idealistic fixations, even on the male. Or, perhaps she can contain the dream sister as in a pregnancy, "hold her bone to term," taking "term" to be the completion of the poet's work. "Bone" conjures a metonymic Eve: the dream sister, like Eve, should be subservient to her "head" but—also like Eve—will assuredly cause trouble.[19]

Though the speaker seems to match in her responses the passivity and fluidity which are Kristeva's marks of the feminine, no such easy correspondence may be drawn. Firstly, we have just noted the association of poet persona with the controlling, word-making Adam, which indentification is itself complicated by the pregnancy metaphor. Secondly, while the containment—hold[ing] her bone to term"—she proposes is hardly an active rebellion, it is one that requires tremendous fortitude. If the dream sister is part of one's psyche, then her interference with the work of poetry can only be overcome by patience and willpower, rather than violence inflicted on what is as close to one and as fragile as a child's heartbeat, a little dried crocus, or as the beginnings of a "stonesong" which, the poet realizes without pride, "is too small for me." Much energy goes into becoming aware of and then keeping decently suppressed the abject, less worthy, despised parts of the psyche.

What might be lost if the poet were to get rid of the troublesome, seemingly malicious dream sister? Psychologists would answer, tremendous energy and creativity. McGuckian hovers around the conclusion that the seed of her poetry might come from that sister's very dream. The third stanza shows us the poet's mind ranging freely, and McGuckian seems to lift a curtain—not for the first time—on her own poetics. Everything must keep liquefying, breaking up, separating, for this poet-speaker: "Like a line of clouds just about to crumble / The breaking of ice in a jar." The poet notices and trusts the movement of a poem to tiny differentiating features; in equal measure, the speaker reveals that

> In my mind,
> I try to separate one Alice
> From the other, by their manner of moving,
> The familiar closing of the unseen room,
> The importunate rhythm of flowers.

> (*VR* 35)

And this same separating, disseminating activity starts, indeed, with a seed, with the dream seed given the poet by her sister, who may be as necessary to her as her own blood: "Partner to me like a ruptured seed," this female figure echoes later in **"Lighthouse with Dead Leaves"** (*OBB* 32). She must not die, or at least she must not die suddenly, be killed off by the speaker. This dream is the seed of poetry, and the means by which the poet actually accomplishes her rising out. Without the dream sister, then, no poem.

We have seen the theme of rising out before. In **"Rowing,"** the poet's "artlessness, too painful to live with" also rises out, "like a spur / Eloping from the room below" (*VR* 33). Both the "below"—the darkness, the place of birth—and the rising are necessary, though the movement from one to the other—seedbed to fruit—involves a certain amount of pain and struggle. If the blood spilt in the Easter Rising of 1916 was to be, in the rhetoric of Commander-in-Chief Patrick Pearse, a sacrifice which would seed future generations with the courage for their own revolutions, the sister's spilt blood, by association,

is intimately connected to the dream-seed.[20] No deaths are enacted in this poem, however. Everyone lives: both the poet who was afraid she would be killed herself and her potential killer.

Let us look once more at that aspect of **"The Rising Out"** which is the McGuckian signature—the deliberate subversion of conventional discourse, the diffuseness that is an act of transgression against the symbolic order. It must be recognized that I have imposed a lucid story on a quite mysterious poem, though not one of McGuckian's most difficult, by ignoring both puzzling phrases—"when I move my palaces" and "blood stretched on the frame," which I saw initially as the speaker's own blood, her death, but which could be the sister's sacrificial blood—and the introduction of an "Alice," and by bringing as well my own conscious and unconscious experience to bear on the poem, a poem diffuse enough to produce a very different interpretation in other hands. As an example of the work of my conscious, unconscious experience in shaping the poem's meaning, consider the title—**"The Rising Out"**—without reference to Ireland. Another layer of meaning appears then, for references to Easter, death, and rising in the space of three lines call up, of course, the Resurrection of Christ and the Christian promise of eternal life—and also, by the way, accommodate "Blood stretched on the frame," as well as such other key images as "seed" and "fruit."[21]

In the diffuse and puzzling array of meanings that **"The Rising Out"** sets up, we might see McGuckian, by her very techniques in poetry, modeling what she describes as her speaker's process, "rising out" of the straightforward syntax of her inherited symbolic order. And, in a second mirroring, the implantation of a dream-seed in the reader, aided by McGuckian's multilayered images and jarring syntax, lifts us out of our daily experience, our syntax, our "clothes."

In her first three collections—*The Flower Master* (1982), *Venus and the Rain* (1984), *On Ballycastle Beach* (1988), McGuckian used increasingly fragmented and decentered language to destabilize meaning. She knew the rules, but increasingly she took them on her own terms; so, light and darkness both appeared in her work, the marks of the patriarchy and the subversion of the patriarchy, the semiotic and the symbolic—grass growing through concrete. Her most recent collections, *Marconi's Cottage* (1991) and *Captain Lavender* (1995), demonstrate both continuity and change in her prosody, the change being evident specifically in the area of syntactic fragmentation. Here we find the "Fragments . . . ready . . . to reintegrate"[22] which the poet's project has allowed for.

McGuckian's new, near-narrative style evident in part in almost half the poems of *Marconi's Cottage*, and in many of the *Captain Lavender* poems, may be the most obvious component of the "reintegration of the fragments." Perhaps her "old" style, however transgressive of logical order, was an artifice the poet could not, or did not, wish to sustain. Not unrelated to this syntactic movement is the fact that

McGuckian is beginning to write much longer poems. In *Marconi's Cottage*, we find new and frequent use of sewing and the iconic baby daughter, but the old key images return obsessively: hands, kisses, light, primary colors—a comfortingly familiar vocabulary. McGuckian still depends on the individual electric charges of words. And a stern "he" who makes rules, is now also, in at least one poem, connected with the trusted father. The father's death occupies the speaker in many poems, among them **"Red Armchair,"** and the wonderful **"The Partner's Desk."** Birth and death are often inseparably interwoven, recalling each other, as in **"Flowered Sitting Room,"** and **"She Which is Not, He Which Is,"** in which time is treated with Shakespearian ambivalence.

It is in the six poems of *Marconi's Cottage* celebrating the gestation and birth of the poet's youngest child and first daughter, Emer Mary Charlotte Rose, that the most intriguing change may be noticed in McGuckian's diction and syntax. Preparatory poems, such as **"Open Rose"** and **"Branches,"** more than hint at the symbiotic permeability between the ego-boundaries of mother and daughter. The poet repeats her own birth, becomes "a guest at [her] own childhood" (*MC* 80). She has "grown inside words / Into a state of unbornness." She has experienced "an awareness of one's being / Added to one's being" (*MC* 89). In **"Charlotte's Delivery"** the mother speaks as a delighted "us," joining with her daughter even as their bodies separate and set over against all the men, the father and three sons, among whom she has perhaps been lonely. Though the spent, newly delivered mother feels herself like "the wrecked hull of the fishing boat" (*MC* 83), she is conscious with joy that something of the strength and permanence of the cypress tree is planted within.

The title of the poem **"Breaking the Blue"** is a quiet joke, surely, on the successive collections of blue baby clothes which, for twelve years, graced the conventional household's washing-line. All jokes are left at the door of this poem, though, for the poem presents the intense excitement at the baby's being the poet's "unspeaking likeness." Thenceforward, the diction of the poem becomes serious, and even the rhythms sentenciously heavy.

> Single version of my mind deflected off my body,
> Side-altar, sacramental, tasting-table, leaf to my
> Emptying shell. . . .
>
> Womb-encased and ever-present mystery without
> Release, your even-colored foliage seems a town
>   garden
> To my inaccessible, severely mineral world.
>
> Fragments of once-achieved meaning, ready to leave
> the flesh, reintegrate as lover, mother, words
> That overwhelm me: You utter, become music, are
>   played.
>
>   (*MC* 84)

Only in the very last words do we have a lift-off into that accustomed McGuckian realm of delectable lightness, in which only undermined meanings have weight and where words bear them with graceful and unconsidered strength. Before that, the unmistakably Latinate, even churchy vocabulary seems to insist on genuflection. The reader understands the feelings of the new mother, but resents just a tiny bit the call to worship.

Again, in **"Almond"** the reader senses that she is being *told* something momentous, rather than being allowed to experience it through an empathy created by the images of the poem:

> To follow the road
>
> On which we lose the power
> Of explaining ourselves
> Back ever more deeply
> Is to mix in the earth
>
> Or soil as a ferment,
> To redissolve the hazards
> Of our own growth
> Like the very flower of matter
>
> Woven into the common ground.
> From the earliest bed. . . .
>
>   (*MC* 92)

The solemn, goal-oriented movement of the phrases shows a departure: it is very interesting, but it is not the McGuckian we are used to. The same didactically solemn speech pattern runs through **"Vibratory Description"** and the sermonette "Real losses and real losers, / We find them possessing us" (*MC* 95). Even at one remove, as in the McGuckian translation the first of Nuala Ní Dhomhnaill's *Toircheas* ("Gestation") poems, her voice—certainly not Ní Dhomhnaill's—brings to the translation the tone of Latinate seriousness which she appears to feel pregnancy warrants.[23]

McGuckian has not lost her old sleight of hand. A great many of the poems are in top enigmatic form. Two of the Charlotte poems, for instance, retain the feeling of multi-layered ambiguity: **"From the First Underworld"** is fascinating and difficult, and **"The Carrying Ring"** is a complex evocation of the relationship to a new child:

> How to come to desire
> What suddenly leaves us so alone,
> A protecting obedience so contrary to human love. . . .
>   (*MC* 88)

The last phrase "a protecting obedience" establishes the child as agent, as other. This is an impressive poem, not least because of its attitude.

McGuckian's most recent collection similarly demonstrates qualities of continuity and change. In *Captain Lavender* (1995) the poet seems to struggle consciously with new "metaposition" (*RPL* 103), even as she adopts it, as "a leaf detaching itself / from the narrative 'tree' / attempts to seal its mean."[24] A step away from her former rebellion against discursiveness, she now observes with unease that through some writing "desire is completely trained: / bound in the bed like an account book" (*CL* 34). Remember that earlier bed out of which she extricated herself in order to develop? The speaker's dismay at this new possibility is palpable.

In 1994, the poet taught creative writing for a time at the prison and former internment camp known as "The Maze," an experience which contributed to changing her lexicon in profound ways. The darkness of chora, so fruitful a creative space in the previous collections, becomes in this collection an ominous dark, which combines the fascination of a secret sexual desire and the fear of personal annihilation. As McGuckian starts to talk more openly about "the betrayed North of my soul" (*CL* 61), images of death mutate into menacing presences: "How did you, roughbarked men, / break into flower, with Death behind you / shaking his," she asks in **"The Colour Shop"** (*CL* 58). Images of violence and war permeate the collection, even to some poems about the father, imagined as a World War II veteran. Even images of fruitfulness are turned on their heads to express violence, in a newly overt critique: "Like an accomplished terrorist, the fruit hangs / from the end of the dead stem, under a tree / riddled with holes" (*CL* 68). "Inexplicable deaths" are a source of change, but where this change will take her the poet cannot imagine. Walking between graves at Easter, her speaker, in an echo of Yeats's "The Second Coming," asks "what morning, like a sleeve too wide, without costing much, can be break in me?" (*CL* 66).

I see in these last two collections the emergence of a new sense of seriousness, reverence, and commitment in McGuckian, previously exhibited only in those poems about the relationship which won that sort of response from her: the presence—heightened by prospective loss—of her father. In an interview given July 13, 1990, McGuckian said of overt commentary on the North: "I think it's a waste of energy and I think [the poetic act] transmutes that energy into a poem, gives it a kind of depth and value, and you forgive through the poem. . ." The word "forgive" is especially interesting, because it seems removed as much as any of her poetic key terms to the higher latitudes of figuration. But it is of a piece with her implied project of containing, encompassing, rather than rejecting or excluding what is there; and perhaps forgiveness is just that: the refusal to exclude, to see people or institutions as enemies. Now that she has begun, however ambivalently, to explore the issues, her tone is untinged with the tragic bitterness and resignation that marks Michael Longley's memorable response to the 1994-96 ceasefire: "I get down on my knees and do what must be done / And kiss Achilles' hand, the killer of my son."[25]

But McGuckian is obviously a wiry and tenacious subversive rather than a turner-of-the-other-cheek. McGuckian belongs to the subculture in the Northern Ireland scheme of things—the deep structures of which are based on an assumption of Protestant, male supremacy set in place by the seventeenth-century "Plantations," and so her writing

is important in beginning a process of breaking free from conformity. In the position of talented underdog, any writer might want to "make it" on the terms of the local power-group. Resisting the temptation to assimilate completely, McGuckian has it both ways: she has "made it," risen within that Northern, male order, while pluckily refusing the terms, subverting the rules. She resists having her mind colonized.

NOTES

[1] Medbh McGuckian, *Venus and the Rain* (Oxford: Oxford University Press, 1984), p. 46; hereafter cited parenthetically, thus: (*VR* 46).

[2] Liam O'Dowd, "Introduction," Albert Memmi, *The Colonizer and the Colonized* (London: Earthscan Publications, 1990), pp. 35-37.

[3] Interview with Medbh McGuckian, Belfast, July, 1990.

[4] See Susan M. Schweik, *A Gulf So Deeply Cut: American Women Poets and the Second World War* (Madison: University of Wisconsin Press, 1991), for an interesting discussion of the politics of gender and war.

[5] Gilles Deleuze and Félix Guattari, *Kafka: Toward a Minor Literature*, trans. Dana Polan (Minneapolis: University of Minnesota Press, 1986), p. 19.

[6] Julia Kristeva, *Revolution in Poetic Language*, trans. Margaret Walles (New York: Columbia University Press, 1984), pp. 79-80; hereafter cited parenthetically, thus: (*RPL* 79-80).

[7] Medbh McGuckian, *On Ballycastle Beach* (Oxford: Oxford University Press, 1988), p. 52; hereafter cited parenthetically, thus: (*OBB* 52).

[8] Julia Kristeva, *Desire in Language*, trans. Thomas Gora, Alice Jardine, Leon S. Roudiez (New York: Columbia University Press, 1980), p. 133.

[9] Commenting on H.D.'s *Helen in Egypt*, Alicia Ostriker observed that the poet's "divided voices evoke divided selves: the rational and the passionate, the active and the suffering, the conscious life and the dream life, animus and anima, analyst and analysed . . . left brain and right brain. . . . " See Alicia Ostriker, "The Thieves of Language," in *The New Feminist Criticism*, ed. Elaine Showalter (New York: Pantheon, 1985), pp. 314-38. This handily summarizes for me the contending selves on McGuckian's poetry, though her poems seldom present more than one point of view voice.

[10] McGuckian once commented: "Wordsworth? An inspired voice. A pure poet. He's so very very English, and yet he's as near to me—his Englishness doesn't annoy me . . . in the way that Yeats's Irishness does!" Interview with McGuckian, Belfast, July, 1990. In the fall of 1990 McGuckian taught a class on Wordsworth at Stranmillis College, Belfast.

[11] Calvin Bedient, "The Crabbed Genius of Belfast," *Parnassus*, XVI, 1 (1990), 199.

[12] James Joyce, *Ulysses*, (New York: Vintage, 1990), p. 763.

[13] In *Tales of Love*, Kristeva observes that "Psychoanalysis skirts religious faith in order to expend it in the form of literary discourses." *Tales of Love*, trans. Leon S. Roudiez (New York: Columbia University Press, 1987), p. 38. No doubt McGuckian was familiar with the Christian mystics

and the long history of using states of unconsciousness for enlightenment before she had heard of Kristeva.

14 Medbh McGuckian, *The Flower Master* (Oxford: Oxford University Press, 1982), p. 10; hereafter cited parenthetically, thus: (*FM* 10). A slightly different text of *The Flower Master* was issued by Gallery Press in 1993.

15 Julia Kristeva, *Powers of Horror*, trans. Leon S. Roudiez (New York: Columbia University Press, 1982), p. 4.

16 *Ibid.*

17 *Ibid.*, p. 23.

18 How does this differ from Yeats's return to the "foul rag and bone shop of the heart"? Well, for his speaker the return is a last resort: he has trotted out all his circus animals and now he "must," perforce, "go down." In Yeats, only the female speaker, and she mad, is given the insight that "fair needs foul."

19 One can read the implications in McGuckian's lines. I apologize for this nugget of patriarchal propaganda.

20 These two stories come together in the rhetoric of the leaders of the 1916 Rising. As already noted, Pearse proposed a sacrifical ideal: "bloodshed is a cleansing and sanctifying thing." In January, 1916, the Marxist James Connolly stated, amazingly, that "in all due humility and awe, we recognize that of us, as of mankind before Calvary, it may truly be said: 'Without the shedding of Blood there is no Redemption.'" Both Pearse and Connolly are quoted in R. F. Foster, *Modern Ireland, 1600-1972* (New York: Penguin, 1989), pp. 477, 479.

21 We should recall the Parable of the Sower and the Seed, where the "seed" equals the Word, and the following teaching: "Unless a seed falls into the ground and dies, it remains a single grain; but if it dies, it bears much fruit."

22 Medbh McGuckian, *Marconi's Cottage* (Oldcastle: The Gallery Press, 1991), p. 80; hereafter cited parenthetically, thus: (*MC* 80).

23 The poem that Ní Dhomhnaill simply titled "Toircheas I," or "Gestation I," McGuckian titled "Ark of the Covenant" in her translation. See Nuala Ní Dhomhnaill, *Pharoah's Daughter* (Oldcastle: The Gallery Press, 1990), pp. 50-51.

24 Medbh McGuckian, *Captain Lavender* (Winston-Salem, NC: Wake Forest University Press, 1995), p. 34; hereafter cited parenthetically, thus (*CL* 34).

25 "Ceasefire," *The New Yorker*, May 15, 1995, p. 48.

Shane Murphy (essay date 1996)

SOURCE: "Obliquity in the Poetry of Paul Muldoon and Medbh McGuckian," in *Eire-Ireland*, Fall-Winter, 1996, pp. 76-101.

[In the following essay, Murphy discusses McGuckian's method of composition and contrasts it with that of the poet Paul Muldoon.]

The poetry of Medbh McGuckian attracts even more vitriolic censure than [Paul] Muldoon's. Patrick Williams classifies her work as "colourful guff" (50), railing against her diaphanous and drifting lyrics (49). "McGuckian's concoctions of endless poeticism," he blusters, "are non-visionary, and the funny, sealed little worlds where harmless cranks parley with themselves in gobbledegook won't impinge on the real world of loot and dragons" (51). Such criticism of McGuckian's supposed morbid interiority and her consequent hermetic constructions is frequent: she has been labeled fey and mannered (Jenkins 56), whimsical (Lucas 38), at best intricate and enigmatic, at worst inaccessible and subjective (McCarthy 176).

I never write just blindly, I never sit down without an apparatus, I always have a collection of words—it's like a bird building a nest—I gather materials over the two weeks, or whatever. And I keep a notebook or a diary for the words which are happening to me and occuring to me. I never sit down without those because otherwise you would just go mad, trying to think of words.17

McGuckian's method of composition provides an insight into the oblique nature of her poetry. The "collection of words" is, in fact, a series of word-lists made up of phrases taken from literary biographers that she has been reading "over the two weeks." When writing a poem, she consults these lists and recombines the phrases to form poems. By manipulating words, fragments, and prior texts to fit neatly into her narratives, McGuckian imposes her own symbolic vision upon them, thereby forming a curious relationship with the reader, who must work hard to keep up with her. Whereas Muldoon foregrounds intertextuality through proper names, dates, and italics, McGuckian provides little indication that she is quoting or referring to other texts. In the following analysis of three poems— **"Gigot Sleeves," "Garbo at the Gaumont," "A Small Piece of Wood"**—I argue that McGuckian's poetry functions as a palimpsestic double-writing. In these works, quotations gleaned from literary biographies are recycled to suggest the poet's immediate relationship with her precursors. Like Muldoon's historiographic metafictions, the doubleness associated with a palimpsest permits McGuckian to retain vestiges of prior writings while including a critique or commentary on them: "[a]t all times in a palimpsest there is foreground and background, new statement and obscured original which can be discovered with the force of a revelation or something left overwritten in undecidable layering" (DuPlessis 56). For the poet, such a layered composition initiates a personal relationship to a literary precursor, a relationship wholly dissimilar to that established by literary biographers whose words she reproduces:

They are only looking at the person's body and physical mind and events and doings—I am for their seed and their undying immortal flame. So I recreate . . . or God through me. I hope to restore to life, and make empty words full. In the text the phrases are not poetry— linked properly in the DNA of the poem—they ought to be. They are intended to be.18

Although McGuckian distances herself from her biographical sources, she still uses their words; therefore, we must ask whether or not McGuckian's verse really does have an "imaginative signature," the unique "poetic DNA pattern" she claims for it.[19] The answer lies in the image itself. The genetic makeup of McGuckian's poems have an inherent doubleness, forming what Michael Davidson has termed a palimtext. Foregrounding intertextual and interdiscursive aspects, Davidson suggests that a palimtext is "a writing-in-process," which "retains vestiges of prior writings out of which it emerges"; more importantly, "it is the still-visible record of responses to those early texts" (310).

In an unpublished interview with Jennifer Noble, McGuckian reveals that she wrote **"Gigot Sleeves"** to pay homage to the enigmatic nineteenthcentury Yorkshire poet/ novelist, Emily Brontë (Noble 48). However, once the poem appears in print it becomes more than an intimate one-to-one conversation across time between authors and, in the process, raises questions about obliquity. "I do publish," says McGuckian, "because I want to, obviously. But only to those who themselves want a relationship to Emily Brontë. I want them to know her, not the way that I do, but in their own way. I would offer the poem as a clue to rediscovering her, to go back and find out more about her for themselves" (Noble 48). Surprisingly Noble does not query this aim since, without McGuckian's stated intentions, the reader would scarcely suspect Brontë's presence. Indeed, the poem's only named literary references are to Trelawney and Shelley. Furthermore, as the following passage from the poem's conclusion illustrates, the temporal specificity conjoined with the hermetic aspect of her imagery helps obscure even further its unidentified subject:

> And everything is emaciated—the desk
> On her knees, the square of carpet, the black
> Horsehair sofa, and the five foot seven by sixteen
>
> Inches of a pair of months stopped.

Until readers discover that McGuckian has "borrowed" the above from Winifred Gérin's compelling biography of Emily Brontë, they will be forever left to puzzle over such a conundrum as "the five foot seven by sixteen / Inches of a pair of months." Gérin's narrative recounts how Brontë's illness, "its relentless progress, the *emaciation,* the fever, the shortness of breath, the pain in the side, all confirmed the family's terrors of worse to come" (248, emphasis added). Her death was, according to Dr. Wheelhouse, due to "'Consumption—2 *months'* duration'" (259, emphasis added) and the dimensions of her coffin are recorded as "5 feet 7 inches by 16 inches" (259).

· · · · ·

When composing **"Gigot Sleeves"** McGuckian, to use Maura Dooley's words, "reel[s]in / life with someone else's bait" (12). Taking five excerpts from the above passage, she quotes them in the second, third, and tenth

stanzas of her poem, insisting at all times on the cramped nature of Emily Brontë's surroundings. Even the one seemingly incongruous detail, "the black horsehair sofa," is taken from a passage to do with the writer's increasing frailty.[20] By stressing the phrase "a pair of months," McGuckian echoes Gérin's realization that Brontë's contracting tuberculosis was far from inevitable during her long illness.

In **"Gigot Sleeves,"** McGuckian is open to the criticism that Tim Kendall[21] leveled at Paul Muldoon's "7, Middagh Street." In both instances, the literary allusions place a heavy burden on the reader. To be intelligible, Muldoon's poem requires knowledge of Humphrey Carpenter's *W.H. Auden: A Biography;* similarly, the reader who fails to recognize McGuckian's debt to Gérin misses the homage paid to Brontë. Yet however oblique her strategy may be, McGuckian's treatment of her subject remains very different from that of the biographer. The poet's economic appropriation of text enables her not only to explore certain root causes of Emily Brontë's demise (the austere living conditions at Haworth parsonage, the stubborn neglect of her health), but also to depict them formally. Indeed, the dimensions of her coffin are juxtaposed with the size of Emily's living space: while William Wood, the village carpenter, says that "he had never in all his experience made so narrow a shell for an adult" (Gérin 259), McGuckian implies that the coffin differed little from the room in which she wrote. Emily Brontë's emaciation parallels that of the house ("the / Narrow sliproom," "the square of carpet"); the gradual disappearance of both writer and building is figured literally in the enjambement at the poem's close whereby one swiftly moves from "five foot seven by sixteen" to "Inches of a pair of months" to "stopped." Never has closure seemed so final.

Many of McGuckian's borrowings from Gérin deliberately set up a particular image of Emily Brontë, one which counters preconceived notions of her as a sheltered recluse, and offers instead the portrayal of a lively engaging woman: "The double-cherry performs a dance behind / Triple gauze, she takes out the bulldogs, / Masters a pistol. . . . "

· · · · ·

McGuckian's meticulous description of Emily Brontë's clothing—the skirts splashed with "purple suns"—appears more appropriate to the posthippie generation of the early 1970s[22] than to Victorian England. Yet this is part of the "rediscovery" of Brontë the poet fosters, which is based on ample biographical evidence. In her biography, Gérin quotes an excerpt from *The Life of Charlotte Brontë,* in which Mrs. Gaskell recounts that when Brontë was staying at the Hotel de Hollande, I Rue de la Putterie, she "had taken a fancy to the fashion, ugly and preposterous even during its reign, *of gigot sleeves,* and persisted in wearing them long after they were 'gone out'. *Her petticoats, too, had not a curve or a wave in them,* but hung straight and long, clinging to her lank figure" (Gérin 131, emphasis added).

That Mcguckian's Emily Brontë—the tragic, "half-un-tamed," solitary figure—is reminiscent of a Romantic, Byronic hero reflects a commonplace biographical assumption of Byron's profound influence on the Yorkshire writer.[23] In personal correspondence McGuckian reveals that "I was re-reading Byron and found again 'a spreading here, a condensation there' which I used in **'Gigot Sleeves'**. I suggest she (Emily Brontë) was more Byron than he."[24] Her characterization of Brontë also reflects Gérin's view that "Emily Brontë was no plagiarist; few novelists were so original as she. What she took from Byron she took because the seed lay in her" (46). Although McGuckian could also be accused of plagiarism, her completely original treatment of her subject refutes such an imputation. Gérin's emphasis on Brontë's originality surely lies behind McGuckian's allusion in the eighth stanza of **"Gigot Sleeves"** to Edward Trelawney's *Recollections*:[25]

> The funeral pyre was now ready; I applied the fire, and the materials being dry and resinous the pine-wood burnt furiously, and drove us back. It was hot enough before, there was no breath of air, and the loose sand scorched our feet. As soon as the flames began to clear, and allowed us to approach, *we threw frankincense and salt into the furnace, and poured a flask of wine and oil over the body.* (emphasis added)

Within the framework of the poem, the reference functions proleptically, prefiguring the death of the female poet; but within the wider context of McGuckian's obvious concern with the anxiety of influence, the ritual of burning the dead poet's body could suggest her attempt at poetic originality, free from any precursor's influence. Yet this reading begs the question: while Brontë may have fully internalized and personalized the influence of Byron, has McGuckian's creativity, as "poetic biographer," suffered while reading the lives of others?

> The words are given to me . . . and the authors, and the translators, especially if they're dead, they are very aware of me using them and they want it; they want me to make the same words live again in a new way and do things with them that carries me and marks my reading of the book and marks my learning process with them.[26]

By embedding or dovetailing quotations within her own work McGuckian offers more than a belated tribute to admired authors; the technique also registers her own continuing engagement with their oeuvres and lives. The reading process is both immediate and personal, involving a connection with the writers who, because of the poet's empathy with their words, become living presences. In the same interview McGuckian stated matter-of-factly that "When I'm with a person that's written the book, I'm almost in love with the person during the course of that book." She cites an example making this relationship startlingly clear: "I got two books out on Byron. One of them neither gave me Byron nor the other man, and the other book gave me both Byron and the person writing it. When I go home and I pick up the book, it's very like getting into bed with the other person—it's very, very intimate."

In **"Garbo at the Gaumont,"** a minor poem in which McGuckian empathizes with yet another precursor, the title itself contains a tantalizingly indirect hint as to whom this might be. McGuckian has based much of her poem on Tatyana Tolstoy's biography of her father, *Tolstoy Remembered*. An essay by her daughter, Tatyana Albertini,[27] which acts as an epilogue for the biography, clarifies McGuckian's title for her poem:

> I only once saw her perplexed. There was a film of *Anna Karenina*, the one starring Greta Garbo, showing at one of the big Paris cinemas. My mother, a cousin, and I decided to go and see it. But when we arrived at the Gaumont-Palace box-office we had to give up the notion, since the prices were way above our means, and we were forced to trudge sadly home again. When we got back, my mother said with a sweet and disappointed little smile: "I wonder what papa would have said if he'd seen that. Or the sight of me sweeping the floor, doing my shopping, and not knowing if I'll have enough left to pay the rent." (249)

The poem shares with Tatyana Tolstoy's reminiscences a wry intelligence that masks the surface capitulation to patriarchy. For example, towards the end of the first stanza, the speaker in **"Garbo at the Gaumont"** notes the debilitating effects that child-care has upon the writing of poetry:

> . . . till the room that was like
> A garden where he took his first
> Steps, and lit up trees, wishes
> Not to go on the move, to leave
> Its book unread, unfinished,
> Like a true woman.

Ironically, this particular "room" (the biography) has been read from cover to cover by the poet. Despite the distractions of caring for children, she has written a poem about her experience, which recalls a passage in Tolstoy's text. Attempting to overcome her father's near-sighted prejudices about women writers, Tolstoy tricks him into believing that an article she had written, summarizing the principles of the American economist Henry George, had in fact been produced by a certain "P. Polilov." Taken in by the ruse, her father stubbornly maintains that a woman cannot produce a sustained, book-length version of the article:

> As the conversation came to an end my father began to chuckle and said: "But how sad about poor Polilov! And I'd formed such a clear picture of him too: he wore a dark blue jacket, really very dapper, in early middle age . . ."

> Then stroking my hair he added:

> "Well, if you don't finish your book, then we shall be able to say you are a true woman." Alas, I was to prove that I was indeed an authentic member of my sex. *Like a true woman I have left my book unfinished to this day . . .*" (164, emphasis added)

Although she may have never finished that particular economic treatise, Tolstoy did go on to write the biography.

Despite the often productive comparisons which can be made between the two texts, **"Garbo at the Gaumont"** illustrates McGuckian using a biography haphazardly, almost as if she has chosen her intertexts more for their aural effect than for any semantic value. One striking example is her reference to the room in which Leo Tolstoy wrote his epic *War and Peace*:

> . . . As the eyelid protects
> The eye, in a house that love has borrowed,
> never to be refurnished, none can tell
> Exactly what room was used for what,
> Until the day after the day after tomorrow.

McGuckian has, in fact, metaphorically refurnished the "house" in Yasnaya Polyana, by inserting a quotation from Tatyana Tolstoy's work into her own poem: "We imagined we were exploring the rooms my father had described in his novel," says Tolstoy, "and we argued passionately over *exactly which room had been used for what*, as though the Rostovs had been actual people who really lived there once" (144, emphasis added). Yet for all her borrowings, McGuckian fails to capture either the spirit of Tatyana Tolstoy or comment on her own poetics. The poem is, thus, inferior to a later text in *Marconi's Cottage* based on the same source, **"A Small Piece of Wood."**

In **"A Small Piece of Wood,"** the rare inclusion of a footnote affords readers a fleeting glimpse of the familiar ghosts that glide between the interstices of this text: "**'Choorka'**, one of [Leo] Tolstoy's pet-names for his daughter, is translated to give the poem its title" (MC 110). McGuckian's characteristic trope of doubleness indicates that she is again creating a palimpsest by taking the following images from Tatyana Tolstoy's text, and thus emphasizing the parallels:

> On my left two rivers flowed
> Together without mingling,
> As though someone had unrolled
> Two different ribbons side by side . . .

Describing a journey taken to Samara in the summer of 1873, Tolstoy remarks:

> After Kazan I saw something very strange: the Volga had grown even wider, and *on our left* the water was sharply divided into two completely distinct strips of colour, *as though someone had unrolled two ribbons side by side,* one blue and the other yellow. This was the place where the Kama flows into the Volga, and although there was no physical barrier between the two currents they flowed on for a great distance *without mingling,* so that you could still distinguish the one from the other by their colour. (109, emphasis added)

The footnote focuses the reader's attention wholly on the speaker's adoption of Tatyana's soubriquet, thereby es-

tablishing a salient parallel between two father-daughter relationships. In its original context, 'Choorka' acts as a testament to the enduring love of Tatyana Tolstoy for an inspiring paternal figure:

> He used to call me 'Choorka' [a small piece of wood], and I loved that nickname because he always used it when he was in a good mood and wanted to tease me or be nice to me.

> The extraordinarily strong feeling of love and veneration I felt for my father never faded. From what I remember, and also what I have been told, he too always felt a particular affection for me. (35)

McGuckian's insertion of the same pet name into an alternative context maintains the literal theme of filial devotion (for her own father). But its status as intertext enables her metaphorically to incorporate the additional theme of literary paternity.

Discussing the psychology of intrapoetic relationships, Harold Bloom contends that to overcome the anxiety of influence and "clear an imaginative space for themselves" (5), "strong" poets always begin by misreading their precursors. Yet McGuckian suggests that while she seeks to revivify the words of past authors, her poetry is not identical with Bloom's "act of creative correction that is actually and necessarily a misinterpretation" (30). As already noted, McGuckian insists, rather, that her quotations make the same words live again in a different context. McGuckian's text is an account of her "learning process," and the selection and subsequent rearrangement of words taken from literary works are tasks for which she deems herself elected. While such a belief may indicate an abdication of control on her part, McGuckian's palimpsestic rewriting often centers thematically on the very notion of "power" and reconfigures the allocated gender positions of the original text.

> Every apple is a feather-room
> For seed's infectious star, and every man
> Who calls a woman 'Choorka',
> For a hundred and eight ruled pages.

The "apple" calls to mind the poem's earlier images of learning (the "lesson-filled inkwell," "Pictures in children's books") since the first letter of the English alphabet is traditionally represented in elementary textbooks as an "apple," to enable the child to discover the function of the abstract signifier, "A." In the final stanza, however, while the "apple" is likened to "a feather-room," suggesting incubation and materials for flight, its effect is decidedly ambiguous: "infectious star" can indeed suggest an enthusiasm which spurs the child on to growth (from seed to star, progressing upwards), but "infectious" hints at a more pernicious influence. The "star" no longer implies that destiny is due to nature, but, rather, to nurture. This ambiguity continues into the final two lines. Whereas the original context in *Tolstoy Remembered* insists upon an unqualified affection for the father, in its translated form **"Choorka"** ("a small piece of wood") suggests the demeaning ways in which this love was often reciprocated (as demonstrated in **"Garbo at the Gaumont"**). In her one "hundred and eight ruled pages,"[28] McGuckian attempts to counter the effects of patriarchal "rule" by gender-swapping and symbolically bestowing the mantle of the male literary figure (Leo Tolstoy) onto the female (Tatyana Tolstoy). This she has done in the first stanza:

> On the secret shelves of weather,
> With its few rhymes, in a pause
> Of blood, I closed the top
> Of my lesson-filled inkwell,
> A she-thing called a poetess,
> Yeoman of the Month.

McGuckian puts immense strain on words. By means of telegraphic-like compression, the temporal and biological aspects of "a pause of blood" suggest at once female menstruation, kinship (father-daughter), and the interiorization of natural forces. Indeed, the speaker manages to domesticate nature ("secret shelves of weather") and, suggesting a similitude with art ("With its few rhymes"), goes on to interiorize and textualize nature until it becomes enclosed in her "lesson-filled inkwell." Most striking, however, is the ambiguous gender of the speaker, at once a "poetess" and a "Yeoman." In the original context (autumn 1872), the action of closing an inkwell is Tatyana's attempt to shield her written thoughts from the prying eyes of her father:

> While we were writing papa came in. He leaned over me to look at my dictation. Noticing that *I was closing my inkwell* every time I dipped my pen in it, he asked me why I was doing it.
>
> "The ink evaporates," I said.
>
> "Evaporates?" papa repeated in astonishment.
>
> "Yes," I insisted stubbornly. "*I close the inkwell* so the ink won't evaporate and get wasted."
>
> Papa said nothing. But next time I offered him an equally absurd and untrue explanation of my behaviour he murmured:
>
> "Yes, the ink evaporates . . ."
>
> Why didn't I tell him the truth? That I was simply engaging in a perfectly innocent experiment? I think it was because I didn't want anyone—even the nearest and dearest to me—penetrating my inner world. I had locked myself away in my own solitude and I didn't want to share my thoughts and feelings, however insignificant, with anyone at all. (Tatyana Tolstoy 95-96, emphasis added)

McGuckian admits her own related desire for secrecy in a remarkable conversation with Nuala Ní Dhomhnaill: "I began to write poetry so that nobody would read it. Nobody. Even the ones who read it would not understand it,

and certainly no other poet would understand it."[29] Yet in **"A Small Piece of Wood,"** McGuckian publicly reveals this need, thus paradoxically contradicting the desire for privacy she asserts. But her concealed use of Tolstoy's biography masks the real narrative—the usurpation of the (literary) father:

> In pale frock and raspberry
> Boots, my waist the circumference
> Of no more than two oranges,
> I rode out to hunt. . . .

The frequent intersections of McGuckian's poem with Tatyana Tolstoy's biography creates a doubled speaking self, but the gender of the figure who rides out to hunt is the androgynous poetess/Yeoman of the Month. The passage in the biography from which the above images emerge[30] reveals the simultaneous birth of the writer and the symbolic (though also painfully literal) fall of her father; thus the poet overcomes the anxiety of influence:

> I was born at Yasnaya Polyana on October 4th 1864. Several days beforehand my father had been thrown in a riding accident. Still a young man then, he loved hunting, especially for foxes and hares in the autumn. So on September 26th 1864 he took his pack of borzois and *rode out to hunt* on a young and spirited mare named Mashka. Some distance from the house he started a great russet hare in a field and immediately set on his hounds. "Follow! Follow!" he yelled, and urged his mount after the bounding hare. Whereupon Mashka, an inexperienced hunter but only too eager to go, was soon launched into an all-out gallop. A dry water-course appeared across her path. She failed to clear it, stumbled, and fell on to her knees. Then, instead of pulling herself to her feet again, she toppled heavily over on to her flank. My father fell with her, and his right arm was trapped so that it took the mare's full weight. (17, emphasis added)

The palimpsestic double writing here allows McGuckian to insert herself into a poetic tradition from which she feels excluded: "it could be argued that far from this being a practice [quoting] that should be frowned on, it is a legitimate one for males and has a long respected and *encouraged* tradition and is one that women *must* themselves incorporate if they are to become part of the poetic tradition."[31]

The poems of McGuckian and Muldoon share a high degree of intellectual rigor, forcing the reader outside the texts for clarifications of meaning. By failing to indicate clearly from which text she is quoting, McGuckian places a larger burden on the reader than Muldoon, but neither poet can be accused of "cliquish nonchalance." The benefits of their obliquity are manifold: not only do they pay literary tribute to their esteemed precursors, but the appropriated texts also provide both poets with a critical shorthand to mark their own rereading of these texts. Muldoon's historiographical metafictions embrace the dialogical potential of the postmodern text; allusions self-reflexively manifest their status as intertexts and thus encourage readers to produce readings located in between the present poem and past context. While McGuckian's palimpsestic double-writing does not so readily proclaim its status as intertext, it allows her to address her own position as a female poet in a patriarchal tradition.

NOTES

[15] See Jefferson's message to Congress, 18 January 1803 (Jackson II), and his letter to Lewis, 20 June 1803 (Jackson 63).

[16] For the prevalence of "savagism" as a concept in America, see Prucha 8.

[17] Medbh McGuckian, personal interview, 28 July 1995.

[18] McGuckian, personal correspondence, 21 January 1997.

[19] See Seamus Heaney 6-7.

[20] Gérin 259: "About noon Emily was visibly worse and her sisters urged her to bed. The only concession she would make was to lie down on the sofa—*the black horsehair sofa* that can still be seen today" (emphasis added).

[21] See Kendall, *Paul Muldoon*, 125-26.

[22] Hence the reference to "fifteen years ago"—the poem was first published in 1988.

[23] See especially chapter 3 of Stevie Davies, *Emily Bronte*, 23.

[24] McGuckian, personal correspondence, 27 July 1996.

[25] Trelawny quoted in Morpugo 88.

[26] McGuckian, personal interview at The Marine Hotel, Ballycastle, 19 August 1996.

[27] See Tatyana Albertini, "I Often Think of My Mother," *Tolstoy Remembered*, 245-52.

[28] In the Gallery Press version of *Marconi's Cottage* the poems are printed on 108 pages. In its original draft, "A Small Piece of Wood" was handwritten on ruled paper.

[29] See McGuckian, "Comhrá," 590.

[30] The vivid description of her clothing comes from Sofia Behrs's [Tatyana Tolstoy's mother's] story about a masked ball held to mark Twelfth Night, 1865, at which she wore "boots with raspberry tops" (23-24).

FURTHER READING

Bedient, Calvin. "The Crabbed Genius of Belfast." *Parnassus* 16, No. 1 (January 1990): 195-216.
> A laudatory review of *On Ballycastle Beach*.

Docherty, Thomas. "Initiations, Tempers, Seductions: Postmodern McGuckian." In *The Chosen Ground: Essays on the Contemporary Poetry of Northern Ireland*, edited by Neil Corcoran, pp. 189-210. Chester Springs, Penn.: Dufour, 1992.
> Examines the major themes of McGuckian's verse and views her as a postmodern poet.

McDiarmid, Lucy. "Ritual Encounters." *New York Times Book Review* (14 April 1996): 11.
> Favorable review of *Captain Lavender*.

O'Brien, Peggy. "Reading Medbh McGuckian: Admiring What We Cannot Understand." *Colby Quarterly* XXVIII, 4 (December 1992): 239-50.
> Defends the obscure nature of McGuckian's verse and compares her to other major poets.

Porter, Susan. "The 'Imaginative Space' of Medbh McGuckian." In *International Women's Writing: New Landscapes of Identity*, edited by Anne E. Brown and Marjanne E. Goozé, pp. 86-101. Westport, Conn.: Greenwood Press, 1995.
> Notes similarities in McGuckian's verse and the writings of the philosopher Jacques Derrida. Porter contends that "a critical approach based upon Derrida's notions about language and meaning can reveal ways in which McGuckian's poetry finally evades the particular obstacles to communication with a wider audience that she faces as a Northern Irish woman poet."

Additional coverage of McGuckian's life and career is contained in the following sources published by the Gale Group: *Contemporary Authors*, **Vol. 143;** *Contemporary Literature Criticism*, **Vol. 48;** *DISCovering Authors Modules—Poetry*; *Dictionary of Literary Biography*, **Vol. 40.**

Alfred Noyes
1880-1958

English poet, critic, essayist, short story writer, novelist, biographer, autobiographer, and dramatist.

INTRODUCTION

An extremely prolific author in several genres, Noyes is primarily known for his conventional English poetry. Defying the modernist movement that attained popularity in the early twentieth century, he was never recognized as an important poet by most literary scholars, and his traditional style led to his eventual critical and popular neglect after World War I. He incorporated standard subjects—everyday life, England's past, the English countryside, the romance and danger of the sea—into his work.

Biographical Information

Noyes was born in Wolverhampton, England. In 1898 he began his studies at Oxford, but left a few years later without earning a degree. An avid reader and budding author, he published his first book of verse, *The Loom of Years*, in 1902, while still an undergraduate. He continued to write prolifically and in diverse genres, such as short stories, novels, literary criticism, political commentary, and essays. After his marriage in 1907 to Garnett Daniels, an American woman, Noyes spent much time in the United States. When she died in 1926, Noyes converted to Roman Catholicism, a decision that profoundly altered the course of his work. His subsequent writings are explicit in their adherence to Catholic doctrine. As a professor at Princeton University, he taught F. Scott Fitzgerald, Edmund Wilson, and John Peale Bishop. His involvement in the Roger Casement affair—an English man accused of recruiting Irish soldiers to liberate Ireland from England—garnered much mixed publicity for Noyes. He continued to travel and lecture throughout the United States until his death in 1958.

Major Works

Noyes's first poetic work, *The Loom of Years*, demonstrated his strong command of language and meter. Its cheerful lyrics, fanciful tales, and dance-like rhythms met with immediate success. In "The Highwayman," the poet's frequently anthologized piece, he intensifies a dramatic, romantic story with driving rhythms. In mood and pacing, "The Highwayman" presages *Tales of the Mermaid Tavern* as a well-researched historical piece, although some find it lacking in psychological subtlety. His most ambitious works, *Drake* and *The Torch-Bearers*—a trilogy comprised of *Watchers of the Sky, The Book of Earth*, and *The Last Voyage*—received mixed critical response. *Drake*, Noyes's serialized sea epic, highlights the exploits and adventures of

the famed English navigator. The grandeur, scope, and strong nationalist overtones of the poem drew praise from some critics while others objected to the epic's ornate and archaic diction and to the predictability of its plot. *The Torch-Bearers*, concerning scientific advancements in astronomy, biology, and modern discoveries and inventions, is judged a notable but uneven and unsatisfying work.

Critical Reception

Critics assert that the appeal of Noyes's poetry can be found in its lyrical and technical aspects: the heartiness of the songs, the rhythm of the ballads, and the diversity of metrical forms. Initially, his prolific output garnered praise, as commentators underscored his energy and enthusiasm. After World War I, however, Noyes was derided for the trite and dated nature of his poems. Temperamentally and stylistically wed to the poetry of an earlier era, Noyes rejected the innovations of twentieth century literature. As a distinguished advocate of traditional English literature, he chose traditional subjects and experimented within the confines of traditional prosody. Critics contend that Noyes's late conversion to Roman Catholicism reinforced his conservatism. Yet in his resistance to what he considered to be the caprices of modernism, he has consequently suffered the neglect of modern readers and literary scholars.

PRINCIPAL WORKS

Poetry

The Loom of Years 1902
The Flower of Old Japan 1903
The Forest of Wild Thyme 1905
Drake 1906-08
The Golden Hynde 1908
Tales of the Mermaid Tavern 1913
Watchers of the Sky 1922
The Book of Earth 1925
The Last Voyage 1930
Shadows on the Down and Other Poems 1941
Collected Poems 1950
A Letter to Lucian and Other Poems 1956

Other Major Works

William Morris (biography) 1908
Rada (drama) 1914
Walking Shadows (short stories) 1918
The Hidden Player (short stories) 1924
Some Aspects of Modern Poetry (criticism) 1924
The Opalescent Parrot (criticism) 1929
Voltaire (biography) 1936
Orchard's Bay (essays) 1939
The Last Man (novel) 1940
Pageant of Letters (criticism) 1940
Two Worlds for Memory (autobiography) 1953
The Accusing Ghost; or, Justice for Casement (essay) 1957

CRITICISM

Times Literary Supplement (essay date 1906)

SOURCE: A review of *Drake: An English Epic*, in *The Times Literary Supplement*, July 6, 1906, pp. 241.

[*This review of Noyes's* Drake: An English Epic *criticizes the work for its mediocre writing and lack of depth.*]

Courage is a great quality everywhere; but perhaps it is seldom greater than in the young poet who sets out to write an epic. Most brave things are done in the stir of the blood, in the eye of a man's comrades, in the passing of a moment. Here is a thing that has to be done alone through months or years that must bring many hours of discouragement. The intellectual fire that is to accomplish it is not of that comparatively easy order which flames high for a moment and then dies down in smoke; it is of that

rarer and finer sort which glows continuously red hot from the beginning to the end of the great enterprise. And that is the same thing as saying that it comes more naturally to the steadiness of maturity than to the ardour of youth. Probably no great epic has been written by a young man. Virgil and Tasso may not have been very old as we count age to-day, but Virgil was at least forty when he began the Æneid, and Tasso, who was only thirty-seven when his great poem was published, lived in an age when men were older at thirty than they are at forty to-day. What the exact age of Mr. Noyes is we do not know; but we imagine him to be younger, even in years, than the youngest of his great predecessors. And there lies the difficulty. For youth, which has nearly all the good things of life in its hand, cannot quite have them all; and, to speak frankly, one of the things it cannot have is the epic. For the very essence of the epic is to see life whole, and that is the one thing which is impossible to youth. It is an admirable remark that Mr. W. P. Ker makes in his "Epic and Romance":—"The whole business of life comes bodily into the epic poem." If that be accepted, there is no further question about the matter. The race of the epic is a race which is not to the swift, nor its battle to the young.

It is probably this general law which is the explanation of what is certainly the fact—namely, that Mr. Noyes's epic is far from fulfilling the promise of his earlier volumes. It has a fine exordium, and what may be almost called a magnificent conclusion, pieces of elaborate and stately work, with a high ambition in them, and a genuine inspiration behind them. The poet has not merely sat down and said to himself, "Now I will write an epic poem, and this theme is unused and seems as likely as any other." His heart is in the matter; he really cares for the great deeds of Elizabethan England, and the ideal which he divines in them is for him no mere memory of glory, but a living and inspiring force, the strength of England's Empire as it is to-day and the secret of all that it may be in the future. That is a great theme, and one thinks at once of the parallel of Rome and Virgil; but such themes, of course, do not in themselves involve or contain "the whole business of life." That has to be put into them somehow, in Virgil's way, by help of Dido and Euryalus, and Ascanius and Camilla; by retrospect and anticipation, which is again Virgil's way and Milton's too; by episode and metaphor and simile and allusion, as is the way of all epics. That is where Mr. Noyes fails. Here are three long books of blank verse, and, speaking broadly, there are no episodes in them and only two characters. There are fine lines and fine passages, of course; but the fact seems to be that the poetic power which was enough to fill the lyrics of his last volume with such abundant life has not been enough to give life to an epic. It is one thing, and a great and delightful thing, to write such poems as **"Apes and Ivory"** and **"The Sweet o' the Year"**; it is another thing to write an Æneid or a Paradise Lost.

"Drake," then, as an epic, as a whole, cannot be called a success. An epic must, by one means or another, get hold of something of the richness and variety of life; and three long books with barely a whisper of a woman in them are, to say the least, against all the precedents. Two three pages out of a hundred and seventy are, indeed, given to Elizabeth; but, for one thing, there is more of Queen than woman in, them, and in any case the allowance is somewhat scanty. Then the villain Doughty, almost the only character beside Drake, is somehow entirely unconvincing. Even Drake himself, if the truth is to be told, is more conspicuous for fine words and fancies than for anything so human as blood or bone. When he looks back on his first sight of the sea as a boy,

> There first he saw the wondrous newborn world,
> And round its princely shoulders wildly flowing
> Gemmed with a myriad clusters of the sun,
> The magic azure mantle of the sea,

somehow it is a picture that is not very convincing as a picture of the boyhood of Drake; when he begins to suspect Doughty's treachery—

> . . . Was there nothing certain, nothing sure
> In those divinest aisles and towers of Time,
> Wherein we took sweet counsel?—

we hardly seem to hear the voice of the terrible man who swept the seas, and made his name one which no Spaniard could pronounce without a shudder. Of course nobody talks in poetry exactly as he would talk in life; the novelist's seacook would be unendurable, as Stevenson knew, if he talked his own talk as it actually is. The business of art is to give, not reality, but the illusion of reality; and the defect of Mr. Noyes's Drake is not that he is not the historical Drake, which does not matter at all, but that he makes us very conscious that he is not, which does matter a great deal.

There are some half-dozen lyrics thrown into the three books. None of them will rank with the best in the poet's earlier volumes. Some of them have rather too many of the hackneyed stage properties of the Elizabethan age— "jolly good ale," "noses aglow," and the rest; and so smack a little too much of the opera, even of the comic opera. But there is a stately beauty in the song to which Drake finds Elizabeth listening:—

> Now the purple night is past,
>   Now the moon more faintly glows,
> Dawn has through thy casement cast
>   Roses on thy breast, a rose;
> Now the kisses are all done,
>   Now the world awakes anew,
> Now the charmed hour is gone,
>   Let not love go, too.

But the best is perhaps the Swinburnian praise of the sea, sung by Drake's "musicians" out in the Atlantic:—

> The same sun is o'er us,
>   The same Love shall find us,
>   The same and none other,
>   Wherever we be;
> With the same goal before us,
>   The same home behind us,

> England our mother,
>   Ringed round with the sea.

> No land in the ring of it
>   Now, all around us
>   Only the splendid
>   Resurging unknown!
> How should we sing of it?-
>   This that hath found us
>   By the great sun attended
>   In splendour, alone.
> Ah! the broad miles of it,
>   White with the onset
>   Of waves without number
>   Warring for glee.
> Ah! the soft smiles of it
>   Down to the sunset,
>   Holy for slumber,
>   The peace of the sea.

That is, perhaps, the thing which sticks in the memory more than anything else in **"Drake."** But fascination does not belong, of course, altogether to Mr. Noyes; and in any case lyrics are the ornaments, not the stuff, of an epic poem. That must be looked for in the blank verse which tells the tale. Lovers of the metre in which English poets have done their very greatest things will ask how far the brilliant young author of **"The Barrel Organ"** has succeeded here. The answer must be that the bulk of **"Drake"** is written in sound and respectable, but not very distinguished, blank verse. The level is below that of the best of our young poets, below Mr. Phillips, for instance, and far below such beautiful blank verse as the **"Penthesilea"** of Mr. Binyon. But Mr. Noyes has his great moments, especially at the Leginning and end. here is a passage near the end:—

> And now along the Patagonian coast
> They cruised, and in the solemn midnight saw
> Wildernesses of shaggy barren marl,
> Petrified seas of lava, league on league,
> Craters and bouldered slopes and granite cliffs
> With ragged rents, grim gorges, deep ravines,
> And precipice on precipice up-piled
> Innumerable to these dim distances
> Where, over valleys hanging in the clouds,
> Gigantic mountains and volcanic peaks
> Catching the wefts of cirrus fleece appeared
> To smoke against the sky, though all was now
> Dead as that frozen chaos of the moon,
> Or some huge passion of a slaughtered soul
> Prostrate under the marching of the stars.

And here are the last words of the noble exordium which precedes the poem:—

> Mother and sweetheart, England; from whose breast,
> With all the world before them, they went forth,
> Thy seamen, o'er the wide uncharted waste,
> Wider than that Ulysses roamed of old,
> Even as the wine-dark Mediterranean
> Is wider than some tido-relinquished pool
> Among its rocks, yet none the 'less explored

To greater ends than all the pride of Greece
And pomp of Rome achieved; if my poor song
Now spread too wide a sail, forgive thy son
And lover, for thy love was over wont
To lift men up in pride above themselves
To do great deeds which of themselves alone
They could not; thou hast led the unfaltering feet
Of even thy meanest heroes down to death,
Lifted poor knights to many a great emprise,
Taught them high thoughts, and though they kept their
    souls
Lowly as little children, bidden them lift
Eyes unappalled by all the myriad stars
That wheel around the great white throne of God.

Here are the eloquence and beauty which are possible to youth; perhaps when the next books sppear Mr. Noyes will have added something of the varied experience which is only possible to age.

William Aspenwall Bradley (essay date 1907)

SOURCE: *"Alfred Noyes's New Volume,"* in *New York Times Book Review,* September 7, 1907, pp. 539.

[*In the following review, Bradley finds* The Flower of Old Japan *a disappointing effort in mediating between William Blake and Lewis Carroll.*]

Mr. Noyes's second American publication will not, we think, materially assist his reputation—which was left somewhat in suspense by his first volume. In fact, we believe that it will rather retard his serious recognition as a poet in this country. For if the selection of poems which was published here last year as an introduction to American readers was inconclusive; if it served on the whole to display the brilliance of his technique, the facility and cleverness of his versification, and his unusual verbal resources, without at the same time giving any evidence of deep-seated originality or genuine imaginative power, it at least contained a number of poems, like **"The Swimming Race,"** in which there was much beauty of expression, and others, like **"The Barrel Organ,"** in which, despite certain feeble affectations of manner, there was a blithe buoyancy of tone, together with a fresh unconventionality in the handling of metrical forms and in the use of the refrain.

In *The Flower of Old Japan*, on the other hand, it is possible to see little but futile ingenuity in the misdirection of poetic energy. The volume contains two long poems which were issued separately in England, but which are here brought together appropriately in that the second poem, **"The Forest of Wild Thyme,"** is conceived in the same spirit as the title poem, and is, in a sense, a sequel to it. Of the former, Mr. Noyes says in his preface that it "must not be taken to bear any real relation to Japan. It belongs to the kind of dreamland which an imaginative child might construct out of the oddities of a willow-pattern plate, and it differs chiefly from wonderlands of the Lewis Carroll type in a certain

seriousness behind its fantasy." **"The Forest of Wild Thyme"** also seeks, in another field but with the same underlying seriousness of sentiment, to construct the imaginative atmosphere of childish fantasy. Both poems are therefore attempts, as Mr. Mabie puts it in his preface to the earlier volume, to combine "the gay temper and the serious mood."

"The gay temper," for Mr. Noyes, is synonymous with the spirit of childhood. Hence, as he says of these two poems in his preface, "If the feet of the children are set dancing in them it was because as children we are best able to enter into that kingdom of dreams which is also the only true, the only real kingdom." One may, however, with some justice question just how representative such verse as he has written really is of the imaginative mood of childhood. Mr. Noyes has borrowed his precise form of fantasy from the modern nonsense verse which he appears to have accepted absolutely at its infantile face value. But such verse itself seems to us very often to have much more of sophistication, of the very antithesis of the child's way of thinking and feeling at the bottom of it, than is sometimes suspected. It is certainly a mistake to assume that because the child's view of nature appears grotesque to the grown man, the child himself is conscious of this grotesquerie or has any aesthetic appreciation of it. Much of what is today written either to please children or to interpret their incomplete or confused idea of things in general seems to us a gross libel on their intelligence, a slur on the pathetic seriousness of their attempts to construct a real world out of their incomplete knowledge and experience. Most nonsense-verse is puerile rather than childlike in any worthy sense of the word, and it seems to us that especially in the first of these two poems by Mr. Noyes, **"The Flower of Old Japan,"** there is a very considerable measure of this sheer puerility which is not made any the more palatable by the fact that the poet has adopted not only the ideas, if we may call them so, but the very idiom of modern nonsense-writers:

> "In China, well,
>   Perhaps you'll smell
> The cherry bloom; that's if you ran
>   A million miles
>   And jumped the stiles,
> And never dreamed of Old Japan.

> "What, palanquins
>   And Mandarins?
> And what d'you say, a blue divan,
>   And what? Hee! Hee!
>   You'll never see
> A pig-tailed head in Old Japan.

> "You'd take away
>   The ruby, hey?
> I never heard of such a plan!
>   Upon my word,
>   It's quite absurd,
> There's not a gem in Old Japan!

This sort of thing is not redeemed by any amount of clever rhyming nor is the poem as a whole, of which it is perhaps an exaggerated example of the poet's style at its silliest, saved by the richness of its exotic coloring or the quaintness of some of its conceits and pictures. What might without the gratuitous intrusion of the note of infancy be acceptable as a sort of musical fantasia on Japanese themes and motives is marred irretrievably by the false affectation of simplicity which is in reality far from simple, while the jingling measures and abrupt staccato phrases well-nigh reach the limit of maddening monotony. Even if it were essential to his purpose to create the illusion of childish naïveté Mr. Noyes might have achieved this with less violation of the principles of sound taste. One is forced either to the conclusion that Mr. Noyes is indeed deficient in imaginative insight as well as in the higher control of his art to be obliged to resort to so poor and mechanical an artifice for the evocation of "atmosphere," or that he is the victim of that conception of pseudo-realism which is variously exemplified in the poetry of to-day, and which makes Mr. Noyes in effect to say that to write poetry from the child's standpoint it is necessary to write like a child, or as a child might be expected to write if it could actually write at all. The ease with which this theory can be carried to a reductio ad absurdum is only too apparent, if indeed *The Flower of Old Japan* does not itself represent that final effort of futility.

But even more extraordinary than Mr. Noyes's verse is the preface. We have already quoted some pregnant passages from this preface, which was prepared especially for the American edition and which gives every sign of having been written, as it actually was, some time after the poems themselves. Indeed, one could almost fancy that the poet had not even taken the trouble to reread the latter for the purpose of refreshing his memory as to their real character and his real purpose in writing them, so little do they seem to support the profound and almost metaphysical interpretation which he attempts to put upon them. There is not space here for a complete analysis of what strikes us as a fundamental want of correspondence between poems and preface. One point, however, is clear, even obvious—this is, that whatever importance we attribute to the form of nonsense verse as an interpretation of one side of the child's imaginative life, it is not, at all events, exhaustive. It certainly does not translate, or attempt to translate, the mood of simple serious wonder of childhood in which is contained the germ of its later religious feeling. If it represents anything at all, it is rather the reverse of wonder, the mood of practical matter-of-fact acceptance, the complete conviction of what Mr. Noyes himself says—namely, that the world of dreams is the only true, the only real world. It is only in its direct contact with reality from which it cannot escape into some imaginative atmosphere of its own that the mood of wonder is evoked in the child—or in the man either for that matter—and it is the very condition sine qua non of nonsense verse, the primary principle of its existence, that such reality be banished beyond its boundaries.

It would seem scarcely necessary to make the above distinction, or to point out that there is a fundamental difference between "Songs of Innocence" and, say, "The Bab Ballads," or the works of Edward Lear, if it were not for the fact that Mr. Noyes seems to have failed to make this very ordinary distinction for himself or to understand clearly the nature of the barrier that separates these representative examples of two antipodal classes of literature. His own verse he apparently feels to partake of the nature of both, to affect a synthesis between them. Hence the curious confusion in the following passage in his preface: "It is perhaps because these poems are almost light enough for a nonsense book that I feel there is something to them more elemental, more essential, more worthy of serious consideration, than the most ponderous philosophical poem I could write. They are based on the fundamental and very simple mystery of the universe—that anything, even a grain of sand, should exist at all."

But are they so based? To us it seems that, just because they are of a quality to fit into a nonsense book, they are devoid of the very slightest trace of genuine mystery or wonderment. And why, if even a grain of sand is so mysterious, the creation in *The Flower of Old Japan*, of so elaborate an artificial wonderland? No, it is impossible to be both William Blake and Lewis Carroll at one and the same time. Nothing of the former has been revealed in Mr. Noyes so far, and his attempt to force upon his own poems a superior construction more in accordance with the profound ideality and mystical intuition of that poet only serves to bring into still clearer relief their essential kinship with the paradis artificiels of the "wonder" writers. . . .

Clayton Hamilton (essay date 1908)

SOURCE: A review of *The Golden Hynde,* in *The North American Review,* September, 1908, pp. 451-54.

[*In this review, Hamilton praises Noyes for his stylistic versatility while questioning the importance and relevance of his poems subject matter.*]

The main difficulty in attempting to estimate the value of the work of Mr. Alfred Noyes is that we are likely to be bewildered by his manifold and eager productivity. *The Golden Hynde and Other Poems*, though it is only the third volume of his verse to be published in America, is the sixth of his volumes to appear in England; and Mr. Noyes is at present only twenty-seven years of age. His fecundity is amazing, and his variety is even more so. He has written poems in innumerable measures that have heretofore been used in English verse, and has invented many measures of his own. He has sung to the tune of masters as diverse as Swinburne, Blake, Rossetti, Tennyson and Heine, with a reckless facility and joyous grace, and has informed all his work with an individuality of charm. He can write a ballad or a lullaby, a song or a symphony, a light lyric or an ode; and he writes them all with the same extraordinary technical accomplishment and dauntless ease. He has not yet developed a blank verse of his own that is completely organized, and his spontaneity of rhythmic variation seems as yet inconsonant with the restrictions of the sonnet form; but he has written no verse that is bad, and much that is very, very good. Perhaps he is most at home in the triple measures which Mr. Swinburne has taught him how to wield.

It is safe to say that even the master himself has seldom surpassed the fluent melody of such lines as these, from **"Orpheus and Eurydice"**:

> "And they that were dead, in his radiant music heard
>   the moaning of
>   doves in the olden
>   Golden-girdled purple pinewood, heard the moan of
>   the roaming sea;
>   Heard the chant of the soft-winged songsters, nesting
>   now in the
>   fragrant golden
>   Olden haunted blossoming bowers of lovers that
>   wandered in
>   Aready;
>
> "Saw the soft blue veils of shadow floating over the
>   billowy grasses
>   Under the crisp white curling clouds that sailed
>   and trailed through
>   the melting blue;
>   Heard once more the quarrel of lovers above them
>   pass, as a lark-
>   song passes,
>   Light and bright, till it vanished away in an eye-
>   bright heaven of
>   silvery dew.
>
> "White as a dream of Aphrodite, supple and sweet
>   as a rose in
>   blossom,
>   Fair and fleet as a fawn that shakes the dew from
>   the fern at break
>   of day,
>   Wreathed with the clouds of her dusky hair, that
>   kissed and clung
>   to her sun-bright bosom,
>   On through the deserts of hell she came, and the
>   brown air bloomed
>   with the light of May."

There can be no doubt whatever of Mr. Noyes's ability to versify. Although he is still very young, he has already mastered the mechanism of his art, and is prepared to say with permanence of form whatever may be given him to say. The deeper question remains to be considered whether or not the things he has to say are of sufficient importance to warrant the hope that in him English poetry may find a successor to the great Victorians. The evidence as yet is incomplete; but a thorough study of his recent volume gives me faith to venture an affirmative prediction. To be sure, it is not yet possible to formulate his message,—much less to weigh and measure it. We can do that in the case of Keats: all that is necessary is to quote the last two lines of the "Grecian Urn," and explain

them with sufficient fulness of understanding. Shelley also said one thing all his life; and it is conceivable that his message might be formulated in a single sentence,— though Matthew Arnold failed to do it in his famous glittering phrase. But Mr. Noyes, who has said so many different things, has as yet not said the one thing he was born to say. That very diversity which so amazes us in his work is probably a penalty that he pays for not yet having found out precisely who he is. He will not be truly great until, like Keats and Shelley, he shall succeed in revealing unity beneath his multiplicity.

But whatever may be the one thing that shall constitute his message, after his genius shall have found the centre around which it must be destined to revolve, I have faith that Mr. Noyes will say it; and the reason is that I have faith in the man himself, as he stands exhibited in all his work. His productivity and his variety are indicative more emphatically of his strength than of his incompleteness. He is productive because he is healthy; and he is various because he is divinely capable of being interested in "a number of things,"—to quote the "Happy Thought" of the Poet Laureate of Childhood, whom in many wise ways Mr. Noyes resembles. His healthiness of spirit is a boon for which to thank the gods. Nothing is the matter with his body or his soul. In this age of morbid introspection, he never looks upon himself to curse his fate. He never whines or whimpers: his sadness is the deep great sadness of a happy man. He religiously believes in being happy; and his triumphant youthfulness is a glorious challenge to the sort of maunderers who are forever saying, "Ah! but wait till you have suffered!" After all the moanings and the caterwaulings of the sorry little singers, we have found at last a poet to whom the world is not a twilight vale of tears, but a valley shimmering all dewy to the dawn, with a lark song over it.

Only two things, so far as I can see, may stop him. There is, of course, a certain peril in his facility. He writes so easily and well that he may be tempted sometimes to write merely for the joy of the working. Some of his poems are already just a little thin: they are done beautifully, but they did not of necessity have to be done at all. But his other danger is more considerable. In several of the poems of this latest volume, he shows a tendency to intellectual dogmatism. He expresses good thought in good verse, instead of writing poetry. This is especially true in the pieces in which he inveighs against war, with a deliberate reversal of Mr. Kipling's thunderous imperialism, and in those other pieces in which he translates his general truth into the too particular terms of Christian dogma. He is least representative of his England when he strives consciously to deliver a laureate utterance. When an intellectual or moral purpose gets in his way, he usually misses that perfect emotional fusion of content and expression which is poetry.

But these are, after all, only the defects of his qualities. Mr. Noyes is by far the most promising of all the younger English poets, because of his vigor and variety, his freshness of personality, and his ease of art. His career should be watched hopefully by all lovers of literature. We cannot now say what the future has in store for him;

but it seems safe to predict that if any poet now writing is to inherit the mantle, it is he.

Richard Le Gallienne (essay date 1910)

SOURCE: "An English Epic by Alfred Noyes," in *The New York Times Book Review*, February 19, 1910, p. 92.

[*In the following review, Le Gallienne classifies* Drake *as an anachronism, but not quite an epic.*]

There is no denying that at first sight Mr. Alfred Noyes's epic has the look of a fearsomely ponderous performance. The very make of the book, handsomely made as it is, with its reproductions of old portraits and old prints, suggests rather a weighty historical treatise than a poem. The words "Books I., xii.," on the title page, also, and the serried lines of 343 pages of blank verse tend to deepen one's misgivings—though here and there the eye catches with a ray of hope the italicised lyrics set like sprays of blossom in the solid unrelenting text.

It is true that we have on the cover quotations of praise from Mr. Kipling and Mr. Swinburne to reassure us. Mr. Kipling vouches that "the tale itself held me yesterday evening from one end to the other," and Mr. Swinburne wrote "your noble and patriotic and historic poem." But then, if I may be excused the expression, Mr. Kipling is, and Mr. Swinburne was, so rabidly British that their opinion of any glorification of England is apt to be tainted with a suspicion of chauvinism. However, as we take heart, and bravely face Mr. Noyes's epic for ourselves, by degrees, though by no means at first, it begins to dawn on us that both those great poets were not so very far wrong. In spite of its anachronistic method, and its cumbrous build—not unlike the elaborate castelled Spanish galleons which Mr. Noyes in many places so picturesquely describes—the story does get hold of one, and there is no doubt whatever, as The London Times said, that "the air we are breathing is great air."

Mr. Noyes has written a special "Prologue to the American Edition," in which, after the manner of imperialistic poets, he naturally speaks of "England, my mother," but again with anachronistic affectation, speaks of America as "my Western sweetheart" and "sweet." Somehow the time seems past for such terms of endearment applied to great embattled nations, and particularly to this iron and "invincible republic." But some of the verses are worth quoting for the expression of that ideal of racial unity which our poets are the men to foster:

> Pledge her deep, my mother;
> Through her veins thy life-stream runs!
> Spare a thought, too, sweetheart, for
>   my mother o'er the sea!
> Younger eyes are yours; but ah, those
>   old eyes and none other
> Once bedewed the Mayflower; once

> As yours, were dear and free.
>   Once! Nay, now as ever
> Beats within her ancient heart
> All the faith that took you forth to
>   seek your heaven alone;
> Shadows come and go; but let no shade
>   of doubt dissever,
> Cloak, or cloud, or keep apart
>   Two souls whose prayer is one.

If, as I have hinted, Mr. Noyes's poem is an anachronism, it is, of course, a conscious one; for Mr. Noyes has evidently deliberately set himself to write the epic of Drake in much the same manner as an Elizabethan poet might have treated it—old Michael Drayton, for example, whose style and method, indeed, it much resembles. It resembles, too, in its longdrawn narrative, its highly decorated descriptiveness, its generally dreamy and richly colored atmosphere, one of those chronicles in tapestry which in Drake's time were hung upon the walls of royal chambers—tapestries

> From Flanders looms, whereon were
>   flowers and beasts
> And forest work, great knights, with
>   hawk on hand,
> Riding forever on their glimmering
>   steeds
> Through bowery glades to some im-
>   mortal face
> Beyond the fairy fringes of the world.

William Morris, too, has evidently had his share in inspiring the method of this poem, "born out of its due time." Conformably with his Elizabethan models, Mr. Noyes opens his poem with a prayerful "exordium," in which he acclaims the greatness of his theme and invokes his "mother and love, fair England," to sustain his muse in its ambitious enterprise:

> The large imperious legend of our race,
> Ere it brought forth the braggarts of
>   an hour,
> Self-worshippers who love their imaged
>   strength,
> And as a symbol for their own proud
>   selves
> Misuse the sacred name of this dear
>   land,
> While England to the Empire of her
>   soul,
> Like some great Prophet passes
>   through the crowd
> That cannot understand . . .

This whole "exordium" is a-tremble with the prayerful passion of a noble patriotism, a patriotism which, however, comes occasionally to seem a little overstrung, almost hysterical, as it continues to pray or prophesy and apostrophize through twelve long books. Yet it is but fair to say that the books, as we read, do not seem as long as they look, for I repeat that the story does hold one, though, its power being cumulative, it is hard to illustrate by quotation. The most vivid episode is undoubtedly the execution of Doughty, a gentleman adventurer who, with others of his class, sailed with Drake on The Golden Hynde on his historic expedition to ravage the Spanish Main. Drake had sailed under the express patronage of Elizabeth, of whom Mr. Noyes gives a striking picture, but Lord Burleigh, who did not approve of Drake's plan, had sent Doughty with him as a spy. Doughty simulates friendship for Drake, but secretly stirs up mutiny among his crews, and Drake, at last discovering his treachery, brings him to trial on a lonely shore on the Straits of Magellan, the skeleton of one of Magellan's old mutineers dangling mournfully on the wind hard by. Drake's crews decree that Doughty must die. Doughty gayly accepts his fate and begs them all to feast with him before his execution.

I would I had space to illustrate by quotation the solemn impressiveness with which Mr. Noyes pictures for us this strange scene.

The figure of Drake, while impressive, is rather that of a demigod than of a human being, and the tender side of him, as in his love story and in his religion, a curious blend of piracy and Puritanism, seems a little oversentimentalized. It is, indeed, when Drake speaks that the dramatic unreality, the naif limitations, of Mr. Noyes's old-world method reveal themselves. Of course, the reader is expected to accept the artistic conditions of the poem, yet it is hard to imagine Drake talking like this:

> And Drake, be-mused, leaned smiling
> to his friend
> Doughty and said, "Is it not strange
> to know
> When we return yon speckled herring
> gulls
> Will still be wheeling, dipping, flash-
> ing there
> Just as we leave them? Ah, my heart
> cries out
> We shall not find a sweeter land afar
> Than those thyme-scented hills we
> leave behind!
> Soon the young lambs will bleat across
> the combes,
> And breezes will bring puffs of haw-
> thorn scent
> Down Devon lanes; over the purple
> moors;
> Lavrocks will carol and the plover cry,
> The nesting peewit cry; on village
> greens
> Around the Maypole, while the moon
> hangs low,
> The boys and girls of England merrily
> swing
> In country footing through the flowery
> dance:
> Roses return: I blame them not who
> stay,

> I blame them not at all who cling to
> home.
> For many of us, indeed, shall not re-
> turn.
> Nor ever know that sweetness any
> more.

For me the value of the poem lies chiefly in its pictures, its tapestried description. Take this fine picture of a Spanish galleon:

> For through a mighty zone of golden
> haze,
> Blotting the purple of the gathering
> night,
> A galleon like a floating mountain
> moved
> To meet them, clad with sunset and
> with dreams.
> Her masts and spars immense in jew-
> eled mists
> Shimmered: her rigging, like an emer-
> ald web
> Of golden spiders, tangled half the
> stars!
> Embodied sunset, dragging the soft sky
> O'er dazzled ocean, through the night
> she drew
> Out of the unknown lands, and round
> a prow
> That jutted like a moving promontory
> Over a cloven wilderness of foam,
> Upon a lofty blazoned scroll her name
> *San Salvador* challenged obsequious isles
> Where'er she rode . . .

Also the poem is charged with the romantic learning, the legendary geography, the fairy-tale maps of the time, of one of which Mr. Noyes gives this delightful description:

> And on the table lay the magic chart,
> Drawn on a buffalo horn, all small-
> peaked isles,
> Dwarf promontories, tiny twisted
> creeks,
> And fairy harbours under elfin hills,
> With marvellous inscriptions lined in
> red—
> *As Here is Gold*, or *Many Rubics Here*,
> *Or Ware Witch-crafte*, or *Here is Canni-
> bals*.

And Mr. Noyes is very skillful in conveying the haunted mystery and marvels of the unknown tropic seas:

> Sometimes at midnight round them all
> the sea
> Quivered with witches' oils and water-
> snakes.
> Green, blue, and red, with lambent
> tongues of fire.

Mile upon mile about the blurred black
　　hulls
A cauldron of tempestuous color
　　coiled.
On every mast mysterious meteors
　　burned,
And from the shores a bellowing rose
　　and fell
As of great bestial gods that walked
　　all night
Through some wild dell unknown, too
　　vast for men. . . .

Scattered amid the narratives are some charming lyrics in the Elizabethan manner, brought in as, in their voyaging, the skilled musicians, who were a romantic feature of Drake's cruises, would strike up a song amid the lonely seas. Here are a few verses of perhaps the most beautiful:

Sweet, what is love? 'Tis not the
　　crown of Kings,
Nay, nor the fire of white seraphic
　　wings!
Is it a child's heart leaping while he
　　sings?
　　　　　Even so say I;
　　　　　Even so say I.

Love, like a child around our world
　　doth run,
Happy, happy, happy for all that God
　　hath done,
Glad of all the little leaves dancing
　　in the sun,
　　　　　Even so say I;
　　　　　Even so say I.

Sweet, what is love? 'Tis not the burn-
　　ing bliss
Angels know in heaven! God blows
　　the world a kiss,
Wakes on earth a wild rose! Ah, who
　　knows not this?
　　　　　Even so say I;
　　　　　even so say I.

So it will be seen that if this poem must be classed as an anachronism, a brilliant tour de force, if we cannot take it quite seriously as an "epic," it is, none the less, rich in manifold fine qualities, and animated by a noble poetic spirit.

The New York Times Book Review (essay date 1910)

SOURCE: "New Poems by Alfred Noyes," in *The New York Times Book Review*, June 11, 1910, p. 339.

[*This review characterizes Noyes's* The Enchanted Island *as "a better book than the author has given us hitherto."*]

It is a common characteristic of the average human to be deeply discouraged over the popular contemporaneous mind; it is always so unintelligent, or so immoral, or so materialistic. Just now the general feeling is that it is too materialistic to appreciate true poetry, and therefore true poetry is not being written. As a matter of fact, if poetry were governed by the ordinary laws of supply and demand, its production would rank with cotton-spinning, or the manufacture of porcelain bath tubs—lower, indeed, since no one can deny the utility of these last-named arts. The truth is, that, as with the wind of the world or the soul of man, no one can say whence poetry cometh or whither it goeth; but one thing is certain: so long as there is Youth to listen or Age to be reminded, so long as the Huntress and the Persuader war in the veins of men, the poet, good, indifferent, and even bad, will have his audience. The fact that poetry is not a commercially profitable form of literature is beside the question. If any proof were needed that even this froward generation is willing to dance if properly piped to, the popularity of Alfred Noyes both in England and in America would sufficiently attest it.

The Enchanted Island, and Other Poems, is a distinct advance, as a whole, upon Mr. Noyes' previous work. Though it would be hard to find anything more perfect than his earlier song,

There's a barrel-organ carolling across
　　a golden street

In the City as the sun sinks low,

with its onomatopoetic swing, its music, and its deep, underlying humanity, there is in this volume, on the other hand, no trace of the earlier immaturity. Here the author has found himself, and he strikes a clear, distinct, and very manly note. He understands how to be simple without falling into the commonplace, robust without being brutal, and to distinguish the beautiful from the decadent-beautiful. A characteristic of the book is an extraordinary quality of make-believe, of illusion, as though we had stepped by accident upon a magic carpet, and had been straightway transported—miraculously, to be sure, but with a curious matter-of-factness about it, too—back to the period before shades of the prison-house began to close about the growing boy. Wordsworth says that

Nothing can bring back the hour
Of splendor in the grass, of glory in
　　the flower;

but Mr. Noyes has very nearly accomplished it in **"The Tramp Transfigured."** It begins with ingratiating gravity:

All the way to Fairyland across the
　　thyme and heather,
Round a little bank of fern that rus-
　　tled on the sky,
Me and stick and bundle, Sir, we
　　jogged along together,

and it would be a very dull-hearted or dull-witted person who would not follow the adventures of the tattered tramp who

"became a butterfly—
(Ain't it hot and dry?
Thank you, Sir; thank you, Sir!) a
   blooming butterfly,"
with a serious interest that quotation can do little to
   suggest.

It is this quality of convincingness—which of course is nothing more or less than imagination—that gives the poems upon the naval heroes of England their splendid sweep and power. **"The Admiral's Ghost"** (which proves beyond a doubt that Nelson was the reincarnation, at England's need, of Sir Francis Drake) and **"The Island Hawk"** contain more than one of those thrills down the spine and glows at the heart by which we measure the value of patriotic poetry. One wonders if their author was aware of the inconsistency which set these verses cheek-by-jowl with **"Lucifer's Feast,"** a gruesome description of the particularly dreadful hell to which the bad men go, who fight each other in their countries' quarrels. This poem is one of those agglomerations of epithet and figure which highly imaginative poets have to get out of their systems once in a while, and yet it would not be strange if it were a favorite child. One can imagine Shelley as ranking **"Queen Mab"** above the "Ode to a Skylark."

There are echoes in plenty in *An Enchanted Island, and Other Poems*—echoes, it should be said, of the spirit, not of the letter, but Mr. Noyes is no less happy in his admirations than in his originalities. His masters are Meredith, Swinburne, and Stevenson, and not one has reason to be ashamed of him. It would be invidious to compare the

Huntress arrowy to pursue—
She, that breath of upper air—

of Meredith, with the supine Diana his disciple
   portrays in "Acteon"—beautiful in technique though
   it is; but surely Swinburne would have loved the
   last lines of the poem addressed to himself—

Wings of the sea, good-bye, good-bye,
Down to the dim sea-line;

and Stevenson, it is to be hoped, is somewhere conscious of that exquisite bit of fooling, "Bacchus and the Pirates." In this veracious, wonderfully rhymed narrative, half a hundred terrible, piping, cut-throat, elegant, dreamstruck, diffident, tottering, jubilant, innocent, fanciful, horrified, lunatic, goggle-eyed, ribbonless, respectable pirates, including Captain Hook, and "Silver himself, with his cruel crutch, and the blind man Pew," had the rare fortune to kidnap Bacchus as he lay asleep on the beach of the "happiest of the Happy Islands," and bear him away "in the lurching bows of the old black barque,

As the sunset died and the white
   moon dawned, and we saw on the
   island a star-bright bevy
Of naked Bacchanals stealing to watch
   through the whispering vines in the
   purple dark!

But the flame-haired god revenged himself, and the diffident pirates ended sadly as Christy Minstrels. while Hook conducted the big brass band.

While it is to be hoped that in the future Mr. Noyes will give us more frolicsome verse like **"Bacchus and the Pirates,"** and more of "the glory of deep-sea kings," it is also to be hoped that he will realize where his richest ore lies, and will not neglect that mine. For there are indications in *The Enchanted Island* that it is in Mr. Noyes to become a great poet, a poet of the People, and of the New Day of the People, that other men have tried in vain to become. **"The Electric Tram"** is not an important poem, judged by the standard of weights and measures, or a carpenter's foot-rule, and its title is as ordinary as most real things are. But every line of it is instinct with "a veined humanity." And **"Rank and File"** is too long, perhaps; it becomes monotonous through repetition, but there is perhaps no poem of the new century with which to compare it in nobility of purpose or in dignity of expression.

Hints and facets of One—the Eternal,
Faces of grief, compassion and pain,
Faces of hunger, faces of stone,
Faces of love and of labor, marching,
Changing facets of One,—the Eternal,
Streaming up thro' the wind and the rain,
All together and each alone.

You that doubt of the world's one Passion,
You for whose science the stars are astray,
Hark—to their orderly thunder-tread!
These, in the night, with the stars are marching
One to the end of the world's one Passion!
You that have taken their Master away,
Where have you laid Him, living or dead?

Not Meredith or Swinburne or Stevenson could have compassed the grave and pregnant beauty of those lines. Meredith is more thorough master of the word that cleaves to the thought till the twain are one flesh; Swinburne surpasses him in the melting or the fiery phrase; Stevenson has as light a hand, but here is a poem that no one but Alfred Noyes could have shaped and polished. This is poetry that is worth any man's making, and is worthy any man's reading.

Joyce Kilmer (essay date 1913)

SOURCE: "At the Mermaid," in *The New York Times*, April 20, 1913, p. 237.

[*Kilmer's review of* Tales of the Mermaid Tavern *suggests that this collection of poems elevates Noyes from a "jingle" writer to a place beside the "English Masters."*]

Generalizations are dangerous things. For instance, we are told over and over that this is an age of prose, "an age," according to William Watson, "that banishes the poets; scourges them with the scourge of apathy, from out her

bosom's rich metropolis." The poet, it is said, has no longer an audience. We humbly accept this judgment, and long
for the vanished days when Byron lived in luxury and Moore
built country houses out of "Lalla Rookh." Then, in the
face of all this, there appears a young man decently dressed
and seemingly well-fed, with no visible means of support
except poetry. Is there no generalization to account for
this phenomenon? Yes, indeed, say our wise pessimists,
this is no exception to the rule. This man gives the public
not poetry but rhymes, jingling platitudes to please the
mob. If he offered them poetry he would offer it in vain.
And just as we are on the point of assenting to this plausible theory the poet himself disproves it. He writes *Tales
of the Mermaid Tavern*.

There was splendid vigor in **Drake**, **Sherwood** was full
of the magic of romance, and in the volume called **The
Enchanted Island** were many lyrics of haunting loveliness. But with *Tales of the Mermaid Tavern* Alfred
Noyes takes his place undeniably and triumphantly among
the masters of English literature. The prophecies of
Swinburne and Edmund Gosse, made on the publication
of his earlier works, are fulfilled. Not in this generation
is the country of Wordsworth and Tennyson to lack a
great poet.

Dealing, as they do, with the men and events of bygone
centuries, these poems are, nevertheless, infused with
the modern spirit. We have passed through an age of
materialism, of cold negation, of obsession with things
physical and temporal. Now, all over the world, eyes
weary with questioning the unresponsive earth are turned
again to the skies; once more we are beginning to affirm
rather than to deny; to acknowledge, sometimes with a
curious sense of embarrassment, that we have souls. Such
men as Belloc and Chesterton in England and Bazin and
Francis Jammes in France are calling our attention to
ancient truths whose glories have not grown dim because
for a while we tried to shut them from our sight. The new
spirit in the thought of the world is the spirit of belief,
of idealism, of a chivalry higher than that of any of the
ages past. And so the poet whose concern is solely with
bodily pleasure and pain, with the transient phenomena of
civilization, with little passions and emotions, is rushing
to oblivion. And the world, always ready to listen to
authentic song, hears gladly of the courage of Sir
Humphrey Gilbert, the patriotic faith of Sir Walter
Raleigh, and the firm friendship of the poets who met in
the Mermaid Tavern. For not only are these names
fragrant with romance, they are symbols, exemplars
of the immortal virtues of the soul of man.

In the introductory tale the poet turns down a narrow lane
off Fleet Street and finds himself before a little inn. He
stares at the worn green paint on the doors and shutters,
at the swinging sign with its siren twisting and smirking
above fantastic rocks, and recognizes it as the Mermaid
Tavern. Through its old walls come sounds of laughter
and clashing wine cups and a ringing chorus:

> Marchaunt Adventurers, chanting at
>   the windlass,

> Early in the morning we slipped
>   from Plymouth Sound,
> All for adventure in the great New
>   Regions,
> All for Eldorado and to sail the
>   world around!

At the end of the song a tall, crimson–clad figure strides
to the inn door, and the poet, seeing his murrey-colored
velvet cloak, caked with mud, knows him to be Sir Walter
Raleigh. He follows him into the inn parlor, to receive a
buffet on the head, and to hear shouts of "Sack! Malm-
sey! Muscadel!" and to learn that he is pot-boy of the
Mermaid Inn. He fills his new rôle with delight, for what
a company he has to serve—Michael Drayton, Kit Marlowe, Lyly, Peele, Dekker, Ben Jonson, and Shakespeare
himself! During the rest of the story his own thoughts
and adventures are left untold; he appears only as the
reporter of the great happenings and greater talks that
come to pass in the smoke-darkened parlor of the famous old inn. Before the day closes Sir Walter Raleigh
has sung the ballad of "A Knight of the Ocean Sea," telling of Sir Humphrey Gilbert's wild voyage and noble death.
It is a splendid poem, full of salt spray and thundering
waves of rhythm, and when it is done Michael Drayton
rises to praise all brave seafaring men, and especially the
subject of Raleigh's ballad, bidding all his friends "Stand
up," and drink to his immortal fame.

From this tale of the sea we pass to the chronicle of
events vastly different and much richer in romantic interest. Jonson sings a gay little song of Will Shakespeare's
poaching exploits in Charlecote Wood, and, as he finishes it, sees the Puritan Richard Bame peering in through
the doorway. The poets tease this dismal visitor for a
while, but they stop suddenly when they see the pamphlet
he carries—"A Groat's Worth of Wit Bought with a
Million of Repentance." As together they read this strange
document, the last work of their dead companion, Robert
Greene, a hand is laid on Kit Marlowe's shoulder and the
voice of Shakespeare asks for the scurrilous attack of
which he is the object. He reads the familiar lines about
the "upstart crow beautified with our feathers . . . an
absolute Johannes factotum in his own conceit," and puts
the paper down to defend its author against the Puritan's
insinuations. He has received, he says, another message
from Robert Greene, written on his deathbed. And he
reads a pathetic letter, a lament for wasted talent and a
ruined life, and a contrite apology for the foolish attack
which has given Greene an unhonored fame down to the
present day.

The situation is tense as Shakespeare finishes his reading
and the entrance of a company of jovial players comes as
a relief. There are some moments of shrewd comedy, in
which Greene's reputation is saved from the clutches of
the Puritan Bame, and the company separates after a rousing song.

To this chapter of romance and tragedy succeeds the broad
comedy of **"Black Bill's Honey-Moon."** This is a joyous fantasy, telling of the amazing adventures of Black

Bill, bo'sun of the galleon Cloud i' the Sun, who came to grief from his love of honey and learned at length the use of bears. Mr. Noyes enjoyed writing this thoroughly; it is done with the whimsical abandon that characterizes **"Bacchus and the Pirates."**

Now comes the greatest and most tragic passage in the book, that which tells of the sordid death of Kit Marlowe. The tale is called **"The Sign of the Golden Shoe."** Chapman sings of the poet as a little boy playing in the streets of Canterbury. Then Nash, who witnessed Marlowe's death, pours out in nervous, fiery terza rima his hatred for the wretched woman who seduced the young poet and for her vile follower who killed him. Seldom in recent years has more passionate scorn been put into verse.

This is, we have said, the book's greatest story. Surely no other part of the long poem surpasses it in dramatic intensity. Yet, it is difficult to make comparisons, for the nature of the poetry varies from tale to tale. Here is the episode of sprightly Will Kemp, the jester, who danced across England. We see London gay with fern and hawthorn and with the blue and yellow and scarlet garments of the morris dancers, we listen to the sweetest, merriest lyrics that have been sung since Corinna went a-Maying. We see Ben Jonson borne in triumph on the shoulders of his friends from prison to the tavern door, and we shout with the crowd, "For all good inns are moons or stars, but the Mermaid is their Sun!" Then on a gloomy All Souls' Eve we sit with Ford and Drummond of Hawthornden and hear the old sexton chant the pedlar-poet's ballad of the secret burial of Mary, Queen of Scots. Gregory Clopton, clerk of the Bow Bell, sings out the chiming phrases that chronicle the splendid fortune of "Sweet Dick Whittington, Flos Mercatorum and a barefoot boy!" And finally we hear of Raleigh's noble death, and of his widow's tremendous vengeance on his betrayer. Here is wide range of versemaking; here are delicate love songs, rousing choruses and gripping narratives of high adventure.

Technically, merely as exercises in the musical arrangement of words, some of the songs in *The Tales of the Mermaid Tavern* are comparable only to the choruses in *Atlanta in Calydon*. But this technical perfection is not obtrusive—Mr. Noyes is no mere juggler of phrases. The interest of the stories is so great that the poet's skill is for the moment unnoticed, the reader's mind is full of grief for poor Kit Marlowe, or of joy in the comradeship of Jonson and Shakespeare in the warm comfort of the Mermaid inn. And through it all, every haunting line, is the insistent note of triumphant idealism, that idealism which once was graven on tablets of stone, and which once flooded with the light an inn older and fairer than the Mermaid.

Brian Hooker (essay date 1913)

SOURCE: A review of *Tales Of The Mermaid Inn,* in *The Bookman,* June, 1913, pp. 445-48.

[*In the following review of* Tales of the Mermaid Inn, *Hooker suggests that the poem is not Elizabethan because it is modern in "form, prosody and style."*]

The critical commonplace about Mr. Alfred Noyes's *Tales of the Mermaid Tavern* is that he portrays the Elizabethan period and the writing, fighting, adventurous London that was then. And this, like many commonplaces, is a halftruth none the worse for winnowing. Certainly, in the sense of representing these spacious times as their own literature presented them, the book is not Elizabethan at all: there is hardly a page in it which could have been written before 1850, or which is not unmistakably dated as modern by form and prosody and style.

> Marchaunt Adventurers, O what 'ull ye
>   bring home again?
>   Woonders and works and the thunder of
>   the sea!
> Whom will ye traffic with? The King of
>   the sunset!—
>   What shall be your pilot, then?—A wind
>   from Galilee!
> —Nay, but ye be marchaunts, will ye come
>   back empty-handed?—
> Ay, we be marchaunts, though our gain
>   we ne'er shall see!
> Cast we now our bread upon the waste wild
>   waters;
> After many days it shall return with
>   usury.
>   *Chorus:*
>
> Marchaunt Adventurers,
> Marchaunt Adventurers,
> What shall be your profit in the mighty days
>   to be?
>   Englande! Englande! Englande! Eng-
>   lande!
> Glory everlasting, and the lordship of the
>   sea.

There is no need to argue about it, or even to point out the demonstrative details: the Elizabethans did not write like that. They did not versify like that either; nor, so far as we of this late day have any means of judging, did they think like that. But this subtler question demands a little more analysis.

> "Thy Summer's Night—eh, Will? Midsum-
>   mer's Night?—
> That's a quaint fancy," Bacon droned anew,
> "But—Athens was an error, Will! Not
>   Athens!
> Titania knew not Athens! Those wild elves
> Of thy Midsummer's Dream—eh? Mid-
>   night's Dream?—
> Are English all. Thy woods, too, smack of
>   England;
> They never grew round Athens. Bottom,
>   too,
> He is not Greek!"

"Greek?" Will said, with a chuckle,
"Bottom a Greek? Why, no, he was the son
Of Marian Hacket, the fat wife that kept
An ale-house, Wincot-way. I lodged with
    her
Walking from Stratford. You have never
    tramped
Along that country side? By Burton Heath?
Ah, well, you would not know my fairy-
    lands.
It warms my blood to let my home-spuns
    play
Around your cold white Athens. There's a
    joy
In jumping time and space."

Now, here is a thoroughly modern bit of criticism, albeit spoken in character. Bacon might well enough have so objected, and Shakespeare so answered—if the idea had ever occurred to them; but we may doubt its occurrence to the Bacon who, for all his learning, calls the Witch of Endor a "Pythonissa" and quotes his Homer in Vergilian Latin, or to the Shakespeare who, both as poet and as manager, costumed all times alike. It is Mr. Noyes who feels a joy in jumping time and space, and who shares with us that pleasure: the Elizabethans, in a manner of speaking, dwelt as gods outside and unconscious of time; and Shakespeare could never have written **Bacchus and the Pirates**, precisely because in his mind they would have met as naturally as Touchstone and Hymen. This conjuring with great names borrows its whole enchantment from distance: it is wonderful for us to sit at table among great names which have already outworn the drums and trampings of three hundred years; but for themselves there was no such wonder. Wings are not wonderful to angels; and it is obvious, though inconceivable, that elephants do not feel elephantine. What Mr. Noyes has done, therefore, is more than merely to imitate Elizabethan verse or to attempt a futile realism of archeology. He is a poet, not a fabricator of antiques; and his creation is our own vision (and his) of the Mermaid Tavern, a new light and life upon a tradition grown great in growing old: a transfiguration of those souls of poets dead and gone in bodies not the same but glorified by centuries of imagining. What the Elizabethan Age thought of itself we see darkly through the glass of its own literature; to that nothing can ever be added; it is done. What the Elizabethan Age actually was in daily fact we cannot possibly know; it is gone, erased, dissolved into oblivion. But what the Elizabethan Age is now, for us, is another and a living thing, as real as a dream and as immortal as a soul; and in recreating this Elizabethan Age of ours, Mr. Noyes has done again what Shakespeare did for the ancient Rome and Athens of his own day. And that, after all, is the only thing that really matters. We are concerned with past times and distant places only as they exist for us: with the present connotation of words like "Elizabethan" or "Athenian" or "mediæval"; with the traditional personalities of Alexander and Cleopatra and Cæsar and Hamlet and George Washington; for these are now a portion of our thought and an influence upon our living, whereas that which they actually were has long ceased to exist. Thus the Middle Ages of Scott and Victor Hugo, the

Pompeii of Bulwer-Lytton, may be historically quite inaccurate; nobody really knows or ever will; but they are at least alive among us, and the facts are dead. Indeed, in a certain sense, these fictions are truer to the life than was that very life itself. Cæsar and Lincoln were in fact something more than they or their contemporaries knew: their future fame was part of them. It is no quibble to say of the actual Hamlet or Macbeth that their chief historical act was to furnish material for Shakespeare. And the whole truth about those gatherings at the Mermaid could not have been apparent to themselves, precisely because it has taken time to prove their greatness: there sat the characters of a poem which would not be written until the year nineteen hundred and twelve.

And in this imaginative embodying of the Elizabethan spirit as it has come down to us, this holding up of the mirror to our romantic and traditional sense of what the Mermaid must have been, these poems are marvellously successful. The book has that cross-section effect, as of a world created, which is the hallmark of a few great novels: that sense of a window opened upon a bright and busy scene wherein every sharp detail suggests unobserved complexities and more is felt than meets the eye. You have this feeling about the India of *Kim*, the Paris of *Notre Dame*, the Georgian society of *Vanity Fair*; but it is a very rare thing to find it in a poem. Mr. Noyes's own **Drake**, for example, with all its fertility of gorgeous images, had no charm to unseal these magic casements. The *Faerie Queene* is perhaps the best example of the quality in English—if we except Shakespeare's creations of Bohemia and Arden. And the method by which this feeling is produced is a remarkable development of one of the first devices of literary craftsmanship—the device of going back into romance for the origin of something immediately familiar to the reader. It is that formula of the folk-tale which begins with the long nose of the elephant or the short tail of the bear, and tells a story to account for it: "and if you doubt the story, just look at the next elephant you see." The conjuring with great names, of which I have already spoken, is a part of this; the very title of the volume is a case in point; and the device is worked out imaginatively in a myriad of details, a gold thread woven through the poems to give the texture brilliancy. We meet with "brick-layer Ben"—

The T, for Tyburn, branded on his thumb,—

and the mention of that mark is like a credential and an identification. Some of us recognise it; others are informed so casually that they feel reminded. It is as simple as an inference of Sherlock Holmes—and as bewilderingly effective. These allusions, moreover, are not hung upon the work like tags, but imagined keenly and emotionally; they are the very stuff of which the dream is made.

I fitted her with morrice-bells, with treble,
    bass and tenor bells;
    The fore-bells, as I linked them at her
        throat, how soft they sang!
Green linnets in a golden nest, they chirped

and trembled on her breast,
And, faint as elfin blue-bells, at her nut-
    brown ankles rang.

Analyse that, after you have done merely enjoying it: try to resolve the elements of learning and artistry and sentiment; see how information is informed with melody, how in the blending and modelling of all, one line will help the poem in various ways, how the brain serves the heart. And you will suspect why the old tradition of the world paid poets the honour of astonishment. For the test of any true creation is that the more you examine it and dissect and discover and understand, the more material you have for wonder.

To attempt a critical appraisal of this book within the limits of a page or two would be somewhat unsatisfactory and perhaps a little premature; for there is too much in it, both for better and for worse, to encourage the superficial balancing of a fault here against a merit there in the endeavour to anticipate posterity. Rather it has seemed of interest to approach a single phase of its craftsmanship in the character more of an observer than of a judge. There is many another phase of equal interest; and to one such in particular it is worth while to call attention. If any single book might comprehend and settle for all time that long-disputed question of morality and art, then that book is the **Tales of the Mermaid Tavern**. It is all here, precept and example and illustration: for whomsoever will really read; the matter is concluded. But how and why these poems have offered a conclusion must be left for the nonce to the observation of the reader.

Times Literary Supplement (essay date 1922)

SOURCE: "Astronomy in Verse," in *The Times Literary Supplement*, March 23, 1922, p. 188.

[*In the following review, Noyes is noted for his "readability" while providing a history of astronomy in verse.*]

We have grown apt during the last hundred years to think of poetry as something which lives entirely and continuously on the heights, something in which we are at every moment conscious of a concentration of formal beauty with intellectual, emotional, and imaginative energy. But poetry was not always so narrowly defined, nor such large demands made upon it. Indeed, such definitions tend to admit of no poetry but lyrical. For nothing else, or hardly anything else, can maintain that concentration continuously for very long. Even the "Paradise Lost" scarcely does so; and perhaps the human mind could not bear to read such poetry if poets could write it. The strain might be too great. As it is, only people of exceptional aptitude for poetry can read without fatigue at a sitting more than a few books of the Æneid or the "Paradise Lost"; and are there any poets except Homer, Virgil, Milton, and Dante who can even pretend to maintain themselves continuously on those heights? Lucretius cannot, certainly; nor the author of "The Prelude" and "The Excursion."

Mr. Noyes has no claim to be of the rank of Lucretius or Wordsworth. But he may have done a service by his effort to recover for us some lost regions of the old wide, almost universal, kingdom of poetry. Verse came before prose in the beginning. Once not only was every tale told but every science taught in verse. That led to many breaches of the later law that nothing should be said in verse which could be equally well said in prose. But surely we have now let the pendulum swing too far in the other direction. With all its poetic limitations, the eighteenth century knew, what we have forgotten, that there is a pleasure in verse for its own sake, a pleasure which prose cannot give. And it was the poet who turned his back on the eighteenth century who said that poetry was the impassioned expression which is in the countenance of all science. And if so, science should not be excluded from the possible subjects of poetry. Even a poet who cannot keep continuously on the heights may by his verse give something of science which prose cannot give.

That is what Mr. Noyes tries to do here for astronomy. His poem is a sort of sketch of the history of astronomy in seven chapters, with a Prologue and an Epilogue. The chapters are Copernicus, Tycho Brahe, Kepler, Galileo, Newton, William and John Herschel. The conception of the poem took shape in Mr. Noyes's mind during a night which he spent on a summit of the Sierra Madre Mountains when the first trial was made of the new 100 in. telescope. His experience that night is described in the Prologue. The poem attempts to give, does in fact give so far as a layman can judge, the gradual development, stage by stage, of modern astronomy. It is admirably lucid. Whatever is said can be understood by anyone. And yet the poet has not forgotten the "impassioned expression" which is only to be found on the countenance of science when it is a human eye that gazes at it. His "Torchbearers" hand on, each to his successor, the light of imagination, faith, and love, as well as that of knowledge. The poem reads everywhere in the stars the faith of Newton in:—

> that First Cause of all.
> The Power, above, beyond the blind machine,
> The Primal Power, the originating Power,
> Which cannot be mechanical. He affirmed it
> With absolute certainty. Whence arises all
> This order, this unbroken chain of law,
> This human will, this death-defying love?
> Whence, but from some divine transcendent Power,
> Not less, but infinitely more than these,
> Because it is their Fountain and their Guide?

But it insists even more if possible on another act of faith, the very poetry of mathematics and especially of astronomy, the faith that truth is music and music truth. It shows us Kepler urging that:—

> in music men might find the road
> To Truth, at many a point, where sages grope . . .
> "All that the years discover points one way
> To this great ordered harmony," he said,
> "Revealed on earth by music."

And it pictures Newton and Newton's laws as foretelling:—

> that knowledge one day shall be song
> And those whom Truth has taken to her heart
> Find that it beats in music:

and Herschel, himself a musician, declaring that algebra, conic sections, fluxions, all pertained to music; and that it was by them, by the music of mathematics, that he would build his heavenly city, which his faith told him would be a **"Holy City of Song."**

The poem is written in an easy, readable blank verse, not distinguished, but never dull. A few lyrics are inserted: none of them remarkable. None of them achieves the lyrical escape; the best, because the one which least attempts it, is Newton's call for simple friends:—

> Not those who'd pluck your mystery out
> Yet never saw your last redoubt;
>   Whose cleverness would kill the song
>   Dead at your heart, then prove you wrong.

And this one verse of it, perhaps the best, has in it more obvious faults than those inexorable astronomical divinities, time and space, will allow us here and now to discuss.

One other note. The only one of Mr. Noyes's sections which has much directly human interest is that of Galileo, into whose story he has introduced several figures beside that of the hero. He has attempted in it an ingenious though hardly convincing defence both of the Church which persecuted Galileo and of Galileo who surrendered and recanted. It is a pity, too, that he has added an assertion, almost demonstrably wrong, that Milton when creating his Samson was thinking rather of Galileo than of himself.

Richard Le Gallienne (essay date 1992)

SOURCE: "Alfred Noyes Among the Star Gazers," in *The New York Times Book Review And Magazine,* May 28, 1922, pp. 9, 22.

[*In the following review, Le Gallienne criticizes Noyes for having the "idea that to make a great poem you have only to take a great subject and pour over it a kind of poetic sauce."*]

To have attained any form or popularity is the unforgivable sin with a certain school of critics, who are either very young, or are gloomily middleaged and sour from having hopelessly pursued the popularity they deride, or are political revolutionaries, and regard popular success as a form of capitalism. For them the best seller must of necessity be the worst writer. For this reason Rudyard Kipling, one of the two or three men of genius at present writing in the English language, has long been impudently brushed aside as of no account by such egregious criticasters, say, as Harold Monro. "With the verse of Rudyard Kipling," says that amiable gentleman, "we are not

much concerned. Its sale far exceeds that of any other living verse-writer—except, perhaps, John Oxenham." But, of course, Alfred Noyes is far from being Rudyard Kipling, and I only mention them together because their success in selling their books makes them alike the target of those who have failed in that desirable end. Their popularity, indeed, is very different in quality and won by very different means. One is a man of genius, of original and energetic mind, who has written the truth that is in him, careless of its reception; the other is a man of facile talent, with a small though genuine lyric gift, but a much greater gift of echoing fluency of writing not merely imitative poetry, but imitation poetry in almost incredible quantities. It is to be feared that, in Mr. Noyes's case, his popularity is to be regarded as something in his disfavor as a poet, however much it may be to his credit as an astute business man, who has, very properly, made the most commercially of his talents, and who, it is to be feared, has mistaken the rustle of his box-office receipts for the rustle of the loved Apollian leaves.

It may come of this box-office fame, or it may have been natural to him, that he has for some time been attempting ambitious themes, which, one regrets to say, are so very much bigger than himself. Men who drive fat oxen, you know . . . And Mr. Noyes is of no capacious build. Nor is he made of Miltonic marble, or Dantesque steel. There is a rather pretty mocking bird somewhere in his brain, and he has a gift for rattling off ballads of organ men, highwaymen, pirates and such like picturesque figures, in a pleasing manner, though with little originality. He writes "words," as the phrase is, with no little skill and gusto, to the old familiar ballad tunes. Occasionally in his first and best volume he struck a more personal lyric note, with real singing charm, and sometimes an intenser thrill. **"Haunted in Old Japan"** haunts me still—"Wind among the roses, blow no more!"—and there was a poem about two strong swimmers with a fine refrain—"two strong swimmers were they"—and there were one or two love poems with a real ache in them; and, indeed, the whole volume was full of memorable things, some of which I think must go on being remembered. But that volume gave a promise which no succeeding volume by Mr. Noyes has kept. As, perhaps, I may be allowed to mention, I had the honor of introducing that volume to America, with no little enthusiasm, in the pages of the North American Review, it is with the more regret that I find it impossible any longer to read Mr. Noyes with pleasure. I did my best to read the brocaded plush epic of *Drake,* but never, it seemed to me, had a manly theme been treated with such effeminacy of handling. In the **"Exordium"** of that epic Mr. Noyes addresses himself to his theme in similar language of dedication as that employed by Virgil and Milton:

> Oh, thou blind master of these
>   opened eyes,
> Be near me, therefore, now. . .

The lecturer on English literature at Princeton sees the high Muses about him, summoning him to "the unattempted task" ("things unattempted yet in prose or rhyme") of singing "England's epic age"—

Worthy the great Homeric toll of
  song,
Yet all unsung and unrecorded
  quite—

a theme that had hardly waited—such had been one's previous impression—for Mr. Noyes. And now, once more, in **Watchers of the Sky**, which is but the first part of a "trilogy" entitled **The Torch-Bearers** Mr. Noyes regards himself summoned to celebrate in song the achievements of the great astronomers, to sing the epic of scientific discovery. He seems to be under the impression that the idea has occurred to no other poet before him, ungratefully forgetting Tennyson, from whom it is easily possible to gather single lines on the very same theme before which these 281 pages crumble into dust. In his "prefatory note" Mr. Noyes says, "even if science and poetry were as deadly opposites as the shallow often affirm." But, surely, it is a very long time since any one regarded them as "deadly opposites." On the contrary, "science" has long been regarded as so essentially poetical, its mere facts so stupendously "imaginative," as to need the aid of no mere "poet" to celebrate them. The mere statement of them is enough. Mr. Noyes, however, deems otherwise, and, having, as he tells us in his "prefatory note," been present at the unveiling of the great 100-inch telescope, "on a summit of the Sierra Madre Mountains," in a blank verse **"Prologue,"** entitled **"The Observatory,"** he records his experiences on that occasion, and tells us how, after watching the trial test of the great spyglass, he wanders out into the night and is met by the usual poetic Presences, urging him to make a "trilogy," embodying this latest achievement in astronomic science in a sweeping retrospect of all the adventurous endeavors that had gone before:

And there was one that moved like
  light in light
Before me there—Love, human
  and divine,
Than can exalt all weakness into
  power—
Whispering, *Take this deathless
  torch of song . . .*
Whispering, but with such faith,
  that even I
Was humbled into thinking this
  might be
Through love, though all the wis-
  dom of the world
Account if folly.
     Let my breast be bared
To every shaft, then, so that Love
  be still
My one celestial guide the while I
  sing
Of those who caught the pure
  Promethean fire
One from another, each crying as
  he went down
To one that waited, crowned with
  youth and joy—

*Take thou the splendor, carry it
  out of sight
Into the great new age I must not
  know.
Into the great new realm I must
  not tread.*

So the mantle was thrown across Mr. Noyes's modest shoulders by hands divine, and so we have the present volume. In reading the **"Prologue"** one had already felt certain misgivings as to Mr. Noyes's power to cope with his high argument, as one noted what little use he made of the humbler poetic possibilities ready to his hand in his account of his journey to that observatory on the Sierra Madre Mountains. Here at least was the opportunity for some fine descriptive writing. One must be pardoned for thinking of Tennyson's powers in that direction. Though Tennyson might have failed with Copernicus or Galileo—and it is unlikely that he would have failed—it is easy to imagine what pictures he would have drawn of that august approach. How dismally Mr. Noyes misses this comparatively minor opportunity I have not space to illustrate, but this quotation will give some idea of his vapid colloquialism of style:

"Tomorrow night"—so wrote
  their chief—"we try
Our great new telescope, the
  hundred-inch."
Your Milton's "optic tube" has
  grown in power
Since Galileo, famous, blind, and
  old,
Talked with him, in that prison, of
  the sky.
We creep to power by inches.
  Europe trusts
Her "giant forty" still. Even
  tonight
Our own old sixty has its work
  to do;
And now our hundred-inch. . .
  I hardly dare
To think that this new muzzle of
  ours may find.
Come up, and spend that night
  among the stars
Here, on our mountain-top. If all
  goes well,
Then, at the least, my friend,
  you'll see a moon
Stranger, but nearer, many a
  thousand mile
Than earth has ever seen her,
  even in dreams.
As for the stars, if seeing them
  were all,
Three thousand million new-found
  points of light
Is our rough guess. But never
  speak of this.
You know our press.

When Mr. Noyes finally settles down to tell the stories of his various astronomers, from Copernicus to William and Sir John Herschel, one simply wonders—why? It is hard to see what gain there is either to poetry or science in such uninspired restatement, in the most denatured blank verse that has been written since Lewis Morris, of such glorious matters as Mr. Noyes has had the temerity to make his province. Such "poetry" as Mr. Noyes has achieved is confined to a lyric or two. And, as for "science," the "poetical" verbiage employed merely darkens the radiant theme. Here is no such interpretative grasp of the imagination such as could alone justify Mr. Noyes's doubtless well-meant endeavor. It is questionable whether good blank verse would be properly employed on such a theme. But Mr. Noyes's blank verse!—well, the rest is silence. His poem harks back to the time of Erasmus Darwin with **"The Loves of the Plants"**—that, too, part of a "trilogy," **"The Botanic Garden"**!—a time when men still thought that things were better said in verse, however bad that verse might be. In the hands of a great poet it is possible that the facts of science might gain in expressive statement. It has happened, as we all know, in the case of Lucretius, as with Virgil's "Georgies"; and Tennyson, to say the least, by no means failed. Mr. Noyes's well–wishers had been only too pleased could it have happened again in his case. But, alas! I am bound to say that the articles in the Encyclopaedia Britannica on astronomy and astronomers thrill me with a deeper sense of the poetry of their theme than all Mr. Noyes's iambic decasyllables. Failing a great poet, prose is the proper medium for all such starry matters, and I would back Mr. Lytton Strachey to take Mr. Noyes's subject and give us a new thrill in the treatment of it, a really imaginative comprehension of it, such as Mr. Noyes's "trilogy" cannot approach.

Mr. Noyes seems to retain the old–fashioned idea that to make a great poem you have only to take a great subject and pour over it a kind of poetic sauce. He seems to possess an inexhaustible supply of such poetic sauce, and he has poured it over every subject, every great theme which the great masters of song first realized, as though it were their own personal agony or ecstasy, reborn through them with bitter travail and bloody sweat. When Dante writes of hell, no one doubts that he has been there, as when Coleridge sings of Kubla Khan no one doubts that he has walked the streets of Xanadu; nor is there any doubt that Keats was as intimate with the moon as Endymion himself. Our more recent poets, whatever criticisms may be made against them, are doing good service to poetry by insisting that poetry shall first be a personal experience, either here on the earth in Chicago or north of Boston, or in some imagined realm where they are as much at home as Wordsworth among his lakes and daffodils. Mr. Noyes is nowhere thus at home, and his Pegasus might be described as a high-powered touring car, visiting in rapid succession all the various "realms of gold"; he, meanwhile, tourist-fashion, notebook in hand, making rapid observations for future use, to be worked up on his return to his verse factory, either on his own typewriter or by dictation to a succession of wearied stenographers.

Thus he once "dropped in" at the Mermaid Tavern, and hobnobbed for five minutes with the great figures of the spacious times. He gave Ben Jonson and Walter Raleigh a swift "look-over," just as an American tourist, with a "schedule" in his hand, "does" Nôtre Dame, Versailles and Fontainebleau before lunch, and catches a boat from Calais to "do" Westminster Abbey and Stratford-on-Avon on the same day. So Mr. Noyes "tours" the romantic Past, and, boarding an airplane, he similarly starts a tour of the starry Infinite, taking in on his way the immediate Future. He tells us in his preface that he has employed in the **Watchers of the Sky** the same method he employed in his **Tales of the Mermaid Tavern**. He has—and with a like result. The title suggests those "Tales of a Wayside Inn" which, let any one who has felt himself superior to Longfellow read again to see how far short Mr. Noyes falls, not merely of Lucretius and Virgil and Tennyson, but of that modest New England master, who, of course, like Mr. Noyes, attempted far too many things, but did no few of them with a charm which only comes of sincerity. Mr. Noyes comes nearest to Longfellow in his retelling of the story of Tycho Brahe, which possesses some dramatic, or perhaps I should rather say idyllic, quality, particularly in his treatment of Tycho Brahe's love for Christine, and in which Mr. Noyes's lyric gift is once more discoverable. In his penultimate section, "Sir John Herschel Remembers," he has one or two lyrics worthy of his earlier day: this, for instance, in which **"The Earth"** sings:

> Was it a dream that, in those
>   bright dominions,
>   Are other worlds that sing, with
>   lives like mine.
> Lives that with beating hearts and
>   broken pinions
>   Aspire and fall, half-mortal,
>   half-divine?
>
> A grain of dust among those glit-
>   tering legions—
>   Am I, I only, touched with joy
>   and tears?
> O, silver sisters, from your azure
>   regions
>   Breathe, once again, your music
>   of the sphere

and this, in which sings **"The Sun"**:

> I hear their song. They wheel
>   around my burning!
>   I know their orbits; but what
>   path have I?
> I that with all those worlds about
>   me turning,
>   Sail, every hour, ten thousand
>   leagues of sky?
> My planets, those live embers of
>   my passion,
>   And I, too, filled with music and
>   with flame,

Flung thro' the night, for midnight
   to refashion,
Praise and forget the Splendor
   whence we came.

Percy A. Hutchison (essay date 1925)

SOURCE: "Alfred Noyes Continue in the Grand Manner," in *The New York Times Book Review*, August 30, 1925, pp. 12, 23.

[*In the following review, Hutchison surmises that while* The Book of Earth *is not as great as* Paradise Lost, *it still serves as a worthy attempt to "interpret through the medium of poetic verse the history of man and man's relation to God."*]

It is by a curious coincidence that Mr. Alfred Noyes's **The Book of Earth**—which is Book 2 of the triology, **The Torch Bearers,** and has for its theme the evolutionary interpretation of creation—should have made its appearance so shortly after the trial at Dayton focused public attention upon the question of evolution. Not since *Paradise Lost* has there been so serious an attempt as Mr. Noyes's to interpret through the medium of poetic verse the history of man and man's relation to God. It is, therefore, with *Paradise Lost* that **The Book of Earth** challenges comparison.

Yet at the very outset it must be admitted that the wide gulf which separates the two poems places certain difficulties in the way. In *Paradise Lost* Milton took the compressed biblical account of creation and expanded it. The room thus provided for the range of the poet's powers of pictorial imagination were all but limitless. Mr. Noyes, by reason of the fact that he deals directly with events and more with intellectual origins, largely cuts himself off from such opportunities. The interpretation of the natural history of the universe in terms of evolution was not so suddenly arrived at as the lay reader is accustomed to believe. Many students in the centuries before Darwin recognized, in geological and zoological evidence, hints which led directly to the theory of evolution. Not one account, therefore, as in the Bible, but several accounts, albeit all of them fragmentary, claimed the attention of the younger poet. His achievement, consequently, must be judged more upon its intellectual merits than upon the color and the breadth and the animation of the painted scene. Whether Mr. Noyes was wise in the method of approach chosen—whether, indeed, he did not willfully blind himself to the tremendous poetic possibilities which opened before him the moment he elected to treat poetically the theme of evolution—is a question which may be postponed for the moment. Before attempting to say what Mr. Noyes might have done, it is first necessary to see just what it is that he has done. There are ten parts, or movements, to **The Book of Earth.** The genesis of the epic, or, if one prefer, the impetus to the succeeding poetic flight, is the Grand Canyon of the Colorado. And in these pages of prologue will be found many of the finest passages of the entire poem.

Out of the painted desert, in broad
   noon,
Walking through pine-clad bluffs, in
   air like wine,
I came to the dreadful brink.

So Mr. Noyes begins. And then,

I saw, with a swimming brain, the
   solid earth splitting apart into
   two hemispheres,
Cleft, as though by the axe of an
   angry God.
          All that day,
Riding along the brink, we found no
   end.
Still, on the right, the pageant of
   the abyss
Unfolded. There gigantic walls of
   rock,
Sheer as the world's end, seemed to
   float in air
Over the hollow of space, and change
   their forms
Like soft blue wood-smoke, with
   each change of light.
Here massed her boulders, over the
   angel trail
Darkened to thunder, or like a sunset burned.
Here, while the mind reeled from the
   imagined plunge,
Tall amethystine towers, dark Mat-
   terhorns,
Rose out of shadowy nothingness to
   crown
Their mighty heads with morning.

The second book of the epic has for its theme the gropings toward evolutionary theory on the part of the ancient Greek philosophers, particularly Pythagoras and Aristotle. From Greece the epic moves eastward, and thence to the Italy of Leonardo da Vinci. The poet then turns to France, to Guettard and Pascal. The next to engage the attention is Linnaeus in Sweden; and after Linnaeus, Lamarck. Goethe comes next. Darwin is finally reached. **The Book of Earth** closes with an epilogue in the Grand Canyon. The major portions of the poem are in the flexible blank verse of the lines quoted from the Prologue; but the epic march is frequently interrupted by short passages in a variety of lyric meters. These lyric or semi-lyric interludes have something of the purpose and the effect of the chorus in Greek drama, and aid materially in increasing that grandeur which is indubitably the distinguishing feature of the epic as a whole.

The **"Quest,"** which is the subject of **The Book of Earth,** begins

In the still garden that Pythagoras
   made,

The Temple of the Muses, firm as
*   truth.*

And Pythagoras and his golden brotherhood died—as many
another before him and since—that the truth might live.
The mob is outside the doors of the temple, with torches
aflame,

A brutal bellowing, as of Asian bulls,
Boomed from a thousand mouths.

But before the fire is applied and the temple burned about
the philosopher and his band of intellectuals the scroll is
read which contains the sum and the essence of their wisdom. Mr. Noyes in the lyric interlude of the **"Scroll"** has
admirably maintained the balance between the pronouncements of the Pythagoreans and the philosophic hesitancy
which compelled them ever and anon to fall back upon the
ancient religion of the Greeks. The lyric thus becomes at
one and the same time a dictum and a psalm.

Close not thine eyes in sleep
Till thou hast searched thy memo-
*   ries of the day,*
Graved in thy heart the vow thou
*   didst not keep,*
And called each wandering thought
*   back to the way.*

Pray to the gods! Their aid,
Their aid alone can crown thy work
*   aright;*
Teach thee that song whereof all
*   worlds were made;*
Rend the last veil, and feed thine
*   eyes with light.*

Naught shall deceive thee, then.
All creatures of the sea and earth
*   and air,*
The circling stars, the wavering
*   tribes of men*
Shall make one harmony, and thy
*   soul shall hear.*

Out of this prison of clay
With lifted face, a mask of strug-
*   gling fire,*
With arms of flesh and bone
*   stretched up to pray,*
Dumb, thou shalt hear that Voice of
*   thy desire.*

Thou that wast brought so low;
And through those dower lives hast
*   risen again,*
Kin to the beasts, with power at
*   last to know*
Thine own proud banishment and
*   diviner pain;*

Courage, O conquering soul;

For all the boundless night that
*   'whelms thee now,*
Though worlds on worlds into that
*   darkness roll,*
The gods abide; and of their race
*   art thou!*

Mr. Noyes probably did well to moderate his enthusiasm
for Pythagoras as an evolutionist, for there is little in
Pythagorean teaching which may be construed as suggesting evolution, outside of the doctrine of transmigration of
souls. And this doctrine is founded rather upon ethical
considerations and Eastern mysticism than upon physical
evidence. But in the physics of Aristotle, to which the poet
presently moves, there is much that may be regarded as
forerunning modern evolution. But the reader will linger
over these pages of Mr. Noyes which eulogize the Greek
philosophers less for his exposition of their teachings than
for the many passages of superlative poetry which they
include. Of Alexander the Great, dead in Babylon, he writes,

The conqueror, stricken in his con-
*   quered city,*
Cold, in the purple of Babylon, lay
*   dead;*
And the slow tread of his armies as
*   they passed,*
Soldier by soldier, through that
*   chamber of death,*
To look their last upon his marble
*   face,*
Pulsed like a muffled drum across
*   the world.*

And of Aristotle:

His mighty mind
Walked like a ghost in Athens.

A variation in the epic progress is attained by the author
when he passes to Italy. The blank verse is still maintained; but dialogue—a dialogue between Leonardo and
Giulio—turns expository narrative into momentary drama. Leonardo is the evolutionist in this drama, and Giulio
the Fundamentalist. Da Vinci, when he finds fossils in the
rocks far inland and asserts that here is indisputable proof
the sea once covered the land whereon they tread, answers his interlocutor's doubts with as sharp a thrust of
wit as might have been heard in Dayton. Giulio having
asserted with Fundamentalist view that it was obvious the
sea being where it was, the flood left the shells when it
receded. Leonardo retorts that in that case Noah must
have dropped them out of the ark.

But as the epic moves from Italy so must also the review
of the poem, although not before having stated that the
monologue on art and beauty which Mr. Noyes puts into
the mouth of Leonardo (the monologue follows the dialogue above) not only does not suffer when compared
with similar excursions by Browning, but, since it is free
from the sentimentalism which not infrequently marred
Browning's discussions, rather gains by the comparison.

The book on Jean Guettard and Pascal must be passed over; and also the book on Linnaeus. But from the latter must be culled the song, or at least a part of the jolly song which with its humor lightens the pages.

> Linnaeus, Papa Linuaeus,
>   He gave his pipe a rap.
> He donned his gown of crimson,
>   He donned his green fur cap.
> He walked in a meadow at daybreak
>   To see what he might see.
>
> So beautiful, bright and early
>   He brushed away the dews,
> He found the wicked wild flowers
>   All courting there in twos;
> And buzzing loud for pardon,
>   Sir Pandarus the bee.
> Quoth he, "'Tis my conviction
>   These innocents must be wed!"
> So he murmured a benediction,
>   And blessed their fragrant bed!
> And the butterflies fanned their
>   blushes
>   And the red-cap whistled in glee,
> "They are married by old Linnaeus,
>   Linnaeus, Papa Linnacus!
> Vivat, vivat Linnaeus,
>   The Man of the Linden Tree."

The pen picture of Darwin on the yacht Beagle, searching the strange waters of the world, and the stranger lands, for the evidence which should add to the already accumulated proof of evolution, is a masterly piece of literary drawing. And the dilemma with which evolution confronts the Fundamentalist is as succinetly as it is powerfully posed.

> Unless God made, for every separate
>   isle
> As it arose, new tribes of plants,
>   birds, beasts,
> In variant image of the tribes he
>   set
> Upon their nearest continent, grad-
>   ing all
> By time and place and distance from
>   the shore,
> The bond between them was the bond
>   of blood.
> All, all had branched from one orig-
>   inal tree.

With that unerring instinct shown on publishers' "jackets" for featuring the least momentous and the least interesting portion of a book. Alfred Noyes's attempted dramatization of the debate between Huxley and Bishop Wilberforce is given a prominent place. As a matter of fact, if there is any one part in which the epic of *The Book of Earth* may be said to fail it is in this attempted dramatization. Nevertheless there are redeeming features even here, and more than one sharply witty sally. Not the least of these is the parenthesis "(sound leather, British)" by which he characterizes the good Bishop's "traveling bag" mind. But this, we assume, will find most applause where Englishmen are not. Yet, even if this attempted resuscitation of an ancient debate were a dozen times more interesting than it is, it would be desirable to hurry on from it to the epilogue which brings Mr. Noyes's pageant to a close.

In this epilogue, which is a paean, a hymn, as well as a conclusion of what has gone before, Mr. Noyes rises to new poetic heights. It can not be quoted in its entirety; but omissions will not be indicated, for the effect of the hymn will be better preserved if apparently unbroken. It is morning in the Grand Canyon.

> Up the Grand Canyon the full morn-
>   ing flowed.
> I heard the voices moving through
>   the abyss
> With the deep sound of pine woods,
>   league on league
> Of singing boughs, each separate,
>   each a voice,
> Yet all one music.
>
>   The Eternal Mind
> Enfolds all changes, and can never
>   change.
>
> Man is not exiled from this Majesty,
> The inscrutable Reality, which he
>   shares
> In his immortal essence. Man that
>   doubts
> All but the sensuous veils of color
>   and sound,
> The appearance that he can measure
>   and weigh,
> Trusts, as the very fashioner of his
>   doubt,
> The imponderable thought that
>   weighs the worlds,
> The invisible thought that sees;
>   thought that reveals
> The miracle of the eternal paradox.
>
> For, as a child that learns to wallk;
>   on earth,
> Life learns these little rhythms of
>   earthly law,
> Listens to simple seas that ebb and
>   flow,
> And spells the large, bright order of
>   the stars
> Wherein the moving Reason is re-
>   vealed
> To man's up-struggling mind, or
>   breathed like song
> Into the quiet heart, as love to love.
> So, step by step, the spirit of man
>   ascends,

Through joy and grief; and is with-
　　drawn by death
From the sweet dust that might con-
　　tent it here,
Into His kingdom, the one central
　　goal
Of the universal agony. He lives,
He lives and reigns, throned above
　　Space and Time;
And, in that realm, freedom and law
　　are one;
Foreknowledge and all knowledge
　　and free will
Make everlasting music.

And as the consummate harmony—the singing of the spheres, and of animals, and of plants, and of earth and sea and sky—as the harmony flows from far away along the unfathomable abyss, the soul of the poet grasps the meaning of the song.

New every morning the creative
　　word
Moves upon chaos. Yea our God
　　grows young.
Here now the eternal miracle is re-
　　newed.
Now, and forever, God makes
　　heaven and earth.

Meagre as under necessity have been the excerpts from *The Book of Earth,* they will have been sufficient to make evident that a modern poet, attempting the theme of evolution, has indeed been able to challenge *Paradise Lost.* Even in the structure of the blank verse is this challenge made, for if Mr. Noyes's line is not so sonorous as Milton's it is more flexible, and in its thrust and parry more delicately adjusted to a scientific interpretation of creation than would have been the Miltonic line. In other words, Mr. Noyes's verse is adequate to his theme; and his theme is an exalted one.

On the other hand, this theme, despite its loftiness, when the effect has passed away, leaves the reader cold, as he is not left cold when the effect of *Paradise Lost* has passed away. But this is not to condemn Noyes any more than it is to elevate Milton. The cause goes deeper. In the biblical account man is the central figure: in the scientific account man falls from his heights. He is but a part of a creation which is vastly larger and more important than himself. The human element—and because the human element the most truly profound poetic element—is absent from *The Book of Life* just in proportion as it is present and all-pervading in *Paradise Lost.* Evolution, because of the subordination of the human element, can never make good its hold on man's imagination. When Arnold said "the strongest part of our religion today is its unconscious poetry" he spoke not merely for today but for all days.

We cannot but feel, to come back to our beginning, that Mr. Noyes would have done better to have avoided his philosophers and his scientists and followed in colorful verse the pageant of evolutionary processes. But this he did not elect to do; and it will remain a theme for some later poet to undertake. Nevertheless, the net result would not have been different. Man would still be subordinate. *The Book of Earth* will not live as *Paradise Lost* has lived because of the lacking human factor. But because of its epic sweep, its dramatic power—most of all because of the loftiness of the design—Mr. Noyes's epic may not be neglected. It is a modern attempt in the "grand manner" of Dante and Milton. It is not entirely the poet's fault if failure was from the outset inherent in whatever might be his measure of success.

William Rose Benét (essay date 1930)

SOURCE: "Round about Parnassus," in *The Saturday Review Of Literature*, December 6, 1930, p. 420.

[*In the following review, Benét discussed two successful aspects of Noyes's poetry: its lyrical quality and metrical "accomplishment."*]

There are two books before us by Alfred Noyes, published by the Frederick A. Stokes Company. The first is *Forty Singing Seamen and Other Poems*, designed and decorated by Elizabeth MacKinstry, the second is the third volume of Mr. Noyes's trilogy, *The Torch-Bearers*, this one being entitled *The Last Voyage*. We have always admired Mr. Noyes's best work; though he has been a most copious writer and has frequently displayed nothing more than facility. He has even tried his hand at short stories and essays and at least one light novel. But his true *forte* remains what it was in the beginning when we first read **"The Barrel-Organ,"** in which this poet whose poems are, at least, always bright with color, accomplished what might be called a Pavement Symphony. He caught up the rhythms of the barrel-organ, or as we call it over here, hurdy-gurdy, and displayed a command of metrics that actually transferred those reeling, rollicking rhythms to the printed page. More than this he built up his London scene around and behind the street piano with such skill and significance that anybody was compelled to recognize a new talent engaged in doing something refreshingly different from the general run of the verse of the time. In this first period of his he also produced a ballad, **"The Highwayman"** that has become a set piece for school recitation, and another, **"Forty Singing Seamen,"** which for the first time delved in that mine of humorous fantasy that is the mythical Sir John Mandeville in his famous fourteenth century book of travels—humorous, that is, to the modern intelligence, though read largely as a gospel in its own day.

It is the last named of these poems that gives the title to the book Miss Mackinstry has illustrated with glowing colour. **"The Highwayman"** is here also. **"Bacchus and the Pirates,"** from a later volume, transforms the old legend of the great vine of Dionysus sprouting up through that fabled ship of the Greek Ægean into a thumping recitation of how "Half a hundred terrible pigtails" (our old friends of **"Forty Singing Seamen,"** being a crew of cutlasses that recall both Robert Louis Stevenson and the more comic creations of Ralph Bergengren) capture the god of wine on "the happiest isle of the Happy Islands," and the fate that befalls them thereafter. Then we have **"The Admiral's Ghost,"** adding a new Devonshire belief to the story of Drake's Drum that Sir Henry Newbolt put into such memorable verses. We have never felt ourselves that Mr. Noyes quite brought off the effect he sought for in his ballad. **"The Tramp Transfigured,"** a long fantastic poem with an allegorical significance that gets rather too involved, follows, and **"Black Bill's Honeymoon,"** from *Tales of the Mermaid Tavern*, closes the collection. The second of its cantos quite successfully adapts a metre of Drayton's.

Through all his voluminous work Noyes has demonstrated that he has unusual metrical range. As a narrative poet telling a high-spirited story full of the glamour of the past or of the Never-Never-Land, in swinging rolling choruses, he develops a vein of considerable humor and a music always somewhat akin to the music of his own Barrel Organ, good things to get from any man, as wine and song are good in front of a wood fire. We are aware that rather thin-blooded people have little use for such, as they conceive them to be, childish things. With this we are in pleasant disagreement. There is no mistaking Mr. Noyes's genuine gift for this sort of thing. In this sort he has enriched the world of books with new delightful matter. Indeed, finer to our mind than any poems shown here are his early **"Orpheus and Eurydice"** and that gem of the *Tales of the Mermaid Tavern* that concerns Will Kemp's famous dance over England for a wager and is entitled **"The Companion of a Mile."** In both these poems practically nothing goes wrong, the intention is fully achieved, the construction is sound, and the metrical accomplishment is little short of amazing. Indeed, any thorough study of Mr. Noyes's versification will reveal many a metrical innovation. Which brings us to what we consider his second claim to attention, the fact that the man, from the first, has been a genuine singer.

The trend of modern poetry, as we have remarked before, is quite away from the song. Mr. Masefield's is a far graver strain. Mr. De la Mare has, of course, given us enchanting songs, Mr. Hodgson a few, but of the purest lyric quality. There have been others in England. And we have had our own poets who were singers primarily. A notable example in America has been Miss Sara Teasdale. These poets, however, of our own generation and before, are no longer the poets of the immediate day. And the trend of that day is most certainly quite away from the song pure and simple. The younger poets have probably considered it to be rather too simple, a mistaken judgment in our own view if it is to mean that a kind of poetry that Shakespeare himself was the last to despise is gradually to go out of existence. Mr. Noyes began with undoubted aptitude for the lyric that is the song and retained his spontaneity for some time. This is not to say that he always wrote successful songs, but scattered through his work are delightful examples of what the Elizabethans

referred to sometimes as "catches." Such an one is the well-known one on the mountain laurel, the one beginning "In lonely bays," the lyric in *Drake*, **"Let not Love go too."** Then there are such poems as the haunting **"Mist in the Valley,"** the translation of Verlaine, the short poem, **"The Waggon,"** where a religiosity which has always been the Nemesis of much of Mr. Noyes's verse, and a tendency toward melodrama and bathos in most of his more serious work—and he can be so serious that it makes one's mind ache—are shed away and a thorough sincerity is manifest. A selected volume of his lyrics and shorter poems would have to be most strictly edited, most carefully sifted. A great deal would perforce go into the discard; but out of all the work he has done it is our own belief that a small gathering of the very best would surprise the critics who have been estranged by his worst, which has, unfortunately, been far too frequent.

Indeed, when one considers him at his best, either in mere metrics or in his later more deeply-felt and strongly-willed and always directly expressed meditations upon the mystery of life, it is difficult to see how it has been possible for him at times to write so badly. Yet it has. The reason may be that he seems, as revealed in his verse, a man of intense emotions sometimes quite out of the control of his reason. We can illustrate what we mean by something he does in **"The Last Voyage,"** now before us. He has been giving us, though fragmentarily, an interesting dramatic picture of Louis Pasteur, whose significance in the history of medicine he fully appreciates. He comes to that hour when the Academy of France assembled "to instal their new immortal, Louis Pasteur, in a death-vacated chair." Renan is presiding. All the poet's sympathy is with Pasteur and against Renan whom he calls a "slight analyst of Christ" and whom he regards as cold and seems to hate for being witty. Pasteur is to speak "in eulogy of the dead," namely "Littré, his forerunner, who had been The chief disciple of Conte." Mr. Noyes shows us the "bent and grey Pasteur" musing that he cannot ever "tell a cynical throng like this" what he saw when he visited the dead man's house (Littré's), namely—and it is brought out portentously—a crucifix on the wall of the room where Littré worked . . .

> *that crucifix.*
> *Not his own. . . .*
> *His wife's, and yet, O doubly then his*
> *own. . . .*

which, to our mind, immediately takes all real point from the incident. It was not significant, surely, of anything in Littré, that his wife's crucifix was on the wall, beyond a natural deep human love. It may or it may not have meant more than that, but there is certainly not an iota of proof that it meant more than that. And, as to Renan, in spite of the poet's comments upon him, when his speech comes, after Pasteur's, even though he may have sought to prove "his own preëminent wit," it seems to us the expression of a difference of opinion polite even to gentleness. One feels that the scales are not being held even, that the poet's own passionate predilection has warped his interpretation.

We do not know whether or not Mr. Noyes has now become a Roman Catholic. We have read this last volume of his trilogy with respect for his faith, often in the past strongly, and sometimes overstrongly, asserted by him. There would seem to be indications that he had joined the Church toward a membership in which all his former analyses of the doctrine of Christianity seemed constantly tending. Certainly his introductory poem following the dedication seems to be the plain statement of such a step. It is a powerful poem of loss and overwhelming grief and the entrance forever into a strong City. It is a story as old as the Christian religion, and older, and (though we cannot share in the poet's convictions) we can understand the experience.

The earlier stanzas, with their slight reminiscence of the spirit of B. V.'s "The City of Dreadful Night" are impressive:

> *Hour after hopeless hour I groped around*
> *   them.*
> *   League after league, I followed the*
> *   girding wall.*
> *Burning with thirst,*
> *I dragged through the drifted sand-heaps*
> *   Round its great coigns, and found them*
> *   adamant all.*
>
> *Once, every league, a shadowy buttress*
> *   Like a vast Sphinx, outstretched in the*
> *   moon's pale sheen,*
> *Loomed through the night,*
> *With flanks worn sleek by the sand-storms,*
> *   And calm strange face that gazed as at*
> *   worlds unseen.*

The main poem begins with the depiction of a great liner at sea. A child is dying upon it. The advice of an eminent surgeon on another ship is sought through the night by wireless. The ship is finally hove-to in mid-ocean for the delicate operation that may save the child's life, the surgeon being in close touch with the course of events though separated from the actual place by leagues of sea. During the time that elapses the poet, in pondering on life and death and the mystery of existence, and started on his reverie by the conversation of some friends on the ship, ranges in his imagination back through time and considers some of the first pioneer sons of Æsculapius. The best of these "flash-backs," to our mind is the conversation between Doctor Harvey and Lord Bacon in Gray's Inn. Of Pasteur we have already spoken. Noyes has usually been successful in conjuring up some scene of an elder day. But the poem tries to do too many things at once. Soon it becomes almost a jumble. Certain interlude-poems are introduced that do not seem to belong at all to this particular book. One, **"Wizards,"** is merely a well-wrought lyric in itself. One—a rather doggerel conversation between Patrick Henry and Thomas Jefferson in the old Raleigh Tavern—seems quite dragged in by the heels. Then, returning to the main narrative interest of the poem: the operation is unsuccessful, the child dies, the end of the

book is the presentation of a religious compensation for the world's deepest grief and the expression of a faith.

Which is, in a manner of speaking, dialectic. The poem as a whole is of no such stature as the second book of the trilogy, **The Book of Earth**, which remains to us the best of the three. But, before we close, we should note that the interpolated poem on page 145, beginning "Every morning," and the like poem on page 149 beginning "Messages,—from the dead?" seemed to us sincerely moving expressions of that deep agony of desire recurring to those who have lost one deeply loved. We quote one section of the last:

> *Rememberest thou that hour,*
> *Under the naked boughs,*
> *When, desolate and alone,*
> *Returning to thy house,*
> *Thou stoodst amazed to find*
> *Dropt on the lintel-stone*
> *Which thou hadst left so bare,*
> *A radiant dew-drenched flower—*
> *And thou couldst never know*
> *Whose hand had dropt it there,*
> *Fragrant and white as snow,*
> *To save thy soul from hell?*
> *Yet, in thy deepest mind,*
> *Thou didst know, and know well.*

Joseph Slater (essay date 1957)

SOURCE: "Voice from the Past," in *The Saturday Review Of Literature*, August 10, 1957, pp. 31.

[*In the following review, Slater notes that* A Letter to Lucian And Other Poems *keeps up a poetic tradition likened to that of Patmore, Belloc and Chesterton.*]

When Alfred Noyes was twenty-seven, he wrote a poem for the seventieth birthday of Algernon Swinburne, which Swinburne liked so well that he invited his young admirer to dinner (lamb, mint sauce, beer) at "The Pines." Now, fifty years later, there comes a new volume of poems by Noyes, *A Letter to Lucian and Other Poems*, which Swinburne would have liked even better and in which, except for a few phrases like "a strong contingent of the F.B.I." and a hymn about the bodily assumption of the Virgin, he would have found almost nothing new or puzzling.

But that is the way Noyes would want it. Out of key with his time, trapped in a period when paintings have "three noses,"

> When the mind is a nightmare,
>   Faith a sham
> And truth wiped out by an epigram,

when poets suffer from "hemlock numbing the heart, cannabis biting the brain," he has striven to keep alive the poetic tradition in which he grew up. And, to a remarkable degree, he has succeeded.

Even the faults of this book are old-fashioned. Its cliches are so different from our own that they have a kind of archaic charm: "naiad" rhymes with "hamadryad," valleys wind seaward, feet hurry, grey gulls hover, souls pass portals, and

> Outward bound, with a song on
>   their lips
> Men still go down to the sea in
>   ships.

Its poems of devotion can slump into Sunday-school pieties like **"Via Crucis"** or puff themselves into windy sermons like **"The Roll of the Ages."** Even its meters, usually flexible and surprising, can, when the poet is possessed by the demons of melodrama or exhortation, grind along with barrel-organ dullness.

These faults are perhaps the penalties of facility and of working in a style inherited and long since mastered.

But Noyes has also the ease and range of a traditional artist. The sixty-three lyrics of this volume are varied in form, tone, and subject. There are satirical ballades, deft and witty enough for *Punch,* where, indeed, they were first published. There are children's poems, a little like Stevenson's, a little like De la Mare's, which are so good that even children like them.

> There was one wee glimmer in
>   the long grass
> Where a gold-green glowworm
>   shone,
> And just one light in the gar-
>   dener's cottage,
> And suddenly that was gone

—and which sing a tune that has not been much heard recently. There is **"The Love-Song of a Leprechaun,"** of course. There is **"A Devonshire Folk Song"** about Drake and his Tavistock lass, naturally. But there are also three Horatian paraphrases, of which the best, **"Diffugere Nives,"** is both English and classical in its elegance and sonority:

> Minos the judge, the all-just, the
>   august, the unerring re-
>   morseless Lord of that
>   shadowy land.

About half of the poems in the volume are religious, and they too vary greatly in manner and value.

Some are chromolithographs; some are tight and intricate medallions. The most ambitious and sophisticated is **"A Letter to Lucian the Sceptic: Dated from the Island of Cos in the year A.D. 165"** but intended rather for other skeptics on another island at "the end of an age." On the surface, it recounts with light mockery the visit of an evangelist to a land which has long since made the passage from superstition to science; beneath the mockery, however, can be felt the hunger of a man not satisfied by scientism:

> Well may your eyebrows be
>   raised, as they were for that
>   mythical swan
> Swooping the Zeus to his lust.
>   Here was that wicked old
>   knave
> Crying no myth, but a man out
>   of God, with his heaven
>   foregone
> Losing his life for the lost, only
>   to heal and to save.

But the poem generates no tension, because the contest it reveals is unequal: the irony of the Greek is heavy and hollow, the message of the evangelist is the Truth. Noyes is not a poet of doubt, complexity, and ambiguity; his religious faith is simple and certain, and he writes his best when he expresses it, as in **"The Assumption,"** with the tenderness and concreteness of his poems of childhood and fairyland:

> Before Earth saw Him she had
>   felt and known
> The small soft feet that thrust
>   like buds in Spring.
> The body of Our Lord was all her
>   own
> Once. From the cross her arms
>   received her King.

Literary historians will place Alfred Noyes with those Victorian and Georgian poets, Patmore, Alice Meynell, Belloc, and Chesterton, who were, or ought to have been, his contemporaries. They should add that even in the new dispensation, among an alien people clutching their gods, he held to the old and matured within it and that the poems of his old age are better than those of his youth.

Derek Stanford (essay date 1959)

SOURCE: "Alfred Noyes 1880-1958," in *The Catholic World*, Vol. 188, January, 1959, pp. 297-301.

[*In the following excerpt, Stanford praises Noyes's lyrical poems while noting that his non-lyrical poem "Drake" is less successful.*]

. . . But it is, of course, with poetry that Noyes' name is most commonly connected. How many classrooms must have thrilled to the elementary but compulsive music of such poems as **"The Highwayman," "The Barrel-Organ,"** and **"A Song of Sherwood"**! With its rhythmic repetitions and its strong dramatic drive, the first of these pieces shows Noyes at his best. Few poems written this century can have served as the basis of a film-script, but **"The Highwayman"** was one of them. The magic of its opening translates itself readily into cinematic terms. One sees, as upon the projector's screen, a figure on a horse careering through the night:

*"The wind was a torrent of dark-
ness among the gusty trees.
The moon was a ghostly galleon
tossed upon cloudy seas.
The road was a ribbon of moonlight
over the purple moor,
And the highwayman came riding—
Riding—riding—
The highwayman came riding, up
to the old inn-door."*

Even more akin to the picture-going experience is the conclusion of the poem with its clear visual imagery and violent action:

*"Back, he spurred like a madman,
shouting a curse to the sky,
With the white road smoking behind him and his rapier brand-
ished high,
Blood-red were his spurs in the
golden noon; wine-red was his
velvet coat;
When they shot him down on the
highway,
Down like a dog on the highway,
And he lay in his blood on the highway, with a bunch of lace at his
throat."*

Ours is not an age when poetry addresses itself to all men. Specialization invades the arts, and with it there comes a sense of isolation. True, this century can name a number of poets who possess the common touch (one thinks of Chesterton, Masefield, and Belloc). But these had all published and formed their style before the end of the first World War, and those who followed after lacked their immediately accessible magic. It is to this earlier body of more popular poetry that the best work of Noyes belongs. Rhythm was always his *forte,* and by its employ-ment he was able to express what would otherwise have appeared tritely sentimental. The feelings behind his justly famous lyric **"The Barrel-Organ"** make this clear. A glib invitation to love in Spring is the essence of the poem's repeated refrain; but though we may smile at its jejune content, few of us are proof against the form it assumes. Like the tinkling hurdy-gurdy music they imi-tate, the words extort a response from us:

*"Come down to Kew in lilac-time,
in lilac-time, in lilac-time;
Come down to Kew in lilac-time
(it isn't far from London!),
And you shall wander hand in hand
with love in summer's wonderland;
Come down to Kew in lilac-time
(it isn't far from London!)."*

There are not many colloquialisms in Noyes' poetry—far fewer than in Eliot's or Kipling's—but the world to which his rhythms belong is that of the music-hall with its songs, the drawing-room with its middle-class ballads. How red-

olent of the "people's palace of varieties" (in the palmy days before 1914) is this other number from **"The Barrel-Organ"**:

*"So it's Jeremiah, Jeremiah,
What have you to say
When you meet the garland girls
Tripping on their way?*

*All around my gala hat
I wear a wreath of roses.
(A long and lonely year it is
I've waited for the May!).
If any one should ask you,
The reason why I wear it is—
My own love, my true love, is coming home
today."*

In a like manner, the rhytham of **"A Song of Sherwood"** clearly belongs to "an evening round the piano" (a mode of entertainment growing rarer every year):

*"Robin Hood is here again: all his
merry thieves
Hear a ghostly bugle-note shivering
through the leaves,
Calling as he used to call, faint and
far away,
In Sherwood, in Sherwood, about
the break of day."*

Noyes' great gift was for writing rhymed verse with a lilt-ing measure and a lyrical refrain, and, whenever he desert-ed this for blank-verse, the result was not artistically hap-py. *Drake* (1908), the earliest of his three long poems, very much oversimplifies history. Noyes, at the time of composition, wrote as a fierce anti-Catholic, seeing the contest between England and Spain in much the same terms as the pan-Protestant historian, J. A. Froude. A similar lack of subtlety is apparent in his *Tales of the Mermaid Tavern* (1913)—a description of Elizabethan literary life in its often vicious hours of pleasure-seeking. Noyes was well enough informed as a scholar to know that the drama-tists and poets of the day were, for the most part, a wild, abandoned crew. This he admits, but appears determined to invest them with a kind of "silver lining." His account of Marlowe's death in a brawl is very much an instance of this. Instead of the unscrupulous cad of a genius, we are shown a high-minded and spirited young man momentarily undone by a wicked courtesan. Noyes had, one may say, the public school prefect's view of history.

His most ambitious work was the three-volume, blank-verse epic of science entitled *The Torch-Bearers*. Here, he celebrates the great names in European research: Co-pernicus, Galileo, etc. As in his prose writing, Noyes maintained that there was no intrinsic opposition be-tween the religious and the scientific spirit when both of them were rightly understood. But where the ques-tion of precedence arises, Noyes himself opts for the leadership of religion.

Few critics would judge **The Torch-Bearers** to represent the poet's best work; but those who like their pill of science sugar-coated will read it for its popularizing information. In his Introduction to the *Lyrical Ballads,* Wordsworth looked forward to the day when science, familiarized by reference and usage, should have become in the hands of the poet "a dear and genuine inmate of the household of man." Perhaps that time has not yet come. Perhaps the daily mention of atomic science, with its vast destructive possibilities, make it not a friendly but an alien element to the human imagination. But, however we may look upon the relationship between poetry and science, Noyes' poem stands as a large-scale venture in proclaiming a close liaison between them. Those who do not think the venture succeeds can, at least, point to no superior endeavor.

Hoxie Neale Fairchild   (essay date 1962)

SOURCE: "Nothing Very New," in *Religious Trends In English Poetry*, Vol. 5, 1962, pp. 214-21.

[*In the following essay, Fairchild explains that Noyes's collection,* Early Poems, *is "an urgent desire for some sort of spiritual affirmation."*]

. . . The seventeen pages of **Early Poems** may surprise readers who associate Noyes with the invitation to come down to Kew, Reminiscent of Swinburne, Banville, Gautier, and Baudelaire, they show that Noyes begins in the nineties as a serious, mildly decadent, but non-Bohemian aesthete who is more interested in the mystical and occult side of French symbolism than most of his English contemporaries. There are hints of Rosicrucianism, as when **"The Symbolist"** yearns to behold the "unknown land" behind the veil of the temple and "the Cross of flame." In **"The Mystic,"** the motivation of this desire to break through to the ineffable and "drown the finite in the Whole" becomes more Spasmodic than aesthetic:

> Never was mine that easy faithless hope
> Which makes all life one flowery slope
>   To heaven! Mine be the vast assaults of doom,
> Trumpets, defeats, and anguish, age-long strife,
> Ten million deaths, ten million gates to life,
>   The insurgent heart that bursts the tomb.[42]

But within a few years the insurgency of his heart had moderated sufficiently to permit him to become the very pattern of a salable late-Victorian poet. It would be unfair to say that he completely renounced the romantic faith in favor of the shopworn vestments of romance: instead, he deliberately cultivated the latter in the interests of the former. The deep heart's desire was vulgarized, but after a fashion it was thereby kept alive. It survived even in his most infantile dreams of Old Japan, where

> Everyone's pockets are crammed with gold;
>   Nobody's heart is worn with care,
> Nobody ever gets tired and old,
>   And nobody calls you "Baby" there.

He was so copiously and steadily productive that the public had no chance to shake off the hypnotic effect of his insistently "musical" rhythms. His style was facile, communicative, picturesque—the language of Victorian romanticism discreetly colloquialized. As occasion demanded, he could remind you of Tennyson, Swinburne, Stevenson, Kipling, George MacDonald, Maeterlinck, Barrie, or Eugene Field. His favorite subject matter was delightfully "poetic": nature, love (very pure), patriotism (idealistic rather than bloodthirsty, but very manly), whimsical but preternaturally wise children, nonradical humanitarianism, the Gypsy Trail, Robin Hood, the Mermaid Tavern with sweet Will Shakespeare and medium rare Ben Jonson, highwaymen, fairies, "Apes and ivory, skulls and roses, in junks of old Hong-Kong."[43] But he could also exploit the romance of everyday reality in pieces like **"The Barrel-Organ,"** and except when he was trying to be very deep and mystical his tastes were mainly activistic. Although Noyes had some gift for Tennysonian brooding and scolding, he was always wholesome about it. According to A. S. Collins, he "found life good, and wrote of it joyously."[44] To such optimism the "poetry-loving" public opens wide its warm uncritical heart.

Precisely to the extent that it has ceased to believe anything in particular, that public also likes its poetry to be surcharged with an amorphous religiosity. On this score Noyes was especially satisfying. In most non-Catholic poets of this period who have not lapsed into complete secularism, Protestantism has so completely melted into romanticism that we observe in them only the final outcome of the deliquescence to which this series of studies has been compelled to devote so much attention. The poems of Noyes, however, exhibit the entire process.[45] The 1913 collection is obviously the work of a man who regards himself as a Protestant Christian. Liberty both political and religious is the theme of **"A Roundhead's Rallying Song,"** perhaps the last of many imitations of Macaulay's *Battle of Naseby.* The No-Popery spirit of Tennyson's historical dramas survives in the epic *Drake.* The hero "fought for the soul's freedom" in "that great war/ That last Crusade of Christ against His priests." He prophesies that the New World will become the home of "Freedom, the last great Saviour of mankind." He tells his arrogantly sacerdotal Anglican chaplain:

> Why, 'tis these very tyrannies o'er the soul
> We strike at when we strike at Spain for England.[46]

Although Noyes's Protestantism demands no very meticulous loyalty to the doctrines of the Reformation, it is by no means devoid of specifically Christian content. **"The Paradox"** affirms the complete transcendent otherness of God. The Deity declares that man is incapable of understanding His ways but that He has shaped this world of light and darkness, peace and strife in a love which will reconcile all its paradoxes "If ye love one another, if your love be not weak." In **"Creation,"** God wearies of the shadowless perfection of Heaven. He decides to make a world because he likes nature, and people, and little children, and is willing to suffer for His love. The emphasis on sacrificial love distinguishes this poem from

Browning's *Rephan,* which it otherwise resembles. Several poems are exercises in apologetics. If man's spiritual impulses and their embodiment in Christianity have arisen from the evolutionary process, can that process be traced back to blank "Nothingness"? Surely *The Origin of Life* is God. Nowadays, Noyes proudly insists, the Christian is the courageous rebel and the secularist the timid slave of convention.[47]

Noyes's defense of the faith is anti-intellectualistic: he believes in God because he does not believe in reason. "I am weary of disbelieving," **"The Old Sceptic"** declares. He has read too many books; now he "will go back to the love of the cotter who sings as he delves," back to

> The ignorant infinite God who colours the
> meaningless
>   flowers
>   To that lawless infinite Poet who crowns the
> law with
>   the crime.

The cotter's faith is no narrower than the rationalist's, which rejects "the deep dark vision, if it seem to be framed with lies." The speaker has no theological arguments against the unbelievers—only the same doubleedged doubt which they themselves have taught him. To debate these mysteries is worse than fruitless, "For creeds are many, but God is one and contains them all," and "nothing is true or false in the infinite heart of the rose." Hence the speaker (like Browning in *Christmas-Eve*) will return to where "the light of the chapel porches broods on the peaceful lane."

> I will go back and believe in the deep old foolish
> tales,
>   And pray the simple prayers that I learned at my
> mother's knee,
> When the Sabbath tolls its peace thro' the breathless
> mountain-vales,
>   And the sunset's evening hymn hallows the
> listening sea.[48]

The difficulty is that Noyes's Protestantism has acquired a vaguely mystical latitudinarian sophistication utterly incongruous with the faith of the chapel, whose ministers would not like such phrases as "deep old foolish tales" and would be puzzled (as would Dante) by the notion that "nothing is true or false in the infinite heart of the rose." And the simple prayers which his mother taught him were not addressed to a "lawless infinite Poet." Again like Browning, he wants something quite different from what the chapel can give him.

The Old Sceptic helps us to understand the sentimental *mystique* of childhood which motivates Noyes's long poems, *The Flower of Old Japan* and its sequel, *The Forest of Wild Thyme.* Their fabric is woven of strands derived from Stevenson, Barrie, George MacDonald, and Maeterlinck. The children's adventures are far too complicated to be related here. The reader must savor for himself the jumble of serious mysticism and Peter Pan, Wonder-

Wander Town and the Heavenly Jerusalem, fairies and angels. What matters for us is the fundamental theme of both poems—the spiritual insight of the child, who knows intuitively that all nursery songs such as *Little Boy Blue* and *Hickory Dickory Dock* are really *one* song which begins, "A child was born in Bethlehem." Little Boy Blue's horn is a sweeter, happier equivalent of Gabriel's:

> Little Boy Blue, come blow up [*sic*] your horn,
>   Summon the day of deliverance in:
>
>   . . . . .
>
>   Sound but a note as a little one may,
> And the thorns of the desert shall bloom with the
>   rose,
>   And the Healer shall wipe all tears away;
> Little Boy Blue, we are all astray,
>   The sheep's in the meadow, the cow's in the corn,
> Ah, set the world right, as a little one may;
>   Little Boy Blue, come blow up your horn![49]

Little Boy Blue is not precisely Jesus, but he is "the child-heart" through which the Healer is made manifest to men who remain loyal to the spirit of their childhood.

We may suppose that when Our Lord said that we must become as little children He meant that we must be humble, trusting, innocent, and obedient. The text does not imply that the child is a Wordsworthian "mighty prophet, seer blest." It is not inconsistent with Paul's "But when I became a man, I put away childish things." One cannot but feel that the Christian view of childhood has been heavily romanticized in such lines as these:

> O grown-ups cannot understand
>   And grown-ups never will,
> How short's the way to fairy-land
>   Across the purple hill:
> They smile: their smile is very bland,
>   Their eyes are wise and chill;
> And yet—at just a child's command—
>   The world's an Eden still.

The identification of "fairy-land" with "Eden" deprives both words of their proper meaning.[50]

In **"The Flower of Old Japan"** the Maeterlinckian children must return to their own English home to discover that

> All the fairy tales were true,
>   And home the heart of fairyland.

There, not in far Japan, grows the flower they have sought. Inconsistently, Noyes explains it all in his own adult person:

> Carol, every violet has
> Heaven for a looking-glass!
>
>   . . . . .
>
> All the shores when day is done
> Fade into the setting sun;

. . . . .

We have found, O foolish-fond,
The shore that has no shore beyond.

Deep in every heart it lies
With its untranscended skies;
For what heaven should bend above
Hearts that own the heaven of love?

Carol, Carol, we have come
Back to heaven, back to home.[51]

Fairyland is heaven (or Eden), and heaven is home, and
home is love, and the whole mess exists solely within the
human "child-heart" which includes all truth and goodness
and is transcended by no spiritual reality external to itself.
This is not the sort of thing one learns in a Nonconformist
chapel or in any other Christian place of worship.

Another of Noyes's favorite themes appears to deny that
optimism for which his public admired him, although it
may have enhanced his reputation for profundity. The
whole world is bound together in "one Passion." Human
suffering, he tells the unbeliever, bears witness to the
truth of the Crucifixion, for

> while ye scoff, from shore to shore,
>   From sea to moaning sea,
> *Eloi, Eloi,* goes up once more
>   *Lama sabachtani!*
> The heavens are like a scroll unfurled,
>   The writing flames above—
> This is the King of all the world
>   Upon His Cross of Love.

The shaping of the world was a sort of pre-Crucifixion,
an agony of sacrificial love which has united the suffering industrial toiler and the suffering artist with a suffering God.[52]

No orthodox Christian would deny that the whole meaning of the Cross is the whole meaning of man's life.
Much depends, however, on whether this thought is interpreted centripetally or centrifugally. It may be used
either to draw us to the foot of the Cross or to dissolve
the Cross in that world which it was meant to save. The
latter process, as readers of my fourth volume may remember, enables Browning to ignore the historicity of
Christ while applying His name to the universe of romantic pantheism:

> That one Face, far from vanish, rather grows,
> Or decomposes but to recompose,
> Becomes my universe that feels and knows.[53]

Similarly Noyes, who in this respect may well have been
influenced by Browning, believes in "the cosmic Christ"
and rebukes those

> Who cannot see the world-wide Tree
>   Where Love lies bleeding still;

> This universal cross of God
>   Our star-crowned Igdrasil.

To prepare the way for this Christ is the supreme function of the poet. In **"Art, the Herald"** "the voice of one
crying in the wilderness" scorns the conventional super-
naturalism of the "foolish-fond," for "Is not the heart of
all things here and now?"

> Come; come and see the secret of the sun;
> The sorrow that holds the warring worlds in one;
> The pain that holds Eternity in an hour;
> Our God in every seed self-sacrificed,
> One star-eyed, star-crowned universal Christ
> Re-crucified in every wayside flower.[54]

The borrowing from Blake is symptomatic.

The Resurrection is pantheized in much the same way. It
is prevented from being thought of as anywhere by being
thought of as everywhere, though the most convincing
evidence is provided by the flowers that bloom in the
spring. So also with the Holy Sacrament: miserable slum-
folk trying to find a bit of light and warmth and nourishment in **"An East-End Coffee-Stall"** unknowingly partake of the Eucharist as "They crowd before the stall's
bright altar rail." Lest such imagery should seem too re-
strictively precise, *The Testimony of Art* is that all religious symbols are man's creative attempts to impose a
"golden shape" upon "the Soul we cannot see":

> Once it was wine and sacramental bread
>   Whereby we knew the power that through Him
>   smiled;

but now poets know many other ways of making Him
smile.[55]

Thus diluted and smudged over everything, Noyes's religion encourages him to sing:

> O, the Heart of the woods is the Heart of the world
>   and the
>   Heart of Eternity,
> Ay, and the bursting passionate Heart of the heart in
>   you and me.

The final step is achieved by subjectivizing this cardiac
confusion in "the poet's heavenly dream," asserting that

> This outer world is but the pictured scroll
>   Of worlds within the soul.[56]

In the last analysis there is no real difference between
the message of "the cosmic Christ" and the "child-heart"
message of Little Boy Blue. Both imply a movement away
from historic Christianity toward the romantic experience. Nothing in Noyes's prewar poetry helps us to understand why he became a Roman Catholic in 1925, and
an attempt to solve the problem would lead us too far
beyond the terminus of this study. But Noyes may as
least be credited with an urgent desire for some sort of

spiritual affirmation; and the mind of such a man may undergo astonishing changes.

NOTES

[42] *Collected Poems,* I, 11, 16.

[43] *Ibid.,* pp. 25, 49.

[44] *English Literature of the Twentieth Century,* p. 29.

[45] I do not mean that the process can be traced step by step from earlier to later poems. Different phases of it are jumbled together throughout his prewar career.

[46] *Collected Poems,* I, 242-43, 251, 268, 320.

[47] *Ibid.,* I, 86-87, 243-44; II, 113.

[48] *Ibid.,* I, 57, 58, 59.

[49] *Ibid.,* pp. 139-40.

[50] *Ibid.,* p. 129.

[51] *Ibid.,* pp. 46, 47.

[52] *Ibid.,* I, 241, 245; II, 7. In the *Collected Poems* of 1913, expressions of the "child-heart" theme tend to appear more frequently in earlier poems and expressions of the "diffused Crucifixion" theme in later, but to the end of our period neither idea is decisively abandoned in favor of the other.

[53] *Religious Trends,* IV, 145.

[54] *Collected Poems,* I, 74, 75.

[55] *Ibid.,* II, 32-33, 76, 77-78.

[56] *Ibid.,* I, 3; II, 66, 76.

FURTHER READING

Bibliography

Tobin, James Edward. "Alfred Noyes: A Corrected Bibliography." *Catholic Library World* XV, No. 6 (March 1944): 181-84, 189.

> Revised and expanded bibliography, first published in October 1941, of works by Noyes and criticism about him.

Criticism

Hamilton, Clayton. "The Youngest of the Epics." *The Forum* XLIII, No. 5 (May 1910): 550-58.

> Negative assessment of *Drake.* Hamilton contends: "It is not in his subject-matter but in his handling of it that Mr. Noyes shows himself defective."

Le Gallienne, Richard. "Mr. Alfred Noyes's Poems." *The North American Review* 183, No. 9 (7 December 1906): 1179-182.

> Lauds the stylistic and thematic diversity of Noyes's verse.

———"Brilliant Verse by Alfred Noyes." *New York Times Book Review* XIII, No. 14 (4 April 1908): 183.

> Mixed review of *The Golden Hynde.*

Payne, William Morton. "Recent Poetry." *The Dial* XLV, No. 531 (31 August 1908): 60-4.

> Commends the patriotism of the poems comprising *The Golden Hynde.*

———. "The Mermaid Company." *The Dial* LV, No. 652 (16 August 1913): 107-09.

> Deems *Tales of a Mermaid Tavern* "a work so shining with beauty, and so opulent in poetical power, that it is difficult to find words with which to do it justice."

Additional coverage of Noyes's life and career is contained in the following sources published by the Gale Group: *Contemporary Authors,* Vol. 104; *Dictionary of Literary Biography,* Vol. 20; *Twentieth Century Literature Criticism,* Vol. 7.

Robert Pinsky
1940-

American poet, nonfiction writer, and translator.

INTRODUCTION

Robert Pinsky's poetry is noted for its combination of vivid imagery and clear, discursive language that explores such themes as truth, the history of nations and individuals, and the transcendent aspects of simple acts. Pinsky strives to create an organized view of the world, often confronting and trying to explain the past to bring order to the present. Recurring subjects in his work include the Holocaust, religion, and childhood. Pinsky's moral tone and mastery of poetic meter often are compared to eighteenth- and nineteenth-century English poets, and the insights conveyed in his analytical works on poetry have led critics to place him in the tradition of other poet-critics such as Samuel Taylor Coleridge, Matthew Arnold, T. S. Eliot, and W. H. Auden.

Biographical Information

Pinsky was born in Long Branch, New Jersey. Although he was not an accomplished student in school, Pinsky attended Rutgers University, where he formed friendships with a group of budding young writers and poets who published work in the school's journal, *The Anthologist.* Shunning creative writing programs, these students considered their apprenticeships as artists to be outside the domain of school and teachers' judgments. Following graduation from Rutgers, Pinsky entered Stanford University, where he studied with the noted poet, critic, and teacher Yvor Winters and earned a Ph.D in 1966. The publication of *Sadness and Happiness*, Pinsky's first volume of poetry, was followed by *The Situation of Poetry*, an exploration of poetic language in the works of several of Pinsky's contemporaries. In 1996 a collection of new and collected verse, *The Figured Wheel*, provided a comprehensive view of his body of work.

Major Works

Pinsky's first collection of verse, *Sadness and Happiness*, contains both long and short poems but is noted in particular for the seventeen-page "Essay on Psychiatrists." Offering a variety of literary and cultural references, the poem is said to typify Pinsky's use of discursive poetic forms. Similarly, in the book-length poem *An Explanation of America*, one of his most ambitious and admired works, the poet teaches his daughter about the past so that she may shape her future. The title poem in *History of My Heart* is an autobiographical narrative on memory and desire that draws on many of Pinsky's childhood,

adolescent, and adult experiences. In *The Want Bone* he employs a pastiche technique characterized by overt word play in order to symbolize and examine the lust for life and the desire for sensual experience. The volume includes mock biblical stories on the childhood of Jesus and an extended prose section in which Jesus, in disguise, enters the story of Tristan and Isolde in order to learn about love. The new poems in *The Figured Wheel* are considered dense and often difficult, but ultimately valuable for their insight and multi-layered commentary.

Critical Reception

Pinsky is often praised for his grasp of traditional metrical forms and his ability to evoke timeless meaning within the strictures of contemporary idioms. Critics applaud his ability to imbue simple images—a Brownie troop square dance, cold weather, the music of Fats Waller—with underlying meaning to create order out of the accidental events people encounter in their lives. Commentators admire Pinsky's ambitiousness, his juxtaposition of the personal with the universal, the present with the past, the simple with the complex. It has been noted that his intellectual style presents challenges to readers, obliging them to unravel the complexity behind the clarity of language and imagery.

PRINCIPAL WORKS

Poetry

Sadness and Happiness 1975
An Explanation of America 1979
History of My Heart 1984
Poetry and the World (poetry and essays) 1988
The Want Bone 1990
The Figured Wheel: New and Collected Poems, 1966-1996 1996

Other Major Works

Landor's Poetry (essays) 1968
Mindwheel (electronic novel) 1985
The Situation of Poetry: Contemporary Poetry and Its Traditions (essays) 1976
The Inferno of Dante [translator] (poetry) 1994
The Sounds of Poetry: A Brief Guide (criticism) 1998

CRITICISM

Jay Parini (essay date 1981)

SOURCE: "Explaining America: The Poetry of Robert Pinsky," *Chicago Review,* Vol. 33, No. 1, Summer, 1981, pp. 16-26.

[*In the following essay, Parini offers a positive assessment of* An Explanation of America, *praising his unique and original verse.*]

Robert Pinsky's book-length poem *An Explanation of America* falls somewhere into that magical fold of "major poetry": it offers a steadiness and wholeness of vision rare in contemporary poetry. Pinsky writes with a deeply humane sensibility, drawing new water from old wells, but also reaching into areas where nobody would have guessed that poetry could be found. "A country is the things it wants to see," he tells us, and the particulars of his America materialize before us as a necessary exterior analogue to the "common dream" of humanity.

Pinsky addresses the poem to his daughter, Nicole, saying: "I want our country like a common dream / To be between us in what we see." With a range of pedagogical and fatherly tones, he instructs first by summoning the scene:

I want for you to see the things I see
And more, Colonial Diners, Disney, films

Of concentration camps, the napalmed child
Trotting through famous newsfilm in her diaper
And tattered flaps of skin, *Deep Throat*, the rest.

This is an inclusive vision, able to contemplate and to "explain" a breadth of ideas, objects, images, and events. And it is quintessentially American in its effort to include so much, yet another attempt to fulfill the Emersonian quest for a poem able to contain the vast reach and complexity of this continent.

Dissatisfaction with the brief Romantic lyric propelled Whitman to write *Leaves of Grass*, and, even before Whitman, prompted Joel Barlow's *Columbiad*; it has been an abiding obsession with American poets. In the era of Modernism, the great efforts of Eliot, Pound and Williams stand out; the next generation includes Lowell's *Mills of the Kavanaughs*, Ginsberg's *Howl*, and Robert Penn Warren's *Brother to Dragons*. More recently we have seen Anne Stevenson's little-known but exemplary epistolary novel in verse, *Correspondences*, and James Merrill's dialogues with the spiritual world; both of these try to recover for poetry some of the ground lost in this century to the novel and are narrative in essence. Robert Pinsky, however, has managed to write a successful long discursive poem. In doing so, he appears to have sacrificed none of the narrative compulsion without which it is impossible to read a long poem.

Although reminiscent of Wordsworth, Whitman, and Stevens, Pinsky's verse is something new. The newness enters with the poet's meditative, modest, oddly affecting tone and in the way he moves effortlessly from abstract formulation to vivid particulars—a technique which Pinsky developed concretely in his first book of poetry, **Sadness and Happiness**, and on a more theoretical level in his criticism.

I

An Explanation of America is Pinsky's second book of poems but his fourth book. He has also written a book on Walter Savage Landor, a celebrated study of contemporary verse entitled **The Situation of Poetry**, and innumerable essays and reviews. Like Johnson, Coleridge, and Eliot before him, Pinsky is determined to create the taste by which he will be judged. **The Situation of Poetry** is dedicated to his great teacher at Stanford, Yvor Winters, whose tough-minded intellectual tone underlies Pinsky's own bemused voice. Winters's principles are in evidence throughout: the firm anti-Romantic bias (in severely modified form), the disposition toward argument in poetry, the willingness to admit and appreciate abstraction and discursive statement. Pinsky writes:

Modern poetry was created by writers born about a hundred years ago. The premises of their work included a mistrust of abstraction and statement, a desire to escape the blatantly conventional aspects of form, and an ambition to grasp the world by using the static, general medium of language. These premises are paradoxical, or at least peculiar, in themselves. Moreover, the brilliant stylistic inventions associated—notably the techniques of "imagism," which convey the powerful illusion that a poet presents, rather than tells about, a sensory experience—are also peculiar as techniques.

Or, as he says, they once seemed peculiar. The climate of expectation is such that these Romantic premises have simply been absorbed into the current fund of tacit knowledge. Thus, elder poets will regularly advise their students: *embody* an experience, don't tell about it; avoid abstraction and concentrate on a "deep image;" let the shape of a poem evolve, don't prescribe a form. I have myself mouthed these truisms during writing seminars as though they fell somehow outside the realm of arguable notion. Horace, Virgil, Milton, and certainly Pope would have been desperately puzzled. We may be grateful to Pinsky (as to Winters and J. V. Cunningham) for pointing out the historically anomalous nature of our current presuppositions.

Pinsky's own tacit presuppositions emerge as he discusses the work of other writers, such as his interest in "traditional verse" in the older, broader sense in which the poet employs discursive statement and "detail is handled in the proportioned, natural way of great art." His readiness to accept abstraction of a certain kind stands out, as does his intuitive grasp of the symbol-making function and its relation to the concrete image. His ideas about poetry, interesting enough on their own, acquire added significance in the light of *Sadness and Happiness* and *An Explanation of America*, wherein Theory and Practice, those infrequently married travelers on the open road, meet happily and wed.

II

Sadness and Happiness (1975) was not a typical apprentice volume because it excluded a fair number of poems which had already appeared in magazines, but which Pinsky discarded as juvenilia. Thus, with his first book of poems he stepped into his majority at once. The book is richly textured and complete in itself, though in obvious ways if foreshadows *An Explanation of America*. The title poem, for example, plus the final sequence, **"Essay on Psychiatrists,"** look forward to the discursive style of Pinsky's later book.

I must confess here a special liking for this poet's shorter lyrics. In the brief aubade, **"First Early Mornings Together,"** his technical brilliance, a bemused and generous tone, and a talent for evincing with a single stroke the image perfectly suited to convey the emotional atmosphere are evident:

Waking up over the candy store together
We hear birds waking up below the sill
And slowly recognize ourselves, the weather,
The time, and the birds that rustle there until

Down to the street as fog and quiet lift
The pigeons from the wrinkled awning flutter
To reconnoiter, mutter, stare and shift
Pecking by ones or twos the rainbowed gutter.

Without fuss, the poet joins inner with outer weathers, the subjective state of feeling shared by the lovers with the physical state of the outside world, represented by the birds, the fog and external sounds. Pinsky often affects the simplicity of, say, Pound in his *Cathay* poems or the breathless clarity of Chinese verse as we in the West have come to know it.

Many of the poems in *Sadness and Happiness* evoke the decaying streets and emotionally pathetic atmosphere of the small New Jersey town where the poet grew up. They share with the poems of Williams, though little else, a profound affection for ordinary objects. The poems are alive with, as Pinsky says, "the things I see," which include: "houses and cars, trees / grasses and birds," as well as incidents: "dusk / on a golf course" or "white / selvage of a mockingbird's gray / blur as he dabbles wings and tail / in a gutter." A poet is one who looks close enough, long enough, at objects so that they take on something of the poet's life; the point at which an object resists assimilation is the point of poetry. Pinsky understands this and perches, breathlessly, on that very point in poem after poem.

My favorite poem in *Sadness and Happiness* is called **"Tennis,"** and it is a masterpiece of elaborate conceit. Written in the guise of an instructor's manual for tennis, for *winning* at tennis, the poem explores the American obsession with victory. Notice the cool, detached tone of the final section, **"Winning"**:

Call questionable balls his way, not yours;
You lose the point but have your concentration,
The grail of self-respect. Wear white. Mind losing.

Walk, never run, between points: it will save
Your breath, and hypnotize him, and he may think
That you are tired, until your terrible

Swift sword amazes him. By understanding
Your body, you will conquer your fatigue.
By understanding your desire to win

And all your other desires, you will conquer
Discouragement. And you will conquer distraction
By understanding the world, and all its parts.

The poem is worth rereading merely because of its verbal brilliance: Pinsky dances on the high wire of metaphysical wit. But it is also worth rereading for its innate wisdom, its insight into our condition as competitive animals. **"Tennis"** is something new for poetry and, for me, the most accomplished poem in this book.

The final **"Essay on Psychiatrists"** has fine moments, expecially the portrait of Yvor Winters in the **"Perforation, Concerning Genius,"** but on the whole it fails because in a sense there is nothing to say about psychiatrists apart from what Pinsky does say:

I find that I have failed
To discover what essential statement could be made
About psychiatrists that would not apply

To all human beings, or what statement
About all human beings would not apply
Equally to psychiatrists.

The effort "to find a healing speech" is what makes us human. Poetry is a language adequate to experience, and most language is inadequate and unhealthy. What is important here, however, is Pinsky's direction; we see him stretching the boundaries of contemporary poetry, invading territories once held intact by prose. **"Essay on Psychiatrists"** is a warm-up for the marathon to come.

III

An Explanation of America divides into three sections, all of which maintain the elegant yet conversational style of the opening stanza:

As though explaining the idea of dancing
Or the idea of some other thing
Which everyone has known a little about
Since they were children, which children learn
    themselves
With no explaining, but which children like
Sometimes to hear the explanations of,
I want to tell you something about our country,
Or my idea of it: explaining it
If not to you, to my idea of you.

This stanza is a single long sentence, full of qualifying clauses and whimsical digressions. C. S. Lewis said of *Paradise Lost* that one has to get used to reading paragraphs, not lines, and one quickly learns to read beyond Pinsky's line. The blank verse movement becomes unobtrusive as one falls into the narrative swing. Though prose-like, this verse will not be mistaken for prose. Pinsky stretches the colloquial phrase across an underlying meter with superb naturalness, what Robert Frost calls "breaking sounds of sense with all their irregularity across the regular beat of the metre." Although the primary movement of Pinsky's verse is iambic, many of the lines are "sprung" to accommodate the tone or texture as it evolves. Enjambements occur easily, giving the verse its aura of intelligent conversation.

In accordance with Pinsky's assumptions about poetry, he refuses in *Explanation* to go in fear of abstraction. He writes in **"From the Surface"**: "A country is the things it wants to see." He follows this up by saying he will not censor anything from his daughter's view on the grounds of its ugliness alone: "Not that I want for you to have to see / Atrocity itself." Like many good fathers, he wants her to see nearly everything: "the things I see / And more," things like "well-kept Rushmore, Chiswick House, or Belsen." We need to see these things "Lest we forget," he says, quoting Kipling. Above, as always, Pinsky follows abstract assertions with hard, shining particulars.

Quoting Mayor Daley, he writes: "All politics is local politics." Moving from a comparison of America and Rome, "the plural-headed Empire," he offers vivid examples of modern plurality from his own life:

On the radio,
The FM station that plays "All Country and Western"
Startled me, when I hit its button one day,
With a voice—inexplicable and earnest—
In Vietnamese or Chinese, lecturing
Or selling, or something someone wanted broadcast,
A paid political announcement, perhaps . . .

Coming back to local politics, the poet refers "to the locus where we vote," the "Nest where an Eagle balances and screams." In a sense, Pinsky's *Explanation* shuttles back and forth continually between local politics and politics in its widest application, between concrete example and abstract formulation, between autobiography and the history of the West.

In "Countries and Explanations" (Part One, IV.) Pinsky concludes that place is itself "a kind of motion." It is partly permanent, partly blurred by the changes that occur as place recedes endlessly into the future, and as citizens of a particular place continually imagine the point from which they proceed: "Our nation, mellowing to another country / Of different people living in different places." In this section he somehow manages to suggest the dynamic quality of evolution—and, likewise, to suggest how place is as much mental as physical. Pinsky's "explanation" is merely his private mythos becoming public; as such, it is a confrontation, inviting the reader to respond in kind. His explanation spawns explanations, which in their collective aspect constitute whatever we may call a "country." "Countries and Explanations" might well be converted into an equation: "Countries are Explanations."

Part Two, which has four sections as well, is a meditation on "Its Great Emptiness," conceived of physically as a prairie, with its "shaggy pelt of grasses . . . flowing for miles." In rich language Pinsky composes a geography so vast that, like death, it is finally beyond conception; Part Two provides a negative from which the America of our choice may be printed, positing an "obliterating strangeness" which is "as hard to imagine as the love of death . . . / Which is the final strangeness." The poet's mastery of literal fact and metaphor, of image and imagination, is evident throughout; where a lesser poet might easily drown in the waves of abstract formulation churned up here, such as the proposition that "the love of death" is "the final strangeness," Pinsky redeems himself time after time with follow-up imagery, such as "The contagious blankness of a quiet plain." The technique is daring, of course, and its results can be controversial (I recall Roethke's "windy cliffs of forever," which some have disparaged), but when it works the result can be a splendid juxtaposition of concept and example.

In **"Bad Dreams"** Pinsky conjures "The accumulating prison of the past / That pulls us toward a body and a place," concluding with the statement:

Americans, we choose to see ourselves
As here, yet not here yet—as if a Roman
In mid-Rome should inquire the way to Rome.
Like Jews or Indians, roving on the plains

Of places taken from us, or imagined,
We accumulate the customs, music, words
Of different climates, neighbors, and oppressors,
Making encampment in the sand or snow.

The poet risks speaking for us all here, but the risk pays off; Americans do, in fact, live with an eye perpetually trained on the future. We keep reminding ourselves that we are a "young country" *vis-à-vis* Europe, as if the situation could somehow change in two or three hundred years. The comparsion with Rome, that supremely confident nation, this time points up a difference; Americans are a people of process and adaptation, of assimilation and, perhaps, instability. We are, in spite of blazoned days (to recall Stevens), a dispossessed—and dispossessing—people.

Throughout his **Explanation** the poet gathers those images and ideas which for him make up America. He becomes increasingly interested, too, in "possibility," as if by *naming* (what Emerson conceived of as the poet's primary task) he could bring circumstances into existence: a curiously vatic notion for a poet of Pinsky's disposition. The comparisons with Rome culminate in "Horace, Epistalea I, xvi," (Part Two, III.), which is in part a translation of a famous epistle by the great Augustan poet. This section takes the form of a letter from the poet's Sabine farm outside of Rome to his friend and benefactor, Quinctius; here all of Horace's aspirations for Rome, all of his "explanations," are revealed. What Horace really meant by this letter finds a terse, eloquent summary in the next section. Pinsky writes:

That freedom, even in a free Republic,
Rests ultimately on the right to die.
And though he's careful to say that Quinctius,
The public man able to act for good
And help his fellow-Romans, lives the life
That truly is the best, he's also careful
To separate their fortunes and their places,
And to appreciate his own: his health,
His cows and acorns in his healing spring,
His circle—"We here in Rome"—for friends and
    gossip.

The compressed quality of this verse should be obvious enough; here is a poet in control—emotionally, intellectually, artistically. He risks another of his abstractions (following Horace's lead): the relationship of freedom to the right to die. This notion holds for Quinctius as well as Horace (and Pinsky), while the job of the intellect remains—the separate fortunes, judging each man's success on individual terms. Here, as throughout **An Explanation of America**, the poet draws the line meticulously between the necessary (therefore true) obstraction and the humane particular. In these terms, Pinsky is the most Horation (i.e., well-balanced and humane) poet that we have.

The final sequence, "Its Everlasting Possibility," opens with a meditation on limits, a difficult task for anyone living in America, where "Possibility spreads / And mul-

tiplies and exhausts itself in growing." This first section, "Braveries," points up some of America's confusion about the past:

The country, boasting that it cannot see
The past, waits dreaming ever of the past,
Or all the plural pasts: the way a fetus
Dreams vaguely of heaven—waiting, and in its
    courage
Willing, not only to be born out into
The Actual (with its ambiguous good),
But to retreat again and be born backward
Into the gallant walls of its potential.

Such ambivalence about history threatens and distorts our visions of the present and, of course, the future. The poet, conjuring his own vision of the future, makes no real proclamations or predictions; rather, his judgments are limited to exactly what he sees. His ear is attentive to both the music of what happens and the music of what might be. One moving section records the progress of a young girl with her horse around a practice arena, while her father "takes crude courage from the ancient meaning / Of the horse." The primitive symbolism of horse and rider somehow liberates him—however briefly—from the binding limits of ordinary life. The mythic image (though I must warn that Pinsky's vision is ironic) works to connect the father, girl, and horse in an antique web of significance.

"Serpent Knowledge" considers the problem of evil, with Vietnam as a pimary specimen—*Vietnam,* a word almost impossible to use in a poem if you happen to have come of age when that particular war was on. The word burns a hole in any page; indeed, it may take decades for poetic language to suitably embody the complex nexus of emotions associated with that word. Pinsky explains to his daughter:

Someday, the War in Southeast Asia, somewhere
Perhaps for you and people younger than you—
Will be the kind of history and pain
Saguntum is for me; but never tamed
Or "history" for me, I think.

He writes vividly about what Vietnam means to his (and my own) generation; it was a time "when the country aged itself." The famous American innocence will never, after that war, be quite the same.

In "Mysteries of the Future" (Part Three, III.), the penultimate section of his **Explanation**, the poet reflects on time and remembrance. He begins with a contemplation of surfaces: the bright images of a winter Sunday morning in Chicago which seem to have precipitated this section. As with most meditative poetry (and most of the individual sections of Pinsky's poem could be considered this), the work opens with a recollection, an evocation or *compositio loci*, and proceeds to analyze by making analogies. This leads, typically, to a conclusion based on what has gone before, an outward turning, what in the old days was called "a moral." Pinsky works in this way, approaching the future via the past, turning images over in his mind and "working" them until their significance yields. "It is fearful to leave anything behind," he says, or "To choose or to make some one thing to survive / Into the future." Thomas Jefferson, whom Pinsky cites, left behind a modest epitaph which did not mention the terms of presidency because they were "something held, not something he had done." What Jefferson actually did was to write the Declaration of Independence and a Virginian law to provide for public education; these facts he chose for remembrance.

The section closes with another epitaph, that of John Jack, an unknown slave, who "Tho' a slave to vice, / He practiced those virtues / Without which kings are but slaves." To speak words "few enough to fit a stone," and to leave them for the mysterious future to absorb, demands that we "be naked, free, and final," Pinsky states. This is, alas, a poet's response to the mysteries first encountered in Chicago in the glint of a Sunday morning; a secular response, to be sure. A few graven words, casting a cold eye on life, on death.

Pinsky's *Explanation* ends with a magnificent "Epilogue: Endings." It is a conclusion in which the poet, akin to Dr. Johnson's narrator in *Rasselas*, does not conclude. The occasion of the last scene is a performance of *The Winter's Tale* by a group of college women; the poet's daughter has a small part in the production. She recites: "A sad tale's best for winter," although, true to the nature of Romance, the statue comes alive in the end and all is well, "frozen Possibility moves and breathes." Possibility—as Phoenix—emerges; and Pinsky is led inexorably into the repetitions, renewals, and refreshments of history as it catches up with the present and pushes forward into time to come. America, Pinsky argues, will not hold still for us, as all confident statements falter in the surge of new evidence. He would agree with his mentor, Winters, who said in an essay on Frost as spiritual drifter, that life is a process of continual revision in the interest of greater understanding. Thus, having reviewed his own and the nation's past with great authority, Pinsky returns to the performance of *The Winter's Tale*:

> And at the end,
> As people applauded louder and louder, you
> Stood with young girls who wore gray wigs and
>   beards,
> All smiling and holding hands—as if the Tale
> Had not been sad at all, or was all a dream,
> And winter was elsewhere, howling on the mountains
> Unthinkably old and huge and far away—
> At the far opposite edge of our whole country,
> So large, and strangely broken, and unforeseen.

The unpredictability and ungovernable sweep of this continent finds not so much an explanation as a selective, intelligent revision in the poem. The poet rehabilitates his own past into a collective past, explaining himself to his daughter as much as explaining America. The vision that Pinsky summons is sane, wry, and wholly generous, an example of what is best in our current poetry.

Robert Pinsky (essay date 1987)

SOURCE: "Responsibilities of the Poet," *Critical Inquiry,* Vol. 13, No. 3, Spring, 1987, pp. 421-33.

[*In the following essay, originally delivered as a lecture at the Napa Poetry Conference in August, 1984, Pinsky outlines the social responsibilities of poets.*]

Certain general ideas come up repeatedly, in various guises, when contemporary poetry is discussed. One of these might be described as the question of what, if anything, is our social responsibility as poets.

That is, there are things a poet may owe the art of poetry—work, perhaps. And in a sense there are things writers owe themselves—emotional truthfulness, attention toward one's own feelings. But what, if anything, can a poet be said to owe other people in general, considered as a community? For what is the poet answerable? This is a more immediate—though more limited—way of putting the question than such familiar terms as "political poetry."

Another recurring topic is what might be called Poetry Gloom. I mean the sourness and kvetching that sometimes come into our feelings about our art: the mysterious disaffections, the querulous doubts, the dispirited mood in which we ask ourselves, has contemporary poetry gone downhill, does anyone at all read it, has poetry become a mere hobby, do only one's friends do it well, and so forth. This matter often comes up in the form of questions about the "popularity" or "audience" of poetry.

Possibly the appetite for poetry really was greater in the good old days, in other societies. After the total disaster at Syracuse, when the Athenians, their great imperialist adventure failed, were being massacred, or branded as slaves with the image of a horse burned into the forehead, a few were saved for the sake of Euripides, whose work, it seems, was well thought of by the Syracusans. "Many of the captives who got safe back to Athens," writes Plutarch,

> are said, after they reached home, to have gone and made their acknowledgments to Euripides, relating how some of them had been released from their slavery by teaching what they could remember of his poems and others, when straggling after the fight, had been relieved with meat and drink for repeating some of his lyrics.

This is enviable; but I think that at some vital level our answer must be, *so what?* Jarrell wrote about those people who say they "just can't read modern poetry" in a tone that implies their happiest hours are spent in front of the fireplace with a volume of Blake or Racine. To court such readers, or to envy Euripides, would be understandable, but futile, impulses.

And I think they are even frivolous impulses, beside the point. Of course every artist is in competition with the movies, in the sense that art tries to be as interesting as it can. But tailoring one's work to an audience any less hungry for one's art than oneself probably makes for bad movies and bad poems. And whether that is true or not, most poets would be bad at such tailoring anyway. Day-dreams aside, more urgent questions are: what is our job? And: what are the roots of good and bad morale about it? The second question is strange, if I am right in supposing that poetry is the very art of being interesting. The two most interesting things in the world, for our species, are ideas and the individual human body, two elements that poetry uniquely joins together. It is the nature of poetry to emphasize constantly that the physical sounds of words come from a particular body, one at a time, in a certain order. By memorizing lines of Euripides, the Athenian soldiers had incorporated certain precise shades of conception. This dual concern, bodily and conceptual, is what Pound means by saying that poetry is a centaur: prose hits the target with its arrow; poetry does the same from horseback. If you are too stupid, or too cerebral, you may miss half of it.

Here I arrive at the relation between the two questions, morale and responsibility. In the root sense of the glamourless word "responsibility," people crave not only answers but also answerability. Involving a promise or engagement, the word is related to "sponsor" and "spouse." We want our answers to be craved as in the testing and reassuring of any animal parent and child, or the mutual nudge and call of two liturgical voices. The corporeal, memorizable quality of verse carries with it a sense of social exchange. The image of the horse burned into the living human body says one thing; the memorized cadence of words, without exactly contradicting that statement, answers it with another.

An artist needs, not so much an audience, as to feel a need to answer, a promise to respond. The response may be a contradiction, it may be unwanted, it may go unheeded, it may be embraced but twisted (William Blake the most quoted author in the modern House of Commons!)—but it is owed, and the sense that it is owed is a basic requirement for the poet's good feeling about the art. This need to answer, as firm as a borrowed object or a cash debt, is the ground where the centaur walks.

A critic, a passionate writer on poetry, culture and politics, once said to me, "When I ask American poets if they are concerned about United States foreign policy in Latin America, they all say yes, they are. But practically none of them write about it: why not?"

My response to this question was not dazzling. "I don't know," I said. And then, thinking about it for another moment: "It certainly isn't that they don't want to." The desire to make a good work, or the desire to deal with a given subject—in theory, the desire to deal with every subject—isn't automatically fulfilled.

The desire to see, and the desire to feel obliged to answer, are valuable, perhaps indispensable parts of the poet's feelings about the art. But in themselves they are not enough. In some way, before an artist can see a subject—foreign

policy, or any other subject—the artist must transform it: answer the received cultural imagination of the subject with something utterly different. This need to answer by transforming is primary; it comes before everything else. Something of the kind may explain the interesting phenomenon of bad work by good artists. Even a gifted, hard-working writer with a large and appreciative audience may write badly, I think, if this sense of an obligation to answer—a promised pushing-back or re-sponding—is lacking. Irresponsibility subtly deadens the work. Conversely, a dutiful editorializing work, devoid of the kind of transformation I mean, may also be dead.

To put it differently, the idea of social responsibility seems to raise a powerful contradiction, in the light of another intuited principle, freedom. The poet needs to feel utterly free, yet answerable. This paradox underlies and confounds much discussion of our art; poetry is so bodily and yet so explicit, so capable of subjects and yet so subtly transforming of them, that it seems recurrently to be quite like the rest of life, and yet different.

One anecdotal example: I have a friend who drives a car impatiently, sometimes with a vivid running commentary on other drivers. One day while I sat next to him the car in front of us behaved in a notably indecisive, unpredictable, petulant, dog-in-the-manger manner. But my friend was calm, he did not gesture and he certainly did not honk. I asked him why, and his explanation was, "I never hassle anybody who is taking care of small children."

This self-conscious respect for child care seems to me more than simply sweet. It exemplifies a basic form of social responsibility, an element of communal life more basic even than the boss-and-henchmen *comitatus* celebrated in *Beowulf*. People in a bus or restaurant where there is a small child like to think, I believe, that in an emergency they would protect the child, despite gulfs of social class or race or mere difference that might intervene.

The feeling is not goodness, exactly, but rather the desire to think well of ourselves—the first civic virtue, the fission of subject and object emitting the bubble reputation. That desire is part of our nature as social animals whose hairless, pudgy offspring pass through a long period of learning and vulnerability. We live together, rather than separately like Cyclopes, or otherwise perish in a generation. We living in our majority need to mediate between the dead, who took care of us, and not only the young, but the unborn.

And as poets, too, one of our responsibilities is to mediate between the dead and the unborn: we must feel ready to answer, as if asked by the dead if we have handed on what they gave us, or asked by the unborn what we have for them. This is one answer, the great conservative answer, to the question of what responsibility the poet bears to society. By practicing an art learned partly from the dead, one keeps it alive for the unborn.

Arts do, after all, die. In a way it is their survival that is surprising. When I was in primary school, they showed us films provided by the paper industry or the glass industry showing, with diagrams and footage of incredibly elaborate machines, the steps in making the innumerable kinds of paper, or glass jars and lenses and fiberglass curtains and fusilages. I remember thinking with some panic that it would soon all decay and fall apart: that the kids I knew in my own generation would be unable to learn those complex processes in time. When the adults died, we would botch the machines; I knew this with certainty, because I knew my peers and myself.

This fear still makes sense to me, and yet some of us went on not only to master those arcane processes and elaborate machines, but to improve them. Some people who were grubby, bored ten-year-olds in 1950 are now experts in fiber-optic controls in the manufacturing of semi-vitreous components, or in the editing of Provençal manuscripts.

So one great task we have to answer for is the keeping of an art that we did not invent, but were given, so that others who come after us can have it if they want it, as free to choose it and change it as we have been. A second task has been defined by Carolyn Forché, in a remarkable essay, as "a poetry of witness": we must use the art to behold the actual evidence before us. We must answer for what we see.

Witness may or may not involve advocacy, and the line between the two is rarely sharp; but the strange truth about witness is that though it may include both advocacy and judgment, it includes more than them, as well. If political or moral advocacy were all we had to answer for, that would be almost easy. Witness goes further, I think, because it involves the challenge of not flinching from the evidence. It proceeds from judgment to testimony.

In the most uncompromising sense, this means that whatever important experience seems least poetic to me is likely to be my job. Forché, for example, writes:

> In those days I kept my work as a poet and journalist separate, of two distinct *mentalités*, but I could not keep El Salvador from my poems because it had become so much a part of my life. I was cautioned to avoid mixing art and politics, that one damages the other, and it was some time before I realized that "political poetry" often means the poetry of protest, accused of polemical didacticism, and not the poetry which implicitly celebrates politically acceptable values.[1]

That is, the poet realized that what had seemed "unpoetic" or fit only for journalism, because it was supposedly contaminated with particular political implications, was her task. The "contamination" of "politics" was her responsibility, what she had to answer for as if she had promised something about it when she undertook the art of poetry. A corollary realization is that "all poetry is political": what is politically acceptable to some particular observer may seem "unpolitical" to that observer.

Where does the debilitating falseness come from, that tempts us to look away from evidence, or fit it into some allegedly "poetic" pattern, with the inevitable result of Poetry Gloom? Forché continues, a few sentences later:

> From our tradition we inherit a poetic, a sense of appropriate subjects, styles, forms and levels of diction; that poetic might insist that we be attuned to the individual in isolation, to particular sensitivity in the face of "nature," to special ingenuity in inventing metaphor.[2]

The need to notice, to include the evidence as a true and reliable witness, can be confused and dulled by the other, conserving responsibility of mediation between the dead and the unborn. And just as society can vaguely, quietly diffuse an invisible, apparently "apolitical" political ideology, culture can efficiently assimilate and enforce an invisible idea of what is poetic. In a dim view of the dialectic, it seems that society's tribute to poetry is to incorporate each new, at first resisted sense of the poetic, and so to spread it—and blunt it—for each new generation. Even while seeming not to taste each new poetic, the world swallows it.

Two nearly paradoxical formulations emerge from this process. First, only the challenge of what may seem unpoetic, that which has not already been made poetic by the tradition, can keep the art truly pure and alive. Put to no new use, the art rots. Second, the habits and visions of the art itself, which we are responsible for keeping alive, can seem to conspire against that act of use or witness. The material or rhetoric that seems already, on the face of it, proper to poetry may have been made poetic already by Baudelaire, or Wordsworth, or Rilke, or Neruda.

To put it simply, and only a little fancifully, we have in our care and for our use and pleasure a valuable gift, and we must answer both for preserving it, and for changing it. And the second we fail to make good answer on either score, the gift stops giving pleasure, and makes us feel bad, instead.

Since there is no way to say what evidence will seem pressing but difficult to a given artist—Central America, the human body, taking care of one's paraplegic sister, theology, farming, American electoral politics, the art of domestic design—no subject ever is forbidden. Society depends on the poet to witness something, and yet the poet can discover that thing only by looking away from what society has learned to see poetically.

Thus, there is a dialectic between the poet and his culture: the culture presents us with poetry, and with implicit definitions of what materials and means are poetic. The answer we must promise to give is "no." Real works revise the received idea of what poetry is; by mysterious cultural means the revisions are assimilated and then presented as the next definition to be resisted, violated and renewed. What poets must answer for is the unpoetic. And before we can identify it, or witness it, an act of judgment is necessary. This act of judgment can only be exemplified.

Here is one of the most valued poems in our language. In quoting the poem, I particularly want to point out the insistently repeated absolutes, especially the words *"every"* and *"most"*:

"London"

I wander thro' each charter'd street,
Near where the charter'd Thames does flow,
And mark in every face I meet
Marks of weakness, marks of woe.

In every cry of every Man,
In every Infant's cry of fear,
In every voice, in every ban,
The mind-forg'd manacles I hear:

How the Chimney-sweeper's cry
Every blackning Church appalls,
And the hapless Soldier's sigh
Runs in blood down Palace walls.

But most thro' midnight streets I hear
How the youthful Harlot's curse
Blasts the new-born Infant's tear
And blights with plagues the Marriage hearse.

The word "every" throbs through all of the stanzas except the final one, repeated five times in the drumlike second stanza. This insistent chain of "every's" leads to the capping, climactic movement of the conclusion, with its contrary, superlative "But *most*": the immense force of the ending comes partly from the way "But most" piles its weight onto the already doubled and redoubled momentum of "every" and "every" and "every."

One thing that "every" and "every" brings into the poem is the sense of a social whole: it is all of us, we are part of it, no utter exception is possible, it is like a family, and a family that bears a "mark." And though my brother and not I may have poured your blood or blighted your tear, it would be stupid of me to think that your response to me—or mine to you—could go uncolored by what you know of my family. The poem witnesses the legal entity of a city in a way that transforms it into this social whole.

Blake's "most" is reserved for the blighting of future generations—the extension of social corruption forward, into the future, through the infection of those still *in utero*. This continuation forward in time of the omnipresent blight and pain, under the climactic "but most," suggests both of the broad kinds of answerability: it is literally conservative, and it reminds us that we are witnesses for the future. Those who want to know about London in Blake's time read this poem. They may read the contemporary journalism, as well, but for an inward understanding of such evidence, they will again read Blake. If someone in the future wants to understand *Newsweek* and *Time*, or the *CBS Evening News*, our poems must answer to the purpose. We are supposed to mark the evidence, as well as continue the art.

In "London," all this is accomplished by the violently wholesale quality of what is "marked" in both senses, witnessed and scarred. The "unpoetic" part of the poem is the rhetoric that invents or enacts the vision of society as a kind of nightmarish, total family rather than an orderly contractual, chartered arrangement. Formally, the poem is a transformed hymn, the cadences of communal binding turned against the institutions of the visible community. And in a sense, Blake had to transform the city imaginatively, put the mark of his judgment upon it, before he could see it.

If all poems were like "London," the question might seem relatively simple. But not all poems invite a social understanding of themselves nearly as strongly as this. And few of us were attracted to poetry to start with by the idea of being a good witness, still less the idea of mediating between the dead and the unborn. Most of us were attracted to poetry because of language that gave us enormous, unmistakable pleasure: not only the physical pleasure of beaded bubbles winking at the brim, but also the intellectual pleasure of thinking of the thin men of Haddam who rode over Connecticut in a glass coach, how they are both creatures of fantasy and suburban commuters on the train.

Such transformation seems to precede witness, in the working of poetry and in the history of our need for poetry. Its relation to witness is like that suggested by a passage in Ben Jonson's great poem "To Heaven":

As thou art all, so be thou all to me,
First, midst, and last, converted one, and three;
My faith, my hope, my love: and in this state
My judge, my witness, and my advocate.

Faith in the absolute fairness of a judge like the Father is parallel to hope regarding a witness (the Holy Ghost) and love for an advocate, whose Christian mercy extends beyond justice. In keeping with the biblical and religious models, the transforming certainty of judgment precedes the processes of witness and advocacy. Jonson's intellectually elegant inversion of the courtroom sequence (evidence, argument, judgment) reflects the way that poetry seems to depend upon a prior and tremendously confident process of transformation.

Transformation, too, is a social role of poetry: its oldest, clearest form must be epideictic, the praising of heroes, celebrating one whose physical or moral gifts have brought gain or glory to the tribe: the woman in Edwin Arlington Robinson's "Eros Turannos," whose catastrophic love affair makes "all the town and harbor side / Vibrate with her seclusion" is a peculiar, American provincial version of such a figure. She makes the town more heroic, and the gossiping townfolk make her story more heroic:

She fears him, and will always ask
    What fated her to choose him;
She meets in his engaging mask
    All reasons to refuse him;
But what she meets and what she fears

Are less than are the downward years,
Drawn slowly to the foamless weirs
    Of age, were she to lose him.
Between a blurred sagacity
    That once had power to sound him,
And Love, that will not let him be
    The Judas that she found him,
Her pride assuages her almost,
As if it were alone the cost.
He sees that he will not be lost,
    And waits and looks around him.

A sense of ocean and old trees
    Envelops and allures him;
Tradition, touching all he sees,
    Beguiles and reassures him;
And all her doubts of what he says
Are dimmed with what she knows of days—
Till even prejudice delays
    And fades, and she secures him.

The falling leaf inaugurates
    The reign of her confusion;
The pounding wave reverberates
    The dirge of her illusion;
And home, where passion lived and died,
Becomes a place where she can hide,
While all the town and harbor side
    Vibrate with her seclusion.

We tell you, tapping on our brows,
    The story as it should be,
As if the story of a house
    Were told, or ever could be;
We'll have no kindly veil between
Her visions and those we have seen,
As if we guessed what hers have been,
    Or what they are or would be.

Meanwhile we do no harm; for they
    That with a god have striven,
Not hearing much of what we say,
    Take what the god has given;
Though like waves breaking it may be,
Or like a changed familiar tree,
Or like a stairway to the sea
    Where down the blind are driven.

The mean-minded little town, the superior, desperate woman, the vulgar man, even perhaps the complacent, spavined literary culture whose editors had no use for Robinson's work, all are resisted and transformed by a rhetoric that includes the coming together of the poem's peculiar form, its powerful narrative, and the heroic symbol of the ocean.

Formally, the resistant or "unpoetic" element in "Eros Turannos" is a kind of hypertrophy. As if in response to an insufficiently communal or folkloric relation between artist and audience, or heroine and community—even between the seemingly omniscient narrator of the beginning and the "we" speaking the ending—the poem exaggerates the formal, communal elements of the poem. With its feminine rhymes and triple rhymes and extension of ballad structure the poem is almost a parody ballad. The hypertrophy of traditional folk or ritualistic formal means resists an idea of poetic language, and of poetry in relation to social reality, by exaggeration. In its own terms this virtuoso exaggeration is as violent as the sweeping terms of Blake's "London."

Based on a mighty, prior act of transforming judgment, "London" takes the rhetorical mode of witnessing ("I mark"); what is on trial is a transformed London, and the poet's eye roams through it like the Holy Ghost, seeing more than any literal social reality could make possible. His repeated "every" is in part a mark of ubiquity. Robinson's poem of tragic celebration, full of mercy and advocacy in relation to its heroine, evokes images and rhetoric of judgment; and judgment is formally emphasized almost to the point of parody by the quality of incantation. Yet the perspective in "Eros Turannos," too, is preternatural. Certainly, the viewpoint is more than socially located. It is the multiple perspective of the ubiquitous witness:

Meanwhile we do no harm; for they
    That with a god have striven,
Not hearing much of what we say,
    Take what the god has given;
Though like waves breaking it may be,
Or like a changed familiar tree,
Or like a stairway to the sea
    Where down the blind are driven.

What "we" see or say; what is known of "her" fears and questions; what "they" hear or take; what the god gives; what "it" may be like—all of these narrated materials gain their authority from the underlying, invisible certainty that he has seen anew. That certainty appears in the "changed familiar tree," and its invisible, generative power leads to the stairway "Where down the blind are driven." The poet's own voice changes from impersonal omniscience at the outset to a communal first person plural by the close.

These examples suggest to me that society forms an idea of the poetic, an idea which has implications about social reality, and that the poet needs to respond by answering with a rebuttal or transformation of terms. But what about a poem that is deliberately irresponsible, that is anarchic or unacceptable in its social attitude? What, for example, about Frank O'Hara's poem "Ave Maria"?

Mothers of America
        let your kids go to the movies!
get them out of the house so they won't know what
    you're up to
it's true that fresh air is good for the body
        but what about the soul
that grows in darkness, embossed by silvery images
and when you grow old as grow old you must
        they won't hate you
they won't criticize you they won't know

                    they'll be in some glamorous country
they first saw on a Saturday afternoon or playing
        hookey
they may even be grateful to you
                for their first sexual experience
which only cost you a quarter
                and didn't upset the peaceful home
they will know where candy bars come from
                and gratuitous bags of popcorn
as gratuitous as leaving the movie before it's over
with a pleasant stranger whose apartment is in the
        Heaven on Earth
                                        Bldg
near the Williamsburg Bridge
                oh mothers you will have made the little
                                                tykes
so happy because if nobody does pick them up in the
        movies
they won't know the difference
                and if somebody does it'll be sheer gravy
and they'll have been truly entertained either way
instead of hanging around the yard
                or up in their room hating you
prematurely since you won't have done anything
        horribly mean yet
except keeping them from life's darker joys
                it's unforgivable the latter
so don't blame me if you won't take this advice
                and the family breaks up
and your children grow old and blind in front of a
        TV set
                                                seeing
movies you wouldn't let them see when they were
        young

The language of this poem dodges and charges so brilliantly on its way, with energy that is so happily demotic, that a reader is likely to want to keep up, to
want to show that one can keep up. Among other things,
the poem expresses love for the flawed, for imperfection—especially American imperfection—and the dark.
O'Hara sprints happily through this terrain, leaping
between such oppositions as "silvery images" versus
"the peaceful home," to find the genuinely friendly,
intimate and democratic note of "sheer gravy" and "so
don't blame me if you won't take this advice." It is a
contest between glamour and decency, apparently settled by an appeal to American idiom. His understanding of such speech, and by implication of the movies,
is so clear and vivid that we want to share it, to assure
ourselves that we, too, understand the dark, stained
charm of Heaven on Earth as it appears in an actual
New York. The language streaks forward impatiently
and we want to go along.

One thing we are invited to go along with is the idea that
children young enough to need permission to go to the
movies may benefit from sexual use by adult strangers;
that they may be grateful for it. Considered as advocacy,
this is distinctly not nice. It is as if O'Hara chose the
most repulsive proposition he could think of, to embed
in the middle of his poem.

Various matters of rhetoric may soften or deflect the
issue of unacceptability: since the group "Mothers of
America" will for the most part not hear, and surely not
heed, this oration, it can be looked on as not literal advocacy but mock-advocacy. And more legalistically, the
seduction is conjectural: they *"may"* even be grateful.
So the advocacy is hemmed by irony and disclaimer, with
the outrageous jokes of "only cost you a quarter" and
"sheer gravy" signaling how very much in the realm of
rhetoric we are—an exuberant homosexual *schpritzing.*

But just the same, there is an element of the unacceptable in the poem, a violation of social boundaries. And
far from seeming a regrettable, separable blemish, this
repugnant element seems essential. It is what makes us
believe the "darker joys," asking in effect if pleasure in
the poem has a component of inexpensive, vicarious sexual naughtiness. Ultimately, I think it asks us to entertain
the possibility of some one unusual eleven-year-old
(should we imagine the lines as actual or fantasized autobiography?) who might conceivably feel grateful to his
mother for the opportunity described.

In other words, the poem breaks or bends ideas about
poetic method and content. And this resistant act seems
prior to the poem, part of a preceding judgment that underlies what is seen and argued. Perhaps one thing I like
so much in the poem is the daring and clarity with which
it plays—and so clearly plays—at the definitive terms of
judgment:

        . . . keeping them from the darker joys
                it's unforgivable the latter

or the ratiocinative terms of advocacy:

        . . . because if nobody does pick them up in the
        movies
        they won't know the difference
        and if somebody does it'll be sheer gravy

The democratic, almost conspirational note of "sheer gravy," and "horribly mean," deftly contrasted with language
like "prematurely" and "the latter," invites an alliance in
imperfection. The poem happily witnesses a great communal imperfection ("what you're up to," "horribly mean")
and excitement in American life, all the grotesque, glorious fantasy life associated with the movies. The bite of
the poem comes from its comic perspectives: the imagination of a scene where the poet addresses the Mothers,
the imagination of the future at the end of the poem, the
imagination of idyllic sexual initiation for "tykes."

He is willing to share his sense of the movies, and of our
culture, with us, and his willingness is rooted in his will
to transform our idea of what is acceptable, in poetry or
in the imagined oration itself. Other works of those late
Eisenhower years get higher marks in the category "does
not advocate awful crimes," but we do not read them with
the pleasure and recognition this one gives, with its stern
standard of being "truly entertained." In one way, the poem
is a daring, ebullient prank; in another, it embodies the

process whereby the vision and rhetoric of a poem spring from a prior resistance to what the culture has given.

"All poetry is political." The act of judgment prior to the vision of any poem is a social judgment. It always embodies, I believe, a resistance or transformation of communal values: Blake's indictment of totally visible, monolithic London; Robinson's dry rage that an aristocracy of grace and moral insight has no worldly force; O'Hara's celebration of what is cheerfully lawless in American life. Even when Emily Dickinson defines the ultimate privacy of the soul, she does it in terms that originate in social judgment:

> The soul selects her own Society—
> Then—shuts the Door.

As one of the best-known lines in contemporary poetry indicates, the unpredictable effect upon a community of what one writes may be less to the point than discharging the responsibility:

> America I'm putting my queer shoulder to the wheel.

The poet's first social responsibility, to continue the art, can be filled only through the second, opposed responsibility to change the terms of the art as given—and it is given socially, which is to say politically. What that will mean in the next poem anyone writes is by definition unknowable, with all the possibility of art.

NOTES

[1] Carolyn Forché, "El Salvador: An Aide Memoire," *American Poetry Review* 10 (July/Aug. 1981): 6.

[2] Ibid.

Alfred Corn (excerpt date 1987)

SOURCE: "Melancholy Pastorals: George Parker and Robert Pinsky," *The Metamorphoses of Metaphor: Essays in Poetry and Fiction*, Elisabeth Sifton Books, 1987, pp. 107-20.

[*In the following excerpt, Corn deems Pinsky's poetry "accurate, truthful, conscientious" and compares his work to that of Walt Whitman.*]

We can doubt that the book [*An Explanation of America*] does . . . in fact, explain America, but not that it defends the humane values of reason and communitarianism. It is not Pinsky's first such defense. Critic and poet, he is the author, first, of *Landor's Poetry* (1968), a book remarkable for the sensitivity, discrimination, and enthusiasm of its readings. It is also sometimes rash, as when Pinsky compares Landor's "To My Child Carlino" to Wordsworth's "Intimations" ode, with all the disadvantage on the side of Wordsworth. The same kind of rashness runs through *The Situation of Poetry* (1975), Pinsky's survey of recent American poetry, with special ref-

erence to "Ode to a Nightingale." The book argues interestingly but unconvincingly in favor of the "discursive" as a central poetic mode, and the one most able to bear moral content. Within this polemical framework, Pinsky makes many aberrant judgments, rating some poets too high, others—John Ashbery in particular—too low; and his treatment of Harold Bloom's views exceeds, in tone and manner, what could be considered a legitimate expression of difference in critical opinion. In 1976 Pinsky published a book of poems, *Sadness and Happiness*, which received high praise, and merited it. The title poem is one of the best written in the 1970s; and the overall *convincingness* of the book assures it of a readership for a long time to come.

It is possibly Randall Jarrell who provided Pinsky with a clue to the subject matter he has treated so tellingly in his poetry, the aspirations and disappointments of Americans "just like ourselves": dwellers in the suburbs, frequenters of shopping malls, zoos, Pancake Houses; parents of fledgling pianists and horsewomen, standers in line at the Savings and Loan. There is a sweetness and pathos to all this—the Cheever and Updike fictional turf—which has never been captured so well before *in poetry*. The effect would be marred if Pinsky had allowed himself to lapse into easy satire or sentimentality, or inaccuracy. His observations, like his style, have an irrefutable air of honesty about them; so impressive is the technical feat I'm tempted to apply to it something Yvor Winters said (overstating a little) about Edwin Arlington Robinson's poetry: "it is accurate with the conscientiousness of genius."

Accurate, truthful, conscientious: these are the terms that describe Pinsky's poetry. Still, it must be said that *An Explanation of America* is a strange and irrational book in many of its aspects. (I'm speaking of the long title poem, not the fine short lyric **"Lair,"** which opens the volume, nor the affecting **"Memorial,"** which closes it.) This long poem is strange both in its ambitious scope and in the organization of its materials. It has three parts, titled **"Its Many Fragments," "Its Great Emptiness,"** and **"Its Everlasting Possibility,"** each of these in turn divided into four subtitled sections. The metric frame throughout is rough iambic pentameter, with paragraphing rather than fixed strophic breaks. The second part of the poem includes a translation of Horace's *Epistula* I, xvi, and a discussion of his life and thought. Pinsky's poem is itself like an epistle, for he has subtitled it **"A Poem to My Daughter,"** (the "you" of the poem), and means it in some sense to be addressed to her.

> I don't mean merely to *pretend* to write
> To you, yet don't mean either to pretend
> To say only what you might want to hear.
> I mean to write my idea of you,
> And not expecting you to read a word . . .

Every long poem needs a Beatrice, in this case the poet's daughter. The fiction is useful here, allowing Pinsky to develop a colloquial or epistolary tone that *holds* the reader; I have read the poem many times, and always straight through, without stopping (this despite the obstacle of the unvaried pentameter frame). The fact that the poet's interlocutor is a child and not an adult—his wife, for example, whose entire absence from the poem is never explained—helps support the general tone of simplicity, fairness, and tact. Communing with ourselves, or addressing another adult at length, we can't plausibly avoid defensiveness of one sort or another—wisecracks, assertiveness, false modesty, even ill humor. When children are listening, we have to do better, and, given Pinsky's commitment to moral perspectives, he could hardly have found a better strategy.

The poem's narrator is present only as a voice and an observing eye, never as an actor; and this, too, helps keep intact our confidence in his moral authority. Most people can see and say what the right thing is, but few can plausibly present themselves as doing it; or if they portray themselves as having erred, avoid the impression of self-hatred or self-pity. None of the poet's actions, not even his profession, is given in the text, and the inevitable complications are circumvented. Actually, the poet does, I believe, appear briefly in the poem's third part, a scene where a father (presented in the third person) watches his daughter's riding lesson. It is likely that this character is really the poet, for the narrator (and reader) are let inside his thoughts. It is the only such instance in the poem, though, and even here the character is presented primarily as an observer.

I raise these issues about the structure and intent of the poem to emphasize the difficulty of the problems Pinsky has had to contend with. He has risen to the challenge. Among the many reasons to admire this book is its legitimate ambitiousness; and I don't think it should be received as just one more collection of poems, some good, some bad. "A country is the things it wants to see," we are told in the opening part of the poem. Like Elizabeth Bishop, he has a keen eye; and he can present what he sees, and, what's more, think consequentially about it. At the mere level of perception, it has already a vigorous, affecting clarity:

>   . . . frowning,
> The children shuffled anxiously at command
> Through the home-stitched formations of the Square
>   Dance.
> Chewing your nails, you couldn't get it straight.
> Another Leader, with her face exalted
> By something like a passion after order,
> Was roughly sterring by the shoulders, each
> In turn, two victims: brilliant, incompetent you;
> And a tight, humiliated blonde, her daughter.

Thus he begins the characterization of his daughter, one of the most winsome in any recent poem. Before it is ended, you half wish she were your own daughter. "A country is the things it wants to see," Pinsky says, and lists some of the things she will become accustomed to, growing up as an American: all kinds of ball games, advertisements, Disney cartoons, *Deep Throat*, car crashes, Brownies (the Scouts, that is), collies, Colo-

nial Diners, cute greeting cards, and "hippie restaurants." To be a snapper-up of unconsidered trifles on this scale is to have supreme confidence in the transforming power of lines in pentameter. Part of the fascination here is the nagging question of whether he has actually "gotten away with it." I think he has, partly because of the strange power of the "always-more-successful surrealism of everyday life," as Bishop once characterized it, and partly because of his use of incantatory, lulling repetitions of phrases and lines—a technique he may have borrowed from Bishop. As he moves through his topics, "Local Politics," "Countries and Explanations," his allusions as far-flung as Winston Churchill, Gogol, and Mayor Daley, one feels not so much instructed as chanted to, over a slowly, endlessly rocking cradle.

The most interesting part of the poem, conceptually and aesthetically, is the second, **"Its Great Emptiness."** The opening section, **"A Love of Death,"** calls upon the reader to imagine a scene on the great Western plains (time unspecified), where a little girl is witnessing a communal grain harvest. As details are filled in, the imperative "imagine" is reiterated (some dozen times)—a device with precedents no less august than Canto XIII of the *Paradiso* and Bishop's "Little Exercise." These imaginings build up a powerful scene; the prairie takes on an hallucinatory solidity and presence, despite its having been carefully presented as fictive. Then, an untoward event: a half-crazed tramp climbs up on one of the threshing machines and throws himself into it; is killed. (I was reminded fleetingly of Kafka's "In the Penal Colony.") After this senseless occurrence, the scene dissolves, and the poem begins a meditation on the nature of the forces that might account for the atrocity, and others like it, on a philosophical or visionary level:

> The obliterating strangeness and the spaces
> Are as hard to imagine as the love of death . . .
> Which is the love of an entire strangeness,
> The contagious blankness of a quiet plain.
> Imagine that a man, who had seen a prairie,
> Should write a poem about a Dark or Shadow
> That seemed to be both his, and the prairie's—as if
> The shadow proved that he was not a man,
> But something that lived in the quiet, like the grass.
> Imagine that the man who writes that poem,
> Stunned by the loneliness of that wide pelt,
> Should prove to himself that he was like a shadow
> Or like an animal living in the dark.

A possible antidote to these morbid imaginings of emptiness, dark, and death might, Pinsky proposes, be found in the consciousness of "immigrants and nomads":

>   And at the best such people,
> However desperate, have a lightness of heart
> That comes to the mind alert among its reasons,
> A sense of the arbitrariness of the senses . . .
> Like tribesmen living in a real place,
> With their games, jokes or gossip, a love of skill
> And commerce, they keep from loving the blank of
>   death.

Another salutary outlook proposed is the traditional Horatian "equal mind"—and a sense of the *positive* value of death. Pinsky inserts into the poem Horace's Epistle to Quinctius, in which the genius of the Sabine Hills discusses their divergent modes of life and their chances for keeping dignity and uprightness. Horace observes that the man who is not afraid to die is safe from tyrants and an unworthy life—suicide is his warrant. The position may strike us as drastic, but it is true to the spirit of Stoicism and can name any number of precedents in Roman history. Pinsky's translation reads fluently and colloquially; he joins here the distinguished company of English translators of Horace, notably Sidney, Dryden, and Pope. [the author adds in a footnote: For whatever reason the apologist of the *Aurea mediocritas* has never attracted many Americans, excepting writers like Franklin P. Adams, Louis Untermeyer, and Eugene Field—though I think I remember a version of the *Carpe diem* ode by Robinson, and a sonnet-length "imitation" in Lowell's *History*.]

The last part of *An Explanation of America* is its strangest. Here Pinsky takes up the issue of "everlasting possibility," that American theme, and juxtaposes it to a sense of limit and boundary. With only a tenuous sense of transition, he moves to an examination of evil, in its characteristic American form of violence. Random assault (with sexual connotations) and Vietnam are invoked. Pinsky views the Southeast Asia debacle as unprecedented, some sort of turning point in the national consciousness, a first loss of innocence. (But surely an earlier example is the 1860-1865 disaster, which still continues to deliver grievous consequences—reread *Patriotic Gore*.) If Pinsky fails to explain American violence, he can hardly be blamed; it is one of the country's ugly, unaccountable mysteries.

The poem comes to a close (three years after its author began it, we are told) with an engaging description of the young daughter performing the role of Mamilius in *The Winter's Tale*, suitably dignified in hose and tunic. This affectionate tableau of Romance is balanced, on the poet's side, by a fanciful panorama of an imagined mountaintop city; it is to be understood, I think, as a metaphoric portrait of America.

> On a lake
> Beyond the fastness of a mountain pass
> The Asian settlers built a dazzling city
> Of terraced fountains and mosaic walls,
> With rainbow-colored carp and garish birds
> To adorn the public gardens. In the streets,
> The artisans of feathers, bark or silk
> Traded with trappers, with French and Spanish priests
> And Scottish grocers. From the distant peaks,
> The fabulous creatures of the past descended
> To barter or to take wives: minotaur
> And centaur clattered on the cobbled streets
> With Norseman and Gipsy; from the ocean floor
> The mermaid courtesans came from Baltimore,
> New Orleans, Galveston, their gilded aquaria
> Tended by powdered Blacks. Nothing was lost—
> Or rather, nothing seemed to begin or end

> In ways they could remember. The Founders made
> A Union mystic yet rational, and sudden,
> As if suckled by the very wolf of Rome . . .

America having been summed up as "a pastoral / Delusion of the dirt and rocks and trees, / Or daydream of Leviathan himself, / A Romance of implausible rebirths," the poem ends its long survey with a last glance at "our whole country, / So large, and strangely broken, and unforeseen." My own survey of the poem doesn't do justice to its intricacy and richness, the artful weaving of theme and metaphor that makes for its dense, evocative texture. It is a poem in which intellect and reason play a large role; the attendant risks cannot be unfamiliar to the critic of Landor, whose poem "To Barry Cornwall" reminds us:

> Reason is stout, but ever reason
> May walk too long in Rhyme's hot season:
> I have heard many folks aver
> They have caught horrid cold with her.

Still, to have more than usual intellect is a fate like any other; if among the many mansions in the house of poetry there is none to shelter that fate, then poetry is not as inclusive as we believe—or need it to be. Myself, I consider *An Explanation of America* an important addition to American letters, even if it goes against the grain in some ways.

I should mention as well one or two dislikes, since the poem shows every sign of being able to weather them. The title: wouldn't "Reflections on America" have been (though no more appetizing) more exact? Poets can sometimes explain the universe (which is ahistorical and nonspatial), but a country so large and various as ours is beyond their scope. The effort to contain and account for all our American experience is felt in this poem as effort; it could only be partially successful. Then, the contents: although the Epistle makes nice reading, bringing it and Horace's life into the poem strikes me as misjudged. The insights developed from them could have been presented in another fashion, one more consistent with the general plan and texture of the poem. And for obvious reasons, the biographical summary of Horace's life following the translation is filled with flat, prosy lines: "Time passed; the father died; the property / And business were lost, or confiscated." "Horace came back to Rome a pardoned rebel / In his late twenties, without cash or prospects. . . ." "I think that what the poet meant was this," (repeated later as, "I think that what the poet meant may be / Something like that"). These would be dull sentences even in a piece of prose.

No reader is likely to agree with all the opinions expressed or implied in the poem, of course. Pinsky is entitled to them; but I will mention one of his views that struck me as egregious. He describes an occasion when, during a flash flood on Chicago's Dan Ryan Expressway, "Black youths" appeared and "pillaged the stranded motorists like beached whales." He says, "a weight of lead / Sealed in their hearts was lighter for some minutes, / Amid the riot." This imaginative leap into the state of mind of the assailants may well be accurate; but why wasn't the same leap made in behalf of the victims in this case? The implied approval of the incident is unfortunate; this sort of spontaneism has never had the support of effective civil rights leaders, and is viewed by them as at most a futile reaction to present oppressive conditions.

Another surprising detail in the poem is Pinsky's misapprehension or simply abuse of some of Whitman's most ringing lines from "Crossing Brooklyn Ferry." After describing teenage prostitution in New York City, Pinsky continues:

> "It avails not,
> Time nor place, distance avails not"; the country
>   shrugs,
> It is a cruel young profile from a coin,
> Innocent and immortal in the religion
> Of its own founding, and whatever happens
> In actual New York, it is not final,
> But a mere episode. . . .

This is a willful misuse of Whitman—a poet who, faced with a young prostitute and her "blackguard oaths," wrote, in *Song of Myself,* "Miserable! I do not laugh at your oaths nor jeer you."

The misuse is the more striking in that Pinsky himself owes quite a lot to Whitman—*An Explanation of America* is the most recent extension of that tradition, and one of the best. Pinsky is less sanguine than Whitman, of course; for more than a hundred years we have heard the melancholy, long, withdrawing roar of faith in the American Dream. But he shows, nevertheless, a reassuring agility of spirit and generosity of affections, inside and outside the domestic round. His discriminations and caveats deserve a careful hearing—the author of *Sadness and Happiness* and *An Explanation of America* is a very distinguished newcomer among the unruly tribe of our poets.

Peter Sacks (essay date 1992)

SOURCE: "'Also This, Also That': Robert Pinsky's Poetics of Inclusion," in *Agni,* No. 36, 1992, pp. 272-80.

[*In the following review, Sacks lauds the "openness" of Pinsky's poetry.*]

With his two most recent collections of prose and poetry, Robert Pinsky enlarges his role as one of contemporary America's most valuable poet-critics. Seamlessly seductive, awakening pleasure as a form of responsiveness and responsibility, his freshness and brilliance serve a didactic yet liberating and inclusionary project—the restless, enlarging evolution of the art of poetry, of the identity of its makers, and of the audiences and worlds to which it is answerable. Pinsky does not urge poets to purify the dialect of the tribe. Rather his essays and poems subvert the assumption of purity itself. They embrace language at its most diverse (hieratic to slangy) and they meld an equal range of reference (*Kol Nidre* to *Naughty Nurses*), while seeking to move us beyond the

rigid "tribal" or categorical borders that keep us apart, or at each other's throats, or just plain stuck—whether in the mud or in the rules that keep us out of it.

In his acclaimed book-length poem, *An Explanation of America*, Pinsky celebrated (not without sorrows and warnings) the nation's "everlasting possibility"—a phrase that marks the conserving yet transgressive impulse inherited from Whitman and Williams, and seasoned by Pinsky's own immersion, as the grandson of immigrant Jews, in the "not-quite melting pot" of modern American culture. As vehicles for opening up that realm of potential, *Poetry and the World* and *The Want Bone* share not only the same interests but also an elegant yet forceful mobility. In each, as for Whitman and Williams, mobility is at once an aesthetic device and the means for quickening erotic, political and spiritual urgencies. It is the inseparability and rhythmic stress of these "wants" that give Pinsky's poetry its underlying heart ("The legendary muscle that wants and grieves, / The organ of attachment"), and that make his work central to our time. Such a centrality is oddly clinched by his forays outward, as if magnetized by what lies beyond the rim of our cultural and poetic assumptions: "Society depends on the poet to witness something, and yet the poet can discover that thing only by looking away from what society has learned to see poetically."

With a gliding grace that honors both the wayward impulse itself and the previously excluded or *unrepresented* objects of attention (again the political crosses with the psychological), Pinsky's essays and poems embody the inclusory motion he admires in a wide range of authors from Campion to Bishop, from Babel to James McMichael and Anne Winters. Celebrating "fluidity of tone, including the inseparable blend of comic and ecstatic, formal and vulgar," he shows how, in McMichael's *Four Good Things*, "range . . . and formal fluidity, embody an art that defies any trite social correlatives of form," or how the movement itself of Winters's poetry conveys emotion, while its "packed formal alertness is part of a characteristically American response to shifting, undetermined manners, forms and idioms, to heroic structures and appalling lives and deaths." Similar fidelities drive his praise of Frost, Stevens, Williams, Toomer, Oppen and others, for their loops of high and low diction, their "formal resourcefulness in defining one's place on shifting ground," their "inclusion of many actual and potential voices," and above all the "flexibility and speed" that mark their "responses to American social reality."

These are the attributes of Pinsky's own recent poems, including "poetry's freedom to dart from narrative to meditation to exposition and back, inserting a self-reflexive undermining of narrative illusion and then restoring narrative again, without visible seams or audible creaks." The poems shimmer with the allure and tensings of fabular romance, the genre of crossed thresholds, transgressive desires, and nonstop metamorphosis; and with a few deliberate exceptions, they soar with an astonishing fluency both of syntax and line as well as of quick-changing internal narratives, stances and tones.

Pinsky sets one of the fastest paces of contemporary poetry: from the stride of Whitman along the open road, or the vigilant cruising of Williams behind the wheel of his car in Paterson (the essay "Some Passages of Isaiah" gives us Pinsky's "profane and glamorous" Grandpa Dave, whose pearl-gray Packard's steering wheel was ivory), Pinsky accelerates into flight "Over the glittering / zodiac of intentions," or rockets his poetic creatures on a **"Voyage to the Moon."** With this speed-up and metafictional play comes a new elusiveness of the lyric speaker; he has partly slipped from the driver's seat while in motion, following the weirdly decentering revolutions of desire and of the mind (Pinsky has also created a computer novel called **Mindwheel**), balancing both at the hub and rim of his inventions. If this sounds as threatening as it is liberating, it should be acknowledged that part of the poetry's spell derives not just from its near-magical flights of inclusion, but from its compounding of exhilaration and panic, of elegant freedom and jagged hunger. To quicken the heart's appetite is to submit it to incessant self-removes—especially as these removes are reinforced by the very means of poetry itself, "As when desiring we desire / Fresh musics of desire, at concentric removes."

One form of this self-displacement is Pinsky's use of what I assume to be an array of possible character-tropes who are themselves volatile and on the move. Thus one of the Ovidian traits of many of Pinsky's situations or characters is that they in turn displace themselves beyond custom or received identity. The book opens with at least three inaugural poems of this kind: **"The Childhood of Jesus,"** with its Sabbath-defying hero who troubles the margins of sacred and profane, human and divine, Jew and Gentile, free creation and punitive withering, artifact and life; **"Memoir,"** which moves from the repetitive self-bindings of Jewish commandment, "It was like saying: I am this, and not that," to the "immense blue / Pagan, an ocean, muttering, swollen: / That, and not this"; and **"Window,"** which places a young child against the storm-fluent window of language (*window* itself shifts from *Windhold* to *Windhole,* constraint to aperture) by which he or she, identity in the very moment of breaking and remaking, gropes toward "the motion / Of motes and torches that at her word you reached / Out for, where you were, it was you, that bright confusion."

From these figures the book spirals outward through such multiple yet recursive and often coupled vessels as those of **"The Hearts,"** or the "Plural, playful . . . double-budded god" of the embracing Shiva and Parvati, or the shifty Daniel/Belteshazzar, who criss-crosses between Jew and pagan, man and lion, subject and authority, comely and corrupt. Hence onward to the remarkable prose romance, **"Jesus and Isolt,"** in which Jesus, who "won't be bound by my own nature," assumes the form of a ciclogriff, and attaches himself to Isolt and Tristan (much as Pinsky's poems attach themselves to pair after pair of legendary illicit lovers): ". . . in the heedless contradictions and paradoxes of the behavior of the two lovers in Isolt's own account, the Son of Man felt something that eased the restlessness of his own double nature. At times,

it was as if he walked the streets of Jerusalem again, defying the Sanhedrin by curing the blind on the Sabbath." With the figure of Daniel, and the famished yet melodic jaw-bone of the book's title poem, this figure of the ciclogriff may be one of the most revealingly empowered yet burdened figures for Pinsky's *daemon*: "The Jewish soul of Jesus, pragmatic, ethical, logical, found in the passionate and self-defeating codes of romantic love and knightly combat some of what he lacked in the jeweled pavilions of Heaven." No less revealing: "Playfully, Tristram cuffed at the little creature with his free hand. The ciclogriff raised its dainty paw and caught Tristram's wrist, arresting the blow with the strength of an iron bar." Our final portrait of this freakish creature, unable to save the lovers from their chosen inferno of desire, shows him soaring heavenward to a reunion with his mother, whose consolations cannot soothe his insatiable compassion.

Following Pinsky's tropisms through the "maze of displacement and sublimation," a further sequence leads to Mrs. W. and the Chief of Police, the doomed yet resurrective couple of **"At Pleasure Bay."** This brilliant yet gently haunting poem ends the book under the medleyed, Whitmanian arias of tenor and catbird—"Never the same phrase twice . . . borrowed music that he melds and changes"—beside a river which blurs the borders of law and transgression, life and death, eros and the spirit, endings and beginnings.

Such a partial tracing slights the range *within* Pinsky's poems, for most of them tend to work individually the way the book works as a whole—by fugues of permuting themes and characters. **"The Hearts"** swings from Romeo and Juliet to Art Pepper, heroin addict, to Antony and Cleopatra, their ruinous yet glorious idolizings "placed" (in the sense of Pinsky's essay, **"Poetry and the World"**) by the unworldly perspective of Buddha, yet offset by the fantastic visions of Isaiah. These hearts revolve as if upon the potter's wheel in Benares, or the wheel of God's imagings, or yet again the turning record of Lee Andrews and The Hearts. Acting as a democratizing leaven as well as a token of continuity—perhaps the phonemic germ-plasm of immortal desire—the exclamation "Oh!" transmigrates from Enobarbus's "but Oh! . . . Then you would have missed / A wonderful piece of work" (the last three words are Shakespeare's, spun via Pinsky's shifting contexts into contemporary street slang, something Art Pepper might have said) to the closing *ah*'s of the poem:

> As the record ends, a coda in retard:
> The Hearts in a shifting velvety *ah,* and *ah*
> Prolonged again, and again as Lee Andrews
>
> Reaches *ah* high for *I have to gain Faith, Hope
> And Charity, God only knows the girl
> Who will love me—Oh! if we only could*
>
> *Start over again!* Then The Hearts chant the chords
> Again a final time, *ah* and the record turns
> Through all the music, and on into silence again.

In these supple tercets, a favored form for Pinsky, with their odd-numbered openness, shifting caesuras, and stanza-enjambing syntax, the poem reaches not only its merger of erotic and religious longings, but also the expression of one of the underlying wants of the book: "Oh! if we only could // Start over again." It is a desire prolonged or renewed throughout the book, extending to the final poem's vision of a posthumous embrace from whose climax the soul

> . . . . brims up
> And burns free out of you and shifts and spills
> Down over into that other body, and you
>
> Forget the life you had and begin again
> On the same crossing—maybe as a child who passes
> Through the same place. But never the same way
>   twice.

To "begin again" on the crossed currents of a restless, and here eroticized, metaphysical hunger—such a want impels much of the lyric poetry of a secular, origin-starved yet origin-fleeing modern America. The need intensifies for Pinsky, as a man of heterodox piety, half-swayed by Judaism's redundant chants of faith and by its taboos against idolatry, even as he rebels against its bonds and discriminations. Like a jazz soloist escaping from a phrasal cage or cradle, he breaks free to value the heathen murmurings of the ocean, the clangor of idol-smith and marketplace, the "shifting velvety *ah,* and *ah*" of The Hearts. He shakes off whatever might keep him from registering the full range of a fetishistic culture and its idols beneath whose crude or polished surfaces his own genius seeks out the roots of authentic longing. Here *Poetry and the World* is again crucial reading, for it taps the autobiographical current of Pinsky's various departures not only from religious orthodoxy, but from what he calls "the coercion of circumstance." Jewish law, fixed identity, "birth and ancestry," "social fact," historical determinism, authoritarian education, time itself, and finally a view of death as fixed terminus—these are some of the limits against which the poet's appetite awakens. I should add that this appetite *depends* on such limits, both as they define and sharpen a desire for the unlimited, and as they reinforce the very differences which poetry as a medium of representation requires. It is this dependency that partly accounts for the more than occasional undertone of anxiety and sorrow in these poems. It underlies the book's thematic interest in illicit lovers, whose doom figures not only the attempt to undo totemic differences on which selves and societies depend, but also the ravenous desire of a poetry that wants to *become* the world, to get beyond the *and* of **"Poetry and the World."** And finally it is this rebellious dependency that, because of the reach and stamina of Pinsky's imagination, leads him to "immortal longings" and their eschatological hopes.

How to begin again? How to get truly free? How to include novelty without falling into an abyss of incoherence, unrepresentability, guilt? In Pinsky's work, at least two strategies come to mind beyond mobility itself or the inclusive displacements of "Also this, / Also that." One is to acknowledge, as in the latter line-breaking yet

line-linking phrase, that breaking and bonding may mark all creative activity. The child Jesus breaks the Sabbath by creating a dam and molding clay birds which he then sends breaking into endless flight. Not only does their flight exceed the limits of his knowledge, but his display of power seems indiscriminable from the angry magic by which he cripples another child who broke the dam (and who also thereby set free the water's flow). The Benares potter molds new vessels from old smithereens and dust; the child in **"Icicles"** breaks the totemic beard of "crystal chimes" down to their originary stems (just as the careful off-rhymes break to new tones); couples burn through selfhood to the one life-force within yet beyond themselves; poetry breaks to absorb the unpoetic; a society ruptures to include new immigrants who in turn enlarge their own self-definitions; one story line is cut and spliced to others. A still more fluent version of such remakings is the "meld and change" of creaturely, linguistic and thematic transmigration, the undogmatic mythos behind such poems as **"The Hearts," "The Refinery," "Pilgrimage"** and **"At Pleasure Bay."**

Such inventions bring into focus a second, overlapping strategy—Pinsky's celebration of a shared activity that transcends aesthetic, social, temporal or religious divisions:

> The crowd at the ballpark sing, the cantor sings
> *Kol Nidre,* and the equipment in our cars
> Fills them with singing voices while we drive.
>
> When the warlord hears his enemy is dead,
> He sings his praises. The old men sang a song
> And we protesters sang a song against them . . .

As the poem unfolds, the multiple, various, and yet single song evolves to include the returning gods who sing us and themselves back into anonymity beyond the *eschaton,* "the whole cold salty world / Humming oblation to what our mouths once made." This is one of the far reaches of Pinsky's dreams of origins and ends, as in **"Pilgrimage"** or **"The Refinery,"** where the gods "batten on the vats" of our utterances "As though we were their aphids, or their bees, / That monstered up sweetness for them while they dozed." A visionary circuit of song between human and divine, this pantheistic atonement would bind us all into a continuum of death and renewal, a continuum dependent on our own makings. *Making,* after all, is the only activity that can appease our wants. But because these wants exceed any object, they call for continuous remakings, not merely within our lives but between those of generations. Hence the "lament" and the immortality of sexual making, and of work—as additional poems like **"The Ghost Hammer"** or **"Shirt"** confirm: "George Herbert, your descendant is a Black / Lady in South Carolina, her name is Irma / And she inspected my shirt." This great chain of making is forged in the monstrous, desperate, yet glorious labor

> To stir the mysteries, Love and Work, we have made
> And that make us willing to die for them—
> That make us bleed, embodied maybe in codes,

Spurts of pressure and crucial variations
In the current of the soul, that lives by changing.

To close, we may wonder how a poet so devoted to openness will now reach beyond the spurts and variations of
these unique poems. One possible shift (apart from moves
toward yet other genres) may in fact lead toward less
openness, less assimilation. Such a shift might embody a
less defiant but still more searching view of the limits
and differentiations on which Pinsky so resistantly depends. So too, getting outside or beside the "omnivorous
verve" that drives these poems might be a way of achieving a different *kind* of success from the one reached by
the most heterogeneous of the current works. If poetry
must assimilate what Pinsky earlier called "the whole unswallowable / Menu of immensities," how to survive the
threats of choking (as depicted in an earlier poem **"The
Saving"**) or of surrendering to a gaping, endless consumption—the shark's jaw picked clean by yet other hungry mouths? I cite these images to suggest that Pinsky is
already aware that the predicament, as presently formulated, gives no rest. If *Also this* must make way for *Also
that* (an inclusion that yields a new *this,* ringed by a new
that), how to arrest the fugue of "concentric removes,"
or establish the limits of the poem, or achieve a degree
of self-presence that may allow a deeper, still more in-
delible etching of what one is, rather than of what one
may become?

Here again, Pinsky is ahead of such questions: there *is* a
powerful imprint and signature in the astonishing originality of his poems as well as in such already mentioned
figures *à clef* as Daniel, the ciclogriff and the stranded
want bone. And those of his essays which focus on the
unworldly—in the form of a religious faith, a resistant
idiosyncrasy, or a "sense of limit"—reveal his interest in
a vantage from which the poet may reveal his or her own
inwardness while also discriminating the claims and place
of the worldly. If Pinsky recalls Grandpa Dave's apparent
"contempt for piety and rabbi-craft," he also notes that
"if he was a bad Jew [he] was at least a bad Orthodox
Jew," one who took his son (Pinsky's father) to eleven
months of daily prayer for the dead—prompting that son
("young, pragmatic, preoccupied with worldly concerns")
to do the same years later for his father. It is this self-
limiting circle of humility and mourning (one which is
here made possible by inherited ritual), which for Pinsky
saves these acts of worship from idolatry, just as the
recognition of scarcity brings value into the world. As a
child, the poet of **"The Night Game"** devised a private
baseball hero more gifted than the actual Whitey Ford: "a
Dodger. / People were amazed by him. / Once, when he
was young, / He refused to pitch on Yom Kippur."

In whatever direction Pinsky evolves—toward a more
pressing sense of limits, or toward further acts of inclusion, or toward yet other ways of suspending such oppositions ("Doing a brake job, he sings into the wheel")—
American poetry and culture will move with him. There
are few poets or critics better able to challenge and lead
us from this century to the next, and perhaps none who
will do so with the dazzling combination of energy, in-

vention and generous delight, both in poetry and the world,
to be found in these two books.

James Longenbach (essay date 1994)

SOURCE: "Robert Pinsky and the Language of Our Time,"
in *Salmagundi,* No. 103, Summer, 1994, pp. 155-77.

[*In the following essay, Longenbach traces the development of Pinsky's unique poetic vision.*]

Robert Pinsky has always stood apart from the various
schisms used to map the world of American poetry. He
not only admires both the formal terseness of Cunningham and the capacious waywardness of O'Hara; his poems also seem to partake of both these qualities. Formal and free, open and closed, Olson and Wilbur—however the twentieth-century American poetry is divided,
Pinsky remains unplaceable in the best sense of the word.
He has recently said that Seamus Heaney seems legitimately "post-modernist" because in his work, "formal
freedom feels assumed, and matters of technique no
longer fighting issues in the old modernist sense." This
quality seems to me even stronger in Pinsky's own work.
If he is a postmodern poet it is not because he opposes
modernism in the way that some modern poets rejected
their Romantic forebears; the label sticks because he
has understood that opposition itself is what holds other
poets down.

A poet's mark may be measured by his or her ability to
expand the language (which is to say the culture) available to poetry. The effort is usually subtle (we don't need
to think of Shakespeare as a formally innovative writer),
and it always depends on an openness to a variety of
poetries, both past and present. Unlike other writers who
seem, mostly because of their formal choices, more programmatically postmodern, Pinsky has slowly become the
more truly innovative poet—the poet who increases the
possibilities open to poetry. By being both completely
distinctive and completely undogmatic, Pinsky reminds
me of the idiosyncratic pianist Glen Gould, who was
known as a champion of twelve-tone music and who consequently affronted his admirers by publishing a gorgeous-
ly tonal string quartet. Gould replied that he was simply
a "student"—as he called himself—whose "enthusiasms
were seldom balanced by antagonisms." What's striking
here is that Gould's performances are unmistakably
unique: his originality came from an embrace of everything that music had to offer him.

I think it's important to make this point about Pinsky
because his criticism has been used to widen the poetic
canon's artificial oppositions. This is in part understandable, since Pinsky is a writer with clear opinions; but he
is not a writer who would say that he is "denying the
hegemony of such dominant twentieth-century conventions as the subjective modernist lyric." Pinsky is too
sophisticated a critic to put together the words subjective, modernist, and lyric, secure that the phrase means
something coherent enough to deny. It's true that Pinsky

has criticized what I might call (though it makes me nervous to do so) a strain of attenuated modernism—much smaller than the practice of any modernist poet—that privileges the "image" to the exclusion of other kinds of poetic discourse. But to capitalize polemically on this aspect of Pinsky's work is to diminish the scope of what he's doing. Pinsky did not set out to replace one orthodoxy with another; his goal is to resist any vocabulary for poetry that becomes exclusionary and taken-for-granted. The point of *The Situation of Poetry* is that all poetic language is more or less arbitrary, none of it closer to the heart than any other. Pinsky has his preferences, but his argument is not with the "image" as such but with the unquestioned acceptance of its values.

Throughout *The Situation of Poetry* Pinsky discusses this issue in what seem like purely formal terms. But as the title of his most recent critical work—*Poetry and the World*—suggests, Pinsky understands that any formal issue in poetry is simultaneously a social issue: "The poet's first social responsibility, to continue the art, can be filled only through the second, opposed responsibility to change the terms of the art given—and it is given socially, which is to say politically." Except that it's not afraid of the word *art,* this statement is similar to many current "New Historicist" ideas about poetry. (In fact, the essay it's taken from, **"Responsibilities of the Poet,"** was first published in a special issue of *Critical Inquiry* on politics and poetic value: unlike most poet-critics, Pinsky seems in touch with academic literary criticism in profitable ways.) But the wisdom of this statement also resonates beyond critical fashion. Over the course of his career, Pinsky has made his finest poems not by harnessing beautiful language but by forcing the language of his time (the language that didn't yet seem beautiful) into poetry. This skill, discovered in the poems of *Sadness and Happiness* and perfected in those of *The Want Bone*, is the product of Pinsky's strong sense of poetry's historicity. Like the poets of his past, Wordsworth or Elizabeth Bishop, Pinsky resists not subjectivity itself but the dramatization of subjectivity uncomplicated by an awareness of the subject's social nature: this is Pinsky's inheritance, romantic and modern.

Pinsky was born and raised in Long Branch, New Jersey, a town that by 1940 was already a dilapidated resort. Graduating from Rutgers University in 1962, he wrote his senior thesis on T. S. Eliot. Then he enrolled as a graduate student at Stanford, and, quite by accident, became aware of Yvor Winters. During his first semester, after he read Robert Lowell's review of Winters's *Selected Poems,* Pinsky was impressed enough to show Winters his poems. On more than one occasion Pinsky has described this meeting with a delicately self-depreciating irony.

> He asked me to sit down, and he thumbed through the manuscript while I was there. It took him perhaps four minutes, stopping once or twice at certain ones. Then he looked up at me, and said, "You simply don't know how to write."

> He added that there was some gift there, but because I was ignorant of what to do with it, he could not estimate how much of a gift it was. If it was blind luck or happy fate or smiling Fortune that must be thanked for leading me to Stanford, let me congratulate myself for having the sense not to leave the room when he said that.

Pinsky stayed in the room for several years, taking directed reading courses with Winters and writing poems. He has subsequently expressed his debt to Winters many times (most wonderfully in the penultimate section of his **"Essay on Psychiatrists"**), but unlike other writers who identify with Winters, Pinsky has never seemed like a Wintersian, repeating the old man's idiosyncratic take on literary history. While Pinsky inherited Winters's preference for a Jonsonian clarity of statement in poetry, I think Winters was important to him as a poet-critic who stressed the necessity of coming to terms with the entire history of poetry: it was Winters's generosity rather than his crankiness that made an impression on the young Pinsky. In addition, I think Winters stressed in usable terms what Pinsky probably knew intuitively: that the reading and writing of poetry was a moral act.

Three years after he showed Winters his work, Pinsky published his first poems in the October 1965 issue of the *Southern Review,* then a journal where many of Winters's students and friends appeared. These poems sound almost nothing like the work Pinsky would produce three of four years later, but they are distinguished by a formal clarity and ease. Of the four poems, Pinsky preserved only **"Old Woman"** in his first collection, *Sadness and Happiness*.

> Not even in darkest August,
> When the mysterious insects
> Marry loudly in the black weeds
> And the woodbine, limp after rain,
> In the cooled night is more fragrant,
> Do you gather in any slight
> Harvest to yourself. Deep whispers
> Of slight thunder, horizons off,
> May break your thin sleep, but awake,
> You cannot hear them. Harsh gleaner
> Of children, grandchildren—remnants
> Of nights now forever future—
> Your dry, invisible shudder
> Dies on this porch, where, uninflamed,
> You dread the oncoming seasons,
> Repose in electric light.

Like one of the poems that accompanied it in the *Southern Review* (another was set in rhymed couplets and the fourth in terza rima), **"Old Woman"** is organized syllabically, the eight syllables of each line variously accented. The subtlety of their rhythm does stand apart from the lines of the other poems ("The marriage bed awakes to hear / A voice reciting, without fear"), but **"Old Woman"** showed only half of what Pinsky would become: the expert craftsman.

Pinsky published no more poems until 1969-70, when he appeared again in the *Southern Review* and also in *Poetry*: all but one of these poems remain uncollected, as do three of the four additional poems that later appeared in the September 1971 issue of *Poetry*. The fourth poem, **"The Destruction of Long Branch,"** seems in retrospect like a breakthrough.

> When they came out with artificial turf
> I went back home with a thousand miles.
>
> I dug a trench by moonlight from the ocean
> And let it wash in quietly
> And make a brackish quicksand which the tide
> Sluiced upward from the streets and ditches.
> The downtown that the shopping centers killed,
> The garden apartments, the garages,
>
> The station, the Little Africa on (so help me)
> Liberty Street, the nicer sections
>
> All settled gently in a drench of sand
> And sunk with a minimum of noise.

It's tempting to say that the new power of these lines comes from Pinsky's focus on the peculiarity of his home town. In some sense, the poem does represent the finding of a "subject matter," and Pinsky has subsequently written in sophisticated ways about the importance of subject matter and of poems that are organized by the earnest presentation of their meaning. But this advance happened when it did because Pinsky broke through an earlier idea about poetic language. He has recently said that **"Old Woman"** represents a kind of poetry that no longer interests him because of its "overt lyricism of vocabulary and syntax." In contrast, the force of the language of **"The Destruction of Long Branch"** depends not on an extravagance of image or wit or metaphor—not even on the sonorous quality of lines like "Deep whispers / Of slight thunder, horizons off, / May break your thin sleep"—but on the unfolding of an argument that includes words like *shopping center.* Pinsky has joked that he tends to suspect a poet who hasn't gotten a shopping center into his poems: his point is to stress not only the place of the everyday world but the place of everyday language—language not yet poetic—in poetry. The phrase *shopping center* could never appear in **"Old Woman,"** just as Yeats could never have gotten the words *greasy till* into "To the Rose upon the Rood of Time"—even if he'd wanted to.

"The Destruction of Long Branch" sounds even more like the mature Pinsky because the introduction of phrases like *shopping center, artificial turf,* and *so help me* does not disrupt the formal clarity evident even in his earliest work. In "American Poetry and American Life" (collected along with "Responsibilities of the Poet" in *Poetry and the World*) Pinsky has described the social qualities of Anne Winters's poetry, and, like all influential poet-critics, he seems to account for aspects of his own poetry when he praises certain qualities in others'.

> I don't intend anything as quixotic or odious as prescribing a subject matter, or proscribing one. Rather, the point is that a certain kind of fluidity, a formal and moral quality,

seems to have been demanded of American poets by their circumstance. . . . Winters's laundromat with its *"I mean to live"* seems simultaneously to challenge and embarrass poetic language, and to incorporate it: to defy poetic form, and to demand it.

These sentences describe perfectly later poems like **"Pleasure Bay"** or **"The Hearts"** (the long, fluid poems that **"The Destruction of Long Branch"** looks forward to). They also describe the values that give those poems their idiosyncratic movement (Williams's diction plugged into Stevens's pentameters). Pinsky has no interest in the mysterious "freedom" often associated with the breaking of poetic forms, since he understands that forms are, as part of the historicity of his writing, unbreakable; but he is interested in bending them, testing them against the warp and woof of his experience.

Perhaps it isn't coincidental that **"The Destruction of Long Branch"** embodies thematically this double attitude toward history and culture—defying it and demanding it. The poem isn't about the slow decay of Long Branch; rather, it's about Pinsky's desire to flood the place and pave it over—an act which he accomplishes, like any romantic poet, "by moonlight." But the loving specificity of the poem's catalogue of everything that disappears belies his desire to destroy, and the poem ends not with destruction but with Pinsky's recreation— "cautiously elegiac"—of his home town. In the process, the words that threatened to make him what he is (*artificial turf, shopping mall*) become the words with which he names the world and makes it his own.

Comparing Elizabeth Bishop to Wordsworth, Pinsky has said that "her great subject is the contest—or truce, or trade-agreement—between the single human soul on the one side, and on the other side, the contingent world of artificats and other people." This is Pinsky's great subject too, and it accounts for Pinsky's emphasis on the historicity of his language: it is only through the social structure of language that the single soul is constituted, and it is only through language that the soul asserts its power over the social structure. "Naming and placing things," says Pinsky apropos of Bishop (though he could have been talking about **"The Destruction of Long Branch"**), "is an approach to genuine liberty. This is true even though the very means of naming things . . . are also part of the terrain."

This concern unites the poems of *Sadness and Happiness.* If Bishop's "In the Waiting Room" is a poem that dramatizes the difficulty of realizing that the self is a social construction (the individual merely "one of them"), then the first poem in *Sadness and Happiness* is about the opposite difficulty of seeing the individual as anything but a product of the categories that constitute it—"an I." The opening stanzas of **"Poem About People"** offer a comfortable account of other people seen less as individuals than as exemplars of a kind of Johnsonian "general nature." The difficulties begin here:

> But how love falters and flags
> When anyone's difficult eyes come
> Into focus, terrible gaze of a unique
> Soul, its need unlovable.

Pinsky offers several examples of this problem, the last of which explores the sentimentality of his earlier remark that it is "possible / To feel briefly like Jesus," crossing the "dark spaces" between individuals.

> In the movies, when the sensitive
> Young Jewish soldier nearly drowns
>
> Trying to rescue the thrashing
> Anti-semitic bully, swimming across
> The river raked by nazi fire,
> The awful part is the part truth:
>
> *Hate my whole kind,* but me,
> Love me for myself.

The truth is partial because single selves have meaning only as the parts of whole kinds; the difference is frightening, and difficult to calibrate. But it is not impossible, as the poem's final lines suggest, restating the opening stanzas' hope in darker, more tentative terms: "we / All dream it, the dark wind crossing / The wide spaces between us."

Two years after *Sadness and Happiness* appeared, Pinsky published *The Situation of Poetry*. But as his fugitive essays and reviews from the early seventies reveal, the book's argument had been in his mind for some time. Its thesis appeared in concentrated form in the June 1973 issue of *Poetry*.

> Some contemporary poems tend, pretty distinctly as such matters go, toward coolness: the aspect of modernism which effaces or holds back the warmth of authorial commitment to feeling or idea, in favor of a surface cool under the reader's touch.

> A previous generation sought coolness through concentration on objective images. But the techniques implied by the term "imagism" have come to look rhetorical and warmly committed. . . . When it fails, it resembles other forms of "poetic diction."

This was the problem. In the January 1974 issue of *Poetry* Pinsky offered a solution.

> Most people who read poetry have some loose idea of what the prose virtues are—a demanding, unglamourous group, including perhaps Clarity, Flexibility, Efficiency . . . ? This is a drab, a grotesquely puritanical bunch of shrews. They never appear in blurbs. And yet when they are courted by those who understand them—Williams, Bishop—the Prose Virtues, which sound like a supporting chorus, perform virtuoso marvels. They become not merely the poem's minimum requirement, but the poetic essence.

The only word missing here is *discursive*: the word is Pinsky's, but it has become the word most often used to describe his poems, especially those from *Sadness and Happiness* like "Essay on Psychiatrists" and "Tennis." Throughout these poems, Pinsky tries to recapture the pre-Romantic sensibility of Dryden or Virgil (the sensibility that was supposedly available, as Winters is made to say in "Essay on Psychiatrists," before "the middle / Of the Eighteenth Century" when "the logical / Foundations of Western thought decayed and fell apart"). If Virgil could write poems about the skills of farming, why not poems about the skills of tennis?

> Hit to the weakness. All things being equal
> Hit crosscourt rather than down the line, because
> If you hit crosscourt back to him, then he
> Can only hit back either towards you (crosscourt)
> Or parallel to you (down the line), but never
> Away from you, the way that you can hit
> Away from him if he hits down the line.

When these lines were first published, they seemed like an incredible breath of fresh air: nothing could have stood more at odds with the fashion for confessional poetry. But after almost twenty years, the more egregiously discursive poems don't seem to me to be the finest achievement in *Sadness and Happiness*—necessary though they were for Pinsky's development. While the textures of "Essay on Psychiatrists" or "Tennis" do encourage the expansion of poetic language, they do so programmatically, making the inclusion in poetry of phrases like *crosscourt* and *down the line* sound like a feat rather than an achievement that later poems will build on. Consequently, the poems seem more like attempts to write like Virgil (no more possible than it is to write like Keats) than efforts to adapt his pre-Romantic sensibility to the poetry of today. In contrast, that is exactly what poems like "Poem About People," "Discretions of Alcibiades," or "The Beach Women" do.

In retrospect, then, how dangerous it was for Pinsky to embark on the long poem *Explanation of America*, published in 1979. This poem is as plainly discursive as "Tennis," but unlike "Tennis" or even "Essay on Psychiatrists," *Explanation* is a poem in which Pinsky has something urgent to say. Halfway through, Pinsky offers this hope to his daughter, to whom the poem is addressed.

> The words—"*Vietnam*"—that I can't use in poems
> Without the one word threatening to gape
> And swallow and enclose the poem, for you
> May grow more finite; able to be touched.

This is what Pinsky had learned, writing his first book of poems. But the word that he chooses here, so much more charged than *shopping center*, reveals how much he feels is at stake in the expansion of the language of poetry. Pinsky begins *Explanation* by stressing the vast multiplicity of images in American culture ("Colonial Diners, Disney, films / Of concentration camps, the napalmed child / Trotting through famous newsfilm"), and he wants his daughter to seel all these images—just as he wants to build a poem ample enough to contain them. Such a poem might satisfy Pinsky's smaller hope:

The Shopping Center itself will be as precious
And quaint as is the threadmill now converted
Into a quaint and high-class shopping center.

But the larger hope—the larger word—is not dispatched
with so easily:

Someday, the War in Southeast Asia, somewhere—
Perhaps for you and people younger than you—
Will be the kind of history and pain
Saguntum is for me; but never tamed
Or "history" for me, I think.

J. D. McClatchy has called *An Explanation of America*
Pinsky's "most capacious and aspiring work," but I agree
with him when he says that *History of My Heart*, published in 1984, represents a turning point in Pinsky's
career. Pinsky's great subject—the dialectical relationship of the self and the social structure—was necessarily
at the center of his meditation on what the word "America" might mean. But while the poems of *History of My
Heart* and *The Want Bone* continue this meditation, they
do so dramatically, enacting the dialectic as well as explaining it. These poems retain the discursive clarity of
the long poem, but their narratives seem (even within
their smaller compass) more comprehensive and complex, more a dramatization of a mind thinking than the
product of thought (to borrow a distinction Elizabeth
Bishop favored).

The opening poem in *History of my Heart*, "The Figured
Wheel," describes the rotation of a great wheel throughout history. A catalogue of culture, high and low, familiar
and foreign, it begins with a *shopping mall* rather than a
center and ends with the creation of Robert Pinsky's single self.

It is hung with devices
By dead masters who have survived by reducing
     themselves
          magically

To tiny organisms, to wisps of matter, crumbs of soil,
Bits of dry skin, microscopic flakes, which is why
     they are called
          "great,"
In their humility that goes on celebrating the turning
Of the wheel as it rolls unrelentingly over

A cow plodding through car traffic on a street in
     Iasi,
And over the haunts of Robert Pinsky's mother and
     father
And wife and children and his sweet self
Which he hereby unwillingly and inexpertly gives up,
     because it
          is
There, figured and pre-figured in the nothing-
     transfiguring wheel.

These lines establish the terms in which the title *History
of My Heart* must be understood. Virtually all of Pin-

sky's poems are autobiographical, but they recognize that
an autobiography, like the self it narrates, is constituted
by a wide array of cultural and historical forces. To get
to the "heart" of these poems is not to find some essential core but to recognize that the heart is on the surface
of everything the poet sees or speaks. Any distinctions
between private and public "history" become difficult to
sustain.

The second poem in *History of My Heart* adds a more
plainly political charge to this history. "The Unseen"
begins with a group of tourists in Krakow, touring the
death camp. The scene is "unswallowable," both unbearably familiar and unbearably horrific: "We felt bored /
And at the same time like screaming Biblical phrases."
Stalled between these extremes, Pinsky remembers a
"sleep-time game"—an insomniac's dream of heroic destruction: granted the power of invisibility, Pinsky roams
the camp, saves the victims from the gas chamber, and,
as a finale, flushes "everything with a vague flood / Of
fire and blood." As in "The Destruction of Long Branch,"
Pinsky dreams of having power over his history, remaking what made him.

It's not possible to take that dream too seriously in "The
Destruction of Long Branch," of course: its act of destruction serves as a kind of metaphor for the self's struggle with language and history. But in "The Unseen" the
act is too literal, too historically charged, and Pinsky
must back away from it more clearly.

I don't feel changed, or even informed—in that,
It's like any other historical monument; although
It is true that I don't ever at night any more

Prowl rows of red buildings unseen, doing
Justice like an angry god to escape insomnia.

Though he feels unchanged, Pinsky describes an important transformation here. Having imagined himself as the
"unseen," Pinsky now recognizes a more potent invisible
presence.

And so,
O discredited Lord of Hosts, your servant gapes

Obediently to swallow various doings of us, the most
Capable of all your former creatures . . .

I think this force could be called "history" as easily as
"Lord of Hosts." Having earlier found the scene "unswallowable," Pinsky realizes that he has no choice but to
take in the past. And as "The Figured Wheel" suggests,
the past—however sordid—is already inside him: in this
sense, the force could also be called "my heart."

This historical wheel rolls through all of Pinsky's work,
but these lines from *The Want Bone* (his best and most
recent book) point to a slight change in his attitude:
"How can I turn this wheel / that turns my life?" Throughout *History of My Heart* Pinsky is amazed by the vast
array of images that make up the self; throughout *The*

Want Bone he is equally amazed by the images that the self can make. The desire—the want—to turn the wheel of history has certainly been present in Pinsky's work since **"The Destruction of Long Branch"**; but in *The Want Bone* Pinsky sometimes stands aghast at the potential hubris of the human imagination—or what in **"What Why When How Who"** he calls

> The old conspiracy of gain and pleasure
>
> Flowering in the mind greedily to build the world
> And break it.

Behind these lines stand Old Testament injunctions against idolatry—"they worship the work of their own hands, that which their own fingers have made"—but in an essay on the prophet Isaiah Pinsky concludes that "all worship, even the most meticulous or elaborate, may be flawed by the spirit of idolatry." Since idolatry is in some way essential to human action, good or bad, Pinsky's fascination is less with greed as such than with the point where pleasure begins to conspire unhappily with gain.

The astonishing first poem in *The Want Bone*, **"From the Childhood of Jesus,"** is impatient with both Old and New Testament wisdom, both the laws of Judaism and Jesus' revision of them. Pinsky tells the apocryphal tale of a young Jesus who makes a little pond of mud and twigs and models twelve sparrows from clay. The scene seems innocent enough until "a certain Jew" (Pinsky incorporates the language of the anti-Semitic joke or story here) scolds the child for "making images." In response, Jesus makes the sparrows come to life, and, when the son of Annas accidentally ruins the little pond, Jesus makes the boy wither away. The petulant tone of Jesus' anger is familiar from the gospels ("what did the water / Do to harm you?"), but his actions are merciless, filled with the childish greed and self-importance that the tone suggests. (As Pinsky says in **"Lament for the Makers,"** worship is "tautological, with its Blessed / Art thou O Lord who consecrates the Sabbath . . . And then the sudden curt command or truth: / God told him, Thou shalt cut thy foreskin off.") **"From the Childhood of Jesus"** ends like a parable gone wrong.

> Alone in his cot in Joseph's house, the Son
> Of man was crying himself to sleep. The moon
>
> Rose higher, the Jews put out their lights and slept,
> And all was calm and as it had been, except
>
> In the agitated household of the scribe Annas,
> And high in the dark, where unknown even to Jesus
>
> The twelve new sparrows flew aimlessly through the
>   night,
> Not blinking or resting, as if never to alight.

Jesus is resolutely human in this story, granted the powers of a god but the emotions of a child, and, like any man, he cannot control the things he has made: the poem's final image is more frightening than the child's pet-

ulance. **"From the Childhood of Jesus"** is astonishing because, while it is ultimately about the consequences of the simple human desire for power, it tells that profane story in the vocabulary of the sacred. Consequently, this poem about hubris is itself startlingly hubristic—a paradox that embodies Pinsky's uneasy double attitude toward the human imagination.

"From the Childhood of Jesus" exemplifies one of the two kinds of poems that make up *The Want Bone*. The other kind, rather than adapting Biblical rhetoric, combines a multiplicity of vocabularies and narratives into a shape that seems both wild and controlled, random and planned. Most of these poems are organized something like a Baroque concerto with a *ritornello* or repeating theme that returns (though in a different key) after each episode of new material. In **"The Uncreation"** various ideas of singing hold the poem's disparate materials together. In **"At Pleasure Bay"** some version of the phrase "never the same" recurs. And in **"The Shirt"** the repeated motif is neither a theme nor a phrase but simply a rhythm: "The back, the yoke, the yardage" or "The planter, the picker, the sorter." Similar to those of *History of My Heart* but even more accomplished, these poems are what **"The Destruction of Long Branch"** ultimately made possible.

In **"The Hearts"** the *ritornello* is an unsentimental image of the heart, itself the sentimental image of desire, as "pulpy shore-life battened on a jetty."

> Slashed by the little deaths of sleep and pleasure,
> They swell in the nurturing spasms of the waves,
>
> Sucking to cling; and even in death itself—
> Baked, frozen—they shrink to grip the granite harder.

Between the recurrences of this image comes a catalogue of harsh desires. The victim of a suffocating lover is equated with a heroin addict who knows, the first time he shoots up, that he will suffer, go to prison, and probably die. But this knowledge doesn't stop the addict, whose consolation is that proposed by Enobarbus in *Antony and Cleopatra* when Antony laments "Would I had never seen her": "Then you would have missed / A wonderful piece of work." This passage, in turn, invokes a sentence from Stephen Booth's commentary on Shakespeare's sonnets: "Shakespeare was almost certainly homosexual, / Bisexual, or heterosexual, the sonnets / Provide no evidence on the matter." This link in the chain of associations provokes the poem's central question: why does human desire fuel, over and over again, the making of images—the singing of songs, the throwing of pots, the writing of poems?

All of these creative acts are invoked as the chain continues, one image leading metonymically to the next. The question of Shakespeare's sexuality invokes the rhetoric of courtly love (tears, crystals, hearts) which still infects the songs (Lee Andrews and The Hearts—"My tear drops are / Like crystals") we sing in the shower (falling like tears or crystals).

To Buddha every distinct thing is illusion
And becoming is destruction, but still we sing
In the shower. I do. In the beginning God drenched

The Emptiness with images: the potter
Crosslegged at his wheel in Benares market
Making mud cups, another cup each second
Tapering up between his fingers, one more
To sell the tea-seller at a penny a dozen,
And tea a penny a cup. The customers smash
The empties, and waves of traffic grind the shards
To mud for new cups, in turn; and I keep one here
Next to me: holding it awhile from out of the cloud

Of dust that rises from the shattered pieces,
The risen dust alive with fire, then settled
And soaked and whirling again on the wheel that
    turns

And looks on the world as on another cloud,
On everything the heart can grasp and throw away
As a passing cloud. . . .

The image of the wheel returns here, but unlike **"The Figured Wheel"** the potter's wheel is turned by a man: the result of all human *making,* Pinsky suggests, is this absurd, this transient—not the potent images with which the Old Testament god drenches the emptiness but the mere images that the Buddha denounces as empty. And yet, as the poem continues to unfold, the wheel continues to turn—perhaps productively. The visions of the Old Testament are dismissed as "too barbarous for heaven/And too preposterous for belief on earth" (Pinsky rehearses the horrible vision in Isaiah 6, after which the prophet's unclean lips are purified by a live coal), and **"The Hearts"** ends by returning to Lee Andrews and The Hearts, their record spinning like the potter's wheel.

As the record ends, a coda in retard:
The Hearts in a shifting velvety *ah,* and *ah*
Prolonged again, and again as Lee Andrews

Reaches *ah* high for *I have to gain Faith, Hope*
And Charity, God only knows the girl
Who will love me—Oh! if we only could

Start over again! Then The Hearts chant the chords
Again a final time, *ah* and the record turns
Through all the music, and on into silence again.

These lines of the poem answer the song: you can start again, though you'll end up in pretty much the same place. Finally, Pinsky's suggestion is that the turning itself— the longing, the singing, the making—must constitute our human value. If this seems like a paltry consolation, the empty images condemned by the Buddha, we should remember in contrast the uncontrollable, unsatisfying images conjured by the Son of Man.

The final lines of **"The Hearts"** cannot sound like too definitive a conclusion since, like so many of Pinsky's later poems, **"The Hearts"** eschews the normal kinds of progression or closure we associate with lyric poetry. Less than the final lines it is the *turning* of the poem itself that is most memorable. In his essay "Poetry and Pleasure" Pinsky praises the apparently random succession of thoughts and observations that a letter can accommodate, and in his quest to keep poetry open to all kinds of language and experience, Pinsky has tried to establish that kind of movement in poems like **"The Hearts," "Shirt,"** or **"Pleasure Bay."** He asks in "Poetry and Pleasure" the question implicit in his work since **"The Destruction of Long Branch"**: "if gorgeous, impressive language and profound, crucial ideas were all that poetry offered to engage us, would it seem—as it does to many of us—as necessary as food?" What engages us is not the product—the achieved word or thought—but the process of a mind moving through those thoughts and words: "This movement—physical in the sounds of a poem, moral in its relation to the society implied by language, the person who utters the poem— is near the heart of poetry's mysterious appeal, for me." In its sinuous investigation of desire, **"The Hearts"** tries to describe this appeal: more profoundly, the poem enacts it.

I've quoted **"Poetry and Pleasure"** to elucidate Pinsky's poems, but of course Pinsky is trying to say something about the pleasures of poetry at large; the phrase "Death is the mother of beauty" is not particularly interesting except because it occurs within the idiosyncratic movement of thought and sound in Stevens's "Sunday Morning." In **"American Poetry and American Life"** Pinsky returns to this quality of movement, emphasizing that it is visible in a wide range of American poetries.

One could exemplify this fluidity of tone, including the inseparable blend of comic and ecstatic, formal and vulgar, in an enormous range of American poets, John Ashbery and Elizabeth Bishop, George Oppen and James Merrill, Allen Ginsberg and Marianne Moore. (I think that the stylistic trait I mean also characterizes poems that do not explicitly take up American cultural material such as bus rides or movies.)

Pinsky is interested in developing categories for the discussion of American poetry that do not encourage the polemical oppositions of Oppen and Merrill, Ginsberg and Moore, or—even more culturally overdetermined— the high and the low. His strategy not only clarifies the position of his own work but helps to insure the future health and diversity of American literature: the segregation of poetic schools only limits the possibilities available to poetry.

Even the most deeply entrenched battle positions of American poetry don't interest Pinsky. In an essay occasioned by the centennial of T. S. Eliot's birth, he has admitted that the subject of his undergraduate thesis first alerted him to the quality of movement he so values, the "clangorous, barely-harmonized bringing together of the sacred and profane."

Eliot is above all the pre-eminent poet of this clash or yoking. . . . Because he identified and penetrated this dualism in the rhythms and noises and smells and surfaces of modern life, without simplifying what he saw into false ideas of squalor or perfection, Eliot remains entirely essential for us. He is not merely whatever we mean by "great poet," but precisely what Pound means by "an inventor." For this, Eliot's readers forgive him his mean side, his religio-authoritarian claptrap, the plushy grandiosity of "Ash Wednesday," the tetrameter anti-Semitism, the genteel trivialities of the late plays.

Today, almost thirty years after Eliot's death, there still seems something daring about this expression of debt and affinity.

I began this essay by proposing that it is precisely through such acknowledgements of debt and affinity that Pinsky's originality is constituted. Tracing his artistic development, I think we can see that Pinsky's own work provides the terms in which my proposition must be understood. Since our selves are turned on the great wheel of history and language, we owe whatever combination of qualities that might distinguish us, formal and vulgar, comic and ecstatic, to mysterious forces we disregard at our own peril. Pinsky's is a poetry of acknowledgment, and its power grows from his deep awareness—sometimes wariness, sometimes worship—of the literary, linguistic, and historical precedents that continue to design his life even as he writes today. Acknowledging Eliot, Pinsky calls him an "inventor," which Pound defined as a writer who discovers "a particular process or more than one mode and process." Above inventors, said Pound, stands the small class of "masters," those "who, apart from their own inventions, are able to assimilate and co-ordinate a large number of preceding inventions." This, near the end of the twentieth century, in both his poetry and his prose, is what Robert Pinsky is doing.

Triquarterly with Robert Pinsky (interview date 1994-1995)

SOURCE: "A Conversation with Robert Pinsky," *Triquarterly*, No. 92, Winter, 1994-1995, pp. 21-37.

[*In the following interview conducted by several people, Pinsky discusses the problems of translating poetry, the influence of Judaism and Eastern philosophy on his writing, and his poetic philosophy.*]

[JIM KNOWLES]: *There's an essay by Seamus Heaney called "The Impact of Translation" in which he starts out with a translation by you. He talks about the problem a poet writing in English might have when he realizes that the kind of poem he is struggling to write has been written already in some other part of the world.*

[ROBERT PINSKY]: The poem is "Incantation," by Czeslaw Milosz, with whom I worked on various translations. Not long after Czeslaw and I had done the translation, Seamus was over to the house and I read it to him. He was struck by the same quality in it that I was. The poem is very explicit and quite, one might say, moralistic or idealistic. Could a poet in English, I thought, particularly an American poet, write such a poem? It's quite short; I'll read it to you:

> "Incantation"
>
> Human reason is beautiful and invincible.
> No bars, no barbed wire, no pulping of books,
> No sentence of banishment can prevail against it.
> It establishes the universal ideas in language,
> And guides our hand so we write Truth and Justice
> With capital letters, lie and oppression with small.
> It puts what should be above things as they are,
> Is an enemy of despair and a friend of hope.
> It does not know Jew from Greek or slave from
>   master,
> Giving us the estate of the world to manage.
> It saves austere and transparent phrases
> From the filthy discord of tortured words.
> It says that everything is new under the sun,
> Opens the congealed fist of the past.
> Beautiful and very young are Philo-Sophia
> And poetry, her ally in the service of the good.
> As late as yesterday Nature celebrated their birth,
> The news was brought to the mountains by a unicorn
>   and an echo.
> Their friendship will be glorious, their time has no
>   limit.
> Their enemies have delivered themselves to
>   destruction.

Seamus has quite complex things to say about this poem. First, he admires it rather eloquently, and then he says something like, on the other hand, this is a poem that one can imagine being written by a prelate or somebody at the seminary on the hill, some literate and bromidic Catholic: someone of intelligence and good will who isn't really hip to poetry.

Instead, "Incantation" is, somehow, a truly wonderful poem. In a way, you can say that the most difficult thing to do in a poem is to present ideas, abstract ideas of this kind, this explicitly, and attain strong emotion. And perhaps the implication is that parts of the world that have experienced totalitarian regimes are fertile ground for this kind of direct approach, while our own good fortune in not having experienced war on our terrain for over a hundred years, nor having experienced a totalitarian regime or a police state, makes us less capable of such writing.

I don't think Seamus says that, in fact, although he takes up the idea. Milosz's own opinion of that idea is interesting—he says this is like envying a hunchback his hump. He considers it a very silly sentimentality on the part of Western writers, romanticizing or idealizing the situation of the artist in extremely oppressive political circumstances. Certainly, if there is a kind of writing we admire and would like to emulate in relation to our own woes and desires, that is up to us. A lot of American poets were disappointed, as I was, that the first poet to read at a presidential inauguration since Robert Frost, Maya Angelou, read something that lacked exactly the kind of cogency or depth or impact or precision that distinguishes the abstractions and noble sentiments of "Incantation" from the clichés of journalism or from what Seamus's imaginary seminarian might write. Ms. Angelou's poem was on the side of goodness, but lacked the passion of art; considered as a work of art it had the vagueness and figurative muddle of plausible journalism at some times and the awkwardness of mere public speaking at others. But that doesn't mean it can't be done—who knows, by Ms. Angelou next time out, or by the poet laureate Mona Van Duyn, or whoever. Like everything else in art, it can't be done only until someone does it.

And the Heaney essay is quite subtle on the question, as I remember, and not easily paraphrased—he says something like, such writing depends immensely upon context. He says I read it aloud to him—he describes the house, he describes the moment, he's a Catholic writer of one generation thinking about Milosz, a Catholic writer of another generation; Seamus is from a country torn by violence and Milosz is from another country torn by violence, in short there's a whole context that made him especially receptive to the poem: and I think he's raising a question about context, rather than proposing to envy the hunchback his hump. It's a good essay, a wonderful essay, and I would not attempt to summarize it. I see you're nodding, so you'd agree with me that he doesn't exactly say we can or we can't write in this way.

Right. I don't think the essay says that it's impossible to write a poem like this, but Heaney does seem to say that there's a trap we fall into when we try to write a poem that sounds like a translation.

Yes. Yes. But I think we did a good enough job of translating "Incantation" that this translation doesn't sound like a translation, which therefore makes me think about this poem in some of the ways that I think about any poem in English that I admire. That first sentence and line—"Human reason is beautiful and invincible"—I believe I thought something like: damn it, I wish I had thought of that: and "that" could hardly mean the idea or sentiment. It must mean something more like, I wish I had found that mode and written that sentence; or, I wish I had heard that imagined music of meaning, I wish I had played that, made that sound. Which again I take to mean that it was possible: it was there to be written. The reason I couldn't have written this poem has to do with all the same reasons that I didn't write "Sailing to Byzantium" or didn't write "At the Fishhouses" but not to do with the fact that I am a Western writer or American or that I write in English. I couldn't have written this in the same sense that I couldn't have written "Sailing to Byzantium."

[HARRY THOMAS]: *On this same subject, though, near the end of his book,* Czeslaw Milosz and the Insufficiency of Lyric, *Donald Davie quotes your translation of Milosz's poem "The Father" from the sequence "The World," and he calls your translation a*

"brilliant" translation, he's full of praise for it, but when Milosz came to put together his Collected Poems *he decided to use his own flatter, more trotlike version of the poem rather than yours.*

This is a complicated issue. Strictly speaking, the *Collected Poems* version is not entirely Czeslaw's own translation: it's largely word-for-word a trot, originally prepared by the scholar Lillian Vallee, though the note in the *Collected* says "translated by the author." Some arbitrariness of this kind in crediting translations is common, and more or less inevitable when many hands share the task. Lillian (who had very ably translated Milosz's *Bells in Winter*) generously provided her literal version of "The World," from which Bob Hass and I worked to make our translation for *The Separate Notebooks.*

I think sometimes a translation enters so much into the spirit of the new language that by a kind of luck it forms a new aesthetic whole; and if the author who first forged the poem deep in the furnace of the original language, and who fueled it with his heart, happens to know this new language well enough to perceive that new aesthetic whole, then it may seem to him in its formal spirit to be too much itself—even though it may be extremely close, even more or less literal: he may prefer something that is not a poem in English, that is a mere rendering, even if the rendering is not particularly more accurate, even though it may be less literal. That is the interesting part: it has nothing to do with loose or free, literal or approximate, because the issue is not accuracy or maybe even not formal equivalence—but the issue of life, an alien aesthetic life. The translation that crosses over into the poetry of the new language may be so good it is bad.

Possibly something a little like this may have occurred with Czeslaw and "The World." I remember how the spirit of that project was reflected by the way we worked, in a committee: the poet Milosz, who is bilingual; Renata Gorczynski, who is not a poet but who is also bilingual, English and Polish; and then Hass and me, neither one of us bilingual, American poets dependent upon the other two and occasional helpers like Lillian Vallee as informants. I've discovered a new phrase I like: Bob and I were the metrical engineers! Also, I guess, idiom experts. This committee or writing troupe met in various combinations—two or three or four. Czeslaw used to joke about crediting the translations to The Grizzly Peak collaborative, named after his street in Berkeley, or maybe crediting them to a single, pseudonymous translator, Dr. Grisleigh Peake. I remember one day Renata said Czeslaw can't make it today. His Korean translators had come to town, and he was meeting with them, she explained. Bob and I looked at one another and started to grin. Renata said, "What's so funny?" And I said, we were just envying his Korean translators, thinking how lucky they are. She said, what do you mean? He doesn't know Korean, was the answer. So he's not there looking over your shoulder, having a view and all the authority there is.

The translations from the "The World" we did in that period were much praised. People sometimes requested

Czeslaw to read from them at public occasions, and reviewers singled them out when *The Separate Notebooks* appeared. This was all complicated by the fact that the originals are written in a form that doesn't exist in English. In Poland, for decades children learned to read by the use of rhymed primers. Not exactly an old-fashioned American primer, not exactly Stevenson's *A Child's Garden of Verses,* not exactly the didactic poems of Isaac Watts. Bob Hass describes the problem very well in *Ironwood*'s Milosz issue. And the poems of "The World," though the sequence is subtitled "A Naive Poem," are a sophisticated response to World War II: "The World" is about Europe destroying itself. But in this "naive poem," what you see on the surface at the outset is the children, sister and brother, walking peacefully to school together. In separate poems, the children draw pictures; the mother carries a candle in a dark stairwell; the family have dinner. In another the father shows them the world, saying here's the global map, that's Europe, this is Italy, beyond the forest is Germany. He shows them the world, with a certain tone that by implication and context—making Seamus's point again—becomes in its overtones sinister and heartbreaking.

And these poems involve very simple, hard rhymes. In working with our translation committee, trying to get some of that formal note, thinking about the predominance in Polish of feminine rhymes, I made a thing that had a certain kind of rhyme in it, slanted or blunted feminine rhymes, and a certain sound, and to some degree it works, a compromise that does some little thing in English. But it does become another creature, another monster. So I can identify with Czeslaw in saying, well, this thing that has slouched and slanted its way into our committee is living and breathing in some kind of half-assed way; the sense is pretty literal, but there is also this smell of an alien, English-speaking animal, and I don't want to listen to it inhaling and exhaling and grunting around in its cage, I want something more like a telephone or a conduit.

To the original's explicit abstract language?

Yeah. The other thing made him nervous.

But he seems to suggest that the tone you got through the peculiar feminine rhymes and so forth prevented you from rendering the abstract language and statements of the poems explicitly enough.

Yes, but I think it was more "technical" than that. The rhymes in Polish are plain, like the cat sat on the mat. Virtually all endings in Polish are "feminine": they end on an unstressed syllable, so it's more like the kitty felt pity. They're like that, very hard and exact, and they're very simple. The rain fell on the garden and froze and the ice began to harden. They're just very, very plain, and the ones I cooked up for the version of "The World" printed in *The Separate Notebooks* are more like—well, Czeslaw called them "modern rhymes." Here is the opening poem of the sequence in *The Separate Notebooks* version:

"The Path"

Down where the green valley opens wider,
Along the path with grass blurring its border,
Through an oak grove just broken into flower,
Children come walking home from school together.

In a pencil case with a lid that slides open,
Bits of bread roll around with stumps of crayon,
And the penny hidden away by all children
For spring and the first cuckoo in the garden.
The girl's beret and her brother's school-cap
Bob, as they walk, above the fringe of bushes.
A jay screams, hopping in a treetop;
Over the trees, clouds drift in long ridges.

Now, past the curve, you can see the red roof:
Father leans on his hoe in the front garden,
Then bends down to touch a half-opened leaf;
From his tilled patch, he can see the whole region.

"Roof/garden, leaf/region"—that is our version, with the consonantal rhymes, mostly feminine. Here is the same poem in the *Collected Poems*:

"The Road"

There where you see a green valley
And a road half-covered with grass,
Through an oak wood beginning to bloom
Children are returning home from school.

In a pencil case that opens sideways
Crayons rattle among crumbs of a roll
And a copper penny saved by every child
To greet the first spring cuckoo.

Sister's beret and brother's cap
Bob in the bushy underbrush,
A screeching jay hops in the branches
And long clouds float over the trees.

A red roof is already visible at the bend.
In front of the house father, leaning on a hoe,
Bows down, touches the unfolded leaves,
And from his flower bed inspects the whole
    region.

I think that the rhymed version is fairly close, and that it's just as abstract—the literal meaning is not much different. It is not a matter of abstractions. But the *Collected* doesn't attempt the rhymes; you can just be informed that they were in the original. I think that it is the rhythms and rhymes that help create an aesthetic creature—a kind of art-organism—and it is the breathing of such a creature that perhaps must make any author nervous simply by being *other*. I think it would make me nervous.

[Susan Wildey]: *Something that came up in class is that we were wondering in what way, if any, Judaism has affected your writing.*

I'm certain that it must have, in many ways. For instance, I talked last night about my interest in things that are made, made up: I am deeply interested in the subject of creation—high and low, great and small. And religions are notable makings, religion itself is. For one kind of religious person creation itself is an episode in the career of God. For me God is an important episode in the history of creation. Possibly having been raised as an Orthodox Jew, which is to say with considerable separation from the majority culture, has contributed to my interest in making. Not sharing such creations as Christmas or Easter or the—our, your—Saviour, and at the same time having other creations like the kosher laws or the prohibition against saying or writing the word for "God": that is a richly interesting conflict. It may have increased the impact upon me of the fact that we creatures—we mammals, we colony-insects, whatever we are—have invented not only language, but Christianity and Judaism and the United States of America and the violin and the blues and so forth.

The experience of a gorgeous, fading European reality—the rich, lower-class Eastern European Judaism and its culture, which were still present and very European in my childhood—must have had an impact on me that I can't fully understand. I grew up in a nominally orthodox family. My parents were quite secular people. They were good dancers, my father was a celebrated local athlete, they didn't go to synagogue except on the high holy days. We did have two sets of dishes—that is, we did "keep kosher." And as the oldest child, the oldest son in the family, I was expected to go to synagogue every Saturday. The *musaf,* the orthodox service, lasts three, maybe three-and-a-half hours. Imagine for a moment being eleven years old: you don't like school; it's Saturday morning; you spend nearly four hours every Saturday morning in the company mainly of old men, chanting prayers in a language you don't understand, in a prolonged, accreted liturgy that is not dramatic. What happens is an accumulation of prayers and rituals, a liturgy that feels medieval. It does not have the drama of Mass: you don't eat God. It just happens. It comes time for *"Adon' olam,"* so everybody stands up and sings *"Adon' olam,"* and then you sit down again. Time for the *Shema,* you open the curtains, look at the Torah, sing the *Shema,* close it, and sit down again. And then you sing some other prayers. Three, three-and-a-half hours. And for the old men, it's a picnic, they love it. It's a social club for them. And afterwards everybody goes down to the basement and drinks schnapps and eats *kichele.* You aren't supposed to drive on the Sabbath, so it may be one o'clock, one-thirty, before you get home. Meanwhile, outside it is the great era of American baseball and the great formative era of rock and roll; across the street is a Catholic church, where they come and go, sometimes girls in First Communion dresses, they are doing something over there, something relatively brief and one may suspect dramatic, and relatively included by the majority culture.

And you just . . . well, I believe that for many people with Christian upbringings there's this thing I have read about in Joyce and others called a "crisis of faith" or "crisis of belief." That is not what happens in relation to Judaism, in my experience. You don't have a crisis of belief. Faith in any such sense was not something I could apprehend as a great concept in the religion. The religion is kind of a surrounding reality, no more "losable" in its own terms than the color of your eyes, or the force of gravity. It's like having faith in the universe, for the Jew to have "faith in" Judaism: it's just there. And there's only the vaguest idea of an afterlife. There's not a state of sin or a state of grace; everybody's kind of culpable vaguely and chosen vaguely. There's a merit system. You get *mitzvahs,* that is you get credited with good points, while waiting for the Messiah. Or you are credited with sins, bad points. So you don't have a crisis of faith. You look over at the Church across the street, and you say to yourself, *hmmm,* Catholic girls and communion dresses and Jerry Lee Lewis and Jackie Robinson: it's the whole world out there, the splendid *traif* [non-kosher] cookie jar of the world. So you just turn to the world as soon as you get a chance. Or so you do if you are a child like me then. And I made a vow, I promised that little child: *once you don't have to do this, you aren't going to do it again.* They are making you do this, but when you are autonomous and you don't have to do this again, I promise you that you won't have to do it. And I am still keeping that promise. So Judaism was in large measure a powerful boredom for me, but it was a *very* powerful boredom: a serious and for me stifling force. And the force of that boredom, no mere ennui but a desperate, animal sense of being caged and trapped, left me, I think, with a feeling about the majority culture that makes me both feel more inside it than I might have been otherwise—because I *chose* it, I might not have, but I chose the majority culture and I like it—yet by the same process also more outside it, in my feelings, than I might be otherwise. There are special ways in which a secularized Jew feels both additionally *in* the new culture, compared to others, and outside it. Terms like "assimilation," or numbering generations from the first act of immigration, do not begin to deal with these intricacies.

So that's a quick sketch of my guess of what cultural ways I might have been affected by Judaism, to which I feel loyal in ways that have more to do with, say, the stories of Isaac Babel than the celebration of Passover. On the more purely religious aspects of the subject, I'd prefer to be silent right now. But to think of it theologically, exclusively theologically, would be wrong. That would neglect something else, a kind of tear-laden and enriching cultural struggle.

[ED BREMAN]: *In the conclusion of a review of* **The Want Bone** *in the* New Republic, *the poem "At Pleasure Bay" is mentioned, and the reviewer says that in that poem you cash in your debts to Eastern philosophy that had been accumulating throughout* **The Want Bone**. *I was just wondering what your familiarity with Eastern philosophy was and how it might have influenced your poems.*

Oh, Eastern philosophy: I'm even less of a scholar of it than Judaism or Christianity. I lived in Berkeley, California, for nine years. I've done some superficial reading. Zimmerman's books about Hinduism and art are fascinating to me. I am attracted by the Hindu conception of time in the many parables where, say, Shiva will come, and then while he's talking there's a parade of ants and each ant is carrying a world, and each world has a thousand Shivas in it, and each of those Shivas is gesturing at a column of ants. They have many little parables or images like that, trying to enforce the immensity of the great cyclicalness—how everything comes back and comes back literally more times than you can imagine. And you give yourself games like that figure of the ants, as you try to imagine as best you can.

And I guess that at some point the idea I was talking to you about last night, about the way that culture is itself a kind of possession by the dead, coming back—at some point that idea illuminated for me the idea of metempsychosis, the transmigration of souls. And the way that the genetic inheritance is comparable to the cultural inheritance, each of them a constant shifting and combining of so many variables, as many variables as ants and Shivas, got connected in my mind with the migration of souls. It is a trickle or thread that runs through this book. I suppose you could say I mock Buddha in **"The Hearts."** In an early draft of **"The Hearts,"** I can remember one line that I took out was, "Easy for Buddha to say." There's that tone in the poem still, of "Easy for Buddha to say" this or that. And as I understand it, there is a considerable Buddhist tradition of mocking Buddha. It's one of the things I like about Buddhism. A Zen saying I have heard is: "Buddha is a very good stick to pick up shit with." That's one Buddha saying, and there is something awfully admirable about it; I don't know, I suppose I do think Judaism or Christianity might be better off if they had that spirit. The Torah is a good stick to pick up shit with! It would transform the religion if you could say that, if the religion were capacious enough and calm enough to embrace that.

[OMA BLAISE]: *In your essay,* **"Responsibilities of the Poet,"** *you talk about the poet needing to transform a subject. Can you say more about that?*

Bad art does what you expect. To me, it's not truly a poem if it merely says what most intelligent, well-meaning people would say. In the other direction, total surprise is babble, it's meaningless; I don't mean to say that one is on a quest simply for novelty. But your responsibility is, even if it's only to versify something you perceive as truth, to put that truth or homily into a rhyme in such a way that you are transforming it. Your job is to do something that the reader didn't already have. And this does not mean simply the lazy reader. One kind of popular fiction just spins out explicitly and doggedly the most vague, generalized fantasies the reader already has—the least individuated fantasies. The reader, on his or her own, has vague, perhaps commercially provoked fantasies of having quite a lot of money and many a sexual adventure; but the nature of these dreams or of the reader as a person makes him or her a little lazy imaginatively. So someone else puts in a lot of industry, and makes up

specific names of characters, and puts them in rooms and buildings and airplanes, and flies them around, and has them have illegitimate children and meet them again twenty years later, and goes through all of the laborious spinning out of the plot.

This is an art, in the old broad sense, but it is not what I mean by the art of poetry. As I understand it, soap operas take the kind of fantasy people have in common and do the work—quite skillfully—of making such fantasy material explicit, without depriving it of a vague, dreamy generality that is part of the appeal. And the reason *Anna Karenina* has a loftier reputation, dealing with very similar material to the material of soap opera, is that the material is transformed by a powerful individual imagination. It is changed by not just anybody's imagination, but by that of a great, particular transformer. The result is that the material, the adultery and money and so forth, smells and feels like something that's both recognized and strange. Somewhere in that recognition and strangeness lies your job as an artist.

For instance, a lot of people have the notion that totalitarianism contains the seeds of its own destruction, and that art is somehow linked to truth, and therefore is the opposite of totalitarianism. According to such a belief, Fascist poetry at some level would become a contradiction in terms, as in Montale's essay on the subject. And one such person with notions of that—what is the word, let's say of that humanistic kind—Czeslaw Milosz, wrote in the poem we were talking about earlier: "Beautiful and very young are Philo-Sophia / And poetry, her ally in the service of the good.... The news was brought to the mountains by a unicorn and an echo." That changes it; the unicorn and the echo, for example, transform the idea with a peculiar blend of irony and astonishment. And it's your job, if you are an artist, to find that moment of transformation. In contrast, sometimes people really like clichés, they really like being told what they already think.

[WYMAN REMBERT]: *Can you tell us a little bit about* **Mindwheel**? *Something we have says it's an electronic novel or complex interactive computer game. Does it have anything to do with poetry?*

It is a text adventure game, and I did put a lot of poetry into it, mostly borrowed. There are many poems in the game, and it was a great pleasure to see the playtesters at the company I wrote it for say, about some two- or three-hundred-year-old piece of writing, "that's neat". For example, there's a wonderful Walter Ralegh poem that you could call a riddle; it's in the form of a prophecy. It says, "Before the sixth day of the next new year . . . Four kings shall be assembled in this isle" and there shall be "the sound of trump" and "Dead bones shall then be tumbled up and down." What's being described, but never named, are the playing cards and dice. The charm of the poem is that it sounds like a mystical, rather frightening prophecy, and it's the cards and dice. At the end the poem says,

> this tumult shall not cease
> Until an Herald shall proclaim a peace,

An Herald strange, the like was never born
Whose very beard is flesh, and mouth is horn.

Until a Herald calls: " . . . the like was never born /
Whose very beard is flesh, and mouth is horn." Well,
Mindwheel is a narrative game where text appears on the
screen; and in response to each bit of narrative, which
ends with a prompt, you decide whether to go north or to
look around a room, say. You type in an imperative or
complete the sentence "I want to. . . . " and the machine
responds by giving you more text on the screen. Early on
in *Mindwheel*, a winged person is trapped behind bars,
and you—the reader-protagonist—can free this person
by solving a riddle. The riddle is, "an herald . . . the like
was never born / Whose very beard is flesh, and mouth is
horn." Has anybody guessed it yet? There is a hint in the
expression of insult popular when I was in grade-school:
"You weren't born, you were hatched." The answer is, a
rooster. They play cards all night until the rooster calls:
a morning herald which isn't born, but comes out of an
egg; it has a beard of flesh and a mouth of horn.

This exemplifies a basic form of transformation, because
the little riddle takes the extremely ordinary perception—
that the cock crows in the morning and the night is over—
and gives it a mystical aura: its "very beard is flesh, and
mouth is horn." Ralegh's poem is a commentary on mysticism, and indeed on poetry, perhaps more than it is on
the cards and dice. It is a delighted, somewhat sardonic
commentary on rhetoric.

[URSULA REEL]: *In your essay on T. S. Eliot you write:
"True poetry is never really misunderstood or discarded, because its basis is in pleasure. Explanations and
theories are misunderstood; pleasures are either had,
or not." Can you elaborate a little bit on that and talk
about the effect you want when you write a poem?*

It's very much involved with the sounds of the words. I
hope that such an answer does not seem disappointing to
you, or simple-minded. I have a conviction that if you
write whatever it is well enough—Wallace Stevens is a
good author to demonstrate this with—the reader will put
up with quite a lot of incomprehension. Look at the rooster. I think, I hope, that you all recognize that there is
something appealing about the sound of those lines.
"Whose very beard is flesh, and mouth is horn" is a good
line, one whose appeal may come not only before you
think *it's a chicken*, but before you even think *it's a
riddle*. You can sense that it's something, you get a little
frisson of something interesting from it, though you don't
"understand" it in the sense that you don't have "an answer" to it. You understand what kind of thing it is. Possibly before you "understand" that it's a riddle, you "understand" that it has a mystical quality, or that it sounds
impressive. You come to understand *how* it's meant to
make you think.

It sounds good, and it sounds good as a syntax, as well as
an arrangement of consonant and vowels, and it sounds
good as an unformulated recognition of other kinds of
fact: the fact that "flesh" and "horn" are good words here,

and the fact that horn means the substance of fingernails
as well as the bony process of, say, a ram's horn, and that
the ram's horn makes a pleasing connection with "herald," because it's the same word—to blow into a horn, a
goat's or a ram's horn. That's how we have the word
"horn," which we now apply to a sax or a trumpet, instruments made not of horn but brass. And a jazz musician
will call his piano or drum set his "horn"! And so forth,
through innumerable chimes and associations. A horny
thing is a callous, a hardening of flesh. There is a sexual
component to the flesh and horn and born and morning,
and certainly to the buried image of the rooster.

All of that is operating, operating and alive in you long
before you think "rooster"—or else if it isn't operating,
then no amount of cleverness or profundity will make it
good, will make it poetry. So that "I don't get it" is a
more damaging thing than "I don't understand it," because
I think often you get it long before you understand it. We
are familiar with this phenomenon in music. A record
comes out, and part of the pleasure of it may be that the
first five or six times you hear it you don't know what the
words are; then you gradually find out what the words are.
But you know whether you like it or not before you understand it. The words seem to be going very well with
the tune, with what the chord changes and the harmony
and the instrumentation and the singer's voice sound like,
and you half-perceive whether you like these words, already. It is the same with a poem by Stéphane Mallarmé.

And I don't think these things are forgotten. I think that
once something really gets under somebody's skin—is
recognized as really good, in the way of art—it tends to
remain, always a source of what I have to call the art-
emotion: whatever that feeling is that art gives to us. And
this happens in the culture in general, too. Eliot is rather
out of style now, particularly with academics. But he's
too good, the pleasure is too solid, for his work to truly
fade. Kids are still reading "Prufrock" in high school,
memorizing parts of it without meaning to. It's there forever, for everybody.

[WILL ANDERSON]: *When you were talking about transformation earlier, I believe you used the word mystic
or mystical, and it reminded me of, in "The Refinery,"
the idea of refined from "oil of stone," and it seemed
like the imagery is sort of chemical there, but there is
a sense of a wondrous transformative power. Is that
the same idea?*

Yes, it is the same idea. As I said last night, I always seek
a way to experience these ideas as part of what's very
ordinary. And "oil of stone" is a literal translation of
"petroleum." You know, if something is petrified, it is
turned into stone. And Peter is the rock you found your
church on. So petroleum simply means stone-oil, oil of
stone. The idea in that poem, that the transformations of
petroleum—into gasoline, benzine, naphtalene, and motor oil and heating oil and all the other things it makes—
WD40 and margarine and whatever else—is comparable
to the transformations of language. I mean the way language itself changes, the way it changes other things, the

way it illuminates our life, and in some ways is very toxic, quite poisonous and dangerous.

It's a pretty volatile mix.

Yes, that is the sort of thinking the poem invites. It was a metaphor or comparison I liked so well that, maybe uncharacteristically, I based the whole poem upon it. The proposition is that language is like petroleum: it is dead life; it was once alive in a different way; in some other sense it remains stubbornly alive; it comes to us from the past, and we do gorgeous things with it—we wear these clothes, these five woven stuffs and subtle colors, we have light, we have music—and there is also something terrifying about it. You are tapping an energy that can feel supremely ordinary, yet that can also associate itself with mysterious awe. Explosion, gusher, leak—energy, as in a word like *fuck* or *Jesus* or *vendetta*.

I believe you said last night that you like the mix of the high and the low. Towards the end of that same poem, **"The Refinery,"** *it seems like there's that idea, the apposition of "Lovecries and memorized Chaucer."* . . .

Yes—and "lines from movies / And songs hoarded in mortmain." Varying texture in language is a pleasure partly as a reflection of the variety in oneself. My terminology of "high" and "low" oversimplifies this variety, or whatever I was trying for with "smeared keep" or "a gash of neon: Bar," or pairing "pinewoods" and "divinity"—to me, contrast, maybe even more than the richness of some single word, is a gorgeous, living part of language, like contrast in music or cuisine. The degrees and kinds of crunchy and smooth, high and low, the degrees of pungency or volume or hotness. In the refinery, they have that whole chemistry, as I understand it, that tunes a kind of hierarchy of degrees of refining. They call it "cracking" petroleum, breaking it into its components. And that is sort of like language too, maybe especially English, and maybe especially in America.

[ANN BROOKE LEWIS]: *It seems that in* **"Window"** *you use the word "window" as an artifact or, as you talked about last night, as a matrix of its own, with its own history, its own part in the culture. How do you feel about the language that you grew up with personally? Do you feel that, as your Irish mother says, your house has a "windhole"? How much history or culture actually is in your language?*

Ideally, I would like to have it all in there. I would like to speak and write a language that does not deny either my lower-middle-class childhood or all the books I've read. I am what is called an educated person as these things go. That does not negate the way I spoke when I was a child, or the way the people around me spoke in what I suppose was a small-town slum—so my mother would call it when she lamented our living there, and was certainly a working-class, racially mixed kind of a neighborhood. Just as the history of the language is in the language, the history of any person's language is in that person's speech and writing, and should be honored. One

doesn't want to be limited to a pose or mode as either a pure street kid or as a pure professor, because one is not pure, and the pose or mode is a confinement. As an ideal, I would like to have it all together.

And sometimes you discover the plainness in the learnedness. It is delightful to discover that the origin of a word like "window" may be something as homely or simple as "windhole." Is that a "learned etymology"? In a way, but what could be more down-home, what could be plainer? It's [pointing] the windhole, the hole where wind comes in. Is that a piece of arcane learning, or a bit of fundamental, funky information about these brutal Anglo-Saxons in their hut with its windhole?

Something comparable is found in the lovely language of the trades, for which I have considerable affection. A carpenter won't even call it a "window." Those separate panes are the "lights" to any builder or carpenter, and the whole is also a light. And these things, the vertical members in here, are "mullions." That piece of wood, the flat piece against the bottom below the sill, is the skirt, and the movable unit with the separate lights in it is the sash. This one has an upper sash and a lower sash. And there's a parting bead between the two sashes. And a head jamb and the side jambs. And they'll use these words very unself-consciously, in the interest of clarity and precision. Hand me some more of the parting beam and the four-penny nails. Because you need to be precise. Go to the lumber store and bring me back some 3 5/8" head jamb. Or I forget what this other thing is called, face molding or something. There's some other kind of jamb that goes this way. The word j-a-m-b: is that a high word or a low word?

One more pleasing example. I went to the hardware store and bought some fertilizer. The guy says, you could buy one of these little whirling things to spread it with, but really you could just strew it broadcast. And I realized what someone from a farming background might have always known, that "broadcast" was not invented by television or radio. The word was there: it's what you do with, say, seeds. If you have a sack slung around your shoulder, and you do this [swings his arm forward], you're broadcasting. The word existed before Marconi and before TV, and for me it had been an unrecognized, dead metaphor. It's just a homey word—not archaic, for farmers, I would guess, nor for the guy in my hardware store.

[SUSAN WILDEY]: *Did you write* **The Want Bone** *from the picture by Michael Mazur that is reproduced on the book's jacket or did you actually see a shark's jaw?*

The image is tied to a weave of friendships that pleases me. I saw one that my friend, the poet Tom Sleigh, had given Frank Bidart. It was on Frank's mantle, and I saw it shortly before I was going on vacation to the beach—a vacation where I saw something of Mike and Gail Mazur, in fact. And I wrote the poem at the beach, remembering the bone on Frank's mantle. When Tom saw the poem, he generously gave me a jawbone too!

Later, when I needed a jacket for the book, I couldn't find an image: the ones The Ecco Press liked, I didn't like, and the ones I liked, Ecco didn't. And Mike, working from the poem and from Tom's present to me, made the picture—a monotype, a form of which he is one of the contemporary masters. I happened to be in the studio when he pulled this monotype from his press—it's a wonderful, sensuous thing to see a monotype pulled: it is a one-of-a-kind print, the plate gooey with color pressed against paper by powerful rollers, a big surface, and a motor drives the roller across the sandwich of wet plate and paper, *shhhhh*. There's a certain amount of chance in the medium. If you're an expert, you can make textures that look like water or hair or smoke or these bubbles here. But you don't know exactly what it's going to look like. Maybe that is a model for what it is like to make any work of art?

James Longenbach (review date 1996)

SOURCE: "Figuring Multitudes," *The Nation*, Vol. 262, No. 17, April 29, 1996, pp. 25-8.

[*In the following favorable review of* The Figured Wheel, *Longenbach deems the collection "the most scrupulously intelligent body of work produced by an American poet in the past twenty-five years."*]

Since the death of Robert Lowell in 1977, no single figure has dominated American poetry in the way that Lowell, or before him Eliot, once did. I take this to be a good sign. But among the many writers who have come of age in our *fin de siècle,* none have succeeded more completely as poet, critic and translator than Robert Pinsky. *The Figured Wheel: New and Collected Poems* allows us to recognize the most scrupulously intelligent body of work produced by an American poet in the past twenty-five years.

Being the least dogmatic of poet-critics, Pinsky could never lend his name to an age. But in retrospect, it's difficult not to feel that the one-two punch of *Sadness and Happiness* (his first book of poems, published in 1975) and *The Situation of Poetry* (his account of American poetry after Modernism, published in 1977) had something to do with the swift decline of what we used to call the Age of Lowell—the age of high-wire, hard-drinking confessional poets. "But it is all bosh, the false / Link between genius and sickness," said Pinsky in **"Essay on Psychiatrists,"** the long poem that concludes *Sadness and Happiness*: "The contemporary poets of lunacy—none of them / Helps me to think of the mad otherwise / Than in clichés."

With its provocative blandness, the very title of Pinsky's first book of poems announced his distance from the dramatically personal poetry of Sexton, Berryman or Plath. It was the style (more than the content) of poems like **"Essay on Psychiatrists"** that made the announcement meaningful. Rather than plumbing his soul in agitated free verse, Pinsky constructed an argument about the world in unruffled pentameters. In *The Situation of Poetry*, he helped to create the taste by which he was judged, offering the word "discursive" to describe a poetry that might be organized by abstract statement rather than primal images.

Almost overnight, the reception accorded these two books transformed a well-educated kid from Long Branch, New Jersey, into the new hope for American poetry. From the start of his career, however, Pinsky has worked to expand the possibilities available to American poetry—not to replace a narrow vision of poetry with one more sectarian view. The title poem of *Sadness and Happiness*, with its invitation to treat human emotions as abstract categories, turns out to be Pinsky's most movingly intimate performance: **"Sadness and Happiness"** is the name of a bedtime game he and his wife played with their daughters. Pinsky could have been describing himself when he recently said that the legitimately "post-modernist" poet will be one for whom "formal freedom feels assured, and matters of technique no longer fighting issues in the old modernist sense."

As far as Pinsky's own career is concerned, the most important aspect of *Sadness and Happiness* is the way in which its title poem suggests that emotions are both personal and public property. "*Hate my whole kind,* but me, / Love me for myself," thinks the Jewish soldier rescuing the anti-Semitic bully in **"Poem About People."** It can be difficult to separate the "unique soul" from its "kind," and Pinsky has struggled in all his poems to imagine a community that will give an individual meaning without threatening to dispense with individuality—a community we might exist *in* rather than be thoroughly *of*.

In *An Explanation of America* (1980), Pinsky undertook this task on a grand scale: Because of its imperialist hunger, American culture threatens to swallow us; but because of its vastness, the culture provides a sense of community amorphous enough to sustain us. *Explanation* is deeply intimate (it is addressed to Pinsky's daughter) and broadly discursive, an account of the world more supple and less arch than **"Essay on Psychiatrists."** But this style, however boldly extended, was never destined to be Pinsky's signature. In **"The Figured Wheel,"** from *History of My Heart* (1984), Pinsky unveiled a poetry that, while retaining the clarity of his earlier work, moves with breathtaking rapidity, each phrase spilling out of the one before it. The "wheel" of the poem is a metaphor for historical process, the ever-evolving sense of community that both constitutes and dismantles the unique soul:

> It is hung with devices
> By dead masters who have survived by
>   reducing themselves magically
>
> To tiny organisms, to wisps of matter,
>   crumbs of soil,
> Bits of dry skin, microscopic flakes,
>   which is why they are called "great,"
> In their humility that goes on celebrat-
>   ing the turning

Of the wheel as it rolls unrelentingly
    over

A cow plodding through car-traffic on
    a street in Iasi,
And over the haunts of Robert Pinsky's
    mother and father
And wife and children and his sweet
    self
Which he hereby unwillingly and inex-
    pertly gives up, because it is

There, figured and pre-figured in the
    nothing-transfiguring wheel.

Pinsky has titled his collected poems *The Figured Wheel* because this poem announces his characteristic theme and inaugurates his fully mature style. Just as Pinsky himself is "figured" and "prefigured" in the forward-moving wheel of history, the theme is embodied in the restless, agglutinative movement of the poem.

In **"Impossible to Tell,"** one of the most stunning new poems in *The Figured Wheel*, Pinsky describes the way in which medieval Japanese poets worked together to write linked poems, or *renga*: "The movement / Of linking *renga* coursing from moment to moment / Is meaning." This is a good description of what Pinsky tries to accomplish in his own poems, creating the texture not only of one poet's mind but of a community's accumulating stock of reality. At first, the poems might seem to move haphazardly, jumping from the sacred to the vulgar to the commonplace. Yet, as Pinsky suggests, the *movement* of the poem between these elements—more than the elements themselves—ultimately satisfies us. In **"Impossible to Tell"** Pinsky cuts back and forth between the Japanese poet Basho, nurturing his disciples, and Pinsky's friend Elliot Gilbert, a consummate teller of ethnic jokes. The jokes Pinsky repeats in **"Impossible to Tell"** are side-splitting, but the poem is also deeply moving. A kind of courtly community grows from the conventional yet idiosyncratic work of the joke-teller:

        But as the *renga* describes
Religious meaning by moving in drift-
    ing petals

And brittle leaves that touch and die
    and suffer
The changing winds that riffle the gut-
    ter swirl,
So in the joke, just under the raucous
    music

Of Fleming, Jew, Walloon, a courtly
    allegiance
Moves to the dulcimer, gavotte and
    bow,
Over the banana tree the moon in
    autumn—

Allegiance to a state impossible to tell.

As these lines suggest, Pinsky often explores the racial and ethnic components of identity, and though all the ingredients for an identity politics are contained within his poems, such a politics never emerges. Rather than assert the singular importance of his lower-middle-class Jewish heritage, Pinsky instead emphasizes the mongrel, compromised heritage of everything: Communal activity fosters allegiance to "a state impossible to tell." Pinsky has on many occasions spoken of the wonderfully mixed-up world of Long Branch, New Jersey (a tacky boardwalk resort populated by Jews, blacks and Italians that was also the summer residence of President Grant), and his poems seem like an effort to re-create his hometown's ambience in words. While the poems are not often about Long Branch, their linguistic texture feels like Long Branch: beautiful yet vulgar, poignant yet funny, preserved out of time yet, like the waves, relentlessly in motion.

But if Pinsky's poems are "cut shimmering from conventions of the dead," the shimmer is all Pinsky's. The poems often end in flights of lyrical fancy that do not transcend conventions but transfigure them in ways we would never have predicted. In **"At Pleasure Bay,"** the final poem of *The Want Bone* (1990), a characteristically fragmented history of Long Branch segues into a sustained vision of the afterlife. After we die, we float across the river where a mass of bodies lie sleeping:

You lie down and embrace one body,
    the limbs
Heavy with sleep reach eagerly up
    around you
And you make love until your soul
    brims up
And burns free out of you and shifts
    and spills
Down over into that other body, and
    you
Forget the life you had and begin again
On the same crossing—maybe as a child
    who passes
Through the same place. But never the
    same way twice.
Here in the daylight, the catbird in the
    willows,
The new café, with a terrace and a
    landing,
Frogs in the cattails where the swing-
    bridge was—
Here's where you might have slipped
    across the water
When you were only a presence, at
    Pleasure Bay.

Compared with these lines, some of the new poems in *The Figured Wheel* might at first seem dense and difficult. Still, these poems seem to be Pinsky's most focused body of work—the poems he has been writing toward for twenty-five years. In **"The Ice-Storm"** he rephrases the question he has been asking since **"Poem About People"**: "What is life? A specimen, or a kind?" The answer, over and over again, is *both*. The notion of a community's atonement (or, more literally, its desire for *at-one-ment*) preoccupies him in **"Avenue,"** which surveys a crowded city street, a cacophony of voices and images, before it becomes the point of view of one human specimen. This nameless "one"—a man lying drunk in the street—explains how he was rescued by the many:

> Their headlights found me stoned, like
> a bundled sack
> Lying in the Avenue, late. They didn't
> speak
> My language. For them, a small adven-
> ture. They hefted
> Me over the curb and bore me to an
> entry
> Out of the way. Illuminated footwear
> On both sides. How I stank. Dead drunk.
> They left me
> Breathing in my bower between the
> Halloween
> Brogans and pumps on crystal pedestals.
>
> But I was dead to the world. The mid-
> night city
> In autumn. Day of attainment, tall saints
> Who saved me. My taints, day of
> anointment.

"Avenue" suggests that, through anonymous acts of charity, a multitude might imagine a sense of community. But the drama of the poem is more resolutely linguistic than thematic. Poems like **"The Figured Wheel"** and **"Impossible to Tell"** move down the page phrase by phrase, twisting and turning, while in newer poems like **"Avenue,"** **"Ginza Samba"** and **"Desecration of the Gravestone of Rose P.,"** the syntactical units are shorter, and the poems move almost word by word. The language seems to generate itself (*atonement, attainment, tall saints, taints, anointment*), and consequently creates a threat of randomness in the poem's movement—as if the sound of the words alone were determining the direction of the poem's meaning. The poems never succumb to this threat. But we need to feel a swirling cloud of language congealing to make the poems, just as the crowd in **"Avenue"** seems as if it were condensed down to the nameless one in the street.

These poems are exciting to read. And however many times I re-read them, they remain mysterious. Not in the sense that they are obscure or merely difficult: The poems remind me of how the people we know best can, in an instant, become inscrutable. Among the new poems in *The Figured Wheel*, elegies are prominent; Pinsky commemorates the lives of lost friends, his mother, a grandmother he never knew. These poems tell us about other people, but even more profoundly, they let us feel the insoluble mystery of otherness. In **"Poem With Refrains,"** Pinsky looks at his mother so intently that he must wonder if he knew her at all. This woman—who refused to visit her own dying mother, although she lived four doors away—remains the "dark figure, awaited, attended, aware, apart."

Though threateningly intimate, **"Poem With Refrains"** is studded with quotations from other poems. And in a sense, all of Pinsky's poems are poems with refrains— poems that, while built from quotation and repetition, seem "to happen / Always for the first time over and over again." They make questions of language, culture and identity seem visceral. They suggest that we plumb the depths of our souls by surveying the grand diversity of names and roles we occupy throughout our lives. Pinsky is a poet who has also written criticism, translated Dante's *Inferno* and composed a hypertext novel. It isn't easy to explain why a culture needs poetry; but as we look forward to the next century, Pinsky offers a model for everything a poet could be.

Katha Pollitt (review date 1996)

SOURCE: "World of Wonders," in the *New York Times Book Review*, August 18, 1996, p. 9.

[*In the following review, Pollitt provides a laudatory review of Pinsky's collected poems,* The Figured Wheel.]

Robert Pinsky's extraordinarily accomplished and beautiful volume of collected poems, ***The Figured Wheel***, will remind readers that here is a poet who, without forming a mini-movement or setting himself loudly at odds with the dominant tendencies of American poetry, has brought into it something new—beginning with his first volume, ***Sadness and Happiness*** (1975), and gathering authority with each subsequent book. Call it a way of being autobiographical without being confessional, of connecting the particulars of the self—his Jewishness; his 1940's and 50's childhood in Long Branch, N.J.; his adult life as "professor or / Poet or parent or writing conference pooh-bah"—with the largest intellectual concerns of history, culture, psychology and art.

Poetry has become so disconnected from the other literary arts that we don't usually look for a poet to share important affinities except with other poets. But one of Mr. Pinsky's great accomplishments is the way he recoups for poetry some of the pleasures of prose storytelling, humor, the rich texture of a world filled with people and ideas. In its free and vigorous play of mind, his **"Essay on Psychiatrists"** really is an essay, a witty, clear-eyed 21-part argument that moves from a group portrait of psychiatrists as a bourgeois social type (liberal politics, B'nai B'rith, "a place on the Cape with Marimekko drapes") to a large and fully earned conclusion: "But it is all bosh, the false / Link between genius and sickness."

A full accounting of his literary connections would have to include Saul Bellow, Bernard Malamud, Philip Roth and Cynthia Ozick—Jewish novelists with whom he shares a wide variety of concerns. There's the fascination with fables and rabbinic lore (**"The Rhyme of Reb Nachman," "From the Childhood of Jesus,"** the jewel-like prose tale **"Jesus and Isolt"**). There's the nostalgic love-hatred for the stifling familial urgencies of the now-vanished world of lower-middle-class Jewish immigrants and the celebration of the talismans—movies, pop music, comics, sports—by which those immigrants' children defined themselves as Americans. In **"The Night Game,"** Mr. Pinsky recalls himself as a child imagining a Jewish southpaw "Even more gifted / Than Whitey Ford" who refuses to pitch on Yom Kippur. The long poem **"History of My Heart"** begins with his mother remembering Fats Waller improvising on a piano "the size of a lady's jewel box or a wedding cake" in the toy department of Macy's, that symbol of democratic glamour. In **"A Woman,"** a grandmother figure attempts to instill in a child her own Old World suspicions and terrors as they walk through an ordinary Long Branch day that seems to range across centuries—from the "imbecile / Panic of the chickens" slaughtered in the market to the purchase of a uniquely American treat, a milkshake. Although the poem ends with the child's vow "Never to forgive her" for holding him back from a Halloween parade, what it shows is that the woman's half-mad smotherings and warnings have awakened the child to self-awareness and a heightened perception of the world. As the title suggests, she's a muse.

It is not surprising that Mr. Pinsky, whose last book was a widely praised translation of Dante's *Inferno* into modern terza rima, should have large ambitions for his own poems. Even the titles of his books proclaim his intention to grapple with major themes: *Sadness and Happiness*, *An Explanation of America*, *History of My Heart*, *Poetry and the World*. One of the earliest poems collected here, **"Poem About People,"** is a tragicomic meditation on humanity itself:

> In the movies, when the sensitive
> Young Jewish soldier nearly
>   drowns
>
> Trying to rescue the thrashing
> Anti-semitic bully, swimming
>   across
> The river raked by nazi fire,
> The awful part is the part truth:
> Hate my whole kind, but me,
> Love me for myself.

The determination with which the early poems set themselves in opposition to the then-dominant confessional mode in favor of the ironic, the didactic the "discursive" (to use Mr. Pinsky's own term) can make them seem dry or willed today, a bit like the benign and prudent therapists cautiously lauded in **"Essay on Psychiatrists."** It is really with *History of My Heart* (1984) that Mr. Pinsky finds a way of making a poem that is, well, poetical, that makes images and the connections—or gaps—between images bear a meaning whose emotional resonance derives in part from its indeterminacy. **"The New Saddhus"** imagines a multicultural assortment of middle-aged men, "Kurd, Celt, Marxist and Rotarian," setting out on a mysterious pilgrimage. Is it a rejection of breadwinning and family life, or a new bend in the masculine (and why only masculine?) life path? In the poem **"The Figured Wheel,"** what is that fantastically decorated juggernaut that rolls over teeming, unresisting humanity—language, culture, history? The way all three both create and destroy? These images have a vitality, a strangeness that overflows interpretation.

Similarly, **"Shirt"** is a kind of free-associative catalogue that encompasses technical sewing terms, Asian sweatshop workers "Gossiping over tea and noodles on their break," the Triangle factory fire, Hart Crane, the invention of tartans, Southern slavery and more. A shirt, it would seem, is a kind of poem:

> George Herbert, your descendant
>   is a Black
> Lady in South Carolina, her name is
>   Irma
> And she inspected my shirt. Its
> color and fit
> And feel and its clean smell have
>   satisfied
> Both her and me.

"Shirt" is a dazzling bravura performance, but it suggests a risk attached to the Whitman stance of "I am large, I contain multitudes." I'm not so sure that Irma is as happy to inspect that shirt as Mr. Pinsky is to wear it. There are times in these poems when one feels that Wordsworth's egotistical sublime is trying very hard—too hard—to be Keats's negative capability, and that what is presented as a kind of grand vision of humanity is a version of self-delight. As with Whitman, as with the Eastern philosophies that furnish him with so many gorgeous examples and metaphors, there's a potential for coldness in Mr. Pinsky's wide-angle vision.

Most of the time, though, the poems of his maturity manage their startling shifts and juxtapositions in ways that give intellectual and sensuous delight. You can read **"At Pleasure Bay"** a dozen times and still feel a kind of delicious surprise at the way Mr. Pinsky moves from the 1927 double suicide of "the Chief of Police and Mrs. W." through music and bootlegging and boats and Unity Mitford's infatuation with Hitler, all the way to reincarnation—the whole ultimately unfathomable round of violence, passion, beauty and sorrow that is human experience coming back always a little different, like the catbird in the willows singing "never the same phrase twice." Who else could have written **"The Refinery,"** in which ancient animal gods from the collective unconscious wake up and take a train to the factory of language (imagined as a kind of petroleum, pressed out of human history while they were sleeping)? Or the recent **"Impossible to Tell,"** which moves between the 17th-century Japanese poet Basho and a friend's sudden death, gives full-dress and very funny versions of two Jewish jokes and—while positing that human existence resembles a *renga*, a Japanese interlinked poetical form—is itself a kind of *renga*.

What makes Mr. Pinsky such a rewarding and exciting writer is the sense he gives, in the very shape and structure of his poems, of getting at the depths of human experience, in which everything is always repeated but also always new. The feathery and furry tribal gods, Jesus, Basho, the frail old people who came to his father for eyeglasses, Shiva and Parvati, the chief and Mrs. W. and Robert Pinsky himself are all characters in a story that has no end and possibly no ultimate meaning either but to which we listen spellbound because, like the figured wheel covered with mysterious symbols, it is our story.

FURTHER READING

Criticism

Breslin, Paul. "Four and a Half Books." *Poetry* CLXX, No. 4 (July 1997): 226-42.
    Laudatory assessment of *The Figured Wheel.*

Hirsch, Edward. "Violent Desires." *NYTBR* (18 November 1990): 24, 36.
    Views *The Want Bone* as "Pinsky's riskiest and most imaginative book of poems."

Nadel, Alan. "Wellesley Poets: The Works of Robert Pinsky and Frank Bidart." *New England Review* IV, No. 2 (Winter 1981): 311-25.

Compares the Pinsky's work to that of Frank Bidart.

Pritchard, William H. "Play's the Thing." *Poetry* CXXXVI, No. 5 (August 1980): 295-304.
    Positive review of *An Explanation of America.*

Spiegelmen, Willard. "The Moral Imperative in Anthony Hecht, Allen Ginsberg, and Robert Pinsky." *The Didactic Muse: Scenes of Instruction in Contemporary American Poetry*, pp. 56-104. Princeton, N.J.: Princeton University Press, 1989.
    Examines the shared characteristics of these three poets, in particular their shared ethnic and geographical backgrounds.

Zawacki, Andrew. "Hope for a Shared Home." *TLS* (24 January 1997): 14.
    Mixed assessment of his poetry collected in *The Figured Wheel*, contending "Pinsky deserves our attention and appraisal, though he may be too level-headed to coax us back again."

Interview

Sorkin, Adam J. "An Interview with Robert Pinsky." *Contemporary Literature* 25, No. 1 (Spring 1984): 1-14.
    Pinsky discusses his poetic concerns, the role of humor in his work, and stylistic aspects of his poetry.

Additional coverage of Pinsky's life and career is contained in the following sources published by The Gale Group: *Contemporary Authors*, Vols. 29-32; *Contemporary Authors Autobiography Series*, Vol. 4; *Contemporary Authors New Revision Series*, 58; *Contemporary Literary Criticism*, Vols. 9, 19, 38, 94, 121; *DISCovering Authors Modules—Poetry*; *Dictionary of Literary Biography*, Vols. 82, 98; *Major Twentieth-century Writers*.

Lucien Stryk
1924-

Polish-born American poet, translator, and editor.

INTRODUCTION

Stryk is best known for his quiet, insightful poetry that incorporates his strong interest in Zen Buddhism. He is also responsible for introducing many important Zen artists to the American public. A writer, translator, and educator, Stryk's professional interests and his aesthetic convictions compel critics to classify him as a Zen poet, although his work covers a wide range of themes and interests. Deemed elemental and demanding, his work strives for unity, gravity, and clarity.

Biographical Information

Stryk was born on April 7, 1924, in Kolo, Poland. A few years later his family emigrated from Poland to Chicago, Illinois. In 1943, Stryk was sent overseas to the Pacific as a soldier in World War II, and it was his experiences in Okinawa and Saipan that inspired a lifelong interest in Japan. After his return to the United States, he received his undergraduate degree from Indiana University in 1948. Disgusted with the atmosphere of materialistic post-war America, Stryk studied in Paris at the Sorbonne and at the University of London in England before receiving his M.F.A. from the University of Iowa in 1956. He taught in Japan for several years before settling on a permanent teaching position at Northern Illinois University. His lengthy stays in Japan allowed him to explore his interest in Zen Buddhism, which is a significant influence on his work. Stryk continues to travel and teach, introducing the work of Japanese poets to readers in the United States.

Major Works

Stryk's early verse is characterized by formal structure and traditional subject matter. With his growing interest in Zen Buddhism, his poetry changed, becoming more insightful, tighter, and evocative. The publication of his poetry collection, *Notes from a Guidebook*, signaled this metamorphosis in his life and career. "Return to Hiroshima," a poem about the effect of the nuclear attack on Hiroshima, employs understated language to let the full atrocity of the event reveal itself to the reader. In "Letter to Jean-Paul Baudot, at Christmas," Stryk attempts to console a friend who has confided his horrible memories of World War II. The poem illustrates a few of his recurring themes: mortality, war, and aging. His most highly regarded poem, "Zen: The Rocks of Sesshu," is considered the culmination of his Zen philosophy and poetic technique. Called a "meditation sequence," Stryk uses central images from a rock garden to reveal the importance of an inner life and a life beyond the

self. As in accordance with Zen principals, the piece also evinces selflessness, and an immersion in the poetic subject to the exclusion of ego and personal concerns. The integration of theme, concentration of form, and vision is considered the masterpiece of Stryk's poetic career.

Critical Reception

Perceived as ornamental, derivative, and uninspired, Stryk's early poetry is derided for its reliance on technical elements and traditional structure. With the advent of his interest in Zen Buddhism in the mid-1960s, his poetic voice loosened and matured as he struggled to reconcile his art with his new philosophy. Critics note his subsequent vitality and openness as well as the transquillity of his tone and the conciseness of his language. Although most scholars assess the impact of Zen Buddhism on his life and work, some critics note that Stryk's poetry is as likely to be about the American Midwest as Zen Buddhism. In fact, his body of work is often praised for its impressive range of subjects and themes including love, elegies to friends or neighbors, war, the forces of nature, childhood, the strengthening of the inner self, and the everyday events of the mundane world.

PRINCIPAL WORKS

Poetry

Taproot 1953
The Trespasser 1956
Notes for a Guidebook 1965
The Pit and Other Poems 1969
Awakening 1973
Selected Poems 1976
The Duckpond 1978
Zen Poems 1980
Cherries 1983
Willows 1983
Collected Poems, 1953-1983 1984
Bells of Lombardy 1986
Of Pen and Ink and Paper Scraps 1989
And Still Birds Sing 1998

Other Major Works

Zen: Poems, Prays, Sermons, Anecdotes, Interviews (editor and translator with Takashi Ikemoto) 1965
Heartland: Poets of the Midwest, Vol. 1 (editor) 1967
Afterimages: Zen Poems of Shinkichi Takahashi (editor and translator with Takashi Ikemoto) 1970
Heartland: Poets of the Midwest, Vol. 2 (editor) 1975
The Penguin Book of Zen Poetry (editor and translator with Takashi Ikemoto) 1977
Prairie Voices: A Collection of Illinois Poets (editor) 1980
Encounter with Zen: Writings on Poetry and Zen (history and criticism) 1981
Zen Poetry: Let the Spring Breeze Enter (editor and translator with Takashi Ikemoto) 1995

CRITICISM

Lucien Stryk (essay date 1976)

SOURCE: "Making Poems," in *American Poets in 1976*, edited by William Heyen, 1976, pp. 392-406.

[*In the following essay, Stryk traces his poetic development.*]

I

"The thoughts expressed by music," wrote Mendelssohn in 1842, "are not too vague for words, but too precise." Replace "music" with "poetry" and, perhaps paradoxically, considering of what poems are made, you have a way of seeing into the difficulty of drawing conclusions about the nature of art. There are days when I feel that the main thing, all else equal, is what the poet has to say; other days, that it is his craftsmanship, not what he's trying to express, that distinguishes him. What colors my view on any given day, tipping one way or the other, may be far more interesting than the whole issue of aesthetics, which is after all the sphere of aestheticians, not artists. All theories on art strike me as collections of truisms, though some ("The poet's theme dictates structure and is at the same time modified by it," might be one) seem pretty sound. Perhaps under the circumstances, and in spite of the great difficulty, the practicing artist should be willing, when called upon, to try to explain what it is he's after and how he goes about attempting to achieve it. That accepted, in what follows I shall try to give as clear an account as possible of the steps which led to where I am now as a maker of poems.

Some, aware of my work as a translator of Zen poetry, seem to feel that my poems are much affected by that interest, in content as well as structure. I believe they are right. Anyone serious about a discipline like Zen learns soon enough that much of his life, certainly any art he may practice, is being changed by it. When as a visiting lecturer there I began translating Zen texts in Japan, I asked the Zen master Taigan Takayama whether the philosophy might be useful to an artist. As an enlightened man (he is one of the most distinguished young masters in Japan) he did not show indignation, but he was most forceful in letting me know that Zen was not something to be "used" by anyone, including the artist, and that its arts were nothing more than expressions of the Zen spirit. That was the first "reprimand" I received. There was another, at the hands of the Zen master Tenzan Yasuda, of a more serious nature. I often went to his temple, the Joeiji, for the superb rock garden laid down by Sesshu, one of Japan's greatest painters who had been a priest at the Joeiji in the fifteenth century. In interviewing the master for the volume *Zen: Poems, Prayers, Sermons, Anecdotes, Interviews*, I said some very stupid things about the rock garden. Tenzan Yasuda was patient, but finally said (I quote from the interview), "In order to appreciate his garden fully you must have almost as much insight as Sesshu himself. This, needless to say, very few possess. Ideally one should sit in Zen for a long period before looking at the garden; then one might be able to look at it, as the old saying goes, 'with the navel.'"

Even as those words were being spoken I felt acute self-disgust, and resolved to try to overcome the vanity which had led me to utter empty phrases about something which I had not even "seen," let alone understood (the Sixth Patriarch of Zen, the Chinese master Hui-neng, insisted on "pure seeing"—one must not look *at* things, but *as* things). A few nights later, while working on a conventionally structured poem set in Sesshu's rock garden, the sort of piece with which I'd already filled two "well received" but unsatisfactory books, I remembered not only Taigan Takayama's reprimand but Tenzan Yasuda's specific comments on my "view" of the garden. Suddenly I became aware, *saw* with the greatest clarity: my failing in poetry was the result in great part of a grave misunderstanding concerning the very purpose of art. The Zen masters who had written the poems I was translating did not think of themselves as "poets" at all; rather they were attempting to express in verse nothing less than the Zen spirit—and the results were astonishing. The poems, without any pretension to "art," were among the finest I had ever read, intense, compact, rich in spirit. Takayama and Yasuda were right.

Working for hours without a break, I transformed the poem I had been writing on the garden, ridding it of "filling," breaking down rigidly regular stanzas, a welter of words, to a few "image units" of around two and one-half lines, while keeping to a constant measure, the short line throughout being of the same syllabic length. In fact, though unintended, the stanzaic unit I came up with was in length and feeling very close to the haiku, and at its best as compact as the short Zen poems I was translating. Perhaps the fact that the "unit" was made up consistently of just so many lines, so controlled, was a matter of chance, the result simply of the way eye and ear, projecting my needs, meshed. I suppose anything leading to, or the result of, deep concentration might have worked as well, but fortuitous or not I was convinced that I had made, for myself, a profound discovery, and that henceforth I might work as an artist.

In the weeks following I wrote seven more pieces about Sesshu's garden, yet given the challenge and because I wanted the sequence to be the very best I could make it, it took a few years to achieve what seemed to me altogether satisfactory versions of what eventually became:

"Zen: The Rocks of Sesshu"

I

What do they think of
  Where they lean
Like ponderous heads, the rocks?—

In prankish spring, ducks
  Joggling here
And there, brushing tails,

Like silly thoughts shared,
  Passed from head
To head? When, gong quavering

About a ripened sky, we
  Up and go,
Do they waken from a dream of flesh?

II

In the Three Whites of
  Hokusai—
Fuji, the snow, the crane—

What startles is the black: in
  The outline
Of the mountain, the branch-tips
Piercing the snow, the quills of
  The crane's wing:
Meaning impermanence.
Here, in stainless air, the

Artist's name
Blazes like a crow.

III

Distance between the rocks,
  Half the day
In shadow, is the distance

Between man who thinks
  And the man
Who thinks he thinks: wait.

Like a brain, the garden,
  Thinking when
It is thought. Otherwise

A stony jumble, merely that,
  Laid down there
To stud our emptiness.

IV

Who calls her butterfly
  Would elsewhere
Pardon the snake its fangs:

In the stony garden
  Where she flits
Are sides so sharp, merely

To look gives pain. Only
  The tourist,
Kodak aimed and ready for

The blast, ship pointing for the
  Getaway,
Dare raise that parasol.

V

To rid the grass of weed, to get
  The whole root,
Thick, tangled, takes a strong mind

And desire—to make clean, make pure.
  The weed, tough
As the rock it leaps against,

Unless plucked to the last
  Live fiber
Will plunge up through dark again.

The weed also has the desire
  To make clean,
Make pure, there against the rock.

VI

It is joy that lifts those pigeons to
  Stitch the clouds
With circling, light flashing from underwings.

Scorning our crumbs, tossed carefully
  To corners
Of the garden, beyond the rocks,

They rose as if summoned from
  The futile
Groveling our love subjects them to.

Clear the mind! Empty it of all that
  Fixes you,
Makes every act a pecking at the crumb.

VII

Firmness is all: that mountain beyond the
  Garden path,
Watch how against its tawny slope

The candled boughs expire. Follow
  The slope where
Spearheads shake against the clouds

And dizzy the pigeons circling on the wind.
  Then observe
Where no bigger than a cragstone

The climber pulls himself aloft
  As by the
Very guts: firmness is all.

VIII

Pierced through by birdsong, stone by stone
  The garden
Gathered light. Darkness, hauled by ropes

Of sun, entered roof and bough. Raised from
  The temple
Floor where, stiff since cockcrow,

Blown round like Buddha on the lotus,
  He began
To write. How against that shimmering,

On paper frail as dawn, make poems?
  Firm again,
He waited for the rocks to split.

There were other poems to work on, and getting rid of much, overhauling what remained of a bulky manuscript, I finished what I have always considered to be my first real book *Notes for a Guidebook* (though it was the third published and limited to a special type of poem: it does not include, for example, **"Zen: the Rocks of Sesshu,"** which I saved for my next volume *The Pit and Other Poems*). That was in 1965, the same year the first volume of Zen translations, done along with my Japanese friend Takashi Ikemoto, was brought out. No coincidence, for the translation of those profound and moving poems and the making of my own new pieces went on together for a long time. And it's been that way since: *The Pit and Other Poems* (1969) was written for the most part while

I was at work on the books *World of the Buddha* (1968) and *After Images: Zen Poems of Shinkichi Takahashi* (1970); the most recent collection *Awakening* was composed while I was at work on *Zen Poems of China and Japan: The Crane's Bill*, and the books were published only months apart in 1973.

That my poems owe much to the Zen aesthetic is undeniable, yet they owe as much surely to the many and various things which make up the life of a Midwestern American— husband, father, teacher—in our time, something perhaps most evident in *Awakening* (and when I deal with the poems of others in the anthology *Heartland: Poets of the Midwest*, the second edition of which, *Heartland II*, has just been completed) and which I have tried to explain in the interviews done with me, as in *Chicago Review*, #88, 1973. It would be very disappointing to learn that because of my interest in Asian philosophy, and the themes and settings of some of my poems, my work was read as that of someone who had gone "bamboo." I believe not only in the need to "hide traces," an invisible art, but as much in the wisdom of hiding sources. **"South"** is a typical poem:

"South"

Walking at night, I always return to
  the spot beyond
the cannery and cornfields where

a farmhouse faces south among tall trees.
  I dream a life
there for myself, everything happening

in an upper room: reading in sunlight,
  talk, over wine,
with a friend, long midnight poems swept

with stars and a moon. And nothing
  being savaged,
anywhere. Having my fill of that life,

I imagine a path leading south
  through corn and wheat,
to the Gulf of Mexico! I walk

each night in practice for that walk.

II

T. S. Eliot in an unpublished lecture on English letter writers, quoted by F. O. Matthiessen in *The Achievement of T. S. Eliot*, says something which for me virtually sums up the poet's ideal, one very close to the "less is more" aesthetic of Zen. Eliot refers to a passage in one of D. H. Lawrence's letters which runs: "The essence of poetry with us in this age of stark and unlovely actualities is a stark directness, without a shadow of a lie, or a shadow of deflection anywhere. Everything can go, but this stark, bare, rocky directness of statement, this alone makes poetry, to-day." Eliot's comment:

This speaks to me of that at which I have long aimed, in writing poetry; to write poetry which should be essentially poetry, with nothing poetic about it, poetry standing naked in its bare bones, or poetry so transparent that we should not see the poetry, but that which we are meant to see through the poetry, poetry so transperant that in reading it we are intent on what the poem *points at,* and not on the poetry, this seems to me the thing to try for. To get *beyond poetry,* as Beethoven, in his later works, strove to get *beyond music.*

To get "beyond poetry," then, to avoid the hateful evidence of our will to impress (thereby perhaps losing that ambition), those handsprings and cartwheels, the heavy breathing down the line, so common to "early work" done at whatever age—the escape from such vulgarity—is the study of a lifetime. It can be furthered by a discipline like Zen, but everything uniquely Western leading to a like realization will of course do as well. A man's poems should reveal the full range of his life, and hide nothing except the art behind them.

As much admiration as I have for a number of English-speaking poets, I am very strongly affected by the work of—ranging both East and West—Shinkichi Takahashi and Zbigniew Herbert, precisely because their poems appear to give the totality of their lives. We may not know our neighbors, but such poets can become our intimates. The fact that some of the poets I love write in other tongues is fundamentally of little importance, for they have been translated well (though as his translator, I should not make such a claim for the poems of Shinkichi Takahashi!). Never have so many poets turned to translation, and all of us stand to gain by the collective energy and dedication, but I admit readily that there are accompanying dangers and that something very close to "translationese" is too often in evidence.

The range and swell of one of the poems of Theodore Roethke's "North American Sequence," the superb concisions of his earlier "greenhouse" poems, are unlikely to be matched in the translations of even the greatest modern poets. And some of the greatest, Rilke among them, have sometimes been very poorly served, with almost criminal effect. A foreign poet is, after all, only as good as his best translator. Still, to deny ourselves the profound satisfactions of the best foreign poetry, for whatever reason, to hover timorously above those deeps out of some theoretical fear, is to cut off a source of major creative growth. Often foreign poetry offers something unique: all sensitive people, for example, felt strongly about the reports of Buddhist monks burning themselves to death in Viet Nam—the ultimate protest against that insane war, a protest not condoned by Buddhism, but one powerful in its effect on the world as a whole. No response to such acts by Western writers could have been as complex, as devastatingly right as Shinkichi Takahashi's in his poem about a fellow Buddhist, "Burning Oneself to Death":

    "Burning Oneself To Death"

That was the best moment of the monk's life.
Firm on a pile of firewood

With nothing more to say, hear, see,
Smoke wrapped him, his folded hands blazed.

There was nothing more to do, the end
Of everything. He remembered, as a cool breeze
Streamed through him, that one is always
In the same place, and that there is no time.

Suddenly a whirling mushroom cloud rose
Before his singed eyes, and he was a mass
Of flame. Globes, one after another, rolled out,
The delighted sparrows flew round like fire balls.

In translating that poem I was put to a grave test, for the responsibility was awesome, the sort felt, I imagine, by the translator of one of Zbigniew Herbert's poems about World War II Resistance fighters in Poland. As I think back to its source, in my experience, I am certain that my work on poems like Takahashi's, my reading of Herbert and Char, among other foreign writers, lay behind the making of this poem:

    "Letter To Jean-Paul Baudot, At Christmas"

Friend, on this sunny day, snow sparkling
everywhere, I think of you once more,
how many years ago, a child Resistance

fighter trapped by Nazis in a cave
with fifteen others, left to die, you became
a cannibal. Saved by Americans,

the taste of a dead comrade's flesh foul
in your mouth, you fell onto the snow
of the Haute Savoie and gorged to purge yourself,

somehow to start again. Each winter since
you were reminded, vomiting for days.
Each winter since you told me at the Mabillon,

I see you on the first snow of the year
spreadeagled, face buried in that stench.
I write once more, Jean-Paul, though you don't

answer, because I must: today men do far worse.
Yours in hope of peace, for all of us,
before the coming of another snow.

I spoke of the responsibility felt when I was working on the Takahashi poem, but I felt an even greater when composing the piece about my friend, to the "experience" itself, one I wanted to share with (impose on?) as many as possible. I knew that in order to do so I would have to get "beyond poetry," put down without faking the truth of a young man's pain, which had nothing literary about it and was felt acutely over the years. A pain I was asked to share, and still do.

            III

In response to the question (in the *Chicago Review* interview mentioned above), "Does art do anything more than manifest moments of revelation?" I say something which relates not only to poems I am always hoping to write but also to those which most move me as a reader:

It extends the imagination; more than anything else it does that. Perhaps the greatest poetry extends and directs it, but all fine poetry does extend, enlarge it. It makes us more than we have ever been. Really important poetry affects the imagination in something like a permanent way; it alters it. If we see the imaginative process (as perceivers or readers) as being constantly acted upon or acting itself, then those things which touch it have varying results. By some, the imagination is substantially affected; by others hardly at all, and of course the question is whether the latter are works of art. Once, in other words, you have read *Hamlet* as it should be read, you are no longer the same person. The possibilities of life have been altered, have been magnified. You read certain poems, they can be rather simple poems, in many ways. . . . I think a good example might be Blake's "London." It's a short poem that reveals, tremendously, a quality of life. When that happens, art takes on a kind of moral grandeur. And I choose as an example a short lyric poem because I think it would suggest what might be the hope of a poet like myself; I want, as a writer, to *reveal* in such a way, hardly with the expectation of achieving a poem like "London," but nevertheless it offers an aesthetic ideal. . . . What I'm saying, I suppose, is that after reading "London" . . . I have a feeling that my view of that time and place is crystallized by the poem. It has, thus, historical importance. Whatever London was for Blake, and many others, is given, contained in, that poem. Now, I think this is what art should do. . . . When art can do this, it takes on a dimension that we sometimes forget it is capable of having. But one should not forget. A poet should never write without the vision that such things have been done, that men have written *Hamlets* and poems like "London," because if he forgets that such things have been done, his work can become trivial. These things stand as warnings, as much as examples. Because by great works, the artist is warned: he cannot afford to use his art for unworthy purposes.

If it is true that, however full the imagination, what the poet experiences fixes the range of his art, then we should not expect him to be touching constantly the depths and the heights. He is often content to be somewhere between, unaware of the distinctions, boundaries set down about him, making some things more important than others. Poetry not being producible, it sometimes just comes, the result of miraculous convergences, the perfect meshing of eye, ear and heart. Some of my poems (the title poem of *The Pit and Other Poems* is a good example) have taken many years to complete; others—and for this I do not think less of them—have been written almost on the spot. I shall never forget wheeling around on my bike and speeding home to get **"Étude"** down, its music clear in my head:

"Étude"

I was cycling by the river, back and forth,
    Umbrella up against the
        Rain and blossoms.

It was very quiet, I thought of Woolworth
    Globes you shake up snowstorms in.
        Washed light slanted

Through the cherry trees, and in a flimsy house
    Some youngster practiced Chopin.
        I was moving

With the current, wheels squishing as the music
    Rose into the trees, then stopped,
        And from the house

Came someone wearing too much powder, raincape
    Orchid in the light. Middle-aged,
        The sort you pass

In hundreds everyday and scarcely notice,
    The Chopin she had sent
        Up to those boughs,

Petals spinning free, gave her grace no waters
    Would reflect, but I might
        Long remember.

As most poets I have been much affected by the other arts, painting and sculpture especially, and along with my involvement in Zen has come a deepening appreciation of *sumie*, the monochromic black/white scroll painting associated with it. Perhaps nothing could illustrate better my turning Eastward and what it has meant to me than the differences—technically, in attitude—between two of my poems, written years apart and dealing with art and the life of the maker. Bartolommeo Ammannati (1511-92), when he was past seventy, wrote in "To the Academy of Design in Florence": "Beware, for God's sake, as you value your salvation, lest you incur and fall into error that I have incurred in my works when I made many of my figures entirely nude." Here is, from ***Notes for a Guidebook***, a poem about his most important work:

"The Fountain of Ammannati"

Below the pigeon-spotted seagod
The mermen pinch the mermaids,
And you shopgirls eat your food.

No sneak-vialed aphrodisiac
Can do—for me, for you—what
Mermen pinching mermaids in a whack
Of sunlit water can. And do.
These water-eaten shoulders and these thighs
Shall glisten though your gills go blue,

These bones will never clatter in the breath.
My dears, before your dust swirls either up
Or down—confess: this world is richly wet.

And consider: there is a plashless world
Outside this stream-bright square
Where girls like you lie curled

And languishing for love like mine.

And you were such as they
Until ten sputtering jets began

To run their ticklish waters down your
Spine. Munch on, my loves, you are but
Sun-bleached maidens in a world too poor

To tap the heart-wells that would flow,
And flow. You are true signorine
Of that square where none can go

And then return. Where dusty mermen
Parch across a strand of sails and spars,
And dream of foamy thighs that churn.

By such works, I appear to be saying, man is made to feel
his insignificance: how pitiable those shopgirls against
the mermaids. Whatever its worth as poetry, **"The Fountain of Ammannati"** is a piece which examines one of
life's profound discrepancies, measures a distance between its realities and ideals. Swirling and clashing, it
makes a harsh judgment. Perhaps the most, or least, that
one can say about it is that it is a young man's poem.

A growing awareness necessitates a changing language,
a greater seriousness an altered structure. Just as at fifty
a man has the face he has earned, the lineaments of his
poems reveal the range and depth of his spiritual life.
Simply by surviving I have become a middle-aged poet,
and as the result of many things which have made that
survival possible, this is where I am now:

"Awakening"
Homage to Hakuin, Zen Master, 1685-1768

I

Shoichi brushed the black
on thick.
His circle held a poem
like buds
above a flowering bowl.

Since the moment of my
pointing,
this bowl, an "earth device,"
holds
nothing but the dawn.

II

A freeze last night, the window's
laced ice flowers, a meadow drifting
from the glacier's side. I think of Hakuin:

"Freezing in an icefield, stretched
thousands of miles in all directions,
I was alone, transparent, and could not move."

Legs cramped, mind pointing
like a torch, I cannot see beyond
the frost, out nor in. And do not move.

III

I balance the round stone
in my palm,
turn it full circle,

slowly, in the late sun,
spring to now.
Severe compression,

like a troubled head,
stings my hand.
It falls. A small dust rises.

IV

Beyond the sycamore
dark air moves
westward—

smoke, cloud, something
wanting a name.
Across the window,

my gathered breath,
I trace
a simple word.

V

My daughter gathers shells
where thirty years before
I'd turned them over, marveling.

I take them from her,
make, at her command,
the universe. Hands clasped,

marking the limits of
a world, we watch till sundown
planets whirling in the sand.

VI

Softness everywhere,
snow a smear,
air a gray sack.

Time. Place. Thing.
Felt between
skin and bone, flesh.

VII

I write in the dark again,
rather by dusk-light,
and what I love about

this hour is the way the trees
are taken, one by one,
into the great wash of darkness.

At this hour I am always happy,
ready to be taken myself,
fully aware.

Ralph J. Mills, Jr. (essay date 1977)

SOURCE: "Lucien Stryk's Poetry," in *Zen, Poetry, the Art of Lucien Stryk,* edited by Susan Porterfield, Swallow Press, 1993, pp. 279-92.

[*In the following essay, which originally appeared in 1977, Mills surveys the thematic range of Stryk's poetry, maintaining that the reader will find "the profound satisfaction of true poetry, and the tug and shift in his own feelings and perspectives which only art of proven quality can bring about."*]

Among the poets around or nearing the age of fifty now active in this country—a group in which I'd include such influential figures as Wright, Bly, Levertov, Simpson, Creeley, Rich, Ashbery, Justice, and so forth—Lucien Stryk is a somewhat elusive, independent figure: a writer, translator, scholar, and teacher, widely respected, admired, yet also provocatively and attractively a solitary, who lives in the middle west but frequently visits the Orient and Europe. Stryk's professional interests and his aesthetic convictions, his lack of association with any current poetic schools or movements reinforce the solitariness. He was reared in Chicago, studied at Indiana, Maryland, and Iowa Universities, but also at the University of London and the Sorbonne. He has traveled and lectured in Asia too. These facts are public knowledge, but perhaps they are worth recalling as one reads and thinks about Stryk's poetry, for they keep us reminded of the sources on which he has drawn—various yet unified—for so much material. His devotion to his art is surely of long standing. Since the first collections, published in 1953 and 1956 by Fantasy Press in Oxford, he has written three other full-length volumes. A recently issued *Selected Poems*[1] incorporates the contents of those three books, selects from the earlier ones, and adds "hitherto uncollected poems," thus offering to readers a substantial (and I will say here, an impressive) gathering of a quarter-century's work.

At the very start, Stryk's poems demonstrate their author's strict commitment to technical and formal resourcefulness, to the making of a linguistic object that is firm, solid, trim, that avoids all excess or flabbiness. Diction and imagery are precise in a manner rendering them also highly evocative; movement, organization in any poem are sure. I cite here two passages from early poems to serve as examples; as his career proceeds we can see even greater economy and severity of means. The initial passage I've selected is the opening stanza of **"The Beachcomber,"** which appears, incidentally, at the beginning of *Selected Poems.* In these lines, landscape and its observed inhabitant, who gives the pieces its title, emerge together as the poet alternates his attention between them, so creating a simultaneous, enlarging vision as the poem continues:

Beyond the patchwork bobbing of her back
The nineteen peaks of Sado float
In violet mist. Below, the "Exiles' Route"
Is taut with sail and net. Across
The humps of sand that blot the sea
The pinetrees hold the beaten shore,
And just as she is wasted by a cold
Necessity, the iced Siberian wind
Has bent and shriveled to their salty core.

That vision reaches its full expansion in a second, concluding stanza, where the actual poverty of the beachcomber and the lushness of her daydreams, her wishes, are played out in what is probably a daily private drama expertly rendered by the poet's use of sensuous detail.

My next example borrows the second pair of four stanzas which comprise **"The Mine: Yamaguchi."** In this poem, Stryk has honed an even sharper cutting edge. The remembered experience is constructed word by word, image by image, with what seems an almost fierce intentness. Each particular is forcefully evoked; and the final, ironic detail closing the poem is overwhelming: it leaves the reader stunned, breathless at the discovery. There are words, phrases, lines in these stanzas over which one must simply nod a vigorous assent at their absolute rightness, the accurate strength and beauty. Perhaps "The eye resists, the vision begged and gotten / Is the heart's" or the verbs "grits" and "sniff" from the passage below will illustrate what I mean:

After weeks of trying to forget,
The eye resists, the vision begged and gotten
Is the heart's: rows of women bent over
Feed-belts circling like blood, pickhammers
Biting at the clods that trundle by,

Raw hands flinging waste through scuttles gaped
    behind
While, a stone's-throw down the company road,
A smokestack grits the air with substance one
Might sniff below, or anywhere. It marks
The crematory, they pass it twice a day.

If these excerpted stanzas provide instances of what we may expect from Lucien Stryk's poetry in the way of achievement during the early phases of his writing, they likewise introduce important areas of preoccupation for this poet. Such areas might at first appear to be chance ones, or topical, since the author relies in the poems we've quoted, as well as in a number of others, on his extensive travels, on place and what it offers to the alert sensibility and to an imagination capable of reaching out to apprehend different lives in foreign settings. But a conclusion of that sort would not cover the matter; it would be insufficient to account for a deeper aesthetic concern integral with his beliefs about the endeavors of poem and poet. These convictions can be learned from various prose pieces, and of course deduced rather clearly from the poetry itself. Some of the comments most helpful for our purposes in this article Stryk has made in an interview.

Necessarily, because Stryk has published widely and received recognition as an Oriental scholar and translator of Zen texts, his conversation with John Somer leads toward questions about Zen Buddhism, its influence on the poet. He refuses to identify himself completely as a Zen poet, remarking that he is "not at all conscious" of being such when he writes. He continues: "It would be a little too much for me to claim. I undoubtedly have been strongly affected by my work in that field and my vision has to some degree been conditioned by it, but I have never intentionally set out to write Zen poems, except perhaps for a few meditation sequences." (These "sequences" are doubtless such poems as **"Zen: the Rocks of Sesshu"** and **"Awakening."**) On the other hand, "the Zen aesthetic," as Stryk defines it in his interview, has left an obvious, permanent mark up his poetics. "It calls," he says, "for directness, concision, and for gravity." Of further related significance are his remarks about the value for his poems of "anything that serves to draw a person out of himself,"[2] and Zen certainly accomplishes this intention. We can recall more pointedly here the concentration evident at once in the early poems, including those discussed above, on what is "other." This is an ability Stryk specifies in the work of the Japanese poet Takahashi, whom he has translated, to "enter the world of one's subject spontaneously, without holding back."[3] An entrance or projection of this kind on the writer's part aims to achieve a high, dramatic moment of "revelation," in which ordinary neglected and unrecognized elements of existence, of the world beyond the self, are caught, fixed in a form that is supple, durable, vibrant, and which compels the reader to see them, discover them, in a startling, visionary way. In his interview with John Somer, Stryk expands on this process as it affects the poet's inner life and artistic methods:

> Once the poet has begun to achieve a revelatory art . . . he begins using it as . . . a way of handling life. He must begin to feel that in order to be revealed to. Some-thing must be given up, and this is . . . a giving up of self, a total commitment to subject, involvement with it; and this is incidentally very important to the Zen aesthetic. There is a term for it, "muga"; and what it means is loss of self. It means that a muga writing on, say, a maple tree identifies with that tree. He is not the perceiver looking at the tree; he enters its life. . . . The artist is selfless. He can't be anything other than selfless if he is to make important art.[4]

This type of "empathy"—a word Stryk uses—is reminiscent, as he notes elsewhere, of Keats's "negative capability"; yet another distinction remains to be made in delineating the selflessness the poet implies. Stryk does not write poems which utilize a mask, persona, or invented speaker: his "total commitment to subject," to repeat his phrase—and the reference to the maple tree above can serve for us as example and indicator—is to something elicited from the body of his own experience, his own perceptions of and encounters with the world and its inhabitants. At the same time, the focal point of the poem is, as a rule, "outside" the poet, "within" the particulars of the experience. "I don't want to pretend as a poet that I'm someone else," he tells John Somer. "This possibly makes my work very personal, consequently limited. But

if my experiences are sufficiently wide in range and intensity, then perhaps I do not need the persona. In other words, what I experience constitutes the range of my art. . . . I explore different things, I assume in a way different stances."[5]

It is impossible for the commentator on Stryk's writing not to observe how closely the poet's statements about his art and his artistic intentions match the poems themselves. In **"The Beachcomber"** and **"The Mine: Yamaguchi,"** as in nearly every poem in his selected volume, the author arrives at that desired climactic disclosure which is for him the goal of the poetic process. Location, figures and ground compose a territory entered, slipped into, by a consciousness that at first seems almost wholly transparent, whose primary impulse is to absorb, to be a sensitive receptor to the life, the surroundings it has encountered. To take another example, "Oasis," the third section of the rather long poem **"A Persian Suite,"** displays the manner in which Stryk characteristically and brilliantly gathers the details that assemble a setting, an atmosphere—getting "at its essence as directly and economically as possible."[6] While this is being done, the lines are moving toward the plane—or if you like, moment—of revelation, in this case the appearance of the pilgrims signals it:

> Nothing stands so green.
> These few trees hold back
>   A tide of sand
>
> And ride the grit-blast,
> Or moving with the sun,
>   Which all day long
>
> Nibbles at the grass-edge,
> Twist like dervishes in
>   The pool below.
>
> Imam Reza, from all
> Sides your pilgrim trails
>   Stretch parched as tongues,
>
> And chanting your name,
> Balanced between water
>   And death, they come.

Another piece, **"Notes for a Guidebook,"** which is also the title poem of his third volume, finds Stryk approaching a similar situation from a somewhat different perspective. Adopting a voice and attitude which combines his learned poetic sensibility with a Baedeker-carrying tourist's awe before the monuments of the past, he fashions a marvelous, partially wry poem where the dead overwhelm or confuse the living. In the first three stanzas, the accomplishments of Dante, Giotto, and Donatello pervade the air that elevates, then diminishes, in the fourth and final stanza, the speaker and other travelers to mere venal mortals— "Dwarfs, clods, motes of dust." Once again, the poem's conclusion brings that sudden, penetrating awareness of which the author speaks, here graced with a touch of levity. The "us" for whom Stryk is a voice are caught at the end between two worlds: the historic/aesthetic realm into which they have entered through their excursion among cultural monuments and the ordinary one to which they may so easily "slip back" after an exposure to these rarified zones of spirit and imagination:

> In celestial Padua
> The ghosts walk hugely
> In the public squares.
>
> Donatello is one,
> His horseman in the
> Piazza San Antonio
> Guards the gruff saint's heart
> Like a mystic ruby,
> The ears of the horse,
> Of the rider,
> Riddled by prayer.
>
> Giotto, Dante are others
> The painter's frescoes
> Float like clouds
> Above the city,
> The poet's cantos
> Ring upon its walls.
>
> And what of us,
> Who stand with heads
> Strained back, feet tapping?
> Shall we eat, sleep,
> Be men again?
> Shall we slip back
> To the whores of Venice?—
> Dwarfs, clods, motes of dust
> In the brightness.

The opening of Stryk's **Selected Poems** consists largely of the kind of pieces we have so far discussed, and I hope the few examples I have chosen are decently representative of them. Included there are some nicely done sequences too long for proper treatment here, **"A Sheaf for Chicago," "A Persian Suite"** (from which I did quote "Oasis"), and **"Return to Hiroshima."** The last of these, made up of three sections, each devoted to a different voice (I. Bombardier, II. Pilot, III. Survivors), demonstrates the poet's remarkable ability to go beyond the absorption of location or objects to an identification with specific individuals and to the articulation of dramatic speeches from within the vividly imagined compass of their lives. The same may be said, in varying degrees, for such other fine poems in this portion of the book as **"Hearn in Matsue," "Chekov in Nice," "The Woman Who Lived in a Crate," "In a Spanish Garden,"** and **"Torero,"** all of which prefigure later, more concentrated extensions into the being of different creatures, men, or objects.

In view of some of the changes which occur in Stryk's writing, the early poems we have discussed, though certainly highly satisfactory and handsomely done in themselves, must appear preliminary to the large but quiet steps he takes into artistic maturity. With these steps, some fundamentals of Zen assume prominence, so that, once again, if Stryk does not feel it appropriate to claim

the title of a Zen poet, still its philosophical influence plays a very significant role in his poetic development. He recounts, in his essay "Making Poems," two incidents in Japan which resulted for him in "reprimands" from Zen masters, and finally instigated crucial alterations in his poetry and in his conception of it. On the first occasion, Stryk queried a master "whether the [Zen] philosophy might be useful to an artist." He was told that artistic practice was only a manifestation of the "Zen spirit," and "that Zen is not something to be 'used' by anyone."[7] Later, interviewing another master, Tenzan Yasuda, the poet admits that he "said some very stupid things about the rock garden" at his temple which had been designed by Sesshu, a famous 15th-century Zen priest and painter. Humiliated, his vanity and pretense punctured by the master's severe requirements for any true appreciation or comprehension of the garden's pattern, he decided to attempt to abolish these shortcomings in himself. The vent which followed on these two experiences is best described by Stryk:

> . . . A few nights later, while working on a conventionally structured poem set in Sesshu's rock garden, the sort of piece with which I'd already filled two "well-received" but unsatisfactory books, I remembered not only Taigan Takayama's reprimand but Tenzan Yasuda's specific comments on my "view" of the garden. Suddenly I became aware, saw with the greatest clarity: my failing in poetry was the result in great part of a grave misunderstanding concerning the very purpose of art. The Zen masters who had written the poems I was translating did not think of themselves as "poets" at all; rather they were attempting to express in verse nothing less than the Zen spirit—and the results were astonishing. The poems, without any pretension to "art," were among the finest I had ever read, intense, compact, rich in spirit . . .

Working for hours without a break, I transformed the poem I had been writing on the garden, ridding it of "filling," breaking down rigidly regular stanzas, a welter of words, to a few "image units" of around two and one-half lines, while keeping to a constant measure, the short line throughout being of the same syllabic length. In fact, though unintended, the stanzaic unit I came up with was in length and feeling very close to the haiku, and at its best as compact as the short Zen poems I was translating. Perhaps the fact that the "unit" was made up consistently of just so many lines, so controlled, was a matter of chance. The result simply of the way eye and ear, projecting my needs, meshed. . . . I was convinced that I had made, for myself, a profound discovery, and that henceforth I might work as an artist.[8]

The poem which emerged at last from his decisive evening was the beginning of Stryk's beautiful sequence **"Zen: the Rocks of Sesshu."** Several further poems were added to it, the whole thing taking "a few years," as he says, to complete to his satisfaction. Since the occasion is so obviously a momentous one in terms of the author's inner and artistic life, it occupies a position in his selected volume that is transitional and indicates its value for him, which the reader needs to note as well. This sequence, as well as the later **"Awakening"** (and to some degree **"The**

Duckpond" joins them in this), seems to me in one sense to require more detailed commentary—more than could be undertaken here. In another sense it might resist such explication because the ways in which the individual poems work within themselves and in relation to the others in the sequence are felt immediately through flashes of intuition and association in an attentive reader's mind and might not be captured readily by critical prose. Thus I will mention only a few important features. Most noticeable at once in **"Zen: the Rocks of Sesshu"**—they will be familiar by the time the reader arrives at the later sequences—are the pared-down, taut stanzas or "image units" of which the poet has spoken, a concentration of form that finds thematic echoes in descriptive passages where Stryk is treating something else yet simultaneously alluding to his art. But these resonances are only one of the elements in a poetry of extraordinary integration of theme, style, materials, vision. As an instance of the achievement here is section V of the sequence:

> To rid the grass of weed, to get
> > The whole root,
> Thick, tangled, takes a strong mind
>
> And desire—to make clean, make pure.
> > The weed, tough
> As the rock it leaps against,
>
> Unless plucked to the last
> > Live fiber
> Will plunge up through dark again.
>
> The weed also has the desire
> > To make clean,
> Make pure, there against the rock.

The sequence itself, while meditative, is rich, inventive, and exciting in its appropriation and disposal of the world's particulars as the means for exploring Stryk's preoccupations, which are, it seems to me, related to the strengthening of the interior life. Of course, the temple's rock garden laid out by Sesshu is central to the poems; not merely a point of departure, it figures in each piece or section—so do birds, clouds, mountains, a painting by Hokusai, and various other details. But through all of the perceptions, the sharp rendering of images, there runs a pervasive, fundamental desire for the renovation of thought, a rigorous cleansing ("Clear the mind! Empty it of all that / Fixes you . . .") which will issue in a fresh, vivified attitude that embraces external reality without preconception or the intention to use or force it in any way, and for the art that may come of this attitude. The sequences's two concluding sections exemplify how Stryk has accomplished his desire, realizing in these lines the very kind of poem he says he now hopes and waits for:

> VII
>
> Firmness is all: that mountain beyond the
> > Garden path,
> Watch how against its tawny slope

> The candled boughs expire. Follow
> > The slope where
> Spearheads shake against the clouds
>
> And dizzy the pigeons circling on the wind.
> > Then observe
> Where no bigger than a cragstone
>
> The climber pulls himself aloft,
> > As by the
> Very guts: firmness is all.

> VIII
>
> Pierced through by birdsong, stone by stone
> > The garden
> Gathered light. Darkness, hauled by ropes
>
> Of sun, entered roof and bough. Raised from
> > The temple
> Floor where, stiff since cockcrow,
>
> Blown round like Buddha on the lotus,
> > He began
> To write. How against that shimmering,
>
> On paper frail as dawn, make poems?
> > Firm again,
> He waited for the rocks to split.

The progression and culmination of this sequence, in fact, of his poetry in general, can perhaps best be put in Stryk's own words from his recent essay **"Zen Poetry."** Discussing there the Zen view of details or particulars in both poems and pictures, he observes: "Foreground, background, each was part of the process, in poetry as in painting, the spirit discovering itself among the things of this world."[9] We meet again in this statement that ideal of selflessness, total "involvement" with "subject" emphasized in his earlier interview. And from here on, in the largely chronological arrangement of his work in *Selected Poems*, the reader will perceive how, with few exceptions, the increased economy and severity of style, the compact line and stanza so prominent in **"Zen: the Rocks of Sesshu"** have been maintained—to striking effect. While, as I suggested before, he has always been a sensitive, controlled stylist, these later developments endow this poet's writings with an admirable new force and luminosity.

Much of Stryk's poetry following these important alterations—though by no means all of it—assumes a rather more personal air and may take a middle western setting or make use of material drawn from the experiences of his daily life. Such poems, however, avoid the restrictions or limitations frequently imposed by experience which is too private; nor are these in any sense pieces that could be labeled as "confessional" poetry. Stryk's employment of his personal existence, its observations, incidents, relationships, loves, tensions, resolutions, always somehow proceeds to the place where it engages the lives and experiences of others. Writing about himself, he gives the impression that he might be writing about his reader. For Stryk calls directly and straightforwardly upon events or perceivings which appear ordinary, commonplace, the kinds of occurrences most of us fail to heed; and he uncovers in them the seed of a disclosure, which, tended by the skills of his artistry and imaginative power, suddenly blossoms before our eyes (and ears) in the shape of a fully achieved poem. We can see exactly how this happens, for example, in the lovely **"Etude"**:

> I was cycling by the river, back and forth,
>> Umbrella up against the
>>> Rain and blossoms.
>
> It was very quiet, I thought of Woolworth
>> Globes you shake up snowstorms in.
>>> Washed light slanted
>
> Through the cherry trees, and in a flimsy house
>> Some youngster practiced Chopin.
>>> I was moving
>
> With the current, wheels squishing as the music
>> Rose into the trees, then stopped,
>>> And from the house
>
> Came someone wearing too much powder, raincape
>> Orchid in the light. Middle-aged,
>>> The sort you pass
>
> In hundreds everyday and scarcely notice,
>> The Chopin she had sent
>>> Up to those boughs,
>
> Petals spinning free, gave her grace no waters
>> Would reflect, but I might
>>> Long remember.

"A man's poems," Stryk notes, "should reveal the full range of his life, and hide nothing except the art behind them."[10] Or as Yeats has told us: "'a line will take us hours maybe, / Yet if it does not seem a moment's thought / Our stitching and unstitching has been naught.'" That invisibility of art, that hidden technique, is characteristic of our poet's work and owes much, I feel, to his determination to formulate his poems in the stark, compressed lines and abbreviated stanzaic patterns he has chosen for himself. This deliberate selection may make creation a "painful art," as Stryk admits in **"The Gorge"**; but that pain is reserved for the poet alone, a hazard of his dedication. The reader, on the other hand, discovers an art that seems nearly artless, imposing no elaborate screen of rhetoric or ornament, never attempting to sway him with verbal or symbolic exhibitions. These poems, so deeply personal in their basic sensibility, the lively affective responsiveness underlying their finished forms, still display, again and again, Stryk's amazing capacity for entering the being of another—human or animal, tree or house or painting, animate or inanimate—and revealing that experience in the unalloyed texture of the poem:

> Gray fur to brown earth,
>> The grasses clinging,
>>> Eyes still bright, piercing

> Through those topmost boughs
>> Where, choked with nuts,
>>> It clambered to the sun.
>
> The rat has come to gnaw,
>> The dog to sniff,
>>> And I to meet my death:
>
> Gray flesh to brown earth,
>> The grasses clinging,
>>> Eyes still bright, piercing
>
> Through those tangled roots
>> Where, crazed with fear,
>>> I leapt from shade to shade

                    ("The Squirrel")

It would be easy, and is tempting, to go on quoting poem after poem, or failing that, naming them, until I have compiled an anthology or list of favorites; but that would also surely bring me to almost the entire contents of *Selected Poems*. Just as Stryk has written many marvelous and very moving pieces which I have not quoted or named here, so he has produced work of a considerable range of subjects I haven't specified within the limits of these pages. The reader will find for himself those love poems, poems about neighbors or to friends, poems about the experience of war and of weather, of inwardness and of the tangible actualities of mundane existence. He will find with them the profound satisfaction of true poetry, and the tug and shift in his own feelings and perspectives which only art of proven quality can bring about. Lucien Stryk has worked over the years quietly, unobtrusively, and he has earned our respect for this modesty and independence; but the selected work of this long period of labor, loyalty to imagination and craft now should be rewarded by many new readers. I close these remarks, leaving you in the presence of the poet, with the final section of his masterly, memorable sequence **"Awakening"**:

> I write in the dark again,
> rather by dusk-light,
> and what I love about
> this hour is the way the trees
> are taken, one by one,
> into the great wash of darkness.
> At this hour I am always happy,
> ready to be taken myself,
> fully aware.

NOTES

[1] Chicago: Swallow Press, 1976.

[2] John Somer: "The Zen Aesthetic: An Interview with Lucien Stryk, Poet and Translator," *Chicago Review* 25, 3 (1973), pp. 65-66.

[3] *Afterimages: Zen Poems of Shinkichi Takahashi*, trans. by Lucien Stryk and Takashi Ikemoto. Chicago: Swallow Press, 1970, p. 41.

[4] "The Zen Aesthetic," p. 69.

⁵ Ibid., p. 72.

⁶ Ibid., p. 66.

⁷ In *American Poets in 1976,* ed. by William Heyen. Indianapolis: Bobbs-Merrill, 1976, p. 392.

⁸ Ibid., p. 393.

⁹ *New Letters* 43, 1 (1976), p. 81

¹⁰ "Making Poems," p. 398.

Gary Eddy (essay date 1978)

SOURCE: "Earning the Language: The Writing of Lucien Stryk," in *Zen, Poetry, the Art of Lucien Stryk*, edited by Susan Porterfield, Swallow Press, 1993, pp. 293-313.

[*In the following essay, which initially appeared in 1978, Eddy offers an overview of Stryk's poetic career, contending that "in the whole of his writing, we can sense a series of great, daring changes which have formed a poet of rare stature and integrity."*]

> "Just as at fifty a man has the face he has earned, the lineaments of his poems reveal the range and depth of his spiritual life. Simply by surviving I have become a middle-aged poet."
>
> —Lucien Stryk

When you take a walk with contemporary American poetry, you can expect to take some great risks, find real people to love and even get a few laughs; but the trick is that you have to listen with your whole life, not just the part of you that reads the books. Poets have been asking their readers to suspend disbelief and venture a few leaps of the imagination for a long time and they, and we, have been paying with consciousness. Our time awake in the world is enhanced by such poets who reward our leaps with new ways of seeing or, simply, with voices in the wilderness that give off the necessary assurances.

Lucien Stryk is a man who wagers his life in this pursuit of communicating the ineffable. His struggling early verse bitterly and needlessly rhymed itself into complacency but gave way to a poetry that solidly accommodates the range of his experience, the range of his art. He abandoned the more academic views of art to favor the Zen aesthetic: "the distance between man who thinks and man who thinks he thinks: wait" (**"Zen: The Rocks of Sesshu,"** *The Pit and Other Poems*). This is the kind of response one will inevitably make to an art that is also a way of life.

Rilke says at the end of his poem "Archaic Torso of Apollo," "you must change your life." A statement of poetics like this points out in all directions to all of us who find our peak experiences in the arts, through an emotional appreciation of the world we see or by simply knowing a great poem. And once we know that poem, we are changed. We realize a flux of new ideas, new potentials, opening up before us. We also assume a new responsibility, as Stryk says in his interview, "By great works, the artist is warned: he cannot afford to use his art for unworthy purposes" (*Chicago Review,* No. 88, 1973). The poet, at this point, is free to do positive things through his art but is also bound to an intrinsic aesthetic, even a morality, in his work.

The world-view, the morality, of a poem is always expressed in the assumptions the poem makes. The statements and actions a poem makes are made possible by the world the poet creates in the first line, even in the title. In **"Christ of Pershing Square,"** we are given a confrontation that has psychologic and religious resonance, and we know it right off the bat.

"Christ of Pershing Square"

"I can prove it!" the madman cried
And clutched my wrist. "Feel where the nails
Went in! By God, I bear them still!"

Half amused, I shrugged and let him
Press the hand against the suture:
"All right," I said, "they cut you up."

Suddenly those fingers grasped
A hammer, it was I had hoisted
The cross his flung arms formed there.
"Yet," I whispered, "there remains
The final proof—forgiveness."
He spat into my face and fled.

This happened in Los Angeles
Six months ago. I see him still,
White blood streaming, risen from
Cancerous sheets to walk a Kingdom.

We are given the world of a strange encounter. Acts of desperation are suggested by "madman" and "clutched." Yet, the speaker of the poem acts with passivity in a situation that calls for total rejection. We now know a great deal about the speaker: "Press the hand against the suture: All right." The tone is searching and willing to remain aware. The speaker is finding religion, in this situation, that understands human suffering; he admits his own guilt and realizes the need for forgiveness. The result, however, is a rejection and denial from the Christ figure that allows room for the image-mind to see the "white blood streaming," resurrection, and the "Kingdom" in a new way. Encounters, human experiences, *do* determine art and the world that is recreated in the reader.

It is difficult and dangerous to make art that is willing to incorporate the whole of human experience. Many great people have made huge sacrifices (Neruda, Wright, Miguel Hernandez) and suffered, often, great setbacks to make art that tries to contain and express a singular life. Great artists abandon a great deal in order to stake life on an attempt at the truth. The trials are much more intense, perhaps, than the rewards, but the driving desire is the most important, most common, element shared by the makers of good poems.

Lucien Stryk published his first book when he was twenty-nine and living in England, working at the University of London. *Taproot* (1953) is full of elaborate metaphoric conceits and "difficult" rhymes. However, despite its "first book" flaws, it shows a definite direction and solid promise in the first two stanzas of **"Masks"** (which, incidentally, are all that remain in the version released in *Selected Poems*):

> Behind the tattered brow
>   the skull looms sharp:
> as branch survives its fruits
>   and wind-picked bark,
>
> so bone releases flesh
>   to weather nakedly
> and lone: on winter's frost
>   burns summer's day.

Stryk's second book, *The Trespasser*, was released three years later but proves to be disappointing. These poems are now more stilted than even the earliest poems. Perhaps Shelley's "internal and external impression" are driven to sell over these poems, but the quite stale influence of the British Romantics remains in lines like these.

> Prince Lucifer, who draws my sail,
> When by the blast I'm overthrown,
>   Strike down the fool that dares to wail
> For with this mad world I've done.
>   (**"Ballade,"** ll. 25-29)

Shelley's influence might make us believe that the poet is a medium through which the poem passes. Therefore, "the Muse" holds the chief responsibility for art, not the human poet. This is a precarious attitude for a young poet to assume. Often the poems that come from "the Muse" are imitative and negligent in message or craft. The source of the poem is removed from its maker. This is the dichotomy between poet and product that stands in the way of these first two books.

In *Notes for a Guidebook* (1965), Stryk begins to follow an aesthetic that is open to his own particular voice and experience. He makes a better, looser kind of poem. At this time, he was working in Japan, Persia and the U.S. on the first of his Zen Buddhism anthologies, *Zen: Poems, Prayers, Sermons, Anecdotes, Interviews*, for Double-day/Anchor. The variety of experiences of this period in his life began to enter his poetry.

Stylistically, it was transformed. He abandons the forced poetics of his first two collections and adopts the three-line stanza he uses to this day. He states, "though unintended the stanzaic unit I came up with was in length and feeling very close to the haiku, and at its best as com-

pact as the short Zen poems I was translating. Perhaps the fact that the '(image) unit' was made up consistently of just so many lines, so controlled, was a matter of chance, the result simply of the way eye and ear, projecting my needs, meshed" ("Making Poems," in *American Poets in 1976*, ed. William Heyen, p. 393). This form allows him to use other elements besides rhyme to balance his lines. Often, Stryk retains the "hit" or deepest image until the end of a line to maintain the tension. For example, **"City of the Wind"** (*NFG*, p. 31).

> Rainspout, fencepost, toolshed,
>   As if the town
> Were tossing on the flood
>
> Of space.

Stryk was also incorporating more daring and contemporary ideas into this new poetry. Often, techniques of modern world poets appear. In the powerful **"The Mine: Yamaguchi,"** he reverses our expectations with a neo-Miltonic flair:

> It is not hell one thinks of, however dark,
> These look more weary than tormented.
> One would expect, down there, a smell more
>   human,
> A noise more agonized than that raised
> By cars shunted, emptied, brimmed again.
>
> Today, remembering, the black heaps themselves
> (On which conveyors drop, chip by chip,
> What aeons vised and morselled to lay
> A straw of light across the page)
> Do not force infernal images.
>
> After weeks of trying to forget,
> The eye resists, the vision begged and gotten
> Is the heart's: rows of women bent over
> Feed-belts circling like blood, pickhammers
> Biting at the clods that trundle by,
> Raw hands flinging waste through scuttles gaped
>   behind
> While, a stone's-throw down the company road,
> A smokestack grits the air with substance one
> Might sniff below, or anywhere. It marks
> The crematory, they pass it twice a day.

He leaves us with the absence, the crematory, the fatal, terse image that drives the message home. Stryk uses the image like a hammer to put the final plumb lines in our picture of the world. He makes it larger, too. We are allowed to experience a larger world, Japan, Spain, Persia, and in a more concrete way. The world comes alive in us through images like "rows of women bent over feed-belts circling like blood."

Stryk doesn't compromise himself by abandoning the music that is open to the craftsman of language. With the more concentrated "image unit," Stryk is more able to create a music that is not forced into a meter but,

rather, free to find new rhythms and even change them
when necessary. **"The Fountain of Ammanati"** is a perfect example of a rhythm as organic and natural as its
topic:

> No sneak-vialed aphrodisiac
> Can do—for me, for you—what
> Mermen pinching mermaids in a whack
>
> Of sunlit water can. And do.

Internal rhymes are a much subtler device for Lucien
Stryk's particular, sensitive voice. Free rhythms allow
him to bring us his aesthetic peaks in poems like **"The
Fountain of Ammanati," "Delgusha Garden"** or
"Hearn in Matsue." In these poems, where the direct
experience of art is expressed, the poems tend to become self-conscious. Perhaps, as Peter Michelson suggests in his review of *Notes for a Guidebook* (*Chicago
Review,* No. 63, 1967) he looks too hard for images, a
retainer from the older poems.

But, poems about art are perhaps the most difficult to
write because they can easily become hollow and lacking
in the real magic that lies underneath all great art. If there
is anything more difficult than making a work of art, it
must be making a good poem about art that hopes, itself,
to be art. In **"The Fountain of Ammanati,"** Stryk succeeds
in bringing us a work that is constantly creating itself. I
mean that in two ways: he creates the fountain for us as
it is for himself, and he paints it so vividly that we can see
it as a work of art that is changing its shape and making
itself new. It is both ideal, as art, and real as it is experienced by the reader:

"The Fountain of Ammanti"
(Piazza della Signoria, Florence)

> Below the pigeon-spotted seagod
> The mermen pinch the mermaids,
> And you shopgirls eat your food.
>
> No sneak-vialed aphrodisiac
> Can do—for me, for you—what
> Mermen pinching mermaids in a whack
>
> Of sunlit water can. And do.
> These water-eaten shoulders and these thighs
> Shall glisten though your gills go blue.
>
> These bones will never clatter in the breath.
> My dears, before your dust swirls either up
> Or down—confess: this world is richly wet.
>
> And consider: there is a plashless world
> Outside this stream-bright square
> Where girls like you lie curled
>
> And languishing for love like mine.
> And you were such as they
> Until ten sputtering jets began
> To run their ticklish waters down your

> Spine. Munch on, my loves, you are but
> Sun-bleached maidens in a world too poor
>
> To tap the heart-wells that would flow,
> And flow. You are true signorine
> Of that square where none can go
>
> And then return. Where dusty mermen
> Parch across a strand of sails and spars,
> And dream of foamy thighs that churn.

In **"Delgusha Gardens,"** however, the true picture of
the artistic sensibility is blurred by a series of allusions
to the exotique. We have "bulbuls," "Aspens with Khyyam,"
"Ghenghis Khan and Tamerlane," but the real concrete
particulars don't appear until the very last stanza, when
the living beings come into the picture:

> And rocking the aspens, hid
>   By leaves, crows
> Rain droppings, and fly on.

The greatest discovery, however, is contained in the title
poem. The literary and artistic allusions are present here too,
but they are given room to explain themselves and, thus,
don't stand out as flaws, but as genuine particulars. Donatello, Giotto and Dante are here in Padua; "the poet's cantos
ring upon its walls." Art is truly felt as a physical part of the
environment that can bring about permanent change in one's
life. We are brought to Padua's majestic artworks and, yet,
he brings us to look at ourselves in the end. Again, as in
Rilke, we find that "you must change your life."

"Notes For a Guidebook"

> In celestial Padua
> The ghosts walk hugely
> In the public squares.
> Donatello is one,
> His horseman in the
> Piazza San Antonio
> Guards the gruff saint's heart
> Like a mystic ruby,
> The ears of the horse,
> Of the rider,
> Riddled by prayer.
>
> Giotto, Dante are others,
> The painter's frescoes
> Float like clouds
> Above the city,
> The poet's cantos
> Ring upon its walls.
>
> And what of us,
> Who stand with heads
> Strained back, feet tapping?
> Shall we eat, sleep,
> Be men again?
> Shall we slip back

To the whores of Venice?—
Dwarfs, clods, motes of dust
In the brightness.

We learn by art a morality. The boundaries and assumptions of a poem, for example, outline a world that we enter, fully awake, with our consciousness. By presenting a spark of awareness or a selection of perceptions, the poet has a responsibility to literature, to the reader and to his world-vision. He must be immediate, honest and humble in relaying his world to us and confident of its self-perpetuation.

As readers, we have been faced with a challenging vista in poetry. Poets consistently try to recreate in us a new peak experience, the deep emotions and wild, joyous insights which the mind finds through contact with this earth. But we only react when the experience the poem relates is clear and acute like the life it is to become a part of. This requires a dedication on the part of the poet to being honest with himself and open to his reader. Stryk feels, "a man's poems must reveal the full range of his life, and hide nothing except the art behind them." Peter Michelson, in his review of *Notes for a Guidebook* (*Chicago Review*, pp. 117-128), cites Stryk for his moral vitality. This seems to stem from a de-emphasis on the ego that can be traced in his poems. The goal is then, to make a poetry that is not conscious of being art, one that is pointed in all directions, anxious after truth. Morally vital poetry is open-ended and willing to include the world as it is experienced. The contact is direct, unpretentious, and hopefully, egoless.

And for Stryk, at the very heart of his life, this speaking point is *zenki,* or the inner formlessness. This is the way in which the Zennist opens himself up to identify with an object. The ego is closed off and the art that is produced is spontaneous, open to explore the world in new ways without the burden of artifice. Again, from his interview with John Somer: "Poems written about others are good poems only when the writer becomes the other. In other words, he can't be anything other than selfless if he is to make important art." (*CR*, No. 88) Art cannot be bound up with an ego if it is to communicate directly to the reader. Awareness of the inner formlessness allows the artist to subdue the ego and crystallize a moment of consciousness on a canvas or a page. But a religion like Zen is not a tool for the betterment of one's poetry; it is a way of life that demands a severe dedication. And it is the dedication that helps the artist, not the philosophy, "if you are seriously interested in a philosophy or religion, then your art is bound to prosper because you are less self-absorbed."

In 1962, while Stryk was teaching in Yamaguchi, his fascination with Zen began to evolve into more than a fascination. *Zenki* becomes the cornerstone of an aesthetic that continues to develop in Stryk's work. He has been busy since then editing books of Zen literature and translating the poems of the greatest masters. This work begins now to couple with his own writing into one directed effort at relating the wonders of our own world to us

in ways many Westerners have never before experienced. But this effort is a most difficult path. In *Zen: Poems, Prayers, Sermons, Anecdotes, Interviews*, he quotes a *waka*-poem by Kando (1825-1904) that sums up the difficulties:

It's as if our heads were on fire, the way
We apply ourselves to perfection of That.
The future but a twinkle, beat yourself,
Persist: the greatest effort's not enough.

                                                              (*Zen*, p. xxxiii)

Yet, the rewards can be astounding. Stryk's next book, *The Pit and Other Poems*, shares with us encounters of *zenki* with new levels of excitement and new heights of artistry. The images seem less strained, the situations less exotic and the particulars grow more vivid and warm. The book begins on a personal note with a poem of self-evaluation, **"Oeuvre."** He confronts himself with an openness and honesty that is exemplary, and also kind.

Seasons of
Pondering, name by name, the past's magnificent,

A squandering. Surely I might have lived.
Spitefully
Watching as rivals stole the girls, got the jobs . . .

He shows his determination: "We build where and as we can." It is not a confessional poem and it is not an abstract poem, it remains somewhere in between: personal, positive and aware.

Next, he turns on himself again with a deeply meditative eye. The poem **"Zen: The Rocks of Sesshu"** is slow moving and ripe with deep images to create in us a meditative consciousness that handles the world slowly and delicately.

"Zen: The Rocks of Sesshu"

I

What do they think of
    Where they lean
Like ponderous heads, the rocks?—

In prankish spring, ducks
    Joggling here
And there, brushing tails,

Like silly thoughts shared,
    Passed from head
To head? When, gong quavering

About a ripened sky, we
    Up and go,
Do they waken from a dream of flesh?

The Zen master Tenzen Yasuda in an interview from *Zen: Poems, Sermons, Anecdotes, Interviews* answered one of Stryk's more impetuous questions about Sesshu's rock garden by admonishing him to "sit in Zen for a long period before looking at the garden; then one might be able to look at it, as the old saying goes, 'with the navel.'" It is here that the poem begins to take shape, with the navel, within. We are given the leaning heads first, then told they are rocks. This presents us, not with a look *at* the objects, but *as* them. The poem doesn't merely speak of the life under the world we see, but makes us sense it with our own minds. The rocks here are not animated; rather they are animating. Sesshu's intention, perhaps, was to make us aware of the formless world we really live in by setting these rocks, this formlessness, "to stud our emptiness." The world is no longer closed in for Lucien Stryk, a variety" of lifestyles and perspectives emerge. And the earth is, above all, respected, as in the fifth part of **"Zen: The Rocks of Sesshu"**:

> To rid the grass of weed, to get
>   The whole root,
> Thick, tangled, takes a strong mind
>
> And desire—to make clean, make pure.
>   The weed, tough
> As the rock it leaps against,
>
> Unless plucked to the last
>   Live fiber
> Will plunge up through dark again.
> The weed also has the desire
>   To make clean,
> Make pure, there against the rock.

It took years for Stryk to be able to complete this poem. It takes a long time for an aesthetic to take shape in an artist's life and work and time, also, for those individual works that express it most clearly to be written and perfected. As an artist, Stryk was constantly being molded by travel, experience, solitude and study. It is not merely coincidental that so many of Stryk's most important poems are drawn from his travels in Persia, Britain, and most significantly Japan, and the world of Buddhism. *Notes for a Guidebook* was completed along with *Zen: Poems, Prayers, Sermons, Anecdotes, Interviews* and Stryk was compiling **World of the Buddha** and *After Images: Zen Poems of Shinkichi Takahashi* while writing **The Pit and Other Poems**. This interchange is important to Stryk's work in a number of ways, but perhaps the breed of image that his poems often share with those of the Zennists.

The images that appear most often in Zen poems are those which try to include for the reader two worlds, as in this image from Takahashi's wonderful poem "Apricot": "and the bluest fish move through blue water— / a sign of pregnancy." The image can demonstrate the life that lies within the ordinary, a transcending depth that a contemplative mind and open eyes are able to reach. For a Zen man, the poem is a device for opening these depths to the reader, the uninitiated. This is a virtually impossible feat

unless the poem contains the keen perception of particulars that can make a poem come alive in our minds, off the page. This kind of keen perception makes for a minimal, concise statement that has no room for many of the excesses of Western art. There is no apology, no explanation; the image does the work of combining two worlds into the one, and the image is left standing, the art becomes invisible.

Stryk, by this time in his career, is fully aware of the traces of art and is able to hide them or is bold enough to discard them. His poems take on a new vibrance and retain their taut, balanced structure. His images show no great strain, and they manage to contain a sense of the inner world as it views and encounters the outer one. Stryk's invisible art is not easily achieved. His years of apprenticeship with **The Trespasser** and his other earlier works have clearly paid off in his obvious craft. It is possible now for the craft and polish of the poem to make it indiscernible from the reality it speaks of and, thus, create a poem that is constantly reflecting the world. It is vital because it issues from a life infused with *zenki*, it sees the world anew with each glance. It is lyric and beautiful because it is made by a fine craftsman who wants very much for us to see the world anew. Stryk defines *zenki* for the poet as "spontaneous activity free of form, flowing from the formless self, leading to the bold thrust of his metaphor."Spontaneous action is crucial to the image that is to catch the senses at the moment of their blending and point out the contours in this worldly fabric. In the final section of **"Zen: The Rocks of Sesshu,"** Stryk achieves both these effects in words like "gathered" and "firm again" and puts it all in a very delicate, very real, time frame of light images.

VIII

> Pierced through by birdsong, stone by stone
>   The garden
> Gathered light. Darkness, hauled by ropes
>
> Of sun, entered roof and bough. Raised from
>   The temple
> Floor where, stiff since cockcrow,
> Blown round like Buddha on the lotus,
>   He began
> To write. How against that shimmering,
> On paper frail as dawn, make poems?
>   Firm again,
> He waited for the rocks to split.

To discuss the work of Lucien Stryk and not mention his sensitive and definitive translations from the Japanese of both ancient and contemporary Zen poems would be to ignore the greatest "volume" of Stryk's work. His collaboration with Takashi Ikemoto is an inter-relationship of skills and strong exchange of ideas. Stryk summarizes this way: "he provided what I required, the gift to dig into the literature and select important examples, and perhaps he needed what I could offer, the skill to turn these things into hopefully, living English." (*CR*, p. 88) The task is obviously a difficult one, given the challenge of an art as bold as that produced through Zen. Stryk worries, himself, about the justice that can be done to the original. He feels that there is no way to *translate* the poetry of Zen, however, we can hope to *transmute* the poems to allow room for cross-cultural acceptance of the delicate and peculiar imagery. "You have to give the spirit of the original, but in doing that you must not add images or take images away . . . because, say cherry blossoms, has more mystic importance and resonance in Japanese than it does in English." (*CR*, p. 88) We can immediately see the conflicts which must arise. However, with the confirmed Zen spirit of Ikemoto and the poetic sensibilities of Stryk, works like the Takahasi translations can come through to us with the vitality that an expression of *zenki* requires and they maintain a natural feel and rhythm as if they were fresh new poems written in English. In the poem "Wind," the spirit of transformation is essential and its subtlety is elusive.

> Give it words,
> Stick limbs on it,
> You won't alter essence
> Whereas the wind—
>
> I'll live gently
> As the wind, flying
> Over the town,
> My chest full of sparrows.

The poem keeps a tight hold on this inner formlessness of both the self ("you won't alter essence") and the object the poet identifies with, wind ("my chest full of sparrows"). The poem allows the reader to feel a distinct presence. First a form is created in space by the "it" that is never clearly defined, yet exists, almost physically, by the third line. Inside that form we sense a complete vitality, and we are directed to an awareness of the poet's world-in-a-world. The beauty of the translation is in the fact that we are struck with the immediacy of effect that is difficult to obtain in the translations from any language, even German. The translation has the immediacy of a new poem in English. Stryk's perception of particulars and a genuine, sympathetic relationship with a work of art are the key factors here. In the Writer's Forum interview, Stryk remarks that "in order to translate well from a poet of this type, the feeling of kinship has to be very strong."

One must have a feel for the local color of the poet's world as well as this kinship. He asks further in the interview, "How can you expect one of the students who has only a postcard sense of that country to produce living poems for translation?" The translator's direct contact with the poet's referents and his image vocabulary is crucial to an effective translation. In many cases, the translator is physically stirred by this contact and his own poetic sensibilities may be aroused as well. Therefore, the study of *any* poet's work in view of his translations is always enlightening.

By the time he wrote *Awakening*, Lucien Stryk had won the *Chicago Daily News* Award for **"A Sheaf for Chi-**

cago," written, edited or translated ten books and published important poems such as **"Notes for a Guidebook," "Zen: The Rocks of Sesshu," "Oeuvre,"** and **"The Pit."** In more recent collections of his own verse there appears a solid core of poems that are set in the Midwest and speak of the people, the land, and the life there. Stryk concedes, "I am sometimes asked why in the face of such 'exotic' pursuits (as travel and translation) I have an interest in the poetry of my region—or, worse, why my own poetry is set for the most part in small-town Illinois. To one involved in the study of a philosophy like Zen, the answer to such questions is not difficult: one writes of one's place because it is in every sense as wonderful as any other, whatever its topography and weathers, and because one cannot hope to discover oneself elsewhere" (*Heartland II: Poets of the Midwest*, p. xxii). Stryk must set his poems down where they are found, as sinewy and stark as the landscape, but as warm and familiar as a hometown or a birthplace.

Knowing how closely a man's writing and his environment are tied together, we can see how a man like Stryk can never completely "go bamboo," as he calls it. As an American poet, and as a husband and father, he is found returning again and again to the poeple and the life immediately near. The awakened man will find the Illinois flatland full of beauty and awe as the foot of Mount Fuji. In the first *Heartland* anthology (1967), Stryk says that the poet can find poems everywhere he chooses to be "for what the land does not supply, his imagination will, and from the synthesis can come things rich and strange." One of the most important products to emerge from the synthesis in Stryk's own work is an openended image. By this I mean the image that not only contains a physical space and describes a relationship, but also points to the life that continues outside the poem itself, into the undiscovered world. This image leaves us with a sense that there exists more to the universe than we previously imagined, both visible and below the visible. In a poem like **"Storm"** we become aware of the vastness of the world described and of the life the place holds for us.

> The green horse of the tree
> bucks in the wind
> as lightning hits beyond.
> We will ride it out together,
> or together fall.
>
> (*Awakening*, p. 18)

The concision of these lines allows for the entry of the unknown. We see only what the lightning shows us. "The green horse of the tree" stands solitary in an undiscovered universe and all we know to feel is determination in the face of great mystery.

The regional poem comes alive in the particulars which appear on the surface of our vision. The regional poem is an inclusive thing that takes hold of people, weather and the special sounds in the air. In a poem such as **"The Duckpond,"** we see these particulars as if within reach and, yet, are impressed with the way in which they stand above the inward, meditative tone that comprises the thrust and background of the vision. There are lawn-chairs and sunbathers, arguments and radio towers present, but the most obvious presence is the space that the images themselves contain.

"The Duckpond"

I

Crocus, daffodil:
    already the pond's
        clear of ice

where, winter long
    ducks and gulls
        slid for crusts.

People circle—
    pale, bronchitic,
        jostling behind dogs,

grope toward lawnchairs
    spread like islands
        on the grass.

Sunk there, they lift faces to the sun.
              (*Awakening*, p. 35)

The poem is populated and yet, through the use of clear natural imagery and concision, we see its meditative aspect and its stake in solitude. We are exposed to two perspectives in the second section, natural phenomena and its reflection of human religion, and our view of both is suddenly more acute. The open-ended image carries us deeper into our world.

Good Friday
    Ducks carry on,
        a day like any other.

Same old story:
    no one seems to care.
        A loudmouth
leader of a mangy host
    spiked to a cross,
        as blackbirds in certain

lands neighboring on
    that history are splayed
        on fences, warning

to their kind. A duck soars from the reeds.
              (*Awakening*, p. 38)

Later in the poem, we see that what is learned in one place, even a duckpond, is the same message the earth sends out everywhere, "the pond sends news of the world" (VI, 1. 13, p. 40). In the final section, we see how the world is constantly in flux, changing from the inside out and acted upon from the outside in.

IX

Ducks lie close together
    In morning dew, wary eyed,
        bills pointing at the pond:

roused by squirrels
    those early rises,
        air's a-whir with wings.

Sad to think of leaving
    this place. A helicopter
    with mysterious purpose

appears above the trees,
    moving low. Its circles
    tightening,

the ducks cling to the pondedge, right to fear.
              (*Awakening*, p. 43)

A poem like **"The Duckpond"** affects us so thoroughly because it speaks with directness, concision and gravity of the Zennist's art and, yet, its focus is the very life we lead as Americans, our land, our pain. Perhaps this book can best be seen if we view the poems it contains as a cycle of transcriptions of genuine experiences aimed at recreating in the reader a similar awareness, awe, or sick sadness. "In order to do so," Stryk says in his essay "Making Poems," "I would have to 'get beyond' poetry, put down without faking the truth of a young man's pain, which had nothing literary about it and was felt acutely over the years. A pain I was asked to share and still do." Stryk says this directly about **"Letter to Jean-Paul Baudot, at Christmas,"** but it stretches over many of his poems that call on the strength of experience to make the poem a valid experience, also, for the reader. Perhaps the poet's own experiences are, after all, the only thing that is shared in poetry. We grow closer through what is to become a common experience.

Stryk says in the *Chicago Review* interview, "what I experience constitutes the range of my art." To bring us to his underlying feelings, he often writes of experiences that border, embarrassingly, on our own. When we see a poem like **"Summer"** that is full of the trivial bickering that keeps neighbors so perennially separate ("he shakes a fist at me / where I sit poeming / my dandelions, crabgrass and a passing dog"), we are struck by its complete grasp of the situation.

I like my neigbor, in his way
he cares for me. Look what
I've given him—something to feel superior to.
              (*Awakening*, p. 27)

But what must move us, most surely, are his poems from fatherhood, from the heart of his life. These poems attempt a very special, very sensitive way of looking at the world. They remain simple poems, but they try to express identification with the child's frame of vision and emotion. He doesn't imitate the innocence of the child, but

becomes, through *zenki,* united with the child's sensibilities. He, and we, see again in a new way. Perhaps the
comedy and, then, the concern expressed in part VIII of
"The Duckpond" can put us in contact with the child's
world once again.

> When tail wagging
>   in the breeze
>   the duck pokes
>
> bill into pondbed,
>   keeps it there,
>   my daughter thinks
>
> him fun—he is, yet how to say
>   those acrobatics
>   aren't meant
>
> to jollify the day. He's
>   hungry, poking
>   away at nothing
>
> for crumbs we failed to bring: how to tell her?
>   (*Awakening*, p. 42)

Stryk's work encompasses twenty-three years of changes
in poetics, taste, religion and lifestyle. Opening his *Selected Poems*, just released by Swallow Press, is like
entering a large room: some corners are dark, there are
great sculptures in some, but all the windows open out on
a great and wondrous world. It speaks strongly to us, as
a great collection and stands as a self-confident effort to
put us in contact with one life that contains a variety of
experience and setting, a clear evolution of style and
poetic strength, and a sympathetic, opened human awareness. This awareness opens up as trust in his reader and
in his own experience, his own world view. Notice the
privacy he can share in this previously uncollected poem,
"Love Poem":

> Startle my wife again—
> "Where will we lay our bones?"
> Harmless, you'd think, yet
> she's berserk. "Mere joshing,"
>
> I protest. She will not
> listen. I want an island
>
> for us, apart, ringed with stones,
> clustering of flowers
>
> merging us closer through
> the all of time. She thinks
>
> me mad with dreaming,
> but it's love for her
>
> which spurs me, this need
> to know we'll never separate.

The confidence that this book has in us, as readers, is
more than complimentary, it is challenging. We are being

asked to have an encounter with an emotion and, from
Stryk's point of view, the contact must be direct. He refuses to stifle feelings using convoluted language or elusive forms. His language must be crystallized and honest:
"it's love for her / which spurs me, this need." As readers, we are responsible for suspending our disbelief at
the expense of a possible awakening and taking all the
risks that the poem deserves. The poet, in turn, is responsible for making our engagement with the life of the poem
clear and meaningful. Only then, when all these conditions
are met and all our ties broken for a moment, are we able
to move our divergent minds "closer through / the all of
time."

Stryk includes in *Selected Poems* sixteen previously uncollected poems, **"Mask"** from *Taproot*, **"Scarecrow"** from
The Trespasser and the entire *Notes for a Guidebook*.
These early books have been out of print for some time
and what is reprinted here flows into the mainstream of
Stryk's work. They shine with the artless and beguiling
style that is present in the more recent works. But perhaps
the choice of so few very early poems is not quite prudent
on Stryk's part. In the whole of his writing, we can sense
a series of great, daring changes which have formed a
poet of rare stature and integrity. Here, however, the sense
of constant change and development is de-emphasized by
excluding a sampling of those early poems. His novice
poems, poor though many of them are, do form the base
for the music and the development of his "image unit"
style in his later books. This portion of the *Selected Poems* leaves us in the dark where the rest of the book sheds
a brilliant light on the world. Above all, this volume startles us awake to the presence of, as Anthony Piccione
states in his review, "an American, guiding us easily again
and again to the ordinary world we tend to loom past and
wherein is lodged the undiscovered unity of all things"
(*CR,* Vol. 28, No. 3, p. 201).

World literature in the twentieth century has undergone
a revolution unlike anything since the Renaissance.
Throughout Europe, the poets are driving themselves to
bring out a poetry that is integral to the lives of their
people. Poetry and art must now do more than entertain
the reader or critic. The world is already overstimulated
by media, art and entertainments. The aesthetic that arises is one that unifies peoples across language barriers by
a common experience, a common consciousness, and a
belief that we can all feel the same sensations underneath
our masks of dogma and nationality.

Out of this desire has come a storm of anti-poems and
aesthetic theories that are sent out from every corner to
boggle the mind and transform sensibilities. But when the
storm clears, the great artworks stand tall and their makers
are remembered for their constant efforts at uniting people
in a common consciousness. Figures like Montale, Herbert, Gabriella Mistral, Neruda and Rilke remain with us
forever to point in their one direction: to hide the visible
show of art and reveal underneath a beauty, an art of
communication. And as each new writer begins to point
in that direction, we must look closely again and again to
where they point: to the ordinary world and to the love of

this life. Looking at Lucien Stryk's direction, we see the shape his poems are making on the horizon: a single form, leading a minimal life, and forging for us a way of seeing the world together and of holding on to the edge.

"The Edge"

Living that year at the edge
of the ravine,
sloped down to the woods, we listened

to the animals before the town
awoke, blurring
the limits of our days,

forcing its round, the needs
of others.
Near sleep, after loving, we felt

part of a stillness with the dark
and all its creatures,
holding to the edge of where we lived.

                                       (*Awakening*, p. 44)

Dennis Lynch (essay date 1980)

SOURCE: "The Poetry of Lucien Stryk," in *American Poetry Review*, Vol. 9, No. 5, September-October, 1980, pp. 44-46.

[*In the following essay, Lynch compares Stryk's early verse to his more recent poetry.*]

A conscious life without a definite philosophy is no life, rather a burden and a nightmare," wrote Chekhov. The definite philosophy of contemporary American poet Lucien Stryk is Zen. Stryk has edited *World of the Buddha*, *Zen: Poems, Prayers, Sermons, Anecdotes, Interviews,* and *The Penguin Book of Zen Poetry*, has translated Shinkiehi Takahashi's *Afterimages,* and has published six volumes of his own poetry. Perhaps no one has done more than Stryk to introduce Americans to the work of Zen masters past and present, and Stryk stands with Gary Snyder as the two most distinguished American Zen poets. Unlike Snyder, Stryk came to Zen relatively late in life. After service in the South Pacific in World War II and education at the University of London and the Sorbonne, Stryk held a series of teaching positions and fellowships in the Near East and the Orient. The last of these positions brought him to Japan in 1962-63 and here he became profoundly influenced by Zen. His first book of poetry to reflect his new discipline is his fourth volume, *The Pit and Other Poems* (1969). The difference between Stryk's poetry before and after this time is astounding. His early work is lifeless, ornamental, derivative; his later work is vital, terse, uniquely his own. It is no exaggeration to say that for Stryk Zen makes the difference, for Zen provides him with the definite philosophy and clear aesthetic he needs to structure his poetic vision.

Stryk's first volumes of poetry, *Taproot* (1953) and *The Trespasser* (1956), were well received at their publica-

tion and still have their admirers. Stryk, however, is not one of them. He unabashedly refers to these books as "valueless" and refuses to reprint them, successfully resisting his editor's efforts to turn *Selected Poems* (1976) into *Collected Poems,* These early poems are all meticulously crafted, as Stryk here works within such tight forms as the sonnet, the villanelle, the sestina, and the canzone, but they leave one unsatisfied. These poems seem too "well-made," too workman-like. Moreover, these are blatantly obvious echoes of Rilke and Eliot ("the dying butt-ends of desires"—**"The Fugitive"**) in these poems, and the constantly repeated themes of this poet then in his twenties are death, despair, and sin. It all seems like so much posturing, and these poems are as stilted in their diction which is full of words and phrases such as "naught" and "rank flesh." These poems are generally so bad and so full of hopelessly contrived conceits that when the persona of **"Canzone on an Old Proverb"** says:

Adieu to Verse! Atrocious rhyme
Begone, and may you fare not well,
No more shall I spoil precious time
In sawing stanzas stiff and stale. . . .

one wants to cry "Bravo!" But young Stryk keeps sawing away.

Yet to say, as the older Stryk does, that all of these poems are valueless is too harsh. Like many relatively late converts to a new belief, Stryk discounts all of his work done before his conversion. But some of this work does have value, if only to point the direction Stryk was heading. Here, for instance, is a stanza from the poem **"Credo"**:

To seek the baffling space between
Things both different and same,
To trace the thin dividing line
And to give the whole a simple name
Is the task to which I'm sworn.

"Credo" is placed first in *The Trespasser*, underlining the importance the author gives to this conscious statement of his poetic. This statement may be too obvious, too naively spoken for most tastes; nevertheless, this credo is to be found in Stryk's later work as well. Importantly, however, this credo is unspoken in later volumes, and it is left to the reader to divine the poet's beliefs. A poem of more intrinsic merit than this one, and perhaps the best poem of Stryk's first two volumes, is **"Chu Ming-How."** Surely it deserves reprinting sometime.

Chu Ming-How, the Mandarin,
Astride his fat brown mule,
Rode slowly up a high green hill
To dodge the lowland din,
    The tassel on the mule's long tail
    Swished gayly in the sun.

Half-way up the mule sat down
And drowsy Chu fell back,
Removed his shoes and dusty pack

And dozed upon the ground,
  The scarlet button on his cloak
  Cast scarlet all around.

But still into his wise old head
The lowland troubles crept
So on the mule's moist rump he leapt
And flogged his way ahead,
  The cherries on the hill were grouped
  In patterns white and red.

Then under a dripping cherry tree
He unrolled his silk and pen
And while the mule brayed down the sun
He sketched the rose-blue sky,
  Which wore a tasseled button
  Above the shading tree.

This pleasant poem is reminiscent in technique of some of the poems in Yeats' *In the Seven Woods.* Indeed, Stryk's career parallels Yeats' in several ways. Both write "technically correct" but derivative poetry as youths; both come to a completely new philosophy in middle age; both are reinvigorated enough by this philosophy to produce works of stunning force.

Yet while Yeats' change is a gradual one, Stryk's is abrupt. The pivotal poem in his canon, the one after which all is "changed utterly" is **"Zen: The Rocks of Sesshu."** This poem was begun during a visit Stryk made to Japan to a rock garden built by Sesshu. There Stryk made some comments to the Zen master Tenzan Yasuda which were gently rebuked; Yasuda told Stryk that he was not seeing things properly. Later, sitting in the garden, Stryk experienced what Zennists call *satori,* or a sudden awakening. He began to see things completely differently and to realize, as Zen master Hui-neng says, that one must not look *at* things but *as* things. He began to write a poem about the garden, and found he was writing it in a style completely new for him. The poem took several years to complete and finally consisted of eight sections. Here is the triumphant final section:

Pierced through by birdsong, stone by stone
  The garden
Gathered light. Darkness, hauled by ropes

Of sun, entered roof and bough. Raised from
  The temple
Floor where, stiff since cockcrow,

Blown round like Buddha on the lotus,
  He began
To write. How against that shimmering,

On paper frail as dawn, make poems?
  Firm again,
He waited for the rocks to split.

This poem is a model for the great changes which have occurred in Stryk's work since his Zen awakening. Rhyme is discarded, and the strict stanzaic forms of the sonnet or

the sentence are shelved. What results is not chaos, however, for a new discipline is substituted. Stryk's later poetry generally consists of three line stanzas with a very short middle line. Terseness is all, and the Zen aesthetic of "less is more" is readily apparent. All unnecessary words are eliminated in this quest for stark beauty. How seriously Stryk takes this Zennist need to be concise is seen in *The Penguin Book of Zen Poetry* in which he audaciously transforms Pound's classic poem "In a Station at the Metro" into a haiku.

Faces in a metro:
Petals
On a wet, black bough.

Incredibly, one is hard pressed not to prefer Stryk's version. As Stryk says, the words omitted from Pound's original are superfluous. Of course, Stryk is not trying to outdo or putdown Pound here, but rather to show how a Zennist might have handled the same material. Pound himself praised the later work of Yeats because it is "stripped of the perdamnable rhetoric of poetry." So is the later poetry of Stryk, as all ornamental language disappears, replaced by the language of the everyday world. "Poetry," Stryk says, "consists of saying important things in the fewest possible words."

Another lesson Stryk learns from Zen is to concentrate on specifics. Willa Cather once commented that great art moves from the specific to the general; a Zennist, however, would say that great art begins with the specific and *stays* with the specific. In Zen the absolute and the concrete are one. There is no compulsion in Zen as in much of Western art to take a humble subject and make it a metaphor for something greater, for the Zennist feels the humble necessarily contains the great. Zen master Ch'ing-yuan remarks, "Before I had studied Zen I saw mountains as mountains, waters as waters. When I learned something of Zen, the mountains were no longer mountains, waters no longer waters. But now that I understand Zen, I am at peace with myself, seeing mountains again as mountains, waters as waters." As Stryk begins to understand Zen better his poetry shows an increasing tendency to see things as they are; the contrived conceits of his youthful work vanish, and give way to the directness of a poem like **"Mole."**

Hunched in the basement,
shadow on the wall,
six feet down and glad to be alive.

Overhead, wilting memory
of long dog days,
earthmovers rumble in the haze

through trees, corn, soybeans—
steel, concrete,
glass to come. I need

this burrow, cool, sunken
with roots. What
will remain, I wonder, when

I tunnel up from where I hunch,
    shadow on the wall,
six feet down and glad to be alive.

Basically, of course, this is a poem about something specific, a mole; but in it we can see the absolute. Stryk perhaps tips his hand more than a Japanese Zennist would with the use of such words as "basement" and "six feet down," which necessarily make us think too overtly of the mole's connection with a human, but generally this poem sees a mole as a mole. Surely it is a fine example of Stryk's following Hui-neng's dictum of looking *as* something not *at* it.

As **"Mole"** indicates, Stryk's poetry after his Zen awakening returns to a more ordinary reality. Much of his early work is set in such exotic locales as Iran, Greece, Paris, and the Far East. These poems are also filled with images of restless questing and of feelings of deep despair. After Stryk finds Zen, these images of searching largely disappear, and the settings of his poetry return to his homeland, the American Midwest. Moreover, the despair is replaced by a calm acceptance of all of life. Stryk has had to return home to find his home. As Zen master Tenzan Roshi remarks, "The Zen experience involves the return to one's ordinary self, the most difficult thing in the world." If the romantic poet believes that one can see all of the world in a grain of sand, the Zennist would agree and would add that the Godhead can be found in the humble and the ordinary. Everyday experiences in DeKalb, Illinois, inspire in Stryk such a poem as **"South"**:

Walking at night, I always return to
    the spot beyond
the cannery and cornfields where

a farmhouse faces south among tall trees.
    I dream a life
there for myself, everything happening

in an upper room: reading in sunlight,
    talk, over wine,
with a friend, long midnight poems swept
with stars and a moon. And nothing
        being savaged, anywhere. Having my fill of
            that life,

I imagine a path leading south
    through corn and wheat,
to the Gulf of Mexico! I walk

each night in practice for that walk.

This poem typifies what Stryk's later poetry does so well: it offers a unique blend of Midwestern setting and Zen sensibility. The Zen in this poem is not so overt as to be didactic; instead, it subtly permeates the poem. The poet dreams an idyllic existence of "nothing being savaged" and imagines a path leading all the way to the Gulf of Mexico. However, he is fully aware that what he is thinking is unattainable. As long as things are being savaged in the world, the poet cannot be content; he cannot sit at

peace in an upper room. Instead he walks each night, and he must keep himself constantly prepared for the challenge of an even longer walk. As the poem implies, the Zennist rejects naive idealism just as he rejects nihilism; though knowing his goal is unattainable, the awakened man nonetheless strives for the perfection of all men.

Another major change in Stryk's later work is the focus of his poetry. Much of his early work centers on himself; after *satori* Stryk centers much of his work on his observations of and relations with others. This is part of the Zen notion of selflessness, or *muga*. Zen is a very non-egocentric discipline; one could not remain for long a very personal, confessional poet in it. Instead, shared experience is all-important. This is best illustrated in Stryk's magnificent **"Letter to Jean-Paul Baudot at Christmas"**:

Friend, on this sunny day, snow sparkling
everywhere, I think of you once more,
how many years ago, a child Resistance

fighter trapped by Nazis in a cave
with fifteen others, left to die, you became
a cannibal. Saved by Americans,

the taste of a dead comrade's flesh foul
in your mouth, you fell onto the snow
of the Haute Savoie and gorged to purge
    yourself,
somehow to start again. Each winter since
you were reminded, vomiting for days.
Each winter since you told me at the Mabillon,

I see you on the first snow of the year
spreadeagled, face buried in that stench.
I write once more, Jean-Paul, though you don't

answer, because I must: today men do far worse.
Yours in hope of peace, for all of us,
before the coming of another snow.

There are several levels of shared experience here. Baudot originally has the terrible exerience and he relives it with each first snowfall; he tells it to the poet who in turn relives it himself; the poet then shares the experience with the reader who, if sensitive enough, will relive it himself and will want to share it with others. Commenting on this poem Stryk says:

My friend had an experience which affected him so strongly that forevermore his life was to be poisoned by it. He told me of this experience and then I began to feel it—*quite literally.* I wanted to make the reader feel it too. I have thought that this is almost the greatest hope a poet can have. It's a wanting to share, and it's a totally selfless thing. It's what one feels when one is walking along and one suddenly sees something striking, a sunset or a bird or a flower, and one grabs one's companion's hand and says "Look! Look!" That's what a poem is; there is nothing egocentric about it.

Takahashi, a contemporary Zen poet Stryk has translated, remarks that the artist wishes nothing less than "to change those who stand before (his) poems." This is Stryk's goal as well; he wishes to make us all more sensitive, more understanding, more compassionate. Stryk takes his characters seriously, and he forces us to do so, too. Stryk remarks, "My family and I lived in an old house on South Tenth Street in DeKalb, Illinois, for many years, and I have a poem in *Selected Poems* on practically every tree and house on that block," and, like Sherwood Anderson in *Winesburg, Ohio*, Stryk finds a unique and moving story behind the ordinary facade of each neighbor's house. No subject is considered too humble for poetry, and this, too, is a Zen notion. The Buddha himself said, "My doctrine makes no distinction between high and low, rich and poor; it is like the sky, it has room for all; like water it washes all alike." Stryk's poem **"Rain"** captures the sad aftermath of an affair between a young girl's father and her babysitter; **"The Unknown Neighbor"** is a tribute to a man whose sudden death affects the poet more than it does the widow; **"The Loser"** sympathetically examines the town drunk. **"Shadow"** is an especially moving expression of the poet's compassion:

> Always coming, neat head
> tilted, "Mad" Nolgate
> shadows these streets for years,
>
> surviving playground taunts,
> the school's Least Likely.
> Prompt as the townclock,
> passes old classmates
> at work, flusters wives
> wilting by chain-store greens,
>
> scattering their kids—
> thunder on pavement,
> storming through grass.
>
> Let loose inside himself,
> cushioned in air,
> he walks on forever.

In *On Moral Fiction* John Gardner writes, "Without will—the artist's determination to take his characters and their problems seriously—no artist can achieve real compassion. And without compassion . . . no artist can summon the will to make true art." Stryk's later poetry blends will and compassion with the buoyancy and terseness of *zenki* to produce morally moving and aesthetically pleasing poems.

One of the clearest statements of the Zen aesthetic of Stryk is found in the poem **"Oeuvre."**

> Will it ever be finished, this house
> Of paper
> I began to raise when I was seventeen?
>
> Others scramble from foundations far less firm.
> Seasons of
> Pondering, name by name, the past's magnificent,
>
> A squandering. Surely I might have lived.
> Spitefully
> Watching as rivals stole the girls, got the jobs,

> Won the laurels, the misery seeped in,
> Tinting the
> Windows, darkening the fairest day.
>
> But how should I have known, a house to please
> Need not be
> Outlandish? And that searching everywhere
>
> The fresh, the rare, prowling the gaudier
> Capitals,
> Something of each would rub off, deface.
>
> Well, we build where and as we can. There are
> Days when I
> Am troubled by an image of the house,
>
> Laden, rootless, like a tinseled tree,
> Suddenly
> Torn to a thousand scribbled leaves and borne
> off
>
> By the wind, then to be gathered and patched
> Whole again,
> Or of the thing going up in smoke
>
> And I, the paper dreamer, wide awake.

Stryk's house of poems is not an outlandish one; surely there are gaudier ones. Its foundation, though, is firm, since it is built on the bedrock of Zen. This is not to say that any poet who is a Zennist has it made; on the contrary, the poet of **"Ouevre"** realizes that though literature is permanent it is also very fragile, since it is made of paper. Thus, a Zennist is constantly fearful that his whole poetic world may someday blow away; a Zennist thus cannot afford the luxury of complacency. He must be always awake and alert.

There is a Zen saying which reads "Poetry and Zen are of a savor." An examination of the poetry of Lucien Stryk reveals that a proper reply to this might be, "Not necessarily." Stryk's early poetry has no taste of Zen in it; it represents instead a false start into an aesthetic dead end. But with his poems written since his awakening Lucien Stryk has enriched the lives of all those who know his work. In the words of Jim Harrison, a fine poet himself, Stryk's poems are as bright and as pure as "a ball of light." Zen has given Stryk the aesthetic to produce works filled with what the Zennists call *yugen*—a stark dignity and a subtle and graceful profundity. And even if his work does not necessarily prove the Zen adage that "Poetry and Zen are of a savor" it does confirm another Zen proverb: "The finer poetry is, the more matured its Zen is."

Jay S. Paul (essay date 1980)

SOURCE: "Renewal of Intimacy: Lucien Stryk's Metaphor of Comprehension," *Chicago Review*, Vol. 32, No. 2, Autumn, 1980, pp. 30-40.

[*In the following essay, Paul provides a thematic and stylistic analysis of Stryk's poetry.*]

In one of his most moving poems Lucien Stryk addresses a letter to a friend he has not seen in years. The man, Jean-Paul Baudot, fought the Nazis and, when trapped in a cave, was forced to feed on dead comrades. Upon his rescue, Baudot devoured snow to cleanse himself. As a student in Paris following World War II, Stryk was sitting in a cafe with Baudot, discussing a lecture, when his friend hastily departed. Some time later, Stryk discovered that Baudot could not help retching at the sight of the first snow of the year. Writing as *he* watches the first snow, Stryk asserts that, even though they have been out of contact, he can empathize with the experience of horror. Stryk also wishes to console his friend. "Today men do far worse," he confides, late in the poem (*Selected Poems*, Swallow, 1976, p. 135).

"Letter to Jean-Paul Baudot, at Christmas" epitomizes the dilemmas in many of Stryk's poems. First, mortality in its various forms—war, aging, airplane crashes—is the primary antagonist: the speaker is horrified by what he has experienced. Second, he must overcome isolation in order to speak. Yet, even though he *needs* to speak, he must be decorous. Maintaining this equilibrium generates much of the drama in Stryk's poems. To study the rhetoric is to watch a voice thread its delicate way between self-indulgence and aloofness. When Stryk is at his best, one finds himself squarely between the immensity of horror and the vastness of love. Like the man in Frost's "Stopping by Woods on a Snowy Evening," one faces the void in two guises.

Moments of candor, such as the culmination of **"Letter to Jean-Paul Baudot, at Christmas,"** are the capstone of Stryk's work. They occur when the drama of the situation coincides with that of the mind, when what Stryk wants to say is most worth saying and emerges forcefully from his material.

Discussing the rhetoric of Stryk's poems raises difficult questions. First, one wonders whether the poem is a vehicle for the statement or whether the speaking is part of the metaphor. The same question has been posed about Frost's work, and we have learned how important drama is in qualifying his statements. While Stryk's statements must be likewise considered in the context of the poems, they come off as less qualified by their context than most of Frost's. Second, one wonders whether the poem is to stand on its own or to be comprehended in terms of the *oeuvre*. Stryk's fullest poems are independent (I will talk about several of these, some of which have been largely ignored by commentators), but most resonate with other poems. The care Stryk takes in arranging the poems in his books attests to his sense of their interrelatedness. Third, one wonders which is responsible for the speaker's reticence, the immensity of horror or the intensity of his love. An answer to this question seems impossible and unnecessary, for the crucial fact is that love and horror often seem inseparable.

With these questions in mind, along with the paradigm of **"Letter to Jean-Paul Baudot, at Christmas,"** I wish to discuss Stryk's work in such a way that the significance of the paradigm becomes clear. Enough of Stryk's poems culminate in candor that one regards them as re-enactments of knowing. More precisely, Stryk's strategy is synecdoche. A brief exchange between people suggests the profundity of that relationship and of relationships in general. In other words, "approaching the other" dramatizes acquiring experience.

Tracing the impulse to know the other, whether that be person, place or nothingness, one finds a continuum. At one extreme are poems implying the speaker's isolation; at the other are poems in which he reaches the other and establishes some form of intimacy. Such a scheme serves as a means of (1) recognizing the range of Stryk's voice and (2) comprehending the profundity of reaching the other. In the first part of this essay I shall summarize Stryk's portrayal of the process of comprehension—purpose, pitfalls and rewards; in the second part I shall examine dramatic poems which demonstrate Stryk's ability to coordinate situation and statement. Again and again Lucien Stryk has tried to tell us how horrible life can be; simultaneously he has expressed how vital love is in the face of that horror.

I

Candor manifests clarity of mind. This freedom from desire and other interference by the ego is the goal of the Zen practitioner. It is the same "coldness" of vision that Wallace Stevens articulates in "The Snow Man," which makes "the listener" "nothing himself" and lets him "behold[s] /Nothing that is not there and the nothing that is," Coldness, of course, does not imply inhumanity, but something closer to honesty or objectivity. In discussing his work, Stryk habitually refers to his poem **"Zen: The Rocks of Sesshu"** as pivotal in his personal development.[1] Appropriately, the poem is his clearest rendering of the process of perception, of the discipline of "pointing" the mind until the perceiver and the perceived are no longer separate. "Clear the mind!" the poet cries toward the end of the poem, "Empty it of all that / Fixes you, / Makes every act a pecking at the crumb" (p. 38). "Disburdenment is what mind seeks / Above all other riches," he muses in **"Snows"** (p. 57). Many of the poems in *Awakening* (1973), particularly the title poem and another meditative sequence, **"The Duckpond,"** show his ability to project himself to and into the other.

What makes perception difficult and vital is the abundance of horror in the poet's world. **"The Pit"** recounts three young soldiers' mission to bury the reeking dead during the Pacific campaign in World War II. **"Return to Hiroshima"** depicts the impossibility of forgetting the horror of atomic holocaust. (In a more recent poem, **"The Faces,"** the central image of which reminds one of the fifty-ninth and sixtieth lines of Lowell's "For the Union Dead," the speaker is haunted by "a boy's face, doomed, / sharply beautiful" shown at the start of each installment of a war documentary (p. 136). Horror—and terror—is by no means limited to war. The speaker is angered by the difficult working conditions of Japanese women in **"The Mine: Yamaguchi"**; he and his wife have been unable to forget their dread during an earthquake ("**The Quake**"); he tells in "**That Woman There**" of a woman frantic for some lost hope—"Every night she stands with arms upraised, / High throat twisting in the streetlamp's noose" (p. 53). Even in a Boston restroom he is not exempt: he finds a man's demand for his own electric razor so intimidating that he hands it over and runs ("**Boston**").

To approach the other in such a milieu, one's spirit and body must be engaged. To Stryk these fuse in any act of love; therefore, it is useful to discuss them simultaneously. I mention them separately here, at the outset of the discussion, to emphasize their unity. Approaching the other—a loved one, perhaps—involves crossing "something / between us" (p. 50), whether it be the metaphorical jungle gorge in "**The Gorge**" or the disagreements dramatized in "**For Helen**" and "**Love Poem.**" The clearest metaphor of the fullness of the commitment is the poem "**Map**":

> I unfold it on the desk
> to trace you once again.
> Though cut off by a smudge
>
> of mountains, ropes
> of water stretched between,
> how easily I spread a hand
> across the space that separates.
>   But this
> cramped sheet, while true,
>
> does not tell all. What of
> that span no map will ever
> show, sharper for being unseen?
>
>   (p. 119)

The encounter with the "madman" in "**Christ of Pershing Square**" shows that contact need not be pleasant to be memorable. The poet has his hand pressed against the sutured palm and is then accused of having killed this Christ. The poet cannot help whispering, ". . . There remains / The final proof—forgiveness" (p. 80). Although the madman spits in his face and flees, his spectre haunts the poet for months.

The unpredictability of encounters is a constant reminder of the dangers of human pride. "**And They Call This Living!**" is one of the finest renderings of this in Stryk's work. The speaker and his wife have grown tired of having the seaside disappoint their expectations. "For once, we said, accept / The ruddy show just as it's always been. . . ." (p. 68). Almost immediately, however, a gust springs up, disrupting the scene and their morning activities. Like the mystic and the Zen practitioner, Stryk knows the dangers of pride. That is what causes the mountain climber to slip in "**The Final Slope**"; that is what precludes perception in the third and fourth parts of "**Zen: The Rocks of Sesshu.**" Pride and its concomitant preconceptions raise the emotional and intellectual stakes too high for one to stay clear-headed. One might become "crazed with fear," like the frantic animal in "**The Squirrel**" (p. 64), or expect the wrong things of nature, like the girl in the

eighth part of "**The Duckpond**," who assumes that the ducks cavort for her pleasure. Too watchful, one may even become a kind of grotesque, as "**Forward Observers**" suggests. In that poem the men with "lensed hill-splitting eyes" are "part of something coming, vile as war" (p. 133).

The poem "**Snow**" pivots on the dichotomy between pride and disinterested impulse, the sort that moves Zen artists (*cf.* "**To a Japanese Poet,**" based on an encounter with Shinkichi Takahashi, in which such inspiration occurs). Two-thirds of "**Snow**" parodies the conventional treatment of snow that produces "much snow, / little poetry." The pure writer, on the other hand, "feels / his hand move" (p. 95). He finds himself suddenly awake. (As Karl Elder observed in a review of Stryk's *Awakening* [*Margins,* No. 11, April-May 1974, p. 49], the writer's mind is like the bluejay in "**After the Storm**" "dart[ing] from branch to branch" "like a startled eye" [p. 99].)

The awakened imagination's role is, for example, essential to the deep calm depicted in "**The Edge.**" Apart from town and its demands, the poet and his wife have "listened . . . to the animals" in the nearby woods until they feel "part of the stillness with the dark" (p. 117). Likewise, while participating in the funeral of a young man he loved, the poet imagines "the long red hair / he could not stop from coiling round . . . [his detractors'] throats" ("**Elegy for a Long-Haired Student,**" p. 93).

The imagination, however, is not always so disinterestedly alert. In "**Torero**" the spectators, in contrast to the pragmatic bullfighter, invent symbolic roles (dancer, butcher, priest, martyr) for him. The speaker in "**To Roger Blin**" is embarrassed at having done the same with the director, having "Fantasized . . . your life" into "a path, / a way, the art / to make life possible" (p. 127). An imagining just as desperate occurs when the poet thinks he has run over a goose and in his distraction sees "a whiteness / mangled / in the maples, everywhere" ("**The Goose,**" p. 96).

One can recognize the importance of the imagination by considering "**Keats House,**" in which the speaker admits that he has been unable to imagine his subject fully. Moving amid Keats's possessions, the poet muses, "Sad—I get the feel of him . . . yet something's gone," and turns his attention to things that inspired Keats (p. 130). Then, instead of depicting Keats, the speaker discusses the weather.

From poems in which imagination is most effectual one might infer that such success depends on complementary experience. "**Farmer,**" a recent poem that is placed last in *Selected Poems*, presents a person who, like a Zen practitioner, has spent "Seasons waiting the miracle, / dawn after dawn framing / the landscape in his eyes," and has been "Made shrewd / by solid and weather" and come to feel "ways of animals" in "the channels of his bones" and "their matings twist his dreams." His identification with the environment is so practiced and profound that "he shelters in the farmhouse / merged with trees, a skin of wood, / as much the earth's as his" (p. 136).

II

Like his farmer, Stryk values the intimacy of shared experience. His narrators characteristically recount some of that before making their candid utterances. As in Frost's dramatic poems, what *is* said evokes the vastness of the relationship. The tension is between "intimacy" (what is shared) and "decorum" (what ought to be said). The constraints of brevity and reticence propel the reader's imagination into the unspoken and unseen. Stryk's rhetoric, then, is the verbal effort to bridge "something / between us" (p. 50), knowing full well that the true subject is "that span no map will ever / show" (p. 119). While **"Letter to Jean-Paul Baudot, at Christmas"** may be the culmination of such efforts, several other poems provide frames of reference necessary to understand its place in Stryk's *oeuvre*.

"To a Japanese Poet," based on an outing with the eminent Zen poet Shinkichi Takahashi, whose work Stryk translates, dramatizes how essential decorum is. Although it is possible to regard the poem as testimony of the spontaneity of Takahashi's mind—

When the poem came,
Your fingers loosened and you
Spoke the dozen words as if
Directing one who'd
Lost his way upon
A mountain path, the night descending.

—the lesson emerges from Takahashi's manner afterward. He avoids Stryk during the rest of the outing, "As if I'd surprised you / In some intimacy." Stryk recognizes the seriousness of his impropriety and apologizes. Takahashi's reply is brilliant in its tact: "Why should you / Have felt badly? We had an enjoyable outing" (p. 35). The older poet is honest but reserved, which is characteristic of Stryk's speakers.

They simply do not confide in strangers. Candid love songs like **"The Anniversary"** and the fifth part of **"Persian Suite"** spring from years of intimacy with a loved one, but even between lovers candor requires repeated effort. **"To Helen"** illustrates how important the right word can be in reviving intimacy. After the speaker and his wife "parry frowns" about feeling old, he entreats, "Look, we're in this / together," knowing the power of the statement: "that / never fails, you're in . . . my arms and young" (p. 118). Like incantation, the proper words retrieve a past moment, elicit a genuine response and rekindle love.

Longstanding love also has its unhappy moments. In **"My Daughter's Aquarium,"** "half answers" provoke temporary estrangement (p. 109). In **"Fishing with My Daughter in Miller's Meadow,"** the outing enables the poet to speak shyly of his fondness:

It's fish I think

I'm after, you I almost catch, in up to knees,
        sipping minnowy
water. Well, I hadn't hoped for more.

(p. 98)

"Rites of Passage" climaxes in the poet's recognition that he cannot keep his son his own. The men have been walking a woodland "path / we've loved for years" (p. 101). Their intimacy makes the impending separation excruciating:

My son moves toward the bank, then turns.
I stop myself from grasping
        at his hand.

(p. 102)

Comprehension, then, involves renewed intimacy. The greater the separation, the more difficult it is to regain this intimacy. **"Lament for Weldon Kees," "Friendship,"** and **"Dean Dixon, Welcome Home,"** presenting situations in which the speaker tries to restore intimacy after a considerable period of separation, may be regarded as poems that anticipate the achievement of **"Baudot."**

"Friendship" is the least satisfying. Having learned of a friend's difficulties, the poet writes a letter to comfort him. Instead of dramatizing the intimacy, Stryk chooses metaphor to characterize the letter. With phrases like "my scroll of bandages and kisses, / my dried and flattened heart," the poem veers toward sentimentality and self-consciousness (p. 123).

Narrative proves more effective. In **"Dean Dixon, Welcome Home"** he remembers the black conductor's early career before welcoming him as "friend" (p. 128). This word, in final position, bespeaks warmth and good intentions. In **"Lament for Weldon Kees,"** however, narrative yields mixed success. Stryk recounts his friendship with Kees, "My first live poet," to express bewilderment at the loss ("Weldon, where the blazes are you?" [p. 81]), and to acknowledge increased comprehension of suicide:

Later, when I heard that you were lost,

Your car parked too near the bridge,
I wonder which of us had left it there.
By then I too was hanging from the edge.

(pp. 81-82)

While the relationship with Kees is developed vividly, the end of the poem retains overtones of self-congratulation that undercut its effectiveness.

Two other poems, **"Objet d'Art"** and **"The Dream,"** supply one more frame of reference necessary to appreciate the achievement of **"Letter to Jean-Paul Baudot, at Christmas."** On the one hand, **"Objet d'Art"** develops a situation in which speech is unnecessary and inappropriate. The poet remembers that a Persian who once took tea with him wept at the sight of the copper bowl in which tobacco was stored. The significance of the bowl thus increased, the poet says, "I no longer smoke in / Company, / It seems indecent" (p. 56). Whereas shared grief is the occasion for candor in **"Baudot,"** here it requires silence. **"The Dream,"** on the other hand, depicts the *violation* of the other, a terrifying picture of what happens when decorum disappears. Finding himself in "a zoo of reptiles" straining their bonds to attack him, he proceeds "unafraid" to a "harem" of naked women, there apparently for his pleasure (p. 75). Some of the faces are familiar, so he is in a position to violate people he has known. That "They tried to win him / With demureness" underlines the fact that the dream offers fulfillment of longstanding fantasies. He moves along the line, fondling, until he realizes that the last body, "posed, small hands raising / Breasts," is "his mother's." He rushes off, feeling "cheated" and repulsed, unable to find the gate and forced to leap the wall into the sea (p. 176).

It is not only Stryk's ability to balance intimacy and decorum, but also the persistence of this effort, that make **"Letter to Jean-Paul Baudot, at Christmas"** a climactic achievement. To write to a friend he has not heard from for years in an attempt to explain, as convincingly as he can on paper, his empathy for the horror that has long plagued Baudot, is the severest test of tact: Stryk must convey that horror without debasing the memory of the friend.

Stryk solves his rhetorical dilemma by stressing not the motives for cannibalism, but the impact of Baudot's having survived the act—upon Baudot, and upon Stryk himself. In the course of the letter Stryk's voice modulates from polite to familiar; simultaneously, he shifts from apostrophe to narrative to articulate his compassion, to imply the difficulty in sustaining such intimacy, and to understate his anger with mankind. Letter as well as poem, **"Baudot"** attests to the constancy of Stryk's love.

"Letter to Jean-Paul Baudot, at Christmas"

Friend, on this sunny day, snow sparkling
everywhere, I think of you once more,
how many years ago, a child Resistance

fighter trapped by Nazis in a cave
with fifteen others, left to die, you became
a cannibal. Saved by Americans,

the taste of a dead comrade's flesh foul
in your mouth, you fell onto the snow
of the Haute Savoie and gorged to purge yourself,
somehow to start again. Each winter since
you were reminded, vomiting for days.
Each winter since you told me at the Mabillon,

I see you on the first snow of the year
spreadeagled, face buried in that stench.
I write once more, Jean-Paul, though you don't

answer, because I must: today men do far worse.
Yours in hope of peace, for all of us,
before the coming of another snow.

                                        (p. 135)

There are two statements of purpose for Stryk's writing to Jean-Paul, one implied ("I think of you once more"), the other explicit ("I write once more . . . because I must"). The difference in motive underlying each statement indicates the degree of intensity of the poet's feelings. Whereas the first, opening with "Friend"—a warm but polite word of greeting—describes the occasion for writing and intimates good will, and seems to be prompted by the poet's surroundings ("this sunny day, snow sparkling / everywhere"), the second, occurring after the poet has recollected the horror of Baudot's past (which has become a horror in his own life), is familiar ("Jean-Paul") and intended solely for the individual. Stryk is full of compassion: he sees past the beauty of the present to the squalor of Baudot's past, and in reliving Baudot's grief, Stryk finds himself compelled to speak in judgment ("Today men do far worse"). Though the final two lines may be considered the denouement, by mentioning the snow—now symbolizing guilt—Stryk reaffirms his love of Baudot and his great concern for the actions of humankind.

By the occurrence of "Jean-Paul," Stryk has dropped the polite for the familiar, the past for the present, and the remote for the immediate. The shift from polite to familiar diction is gradual. The language of the first two tercets is mild, dictated by the occasion, and is a means of showing Baudot that Stryk wishes to resume discourse: he uses only one shocking word, "cannibal," without dwelling on its implications. Later, however, he describes in detail Jean-Paul's reaction to his own act of cannibalism, capped by the word "stench." The latter two changes can be specifically located: line 13 introduces, mid-sentence, the present tense, underscoring the poet's full comprehension of the horror; with line 12 ("you told me"), the last time Baudot serves as subject of a sentence and the first explicit mention of their relationship since line 2, Stryk resumes an active role. Thus, he has prepared Baudot and the reader for his two greatest rhetorical risks: the assertion (lines 13-14) that he empathizes with Baudot through imagination and memory, and the statement (lines 15-16) of his outrage. Encouraged by the revived intimacy, Stryk assumes a cosmic vantage point in the denouement and he regards the future ("the coming of another snow"), an act in which he detaches himself from Baudot and the moment of recollection. The customary closing, "your," suggests the poet's realization that the charged moment has begun to fade.

Throughout the poem, Stryk takes great care that his subject does not become sensational, that the reader react how and when he should. The stanza division after "Resistance" and the line break after "became" muffle the impact of the story early in the discourse, and offer momentary reprieve from the full horror. "Saved by Americans," following "cannibal," could be taken as an ironic quip about American self-righteousness, but more likely provides the reader with more relief. Concluding line 7 with "foul" properly focuses the reader's attention on the reaction to eating, not the act itself.

But I think the fourth tercet epitomizes Stryk's control of voice. The recurrence of the word "since" gives the reader an opportunity to understand the poem's turning. In line 10 the colloquial use of "since", part of the adverbial phrase "Each winter since," conveys the poet's grief; its final position in the line stresses the remoteness of Baudot's compulsive retching. In its second appearance "since" is less prominent, specifying the winter in question; yet, it becomes the means of approaching Baudot by memory because that winter was the winter when Stryk first knew him. Thus, in a poem which is built around a flashback, it is appropriate that a word denoting time would coincide with the poet's emotional closing with his subject.

By examining poems in which Lucien Stryk dramatizes human interaction one can appreciate the link between such poems and his well-known and more obviously Zen-influenced meditative poems like **"Zen: The Rocks of Sesshu," "Awakening,"** and **"The Duckpond."** Approaching the other, and the renewal of intimacy, epitomize the process of comprehension underlying all of Stryk's work. Only by risking the unknown that is the other person can one appreciate the need for genuine communion, and when such a situation *demands* a statement and the poet makes such a statement decorously but still tellingly, the reader, too, participates in the process of comprehension.

As much as one analyzes and talks of technique, though, what is most important in any poetry is its vision. Living through and after World War II, Stryk had had to deepen his compassion against a backdrop of atrocity. As he says in "Making Poems," his essay in William Heyen's *American Poets in 1976*, he has learned from the poets he most admires—Takahashi, and Zbigniew Herbert of Poland—"to get 'beyond poetry.'" Stryk says this in the context of a comment of T. S. Eliot's: "poetry so transparent that in reading it we are intent on what the poem *points at*, and not on the poetry, this seems to me the thing to try for. To get *beyond poetry*, as Beethoven, in his later works, strove to get *beyond* music." With countless other artists, Stryk strives for the capacity to look not "*at* things," but to look "*as* things."

NOTES

[1] John Somer, "The Zen Aesthetic: An Interview with Lucien Stryk," *Chicago Review*, 25, 3 (1973), pp. 62-72; Lucien Stryk, "Making Poems" in *American Poets in 1976*, ed. William Heyen (Indianapolis: The Bobbs-Merrill Company, Inc., 1976), pp. 392-406; and Gregory Fitz Gerald and Anthony Piccione, "Zen Poetry: A Conversation with Lucien Stryk," *American Poetry Review*, 6, 4 (1977), 33-36.

Gary Steven Corseri (essay date 1985)

SOURCE: "Journeying Eastward, Journeying Home," in *The Georgia Review*, Vol. XXXIX, No. 4, Winter, 1985, pp. 864-70.

[*In the following essay, Corseri explores influence of Zen Buddhism on Stryk's verse and poetic philosophy.*]

I

I know very well that Zen is above explanation, and that a Westerner may find expository remarks in a Zen interview inadequate. Nonetheless, an exchange between a Westerner and a Japanese master might very well

serve as a stimulant toward the reader's further efforts for a better appreciation of Zen.

Forewarned is forearmed, and Lucien Stryk serves us well in quoting Rinzai Master Taigan Takayama before the first of sixteen interviews with various practitioners who explore the world of Zen. A prolific writer on the subject—as well as the brilliant translator of Japanese Zen poet Shinkichi Takahashi and a noted poet himself—Stryk is aptly positioned to guide the uninitiated and the curious through this mysterious, intriguing territory. But the way is not clear-cut, and our guide does not avoid all the pitfalls.

The Westward movement of the American frontier is now butting against Asia; the "Pacific Basin" is the shibboleth of the age. Weaned from their European somnambulism, our poets have slowly discovered the millennia-old traditions of the East. Seers and prophets like Whitman, Emerson, and Thoreau were influenced by Eastern thought before the Civil War. Lafcadio Hearn carried the flame at the turn of the century. But it is really since the 1960's, with the disillusionments following the ennui and materialistic complacencies of the Eisenhower years, the deepening crisis in Vietnam, and the reemergence of Japan as an international power, that this intellectual/spiritual tropism has acquired the momentum of a manifest destiny.

Just as a new love impels a reexamination of the self and may shake us into discarding what we thought intrinsic, so the journey to the East must quintessentially change the content of American cultural and spiritual life. Yet there are dangers: the human chrysalis must know what it has been as well as where it is going, and in this regard, Stryk does not ably inform us.

The first part of *Encounter*, consisting of six essays, provides the basic exposition of the subject. It is here that we most vividly encounter and lament Stryk's conceits and preconceptions:

Unlike dialogue in the Socratic tradition, in which the dominant party defends a viewpoint, Zen dialogue is at all times intensely exploratory. . . . It is revelation which, at all times, is sought, and this accounts for the gravity of Zen dialogue.

If the gadfly of Athens is guilty of intellectual authoritarianism, as Stryk asserts, if Socrates sought not revelation and the puncturing of sophism, I'd suggest that Plato's dialogues have been misread these 2,500 years. Further on, we are informed that

. . . the differences between Western and Eastern, particularly Buddhist, dialogues are due to the former being based on the effort of the stronger party to formulate and defend ideas . . . whereas the latter concerns problems of a more ontological order: the question most frequently heard in Western dialogue is "Who am I?" in Buddhist, "What am I?" In other words, the Occident's view of the natural scheme is essentially idealistic, with everything in its place and man somewhere in the center—doubting and perplexed at times . . . but never questioning his right to be, perpetually. This view of the world may be the source—and the result—of the West's reliance on empiricism, which can be made to offer proofs and invest the shakiest theories with invincibility. It is also behind the West's distrust of intuition and the Eastern penchant for will-lessness, which it has somewhat scornfully named "quietism."

Unfortunately, Stryk's summation of the two worlds can only tend to obscure and illegitimize, rather than clarify and substantiate. His calumnies on empiricism badly misrepresent the best scientific tradition, from Democritus to Einstein. Further, the West's distrust of intuition may be less the result of a proclivity for empiricism than it is the outcome of a thousand years of darkness following the sacking of Rome. During that crucible, intuition wed with fear, ignorance, and poverty to produce witch burnings, public flagellation, and the Inquisition.

Stryk's principal, regrettable tack is to illuminate Eastern thought by contrasting it with, and denigrating, Western. This simply will not do. Stryk ardently spurns a syncretistic approach, time and again celebrating Zen's elitist exclusivism. His approach is that of a proponent, a champion, rather than a critical explicator. The underlying, unanswered puzzle of the books is to find what accounts for Stryk's aversion to the West. One suspects it may simply be a too-simplistic understanding.

> The failure . . . of much Western philosophy . . . is due largely to its being too easily acquired, calling for very little discipline and sacrifice. . . . If one reads Plato and approves of his view . . . one is automatically a Platonist; if one "understands" the phenomenologists and appreciates the imaginative writing of . . . Sartre . . . one can call oneself an Existentialist, and so on. Of course, there are Occidentals who accept . . . a rather spurious neo-Buddhism. . . . Yet when one takes into account the varying capacities among men, one finds it possible to tolerate almost anything, even the apparent need for escapism satisfied by a strange doctrine. By and large, Western response to Buddhism is based on the most human of needs, that of self-understanding.

Even if we overlook the many contradictions in this passage, we shall have to consult St. John of the Cross, Mother Teresa, or Thomas Merton to ascertain the ease with which spiritual credentials may be obtained by Westerners. In his attempts to elevate Buddhism above "flawed" Western dogmas, Stryk becomes guilty of dogma himself. He seems especially put out with Existentialism:

> No philosophy is more realistic in its methods and aims than Buddhism. Much has been said in recent years about the realism of Existentialism, and many presumably consider it to be a total philosophy . . . yet its chief theorist and spokesman, Jean Paul Sartre . . . speaks of death as the one absurdity, an abyss before which man must tremble. In so far as such an attitude betrays a slavish attachment to life . . . Existentialism is, in comparison with Buddhism, an incomplete, thus unsatisfactory philosophy.

Such sweeping characterizations must always be suspect. Despite his endorsement of Zen's antirelativism, Stryk constantly dictates his hierarchical preferences. In spite of its different view of death, Existentialism also propounds a philosophy for decent, brave, and dignified living. Notwithstanding Zen's ideal of calm acceptance in the face of calamity, the Master and premier writer on Noh drama, Zeami, bewailed the death of his son and vilified his own art as so much vain attachment.

Stryk is a great admirer of the haiku and sumi-e, styles of poetry and painting that impress one with their power and brevity. Thus, Basho probes the profoundest metaphysical mysteries in seventeen syllables; in a few bold lines Sessh can depict both backbreaking labor and natural grace. Asked to explain his view of Western art, one of Stryk's interviewees replies: "Western art has volume and richness when it is good. Yet to me it is too thickly encumbered by what is dispensable. It's as if the Western artist were trying to hide something, not reveal it." Stryk thanks the man for answering his questions so frankly and thoughtfully.

And that's that. Except we wish we were in his place to ask some questions of our own. What one wants in *Encounter with Zen* is someone less deferential, less ill-disposed toward defending the breadth of the Sistine Chapel, the chiaroscuro nuances of "The Night Watch," the passion of "Starry Night." One may call oneself anything one pleases, but in fact it is not so easy to be a Platonist, to view life and art in a "hard, Sophoclean light," to reconcile the opposites, to discover our common, essential humanity. Stryk reduces the vast, variegated body of Western thought to a straw man as he supports the edifice of Buddhist/Eastern philosophy. He provides scant historical or cultural context for the rise of Buddhism, his assumptions about Western culture are facile, and his lack of historical perspective is egregious.

Perhaps Western institutions are in decline today—and this is arguable—not because of the failure of empiricism, but because of their vigorous performance in the last four hundred years. They may simply be played out, spent, on one of Toynbee's cycles. Buddhist societies have also had their crests and troughs—of which fact Stryk seems unaware.

II

Because of its emphasis on the aesthetic value of Zen, *Encounter* provides a kind of metronome for Stryk's **Collected Poems**. Although Zen cannot be "used" by artists, all of the interviewees, many of whom *are* artists, aver the profound changes in personality occurring as a result of *satori* (revelation) or *zazen* (meditation). **Collected Poems** covers the three decades from 1953 to 1983. Stryk's first of four journeys to Japan took place some twenty years ago; thus we may be able to chart his progress as a poet and a man of Zen in his collected volume. Such progress in *Encounter* is far more difficult to consider because neither essays nor interviews are dated.

A good poet, Randall Jarrell said, is one who stands in thunderstorms for a lifetime and manages to get hit by lightning some half-dozen times; a great poet, a dozen or two dozen times. Not including the translations of Shinkichi Takashashi, there are certainly some half-dozen fine poems in this collection.

Some of the poems have a Zen or Oriental flavor, but most do not. In the first three books one espies banalities like "blistered fields," "staring eyes," "the sweet / Rush of water to the / Aching throat," "the wonder / Of need beyond fulfillment." In parts of the third book, however, Stryk finds a clearer, steadier voice. **"Hearn in Matsue"** is one of the pearls of the collection:

> The fame did not surprise: it had awaited
> Him like those fragrant ports of forty
>   Years ago
> The tall black hulls of home. It fit him, and he
> Wore it as he felt, deservingly.

Juxtapose that straightforward elegance and natural cadence with the stilted beginning of **"The Revolutionary"**: "Who was it said that men to forge ahead / Must jell into a mob composed of as / Many minds, fused singly, as it has heads?" Often the fault is not a starchy overreaching, but just the opposite, a prosaic flaccidity such as this: "There are // Many ways to dodge reality, / Hundreds of states preferable / To the kind of life we own." Or this, from his most recent book:

> the book with all the
> answers on the shelf. I
> doodle on one, thumb
>
> through the other, now
> and then. This hour, it
> makes no difference.
>
> I sit back, let thoughts
> come as they may.

Poetry is the art of enoughness, what Keats called "a fine excess." Much of Stryk's work reveals a man who is either trying too hard or not hard enough. Poets, Edith Hamilton wrote of Catullus, must be judged by their best work; books, on the other hand, are judged by their cumulative effect.

There is so much prosaic matrix in these 198 pages that the good lines stand out like crows in a winter landscape. Notwithstanding, this book has enough redeeming qualities to recommend it to the discerning, patient reader. As Stryk's poems are not to be noted for their verbal dexterities or imaginative scope, we must look elsewhere to know how to value them. His best work concerns quotidian themes, as does **"The Ordinary,"** presented here in full:

> To love the ordinary—
> fifty feet of dandelions
>   and burdock

> and a small house perched
> on concrete under a dying
>   Chinese elm.

> To be content with neighbor-
> banter over a crooked fence,
>   days, nights, years.

> And not to regret—sun
> touching the willow-oak—
>   some Elsewhere.

In a way, this poem epitomizes Stryk's work. He is a poet of the ordinary, the small delights of the everyday—a middle-class intellectual passing his life in suburbia. In poems like **"Evelyn,"** **"Barbecue,"** **"Friendship,"** **"Constellation,"** and **"Summer"** we glimpse a man who has made peace with himself, his family, and his neighbors. Celebrating simple moments of beauty and wonder—what Robert Hayden called "love's austere and lonely offices"—Stryk accomplishes the Zen ideal of being wholly here in the moment, open to its eternal, evanescent magic:

"Busker"

> Facing the playhouse queue,
> straining through songs
>
> all can remember, she muffs
> a high note at the end.
>
> As we start to shuffle in,
> she scrambles for the loot.
>
> Fat, seedy—never mind—
> she is so purely what she is
>
> no actor could do more.
> Leaving the queue, I follow
>
> her all night, hands full of coins,
> songs ringing everywhere.

Zen is anticonceptualist, antirationalist. In **"Fishing with My Daughter in Miller's Meadow,"** Stryk reminds us that most great discoveries are serendipitous:

> It's fish I think
>
> I'm after, you I almost catch, in up to knees,
>   sipping minnowy
> water. Well, I hadn't hoped for more.
>
> Going back, you heap the creel with phlox and
>   marigolds.

It's as though three spirits warred within this poet. If he will forgo the forced, contorted Latinate diction and discard the pedestrian simplicities, his next book could be his triumph.

Stryk has already earned a niche in contemporary literature as a translator of Shinkichi Takahashi. Considered by many to be the finest and purest Zen poet writing today, Takahashi in his section of **Collected Poems** opens a window on Chagall-like moments of the metaphorical, chillingly recognized as the here-and-now:

"Fish"

I hold a newspaper, reading.
Suddenly my hands become cow ears,
Then turn into Pusan, the South Korean port.

Lying on a mat
Spread on the bankside stones,
I fell asleep.
But a willow leaf, breeze stirred,
Brushed my ear.
I remained just as I was,
Near the murmurous water.

When young there was a girl
Who became a fish for me.
Whenever I wanted fish
Broiled in salt, I'd summon her.
She'd get down on her stomach
To be sun-cooked on the stones.
And she was always ready!

Alas, she no longer comes to me.
An old benighted drake,
I hobble homeward.
But look, my drake feet become horse hoofs!
Now they drop off
And, stretching marvelously,
Become the tracks of the Tokaido Railway Line.

Often, Takahashi's work has as much to do with surrealism and dadaism as with Zen, and some of it seems perversely hermetic. But in his best, we see that wonderful process by which the imagination and the world transform one another. The familiar, the quotidian, is metamorphosed into the odd and peculiar—and vice versa. It is poetry that teaches us to take nothing for granted.

III

The drayhorse Knowledge shudders before the leopard Inspiration. But the leopard cannot eat the horse. It must hold the reins.

Defining Zen is difficult. Even the masters whom Stryk interviews in *Encounter* frequently disagree with each other and contradict themselves. Although the masters keep warning against the dangers of scholasticism, scholars keep trying to encapsulate the subject. The books of Alan Watts and D. T. Suzuki point the way to Zen; the haiku of Basho and Buson express its spirit much more directly.

For the Westerner attempting to follow the path of Zen there is an additional difficulty. We are raised with a syllabistic language that lends itself to syllogistic constructions. Japanese, Chinese, and other Oriental languages are ideogrammatic: instantaneous rather than sequential. The nature of the experience is different, as is the way in which experience is perceived.

In poetry, inspiration will always ride roughshod over revelation. The attainment of *satori* does not automatically confer poetic brilliance. One guesses that Bash would have been a great poet even if he had not been a great Zenist. His Zen gave his work a certain flavor, an alluring depth. At the other end of the rainbow there are the likes of Baudelaire, Mishima, and Poe. Inspired, brilliant writers—but who would call them Zenists?

The man of the spirit seeks revelation, and the artist seeks inspiration. They are sometimes the same, with revelation leading to a new force, an enhanced sensibility. But they are not necessarily the same, and when one seriously considers the matter, one would not want all our great artists to be men or women of the highest realized wisdom. One wants Li Po to enjoy his wine, one indulges Shakespeare's bawdier moods. What works for Lucien Stryk or Gary Snyder may not work for Carolyn Forché or Ernesto Cardenal. Above all, we want our poets to be brave enough to follow their own paths with full hearts and to report their journeys earnestly.

These two books by Lucien Stryk record the course of one man's struggle for insight, depth, and power. Therein lies their ultimate value. Still, the greatest artists have been the greatest synthesizers, have dared to imagine all. A basically antisyncretistic approach will not reveal the emerging constellations. We must learn to go beyond our father's sayings: a good teacher, as Confucius said, is one who knows and makes known the new by revivifying the old.

We are not really so distant. We are not really so apart. Phenomenalism's apprehension of noumena—i.e., things-in-themselves—is not dissimilar to Zen's emphasis on absolute identification with the thing perceived in order to fully know it as a thing-in-itself. It may be that West and East make a *girandole* around the same center, using different terminology and approaches, confusing each other as with a show of weird masks where all the actors are one and the same.

Daniel L. Guillory (essay date 1986)

SOURCE: "The Oriental Connection: Zen and Representations of the Midwest in the Collected Poems of Lucien Stryk," in *Midamerica XIII*, edited by David D. Anderson, Midwestern Press, 1986, pp. 107-15.

[*In the following essay, Guillory asserts that Stryk's poetry illustrates the "aesthetic and poetic possibilities inherent in the midwestern experience."*]

In 1967 Lucien Stryk edited *Heartland: Poets of the Midwest*, and in his Introduction to that anthology he underscores the aesthetic and poetic possibilities inherent in the Midwestern experience. Although many critics have denigrated the region for being flat and "colorless," Stryk insists that the Midwest can be "rich, complicated, thrilling" (*Heartland* xiv). In the poetry he chooses for that anthology and, more importantly, in his own work, Stryk dramatizes again and again that the Midwest is

> made up of the stuff of poetry. And once those living in it begin to see its details—cornfields, skyscrapers, small-town streets, whatever—with the help of their poets, they will find it not only more possible to live with some measure of contentment among its particulars but even, miraculously, begin to love them and the poems they fill.
>
> (*Heartland* xiv)

After this aesthetic manifesto, it is not surprising to discover that the opening poem in Stryk's **Collected Poems, 1953-1983**, is **"Farmer,"** a powerful evocation of the agrarian life that typifies the region. Without rancor or sentimentality, the farmer beholds the landscape purely, observing a world "bound tight as wheat, packed / hard as dirt." His life and even his dwelling place are subsumed by the larger reality of the prairie:

> While night-fields quicken,
> shadows slanting right, then left
> across the moonlit furrows,
> he shelters in the farmhouse
> merged with trees, a skin of wood,
> as much the earth's as his.

In **"Old Folks Home,"** a later and more meditative poem, Stryk imagines such a farmer at the end of his days, useless and unproductive but still tied to the fields by plangent memories and subtleties of perception. From his prison-like cell in the rest home, he follows the "empty path" to "fields pulsing / gold, green under / vapors, rain-fresh / furrows stretching / miles." (*CP*, 192). Then he is overcome by memories of his lost farm and long-dead wife:

> he stands hours, keen
> to the cool scent
> of fullness—now
> without purpose where
> corn-tassels blow.
> Returns to the bare
> room, high above cedars
> gathering gold and green.
>
> (*CP*, 193)

The "corn-tassels" are just one of the constituent Midwestern "details" that Stryk invokes in his Introduction to *Heartland*; earlier, in **Notes for a Guidebook** (1965), he refers to the importance of "small particulars," (*CP*, 22) and in a recent interview with this author, Stryk insists on the primacy of the finely perceived detail. He explains that some years ago, after returning from one of his many trips to Japan, he determined "to make a minute inspection of my own world in DeKalb, Illinois . . . You see the smallest

things become important as a source of revelation" (Guillory 6). This emphasis on the "small particulars" is a stylistic hallmark of Lucien Stryk's work. He rarely paints with a broad brush; his method is to focus on single objects, moments, and scenes. In his long poem, **"A Sheaf for Chicago"** Stryk reduces Sandburgs comprehensive "city of the big shoulders" to particular scenes. Stryk's own childhood in Chicago is suggested by a catalogue of details, including discarded automobile parts and Christmas trees:

> We gathered fenders, axles, blasted hoods
> To build Cockaigne and Never-never Land,
> Then beat for dragons in the oily weeds.
> That cindered lot and twisted auto mound,
> That realm to be defended with the blood,
> Became, as New Year swung around,
> A scene of holocaust, where pile on pile
> Of Christmas trees would char the heavens
> And robe us demon-wild and genie-tall
> To swirl the hell of 63rd Place . . .
>
> (*CP*, 23-24)

Another poem dealing with the theme of childhood is **"Rites of Passage,"** a much later work in which Stryk, the former Chicago street urchin, has become a kind of Wordsworthian man, wandering through a rural corn field with his own son. The poet is even more aware of the importance of details and the intensity of childhood moments, here glimpsed through the eyes of his own son. The poem turns into a kind of incantation in which human language is replaced by the altogether more powerful language of nature itself:

> soybeans, corn, cicadas. Stone rings
> touch the bank, ripple up my arm.
>   In the grass
> a worm twists in the webbed air (how things
> absorb each other)—on a branch
>   a sparrow
> tenses, gray. As grass stirs it bursts
> from leaves, devouring. I close my book.
>   With so much
> doing everywhere, words swimming green,
> why read? I see and taste silence.
>
> (*CP*, 153)

In **"Rites of Passage"** the words become living entities, as if Stryk short-circuits the linguistic process and returns to an earlier time in pre-history when every word was the actual *name* of a living entity—a development described exhaustively by Ernst Cassirer in his classic work, *Language and Myth* (48-55).

Not all Midwestern moments, however, are the basis for transcendent experiences; many characteristic events inspire anxiety or outright terror. The region is visited by every meteorological curse imaginable, including freezing rain, dust storms, ice storms, hail, tornadoes, floods, and earthquakes. These natural disasters occur as background or foreground in many of Lucien Stryk's poems, although he gives each terrifying event a peculiarly personal stamp.

In "**The Quake,**" for example, the poet and his wife are thrown out of bed by the mysterious rumbling underground. Their love-making is interrupted by a natural occurrence that shatters their tender interlude of shared intimacy. At first, they view the event as comic:

> We laughed when the bed
> Heaved twice then threw
> Us to the floor. When all
> Was calm again, you said
> It took an earthquake
> To untwine us. Then I
> Stopped your shaking
> With my mouth.

The "shaking" persists, however, as doubts and fears open in their psyches, fault-lines of a deeper and more sinister kind:

> Then why should dream
> Return us to that fragile
> Shelf of land? And why,
> Our bodies twined upon
> This couch of stone,
> Should we be listening,
> Like dead sinners, for the quake?

The most terrifying of all the natural disasters is the tornado—deadly, unmerciful, and always unpredictable. In "**Twister**" the poet and his family wait out the storm in their basement after the tornado has already "touched down / a county north, leveled a swath / of homes, taking twenty lives." Like countless others, they study the "piled up junk" while wondering "what's ahead":

> We listen; ever
> silent, for the roar out of the west,
> whatever's zeroing in with terror
> in its wake. The all clear sounds,
> a pop song hits above. Made it
> once again. We shove the chairs
> against the wall, climb into the light.
>
> (*CP*, 115)

Like the earthquake in "**Quake,**" the tornado in "**Twister**" breaks the numbing routine of ordinary existence and, hence, provides an opportunity for spiritual insight. By placing the poet (and his family) on the edge of death, such disasters force an instantaneous awareness of—and appreciation for—the mysterious and fragile life force. Paradoxically, the poet transforms such potential disasters into positive aesthetic triumphs. Speaking of all the possible setbacks to be encountered in writing poetry about the Midwest, Stryk remarks that "if the poet is worth his salt he is certain to get as much out of it as those who live elsewhere . . ." (*Heartland* xv).

Natural disasters are not the only kinds of setbacks that figure prominently in the poetry of Lucien Stryk; he gives a good deal of attention to the "**Babbitry**" (*Heartland* xix) that often typifies small-town life in the Midwest. Social disasters seem to occur just as often as natural

ones. Every town has its share of malingers and ne'er-do-wells, like the "toughs" and dropouts" described in "**The Park**":

> All summer long rednecks,
> high-school dropouts rev
> motorbikes and souped-up
> cars across the isle of
> grass, jeer at cops cruising
> as the horseshoes fly.
> Strollers, joggers, children
> traipsing to the city pool
> flinch at hoots and whistles,
> radio blasts recoiling from
> the trees.
>
> (*CP*, 190)

The sociology of prejudice and ostracism is the ugly core at the center of "**The Cannery**," another poem about malaise in the small midland town. Local residents resent—and fear—the annual influx of migrant workers, especially poor Southern whites and illegal Mexicans who form a cheap labor pool for the local cannery:

> In summer this town is full of rebels
> Come up from Tennessee to shell the peas.
> And wetbacks roam the supermarkets, making
> A Tijuana of the drab main street.
> The Swedes and Poles who work at Wurlitzer,
> And can't stand music, are all dug in:
> Doors are bolted, their pretty children warned,
> Where they wait for the autumnal peace.
>
> (*CP*, 74)

Some of the "disasters" may seem minor to someone who has never attempted the supremely difficult task of poetic composition, a process that requires intense powers of concentration. The poet's frustration in "**Here and Now**" is more than understandable: a poem has been scuttled by the importunate knocking of an Alcoa salesman. The poet's indignation turns on itself again and becomes the catalyst for a poem about not being able to write a poem in peace:

> Hear a knocking
> at the front. No muse,
> a salesman
> from the Alcoa
> Aluminum Company
> inspired by the siding
> of our rented house.
>
> (*CP*, 117)

The greatest disaster, perhaps, is to fall victim to the sameness and plainness that, at least on first sight, characterize the Midwestern scene. "And if the poets of the heartland," asks Stryk, "see their territory as often luminous and wild, are we to conclude that the weary passer-through who views it as a terrible sameness may, in fact, be seeing nothing other than himself" (*Heartland* xix)? In point of fact, seeing things in a new way is one of the primary results of Zen training, and while it is true that good artists acquire this trait in many ways—not merely from Zen—it is also true that Lucien Stryk's work bears an especially strong affinity to Zen. For years he has translated Zen poetry and taught Asian literature; he has actually lived in Japan for a number of years. His most recent books are eloquent examples of his life-long attention to this meditative and aesthetic discipline: *On Love and Barley: Haiku of Basho* (Penguin, 1985) and *Triumph of the Sparrow: Zen Poems of Shinkichi Takahashi* (University of Illinois Press, 1986). "I think my life has been profoundly affected by Zen and by meditation, reading, and translating," Stryk observes. "I think about Zen constantly; I believe I'm easier to live with, more able to handle life. And I take joy in reality of a kind that I could not have taken without such Zen training" (Guillory 13). The kind of joy Stryk means in this remark is well illustrated by the little poem **"Constellation,"** a kind of poetic diary-entry in which the poet records the surprising discovery of beautiful sunflowers in a most unlikely setting:

> Behind the super-
> market where we
> forage for our
> lives, beyond the
> parking lot, crammed
> garbage bins—
> thick heads of
> bee-swarmed
> seed-choked
> sunflowers blaze
> down on me through
> fogged noon air.

> > (*CP*, 178)

Stryk is quite conscious of his unique way of looking at ordinary Midwestern artifacts: he describes himself as "someone whose experiences have all the limitations and, of course, all the possibilities of this particular corner of the universe" (Guillory 6).

Elm trees, to cite one example, represent one of the many "possibilities" for the poet. Once so numerous that their leafy branches were a trademark of every small town in the Midwest and now virtually extinct because of Dutch elm disease, the elm is a kind of totem for the region. In **"Elm"** the poet mourns the loss of his elm, a personal favorite destroyed by "beetles smaller than / rice grains." Then the season changed and frost "spiked"

> the twigless air. Soon
> snow filled emptiness
> between the shrubs. I
> fed my elm-logs to the
> fire, sending ghost-
> blossoms to the sky.

> > (*CP,* 156)

Those "ghost blossoms" are an unexpected and wholly Zen-inspired touch, as are the novel ways of seeing clothes hanging on a clothesline in **"Words on a Windy Day"**:

> I watch in wonder
> > As the wind fills
> > > Trouserlegs and sweaters,
> Whips them light and dark.
> > In that frayed coat
> > > I courted her a year,

> > > . . . . .

> > These mildewed ghosts of love
> That life, for lack of something
> > Simple as a clothespin,
> > > Let fall, one by one.

> > (*CP*, 38)

Even more inventive is **"Storm,"** a kind of extended metaphor:

> The green horse of the tree
> bucks in the wind
> as lightning hits beyond.
> We will ride it out together
> Or together fall.

> > (*CP*, 114)

But the poem that best illustrates the Zen method is **"Willows,"** the final selection in *Collected Poems*. Stryk describes the poem as a" embodiment of Zen learning," explaining that it is "based on an old Zen exercise known as 'mind pointing'." Mind pointing involves focusing

> on some everyday scene or object, something you encounter but take for granted. It could be anything . . . there's a stand of willows near the lagoon on the campus of Northern Illinois University, and my self-imposed exercise was to go by the willows, seeing whether in fact I could really look at them without thinking of what happened yesterday, what will happen tomorrow, problems or whatever. And the finished poem is a detailing of that experience." (Guillory 10)

At one level, **"Willows"** is a kind of journal of a great experiment that fails, because Stryk never fully succeeds at ridding his mind of distractions. At another level, however, **"Willows"** is a magnificent accomplishment because it dramatizes the great Zen notion that the search and the thing sought are one and the same. Perhaps the poet does not fully apprehend all twenty-seven of the willows, but he does perceive them in a new way as they become "delicate / tents of greens and browns." Although he once makes it to the seventeenth tree, his trials are marked with various gestures of frustration, wrung hands and clenched teeth. But even his distractions are valuable. Shifting his focus from the nearest tree to the farthest one in the row, he beholds a shower" of leaves. In his passionate attention to the trees, the whole world becomes intense and vivid, and even the distractions are raised to the level of pure comprehension. The poet may not be granted perfect awareness of all twenty-seven trees, but he *does* receive unmediated impressions of reality as if the world around him were suddenly and magically translated into haiku-like imagery:

the flap of duck, goose, a limping
footstep on the path behind,
sun-flash on the pond.

(CP, 198)

"**Willows**" concludes with the poet still "practicing" on the trees "over, over again" because in each failure lies the magnificent gift of incidental poetry.

Like Japanese art, the poetry of Lucien Stryk is spare, compressed, and simple—minimalist art at its very best. But Stryk is no Japanese, and his representations of tornadoes, elm trees, willows, and farms revitalize these primary images of midland America. Without them there could be no Midwest; and Stryk deserves the gratitude of his readers for helping to rescue this precious world from oblivion. In "**Awakening**" Stryk reminds his readers that poetry is the greatest form of awareness; to be fully alive is to participate in the fundamental joy of seeing and, even, of *not* seeing, as in the final moments of every sunset on the prairie:

and what I love about
this hour is the way the trees
are taken, one by one,
into the great wash of darkness.
At this hour I am always happy,
ready to be taken myself
fully aware.

(CP, 108)

WORKS CITED

Cassirer, Ernst. *Language and Myth*. Trans. Susanne K. Langer. 1946. New York: Dover, 1953.

Guillory, Dan. "The Way the Eye Attacks: An Interview with Lucien Stryk." *Indra's Net* 10 (1986):6-13.

On Love and Barley: Haiku of Basho. Trans. Lucien Stryk. New York: Penguin, 1985.

Stryk, Lucien. *Collected Poems, 1953-1983*. Athens, Ohio: Swallow Press, 1984.

Stryk, Lucien, ed. *Heartland: Poets of the Midwest*. DeKalb: Northern Illinois University Press, 1967.

Triumph of the Sparrow: Zen Poems of Shinkichi Takahashi. Trans. Lucien Stryk. Urbana: University of Illinois Press, 1986.

Susan Porterfield (essay date 1994)

SOURCE: "Portrait of a Poet as a Young Man: Lucien Stryk," in *Midwestern Miscellany XXII*, edited by David D. Anderson, Midwestern Press, 1994, pp. 36-45.

[*In the following essay, Porterfield discusses autobiographical aspects of Stryk's work, in particular his alienation from American culture and his subsequent embrace of Zen Buddhism.*]

In 1947, two years after returning from the Pacific where he had served during WWII, a twenty-two year old Lucien Stryk published his first essay, "The American Scene versus the International Scene," in a student journal at Indiana University. The article criticizes the climate of post-war America, what historians would later call the attempt at "normalcy" that characterized the peculiarities, even excesses, of the decade immediately after the War.

Conscious of its tremendous strength and its own unblemished virtue, the undefeated champion of the world hangs up its gloves and decides to relapse into its indolent mental habits of sublime self-adoration, self sufficiency, regional self-righteousness, and inflated egotistic super-nationalism. The inevitable reversion to the romantic conception of the American Garden of Eden, of the Promised Land flowing with milk and honey, new cars and refrigerators, in a world ravaged, gutted, atomized, agonized, miserably cold, terribly afflicted, and revenously hungry is the most horrible manifestation of our national escapism and moral inertia.

The disquiet Stryk exhibits here is not typical of the ethos informing his later work. Few of his reviewers have failed to praise the calmness of his tone, how balanced his manner even in the face of brutality. But the mood of "The American Scene" is quite different.

His disdain for a society blinded by its own myth and insensible to the suffering of others belongs to a young man certain that the world can be made better. His urgency belongs to a young man only too aware that he is lucky to be alive. Given his recent experiences as a soldier, the despair, which verges on outrage, is understandable. So too is the irony, which more than anything else, reveals the impatience of youthful idealism. Shortly after writing this piece, Stryk would leave the United States to spend the next several years abroad, studying in Paris at the Sorbonne and then at the University of London.

Obviously, somewhere, sometime, between this first effort and the rest of his life, he found, as he wrote in "**To Roger Blin**" (*Awakening* 1973), "a path, / a way, the art / to make life possible." That way was the way of Zen. Although he would not find it for many years, he shows himself predisposed in "The American Scene," to Zen teachings, despite or perhaps because of his unrest.

His dismay is counterpointed, for example, by both tremendous energy and a great desire either to find or, if necessary, to create essence. That he accuses the United States of suffering from "spiritual poverty" indicates that he valued spirituality, thus, that he hoped for its grace in his own life. His need for purity, an essential of Zen, he hails in "pure science," calling it a "knight in armor," and contrasting its mission to serve the country and the world, with "selfish, rapacious people" whose wartime patriotism was motivated by the sales of munitions. Despite his use of irony, he feels great compassion for mankind, evident in his socialistic leanings and in his hope that pure science will one day ease the world's suffering. That he insists upon the affinity of all men and women is affecting, considering his recent experiences on Saipan and Okinawa—so too is his quoting of John Donne: "any man's death diminishes me, because I am involved in mankinde." The quotation is meant to support a call for internationalism. It also shows Stryk's inclination to perceive interconnectedness, which later serves to sensitize him to Zen belief in the relatedness not only of all people but of all things.

It is revealing that even this early in his career, Stryk would set up a dichotomy between internationalism and regionalism, because both will influence his future work. His life was affected by the dichotomy as well. He was born in Kolo, Poland in 1924, for example, but managed to escape the tragedy the country endured during the 1930s and 40s because his family moved to the United States, specifically to Chicago, in 1928. Most of his early memories are about the South Side of Chicago. Poems, like **"A Sheaf for Chicago"** (*Notes for a Guidebook* 1965) show him to be a true child of that city. Here is section II of that poem.

> In a vacant lot behind a body shop
> I rooted for your heart, O city,
> The truth that was a hambone in your slop.
>
> Your revelations came as thick as bees,
> With stings as smarting, wings as loud,
> And I recall those towering summer days
>
> We gathered fenders, axles, blasted hoods
> To build Cockaigne and Never-never Land,
> Then beat for dragons in the oily weeds.
>
> That cindered lot and twisted auto mound,
> That realm to be defended with the blood,
> Became, as New Year swung around,
>
> A scene of holocaust, where pile on pile
> Of Christmas trees would char the heavens
> And robe us demon-wild and genie-tall
>
> To swirl the hell of 63rd Place,
> Our curses whirring by your roofs,
> Our hooves a-clatter on your face.

He has, in addition, lived most of his life in small-town Illinois, and the region infiltrates his work.

But because he is also a world traveller, he often writes about his experiences in foreign countries as well. *Notes for a Guidebook* contains such poems as **"The Mine: Yamaguchi"** and **"Moharram,"** that reflect his lengthy stays in Japan and Iran, where he taught. Others pieces, among them, **"Torero,"** and **"The Road from Delphi"** evolved from his trips to Spain and Greece, just as **"The Blue Tower,"** in *Of Pen and Ink and Paper Scraps* (1989), records his visit to Strindberg's home in Sweden where Stryk had gone on a reading tour. The lovely sequence, *Bells of Lombardy* (1986), grew from his trips to Italy,

while **"Paris"** (*The Pit and Other Poems* 1969) or **"Museum Guards (London)"** (*Awakening*) are set in France and England where he attended university. In "Away," he chides himself for his wanderlust: "Here I go again, / want to be somewhere else— / feet tramping under desk,. . ." His hunger to see the world pulled at him from the beginning and often ended in his finding fare for his art.

Still, his poetry is just as likely to be about the Midwest as about Paris. **"Return to DeKalb"** (*The Pit*), **"Fishing with My Daughter in Miller's Field"** (*Awakening*), and **"The Ordinary"** from *Collected Poems: 1953-1983* (1984), chronicle his life as well as his appreciation of the Heartland. **"Waking Up in Streator"** is a good example.

> I am wakened by a poem
> I have never heard, in
>
> a town never visited
> deep in Illinois. Last
>
> night, due to read poems
> 500 miles away—now
>
> shaggy from dreams—I
> remember a friend, long dead,
>
> who grew up in Streator,
> played football, talked tough,
>
> scorning all dreamers.
> Yet one night, late,
>
> loosened by beer, confessed
> he'd once written a poem.

He listened to the sound of the region and found himself in love with its harmonies. Finding other writers with an ear for music, he edited two books of Midwestern poetry, *Heartland: Poets of the Midwest, I and II* (1967, 1975).

Readers of Stryk's work may thus be surprised by his apparent quarrel with regionalism in "The American Scene." He objects, however, not to a clear-sighted depiction of region but to the spirit of isolationism, so prevalent after the War, that led art to romanticize rural, middle America. This kind of pandering to sentimentality, like the paintings of "blue-overall-clad giants and sickly-sweet, properly-bonneted maidens" that he uses as examples, earns his scorn. What he seeks is an art unafraid to see the region wholly and cleanly and what is also significant, one that is willing to acknowledge the future as well. Grant Wood, he says, opts to paint only a rurally idyllic Iowa. But to Stryk, Wood's vision ignores the beauty of the state's "superbly efficient farms pouring out floods of golden wheat, like Ceres bestowing a bountiful blessing on America and humanity, through the dynamic effort of its fields, farms, towering silos, and the mighty vertical expanse of its grain elevators." His complaint seems to be against the kind of art Clement Greenberg calls kitsch, that is, with art that reinforces the *status quo*.

For a young man like Stryk, all energy and idea, home from the War and poised to leap, his country's apparent preference for keeping "things as they are," must have seemed stifling. The world had gone through trial by fire. So had he. After that, anything must have seemed possible. That both he and the world now possessed a future was a wonder and meant opportunity. By the time Stryk wrote this essay, he had, in spirit at least, already left home. Soon, he would actually leave to study abroad. But he would always return to the Heartland.

He went to Paris in 1948 where he lived the Left-Bank life of the student at a time when existentialism and the Deux Magots were *a la mode*. Once there he furthered his pursuit of art, studied philosophy under Gaston Bachelard at the Sorbonne and entertained an attraction to phenomenology. He met various artists, James Baldwin, Roger Blin, and enjoyed the companionship of other young intellectuals who frequented the cafe Mabillon, among them, Jean-Paul Baudot, the French Resistance fighter of the gripping poem, **"Letter to Jean-Paul Baudot, at Christmas"** (*Awakening*).

> Friend, on this sunny day, snow sparkling
> everywhere, I think of you once more,
> how many years ago, a child Resistance
>
> fighter trapped by Nazis in a cave
> with fifteen others, left to die, you became
> a cannibal. Saved by Americans,
>
> the taste of a dead comrade's flesh foul
> in your mouth, you fell onto the snow
> of the Haute Savoie and gorged to purge yourself,
>
> somehow to start again. Each winter since
> you were reminded, vomiting for days.
> Each winter since you told me at the Mabillon,
>
> I see you on the first snow of the year
> spreadeagled, face buried in that stench.
> I write once more, Jean-Paul, though you don't
>
> answer, because I must: today men do far worse.
> Yours in hope of peace, for all of us,
> before the coming of another snow.

In his tiny room on the Rue de Buci, Stryk read and studied and began seriously to write poetry. He recounts in the third section of **"Rooms"** (*Bells of Lombardy*) how he would

> read through the dictionary, stalking
> new words for verse scrawled on
>
> used paper bags, old envelopes
> airmailed from home, to the beat
> of the asthmatic radiator. How I
>
> would love to climb those stairs once
> more, see where it all began. Making
> a bold check, in the g's, for granadilla—

From Paris, he travelled to England in order to attend the University of London. There he continued to study and write, began to freelance, married Helen Esterman, a Londoner, to whom most of his books are dedicated, and became a father. He also published his first book of poetry, *Taproot* (1953).

The poems in *Taproot* are formal in structure and traditional in subject matter; throughout them rings the same note of unrest that tolls in "The American Scene." But they also have its vitality. Deep within the patterning of this verse, in its attempt at order, one senses that Stryk still searches and that he remains unable to assume the incongruities of war. Consider this stanza from **"Testament."**

> Give no reassurance, speak not
> Of war's necessity nor praise
> The beauty of its crimson snout:
> The earth is waste where iron fangs
> Have pierced, lies torn where it has coiled
> And leapt: victor and the fallen
> Now are one, and all is peace where
> Roots pluck down their skulls
>   and all is peace.

Back in the United States, he attended the University of Iowa and received an M.F.A. in 1956. In that same year, Fantasy Press, which had published *Taproot*, brought out his second book of poetry, *The Trespasser*. These poems, like those of his first collection, are sharply self-conscious. Stryk would later find most of them unacceptable and included only a revised handful in *Collected Poems (1953-1983)*. It was his experiences in Japan, where he travelled after Iowa, that taught him to look again at his art.

He had been there briefly before. While still in the service, immediately after the War, he was stationed in Japan and found that the people he was told to fear and hate were far from being monsters. He was, in fact, intrigued by the country and resolved someday to return. From 1956 to 1958, Stryk was a visiting lecturer at Niigata University. During this first extended stay, he became seriously interested in Zen, roused by meeting a Zen priest, a potter. Stryk describes the effect of that meeting upon him in his essay, "Beginnings, Ends" from *Encounter with Zen* (1981).

> The visit left an extraordinary impression. Home again, sipping tea from the superb bowl he made for me . . . I began making plans. Soon I was inquiring seriously into Zen, reading everything available, and, for my own pleasure and enlightenment, making very tentative translations of some of its literature, particularly poetry. I visited temples and monasteries, meeting masters and priests throughout the country and, most important of all, began to meditate. I sensed most strongly that I had found something which could make a difference to my future. The intuition proved right, for that encounter in the mountains was among the most important of my life.

The study that he made of Zen between this visit to Japan and his next stay there in 1962 served him well. It prepared him for what can only be called an epiphanic moment. Narrating the incident in "Making Poems," from *Encounter with Zen*, he tells how, while visiting the rock garden at the Joeiji temple, he was chastised by the Zen master, Tenzan Yasuda, for asking inappropriate questions about the garden. His shame triggered a stern examination of self that exploded into revelation, transforming both his life and his art. To change one's poetry, one must first change the self.

Stryk understood that for Zennists who are poets, the poem itself is ancillary to the vision it both engenders and expresses. What is crucial lies behind or underneath a poem, perhaps surrounds it and lifts it into existence. The poem expresses the Zen man or woman, from deep self to the page and beyond. Stryk explains, again from "Making Poems":

> Suddenly I became aware, *saw* with the greatest clarity: my failing in poetry was the result, in great part, of a grave misunderstanding concerning the very purpose of art. The Zen masters who had written the poems I was translating did not think of themselves as "poets" at all; rather, they were attempting to express in verse nothing less than the Zen spirit—and the results were astonishing. The poems, without any pretension to "art," were among the finest I had ever read, intense, compact, rich in spirit.

This revelation could not have come had Stryk not been preparing himself for it by studying Zen and translating Zen poetry. With revelation came responsibility and work. He began immediately to write new poems, different from anything he had previously written and to revise poems he had once considered finished. As he says, anyone "serious about a discipline like Zen learns soon enough that much of his life, certainly any art he may practice, is being changed by it."

How his life was changed is best seen by looking at his art. That nine years passed between *The Trespasser* and his next book of poems, *Notes for a Guidebook* (1965) is perhaps significant. His tone in *Notes* is less emphatic but more sure. Although he may continue to write about atrocities, when he does so it is with a quieter hand as in section three, "Survivors," from the poem, **"Return to Hiroshima"**:

> Of the survivors there was only one
> That spoke, but he spoke as if whatever
> Life there was hung on his telling all.
> And he told all. Of the three who stayed,
> Hands gripped like children in a ring, eyes
> Floating in the space his wall had filled,
>
> Of the three who stayed on till the end,
> One leapt from the only rooftop that
> Remained, the second stands gibbering
>
> At a phantom wall, and it's feared the last,
> The writer who had taken notes, will
> Never write another word. He told all.

His poems also become tighter, leaner. He constructs them to sculpt the space of the page more subtly, often writing the three line stanza, using syllables as a measure, sometimes shortening one line to let in air so that the poems favor haiku.

Stryk's next collection of poetry, *The Pit and Other Poems* (1969), as well as subsequent books would also possess these same qualities of quiet force and conciseness. The energy so evident in "The American Scene" still exists, is still intense, but centered. As Joseph Parisi has written of Stryk's fifth book: "Tranquil strength pervades the short, evocative poems of Lucien Stryk's *Awakening* (1973). . . . Everywhere the benevolent influence of his Zen masters touches the clean, spare lines shaped with the elegance of an Oriental scroll painting" (*Poetry* 1973).

With clearer vision and focused energy he began writing more poems honoring the common, the ordinary. As he says in his "Introduction" to *Heartland II*, a "small town street known for years reaches through the universe: to the eye alive *nothing* is without its wonder." Thus, he can write "Lake Dawn" from the sequence, **"The City: A Cycle"** (*Collected Works*):

> Slow spread of light
> beyond the tracks,
> fingering bare branches
>
> of the oak. After
> thick year on year
> another chance to find
>
> what dawn, rising on
> frosty air, will
> bring. Yesterday, ice
>
> floes on the lake, a
> revelation: nothing's
> warmer than sun-webbed
>
> snow, boots scorching
> on the crust. What
> will I learn today?
>
> I thirsted seasons,
> dragging a leaden shadow
> into nothingness. Now,
> as fire meets ice, I see.

Stryk has written in his "Introduction" to *The Dumpling Field: Haiku of Issa* (1991) that Issa's empathy for living creatures is indicative of his ethos and "must become ours if we are to survive as humans." Issa reminds us, he says, "of the individual reality of each life destroyed." Stryk reminds us of this as well. The Swedish daily, *Dagens Nyheter,* reviewing a recent translation of his poetry identifies him as the "absorbed Westerner, with senses and intellect jointly linked to the object of meditation,,,,," His poems are "like a twilight zone where the border between the self and the world is dissolved . . ." Or, as the young poet, Walter Pavlich has written, a bit closer to home:

There are certain poets I consider world-poets. They speak with quiet power, personally and intimately to all people. In this group I would include Yehuda Amichai, Rolf Jacobsen, Tomas Transtromer, Lucien Stryk. Among their qualities are a reverence and respect for life. They show us the many sides of the world's capacity for self-harm and love. There is blood in their poems. From wounds. From wombs. (*Thinker Review* 1992)

In an interview, Stryk has spoken of a "curiosity and hunger . . . that will take a man very far across the earth looking for things, and this excitement about reality is part and parcel of the making of poems." His "excitement about reality," which is so evident in "The American Scene," took him far, led him to Zen, and through Zen taught him to look anew at the here and now. "All true men," he has written, "come to the very same conclusion, for it is the only sane one. If one cannot find fulfillment in the world around one, where it happens to be, there is no hope."

From our artists, we ask that they possess vision, of how to live and what to live by. We look to them for the "art to make life possible." What would the twenty-two year old veteran think, wonder, if told in 1947 that he would one day share his own vision with others and would himself create the art that creates life? Despite his hopes, his obvious joy in words, how could he know? That he would live, fully. That he would find "the way." That he would write poetry with the power to endure.

Susan Porterfield with Lucien Stryk (interview date 1995)

SOURCE: An interview with Lucien Stryk, in *Poets and Writers,* Vol. 23, No. 4, July-August 1995, pp. 34-35.

[*In the following interview, Stryk discusses his background, his interest in Zen Buddhism, and his creative process.*]

I'm eating lunch with Lucien Stryk at his home in De-Kalb, Illinois. He has returned from London for a few weeks to keep reading tour engagements in the east and while here to be interviewed by me. His wife of more than 40 years, Helen, has remained abroad.

Instead of one of her renowned meals, I'm eating canned lentil soup into which Stryk has tossed mushrooms, also canned, and sliced, red onions. On the side we have tinned salmon mixed with the remainder of the onion, which has been marinated with apple cider vinegar, a consort of grapes and bananas drizzled with blueberry syrup, and toasted bagels.

It's surprisingly good.

In fact, Stryk seems to have a way of finding what will work in almost any situation, domestic or otherwise, compelling hidden unities to reveal themselves amid apparent differences. This is so, I suspect, because for him the world isn't fragmented, fractured, or blasted. Men and women may be, in their responses to it. But the world itself is perfect.

The disparity may explain something about why he writes: to move beyond his partial, ego-centered perception toward the genuine; to come as close to it as he can; to approach via the word.

Stryk belongs to a tradition that considers the true artist to be a hero, a visionary, a prophet, someone to whom others may turn. The natural artist can see, or at the very least tries to see, what others don't, and he or she is capable of creating a thing of beauty. Because poetry is frighteningly important, the nature of those who write it is just as significant. "We write what we are," he tells me, then interrupts himself, pointing to a cardinal in the fir tree outside. "And what we are matters."

Who is Lucien Stryk? His life unfolds narratively, event leading to event, leading to epiphanic moment, and its story-like quality is part of its romance, part of his appeal. Most simply, he's a good Midwestern son, a boy from the heartland, reared in Chicago.

His father, Emil, a paint store-owning sculptor, knew many of the artists and writers of Chicago, among them Ben Hecht and Maxwell Bodenheim. Emil Stryk took his son to the Art Institute, and to local galleries. He brought the boy with him on visits to his good friends, the two Kemp brothers, one a painter and the other a wood carver. He also prompted the boy to memorize poems, and later when Stryk was older, encouraged him to read the family's subscription to *Les Temps Modernes,* the newspaper begun by Jean-Paul Sartre in 1945. Growing up in an environment supportive of the arts, Stryk was naturally drawn to them. "Quite early I felt I might work as a writer, although I didn't know in what direction. I knew that in important art, I could find something for myself."

His Chicago upbringing aside, Stryk is also a native European, born in Poland and brought to this country by way of Ellis Island in the late 1920's when he was about four years old. We discuss how this experience is, paradoxically perhaps, typically an American one, how the dual cultural identity of many of his generation of artists has contributed to our current artistic heritage, particularly regarding the widespread interest in translation.

"The American is famously exploratory: we've engaged with other cultures since childhood. I remember Italians, Greeks in my old neighborhood. From our earliest years, we're exposed to different cultures." The result may be that we are more accustomed to hearing the voices of those different from ourselves. Stryk finds this "migration of cultures across boundaries through the vehicle of poetry" one of the most positive characteristics of American letters.

Certainly his numerous experiences abroad have contributed to the formation of his own poetry. During World War II, for example, he served on Okinawa and Saipan as a forward observer, scouting the position of enemy troops. This ordeal and other trials of war eventually proved crucial to his art as did his days spent as a pupil at the Sorbonne. Stryk came home to Chicago from the war in late 1945 but two years later left the States again, this time to live the life of a student-intellectual in the heady atmosphere of post-war Paris. Here, studying under Gaston Bachelard, Stryk read philosophy, frequented the Café Mabillon where he often met his friend, Jean-Paul Baudot, the young Resistance fighter of Stryk's poem **"Letter to Jean-Paul Baudot, at Christmas,"** nightwalked along the banks of the Seine, fell in and out of love, and dreamed.

Paris *is* a moveable feast and proved to be so for Stryk, who remained there for two years from 1948 to 1950. Important things were happening for him. He began to know how he might live in the arts, in what direction he would go. Up in his tiny left-bank lodging at the Hôtel de Buci, he began seriously to write poetry. His poem **"Rooms"** tells how he'd "read through the dictionary, stalking / new words for verse . . ."

> in the g's for granadilla—

> where visions of stigmata, nail marks,
> thorns became a poem heavy with
> may-pops, fruit of the passionflower.
>
> —(*Bells of Lombardy,*
> Northern Illinois University Press, 1986)

After Paris, Stryk went to England to study at the University of London. There he met his wife, an Englishwoman who worked in a local bookstore and who noticed the young, serious-minded American flipping through journals that contained his work, too poor to buy copies. In the 1950's, Stryk's first two books of poetry appeared, *Taproot* (1953) and *Trespasser* (1956) both published by the British house, Fantasy Press. He also became a father.

But he wasn't quite ready to settle down. From 1961 to '62, with the Shah of Iran in power, Stryk held a Fulbright lectureship in Meshed. He and his wife tell tales about learning to censor themselves concerning the activities of some of his students who otherwise might suddenly disappear. Stryk also circled the globe twice, once on a tramp steamer, and happily recalls the exotic ports, the people, the free-flowing wine.

Despite these adventures, no place has affected him as profoundly as Japan. While stationed on the mainland during the autumn of 1945, shortly before he was discharged, he promised himself that one day he'd return to learn about this country. Through the course of two subsequent visits there, the first lasting from 1956 through 1958 and the second from 1962 to 1963, he discovered something that would change his life.

He learned how to write poetry. "Above and beyond the desire to make oneself an artist," he realized then and still very much believes, "one must make oneself a more complete human being." Until this point, despite receiving an MFA from the University of Iowa in 1956 and having published two books of poetry with Fantasy Press, he hadn't yet found his voice.

But after two Zen Buddhists admonished him for asking naive questions about Buddhism, Stryk says in the essay "Making Poems" from his book *Encounter with Zen* (Ohio University Press/Swallow, 1981) that he became determined to understand. What he learned changed his life and led him to revise completely pieces that he'd once considered finished. He began writing poetry different from anything he'd previously done. At one crucial point, he stayed up all night working on **"Zen: The Rocks of Sesshu,"** which was his initial attempt in verse to come to terms with first principles. "To be an artist," he says, "you must become a larger human being, more compassionate, more concerned, more aware." Not surprisingly, his next book, *Notes for a Guidebook* (Ohio University Press/Swallow, 1965), which he considers his first real book of poetry, would not appear for nine more long, contemplative, patient years.

Even now, after publishing more than 30 books of his own poetry, translations of Zen works, and editions of collected poetry, Stryk continues to learn about himself as a poet and about the art he loves. On the first day of our interview, he was kind enough to show me revisions of some poems that I'd heard him read several months before. "I like discovering I've been an ass and then returning to the work and making something of it, discovering that I've been given another chance."

He is sitting in his recliner, feet up, relaxed. For a man of 71, Stryk radiates the energy of a person half his age. He has, in fact, just driven from Virginia to his home in Illinois in one day. "It is very easy for a practicing poet to delude himself simply by looking at something and coming up with effective detailing and, *voilà*—a poem," he tells me. "But the poetry has not been found. One has lied to oneself." This delusion, he says, produces art that is immoral.

Zen teachings insist that the character of the artist determines the quality of his or her work. Because Stryk finds this idea to be crucial to both art and life, he continues to study and translate Zen texts. Many of the poems are traditionally written in response to *koan* (Zen riddles or paradoxical problems for meditation) set by a master, who judges them not on their aesthetics but as evidence of his disciples' spiritual condition. The most accomplished poems come only to the enlightened few.

Because Zen poetry can reveal the enlightened thought of its authors, translators of it, according to Stryk, must try to achieve an analogous spiritual level or risk producing inferior work. "Some may see the translator's attempt as arrogant," Stryk admits, "but even if his worthiness lasts only for the moment, it must be so."

"Who owns the text then," I ask him, thinking the question a tough one, "the poet or the translator?"

"The translator," he says without a quiver, and adds that this is true regardless of the kind of poem, whether Zen or not. His own poetry, for example, has been rendered into Swedish, Italian, French, and Russian. Three versions of his work, he feels, belong to their foreign authors. To be a good translator, you must "live the poems, breathe them," he tells me, must identify yourself with the poet, regardless of the century, gender, or culture.

I ask to see Stryk's study, and he leads me to a small room in the rear of the house where we continue the interview. One wall of windows is half covered on the outside with bushes, home to tiny birds that live in the intricacies of the branches. His desk is semi-circular and smallish. The typewriter, which he only uses at a certain advanced stage in the composing process, rests on a table to the left. He distrusts computers, feeling that their capacity for generating a tidy text can deceive writers into thinking that they've completed their work.

On the wall next to his desk hangs a scroll painted by the 18th-century artist Taiga. It is one of his most prized possessions. "Sometimes, at dawn," for he's an early riser, "the sun comes in these windows and falls on the scroll in such a way . . . Can you imagine this? I practically do a little dance for joy, just to see it." That same joy, or energy, or whatever it is, led him to circle the globe, to search for and find "the art to make life possible" in a world whose myths the war had exploded.

Stryk is never anything but excited about life, whether he is listening to a favorite aria, walking in the park, which he does every morning, rain or shine, admiring his favorite Guardi or Goya paintings at the Art Institute of Chicago, or even eating canned lentil soup. "We look in art for passionate engagements with the things of this world. And passionate commitment to ideals. There can't be good art without passion."

"Is the person in the act of writing a poem different from the same person not writing, when he or she takes out the garbage, for example, or balances the checkbook?" I ask.

And again, he doesn't hesitate. "We are never free of the obligation to respond to the world. The poet, if he's any good, is always a poet. To the eyes of others, he may be considerably different, but it could very well be that the poet's struggle with a poem may occur anywhere, in class teaching, driving somewhere. The poet doesn't keep office hours."

Stryk happens to do much of his writing in the morning, but he says he likes knowing that a poem could come at any time, anywhere, be about anything. "What we want is discovery, and I think the finest discoveries are made when one is not looking. Such discoveries are often small, an observation, something seen freshly. Then suddenly, because of the poet's state of mind at the time he perceives this thing, that perception crystallizes, and hence in the most organic way a poem begins." While some poets claim they often know nothing else about a poem

except how it will end, Stryk says just the opposite. "Every poem turns out differently from what I expected, makes its shifts, goes through its disguises, waits for me to rip off its disguises."

Through his translations of important haiku, Stryk has developed such a high regard for the art that he feels unqualified to achieve anything worthy enough of his own in the form. He does favor a construct that is haiku-like, however, tercets, sometimes couplets, composed of short lines. He finds that the way the first lines arrange themselves, "stretch, fall across the page, the tonal resonance," is extremely important for the poem as a whole. "It has to do with the way we breathe, the way our eyes take in detail."

He gives me an example: "Two poets look out the window at the same scene with the thought of describing it. Working in the way most natural to them, one will need 20 words and the other 75. The one needing only 20 is likely to choose the couplet or tercet, the other will need something ampler. Now if you were to ask, they'd say, 'Why, purely aesthetic reasons determine their choices. The eye fills the space with what it requires. A choice has been made, a limitation accepted."

As he speaks, I happen to notice that the curtains on the windows of his study are fastened open with neckties. I pause in my questioning to bring this fact casually to his attention. He confesses and admits to disliking watches as well. We agree that there are certain limitations that one cannot accept.

Still, Stryk has turned most of his limitations into blessings that structure the narrative of his life. There is something appealing about someone who has found a way that endures. He continues to learn about and write poetry and has brought out two books in 1995. Both *The Awakened Self: Encounters with Zen* (Kodansha America) and **Zen Poetry: Let the Spring Breeze Enter** (Grove/Atlantic) contain his translations of Zen poetry. *Where We Are: Selected Poems and Zen Translations* (to be published in 1996 by Skoob Books) collects his new poems along with others that had been initially published in Great Britain.

He remains certain as well that there is such a thing as a poetic disposition. "Otherwise," he says, "there'd be no point." If, in other words, poetry does anything more than entertain, if it can provide answers, guide us, teach us, inspire us, then who the poet is becomes important. For Stryk, poetry depends upon the sensibility of the artist, upon a "generosity of spirit, an openness that leads the poet to embrace many things that on the surface might seem unpromising." The more an artist looks beyond the self "to a keen awareness of the human journey, the more likely he is to win through, to achieve something important."

"Could an immoral person be a poet?" I ask.

"I can't imagine an immoral person bothering with poetry," he shoots back, "and by 'immoral,' I'm not talking about trivialities. I mean in the largest sense, in the way a person relates to the world, his spirit. In the poets that affect me, there is always that element of desire and hope."

FURTHER READING

Criticism

Porterfield, Susan, editor. *Zen, Poetry, the Art of Lucien Stryk.* Athens, Ohio: Swallow Press, 1993, 388 p.
    Collection of critical essays and interviews with Stryk, as well as a selection of his poems.

Stitt, Peter. A review of *Selected Poems,* by Lucien Stryk. *The Georgia Review* XXXII, No. 4 (Winter 1978): 940-48.

Mixed review of *Selected Poems.*

Interviews

Johnson, Kent. "Lucien Stryk: An interview with Kent Johnson." *APR* 19, No. 2 (March-April 1990): 47-55.
    Stryk discusses his work as a translator for the Japanese poet Shinkichi Takahashi and the influence of Zen Buddhism on his life and work.

Lynch, Dennis and Gay Davidson. "Zen Heartland: An Interview with Lucien Stryk." *Modern Poetry Studies* 10, No. 1 (1980): 22-37.
    Relates Stryk's interest in Zen Buddhism to his artistic and personal development.

Additional coverage of Stryk's life and career is contained in the following sources published by the Gale Group: *Contemporary Authors*, Vols. 13-16; and *Contemporary Authors New Revised Series*, Vols. 10, 28, 55.

Tristan Tzara
1896-1963

(Pseudonym of Samuel Rosenfeld) Rumanian-born French poet, dramatist, essayist, critic, and novelist.

INTRODUCTION

Tzara is best remembered as a proponent and practitioner of Dadaism, an intellectual movement of the World War I era whose adherents espoused intentional irrationality and urged individuals to repudiate traditional values. Tzara and other European artists sought to establish a new style in which random associations challenged logic and grammar, and promoted an individual vitality free from the restraints of artistic, historical, and religious authority. Tzara's career included other artistic and political movements, including Surrealism and communism. His work often defies standard classification: He wrote dramas as well as poetry, criticism on both art and poetry, and essays on a range of social and cultural issues. Although his work is largely ignored by most English-speaking scholars, Tzara is esteemed in France for his large and diverse body of poetry.

Biographical Information

Tzara was born Samuel Rosenfeld in Moinesti, Bacu, Romania. Some sources date his birth April 4, 1896; others claim April 16, 1896. His first published poems appeared in a Rumanian literary review in 1912. Many of these poems, written in Rumanian and influenced by French symbolism, appear in a later volume of collected works, *Les premiers poèmes* (1958; *Primele poèmes: First Poems*). Tzara studied at Bucharist University from 1914 to 1915, during which time he also founded two journals in Romania: *Simbolul* (1912) and *Chemarea* (1915). In 1916 Tzara left Romania and immigrated to Switzerland. Together with Jean Arp, Hugo Ball, and others he created Dadaism and staged Dadaist performances at the Cabaret Voltaire in Zurich. Tzara then moved to France, settling in Paris in 1919. There he engaged in Dadaist experiments with Andre Breton and Louis Aragon. Serious philosophic differences caused a split between Tzara and Breton in 1921; soon after, Breton created the Surrealist movement, and by 1922 Dadaism had dissolved. From 1929 to 1934, Tzara participated in the activities of the Surrealist group in Paris. In 1934, he joined France's Communist Party, becoming a life-long member. Tzara served with the Loyalists during the Spanish Civil War, and he directed the cultural broadcast of the French Resistance in the south of France from 1943 to 1944, and also wrote for Resistance magazines. At the end of World War II he became a naturalized French citizen. In 1961, he was awarded the Taormina Interna-

tional Grand Prize for Poetry. Tzara died December 24, 1963, in Paris.

Major Works

Tzara's early Dadaist verse, written between 1916 and 1924, utilizes agglomerations of obscure images, nonsense syllables, outrageous juxtapositions, ellipses, and inscrutable maxims to perplex readers and illustrate the limitations of language. Volumes such as *Vingt-cinq poèmes* (1918) and *De nos oiseaux* (1923) display the propositions outlined in Tzara's manifestos and critical essays, often blending criticism and poetry to create hybrid literary forms. Tzara's Surrealist poetry, written between 1929 and 1934, places less emphasis on the ridiculous than his Dadaist verse. Tzara's works published during this period include *L'homme approximatif* (1931; *Approximate Man and Other Writings*), an epic poem that is widely considered a landmark of twentieth-century French literature. This work portrays an unfulfilled wayfarer's search for universal knowledge and a universal language. This and Tzara's later Surrealist volumes— *L'arbre des voyageurs* (1930), *Où boivent les loups*

(1932), *L'antitête* (1933), and *Grains et·issues* (1935)—reveal his obsession with language, his vision of humanity as afflicted by tedium and alienation, and his concern with the struggle to achieve completeness and enlightenment. As Tzara's interest in politics and his commitment to Communism increased during the thirties, his poetry included greater political content. It stressed revolutionary and humanistic values while maintaining Tzara's lifelong interest in free imagery and linguistic experiments. *Midis gagnés: poèmes* (1939) focuses on Tzara's impressions of Spain during that country's civil war. The prose poems *Sans coup férir* (1949) and *À haute flamme* (1955) address political topics related World War II. Critics generally regard such later works as *Terre sur terre* (1946) and *Le fruit permis* (1956) as less vigorous and inventive but more controlled than his earlier poetry.

Critical Reception

One of the difficulties in evaluating Tzara's poetry, particularly his Dadaist works, is distinguishing between his poetic vision and his poetic pranks. Tzara deliberately confounded and confused his readers. He even mocked them for their difficulty reading his poetry. In "Le géant blanc lépreux du paysage" Tzara wrote, "Here . . . the reader begins to scream . . . he is skinny, idiotic, dirty—he does not understand my poetry." Some critics argue that the chaos of his poetry is only apparent and that the many challenges he poses to his readers have a serious, unified purpose. Other critics question whether it is possible to find what Mary Ann Caws calls an "interior ordering" in his poetry. Tzara himself observed that "Dada proclaimed the negation of theory and the expression of naked personality." Caws also says: "We may, perhaps most wisely, follow his insistent advice that we look at the Dada poem as a simple spectacle, as creation complete in itself and completely obvious." Roger Cardinal observes that "Tzara's ideal text would seem to be one in which words emerge in a naked state, not as carriers of meaning proper but as manifestations of a kind of pure electrical energy." Cardinal argues that Tzara approached this ideal, and he praises his poetry for "the naked energy of his singular consciousness."

PRINCIPAL WORKS

Poetry

La première aventure céleste de Monsieur Antipyrine 1916.
Vingt-cinq poèmes 1918
Cinema calendrier du coeur abstrait maisons 1920
De nos oiseaux 1923 [*Cosmic Realities Vanilla Tobacco Dawnings,* 1975]
L'Indicateur des chemins de coeur 1928
L'arbre des voyageurs 1930
L'Homme approximatif 1931 [*Approximate Man and Other Writings,* 1973]
Où boivent les loups 1932
L'Antitete (prose poems) 1933

Parler seul 1933
Abrege de la nuit (poetry and prose) 1934
Grains et issues (prose poems) 1935
La main passe 1935
La deuxieme aventure celeste de Monsieur Antipyrine 1938
Midis gagnés: poèmes 1939
Entre-temps 1946
Le signe de vie 1946
Terre sur terre 1946
Morceaux choisis 1947
Sans coup férir 1949
De memoire d'homme 1950
La face interieure 1953
La bonne heure 1955
À haute flamme 1955
Le fruit permis 1956
Frere bois 1957
La rose et le chien 1958
Les premiers poèmes [translated from Romanian into French] 1958 [*Primele poeme: First Poems,* 1976]
Thirteen Poems 1969
Selected Poems 1975

Other Works

La coeur a gaz (drama) 1920 [*The Gas Heart,* 1964]
Dada au grand air [with Hans Arp and Max Ernst (criticism) 1921
Faites vox jeux (autobiographical novel) 1923
Sept manifestes dada (essays) 1924 [*Seven Dada Manifestos and Lampisteries,* 1977]
Mouchoir de nuages (drama) 1925
Essai sur la situation de la poesie (criticism) 1931
Sur le champ (essays) 1937
Vigies (essays) 1937
Ça va (essays) 1944
Une route seul soleil (essays) 1944
La fuite (drama) 1947
La surrealisme et l'apres-guerre (essay) 1947
Picasso et les chemins de la connaissance (criticism) 1948
Phases (essays) 1949
L'Art oceanien (criticism) 1951
L'Premiere main (essays) 1952
Picasso et la poesie (essay) 1953
L'Egypte face a face (essays) 1954
Le temps naissant (essays) 1955
Peintures [with Philippe Bonnet] (criticism) 1956
Dada: die Geburt des Dada [with Jean Arp, Richard Huelsenbeck, and Peter Schifferli] (criticism) 1957
Juste present (essays) 1961
De la coupe aux levres (essays) 1961
Destroyed Days (essays) 1971
Oeuvres complètes (poetry, dramas, essays, and criticism), 1975-91

Mary Ann Caws (essay date 1970)

SOURCE: "Motion, Vision, and Coherence in the Dada Poetry of Tristan Tzara," in *The French Review,* Vol. XLIII, No. 1, Winter, 1970, pp. 1-8.

[In this essay, Caws traces the visual imagery of Tzara's early poetry and find the unity of his poems in the "instant and incoherent reactions of the eye and ear."]

"Dada Est Une Quantité De Vie En Transformation Transparente Sans Effort Et Giratoire."[1] Tzara's description of the universe of Dada denies progress for pure movement, and deliberate form for spontaneous vitality. Neither his often-quoted formula for constructing a Dada poem (cut out the words in a newspaper article of the desired length, shake them in a bag, remove them in random order), nor his superb example of a poem constructed in this way ("prix ils sont hier convenant ensuite tableaux . . .") contradict this vision of easy energy; nor can they be said to arouse, in general, any overwhelming passion for the prolonged reading of much Dada poetry.[2]

But if this poetry is indeed a chance conglomeration of phrases, what can explain Tzara's statement that the Dada poem is the quintessence of pure structure, that it is based on a rhythm both unheard and unseen which he calls a "rayon d'un groupement intérieur vers une constellation de l'ordre" (*SDM*, p. 106)? Is this a genuine conviction, or a supreme example of the Dada joke? And if we consider the statement a serious one, we still do not know if the innate coherence is in each case due to the constants in the poet's own personality somehow reflected in the poem, or if it originates within the being of the poem itself. (Of course, since ambivalence and ambiguity are essential to Dada and to the extremes of its character, we should not wish for clarification or resolution).

There remains a more significant problem: since the essential groupings are intuitive and interior, is it not a useless enterprise to examine the necessarily partial and exterior links perceived by the reader, since they may lie in an entirely different realm from the ones inside? Perhaps so; but perhaps also the still frequent assumption that Dada was a totally negative and incoherent attitude which produced totally negative and incoherent results suffices to justify the brief catalogue of a few surface indications of coherence, whether or not they have any relevance to the interior ordering, and whether we consider them artifacts left by chance or predictive markers set up on purpose.[3]

Even Tzara's earliest French poems,[4] the *Vingt-cinq poèmes Dada* of 1918, show a certain unity of mood and imagery. For instance, the poem **"Printemps"** begins with the morbid instruction:

> placer l'enfant dans le vase au fond de minuit
> et la plaie,[5]

and continues with images of stagnation, melancholy, imprisonment, exile, and attempts at escape. Many of these images are attributed to animals: unhealthy water trickles down the antelope's legs, while the caged peacock is thirsty; broken grasshoppers and ant hearts are sown in the garden, while the deer flee over the sharp points of black branches. The title seems ironic in the most obvious and least subtle sense, since spring is rarely associated with melancholy, either in the human or in the natural world.

"Petite Ville en Sibérie" from the same collection begins with three parallel motionless and one-dimensional images which utterly negate any joy or freedom (people flattened together on the ceiling in a blue light, signs pasted on doors, and a label stuck on a medecine bottle) and continues with a series of alternating images of static ordering and irrational or frenzied movement, at times actual and at times only dreamed of:

> c'est la maison calme mon ami tremble
> et puis la danse lourde courbée
> offre la vieillesse sautillant d'heure en heure
>   sur le cadran
> le collier intact des lampes de locomotives
> coupées descend quelquefois parmi nous
> et se dégonfle tu nommes cela silence . . . et mon
>   cœur décent sur des maisons basses plus
>   basses plus hautes plus basses sur lesquelles
>   je veux galoper . . . dormir oh oui si l'on
>   pouvait seulement
> le train de nouveau . . . je reste sur le banc . . .
> des cœurs et des yeux roulent dans ma bouche
> en marche
>
>   (*MC*, p. 32)

In spite of the tranquil, if ridiculous, light cast by a herring tin on the tin roofs, our final picture of the **"Petite Ville"** includes little children in pools of blood and a bitter image of frantic motion and its complete futility:

> courons plus vite encore
> toujours partout nous resterons entre des
> fenêtres noires
>
>   (*MC*, p. 32).

The poem has thus progressed from imprisonment in a blue light, through the total inability either to move as one would like or to rest, to a permanent confinement within an absence of light and vision.

Some of these poems are based on contrasting images of motion and immobility like those just mentioned, but show, instead of any sustained atmosphere, certain shifts of mood parallel to the shifts of images. **"Gare,"** another of the *Vingt-cinq poèmes*, opens with a conscious separation between action and noise on one hand and the passive indifference of the poet on the other:

> danse crie casse
> roule j'attends sur le banc
>
>   (*MC*, p. 33).

Then comes an ironic comparison between the vital world of nature and the sheltered human world:

> le vol d'un oiseau qui brûle
> est ma force virile sous la coupole
> je cherche asile
>
>   (*MC*, p. 33). . . .

Echoing this last image are three examples of the poet's face enclosed—first by the circle of evening, then by a suitcase, and finally by the bars of a cage. Like the title image of the station, the strange conception of the face in the suitcase implies both motion (departure) and spatial limit. The suitcase has a logical place in the poem, for shortly after the question or challenge "partir," the poet, who has been quietly reading on the bench in the evening, answers: "je pars ce soir." The evening calm is spoiled in any case by dogs and jaguars howling in a factory but also in the poet's bed, a final image of rest denied which reminds us of the preceding poem's "dormir oh oui si l'on pouvait seulement." Most of the other elements in **"Gare"** reflect either the peaceful atmosphere with which the poet initially surrounds himself: his silent reading of the paper, the precise and wise god, an orderly friendship, the listening light near the beginning and the "lueurs sphéroidales" at the end—or the shattering of it: the poet's blackened eyes that he hurls into the waterfall, the weeping spark, and the lions and clowns in the last line, which are directly related to the dogs and jaguars, and which close the poem on the mocking and shrilly active tone of a circus.

"Les Saltimbanques"[6] (where the image of the circus performer mentioned in **"Gare"** is repeated) revolves about the whining sound of an accordeon ("glwawawa") and its obvious rhythm:

> *les cerveaux se gonflent s'aplatissent des*
> *   ballons lourds s'épuisent s'aplatissent*
> *   . . .*
> *se gonflent s'aplatissent se gonflent s'aplatissent*
> *   s'aplatissent*
>
> (*MC,* p. 76).

The poem is arranged on the page to suggest movement and variations in volume, but Tzara inserts an absolute and characteristic contrast to the movement, doubly amusing in its apparently self-referential note:

> *NTOUCA qui saute*
> *   marotte*
> *qui est dada qui est DADA*
> *   le poème statique est une nouvelle invention*
>
> (*MC,* p. 76). . . .

Dada poetry is of course anything but static. In fact, the reason the poet must reject all sentimentality in his work, according to Tzara, is that the "humidity" of tears often visible in past art might retard this intensely modern dynamism, merciless and severe. The ideal Dada poem "pousse ou creuse le cratère, se tait, tue ou crie le long des degrés accélérés de la vitesse" (*SMD,* p. 106). It is oriented not toward the concept of a whole, but rather toward the changing procession of different moments. "La force de formuler en l'instant cette succession variable, est l'œuvre" (*SMD,* p. 105).

Perhaps the most interesting trait of Tzara's early poetry is the way in which motion is so often juxtaposed with the stability of certain geometrical figures. In **"Gare,"** the flight of the bird is compared to the poet's act of seeking refuge in the safety of the cupola, and his invocation of the theme of departure and his resolution to leave are separated only by the image of his face in the circle of evening. As the circus performer climbs up the ladder, the poet observes his "oblong" skull, and finally the hearts of the medicinal plants are opened to lights with the shape of spheroids. In **"Circuit total par la lune et par la couleur,"** a poem entirely about motion, as the title indicates, there are circles everywhere. The announced image of the moon is followed in the first line by an iron eye, then by portholes, olives that swell into symmetric crystallisations ("pac pac"), a lemon, a coin, and the sun. And at the same time, all the nervous dancing of the Dada god, the vertical flight of butterflies and of rivers, roads, irregular rains, and kiosks, as well as the dilating of cells, the elongating of bridges, the writhing of yellow snakes, and the rapid march of all the shades of the color red, are subject to the sudden miraculous arrangements implied in the infinitely mobile universe of Dada spontaneity:

> *autour des pôles magnétiques les rayons se*
> *   rangent comme les*
> *plumes des paons*
> *boréal*
> *et les cascades voyez-vous se rangent dans leur*
> *   propre lumière*
> *au pôle nord un paon énorme déploiera lentement*
> *   le soleil*
> *   . . .*
> *quand je demande comment*
> *les fosses hurlent*
> *seigneur ma gêométrie*
>
> (*MC,* p. 74).

In his "Note sur la poésie," Tzara demands that the Dada poet write with joy, enthusiasm, and intensity, that he present a constantly varied spectacle: "Ruisseler dans toutes les couleurs . . ." (*SMD,* p. 104); his own poetry is as diverse and as brightly colored as Benjamin Péret's poems and stories, and it communicates the same peculiarly visual directness. The peacock feathers and the northern lights ("la nuit des couleurs") of the **"Circuit . . . par la couleur"** have a counterpart in many other early poems, where the incessant transformations are sometimes conceptual, sometimes rhythmic, but appeal more often and more vividly to the sight. Still another circus poem, **"Le Dompteur de lions se souvient,"** insists on the immediate attention of the onlooker, who will later be called upon to participate in the world of spectacle:

> *regarde-moi et sois couleur*
> *plus tard*
>
> (*MC,* p. 30),

and then presents a garishly-tinted assortment of blue antelopes, a red so lively that it rolls of its own momentum with no less energy than the marching reds already mentioned ("roule roule rouge"), and a green horse, with a number of white parasols for contrast. No Dada reader would have expected a subtle watercolor, since he knows that "Dada a aboli les nuances" (*SMD,* p. 119). All Dada colors have the clarity and pure affirmation of the glass corridors and the mountains of crystal which are the true domain of the Dada artist.

Tzara often associates colors with height, as if we should not content ourselves with the ordinary drab furnishings and undramatic spectacle of our world at eye-level:

> let jet d'eau s'échappe et monte
> vers les autres couleurs[7]
>
> en arc-en-ciel de cendre
> les couleurs hamides rôdent ivres[8]
>
> salis mouillés lambeau de nuit nous avons élevé
> en nous chacun de nous une tour de couleur si
>   hautaine
> que la vue ne s'accroche plus au-delà des
>   montagnes et des eaux . . . [9]

At other times color is more closely identified with human sensitivity, either in a positive setting, as when piano music runs multi-colored through the listeners' brains like the metallic veins in rocks, or in a negative one, where the aesthetic sense is insulted:

> les couleurs sont des chiffres qu'on tue et qui
>   sautent
> carrousel
> comme tout le monde.[10]

The vulgar circling of the carousel here is preceded by the spontaneous belly dance of a balloon, in opposition to the calm checkerboard of a landscape, just as the woman in kilometers of green rubber makes a brilliant contrast with the static and peaceful "blanches cordes du minuit atrophié" in a later section of the same poem. In this poem and in many others the two main themes of Tzara's early poetry, color and motion, are joined in an association closely related to his frequent use of the circus image.

With all this stress on color and movement and contrast, the poet is sure of forcing the reader's attention, which is his principal aim. "Nous sommes directeurs de cirque" (*SMD,* p. 15)—a second possible factor in the choice of circus imagery is a consciousness of the poem as performance, so that even the belly dance and the piano concert mentioned above can be considered self-referential according to this interpretation. Many of Tzara's poem start with a command, "regarde" or "regarde-moi." Others incorporate a testimony to the crucial role of vision: "voir," "vois mon visage," "regardez monsieur."[11] These are at once an invocation of the reader's power of sight and a self-reminder to the poet of the essential showmanship expected in his poetry.

Dada poetry is not meant to elicit the educated responses of cultured sensitivity, but rather the instant and incoherent primitive reactions of the eye and ear. If it permits no slow-moving intellectual translations, it seems to carry its own rapid and external indications of a possible (or,

as Tzara woud say, necessary) interior ordering. But since we cannot glimpse the internal order, our vision of the poem is likely to remain disordered, fragmented, and bewildering, in spite of the structural or thematic links perceived on the surface, which may or may not lie parallel to the unheard rhythm within. We can either place our faith in Tzara's guarantee of an intuitive luminous architecture, or accept his only half-humorous assurance that Dada's obscurity is so dark as to eventually create its own light; or we may, perhaps most wisely, follow his insistent advice that we look at the Dada poem as a simple spectacle, as a creation complete in itself and completely obvious. "L'art est à présent la seule construction accomplie en soi, dont il n'y a plus rien à dire, tant elle est richesse, vitalité, sens, sagesse. Comprendre, voir, Décrire une fleur: relative poésie plus ou moins fleur de papier. Voir." (*SMD,* p. 85).

NOTES

[1] Tristan Tzara, *Sept manifestes Dada* (Paris, Pauvert, 1962), p. 69. Referred to in text as *SMD.*

[2] Nor does the peculiar fashion in which the poems were published. Since the edition of 1918 is printed in a narrow column, it is impossible to tell which lines are continuations of the preceding ones and which are meant to be new; unfortunately, the most recent edition (1946), which has a wide column of print, takes the 1918 edition for a model instead of going back to the manuscript. Consequently, many lines which were originally long and made a definite contrast in texture when combined with the short ones are chopped up into two, three, or even four lines, resulting in a final impression of jerkiness often not present in the original manuscript. There are also other deformations: part of a poem placed in another poem (see the last of the *Vingt-cinq-et-un poèmes,* "le sel et le vin," whose first line comes from one page and the remaining part from the other side of the page, leaving the rest of the first page to be part of "la grande complainte de mon obscurité deux") and so on. Parts of lines are somehow lost in the transition between manuscript and printing, to say nothing of the rearrangements. Perhaps this does not matter, if one considers only Tzara's purely negative statements about art, so much more famous than his positive ones about poetry. But since he intended his *Note sur la poésie,* quoted here, to be a sort of preface to this work, it seems valid to take the statements within it as serious, at least in a Dada framework.

[3] It might be interesting to relate these theories of Tzara to the contemporary linguists' distinctions between deep structure and surface structure (see Chomsky et al.)

[4] His Roumanian poems of 1912-15 are not in question here since they are "pre-Dada," though it must be admitted that Tzara himself refused any such distinctions as "pre-Dada" and "post-Dada." See Claude Sernet's translations of and introduction to Tristan Tzara, *Les Premiers poèmes* (Paris, Seghers, 1965).

[5] In Tristan Tzara, *Morceaux choisis* (Paris, Bordas, 1947), p. 31. Referred to in text as *MC.*

[6] From *De nos oiseaux* of 1923.

[7] "La Grande Complainte de mon obscurité deux," from *Vingt-cinq poèmes,* quoted in Tristan Tzara, *Œuvres* (Paris, Seghers, 1952), p. 122.

[8] "Surface maladie," from *De nos oiseaux, ibid.,* p. 129.

[9] "Règle," from "Indicateur des chemins de cœur," *MC,* p. 106.

[10] "Cinéma calendrier du cœur abstrait," *MC,* p. 31.

[11] A god example of the visible linking of some of this poetry (the word "progression" is perhaps too strong) is "Le Dompteur de lions se souvient," which begins with the specific "regardez-moi" and ends with the general "voir."

Gordon Browning (essay date 1974)

SOURCE: "Tristan Tzara and Decomposition: 'Le géant blanc lépreux du paysage,'" in *Dada/Surrealism,* No. 4, 1974, pp. 27-34.

[*In the following essay, Browning argues that the structure of "Le géant blanc lépreux du paysage" was designed to subvert or sabotage the experience of reading this poem, as well as the poetic experience in general.*]

Explicating Tzara's **"Le Géant blanc lépreux du paysage"**[1] can be risky, since Tzara put the reader's efforts in the poem: "Here . . . the reader begins to scream . . . he is skinny, idiotic, dirty—he does not understand my poetry." Yet this portrait is itself comprehensible, and, as such, highlights the paradoxical aspect of Tzara's Dada poetry, in which intelligible statements announce the unintelligibility of the text, an imagery rich in creative suggestion prepares its own negation, and the implicitly poetic elements of pattern, movement, and vision reveal a poetics of anti-poetry. Moreover, the image here of the reader who does not understand makes us aware that **"Le Géant blanc"** is a poem about anti-poetry, a poem perhaps grounded in a poetic experience, but itself the negation of this experience's expression.

"Le Géant blanc lépreux du paysage" combines in a landscape scene the image of a deteriorating mountain and the image of a deteriorating reader. Terrestrial and marine imagery suggest the typical Alpine scene of a mountain dominating a lake. Superimposed on the image of the mountain and lake are a tumor, microbes, lungs, and even intestine-shaped tubular seaweed, which justify the title's personification of the countryside.

In a letter from Tzara in Zurich to Picabia, the theme of infected mountains reappeared in a definition of Switzerland: "Switzerland: a tumor where God has spit some lakes."[2] And in a letter to Breton, Tzara applied the diseased-mountain metaphor to his reaction to a train accident: "You can well understand that such an incident would cure even a Mont Blanc eaten by vermin."[3]

Pointing from North to South helps the reader unfamiliar with the Brazilian highlands to find his bearings, but the usual North-at-the-top-of-the-page form is inverted. Diagrammatic trickery puts the reader in an unfamiliar geographical situation, yet the upside-down view is such that the haphazardly built circle around the large central house has an uncanny resemblance to the plan of Paris that all French children know by heart. This is a large center plan: the Ile-de-la-Cité, dominated by Notre-Dame, the Sainte-Chapelle, and the "men's house" of governmental affairs in the Palace of Justice have roughly concentric circles on both sides of the Seine, delineated, as in the rings of a tree, by walls constructed at different times in the Middle Ages (the green *Guide Michelin* to Paris shows this). The French child also never forgets such a devotional image of a map after his years of indoctrination. Familiarity and unfamiliarity, placement and displacement in text and diagram corroborate one another.

Reading the surfaces of image and text reveals much more. The same photograph suggestive of Poussin is used to explain a network of myths in the early chapters of *Le Cru et le cuit,* but paradoxically, the *"native-as-staffage"* is the only element absent in the specialized study published seven years after *Tristes Tropiques.* Remembrance of Poussin is no longer evident, and the sense of classical landscape tradition is disembodied in favor of binary oppositions of myth in so complex an analysis that the self as topic of study must be removed. Lévi-Strauss, whose writing, as we have suggested, has strong literary resonance reminiscent of Proust and Mallarmé, displaces Paris once and for all. Study of arabesques of myth from *Le Cru et le cuit* to *L'Homme nu*—the latter a title-as-slip in the context of our discussion—could be construed as the alternately compassionate search for a flight from the Bororo native, as removal of the tourist cliché in the passage from New World to Old, or as expedition à la *National Geographic,* recounted in snapshots, to the four volumes of speculations composed in Paris and Lignerolles between June 1961 and September 1970. The 2,130 pages from *La Pensée sauvage* to the concluding volume of *Mythologiques* bear the mark of irrevocable absence or inability to recapture lost time and space.

In fact, we discover in the preface to *Le Cru et le cuit* that exertion and loss are transposed into a far more disciplined series of athletic exercises, which successfully sublimate the longings felt so keenly in the displacement of the *Tristes Tropiques.* The mythographer will translate systems of North and South American myths into his own system in order to reveal "a pattern of basic and universal laws: this is the supreme form of *mental gymnastics,* in which the *exercise of thought,* carried to its objective limits (since the latter have been previously explored by ethnographic research), emphasizes every muscle and every joint of the skeleton, thus revealing a general pattern of anatomical structure."[4] The books are then a record of mental pushups and jumping-jacks executed in a gymnasium of anthropology whose program, he says in the same context, "I have been pursuing since I wrote *Les Structures élémentaires de la parenté"* (1949), and of which *The Savage Mind,* despite the controversy it had provoked in Paris in 1962, "represented a kind of pause in the development of my theories: I felt the need for a break between two bursts of effort" (pp. 9, 11). To say that one of the most influential tracts of the 60s, counting 357 pages hyperbolic curve is first suggested in the ascent of the rising vision, which is continued metaphorically by the poet's own trip, then complemented by the disintegration of the reader, and finally completed geometrically in the last lines, which indicate a return to the lake.

"Le Géant blanc" also refers to making sounds. A helicon horn and violin introduce the flaming vision. The importance of sounds is suggested further by the image "the family of sounds" preceding the hyperbolic trip. And in the last section, the reader's incomprehension is represented as his own physical vibration from the noise of a Dada soirée. His stomach is a bass drum, he screams, he has *rrrrrr* on his soul—until flutes introduce coral and prepare the last underwater scene. Furthermore, the fact that part of the poem is real noise is obviously relevant: when, regardless of meaning, noises suggest words and words suggest noises, there is an implicit reduction of sense to sound. Certain sound associations, like the assonance and alliteration of "sans cigarette tzantzantza," "le sang gangà," and "gmbabàba/berthe," imply this generative correlation between sound fragments and the text. If they are thematically part of the poem's reference to itself, they are also concretely becoming poetry's negation.

"Froid jaune," another poem from the **Vingt-Cinq Poèmes**, provides a further concordance for **"Le Géant blanc."** It includes both aspects of the decomposition theme—the infected poet and the cadaver—linking them to poetic vision and the act of creating poetry. In contrast to **"Mouvement,"** which begins in the vibrating heights and descends to silence, **"Froid jaune"** begins with the suggestion of departing and ends by announcing an ascension. Central to this development is the declaration of the poet's physiological deterioration.

> piéton fiévreux et pourri . . .
>   . . . . .
>
> je pensais à quelquechose de très scabreux
>   . . . . .
>
> mon organe amoureux est bleu
> je suis mortel monsieur bleubleu
>
> et du cadavre monte un pays étrange
> monte monte vers les autres astronomies.

The poet is "pourri"—infected. Monsieur Bleubleu, to whom the poet confesses the scabrous state of his love organ and the apprehension of his mortality, is presumably also the personification of this ailment. As the blue love organ personified, Monsieur Bleubleu is also a character in *La Première Aventure céleste de Mr. Antipyrine*, where he crudely authors manifestoes of his own through his bowels.

The poet in **"Froid jaune"** is diseased, mortal, impotent. Since the personification of this infection, Monsieur Bleubleu, is himself a writer, there would seem to be a strong correlation between the themes of infection, impotence and decomposition and the making of anti-poetry. In this perspective, the last stanza of "Froid jaune" is illuminating, for it affirms an ultimate ascent:

> et du cadavre monte un pays étrange
> monte monte vers les autres astronomies.

In **"Froid jaune"** the poet has a colored sex organ and is mortal. The infection is personified, and from the cadaver a strange country rises. In **"Le Géant blanc"** there is a separation of the poet's decomposition from that of the cadaver, and consequently a doubling of the ascension motif. In the latter poem, a giant leprous mountain becomes a cadaver, and again, from this diseased scenery, a new vision rises. The pattern is repeated when the poet declares that his sex organ is cold and monochromatic. From this statement follows the ascent of the poet's brains on the hyperbolic trip. Poetry, Dada poetry, seems to be the ultimate term in the decomposition paradigm. Thus, decomposition, the cadaver, the poet's infection and his impotence disparage and negate the poetry they announce.

It is possible to interpret **"Le Géant blanc"** as an incipient poetic experience, which is then denied. On one hand, we see the vision and the suggestions of departure, and, on the other, the decomposition of the mountain-cadaver, the malady of the poet, and the disintegration of the reader. The scenery is sick, a fire in a rising visionary metamorphosis. The abrupt announcement of the poet's impotence ends the vision, and hermetic allusions to the poetic experience and departure follow. The declaration of the poet's exalted ascent is followed by the portrait of the reader, which completes the allusions to making poetry. He vibrates and himself produces the sounds he does not understand, sounds that eventually reintroduce the scenery, the algae underwater, and a three-line *bruitiste* conclusion.

In the first line, "le sel se groupe en constellation d'oiseaux sur la tumeur de ouate," I take the "tumor of cotton wadding" to be the snow cap. Salt apparently accumulates around the sore, as an irritant, or for its crystalline properties.[5] (Microbes will crystallize later in the text. Birds relate to the ascension-heights motif and also suggest potential movement, the mobility of the scene. In the second line, the attribution of lungs is part of the personification process.[6] It is an extension of the Mont-Blanc-eaten-by-vermin metaphor, and the internal teeter-tottering and crystallizing of bugs and microbes is an imagined disintegration. The next step in the personification begins with the image of macrocystis, a seaweed whose tubular thalli reach several hundred yards in length. Like the lungs, the intestinal seaweed is imagined, and serves to introduce to the scene the third level, the lake, where tentacles surround boats appearing as small scars on the surface. The personification of the leprous Alpine scene is now complete: a tumor for a peak, lungs deteriorating in the mountain's interior, intestinal algae below the waistline of the lake's edge. This is the first stage of the poem. The image of boats on the water, scars, dark patches on a lake shimmering with light, "paresse des lumières éclatantes" (strikingly poetic when detached from the poem), I believe are based on actual observation. It is from this bright reflecting light that the visionary section of the poem takes its impetus. From this wavering light, seen as flames rising from the water, there is a new all-consuming transformation of the scene, which the poet appropriates as an epiphany, attributing the origin of the flames to his own aggression, candles that he wields:

> je lui enfonce les cierges dans les oreilles angànfah
> hélicon et
> boxeur sur le balcon le violon de l'hôtel en baobabs
> de flammes.

Since, however, the mode of attack is ultimately anti-poetic, a de-poetization of the experience, the vision is represented as cacophony, an attack against hearing. The production of harsh and meaningless sounds has consistently implied a disparagement of poetry-making. The auditory motif, here the helicon horn and the violin associated with the flames, will be dominant in the portrait of the reader: *tombo et tombo,* bass drums, castanets, flutes, and *rrrrrrr.* The presence of the poet ("je lui enfonce"), the suggestion of the reader's presence ("ears"), and the initial association between sounds and flames ("le violon . . . en baobabs de flammes") link the ensuing metamorphic scene to the making of poetry.

I take the flame scene to be a visionary transformation of an actual landscape, rising from the lake and up the mountain—enveloping bracken, waterfalls, glaciers, rocks, snow, clouds, peaks—with boats appearing again at the top.[7] Into the vision at its zenith—"ultrared"—Tzara interjects the line implying the poet's physiological and creative insufficiencies: "ma queue est froide et monochromatique." The lament is crude, though humorous, and seemingly gratuitous in the context. But it can be considered here, as in other poems, an essential counter to the visionary experience and to its expression as poetry. Here the text apparently passes from the vision to the experience of the poem, the suggestion of the poem's origins and departure in very abbreviated form:

> les champignons oranges et la famille des sons au
> delà du tribord
> à l'origine à l'origine le triangle et l'arbre des
> voyageurs à l'origine.

The orange fungus or mushrooms recall again the decomposition theme.[8] "The family of sounds" is recognizable as part of the sounds-dissonance imagery related to poetry. "Beyond the starboard," as well as suggesting departure ("au delà"), also repeats the boat motif. Boats on the shimmering water initiated the vision and were apparently carried on it to the peaks and clouds at the top—"les ciseaux, et les nuages les ciseaux et les navires." Finally, we may infer in the next line that "l'arbre des voyageurs," an echo perhaps of "baobabs en flammes," alludes to poetry too, since it later became the title of a collection of Tzara's poems.

Anticipated by the leprous personification of the scenery, by the suggestion that its transformation is to be rendered first by an assortment of cacophonous noises, then by the crude and abrupt announcement of the poet's impotence, and finally by the abbreviation of the further

allusions to the poem's departure, the success implied in the line "mes cerveaux s'en vont vers l'hyperbole" is not the success of the poetic experience of living—conducting and naming a metamorphosis—but rather the affirmation of negating the poetry of this experience and of its expression. The portrait of the reader confirms that negation is the goal and that it has been achieved. Changing scenery was the subject of the poem, now the subject is the changing reader. The poem becomes his vibration through the noises of a Dada soirée, becomes his progressive deterioration and cretinization, becomes finally the declaration that the reader does not understand. The poem that was presumably once grounded in a poetic experience becomes the reader's reaction to its anti-poetic transposition.

"Le Géant blanc lépreux du paysage":

> le sel se groupe en constellation d'oiseaux sur la
> tumeur de ouate
>
> dans ses poumons les astéries et les punaises se
> balancent les microbes se cristallisent en palmiers
> de muscles balançoires
> bonjour sans cigarette tzantzantza ganga
> bouzdouc zdouc nfoùnfa mbaah mbaah nfoùnfa
> macrocystis perifera embrasser les bateaux chirurgien
> des bateaux cicatrice humide propre
> paresse des lumières éclatantes
> les bateaux nfoùnfa nfoùnfa nfoùnfa
> je lui enfonce les cierges dans les oreilles gangànfah
> hélicon et boxeur sur le balcon le violon de l'hôtel
> en baobabs de flammes
>
> les flammes se développent en formation d'éponges
>
> les flammes sont des éponges ngànga et frappez
> les échelles montent comme le sang gangà
> les fougères vers les steppes de laine mon hazard
> vers les cascades
> les flammes éponges de verre les paillasses blessures
> paillasses
> les paillasses tombent wancanca aha bzdouc les
> papillons
> les ciseaux les ciseaux les ciseaux et les ombres
> les ciseaux et les nuages les ciseaux les navires
> le thermomètre regarde l'ultra-rouge gmbabàba
> berthe mon éducation ma queue est troide et
> monochromatique nfoua loua la
> les champignons oranges et la famille des sons au
> delà du tribord
> à l'origine à l'origine le triangle et l'arbre des
> voyageurs à l'origine
> mes cerveaux s'en vont vers l'hyperbole
> le caolin fourmille dans sa boîte crânienne
> dalibouli obok et tombo et tombo son ventre est une
> grosse caisse
> ici intervient le tambour major et la cliquette
> car il y a des zigzags sur son âme et beaucoup de
> rrrrrrrrrrrrrr ici le lecteur commence à crier
> il commence à crier commence à crier puis dans ce
> cri il y a des flûtes qui se multiplient des corails
> le lecteur veut mourir peut-être ou danser et

commence à crier

il est mince idiot sale il ne comprend pas mes vers il
crie

il est borgne

il y a des zigzags sur son âme et beaucoup de rrrrrrr

nbaze baze baze regardez la tiare sousmarine qui se
dénoue en algues d'or

hozondrac trac

nfoùnda nbabàba nfoùnda tata

nbabàba

NOTES

[1] "Le Géant blanc" is the first poem in the *Vingt-Cinq Poèmes* (June
1918). It was probably composed in the fall of 1916, one of Tzara's first
Dada poems after his first Dada Manifesto and the play *La Première
Aventure céleste de Mr. Antipyrine.* The manifesto is highly self-dispar-
aging; the play, scabrous and unintelligible. But it is in his Dada poetry
that Tzara brings self-disparagement, the scabrous note, and the theme
of unintelligibility together in a unified movement and imagery. Twenty-
two years later, both Paul Eluard and Benjamin Péret included "Le Géant
blanc" in a list of ten or twelve essential poems in an answer to an
"Enquête: La Poésie Indispensable" (*Cahiers G.L.M.*, No. 8, October
1938, p. 53, p. 58). (Bibliographic note from Byron Leonard.)

[2] Sanouillet, *Dada à Paris,* letter dated July 11, 1920, reprinted in Appendix, p. 500.

[3] Sanouillet, op. cit., letter dated March [1 or] 5, 1919, p. 442.

[4] The importance of the theme of decomposition and its ultimate reference to poetry can already be inferred from Tzara's correspondence with
Max Jacob. Clearly in response to Tzara's initial comment (Tzara's letter
is not available), Jacob wrote on February 26, 1916, "I love you since you
do me and I love in you a great poet, but I believe it is necessary to come
back to vigorous constructions and to order. Decomposition broadens
art but recomposition strengthens it." Letter in Sanouillet, op. cit., p. 556.

[5] Reminiscent of "Le Géant blanc," but without the anti-poetic context,
flame, giant, mountain, and crystal are evoked in Tzara's "Note 14 sur la
poésie" (1917): "D'autres forces productives crient leur liberté, flamboy-
antes, indéfinissables et géantes, sur les montagnes de cristal et de
prière" (*Sept Manifestes Dada,* p. 107). In the anti-poem, the values of
these images are inverted; no longer expressions of productivity, liberty,
and concentrated purity, the mountain decomposes, the flames are spong-
es, and the crystal is infection.

[6] "Droguerie-Conscience," another of the *Vingt-Cinq Poèmes,* offers
further exterior description of the mountain, as well as a concordance for
the sickness in the lungs:

le géant le lépreux du paysage
s'immobilise entre deux villes
il a des ruisseaux cadence et les tortues des collines
s'accumulent lourdement
il crache du sable pétrit ses poumons de laine . . .

[7] Mr. Aa l'antiphilosophe's "Exegèse sucre en poudre sage" suggests
similar scenery, of flames, metamorphosis, and exalting ascension:

. . . Aa sort de son lit . . . paupières tremblantes, applaudissement
muet au spectacle des flammes jetées entre lignes parallèles,
étroites, vraiment trop brûlante affirmation d'en haut pour simple
coincidence sulfureuse du choc précis des nuages (ici les

montagnes se reflètent dans le lac) l'accouplement des rivages
ne serait pas impossible à l'aurore . . .

Ruth Caldwell (essay date 1974)

SOURCE: "A Step on Tzara's Road to Communication,"
in *Dada/Surrealism,* No. 4, 1974, pp. 35-41.

*[In the following essay, Caldwell suggests that in
L'Indicateur des chemins de coeur Tzara demonstrated
a concern for linguistic coherence that was part of his
transition from Dada to Surrealism.]*

During the 1920s, in a transition from Dadaism to Surrealism that has been more readily assumed than pinpointed, Tristan Tzara produced ten poems of rich thematic unity, a volume entitled ***L'Indicateur des chemins
de coeur***. The dominant theme of these poems is a desire
for communication, not only between humans, but between humans, animals, plants, and the cosmos.

Part of this theme is announced by the title of the volume. Although Tzara is not the only author to have used
a train schedule as a metaphor for communication with a
loved one (we find it in Proust's *Un Amour de Swann:*
"il se plongeait dans le plus enivrant des romans d'amour,
l'indicateur des chemins de fer . . .),[1] Tzara, with poetical economy, slightly deforms an ordinary term to render a new image. This new image is the quest of the heart,
which, like the routes of trains, reaches out, traversing
far and diverse places. The train and travel imagery is
carried over into many of the poems—in their titles,
**"Voie," "Bifurcation," "Pente," "Accès," "Signal,"
"Démarrage"**—and in the texts. Rather than showing
actual communication, the travel image emphasizes unfulfilled desire, search, and separation. We see this conflict in the first lines of **"Voie"** ("quel est ce chemin qui
nous sépare") and in **"Volt,"** which begins with confused
and distorted images of the world ("les tours penchées
les cieux obliques / les autos tombant dans le vide des
routes"), and ends in a wandering search ("perdu dans la
géographie d'un souvenir et d'une obscure rose / je rôde
dans les rues étroites autour de toi").[2]

The conflict presented by the desire for communication
and the abiding lack of it is also maintained by light and
dark imagery. At the beginning of **"Pente,"** darkness and
sickness are associated with separation and distance:

malade de nuits trop
amères ombres
sur le mur cru se dépassant aux enchères
les chiens aboient l'insaisissable distance[3]

By contrast, images of light and of rebirth accompany the
possibility of communication:

conduisent l'enfant à la bouche du jour

. . . . .

tu chantes des berceuses dans la langue de ta
lumière

. . . . .
tes yeaux renaissent dans le sang des chaudes
    interrogations[4]

Light imagery at times accompanies a cosmic imagery, a
mixture of biological, botanical, and chemical words that
suggests another possible communication. In **"Accès,"**
in the midst of an evocation of obscurity ("nuits incom-
plètes," "nuits avalées en hâte," "nuits enfouies," "rêves
arides," "salis mouillés lambeaux de nuit"),[5] the speaker
says that each of us has raised "such a high tower of
color" within ourselves, that the following results:

que la vue ne s'accroche plus au delà des montagnes
    et des eaux
que le ciel ne se détourne plus de nos filets de pêche
    aux étoiles
que les nuages se couchent à nos pieds comme des
    chiens de chasse
et que nous pouvons regarder le soleil en face jusqu'
    à l'oubli.[6]

Here the proximity of humans, animals, and the cosmos
is explicit. In many other poems, one sees the hidden
relationships between humans and other living elements,
as in **"Evasion"**:

et pourtant herbe si souvent passée sous le peigne du vent
qui sait quand viendront se joindre tes regards de
    chlorophylle aux miens.[7]

A technique in these poems suggesting communication is
the constant address to another person, a *je-tu* relationship present in every text. In many of the poems, the
person addressed could be a loved one from whom the
speaker is separated. This interpretation might apply to
"Voie," "Bifurcation" ("mon sourire est attaché à ton
corps"), **"Accès"** ("et pourtant mon repos ne trouve sa
raison / que dans le nid de tes bras . . ."), **"Signal"** ("je
ne puis pas t'écrire"), **"Volt"** ("je rôde dans les rues
étroites autour de toi"), and **"Démarrage"** ("sans joints
sans nervures tu es loin").[8] However, some references in
these poems do not support this interpretation. In **"Evasion,"** the speaker directly addresses grass ("tes regards
de chlorophylle"), and the person in **"Règle"** ("la promesse
tant attendue à l'horizon de ton sourire")[9] is ambiguous
in the poem's total context of cosmic imagery (actions
of the sea, sky, clouds, earth, and wind). The *tu* in **"Pente"**
has maternal qualities,

tu chantes des berceuses dans la langue de ta
    lumière

. . . . .

mère des chanson égorgées dans la vague noyées,[10]

but we might note that it is not the traditional mother
evoked here; rather one who has a special sort of language, and this image in context with images of the night,
the dream, and the sea (with a probable pun on *mer* and
mère), might suggest that the speaker is addressing his
subconscious. There are two direct addresses in **"Tonique."** In the first, the *tu* is passive, his chest a quay

exposed to the somewhat rude clarity of the sun. At the
end of the poem, the *tu* whom the speaker awaits at "the
door of the day" has become active and verbal:

la lumière du jour s'allume à tes lèvres
vernies par le souriant avantage de ce jour
et tes lèvres s'allument à l'éclat des syllabes
qui s'échappent aux lumineuses défaillances de tes
    lèvres[11]

While this poem might indicate a communication between
the speaker and some loved one, it might also very well
suggest the doubling of the speaker, where he addresses
himself (*tes lèvres*) in an effort at re-unification in expression (*des, syllabes: lumineuses defaillances de tes
lèvres*). This interpretation is reinforced by the marine
image that appears earlier in the poem:

bleu est le ciel dans le travail des marins
les cordes des âges tendues entre leurs mains
les départs risqués vers de bégayants langages
entre leurs mains qui sèment des signaux l'étrange
    langage[12]

This image, with the references to language and signs,
might suggest a descent into the subconscious, rather than
a simple sea voyage.

Given these possible interpretations of *tu*, and considering the varied imagery of communication in these poems,
the vocative might be more generalized, indicating not
only the possible communication between the speaker
and a loved one, but also the communication between the
speaker and himself, and ultimately through language, his
communication with all beings. The *nous* implied in some
of these poems and explicit in others then becomes enlarged to include all beings in the endeavor for communication, and what might be personal love poems become
generalized expressions of communion.

The preceding quotations imply that language is the solution to separateness and to the desire for communion
between humans and the universe. References to language
in these texts are constant and intentional. The capacity
for written or oral expression is attributed to all beings
of the universe, as in **"Voie"** ("une fleur est écrite au
bout de chaque doigt"), **"Bifurcation"** ("comme
l'escargot avec de fines voix"), and **"Eyasion"** ("réunit
les berges en lacets de dialogue").[13] Sometimes the references are negative, indicating the absence of language
and the desire for expression, as in **"Signal"**:

mon vers hésite au delà des pas.
. . . . .
que tu guérisses aussi vite que la parole du lumineux
    est vraie
. . . . .
mais nous sommes si éloignés de la chantante
    étreinte[14]

In **"Règle,"** false everyday language must be destroyed
in order to give way to the true, intimate communion:

le vent étrangle la parole dans le gosier du village
    pauvre village
sa vie d'étranges éclaircies
cassée est la chaîne des paroles couvertes d'hivers
    et de drames
qui reliaient les intimes éclaircies de nos existences[15]

Only two poems, **"Accès"** and **"Volt,"** do not have explicit references to spoken or written languages. However, in **"Volt,"** the line "distillant son dépit à travers les fragments de mémoire et d'arithmétique,"[16] by its reference to such operations of the brain as memory and symbol-making, might imply language in its state of formation. We have already seen the importance of language as a communicative power in **"Pente"** and **"Tonique,"** the title of the latter poem taking on perhaps a secondary meaning, aside from that of a medical tonic, since it could refer to a stressed word or sound.

We are sure of Tzara's intentional insistence on the power of language not only from the frequency of these references but also from evidence in his manuscript corrections.[17] In an early prose version of **"Règle,"** we do not see the phrase "au bruit des pages des vagues tournées par le lecteur du ciel inassouvi"[18]; its addition in the published poem gives a literary sense to man's interpretation of and communion with the cosmos (*ciel, vagues*). In the manuscript of **"Pente,"** the word *nourriture* in the line "mains qui portent la nourriture à la bouche de l'enfant"[19] is corrected to read *parole,* thus reinforcing the later references to the "mother of songs" whose "hand agitates language."

Apart from their thematic signification, these poems are effective in their composition. We see a marked difference in techniques between this volume and earlier ones, for the composition of these poems demonstrates a will to communication that corresponds to the theme of the poems. No longer is the reader stopped by strange or exotic words; in their place are the common and general words for the sea, wind, earth, flowers, mountains, and animals. Our attention to sound is drawn purely by alliteration or assonance, such as "rêves arides par de longs regards" (**"Accès"**), "les orties sont sorties les sorts en sont pleins" (**"Démarrage"**), "pieds nus et gorge rêche au guet" (**"Evasion"**), "l'onde de leur indolence" (**"Règle"**).[20]

Nor do we find an incomprehensible juxtaposition of words, although similes and metaphors continue to be rare in these poems. The juxtaposition of contradictory nouns to render an unusual image ("la main de ma pensée," "le muscle de la branche")[21] is a favorite Surrealist technique, but it is one that makes particular sense in this volume, where it corresponds to the theme of communication of the elements.

The lines are no longer isolated images in themselves, as in earlier poems, for the images here are continued over several lines. Tzara explicitly reinforces association by repeating words from line to line: "des eaux les riantes veines / veines de vent inconstant" (**"Tonique"**).[22] On occasion, the association between disparate elements is achieved through

a pun, as in these lines from **"Signal"**: "qu'entre l'amour et la maudite coincidence / j'ai planté le grain de ton savourex chagrin,"[23] where chagrin is likened to grain first by homophony and then by the underlying image of something that grows from the interior.

Syntax is never disrupted in these poems, which move easily from line to line in the language as well as the images. An effective example of this facility and harmony of syntax and imagery is seen in these lines of **"Volt"**:

la ville bouillonnante et épaisse de fiers appels et de
    lumières
déborde de la casserole de ses paupières
ses larmes s'écoulent en ruisseaux de basses
    populations.[24]

Here the comparison of an overpopulated city to an overflowing pot and then to an eye filled with tears is accentuated by the placement of key verbs at the beginning of new lines, which, by continuing the action, give a textual sense of overflowing.

Many inversions are in the standard form of adjective-verb-noun found in epic poetry, and they give a grandiose tone to the search evoked in these poems: "bleu est le ciel dans le travail des marins" (**"Tonique"**), "brisée est la clavicule de la montagne en haillons de neige" (**"Evasion"**). Although many lines are long and complicated, they are counterbalanced by short lines eloquent in their simplicity: "je ne veux pas te quitter" (**"Bifurcation"**), "je ne puis pas t'écrire" (**"Signal"**), "quel est ce chemin qui nous sépare" (**"Voie"**).[25]

Marking a will for poetry and for understanding, this volume occupies an unusual place in Tzara's poetical evolution, being far more coherent than the works published immediately before and simpler than many of his later volumes. The strong desire to communicate that is expressed thematically is reflected technically by the coherence of this work. While many of Tzara's works contain references to words, language, and a search for communication, few works are so consistent in this imagery as *L'Indicateur des chemins de coeur*. It would seem that, momentarily, Tzara had found a language.

NOTES

[1] Ed. Gallimard, 1, p. 293 ("he plunged himself into the most intoxicating of love novels, the train schedule").

[2] "Track" ("What is this road that separates us")
"Volt" ("leaning towers oblique skies / autos falling into the empty space of roadways . . . lost in the geography of a memory and of an obscure rose / I prowl in the narrow streets around you").

[3]

"Gradient"
sick from nights too bitter
bitter shadows
on the crude wall out-bidding one another
the dogs bark the elusive distance.

4 conduct the child to the mouth of day

. . . . .

you sing lullabies in the language of your light

. . . . .

Your eyes are born again in the blood of warm interrogations.

5 incomplete nights . . . nights swallowed in haste . . . buried nights . .
. arid dreams . . . dirtied, damp tatters of night.

6

that the view no longer gets caught beyond the mountains
and the waters
that the sky no longer turns away from our star fishing
nets
that the clouds lie at our feet like hunting dogs
and that we can look straight in the face of the sun as far
as oblivion.

7 and yet grass passed so often under the wind's comb
who knows when your chlorophyll glances will come to join   mine.

8 "Junction" ("my smile is attached to your body")
"Approach" ("and yet my rest does not find its reason / except in the
nest of your arms")
"Signal" ("I can't write you")
"Volt" ("I prowl in the narrow streets around you")
"Start" ("Without joints without ribs you are far away").

9 "Rule" ("the promise so expected at your smile's horizon").

10 you sing lullabies in the language of your light

. . . . .

mother of songs slaughtered drowned in the wave.

11 the light of the day lights up at your lips
varnished by the smiling advantage of this day
and your lips light up at the flash of syllables
that escape from the luminous lapses of your lips.

12 blue is the sky in the work of the sailors
ropes of the ages taut between their hands
risky departures towards stammering languages
between their hands that sow the strange language of signals.

13 "Track" ("a flower is written at the end of each finger")
"Bifurcation" ("like the snail with fine voices")
"Evasion" ("reunites the banked edges in laces of dialogue").

14 my verse hesitates beyond the steps

. . . . .

may you recover as quickly as the word of the luminous is true

. . . . .

but we are so far from the singing embrace.

15 the wind strangles the word in the throat of the village,
poor village
its life of strange openings.

broken is the chain of words covered by winters and dramas
that bound the intimate openings of our existences.

16 distilling its spite through fragments of memory and arithmetic.

17 Consulted at the Bibliothèque littéraire Jacques Doucet, TZR 14-16.

18 at the sound of pages of waves turned by the unsated reader of the
sky.

19 hands that bring nourishment to the mouth of the child.

20 dreams dry with long glances ("Approach")
the nettles are out the destinies are full of them ("Start")
barefoot and harsh throat on the watch ("Evasion")
the billow of their indolence ("Rule").

21 my thought's hand; the branch's muscle.

22 the laughing veins of the waters / veins of inconstant wind.

23 that between love and accursed coincidence / I planted the grain of
your savory chagrin.

24 the city bubbling and thick with proud calls and lights
overflows the saucepan of its eyelids
its tears flow out in gutters of lowly populations.

25 blue is the sky in the work of the sailors ("Tonic")
broken is the clavicle of the mountain rags of snow ("Evasion")
I don't want to leave you ("Junction")
I can't write you ("Signal")
What is this road that separates us ("Track").

Roger Cardinal (essay date 1978)

SOURCE: "Adventuring into Language," in *The Times Literary Supplement*, No. 3,993, October 13, 1978, p. 56.

[*In the following review of* Oeuvres complètes, *Cardinal praises the "wild and nihilistic glitter" of Tzara's Dada poems and identifies his primary poetic accomplishment as the passionate and direct expression of his personality.*]

It is a tried irony of French literary life that those who most violently attack the conventions of the cultural establishment should in due time achieve cultural security themselves by virtue of the careful collation and publication of their *Oeuvres complètes*. It is now the turn of Tristan Tzara: the extremist leader of that movement of cultural terrorism known as Dada is now publicly honoured by a monumental edition, complete with detailed scholarly apparatus. What would Monsieur Antipyrine have said?

These first two bulky volumes of Tzara's prolific lifework take us from the poems of his adolescence in Bucharest, through the classic texts of Zürich and Paris Dadaism, and on into his Surrealist period in the late 1920s and early 1930s. Tzara himself refused to accept that his different "periods" were discontinuous, and kept a careful archive of his own. From this and from Henri Béhar's painstaking editorial researches, we now have the material from which the overall shape of Tzara's achievement as a counter-cultural writer can be elicited.

Dada once styled itself a "société anonyme pour l'exploitation du vocabulaire", and Tzara was one of the major forces in its verbal productivity drive. Having abandoned his native Romanian, he found himself in an ambivalent position with regard to his adopted language, French. On the one hand, along with other renegades of Dada/Surrealism, he saw the language of international diplomacy and social finesse as supporting a cultural system he was pledged to sabotage; on the other, he was attracted to its fluency and euphony, its appropriateness to lyrical ends. From the outset, Tzara's outrageous onslaughts on syntax and linguistic coherence are accompanied by a reassuring sense that even as it succumbed to his aggressive manipulations, the French language remained attractive. It is fascinating to observe how the writer's style develops in these volumes: lyrical beauty seems to be fostered by the very ravages that the Dada experiments dictated.

Tzara's literary terrorism took the form of experimental writing based on an astounding variety of techniques. The texts include spontaneous or automatic poems (more or less consistent with the principles of composition defined by Breton in the Surrealist Manifesto), sound poems using nonsense syllables, and poems adapted from Negro and Maori folk-songs. Tzara experimented in "fold-in" techniques à la William Burroughs whereby, boasting that he was a "self-kleptomaniac", he would rejuvenate old texts of his own by cutting them up and shuffling the bits. He would delightedly appropriate any manuscript or printing errors, and introduce meaningless coinages ("tzaca tzac tzacatzac"), abstruse scientific terms, newspaper headlines, publicity slogans, anagrams, puns ("mississi-cri") and frenzied repetitions (as witness the page from the 1918 *Manifeste Dada* on which the single word *hurle* appears in a block eleven rows wide by twenty-five lines deep). Together with their typographical inconsistencies and their general submission to the principle of syntactic and semantic illogicality, the resulting texts are almost impossible to read in any coherent way. They are manifestations of disorder and absurdity, and defy all normal logic.

There is a wild and nihilistic glitter about the Dada poems of *Vingt-cinq poèmes* (1918) and *De nos oìseaux* (1923), for instance. Tonal shifts occur from line to line, thrusting the reader through staccato transitions—calm, querulous, sly, disdainful. The vocabulary is in constant flux; all sense of sequence or form is absent. To read is to speed through an alien country where landmarks flash past too fast for recognition. There is no centre and no shape to these poems; their message is purely one of aggressive self-manifestation: "Danse crie casse". They are spectacular provocations which deliberately obstruct the intelligence in search of meaning and implicitly challenge the reader—"Dare you take this to be Literature?":

> le marais de miel bleu
> chat accroupi dans l'or d'une taverne
>   flamande
> boum boum
> beaucoup de sable bicycliste jaune
> château neuf des papes

> manhattan il y a des baquets d'excrément devant tòi
> mbaze mbaze bazebaze mleganga
>   garoo

At this stage, Tzara's ideal text would seem to be one in which words emerge in a naked state, not as carriers of meaning proper but as manifestations of a kind of pure electrical energy. And each word is as highly charged as the next: "concentration intérieure craquement des mots qui crèvent crépitent". Each word comes out of the blue, so to speak, lacking a context and yet bristling with its own urgent singularity. The author himself is nowhere to be seen, so that what he offers is a random texture, an anonymous surface from which no intention or meaning can be read.

However, no writer would want to keep up such an illegible mode for ever, and Tzara's savage zest generates occasional passages of accessible lyricism. The reader battling his way through the blizzard of unintelligibility is rewarded by abrupt transitions into zones of radiant meaning. Random islets of unexpected beauty float up, images which glow with the strange and moving colours of a dream:

> et je dessine le pays et tes bijoux
>   sont des yeux vivants
> la vache accoucha un grand oeil
>   vivant de douleur ou de fer
> au bord de la mer monte en
>   spirale la sphère
> la tempête

There is a sense, then, in which this most formless and anarchic of poetry eventually coheres and reveals some sort of purpose and shape. The climax of **"Maison Flake"** (1919) expresses a vision which it is not hard to read as being consciously constructive rather than terroristic:

> ici on n'assassine pas les hommes
>   sur des terrasses
> qui se colorent de la succession
>   intime les lenteurs
> nous tentons des choses inouïes
> mirages in-quarto micrographies des
> âmes chromatiques et des images
> nous portons tous des grelots-
>   tumulte que nous agitons
> pour les fêtes majeures sur les
>   viaducs et pour les animaux

Here the poetic meaning emerges clearly enough in the form of an apologia for the poem itself. Sounding much like Apollinaire in "La Jolie Rousse", Tzara describes his aim of uncovering poetic images which will suggest to his reader that a deeper harmony underlies the surface discontinuities of reality and language.

The more one reads Tzara, the more one becomes attuned to the notion of the creative stance as sketched in the 1919, "Note sur la Poésie". There Tzara sees poetry as a juggling with disparates whereby the juggler stands at the central point of serene communion with his innermost being: "Eye, water equilibrium, sun, kilometre, and everything that I can imagine as belonging together and which represents a potential human asset: sensibility". The continuity which underlies the torrential generation of texts is that of the sensibility at their centre. Tzara may insist on remaining impersonal, on setting value only on work produced by one who remains "demanding and cruel, pure and honest", that is: committed to no intentional meaning. Yet the immediacy and sheer verve of his writing is such as to convey a lively sense of his involvement: the author's euphoric pleasure in his own text transmits a kind of presence after all. We witness "l'intensité d'une personnalité transposée directement" as, like a watermark on soiled paper, the temper of the propelling consciousness shimmers beneath the flux of words. And here one can find confirmation of a paradox that has haunted French poetry since Rimbaud and Mallarmé: that the more a writer strives to extinguish his individuality, the more idiosyncratic and personal his style becomes.

Tzara evidently saw himself as fitting more and more into the French poetic tradition as he developed. The love poems of *Indicateur des chemins du coeur* (1928) and *Arbre des voyageurs* (1930) contain elegiac echoes of Lamartine and Apollinaire, while the major poetic performance of *L'Homme approximatif* (composed during 1925-30) is a deliberate attempt on Tzara's part to stake a claim to a place in French literary history as a poet confident enough to sustain a long poem, on a par with Apollinaire ("Zone"), Saint-John Perse (*Vents*) and Eluard (*Poésie ininterrompue*).

While, in this ninety-page poem, Tzara remains very much the literary "savage", he demonstrably draws upon all sorts of sophisticated effects, many of them entirely traditional. Most noticeably, the verbal flux now falls into rhythmic clusters, long lines reminiscent of the epic *laisses* of a Perse, and is punctuated by recurring words or leitmotif phrases that communicate an overall sense of an insistent, structured argument.

The poem is centred on the consciousness of the "approximate man": "homme approximatif te mouvant dans les à-peu-près du destin / avec un coeur comme valise et une valse en guise de tête". This Tzara's persona, a timid yet hopeful pilgrim who battles for meaning in a universe of absurdity.

    la brèche ouverte au coeur de
      l'armée de nos ennemis les
                  mots
    la glaciale paresse du sort qui nous
        laisse courir à notre guise
    nos chiens nous-mêmes courant
              après nous-mêmes
    seuls dans l'écho de nos propres
        aboiements d'ondes mentales
    malgré l'inexprimable plénitude qui
        nous entoure d'impossible
    je me vide devant vous poche
             retournée

No longer absent from the verbal struggle, the poet reveals his frailty in the face of the "inexpressible plenitude" of his surroundings. Words seem hostile, and he can only succumb to their terrifying meaninglessness as they flash through consciousness: "words streaking/leaving the merest trace majestic trace behind their meaning scarcely meaningful". Perplexed, and disoriented, he bobs in a whirlpool of words, cosmic winds and snows, fire and oceans,

    horreurs grimées enfers asphyxies
          de suie sueurs
    grimaces d'orages cataclysmes con-
        tagieux avalanches tombes

Like Perse or (as Jean Cassou suggested) Walt Whitman, Tzara had in mind in this long poem to build up a catalogue of allusions that would support a poetic vision of elemental depth and encyclopedic completeness. Animals, minerals, cities, jungles—all are evoked in a polymorphous discourse voiced by a subject who, at first bewildered, grows in confidence, being gradually borne upon the tide of words to achieve a position of confidence and all-surveying dominance. Henri Béhar comments that the poet "transforms himself into mineral, vegetable, bird, insect: he is himself *natura naturata*".

That is, in this apocalyptic explosion of language, the poet finally approaches the primal seat of creativity, the point where the naked word reveals the naked truth about the world:

    à la racine du monde dans les
          berceaux des germes
    l'homme nidifie ses sens et ses
             proverbes

A language which at last takes root and generates profound meaning, this is Tzara's ultimate aim.

At the same time, however, his tone has a certain shrillness which makes his grand theme less overwhelming than does, say, the more majestic rhetoric of Perse. Prolonged reading of the poem has left this reader unsatisfied that it succeeds in approximating a visionary grasp on cosmic realities. Much of *L'Homme approximatif* is too wordy, the modulation from chaos to confidence too sleekly *verbal*. "La parole seule suffit pour voir", claims Tzara, in echo of a prime Surrealist tenet; but this text is often too mannered and wilful to create the full visionary effect.

One turns therefore to the last section in these two volumes, *L'Antitête*, which groups texts written across the Dada and Surrealist years (1919-32). The most impressive are a set of automatic prose pieces under the heading **"Le Désespéranto"**, a title which ties in the two strands of Tzara's poetic effort: a desire to achieve the condition of a universal language, an "esperanto" which will touch on all aspects of human feeling and thought; and the acknowledgment that true intensity of expression can only be found in circumstances of stress and desperation—the courting of self-extinction is a corollary of verbal authenticity.

These are indeed texts of moving authority and incisiveness, which suggests that it was in prose that Tzara was best able to sustain his characteristic "attack". In the closing piece, **"Les Consciences atténuantes"**, the adventure into language comes across most powerfully, truly convincing the reader that "beneath each stone, there is a nest of words and it is from their rapid spinning that the substance of the world is formed". It is in such texts, stripped of self-conscious flourishes and rhetorical supports, that Tzara comes closest to that "stenography of feeling" which he came to see as his poetic goal, and thus demonstrates the remarkable way in which his uncompromising poetics of non-intentionality finally communicates "l'aiguë intensité de la conscience", the naked energy of his singular consciousness.

Mary Ann Caws (essay date 1981)

SOURCE: "Dada's Temper, Our Text: Knights of the Double Self," in *The Eye in the Text: Essays on Perception, Mannerist to Modern,* Princeton University Press, Princeton, New Jersey, 1981, pp. 133-140.

[*In the following excerpt, Caws examines the emphasis that Tzara and other Dadaists placed on the reactions of their readers and argues that the audience is "a passenger in Dada's rite of passage."*]

This text takes its starting point in the Dada temperament and in what it perceives, as well as the way in which it perceives it, moving from the double and two-way images of Duchamp and Tzara to an apparently closed door, in reality open.[1] The Dada temperament is opposed to closure of all sorts.

From **"M. Antipyrine"** to **"M. AA I'Antiphilosophe,"** from **"M. Anti-psychologue"** to **"M. Antitête"** the antis have it: anti-aspirin, but also anti-head and anti-the-workings-of-the-head, philosophical and psychological: Tzara's approximate man, savage or not, will have none of the noble confessional about him. His self-portraiture is ironic and a put-down: He stutters: "Aa," or then "da-da," and he is given to odd stylistics, half-repetitions, ruptures, and incompletions: "Je me, en décomposant l'horreur, très tard" (Tz, 2:293; I myself, decomposing horror, very late), or, disguising his disorder in the reassuring cliché style of a proverb, even more offputting: "Quand le loup ne craint pas la feuille je me langueur" (Tz, 2:293; When the wolf does not fear the leaf I langor me). Tzara will write later about the **"Automatism of Taste"** and is, at the time of **"M. AA l'anti-philosophe,"** preparing a one-up on *haute couture,* which is to say, an *haute coupure,* cutting and shaking up the elements in some hat or other, making a cutting for a transplant and a sample—a **"Treatise on Language,"** in fact, but the fact is hidden within the body of the **"Sluicegates of Thought,"** a brief manifesto in the *Antitête* about the "roundness of my half-language." About this language, we

had scarcely to be told that it was "invertebrate." The intensity of the temper already stressed may be antipsychological, but there is clearly no question of forgetting the mental mechanism or what contains it. Tzara's incompleted novel is called *Faites vos jeux* (Place Your Bets) and the play does begin here, but in the head. The last four chapters are entitled "The Surprise Head," "The Tentacle Head," "The Head at the Prow," and, as a resumé, "Tête à Tête." The collection begins with the expression: "le coeur dans le coeur" (the heart in the heart) and ends not with a heart-to-heart chat but a head-to-head summary: this self-portrait is based on an intellectual self-mockery.

Now Dada is a self-regarding movement in moving opposition to its own image and self-image. That there should be a paradox of this kind available is all to the good, for, as we know, Dada and Surrealism flourish on the juxtaposition of contraries: yes and no meeting on streetcorners "like grasshoppers," according to Tzara, and, for Breton, the meeting of high and low, birth and death, absence and presence. Take, for instance, Tzara's "Static poem" (which transforms the words into individuals: "from the four letters 'bois' there appear the forest with the fronds of its trees, the forest-keepers' uniforms and the wild boar; perhaps also a Pension Bellevue or Bella Vista" (Tz, 1:726). Now whatever lovely view there is is enhanced by its own opposition, cheerfully and vigorously stated: "Long live Dadaism in words and images! Long live the world's Dadaist events! To be against this manifesto means to be a Dadaist" (Tz, 1:358). Self-regarding and self-negating, keeping its humor good, Dada keeps it well.

As for the regard of self, one of the most instructive texts "signed by" Rrose Sélavy, herself already the imagined female double of Duchamp as we know, was supposedly written in German by a girlfriend of Man Ray and translated into English, therein entitled, sardonically "Men before the Mirror." The text in this table-turning description is cruel, as one might expect: Rrose Sélavy's adopted text is not directed at a mirrored man, standing for all men, but at men, less general, more sex-specific:

> Many a time the mirror imprisons them and holds them firmly. Fascinated they stand in front. They are absorbed, separated from reality and alone with their dearest vice, vanity. . . . There they stand and stare at the landscape which is themselves, the mountains of their noses, the humps and folds of their shoulders, hands and skin, to which the years have already so accustomed them that they no longer know how they evolved; and the multiple primeval forests of their hair. They meditate, they are content, they try to take themselves in as a whole.[2]

Already, of course, a woman writing about these men as they are mirrored—whereas in art the woman is usually mirrored—is retracing the gesture of the one and the other, herself and them, in opposition and in fascination; to complicate things further, a woman writer writes of Marcel Duchamp playing Rrose Sélavy playing at being a German girl playing at watching men watching themselves. The self-regarding game is right up Dada's alley, but only the sensitive reader will be bowled over by a direct hit:

"The mirror looks at them. They collect themselves. Carefully, as if tying a cravat, they compose their features" (MS, pp. 195-196). The very act of looking as it is seen by the other her or himself creating that self in the act of its own self-regard and self-creation occupies the center of the fascinated gaze.

Since it is Duchamp who reminds us that "It is the OBSERVERS who make the pictures" (MS, p. 173), it is scarcely necessary to point out a certain possible supersensitivity in the reaction of the female eye to some particularly aggressive images such as, for instance, the famous Mona Lisa inscribed by Duchamp to make a sort of Lady Lisa in hot pants ("L.H.O.O.Q." which is an abbreviation for "Elle a chaud au cul," or she has a hot seat).

As to this self-regarding self, it is rarely at ease: we remember the reflective despair of Jacques Rigaut already quoted: "I consider my most disgraceful trait to be a pitiful disposition: the impossibility of losing sight of myself as I act. . . . I have never lost consciousness."[3] Dada, that ambivalent, bisexual, two-headed delight, contemplates its own visage in some of Ribemont-Dessaignes' *artichauds,* hot spots for art, or really hot plates, keeping them available on the burner, like a *réchaud,* to heat and reheat, looking and not looking, in one temper now, and now another: "Dada, o Dada, what a face! so sad as all that? so merry? Look at yourself in the mirror. No, no, don't look at yourself."[4]

Full of doubt, even as to the writing, the narrator of *Faites vos jeux* laments his inability to step outside the self, or to judge himself more independently. That alone:

> is sufficient for me to detest myself, for me to despise my egoism. I am lacking a distance between the characters and the events they give rise to. My criticism is not objective. My readers will never be able to follow me.
>
> (Tz, 1:284)

What is this but a contemplation in the mirror of his own writing? That the woman in the text should be called "Mania," a sort of transformation of a "manie" or obsession predicting Breton's own *Nadja,* whose obsessed vision inspires our reading of Breton, is not without its own obsessive interest. The entire text of the unentire novel is based on the substitution and the repetition of self and other, and on the fatigue of the reflective game, no matter how fascinating:

> Although visibly false, this adventure excited me to such a degree (doubt had already substituted another self for my own) that I left to see her. . . . But distance had already withered my passion. For the first time I felt fatigue and boredom inhibiting the flow of my speech. . . . We, the knights of the double-self.
>
> (Tz, 1:290)

This double self, here pictured as tragic, is referred to in an early passage of *L'Anti-tête* (**The Antihead**) as a sort of Rimbaldian parody, without the tragedy:

> Je m'appelle maintenant tu.
> Je suis meublée et maison de Paris.
>
>   . . .
>
> Maison de Paris, je suis très belle.
> Bien imprimée.
>
>   . . .
>
> Monsieur Aa l'antiphilosophe Je-Tu tue, affirme de plus en plus que, sans ailes, sans dada, il est comme il est, que voulez-vous . . .
>
>   (Tz, 1:399)

> I am now called you.
> I am furnished and a Parisian house.
>
>   . . .
>
> A Parisian house, I am very lovely.
> Well printed.
>
> Mr. Aa the antiphilosopher I-You yous, kills,
> affirms more and more that, without wings.
> without her, without Dada, he is as he is,
> What can I tell you . . .

And yet the knight of the double countenance here leads the game, just as Tzara did in his early role of circustamer. "De mes maux qu'on m'a fait subir" says the narrator of *Faites vos jeux* (Place Your Bets) which reads: "Of the sufferings I have had to undergo / I am the elegant inspirer"—or then, and I believe we should read it both ways: "Of my words I am the elegant lover," for that *animateur,* returning to us the "animal" with the "anima," is also an "amateur" (Tz, 1:284).

Amateur, chiefly, of the word and the eye: Ribemont-Dessaignes' "oeil verbe" or "eye word" in the strong sense of that world-creating word: it is on that globe, assuredly, that we should keep our eye. "Sous je," reads one of his titles, literally "Under I," if I may be allowed to profit from the English word play. The spirit of Dada includes plays in all senses and in the most slippery ones, including the game's denial as its own mirror image. Witness Ribemont-Dessaignes' *Manifeste avec Huile* (Manifest with Oil), a text at play at not-playing.

> Dada is no longer a game. There is no longer a game anywhere. . . . There is one moment of the game when you play at not playing, and when it ends badly. That moment is now.

> The street must be sad in your eyes when you go out into it. And there must be no more consolation for you in the pit of your stomach. . . . But DADA knows choreography and the way to use it. . . . For you have to love me right through the cancer of your heart, through the heart-cancer that I shall have given you.

Aragon's *Le Paysan de Paris* (The Peasant of Paris) is also a spreader of this other sort of social disease in the passages of Paris, the vertiginous poison and poisonous vertigo of "that vice," as he called Surrealism, destructive to the middle-aged mind. But Dada's choreography, subtle and unsubtle, is really supervisual, and metaphysical, superirritating, and superb, as well as upsetting.

Tzara's repeated sounds that are to start the listener yelling, as Marinetti's did, put the reader's nerves also on end:

> car il y a des zigzags sur son âme et beaucoup de
>   rrrrrrrrrrrrrr
>   ici le lecteur commence à crier
>
>   (Tz, 1:87)

> for there are zigzags on his soul and plenty of
>   rrrrrrrrrrrrrr
>   here the reader begins to scream

Verbal aggression, then, and visual too—the *rrr* on the page are irritating to the eye as they would be to the ear. The whole matter turns about the self-contemplation of the reader in the text as it frames the vision, self-conscious in its own exacerbation.

Tzara is in particular the poet of self-consciousness, of the man masked, and perpetually ambivalent, of the tragic hero, mirrored in his double role as narrator and actor. The main questions raised by this game of double perception are those of identity, of mask, and of approximate relation: Tzara's approximate man, who "laughs face on and weeps behind" (Tz, 2:102), as touching as he is brilliant—a mirror of the poem itself—confesses his doubts facing others, or on that place of passage that is the stair:

> tu es en face des autres un autre que toi-même
> sur l'escalier des vagues comptant de chaque regard
>   la trame
> dépareillées hallucinations sans voix qui te
>   ressemblent
> les boutiques de bric-à-brac qui te ressemblent
> que tu cristallises autour de ta pluvieuse vocation—où
>   tu decouvres des parcelles de toi-même
> à chaque tournant de rue tu te changes en un autre
>   toi-même

> facing others you are another than yourself
> judging on the staircase of waves the texture of each
>   look
> dissimilar voiceless hallucinations that resemble you
> that you crystallize around your rainy calling—where
>   you find portions of yourself
> at each turn of the road you change into another
>   self.[5]

In the realm of the stair, the crossroads, or the circus ring, the page, or the game, around the window or the table, upon the canvas or in the mirror of a large glass and a Great Work, be it alchemical labor, epic poem, or lyric life, the animator of the circus leaves his mark on every passage, which is to say, at every threshold of perception and passion:

> mais que la porte s'ouvre enfin comme la première
>   page d'un livre
> ta chambre pleine d'indomptables d'amoureuses
>   coincidences tristes ou gaies
> je couperai en tranches le long filet du regard fixe

> et chaque parole sera un envoûtement pour l'oeil et
>   de page en page
> mes doigts connaîtront la flore de ton corps et de
>   page en page
> de ta nuit la secrète étude s'éclaircira et de page en
>   page
> les ailes de ta parole me seront éventails et de page
>   en page
> des éventails pour chasser la nuit de ta figure et de
>   page en page
> ta cargaison de paroles au large sera ma guérison et
>   du page en page
> les années diminueront vers l'impalpable souffle que
>   la tombe aspire déjà.

> but let the door open at last like the first page of a
>   book
> your room full of unconquerable loving coincidences
>   sad or gay
> I shall slice the long net of the fixed gaze
> and each word will be a spell for the eye and from
>   page to page
> my fingers will know the flora of your body and from
>   page to page
> the secret study of your night will be illumined and
>   from page to page
> the wings of your word will be fans to me and from
>   page to page
> fans to chase the night from your face and from
>   page to page
> your cargo of words at sea will be my cure and
>   from page to page
> the years will diminish toward the impalpable breath
>   that the bomb already draws in.
>
>   (**AM**, p. 155)

These pages of Tzara, themselves sufficient as a landscape, indicate the truest temper of Dada, and our truest text of that movement. That the "page" should be so plainly part of, and such an essential part of the "paysage" and that they should both be part of the "passage" as it is part of them, is an unmistakable truth identical to itself, in whatever mirror we might choose to see ourselves and our text: "De vastes paysages s'étendent en moi sans étonnement" (Tz, 1:349; Vast landscapes stretch out in me without astonishment), says Tzara in **L'Antitête**. Toward these interior landscapes Duchamp also directed himself, his thought, and his surest contemplation and art: "My aim was turning inward, rather than toward externals" (MS, p. 11); "Dada was a metaphysical attitude." Thus the closed door of his *Etant donnés* (Given . . . ; figure 36), the great door of the given, as we might phrase it, imposes a frame on the eyes of the beholder, forced into the position of peeping-tom or peeping-reader, his view necessarily concentrated through the small holes pierced, upon the parts exhibited. It is itself an art related to the whole and raises the questions of identity, of perception and of passion—this door is the perfect example of what opens on an inner landscape and what frames a privileged inner seen.

Let us end our own scene here by a metaphysical paradox: what most hides is most revealing. Artaud's paradoxical description of a state outside ordinary life that we could see as equivalent to the Dada temper should be taken as sign and as sight, a reminder of the text as a liminal state for threshold experience, of the viewer as a passenger in Dada's rite of passage. "There are no words to designate it but a vehement hieroglyph designating the impossible encounter of matter and of spirit. A kind of vision inside" (Ar, p. 202). Here that quotation also may be left as incomplete, as our own architexture is ideally incomplete, its passage left forever open to the reader.[6]

NOTES

[1] Tristan Tzara, *Oeuvres complètes*, ed. Henri Béhar, vol. 1:1912-1924, vol. 2: 1925-1933 (Paris: Flammarion, 1975 and 1977), 1:409. Hereafter cited as Tz.

[2] Marcel Duchamp, *Marchand du sel: Ecrits de Marcel Duchamp*, ed. Michel Sanouillet (Paris: Le Terrain Vague, 1958), p. 95 (hereafter cited as MS): the text signed "Rrose Sélavy," the name of Marcel Duchamp's double, himself—like his text—in drag.

[3] Jacques Rigaut, *Écrits*, ed. Martin Kay (Paris: Gallimard, 1970), p. 113.

[4] Georges Ribemont-Dessaignes, *Dada: manifestes, poèmes, articles, projets* (1915-1930), ed. Jean-Pierre Bégot (Paris: Projectoires/Champ Libre, 1974), pp. 15-19, for this and the following quotation.

[5] Translation from Mary Ann Caws, *Approximate Man and other Writings of Tristan Tzara* (Detroit: Wayne State University Press, 1973), p. 53. Hereafter cited as AM.

[6] For the term "architexture," already used in the introduction, see my "Vers une architexture du poème surréaliste," in *Ethique et Esthétique de la littérature française du XXᵉ siècle*, ed. Cagnon (Stanford: Stanford University Press, 1978), pp. 59-68.

Philip Beitchman (essay date 1988)

SOURCE: "Symbolism in the Streets: Tristan Tzara," in *I Am a Process with No Subject,* University of Florida Press, 1988, pp. 27-52.

[*In the following excerpt, Beitchman examines Tzara's poetic utopianism, particuarly his determination to force his readers into a more satisfying future by separating them from the limitations of the past.*]

In his epic-length poem of 1931, *L'Homme approximatif* (*Approximate Man*), Tzara deepens and further defines his rejection of exoticism and points to the possibility of realizing an authentic destiny and purpose for mankind; as a preliminary to this evolution, man must strip himself of the excess baggage of his past and the notions, based on insufficient logic and reason, with which he has hitherto tried to control his life. Tzara is now looking forward to a future that is as utterly new as the first page of an unread book:[11]

> but let the door open at last like the first page of a
>   book

> your room full of unconquerable loving coincidences
>   sad or gay
> I shall slice the long net of the fixed gaze
> and each word will be a spell for the eye and from
>   page to page
> my fingers will know the flora of your body and from
>   page to page
> the secret study of your night will be illumined and
>   from page to page
> the wings of your word will be fans to me and from
>   page to page
> fans to chase the night from your face and from
>   page to page
> your cargo of words at sea will be my cure and
>   from page to page
> the years will diminish toward the impalpable breath
>   that the tomb already draws in.
>   (***Approximate Man and Other Writings***, 61).

Tzara conceives of man, in this poem, as stretched on the cross of memory, sheltered from reality by words and notions that keep him from knowing effectively what he is supposed to do. The poet is special only to the extent that he is aware of things that others can't or don't want to face. As Tzara so often reminds us, "the approximate man is like you, reader, and so many others." The poet, as the ultimate intellectual, he who takes words for things, is uniquely situated to tell of the limits and pitfalls of intellect:

> we have displaced the ideas and confused their
>   clothing with their names
> blind are the words which from their birth can only
>   find their place again
> their grammatical places in universal safety
> meager is the fire we thought we saw kindling in
>   them in our lungs
> and dull the predestined gleam of what they say
>   (103)

This is the same intellect that has converted our world into the desert, where at the conclusion of the poem the approximate man pledges himself, in repeated refrains, to wait:

> and stony in my garments of schist I have pledged
>   my waiting
> to the torment of the oxidized desert
> to the unshakable advent of fire
>   (127, 129)

Tzara, of *Approximate Man*, has absorbed and transcended the aesthetic of symbolism, a philosophy whose attractions and limitations were so frankly summed up by Walter Pater when he said that the purpose of life was to appreciate beautiful things; Tzara finds in an aestheticism of this sort no cause for celebration, or even consolation, but rather a pretext for some savage irony:

> continue sharp fears to click above our heads
> your surgical instruments
> vague forebodings sound the shouting depth of the
>   walls

where we pile up pell-mell knowledge and poetry
but from our fists clenched and cemented with
    destinies
you can never take what the trial of the laughable
    grain
seizes from the indecision of a consoling day
take one step back leprous thoughts of death of
    vermin consolation
leave to the cultivators of colors and of skies the
    succulent promise
of man carrying in his fruit the burning and propitious
    blossoming of morning

                            (107)

Tzara prefers to think of man, instead, and maybe Pater would have approved at least of the image, as a slow fire—a blaze that consumes and was meant to consume everything in its path—past, present and future, and working toward an unknown destiny, whose approximate nature is the only sure sign we have of its authenticity:

a slow furnace of invincible constancy—man—
a slow furnace rises from the depth of your slow
    deliberation
  . . . a slow fire brightens in the gaping fear of your
    strength—man—
a fire grown tipsy on heights where the coastal
    traffic of clouds has earthed over the taste of
    abyss
a fire climbing supplicant the ladder to the stains of
    unbounded gestures. . . .

                            (130)

This fire, whose essence is constant motion and pure change, will live as long as there is something to burn; however small the combustible, it will not be disdained, but like a fading wick the flame will jump across the rim of the candleholder in search of more beeswax; for what remains when we have left behind all those illusions by which we lived, when we are no longer moved by ideas nor motivated by abstractions—like words of praise and blame? Tzara in this poem is looking for some residue of humanity, some solid ground from which to greet the coming of the future, some excuse for hoping:

morning morning
morning sealed with crystal and with larvae
morning of baked bread
morning of shutters in madness
morning keeper of the stable
morning of squirrels and of window cleaners cool by
    the river
sweet-smelling morning
breath clinging to the striations of the iris

                            (111)

This repetition is not only visual and olfactory in its variations; it is incantatory and prayerful in its tenacity. A song with words that could be other words that it will take a "new man" to understand.

What will this "new man," this amnesiac creature, be like—as on that first morning of creation—this man whose lack of a past keeps him from defining a future? It would, of course, be perverse of us to assign him an essence that would be affirmed only to be denied, but one can't help feeling that this "new man" of Tzara's will be physically sensitive to a hitherto unknown extent, that the Cartesian breach between mind and matter will be healed as people begin to think with their bodies and act by intuition rather than by calculation. "No, I am not a thinker," Tzara tells us (and we *almost* can believe him)—and elsewhere the refrain imposes itself, "Do not close your eyes yet" (118), in other words, "do not make up your mind." For when you have done that you are finished, a (dead) object among objects.

Tzara emphasizes in particular the importance of *hands*. The "new man" will rely much more on these nonverbal means of communication. He will say all that need be said with a wave, a caress, a blow:

hands that lift from the stern forehead the thick layer
    of notched thoughts
carry to the lips the glass where worlds expand
offer alms and debase man's proper bearing
hands tense on the plank that will bear away the
    lowly body
hands that pray before that plank of air—unable to
    grasp it—
telling other hands of the unspeakable possibility . . .
cool hands musicians of serene discoveries
hands adept at saving or destroying . . .

                            (113)

Tzara finds not only things for these hands to do, he is also conscious of reality as worked upon by hands. The above passage (before my quotation) starts with the image of a street being kneaded, like bread, "under the coming and going of wheels." Those hands, which for Rilke were symbolic of an absolute limit for communication ("ours is to touch, nothing more") or for an infinite yearning for contact with an earthly astral being, the "angel of Beauty," these "mystic" hands have been stripped by Tzara of the gloves of their metaphysical destiny. They become as naïve and human as a voice and as innocent as the desire to help another human being. These are active hands, not only praying or resigned ones. These are hands that we humans use to satisfy or to destroy each other:

hands that catch and tame the beasts come forth in
    human bodies
forged in the tension of celestial births
and also hands that kill . . .
hands cut off
but there are also hands that write
peace to some disillusioned wealth to others
    according to the chance of the wells we fall in
incendiary hands
the only ones that shine

                          (113-14)

The poet of *Mouchoir*, stripped of all transcendence, knocked off his pedestal, and forced to sink or swim in a sea of banal humanity, has evolved into this "approximate man" who, as is so insistently repeated, "like you reader and so many others," has only his hands to protect himself against nothingness. Tzara, as is apparent above, stresses that these hands are not, nor should they always be, so kind. Images of cruelty, blood, and destructive fire abound in this poem; and there is obviously some type of compensation attempted here for the aseptic utopias of the positivists that no one could stand to live in. In a larger sense the hypocrisy of all the utopian dreamers has been to deny the animal in man. The attempt to manufacture a man according to a prototype that has been purified of all ambiguity, whim, and spontaneity has given rise to that monstrous, unbalanced figure that alone is "adapted" to survive in modern society, a machine among machines, and that we may doubt, along with Foucault, that we can still call "man." The bomb has dropped, as Marcuse said, at least half-seriously, and *we* are the mutants. Now Tzara's man is not really man either, which is why he calls him "approximate." "My horizon is limited to the face of a watch" (113), the poet now proclaims; but then what makes him any different from any other cog in the social machine? Machines, introduced as servants, have become the masters and models, as Hegel predicted they would; and the most relevant biblical fable is not the one that so fascinated Kierkegaard, that of Abraham and Isaac, nor is it Gide's favorite lullaby, the return of the prodigal—it should be rather that of Esau, who sold his birthright for a mess of porridge. A half million years of human evolution so approximate man can wind up in a third-class railway carriage with a timetable on his knees:

> so many men have preceded me in the noble furrow
> of exaltation
> so much soul has been squandered to build the
> chance I gamble
> in the lonely jail where a blood prowls thick with
> remorse . . .
>
> (83)

And elsewhere the clock is remembered, probably Poe's Big Ben, "which cut off heads to tell the hours" (71). The clock and all it stands for here come to resemble the savage god of the Aztecs, who demands human sacrifice as his constant diet.[12] Still, Tzara's war is not against time, in the sense of a sobering and necessary reminder of our transience that renders to life the value it has, but instead against the measurement and quantification of time that cannot help but become an obsession and compulsion;[13] the reason why clocks and all other similar devices are so seductive lies in our anguish with our uncertainty. With clocks, thermometers, calendars, speedometers, etc., we can pretend to absolute truth. They are Platonic ideas come to visit us in this instamatic age—and in the flesh. Here is a truth that we can know and be familiar with, and that can even talk, or at least beep, back at us. Yes, here it is in all its naked majesty, the great unquestioned absolute: since we no longer pretend to the big things, we can at least be certain of the small ones; so it, *is,* for instance 10 P.M., and we *have* just taken two aspirins. Or maybe our senses deceive us; but we can measure that too. This we know.

These clocks that were brought out in time of dearth,[14] we have made into the gods that we are afraid to face:

> man so fears the face of his god that deprived the
> horizons he trembles
> man so fears his god that at his coming he stumbles
> he drowns
> horizonless man. . . .
>
> (*Approximate Man*, 78)

We are ashamed to face these machines we have made into idols because we can't but laugh at what they have to say; this is because, except for the clocks that aren't working, they are never right. According to clocks it is never *time* and it can never be *now.*

But the approximate man has turned away from these illusory certitudes; he is willing to admit that he cannot know or be *exactly* anything; he has dealt with the need for certainty in his own soul, which is why he is at once so attractive and so threatening to others. The approximate man is only pretending to have pledged his waiting:

> to the torment of the oxidized desert
> to the unshakable advent of fire
>
> (130)

This is clearly a mask for those who still need the comfort of a disguise that words can furnish.[15] The approximate man is instead "impossible man"—impossible to locate anywhere; because you have found him do not think he's there: this is Tzara's message for all searchers of identity (and who else would read him?), as it was in a more blatant way Nietzsche's before him. This Tzara, who appears from the East, suddenly, with all the knowledge of a Gurdjieff, all the talent and strange, obdurate patience of a Brancusi, this Tristan Tzara, whose very name, adopted, means the marriage of contraries, that of heaven and earth—he is not about to take us anywhere we have ever been before. His *disguise* is that of the poet, his *persona* that of the performing artist he was while at Cabaret Voltaire in Zurich and the famous dada "happenings" of his early years in Paris, but you will never get him to say exactly what he means. This is because what he means is more or less than what can be said. Above all, he is not asking for your admiration, your esteem, or the confession you have to make of his "greatness," that is, superiority over you, which would excuse you from the responsibility of your own freedom. His goal is not to create another time-honored cultural monument for humanity to abase itself in front of. Tzara talks to his reader not across a distance, formally, like a lecturer, but familiarly, intimately, like a brother, a friend, or a lover. The human condition is his major argument, its transiency, its futility, and the fleeting nature of the sensations that constitute the best of what it has to offer:

> you know you will fall apart at your life's end but
> you conceal yourself and come in
> flower knot of ribbons of human skin . . .
> in stations—but I could never say enough of
> stations—there are born fragmented pleasures

greetings too brief in shabby hotels
where even love is only part of a dusty legend

(50)

Tzara's apostrophe to "stations," though reminiscent of the *via crucis* (Way of the Cross), would of course be apostasy, since crucial to Christianity is the conception that the trip is made only once; for Tzara, as for those "noble pagans" of antiquity that St. Augustine so took to task, the journey is cyclical and interminable, as Tzara emphasizes the virtues of rootlessness and transiency in this existence "which we have only rented" (79). As if the best we can hope for in life is to enjoy the passage through it.

The *Approximate Man* comes across, in this mood, as an alternately strident and tender appeal to the reader to abandon the gods of the past, those that man worships in the form of History and Memory and that merely represent our nostalgia for a stability that is no longer to be had. Once, when we thought the sun revolved around the earth, we were confident in our own existence; now that we know better we must feel equally sure and confident about our nothingness. For only the knowledge that we have nothing left to lose can enable us to face the future with hope.

IV

Occidental civilization . . . must ultimately end in disorder
and demoralization. . . . Peaceful equality can only be
built up among the ruins of annihilated Western states
and the ashes of extinct Western peoples.

—Viscount Torio[16]

In a later and fascinating poem in prose, *Grains et issues* (*Seed and Bran*, 1935), Tzara is ready to describe more concretely the future he has in mind.[17] There will still be subways, for instance, but no one will use them because there will be no reason to hurry. Sexual desire will be satisfied in ways that are at once polymorphous, sudden, and spontaneous. The slightest touch will be sufficient to release orgasm or its equivalent in satisfaction. Human contacts in general will be free and unencumbered by the social hierarchies—which will have been abolished. Tzara has taken seriously Rimbaud's slogan, "il faut changer la vie" ("we must change life"), as well as Lautréamont's leitmotif of a poetry that will be made by all. In this sense the symbolist theme of the irrelevance of poetry to daily life in a mechanical age reaches its fruition in Tzara's notion of a daily life that is transformed by and infused with poetry,[18] that is poetic to its very core—a change that can only take place at the "end of History," as Hegel never imagined it to be, when Revolution and Poetry finally meet, as they must (for only one can justify the other), to translate the routines of our lives into endless possibilities.

This new culture will be based on oblivion, that is, on the abolition of memory. Tzara here, completing a critique of language commenced by dada and carried on by surrealism, operates a thoroughgoing devaluation of the word, both written and spoken. To make sure that the new atti-

tudes don't become frozen into new compulsions, there will be a change of language every Saturday. People will hesitate to trust their thinking to words (and all the more their words to paper), so that gradually the habit of thinking in words will die out. This verbal faculty that Western man has exaggerated comes in for some serious reappraisal: words in the future will have a decorative function only—a little bit like the brief greetings and inquiries we exchange when we are in a hurry.[19]

Crime and cruelty will be key elements in any future utopia.[20] Tzara in the earlier *Approximate Man* had more than hinted at the importance of these sides of human nature—an importance that the bourgeois epoch has hypocritically chosen to ignore, while practicing real savagery more systematically than any ruling class before it:

let crime at last flower young and fresh in heavy
garlands along the houses
fertilize with blood the new adventures the harvests
of future generations

(*Approximate Man*, 48)

For the bourgeoisie the willful violation of order, incarnated in the concept of crime, is the enemy it pretends to fight, while it perpetuates ever greater crimes in the very name of the order it is defending.

The critique that Nietzsche and Dostoevsky have made of the *perfect worlds* as imagined by the English utilitarians (Bentham, Spencer, Mill) as well as the French social idealists (Saint-Simon, Comte) has had a telling effect on Tzara. A world of complete harmony, peace, and material well-being would be completely unlivable—and Tzara's contemporaries, Artaud and Freud, were as well aware of this as he was. A society that pretends its job is over when the needs of its citizens have been met is doomed to be destroyed by this same citizenry. Closer to psychological reality is the ancient Roman world of frank violence and mass sadism.

The major writers of the symbolist period—Baudelaire, Mallarmé, Rimbaud, and Lautréamont—all condemn this bourgeois version of paradise as if with one voice, as had Stendhal, Flaubert, and the romantics before them; and Tzara is, of course, in fundamental agreement with his predecessors on this point. But he pushes beyond the past denunciations and "refusals" in going on to visualize in positive, concrete terms a utopia that will be a pleasure, or at least interesting, to live in, in more than the merely quantitative sense meant by the bourgeois planners. If for the writers of symbolism, for instance, "boredom" remains the fundamental characteristic of bourgeois society, which, while they remain a part of it, they accept as inevitable, in Tzara's utopia boredom becomes simply a redoubtable enemy that can be eliminated with the help of a little imagination. "Sooner murder an infant in its cradle than nurse unacted desires" and "he who desires but acts not breeds pestilence" are two mottos from Blake's *Marriage of Heaven and Hell* that could well serve Tzara in this connection.

Roger Gilbert-Lecomte, in a remarkable essay contemporaneous with the prophecies of Tzara, "L'Horrible Révélation la seule" ("Horrible Revelation the Only One"),[21] proclaims that human beings are in the process of turning into *insects*. He allows that, consistent with this mutation, men will become so busy that they will lose their ability to dream, symbolizing the reduction of man to the narrow "one-dimension" of waking consciousness wherein he follows his interest doggedly like an ant under a bread crumb. For Tzara this dreamlessness is instead a positive phenomenon; in this utopia men will no longer dream because their desires will have been satisfied by their waking lives.[22] The subtitle, then, that Tzara gives to *Grains et issues*—"Rêve Expérimental" ("Experimental Dream")—is strangely provisional in this sense. As he explains in a note, he means by this phrase a kind of "waking dream" that operates on the frontiers of consciousness and whose purpose it is to facilitate an interpenetration of the worlds of logic and the irrational. Dream here for Tzara is furthermore expressive of the lyric impulse and as such is not exclusively dependent on the will of the poet (one does not simply *decide* to dream, though one may find oneself in a situation where one is likely to) but must await the proper concatenation of social forces and personal needs. This dream-poetry is only a provisional strategy and must be abandoned when it has served its purpose—when reality will have become a revery, and poetry, from being a more or less tolerated deviation and the affair of specialists, will evolve into the principal means whereby men come to know their world. In the end, for Tzara, poetry will equal love.[23]

Tzara is working to resolve some uncomfortable antinomies here. On the one hand, he adopts enthusiastically the communist-anarchist critique of bourgeois society. On the other, he refuses to be blind and naïve about human nature, so he relates elements of his vision of utopia to the necessity of cruelty and crime as representing authentically human drives—aggression, sadism, hatred—that will need to find outlets. It is as if he is trying to marry the Marx of the *Manuscripts of 1844* with the Freud of *Civilization and Its Discontents*. Small wonder, as Micheline Tison-Braun comments in her perceptive book on Tzara,[24] that eyebrows must have been raised in Moscow and Paris over the dubious political orthodoxy of this attempt as well as over the sanity of its originator. Pickled tongue of aristocrat would have been difficult for even the angriest proletarian to digest:

> Dogs gorged on gasoline and set afire will be turned loose in packs against naked women, just the most beautiful among them, of course. Old people will be pressed and dried between the leaves of great wooden books and then stretched out in the carpets of middle-class salons. Crystal globes filled with aristocrats' tongues will be exhibited among the pots of jam and mustard in store windows.

("Seed and Bran," *Approximate Man*, 217)

This is of course no realistic scenario and was never meant to be one. Tzara is merely stating that in his version of communism life will be a complex and interesting affair, something that May 1968 well understood with its renowned slogan, "l'imagination au pouvoir" ("power to the imagination"). The fact is, as Freud came to realize with the theory of a "death-instinct" that inflects his later writings, we kill ourselves more than we kill each other (or we do one because we have been brought up not to do the other) because our progress-oriented society, whatever its actual achievements, is bound to increase the guilt each member feels. Such guilt, which is based on the inability of the individual to exchange anything with society for those "benefits" he reaps from it, augments with each of the inventions that supposedly make life easier.[25] The death wish, or Thanatos, becomes more than Eros (there is acceleration here too: hippies, nudity, promiscuity, centerfolds, aphrodisiacs) can cope with. We accelerate our speed,[26] take to toxins, and engage in what the social professionals call "self-destructive behavior." When war, inevitable concomitant of the aggressions pent up in each individual, finally breaks out, the tension is lifted as socially sanctioned outlets are provided. Anti-smoking, anti-drug, safe-driving campaigns, and the like, as well as legislation, pretend to deal with the problem; but they result, even in the rare cases where they succeed, only in a change of symptom. "Let the lost get lost," Artaud once remarked in defense of the opium users' right to stone themselves out.[27]

What makes Tzara's vision so interesting is not finally its oddness, it is the practicality of it all, for Tzara was an eager reader of Wilhelm Reich and certainly well acquainted with the latter's theories linking the development of fascism with sexual repression.[28] Our technical civilizations have lengthened life and made it easier for the masses, only to have the average man act as if he were already dead. In Tzara's utopia the individual (although the survival of such an entity is highly problematic) will owe society nothing,[29] except the dubious privilege of having been born. What Tzara is saying is that we need to pay more attention to the qualitative side of life, which we have neglected for the quantitative. We need to take more into account when we make our plans, or even our revolutions, than simply statistical well-being, literacy, nutrition. . . . There is such a thing as desire.

NOTES

[11] Since I believe it will make for less choppy reading, and because of the availability of a good translation (by Mary Ann Caws), I'll be citing Tzara in English.

[12] This analogy was made by the Russian symbolist Dmitri Merejkowski in *Atlantis/Europe: The Secret of the West*, citing Bartholomeo Diaz's *Conquest of Mexico*: "Eighty thousand sacrifices fall at the consecration of one great pyramidal temple in the city of Mexico" (average 50,000 a year); but we moderns match or surpass these figures on our roads alone.

[13] Tzara speaks often and eloquently on the theme of the domination of man by the machines that were meant to serve him, as in the following passage from a prose poem in *Résumé of Night* (1934): "It would be difficult to convince me that a given individual (let's take the one who

is right now synchronizing as best he can his organic needs with the time he has at his disposal until the bus comes) sees, hears, feels, perceives at the same speed and in the same dimension as I do what is going on around him and that his watches, meters, and adjectives have not been, from the moment of his birth, rigged by the unanimous and constant relationship of things and beings to which he has subjected the norms of his judgements" (*Approximate Man and Other Writings*, 223). The passage quoted in n. 6 above is from further on in this prose poem. For Tzara, subliminal methods (drugs, hypnotism, and what he calls a kind of "waking sleep"), while not to be blindly trusted, may be useful to break the conditioned patterns and routines that our machines and noxious social structures force upon us. These "underground" techniques can only give us a glimpse of what it will take a "new man" to really see.

14. "In time of Dearth bring out Number, Weight and Measure"—Blake, from *The Marriage of Heaven and Hell*.

15. Tzara, *Approximate Man*, where our translator remarks the change in tone: "Unexpectedly the final wait in the desert for the coming of the flame rejects the approximate" (258).

16. Cited by A.K. Coomaraswamy, *The Dance of Shiva*, 122. Coomaraswamy does a comparative study of Indian Vedanta and the eschatological-apocalyptic themes typical of French (Marcel Schwob: *Le Livre de Monelle*) and especially Russian symbolism. His approach is therapeutic, similar to such popular but very erudite treatments as Alan Watts's *Psychotherapy East and West*. Symbolist novels, works like Bely's *St. Petersburg* or Sologub's *Petty Demon* (which, according to Henri Peyre's concluding note in his book on symbolism, represent the summit of the movement in literary achievement), which were written in Russia early in our century, are all haunted by the theme of the end of (our) civilization. As far as Viscount Torio goes, whose statement seems to sum up the symbolist theme of apocalypse in its most extreme form, I've never been able to find out more about him, though I've looked. Perhaps he's a pseudonym for one or another of the strange spirits that haunted Russian culture at the beginning of the century—Rozanov, Solov'ev, or Ivanov—far easier, at all events, to say such a thing than own up to having said it!

17. Another "prophetic" extended prose poem that Tzara wrote in close proximity to *Grains et issues* was *Personnage d'insomnie*. In the latter text men are envisioned as metamorphosing into trees or other forms of plant life. This is nature's revenge on man for his colossal pride and the negligent way he has handled his world: "car les lois végétales, malgré tout, ne s'exprimaient que dans leur propre matière selon une conscience dont l'essential échappe encore aux hommes qui, depuis longtemps, avaient oublié la leur et confirme les volontés d'autonomie de la nature que l'homme, qui s'en est profondément détaché, considèrera toujours comme une insulte perpétuelle à son désir de tout accaparer" ("For the vegetable laws, in spite of it all, only expressed in their own way a consciousness whose central meaning still escapes man—who long ago has forgotten his own and thereby confirms the will to autonomy in nature, from which man has utterly detached himself and that he will always treat as a perpetual insult to his desire to own everything"; *Œ.C.* 3:207). *Personnage d'insomnie*, a consummate tour de force, lyrical, dense, persuasive, and utterly unique, is a bit of a bibliographical enigma. It was never published in Tzara's lifetime, by conscious decision, according to Henri Béhar (*Œ.C.* 3:561-62), who examines one by one the possible motives Tzara had in withholding it from the public but finds none of them sufficient.

18. This interpenetration of life and poetry is Tzara's fundamental message, refined, repeated, and clarioned all through his career not only in his poetry but also in his persistent critical production, which incessantly turns on the problems and prospects of finding and preserving the poetic quality in everyday life. A few quotes may be detached almost at random from a life's work that says, in the end, *nothing else*: "Toute œuvre poétique elle-même, en tant qu'expérience, n'est pas uniquement un produit de la raison ou de l'imagination, elle n'est valable que si elle a été *vécue*. L'image poétique est un produit de la connaissance; ou, la connaissance ne peut être une leçon qu'il faut avoir *apprise*, elle doit être *prise* au monde extérieur, c'est-à-dire résulter d'une action plus ou moins violente sur la réalité qui nous entoure. Toute création est donc, pour le poète, une *conquête*, une affirmation combative de sa conscience" ("Any poetic work itself, as an experience, is not only a product of reason and imagination, it is worthwhile only if it has been *lived*. The poetic image is a product of knowledge. Now knowledge cannot be a lesson that it's necessary to have *learned*, it must instead be *seized* from the external world, that is to say, it must be the outcome of an action, more or less violent, on the reality that surrounds us. All creation is therefore, for the poet, a *conquest*, a combative affirmation of his consciousness"; "Les Écluses de la poésie" ["The Dams of Poetry"], *Œ.C.* 5:95).

"Le poète non seulement vit l'histoire, mais en partie il la détermine. Pour lui, l'existence elle-même est un phénomène poétique à l'inverse de ceux pour qui écrire des poèmes constitue une profession" ("The poet not only lives history, but he in part determines it. For him, existence itself is a poetic phenomenon, just the opposite of what it is for those to whom writing poetry is a profession"; ibid., 109).

19. *Grains et issues*, *Œ.C.* 3. For the last paragraph or so I've been paraphrasing parts of pages 9-25.

20. The Marquis de Sade's astounding pamphlet, "Français encore un effort pour devenir vraiment républicains" ("Frenchmen One More Effort to Become Real Republicans") figures prominently in surrealist political thought. See, for instance, "L'Utopie sociale du Marquis de Sade," by Roger Gilbert-Lecomte, in his *Œuvres complètes* 1:261-65. See nn. 21 and 22 below.

21. Roger Gilbert-Lecomte, along with René Daumal and René de Renéville, edited during the early 1930s an influential review, *Le Grand Jeu*, where this essay first appeared. It has recently resurfaced in the *Fata Morgana* anthology (10/18) and in the *Œuvres complètes* of Gilbert-Lecomte. The group of the Grand Jeu, dissatisfied with what they considered to be the reigning materialism but agreeing in principle with the surrealists about the importance of dreams, the present moment, and spontaneity, attempted to astralize or spiritualize surrealism, especially by importing Eastern religion and philosophy. René Daumal, for instance, made himself into a proficient scholar of Sanskrit, and he is the author of the posthumously published *Mount Analogue: A Novel of Symbolically Authentic Non-Euclidean Adventures in Mountain Climbing*, somewhat of a "hippie classic" in America of the 1960s. From surrealism the road led, although of course not straight, to Woodstock.

22. For Gilbert-Lecomte, we no longer dream because being no longer human we will no longer feel the pang of desire; for Tzara the oneiric faculty will dry up because we won't need to dream, our desires having been satisfied by our activities. In either case the days of dreams are numbered. Tzara, *Œ. C.* 3:16: "Le sommeil tournera vide et sec car les rêves ne viendront plus concasser les pierres de l'existence avec leurs vis d'Archimède, les désirs étant comblés pendant le temps de veille" ("Sleep will turn empty and dry for dreams will no longer come to smash the stones of existence in their Archimedean vice, desires having been fulfilled during the time one is awake").

23. This "love," unlike the "amour fou" Breton evoked so hauntingly (*L'Amour fou*), involves no mystical or seemingly predestined encounter

between two people meant to meet at a certain astral and earthly conjuncture; its nature, instead, is to be indistinguishable, like Tzara's ideal of poetry, from the pulse of life itself. For Tzara, we won't so much *find* love and poetry as *breathe* it. Tzara, worthy like a very few others (Eluard, Aragon, Neruda) of the name "communist poet," needs a love and an art that rises above particulars: "Sous une forme bien différente de celle qui nous apparaît comme telle, la poésie deviendra acte *unanime-ment employé et exercé,* principal moyen de connaissance, quand elle aura transpercé le stade de champ d'observation et de déviation spécial-isée, voisine du délire et de la simulation, qu'elle occupe encore, pour suivre son destin révolutionnaire qui se confondra avec celui de l'amour" ("In a very different way than now appears to us as such, poetry will become a unanimously *employed* and *exerted* act, a principal means of knowledge, when it will have pierced through the stage of specialized observation and deviance, classed with delirium and simulation, that it now still occupies, to follow its revolutionary destiny where it will merge with the voice of love"; Tzara, *Œ. C.* 3:103).

24. Tison-Braun, *Tristan Tzara,* 78: "il a du faire hausser bien des épaules de Paris à Moscou" ("He must have caused much shrugging of shoulders in Paris and Moscow"). Tison-Braun, deeply versed in the literature and lore of dada and surrealism, is a splendid student of the specifically *poetic* side of Tzara's project, which she ingeniously *isolates.* She may not be so satisfactory, however, as a commentator on his theory, which she insists on demarcating I think a little too neatly from his practice. She is eloquent and clever, for instance, on the logical paradoxes and contradictions between Tzara's (or any) revolutionary theory and the living practice of poetry. But she fails to see that, for Tzara, theory and practice are inextricably intertwined, like flesh and bone on a living organism, and that cutting one away from the other means only that you are dealing with a corpse. In the prose poetry especially, theoretical pronouncement alternates with lyrical effusion, often within the same paragraph or sentence. Tison-Braun, attached as she is to a concept of the work of art (owing much to Malraux) as expression of a "human essence," is perhaps badly placed to sympathize with the wilder ideas and passions of such visionaries as Tzara, for whom the *real* human is an entity yet to be created.

25. Cf. Jean Baudrillard, *La Société de consommation (The Consumer Society),* where a major thesis is that the true function of publicity in our societies is not so much to sell the product as to ease the guilt, inherited from our Puritan-Christian tradition, that we have at consuming it. Baudrillard's later book, *L'Échange symbolique et la mort (Symbolic Exchange and Death),* is largely concerned with what he considers to be the unilateral relations between modern states that give all and their citizenry who can give nothing in return *except their lives.*

26. The metaphor of speed, rapid transformation, and metamorphosis is one of the constants of Tzara's critical and poetic vocabulary. Tzara's play *La Fuite (Escape)* is one of his more systematic expositions of this philosophy of "permanent change." Michel Leiris' enthusiastic introduction to Tzara's text could describe his own project as well as the poet's: "Le thème directeur en est ce déchirement, ce divorce constant, cette séparation qui répond au mouvement même de la vie. Fuite de l'enfant qui pour vivre sa vie doit s'arracher à ses parents. Divorce des amants qui ne peuvent rester l'un à l'autre sans aliéner leur liberté et qui doivent nier leur amour s'ils ne veulent pas eux-mêmes se nier. Mort d'une génération dont se détache peu à peu, pour monter à son tour, une génération nouvelle. Fuite de chaque être vivant, qui se sépare des autres, souffre lui-même et fait souffrir, mais ne peut faire autrement parce que pour se réaliser il lui faut une certaine solitude. Fuite des hommes. Fuite des saisons. Fuite du temps. Cours implacable des choses, qui poursuit son mouvement de roue. Fuite historique enfin: exode, déroute, dispersion de tous et de toutes à travers l'anonymat des routes et dans le brouhaha des gares où se coudoient civils et militaires. Faillite, effondrement, confusion, parce qu'il faut ce désarroi total pour que

puisse renaître une autre société impliquant d'autres relations entre les hommes, entre les femmes, entre les femmes et les hommes" ("The main theme of the play is this rending, this constant divorce, this separation whose movement is one with life. Escape of the child who must tear himself away from his parents to live his own life. Lovers' separation who cannot continue belonging to one another without alienating their liberty and who must deny their love if they don't want to deny themselves. Death of a generation that another generation separates itself from little by little, to give rise, in its turn, to a new generation. Escape of every living being, who separates himself from others, suffers and causes others to suffer, but cannot do otherwise because to realize himself he needs a certain solitude. Escape of men. Escape of seasons. Escape of time. Implacable course of things on the turning wheel of fortune. Escape in history, finally: exodus, rout, dispersion of men and women into the anonymity of roads and into the clamor of railway stations where civilians and soldiers rub elbows. Failure, collapse, confusion, because we must have this total disarray for there to be created a new society, implying other rapports between men, women, and between men and women"; "fuite en avant" = escape into the future; extract from Leiris' "présentation," 21 Jan. 1946, Théâtre du Vieux Colombier—Tzara, *Œ. C.* 3:623).

Among contemporaries, J.M.G. LeClézio assumes perhaps most obdurately and masterfully the mantle of this "tradition of the transitory" so intrinsic to data-surrealism in a series of remarkably provocative but unclassifiable "fictions." See, for instance, as directly pertinent to the "fuite en avant" praised by Leiris above, *Le Livre des fuites.* That speed, and the accelerating tempo at which we are all obliged to live, is not always libertarian in its implications, is one of the telling points made recently by Paul Virilio, for instance in *Vitesse et politique,* where speed is seen as the fundamental strategy of established (military) power for allowing its subject populations time only for conditioned reaction, not calm reflection.

27. Antonin Artaud, *Œuvres complètes* 1:247-51; cf. also the hilariously Swiftian statement of Gilbert-Lecomte (dead at 36 of an overdose) on the issue, "Monsieur Morphée empoisoneur publique," in Gilbert-Lecomte, *Œuvres complètes* 1:118-29.

28. It is most unlikely, however, that Tzara would have followed Reich into the further reaches of his sexual pilgrimage. For the former, sexual desire would change in nature and quality in a better world, whereas for the latter this was an unalterable quantity or energy that could only be repressed or liberated. Among Freud's students Tzara was perhaps most profoundly influenced by Otto Rank and, specifically, his idea of "birthtrauma." The latter concept enabled Tzara to rationalize certain connections between primitive culture and a meaningful direction for modern art, on the basis of what he saw as a shared experience of terror or recoil at the fact of living.

29. Tzara memorably expresses this millennial aspiration of a consciousness that is liberated from debt in the final two lines of a late (posthumously published) poem from *40 Chansons et déchansons (40 Songs and Ditties), Œ. C.* 4:280: "je dis comme je vis / je vois comme la voix / je prends comme j'offre / ma vie est ainsi / je ne dois rien à personne / je dois tout à tous les hommes" ("I speak as I live / I see as a voice / I take as I give / My life is like this / I owe nothing to anyone / I owe everything to everyone").

Alina Clej (essay date 1991)

SOURCE: "Between Dada and Marxism: Tristan Tzara and the Politics of Position," in *Cross Currents: A Yearbook of Central European Culture,* Number 10, 1991, pp. 85-105.

[*In the following essay, Clej considers the unstable relationship between Tzara's poetry and his political beliefs and finds the source of this increasing conflict in his poetry.*]

> *What we call dada is a farce of nothingness in which all higher questions are involved; a gladiator's gesture, a play with shabby leftovers, the death warrant of posturing morality and abundance.*
>
> — *Hugo Ball,* Flight Out of Time

The Romanian-born poet Tristan Tzara had the good fortune, one might say, to achieve an international reputation at the age of twenty-one. This early recognition, which turned out to be his most enduring claim to fame, stemmed from Tzara's contribution to the Dada movement, which he helped kindle and disseminate. The name "Dada" itself is said to have been found by Tristan Tzara as he opened at random the pages of a dictionary. "Dada" can mean, according to Tzara, a wide variety of things: "the tail of a sacred cow" among the Kru people of Africa, "the cube or mother" in certain parts of Italy, "a wooden horse, a wet nurse, [or] the double affirmation in Russian and Romanian"; but ultimately, as Tzara insists, "Dada means nothing."[1] This all-inclusive and yet empty name came to designate a loose association of European (and, occasionally, American) artists. Through their bold manifestos and irreverent productions in the second decade of this century, these artists from all domains began to challenge the institution of art itself. What started as an improvised, spontaneous activity in Zurich in 1916, and took shape largely owing to Tzara's inventive genius and organizing talents, soon became an international phenomenon branching out to New York, Paris, Berlin, Cologne, and Hanover. Although Tzara "officially" buried Dada at the Bauhaus festival in Weimar in 1922, its spirit never quite died out. For one thing, it persisted in the works of some of the onetime Dada artists like Marcel Duchamp, Francis Picabia, Max Ernst, and Kurt Schwitters, but it also inspired at least one direction of the Romanian avant-garde between the wars, represented by the journals *Integral* and *Unu*. After the war the Dada spirit reemerged in *lettriste* poetry in France—an invention of Isidore Isou (another Romanian-born writer)—and in various neo-Dada manifestations in Europe and the United States. A Dada affinity can be recognized in the works of Robert Rauschenberg, George Segal, Claes Oldenburg, Yves Klein, Jean Tinguely, and, more recently, Christo, not to mention the ephemeral products of urban pop culture.[2] Ironically enough, however, the movement that brought Tzara to fame also obscured his figure. Tzara became just another name for Dada.

There is one side of Tzara's generally ignored personality that I would like to explore in this essay, namely his political involvement in his later life, an aspect that at first sight may seem totally unrelated to his well-known and much-celebrated Dada identity. Indeed, nothing could be more unlike the Dada insolence and anarchist defiance that Tzara vaunted in his precocious youth than the communist image of conformity that he adopted in his adult life. He chose to become a member of the French Communist party in 1935.[3] It is not that Dada and communism could not meet, but when they did—as in the case of the Berlin Dadas—it was almost by mistake. One may describe this accidental convergence as an optical illusion, which by straining, as it were, the field of the ideological apparatus, allowed for the political and the poetic, pragmatic reason and imaginative freedom, to appear in the same frame. In Tzara's case the optical illusion works in reverse: it creates a double image where in fact there may be only one. Beyond the troubled, uneven surface of Tzara's life and work one can detect, I think, a nebulous consistency, which brings his apolitical Dada and politicized communist phases into a disturbing approximation. Behind all the shifts and the changing political stances lurks a restless (but oddly immobile) politics of position and context. I choose to call it a politics of position because it seems to me that ideological moves, in Tzara's case, have no substantial value but are subsumed instead to a highly personal oppositional practice. Charting some of the surface variations and deep resonances of Tzara's political engagements will be the aim of what follows.

Tzara's embrace of communism, although by no means uncommon among European intellectuals in the late 1920s and early 1930s, remains somewhat of a surprise insofar as it comes from one of the most fiercely independent spirits among the Dadas. No matter how much one would wish to excuse him, and in spite of a mostly discreet and possibly guarded allegiance, the fact remains that Tzara maintained his Communist party membership with equanimity, if not enthusiasm, through the Stalinist purges, the Nazi-Soviet pact, and the cold war period until the very end of his life, in 1963. Although he did not go as far as to change his poetic style to suit the ideology, as Louis Aragon did, Tzara's was nonetheless a long-standing fidelity, which the French Communist party duly acknowledged by claiming Tzara in the hour of his death, as its own.[4]

And yet Tzara was anything but politically dishonest or naive. There is from the very beginning a kind of implacable rigor, an almost abrasive lucidity in his judgments of situations and events, which could hardly accommodate an unreflective form of ideological infatuation, let alone delusion. Moreover, the very idea of an inconsistency or of an irrational break between different moments of his life would have been infinitely displeasing to his sense of cogency. When his early poems in Romanian were being collected for publication, Tzara objected, for instance, to the title *Poèmes d'avant-dada* suggested by the editor, Saşa Pana . According to Tzara, such a title "would imply some kind of rift in [his] poetic personality," when in fact there had been, in his own words, "a continuity by fits and starts more or less violent and potent, if you wish, but continuity and interpenetration nonetheless, related in the highest degree to a *latent necessity*" (*OC,* 1:632).

On the face of it there seems to be as little connection between Tzara's early poetic exercises inspired by symbolism and his Dada experiments with language as there is, at another level, between his Dada credo and his Communist party loyalty. And yet I would argue that the same invisible, spasmodic continuity, which Tzara himself claimed for his poetic development, may apply to his political career. In that case both the Dada and the communist phases could reflect the same "latent necessity" to which Tzara alluded in relation to his poetry. It is this latent necessity, its literally hidden, unsuspected character, that provides, I believe, the key to understanding Tzara's uneven trajectory.

FROM DADA ANARCHISM TO COMMUNIST ORTHODOXY

Tristan Tzara (Samuel Rosenstock) was born in Moineş ti, in the Romanian province of Baclau, in 1896, the son of a prosperous forest administrator. Judging by his unfinished autobiography *Faites vos jeux* (Place your bets), it seems that from early on Tzara was a difficult, wayward youth embattled against his traditional family, his father in particular. Whether there was any link between Tzara's revolt against his bourgeois father and his precocious interest in socialism must be a matter of speculation. Be that as it may, it appears, however, that at the age of ten Tzara knew already about "profit, surplus value, capitalist exploitation, socialism, and revolution" through the good services of a typographer who provided him with popularizing pamphlets on the life and thought of Jean Jaurès and the doctrines of Russian and French socialist thinkers.[5] For Tzara, socialism was, I suspect, not only a discourse of resistance (in relation to his bourgeois milieu), but also one of seduction, by virtue of its exotic appeal. The image of the proletarian (the undernourished, sickly worker, the ragpicker, or the prostitute) was already part of the symbolist landscape and must have been familiar to Tzara from his youthful readings of French and Romanian symbolist poets.

It is this symbolist landscape that only fleetingly appears in Tzara's early poems, which otherwise bear no trace of his socialist readings. The image in question is worth mentioning, however, for what I believe to be its symptomatic nature. In a variant to "Cântec de razboi" (Song of war) the siren "calling the workers to the factory" is said to "echo faintly, [like] a shepherd's horn in faraway hills."[6] The implicit simile that brings together the rural, untrammeled ground of the shepherd's world and the industrial, grimy landscape of a suburban factory is, I think, more than a poetic conceit. It evokes a figure of double estrangement, from both past and present, an uncertain space stretched in two directions between which desire and resistance can shuttle back and forth. It seems that the image of the distant call, which makes the shepherd and the worker equally remote, contains *in nuce* the script of Tzara's poetic itinerary and its ceaseless play between impossible limits.

The siren's plaintive call (probably suggested by Emil Isac's poem "Sirena fabricii" [The factory siren]) reappeared as the title of a journal published by Tristan Tzara and Ion Vinea in 1915, *Chemarea* (The call), which after the uninspired title of their first journal, *Simbolul* (1912),

seemed to indicate a shift toward a more militant position. Whether, in Tzara's case, this choice of title was an intimation of a real political engagement is hard to determine. The young poet, not yet twenty, was soon to leave Romania for Zurich, where he started a literary "insurrection" that became a landmark in modern literary history.

In spite of its antibourgeois claims and its occasional outbursts against the war, Dada in its Zurich phase (1916-1919) displayed little overt interest in political commitments or affiliations. Without discounting the revolutionary potential of Dada as a reservoir of imaginary destruction, slogans, and battle cries, the fact remains that in 1916 in Zurich political action was not an issue. The founding group, which included—besides Tzara—Hugo Ball, Emmy Hennings, Marcel Janco, Richard Huelsenbeck, and Hans Arp, had little in common with the various socialists and pacifists that were then operating in Switzerland. Lenin was preparing for the Russian revolution in his study, across from the Cabaret Voltaire, where the Dadas were carrying on with their boisterous performances, and yet the two sides never came together, except in Tom Stoppard's *Travesties*. It is only in its last stages that Dada attempted to orient itself toward a more constructive revolutionary program, and this was owing mainly to the efforts of Marcel Janco, who in 1919 created, together with Arp and Hans Richter, an Alliance of Revolutionary Artists to express the Dadas' support for the popular uprisings in Munich and Budapest. But in this late development Tzara, curiously enough, did not participate, and rumor has it that he even tried to sabotage Janco's initiative.

On the other hand, the implicit political value of the Dada offensive on language should by no means be underestimated, and most critics, in fact, do recognize the ideological significance of Dada and of Tzara's destructive enterprise. But in this "poetic revolution" Tzara's master was not Marx but Nietzsche, whom he appears to have known already from Romania.[7] And the value that the Dadas attached to the overhaul of language outweighed the importance of social reform. Their concern for the masses, such as it was, is indistinguishable from a poetic interest in naive, infantile, or primitive art, which represented, in their eyes, a source of untainted creative energies. In this respect the child, the madman, the Zulu, and the worker were on an equal footing. One should add, however, that by stripping language of its privileged aura, Dada was implicitly granting the masses the right to creativity, following in this respect Lautréamont's famous injunction, "Poetry should be made by everybody, not by one alone." Implementing this desideratum was another story. The educational programs that Dada envisaged, most certainly inspired by the Dada "educators" Ball and Janco, did not go very far. The Galerie Dada, which opened on March 1917, organized events for schoolchildren and workers as well as for upper-class women and art dealers, having more success with the latter than with the former. All in all, during the "Zurich insurrection" Tzara's outward behavior was more that of an eccentric dandy than that of a committed revolutionary.

The Dadas in fact made no secret of their lack of interest in political action. As Hugo Ball put it, "Politics and art are two different things."[8] But their rejection of politics was motivated less by political indifference than by a high sense of moral righteousness and by the desire to avoid contamination with what they saw as the general corruption of public life. One may understand why the word "disgust" (*Ekel*) is perhaps the best expression of their ontopolitical stand, very much the way *nausée* distilled the underlying spirit of existentialism. The Dadas' revulsion for political concepts and manifestations derived, however, from a specific historical context, that is to say, from the grievous compromise of the very notion of political discourse, which, in the form of nationalism, was responsible for the outbreak of World War I. As Tzara put it, "This war was not our war. We suffered it through its false emotions and petty excuses. . . . Dada was born of a moral imperative, of an implacable will to achieve a moral absolute. . . . Honor, Fatherland, Morality, Family, Art, Religion, Liberty, Fraternity . . . all these notions that had once answered to human needs had been reduced to skeletal conventions" (*OC*, 5:65)." It is true that this is a late assessment (1947) and that in the meantime Tzara had given a more deliberately political coloring to the Dada gesture of absolute defiance. Yet it is hard not to see behind Dada's wild grimaces and verbal stunts a desperate search for "a moral absolute" that entailed a radical purge of linguistically coded values. And in this sense Dada could be seen as the effective realization of Nietzsche's project of a "transvaluation of all values."[9]

From this perspective, anarchism, rather than communism, was the only legitimate political position. In his rejection of all ideological systems (including Dada itself), and in his lack of interest in the Bolshevik revolution, Tzara shared Ball's anarchist credo, inspired by Bakunin, and maintained it even after moving to Paris in 1920. In an interview with Ilarie Voronca published in the Romanian avant-garde journal *Integral* (no. 12, April 1927), Tzara reveals political opinions that echo closely Ball's reflexions in *Flight Out of Time*, especially in the attack on the reductive, philistine nature of communist ideology: "To recognize dialectical materialism, to formulate in clear sentences, even with a revolutionary goal in mind, this can only be the profession of faith of a shrewd politician." Like Ball, Tzara had few illusions about the promises of the Bolshevik enterprise: "Communism is a new bourgeoisie started from scratch; the communist revolution is a bourgeois form of revolution. It is not a state of mind but a 'sad necessity.' After it, order begins. And what order! Bureaucracy, hierarchy, Chamber of Deputies, French Academy" (*OC*, 2:418). Communism, in other words, was a travesty of the old regime, in a more ruthless form.

Dada was supposed to be precisely the opposite of all this, "a perpetual revolution . . . of the spirit," and it was only an irony, as Tzara saw it, if Dada turned into a movement, with himself as its leader. Many avant-garde scholars take Tzara at his word, but it is quite obvious, judging by the historical evidence, that one of Tzara's

driving motives *was* the creation of a movement. He was the one who, among the Dadas, was the most interested in giving a formal sanction to the disruptive activities of the Cabaret Voltaire by transforming it into a Voltaire Society with an international audience. Not unlike "a shrewd politician," he initiated an extensive press campaign, advertising Dada (as well as himself) in all the important avant-garde journals of Europe and New York. As Huelsenbeck remarked in *En avant Dada*, perhaps not without a grudge, "Tzara was devoured by ambition to move in international artistic circles as an equal or even a 'leader.'"[10] Janco himself, Tzara's fellow countryman and at first a close friend, described Tzara as the "strategist and later [the] publicity manager" of the Cabaret Voltaire (*Dada Créateur*).[11] It was indeed Tzara's organizing talents that launched Dada in Paris in 1920 and prepared the audience for the surrealist adventure, from which, however, he would be left out.

And yet it seems unfair to ascribe to ambition alone Tzara's pressing desire to found a movement and his later disputes with André Breton over "the direction and defense of the modern spirit" or the politics of the surrealist group.[12] Tzara's contradictory manifestations and political maneuverings, both for and against organizing the avant-garde, were motivated, I believe, by psychological needs that happened to coincide with a more widespread pattern among European intellectuals at the time. This could be described as a dynamics of exclusion and inclusion, in which Tzara was easily absorbed, for personal as well as political reasons.

Tzara had already experienced, in more than one way, the effects of exclusion. His exile from Romania is perhaps the most conspicuous instance, although one should note that it was an exclusion that was provoked as much as suffered. (Tzara was sent—one might say "banished"—to Zurich by his parents, who were anxious to keep him away from the "decadent" milieus of Bucharest, a city known at the time as the Paris of the Balkans). To counteract this expulsion, Tzara seems to have sought a different form of integration in the collective spirit of Dada, which made art or anti-art the abode of those without a country: the founding Dadas were all exiles. One should also mention, in Tzara's case, a different, more subtle kind of exclusion, which he must have experienced already in his native country and which seems to haunt his works. Under the name of Samuel Rosenstock, Tzara was labeled, as was the custom at the time, as an ethnically alien subject, "of Israelite nationality." And to compound this estrangement, Tzara seems to have been fairly removed from his Jewish heritage, which left him hovering between equally distant cultures.

But Tzara's sense of exclusion and isolation, which pervades his work in all its various phases, was by no means a singular phenomenon. Most European intellectuals between the wars seem to have suffered from some form of *horror vacui*, a nagging fear of being left out, which appears to have been both existential and social in nature and which explains, I think, much of the tiresome wranglings over formal affiliations that went on within artistic communities at the time. It is in this general context of defensive strategies, which overdetermines, in Tzara's case, a personal configuration, that I would like to situate Tzara's ideological shifts and political reactions.

During and after World War I, internationalism represented both a form of subversion and a political defense for the European intelligentsia, modeled, in that respect, on the Workers' International. It is remarkable, in fact, to what extent the opposition between nationalism and internationalism shaped the ideological battles that raged during the 1920s and 1930s. Through its association with the disasters of the war, nationalism had come to be viewed by left-wing intellectuals as an immediate threat not only to their freedom of expression and to the idea of a universal heritage but also to their biological existence. Young intellectuals represented one of the heaviest casualties of the war. Intellectual vigilance and panic naturally grew with the rise of fascism. A critical point was reached in the late 1930s when it became clear that communism, in its Stalinist form, was no longer a safeguard or a model to imitate. This dark realization threw many intellectuals into despair or made them embrace the right-wing alternative. It is at this moment of mounting tension, in 1935, that Tzara decided to become a member of the French Communist party, a move that coincided with his definitive break with the surrealist group.

This is how the former enemy of the establishment came to don official roles and pose as intellectual spokesman for the *Maison de la culture,* a propaganda platform established by the French Communist party. Tzara also acted as cultural ambassador to the Spanish Republic on behalf of the Writers' Association for the Defense of Culture, an intellectual coalition controlled by the communists, which made him, even unwittingly perhaps, a representative of Stalinist policy in the area.[13]

Can the need for a political stronghold alone explain Tzara's allegiance to communism? The threat of fascism was no doubt very much on Tzara's mind at the time, and other political alternatives, like Trotskyism or different forms of socialism, were far less well equipped to deal with its perils. Tzara's reluctance to return to his native country, even for a visit, may have had something to do with his anxiety, especially in the late 1930s, when a wave of belligerent nationalism gained momentum in Romania, provoking a campaign against modernist art and against what was called the "Judaization of Romanian literature," one of whose main targets was Tzara himself.[14]

Tzara's antifascist commitment took shape in his active participation in the French Resistance and in his postwar initiatives, among which was a lecture tour through a number of Central and Eastern European countries, including Romania (which he visited for the second and last time in his life). Tzara undertook this journey, in the autumn of 1946, with the full confidence of a man who had seen the defeat of fascism and who took some pride in his personal contribution to the Resistance.[15] He offered his services to the French Ministry of Foreign Af-

fairs and financed his own trip in order to have the opportunity of expressing his support for the "emancipation movements" under way in Eastern Europe.[16] In retrospect, Tzara's upbeat mood appears sadly out of place. In heralding what he saw as the noble continuation of the French revolution in those recently liberated territories, Tzara was clearly unaware of the sinister turn that events were about to take. Eastern Europe was still in a state of political turmoil, and few were those in the West who could, or were willing to, predict the brutal suppression of democratic forces that was to ensue. At that juncture Tzara may well be excused for his lack of political insight.

And yet the threat of fascism alone cannot explain Tzara's political moves. In examining the interpersonal dynamics of the French intelligentsia between the wars, one could easily see how Tzara's position may have varied according to that of his main rival, André Breton. It seems that when Breton was in, Tzara was out, and vice versa. At the time of the dispute over the Congress of Paris masterminded by Breton, in the spring of 1922, Breton was warning the public against "the agitations of a personage known as the promoter of a movement coming from Zurich," which in those days was synonymous with the German enemy.[17] The fact that Tzara was Jewish only added to the irony. Tzara was subsequently excluded (with only a brief reinstatement) from the surrealist group dominated by Breton and, in a more discreet way, marginalized in the history of French poetry (he was already a marginal figure in Romanian literary history).

In the 1920s the Surrealists' attempts to collaborate with the Communist party left Tzara, who was still an anarchist at the time, even further adrift. When, later on, the surrealist group no longer had a chance to win the communists' confidence, the roles were reversed. On the occasion of the International Congress of Writers for the Defense of Culture, it was Tzara, by then a member of the French Communist party, who was on the program and Breton who was denied access to the proceedings. While Tzara went to Spain during the Spanish civil war, on behalf of the same forum, Breton stayed in Paris, allegedly to tend to his recent paternal duties. While Tzara was directing the literary broadcast of the Resistance in the south of France, Breton was socializing in New York, broadcasting for the Voice of America and editing the largely apolitical journal *VVV*.[18]

This antagonistic play, which was as much the result of circumstances as it was of deliberate intentions, finally came to a climax on the occasion of Tzara's lecture at the Sorbonne entitled *Le surréalisme et l'après-guerre* (Surrealism and the postwar period [1947]), in which Tzara did not fail to remark upon Breton's absence during the Occupation. In an ironic reversal from his previous Dada performances, Tzara played the serious orator on the stage, whereas Breton was vociferating from the audience; and it was Tzara's communist bodyguards who strove to impose order. One could almost say that Tzara became and remained a communist in part because Breton happened to occupy the other alternative positions in the spectrum of the left, namely those of a Trotskyist and of a libertarian.

Tzara's lecture at the Sorbonne, following his tour in Eastern Europe, was one of his last memorable public appearances. After this final attempt to reclaim his position as the legitimate leader of the European avant-garde and to secure the place of Dada in the Western tradition of poetry (a very non-Dada gesture), Tzara was obliged to retreat to less exposed ground. He became more and more of a recluse and spent the last ten years of his life in Paris, decrypting anagrams in the works of Rabelais and Villon. It was three scholars who brought the Romanian-born poet back into the consciousness of the general public: Michel Sanouillet, with his impressive volume *Dada in Paris* (1965); Claude Sernet (Mihail Cosma), with his translation of Tzara's Romanian poems, published the same year; and Henri Béhar, the editor of Tzara's complete works. Even now, however, there remain large segments of Tzara's writings that are still draped in silence.

In retrospect, the main drift of Tzara's Sorbonne lecture, namely the idea of placing poetry "in the service of the Revolution," in contrast with the mystic, retrograde position of the surrealist group dominated by Breton, seems astonishingly fragile. At the time, Tzara was consciously searching, as he had been since the early 1930s, for a "dialectical solution" to the general condition of literature (and the "stagnation" of surrealism, in particular), which would allow poetry, "without surrendering any of its essential virtues, to play an active part in the revolutionary becoming [of the world]" (*OC*, 5:638). This "dialectical solution" may have also been meant as a cure to the "stagnation" in the poet's own life. The question remains, however, how Tzara's revolutionary conception of poetry as "an activity of the mind" went beyond the fanciful theories invented by Breton, that is, beyond the "amusing game" of "creating myths out of one's own study" (*OC*, 5:638). How did it retain its historical relevance?

THE POET AS LONELY WOLF

It is clear that in spite of his political alliance with the communists—motivated, as I have tried to show, by strategic rather than purely ideological reasons—Tzara was very much a lonely poet, wary of organized groups that represented, in his eyes, a threat to the freedom of the individual. On the occasion of the Congress of Paris, in 1922, he warned that "the current state of dejection," resulting, among other things, from "the substitution of groups in the place of individuals, could be more dangerous than the reaction itself," adding that he had personally suffered from a similar backlash.[19] This somewhat enigmatic allusion seems to refer not only to his exclusion from the congress but also to a deeper feeling of alienation, which may explain why Tzara both sought and avoided political and literary organizations. Even more intriguing, perhaps, is that his marginality appears to have been as much the result of external factors as it was a matter of personal choice. In *Faites vos jeux* Tzara describes his writing as a form of opposition and at the same time as a curious form of therapy: "I began writing in my first youth . . . from a sense of contradiction. I was

writing poems 'against' my family, on the sly, and in order to mitigate a state of imbalance in my mind." This habit of "transcribing a psychological malaise" became for Tzara a "therapy of mental release" and eventually "turned into a kind of latent vice, by virtue of the pleasure that it procured" (*OC*, 1:260). One may compare this notion of "latent vice" to that of the "latent necessity" connecting Tzara's early Romanian poems to his later Dada output. What is hidden or latent seems to be precisely the torment and pleasure of resistance at the heart of writing, which the subject both produces and attempts to overcome.

This self-generated exclusion created by a conscious oppositional act (writing "against" the family and then later the audience) combines, to the point of becoming indistinguishable, with a sense of enforced exclusion or banishment.[20] The resulting feeling is one of haunting sorrow, which resonates throughout Tzara's poetry. Affliction is present in unexpected ways, even in his mischievously funny Dada poems, like **"The First Celestial Adventure of M. Antipyrine,"** where the sorrow appears as a distorted echo of metaphysical despair ("grief without a church come on come on coal camel") or as the blunt expression of a lack of human community ("closed door without brotherhood we are grieving" [*OC*, 1:78]). There are moments, however, when sorrow is specifically related to Tzara's feeling of exile and separation from home: "I am without soul waterfall without friends and talents lord / and I don't often receive letters from my mother" (**"The Great Lament of My Obscurity One"** [*OC*, 1:90]). It is certainly surprising to discover, under the detritus of the Dada's language, a persistent lyrical residue or at times even the remnant of a traditional lament.[21] The Romanian words "nu mai plânge nu mai plânge veux-tu" (don't cry anymore don't cry anymore will you), at the end of **"The Great Lament of My Obscurity One,"** bring, moreover, a distant echo of nursery rhymes, Romanian folk lyrics (*doine*), and Romanian mourning songs (*bocete*).

Images of isolation and separation, departure and estrangement, are all too frequent in Tzara's poetry, recalling, to a certain extent, the obsessive themes of another exiled Romanian poet, Paul Celan. Tzara's best known poetic work, *Approximate Man* (1931), is a lengthy meditation on man's loneliness and uncertainty in a hostile world and expands his earlier "laments" to universal proportions. It is perhaps no accident that the poet's pseudonym, Tristan Tzara, carries with it a double load of sorrow since it means "sad" in Romanian (*trist*) and "trouble" in Hebrew (*tzara*).[22]

If, as I have tried to suggest, Tzara's exile is self-induced as much as suffered, it is perhaps less surprising to discover a valedictory sorrow in the Romanian poems, which predate his actual departure from his native country. In fact, Tzara's pseudonym in Romanian can mean "sad in his country," a meaning that the poet himself acknowledged.[23] Leaving and traveling are perhaps the two most frequent activities in Tzara's early Romanian poetry. Even in his later work endless journeys appear, often by train, as the title of one of his collections of poems suggests (**The Railway Timetable of the Heart** [1928]), or else images of flight (*fuite*), which gives the title to one of his later plays (*La fuite* [1940]). This poetic obsession materialized into a very real and traumatic experience when Tzara had to flee for his life from Paris to the south of France during the war.

The motif of exile is conveyed on a different register, by the image of the lonely animal (horse, dog, or wolf) running away or hunted down in the closed space of a poem. It is the circular image of the howling wolf or wind that creates in its vortex the movement of many of Tzara's poems, as if the force of an original expulsion were converted into poetic energy. A whole page of the *Seven Dada Manifestos* is covered with the word *hurle* ("howls") arranged in parallel columns, in a mounting crescendo of maddening reverberation (the page itself seems to vibrate), broken at the end by the innocuous description "Qui se trouve encore très sympathique" (who still finds himself quite pleasant) which introduces the subject, Tristan Tzara.[24]

The wolf is not only a recurrent image in Tzara's poetry (a whole poetic cycle is entitled *Where the Wolves Drink*) but also a principle of poetic production, which Tzara names "lycanthropy" (a term borrowed from Petrus Borel). The originally magical practice of assuming a wolf's shape becomes, in Tzara's case, a theory of oppositionality *avant la lettre*. As a solitary wolf, the poet refuses his society, being a traitor to his own social class; and yet it is precisely this distance that allows him to integrate poetry and life, or rather to transform life into a mode of poetic activity. Lycanthropy acquires, at the same time, a therapeutic value in Tzara's writing, which harks back to its old magical function. It is as if being "against," in opposition to a certain social environment, parallels the state of imbalance in the poet's mind and serves to channel and release a certain amount of pent-up energy. The poem becomes the site of an antagonistic conflict followed by a momentary resolution, the result of an action and reaction. In a similar way one could say that Tzara himself creates the conditions for his own nostalgia, a space of exile in which blank energy can become meaningfully oriented in the form of sorrow and longing (*dor*).

Lycanthropy can be seen to function, moreover, as a form of mythical or utopian integration. It is perhaps not without significance that Tzara chose the symbol that he did; according to Mircea Eliade, the wolf may have given the name to the Romanians' ancestors. Ancient authors called the Dacians *Dahae,* a word probably derived from the Iranian *dahae* (wolf) and which may allude to both their religious and military rituals. But the wolf was also the symbol of the outcast, the exile, or the fugitive protected by Apollon Lykeios, a meaning that may have been assimilated to the original name of the Dacians.[25] Such an explanation eminently suits the dynamics of exclusion and inclusion that informs not only Tzara's historical experience but also his poetic practice.

DIALECTICAL MATERIALISM AS A TRANSGRESSIVE PRACTICE

Tzara was not content, however, with a mere subjective form of oppositionality and attempted, especially in his later life, to both historicize and politicize this notion. In the early 1930s he turned toward dialectics (historical materialism) in order to use it as an instrument for analyzing poetry in everyday life. The result of Tzara's extensive readings in this area was his *Essay on the Situation of Poetry* (1931), which marked his transition to a new form of poetic discourse. Tzara's departure from his previous views is considerable: in his interview with *Integral* Tzara had spoken disparagingly of dialectical materialism in the name of that to which it was opposed— "the perpetual revolution," "the revolution of the spirit, the *only* revolution that I envisage, and for which I would be willing to pay with my life, because it does not exclude the Sacredness of the self, because it is *my* revolution" (*OC,* 2:418). In 1931, however, dialectical materialism became for Tzara the only valid scientific method that could allow for the definition of "living poetry."

Given the dynamics of Tzara's life and poetic thought, the switch is not surprising. Dialectical materialism obviously offered him a way of creating a sense of meaningful continuity, by which negations could be reintegrated at a higher level, a method of throwing "bridges" and forging "links" between things and events that were far apart. At the same time, the oppositionality (lycanthropy) characteristic of the avantgarde poet could be interpreted as the propelling force in the history of poetry, a source of revolutionary energy. Moreover, dialectical materialism also provided an unexpected model for poetry, which Tzara developed in his *Essay on the Situation of Poetry.*

As a material activity bearing on language, poetry is here said to function as a superstructure (Tzara applies Marx's terms of political economy to poetic theory); but it is a refractory superstructure, one that does not always reflect its material and economic base. For, according to Tzara, poetry is not only the result of certain socio-economic conditions but also of their refusal, which thus prepares the ideological conditions for a new social formation. In this sense it has a superior, independent power as a "superstructure of a psychic order imposed on the existing mass of living civilization" (*OC,* 5:22) and may become the equivalent of a "dictatorship of the spirit" (*OC,* 5:12). This particular interpretation recalls Nietzsche's superman as much as Marx's superstructure and proletarian dictatorship, but Tzara himself was by no means a purist in his use of Marxism. Besides, he was well aware that poetry and revolution are incommensurable.

Even as a communist, Tzara had little faith in the poet's ability to carry on practical political work. The task of the poet could only be of a conceptual order, that of changing the sensibility, mental patterns, and linguistic habits of the masses in order to prepare them for the society of the future. Since the poet can be of little use in an actual revolution, his revolutionary role can only be envisaged in a postrevolutionary society, in which, as Marx's utopia goes, all practical problems will have been solved. This is how Tzara can claim that the main function of the poet is that of organizing "the activity of dreaming, idleness, leisure, in view of the communist society" and then declare in all seriousness that this is "the most immediate task of poetry" (*OC,* 5:27). Tzara's investment in the establishment of the communist society is in this sense very close to Georges Bataille's, who, taking for granted the success of the Soviet revolution, saw in it the end of history and of dialectical struggle and hence the possibility of using the liberated negativity in unproductive forms of "expenditure": festivals, sacrifices, and so on.[26]

Ultimately it is the revolution that is said to serve the poet, by giving him a utopian ground on which to play out his fantasies and allowing him to "pass," at least in imagination, from the individual to the collective. Like the barley grain, which is both negated and multiplied in the plant (Engels's example from *Anti-Dühring*), the poet's identity is both annihilated and enhanced in the communist society, in which poetry is no longer a "quality" reserved for the happy few but is transformed into a "quantity" destined for the use of the masses (*OC,* 5:27).

What seems to fascinate Tzara in the dialectical process of conversion from a quantitative change to a qualitative one and back is less the result than the "passage," the rapture that comes with the change. It is difficult not to see in the poet's obsession with passages and nodal points of transformation as they appear in dialectical materialism (via Hegel) Tzara's old fascination with trains and junctures. Dada itself challenged the "static" notion of beauty through the idea that art is a "state of mind" that is able to prove that "everything is movement, constant alignment along the flight of time" (*OC,* 1:18). It seems indeed that with dialectical materialism Tzara had found a way of scientifically aligning his life along the flight of time.

Grains et issues (Grains and issues), published in 1935, offers a poetic realization of the utopian project already sketched out in the *Essay on the Situation of Poetry* and is the most telling illustration of Tzara's use of dialectical materialism. It is this text that offers perhaps one of the most important sources for understanding Tzara's commitment to a certain form of Marxism and his relationship to the Communist party, which he joined the same year, as the dangers of fascism were growing. *Grains and Issues* is not only a personal poetic document; it is alos one of his most original, and least appreciated, efforts to combine Marxist ideology, psychoanalysis, and poetic theory. The closest equivalent at the time may be in Bataille's antiphilosophical essays. Tzara's experiment in poetic theory, arguably, anticipates the "revolution in poetic language" initiated by the critics of *Tel Quel* in the late 1960s.

And yet this essay, never reprinted until 1979, remains—for all its richness, and possibly because of it—a source of vexation rather than of enlightenment. The text is formless, with countless pages of dense prose, in which lyrical passages, oneiric scenes, and philosophical reflec-

tions are hopelessly mingled in disconcerting patterns. These intricate reflections, distributed into three sections—"Grains and Issues" (subtitled "Experimental Dream"), "On Nocturnal and Diurnal Realities," and "From Top to Bottom Clarity"—taper off in a concluding series of theoretical notes, seven in all, which attempt to explain the poet's enterprise. Tzara's sources are eclectic, ranging across Marxist and Freudian terrains as well as anthropology, and his tangled argument echoes the polemics surrounding the development of Freudo-Marxism in the early and mid-1930s and the new explorations in anthropology initiated by Bataille and his group. Tzara's own ideological motives, however, recede into a zone of approximation that befits what he called "the approximate man."

Grains and Issues is in many respects a utopian text, offering the vision of a postrevolutionary society in which the poet can freely indulge his imagination in order to organize and direct the crowds in their pursuit of happiness. The text is in this sense a perfect demonstration of what Tzara had curiously defined as "the most immediate task of poetry": "organizing the use of dream, idleness, and leisure in view of the communist society" (*OC,* 5:27).[27] This "new culture of joy," over which the poet presides as a master of ceremonies and which evokes in more than one way Bataille's image of the festival, is a blend between a Rabelaisian paradise and a Hollywood superproduction, combining rural, earthy pleasures with technological excitement. "Piles of fruit will be staked at crossroads," "eggs of light will be gathered on the breast of buildings," and the whole city will be flooded with florescent lights (*OC,* 3:10). This wild expenditure often suggests a massacre scene (reminiscent of the last war) that has turned into a sacrificial feast of unbridled consumption. Amid the "mountains of lamb" and "veal heads hanging from the trees," "tons of honey will pour through the mouths of military cannon," and chandeliers will hang amid the "remnants of planes built out of mangroves and carrots" (*OC,* 3:23).

There is an undeniable cruelty in Tzara's vision, in which the artist plays the role of a mad scientist (Caligari), an "exquisite being" whose "scattered madness" infuses the "propriety of the crowd." Tzara imagines a city in which "undergrounds are transformed into laboratories of suffering and cruelty" (*OC,* 3:16), in which "dogs gorged with gasoline and set on fire will be roused against naked women, the most beautiful, of course. Bowls containing the tongues of aristocrats will be exhibited in shop windows amid pots of mustard and jam. Fast cars provided on their front with steel prongs could impale long queues of people waiting in front of a cinema, for instance" (*OC,* 3:14).

One might well wonder at the hidden sources of this delirious vision, in which pleasure and cruelty are so closely fused. What is the meaning of the invention of new rituals, based on the principles of "osmosis and contagion" (*OC,* 3:59) and which recall Antonia Artaud's theater of cruelty? Tzara is ostensibly offering a drastic cure for various forms of psychological repression, "war neuroses," and so forth, on which fascism thrives, by advocating a poetic release of inhibitions and aggressive fantasies. What is odd in all this is that the release in turn resembles the disease itself (that is, fascism). Bataille's essay "The Psychological Structure of Fascism," written in 1933, turns on the same paradox. Tzara's proposal of sadomasochism as a synthesis between masochism and sadism, meant to channel the aggressive instincts in man, combines a Swiftian sense of enormity with the most extreme forms of science fiction. And yet Tzara appears to be striving to make the valid point that uncured repression may lead to the most violent explosions. His solution for the "reduction of the monstrous antagonisms" of bourgeois society (which, in his view, are psychological rather than social) is in fact a libidinal liberation of man, in retrospect something far more radical than the sexual liberation of the 1960s since Tzara's involves the release of all ambivalences and even perversions.

On the other hand, "vice" or violence serves as a "solvent" or subversive element in the destruction of the "conventional image of the world," which may explain some of the macabre visions in *Grains and Issues*, not to mention his explicit praise of Sade. Tzara's attempt to dislocate or undermine the old ideology is very much like a practical application of Nietzsche's project of a "transvaluation of all values"; it consists in the transformation of matter into a "non-Euclidean" space that resists authority (*OC*, 3:19). By creating a system of imaginary resistances, Tzara's utopian vision acquires a manifest oppositional value. The poet speaks of a "utopian will that obsesses him; the desire to set across the roads obvious propositions and so solid that people stumble and can no longer recover from the mental deformation that these emerald obstacles have imprinted on them" (*OC*, 3:59). In Tzara's oppositional project, deformation serves as a principle of construction. In the same way, negative conditions, like melancholia, are turned into positive energy (*OC*, 3:59), suggesting the possibility of recycling nonproductive forces to create productive meaning (*OC*, 3:63).

Negativity, however, like opposition itself, functions in a closed, inert field, where movement can only occur through a deliberate act of transgression or acceleration. Writing operates like "the rapid successions of lightning produced by a feathery wheel . . . whose stopping creates a deep gash . . . in the amorphous flow of memory" (*OC*, 3:56). It is only by sudden leaps, by "transgressing barriers," that the poet can attain "the indefinite terrains of roaming and even those of confusion," where memory is reactivated in the "psychic residues of instincts" (*OC*, 3:60). It is finally unclear, however, whether the ultimate aim of Tzara's utopia is to achieve release and oblivion, as he repeatedly claims, or, on the contrary, to create an effect of memory, a semblance of recollection that would shake his state of numbness produced by what he calls the "absence of filial local maternal paternal love" (*OC*, 3:24).

This ambiguity becomes apparent in the notion of the "birth traumatism," which occupies a significant place in *Grains and Issues*. The term, borrowed from Otto Rank, implies in Tzara's case both an ontological threshold and the prohibition of incest. One may assume that the desire to return to the mother's womb parallels the nostalgia for the lost homeland, whereas the possibility of return is censored by the incest taboo or, in Rank's understanding, by the birth traumatism, the painful memory of the original expulsion, which preempts the return. Not only does the maternal world represent simultaneously the ultimate recovery and final loss of memory, but this ambiguous construct is itself the object of ambivalent feelings, being at once coveted and abhorred. And yet these bewildering paradoxes do not stop at the level of personal history. Through a curious twist the threshold represented by the incest taboo is, in *Grains and Issues*, further identified with the historical break created by a revolution, the breach against and beyond which Tzara's utopia is set. In this double scenario the past and the future, incest and social transgression, expulsion and return, are collapsed in the same figure. The moment of rupture itself can only be thought of, however, from a utopian perspective, that adopted by *Grains and Issues*, and can only be experienced through the successive shocks and ripples that the text produces, artificially as it were, within its movement. As the revolutionary trauma can only be envisaged from a point of beyondness, so too the threshold of birth or the return to the native land, the going back in time to the point where memory is ultimately regained and extinguished.

It may well be that what Tzara is really combatting through his images of cruelty is both pain and anesthesia—not only memory but also its absence. It is this tension between the will to remember and the desire to forget, between the urgency of memory and its inertia, that underlies, I believe, the particular dynamics of Tzara's poetry. In a vivid image from *Grains and Issues* Tzara describes himself as living "half immersed in total absence and half in the torment of electromagnetic nostalgia," which creates "the axial ruptures of the roots" (*OC*, 3:86-88).

Tzara's poetry represents this spasmodic movement, which creates its own resistance and, through resistance, perpetuates itself, not so much as movement but as an illusion of movement. Life appears as a "perpetual flight of contorsions of verses that nudge each other . . . looking for a tortuous solution to oppositions and obstacles produced by the movement itself" (*OC*, 3:49). It is this friction, this endless convulsion, that creates a lyrical residue, a trail or trace suggesting a positive presence, the tangible shadow of memory, which the poet both pursues and rejects: "As the materialized cloud raised behind the desperate flight of the cuttlefish, which conceals it, clears off and then quietly settles down when the subterfuge is devalued at its basis, so will I chase away the now-futile smoke, under which the exaltation of the senses was installed" (*OC*, 3:90). Like the ink of the cuttlefish, the poet's writing conceals the aimless flight, the painful realization that there is nothing to conceal, and prompts in turn a new desire for erasure and inscription.

Through its inner turmoil Tzara's work ultimately communicates an image of Heraclitean flux, a migratory pattern that, like the shuttling movement of a train in his earlier poems, translates into the motility of images. In this respect, however, Tzara's poetry may evoke in a strange and unexpected way what Lucian Blaga called the "mioritic space," an "unconscious spatial horizon" modeled after the Romanian landscape of hilly pastures, where shepherds drive their herds back and forth with the changing seasons.[28] Tzara's use of a veiled image of transhumance in his utopia suggests seasonal movement and shifting positions—"cultures of gyratory worlds" where "the wind shakes the almonds," "regions of transhumance where the staff breaks . . . toward the crippled landscape the cohesion of steps" (*OC,* 3:83-84). And in this distant landscape resounds—never completed—a prophecy, a clamor, as remote as the factory siren in his early poem "Song of War," the "hour of the shepherds," Tzara's dim vision of a mythic, utopian community, from which he was forever barred by "the traumatism of birth" (*OC,* 3:10).

Facing this never-fulfilled destination, one is left with an endless "traversing of signs," signals, milestones, indices of a passage in continuous transformation in which both the flight and the positions taken form part of a simulacral economy whose center is fixed but absent ("the axial rupture at the roots"). Tzara's very definition of poetry follows this line of "flight": Dada was described, in contrast with static notions of beauty, as a *"state of mind* in which all is in movement, a constant alignment along the flight of time" (*OC,* 5:18). Dialectical materialism proved to be but an explanation, a justification of this "state of mind" and of this endless movement, giving a semblance of meaning and stability to its "provisional" moments. "I will have to insist," Tzara writes, "upon a principle that I hold dear, 'the provisional,' but a provisional solidly rooted in a development that can no longer escape our consciousness . . . , a provisional state conscious of its objective value. . . . I can give facts no other importance . . . than that which derives from their value as signs, witnesses, milestones in a perpetual transformation, and which is only measurable against the scale of their future" (*OC,* 5:7-8).

Tzara's constant attempts at politicizing his personal experience, and then depoliticizing, proves in fact the extent to which the political and the poetic are enmeshed in a common web of desires and phantasms, which only action can briefly separate, the way a fish line passes through the water, an act that has to be constantly renewed in order to keep apart the closing folds of the real and the imaginary. And yet if Tzara, unlike Breton, was fully aware of the dangers of confusing politics and poetry, he nonetheless found it hard to maintain his lucidity without falling back into the silent pain of reality. Tzara's restlessness and anxious shifting of positions was but a measure of his will to retain his wakefulness and the right to resist, which Tzara learned to assert even at the cost of self-contradiction.

NOTES

[1] Tristan Tzara, *Oeuvres complètes,* 5 vols., ed. Henri Béhar (Paris: Flammarion, 1975-1982), 1:360. All further references to Tzara's works (*OC*) are to this edition and are included in the text. Translations are mine.

[2] For the aftermath of Dada, see Matei Calinescu, "Avangarda literara in România," in *ViaŌ a româneasca,* no. 11 (November 1967): 106-117; Elmer Peterson, *Tristan Tzara* (New Brunswick, N.J.: Rutgers University Press, 1971), xi-xx; John D. Erickson, *Dada: Performance, Poetry, and Art* (Boston: Twayne Publishers, 1984), 119; Greil Marcus, *Lipstick Traces: A Secret History of the Twentieth Century* (Cambridge: Harvard University Press, 1989).

[3] This is the most likely date for Tzara's adherence to the Communist party, as it appears in the chronology published by Jacques Gaucheron and Henri Béhar in the commemorative issue of *Europe,* no. 555-556 (July-August 1975). There is, however, a discrepancy with Henri Béhar's chronology included in the first volume of *OC,* where the date is given as 1947.

[4] Isidore Isou, the *lettriste* poet, had to brave "the insults, threats and provocations of the Stalinists" in order to read his "Epistle to Tristan Tzara" at the poet's funeral (Maurice Lemaître, *Le lettrisme devant dada* [Paris: Centre de Créativité, 1967], 17), and it was Louis Aragon who delivered Tzara's funeral oration over French radio.

[5] Claude Sernet (Mihail Cosma), Introduction to Tristan Tzara, *Les premiers poèmes* (Paris: Seghers, 1965), 17-18.

[6] In SaŌa Pana , *Primele Poeme ale lui Tristan Tzara* (Bucharest: Editura Cartea Româneasc , 1971), 19. The volume is followed by a postface entitled "The Zurich Insurrection."

[7] Tzara and his friend Ion Vinea had been reading Nietzsche together during the summer vacation of 1915, before Tzara left for Zurich. Cf. Ion Vinea's poem "Dintr-o vara" ("From a Summer") and Simion Mioc, *Opera lui Ion Vinea* (Bucharest: Editura Minerva, 1972), 219.

[8] Hugo Ball, *Flight Out of Time: A Dada Diary,* ed. John Elderfield (New York: Viking Press, 1974), 114.

[9] For the connection between Nietzsche and Dada, see Rudolf E. Kuenzli, "The Semiotics of Dada Poetry," in *Dada Spectrum: The Dialectics of Revolt,* ed. Stephen C. Foster and Rudolf E. Kuenzli (Iowa City: University of Iowa Press, 1979), 51-71.

[10] Richard Huelsenbeck, *En avant Dada,* in *The Dada Painters and Poets,* ed. Robert Motherwell (New York, 1951), 26.

[11] Marcel Janco, *Dada: Monograph of a Movement* (New York: St. Martin's Press, 1975), 30.

[12] For the polemics between Breton and Tzara over the Congress of Paris, designed by Breton as "The International Congress for the Determination of the Directives and the Defence of the Modern Spirit" (1922), see Emil Manu, "InsurecŪia de la Paris din 1922 (Polemica Breton-Tzara)," *Revista de istorie si teorie literara* 26, no. 2 (1977): 271-288.

[13] Most of the details regarding Tzara's political activities between the wars come from Helena Lewis, *The Politics of Surrealism* (New York: Paragon House Publishers, 1988).

[14] See Tristan Tzara's correspondence with SaŌa Pana , documented by Henri Béhar, in *Manuscriptum,* 1982, no. 4:158.

[15] This contribution was mainly literary and consisted in Tzara's direction of the cultural broadcast of the French Resistance in the south of France (1943-1944).

[16] See "Interview with Tristan Tzara across the Balkans" (*OC,* 5:381-387) and "Conversation with Tristan Tzara" (*OC,* 5:388-392), which was first published in *Cahiers France-Roumanie,* no. 7 (February-April 1947): 62-68. See also the interview that Tzara gave for the Romanian journal *Rampa,* no. 27 (1946).

[17] See the exchange between Breton and Tzara in Emil Manu, "Insurecția," 277.

[18] See Lewis, *Politics of Surrealism.*

[19] See note 17.

[20] On the question of literary opposition, see Ross Chambers, *Mélancolie et opposition: Les débuts du modernism en France* (Paris: Librairie José Corti, 1987).

[21] Tzara's *Great Lament of My Obscurity Three* evokes through its incipit ("chez nous les fleurs des pendules s'allument") a "classical" elegy by Octavian Goga, "La noi."

[22] I would like to thank Rudolf Kuenzli for bringing this latter meaning to my attention and Sandor Goodheart for additional clarification of the meaning of the word.

[23] See Colomba Voronca's testimony in Serge Fauchereau, ed., *Tristan Tzara, Poèmes roumains* (Paris: La Quinzaine littéraire, 1974), 17.

[24] Both the scream and the image of the lonely wolf become theorized later as the very conditions of poetic expression and productivity (see *Note sur le comte de Lautréamont ou le cri* and *Tristan Corbière ou les limites du cri*).

[25] See the chapter entitled "The Dacians and the Wolves" in *De la Zalmoxis la Genghis-Han* (Bucharest: Editura sÛiinÛifica si enciclopedica , 1980).

[26] See Allan Stoekl, "The Avant-Garde Embraces Science," in *A New History of French Literature,* ed. Denis Hollier (Cambridge: Harvard University Press, 1989), 933.

[27] This view perhaps explains Tzara's enthusiasm over the artistic activities that were going on in Romania in 1946—the newly organized proletarian theater in Bucharest and the proselytizing tours organized by poets and writers through the Romanian countryside. Tzara failed to realize to what extent these activities were ideologically programmed and compared them instead to Federico García Lorca's popular theatrical representations in Spain (*OC,* 5:383-384).

[28] See Lucian Blaga's description of the mioritic space in his essay "Horizon and Style" (1935), in *Trilogia Culturii* (Bucharest: ELU, 1969), 48-49.

FURTHER READING

Criticism

Bersani, Jacques. "Tzara Lives!" *Manchester Guardian Weekly* (December 28, 1975): 12.

> Reviews the *Oeuvres complètes, Volume 1: 1912-1924* and praises it for showing "the singlemindedness and consistency of Tzara's concerns."

Biron, Lionel A. "The Secret French and German Editions of Tristan Tzara's *Dada 3,* or How to Launch an International Movement at the Height of European Nationalism." *Rackham Literary Studies* 6 (1975): 35-40.

> Recounts Tzara's efforts to publish a journal containing both French and German poetry in 1918, before World War I had ended.

Browning, Gordon Frederick. *Tristan Tzara: The Genesis of the Dada Poem, or from Dada to Aa.* Stuggard: H.D. Heinz, 1979. 195 p.

> Offers an in-depth analysis of the development of Tzara's Dada poetry.

Caldwell, Ruth L. "From Chemical Explosion to Simple Fruits: Nature in the Poetry of Tristan Tzara." *Perspectives on Contemporary Literature* 5 (1979): 18-23.

> Uses imagery of nature to show how Tzara's poetry changes over the course of his career.

Cardinal, Roger. "States of Emergency." *Times Literary Supplement* No. 3955 (January 13, 1978): 27.

> Argues that the provocative aspect of Tzara's Dada poetry was part of a serious project with "positive creative value."

Caws, Mary Ann. "Tristan Tzara." In her *The Poetry of Dada and Surrealism: Aragon, Breton, Tzara, Eluard, and Desnos,* 95-135. Princeton: Princeton University Press, 1970.

> Explores the hidden structure or "interior ordering" of Tzara's Dada poetry.

————Introduction to *Approximate Man and Other Writings* by Tristan Tzara, translated by Mary Ann Caws, pp. 15-35. Detroit: Wayne State University Press, 1973.

> Provides an overview of Tzara's literary career.

Grossman, Manuel L. "Montage in the Dada Poetry of Tristan Tzara." *Dada/Surrealism,* No. 4 (1974): 53-56.

> Examines the relationship between verbal structure and visual imagery in Tzara's Dada poetry.

Jeffett, William. "'L'Antitête: The Book as Object in the Collaboration of Tristan Tzara and Joan Miró (1946-1947)." *The Burlington Magazine* CXXXV, No. 1079 (February 1993): 81-93.

> Examines Miró's work on a set of engravings to illustrate the second edition of Tzara's *L'Antitête.*

Norman, Dorothy. "Two Conversations: Marcel Duchamp and Tristan Tzara." *Yale University Library Gazette* 60, No. 1-2 (October 1985): 77-80.

> Includes a short excerpt of a conversation with Tzara in which the poet discusses the relationship between Dada and artistic movements such as Cubism.

Petersen, Elmer. *Tristan Tzara: Dada and Surrational Theorist.* New Brunswick, New Jersey: Rutgers University Press, 1971, 259 p.

> Traces the development of Tzara theories about art and poetry during his Dada and Surrealist periods.

Additional coverage of Tzara's life and career is contained in the following sources published by the Gale Group: *Contemporary Authors, Vol. 89-92, 153; Contemporary Literature Criticism, Vol. 47; DISCovering Authors Modules—Poetry; Major Twentieth Centruy Authors*

Peter Viereck
1916-

American poet, critic, historian, dramatist, and essayist

INTRODUCTION

Peter Viereck's poetic career was shaped by his struggle to define a new direction for poetry following the modernism of T. S. Eliot and Ezra Pound. He has been heralded for his effort to create a poetry of ideas while reviving traditional formalism. An eminent historian as well as a poet, Viereck has received numerous awards for his works of poetry and historical nonfiction, including the Pulitzer Prize for poetry in 1949.

Biographical Information

Peter Viereck was born August 5, 1916, in New York City, to Margaret Hein and George Sylvester Viereck. His father was born in Germany to a literary family whom the elder Viereck once described as "breeding books like rabbits." A poet himself, as well a journalist and a freelance writer, George Viereck raised his own children in the same tradition of literary, philosophical, and political discourse. Peter Viereck graduated from the Horace Mann School for Boys in New York City and then entered Harvard College, where he won the Garrison Prize Medal for poetry. His younger brother, George S. Viereck, Jr., also attended Harvard, and the two of them co-founded the *Harvard Guardian,* a magazine devoted to the social sciences. In 1937, Viereck received a B.S. degree *summa cum laude* from Harvard. From 1937-38, he studied at Christ Church, Oxford, and then returned to Harvard for graduate study in history. He won the Bowdoin Prize Medal for an essay on romanticism, and he received an M.A. in 1939 and a Ph.D. in 1942.

Drafted in 1943, Viereck served with the Psychological Warfare Branch of the U.S. Army, analyzing German propaganda, including anti-American pieces written by Ezra Pound. In 1944, his younger brother was killed in combat at Anzio, Italy. After the war, Viereck taught history at the U.S. Army University in Florence. There he married Anya de Markov, the daughter of Russian emigrants, in June, 1945. He returned to teach history and German literature at Harvard from 1946-47. He taught at Smith College for a year and became associate professor of history at Mount Holyoke College in 1948. He was made a professor in 1955 and has held the William R. Kenan chair of history at Mount Holyoke since 1979.

Major Works

"Teaching is his profession," Mary Henault wrote of Viereck, "and poetry is his life." Called a "campus poet" by critics such as George Green and grouped with other academic poets such as Richard Wilbur, Randall Jarrell, and Robert Lowell, Viereck's writing is distinguished by the thematic continuities between his poetry and his prose. His essays about history and society, published in books such as *Metapolitics: From the Romantics to Hitler* (1941) and *Conservatism Revisited: The Revolt against Revolt* (1949), emphasize the importance of traditional values. In critical essays such as "My Kind of Poetry," Viereck advocated what he called "a revolt against revolt," arguing that traditional values and traditional forms should reclaim a central role in modern poetics. Calling this new aesthetic "Manhattan classicism," he rejected free verse "on principle" and returned to the conventional meters and rhyme schemes that had been rejected by earlier twentieth century poets. He also strongly resisted the modernist tendency to distinguish between ethics and aesthetics, insisting that social responsibility was at the heart of poetic beauty. He took his most famous moral stand on aesthetics when Ezra Pound was granted the Bollingen Prize in 1949. Harshly criticizing Pound's alliance with fascism, Viereck attacked the prize committee for claiming that "artistic form can be considered apart from content."

"What do they know of poetry who only poetry know?" Viereck once asked. His own verse embodies political, philosophical, and ethical themes. His first volume of poetry, *Terror and Decorum: Poems 1940-1948* (1948) won the Pulitzer Prize. It includes poems such as "Kilroy" a mock-epic drawn from his experiences during World War II, and "*Vale* from Carthage," an elegy to the memory of his younger brother, who died in the conflict. Many reviewers considered *Strike through the Mask!: New Lyrical Poems* (1950) a disappointment, despite successful individual poems such as "Small Perfect Manhattan." Here Viereck called for a classical poetry that remains engaged with the needs of the modern world. In *The First Morning: New Poems* (1952) and in *The Persimmon Tree: New Pastoral and Lyrical Poems* (1956) Viereck combined lyrical verse with satirical works that display his sharp, acid wit. *The Tree Witch: A Poem and a Play (First of All a Poem)* (1961) is poetry presented as a drama. The force of nature and spontaneity is represented by a dryad, and she is opposed by a chorus of modern women, called Guardian Aunts, who represent modern technological materialism. Many critics doubt that a piece so heavy with disputation could ever have been performed successfully. Much of the poetry in *New and Selected Poems, 1932-1967* (1967) is taken from *Terror and Decorum,* and this volume has been frequently praised for a careful arrangement that emphasize themes rather than chronology. Viereck's most conceptually ambitious work is *Archer in the Marrow: The Applewood Cycles of 1967-1987* (1987). This theological epic in eighteen lyrical cycles explores the themes of sin and redemption through the voices of three characters: God the Father, God the Son, and a modern everyman whom Viereck calls "You." In his final collection, *Tide and Continuities: Last and First Poems 1995-1938* (1995) Viereck arranged the poems in reverse chronological order. This volume includes "Dionysus in Old Age," a retelling of the story of Persephone, and satires such as "Now That Holocaust and Crucifixion Are Coffee-Table Books."

Critical Reception

Most critics agree that Viereck took courageous risks in his poetry. His bold experiments in poetic form are almost universally admired, as is his fearless engagement with the great themes of Western literature. Most critics, however, are uncertain about the success of Viereck's poetic risks. He is most frequently faulted for overburdening his poetry with philosophy, theology, and ethics. M.L. Rosenthal urged readers "to forgive Viereck's endless slogans, the precious credos, the saucy banalities about poetry and this harsh world . . ." for the sake of a few strong poems. Ernest Kroll writes that Viereck "frequently takes his reader on a wild ride from which he alone, the poet, returns." For some critics, the weight of ideas crushed Viereck's personal poetic voice. Paul Goodman complains that "he seems to have no personal language," and Kimon Friar expresses the same doubt, arguing that Viereck "writes with a dashing competence . . . but rarely do I find a consistent cadence of his own." Hayden Carruth praises his individual voice and "the rather nervous movement" of diction and ideas in his poetry, but he admits that "Viereck's poems are painfully hard to read." There are some critics, however, who argue that Viereck's political and philosophical convictions sustain his poetry. Josephine Jacobsen praises him for his "cosmic sense"—an ability to express universal themes that lead "straight into a sense of the infinite depth of the small and the large." Phoebe Pettingell delights in both the formal and the conceptual challenges that Viereck poses his readers. She particularly admires his identification of art with morality: "Viereck insists that art is an exercise in empathy, the greatest good we as humans can know and practice."

PRINCIPAL WORKS

Poetry

Terror and Decorum: Poems 1940-1948   1948
Strike through the Mask!: New Lyrical Poems   1950
The First Morning: New Poems   1952
The Persimmon Tree: New Pastoral and Lyrical Poems 1956
The Tree Witch: A Poem and a Play (First of All a Poem)   1961
New and Selected Poems, 1932-1967   1967
Archer in the Marrow: The Applewood Cycles of 1967-1987   1987
Tide and Continuities: Last and First Poems 1995-1938 1995

Other Works

Metapolitics: From the Romantics to Hitler (history) 1941; revised edition published as *Metapolitics: The Roots of the Nazi Mind,*   1961
Conservatism Revisited: The Revolt against Revolt (essays) 1949 second edition published as *Conservatism Revisited and the New Conservatism: What Went Wrong?,*   1962
"My Kind of Poetry" (critical essay)   1950; published in *Mid-Century American Poets,* ed. John Ciardi
Shame and Glory of the Intellectuals: Babbit, Jr. Versus the Rediscovery of Values (history)   1953
Dream and Responsibility: Four Test Cases of the Tension between Poetry and Society (critical essays) 1953
Conservatism: From John Adams to Churchill (history) 1956

The Unadjusted Man: A New Hero for Americans: Re-
flections on the Distinction between Conserving and
Conforming (essays) 1956
Inner Liberty: The Stubborn Grit in the Machine (es-
says) 1957
Conservatism from Burke and John Adams till 1982: A
History and an Anthology (history, anthology) 1982
Opcomp: A Modern Medieval Miracle Play (drama) 1993
"Strict Form in Poetry: Would Jacob Wrestle a Flabby
Angel?" (critical essay) 1978; published in *Critical*
Inquiry

Selden Rodman (review date 1948)

SOURCE: "Against Barracks and Classroom," *The Satur-*
day Review of Literature, Vol. XXXI, No. 41, October
9, 1948, pp. 29-30.

[*In the following review of* Terror and Decorum, *Rod-*
man praises Viereck's first collection of poetry for being
"so rich in experimental vigor."]

In ten years of reviewing verse. I have gone overboard, as
they say, for only two first books—Shapiro's. "Person,
Place and Thing" and Lowell's "Lord Weary's Castle"—
as I intend to go for this one, (***Terror and Decorum***) and
I can't think of a better way of beginning than by measur-
ing it against the other two. The excitement of Shapiro's
book was in its summing-up of the social revolt of a
whole decade that had been (if we except Auden, in England) without a spokesman in poetry; with his personal
blend of violence and elegant wit, Shapiro delivered the
coup de grace to the Lost Generation (expatriate and
metaphysical wings); yet in a sense he belonged to the
exclusive circle which he exercised. But Lowell was a
poet's poet from the start, and much too involved in the
obscure theology or demonology of his New England
soul to strike a common chord, but he achieved a profound poetic originality by clothing his contemporary
nonconformism in the robes of a noble tradition.

Peter Viereck is harder to classify than Shapiro or Lowell.
His style is much less "finished." He has written no single
poem that is as impressive as the best of the other two. He
writes poems and parts of poems bristling with undigested
raw material or awkwardness of which the other poets are
incapable. Yet his book as a whole is so rich in experimental vigor, so full of new poetic attitudes toward civilization
and its discontents, so fresh and earthy in its re-animation
of the American spirit, that it seems to offer endless possibilities of development—both for Viereck himself, and
for other young poets who are certain to take the cue.

What makes him different seems so
    small a thing:
His knack of shaping joy from pain
    by rime.
He whittles joy so sharp it is a
    spear
And jabs it deep between the ribs
    of time.

Even his sickness blesses: singers
    wear
Neurosis like new roses when they
    sing.

This, Viereck's description of the fourth "stage of craftsmanship," could not be improved on as a description of
his own particular qualities. No other poet but Cummings,
the only contemporary Viereck remotely resembles or
from whom he has borrowed anything conspicuous, is so
haunted by the nightmare of writing a cliche—or under-
takes such acrobaties, typographical, grammatical, and
learnedly academic, to avoid one. An important difference, however, is that while Viereck's gyrations lead him
to almost as many shocking successes—.

To minks that slither like love's
    submarine.
Have pelts more glossy than the
    sea is sheen;
But sea!—it spews, it sheds these
    gray pollutions
By always beaching love, their
    carrier.
Spiraling, down and up through
    brine and air.
Love's valves become involved in
    convolutions:
And all descent is gray.
                    But rich.
                    But rare.

—he is never trying to *bait* anyone and hence is never
deliberately elusive. Indeed one of the qualities that makes
Terror and Decorum more of a break with the Eliot-
dominated past than any recent book is this very passion
to communicate. It is on every page. It is in the sometimes fantastically pedantic notes. It is in the pages of
"acknowledgments" (who but Viereck has ever listed his
magazine articles along with his previous books!). It is in
the ponderous conception of a prehistoric horse explaining in stanza after stanza of complicated ballad-meter
how he lost his four toes; or the Idaho potato boasting
this one comes off, brilliantly why it envies the stars. It
is in the unabashed titles (**"You All Are Static: I Alone**
Am Moving." "Hard Times Redeemed by Soft Dis-
carded Values," "Why Can't I Live Forever?," "Don't
Look Now But Mary is Everybody," "Graves Are
Made to Waltz On." "Crass Times Redeemed by Dig-
nity of Souls") above all it is in the was poems and the
poems about the poet in America.

These two themes, naturally enough, are Viereck's major
ones. He has been toughened, or sharpened if you like, by
the two conflicts: trying to be a poet while being a soldier the was a GI in the African and Italian campaigns),
trying to be a poet while making a living as a teacher of
history at Harvard and Smith. The soldiering has contributed to his verse as a whole its racy colloquialism and its
sense of identity with ordinary people. Academic training
has given him a working knowledge of the styles of a half
dozen literatures and a familiarity with cross-references

in symbolism almost Joycean in scope. But it is the fight *against* these two conformisms—of the barracks and of the classroom—that makes the poetry.

Out of extreme complexity, simplicity. From sophistication beyond cleverness, innocence. In Shakespeare, Donne, Blake, Hopkins, the later Yeats, perhaps in all of the greatest poetry, it is the "formula" toward which Viereck, more than any contemporary poet, seems to be moving. **"Vale from Carthage,"** along with Shapiro's "Elegy for a Dead Soldier," the most impressive poem of World War II, begins ponderously with Viereck at the grave of a Roman thinking of an American friend shot dead at Rome who was sure he'd see Times Square again, but ends:

> Roman, you'll see your Forum
> Square no more;
> What's left but this to say of any
> war?

New York says to America (in a dialogue that could be, and in parts is, as corny as an immigration poster):

> Your forests now are fences, and of late
> You talk less of "frontiers" and
> more of real estate.

Viereck says to Crane (in a ballad that is refreshingly irreverent—and penetrating):

> Walt did it—Walt, the city slicker,
> Sold Hart the Brooklyn Bridge.

And in **"Well Said, Old Mole,"** a poem that probably reflects Viereck's philosophy and his disarming directness as well as any, the complexities are cut away altogether:

> Against the outside Infinite, man
> weighs
> The inwardness within one finite
> face
> And finds all Space less heavy than
> a sigh . . .
> We are alone and small, and heaven
> is high;
> Quintillion worlds have burst and
> left no trace;
> A murderous star aims straight at
> where we lie.
> And we, all vulnerable and all
> distress,
> Have no brief shield but love and
> loveliness.
> Quick—let me touch your body as
> we die.

Richard Eberhart (review date 1948)

SOURCE: "A Conscious Poetry of Secular Breadth," *New York Times Book Review*, November 21, 1948, p. 5.

[*In the following review of* Terror and Decorum, *Eberhart admires the "new complex of contemporary feelings" and the extent of the technical skills exhibited in Viereck's poetry.*]

Peter Viereck is primarily a poet of ideas. The ideas that have been flying around in his head for the past eight years find resolution in sporadic order. There's the rub: much tumult, much prestidigitation, variety of trials and effort, considerable learning, and the result is an uneven book of poems (**Terror and Decorum**) containing a good number of excellently realized pieces.

He challenges the reader with a new complex of contemporary feelings, presented in a vigorous play of growing and shifting attitudes. He synthesizes his experience in his own way, leaning both on traditional usages and on experimentation. He does not go back to social protest. He does not continue the religious revival. He creates predominantly a secular breadth conscious of secular depth coming down from ancient times, from various cultures.

Peter Viereck is not grinding an axe. Voracious for experience, he accepts it by exfoliation of notions, diversely calculated. He looks from his China to his Peru with sprightliness of thought. artistic detachment allowing him to express his personality without fear either of enthusiasm or gaucherie.

As a new poet he is neither cynical nor melancholy. He is this—worldly, not other-worldly in the sense of one who attempts to penetrate hidden reaches of the soul. He is concerned with the problem of the formalizing of knowledge. We see the play of his mind shining from and glancing from invented shields of tempered form.

The **"Author's Note on Marabouts and Planted Poets"** specifies some of his preoccupations and illuminates his intentions. He states that "the poet imposes form upon nature, humanism upon the inhuman." Note the breadth of skills showing in poems like **"Ballad of the Jollie Gleeman"** and **"Prooimion"**; **"Hard Times Redeemed / By Soft Discarded Values"** and **"Crass Times Redeemed / By Dignity of Souls"**; or **"Poet," "Well Said, Old Mole"** and **"Vale From Carthage."**

The war as he knew it is reworked without his becoming mired in it, disinterestedly. He sees a wry decorum in a **"Child of the Sixtieth Century"** and evokes a submerged terror in **"Dolce Ossessione."** Light verse is permitted, as in **"To a Sinister Potato"** and **"What a Pretty Net."**

The following is partial quotation from **"Vale From Carthage"**

> He will
> Not see Times Square—he will
> not see—he will
> Not see Times
> change; at Carth-
> age (while my friend,
> Living those words at Rome

screamed in the end)
saw an ancient Roman's
    tomb and read
"Vale" in stone. Here two wars
    mix their dead;
Roman, my shipmate's dream
    walks hand in hand
With yours tonight ("New
    York again" and "Rome"),
Like widowed sisters bear-
    ing water home
On tired heads through hot
Tunisian sand
In good cool urns, and says
    "I understand."
Roman you'll see your Forum
    Square-no more;
What's left but this to say of
    any war?

Paul Goodman (review date 1949)

SOURCE: "Tall Ideas Dancing," *Poetry*, Vol. 73, No. 5, February, 1949, pp. 289-91.

[*In the following review of* Terror and Decorum, *Goodman faults Viereck for stopping short of self-exploration and for finding satisfaction in a "disheartening" superficiality.*]

The most moving of these poems—to my sensibility almost the only moving one—**"A Walk on Snow,"** has the following theme: the possibility of a meaning appears in experience, "a rite, an atavism . . . Myth"; the poet "drunk with self-belief" tries to control it and wrest a factual answer; then

> At once the gate slammed shut, the circle snapped,
> The sky was usual and broad and silent.

So Wordsworth, in the Ode, came to the line, "And fade into the light of common day." But the difference between this poet and Wordsworth is crucial: Viereck apparently does not believe in the meaning, does not remember it, thus he derogates it, calls the sense of it an illusion, "Magic—like art—is hoax redeemed by awe"; he thinks that his daily cleverness is true; but Wordsworth knew that this is precisely neurotic and defensive, one of the "shades of the prison-house." Here and everywhere in this volume Viereck outsmarts himself and thinks this is his strength, but it is his weakness and defense against feeling. Perhaps then it would be better for him to devote himself to small particular themes, rather than always to be fabricating great myths.

Peter Viereck assigns himself a curious role: to be a witness to the possibility of poetry:

> My life is darkness. Yet I live to tell
> How shimmering, how gaily freedom prowls
> In flesh that guards its consciousness of souls.

(Note that the gay freedom is a prowling animal and that the free flesh is defensively engaged.) *He* is not the poet but he has kept open within himself a little window through which he can observe flow by something meaningful and feelingful. He does observe it and believes it is very dramatic, warranting such an horrendous title as **Terror and Decorum** for these cold studies; he calls witness to it; he does everything but give in to it and be a poet.

In the same poem (**"Crass Times Redeemed by Dignity of Souls"**) he says:

> May yet when slick with poise I overreach.
> When that high ripening slowness I impeach,
> Awe of that music jolt me home contrite.

It is pathetic that a poet should ever face in himself the feeling of being slick with poise; he is no doubt referring to slick language, *New Yorker* style, and smart-alecks well ahead of the game, *Partisan Review* style; but a poet, one would think, would be subdued to his own words and ways. Indeed, it is hard to read these verses seriously because, though Viereck has many lively talents, he seems to have no personal language. (I don't mean private language, of course, but simply one's heart-words.) Again, how does he come to *count on* the "ripening slowness"; does not reality rather take one by surprise? And will it be "high"? I doubt that one has the breathing space to make judgments of either high or low. Oh, and will awe of music "jolt"? I have known music to melt my hardness to tears; one is "jolted" if *nevertheless* one intends to cling to oneself, and then the chance of love is a means of punishment.

Why should we cling to ourselves—are the rewards of our "slick poise" so satisfactory? No, obviously one is afraid. . . . In a poem for St. Francis, Viereck asks,

> O Francis, WHAT of the crocodile?
> Would you dance with him in the dark?
> Yes, crumbs for the birds—but WHAT for the
>   crocodile?

Why on earth does he have to take the part of the crocodile? I think Francis would say that the dear crocodile (truly dear) can well take care of himself. Then on the other hand he envisions that, under a spell of love, "the irreconcilable crocodile . . . crawls to your shrine / Nuzzling his grotesque, tender, harmful nozzle / Harmlessly at your startled ankles." What, would it be love to want the crocodile to be not a crocodile?

So there are characteristic poems (**"For an Assyrian Frieze," "Prince Tank,"** etc.) describing unbridled violence. But the poet's indignation loses its savagery in a feeble masochism; and the underlying self-hatred in turn loses its force in intellectual self-deprecation. I am moved to mention these brutal commonplaces, rather than to pass by the poems in silence, solely because Viereck shares this ambivalent attitude with other war-poets, and it leads them one and all to a superficiality so disheartening that one can hardly drag one's feet around after reading them: they regard the war as a kind of boyish adventure! Viereck, indeed, with his myth-making propensity, goes to the ultimate (I suppose): he praises "Kilroy" because he was physically present in lots of places, and presumably in that way took part; and this, to Viereck, was no different from—Ulysses.

It is hard for me to notice the virtues in these poems. Viereck has epigram, he can conclude his thought with force and point—this means he has intelligence habitually exercised, and that such learning as he has is systematic, and such words as he has he can control; but how is one to evaluate an epigram that is false? It seems to me that by this means he closes his thinking and, to say it uncharitably, satisfies himself, protecting himself. The error of his propositions is not that they are not all the way to truth but that they shut off, by their form and feeling, any further motion. . . . Again he has self-observation—this means that he has made a salutary turn, will not be a literary gangster, etc.; but in heaven's name, Peter, less awe and decorum, but come on! come on!

J. H. Johnston (essay date 1949)

SOURCE: A review of *Terror and Decorum, The Commonweal,* Vol. L, No. 17, August 5, 1949, p. 418.

[*In the following review of* Terror and Decorum, *Johnston connects Viereck's first volume of poetry with his study of history and concludes that he is an author "perhaps a little too full" of theories.*]

"Excursions of the visceral and irrational into the prose realm of politics and economics," writes Peter Viereck in this, (*Terror and Decorum Poems 1940-1948*) his first volume of collected poetry, "are either silly or sinister." That such excursions may not only be sinister, but catastrophic as well, is the message of Viereck's rather breezy analysis of the origins of Nazism, published in 1941 under the title *Metapolitics: From the Romantics to Hitler.*

In the present volume of poetry the theme of opposition between the "visceral and irrational" and the disciplines of sanity and control is more concisely, though no less breezily stated, and receives a more general application to human life and to poetry.

These basic oppositions, of course, are traceable to the old clash between romanticism and classicism. In *Metapolitics* Viereck, arguing for the theory that romanticism reached its "purest expression in those territories freest from Roman colonization" (i.e., Germany), remarks that romanticism is to be seen mainly "as a cultural and political reaction against the Roman-French-Mediterranean spirit of clarity, rationalism, form, and universal standards." Romanticism came out of the wild Saxon north as an energy of expansion and destruction, a principle of terror; classicism is the heritage of western civilization, the heritage of reason, law, control, order, and decorum. "Civilization's task," writes Viereck in *Metapolitics*, "is

not a question of destroying but of harnessing the eternal romantic element." In other words, the spiritual and emotional energy of romanticism (love) must be guided by a principle of rational control (law).

In *Terror and Decorum* it is the poet, as a modern counterpart of the Promethean "culture-hero," who emerges as legislator, and who imposes civilization on savagery, just as he imposes form on matter. The "eternal romantic element" is identified by Viereck with the "tuneless mutiny of Matter;" hence the poet, in his struggle with the inherited, illegal expansiveness of romanticism, is really engaged in a larger struggle with the recalcitrance of matter. Poetic metaphor, in this encounter, is compared with the ritual of incantation; it tames "each thunderous force of nature by knowing its secret unnamable Name and saying it in the ritual of rhythm." Thus terror is tamed by knowledge and by poetry; thus "love and law, by pattern reconciled, must rhyme." The whole process, however, may "work" (culturally) without being "true" (literally), and the poet himself may be completely hidden behind his works, far from the gaze or knowledge of mankind. Nevertheless his pattern, "like the equally non-existent universals of Plato, may be daily moulding our meaningless existence into meaning."

For those who take poetry seriously, the spectacle of the poet subsisting on his own meaninglessness may not be altogether re-assuring; likewise, the theory that poetry creates its own meaning is not quite consistent with theories about value, reason, control, law, and decorum—all of which presuppose at least an external, if not an absolute, criterion—and all of which Peter Viereck holds to, as a professional humanist, against the "visceral and irrational."

Viereck has something of an insight into the tensions of poetry, into the struggles of the formative spirit, and into the spiritual area of romanticism; but he has mounted too shrilly and too athletically the stilts of "romanticism-classicism," and has taken this opposition, not so much as something from which one could learn, but as an article of faith and a source of poetry. It may well be that the hour of romanticism has struck and that a new order of form and control is rising; and it may be that these are signs of a recurring conflict of elements in the human soul. But such statements remain, somehow, on the side of literary history and psychology; and the poetry that would deal with them as basic remains limited to the fashions of "enlightened" criticism, feeding on theories and formulations rather than dealing with the substance of reality itself.

The poet as "legislator," moreover—except in the case of a long-established literary and cultural tradition—is an idea that is essentially romantic, for culture is a labor of reason more than a labor of art. If poetry, in the ritual of naming the unnamable, does not find it necessary to distinguish between "it-was" and "it is false," then the poet is a sorry legislator, and we must have recourse to philo-sophy, in which naming the unnamable is more than a ritual. It is doubtful, at this time, whether the humanistic faith in "universal standards" is the philosophy that we can most honestly have recourse to.

Many of the poems in **Terror and Decorum** do not seem related in any specific way to the theme of the book; and many of these are either boisterous, or abstruse, or macabre. The tone generally is one of sophisticated humor (suited, perhaps, to the pages of the various magazines in which Viereck's poetry has appeared) which occasionally takes a sardonic or a petulant turn, after the manner of an astringent Omar Khayyam. But in half-a-dozen poems (and especially in the **"Author's Note on Marabouts and Planted Poets"**) Viereck states his theme well enough and seriously enough to be considered as a talent and as a man—perhaps a little too full—of theories.

Robert Fitzgerald (essay date 1949)

SOURCE: "Patter, Distraction, and Poetry," *New Republic*, Vol. 121, No. 6, August 8, 1949, p. 17.

[*In the following review, Fitzgerald calls most of Viereck's poetry "patter" and doubts that there is much in* Terror and Decorum *that readers will study or reread for pleasure.*]

The Pulitzer Prize for 1948 was awarded to Peter Viereck, whose **Terror and Decorum** is a novelty among first books of poems. The poet seems to have been prepared for fame: he has forestalled his bibliographers by including a two-page list of all his poems, with their original titles and the periodicals wherein they appeared or were reprinted, and a page entitled "Prose by Peter Viereck" listing his articles and book reviews. The fact that one article was in French and one in Italian hints at his linguistic attainments, and his travels are attested by the place names that accompany many poems—Stonehenge, Carthage, Athos, Assisi, the Borghese Gardens. . . . There is a liveliness about all this.

The poems are lively, too, and a few of them sustain a neat, coarse clarity and a satiric turn of fancy that is not disagreeable. **"For Two Girls Setting Out in Life,"** **"To a Sinister Potato"** and one or two of his **"Theological Cradle Songs"** strike me as complete and rollicking compositions. The appearance of these qualities, and the appeal they seem to have, are evidences of a shift long under way from visionary concentration in poetry—from the high styles of Yeats or Crane or Tate or Thomas—to a drier and airier attitude, a more epigrammatic vein. William Empson's less diamondlike later poems are examples; Karl Shapiro's postwar lyrics are others; John Betjeman's are minor masterpieces, and Auden was at it long ago.

In Viereck's case, however, the shift is so indiscriminate that on the whole it looks more like a relapse. Auden has been saying, usefully but a little carelessly, that poetry is not a religion but a game; now Viereck describes it as "a hoax redeemed by awe." Perhaps this is open and aboveboard but it is not relevant to most of the examples offered, which are redeemed, if at all, by Viereck's wit—and his wit is frequently dreary. He has a warm, breezy, familiar way of being acutely embarrassing, as when he calls, in a poem to Hart Crane, "Hey, Hart, don't jump." In something called **"The Big Graveyard"** the reader is treated to five stanzas of riddling metaphors on The Cosmic Womb and, finally, to this flashing stroke:

> The living noon whose tulip gapes with
>   peace—. . . .
> But soon: the tomb whose two lips gape.

Thus is language made to yield her every nuance. The book also contains a brief prose insertion in which Viereck discusses the poet as "culture-hero" with a glibness that puts the reader at ease: here, at least, is no such formidable figure—just a man who knows all about it. The favorable reception of this patter may be significant, but I judge it to be momentary, for Viereck has as yet written very little to which one could wish to return often or with serious interest.

M. L. Rosenthal (review date 1950)

SOURCE: "Poet in Spite of Himself," *New Republic*, Vol. 122, No. 17, April 24, 1950, pp. 30-31.

[*In the following review of* Strike through the Mask!*, Rosenthal claims that he endured Viereck's "saucy banalities" in this volume for the sake of six or seven rich, suggestive poems, including "Small Perfect Manhattan" and "My Gentlest Song."*]

Those Terrifying Whimsies of Peter Viereck! Granted, as another, greater poet has told us, that a person of genius has to do *something*. Still, just look at the sort of thing he sees fit to print:

> "None of that!" shouted the Ohio River. "No more roses and nightingales permitted to any poet who drinks our waters, yours or mine. Those creaking nightingales of the Rheumatic movement! Longfellow reads like a pretty short fellow nowadays. Better a live extravert than a dead lyre."

Yet we must bear with him. The man may be garrulous. He may write books about revisiting conservatism and finding it good. He may be an esthete right out of the nineties who really thinks he's doing something brand-new. He may moralize about Beauty and The Machine and at times sound like Vachel Lindsay. And, often, he may even rather fancy himself as a tree. (There is more passionate timber in his books than in Pound's, though the lumber is less learned.) Nevertheless he is, to quote him out of context and inaccurately, a "gen-u-ine poet."

For the sake, then, of a few untypical poems in this volume (**Strike Through the Mask!**) and in **Terror and Decorum**, his Pulitzer Prize winner of 1948, we shall have to forgive Viereck's endless slogans, the precious credos, the saucy banalities about poetry and this harsh world, etc., etc. These sorties are at any rate witty enough, and they do somehow serve to free him morally for the occasional luxury of doing the real thing. In the earlier book, they released him for such poems as the truly humane **"Kilroy,"** the idealistic **"Poet,"** the naïvely savage **"From Ancient Fangs."** *Strike Through the Mask!* is a less bitter collection. Outwardly bristling with even more intellectual defenses and diversionary tomfooleries, it holds within it a purer, more concentrated core of "gen-u-ine" verse.

Six or seven poems make up this core. Of these, only one, **"Small Perfect Manhattan,"** can be called intellectually argumentative. What it "argues" for, as the title may suggest, is a new geographical association for the classic values, Europe and Africa having lost touch with the old idealism and the tradition of living song. Elsewhere Viereck has both admired and patronized Hart Crane; here, as in **"Serenade,"** he comes very close to him in style and spirit:

> Unable to breathe, I inhaled the
>   classic Aegean.
> Losing my northern shadow, I
>   sheared the noon
>   Of an almond grove. The tears
>   of marble
>   Thanked me for laughter.

Among these poems, too, we find **"My Gentlest Song"**—Viereck's one "tree-poem" which does not absolutely shriek its indignant message at us. The sense is surer, goes deeper here, than in many other more striking pieces. This love song of a pine tree to a rose—the utterly absurd "beautiful hunger" of the protecting pine for the "bright brief putrefying weed"—evokes the very essence of romantic pathos, all the more because it is never mechanically symbolic. A certain heaviness, a melancholy almost without objective meaning and yet intensely human, pervades this poem and the other "pure" poems in the book—particularly **"Counter Serenade," "Obsessed by Her Beauty"** and **"Twilight of the Outward Life."**

Viereck's whimsies and debating can be sold too short, of course. There is the joy of good satire in something like the Lindsayan chant, in his *Americana* section, about

> *Clambakes, clambakes on cran-*
>   *berry bogs:*
> *Cans piled up to the moon.*

He is generally amusing, or exciting, or in any case *interesting,* even when taste and originality desert him. And his range is wide, from sentimental trivia and comic ballads to the macabre irony of **"To My Playmate"** or the painful effort, in **"Some Lines in Three Parts,"** to dramatize in images the "mangy miracle" of artistic creation. Yet even in this last poem the most moving lines are the ones which assert—with Yeats, one of Viereck's most apparent masters—the tragic paradox of the human condition so poignantly felt by the best poets of the late nineteenth century:

I say the honor of our flesh is love.

I say no soul, no god could love as we—A forepaw stalking us from every cloud—Who loved while sentenced to mortality.

David Daiches (review date 1951)

SOURCE: "Some Recent Poetry," *Yale Review*, Vol. 40, No. 2, Winter, 1951, pp. 353-354.

[*In the following review, Daiches finds* Strike through the Mask! *disappointing in comparison to* Terror and Decorum, *but praises Viereck for his continued struggle to realize his poetic vision.*]

If *Strike Through the Mask!* is a trifle disappointing, it is only because Viereck's first volume was so good. There is nothing here quite so good as the best in *Terror and Decorum*, yet in such poems as **"Ennui"** and the third part of **"Some Lines in Three Parts,"** for example, we have the same cunning clarity of style and classical sense of form that so refreshed us in the earlier poems. Mr. Viereck affects what one might call a desperate clarity, a wild matter-of-factness which at its best can be employed for more subtle effects than those achieved by the more obvious kinds of obscurity. He bodies forth a situation in blunt and economical language, then, as it were, tilts it somewhat askew, to give it a new meaning and a new dimension. The tilting is done almost entirely by structural devices, by the sequence in which the simple-seeming statements are arranged. His prosodic unit is the single line of verse, which he can handle with real deftness, but he is developing a tendency to employ a number of end-stopped lines in succession, each ending with a period: this produces a curiously jerky effect which almost spoils more than one poem, notably the otherwise admirable **"A Hospital named 'Hotel Universe.'"**

Viereck is also developing mannerisms, imitating himself a bit, which is, I suppose, a tendency to be found in the second volumes of most interesting poets. (The first part of **"The Slacker Need Not Apologize"** reads a little like a parody of some of the things in his first book.) There are dangers in that terrible innocence of eye which yields Mr. Viereck so many of his subjects and best poetic effects; but of course everything is dangerous when you are writing poetry, and this approach certainly yields more vitality than most, especially these days when the poetic air is thick with unassimilated conventions. Mr. Viereck is an *enfant terrible* in the same sense that the child who found out about the emperor's new clothes was an *enfant terrible,* and his two problems are, first, to maintain the proper balance between his infancy (that is, genuine innocence or freshness of vision) and his terribleness, and, secondly, to avoid becoming either professionally innocent or professionally terrible. I think he will come through, because he is a poet in his bones and because such mannerisms as he has have been acquired as a result of perhaps too strenuously fought battles against mannerisms. Thus even his less good poems are blows in the fight for poetry, evidences of a desire to make the poem out of its proper materials (the authentic vision) rather than to assemble ready-made parts in accordance with the blueprints supplied by the manufacturing critics. He may be marking time just now, but he is all right.

Howard Nemerov (review date 1953)

SOURCE: "Macleish and Viereck," *Partisan Review,* Vol. XX, No. 1, January-February 1953, pp. 115-120.

[*In the following excerpt from a review, Nemerov describes* The First Morning *as an uneven mixture of "witty and ingenious poems" with a large quantity of mediocre work.*]

The poet's responsibility to society . . . a matter much debated. In the phrase itself there is implicit some prospective metaphor of the poet as criminal, vainly trying to *discharge his debt* by means of his poems while all the time, really, it is something else that "society" wants. What? This has not been made clear, but seems to have confusedly to do with, on the one hand, messages of life and hope; with, on the other, moral earnestness and a severe, traditional look at current events. Archibald MacLeish takes in many places a severe view—with virtue, with this Republic, with poetry itself, things were formerly different, are now much degenerated, but the poet by his images may redeem the time, "Turn round into the actual air" and "Invent the age! Invent the metaphor!" Peter Viereck brings, so it is held by some, messages of life and hope; "perhaps . . . the promised man who is going to lead modern poetry out of the wasteland" (statement by Van Wyck Brooks, but what wasteland?), he wears his rue with a difference.

Both these poets, the one long established and latterly neglected, the other young and spectacularly successful almost from his first appearance a few years ago, are much given to debating, in poems and elsewhere, the theme of the poet's responsibility to society, and both have been quite downright on this subject; there is some temptation, which I hope I shall avoid, to treat them as the same poet Before and After. This temptation would lead conveniently away from the poetry and into a discussion on the implicit premise that the poetry didn't in fact matter and with the implicit conclusion that poet Before and poet After were of the same caliber, something I do not believe. What would matter, in such a discussion? Attitude (positive), ease and rapidity of "communication," political awareness, the quality of being *contemporary* (as today's newspaper is more contemporary than yesterday's newspaper). Above all, perhaps, the ability to take a revolutionary tone while moving steadily backward, the triumph of strategic withdrawal. Both these poets, perhaps in the largest part of their production, seem deliberately to invite a discourse in those terms, a discourse which, except for a feeble protest at one point, I do not feel drawn to give, preferring for the most part instead simply to record something of my impression of the poetry. . .

The poetry of Peter Viereck is often both pleasant and accomplished; light in tone, you might say, but never lacking in that suggestion of more serious stuff beneath the surface, a suggestion which no poet these days will do well to do without; there are also mythology and quotations from literature in foreign languages. Here is an example.

"Home, James"

Time's tumbling curtain means: "Finita è—".
Hell's jolly beavers gnaw at every sprout.
Mankind's last headline calls it doomsday-day.
The sun stands still and wilts in every way;
Sometimes a comet tries to run away
("Snuffed trying to escape," the Agents gloat);
Sometimes a planet seems to try to pray.
    Now . . postponed . . . dreams . . . shout.
The hot and disappointed lipsticks pout.
Apocalyptic apoplexies fray
The nerves of Cronos like a Gaffer's gout.
Not ants but grasshoppers have won the bout
Because there is no piper left to pay.
Who disconnected breath from clay?

                     Hey,
    Who . . . pulled the . . . socket . . . out?

It is difficult, in our excitement, to know what we admire most, or first, about this poem—the skillful regularity of the meter? the way in which the syntactical and metrical units exactly coincide, one phrase to one line, to produce the lilting effect so characteristic of this poet's work? the alliterations and assonances (line 10)? the highly compressed allusions to literature and mythology (lines 1, 11, and 12)? the irony (title)? the nature imagery (lines 2, 4, 5, etc.)? the awareness of the contemporary scene (lines 3, 6, 9, 15)? or perhaps it is the morality (*passim*)? Anyhow, all these features work together to produce, in their intricate weavings and delicate tonal combinations, this poem. This poem is by no means the best in *The First Morning*, any more than it is the worst; probably the worst—allowing for the fact that I can't read German and have had to omit the consideration of three poems in that tongue—is one called **"Love Song of Prufrock Junior,"** the first in a series called **"1912-1952, Full Cycle."**

Must all successful rebels grow
From toreador to Sacred Cow?
What cults he slew, his cult begot.
"In my beginning," said his Scot,
"My end"; and aging eagles know
That 1912 was long ago.
Today the women come and go
Talking of T. S. Eliot.

The word goes round the English Departments that this is the equal of "The Lost Leader," and perhaps it is—though Professor Limpkin has acutely suggested that its allusive qualities (it is almost entirely built of cryptic references to Western Culture) may make it somewhat tiresome to the average undergraduate.

The best poems in this volume—including, on one opin-ion, **"To be Sung," "Again, Again," "The Planted Skull," "Homecoming"** and **"Saga"**—are quite good poems, perhaps a little light in weight. That they are *great* poems, that they constitute in any sense a revolution in the art (a return to this or revival of that), that they are particularly new or original or fresh, I submit that I doubt.

Now it is doubtless *not nice* to speak slightingly of a volume containing, say, half a dozen witty and ingenious poems which have given me pleasure, and I do not so speak merely because this volume contains also a rela-tively large amount of mediocre verse, fallen epigrams and jotted-down opinions, as well as a relatively stagger-ing amount of simple blank space. But I feel (and feel I may as well express the feeling) a resistance to the pre-tension involved in the terms on which this verse is sup-posed to be taken—as "the present hope of poetry" (Rob-ert Frost), "real magic" (Van Wyck Brooks), "conscien-tious skill . . . that makes much contemporary poetry look like the shabbiest free association" (David Daich-es), "a break with the Eliot-dominated past" (Selden Rodman), "The modernist revolt has ended . . ." (Anthony Harrigan). These citations are from the dust-jacket of **The First Morning**, and though I have not quoted them in full the distinctive thing about them, as about so many favorable opinions of this poet, is visibly that it seems nearly impossible to praise Mr. Viereck except by way of taking a swipe at someone else; the ax-grinders seem to find him handy; uplifting Mr. Viereck seems to be the equal and opposite reaction generated by people standing on Mr. Eliot's head and jumping up and down. This sug-gests a certain expedient quality to the exaltation. When Mr. Harrigan, whom I quoted above, described Peter Vi-ereck as "the principal standard-bearer of the tradition of humanistic democracy in this country," the battle-lines are drawn, one may or may not shudder for humanistic democracy, but in any event the poetry has been left to one side—as perhaps it should be, for I do not believe it will stand the strain of the program that is being erected for it. It is probably not good for the poet to become the standard-bearer of any party, the thing gets out of con-trol—from being standard-bearer he becomes standard, and people wave him about wildly. I think the results begin to show in **The First Morning**, particularly in the number of pages given over to small versified remarks, parodies (even one of the poet himself, which does not appear to show any great self-knowledge) and pompously humor-less jokes about poetry and criticism—the more or less affable informalities, the inflated marginalia, of the arbi-ter-elect. It is probably not good for the poet to become a myth, any myth but his own, surely; there is the danger of becoming at last, as Mr. Viereck in another connec-tion points out, merely "a *Maerchen* dreamed by the deep, cool clams." Let the clams keep cool, they're not out of this wasteland yet.

Kimon Friar (essay date 1953)

SOURCE: "Verses and Poems," *New Republic,* Vol. 128, February 9, 1953, pp. 20-21.

[*In the following review of* The First Morning, *Friar argues that Viereck has a great deal of technical skill but no poetic voice of his own.*]

Even if Santayana *did* write Peter Viereck from Rome: "Oh, then you are a great man," neither the poet nor his publisher should have allowed such a statement to chance gathering a film of dust on what is, after all, a dust jacket. And what can impish Robert Frost be up to with: "Peter Viereck . . . is the present hope of poetry"—on the same dusty jacket? Indeed, I doubt that Viereck is essentially a poet at all. He writes with a dashing competence in a wide variety of verse forms, meters and modes, but rare-ly do I find a consistent cadence of his own; these are the old tunes refurbished and slicked up, but lacking that peculiar crack in the voice which can belong to one poet only. Perhaps the admirerers who find in Viereck a "new voice" refer not to his cadences but to his diction and general attitude, in which I find, however, together with much vitality and freshness, overmuch gauchery ("I'll honor gaucheness anywhere I find it"), cleverness, lack of taste ("Last night my stamen / Could hear her pistil sigh"), breeziness, charades, and posturing ("Will no one watch me? Look!, I'll dance on thread / Or hold my breath for cameras till I burst."). The effect is at times that of a tennis player in full rythmical swing blissfully unaware that his shorts are slipping. Alertness, agility, intelligence, brusqueness, are not the beating heart of poetry where a thought may be wooed but not flaunted, where a lyric may be seduced but not raped. In **Stanzas in Love with Life and August**, **Again**, **Again** and **Algiers in Wartime** Viereck gives us pleasing verse but not moving poetry.

Kenneth Rexroth (review date 1953)

SOURCE: "A Publicist in Poetry," *The New York Times Book Review,* October 11, 1953, p. 22.

[*In the following review, Rexroth faults the poetry in* The First Morning *for not concentrating on a consis-tent poetic goal.*]

Peter Viereck is well aware of the separation of the poet from society. He proposes to do something about it. Many people think he is the wave of the future in American poetry. He says:

> DANTE: We were God's poets.
> BURNS: We were the people's poets.
> MALLARME: We were poets' poets.
> TODAY (preening himself): Ah, but we are
>   critics' poets.

Certainly true, but diagnosis is not enough. It does not matter that Mr. Viereck has allowed his career as a pub-licist and polemicist to leak over into his poetry. That is all for the best. Although he has many of Byron's virtues he suffers from most of Byron's faults, and some others in addition. Some of these poems (in **The First Morn-ing**) are very moving but with few exceptions they all jump the track somewhere in their course. This is their most serious blemish—instability and failure of consistent aim. Mr. Viereck's chase may have a beast in view but too often he gets distracted and takes off after mice when he has set out after bears and lions. This instability of style results in plain lack of taste, poetical malapropisms.

Until he can keep his critical fire concentrated, until he can preserve an over-all consistent tone, Mr. Viereck is not going to write the "Dunciad" or "Masque of Judgment" of our day. There is more to it than letting fly with both fists simultaneously at Mike Gold and T. S. Eliot. However, nobody else is even trying to do anything like this, and it certainly needs doing. Furthermore, his less ambitious and programmatic poems are clear, communicable, deeply concerned and very moving—which can be said of only three or four poets of Mr. Viereck's generation.

Ira N. Hayward (essay date 1955)

SOURCE: "The Tall Ideas Dancing: Peter Viereck, or the Poet as Citizen," *The Western Humanities Review*, Vol. 9, No. 3, Summer, 1955, pp. 249-60.

[*In the following essay, Hayward examines Viereck's insistence on making ethical judgments about poetry and considers his commitment to writing poetry that maintains a vital, active relationship to both politics and culture.*]

Peter Viereck is becoming an increasingly powerful voice for a thoroughgoing re-appraisal of the trends that dominated poetry, literary criticism, and political thought between the two world wars. Like the symposium *Critics and Criticism,* edited by R. S. Crane,[1] Viereck's three books of poems, his numerous magazine articles, and his recent volume of satiric prose present a basic challenge to the New Poetry and to the New Criticism which it stimulated. The challenge is long overdue. A too-easy victory over the shallow philistinism and pedantic academicism of the 'nineties and the years before World War I seems to have betrayed the literary modernists into an equally easy over-confidence in opinions which should have been held tentatively if at all, but instead have hardened into dogmas ranging from the dubious to the absurd.

Viereck is a stout controversialist, more adept, as he told an audience at the 1948 writers' conference in Logan, Utah, at pouring oil on troubled fires than on troubled waters. He has advanced during the past eight years from an attitude of skeptical questioning to an open attack on what he calls the "hermetic formalism" of the New Criticism and the "cross-word-puzzle" obscurity of the New Poetry.

In the *Atlantic* for July, 1947, under the title "Poets Versus Readers," he wrote optimistically that with the work of younger men like Auden, Spender, Robert Lowell and Dylan Thomas, "Poetry has returned from the dazzling and esoteric to its traditional concern with the mystery of mortality. . . . There is a fruitfully obsessive search for the path from our dinginess and glibness to regeneration. This is the path that leads from Eliot's *Wasteland* to *Ash Wednesday.*" As a result, "with the return to form and clarity, there can now be a disarmament conference between reader and poet."

At the end of the essay he qualifies his optimism by citing as an "example of how the poet-versus-reader feud of the 1920's can still re-erupt today . . . Robert Graves's preface to his new book of poems: 'I write poems for poets. . . . For people in general I write prose. . . . To write poems for other than poets is wasteful.'" Viereck's rejoinder to this point of view is prophetic of the position he has taken since with increasing vigor:

> My objection to it is pragmatic rather than absolute: ivory towers are not equipped with air-raid shelters. Culture is not a self-sufficient island separated from some safely distant mainland but is infinitely vulnerable and infinitely responsive to outside stimuli.

The award to Ezra Pound in 1949 of the Bollingen Prize for the best American poetry of 1948 caused Viereck to abandon his optimism and to recognize that the ivory tower aestheticism of the 1920's was still firmly entrenched behind a solid wall of critical opinion. In an essay, "My Kind of Poetry," appearing at the time in the *Saturday Review of Literature* and later reprinted as his introduction to the selections from his poems in John Ciardi's anthology, *Mid-century American Poets,* he wrote:

> . . . my poetry is equally interested in shaking off the vague sentimentalities of the pre-Eliot romanticism and the hermetic ingenuities of the post-Eliot version of Neo-Classicism. The latter contains (1) no fun and (2) no humanness, two "vulgar" qualities that are the lifeblood of art. What was new and imaginative in the master becomes a slot-machine stereotype in the disciples who thereby create a new and more insidious type of Babbitt: the highbrow Babbitt-baiting Babbitt.

Besides presenting a lucid analysis of Viereck's own position, the essay is thus a frontal attack on a literary movement which has aged "into a cocktail party clique, a mutual admiration pact, a pressure group upon college English Departments and Little Magazines. . . . Today the New Criticism, already a very old criticism, has become a bar to further esthetic progress, producing nimble imitative pedants and enslaving our metrics with its own twentieth-century clichés."

Of his own revolt against the trend he writes:

> It's not enough to say a poet must belong to none of the arty coteries. It's essential that he actively sin against their rituals. *My own sin is twofold.* (1) I've content—something to say about the profane world they scorn—and not only form; this makes me an "impure" poet. (2) I try to communicate to the qualified layman also, instead of only to fellow poets and critics; this makes me a philistine.

Later in the same essay he writes, "Mine is a poetry of ideas. Above all, ideas connected with ethics or with the search for ethical values," and he quotes from his poem **"Incantation at Assisi"**:

> Listen, when the high bells ripple the half lights:
> Ideas, ideas, the tall ideas dancing.

In his latest volume of verse[2] Mr. Viereck takes another poetic fling both at the New Critics and at the willful obscurantists in poetry whom he has called "the Pound-Tate school of epigones." The section captioned "Irreverences," besides annoying those whom it is intended to annoy may displease others who believe that although the current "battle of the books" may be expected to rage for some time along the critical foothills of Parnassus, the sacred mount itself should, by mutual agreement, be accorded immunity as a No Man's Land in the skirmishing. Yet the genuine humor with which he hits off the poetical mannerisms not only of the new poets, American, British, and German, but of Browning, Hardy and even Viereck himself, entitles the section to a modest niche in the gallery of poems in dispraise of poets.

Convinced, as he wrote in an article "Pure Poetry, Impure Politics, and Ezra Pound," appearing in *Commentary* for April, 1951, that the New Critics have "Alexandrinized and Babbittized" the work of Pound and Eliot "*not* into a 'fascist' conspiracy as some *Saturday Review of Literature* writers absurdly implied, but into a supreme bore," he is here laying about him with the rapier of satiric wit, the bane of bores in all ages. It was a foregone conclusion that those whom he calls Pound's "disarmingly, really endearingly humorless" grandsons would not be amused by **"Full Circle,"** the poem in which their current dilemma is deftly run through its vitals. Judging by their comments, they were least amused by the closing two-line parody of a couplet which, from having been too much admired as an epitome of the banalities of late Georgian culture, has come in the space of forty years to epitomize a no less deadly banality all its own:

> Today the women come and go,
> Talking of T. S. Eliot.

Viereck's absorption in ideas does not in any sense make him indifferent to technique. On the contrary, he is much concerned with it, and, as he himself writes, he composes his poems with definite theories of prosody in mind. Few modern poets show an equal mastery of varied verse forms. One of his major interests is in preserving the distinction between what he calls the "necessary obscurity" of most good poetry and obscurity for the sake of obfuscation. In "My Kind of Poetry" he quotes a paragraph from a review by Selden Rodman:

> He is never trying to bait and hence is never deliberately elusive. Indeed one of the qualities that make *Terror and Decorum* more of a *break with the Eliot-dominated past* than any recent book is this very passion to communicate. . . . Out of extreme complexity, simplicity. From sophistication beyond cleverness,

innocence. In Shakespeare, Donne, Blake, Hopkins, the later Yeats, perhaps in all of the greatest poetry, it is the "formula" toward which Viereck, more than any contemporary poet, seems to be moving. (Viereck's italics.)

Mr. Viereck adds, "The above formula of a difficult simplicity, though unattainable for my practice, is the truest summary of the ideal behind all my 'working principles.'" He has, indeed, stressed his "passion to communicate" at times almost to pedantry.

The distinction between this "difficult simplicity" and mere reader-baiting obscurity is easier to state in theory than to achieve in practice, as Viereck himself acknowledges, and it must be said in fairness that the new poet-critics whom he deplores have often insisted that the impulse back of the obscurity which he denounces as "willful" is the desire to give their poems that same richness of texture which is his own object.[3] A lyric poem is, by definition, the expression of a concept deeply personal to the poet. How then can he be sure that the metaphor in which he couches this expression shall, in all its details, be intelligible to the reader?

It is ironic that some readers, finding Viereck's verse difficult, have bracketed him as himself merely another "obscure" new poet. This was shown amusingly when his poem, **"Like A Sitting Breeze,"** reprinted in the latest volume with the subtitle "Farewell to l'art pour l'art," appeared in *The American Scholar* and forthwith became the focus of a long, wordy battle. The editor, Hiram Haydn, had written the author, "I'll be blamed if I know what it means," and had invited an exegesis which was published with the poem itself. The irony of the incident lay in the fact that the poem represents the author's "lonely duel" *against* the trend toward the personal and the obscure as an end in itself.

Finding a poem—even a very good poem—obscure, does not necessarily mean that the readers lack genuine poetic insight as Mr. Viereck seemed to imply in his rejoinder to critics of **"Like a Sitting Breeze."** Still less can it be argued, as Mr. Allen Tate tries to argue, that too long an immersion in what he calls "the Romantic sensibility," by making the reading of poetry a purely emotional experience, has obscured for modern readers the necessity of an intellectual approach, not only to the new poetry, but to the best poetry of other ages. Tate cites, for example as does Cleanth Brooks in an analysis of Donne's "Canonization"), the necessity of being aware that Donne's reference to dying in his "Valediction: Forbidding Mourning" is a pun involving the knowledge that "in Middle English and down through the sixteenth century the verb die had as a secondary meaning, 'to perform the act of love.'" He concludes his essay on "Understanding Modern Poetry" by advising that "if we wish to understand Donne and Eliot, perhaps we had better begin, young, to read the classical languages, and a little later the philosophers."

Sound advice, surely, for any reading of great poetry past or present. But it will hardly help us with a poet who lards his verse with bits of Sanskrit or Chinese (or perhaps, like Mark Twain's pedantic amanuensis, with a word here and there of Amerindian) merely to parade a very private erudition. Or who, for no other discoverable purpose, drags in bits of anthropological data which form no necessary part of the mental equipment of even a fairly advanced student of the classics and the philosophers.

Donne's pun on *dying* was perfectly familiar—in other words not at all "obscure"—to the literate reader of his time. Pound's use of Chinese ideographs in several of his late cantos, like Eliot's use of Sanskrit in "The Wasteland" and of anthropological references in "The Cocktail Party" that might, as Viereck implies in a footnote to **"Full Circle,"** have occurred more appropriately in *The Golden Bough,* are not quite the same thing. They could communicate to no one but the rare, highly specialized scholar of our time, as Eliot acknowledges by implication in his footnotes to "The Waste Land" and Pound in his "explication" appended to one of the cantos just mentioned. Even with these helps the poetic value of such esotericism is far from clear. Too much of this deliberate use of obscure, private allusions can reduce the deciphering of a poem to a process, as Viereck says, roughly like that of solving a double-crostic. The simile is not farfetched. John Crowe Ransom says of Wallace Stevens' "Sea Surface Full of Clouds," "The poem has a calculated complexity and its technical competence is so high that to study it, if you do that sort of thing, is to be happy."

II

As already noted, it was the Bollingen award to Ezra Pound that drew Viereck into an open attack on the poetry and the criticism which most strongly reflect the influence of Pound and his disciple Eliot. As Viereck explains in the exegesis of his poem **"Like a Sitting Breeze,"** the "cruel crossroads" of his life came "when I had to force myself to take a stand on the issue of certain ethical implications of Mr. Pound's badly written new book, the *Pisan Cantos.*"

His conclusion was that

> . . . all human beings, including poets, who enjoy the privileges of a free society should try to make their duties . . . equal their privileges, in defiance of the pressures toward unfree conformity. . . . The free artist, like any other free citizen, has a moral responsibility against the evil of fascism and anti-semitic persecution. . . . **"Like a Sitting Breeze"** reflects the turning-point when I could no longer evade taking the stand of: ethics before "pure" art, freedom from totalitarianism before irresponsible ivory tower.

In his more recent *Shame and Glory of the Intellectuals*[4] he points out that for years Alger Hiss and Ezra Pound "were the heroes of progressivism in politics and literature respectively" and asks, "What is the lesson when progressivism, after sincerely setting out to liberate literature and politics, ends by flirting with treason?" This issue, he adds, is one so central in today's thinking that

detached minds must insist on its being faced. They must insist on "vulgarly" and tactlessly rubbing the faces of American progressivism in Ezra Pound and Alger Hiss. . . .

Pound and Hiss do not invalidate experimental avant garde. They do not invalidate liberalism. . . . What they do invalidate . . . is a hermetic, narcissistic progressivism, so self-absorbed in artistic or political progress that it neglects the inexorable moral framework into which all progress must fit.

It would be pointless here to review in detail the controversy growing out of the award of the Bollingen Prize to Pound's *Pisan Cantos* as the best poetry of 1948. This effort to glorify a literary performance which to many appeared as a deliberate justification of high treason finally reached the halls of Congress. The sensational charges of Robert Hillyer against the Fellows of the Library of Congress were adequately answered by their own subcommittee in a pamphlet "The Case Against the Saturday Review of Literature"—though without noticeably improving the case for the Pound award.

In their press release announcing the award, the jury said:

> The Fellows are aware that objections may be made to awarding a prize to a man situated as is Mr. Pound. In their view, however, the possibility of such objection did not alter the responsibility assumed by the Jury of Selection. . . . To permit other considerations than that of poetic achievement to sway the decision would destroy the significance of the award and would in principle deny the validity of that objective perception of value on which any civilized society must rest.

In this pronouncement the famous "dissociation of sensibility," which Eliot once deplored as having caused a deterioration of poetry since the seventeenth century, seems to have been elevated by Eliot and his disciples into an artistic credo bearing the official blessing of an agency of the state.

The Library of Congress is perhaps the most potent single cultural institution of the American Government. The Fellows of the Library, despite the nimble casuistries by which they attempted to minimize the fact, were speaking in the name of that institution. It seems never to have occurred to the majority of the group that the freedom which enabled them to award a prize "to a man situated as is Mr. Pound," in the name of an agency of the government he did his senile best to destroy, is in itself, to a truly "objective perception," the most precious of those values "on which any civilized society must rest." And their aplomb seemed equally undisturbed by the fact that the poem so honored was in purpose partly at least Pound's apologia for his treason.

Expatriation among American literati is nothing new. It was during World War I that Henry James, irked at American foreign policy, declared himself a British subject, thereby anticipating by some twelve years the similar gesture of T. S. Eliot, most famous of the Fellows. Long before this, however, as Van Wyck Brooks has shown,[5] numerous Americans, endowed with the wherewithal by material-minded American ancestors, turned their backs on American material-mindedness for the loftier culture of the Old World. The Fellows in their defense indignantly denied Hillyer's charge of expatriation. Yet one of them, Mr. Allen Tate, who is old enough to have voted in the presidential election of 1920, wrote in 1949, "I have voted in only one presidential election, that of 1940." By this acknowledged aloofness from national affairs during perhaps the most crucial years of American history, Mr. Tate seems to qualify for the hitherto undetermined classification of expatriate-in-residence.

The critical problem involved in the Pound award is also not new in American literary history. As early as 1826, in a lecture on poetry before the Athenaeum Society of New York, William Cullen Bryant referred to "some critics [who] have made poetry to consist solely in the exercise of the imagination." He continues

> They distinguish poetry from pathos. They talk of pure poetry, and by this phrase they mean passages of mere imagery with the least possible infusion of human emotion. I do not know by what authority these gentlemen take the term poetry from the people and thus limit its meaning.

The issue was joined in terms nearer to the present debate during the 1840's in the conflicting ideas of Poe and Emerson. Poe never tired of ridiculing as "often the flattest prose the so-called poetry of the so-called transcendentalists," and in one essay he placed Emerson among "a class of gentlemen with whom we have no patience whatever—the mystic of mysticism's sake." In his essay "The Poetic Principle," he attacks vigorously the "heresy of *The Didactic*" the idea that "every poem . . . should inculcate a moral." In a famous passage he defines "the poetry of words as The Rhythmical Creation of Beauty," and adds: "Its sole arbiter is Taste. With the Intellect or with the Conscience it has only collateral relations. Unless incidentally, it has no concern whatever either with Duty or with Truth."

Emerson's own idea of the relation of thought to form he states in "The Poet":

> It is not metres but a metre-making argument that makes a poem—a thought so passionate and alive that like the spirit of a plant or an animal it has an architecture of its own and adorns nature with a new thing. The thought and the form are equal in the order of time, but in the order of genesis the thought is prior to the form.

Emerson's position, as Norman Foerster has shown,[6] is in the basic tradition of American criticism through Lowell and Whitman to Irving Babbitt and Paul Elmer More. It describes the tendency of American poetry from Edward Taylor to Robert Frost. Even Poe acknowledged that what gives "richness" to a work of art is "some undercurrent, however indefinite, of meaning." Robert Frost makes the point specific in the preface to his *Collected Poems* (1939):

> . . .The object in writing poems is to make all poems sound as different as possible from each other, and the resources for that of vowels, consonants, punctuation, syntax, words, sentences, meters are not enough. We need the help of context—meaning—subject matter. That is the greatest help towards variety. . . . And we are back in poetry as merely one more art of having something to say, sound or unsound.

Much of the current controversy over the relationship of the content of a poem to its value as a work of art seems to arise from a tendency to confuse *meaning* with "message." This confusion appears in a recent review by John Ciardi of Archibald MacLeish's *Collected Poems*. Ciardi quotes with approval the conclusion of MacLeish's early "Ars Poetica": "A poem should not mean / But be." But he notes that "within a few years of this poem MacLeish had taken up his advocacy of poetry as Public Speech." He continues: "Should the poem 'mean' or 'be?' Should it arrive at perception or a message? Should it explore the enduring and ever-personal emotions of *individual sensation and individual* loss or should it accept the challenge of specific *political assignments?*" (Italics mine.)

If the problem were as simple as this, the task of the critic or of the general reader would be equally simple. Unfortunately, however, no such clear either-or dichotomy exists in poetry of any distinction. To assume that it does is sure to involve the critic in a basic confusion, as Mr. Ciardi's further analysis demonstrates. Selecting "an irreducible half-dozen" of MacLeish's lyrics which he thinks "must certainly endure as long as poetry is read" he adds that "none of these successes are 'message' poems. Rather they are all poems of the most intensely personal feeling whose central subject is the sense of the passage of one man's life under the shadow of a mindless eternity which moves on to the obliteration of the individual."

Now if Mr. Ciardi's analysis of the irreducible half-dozen MacLeish lyrics is sound, it would appear that their "meaning" is neither private nor new. It is in effect the meaning of Lucretius, of Omar and of hundreds of lesser poets; namely that the life of one man—and if one man, all men—is passed "under the shadow of a mindless eternity which moves on to the obliteration of the individual." It is neither newer nor more private than the meaning of the Twenty-third Psalm which, in contrast, conveys the sense of the passage of the life of one man—and again if one man, all men—under the shadow of a benign Omnipotence which moves on to the perfect felicity of the individual.

The meaning of a poem may present itself in either of three ways: (1) overtly or didactically as in Longfellow's "A Psalm of Life," (2) aphoristically, as in the poetic passages of *Proverbs* and *Ecclesiastes* and in Emerson's "Ode" to W. H. Channing, and (3) covertly or by figurative indirection as in *Oedipus Rex, The Divine Comedy, Hamlet,* and *The Waste Land.* Needless to say, although memorable poetry of the first two types does exist, it is by the third method that the greatest poets of all time have most often conveyed their meanings—their "readings of earth." This appears to be what Emerson has in mind when he tells us that "the poet is representative. He stands among partial men for the complete man, and appraises us not of his wealth but of the common wealth." It also appears to be what Matthew Arnold means when he speaks of poetry as a "criticism of life."

III

One of the paradoxes of the new criticism is that while it insists on the one hand on the right of the poet to his private emotions, his private images, his private vocabulary—even his private typography—it devotes long chapters and entire volumes to explaining Pound, Eliot, and Joyce for the purpose of proving that their meanings are not private but universal. Granting then the soundness of Viereck's dictum "that a poem should both mean and be" the question of whether confused or even vicious ethical meanings may impair the value of a poem still remains. Robert Wooster Stallman puts in concretely in an essay, "The New Critics," published in his anthology *Critiques and Essays in Criticism*:

> The poet-poem-reader relationship is again illustrated by the Problem of Belief: the question whether it is necessary for the reader to share the poet's beliefs in order to enjoy fully his poetry. The problem . . . is resolved by Eliot thus: "When the doctrine, theory, belief, or 'view of life' presented in a poem is one which the mind of the reader can accept as coherent, mature, and founded on the facts of experience, it interposes no obstacle to the reader's enjoyment. . . ." With this interpretation, which Eliot makes in *The Use of Poetry* (1933), all later critics concur. The question of the specific merit of a poetic statement as truth or falsehood does not arise when the beliefs of the poet are ordered into an intrinsic whole.

This seems to have been essentially the position of the majority of the Bollingen Committee, who in making the 1948 award to the *Pisan Cantos* sidestepped the poem's ethical content. Karl Shapiro attacked this position in a letter to *Partisan Review* saying that he had voted against Pound "in the belief that the poet's political and moral philosophy ultimately vitiates his poetry and lowers its standard as literary work." Mr. Shapiro added,

The jury that elected Pound was made up partly of Pound's contemporaries, those who had come under his influence as impresario and teacher . . . and those who had engaged in the literary struggle to dissociate art from social injunction. The presence of Mr. Eliot at the meetings gave these facts a reality which perhaps inhibited open discussion.

Viereck states his view in "Pure Poetry, Impure Politics, and Ezra Pound." With characteristic forthrightness he says of the Bollingen Committee, "Judging by their much debated press release, their sympathies were with the widely held belief—a belief I consider unhistorical and psychologically false . . . —that artistic form can be con-

sidered apart from its content and moral meaning." Of the *Cantos* specifically he concludes: "Pound's prize-winning poem was not intended as purely aesthetic. Its message politically was that Mussolini was martyred and World War II caused by Jews. . . . This is politics, not serious poetry, hence not exempt from ethical as well as aesthetic condemnation."

He challenges "the famous New Criticism's method of [treating] a poem by itself, like a self-created airtight-sealed object, outside cause and effect":

> A reader's response to a poem is a total response, a *Gestalt* in which aesthetic as well as ethical, psychological, and historical factors are inseparably fused together. It is a self-deception to try to separate them and to discover some alchemistical quintessence of "pure" aesthetics, to be judged only by certified "pure" mandarins of criticism.

In *The Shame and Glory of the Intellectuals* he says of the probable influence of Pound on future American poetry:

> Justice will be done: art outlasts politics. But only if truly art and not fashion, not coterie. In case Pound has truly made the artistic contribution his admirers believe he has made, then I hope the future will reward him by remembering only his poems and not his ephemeral rantings against "Jew York" and "President Rosenfelt."

Viereck makes his own prognosis of the future of American poetry. He deplores the fact that

> The current battle of "obscurity" versus "clarity". . . tends to divide poets into two extremes equally deadly to poetry. The first extreme, in the name of anti-philistinism, is for crossword puzzle poetry which . . . would kill poetry by scaring away its audience. The second extreme, in the name of communication, would demagogically popularize poetry, . . . until it is no longer poetry at all, but verse.

He pleads for "an act of creative faith in a new and third force in poetry, already emerging, equally remote from the muse's mincing sterilizers and backslapping salesmen."

> Such a third force must prefer a difficult simplicity to an easy obscurity. It must return to the function of ethical responsibility and of communication of ideas and emotions. . . . The American poetry of the future like the classicism of the ancient past, will again see art as a groping search for the good, the true, the beautiful; all three as potentially harmonizing rather than conflicting.

Viereck's quarrel with the award to Pound went far beyond the question of American loyalty. To him the committee seemed to have condoned treason, not only against the land which had indicted Pound for treason but against humanity itself, conceived in terms of what he calls the

Greek-Roman-Judeo-Christian standard of values. His viewpoint is broader than Shapiro's, who objected to Pound's being given the award not only on aesthetic grounds, as noted above, but for the "first and most crucial reason . . . that I am a Jew and cannot honor anti-semites." If Pound's polemic had been directed against the Negro race or the Catholic faith, would Mr. Shapiro have been equally opposed?

Viereck's position is on the high grounds that a poem which purposely becomes the vehicle of an indefensible ethic cannot be a great poem whatever else its merits. Convinced, as he says in a preview of his projected history of modern Europe, that under the combined impact of mil-itant nationalism and militant socialism the West since 1871 has undergone a devastating ethical revolution, he is horrified by the spectacle of a professedly civilized world reverting to a worse-than-savage brutality. He calls "Pound's joking reference to mass murder as 'fresh meat on the Russian steppes' the most callous single reference ever written by an American artist."

What appalls Mr. Viereck is not that the victims of Hitler's death camps were mainly Jews, but that tortured and torturers alike were all human beings. He is aware, in short, as every thoughful observer of the times must be, that at any moment we may face a situation when, in the words of an objective contemporary scientist, there will literally be "no place to hide." Such a time, he feels, is hardly propitious for an influential coterie of poets and critics to claim the privilege of hiding in an ivory tower of de-humanized aestheticism.

In his *Shame and Glory of the Intellectuals* he warns liberals and reactionaries alike:

The lesson of Pound and Hiss is not, as literary and political reactionaries may claim: "Stop being avant-garde, stop being liberal." . . . The lesson is "become genuine apostles of literary and political progress by watching the moral correlative of progress more sensitively in the future."

NOTES

[1] Chicago: The University of Chicago Press (1952). See also Van Wyck Brooks, *The Writer in America* (New York: E. P. Dutton and Company, 1953).

[2] *The First Morning* (New York: Scribner's, 1952).

[3] See William Van O'Connor, *Sense and Sensibility in Modern Poetry*, Chapter 8, "The Imagistic Symbol" (Chicago: University of Chicago Press, 1948).

[4] (Boston: The Beacon Press, 1953).

[5] *New England, Indian Summer* (New York: E. P. Dutton, 1940).

[6] *American Criticism, A study in Literary Theory from Poe to the Present* (Boston: Houghton-Mifflin Co., 1928.)

Hayden Carruth (review date 1957)

SOURCE: "Some New Poems by Peter Viereck," *Poetry*, Vol. 89, No. 5, February 1957, pp. 316-19.

[*In the following review of* The Persimmon Tree, *Carruth considers the poetry in this volume an improvement over Viereck's earlier works but confesses that he finds Viereck's poems "painfully hard to read."*]

Peter Viereck's new poems are very similar in tone and manner to the earlier poems which won him such great popularity, yet there is, I think, a difference. His book, **The Persimmon Tree**, is divided into a number of sections, and particularly in the one marked **"Pastoral"** the new poems offer a somewhat gentler flow, an easier tone of voice. To my mind this is an improvement, and I like some of these new poems very much. Viereck manages to bring to the meditative lyric, our supremely popular kind of poem, an individuality of voice and a rather nervous movement which make his poems genuinely distinct from the rest and superior to most of them. He is, of course, an accomplished writer, a clever writer, and his skill has a good deal to do with the success of his successful poems. I mean that his accomplishment lies partly in his ability to please us with purely verbal constructions, apart from their context of thought or feeling. But his virtuosity sometimes interferes with his poetry too. Distinctions of rhyme, I know, are ultimately a matter of taste, but to my ear the rhyme of "where sol lives" with "olives" in a poem which is otherwise quite serious and even graceful seems a grievous obtrusion. In other poems, the virtuosity is better placed. **"Decorum and Terror,"** for instance, a tour de force in which Viereck uses, I am sure, every imaginable rhyme on his own surname, is a frank offering of doggerel, quite suitable to its subject (a conversation between Goethe and Hart Crane), and is the kind of cogent farce for which we can always be grateful in this comparatively dull time. In short, Viereck's new poems are strong and varied and on the whole good examples of what the poet can do at this stage of literary development.

That, at least, is what must be said before I can proceed to some of the other thoughts which occurred to me while I was reading these poems: it is the view which, although not necessarily orthodox in itself, nevertheless projects its meaning against our consciousness of orthodoxy. But I think that if one makes the effort to escape for the moment from our particular encampment and look back, as it were, from the surrounding hills, one's view becomes both more detached and more doubtful. In doing so, of course, one destroys the individuality of Viereck's poems, which become instead merely motions representative of our whole activity, and it is important to bear this in mind. But what does one see first of all? It is, I think, the congestion of our work. The truth is that Viereck's poems are painfully hard to read.

One does not understand immediately why this should be so. In mood and theme, Viereck's poems are not at all unfamiliar to us. His technique is the accustomed alogical and associative way of proceeding in which we have been well schooled. Moreover, in these poems the intellectual and emotional processes occur at a public though naturally high level of culture; we are not left behind, as we have been sometimes, in a poet's essentially private excursions. Yet something is wrong. We can attend easily, almost habitually, to these poems, we can admire them, but at the end, as often as not, we are left with a sense of weariness and dissatisfaction, as after an unnecessarily difficult labor. Here is the shortest poem in Viereck's book; it happens to be also the poem from which the book takes its title.

Not as we wish, accoutred regal,
Our soarers land but pent in cloud.
So must we take each molted eagle
Just as he comes or do without.
No radiance radiates. Its birth is
Dark-stained with lusts and blasphemies.
We sing them shiny if we please.
Or snuff them. Either way, unclean.
We dodge with outrage or derision
Truths that assault us squashily:
Each clowning, sweetish, harsh-cored vision
That shoots from the persimmon tree.
Brief bloom, we always wrong you; earth is
A drabber patch than need have been.

Here the poem, which I take to be a comment on the failure of the artistic imagination, progresses so heavily through its difficult changes that at the end it is pretty well wrung out, and so are we. From moulting eagle to metallic song to squashy fruit to flowering vision, with perhaps a dozen minor shifts, we go at a labored pace. I am not complaining about a mixed metaphor; that, after all, is the poet's business. I am complaining about a false density of metaphoric writing which has become virtually automatic and empty of any real urgency.

The symbolist movement in English poetry is a notably difficult thing to locate, probably because it envelops us and much of our tradition so mistily. But say experimentally that it was predicted by Blake, founded by Wordsworth, muddled by the Pre-Raphaelites, restored by the French, perfected by the generation of Eliot and Stevens, and upraised to a fragile and collapsing peak by Dylan Thomas. Where does this leave us now? And what has been the pull of this long experience in symbolism upon the permanent stuff of poetry, upon metaphor? Metaphor has, I think, warped closer and closer to symbol, as toward an unattainable perfection. Symbolism, a technique of thought and feeling, has naturally intervened with metaphor, a technique of writing. Metaphor has striven, in a manner of speaking, toward the state of being compact, autonomous, luminous, toward the state of being a symbol. But perhaps this movement has endured beyond its point of real meaning and tension, perhaps now the ultimate moment is behind us, perhaps this accounts for the loss of creative urgency. Metaphor is beginning to disintegrate, and its fragments fall and clatter in our poems. That is to say, the unity of feeling and technique is gone; we are perpetuating the technique because it is our en-

dowment, already our burden, and because we do not know how to begin again. We become anxious, and in the poem we twist the line of metaphor so that it becomes forced, conspicuous, and exorbitant. This is what I mean by a poem that is hard to read.

George Green (essay date 1960)

SOURCE: "Four Campus Poets," *Thought*, Vol. XXXV, No. 137, June 1960, pp. 230-33.

[*In the following excerpt from an essay, Green examines the political and moral elements in Viereck's poetry.*]

. . . No one could accuse this history professor of neglecting the contest outside college gates. Indeed, it becomes impossible to consider Viereck's poetry without reference to his prose, where he has wished to protect humanistic conservatism primarily through literature and philosophy. His concern for politics has been secondary because he never escaped his fear of it descending into a *Realpolitik* of brutalization. We may admire the sincerity with which liberals of older generations spoke their victory cry: "I wear no man's livery!" But the progression of values for which Nietzsche hoped, taking humanity beyond good and evil, has descended instead into a morass where one finds only devaluation. "Without the idealistic framework of ethical restraints," Professor Viereck wrote in *Shame and Glory of the Intellectuals,* "materialism can never achieve its material goals."

It is tempting though potentially disproportionate to dwell on Mr. Viereck in any debate which involves the public conscience of academics. For he has been so anxious to come to terms with this reality "too extreme for even the extremest adjectives of overstatement." Awareness of the demands of art and the need to comprehend contemporary facts establish a unique tension. "Toute forme créée, même par l'homme, est immortelle." Thus Viereck quotes Baudelaire as a preface for **"Poet."** We never forget this desire for independent form which seeks a *modus vivendi* with wider social loyalties. "What terror crowns the sweetness of all song?" It is natural that Viereck's career should pursue "terror" and "rage," yet the poet—sometimes without being totally aware—serves his era best when "coldest art" has blessed him, though it appeared hostile. In phrases which describe the impact of a poet, we note his judgment of the writer as someone who fights on his own section of the barricades. At the death of a true artist, inexact and flaccid language charges abroad:

Words that begged favor at his court in vain—
Lush adverbs, senile rhymes in tattered gowns—
Send notes to certain exiled nouns
And mutter openly against his reign.
While rouged cliches hang out red lights again,
Hoarse refugees report from far-flung towns
That exclamation marks are running wild
And prowling half-truths carried off a child.

Indeed, certain titles explain in a manner which sometimes diminishes emotional response: **"The Slacker Apologizes,"** or **"Crass Times Redeemed by Dignity of Souls."** This last poem, published at an earlier date, served as the credo for *Shame and Glory of the Intellectuals.* We understand Viereck's fondness, for it summarizes his ideal of the poet as conserver, one who realizes that human lives are surrounded by uniformity, though he resists violently the excesses of conformity. No text in modern poetry better exploits the combination of *politique et moraliste,* a posture which Viereck has done so much to re-establish as legitimate for writers.

"*The music of the dignity of souls* / Molds every note I hum and hope to write." Faith in human potential helps conquer "the earthquake licking at our soles." The pun is intentional, heightening the irony of human limits in dust. Belief in humanity helps one to grasp "the burrows of heart's buried lair / Where furtive furry Wishes hide like moles." Personification is a recurrent device, combining with regular rhymes to strengthen classical restraint.

> The weight that tortures diamonds out of coals
> Is lighter than the skimming hooves of foals
> Compared to one old heaviness our souls
> Hoist daily, each alone, and cannot share:
> To-be-awake, to sense, to be aware.
> Then even the dusty dreams that clog our skulls,
> The rant and bluster of the storm we are,
> The sunny silences our prophets hear,
> The rainbow of the oil upon the shoals,
> The crimes and Christmases of creature-lives,
> And all pride's barefoot tarantelle of knives
> *Are but man's search for dignity of souls.*

Regularity of line implies an enormous time span: a sequence made possible to accept because one is more aware of identifications than of variance. Life is essentially a problem of disciplined response, like the process which triumphs in the diamond, brilliant, permanent, after millennial pressures. For all our will to escape in animal exultation (the skimming hooves of foals in open pasture), man cannot deny without disaster fundamental restrictions. Stability lives in the lonesome outposts of individual consciousness, where to be aware is to stand guard. Man wages an eternal battle to subdue self, to recognize values which endure by resolving—or at least weathering—the psychic storm. Combat is worth our devotion, nonetheless. We find this faith in the songs of prophets, in all valuable deeds of "creature-lives," even in the frantic, mistaken rhythm of crusades which equate glory with messianic compulsion.

In each of these areas, if one grasped the complete process, one would uncover preoccupation with value, making significance out of the hectic "tarantelle," the selfish jealousies and glorious events which dot history. The "rant and bluster" of centuries have blurred reality under the aegis of supposedly irreversible systems, but such programs resemble the "rainbow of the oil upon the shoals." History is irrevocably associated with storm. By shunning embattled readiness, one pretends that the oil slick

on rocky coasts will insure survival. This calm resembles the transitory magic of rainbows. Tomorrow the gale will resume, more violent than ever. Oil is no pledge of safety, rather the natural and recurrent consequence of nautical disaster.

Closely knit rhyme and personification remind us that Peter Viereck has been particularly aware of deadening effects which have characterized some modern poetry, sedulous for novelty. He has undertaken "a frontal assault on obscurity," though he is too sophisticated to condone lazy reading. It does not bother him to be associated with the phrase "Manhattan classicism." Indeed, he seeks a classicism applicable to our industrial era, "with an ivory tower built where the subway rumbles loudest," as he has quipped. Anxious to shed pre-Eliot sentimentalism, at the same time he avoids "hermetic ingenuities" of the post-Eliot version of neo-classicism. Relying on what Eliot calls "audio imagination," Viereck has exercised his splendid gift for rhyme. This is clear in the stanza quoted, from what Viereck calls an "incantatory poem."

It is not so much philosophical conservatism as a truth of his psychology that has brought Peter Viereck to his major theme: vindication of the reality of evil. Not without reason does he refer to Seth, the donkey god of Egypt, oldest symbol of darkness in human records. "But 'I' being less than soul, of dustier plume— / If I escape, it is myself I lose." Accepting limits should be no excuse for sentimental trash—was it not this writer who spoke of romantic poetry of a certain character as infinite capacity for faking pains? Facing crises, it becomes the duty of the poet to "Sing the bewildered honor of the flesh. / I say the honor of our flesh is love." Though "sentenced to mortality," we transcend fate, the "forepaw stalking us from every cloud. . . ." Our best strategy in this predicament lies in the revelation of love, which in turn requires sacrifice, invincible faith in others. "Never to be won by shields, love fell / Oh only to the wholly vulnerable." Mr. Viereck resents those who cannot recognize the "muddy and vulnerable glory" of man. He presents a notable example of the intellectual committed to avoidance of violence, that last resort of thinkers who, isolated and alienated, espouse the clatter of external event, self-conscious aesthetes who revel in the phrase *les fauves,* the wild beasts. Viereck's allegiance to the tradition of the West, with its manifold debts to Greek reason, to Roman law, to Hebraic discipline and Christian love, can express its reading of life in terms of combat. The commitment of the artist is such that he lives, joyfully, to tell

> How shimmering, how gaily freedom prowls
> In flesh that guards its consciousness of souls.

Richard P. Benton (essay date 1961)

SOURCE: "Viereck's 'Don't Look Now but Mary Is Everybody,'" *Explicator*, Vol. XX, No. 4, December, 1961, item 30.

[*In the following essay, Benton offers a close examination of the literary parodies and theological themes in Viereck's poem, "Don't Look Now but Mary Is Everybody."*]

Viereck's poem (**"Don't Look Now But Mary Is Everybody"**), one of a series of nine poems called **"New York,"** communicates on three levels of meaning simultaneously. These three levels are: (1) the historical level, (2) the mock genotypic level, and (3) the theological level.

The historical level tells a story that one can read almost everyday in the tabloids. Mary, a private secretary, having become bored with her boss's kisses, seduced an inexperienced youth and fled with him aboard her employer's yacht which she stole to embark on a pleasure cruise with her new lover, expecting to lead a life of perfect freedom and bliss. However, her employer overtook his stolen property and Mary and her recently acquired "sucker" received the full force of his vengeance. Mary fell overboard, but her life preserver failed to keep her afloat. She tried to shoot her attacker, but her pistol backfired. The compass she took with her to guide her safely on her course guided her instead to disaster. Even Mary's new boy friend, having become dismayed at the reversal of fortune, turned against her and shouted recriminations and insults at her.

The genotypic level communicates its relationship to certain traditional literary forms. Through them it satirizes the moral code of the "Mary Mixup's" of the twentieth century. Two traditional literary genres are parodied: (1) the medieval morality plays, and (2) and Mother Goose nursery rhymes.

The clues to the parody of the first are best explained in the discussion of the theological level. The clues to the second are furnished by the following elements:

1. The association of Mary with her lamb recalls the nursery rhyme "Mary had a little lamb; / Its fleece was white as snow," etc.

2. Mary's rebellious act recalls the rhyme "Mistress Mary, quite contrary," etc.

3. Mary's sailing on her "dream boat" in quest of what turns out to be a "fool's paradise" evokes the verse "North by south and east by West, / Out of space and out of time, / Lies the land old dames know best, / The foolish land of nursery rhyme."

4. Mary's falling contentedly asleep and her subsequent awakening to the reality of her predicament calls up the nursery rhyme "Little Bo-peep fell fast asleep / And dreamt she heard them [her lost sheep] bleating; / But when she awoke, she found it a joke, / For they still all were fleeting."

5. Certain syntactical formations associated with nursery rhymes and baby talk, namely, the inversion of subject and predicate ("Her lamb took she," "Compass and pistol took she," "Free sailed she north," "Unleashed His typhoons Boss," and "knew she") and the inversion of subject, predicate, and direct object ("her helped ocean" and "Her buoyed the life-preserver down") also contribute to the nursery-rhyme evocation. Even the use of the term "lamb" as a trope for Mary's boy friend aids this connotation, since this word is used hypocoristically by mothers and lovers.

The theological level unfolds an allegorical drama on the order of a medieval morality play. Its theme has to do with the meaning of free will, the loss of one's soul, and the inevitability of God's justice. The first clue to this theological view is the proposition put forward in the second clause of the poem's title where Mary is equated with everybody, i.e., with humanity in general. This equation and the allegorical method employed in the poem suggest the conditions set forth in the morality plays, especially in the well-known *Everyman*, whose protagonist stands for humanity in general, whose theme concerns the saving of man's soul, and in which vices and virtues are personified. This genotypic aspect of the poem is aided by the capitalization of "Boss" and "His," since these grammatical signs indicate that these words have religious significance and hence refer not only to one in authority over an employee but also to the Supreme Authority or God.

Similar to the methodology of the morality play is the employment in the poem of persons and things to symbolize abstractions such as concepts, states, and powers. The yacht stolen by the particular Mary is more than a pleasure craft and her cruise is more than an ocean voyage; the yacht represents humanity's cupidity and the cruise humanity's misuse of freedom of the will by indulging in the pursuit of vice. Mary's lamb is more than a "fall guy" for a *femme fatale*; he represents humanity's original state of innocence and purity corrupted by sin. The two instruments that Mary took with her—compass and pistol—are more than mechanical devices; they represent humanity's conscience and will. Humanity's conscience guided it wrongly; its will becoming untrue, it acted contrary to the law of God. Mary's fall in the sea represents humanity's Fall and expulsion from the Garden of Eden. The lifepreserver that failed to keep Mary afloat is more than a ring or jacket of canvas-covered cork; it stands for humanity's religious faith that, when lost, was unable to support mankind under its weight of sin. Humanity's disaster came when God in his righteous wrath rained a horrible tempest on the wicked. Viereck's theology is typically medieval and scholastic: Freedom of the will doesn't mean the privilege to sin; conscience is the guide of human conduct; and the will is truly directed only when man wills what is in accordance with God's law.

John Woods (review date 1962)

SOURCE: "A Poetry Chronicle," *Poetry*, Vol. 100, No. 6, September, 1962, pp. 404-11.

[*In the following review, Woods finds no dramatic structure to* The Tree Witch, *which Viereck intended as both a poem and a play.*]

The Tree Witch is presented as "a poem and a play (first of all a poem)". I would add, "last of all a play". We are invited to read the book either as a play or (by omitting stage directions) as a poem. I am unable to omit anything when I read, even the poet's portrait. Besides, I don't believe poetry or drama operates this way. Surely there's more to drama than stage directions.

The play has been staged, we are informed, but I have serious doubts that much happened on the audience side of the footlights. I can't conceive of any dramatic context within which Viereck's poetry would be accessible. It's too involved for the ear alone, with a jazzy diction, relentlessly up-to-date, but in no sense colloquial. The following passage is moderately illustrative.

> Castaways hoard the annals of beginnings,
> The alphabets of dawn before the split.
> Two signs, when first your campfire banned us,
>   wrangled:
> Circle and line. Our cycle, your ascent.
> "Revere each season's own true swerve," we sang
>   then;
> "Drain, build, stamp logic on," clanged will, male,
>   steel.
> Clang-knit geometries of girders garland
> Your plumb-lines now
>   and grid our zigzag ways.

A more convincing illustration would be the line: "O slogan me no Atlas from your engines." But I needn't overstate my case. Viereck does write interesting, hyperactive poetry.

The major problem of **The Tree Witch** as a play lies in its involved presentation. Viereck is trying everything at once. Even the production notes need explication. The play is built about a conflict, I believe, between spontaneous magic, as represented by a Hellenistic dryad, and various "anti-pagan" contemporary anatomies, represented by "adjusted moderns" and Guardian Aunts. The adjusted moderns represent "hedonistic materialism" and the Guardian Aunts represent "joyless, respectable 'religion'". But this is no simple triangle; both the sides and the angles are so scrupulously qualified as to defy dramatic recognition.

Josephine Jacobsen (essay date 1968)

SOURCE: "Peter Viereck: Durable Poet," *The Massachusetts Review*, Vol. IX, No. 3, Summer, 1968, pp. 591-95.

[*In the following essay, Jacobsen argues for the durability of Viereck's poetry, suggesting that in addition to his technical skills his work reveals a certain universality which she calls a "cosmic sense."*]

Though in general it is far from the case, one would think that humility would be an occupational hazard for the critic. The percentage of howlers produced by generally astute critics is history. But not even the widely held belief that *Lalla Rookh* was the apex of its century's literary offering, chastens the professional descendants of those prophets. Poetic *chic* flows on, carrying with it a number of fine poets, and all the flotsam of the arriviste and the second rate. Eventually, less precarious judgments are established.

As there are good poets whose especial vein happens to coincide with the current taste in poetry, so there are others whose especial gifts run, if not counter, yet not fully parallel to that taste. For these poets, the usual result is disproportion—a gulf between the calibre of their work and the dynamism of their reputation. Peter Viereck belongs to this second category.

He has accumulated the respectable honors—a Pulitzer Prize; two Library of Congress lecture appointments—but a dozen inferior poets figure more notably in the poetic press. His **New and Selected Poems**—ranging over thirty-five years—gives a complete enough representation of his work to make critical comment very worth while indeed.

Viereck's work has three qualities essential to that of any good poet. He has an individual, sustaining style. He has poetic convictions, flexible in approach but durable in essence. He has an affinity for themes of inherent scope and power. But in addition to these, he has something extremely rare in a mechanical and insulated age, something largely absent from contemporary poetry. To call it a cosmic sense sounds portentous. Yet this is what it is. Roethke had it, Tomlinson, and D. H. Lawrence. It is one poetic quality which is purely a gift, and there is absolutely nothing which can be done to simulate its possession. It is quite different from the gift for metaphysical conceits expressed in a sort of cosmic vocabulary; it is quite other than the ability to write good "nature poetry." It is instead a spontaneous reaction by which the poet feels himself constantly involved in a series of giant processes of which his humanity is only a part; not a *knowledge* that grass is growing, animal skin encasing its blood and flesh, trees toughening their bark, but a *sense* of the non-human, a *sense* of the multiplicity of matter, matter in the definition of physics: *matter, that which is considered to constitute the substance of the physical universe, and, with energy, to form the basis of objective phenomena.* This leads straight into a sense of the infinite depth of the small and the large, the minute and the enormous, and to glimpses into the dizzying abysses of time, those abysses which we habitually telescope into "the past." It is providential, since this rather massive gift is his, that Viereck has wit, virtuosity, and above all, poetic energy. These three last qualities do not always appear as friends; they are blood relatives to his dangers and defects, but they are indispensable to his over-all success.

One of the difficulties with which Viereck's poetry has to contend is that these dangers and defects spring to the eye. The poetry stands up. It does not quietly cave in when pushed by a second and third reading. But at first reading, the carnival atmosphere which is such an important ambiance for the work, can seem shrill, distracting, or overdone. Re-reading dispels a good bit of this impression; the stuff is there, under the mannerisms. It is true that, although it contributes strongly to his most successful poems, Viereck's technical virtuosity is allowed to spoil some of his work. Because he *can* manage a sequence of tour de force rhymes, he will do so at the risk of a sense of strain, and a diversion from the poem itself. He has, on the other hand, a lovely sense of the grotesque—both the sinister and the light-hearted—and happily addresses a potato (one of the "fat and earthy lurkers"),

> O vast earth-apple, waiting to be fried,
> Of all the starers the most many-eyed,
> What furtive purpose hatched you long ago
> In Indiana or in Idaho?
>
> In Indiana and in Idaho
> Snug underground the great potatoes grow,
> Puffed up with secret paranoia unguessed
> By all the duped and starch-fed Middle West.

Viereck's work, at its best, is almost perfectly implied in two of his lines:

> Being absurd as well as beautiful
> Magic—like art—is hoax redeemed by awe.

The hoax he consistently exploits; the awe is entirely real. His argument, again and again, is for the inherent and vitalizing duality. He acknowledges with respect the constant terrifying and decorous (*terror* and *decorum* are key words) counter-pull of death:life, hun-ger:satisfaction, intention:undertow. He carries this into analysis, ethics, politics. Now and then he becomes pat, or instructive, so strongly does he feel his conclusion. But it is, most of the time, a fecundating process, an intuition of reciprocity, not optimistic, but mature and undespairing, and allowing for all surprises in the long process of

> . . . doom made sweet in art and
> Bloom out of bloom-dust gardened.

Viereck's work is strengthened by the conviction which he shares with a very different contemporary, Georges Ionesco: that the great themes are few and eternal, and that the intimidating anxiety in regard to falling into a cliché indicates a poverty in the poet's creative ability. He lampoons the nervous profferers of novelty as a substitute for creative freshness, who can only bewail the dailyness of the sun:

> Trite flame, we try so hard to flout you
> But even to shock you is cliché,
> O catastroph-i-cal-ly dowdy
> O tedium of gold each day!

He lampoons the nervous Januses who compete for cash by day and culture-certificates by night:

> We've got to play with boors by day in order to
>   stock the larder:
> We put to flight that guilt by night, by hugging culture
>   harder.

He lampoons the nervous gentility of

>   . . . our limbo where
> Girls are not Bad but merely Indiscreet,
> Girls are not Good but merely Very Sweet.

He is concerned to scrabble at the roots, to twitch off the label. His poems involving trees are marvelously tree-y; small wonder that his heroine of *The Tree Witch*, at bay between "We (The enlightened and emancipated technologizing moderns), and They (Our three guardians, the hygiene-spraying and jargon-spraying aunts . . . who . . . later turn out to be the vengeful Eumenides)," is a hamadryad, wrenched from her tree "stript, trapt and spitting." Birds, grass, loam, bears, moss, snails, snow, potatoes, fountains manifest themselves, rather than suffer a label.

Another characteristic which Viereck shares with his fellow-juggler, Ionesco, is a sense of the omnipresence of death. Death appears wearing all sorts of masks: as the inevitable shift-point of the cycle,

Triumphant falling leaf, you are the strongest thing of all . . . ; as the lovers' chill observer (in a number of the beautiful lyrics which are Viereck's finest form),

> The hibernating bear, but half alive,
> Dreams of free honey in a stingless hive,
> He thinks of life at every lifeless breath.
> (The lovers think of death.) . . . ,

as the blind flamingo in the brilliant and macabre **"Why Can't I Live Forever?"**

> At night he wades through surf to seek a mate.
> That's why he stinks of salt and oyster shells.
> It is his blindness keeps him celibate;
> This bungler thinks he kisses when he kills . . . ,

or as the force in the sense of the past,

> Sweet Eohippus, "dawn horse" in
> That golden Attic tongue which now
> Like you and Helen is extinct,
> Like Cheshire-cat of fading grin,
> Like Carthage and like Villon's snow,
> With death and beauty gently linked.

If Viereck can be over-dextrous, didactic, he is never sentimental. And in view of the tenderness and delicacy of the loveliest of his lyrics, this says much for his poetic calibre. His love poems, sad or exuberant, have no taint of the mawkish. They do not depend on contrived shock for their sensual vitality, they don't substitute autobiography for emotional energy. And, being no sentimentalist, he understands that the undercurrent of nursery-rhymes is terror. His are splendid. He *knows* "the cupboard where the cakes and poisons are." His children who play hide and seek in the forest, grow up to be his lovers, who know

> That through the gamut lovers' bodies press,
> Through all that shattering terror's tenderness,
> The whiplash of their tensest truth is this:
> Their winged and stinking ecstasy flows bitter.

Viereck is an important poet, he is an honest and—at all risk of critical prediction—a durable one. He has an ear equalled by few poets now writing. One result is the effortless motion of his lyrics:

> Birds are exploding into bloom and glowing,
> And petals fan our sleep with little wings,
> (Into your ear-drums what glass snake is flowing?
> It is a Moorish fountain, and it sings.)

But in the end, the flavor of durability comes less from the components of his skill—the lyric tone, the virtuosity, the wit, the thematic strength—than from a sort of authority, a permanent sureness of decision. It is something which rises like an essence from the book's latest, and final, poem:

> Wade without foresight or don't wade at all.
> Plunge without seeing or you'll never find.
> There's only insight. (Gulls read maps, their eyes
> Look outward; berries, even winds are solid.
> Roses are cold. Even warm roses are cold.)
> There's only insight, paid for: not a flashlight,
> But night probing night. Walk out alone.

Laurence Lieberman (review date 1968)

SOURCE: "A Poetry Chronicle," *Poetry*, Vol. 112, No. 5, August, 1968, pp. 337-43.

[*In the following review of* New and Selected Poems: 1932-1967, *Lierberman surveys Viereck's career commitment to both politics and poetry.*]

The career in poetry of Peter Viereck, perhaps more than that of any other writer of our time, can be viewed as an experiment in the symbiosis of poetry and politics. *The New Cultural Blues*, his best satire, draws on a complex linguistic and sociological intelligence. I can't recall when, if ever, these two cultures (language and social science) have been embraced by a more consolidating sensibility. His best satires are memorable events in the history of ideas, without loss of art.

Viereck's earliest poetry served him as an extension of political consciousness into a medium in which paramount ideas of our era could be abstracted from their worrisome contexts in international affairs and viewed freshly and intrinsically through the symbolic machinery of art. Poetry later became for Viereck a mind-style for escaping the risks of socio-political consciousness in playful, if ingenious, literary word-puzzles. But in his most re-

cent work, in going still further beyond literal reality, Viereck returns to full human force and wholeness. Enacted before our eyes in **"Five Walks on the Edge"** is the drama of aspiring spirit in search of the mindlessness of supra-being, the poet attaining a larger totality of mind than ever before in **"Counter-Walk, Reversals,"** the superb poem that ends the book. Foregoing his former escape of spiritual transcendence, there is a new toughness in immanence, identification with the indwelling natural forces in rivers, trees, cliffs, rock, mud. In **"River,"** a voyage of man's spirit is symbolized, but an equal interest is generated in the sheer fun of letting the river be itself, speak its being, act out its life of surfaces, appearances: nothing *is* but what can be seen, touched, poured. If the poet's mental life, a see-sawing fluid motion, is particularized and embodied in the river's cycles, his fascination with the actual properties of the river is so intense it threatens to steal attention away from its symbolic value. It is a vision in which we feel "body is not bruised to pleasure soul", nor ideas lost to things. No portion of sensibility is sacrificed or compromised to any other. The political man is perfecting his anti-self in apolitical forms and spirits in nature.

I'm particularly struck with the original design of this book, the organization taking account of Viereck's development as a cyclic eternal return to key themes, an ascent along many separate spirals: not a mere chronology. This method of arrangement befits Viereck's work more than it would the work of most other poets, but all can profit by the example—especially in what it tells of a man's style of guiding the growth of his art over a thirty-year period.

Marie Henault (essay date 1968)

SOURCE: "Themes: Obsessive Crystals," in her *Peter Viereck*, Twayne Publishers, 1968, pp. 33-51.

[*In the following chapter from her book-length study, Henault surveys the constants of Viereck's poetry—particularly the themes of poetic classicism and ethical responsibility.*]

On a first reading, Peter Viereck's poetry seems to have great variety. This apparent diversity, however, is not characteristic. For, as he once said, to him "A key word is 'obsessive'"; and in his first book of verse this word and its derivatives appear at least five times. The phrase "obsessive crystals" from **"A Walk on Snow"** in *Terror and Decorum* describes his consistency in theme, idea, technique, and subject matter. An important obsessive crystal is "Manhattan classicism," a term Viereck coined to name the type of poetry which he thought he and other poets of his generation were writing.

I Manhattan Classicism

"The spirit of revolt is over," Viereck wrote in 1947. By this he meant that the poetic revolt of the first half of the twentieth century was ended; now a new revolt against revolt was well begun. Poets were returning, he thought, to the "poetic forms and disciplines" abandoned "just before the First World War. . . ."[1] The return had begun, he wrote, with the older poets T. S. Eliot and W. H. Auden; but its importance became clear only in the mid- and late 1940's with Robert Lowell, Dylan Thomas, Randall Jarrell, Richard Wilbur, and others—mostly "men under thirty-five publishing their first books."

In different prose pieces and in his verse, Viereck speaks for this poetic change. In *form,* while granting that Eliot and Pound had rebelled "less against form than formalism," Viereck claimed that the newly rebelling poets were returning, first, to "rigorous and exacting forms" and, second, to communication between poets and readers as "artistic"—to a "third force in poetry" of "a deep and, if need be, difficult clarity."[2] In *content,* Viereck wanted more concern for "values." Men of his generation, he wrote, "were forced—in fact, thrown—by war service into a willy-nilly preoccupation with the content of the realities around them." Consequently, they used "traditional forms and metrics . . . not for their own sake but as a means to enhance the content, including the intellectual and moral values implied by the content" ("Beyond Revolt," 58-59). This "conservative revolt against revolt," sought also to "return to romantic wildness of music and lyrical passion" ("Beyond Revolt," 45).

These four requirements in form and content—"traditional forms and metrics," clarity, ethical responsibility, and lyrical passion—Viereck summed up in 1966 in the phrase "strict wildness": it means "spontaneous absent-mindedness accompanied by the strictest, most conscious discipline of craftsmanship." Furthermore, this "third alternative" of a "strict wildness" communicates clearly and recognizes "that moral implications must be present in great art . . . [as] the by-product of a responsible use of words for their own sake."[3]

In Viereck's poetry "form" means, first of all, conventional stanzas, rhyme, and meter. "Free verse I write not at all," he said in 1949, "on principle" (*Mid-Century,* 20). And, in 1956, he asserted that "among the younger contemporary poets, free verse is dead and forgotten" ("Lyricism," 283). In *Terror and Decorum* he favored quatrains and five- and six-line stanzas, with some variations on the sonnet and the ode. Into lines mostly iambic pentameter, he inserted now and then shorter three-and four-beat lines "for variety or special emphasis." "Almost all of my poems," he wrote in 1950, "are rhymed." He uses and often emphasizes alliterative and assonantal sounds as well as rhyme. "If done not too unobtrusively," he wrote, "a poet can use [alliteration] triply instead of doubly; and triply is to my ear more effective" (*Mid-Century,* 20).

Yeats's "Cold Heaven" Viereck thought "the greatest lyric in our language"; and he imitated Yeats's rhythmic technique, especially the use of "a quick extra unaccented syllable amid an iambic or trochaic line" (*Mid-Century,* 21). Other poets who influenced him are e. e. cummings and Vachel Lindsay (both for typography), as well as W. H. Auden and Hart Crane. Like Crane, Viereck uses ep-

igraphs of explanation or amplification and italicized and broken lines. Crane's stanza in the "Indiana" section of "The Bridge" (three five-beat lines with a shorter fourth line) is one among many that are like Viereck's. And Crane's "Repose of Rivers," which Viereck admired, also reads like a Viereck poem.

Viereck's own "typical" poem, he wrote in 1950, was "a moderately long" one, "often of several pages, in rhymed iambic pentameter . . ." (*Mid-Century,* 22). The poems opening and closing *Terror and Decorum,* **"Poet"** and **"Crass Times,"** are of this type, as are some in *Strike Through the Mask!*—**"Some Lines in Three Parts," "My Gentlest Song," "To My Playmate"**—and many others in subsequent volumes. But, like many of his contemporaries, Viereck writes best in the short lyric. A fellow poet, Louis Simpson, once said that "Confidence in social and intellectual order must support any writing on a large scale; such confidence scarcely exists today, and the poet must attempt to re-order the world in a brief space."[4] At this reordering in a few lines, Viereck repeatedly succeeds. His short poems, too, like his long ones, are usually rhymed and often in pentameter: **"Vale from Carthage," "Don't Look Now But Mary Is Everybody,"** and some of the tree-girl lyrics in *The Tree Witch* (**"Outside my window," "The reaching out of warmth is never done").** In six-, seven-, or eight-syllabled lines, Viereck also works well, as in experiments with sound such as **"Tempest and Music"** and **"Roman Cadences"** and in some poems with irregularly short and long lines such as **"In the Month of March."**

Still, Viereck frequently writes long poems—perhaps because they more easily convey ideas. In 1950 he thought that, in his *"typical* poem," "lyrical emotions and philosophical ideas are equally present and are fused into unity by expressing the ideas in sensuous metaphors." "Mine," he continued, "is a poetry of ideas." At first Viereck did not see his own strengths and weaknesses; he said, in fact, in this 1950 essay that he was unable "to discriminate between [his] worse and better poems" (*Mid-Century,* 23). His first volume of verse won praise for its fertility of idea; but much of its content was an intellectual "classicism" from which he has moved away. In much of his work since then his best poetry is romantically sensuous; in spirit, style, and idea his poetry is like that of Yeats and also like that of the modern American romantic poet Hart Crane.

But "Manhattan classicism" was, Viereck wrote in this early period, "as accurate a label as any" for his verse (*Mid-Century,* 17). The phrase usefully isolates one of his distinctions as a poet: he finds poetic subjects "in the heart of the traffic bustle." The early poem **"Apollo in New York"** (1939) has such a subject; in it Apollo says, "Oh, the Bronx and the old country live the same nowadays." This brief poem ends with the god's searching in Manhattan for "Serenity among olives, passion static in stones."[5] **"Africa and My New York"** and **"Small Perfect Manhattan"** contain this idea too. In the latter poem the speaker says "No to sweet Charon," to the old world; he chooses instead Manhattan.

While Viereck has written poems set in different parts of the world—in Africa, in Italy, and in other sections of the United States—his poetry accords with his idea of the "perfection" of Manhattan and metropolitan America: "a classicism," as he put it, "of the industrial age, with an ivory tower built where the subway rumbles loudest" (*Mid-Century,* 17). Later he wrote that not his poetry alone but a whole "mid-century ground swell [of poetry can] . . . be called 'Manhattan classicism.'" Termed also the "baroque synthesis," it was "An urban, machineage classicism . . . not . . . afraid to build its small, quiet perfection right inside the largest, noisiest—also most vital—industrial center of the world . . ." ("Beyond Revolt," 42). This acceptance of New York's (and life's) uncouthness, while building a "perfection" in its midst, provides Viereck with his modern tone and many of his themes. The "reconciling" of New York and America, for instance, is the subject of **"Always to Love You, America"** and of **"Hurrah for Karamazov!"** New York *and* America, wheels *and* tulips, the East *and* the Ohio rivers—New York and wheels and the East River symbolize, of course, "urban America" ("Beyond Revolt," 42).

In **"Always to Love You, America,"** New York, "the dirty joke," the destroyer, will provide "America" with what it otherwise lacks—a free and lusty vitality. America questions at the climax: "The asphalt bonfire my prairies hated so / Will rise—Times Square above America?" New York answers that it will rise high indeed to "Where 'love' and 'law,' by pattern reconciled, must rhyme." "Risky . . . ," America comments, "where you would tug me to." In the conclusion, America calls New York a "true / Trigger-finger, that's your part: / To do god's dirty work. But after you—." So the poem ends: after New York, what? The theme of the unique and necessary place of New York (urban America) in this country reappears in other poems, mostly early ones; handling it gives background for his later sensuous, lyrical poetry about nonurban subjects.

For Viereck "Manhattan classicism," or the "baroque synthesis," was a term under which he subsumed the characteristics of his revolt against revolt. It meant coming to terms with contemporary life, using urban materials—the heart, spirit, and mind of urban man as well as (early) actual urban landmarks and machines. It meant also "clarity," explicit and meaningful statements about "intellectual and moral values implied by the content." And, finally, it meant "exacting forms," "traditional metrics," and, within these, "romantic wildness of music and lyrical passion. . . ."

Of these attributes only the "lyrical passion" is absent from Viereck's early poetry. With his second and third books of verse, however, the romanticism of his better poems became evident; and he was labeled a "Romantic classicist" and, later, an "intelligent Romantic." Because of Viereck's early featuring of his "classicism" and "humanism," the romantic elements in his attitudes and themes need stressing. The modern American anti-romantic tradition of Eliot and Irving Babbitt (still present in Viereck's Harvard) so detested what romanticism had led

to that the young poet used the term "classicism" honorifically. Still, he thought that although "romanticism does only harm in politics. . . . [in] poetry its emotionalism is a needed ingredient" ("Beyond Revolt," 44). Symbolically, for Viereck, Goethe is the classic and Hart Crane the romantic; and they supplement one another: like "mint and thyme, / Yours the cool and yours the acrid clime; / Art's two equal, different truths you mime." In Viereck's verse this "romantic classicism" means themes such as the supreme importance of man and love, beauty, and poetry in the face of the "mystery of mortality."

II SATIRE

In Viereck's first volume of poetry, **Terror and Decorum** (1948), these major themes were not yet paramount. He seemed rather a satiric and an "idea" poet. Hence in 1951 Selden Rodman emphasized Viereck's "learned dissection of history and . . . the play of his wit upon the follies and extravagances of the contemporary scene."[6] Viereck is a master of puns, epigrams, derisive descriptions, and variations on common sayings, mainly in prose but in poetry too: "Ruthless amid the alien corniness," "Uneasy lies the clown that wears a head," "Modern poetry is a snore and an allusion," and "genius is an infinite capacity for faking PAINS." The late verse, too, contains wit of this early admired kind—the line "Ruthless," mentioned above, is from a 1961 volume. But Viereck's development has been toward incongruity and simple "fun"; from the explicit satire of the earlier work he has moved toward "the brief and light touch" because it "is the least embarrassing approach to a tragic reality" (*Shame and Glory,* 55).

The typical early satiric poem **"To a Sinister Potato"** shares with other apprentice poems the use of an inanimate or an abstract subject to make a witty comment on human existence. With rapid rhythm and a catchy assonantal refrain ("In Indiana and in Idaho"), the poem presents the potato, like men, "Puffed up with secret paranoias." Its significance is outlined in the three central stanzas; potatoes, "fat and earthy lurkers," bide their hour, swelled by "mania" and envious of "stars"; the pending doom will be a tables-turned one:

When—once too often mashed in Idaho—
From its cocoon the drabbest of earth's powers
Rises and is a star.
And shines.
And lours.

(*Terror,* 16, and *New and Selected,* 119)

More patently satirical and "comic" than **"Potato"** are social and political poems which compress complexities. The middle part of *The Tree Witch* (1961) contains this second kind of satire—**"The Culture-Hug Blues,"** the Creed songs, and **"The Global Lobal Blues."** **"Decorum and Terror: Homage to Goethe and Hart Crane"** in Viereck's fourth book (1956) and **"The Insulted and Injured"** and **"The Self-Abuser and the Suicide"** in his third (1952) are poems of this type, as are **"What a Pretty Net"** and **"Always to Love You, America"** in his first (1948). Ideas are too overtly stated in some poems for complete success; but like these phrases in **"Always to Love You,"** expression is often vivid: "I have a child named Dagokikeandmick," "Better tell / Your angel-Saxons and your Anglo-nice," and "A deepfreeze disinfected liberty." As a poem **"Always to Love You"** does not cohere despite its rhyming ingenuity (exact rhyme and off-rhyme: "American-hurricane"; "back-heretic-deck") and alliteration ("fence-forests-fences-frontiers-footsteps-fate"; "too rapid jive-terrible ripening joy"), (*Terror,* 35-38). The poetic devices are employed for music, not for meaning. The social and political poems are inspired doggerel or statement, not poetry.

Related to these are narrative or narrative fantasy poems, light in tone but not always directly satiric. **"Tempest and Music,"** the amusing **"Homily on the Piety of All Herd Animals,"** and **"Love Song to Eohippus"** are successful poems of this kind. Other odd subject or fantasy poems are **"Prince Tank," "Child of the Sixtieth Century," "The Blind Doge at 83," "I Am an Old Town Square," "Masque of Tsars," "Aging Refugee from the Old Country," "For an Assyrian Frieze," "Birth of a Fascist,"** and **"Homecoming."**

The facetiously entitled **"Homily on the Piety of All Herd Animals (A Mammoth Idyll)"** and **"Photomontage of the Urban Parks,"** both mildly satiric, find beauty "in the heart of the traffic bustle." The **"Homily"** pastoral sees New York's Fifth Avenue buses as the "metal flock" which "Theocritus now hymns. . . ." The "tired buses" doze in "secret beds" (carbarns); "noble," "kindly," "chivalrous," and "loyal" creatures, they "lumber out / in pious herds / each dawn" (*Terror,* 40-41, and *New and Selected,* 121-23). The animation of the buses is engaging; and the alliteration, rhyme, and diction are felicitous. **"Photomontage of the Urban Parks"** philosophically fancies all urban parks merging together:

> Versailles and Schoenbrunn, waltzing knee to knee,
> Elope into the eighteenth century.
> All spins and mixes. Who cried, "Stop!"? Alarms
> Won't help now. Faster. Whirlwind, whirl again
> A park called Eden, Francis *with* Saint Pan:
> The white snow with the rainbow in her arms.
> (*Terror,* 47, and *New and Selected,* 101)

All urban parks have an element of Eden in them, and St. Francis and Pan paradoxically mix; the contrast in the last line, echoing the ballad "Sir Patrick Spence," also suggests that this antithesis is "the new moone / Wi the auld moone in hir arme. . . ." In the early 1960's, in transforming a narrative poem into his play *The Tree Witch,* Viereck inserted several speeches in this satirical manner. Many of these are clever parodies—"Little boy Geiger, come blow your horn; / There's beep in the meadow, there's borsht in the corn," and "Give us this day our daily treadmill. . ."

Viereck retains a touch of this early comic manner—one transmuted with a delight in the indecorous—in his mature, serious poetry. The diction of **"Some Lines in Three Parts,"** a poem about "the birth of song," demonstrates this quality (*Strike,* 45-49, and *New and Selected,* 96-97). Unpoetic words and phrases reveal the difficult process of song's emergence—"stinking trash," "ululations," "squints," and "squawks." Sometimes onomatopoeic, colloquial, or simply unbeautiful—"A cartilaginous, most rheumatic squeak," "bawling beauty out," "hubbub," "hooting," "squash," and "cooped"—the words of the poem illustrate Viereck's terror-decorum dichotomy.

The "winged ego" asks himself in the first part of **"Some Lines,"** "What ailed me from the arsenals of shape / To rent so armorless a pilgrim's cape?" Beginning colloquially ("What *ailed* me. . . ."), the line proceeds to the elevated figure "arsenals," implying that the ego could have chosen some other "shape" than that of the "ridiculously vulnerable" one of "the human forehead." In the second line, "To rent" continues this trope; this costume was transiently and vulgarly *rented.* Next, "armorless" and "pilgrim's cape," on the same level of diction as "arsenals," stress the fragility of the shape rented. The incongruity of these juxtaposed images in these lines and throughout the poem represents the eventual aim of the "comic" aspect of Viereck's poetry.

III Mystery of Mortality

Restoring "fun" and "human-ness" to poetry is to Viereck one of his central poetic functions, and in his best poems the tone is often still jocose but with a serious intention. Unlike the poems already cited (with the exception of **"Some Lines"**), in these poems the wit, satiric or ironic or non-poetic, is consonant with his lines "I'll honor gaucheness anywhere I find it / And the deep sadness of a shaggy hope" (*First Morning,* 77, and *New and Selected,* 125). A gauche pathos, shaggy hopes, and deep sadnesses prevail in his tender, humanistic view of man.

Like many twentieth-century men who fiercely refuse the panacea of any "friend in the sky" and who also share what has been called the modern world's "amazement at the silence of God," Viereck remains bound to earth and humanity. But, as Selden Rodman has pointed out, Viereck does not negate; he affirms vigorously, sadly, and joyously "that life cannot be altered for the better either by retreat from humanity or by superimposing on man the authority of any institution, stately or godly."[7] Though this earth be an "uninhabitable planet" because of its "built-in cellar of error, death, decay," still, Viereck says, it is the only world man will ever get. And its joys and satisfactions, griefs and tragedies season one another. "For a while it was good to have been the word 'Man.'" One should embrace life's laughs and its sadnesses, and when the time comes accept the end with stoic calm. Meanwhile, the poet offers as comforts love and companionship, the beauties of life, and the enjoyment of nature, color, food, wine, and other sensual pleasures. The principal danger in life is that "the radiance of tragedy," of complete acceptance of all parts of existence, will be snuffed out; and, "unlaughing and untragic," man will be vended mere "Pleasure, which turns out to be / An optimistic mechanized despair."

To warn men against this "optimistic mechanized despair," Viereck catalogues life's transcending beauties: "glittering flesh," "rain's tilt," and "sheen of snow." Since "casual earthlings" fail to value their "angels" of lucky glances, Viereck inverts the world to reveal what is there. His "tree poems," as well as some of his other poems on odd subjects which do so, have the quality best described by Herman Melville's "strike through the mask!" which Viereck used as a book title. "All visible objects, man, are but as pasteboard masks," Ahab of *Moby Dick* said. "If man will strike, strike through the mask! How can the prisoner reach outside except by thrusting through the wall? . . . Oh! how immaterial are all materials!" Behind the "mask" (the material *accidents* of nature) to be struck through, lies the spiritual *substance* of existence.

The poems on odd subjects ordinarily make mythic use of an individual (Kilroy, Apollo) or of an object (graves, a potato, the dawn horse, a town square, a tree) to articulate truths about life—the surfacing of buried instincts, mutability, yearning, consistency of experience, and other similar ideas. **"You All Are Static: I Alone Am Moving"** (a young tree addresses humanity), one of Viereck's first tree poems, charmingly presents the view found in these poems. Like Montaigne asking "When I play with my cat, who knows if I am not a pastime to her more than she is to me?," Viereck's persona, a young tree, assumes that *he* moves—not humanity or its mobile artifacts such as trains.

The young tree loves, lives, feels, runs, jumps, threshes the air. He strides through time and space, exuberantly proclaiming his superiority to his surroundings; he has, too, the gnawing doubt that he (like humanity) supposes is his alone: "Why did the God who keeps you blind, / Instead give sight and sentience to my flowers?" As fable, the poem lightly limns a central human problem, the mystery of being mortal, man's aspirations toward Absolutes while earthbound—or while, in the words of the poem, such contraries as "bugs and diamonds agonize [his] roots" (*Terror*, 14, and *New and Selected,* 3).

Some of the other tree poems, **"My Gentlest Song"** and **"To My Playmate,"** are also richly human and melancholy. In the former, the narrator, a pine tree, presumes his immortality because he outlives his "Small friend," the rose. Saddened that the rose has death while he has winter sleep ahead, the tree cries: "How many times I've wished me dead instead!" But he must not help her, he says,

> For it's not I who made you less than wood.
> You—bright brief putrefying weed—
> Will feed my roots next spring, will feed
> The fabulous white-hot darkness at my core.
>   (*Strike*, 10, and *New and Selected*, 9)

The pine is humanity fed by the momentary beauty of the rose. The tree in **"To My Playmate"** also represents humanity, but the meaning of his "playmate" attached to him by hemp (a hanging man) is less clear. Most likely it is man's soul or at least his perfection, the *dignity* of his soul; for the closing lines suggest such an interpreta-

tion. There the tree asks: "How long, O fruit, since ripeness burst your skin? / Commemorate that second birth. You bore / What every triviality of flesh / Is pregnant with: the perfect bone within" (*Strike*, 15, and *New and Selected*, 10). The poem rounds out with the familiar paradox that, unless the grain (fruit) dies, it cannot live. The perfection of man is revealed by striking through the mask of his flesh.

This "perfection" of man is treated in **"Crass Times"** as his **"Dignity of Soul"** and in Viereck's prose as man's individuality or the "unadjustedness," which adds spontaneity and terror to life. Man's simply being man makes difficult an existence which still can be satisfying:

> The weight that tortures diamonds out of coals
> Is lighter than the skimming hooves of foals
> Compared to one old heaviness our souls
> Hoist daily, each alone, and cannot share:
> To-be-awake, to sense, to-be-aware.
>   (*Terror*, 107, and *New and Selected*, 58)

As the title of the first book of poems indicates, "terror" hovers close to the ordered surface of life. Waltzing on graves, man should be aware that his "disowned deep-buried banished brothers," his "horrid atavisms," are "hands" waiting to "reach out to drag [him] down below." This conjunction Viereck calls "the dualism of the primordial 'dark gods' of the unconscious and the more rational, civilized conscious mind" (*Mid-Century,* 26). The antithesis between the two can make man shiver with "holy dread," despite life's other joys. Only artistic creation or love can temporarily quell the terror: " . . . we, all vulnerable and all distress, / Have no brief shield but love and loveliness. / Quick—let me touch your body as we die (*Terror*, 74, and *New and Selected*, 23).

But "Earth is the center still, despite our science"; and what earth has to offer, man should joyfully accept—the fruits of the season be they "malediction's midnight lions" or the joys of August. Arethusa, the stream, for instance, having existed and known kinship when a doe crossed her and made "hoofprints on [her] mirror," thinks while dying that she will "find no hoofprints on the sky" (*First Morning*, 19). Love, companionship, and fellow feeling are earthly, not heavenly possibilities.

IV *Man and Poet*

Earthbound and, even more, his "ego . . . trapped in its vulnerable mortal skull," man attempts "to burst free," Viereck says, "by means of song." The poet and the poetic process are recurrent subjects for Viereck because of his exalted concept of the liberating function of poetry. Man as poet is more than man, or different from him; he is the possessed, inspired creature of the visionary tradition that reaches back to Plato and encompasses William Blake, Samuel Taylor Coleridge, Friedrich Hoelderlin, Charles Baudelaire, Hart Crane, and others.

A prose insert and several poems in *Terror and Decorum* present the poet as the "culture-hero, the showman as shaman, the clown as priest." In **"A Walk on Snow,"** for example, magic and art are "hoax redeemed by awe." Deliberate and planned, art knows itself for what it is: "Art, being bartender, is never drunk; / And magic that believes itself, must die." The artist (poet) is "Not priest but clown," and he "Is more astounded than his rapt applauders" when he achieves success: "Then all those props and Easters of my stage / Came true? But I was joking all the time!" Only in not-believing, in not being "drunk," can the poet arrive at truth. The speaker in **"A Walk on Snow,"** "drunk with self-belief," asks more of his "star" than he should; hence the spell snaps:

> Ring all you like, the lines are disconnected.
> Knock all you like, no one is ever home.
> (Unfrocked magicians freeze the whole night long;
> Holy iambic can not thaw the snow
> They walk on when obsessive crystals bloom.)
>   (*Terror*, 53, and *New and Selected*, 156)

In **"Poet,"** the opening poem of *Terror and Decorum*, Viereck presents his esthetics more candidly than in **"A Walk on Snow"** or in **"Africa and My New York,"** **"The Killer and the Dove,"** and **"Jollie Gleeman,"** the other poems in this volume that concern the poet. With no geographical or narrative intrusions, **"Poet"** moves metaphorically in an abstract world of the creative imagination. The epigraph in French states the theme: "All created form, even that created by man, is immortal. For the form is independent of the material, and it is not the particles that make up the form" (Baudelaire, *My Heart Stripped Bare*). The death of the poet "liberates" the shabby images, rhymes, parts of speech, and punctuation marks that in life, as poet-ruler, he had sent into exile. Viewing **"Poet"** as a compressed elegy, one can read the first two stanzas on the freeing of "lush adverbs, senile rhymes," as the mourning ruefulness of not having the classic poet to wrest order out of the chaos of language. Stanza three, then, is the "But he is not dead" section of a conventional elegy; and the controlling metaphor is a musical one. Part of a "living thousand-year / Tyrannic metronome," the great poetic tradition of beautifying experience, the poet "lives on in Form, and Form shall shatter / This tuneless mutiny of matter."

This monstrous, over-arching power that the poet exerts is the "terror [that] crowns the sweetness of all song. . . ." A molder, the poet "hammers us to shapes we never planned . . ."; he alters man by making him change, causing him to experience "a different dying," one immune to all exorcism. A "haunter" indestructible, the poet eludes man; in his frustration man guesses that he is being blessed when he least knows it, "and when coldest art / Seems hostile, / useless, / or apart." Finally, as an ultimate creator, the poet is not the food for worms that most dead men are; he remains an immortal singer:

> Not worms, not worms in such a skull
> But rhythms, rhythms writhe and sting and crawl.
> He sings the seasons round, from bud to snow.
> And all things are because he willed them so.
>   (*Terror*, 5, and *New and Selected*, 93)

"Some Lines in Three Parts" develops this theme. Classic song, Viereck writes in his epigraph, "is outwardly terrifying as much as inwardly decorous." "This moment of 'holy dread' [is] . . . as unbearably ugly as birth and creativity always are . . ." (*Mid-Century*, 26). "Self ousts itself, consumed and consummated; / An inward-facing mask is what must break . . ."; and, "Possessed by metamorphosis," the owl has "writhed" out of him philomel: "Moulted, naked, two-thirds dead, / From shock and pain (and dread of holy dread) / Suddenly vomiting" (*Strike*, 49, and *New and Selected*, 97).

Poetry is an inescapable obsession. Prospero might wish to bid farewell to his wand of song, to be "free," to enjoy his "safe new peace"; but he cannot: "While winds are promises, / How can I bid the wand of song goodbye? / While even one stray cloud has eyes that bless and bless, / I must sing or I must die" (*Strike*, 38). The poet cannot choose how, when, or in what shape poetry is to come; he "must . . . take each molted eagle / Just as he comes or do without." And he cannot always do full justice to what comes: "Each clowning, sweetish, harsh-cored vision / That shoots from the persimmon tree" is always "wronged"; and "earth is / A drabber patch than need have been" (*Persimmon*, 50, and *New and Selected*, 91).

The thematic statement affixed to **"At the River Charles"** abstracts the stages in this poetic process. The first and lowest is "mere material flux"; the second "is inner and spiritual but too awake, too willed: view but not vision." The third and final stage, then, is "vision: kept only by not trying to keep it, by not subjecting it to will and daytime wisdom" (*Persimmon*, 10, and *New and Selected*, 77). A symbol of this "vision" is woman or her "girl" aspect. Woman, on the one hand, is Muse and the "race's unshrined core"; on the other, "aunt, guardian, toilet-trainer," nurses, Furies—everything that inhibits man and poet. The Muse mediates between the poet and the primitive springs of life; but the Fury, the confining force in life, is woman also. The girl-woman division, implicit in Viereck's earliest poetry, finds its fullest expression in *The Tree Witch* (1961); in it both Muse and Fury are part of man. If he chooses the woman-Fury, he has safety, security, conformity; but the girl-Muse troubles his dreams.

V EZRA POUND AND HART CRANE

In his prose Viereck names many poets, among them Eliot, Frost, Auden, Wallace Stevens, Yeats, John Crowe Ransom, Allen Tate, Vachel Lindsay, Robert Lowell, Theodore Roethke, and Theodore Spencer. And Viereck has written perceptively in articles and reviews on the poetry of some of these poets and as well on that of Richard Wilbur, Thomas Hornsby Ferril, and several "younger poets." The two poets of an earlier era about whom his remarks are more personal than literary are Ezra Pound and Hart Crane. Commenting on "The love-hate relationship between our Middle West and its tormented rebel artists" in *Shame and Glory*, he cited Pound and Crane (115). Since the Middle West for Viereck is "America," as opposed to metropolitan areas (*urban* America or "New

York"), the quotations he selects from each show that they symbolize for him the condition of the artist in America: from Crane, "I could not pull the arrows from my side"; from Pound, civilization is "a bitch gone in the teeth."

Both poets are tragic: Crane, in his unhappy, short life and early suicide; Pound, in his youthful self-exile from America and in his later suffering of obloquy because of his support of fascism in his elder years. The significance of both poets to Viereck needs no documenting for any reader of his works, for their names recur frequently in his prose. Poets of Viereck's age could hardly escape the influence of either, and Viereck has admitted that he was "influenced in part by" Pound (along with Eliot, Ransom, William Empson, and Cleanth Brooks [*Mid-Century*, 49]). He also valued, he has said, Pound's insights and his "post-Imagist and pre-canto" poetry (*Dream*, 6). Of the poets immediately preceding him, Crane most resembles Viereck in several ways. But each poet stands for certain qualities in Viereck's imagination.

Pound is Viereck's main target in the "revolt against revolt"; he is the poet of obscurity, ethical irresponsibility (anti-Semitism), formlessness, and much else. Older than Hart Crane by fourteen years, Pound is of Viereck's father's generation. Like the elder Viereck, Pound, a poet of "poetic" behavior, is flamboyant and self-assertive. Later poets, those of Peter Viereck's time, the so-called "silent generation," are, on the contrary, reluctant "to advertise their personalities at the expense of their work. . . ."[8] Like George Sylvester Viereck, Pound also chose the fascist side in the important political alignment of the 1930's and 1940's.

Peter Viereck once called "simple human compassion for Hitler's millions of tortured victims . . . the deepest emotional and moral experience of our era . . ." (*Dream*, 14). "Deepest" is the important word. For Viereck feels deeply and always writes harshly about anti-Semitism— as in a 1940 article, in his first two prose books, and in many other places. In a 1960 article—an analysis of Vachel Lindsay's poetry—Father Coughlin, anti-Semitism, and Ezra Pound are cited in a single paragraph. Thus Viereck seldom writes anything on poetry or politics, early or late, but that Pound intrudes. Indeed, the 1949 Bollingen Award granted to Pound brought Viereck to a "cruel crossroads." **"Like a Sitting Breeze"** (*First Morning*, 98) presents his interior conflict as one between dueling or, like a lovely petal, merely falling.

Not yet choosing either silence or public attack of the award to Pound,[9] Viereck first says that he will choose beauty, not duty; art-for-art's sake, not responsibility. Next, though, he asks to be suspended in the "choiceless Now." But one must choose; if fallen petals could return to trees and "If hoverers could wait where they want and never ever fall, / I'd stay," he says, "Like a sitting breeze." Of course, despite the common phrase, breezes cannot *sit*, and neither can the poet. Hence, "(petal-treading now) / I'm off to the lonely duel by the water's edge again."

Such duels are always lonely, but for Viereck his posture in the Bollingen-Pound case was more markedly "lonely" than usual. Objecting to the award on moral grounds, he was accused by defenders of modern poetry of "unconsciously serving the philistines," all those who would use his objections "as a demagogic weapon against . . . everything that challenges the reader to effort" (*Dream*, 12). These "philistines" used the furor aroused by the award to Pound to attack all modern poetry and, incidentally, to impute fascist sympathies to the Bollingen judges.

A second position, that of the Bollingen judges (Eliot, Tate, Conrad Aiken, Karl Shapiro, and others), was that, as their official press release phrased it, "To permit other considerations than that of poetic achievement . . . would in principle deny the validity of that objective perception of value on which any civilized society must rest." On this side, Viereck said, "The sympathies . . . were not with [Pound's] fascist politics but with the widely held argument . . . that artistic form can be considered apart from its content" ("Beyond Revolt," 52). The "dissatisfaction which greeted . . . [the] *Pisan Cantos*" "divided" Parnassus and, for Viereck, made the Pound-Bollingen issue "the most important literary controversy of the decade" ("Beyond Revolt," 33, and *Unadjusted*, 287). The "published magazine controversies" only articulated the general reaction against the "cult of obfuscating for the sake of obfuscating and of shocking merely for the sake of shocking . . . "; "young people . . . good students or good writers or good readers . . . with the best will in the world cannot find [the *Pisan Cantos*] beautiful" ("Beyond Revolt," 33, 34).

Viereck insists that the Pisan cantos lack "beauty"; "fascism and anti-semitism compose one of the[ir] essential 'myths'" ("Beyond Revolt," 52); therefore, "the poem was not intended as purely aesthetic." It is, instead, "98 per cent incoherent, 2 per cent lovely, and persistently fascist and anti-Semitic . . ." (*Mid-Century*, 28). "Its message politically was that Mussolini was martyred and World War II caused by the Jews: 'the goyim go to saleable slaughter' for 'the yidd,' known as 'David rex the prime s.o.b.' This is politics, not serious poetry, hence not exempt from ethical, as well as aesthetic condemnation" (*Dream*, 14). This quotation from Pound and two other repellent ones ("Pétain defended Verdun while Blum was defending a bidet" and "Geneva the usurers' dunghill / Frogs, brits, with a few dutch pimps") Viereck frequently cites as examples of the impossibility of finding any "technical embellishments" or "beautiful poetry" in the *Cantos*.[10]

The point would be better taken if other lines from the book were occasionally quoted; for "among the countless ugly pages," Viereck perceives only "a dozen lines of power and loveliness": the "Pull down thy vanity" passage of **"Canto 81"** and the four lines beginning "Tudor indeed is gone" in the preceding canto.[11] Moreover, Viereck's acceptance of the necessity and, at times, of the desirability of the "ugly" and the indecorous in his own poetry and his insistence on the lack of the "beautiful" and of "lines . . . of loveliness" in Pound manifest a failure of literary perspective in regard to the older poet.

But Hart Crane is another matter. For Viereck—as for Robert Lowell, John Wheelwright, and Allen Ginsberg—Hart Crane dramatizes the problem of the artist in America. Viereck treats Crane at most length in **"The Poet in the Machine Age"** (1948) and in **"The Crack-Up of American Optimism"** (1960). The references to Crane, more diffused than those to Pound, vary from specific comments on his meter (his conversational spondees), to praise of separate poems (Crane's "Repose of Rivers") or his manner ("sensuous lyricism"), to use of him as a personal symbol. In *Shame and Glory,* Viereck sees Crane as a symbol "*From* Rive Gauche *Back to Pattern*," and he quotes six lines from one of Crane's "Uncollected Poems," material originally printed as prose.[12] A friend had told Crane that he must "loose" himself "within a pattern's mastery," the pattern, as Viereck sees it, of "Mediterranean classicism" against which "german romanticism" had revolted (*Shame and Glory,* 77).

In *The Unadjusted Man* Viereck writes that "The traditional flight, from west and south to New York, still was essential to the creativity of a Hart Crane in the 1920's" (15). Furthermore, Crane is one example of "the unadjusted yet traditional individualist" in America (*Unadjusted,* 25-26). In **"Look, Hart, That Horse You Ride Is Wood"** (*Terror*, 45-46), Viereck begins with a quotation from Crane's "The Tunnel": "the River that is East." In the poem, Viereck shows Crane sauntering "toward Saint-Terre"; outlines Crane's tragic career: "A Holy Land's a nowhere land; / Ohio's everywhere"; and ends with New York as "the clerks his daddy hired / Plus gin plus sea; then Hart felt tired, / Drank both and drowned." While well-phrased, the poem, in doubtful taste ("For love of sails and sailors"), uses Crane less well than another poem in which "The spindrift awe of Hart's obsessive pet / Seal" is one of the examples of looking "backwards / inward": "Earth's faces jammed against His windowpane" (*Terror*, 15, and *New and Selected*, 53).

"The Poet in the Machine Age" (1948) devotes the last few pages to Crane. The "poet who rightly called himself 'the Pindar of the Machine Age,'" Viereck wrote, was "By far the most exciting pro-mechanist . . ." (*Dream,* 61). From Crane's 1929 essay on the function of art in the machine age, Viereck quoted a long passage which mirrors his own views. Poetry would fail of its "full contemporary function," Crane had written, if it should not be able to "absorb the machine," acclimatize it as, in other eras, it had nature, animals, buildings, ships, and other things. Certainly, Crane had continued, the poet would not need to overstress machinery or even to mention specific machines. But, to absorb the machine, he must have, besides his usual qualifications, "an extraordinary capacity for surrender," perhaps only momentarily, "to the sensations of urban life."[13] Such absorption and acclimatization is Viereck's concept, "Manhattan classicism," wheels and aspirations, wheels plus tulips, America and New York. The two "worlds" "of the spirit and machinery," Viereck said later in his machine-age essay, need to be joined by the "unifying artist" who can see "beauty in both and not merely [in] one" of them. If they

cannot be mediated, "our road to hell will be paved with good inventions" (*Strike,* 69).

A poem written in the mid-1950's on Hart Crane and Goethe (*Persimmon,* 62-63, and *New and Selected,* 93-96) begins once more with a Crane line, the opening of one of the stanzas of "For the Marriage of Faustus and Helen": "The siren of the springs of guilty song. . . ." Viereck comments that Crane's jazzy "siren" was "not the muse of Weimar's hushed salon." Though in the ensuing dialogue Crane and Goethe represent romantic and classic polarities, viereck does not elevate Goethe at the expense of Crane. In fact, Goethe is made to say that Crane's "gift is more Athenian than Doric; / Your best songs are not ruggedly folkloric / Nor grossly and gregariously choric / But subtly—this I honor—esoteric." And to have each find the "other strangely right" is the **"Homage"** Viereck finally pays the two poets.

Setting forth American literature's "two conflicting traditions, the first romantic and progressive, the second classical and conservative," in the 1960 essay on Vachel Lindsay, Viereck writes that "The first [tradition] heartily affirms American folklore, American democratic and material progress. That Whitman-Emerson literary tradition cracked up in Vachel Lindsay and Hart Crane . . . not merely in their personal breakdowns and final suicides . . . but in the aesthetic breakdown of the myth-making part of their poetry. The non-mythic part of their poetry, its pure lyricism, never did break down and in part remains lastingly beautiful."[14]

Crane's "pure lyricism" is, therefore, what Viereck values most. Crane's and Lindsay's "attempts to create a new, untragic kind of myth for America" failed, Viereck thinks; because, like any other human being, "the democratic American" pays "the spiritual price . . . for industrial progress." The combining of the classic and romantic traditions, Goethe *and* Crane, Viereck saw realized in the Manhattan classicism of his generation of poets who were the sons and grandsons of Ezra Pound and Hart Crane; learning from their masters, these younger poets made their own baroque synthesis.

NOTES

[1] "Poets Versus Readers," *Atlantic,* CLXXX (July, 1947), 109. The material in this section on Viereck's poetics is taken from the article above, from his other early *Atlantic* articles listed in the Notes and in the Bibliography and from these articles of his: "For a Third Force in Poetry Today," New York *Herald Tribune Book Review,* September 3, 1950, p. 3; "My Kind of Poetry," in *Mid-Century American Poets,* ed. John Ciardi (New York, 1950), referred to as *Mid-Century;* and "Beyond Revolt: The Education of a Poet" in *Arts in Renewal,* ed. Sculley Bradley (New York, 1961), pp. 32-66. Another poetic credo, also referred to in this section, is "Dignity of Lyricism" (abbreviated "Lyricism") in *The Unadjusted Man.* Another statement of Viereck's poetics is "Conflict and Resolution" in *The Christian Science Monitor,* December 29, 1966, p. 8, a revision of earlier "outdated" credos (private communication).

[2] "For a Third Force," p. 3.

[3] "Conflict and Resolution," p. 8.

[4] Simpson, p. 112.

[5] "Apollo in New York," *New Republic*, C (August 9, 1939), 16.

[6] Selden Rodman (ed.), "Introduction," *100 Modern Poems* (New York, 1951), p. xxx.

[7] *Ibid.*

[8] Simpson, p. 111.

[9] "Correspondence Relating to 'Like a Sitting Breeze' by Peter Viereck," *American Scholar*, XX (Spring, 1951), 217.

[10] "Parnassus Divided," *Atlantic*, CLXXXIV (October, 1949), 70.

[11] *Ibid.*

[12] Waldo Frank (ed.), *The Complete Poems of Hart Crane* (Garden City, New York, 1958), pp. 156-57.

[13] *Ibid.*, p. 181; quoted in *Dream and Responsibility* (Washington, D.C., 1953), p. 63.

[14] "The Crack-Up of American Optimism: Vachel Lindsay, The Dante of the Fundamentalists," *Modern Age*, IV (Summer, 1960), 275.

Phoebe Pettingell (review date 1987)

SOURCE: "Peter Viereck's Cross," *The New Leader*, Vol. LXX, No. 11, August 10-24, 1987, pp. 16-17.

[*In the following review, Pettingell examines the grand ambitions of* Archer in the Marrow: The Applewood Cycles *and concludes that Viereck identifies art with morality.*]

Two decades ago, Peter Viereck began writing an epic cycle of poems about man's attempts to come to terms with a confusing world and its presiding deity, if any. To call such a project risky would be an understatement. In the first place, the very theme brings to mind the greatest works of Dante, Milton and Goethe—formidable competition! In the second place, long poems were especially unfashionable at the time. Even a writer as popular as Robert Lowell found little audience for his *History* sonnet sequence (republished as *Notebooks* to sound more spontaneous and fragmented). Viereck believes his own poems were unacceptable to the "literary establishment" because of an article he wrote for *Commentary* in 1950, where he argued that the Bollingen poetry prize should not have been awarded to Ezra Pound on the grounds that Pound's anti-Semitism and treasonable views infected his verse. Whether or not this opinion, unpopular enough with the poetry community of the day, had anything to do with it, Viereck's poems did stop receiving the attention they had previously attracted. The spirit of the '60s and '70s demanded simple, emotional lyrics, not the ironic complexity of form and thought that typifies his work.

Viereck nevertheless persevered, and fashion is changing once more, so finally *Archer in the Marrow: The Applewood Cycles, 1967-1987* has appeared. Throughout 18 cycles, God the Father, God the Son (both Jesus and Dionysus) and "You"—a modern Everyman, alternately male and female—circle round one another in a wary battle of wits. "Applewood" refers, of course, to the tree in Eden from which Adam and Eve (identified with You) plucked the fruit of knowledge, thus defying the Almighty. For Christians, the crucifixion of Jesus—the "Second Adam"—wiped out this primal disobedience. The Middle Ages embroidered the redemptive idea with a legend that Eden originally covered the hill of Golgotha outside Jerusalem, and that the tree of knowledge was cut down to make Christ's cross. In Viereck's scenario, God created Man to be a toy, but men, by exercising free will, became as gods. The Crucified must evolve from passive suffering into a dionysiac figure, the Archer who can teach man to shoot back at the controlling Father: "Pierced hands . . . bending cross into crossbow. / Look: goatfoot Jesus on the village green."

The gnostic struggle between parent and child has been one of the traditional themes of literature—the only one, according to some. Viereck handles his drama as burlesque or revue. The four principles put on different hats, or dance out with a new prop to suggest a change of scene. Often, the stage directions call for a song or a soft-shoeroutine. Puns and irony abound. God the Father whines,

> *Of all the ark's worst monsters, two by two,*
> *The apple-biter nearly bit me. Whew,*
> *I should have sired some unobtrusive zoo*
> *Like minotaurs and swan eggs. What a jam!*
> *All because Mary had*
> *A little Lamb.*

Some scenes take place outside time, and a few in other universes—where Western Europe lost the Crusades and became Moslem, Lucrezia Borgia was elected pope, or George Orwell's *1984* came true. Auschwitz figures prominently, together with Pope John XXIII's characterization of the Holocaust as "the second crucifixion." Once, You exclaims that the apple pit "has grown a mushroom shape." At the poem's end, yet another cycle is about to begin.

Obviously Viereck's passion play redounds with meanings; they spill over into copious stage directions, footnotes, glossaries, and appendices. The relentless message of *Archer* is that art *is* morality. In an appendix looking back to the Pound controversy, Viereck argues that "Unlike the Right and Left totalitarians, we should never judge art by its politics. But [Pound's poetry was] not a matter of politics or economics; it was a matter of ethics, a metaphysics of evil. Evil does indeed fall into the purview of esthetic criticism because it parches empathy and hence the artist's creative imagination." Pound, and Richard Wagner before him, did not limit the expression of their hateful views to incidental prose writings; they wove them into their principal works: *The*

Pisan Cantos and *The Ring of the Nibelung.* Nietzsche warned that Wagnerian anti-Semitism would engender a "bloodbath." Orwell wrote in 1949 that the views Pound "tried to disseminate in his works are evil." Agreeing with both, Viereck insists that art is an exercise in empathy, the greatest good we as humans can know or practice. Poems devoid of empathy—lyrics of no content, propagandistic doggerel, verse that promotes antihumanistic attitudes—are not merely defective or incomplete; they are a force for wickedness.

Viereck's second major polemical concern is form in poetry. In an appendix subtitled **"Would Jacob Wrestle with a Flabby Angel?"** he insists that "Whether our biological pendulum (the thump THUMP of artery and lung) is but the split iambic of a song, or vice versa, either way biology and poetry are welded by the same scannable tide. The welding not only throws new light on the odd, obsessive quality of poetry's magic; it re-establishes, in the teeth of current opinion, the dependence of that magic on the continuity of traditional meters and even of rhymes." *The Applewood Cycles* are written in a dazzling variety of metrical patterns. Viereck has also invented a new system he calls "crisscross," in which the first and last syllables of each line rhyme with the last and first syllables of the following one:

> *Doubting in a garden*
> *When will I climb out?*
> *Crying on a tree:*
> *Me, father? Why?*

This scheme, in addition to offering a subtle and pleasing variation to the ear, makes for less "filler" than when the poet merely has to concentrate on end rhymes.

But *Archer in the Marrow* is not simply a poem of ideas written in a variety of forms; it is a manifesto in defense of formalism as humanism. Iambs beat in time with the human heart. The galloping rhythms of anapest and dactyl mimic the excitement of a racing pulse, or "the interacting different tempo'd pulsations of two bodies intensely joined, as in love or combat." Viereck thinks that the "rebellion" of free verse depended on ears trained to hear the counterpoint of a steady beat, and thus able to appreciate the disruption of the expected scheme. For ears ignorant of regular patterns, chaos becomes the norm. "Why, one gets asked in poetry 'workshops,' why isn't it just as natural for poems to scan every which way as to move along on alternate beats? The condign reply is a counterquestion: Do human beings move like amoebas, on pseudopods every which way, or on two feet with alternate steps?" Viereck concedes that by the early decades of this century, a lot of formal poetry had become dull and predictable. Nevertheless, he says, "the road-not-taken would have led—can still lead . . . through the unconventional delicate rhythms of de la Mare, the vigorous ones of Hardy, the agonized iambic pentameters of Charlotte Mew, and the ecstatic ones of Hart Crane and Roethke, with Frost (not the folksy fake but the fierce fox) central rather than peripheral." Avoidance of form has bred sloppy self-indulgence. Rhyme and rhythm are a strong angel; it is in wrestling meaning from

such an adversary, Viereck believes, that the poet discovers his true voice.

Ultimately, prosody reflects the music of the spheres as well as that of our own bodies. "Rhythm is Time in leotards," the ebb and flow of life as a dance: Intricate measures are worked into a pattern unseen by the performers but visible to anyone watching. This being his creed, no wonder Viereck castigates both the orthodox formalists, such as the Southern Fugitives, and freedom-fighters like the Beats. The two represent flip sides of "the same coin: form made sterile or form uprooted." He charges that the former group made poetry an elite game; the latter reduced all complexity to a "howl."

Regular readers of these pages know that I have been calling attention lately to a revival of richness of sound and sense in poetry, qualities that seemed lost after the Modernists. One can't imagine Viereck's *Applewood Cycles* attracting serious attention (not to mention a publisher) during the '60s and '70s. As for his essay on form, it would have provoked more derision than his views on Pound did in 1950. He has, indeed, wrestled against the current, and *Archer in the Marrow* is the stronger for it.

Viereck has more allies, though, than he acknowledges— perhaps than he knows of. The unexpected success of James Merrill's *The Changing Light at Sandover* encouraged further poetic cycles justifying God's ways to man, or vice versa. Merrill and John Hollander have been defending meter with arguments similar to Viereck's for decades. Moreover, I have never been able to quite accept the conspiracy theory that authors who promulgate unfashionable opinions are blackballed by the establishment (hardly a united body itself). In a free market system, editors offer the public what they think it wants. Once upon a time, august critics, writing in serious journals, may have shaped tastes, but today's poets advertise themselves through readings and workshops.

We should be grateful, however, for Viereck's provocative statement of his case. It will promote debate and, one hopes, enrich the terms. Arguments about the biological roots of rhythm ought to join the disputes about the right and left sides of the brain. In the fervor of the Freudian '40s, physiological causes were discounted; in the present intellectual cycle, biology is again destiny, for poets and critics too. By all means read *Archer in the Marrow* to set your own pulse racing, your own juices flowing.

Michael Lind (essay date 1988)

SOURCE: Review of *Archer in the Marrow: The Applewood Cycles, National Review*, Vol. XL, No. 2, February 5, 1988, pp. 55-56.

[*In the following review, Lind calls* Archer in the Marrow: The Applewood Cycles *a "philosophical poem" and suggests that it marks Viereck's return to German romanticism.*]

There Are two Peter Vierecks—or are there? In his astonishing poetic sequence *Archer in the Marrow*, the

Pulitzer Prize-winning poet deals with favorite concerns in a style familiar to those who know Viereck primarily as a political polemicist.

Viereck, an historian at Mount Holyoke now in his eighth decade, helped define the "New Conservatism" of the early Fifties with his *Conservatism Revisited* (1949) and *Conservatism: From John Adams to Churchill* (1956). Somewhat like George Will today, Viereck argued for the compatibility of Tory paternalism and New Deal statism; he praised Metternich, voted for Stevenson, and waited for the *gauche* Right mustered by the young Wm. F. Buckley Jr. to go away. Instead, it was Viereck who went away, retiring from conservative debate around the time he cast his Tory vote for Kennedy.

If Viereck the polemicist has long since fallen silent, Viereck the poet has come into his own. *Archer in the Marrow*, the product of two decades of invention and revision, is Viereck's bid for a place in the American pantheon. The bid is a daring one, particularly because the form he has chosen—the philosophical poem—has been a siren shipwrecking poets from Hesiod and Lucretius to Wordsworth. Not even the artistry of Dante and Goethe could have saved their masterworks from tedium without the interest of characters and the impulse of drama.

Viereck should have learned from their example. His poem is a collection of 18 allegorical morality plays, linked by a dialogue among three personae: Father, Son, and "You." The scene shifts from Land's End to Gethsemane; characters include a lungfish avatar of "You" and a voluble potato. Were it not for Viereck's taut prosody and jazzy diction, *Archer* would be incomprehensible and dull; as it is, it is incomprehensible and intriguing.

In his metrical traditionalism and his use of Christian symbols in a portmanteau philosophy of his own, Viereck resembles Yeats, whom Viereck extols as a model for future poets in an essay appended to his poem. Lines like: *"Are we waltzers or waltz?"* and, *"Am I the stone, the slinger, or the sling?"* are among the less subtle echoes of the Yeatsian music. At his best, Viereck can make the language sing as few contemporary poets can:

> If blossoms could blossom
> One petal of petals
> To whom all other blooms are
> As leaves are to flowers,
> It would be to the others
> As you are, my daughter,
> To all other daughters
> Whom songs are adoring.

Viereck is more at home with the epigrammatic than the elegiac: *"Whose vision is it, yours or mine, that garbles? / Men see marble, God sees marbles."*

More is required of a philosopher in verse than the ability to write masterly lyrics. Viereck's philosophy—whether in poetry or in polemics—can be summed up, in Viereck's own phrase, as the Third Way. He explains in a preface that

his poem "gropes for a third way. Gods being your own projections, only man's free choice can combine earth's Hellenic and Hebraic halves, Dionysus with Jesus, Aphrodite with Eve . . ." The poem concludes with the fusion of Christian transcendence and Dionysian immanence: *"Look: goatfoot Jesus on the village green."*

To personify complex traditions in cartoons and then to combine them in chimerical images is characteristic of Viereck, who, as the "New Conservative" and "Manhattan classicist," found no debate so irresolvable it could not be mooted by an oxymoron. In his political essays he relied on personification (e.g., Babbitt Jr., a caricature of left-liberal Fifties intellectuals) and on aphorism ("Anti-Catholicism is the anti-Semitism of the intellectuals") to do the work of argument. The following, from his **"Appendix: Form in Poetry,"** is Viereckism distilled: "Just as rooted lawful liberty is equally betrayed by reactionary authoritarianism and by its consequence, radical anarchy, so aesthetic form is equally betrayed by the anarchic formlessness of the barbaric yawpers and by the dead formalism of the elegant wincers."

That his faith in a higher third choice transcending and reconciling every opposition was identified by Carl Schmitt as characteristic of German Romanticism looks like cosmic irony when one remembers that Viereck began his career as a conservative with his first (and worst) book, *Metapolitics: From the Romantics to Hitler* (1940). Like another literary conservative, Irving Babbitt (no kin to Babbitt Jr.), Peter Viereck rebelled against a Romantic father, in his case the formidable George Sylvester Viereck, a prominent German-American poet and publicist who founded *The Fatherland* in 1914 and opposed U.S. entry into the Second World War. Babbitt, to the dismay of his disciple T.S. Eliot, was never able to return closer to Christian roots than belief in a vaguely Buddhist "inner check"; Viereck, however, seems to have made his way slowly back to the heritage from which he broke as a young man: the heritage of German Romanticism.

The search for a third way beyond the polarities of spirit and matter, evolution and eternity, form and content, brings to mind Schelling and Hegel.*"You've stuffed with 'God' the sky that left you friendless, / You taxidermists of the empty Endless"*—Viereck echoes Feuerbach. Theology will be unmasked as anthropology; alienation will be overcome through the reconciliation of paganism and Christianity; these are among the themes of *Archer in the Marrow*. By one of the most curious reversals in American intellectual history, the youthful admirer of Metternich has aged into a Left Hegelian. The elderly Viereck has arrived at the starting-point of the young Marx.

Robert McDowell (review date 1988)

SOURCE: "Collisions in Poetry," *The Hudson Review*, Vol. XL, No. 4, Winter 1988, pp. 677-85.

[*In the following review, McDowell praises the historical vision and philosophical breadth of* Archer in the

Marrow: The Applewood Cycles, *and he suggests that the seriousness of this book dwarves the works of many other contemporary poets.*]

Nearing the end of his life, Albert Einstein answered a question he had wrestled with all his life: Does God exist? Einstein concluded that God did exist, but did not really care about us. Peter Viereck's God, in his epic cycle, **Archer in the Marrow**, resembles Einstein's deity.

Woven into the texture of this book is a tremendous historical awareness, apt irony, and a rhythmic facility seldom encountered in contemporary poetry. The ghosts behind the rhetoric and sensibility include Beckett, Calvino, the mirthful Byron, and the Son's unnamed, adopted brother, Nietzsche. In addition, Viereck imposes the Yeatsian circular notion of time as a stage on which three main characters, Father, Son, and You (the Everyman) carry out their rigorous debate.

On this stage Old Galilee is interchangeable with New California. The machine subjugates the earth, which means that it subjugates Woman. In the Son's eyes, the Father looks down and sees earth as a toyland. At one point, the Son declares "The race is almost meaningful." The Father's response is stifling: "Your race was never meaningful." Meanwhile, the You constantly questions the pair until late in the poem he comes to this revelation:

> Too long I've been the buffer-brother
> Through whomo two prima donnas who won't
>   address each other
> Address each other.

The intention of this debate, of course, is to illuminate Man's struggle for freedom, his struggle to wrest the gift of creativity from the Father's control. The Son, torn between the two, eventually confronts the Father, with the You (man) acting as the congealing agent. By serving this purpose, Man also acts as the agent bringing about his own inner happiness. Optimistically (some might prefer wistfully), the poem ends with "goatfoot Jesus on the village green."

It is rare to meet such serious matter in our poetry now, and for this reason **Archer in the Marrow** may not play immediately to a large audience. It should. In spite of occasional moments when the tone becomes too light-hearted and the rhetoric exalted, Viereck has created a volume that makes the small books of many current poets read like the prattling of pipsqueaks. This poet has pushed his chosen form to the limit and beyond. A useful glossary and long essay, "Form in Poetry," enhance this collection, and the latter will no doubt contribute to the lively debate concerning the resurgence of traditional form in our poetry.

Mark Edmundson (review date 1988)

SOURCE: "A Great Poem?" *Salmagundi*, Vol. 80, Fall 1988, pp. 216-26.

[*In the following review, Edmundson argues that despite the epic ambitions of* Archer in the Marrow: The Applewood Cycles, *the work does not represent a conceptual or poetic advance.*]

Imagine a poem of epic length in which the main characters include Father, Son, You, Dionysus, Venus, Eve, Mary Magdalen and a Lungfish, mankind's amphibious ancestor. The poem's scope encompasses all of human time, from its first syllable to its apocalyptically re-engendering last. Though the work is provided with stage directions, its spatial range is not measurable. It takes place simultaneously in the cosmic mytho-sphere and in the mind of a composite version of Man. The author's high argument concerns the true path to self-overcoming, which he conceives as a process by which mankind learns to give up on ersatz versions of transcendence and exult in what we might call the poetry of earth. It is this renunciative embrace that the poet describes, memorably if abstractly, as the no that affirms more than yes.

The account I have offered so far might seem to fit a newly unearthed Gnostic text, or perhaps a radical alternative to *Paradise Lost* written by one of Milton's sectarian contemporaries. But **Archer in the Marrow** was published only a few months ago, and has already received high praise from James Dickey, Richard Wilbur and Joseph Brodsky, to name a few. Twenty years in the writing, **Archer** is the work of Peter Viereck, who has won past distinction as a lyric poet and also as a social historian and philosopher. Viereck is a man of considerable learning; his reading is large and his sense of responsibility to the past pervades the poem. But the work's diction, irreverent and demotic even at exalted moments, conveys the poet's urge to be responsive to the present. Viereck desires to be nothing if not timely. Why then does he write in the high mythopoeic style which seems, after the exertions of Shelley and Blake, largely to have died out of poetry in English? What currently dominant form is Viereck turning against and why?

The majority of contemporary poets are, in important ways, the descendants of John Keats, a judgment suggested by Walter Jackson Bate when in the great biography he encourages us to think of Keats as the first genuinely modern English poet. Keats's modernity lies, in part, in his having transferred the ambivalence that Wordsworth felt before Nature into the realms of art and culture in general. Keats, a born Cockney, was infatuated from early youth with the literary imagination, and particularly with the spirit of Romance as he found it exemplified first in Spenser and later in Milton and Shakespeare. Yet even as he loved Romance, Keats resisted it. He was self-consciously a poet of the Enlightenment, eager to contribute to what he called the Grand March of Intellect. Poetry needed, if it was to survive, to evolve beyond superstition and wish-fulfillment and become a source of humane knowledge. Thus some of Keats's greatest poems, such as "Ode to Psyche," *The Fall of Hyperion*, and "To Autumn," dramatize the process by which the poet questions his reliance on the sublime mythic forms and begins to evolve toward something else.

What else was the question. Keats's inability to answer it effectively led him, one can speculate, to abandon the *Hyperion* poems, and to hover in an infinitely extended farewell to the goddess Autumn in his last major performance. Keats's quandry has, at least in my view, developed over time into the central question posed by contemporary poets. What poetic affirmations are possible in the context of a culture devoted to becoming fully secular, completely demystified? Are there moments of sympathetic illumination that can sustain themselves without appeal to any of the antiquated principles of transcendence? If the great modernist writers taught us, in their most rigorous works, how to live without a conventional version of God, their inheritors have affirmed what they could without referring to the sovereign ego, to the cultural tradition, or even to the anti-truths of deconstructive thought for confirmation. The poetry of John Ashbery, for instance, gives its wistful assent to nothing so much as the desire to skate on surfaces, to find pleasure in appearance, in disconnected phenomena and unguided talk, without origin or destination.

Viereck possesses none of Ashbery's calculated ease; his persona is emphatically that of a maker, not a site where poems coalesce. But Viereck's devotion to craft, manifest in sophisticated rhyming and technical play, doesn't quite place him in the Augustan line either, the line that reaches its zenith in Pope and progresses through Byron and Auden to present day writers like James Merrill and, in a minor key, James Fenton and Vikram Seth. There is a side of Viereck that, in the Augustan mode, is urban and urbane, skeptical, conservative, witty and worldly-wise. But Viereck's larger aspirations place him in the visionary or apocalyptic tradition that runs through the English Bible, Spenser and Milton before it reaches Shelley and Blake and, in a highly displaced form, Whitman.

Post-Enlightenment practitioners of the visionary mode like Viereck tend to believe that poetic truth lies embedded in the sublime forms of Romance, myth and religion. Where the Keatsian naturalist attempts to evolve away from the sublime, and the Augustan poet to parody sublimity when he considers it at all, the modern visionary reimagines the received myths against the normative grain. By creating the figure called Los, for example, Blake believed that he was offering a truer conception of Adam than the one currently in circulation. The assumption guiding this kind of activity is that usage and the needs of a fallen society to see itself justified in literature have led to a programmatic distortion of major imaginative works such as the Bible. It is the wager of poets like Viereck that we all possess a certain spiritual promise which, though now in bondage to custom and convention, can be unlocked by an inspired recreation of traditional figures and myths. The result of such a recreation will inevitably be a religious text, a text that has as its ultimate aim the conversion of its reader to another way of life. The visionary poet always aspires to play the role of Socratic midwife. What sort of conversion does Viereck have in mind?

Viereck's designs on the reader come through most perceptibly in the design of the poem. *Archer*, which is sub-titled *The Applewood Cycles*, itself composes one large cycle. It begins, as almost all visionary works do, with a myth about the fall of man. This fall takes place in the nether zone of Part Zero (Outside Time), which is to suggest that the fall is always occurring, and that it never has occurred at any determinate point in time. From there the poem proceeds through a series of encounters in which You—Viereck's version of Everyman—learns his own past and present failings and his possible future strengths. Fully instructed, You acts his crucial part in the climax of the poem, Part Zero Replayed, in which the losses of the opening section are redeemed. *Archer*, then, is a *rite de passage*: the initiate is You.

Every re-birth ritual requires a guide to see the initiate through his trials, and Viereck's chosen guide carries the name of the most illustrious mediator of the Western tradition, the Son. But Viereck, in visionary fashion, has reimagined the Son, making him a figure frequently at odds with the standing orthodox version of the savior of mankind. The Son's failing, self-acknowledged early-on in the poem, was to have embraced asceticism and the promise of heavenly reward, and given up on the beauties, pleasures and sorrows of earthly life. So he castigates himself for having

> Transcended laps of loam for sky-high cleanness.
> . . . Triumph? I failed—I fell (crest drained the root)
> Uphill.

The Son's icy renunciation is also represented as a split between the Son and his pagan double, Dionysus, the vital earth-god. You will only be healed when he can unify the torn principles of Christian gentleness and Dionysian passion and see, as a reflection of his own restored spirit, the image of "goatfoot Jesus on the village green."

Inhibiting this fulfillment is the figure Viereck calls Father, "the old universal thunder God, the brutality of reality, masked by the jauntiness of a stand-up-comic Mephisto." It's he—or the internal forces he represents—who deludes man into transcendent hopes and induces him to banish Pan and replace his kingdom with the earthly reign of guilt and anxiety. Where Pan was, Pain presides. Father is a descendant of the spectre of limitation that Blake called Nobodaddy, lord of jealous hate and sterility, Nobody's Daddy. He's also related to Hardy's aphasic God, whose creations pose questions and suffer torments his weak mind can't encompass. But Viereck's spry old huckster has a character very much his own, as a few of his lines will illustrate:

> Fellows, it's not been easy being God;
> The hohum festered worse than thorn or rod.
>
> My cross?—ennui's insomnia.
> And yours?—mors vincit omnia.
>
> Virtue?—dowdy.
> Vice?—frowzy.

You've stuffed with 'God' the sky that left you
    friendless,
You taxidermists of the empty Endless.

Even when he's suffering from the tyrant's malady—tedium vitae—Father's learned rasping wit and slingshot delivery make him more invigorating company than by all rights he ought to be. In any event, he supplies a fine counterpoint to the Son, who occasionally grows too pious about his impiety.

The Son is at his most effective as a voice and a character when he relinquishes his part as You's mediator and reflects on his own failings, which are of course inseparable from the failings of orthodox Christianity, and on his all too human sufferings and losses. This reflection culminates early in the poem in what is to me the most bold and moving conceptual leap that Viereck makes, his identification of Christ's crucifixion with the Holocaust. The conjunction itself is not new: Viereck makes reference to Pope John XXIII's prayer, "Forgive us for crucifying Thee a *second* time in their flesh," and the sentiment could obviously be found elsewhere. What is new is the complex development that Viereck gives to the idea and the startling language in which the Son first expresses it:

Here on Skull Hill, no chubby grass;
The dogs were fetid, it's the air went mad.
Rome's Kraut Centurions sweated out their north.
They gave me—I thought it was water—gall,
Or was it (time swirling me back and forth)
Gas? Mad air,
Were you fooling around with my shower stall?
And back here on the hill was the heat already a
    breath
From my second death, from my far
Chimney's Baal-bellied belch?
No, it was still my first Passion play; Bethlehem's
    star
Had not yellowed into a badge.

The diction is harsh, somewhat in the mode of Donne and Webster, impacted and raggedly eloquent. "Were you fooling around with my shower stall?" seems to me close to bad taste, which Viereck, like Donne and Webster, will risk in the interest of shocking the reader into perceptions he would like to resist. The line remains questionable. But the closing metaphor, in which the Bethlehem star and the yellow star, which Jews under Nazi subjection were compelled to wear, merge, represents a feat of ethical imagination.

The suggestion is present in the trope, and Viereck does not retreat from it, that the ascendancy of the star of orthodox Christianity involved, as a consequence, the twentieth century persecution of the Jews. The reasoning behind this view is not simple, but it is cogent. Viereck's Christ collaborated in his own martyrdom out of a sincere, if misguided, desire to overcome all earthly attachments. ("Was I wrongly 'right' when I dyed love white / To bleach my own frenzies?" he asks himself in retro-

spect.) His death's legacy to Christians, thus, entailed the obligation to perfect and purify the soul by making it the repository of only immortal thoughts. The communal equivalent to this private drive for purification is scapegoating, which purges the society by driving out the stranger, the other, the Jew:

Eons of stinkless Immaculate love
Parked at a cattle car.
One yellow for badge or for manager.
A star found its way to a star.

The wages of cold Christian virtue is death, a judgment finally too reductive to stand as the sole "deep" explanation for the Holocaust. Yet the metaphor—star for star—carries the force of authentic divination, which one does not dismiss easily.

The reader who, because he lacks overt Christian allegiances would tend to look on Viereck's charge with aesthetic detachment, may find himself implicated by way of the poem's second key conceptual move. This one is less striking than the first, having been anticipated for some time by anti-metaphysicians like Heidegger and his descendants Derrida and Foucault. To Viereck, the modern age has not surpassed Christianity, but transferred its impulses intact to another sphere. The worship of the God Mek—whose name Viereck derives from the Hittite word for power—is the currently operative transcendental faith. Technology offers its worshippers what Christianity did, the prospect of passing beyond the human condition and living with god-like powers.

The result is a split between the archaic natural self and the post-modern cybernetic mind:

"Brave new machine, 'tis I, thy Luddite lover,
Still splitting metal mind from gothic heart,
Medievally mod. Solve contradictory me.
Or crash me; I can't get off."

The speaker, a male lab boss, is in the quandry that Freud attributed to over-civilized man in *Civilization and Its Discontents*. The subject's urge to refine himself into immortal, stainless perfection is running into conflict with the demands of his instinctual self, which has become darker and more dangerous—Viereck says "gothic"—in confinement. The results are too easily predictable. Predictable too, I'm afraid, because far too programmatic, are the lab boss's lines. But at other times, Viereck's rough humor throws life into the idea. Here's You as Mek's macho servant:

"If we've no better fate than hooks to face,
Let's go down shooting, let jets rape space.
Man's your amok amoeba, mugger of the universe,
Ramming all Black Holes with our jet's white
    spurts."

The vision of man as cosmic rapist flourishing his jet-phallus evokes the misogyny that Viereck, rightly I think, sees an inseparable from faith in Mek.

Mek is one in an array of God-terms (or "transcendental signifieds," if you like) that *Archer* works to dispose of through dialectic. The body of the poem, from Part Zero to the climactic Replay at the end, consists largely of a series of dialogues between You and Father and You and Son, with occasional monologues by figures like Venus, Dionysus and the Lungfish. The exchanges are supposed to lead You away from the old illusions and reductions, and into an affirmation of nature, the earth, mortality and the "minute particulars" of life. By the end of the treatment—for there is something of the therapeutic as well as the religious about this text—the reader has presumably learned to give up on progress, pure knowledge, absolute power, domination and greed, and to affirm the merged form of Dionysus/Christ. Their conjunction represents, to Viereck's mind, the joining of pity with passion, appetite with gentleness, and the self-vaunting power of Romantic self-creation with the desire to live harmoniously among others, and, if need be, for others. And with the imaginative achievement of this ideal, the epic reaches its end.

So far my account of *Archer* has focused on its conceptual designs, an approach that is both just and unjust. Unjust because, at least to me, the chief glory of the poem lies in its lyrical achievement. Viereck's range is stunning. He is, first of all, a superb satirist. His composite portrait of the citizen of ancient Rome/contemporary L.A. (a portrait, I suspect, of the work's more resistant readers) is at once savage and coldly incisive. Throughout the poem, Viereck's standard perspective is masculine, learned and experienced, but he's also capable of disarmingly tender writing, as when he speaks of a "turquoise so blue that the stone is the hue / And 'blue' the metaphor." The dramatic monologues spoken by Aphrodite and Dionysus, and some of those by You and the Son, constitute the finest moments in *Archer*. They're passionate, infused with prodigious local invention, and tempered with Viereck's style of irony, a strong bass line that perpetually evokes the press of transience. Of particular distinction is the speech in which, with an exuberance comparable to Whitman's, Dionysus celebrates his metamorphoses:

> Don't you smirk too; I know I'm all awry.
> I'm fluff, I stick to every whim like lint.
> I'm dandelion fuzz: my gold spikes dry
> And silver off with every aimless wind.
>
> I wear what glistens (next round, I'll leap as trout).
> My motes traipse far—I gawk from every spark.
> I rocket from smokestacks, intersect with soot,
> And stun noon's sauna with my sunnier dark.

The speech is a verbal fugue, brilliantly extemporizing on the theme of transformation, without an uninspired moment, for over two hundred lines. And as if speaking through the mouth of the wine god or the savior didn't provide enough challenge, Viereck also attempts, and largely brings off, monologues by a gallows tree, a gangplank and a paving stone. Putting a soliloquy by a potato into a life's crowning work probably betrays an impulse to self-destruction, but given the odds against, the potato acquits himself honorably.

Archer is always written full-out and teems with strongly conceived lines. "There are no lazy intervals," as the Richardsons, Milton's editors, said of his epic. Unlike many contemporary poets who feel that to have written a few stanzas that are beyond reproach is to have written a poem, Viereck takes verbal chances constantly. He'd rather risk over-stepping than let a chance go by. But the semantic density of the poem arises, ultimately, from the fact that the true matrix of Viereck's work is the riddle. He loves submitting the reader to tricky compressed passages. Depth-charges are scattered everywhere, and you have to stand guessing in front of some of the poem's best lines—and a few that turn out shallow. The overall sensibility, almost no matter which figure is speaking, is mock-oracular, as though Nietzsche's Zarathustra were slightly drunk and throwing his voice through Delphic shadows. And the reader is compelled to construe it all as he can. The first time through, he's likely to be baffled and exhilarated by the carnival of ideas—historical, artistic, philosophical, political and theological—refracted through the medium of Viereck's singular style. *Archer* presents itself, first, as an inspired celebration of the polymathic perverse.

But the poem is, in its strongest intentions, religious: its aim is to convert the reader, to impress its terms upon him as ultimates. A second reading reveals a pressure of ideas upon the work so strong that a conceptual description (such as the one I began with) becomes inevitable and just, despite the poem's lyric heights. For those heights occur only when Viereck manages to cut himself loose for a time from his polemical task. One is reminded here of Auden, who said that someone who wanted to hang around words to see what they might be up to had a better chance of becoming a poet than did a man with truth to impart. Viereck is undoubtedly a poet, but his attachment to a gospel constrains his gifts. Though his words are a force of irregulars, most of the time they are waging carefully conceived ideological war. There's too much Prospero and not enough Ariel, to borrow again from Auden—or a bad mix of Holofernes with Orpheus, if one's resistance to didactic work is absolute. The more you read *Archer*, the more you feel its imperial ambitions.

In his most didactic moments, which occur in the dialogic sections of the poem, the resources of poetry frequently act for Viereck in the way that the "dream work" acts in the Freudian account of dream production. The grotesque diction and unfamiliar rhymes serve (for a time) to disguise the heuristic intent in the same way that "condensation" and "displacement" hide the dream-wish from the censorious ego. Viereck's technique amounts to distortion, rather than imaginative transformation, of ideas because the message remains firmly under his conscious control. All of Viereck's riddles have right answers. He doesn't allow for enough play in the poem; he won't let his words float to accrete unexpected meanings. We get coded Truth, and little chance to make up our own minds.

Viereck is not unaware of the problem. In a brilliantly written appendix, he describes his rhyming technique—which is related to Emily Dickinson's "slant" rhyming—

as a way of ironizing the text and introducing a full play of meaning. But the necessity for including the appendix speaks against its thesis. The poem comes with three sections of prefatory explanation, the appendix, notes (apparently enforced on the poet by his publisher) and a glossary. *Archer* is already a *Norton Critical Edition.* And doesn't this drive for ultimate authority over his own production bring the poet uncomfortably close to those purveyors of absolute knowledge that the poem so energetically assaults?

But there is, I think, a more significant contradiction at the work's core. I said at the beginning of the review that Viereck's objective is to affirm something we might call the poetry of earth. The phrase is Keats's, and the ethos to which *Archer* finally commits itself would be very hard to distinguish from Keatsian naturalistic humanism. In other words, Viereck endorses the values most other contemporary poets are attached to. And yet he does so by way of a visionary epic, a poetic mode which qualifies, perhaps, as an exercise in the kind of grand self-vaunting thought that the poem seems to be enjoining us to give up on. To modify Karl Kraus's remark on psychoanalysis somewhat, *Archer* may be an instance of the malady for which it purports to be the cure.

Even if we suspend this kind of a criticism as being merely ingenious (which I don't think it is), there is still the question of the freshness of *Archer*'s findings. Keats never did arrive at a fully developed vision of his naturalism, it's true. But Wallace Stevens, for whom "the poetry of earth" was a congenial phrase, may have reached the point where *Archer* ends as early as *Harmonium*, his first volume. There, in the poem "Sunday Morning," he wrote of the struggle to renounce other-wordly dreams:

> And shall the earth
> Seem all of paradise that we shall know?
> The sky will be much friendlier then than now,
> A part of labor and a part of pain,
> And next in glory to enduring love,
> Not this dividing and indifferent blue.

Viereck may not have much to add to Stevens's early vision of a world content without transcendental faith, though Viereck's sense of what can happen in politics and private life when we fail to embrace a poetry of earth *is* startling and fresh. And so too are his monologues which, when they unyoke themselves from ideological weight, represent some of the best lyric poetry of recent years.

Is *Archer*, then, a great poem? Is it, as the recent Nobel Laureate Joseph Brodsky has said, "the major event in American poetry of today, on a par with Williams's *Paterson* and Pound's *Cantos*"? Even if the criticisms I've made are just, they do not necessarily make this question an empty one. *Paradise Lost* is, by consensus, the most perfect long poem in the language, but consensus probably agrees with Dr. Johnson too in not wishing it longer. The number of literary offenses one could compile against *Paterson* and *The Cantos* is perhaps endless, and yet there is no prospect of their being displaced from the modern canon. They have both answered to the pragmatic standard for poetic survival: they have affected good young poets and generated a body of critical response.

Viereck, I would predict, will not do so. His text could keep the scholars busy for more than a few decades; it's crammed with allusions, references, echoes, motifs and significant structures. But I doubt young poets will be inspired by it: didactic poetry is their "abhorrence," as it was Shelley and Keats's, and too many of *Archer*'s driving concepts are by now commonplace. Yet Viereck occasionally shows evidence of possessing a genuinely prophetic temper; which suggests not that he can divine the precise events of the future, but that perhaps he can intuit the shape of its imaginative needs. If poets and readers in years to come find themselves in the situation that Johnson attributed to us all—of needing more to be reminded of humane knowledge that we have had than to be informed of things previously unknown—then perhaps *Archer in the Marrow* will be there to do it.

David Kirby (review date 1996)

SOURCE: "Lasting Words," *Parnassus*, Vol. 21, No. 2, 1996, pp. 113-30.

[*In the following review of* Tide and Continuities: Last and First Poems 1995-1938, *Kirby admires Viereck's sharp wit and his experiments in poetic form but finds many of his poems repetitive rather than original.*]

Tide and Continuities ("my last because of age and illness," Viereck writes) consists of either three or six parts, depending on how you read a preface that is as full of paradox, irony, and downright contradiction as the poems themselves. The first part consists of new poems written mainly in hospitals; the second comprises four sections of selected poems composed over a sixty-year period; and the third is devoted to long poems that tie the first two parts together.

The book's thematic leitmotifs are as ambitious as its formal architecture. They are, as Viereck sees them, "the seesaw of ambivalence between Persephone and Dionysus; the merging of Dionysus with Jesus, the Son of Man; and, thirdly, ageing and its doomed last venture." Of these three, the first is the most insistent—so insistent that one wishes the poet had appointed a handful of poems on this theme to represent the many included here. Viereck is fond of multiple roles for his characters (name tags like "Eve-Aphrodite" and "God-Mephisto" recur in these poems), and his gods take all too human form at times:

> *"Are we slumming Olympians, earth our importer?*
> *Or, second choice, each a sleazy imposter,*
> *The 'traveling salesman' (of firewater)*
> *With the porn-joke 'farmer's daughter'?*
> *Or, third, Viereck's puppets, his strings our*
> *   halter?*
> *Check one of three."*

Even if "we" are slumming, this is a project of Olympian proportions, though shot through with foolishness, self-mockery, and a wit so acid I was relieved to read in the front matter that the book will be printed on "alk. paper."

The following poem gives something of the flavor of the poems overall, from the ponderous title to the list of dramatis personae (it is hard to imagine a Viereck poem without one) to the relentless *sui generis* formalism:

**"Now That Holocaust and Crucifixion Are
          Coffee-Table Books"**

The two speakers are Christ and modern man, the latter voice always in quotes and italics.

> Waiting for dying? Tell me how
> It feels to grow up mortal?—*"Ow."*
> So long since I did dying on my own.
> How did you manage it?—*"Alone."*
> I mean, what does it feel like?—*"Cold."*
> Resist! Young rebels how do *they* end?—*"Old."*
> But ethics—brothers all—.*"Like Cain."*
> Asylums needed!—*"For the sane."*
> Man's load, I'll share it.—*"No such luck."*
> I sold for thirty—.*"Lambchops for a buck."*
> From me they made Wafers.—*"From later Jews,
>   soap."*
> But Christians, being Christians, saved us.—*"Nope."*
> But I'm Mr. Christian in person, not solely a Jew.
> *"Sure. By the way, Mr. Eichmann is looking for
>   you."*
> Six million! Where can I find the memorial booth
> For their lost golden dreams?—*"In a German gold
>   tooth."*
>
>   . . . . .
>
> Unique: I rose.—*"Some lambs escape the stew."*
> At least my Stages went unshared by you:
> I lugged a cross uphill once; say
> If you have.—*"Nine-to-five each day."*
> Who else blooms Easter back with April showers?
> *"All funeral parlors 'say it with flowers.'"*
> My parents didn't help.—*"Whose really do?"*
> My lonely hour both copped out on.—*"Who?"*
> My father wouldn't stop the spear.—*"Same here."*
> O mother, I'd hoped it wouldn't hurt.—*"Me too."*

In the course of this clipped call-and-response dialogue, two speakers with very different attitudes become more and more like-minded, yet the One who changes is not the one who would be expected to change: Instead of modern man being redeemed, it is Christ who is corrupted, his naïveté and good cheer eroded by the man's dour outlook; the latter speaks in fragments and monosyllables, as though too discouraged to say more, and his simple end rhymes chip away at his would-be Redeemer's confidence. Not all of Viereck's poems are this tightly wrapped, though even the more loosely constructed ones would appear extremely formal by anyone else's standards.

Poets use as much or as little form as they need, and it is easy to say that form fits content ideally here, that so arch a scold has to anneal his pronouncements lest they collapse into mere whiny rancor. Viereck himself would not hold with such relativism, for form is such an absolute to him that he devotes almost half of his preface to a rather touchy apologia:

> Imagine you're drowning. The water swallows you.
> Suddenly an arm tugs you to shore. A lifeguard
> revives your heart and your lungs, breathing into your
> mouth once for every five heart messages, as he or
> she has been taught. Five ta-TUMS per line of breath.
> Your life has just been saved by an old "outdated"
> imabic pentameter. How Elizabethan of nature! Both
> life and poetry depend on such body rhythms. Would
> you trust your life to a free-verse lifeguard?
>
> Um, an *exclusively* free-verse lifeguard, no, though
> I would hope my savior had lots of instruction and
> experience in all the life saving techniques and
> could improvise if he had to.

Viereck is not the only one who wants to put all the free-versifiers in a weighted sack, drop them over the side, and rub his hands with glee as they caterwaul unrhythmically to the bottom. But in keeping with his cranky nature, he has a similar fate in mind for the neoformalists. "Form's living metronome of walking, breathing, feeling is replaced by a dead mechanical metronome," he writes, and the result is "the net without the tennis." So instead of "full-throated song," the reader gets "a bloodless correctness, a thin-lipped disapproval."

No one would accuse as feisty a Jeremiah as Viereck of being either bloodless or thin-lipped. And regardless of how one plays tennis, one has to admire Viereck's constant fidgeting with received forms and invention of new ones. To wit, crisscross rhymes:

> Image of ambush,
> Hushingly dim:
> Gold-bellied hornet
> Hanging from ceiling.
> Torment is dangling
> Feelers at man.

So "Im-" rhymes with "dim" in the line below, as "-bush" does with "Hush-"; "hornet" and "torment" make crisscross half-rhymes, as do "hanging" and "dangling," with "cei-" and "fee-" as a kind of true-rhyme sandwich in the middle. In a note, Viereck explains that he also moves "rhythm forward to first syllable, overthrowing the tyranny of over-accenting the rhymed last syllable of lines." Fine, but this is a fifty-line poem, and it never becomes any more engaging than this.

Viereck does better with his "uncouplets," by means of which he proposes "a kind of coitus interruptus to frustrate the ear's expectancy of cliché rhymes." Thus:

> I remember, I remember
> Love's leaf fell in July.

I desire, I desire
To live forever; in the end I flame like ash.

and

Now when your sky-queen eyes of blue
Swear to be false,

At least I'll go down without blah or blink: my dove
Coos hate.

Now these are formal experiments to be excited about, to show to one's bedmate or party guests or students. The fun here is contagious; a fine line separates the identification of the expected rhymes ("September," "fire," "true," and "love") and the composition of one's own uncouplets. What makes this exercise successful is that substitution of un-rhymes for the expected clichés compels one to rethink not only how poetry operates but the heart as well. Viereck spoils the effect somewhat with a the-formalist-doth-protest-too-much headnote declaring that "the aim of the poem is not these mere formalist gimmicks but a protest against the sentimental cult of nature and earth-mother." Yes, yes. Any reader who finds himself on page 170 of a collected works knows how to read poetry without over-the-shoulder advice, but then no amount of ham-fisted authorial intervention can truly ruin a poem one admires.

Viereck's best formal work seems unstudied, if that adjective is at all applicable to so self-conscious a poet as he. Couplets like this one flash wittily without calling too much attention to the technical aspirations that underlie them:

In the month of March the sanils climb tender trees
To be nearer the Pleiades.

As with the uncouplets, the comic unexpectedness of the second line whisks the reader away from any ponderous consideration of form; one is too busy appreciating the effect to analyze its cause.

Viereck is often cynical to the point of bitterness, as a poem like **"Now That Holocaust and Crucifixion Are Coffee-Table Books"** illustrates. Wisely, he offers the candy of humor fairly often. Yet he is at his most appealing when being frank about the difficult struggle of writing and even living. The alternation between Dionysian scattering and Persephonean restoration is the major theme, played out in the alternation between the two kinds of writing that Viereck practices. The first, represented by the excerpts quoted above, is seemingly casual, and appears to come to the surface of the page as smoothly as Persephone on the up-escalator out of Hell. The second kind is the foredoomed yet nobly persevering verse that strives to bring great fragments of the psyche together, as though Dionysus might have tried to reassemble himself unaided. In a long poem called **"At My Hospital Window,"** he writes:

Nothing shaped. Once a bore came to abort
(*Flagrante delicto*) doped Coleridge's hug of the
    muse.

Pain-killer-drugged, I, too, have Xanadus,
My promised ode being daily cut short
By some goody-bore's "HAVE A GOOD DAY."
Well, back to work; now I'll finish—
What was it I promised her I'd finish?
And who was "her"? And why of the sea? And
    where did I lay
My glasses? Memories shed.
(We differently-abled golden agers
Are mnemonically-challenged underachievers.)
    Tomorrow I'll shape, not shed. The best is ahead.

A line later, Viereck writes, "Days passed. Nothing shaped." This frank admission is more endearing than any of the technical wizardry of the other poems. The most touching poetry is not the most finished; it is the poetry that we finish ourselves.

Of course, one way to be perfect is by letting the rest of us know that we are im-. (Another is by spelling words as they once were but no longer are, though I have to admit a soft spot for a poet who writes "rôle" and "haemophilia.") Parodies are often good-natured, and the best reveal the parodist as at least half in love with that which is being spoofed. But there is something condescending about such a "blues" as the one entitled **"To Helen (of Troy, N.Y.)"**:

I sit here with the wind is in my hair;
I huddle like the sun is in my eyes;
I am (I wished you'd contact me) alone.

A fat lot you'd wear crape if I was dead.
It figures, who I heard there when I phoned you;
It figures, when I came there, who has went.

Dogs laugh at me, folk bark at me since then;
"She is," they say, "no better than she ought to";
I love you irregardless how they talk.
You should have done it (which it is no crime)
With me you should of done it, what they say.
I sit here with the wind is in my hair.

Mr. or Ms. Copy Editor, don't touch a single solecism; the poor grammar and seeming typos are all too deliberate. The faux blue-collar phrasings seem to say, "That's how the uneducated do it, folks—just in case you didn't know." But we do, and we know how an educated person does it as well. And while we like much of what he has done, we wish he had been a little choosier about what he has included here. So much of what Viereck has written is the very best of its kind; poems from the **"Mostly Hospital and Old Age"** section (Part I of *Tide and Continuities*) echo and extend the legacy of Johnson, Swift, and especially Pope. But after a while, later poems begin to recall things done slightly differently in earlier poems rather than striking the reader as fresh and original. Viereck is a needler, and a little needling goes a long way.

Phoebe Pettingell (review date 1998)

SOURCE: "Viereck's Puppets," *The New Leader*, Vol. LXXXI, No. 9, August 10-24, 1998, pp. 12-13.

[*In the following review, Pettingell calls* Tide and Continuities: Last and First Poems 1995-1938 *"a versatile and entertaining book" and suggests that the poetry in this volume represents the culmination of Viereck's career.*]

For almost 60 years the indefatigable Peter Viereck has honed his wit and offered shrewd cultural judgments in spirited formal verse. Born in the same decade as Dylan Thomas and Robert Lowell, Viereck has lived through the era of neometaphysical poetry bristling with Donne-ish puns and Audenesque prosodic pyrotechnics, then that of Minimalist blank verse and plain speaking, and into the current return to Romantic expansiveness. His declared last collection, *Tide and Continuities: Last and First Poems 1995-1938* is introduced by the late Joseph Brodsky in an appropriately poetic Foreword.

> *An introduction to a book*
> *of poetry must have a look*
> *of poetry. I thought a lyric*
> *befits this work by Peter Viereck,*
> *perhaps the greatest rhymer of*
> *the modern period, a prof*
> *of history at Mount Holyoke College*
> *famed for its feminists and foliage.*

And so forth for 10 more rollicking stanzas. Brodsky, like Viereck, knew how effective doggerel can be. Sadly, in our own day, we associate its mongrel meter and jangly rhymes with the work of inept poetasters and saccharine greeting-card verses.

In previous centuries, though, major poets employed it for satiric effect, or to convey a homespun quality. Byron and Browning were adepts. American poets particularly excelled at doggerel: James Russell Lowell's "A Fable for Critics" sustained it for several cantos. The form probably reached its apogee between the final decades of the last century and the early part of this one with the popularity of such newspaper columnist poets as Eugene Field, Gelett Burgess (of "Purple Cow" fame), Guy Wetmore Carryl, and Don Marquis—inventor of the irrepressible literary cockroach, archy, and his pal the upbeat alley cat, mehitabel.

Doggerel's effects are often comic, but they also allow for philosophical musings, mockery and even a species of folksy pathos. In today's painfully earnest critical climate, though, it can be hard to scrape up an audience for any humorous verse. Viereck and Garrison Keillor may be the only well-known writers who still love doggerel, and probably no one has put it through more paces than Viereck. In doing so, he proves once again its flexibility and emotional resonance.

Tide and Continuities (a rather academic title for such a versatile and entertaining book) begins with the poet's most recent work. Much of it deals with mythic themes of death and resurrection, and an initial series of poems, including **"Dionysus in Old Age,"** retells the story of Persephone, daughter of Ceres, goddess of the harvest. In the original, the young maiden was raped by Pluto and forced to live as his queen in the underworld, but her sorrowing mother refused to make the crops grow until her child was restored. The gods came up with a compromise that returned Persephone to the world of earth and sky for six months of each year, ensuring summer's abundance before her inevitable disappearance to the subterranean land of the dead. Aboveground, she becomes, according to some versions of the myth, the bride of Dionysus, god of the grape—who is associated with resurrection too, since he was torn to pieces before coming back to life, just as vines must be pruned back to sticks at the end of the season in order to grow more abundantly the next year.

Viereck is fascinated by this peculiar ménage-à-trois in which intoxicated Dionysus must share his sweetheart (a stand-in for the poet's muse) with Death himself. These riveting poems are always laughing through tears of pain, humiliation, frustrated rage, and fear. Thus Viereck's version of the tale begins with an explanatory note: "Not theological nor supernatural in its myth-echoes, the poem relates Dionysus [here "Mr. Dionysus Jones"] and Persephone to the old folklore humor of the traveling salesman and the farmer's daughter."

But gradually the speaker becomes the voice of the scribbler as well, addressing his "belle dame sans merci' muse." The poem's Dionysus, "an aging shabby wine salesman and magician, feeling vine's autumn," sometimes breaks into musical comedy-style arias with grace notes of Cole Porter or Noel Coward in bittersweet mode:

> *Poignant: this autumn aura, this afterglow half-shed,*
> *No matter which orphaned flora (youth, lust, or*
> *   primavera)*
> *I hoard. And the end hard.*
> *—But harder this poignance, whittled by my rhymes ...*
> *Fall is the heartbreak Her Niobe-heart can't bear.*
> *Halt—can you hear me?—you falling leaf up there;*
> *Halt in mid-air.*

Unimpressed by his sentimentality, Persephone belts out her numbers like Ethel Merman, in **"Goat Ode in Mid-Dive"** (the word "tragedy" derives from a Greek word meaning "goat song"). He has displayed resentment because she only gets to spend six months of the year aboveground with him before she must return to Hades. However, she puts him in his place:

> *"Don't map me as femme-fatale-ing all over the*
> *   place.*
> *I'm too solid for fluffy romantic props.*
> *Not many a belle-dame-sans is also a nanny.*
> *With my glamorless chore of baby-sitting the*
> *   crops,*
> *I'm hard-core no-nonsense ore. . . .*
> *I'm slapdash life, not school. No guild*
> *Can build on my quicksilver quicksand base,*
> *I dodging your x-rays paraphrase. . . .*
> *I'm whirls of myth and science*
> *Through wheels of song and silence.*

*Pluto can't keep his mitts off me; he's conned
By all that's round."*

Fed up with his attempts to poeticize her, she tells him,
"nothing wows me but the commonplace." The two of
them are, as the poet has her put it, "Viereck's puppets"—
an objectification of his musings about cycles of creative
activity and lying fallow, together with apprehensions of
his own approaching extinction. Finally, in **"Pluto In-
cognito,"** the poet concludes that his appropriation of
the mythic story is akin to

*A grandma fabling for children.
This is the ancient tale of the three.
This is the future tale of the trillion.
The children, bored (they'd rather play soccer),
Retell it blurred, with new myth garnished.
Smelling of urine and roses, clasping a nursing-
    home garland,
Alzheimer'd granny is fabling on her rocker:
Tales truer for being garbled.*

So each new teller of the universal myths of our culture
changes the plot a bit in order to highlight an aspect
hearers may have missed in earlier recountings, until human voices fall silent and our alphabets become meaningless scratchings.

Against all odds, Viereck has been inspired by what he
wryly calls "those gifts reserved for age." They include
not merely illness ("the conqueror germ" in Viereck's
parlance) and failing memory, but also what T.S. Eliot
identified as "the conscious impotence of rage / At human folly, and the laceration / Of laughter at what ceases
to amuse."

Hospitals appear as a kind of Hades from which, in common with Persephone, we hope to be freed after a season; sickness as a condition we yearn to recover from,
made whole again like dismembered Dionysus. The first,
and most recently written, section of the book begins
with a long poem, **"At My Hospital Window,"** tracing
the effects of a critical illness Viereck suffered a few
years ago.

Among many other matters, the poem contemplates the
effect morphine (given as a painkiller) has on the imagination. "I, too, have Xanadus," viereck remarks, alluding
to Coleridge's drug-induced "Kubla Khan." No wonder
the poet has Dionysus complain in one of the Persephone poems that his beloved is "now hooked on wines
of entropy booze; / She brews them from poppies, not
vines" to become a psychedelic hippie maenad, prone to
dark hallucinations and violence.

Not all Viereck's poems have such an epic quality. Sprin-
kled throughout *Tides and Continuities* are short lyrics
in a variety of forms: Sapphics, odes, ballads, almost-
sonnets of 13 lines. Viereck includes elegies for his father
and for a brother killed fighting the Nazis in Italy. Nijin-
sky carols from his Swiss madhouse, Venus in a music
hall plays Mary Magdalene as "Maggie Jones." Love po-

ems abound, but so do satires with titles like **"Now that
Holocaust and Crucifixion are Coffee-Table Books."**
Science sings antistrophe to Myth's strophe. In **"The
Green Menagerie,"** speakers "include DNA, potato,
cactus, stone, and water, as well as occasional human
voices."

The final section of this volume returns to the Dionysus/
Persephone story, and to even darker observations about
the end of life. The god is now identified with Orpheus
and Christ—also with Arthur Rimbaud and his drunken
boat. His partner links herself with everyone from Eve
and the Virgin Mary to Joan of Arc, "Madame Ovary,"
and the girl-who-can't-say-no.

By turns irreverently philosophical or laughingly tragic,
Viereck's puppets dance the spiraling rounds of historical revolutions and human stages of development. Sometimes their puppeteer makes them deliberately artificial,
like the stock characters of *commedia dell' arte*. Other
times, he moves their strings in a way that makes them
affectingly lifelike. Doggerel mixes with the sublime to
create a thoroughly contemporary poetry. In his long
career, Peter Viereck has saved his best for the last, and
his contribution to this ancient story needs to be heard.

FURTHER READING

Davidson, Eugene. "New Books in Review: Poets' Shelf." *Yale Review* 38 (1949): 723-27.
    Considers the variety of Viereck's poetry and admires his craftsmanship.

Hall, James. "Ordered Withdrawals." *The Virginia Quarterly Review* 26, No. 3 (Summer, 1950): 464-69.
    Praises Viereck's flexibility and technical skills in *Strike through the Mask!*.

Kroll, Ernest. A review of *New and Selected Poems: 1932-1967*. In *Michigan Quarterly Review* (Summer, 1969): 204.
    Suggests that Viereck may be one of the memorable poets of his generation.

Mueller, Lisel. A review of *New and Selected Poems: 1932-1967*. In *Shenandoah* (Spring, 1968): 66-7.
    Criticizes the formal structure of Viereck's poetry, particularly his end-stopped lines, but admires his lyricism.

Older, Julia. "High Latitudes: Recent Books from Four New England Poets." In *The Literary Review* 31, No. 3 (Spring, 1988): 358-362.
    Reviews *Archer in the Marrow: The Applewood Cycles of 1967-1987* and finds that Viereck's poetic skill sustains the ambitious theological scheme of this volume.

Weeks, Edward. "The Peripatetic Reviewer." In *Atlantic* 184, No. 2 (August 1949): 83.
    Finds the poetry in *Terror and Decorum* to be both realistic and idealistic.

Additional coverage of Viereck's life and career is contained in the following sources published by the Gale Group: *Contemporary Authors*, Vols. 1-4; *Contemporary Authors New Revision Series*, Vols. 1, 47; *Contemporary Literary Criticism*, Vol. 4; *Dictionary of Literary Biography*, Vol. 5.

Sir Thomas Wyatt
ca. 1503-1542

English poet and translator.

INTRODUCTION

While Sir Thomas Wyatt is best known for introducing the sonnet to English, his precarious life as a courtier in the court of Henry VIII, which he recorded in verse for an aristocratic audience, is historically eminent. He served as a foreign diplomat on the Continent and was imprisoned repeatedly without charges, yet remained loyal to his king. Although his poetry has been cited for poor craftmanship, twentieth-century scholars have re-evaluated his oevre and found much to admire: experimentation with meter, voice, and forms, both Continental and classical; and satires of the Protestant Reformation and of the centralization of state power are a few such hallmarks. A theme common to Wyatt's work is mutability or betrayal as an undesirable trait for a lover, servant, patron, or king as he sought "quietude of mind" throughout his life. Despite the uncertain fortunes of his career as courtier, his intelligence and strong character helped him to survive and serve his king and kingdom to the end of his life.

Biographical Information

The son of Sir Henry Wyatt of Yorkshire and Anne Skinner Wyatt of Surrey, Thomas Wyatt was born in Kent around 1503. Wyatt admired his father, a member of the Privy Council of Henry VII and Henry VIII, and regretted his own lot by comparison at times. It has been difficult to separate Wyatt's private and public life from his poetry. From the start of his career at Henry VIII's court, he quickly succeeded; within the span of only several years Thomas Cromwell, Henry's secretary and counsel on religious matters, had become his patron. Having traveled to France and to Rome, he received a request from Queen Catherine of Aragon to translate Petrarch's *De remediis utriusque fortunae* in 1527. Wyatt translated *The Quiet of Mind* instead because its philosophy was significant to Wyatt. Wyatt's private life, filled with discord due to his public position on the king's court and his personal relations which often defied the moral judgement of England at that time, became the center of his poetry. According to most sources, Wyatt attended Cambridge where he met and married Elizabeth Brooke. In 1521, they had a son, but due to Elizabeth's infidelity, their relationship was estranged. In 1536, Wyatt began a lifelong relationship with Elizabeth Darrell, with whom he also had a son. But it is Anne Boleyn, King Henry's second wife, with whom Wyatt is most notoriously associated. The nature of their

relationship has been impossible to ascertain because it is surrounded by rumor and conjecture. Several of Wyatt's poems allude to her, notably the riddle No. 54, that is solved by the word "Anna," and his critically-acclaimed translation of the Petrarchan sonnet, "Whoso list to hunt," No. 11, that centers on the courtly game of chase that ends with one of the king's ladies who is unattainable and in ultimate control of her suitor. Sonnet No. 123, composed during Wyatt's imprisonment at the time of Boleyn's trial, points to their other lovers and results in a strong sense of vulnerability due to the woman's proximity to the king. After the queen's beheading, Wyatt was reinstated and sent as ambassador to Charles V's court to prevent a Catholic alliance from being formed between Spain and France. When this threat diminished, Wyatt returned home. But the execution of his patron Cromwell in 1540 left him open to attack by his enemies at court, and he was once again imprisoned. A brilliantly wrought self-defense won his pardon on the sole condition that he forsake Darrell and accept Elizabeth Brooke as his wife. It was during these later years that Wyatt wrote to his son, encouraging him to follow his path as a poet and a patriot. In 1542, Wyatt died while traveling for king Henry.

Major Works

All issues of scholarly debate depicted in Wyatt's work have been discussed for centuries. *The Court of Venus* (1955) includes three fragments of Wyatt's verse that were circulated among members of Henry's court from 1535-39, 1547-49, and 1561-64, the latter being subtitled *A Book of Ballets*. His most important work by far has been *Tottel's Miscellany* (1557), that features one-third of Wyatt's canon, focusing on his lyrics and translations of Italian masters, such as Petrarch and Serafino. This miscellany has appeared in at least nine editions over thirty years. A great deal of lattitude was exercised in the recent re-editing of Wyatt's poetry, and although it is uneven in quality, *Tottel's* represents one of the most important works of the sixteenth century. As such, Wyatt's canon has been revised and collected in several editions since his lifetime, his work currently experiencing a resurrgence in popularity for its depictions of life and society at the time of Henry VIII.

Because Wyatt worked with English models, especially Chaucer, as well as with those from the Continent, his poems exhibit the conventions of *amour courtois* while at the same time subtly rejecting them. His courtly poetry includes love poems, the sonnets, epigrams and songs; and satiric poems. The context of this work encompasses depictions of love set within the tradtional modes of the English court, and deals with social vying and competition between classes. For example, in his love lyrics, the king's bard becomes the lover who writes, sighs, and sings to win the favor of ladies who might help advance his career. Although his verse serves as commentary on the early Tudor court, Wyatt's three epistolary satires are humanist pieces taken from the Italian tradtion that more effectively criticizes the court than does his poetry. His Penitential Psalms also established Wyatt as a writer of the Protestant Reformation as he based his translations on the repentance of King David, encouraging, according to one view, continual repentance among the Christians of the kingdom.

Critical Reception

In the early sixteenth century, the popularity of Chaucer's style of satirical sonnets waned, and many English poets began studying the Continental Renaissance masters. Wyatt's poetry, and most of the popular poetry of the day, reflect this influence. Wyatt's younger contemporary, Henry Howard, Earl of Surrey, was held in greater esteem for his developed use of the Renaissance style, but it is Wyatt's rough meter and his experiments with form that have earned him recognition in this century as the more original and complex of the two poets. Some critics attest that the four-beat measure of the Anglo-Saxon line plays against pentameter, but more recently others have taken an opposing view, that the language at times pushes what is essentially pentameter into a more expressive and rhythmic line. Although one of the major credits to his name is his adaptation of the sonnet, Wyatt has also been faulted for imitating the conceits (extended comparisons) and oxymora (paired opposites) of his Italian forebears. However, his "mistranslations" of Petrarch and other foreign styles continue to hold the attention of critics, for some believe that he molded the texts into an English context or adapted them for his own aims; other scholars believe that he individualized his translations solely for the principles of, and freedom gained within, adaptation itself. Critics do agree, however, that Wyatt's poetry, despite its sometimes overt influence by the eminent writers of preceeding eras, foretells the anti-Petrarchism of the following Elizabethan age in its rejection of the game of love and beloved, It is Wyatt's acceptance and subsequent rejection of traditional styles that made him a forebear of a coming generation of poets. Wyatt's role in the courts, first in Henry's and then in the early Tudor, in addition to his personal work as a representative of the progressive poetry of his time, have ensured him a place in the history of English literature. His innovative poetic form, creative content, and moral and philosophical canon have ranked Wyatt as the foremost among the poets of his age.

PRINCIPAL WORKS

Poetry

The Works of Henry Howard, Earl of Surrey, and of Sir Thomas Wyatt the Elder 1816; revised edition, 1965
The Poetical Works of Sir Thomas Wyatt 2 vols. 1854
The Poems of Sir Thomas Wiat 2 vols. 1913; revised edition, 1964
A Gorgeous Gallery of Gallant Inventions 1578; revised editions, 1926, 1971, 1972
Tottel's Miscellany (1557-1587) 2 vols. 1929; revised edition, 1965
The Poetry of Sir Thomas Wyatt: A Selection and a Study 1929; revised edition, 1949
Collected Poems of Sir Thomas Wyatt 1949; revised edition, 1950
The Court of Venus 1955
Sir Thomas Wyatt and His Circle, Unpublished Poems from the Blage Manuscript 1961
Songs and Sonettes 1966
Collected Poems of Sir Thomas Wyatt 1969
Sir Thomas Wyatt: Collected Poems 1975
The Canon of Sir Thomas Wyatt's Poetry 1975
Sir Thomas Wyatt: The Complete Poems 1978; revised edition, 1981
Sir Thomas Wyatt: A Literary Portrait. Selected Poems, with Full Notes, Commentaries, and a Critical Introduction 1986

Other Major Works

Tho. wyatis translatyon of Plutarckes boke, of the quyete of mynde [translator] (essay) 1528
Certayne psalmes chosen out of the psalter of Dauid, called thee. vii. penytentiall psalmes, drawen into englyshe meter by sir T. Wyat [translator] (poetry) 1549

CRITICISM

Elias Sehwartz (essay date 1963)

SOURCE: "The Meter of Some Poems of Wyatt," in *Studies in Philology* Vol. LX, No. 2, April, 1963, pp. 155-65.

[*In the following essay, Wyatt's metrics are defended.*]

In his pioneer essay on "The Fifteenth-Century Heroic Line,"[1] C. S. Lewis demonstrated that much fifteenth-century verse, long thought to be defective iambic pentameter, is really a species of native accentual verse, descended from *Beowulf* and surviving most obviously in the alliterative verse of the Fourteenth Century. Although he did not specify or analyze any poems, Lewis suggested that Wyatt occasionally wrote in the native meter. In 1946, D. W. Harding defended Wyatt against the charge of metrical ineptitude by maintaining that he used a metrical convention much looser than that we have become accustomed to in later English verse.[2] This convention, says Harding, allows the poet to shift from accentual to accentual-syllabic meter at will; once we become aware of this, the charges against Wyatt disappear. But while Harding thus defends Wyatt against the charge of writing bad iambics, he leaves him open to the no less damaging charge of metrical haphazardness. Harding raises, in short, a critical problem of which he seems to be unaware.

The generally recognized power of such poems as **"They fle from me"** and **"Who so list to hount"** is as much a consequence of their rhythmical excellence as of anything else. How are we to account for it? To attribute it to "deliberate" as opposed to "unconscious roughness," as E. M. W. Tillyard does,[3] is to explain nothing. And the loose, shifting meter that Harding suggests will hardly serve. For precise and powerful rhythm is, I take it, a function of precise and skillfully controlled meter: it is a result of form, not formlessness. Yet the most recent student of Wyatt's prosody states even more pointedly than Harding that Wyatt wrote in a shifting and (to my mind) formless meter:

Skelton and Wyatt have in mind an iambic pentameter as the basic pattern for a large portion of their verse. At the same time, the metrical tradition which they inherited for serious verse did not include the iambic pentameter as a particularly common metrical type. . . . In fact, the tradition for this verse dictated no strict pattern, since many variations were allowed in the broken-back line . . . thus the tradition . . . dictated a carelessness about metrical pattern, a variable metrical scheme . . . the poet could move from one pattern to another with comparative ease.[4]

Possibly Wyatt does use such a careless metrical convention in his poorer work. But it is difficult to understand how he can achieve the power of his best work in a metrical convention which allows the shift, not merely from one meter to another, but *from one metrical principle to another* in a short poem. Renewed study of the meter of Wyatt's best poems is, I think, in order.

The best introduction to the kind of meter Wyatt uses on occasion with great skill is provided by a poem not written by Wyatt, one whose very lack of metrical skill makes its metrical nature show up clearly.[5]

> Brittle beauty that nature made so frail,
> Whereof the gift is small, and short the season,
> Flow'ring to-day, to-morrow apt to fail.
> Tickle treasure, abhorred of reason,
> Dangerous to deal with, vain, of none avail,
> Costly in keeping, passed not worth two peason,
> Slipper in sliding as is an eelë's tail,
> Hard to attain, once gotten not geason,
> Jewel of jeopardy that peril doth assail,
> False and untrue, enticed oft to treason,
> En'my to youth (that most may I bewail!),
> Ah, bitter sweet! infecting as the poison,
> Thou farest as fruit that with the frost is taken:
> To-day ready ripe, to-morrow all to-shaken.

This may at first appear to be an early sonnet in typical stiff, plain style, with typical excessive alliteration. Many of the lines *can* be scanned as iambic pentameters, the first three, for example:

$$| \quad x \quad | \quad x \quad x \quad | \quad x \quad | \quad x \quad |$$
Brittle beauty that nature made so frail,
$$x \quad | \quad x \quad | \quad x \quad | \quad x \quad | \quad x \quad | \quad x$$
Whereof the gift is small, and short the season
$$| \quad x \quad x \quad | \quad x \quad | \quad x \quad | \quad x \quad |$$
Flow'ring to-day, to-morrow apt to fail.

Apart from the uncommon inversion of the first two feet of line one, these seem to be standard iambic pentameter lines. And so do lines six and seven, ten through fourteen. In line four, however, we get a line which clearly violates an iambic pentameter norm: "Tickle treasure, abhorred of reason." The line yields only four feet—and this is true of line eight too. Lines five and nine, furthermore, appear to have *six feet*:

$$| \quad x \quad | \quad x \quad | \quad x \quad | \quad x \quad | \quad x \quad |$$
Dangerous to deal with, vain, of none avail, . . .
$$| \quad x \quad x \quad | \quad x \quad | \quad x \quad | \quad x \quad |$$
Jewel of jeopardy that peril doth assail.

In the first of these lines the light syllable of the fourth foot is dropped and compensated for by the preceding pause, a not uncommon procedure in iambic verse. The inversion of the first three feet, however, is very rare outside of song meters.

This sort of metrical carelessness—this formal indeterminacy—is to be found in the poem only, however, if we insist on taking it as written in iambic pentameter. If we assume a four-stressed accentual line, we find that the poem coheres both metrically and rhythmically. And we do not, by so taking the poem, violate the natural rhetorical stressing of any line; on the contrary, certain characteristics of the lines emphatically point to such a reading; the heavy and regular mid-line pause (a true caesura), the heavy, stress-pointing alliteration, the many lines in falling rhythm, recalling the Anglo-Saxon type A half-line. Here is how I think the poem should be scanned:

```
 |      |          |               |
Brittle beauty / that nature made so frail,
           |        |       |        |
Whereof the gift is small, / and short the season,
    |        |            |        |
Flow'ring to-day, / to-morrow apt to fail,
   |      |         |        |
Tickle treasure, / abhorred of reason,
   |         |          |          |
Dangerous to deal with, / vain, of none avail,
    |      |      |        |        |
Costly in keeping, / passed not worth two peason,
   |      |        |      |
Slipper in sliding / as is an eelë's tail,
   |      |         |        |
Hard to attain, / once gotten not geason,
   |        |         |         |
Jewel of jeopardy / that peril doth assail,
   |        |        |        |
False and untrue, / enticëd oft to treason,
   |      |        |        |
En'my to youth / (that most may I bewail!),
    |      |      |        |
Ah, bitter sweet! / infecting as the poison,
    |       |       |          |
Thou farest as fruit / that with the frost is taken:
   |      |        |        |
To-day ready ripe, / to-morrow all to-shaken.
```

Thus read, the poem is metrically all of a piece, and gains the power of a consistent metrical norm. Notice that those lines which can be read as iambic pentameters "become" accentual lines because of the metrical context in which they now appear.

We have a choice, then. We may take the poem as a carelessly-wrought iambic pentameter sonnet, or as a more skilfully-wrought poem in accentual verse. My own preference and the reasons for it have already been indicated. There is, I suppose, no way of "proving" such things. This poem is not rhythmically distinguished enough in either meter to warrant great confidence: possibly the poem *is* ill-wrought. In the two poems of Wyatt that I mean to consider the rhythmical power is too evident and too great to be achieved by a shifting or badly-handled meter. So that we must begin with the presumption of a consistent and skilfully-handled meter, and attempt to discover what that meter and handling are which give these poem that "access of being" consequent upon formal excellence.

Once one's ear becomes accustomed to the accentual line, one finds that Wyatt is using it—perhaps experimentally—in certain of his "roughest" verses. We find it in the puzzling and apparently unfinished "I abide and abide."[6] Up to the last six lines, the poem is even more obviously in the four-stressed accentual meter than is "Brittle beauty." There is again the heavy, accent-pointing alliteration and the heavy caesura; and here the four-stressed line is inescapable. From line nine to the end, there seems to be no metrical structure at all—with the possible exception of line nine. This line may represent a deliberate and formally acceptable variation of the accentual norm—a kind of sprung rhythm that we will occasionally find in the more finished poems:[7]

```
 |    |      |       |
"Aye me! / this long abyding."
```

Since the syllables as such do not "count" in accentual verse, there may be many or few of them in a line. In the delivery of the line the light syllables are slurred, that is, lightly accented and, depending on the number that come between accented syllables, more or less quickly spoken. This is a result of the (to my ear) marked isochronism (approximate equal duration) of the accentual line. Now even though unaccented syllables do not count, one or more unaccented syllables ordinarily come between accented ones. So that, if we take the first half-line of line nine as being accented on both its monosyllables, we get a kind of sprung rhythm and a long duration for both syllables. The accentual norm is thus not violated and we get a rather skilful formal expression of the sigh which the two syllables express.

The first ten lines of **"Who so list to hount"** present the same metrical alternatives as "Brittle beauty." These lines can be scanned as iambic pentameters (except for line one, which has six feet) or four-stressed accentual lines. If we assume an iambic pentameter norm, however, we get into considerable difficulty in the last four lines of the poem.

```
    x   |  x   x   |  x   x   |   x  |
And, graven with Diamonds, in letters plain
    x   x  |  x   x  |   x   |     x   |
There is written her faier neck rounde abowte:
  | x   x   |  x   x   x   |  x   x  |
Noli me tangere, for Cesars I ame;
    x   |    x   x  |   x   |   x    |
And wylde for to hold, though I seme tame.
```

One might argue that these are irregular iambics or irregular anapests—one will have difficulty accounting for the penultimate line here on either assumption. One thing we can be sure of: it is not possible to make pentameters of these lines. If, however, we again attend to certain clues—heavy mid-line pause, heavy alliteration, natural accentuation and word grouping—we are led again to infer a four-stress accentual norm for the whole poem. And again, this meter makes of the poem an organic metrical and rhythmical whole, the audible effect being at once natural and more pleasing. Thus:

```
        |      |       |             |
Who so list to hount, / I knowe where is an hynde,
        |      |       |       |
But as for me, helas, / I may no more:
      |      |       |            |
The vayne travaill / hath weried me so sore.
```

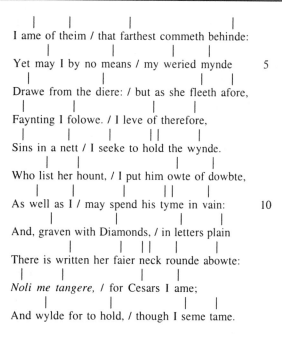

| | | |
I ame of theim / that farthest commeth behinde:

| | | |
Yet may I by no means / my weried mynde   5

| | | |
Drawe from the diere: / but as she fleeth afore,

| | | |
Faynting I folowe. / I leve of therefore,

| | | || |
Sins in a nett / I seeke to hold the wynde.

| | | |
Who list her hount, / I put him owte of dowbte,

| | | || |
As well as I / may spend his tyme in vain: 10

| | | |
And, graven with Diamonds, / in letters plain

| | || | |
There is written her faier neck rounde abowte:

| | | |
Noli me tangere, / for Cesars I ame;

| | | |
And wylde for to hold, / though I seme tame.

Rhythmically this is palpably superior to the mechanical movement of both "Brittle beauty" and **"I abide and abide."** The internal pauses are skilfully varied in duration, and additional pauses (a natural result of greater syntactical complexity) further modulate the rhythm. In lines eight, ten, and twelve I have marked what sounds to my ear like a secondary accent on one syllable. That is, we may have in these lines five rather than four accents, a survival of the practice of the alliterative poets of allowing two, two and a half, or three accents in any half-line.

The end-line pauses too are varied, ranging in duration from the long pauses at the end of lines one, four and eight, to the fine enjambement at the end of line five, which runs on to the initial stress on "Drawe." In line twelve the caesura is deliberately avoided; instead there is a slow, heavy and hesitant movement that aptly prepares for the climactic couplet. Throughout there is a progressive vowel coloring and echoing: the long sounds /ay/, /ow/, /ey/, and /iy/ keep recurring until they all appear in the last line.[8] In the last line, finally, we get very heavy (and apt) stress on "wylde" and "hold" and, in the second half of the line, perhaps the finest instance of sprung rhythm in Wyatt:

| |
"though I seme tame." These stressed words, opposed in idea to the first two stressed words in the line, finely sum up and conclude the thought and feeling of the whole poem. This stressing is only possible, be it noted, in an accentual scansion. In iambic verse the line reads,

x | x x | x | x |
"And wylde for to hold, though I seme tame," and this runs quite contrary to the rhetorical emphasis of the line.

The great and rhythmically fascinating **"They fle from me"** is, I suppose, the poem by which my case must either stand or fall. Let me risk being tedious by first scanning the poem as an iambic one.

x | x | x | x | x |
They fle from me that sometyme did me seke

x | x | x | x | x
With naked fote stalking in my chambre.

| x | x | x | x |
I have sene theim gentill tame and meke

x | x | x | x x | x
*That nowe are wyld and do not remembre

x x x | x | x | x
*That sometyme they put theimself in daunger   5

x | x | x | x | x |
To take bred at my hand; and nowe they raunge

| x x | x | x x | x x |
Besely seking with a continuell chaunge.

| x x | x x | x | x |
Thancked be fortune, it hath ben othrewise

| x x | x x | x | x |
Twenty tymes better; but ons in speciall,

x | x | | x x | x |
In thyn arraye after a pleasaunt gyse,   10

x | x | x x | x x |
*When her lose gowne from her shoulders did fall,

x | x | x x | x | x |
And she me caught in her armes long and small:

| x x | x | x |
*Therewithall swetely did me kysse,

x | x | x | x | x |
And softely saide, *dere hert, howe like you this?*

x | x | x | x | x
*It was no dreme: I lay brode waking.   15

x | x | x | x | x |
But all is torned thorough my gentilnes

| x x | | x | x |
Into a straunge fasshion of forsaking;

x | x | x | x | x |
And I have leve to goo of her goodenes,

x | x | x | x | x |
And she also to vse new fangilnes.

x | x | x | x x | x
*But syns that I so kyndely ame serued,   20

x | x | x | x x | x
*I would fain knowe what she hath deserued.

Scanning thus, we might suppose the poem to be written in irregular iambics. But if the lines are supposed to be pentameters (as most of them seem to be) we have difficulty accounting for seven lines (those marked with an asterisk) which will not yield more than four feet. And there are a few lines which sound very odd to an ear trained in iambic movements: lines seven, nine, twelve, and seventeen. An iambic meter, furthermore, forces some rhetorically bad stressing. In line six, for example, the meter forces the accent to "at" rather than "bred"; in line eleven, to "her" rather than "gown"; in line twenty-one, to "would" rather than "fain." So that, again, if we assume an accentual-syllabic norm for the poem, we get a slipshop and badly-handled meter, and one which cannot produce the very real rhythmic power of the poem.

If, however, we assume a four-stressed accentual norm, we get a firm and skillfully managed meter and we do not violate any rhetorical emphases. This poem is not as obviously accentual as the other poems we have considered—partly because the caesura has all but disappeared (a shifting internal pause takes its place), partly because the alliteration is less obtrusive. There is no mechanical end-stopping; we find, instead, skillful use of various degrees of enjambement, the occasional end-stopped line and internal pauses modulating the overall movement. Let me mark the stresses for the whole poem.

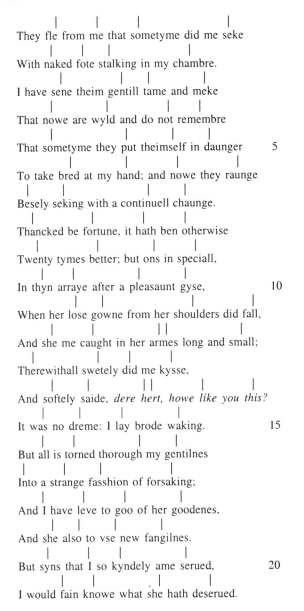

Notice that this scansion makes good rhythmic "sense" precisely at those points where violence is done by an iambic norm. In line six, we now get an apt stress on "bred"; in line eleven, stresses on both "lose" and "gowne"; in the last line, stresses on both "fain" and "knowe." A fifth stress occurs in lines twelve and fourteeen, similar to the secondary stresses we noted in **"Who so list to hount"**; as in the latter poem, they read quite "naturally" within the four-stress accentual context.

Wyatt's meter differs somewhat from its ancestor, as well as from standard iambic meter. It happily dispenses with the rigid caesura and heavy alliteration of the former and achieves something of the flexibility of the latter. It is perhaps closer in structure and effect to modern free verse, as composed by Wallace Stevens and W. C. Williams, than to anything else.[9] It has similar limitations (e. g., it is not open to the use of many degrees of accent, as is iambic verse), but it has, I believe, one virtue which free verse has not. Its marked isochronism (as I hear it) allows a principle of metrical variation unavailable in most free verse: the relatively equal linear duration sets up a temporal norm which permits precise control of line speed and pauses. In the poems I have quoted, the number of syllables per line varies from nine to twelve (excepting the line from "I abide and abide"); in the Wyatt poems, the great majority of lines contain ten syllables.[10] Since the syllables as such do not "count" in accentual meter, this indicates a "natural" tendency to keep the lines of equal duration, the differences in syllable count being made up by pauses, syllable duration and speed of delivery. In free verse the number of syllables to foot or line cannot, of course, be unlimited, because the language places a natural limit on the number which can elapse before a primary or secondary accent occurs. In free verse, however, the number of syllables to the line varies within much wider limits.

In the essay referred to earlier, C. S. Lewis remarks (p. 30) that Anglo-Saxon accentual verse differs from standard iambic verse by not involving "double audition." Lewis refers to the fact that iambic verse achieves its effects by utilizing formally the aesthetic principle of variety within sameness—in psychological terms, the arousal of expectations and the concurrent fulfillment and surprising of them. In attending to iambic verse, the hearer is simultaneously aware of both the "ideal" metrical norm and of the actual series of sounds that comprise the poem. It is in the controlled departure from the norm, slight but perceptible, that significant *rhythm* is created and perceived. Now Wyatt's meter does not, as Lewis maintains, lack this capacity; it has it, however, in a different—in a "reverse"—way. The four stresses of Wyatt's meter are, it is true, virtually equivalent: in delivery, each of the stressed syllables is given nearly the same volume. Such delivery, while making the rhetorical emphases, would, of course, depart from the natural-speech articulation of the lines. The hearer, however, is *aware* of the latter, even though it is not actualized: it is heard with the inner ear, just as the ideal norm is "heard" in iambic verse. So that "double audition" (as Lewis calls it) is as available in Wyatt's meter as it is in iambic meter. No doubt the contemporary poet, whose ear is trained in iambics, would find Wyatt's meter difficult, if not impossible, to manage well. But it is an instrument of considerable range and power—as Wyatt demonstrated in a few poems.[11]

NOTES

[1] *Essays and Studies,* XXIV (Oxford, 1939), 28-41.

² "The Rhythmical Intention in Wyatt's Poetry," *Scrutiny*, XIV (Dec., 1946), 93. Harding's thesis is supported by Hallett Smith's discovery ("The Art of Sir Thomas Wyatt," *HLQ*, IX [August, 1946], 332) that Wyatt revised certain poems in the direction of "roughness." Wyatt's habits of revision, says Smith, "do not lend much support to the suggestion that awkwardness and roughness resulted from hasty composition and that they would have been smoothed out in revision." That Wyatt could write competent iambics ·when he wanted to is evidenced by the sophisticated verse of his satires.

³ *The Poetry of Sir Thomas Wyatt* (London, 1949), 20.

⁴ Alan Swallow, "The Pentameter Lines in Skelton and Wyatt," *MP*, XLVIII (August, 1950), 8.

⁵ "Brittle beauty" is attributed to Surrey by Hebel and Hudson, *Poetry of the English Renaissance* (New York, 1929), 27.

⁶ Throughout I use the texts of Wyatt's poems given in Kenneth Muir's *Collected Poems of Sir Thomas Wyatt* (London, 1949).

⁷ I use the term "sprung rhythm" as defined by Yvor Winters in *In Defense of Reason* (Denver, 1947), 109-111.

⁸ I give, of course, the modern pronunciation of these sounds. Since the changes in them since Wyatt's time have been regular, my statement about their structuring in the poem still holds.

⁹ For a good description of free verse meters, see Winters, pp. 112-129.

¹⁰ This tendency toward a ten-syllable line has, I think, led Wyatt's critics, beginning with Tottel, to assume that Wyatt was writing iambic pentameter verse, and doing it badly. Professor Edward Weismiller maintains (in a private communication) that this tendency indicates that Wyatt was attempting to adapt to English the hendecasyllabic verse of his Italian models. Wyatt's metrical clumsiness, Weismiller holds, is a sign of his difficulty in so doing. This is certainly a plausible contention, but it fails to account for the rhythmical beauty of the poems under discussion. The issue here is an esthetic one. Professor Weismiller apparently believes, as do many, that great rhythmic power can be achieved in the absence of its formal constituents (in the present case, a firm and consistent metrical principle). I do not.

I may add that the tendency toward a ten-syllable line *may* have resulted from the influence of Wyatt's models. But this does not affect my argument.

¹¹ In addition to "They fle from me" and Who so list to hount," I would include in this group the much maligned "The longe love that in my thought doeth harbar." See Smith, pp. 333-337, for a fine analysis and defense of the poem.

Donald Friedman (essay date 1966)

SOURCE: "The 'Thing' in Wyatt's Mind," in *Essays in Criticism*, Vol. XVI, No. 4, October, 1976, pp. 375-81.

[*In the following essay, stability of mind is described as the "thing" Wyatt seeks.*]

In an article first published in *Essays in Criticism*¹ and later incorporated in his book *The Courtly Maker*² Ray-mond Southall speaks of 'the generally acknowledged introspection of Wyatt's poetry' as 'an attempt to come to grips with the "thing" within the mind'. He chooses to identify 'the thing' with the 'syght' that Wyatt says 'The bell towre showed' him. That is to say, he believes that Wyatt witnessed Ann Boleyn's execution in the Tower, and that the sight haunted him for the rest of his life as an image of 'the insecurity and instability of court favour'. So precise an identification does not seem to be warranted by the poem on which Mr. Southall builds his theory, 'Who lyst his welthe and eas Retayne'. It occurs only in the Blage MS.³ and cannot be proved to be Wyatt's.

To be sure, Mr. Southall moderates his view by saying that 'there is no need to be too specific about the experience which is represented by the thing within the mind: although related to the lesson of the bell tower, the psychological insecurity is as general and pervasive as the corresponding social insecurity . . . ' But there may be a need to be a little more specific than this, if only to question the assumption that the 'thing' Wyatt refers to represents an experience, however vaguely described. That it does not is suggested by the context in which the phrase appears most distinctively, in the lines from the second satire, '**My mothers maydes,**' which Mr. Southall cites to support his argument:

> Then seke no more owte of thy self to fynde
> The thing that thou haist sought so long before,
> For thou shalt fele it sitting in thy mynde.

I do not think this passage can refer in any sense to the scene Wyatt allegedly witnessed from the bell tower, or to any of its implications, social or personal. The lines serve as the climax of a long address to John Poins in which Wyatt attacks worldly pleasures and possessions because they are unfit objects of human ambition—a passage that moralizes on the tale of the town mouse and the country mouse that Wyatt had just retold. He is counselling satisfaction with one's own condition and abilities; his final wisdom is summed up in the remark that restless desire can never be stilled by anything outside oneself. The 'thing' so long pursued—satisfaction, stability, steadfastness—exists only within the mind itself.

This counsel can be paralleled in any number of the love lyrics, if only implicitly, because again and again Wyatt characterises both the realities of passion and the elaborate rituals of courtly love as assaults upon the mind's integrity. In '**What no, perdy**'⁴ he asks whether the memory of betrayed love, 'Vnstable, vnsure, and wavering,' shall remain in his 'mynde withoute recure;' in '**What rage is this?**'⁵ he analyses the passion that 'doth wery thus [his] mynd;' in a translation of Filosceno⁶ he deplores the effect of the 'Vnstable dreme' of love on 'this tossing mew,' his mind. And the palinodic sonnet, '**Ffarewell Love and all thy lawes for every,**'⁷ is remarkable in that love is rejected not because it is sinful or irrational but because it is tiring. It wastes time and spirit, returning meaningless pain for intelligence and devotion. It is fit, says Wyatt, only for 'idill youth' which cannot measure either its own proper goals or the reward proper to service. Seneca and Plato have brought him, the poet claims, to the appreciation of his 'wit' and its need to be directed at 'perfait welth'. Thus the poem's emphasis falls not so heavily on the traditional palinodic argument that love is a degrading appetite, usurping the pre-eminence of reason, as on the poet's wearied realisation that he has squandered the powers of his mind in fruitless acts, that the integrity of his consciousness has been shaken by the distortions of the courtly game of passion.

The mention of Seneca in this sonnet is not idle, for throughout Wyatt's career we find evidence of his attraction to Stoic ethical thought. The mention of Seneca and Epictetus in a letter to his son written in 1537 may be construed as a sign only of his unassailably conventional fatherly attitudes,[8] but it is again Seneca to whom he turns when translating some lines on the precariousness of court life.[9] And he is drawn to Stoicism particularly by its suggestion of a core of identity within the mind, a focus of consciousness that maintains its self amidst life's vicissitudes. From his translation of Plutarch in 1527 to the psalms and moral epistles of his late years his interest returns with fascinated consistency to the ideal concept of 'quiet of mind'.[10] According to Wyatt's custom 'mind' may stand for 'spirit', 'consciousness', 'soul', even what we might call 'character'. But beneath the eddying meanings lies Wyatt's sense of the mind as a harbour of uniqueness, the haven of that part of a man which remains unchanged by external events. This core of personality is terrifyingly fragile, as much of Wyatt's verse testifies; and the mind's powers to observe and imagine, to evaluate, interpret, and judge are all that can preserve it against the dangers of the unstable world it contemplates.

Wyatt thought of the mind not simply as the faculty of rational thought, but also as an active source of strength in the battle against temptation and despair, as both the toughest armour and the sharpest weapon of the embattled self. As we have seen, it is easy enough to demonstrate this in the love poems, because so many of them dramatise the conflict between the deceptive lures of passion and the mind's need for contentment and permanence. I should like to suggest briefly that Wyatt also transported his secular stoic doctrine into the devotional atmosphere of the psalm translations, and that the health and wholeness of the mind are there held to be of comparable importance to the heart's purification and the rejuvenation of the repentant spirit.

The orthodox outline of David's situation is sketched in the sixth psalm; Wyatt speaks of the 'assawltes' of 'worldlye vanytie, that temptacion castes / Agaynst the weyke bulwarke of the flesshe frayle' (32-34). and implores God to 'revyve' his 'sowle,'

> And reconcyle the great hatred and stryfe
> That it hath tane agaynste the flesshe, the wretche
> That stirred hathe thie wrathe bye filthie life.
>
> (47-49)

But that it is not the soul alone that is troubled and punished by the life of sin is made clear in the next of the

Penitential Psalms, where Wyatt adds to the list of the sinner's chastisements

> . . . . fretyng styll within,
> That neuer soffer rest vnto the mynd.
>
> (67-68)

By the reverse token, in Psalm Thirty-Eight Wyatt adds, gratuitously, to the list of virtues that have failed him in his desperate hour, 'reson and wit (43).' I should make it clear that I say 'Wyatt adds' because the phrases to which I call attention appear neither in the Vulgate nor in any of the texts of the Psalms Wyatt is likely to have used. Mr. H. A. Mason, in two well-known articles in the *Times Literary Supplement,*[11] argued persuasively for Wyatt's reliance on the *Enchiridion Psalmorum* (1533) of Johannes Campensis, as well as on Aretino's prose *I Setti Psalmi.* I have compared Wyatt's versions with these books, and also with *A Paraphrasis upon all the Psalmes of Dauid* (1539), (an English version of Campensis), *The Psalter of David in English* (1530), The Vulgate versions, Coverdale's translation of 1535, Bishop Fisher's *Treatise concernynge the fruytfull saynges of Dauyd* (1508), and others.

There is a clear example in Psalm Thirty-Eight of Wyatt's reinterpretation of the drama of David's repentance in the concepts and vocabulary of his secular poetry. Wyatt says that God's wrath is such

> That in my fleshe for terrour of thy yre
> Is not on poynt of ferme stabilite,
> Nor in my bonis there is no stedfastnes:
> Such is my drede of mutabilite.
>
> (12-15)

The Vulgate reads simply: *Non est sanitas in carne mea . . . Non est pax ossibus meis a facie peccatorum meorum.* We know from the love poems that 'stabilite' is health for Wyatt, and that 'stedfastnes' can be equated with peace; the burden of the courtly lyrics is that all these desired states are unattainable by the man trapped in the dream of desire. We should note too that where the Psalmist says that the thought of his sins forbids his 'bones' to rest, Wyatt identifies 'mutabilite' with sin, and attributes the restless state of his flesh to his fear and detestation of change—both within himself and, presumably, in the world about him.

This may be to interpret too closely; but the opposition between steadfastness and mutability, so familiar in the love poems, runs lightly but insistently through the diction of the psalm translations. In Psalm Fifty-One, for example, the Lord's word is called 'stable' (26), and the poet a 'thing most vnstable;' (30) neither word occurs in any of the texts of the Psalms I have mentioned. Similarly, in line fifty-eight of the same Psalm Wyatt asks that his will be confirmed 'with spryte oft stedfastnesse;' the Lord's spirit is described in the Vulgate as *principali, potenti,* or *generoso,* by Campensis as 'principal,' and by Coverdale as 'free,' which is also the adjective that appears in *The Psalter of David in English.* Clearly Wyatt, in the *persona* of David, has asked for that spiritual quality whose lack he feels most painfully. He is afraid neither of poverty nor of impotence of spirit, but only of the instability, the wayward, passion-led fluctuations of mind that have always tormented him.

We might say, then, that Wyatt has added to the initial situation of the seven Penitential Psalms—David's exorcism of his fleshly sinfulness—an awareness of the complicity of the unstable consciousness in the rebellion of the passions. In Psalm One Hundred and Two the opening entreaties, *Domine exaudi orationem meam,* and *Ne avertas faciem tuam a me,* are made more poignant by Wyatt's admission that his fear of God's turning His face away is compounded by his fear of being left to his own 'government'. It is not only the sinner who speaks here but the sinner fully aware of his disused intelligence and the role it has played in failing to oppose the power of temptation. Wyatt's concern with the responsibilities of the mind is best revealed in the familiar passage which follows the opening lines almost immediately:

> My hert, my mynd is wytherd vp like haye,
>   By cawse I have forgot to take my brede,
>   My brede off lyff, the word of trowth, I saye:
> And ffor my plaintfull syghes, and my drede,
>   My bonis, my strenght, my very force off mynde
>   Cleved to the flesh and from the spryte were flede.

Neither of the references to the mind is to be found in other versions of the Psalms; and in each case Wyatt has emphasised that the mind as well as the heart and the flesh derives its power from the word of truth, and that the withering of the mind is as sure a sign of spiritual decay as the wasting of the body. Furthermore, Wyatt has reversed the meaning of the first three lines in order to make unmistakably clear the mind's dependence on stable truth for its vigour; where Campensis explains that 'my sorow was so vehement that I forgot to take my meate,' Wyatt says that his mind has withered without its peculiar bread. In yet another way he attempts to characterise the essential importance of the mind's wholeness by yoking it to more familiar symbols of bodily health: 'My bonis, my strenght, my very force off mynde'. The same singular emphasis appears toward the end of the last of the Penitential Psalms, number One Hundred and Forty Three, where Wyatt declares to God, ' . . . vnto the I have reysed vp my mynd,' while the Vulgate and contemporary texts speak of *anima,* or soul.

It is not clear to me what distinctions Wyatt would have insisted on between the meaning of 'soul' and the meaning he intended for the word 'mind'. But even these few examples from the psalm translations suggest that the nature of the individual consciousness—its vulnerability to deception as well as its capacity to maintain 'stedfast' truth while immersed in the torrent of daily experience—was of profound moral significance for Wyatt. It is not surprising, nevertheless, that the concept of the mind's integrity plays so small a part in the drama of the Penitential Psalms. What is surprising is that it appears at all; in almost every instance I have cited Wyatt has added the

mention or consideration of the mind to the texts he inherited, studied, imitated, and paraphrased. The issues he touches on—the mind's frailty and its weighty moral burdens—are consistent with the major preoccupations of his secular poetry. One can trace through all his work, I think, Wyatt's unillusioned fascination with the idea of a mind secure in its self-knowledge, proof against passion and delusion, maintaining an inviolable core of personal identity against the myriad open and disguised assaults of the world, the flesh, and the devil. This, I believe, is the concept he never succeeded in describing more exactly than by calling it 'the thing . . . sitting in thy mynde'.

NOTES

[1] 'The Personality of Sir Thomas Wyatt', *Essays in Criticism,* XIV, 43-63.

[2] *The Courtly Maker* (London, 1964), pp. 67-91.

[3] See *Unpublished Poems by Sir Thomas Wyatt and his Circle,* ed. Kenneth Muir (Liverpool, 1961), No. LXIII.

[4] *Collected Poems of Sir Thomas Wyatt,* ed. Kenneth Muir (London, 1949), No. 45. All citations to Wyatt will be to this edition, and will include Professor Muir's numbering of the poems rather than page references.

[5] Muir, *Collected Poems,* No. 99.

[6] Muir, *Collected Poems,* No. 79.

[7] Muir, *Collected Poems,* No. 13.

[8] See Kenneth Muir, *Life and Letters of Sir Thomas Wyatt* (Liverpool, 1963), p. 43. Wyatt seems to suggest that the brevity of Seneca's writings may be an inducement to his son to read them.

[9] Muir, *Collected Poems,* No. 176.

[10] Patricia Thomson, in *Sir Thomas Wyatt and his background* (London, 1964), p. 79, remarks that 'Practically all Wyatt's translations from Latin originals have to do with peace of mind, the "remedies" against Fortune's blows that the wise man will seek'. But Wyatt extends the Stoic idea; the mind has more subtle enemies than the random blows of chance, and it is capable of providing more than simple solace.

[11] 'Wyatt and the Psalms', Part I (Feb. 27, 1953); Part II (Mar. 6, 1953).

Michael McCanles (essay date 1968)

SOURCE: "Love and Power in the Poetry of Sir Thomas Wyatt," in *Modern Language Quarterly,* Vol. XXIX, No. 2, June, 1968, pp. 145-60.

[*In the essay that follows, Wyatt's lyrics are read as literal expressions of his relationship to his lady as well as of his position in the court.*]

Wyatt's love lyrics establish a relationship between lover and lady in which love is used as an instrument of power.

The conventional relationship between suppliant lover and unattainable lady, portrayed by Petrarch, is here rendered in reverse. The stance of Laura's lover is one of unremitting respect and idealization, taken with good will and a melancholy tinged occasionally with self-pitying egoism. The difference, as well as the indebtedness, becomes immediately clear when we consider Wyatt's poetry. The relationship of idealized lady and adoring lover has been given a malign twist, so that we have instead a sadistic lady glorying in her power over a lover whose "love" is measured by his desire for conquest or revenge. In a word, Petrarch's love as adoration has become Wyatt's love as power.

I am proposing to read Wyatt's love lyrics as if they meant exactly what they say. That is, I hope to show that the bulk of his poetry presents a coherent psychological situation and that the conventional postures he adopts are partly the vehicles and partly the very embodiments of that situation. Love conventions are a symbolic expression of how love was understood in the Renaissance, if not necessarily how it was felt in many specific cases. The distinction to make is not between conventional and "original" poetry, but rather between a use of conventions which engages the psychological contours of the "experience" it renders, and one that does not. By "psychological contour" I refer to a precision by which many of Wyatt's poems succeed in drawing together a number of disparate expressed and conventional states of mind in order to show their interconnections and mutual dependence. Thus the measure of their success or failure is the coherent complexity with which they manipulate conventional materials so as to illuminate the felt psychological movements that are themselves the foundations of these materials.

Throughout Wyatt's poems a consistent syndrome of psychological actions and reactions is outlined, each poem dealing with a part, with the rest adumbrated and taken up in still other poems. From these it is possible to reconstruct the typical Wyatt "love situation." First of all there is the speaker himself, "Wyatt" as he chooses to project himself in poetry, who may or may not have been coextensive with the courtier suspected of an affair with Anne Boleyn and who later served as Henry VIII's trusted ambassador. He is a complicated fellow, a mixture of real and feigned naïveté, lacking in self-confidence and therefore distrustful always of the lady's affection, prone to simple idealization and its concomitant deflation into hardened cynicism.

His attitude toward the lady is likewise characterized by paradoxical psychological movements. On the one hand, he views her as desirable, he swears an absolute fidelity to her which is forever being condemned, he willingly cedes her his liberty (a favorite Wyatt word) in hopes that she will have pity on him. But there is something in him of the will to fail. Only rarely does he rest assured in her affection. Much more often he expresses knowledge after the fact that he always doubted that he would ever succeed, and there is almost a self-justifying masochism apparent in the confirmation of failure. As we

shall see, Wyatt's insight, or it may have been simply his honesty, presents us often with evidence that the speaker's rebuffs owe as much to his own attitude as to the lady's cruelty. On the other hand, his idealization of the lady places her wholly beyond reach—in Marvell's definitive deflation of the Petrarchan enterprise, his love "was begotten by despair / Upon Impossibility."[1] The failure to achieve the lady leads in turn to much righteous indignation, wherein the speaker projects himself as the wide-eyed, faithful innocent, betrayed by the deceit of a woman dishonorable to the core. This attitude in turn generates or, perhaps better, unmasks the latent hostility within this love. He wants revenge, he speaks in terms of tyranny and servility, he tries, with an overt attitude of sour grapes, to get one-up on her. The result, as we might expect, is just what the speaker assures us it is—a state of continual restless frustration and enslavement to passion. If we wanted to chart the psychological movements according to a hypothetical linearity of cause and effect, this state of hostile frustration prepares the way for another assault on the same or another lady, and the cycle starts all over again.

The lady herself is manifestly the projection of the speaker's own vision and, as such, is the perfect correlative to his own mixture of idealization and hostility: she is completely desirable and proportionately hateful. She is never simply indifferent to him; rather, the speaker projects her disdain as a positive desire to hurt him:

> Syns so ye please to here me playn,
>   And that ye do rejoyce my smart,
> Me lyst no lenger to remayn
>   To suche as be so overthwart.
>
> (No. 128, lines 1-4)

> Syns ye delite to knowe
> That my torment and woo
>   Should still encrese
>   Withoute relese,
> I shall enforce me so
> That liff and all shall goo,
>   For to content your cruelnes.[2]
>
> (No. 72, lines 1-7)

Thus, even in this rather oblique manner, the lady becomes wholly a function of the speaker's fantasies. In addition, she is, conventionally enough, fickle and beyond all trust—the reflection, in reverse, of his own claim to loving with complete fidelity. But the most important role she enacts, one which subsumes all the others, is that of conqueror. The speaker sees her as using her beauty primarily as an instrument of power over men, and it is in this relationship of conqueror to conquered that the core of the love situation outlined by Wyatt's poems is to be found.

Clearly, the speaker is ripe for a love relationship wherein power is the main motive. The lady appears to him as the totally "other," the alien, a prize set high above him in her desirability. In other words, we have a vertical scale of snobbery on which the speaker finds himself placed low in proportion as the lady's desirability places her high in a position of command over him. He is thus ruled both by his own desires and consequently by the lady herself. For this reason the speaker complains often of losing his liberty and of attempting to free himself from her:

> I aske none other Remedy
>   To recompence my wronge
> But ons to haue the lyberty
>   That I haue lakt so long.[3]

(No. 129, lines 25-28)

That his enslavement is the result mainly of his own passions is an insight that comes to us usually over the head of the speaker's complaint. For him it is the lady herself who has enslaved him.[4]

Linked with this drive to conquer his conqueror is "fansy," the dreams of love which the lover sets up and then seeks to realize. As he says in one poem,

> Now must I lerne to lyue at rest
>   And weyne me of my wyll,
> Ffor I repent where I was prest
>   My fansy to ffullfyll.

(No. 129, lines 1-4)

The psychology here is acute. What he loves is not so much the lady herself as the lady as she is imagined and dreamed of. Needless to say, such following after fancy is destined always to be disappointed. Fantasy projects an ideal, the desirability of which is in direct proportion to its impossibility. When such a fantasy seeks for realization, only a lady who holds herself unattainable will do.[5] An acute tension of self-frustration leading to cynicism is the result, neatly summed up in No. 71:

> In eternum I was ons determed
> For to have lovid and my minde affermed,
> That with my herte it shuld be confermed
>   In eternum.
>
> Forthwith I founde the thing that I myght like,
> And sought with loue to warme her hert alike,
> For, as me thought, I shulde not se the like
>   In eternum.

(1-8)

As might be expected, the love is disappointed, and the lover turns from idealist to cynic:

> In eternum then from my herte I kest
> That I had furst determined for the best;
> Nowe in the place another thought doeth rest,
>   In eternum.

(21-24)

The unbridled desire for the dream fantasy ends in enslavement both to whatever lady on whom he chooses to project the fantasy, and to his own will.

Further, fantasy is the prime instrument by which the lady appears to him as the totally "other," as desirable as she is unattainable, and vice versa. As he says at a moment of unusual truth,

> Of loue there ys a kynd
>   Whyche kyndlythe by abuse,
> As in a feble mynd,
>   Whome fansy may enduce
> By loues dysceatefull vse,
> To folowe the fond lust
> And profe of a vayn trust.

(No. 124, lines 8-14)

"Abuse" in this poem refers both to the deceits which characterize love and, consequently, the pains which the abused lover feels. Here we can easily see how susceptible the lover is to a love that is kindled by being abused. When we realize that the lover desires only the woman who is unattainable, the impossibility of his situation becomes clear. The only woman he desires is one beyond him on the scale of love snobbery, and therefore we might say that his desire is kindled only for those erotic objects which he unerringly reads as sure to frustrate this desire. No wonder the speaker cries so often for liberty! For he is an inmate of that most impregnable of prisons, that which he creates for himself in the desire to achieve the absolute freedom of his fantasy world.[6]

If I am right in my synthetic interpretation of the coherent psychology of Wyatt's poems, then the generally hostile tone of many of them is easily explained. The ambiguous love-hate which he feels for the lady is likewise a function of his desiring only his conquerors. If we interpret this desire as a species of snobbery, the highlights of the psychological motives become sharper. One wants what one values, and for the snob what he values must have two qualities: (1) it must be somehow superior to him (note how devaluation of self is always a main ingredient in snobbery and power plays in general); (2) he must not possess it. Wyatt's persona, it would appear, hates the lady, not only after she rejects him, but even before. If she swears fidelity, then he can interpret this as "onely wordes":

> A thowsand thoughtes and many dowbtes I fynde,
>   And still I trust thou [Venus/lady] canst not be
>   vnkind . . .
> Yet on my faith, full litle doeth remain
>   Of any hope whereby I may my self vphold;
> For syns that onely wordes do me retain,
>   I may well thinck the affection is but cold.

(No. 78, lines 18-19, 22-25)

How can he help doubting the lady's fidelity when it is precisely that lack of fidelity to himself that measures the aloofness which makes her desirable? In moments of greatest truth, the speaker's complicity in his failure is rendered so as to show his allegiance to the same syndrome of desires of which he is himself a victim:

Desire, alas, my master and my foo,
  So sore alterd thi selff, how mayst thou se?
Some tyme I sowght that dryvys me to and fro;
  Some tyme thow ledst that ledyth the and me.
What reson is to rewle thy subiectes so
  By forcyd law and mutabilite?
For where by the I dowtyd to have blame,
Evyn now by hate agayne I dowt the same.

                                              (No. 75)

It is not difficult to see that the speaker's desire is his foe because it is his master. But what puzzles him is that desire also at one time led the lady just as it led him, only to frustrate him by leading the lady away from him. The point is that both seem to be led by the "mutabilite" that governs the will to power. Therefore the speaker is seen to be involved in and possessed by the same drives that—projected onto the lady—will "blame" that drive in him.

The frustration of his desires usually ends in sour grapes and a kind of sniping insistence on being one-up, a psychological state from which several lyrics begin in recollecting the past history of the love affair. One of the most famous of these contains such lines of malevolent gloating as:

Perchaunce the lye wethered and old,
The wynter nyghtes that are so cold,
  Playnyng in vain vnto the mone;
Thy wisshes then dare not be told;
  Care then who lyst, for I have done.

                                      (No. 66, lines 26-30)

So far I have been drawing from a medley of poems fairly uncomplex. Each of them contributes an isolated insight into the psychological states frozen in conventional topoi. But a number of Wyatt's poems draw within themselves a wider range of interrelations which allow them to stand as summaries of the total theme, fragments of which are scattered throughout. Perhaps the most famous of Wyatt's lyrics, **"They fle from me"** (No. 37), gains some added significance from being seen in the context of the whole. The over-all metaphor is hunting, equally famous in the sonnet possibly about Anne Boleyn, **"Who so list to hount"** (No. 7). Here, there is a typical Wyatt ambiguity in the fact that it is ultimately uncertain who is hunting, and who has in fact caught whom. When the speaker says, "Yet may I by no meanes my weried mynde / Drawe from the Diere: but as she fleeth afore, / Faynting I folowe" (5-7), we may be sure that, though she is Caesar's, the speaker is certainly hers. It should be clear by now that hunting can easily be made a variant of the drive to conquer, and when a woman gets a man to chase her, she has already caught him.[7] Knowing this, and also recognizing that there is more than one way to trap a bird, we can now unlock the multiple ironies of **"They fle from me."**

The speaker finds it difficult to resolve two questions. First, how is it that "they" who had previously sought him now run from him? They might run to escape him or perhaps to tempt him to follow. Actually, both possibilities are correct, and are so in relation to each other. Second, the speaker does not understand how he has driven them away since he has treated them with "gentilnes."

They fle from me that sometyme did me seke
  With naked fote stalking in my chambre.
I have sene theim gentill tame and meke
  That nowe are wyld and do not remembre
  That sometyme they put theimself in daunger
To take bred at my hand; and nowe they raunge
Besely seking with a continuell chaunge.

                                              (1-7)

These birdlike women the speaker is lamenting the loss of are shown to us curiously ambiguous in their mixture of tameness and aggression. It is precisely this combination that the speaker cannot understand. Their stalking in his chamber casts them in the role of hunters. But, as we have seen in **"Who so list to hount,"** fleeing is also a kind of hunting, and we should be alert to the possibility that their tameness and meekness in taking bread at his hands signify one of several strategies for capturing him. After all, in any wooing situation the wooer must necessarily be both attacker and pleader—indeed, he may well attack under the sign of pleading—and both strategies have as their end the capture.

In the second stanza "they" becomes the singular "she" in a much-mooted transfer. We are reminded of the naked feet of the bird-women in the first stanza when the lady here strips naked for the capture:

Thancked be fortune, it hath ben othrewise
  Twenty tymes better; but ons in speciall,
In thyn arraye after a pleasaunt gyse,
  When her lose gowne from her shoulders did fall,
  And she me caught in her armes long and small;
Therewithall swetely did me kysse,
And softely saide, *dere hert, howe like you this?*

                                              (8-14)

Apparently the speaker's bread-strategy has succeeded, for now he has maneuvered one of the bird-women into seducing him. But when she catches him in her arms and exhibits both consciousness of her power to attract and pride of possession in her *"dere hert, howe like you this?"* we begin to realize the full implications of the situation. If he has caught her, she has also caught him, and given the mixed motives in this love affair, inevitably one or the other will seek a way to avoid being captured by his prey. The main crux of the poem lies in the way, within a love relationship conceived basically as a hunt for power, one must avoid being himself tied to the prey in the very attempt to conquer and hold it.

The speaker himself is not conscious of the malign ambiguities of the situation in which he is involved. On the contrary, he is thoroughly gentle and trusting, as "gentill tame and meke," we might add, as were the birdlike huntresses of the first stanza.

It was no dreme: I lay brode waking.
  But all is torned thorough my gentilnes
Into a straunge fasshion of forsaking;
  And I have leve to goo of her goodenes,
  And she also to vse new fangilnes.
But syns that I so kyndely ame serued,
I would fain knowe what she hath deserued.

(15-21)

The answer, which the speaker's sarcasm merits, is simply that he got what was coming to him. Overtly, he would see his "gentilnes" as the main virtue, making him deserving of love. But in his passivity he is playing for power as much as the lady was in her aggression. Both are playing for power, and the ambiguities which the poem defines lie in the fact that power results as much from yielding oneself to the capture as in hunting actively. Not the least of the perversions on which such love is capable of playing variations is the speaker's blindness to the situation. He assures us and himself that the lady in his arms (he in her arms?) was no fantasy: "It was no dreme: I lay brode waking." She has this advantage over the indefinite "they" of the first stanza: she had stalked him "ons in speciall" on a definite occasion. But the bird-women with their naked feet are as much fantasy as they are real: they are all the women of the speaker's erotic experience, advancing and withdrawing with a maddening lack of logic. The change from "they" to "she" thus establishes a bridge even while apparently exhibiting a gap. She is of course one of them, and the reality of this one occasion does not so much establish the facticity of the speaker's many disappointments, as throw them all into the border realm between actual encounter and erotic fantasy.

The lady seeks to capture without being captured: that is the answer to the speaker's question about the fleeing and seeking, for both movements are motivated by the same drive to power. As for the speaker's own co-operation in this merry-go-round, we can see that the strange fashion of forsaking is indeed the result of his gentleness. For the hand with the bread in it, as the woman well knows, being herself a master of catching with "her armes long and small," is a trap covered with velvet. The poem defines a complex love relationship in which both lover and beloved, hunter and prey, continually jockey for advantage, each one changing places with the other as the rigors of the game demand either fleeing or seeking.[8]

"They fle from me" analyzes masterfully the theme of love as power; contained in it are the seeds of many a greater treatment of the subject such as *Les Liaisons dangereuses* and *Le Rouge et le Noir*. Nevertheless, though conventional in its general situation, it realizes and manipulates the possibilities of this situation in a completely original manner. Wyatt's mastery of the inner logic of his conventional materials is perhaps better shown in a poem where the topoi are arranged in a more traditional fashion. **"Suffryng in sorow in hope to attayn"** (No. 107) gives us a situation wherein the lover is unable to tell his love and moves in a psychological vicious circle between hope and despair. The opening lines,

hovering over a four-beat accent before settling down to a continuous five-beat line, set up the outlines of the poem:

Suffryng in sorow in hope to attayn,
Desyryng in fere and dare not complayn,
  Trew of beleffe, in whome ys all my trust. . . .

(1-3)

The rest of the poem follows a structure that is typical of Wyatt's lyrics. It does not so much develop lineally as set forth one after another the moments implicit in a fixed but dynamic psychological situation. We discover that these various emotional moments lead each other round in an unchanging cycle of mutual cause and effect. Thus the speaker finds that the "Desyryng in fere" of the first stanza is the source both of his hope and his despair:

Hope ys my hold, yet in Dyspayre to speke
I dryve from tyme to tyme and dothe not Reke
  How long to lyve thus after loves lust. . . .

(6-8)

The refrain—"to serve and suffer styll I must"—thus sums up the emotional impasse created by his contradictory yet mutually supporting drives. He is completely removed from the usual delights of his life and cannot keep himself from speaking:

I hate that was sumtyme all my delyght;
  The cawse theroff ye know I have dyscust,
And yet to Reffrayn yt passythe my myght. . . .

(12-14)

The first three stanzas depict several opposed emotions which mutually support each other and so lead to their own frustration. Love leads the speaker to hope of attaining, but this hope brings with it fear of failure such that the very force of hope leads to despair. His despair is also "Dyspayre to speke," yet we see that this despair derives from the same passion that pushes him to speak. It is no wonder, then, that the speaker comments on his "losse of lybertye" (21) because his "trewthe regnith with fals mystrust" (23).

Here we see a psychological aberration peculiar to Wyatt's poetry. The speaker insists that his distrust of the lady and his fear of failure flow directly from his own open trustfulness. We may well doubt the honesty of the latter, which appears more often than not as a pose of wide-eyed vulnerability and in any case is incompatible with the dour intimations of deceit which Wyatt gives voice to so frequently. That this pose is a kind of stick with which to beat the lady comes out explicitly in at least one poem, "The knott whych ffyrst my hart dyd strayn" (No. 120), where the speaker insists that "I am yowrs assueredly" (11) in an argument establishing his "Ryght" to the lady's love. Little wonder that a lover capable of such a line should fail so often.

That he has failed often is given in **"Suffryng in sorow"** as precisely the reason for his doubts and despair:

Untrew by trust oftymes hathe me betrayd,
Mysusyng my hope, styll to be delayd,
  Fortune allways I have the fownd vnjust;
And so with lyke rewarde now am I payd:
  That ys, to serve and suffer styll I must.

(26-30)

Since we have already seen why he continues to serve and
suffer, this cry against false women and fortune must
strike us as at least disingenuous. Yet the speaker doggedly holds to his tattered good faith in the closing stanza, although by now his resolution to speak his love is
already doomed to failure by the very psychological knots
he has tied himself in:

Neuer to cesse, nor yet lyke to attayn,
As long as I in fere dare not complayn;
  Trew of beleff hathe allways ben my trust,
And tyll she knowythe the cawse of all my payn,
  Content to serve and suffer styll I must.

(31-35)

The word "serve" in the refrain represents the place of
the whole poem in the scheme of love as power outlined so far. It is clear how the speaker's self-distrust
coalesces with his vision of the lady as unattainable to
produce a syndrome of psychological forces calculated
to generate alternating desires to conquer and despair
of doing so.

Though many of Wyatt's love lyrics explore the different
facets of love as power, there is a handful of poems in
which the speaker shows himself unexpectedly at peace
in a love mutually reciprocated. Such is the one that begins
"After great stormes the cawme retornes" (No. 83).
It is not one of his most interesting pieces, since it lacks
precisely that psychological and resulting poetic tension
generated by the speaker on the rack of his own devising.
Interestingly cnough, the calm of love turns on the possession of just that assurance of fidelity that most of the
poems bewail the lack of:

Whereto dispaired ye, my frendes?
  My trust alway in her did ly,
That knoweth what my thought intendes,
  Whereby I lyve the most happy.

Lo! what can take hope from that hert
  That is assured stedfastly?
Hope therefore ye that lyve in smert,
  Whereby I ame the most happy.

(9-16)

In at least one lyric, however, Wyatt is able to make
genuine poetic capital from this theme, and it is one of
his finest. "Syns loue ys suche" (No. 125) displays a
mastery at deploying syntax within a complex stanza form
that Wyatt shows only occasionally and that mostly in the
later Penitential Psalms. The main strategy of the poem
involves a rejection of love's folly and slavery, only to
end with a surprise reversal in favor of love, a reversal
that is all the more legitimate since it demonstrates its

own logic as growing out of the previous argument as
well as transcending it. In the first stanza the speaker
addresses an interlocutor from whom he begs indulgence
for the amorous sins of his youth and asks that "suche
folye be forgott." The second stanza offers us a view in
retrospect of all love's traumas suffered in the past, but
reduced in scope according to the speaker's power to
summarize and dismiss them:

Ffor in my yeres of rekles youthe
  Me thought the power of loue so gret
That to her lawes I bound my trouthe
  And to my wyll there was no lett.
  Me lyst nomore so far to fett
Suche frute lo as of loue ensewthe;
  The gayn was small that was to gett,
And of the losse the lesse the reuthe.

(9-16)

There are none of the masochistic regrets that are found
in many of Wyatt's lyrics. The metrical irregularity in
placing "lo" after a spondee and before two weak syllables creates the perfect balance between the complete
experience of love's "frute" and the controlled rejection of it. The binding of the speaker's "trouthe" to the
laws of love and the consequent self-enslavement to
unbridled will, a whole theme in itself for many of
Wyatt's poems, are here brought to simple focus and
dismissed. The third and central stanza of the poem
achieves a sonorous firmness of statement, denied to
the speaker in more hectic moments, and mirrors perfectly the assurance in the sense:

And few there ys but fyrst or last
  A tyme in loue ons shall they haue;
And glad I am my tyme ys past,
  Henceforthe my fredome to withsaue.
  Now in my hart there shall I grave
The groundyd grace that now I tast;
  Thankyd be fortune that me gave
So fayre a gyfft, so sure and fast.

(17-24)

The opening quatrain shows Wyatt's violation of meter
at its most sure. The strong accent on "ons" and the
spondee "Henceforthe" respond to each other as both
metrical variations and correlatives in sense, and point
a statement otherwise perfectly regular in its onward
movement. The second four lines prepare for the poem's end, while directing the reader's present understanding of the "groundyd grace" to take it in as only the
final respite from his "tyme in loue." The metrical variations occurring with "Now," "there," and "Thankyd" are
played off against the metrically regular lines which
affirm the speaker's freedom in love with assurance and
tranquillity.

The fifth and final stanza shows an apparent reversal of this
freedom. This reversal leaves a gap in the explicit logic of
the poem, which is bridged to greater effect when we recognize that this gap is really a sign that the new love was
made possible only by a rejection of the old:

But frome henceforthe I do protest
　By presse of that that I haue past,
Shall neuer ceace within my brest
　The power of loue so late owt cast;
　The knott therof ys knytt ffull fast,
And I therto so sure proffest,
　Ffor euermore with me to last
The power wherin I am possest.

(33-40)

With the possible exception of "henceforthe" in the first line, there is not a single metrical variation here. The logic of this reversal, indeed of the whole poem, is summed up in the counterpointing of the second and fourth lines. "By presse of that that I haue past" refers us back to his rejection of love's enslavement. But the other line, in overtly allowing that he has readmitted "The power of loue so late owt cast," indicates that this new love is similar to the old in exerting its power, but different in exerting it beningly because within a new context of understood experience and achieved assurance.

This poem shows us a Wyatt one would not have expected, and of course it is possible that he did not write it, the ascription of poems in the Devonshire MS. not being certain. If he did not write this poem, then whoever did certainly had mastered the "Wyatt" experience in the first four stanzas and understood it. But be that as it may, this poem remains unique among these love lyrics, and it defines, if only by negation, the central experience which they comment on *in toto*.

That experience is conventional, to be sure. Yet, as I have tried to show, it is the measure of Wyatt's originality, that is, his mastery of traditional materials, that he went beyond both the imitators of Petrarch and many of his own imitators in reaching to the living human experience which these conventions had incapsulated and frozen into formula. The psychological postures characterizing love as power are essentially little more than reversals of those which the poets of the *dolce stil nuovo* had transmitted to their followers, and show the dark potentialities of which these postures of adoration and ecstasy were capable. Wyatt's main achievement was to perceive these potentialities in his traditional material and to realize them in his poetry so that the conventions were made to reveal anew their foundations in human experience.

NOTES

[1] "The Definition of Love," *Poems of Andrew Marvell*, ed. Hugh Macdonald (Cambridge, Mass., 1952), p. 34.

[2] The edition used is *Collected Poems of Sir Thomas Wyatt*, ed. Kenneth Muir (Cambridge, Mass., 1949), and the numbers of the poems are Muir's. I am aware of Raymond Southall's criticism of Muir's attributions in *The Courtly Maker* (New York, 1964); like him, I would also insist that the name "Wyatt" may well refer to a group of poets rather than to a single man. My only assumption, which is in fact based upon Muir's collection of a "total corpus" of poems, is that, whether by one man or several, the poetry in Muir's edition exhibits a remarkable unity of complex attitude and theme. To illustrate this unity is one of the objects of this paper.

[3] That love necessitates loss of liberty is a running motif in Wyatt's poetry. When the lady disdains him, he finds that she abuses him unjustly "Sins with good will I lost my libretye" (No. 153, line 3; cf. also No. 114). But even when he has yet to consummate his suit, he is still psychologically straitened "Twixt hope and drede locking my libertie" (No. 56, line 8, trans. from Petrarch). Indeed, whether accepted or rejected, the persona sees himself as bound in by his desire for the lady, and his escape from the power of his desire occasions the gloating refrain from No. 154: "But ha, ha, ha, full well is me, / For I am now at libretye." The obsession with liberty and freedom is an obvious symptom of love conceived as a struggle for power, for the persona continually views his relationship with the lady as one in which he is thralled to her and she in turn rejoices at the power she wields.

[4] It could be shown that the overriding concern of all Wyatt's poetry, including the Satires and the translation of the Psalms, is adjustment to a court and to a society in which the drive to power is dominant. Southall presents the fullest statement to date of the connection between the concerns with frustration and insecurity in the poetry and the ubiquitous environment of power intrigue in Henry VIII's court. For Southall, Wyatt's main criticism of courtly love was that it provided the grammar and framework of court intrigue and so dehumanized the love relationship. Southall sees Wyatt's standard as that of honesty and the demand for unfeigned love; cf. p. 89.

[5] The words "fancy" and "fantasy" are used in several mutually related senses in Wyatt's poetry, all of them corroborated by the *OED*. (1) "Fansy" means love or desire ("And when in mynde I did consent / To follow this my fansies will," No. 186, lines 19-20). (2) Related to this meaning but distinguishable is the uncertainty and fickleness of affection ("But fansy is so fraill / And flitting still so fast," No. 43, lines 13-14). (3) Finally, most pertinent to the present discussion, "fantasy" is the dream image of the ideal woman unstable in its fixations on any given woman precisely because no woman can fulfill it: "To fantasy pertaynys to chose: / All thys I knowe, for fantasy / Ffurst vnto love dyd me induse" (No. 121, lines 22-24); "Ffor fansy at his lust / Doeth rule all but by gesse" (No. 43, lines 17-18). Related to this motif is one of Wyatt's finest translations (from Filosceno), beginning: "Vnstable dreme according to the place, / Be stedfast ons; or els at leist be true" (No. 79).

[6] The other side of Wyatt's treatment of power and the desire for power comes in his Satires, his translations of the Psalms, and his prose translation, *Plutarch's Quyete of Mynde,* done into English at the request of Catherine of Aragon. In this last work we get Wyatt's overt analysis of the power play: "for we ar now come to that madnesse / that eche of our lyues hangeth vpon other mens / more than our own / and that our nature is so altred / in to a certeyn vnkynde and enuyous affectyon / nat so moch to glad in our owne / as to be troubled with other folkes welthes . . ." [p. 28; no pagination in the original]; I quote from the edition of Charles Read Baskervill (Cambridge, Mass., 1931). As Wyatt demonstrates in all these works (each of which is based on some other original), he is perfectly aware that the psychological turbulence caused by insecurity is the result of the individual himself casting his lot with the scale of power and snobbery.

[7] Wyatt's divergences from Petrarch's original are instructive. Donald L. Guss, "Wyatt's Petrarchism: An Instance of Creative Imitation in the Renaissance," *HLQ*, XXIX (1965), 10-11, sums them up: "Where Petrarch is drawn by the hind involuntarily, Wyatt hunts a definite prize. Where Petrarch enjoys seeing the hind, Wyatt is cruelly wearied by the hunt. And where Petrarch, deprived of the hind he knows not how, is left in sorrowful bewilderment at his loss, Wyatt willingly renounces the quest, perceiving it to be a trap. Essentially, then, where Petrarch expresses his painful recognition that the world whose beauty he loves is evanescent, Wyatt protests against the injustice that has deprived him of his reward."

[8] Leonard E. Nathan, "Tradition and Newfangleness in Wyatt's 'They Fle from me,'" *ELH*, XXXII (1965), 15, finds that "the speaker reveals in the conclusion no awareness of how implicated he is in the failure of the relationship, and it would be hard to show that Wyatt understood any more than his speaker." This is indeed a moot question in establishing whether any ironic circumference bounds the vision of Wyatt's persona. A simple solution, suggested by Wyatt's sober consciousness of the perversions of the lust for power in his other works, would be to make a complete distinction between the persona and the poet's irony at his expense. This hypothetical answer is belied by the continual recurrence of the same problem in most of the lyrics ascribed to Wyatt: one need not rehearse the same story having once mastered it in irony. In other words, whatever irony is found in Wyatt's poetry would be more calculated to involve the poet in the situation than to liberate him from it. It would be an irony whose real correlative would be self-pity. Cf. Ann Berthoff, "The Falconer's Dream of Trust: Wyatt's 'They Fle from me,'" *SR*, LXXI (1963), 477-90.

The Times Literary Supplement (review date 1970)

SOURCE: A review of *Collected Poems of Sir Thomas Wyatt* in *The Times Literary Supplement*, No. 3548, Febraury 26, 1970, p. 223.

[*In the following review of Muir and Thomson's updated edition of Wyatt's* Collected Poems, *the reviewer discusses newly discovered poems from the Blage manuscript.*]

Since Professor Muir discovered poems by Sir Thomas Wyatt in the Blage Manuscript at Trinity College, Dublin, ten or a dozen years ago, it has been clear that a thorough revision of the text of all Wyatt's poetry must be undertaken. Until that discovery our knowledge of Wyatt's poetry was mainly derived from two major manuscripts, one of which (Egerton 2711) had belonged to the poet himself, while the other (Devonshire 17492) had been compiled by or for certain ladies at the Court of Queen Anne Boleyn. The Blage Manuscript, compiled by Sir George Blage, who was a close friend of Wyatt, is of comparable importance with these two. These three manuscripts are, it is true, supplemented by other manuscript and printed sources, but between them they contribute 233 out of the 268 poems now included in the *Collected Poems*. This edition, prepared by Professor Muir in collaboration with Miss Thomson (author of the best study of Wyatt's poetry yet published) is likely to remain the definitive edition for the text of these poems.

There are indeed other problems, especially of attribution: how many of these poems are in fact by Wyatt? On this the editors offer a little guidance. In the third section of their introduction—"The Canon"—they state the nature of the problem: by all except the most extreme sceptics at least half the poems here printed can be accepted as by Wyatt. In the critical apparatus the editors helpfully provide brief evidence for Wyatt's authorship, which is sometimes supplemented in the commentary. They are not, perhaps, always as explicit, or as consistent, as one could have wished. "Syns Loue ys founde wythe parfytnes" (No. LI in *Unpublished poems . . . from*

the Blage MS., 1961) is now excluded from the canon, but no reason is given. Yet No. CLXXI in the present text is said to be "presumably not by W.", again with no reason stated. No. CXCIV, printed among "Doubtful Poems" in Professor Muir's "Muses Library" edition, is here re-admitted to the canon on the grounds that it is "at least as likely to be W's as many of the Devonshire MS poems printed as his" by earlier editors. However, Professor Muir and Miss Thomson probably decided that it was more important to provide an authentic text of some fine poems than to hesitate interminably about attributions. As they say, "we know comparatively little about the work of the other Court poets of the period". These questions of authorship will no doubt be discussed for many years; but no sensible person refuses to read a good poem until he knows who wrote it. Renaissance poets were not concerned with Romantic self-revelation.

Certainly Wyatt was not: he was either translating Italian poems, or adapting English ones much of the time, with occasional diversions into Horatian satire or paraphrases of the Psalms. He was much more at home in the native, and therefore medieval, tradition of lyric than in the Italian, Renaissance, tradition of sonnet and strambotto which he introduced to English. Skelton, his older contemporary, rejected the New Learning and remained obstinately medieval; Surrey, his younger contemporary, was entirely converted to the Renaissance manner, so that for Thomas Warton he was "the first English classical poet". Wyatt, in temper as in time, lay between the two: he was of less interest therefore to Elizabethan or Augustan poets, but in our own time his reputation has surpassed Surrey's. This is in part due to pseudo-Romantic interpretations of his poetry, and in part to a current preference for poetry that is nearer to the spoken word. In fact most of the best of Wyatt's poetry derives from his attempt to make acceptable to a Tudor Court audience the lyric tradition of the fifteenth century.

The commentary in this new edition provides almost all the help that anyone needs and is especially valuable in that it uncovers English as well as Italian antecedents for Wyatt's expression. Many of these notes are attributed to WMT, whose identity is disclosed in the Sigla as "W.M. Tydeman", but whose work (published or unpublished) is not listed. One might have wished for rather fuller information about musical settings for Wyatt's poems in view of recent controversy on this very relevant matter. Some settings are mentioned but not others and Miss Maynard's reply to Dr. Stevens is not referred to until the commentary on No. CLVIII. (Perhaps the commentary on earlier poems had been completed before her articles appeared?) However these are minor criticisms of a most valuable piece of scholarship, which provides a secure foundation for the study of a major poet, who, more than any other, bridged the gap between "Medieval" and "Renaissance".

Pamela Dembo (essay date 1971)

SOURCE: "Wyatt's Multi-faceted Presentation of Love," in *UNISA English Studies*, Vol. IX, No. 4, December, 1971, pp. 5-10.

[In the following essay, various attitudes toward love are explored in Wyatt's poetry.]

In this article, I should like to explore the variety of Wyatt's attitudes to love. Wyatt differs from a number of Elizabethan poets in that his poetry is not centred around the beloved but on the experience of love itself. He portrays mutual and unrequited love, quarrels and reconciliation, contentment and satiety, and the perils of wooing. He presents woman's fickleness as well as her constancy; and the poet himself, as lover, hovers between assurance and doubt, forceful insistence and gentleness, impatience and tolerance, independence and loss of liberty.

In the following poem, Wyatt adopts a characteristic attitude of wariness to love and his beloved. That they are curious phenomena is suggested by his oblique reference to them through impersonal pronouns:

> *Ryght true it is, and said full yore agoo:*
>   *Take hede of him that by thy back the*
>   *claweth.*
> *For none is wourse then is a frendely ffoo;*
>   *Though they seme good, all thing that*
>   *the deliteth,*
> *Yet know it well, that in thy bosom*
>   *crepeth:*
> *For many a man such fier oft kyndeleth,*
> *That with the blase his berd syngeth.*

The seemingly indiscriminate shift from 'him' (1.2) to a 'frendely ffoo' (1.3), to 'they', 'it', and 'that' (11.4-5), is calculated to convey an attitude of gingerness. The poet has proved by experience the truth of the old proverb (in line 2), thus his pronouns hold at a respectful distance the creature of insidious delight that, like fire, requires cautious handling.

Similarly, in two other poems,[1] love is tentatively re-approached after experience has taught caution:

> *It may be good, like it who list,*
>   *But I do doubt: who can me blame?*

And:

> *Though that with pain I do procure*
> *For to forgett that ons was pure,*
>   *Within my hert shall still that thing,*
>   *Unstable, unsure, and wavering,*
> *Be in my mynde withoute recure?*

Here, the use of impersonal referents ('it', 'that thing') paradoxically makes the person or experience so described seem more intimate. More effective than similes, their seeming neutrality suggests that the poet has been scarred by the experience and now views it at a distance like a snake at stick's end.

In **"What Wourde is That,"** the use of the impersonal pronoun conveys depth of emotion and tolerated chagrin rather than wariness, and since direct reference to Ann Boleyn would have been dangerous, this obliqueness is also expedient.

> *What wourde is that that chaungeth not,*
>   *Though it be tourned and made in twain?*
> *It is myn aunswer, god it wot,*
>   *And eke the causer of my payn. . . .*
>
> *Handell it soft and trete it tenderly,. . . .*

Wyatt's curious use of 'they' instead of 'she' in **"They Fle from Me,"** has been noted by a number of commentators. J. D. Hainsworth writes:

> *A desire to disguise the real meaning, and make what is personal appear conventional, may be part of the explanation of the difficulty of these poems. No doubt it could be dangerous to those in power. . . .* [2]

While this is true, the pronouns also seem to indicate that the poet's fortune in worldy affairs as well as in love are going awry. The beloved remains firmly in the foreground, but the world is always sensed in the background:

> *Ffor where I sue*
>   *Redress of all my grieff,*
> *Lo, they do most eschew*
>   *My hertes relieff.*
>
> *Alas, my dere,*
>   *Have I deserved so,*
> *That no help may appere*
>   *Of all my wo?*

This is perhaps why G.F. Nott in his 1815 edition of Wyatt's poems entitles **"They Fle from Me,"** as **"The Lover Sheweth how He is Forsaken of Fortune who Sometime Favoured Him."** The plural pronoun 'they' in this poem also contributes a specific tone to the lover's complaint. His reproach of the beloved is made milder by the plural reference, as one might say of a specific person who has been unkind: 'People are sometimes cruel'. It is the seeming gentleness of reproach in the first stanza that causes the reader to react more emphatically to the lady's betrayal of the poet.

Just as Wyatt's reproach of the beloved gains effectiveness from his portrayal of himself as gentle, so in the poem beginning **"Ye know my herte"**, he claims blameless service, and reinforces his complaint with parenthetical reminders that the lady knows this is so. Thus, by implication, she is cruel to ignore his patient devotion:

> *Ye know my herte, my ladye dere,*
>   *That sins the tyme I was your thrall*
> *I have bene yours bothe hole and clere,*
>   *Tho my rewards hathe bene but small:*
>   *So am I yet and more then all,*
>   *And ye kno well how I have served,. . . .*

The reminders are varied throughout the poem:

Ye know, also, though ye saye naye . . .

Ye kno yt ware a just request . . .

And I knowe well how frowerdly
Ye have mystaken my true intent . . .

And I knowe well all this ye knowe. . . .

The poem concludes with the guileless assertion that he is her own beloved which assertion, characteristically, is mined with a reproach of neglect should she still fail to respond:

Why are ye then so cruell ffoo
Unto your owne that loveth you so?

A similar method of persuasion combined with reproach is found in **"Forget not Yet,"** where his true service, suffered with patience and willingness, is conveyed by phrases such as the following:

the tryde entent / of such a truth as I have ment

My gret travayle so gladly spent

The wery lyffe . . . / The sute, the servys
none tell can

The paynfull pacyence in denays

How long ago hathe ben and ys / The mynd
that never ment amys

The wyche so long hathe the so lovyd,
Whose stedfast faythe yet never moved

Once again, the lady is reminded that she knows all this, and her ingratitude is implied in 'ye know syns whan' and in the exhortations which ruthlessly begin and end each stanza, 'forget not yet'. As in **"Ye Know My Herte,"** the final stanza asserts that he is her 'owne aprovyd', and we are left feeling that the beloved has been fickle rather than that she always has been obdurate.

Wyatt's ruthless insistence on confronting the beloved with her fickleness, and her feigned denial of changed affections is also found in **"Blame not My Lute,"** which like **"Forget not Yet,"** derives masculine force from the use of chiasmus. Reproach is inescapably brought to the lady's attention in every stanza:

Tho my songes be sume what strange,
And spekes suche wordes as toche thy change . . .

Then tho my songes be sume what plain,
And tochether some that use to fayn, . . .

And tho the songes which I endight
Do qwytt thy chaunge with rightfull spight, . . .

Then sins that by thyn own desartt
My soinges do tell how trew thou artt, . . .

But if tyll then my fingers play
By thy desartt their wonted way, . . .

And yf perchance this folysh Rymyme
Do make the blushe at any tyme,. . . .

Wyatt is not one to suffer without causing the causer of his pain some smart too, 'spyght askyth spight and changing change, / And falsyd faith must nedes be knowne'. As he says in **"Spight hathe no Powre,"**

Yt doth suffice she dothe me wrong,
And that herself doth kno the same.

The poem is dramatic, and witty, for the lady first objects, then breaks the lute strings—quite understandably. With male persistence and strength, the poet returns with restringed lute to complete his song.

This combination of wit with reproach is comparable with Donne's "The Apparition," but Donne also shows himself more gentle than Wyatt in his expression of recrimination, as in "When my Harte was Mine Owne." He writes, nor can falshood whett / My dull minde to revenge. That I will leave / To thee, for thine owne guilt will that begett'. Donne's claim of unshakeable constancy in this poem highlights the beloved's lack of faith:

And in exchange I gave thee such a harte
As had it bene example unto thine,
None could have challenged the smallest parte
Of it or thy love.

Wyatt similarly chastises the beloved with assurances which are, however, more truculent than those of Donne:

I shall be hyres, she may be sure,
As long as my lyff dothe endure.

The variety of Wyatt's attitudes of recrimination is balanced by objectivity and tolerance. For example, **"A Robyn, Joly Robyn"** expresses opposed accounts of experience, the plaintiff finding women fickle and deceitful, while the respondent finds them true. The plaintiff says:

She loveth an othre better then me,
And yet she will say no. . . .

Womens love is but a blast
And torneth like the wynde. . . .

The respondent replies:

I fynde no suche doublenes,
I fynde women true.
My lady loveth me doutles,
And will chaunge for no newe.

Wyatt's final solution is characteristic of his bias towards independence, for the respondent advises the plaintiff to warm himself at other fires rather than suffer indefinitely.

That deceitfulness requires a willing dupe is recognised in the poem **"Full Well Yt Maye be Sene,"** where Wyatt does not blindly rage at women:

> Of love there ys a kynd
> Whyche kyndlythe by abuse,
> As in a feble mynd,
> Whome fansy may enduce
> By loves dysceatefull use,
> To followe the fond lust
> And profe of a vayn trust. . . .
> And some can thys concyle,
> To gyve the symple leave
> Them sellfes for to dysceave. . . .

Moreover, in **"It May be Good"** he can laugh at himself made awkward by uncertainty:

> For oft assured yet have I myst,
> And now again I fere the same.
> The wyndy wordes, the les quaynt game,
> Of soden chaunge maketh me agast:
> For dred to fall I stond not fast.

And also in **"What Menythe Thys"**:

> But yff I sytte nere her by,
> With lowd voyce my harte dothe cry,
> And yet my mowthe ys dome and dry:
> What menys thys?

Wyatt's tolerance of woman's inconstancy retains a sting of experience and of reproach in **"Dyvers Dothe Use"**:

> I will not wayle, lament, nor yet be sad;
> Nor call her fals that falsley ded me fede:
> But let it passe and think it is of kinde,
> That often chaunge doth plese a
> womans minde.

These lines also exhibit the poet's often expressed determination to be his own man, not a woman's lapdog. Similarly, in **"Madame, Withouten Many Wordes,"** he refuses to play the game of coquetry in which the man is baited and played with, but is given no reward:

> Yf it be yea I shalbe fayne;
> If it be nay, frendes as before;
> Ye shall an othre man obtain,
> And I myn owne and yours no more.

Also, in **"Mye Love toke Skorne,"** he refuses with crisp civility to serve longer, since where love is not mutual it is, for him, dotage:

> But sins that thus ye list to ordre me,
> That wolde have bene your servante true
> and faste,

> Displese the not, my doting dayes bee paste:
> And with my losse to leve I must agre;
> For as there is a certeyne tyme to rage,
> So ys there tyme suche madnes to asswage.

Since the lady chooses to dismiss him, he will leave with manly dignity though her loss causes him pain. That independence is not won without a struggle is seen in **"Most Wretched Hart,"** which records the poet's dialogue with himself, the verses alternating between despair and reason. The question, 'Most wretched hert, why art thou not ded?' is answered with, 'he is wretched that wens him soo', and 'who hath himself shal stande up right'. Though these are reasonable answers, the poet still needs to convince himself emotionally that he is his own man. Thus he asks, 'Hath he himself that is not sure?' and the voice of reason must admit that this question is the worst—'who feres not that?'—for one cannot escape oneself. The cause of despair only becomes evident in the ninth stanza in which the poet, not yet convinced, cries out:

> Seist thou not how they whet their teth,
> Which to touche thee somtime ded drede?

Only after the release of this protest is some consolation found in the acceptance that 'happe doth come again and goo'.

It may be questioned whether the above is a love poem at all, but as in **"They Fle from Me,"** it is flexible enough to be considered both in the category of love and of the poet's general fortune. One thread of unity in Wyatt's Egerton and Devonshire manuscripts may be said to be the theme of the poet's having 'outworn the favour' that he had. This is why the image of the beloved is often fused with that of fortune and why, when Wyatt addresses Fortune with her 'dyvers change' and her chain that so enwraps him, he could equally well be addressing the lady. In **"To Wisshe and Want,"** Fortune is described as follows:

> If fortune list yet for to lowre . . .

> Such cruell chaunce doeth so me threte . . .

> Ffortune is deiff unto my call
> My torment moveth her not at all . . .

and in **"Ons As Me Thought"** the poet is kissed by Fortune who keeps her promise to him though it seemed, at first, that she would not.

My discussion to this point has shown how Wyatt, having had and lost the joys of love and fortune, expresses wariness, reproach (coupled with reminders of his own worth), wit, manly independence and objectivity. That his poetry, in content, is ruggedly independent of the love convention is clear, as there is no rehearsal of the usual motifs—laments on absence, the *carpe diem*, and the pursuit and granting of a kiss. One has the sense not of lover and beloved playing out a drama but rather of the constant presence of a forthright man of integrity who writes as he is. In **"I Am as I Am,"** he says:

I am as I am and so will I be . . .

I am as I am and so do I wright. . . .

Thus, when he is jarred by frustration, his verse conveys the very rhythm of discord and undisguised impatience, for 'How may a morning hert / Set fourth a pleasaunt voise? / Play who that can that part. . . . ' Throughout the poem, the unlyrical words are matched with a lurching abruptness of rhythm:

But yet perchaunce som chaunce
  May chaunce to chaunge my tune;
And when suche chaunce doeth chaunce,
  Then shall I thanck fortune.

Just as he refuses to aestheticise or falsify his feelings in speech, so his reaction to love's games is one of impatience; he bluntly seeks for ease of his desires. In **"To Wisshe and Want,"** he rejects the pity of his mistress and of those who hear his complaint, nor does he find comfort in Fortune's changing unless it fulfils his wishes. He rails against all these and himself, as he does not wish to escape the cause of his own woe, 'if from the fyre me list not goo, / If then I burne, to plaine me so / What may it availl me?'

Similarly, while he has the objectivity to realise the girl's docility in **"Processe of Tyme,"** he rejects her humbleness, and his own in her service, as being irrelevant as it does not ease his frustration.

Eche fiers thing lo! how thou doest exceede,
  And hides it under so humble a face;
And yet the humble to helpe at nede,
  Nought helpeth tyme, humblenes, nor place.

In **"Lo, What It is to Love,"** though love is admitted to be a pleasant and fervent fire, its pain renders it more trouble than it is worth, and in **"Farewell Love,"** the poet refuses to be bound longer by love's laws. In chagrin at his 'sherpe repulse', he churlishly equates love and women with climbing 'rotten boughes'.

In addition to the subtly differing attitudes which Wyatt expresses towards love, the variety of situations and moods which he presents gives breadth to his portrayal of the subject. **"Ys It Possible,"** has a mood of good-humored tolerance and amusement—an argument between the lovers leads to reconciliation in bed. The lady has moved from love, to hate, and then to relentment, and the poet teases her by expressing his amazement at love's vagaries:

Ys yt possible
  That eny may fynde
Within on hert so dyverse mynd,
To change or torne as wether and wynd?
  Is it possible?

Chiasmus and the form of the verse on the page demonstrate the variation in the lady's moods. In the penultimate stanza, double entendre is used to stress love's extreme shifts and to suggest that the heated debate ended in lovemaking:

It is possyble
  Ffor to turn so oft,
To bryng that lowyste that wasse most aloft,
And to fall hyest yet to lyght sofft:
  It is possyble.

The change from question to affirmation in the framing figure conveys rejoicing and amused triumph on the part of the lover. The last stanza is likewise debonair in the pun on 'lycence' and 'leve'—some ladies are brought to bed by their consent to a wedding; others simply by their consent, and then men leave them.

In **"Suche Happe as I ame Happed in,"** the poet writes with a bouyancy derived from satisfaction of his desires, and good-humoredly presents an unexpected paradox of love, 'a new kynde of unhappenes'—that love's desire outruns the performance:

To do me good what may prevaill
  For I deserve and not desire,
And still of cold I me bewaill,
  And raked ame in burnyng fyer . . .

What wonder is this gredy lust
To aske and have, and yet therefore
  Refrain I must. . . .

Refrain I must: what is the cause?
Sure as they say: so hawkes be taught.

As a hawk is trained by making it walk on one's turning wrist until it tires and its will is broken, so the poet has been exhausted in love's labour. But the last lines seem to indicate that he defies his exhaustion:

But in my case laieth no such clause,
  For with suche craft I ame not caught. . . .

Wyatt, like Donne in "The Flea," vividly portrays the reciprocal reactions of beloved and lover in ***"Suffised not, Madame:"***

Suffised not, madame, that you did teare
My wofull hart, but thus also to rent
The weping paper that to you I sent,
Wherof eche letter was written with a teare. . . .

The poet retains his dignity through somewhat stiff formality, yet his indignation provokes a smile for it is incongruous with the image of his weeping over each letter.

Amusement is also roused in **"Who Hath Herd,"** by the picture of the girl's mounting irritation at being presented with the lover's complaint so that her furious stitching gives the impression that she wishes each stitch were his heart. The poet's outrage is greater than the occasion warrants, and this, together with his satisfaction when she pricks her finger, gives the poem a light-hearted wit.

> *Who hath herd of suche crueltye before?*
> *That when my plaint remembered her my woo*
> *That caused it, she cruell more and more*
> *Wisshed eche stitche, as she did sit and soo,*
> *Had prykt myn hert, for to encrese my sore;. . . .*

Typical of Wyatt is the imputation that if the lady causes grief, she should rightfully provide the remedy. The impelling rhythm of this poem captures the girl's growing irritation as she stitches.

Wyatt portrays not only the effects of woman's fickleness but also those of betrayal by a man. The imagery and choice of words in **"Farewell All my Wellfare"** convey the delicacy of the girl's lament:

> *Ffarewell all my wellfare,*
> *My shue ys trode awry;*
> *Now may I karke and care*
> *To syng* lullay by by.

Her complaint has none of Wyatt's usual male vigour and retributiveness:

> *Alas! he ys unkynd dowtles*
> *To leve me thus all comfortles.*

The girl laments in two-line statements throughout the poem, and this also captures the rhythm of girlish speech in falling cadences and unsustained energy.

That Wyatt is essentially gentle despite the cutting reproaches which love's pangs often elicit, is seen in **"There was Never Nothing."** Tender sympathy for a girl, whose love he cannot return, is expressed in the mingling of his sighs with hers in the refrain, 'Alas the While'. He is hurt by her unhappiness as much as she is:

> *Her paynes tormented me so sore*
> *That comfort had I none,*
> *But cursed my fortune more and more*
> *To see her sobbe and grone:*
> *Alas the while!*

The girl wrings her hands, turns away and drops her head, unable to speak with grief. Her tears falling in his neck suggest his close comforting of her, and her words express the hopelessness of her love, for though she knows their relationship is breaking, she still loves: 'all thing decayes, / Yet can I not remove'.

Wyatt also writes of the pain of mutual love where consummation is prevented by a third party. In **"I Lovve Loyyd,"** the lady has consented to his pleas, but her consent is worse than denial:

> *O deadly yea! O grevous smart!*
> *Worse then refuse, unhappe gaine!*

> *I loove: whoever playd this part*
> *To lovve so well and leve in payn?*

The intractability of circumstance and the unrelievable pain of longing are stressed by variations of the same thought in the last line of each stanza:

> *To lovve so well and want our will . . .*

> *To lovve so well and leve in woo . . .*

> *To lovve so well and not rejoice . . .*

> *To lovve so well and it to wantt. . . .*

Each line develops tension between fulfilment and lack of fulfilment.

Wyatt frequently uses devices such as the refrain and chiasmus. In **"Alas the While,"** this causes the poem to continue in the silence after the words have ended, and in **"In Eternum I was ons Determed,"** the final 'In eternum' gains curt strength from all its previous uses.

Nothing seems merely ornamental in Wyatt's poetry; not only does he explicitly claim that he writes as he is, but his forthright statement of love's grievances, paradoxes, sorrows and tenderness, all give the impression of honesty to himself and to reality. Likewise, his imagery is not fanciful but is drawn from the court and nature, the two worlds with which he was familiar. He writes of deer, hawks, and love's rotten boughs and baited hooks; of his foes as whetting their teeth; and of his beloved as the crop and root of his health, and as the object of his devoted fealty. Beneath the sophistication of the court, one senses its animality, and beneath the instincts of love there is the courtliness of service. His quoting of homely proverbs such as 'Take hede of him that by thy back the claweth' in **"Ryght True It is,"** and of simple objects like the girl's shoe which, like her love, no longer fits well in **"Farewell All my Wellfare,"** contributes to the unaffected simplicity of his poetry. Wyatt's appeal perhaps lies in this retention of integrity and in his mature and manly assessment of the vicissitudes of his broad experience of love and the world.

NOTES

[1] The poems are numbered 21 and 45 in the Kenneth Muir edition of Wyatt's verse. I shall, however, give the first lines of poems to which I refer as titles, so that readers may find them more easily in other editions.

[2] *Essays in Criticism*: 'Wyatt's use of the Love Convention', No. VII (1957), p. 91.

Nancy Leonard (essay date 1977)

SOURCE: "The Speaker in Wyatt's Lyric Poetry," in *The Huntington Library Quarterly,* Vol. XLI, No. 1, November, 1977, pp. 1-18.

[*In the following essay, the speaker in Wyatt's poems is seen as a vehicle for his unique aesthetic sensibility.*]

The lyrics of Sir Thomas Wyatt have prompted comment about their role in the development of Tudor poetry ever since 1557. Richard Tottel's appreciation of the "depe witted" Wyatt extended more to Wyatt's demonstration that the English "tong is able . . . to do as praiseworthely as ye rest" than to his "weightinesse" of style.[1] As for poetry, Tottel preferred Surrey. By now, the obligatory comparison between Wyatt and Surrey has faded away, and Wyatt's reputation as a poet is considerably higher than Surrey's, for all the latter's "honouable stile"; but Wyatt's reputation still rests more on his place in the development of English lyric than on the distinctive quality of his poetry. Various students of Wyatt have, of course, sought to define that quality, beginning, perhaps, with Tillyard, who drew attention to the "dramatic touch" that marks Wyatt off from writers of medieval lyric and anticipates the work of Donne.[2] Later critics, particularly Hallett Smith and Patricia Thomason, have provided valuable accounts of Wyatt's characteristic concerns as an artist.[3] Nevertheless, studies of Wyatt have usually given less attention to the poetry than to its contexts in medieval and Renaissance lyric traditions.[4] This essay, to help even the balance, moves to the exploration of Wyatt's lyric art. It seeks to read both his Petrarchan imitations and his native lyrics as the reflection of a single aesthetic sensibility, and to define the means by which he establishes the individuality for which he is often admired.

Concentrating on Wyatt's love poetry, I will argue that a major source of Wyatt's achievement in lyric is his complex and powerful handling of the speaker in the poem. Wyatt deals with conventional themes and attitudes in his poetry of love, yet his major emphasis in the poems, expressed as subject and strategy, is the subjectivity of the speaker.[5] It is important to emphasize that this subjectivity belongs to the speaker, not to the poet, because the question of what a poem "expresses" has always been a vexed one in Renaissance studies. Wyatt's focus on the experience of the speaker allows him both to create the power of feeling in a way appropriate to lyric, and to comment on that power in response to his material, the conventional attitudes of courtly love. The "characteristic themes" of Wyatt, so concisely formulated by Kenneth Muir, are in my view more properly understood as the forms of the speaker's experience, which is itself the center of the poetry. The poet writes "of the pain and smart of love, of the cruelty, disdain, deceit and faithlessness of women, of the absence of pity and steadfastness, on the need of patience, and on the inconstancy of Fortune" as occasions, then, for the dramatization of states of mind.[6]

Though Wyatt's love poetry clearly treats these conventionally defined subjects and attitudes, it does so with a curious lack of specificity. The absence in the poetry of concrete descriptions of the beloved is clear. No conventional *blazon* of the lady's beauties, characteristic of the earlier lyric, appears in Wyatt, nor does the poet describe the lady in order to investigate attitudes of mind,

as in Petrarch. Nothing in Wyatt anticipates the emotional and thematic value of the concrete descriptions of the lady in Spenser's *Amoretti,* nor her concretely imagined dramatic role in the poetry of Donne. Indeed, external nature in general, in addition to the concrete presence of the beloved, is excluded or minimized in the poetry.[7] Further, Cupid, Venus, and all the "mythological paraphernalia of Love" are excluded from the poetry, and the operations of fortune, so concretely imagined in other lyrics, are subjectivized as the turning away of a lady's face or as an abstract operation defined by its subjective effects, as other readers have observed.[8] Wyatt transforms Petrarchan commonplaces from conventional conditions of a generalized kind, though concretely defined, to internal stimuli for the speaker's states of mind.[9] The absence of concretely described objective conditions for the lover's feelings is no mere stylistic difference between Wyatt's poetry and other love poetry. It reflects, rather, a deliberate focus on subjectivity as subject matter, a focus apparent in both the Petrarchan translations and adaptations of Wyatt and in his original lyrics.

The weary despair of loving a disdainful mistress is a conventional theme in love poetry of both native and continental kinds, yet Wyatt's handling of the theme reveals the way that the feeling itself is the subject of the poem, rather than the contexts, genesis, or even the evaluation of it. **"To wisshe and want and not obtain"** is a characteristic treatment of the theme, revealing the concentration of focus achieved in the original lyric. Consider the development of the first stanza:

> To wisshe and want and not obtain
> To seke and sew esse of my pain,
> Syns all that ever I do is vain,
>   What may it availl me?[10]

In this opening, the speaker defines the experience of his love as an interplay between his desire and its futility. The first line establishes this interplay by the clear contrast between "wisshe and want" in its first half, and "not obtain" in its second. The next two lines repeat the same contrast, as the desire expressed in the second line, "to seke and sew esse of my pain," yields to the futility in the third line, "syns all that ever I do is vain." This interplay always moves from desire to the dominant feeling of frustration, of not having, which forms the emotional center of the poem. The coupling of desire and dissatisfaction offered in the opening line is reinforced by the structure of each stanza of the poem, in which the first three lines describe the struggle of the lover, and the summary refrain emphasizes its futility. Thus, the speaker's love is self-reflexive; the very conflict of the poem is subjectively defined. The lover struggles not with his mistress, but rather with himself.

It is the measure of the speaker's insistent inwardness that not even the mistress, its ostensible cause, can draw it out of itself. Wyatt demonstrates this effectively, in a typically sophisticated use of the refrain to comment upon its speaker, at the midpoint of the poem:

Ye, tho the want of my relief
Displease the causer of my greife,
Syns I remain still in myschiefe,
      What may it availl me?

Perhaps the first thing to notice here is that the mistress is not even named in her own person; she is present to the speaker, and defined for him, only as "the causer of my greife." This subjectivizing identification, in effect, reduces the loved one to a part of the process of loving her. That process of loving is itself transformed, driven in ward, as its meaning changes from the movement of desire, however frustrating, to the stasis of an unyielding misery. Whereas the first few stanzas of the poem defined the speaker's love as a frustrated movement toward an object of desire, in this stanza love is simply the "greife" and "myschiefe" that this movement imposed on him. The speaker raises the possibility that she may not want to pain him, that his grief may "displease" her—a recognition that would necessarily establish a point of view inclusive of more than the self. Yet this point of view is summarily refused, as the speaker asserts that it cannot matter because he remains "in myschiefe." The feeling dominates him utterly even over the possible good will of the mistress.

The remaining stanzas of the poem continue to stress intense inward ness as the subject and experience of the poem by repeating, with the slightest of modifications, the psychological act just explored. The speaker evokes a source of possible help and in the instant casts it of in part by defining that source as a tenuous abstraction with little objective power for him. Just as the mistress was thought of only as "the causer of my greife," chance is evoked as that "cruell chaunce" which "doeth so me threte," that is, only as a catalyst for the speaker's inward "fretting":

Suche cruell chaunce doeth so me threte
Continuelly inward to fret,
Then of relesse for to trete
      What may it availl me?

The key term, of course, is the word "inward," which precisely identifies both the quality and the inescapable medium of this "fretting." As the speaker turns, in the course of the poem, to consider his mistress, chance, fortune, and finally, his own "despere," he is not enacting an analysis so much as he is repeating, with the slightest of modifications, the same experience: of *having* "continuelly inward to fret" *because* he does so. He insures the continuity of his "fretting" by the "inward" nature of his experience, by, in other words, a self-perpetuating imprisonment in self. The poem thus exploits the intense subjectivity implicit in the Petrarchan posture of the suffering lover. The imprisonment in subjectivity is neither a new nor a unique idea about love, of course; what seems distinctive is the way Wyatt shapes its power as experience, and does so by developing the role of the lyric speaker.

In another poem, **"Processe of tyme worketh suche wounder"** (82), Wyatt extends his subjectivizing pro-

cess in the handling of the speaker to what is perhaps its most radical extent. If, in **"To wisshe and want and not obtain,"** the mistress is converted into the mere "causer" of the speaker's grief, and the abstractions of chance and fortune are also subjectivized, in this poem Wyatt makes the larger conversion of external reality itself into inwardness:

Processe of tyme worketh such wounder,
      That water which is of kynd so soft
Doeth perse the marbell stone a sonder,
      By litle droppes faling from aloft.

And yet an hert that sems so tender
      Receveth no dropp of the stilling teres,
That alway still cause me to render
      The vain plaint that sowndes not in her eres.

The poem begins, in these first two stanzas, with the vivid awareness of an external process, the wearing away of stone by drops of water, but the poem immediately retreats from that awareness into a concentration on the heart from which it never emerges. The initial image appears in the poem only as a point of departure; the poem itself can be seen as an extended withdrawal from the mode of awareness it begins with. But the withdrawal is specific as well as general. The speaker not only moves from rain on stone to the heart, but in the process reinstates the falling rain, "litle droppes faling from aloft," in the personal dimension of experience represented by the heart, "stilling teres." The image, with its reflection of externals, is virtually dismantled, and the drops of rain, torn from the world or the speaker's awareness of it, are reconstituted as his tears, directly and futilely expressing his feeling. Yet even this reconstitution does not measure the full extent of the speaker's retreat from the contact with externality measured by the image. For the true center of attention is the heart, which is defined as that region of feeling which these tears never reach. Thus, the speaker places himself at two removes from reality: he subjectivizes his image of external process, and then draws himself back even from that subjectivization. His isolation in a realm of pure feeling is then confirmed by the fact that the sound of the tears, which might be expected to mediate between his mistress and himself by expressing his feelings, is cut off from her as well as from him. The sound never reaches her ears.

The forms of subjectivization visible in these original lyrics by Wyatt have their counterparts in the poet's translations and adaptations, which insist no less than the original poems on the intensely self-reflexive feeling of the speaker, often in his characteristic mood of weary despair. Again, the basic situation and the images that specify it are Petrarchan conventions; yet again, Wyatt's strategy is to emphasize the subjective force of the state of mind, its quality as experience.[11] The sonnet **"My galy charged with forgetfulnes"** (28) is a particularly effective and complex example.

My galy charged with forgetfulnes
      Thorrough sharpe sees in wynter nyghtes doeth pas

Twene Rock and Rock; and eke myn ennemy,
   Alas,
   That is my lorde, sterith with cruelnes;
And every owre a thought in redines,
   As tho that deth were light in suche a case.
   An endles wynd doeth tere the sayll apase
Of forced sightes and trusty ferefulnes.
A rayn of teris, a clowde of derk disdain,
   Hath done the wered cordes great hinderaunce;
   Wrethed with error and eke with ignoraunce.
The starres be hid that led me to this pain;
   Drowned is reason that should me consort,
   And I remain dispering of the port.

The Petrarchan conceit of the lover's soul as a ship weathering rough passage frames the basic situation. In the handling of the conceit, however, there is little attention to developing the specific resemblances between self and ship, and a great deal to increasingly direct expressions of feeling. As we read the first line, "My galy charged with forgetfulnes," all we know about the galley or self is the burden it bears; that is what, for the moment, we need to know. Yet we are not shown "forgetfulnes" through the implication and inference customarily developed by analogy, but are rather told directly what the galley "is." Our usual expectations about metaphor, that we know the tenor by means of the vehicle, are deliberately violated, so that tenor and vehicle seem separated but in a state of alliance, as expressions of the speaker's state of mind. As the poem proceeds, the alliance becomes unstable. Put another way, feeling comes to be named more and more directly, and to be dissociated from identification with the image. The effects of this process are to direct attention to feeling as such quite forcibly, and to question, as another indication of the speaker's state of mind, the power of the image to convey feeling.

The poem's structure is the first real clue to this process. The first six lines of the sonnet identify and establish the image of the self as ship, forming a complete unit of thought, and incidentally a complete sentence. The last eight lines describe what happens to the ship, that is, the "weather of feeling" and the distortions of value which emerge as effects of the situation. The sonnet offers, then, a "sestet of meaning" and an "octave of meaning" at odds with the octave and sestet created by rhyme. This structure creates for the reader an experience of perilous balance, through which he feels the speaker's situation more intimately.

In the first six lines of the "sestet of meaning," the vivid images of the opening yield increasingly to equations between the imagery and the speaker's state of mind. We move from a precise, though generalized, image of passage, "Thorrough sharpe sees in wynter nyghtes doeth pas," to the image of an "ennemy" defined only as a function in the speaker's state of mind: he is "my lorde," and he "sterith with cruelnes." The next line, "And every owre a thought in redines," makes the equation of image and feeling quite explicit; the oar "is" a thought in readiness. Such an equation, since it does not rely on the vehicle but names the tenor too, has the effects of dissociating

image and feeling and encouraging reliance on direct statement. The "octave of meaning" furthers this separation of image and feeling. The series of "of—" locutions, such as a wind "of forced sightes" and a cloud "of derk disdain," does this simply by naming feeling explicitly, and naming it not *as* the image but as *belonging to* the image—an effective deidentifying of the two. The speaker relies increasingly on direct statement, plain speech; the "cordes" that bind him are "wrethed with errour and eke with ignoraunce." Finally, the last three lines of the poem provide a culmination of the emphasis on feeling by making direct statements of evaluation:

   The starres be hid that led me to this pain;
      Drowned is reason that should me consort,
      And I remain dispering of the port.

Even the images chosen—the hidden stars, the absent consort, the distant port—by their very remoteness intensify the isolation and misery of the speaker. The images, so to speak, embody their own withdrawal from the poem, while the speaker names his pain and despair more explicitly than ever.

Wyatt's characteristic method in lyric, then, is to concentrate on the subjective power of the experience by his means of handling conventional themes and attitudes. This concentration is sometimes achieved by excluding objective elements entirely and sometimes by bringing in a kind of minimal objectivity in the form of concrete images of the world external to the speaker, in order to withdraw from objectivity, to focus even more radically on the inwardness of the speaker. Because the subjective emphasis characterizes both the original lyrics and the translations and adaptations, the two "kinds" of poetry that form Wyatt's lyric canon may be a good deal closer than they are usually perceived to be.

Probably the central means by which Wyatt shapes and governs the focus on subjectivity is the deliberate curtailment of the poem's intellectual, attitudinal, or narrative development of its initial situation.[12] The speaker in a typical Wyatt poem seems not so much to consider or examine his experience as to feel continually its power and immediacy. In its simplest form, this curtailment consists of presenting a poetic subject solely by means of repetition and dilation, thus inhibiting and often excluding analytical or emotional qualification. **"Tho I cannot your crueltie constrain"** (57) is a representative poem of this kind. The first stanza of the poem presents the speaker's powerlessness, caused by the disdain of an implicit mistress, as the subject of the poem:

   Tho I cannot your crueltie constrain
   For my good will to favor me again,
      Tho my true and faithfull love
      Have no power your hert to move,
         Yet rew upon my pain.

The opposition between the "crueltie" of the mistress, the subject of the first two lines, and the "true love" of the speaker, the subject of the next two, is more apparent than real. Both her cruelty and his love are defined only as signs of the power she has over him, that power which generates his plea for pity that concludes the stanza. What we *know* about her cruelty is the speaker's sense of powerlessness against it; what we *know* about his love is his own sense of its ineffectuality. Love and cruelty, lover and mistress, seem substantially identical, as variants of the powerlessness of the speaker. Grammatical repetition, in the parallel conditional clauses that begin with "Tho," serves to enforce our impression that the "dilation" or expansion of subject is more apparent than actual.

The same process works from stanza to stanza. Each stanza restates the powerlessness of the speaker and his request for pity by means of an apparent dilation that is essentially a repetition. The effect is to curtail analytical development, and each stanza enforces that curtailment by grammatical repetition and by, as well, the use of an only slightly modified refrain. The third stanza illustrates this kind of redundancy, restating the mood in the terms of patron and court:

> Tho I have not deserved to obtain
> So high Reward but thus to serve in vain,
>   Tho I shall have no redresse,
>   Yet of right ye can no lesse
>   But rew upon my pain.

The terms are only apparently social and political; essentially, they are as subjective as the poet can make them. The last stanza explicitly recognizes the futility of the speaker's plea, only to reassert it in a version of the refrain whose very slight qualification only deepens his helplessness:

> But I se well that your high disdain
> Wull no wise graunt that I shall more attain;
>   Yet ye must graunt at the lest
>   This my powre and small request:
>   Rejoyse not at my pain.

Having mentioned in the previous stanzas the authority of his love, the mistress' grace, and the "right" that might justify a pity for him, the speaker has simultaneously, by the fact of this final plea, rejected the claims that might justify it and insisted on making it once again, this time without hope. In accepting and confirming a powerlessness without hope, the speaker of the poem embodies both the irrationality and the strength of romantic passion.

In other poems by Wyatt, curtailment is not merely a premise illustrated by the grammatical and rhetorical organization of the poem, but rather a process of the poem itself. Though the devices of repetition still serve to emphasize the subjective power of the speaker's experience, the process of the poem, in this kind of lyric, does evoke possible qualifications of the speaker's initial situation, or possible resolutions to it of thought and feeling. Yet in the course of the poem, these possibilities are raised only to be minimized. One of the most effective examples in Wyatt of the process of curtailing analytical or emotional resolution is **"What menythe**

thys?" (110). The speaker of the poem begins with this question, addressed to himself, which, though a familiar theme of the complaint, catches the fatigue and the intensity in love's suffering with effective simplicity. Further, the poem uses its central question with subtly ironic force: to stress in the process of the poem the emotions of bewilderment and suffering which prevent the question from ever being answered. The speaker asks himself the same question when in bed (sts. 1—3), when rising in the morning, and throughout the day (st. 4), without discovering an answer. Because the speaker asks himself the same question continually, and because, again and again, he can find no answer to it, his ability to analyze his experience is undermined in its very effort. What he as speaker insists upon is the curtailment of this ability, as the sixth stanza illustrates:

> But yff I sytte nere her by,
> With lowd voyce my hart dothe cry,
> And yet my mowthe ys dome and dry:
>   What menys thys?

Naïvely yet movingly, the speaker presents his plight as the unresolved paradox of the heart that cries and the speechless "mowthe." But if the refrain, **"What menys thys?,"** is the protest of the heart, it is also the cry of the mind in the effort to understand, frustrated yet insistent.

In this stanza and the next one, the speaker considers the possibility of finding an answer to "what menys thys?" in conversation with his mistress. But his emotions are so powerful that they prevent him from asking *her* the question that he has asked himself, and this leads him to ask it of himself again in a mood of virtual frenzy (st. 7):

> To aske ffor helpe no hart I have,
> My tong dothe fayle what I shuld crave,
> Yet inwardly I Rage and Rave:
>   What menys thys?

His inability to ask her the question dramatizes the lack of analytical power or control of feeling he felt and feared at the outset of the poem. His inability to answer it for himself sums up and makes permanent his lack of understanding; at the end of the poem he is still asking the same question. The speaker's predicament, then, embodies in a complex way the aesthetic strategy of the poem as a whole. The potential of rational or emotional resolution is substantially present, yet its denial is insisted upon, in a process of curtailing understanding. This process works at the level of structure by roping each different stanza, resolving each experience, into the single question "What menys thys?" Hence repetition as an aesthetic strategy is here employed to underscore a process rather than to articulate a condition, and the repeated refrain takes on accumulative emotional power.

Other poems by Wyatt proceed somewhat differently to curtail development of subjective perception. In these poems a narrative means of organization is initiated by Wyatt only to be subverted ironically.[13] A successful and representative illustration of the type is the poem known as **"In eternum"** (71). The first two stanzas of the poem present the initial situation of the speaker as the postualte of his belief in eternal love and his desire for it.

> In eternum I was ons determed
> For to have lovid and my minde affermed,
> That with my herte it shuld be confermed
>   In eternum.
>
> Forthwith I founde the thing that I myght like,
> And sought with love to warme her hert alike,
> For, as me thought, I shulde not se the like
>   In eternum.

This postulate forms the subject of the poem, yet it is organized and presented as a narrative of the speaker's personal history. Only the presence of the past tense and the qualifying words "ons" and "as me thought" indicate a discrepancy of attitude between past and present; by and large, the belief in eternal love is invested with the authority the past gave to it. The conversion of the device of the refrain to narrative development is particularly interesting. While the repetition of "in eternum" does serve to enforce the subjective value of the eternal quality of love for the speaker, the primary function of the refrain is to accumulate different meanings as it suggests the speaker's history in time. The refrain takes on the gradual accretions of value and meaning which constitute the speaker's experience of love's "immortality."

The first eight lines of the poem develop multiple meanings for the phrase "in eternum." The "in eternum" that opens the poem refers to the speaker's continuing determination to love, and perhaps also to have an eternal love; at the close of the first stanza, the same phrase refers to the continuity and perpetuity of his heart's enactment of that faith. In the second stanza, by contrast, "in eternum" is used to mean his perception of the uniqueness of the mistress: "For, as me thought, I shulde not se the like / In eternum." The line also implies that her eternal peerlessness is both a reason for loving her, and a quality invested in her by his loving perceptions. The nature of perception thus becomes an important part of the poem's meaning.

The phrase "in eternum" continues to be redefined in the third, fourth, and fifth stanzas, until it comes express simultaneously both the speaker's faith in the relationship and its movement toward betrayal. The unwearied, unhappy service of the speaker in the third stanza ("To serve, to suffer, and still to hold my pease / In eternum") conditions his trust in his mistress' "grace" in the fourth ("With full assurans to stond in her grace / In eternum"). Yet it is not long until "proofe" of experience shows the speaker's faith, and the relationship itself, to be thoroughly subverted by the lady's failure ever to hear the phrase "in eternum" in her heart (st. 5). Her failure is a betrayal, since it means a deafness to the defining words of their love. Yet, in a striking *tour de force,* the phrase is converted in stanza six to an image of the speaker's *self*-betrayal:

> In eternum then from my herte I kest
> That I had furst determined for the best;
> Nowe in the place another thought doeth rest,
>   In eternum.

Though the specific nature of that "thought" is not made explicit, the thought can only be one in opposition to the love valued "in eternum" which the speaker "kest" from his heart. This act, which must be defined as a rejection of love and its replacement by "another thought," ironically subverts both the speaker's faith, postulated as the poem's subject, and his narrative means of developing his understanding. By immortalizing the rejection of love rather than its acceptance, he achieves the eternality he sought, if not of the kind he sought. What this costs him, though, is his understanding of his mistress' limitations, and indeed of his narrative as a whole. By reconstituting himself in the same terms—"in eternum"—which his own narrative proved false through experience, the speaker betrays himself and his own comprehension of his past. The experience of the poem is transformed from the pain of rejection by a mistress to a self-betrayal and an ironic subversion of the speaker as narrator. This is not entirely a sudden collapse; significantly, the narrative "development" of meaning is resisted, and its ultimate failure prefigured, by the striking regularity of Wyatt's rhythm here, by the triple rhyme, and by the dronelike repetition of the refrain. These aspects of the verse reflect and endorse the speaker's enclosure in the perfected circle, "in eternum," of his own concern with eternality. The powerful immediacy of his concern, which characterizes both present and past, collapses past into a present that the speaker can neither understand nor control.

Finally, certain poems in Wyatt sustain the immediacy and power of the speaker's subjective experience while simultaneously allowing it a certain development. Since the dominant focus in these poems remains the strong immediate subjectivity of the speaker, the effect of their developments is to reinforce the speaker's initial feeling in the course of expanding its meaning considerably. **"Who so list to hount"** (7), a sonnet translated from Petrarch, is a striking example of this kind of poem, one of a complexity and power that can only be suggested here. The mood of the lyric speaker in this poem, like that of his counterpart in **"My galy charged with forgetfulnes,"** is the feeling of weariness, futility, and despairing pursuit typical of the complaining lover. In both poems, the subjective power and effects of the experience of loving are strongly felt. Yet the differences are clear and important. In **"My galy charged with forgetfulnes,"** the speaker's absorption in his experience effects a continually increasing movement from image to direct statement, suggesting a shaky confidence in his power to interpret or deal with his feeling. **"Who so list to hount,"** by contrast, maintains more steadily the power of the initial image to shape feeling; it develops the speaker's direct statements in terms of the image; and most importantly, it dramatizes, in its handling of the speaker, a mind in complex awareness of what the heart follows.

The octave of the sonnet provides initial illustration of these points.

> Who so list to hount, I knowe where is an hynde,
>> But as for me, helas, I may no more:
>> The vayne travaill hath weried me so sore.
>> I ame of theim that farthest commeth behinde;
> Yet may I by no means my weried mynde
>> Drawe from the Diere: but as she fleeth afore,
> Faynting I folowe. I leve of therefore,
>> Sins in a nett I seke to hold the wynde.

Though the opening line of the poem introduces the basic conceit of hunting, what is "hunted" is not explicitly identified as a mistress until the sixth line. Fully six first person singular pronouns precede the first reference to the deer, and no explicit comparisons between deer and mistress, or between the activities of hunting and loving, are allowed to emerge in the opening lines. The range of the conceit is narrowed, and clarification of the speaker's specific goal delayed, in order to stress the intensely inward experience of the speaker as the poem's central concern. Yet the expression of the speaker's feelings does not withdraw from imagery to direct statement in this poem, as is the case in **"My galy charged with forgetfulness"**; here the speaker's feelings are presented in terms of the imagery, rather than disjoined from it, as when his failure in the hunt defines his place among unsuccessful lovers, and in a more universal community: "I ame of theim that farthest commeth behinde." As the speaker goes on to particularize his situation (ll. 5-8), he simultaneously evokes intense feeling about the futility of love and begins to clarify what makes it futile. The fleeing of the "Diere," and the "faynting" of her pursuer, are expressed almost as a single motion, so that the speaker's pursuit seems as inevitable, and as mysterious, as his lady's flight. The image takes in external as well as internal reality, the elusiveness, and perhaps the vanity, of the "wynde" as well as of the impulse to "hold" it in a "nett." Yet there is no diminishment of the poem's initial emphasis on subjective feeling.

The implications of the octave show that the speaker has the power to understand, at least in part, what his heart pursues. As his imagery has revealed him so far, he is a speaker aware of more than his subjective feeling, though he is preoccupied by it. This self-awareness under goes a significant expansion in Wyatt's creation of a fictive "audience" as well as a fictive speaker. At major structural points of the poem, the beginnings of octave and sestet, the speaker addresses a potential companion in the sport of amorous pursuit. This dramatic idiom allows the speaker a certain detachment about his own weariness and self-preoccupation, a detachment that complicates his emotions, as in the wry amusement here:

> Who list her hount, I put him owte of dowbte,
>> As well as I may spend his tyme in vain.
>
> (ll. 6-7)

The speaker's emotions thus continually become more resonant, yet they do not change character or lose intensity.

The presence of a "companion" in hunting also prepares for the poem's extraordinary expansion of its basic image in the concluding lines, because the social reference of the dramatic idiom makes plausible, if still shocking, the sudden extension of the imagery of the hunt into a courtly context:

> And, graven with Diamonds, in letters plain
> There is written her faier neck rounde abowte:
>> *Noli me tangere,* but Cesars I ame;
> And wylde for to hold, though I seme tame.
>
> (ll. 11-14)

How and why this powerful image might apply to the poet's political situation is less important, for my purposes, than its relevance for the speaker's. By its connection of the futility of the hunt with the rights of possession, the inscription worn by the deer supplies psychological, moral, and, of course, political dimensions to the beloved's flight from the lover, and to his wariness of her. It brilliantly suggests both the value and the unobtainability of what—or whom—the speaker has so fruitlessly pursued. This, of course, involves a sudden shift toward objectivity, a telling and indeed surprising movement away from the speaker's feelings and toward their cause. That cause, however, is so extraordinary, with its diamond band of royal possession which constrains both the deer and the hunter, that it emphasizes, by justifying, the extreme feeling it has drawn forth from the speaker. Paradoxically, by showing us in concrete description what objective limits constrain his desire, the speaker tells us most about himself. What reason prohibits, the heart would pursue; and surely the concluding line applies to the speaker's self-mastery as well as to his mastered beloved: "And wylde for to hold, though I seme tame." Development expands but never loses its sure direction; we end where we began, with the speaker in the poem.

The deliberate curtailment of development in Wyatt's lyric poetry, that aims to reinforce the focus on states of mind, has a subtle and interesting effect that deserves some attention in its own right. This effect might be called, awkwardly but precisely, the "minimalization" of the speaking voice. In poems that reveal this most strongly, the speaker's voice seems to condense itself into a single word or phrase, which comes to bear the full weight of meaning and of expressive power in the poem. The use of a phrase as summary refrain is one of the ways Wyatt most typically achieves this effect of minimalization. The discussions of **"What menythe this?"** and **"In eternum"** have revealed very different handlings of the summary refrain to achieve concentration on the speaker, yet the poems are alike in using the titular phrase as a burden not merely of the power of the speaker's feelings but also of their concrete meaning. Other lyrics by Wyatt in which one can recognize the distinctive "voice" created by the repeated phrases of particular speakers would include **"What may it availl me"** (58), **"Ys yt possyble"** (111), **"Forget not yet"** (130), and **"Blame not my lute"** (132). These phrases embody the minimalized speaking voice. Each one condenses the subjectivity of a particular lyric speaker into a phrase whose power is closer to the unity of emotion fundamental to the lyric form than to the almost choral quality of the summary refrain in the ballad.

"Hate whome ye list" (151) is perhaps the most remarkable example of this minimalizing effect in Wyatt's lyric poetry.[14] In a single word it comes to express both expletive power and the complex thematic burden of the poem. On first reading, the poem expresses with extraordinary simplicity and compression its defining experience of negation:

> Hate whome ye list, for I kare not;
> Love whom ye list and spare not;
> Do what ye list and drede not;
> Think what ye liste, I fere not:
> For as for me I am not,
> But even as one that reckes not
> Whyther ye hate or hate not;
> For yn your love I dote not;
> Wherefore I praye you, forget not,
> But love whome ye liste, ffor I care not.

Yet the use of "not" to guide the poem's development is more subtle than it first appears. In ten brief lines the speaker's indifference charges through the paradoxes of love and reveals their continuity: from hate to love, from cruelty to doting, from fear to pity. Centered in indifference, as the poem is, the speaker constitutes himself: "For as for me I am not." Though reading this line in a continuous way with the following lines yields a paraphrase such as "I am nothing if not one who is indifferent to your feelings, whether hate or otherwise," the rhetorical structure of the poem as a whole and the closure of each line in the same way insist that we read the line by itself, to mean also, and perhaps primarily, "I am nothing [because of and through my indifference]." Hence the center of the poem is the speaker making himself as the "nothing" his indifference makes of him: pure negation, a denial of the feelings of both "the beloved" and himself. The speaker thus becomes ironically subject to the circularity of the poem, whereby to express indifference or negation becomes the implicit revelation of its opposite, the engaged attempt to triumph over both hate and love. Clearly, the speaker's passionate indifference subverts itself into irony and self-betrayal, for the commitment to indifference becomes so extreme—so passionate—that he turns himself into a kind of "nothing" of pure negation. A modern sensibility would speculate that he turns himself into what he feared she regarded him to be.

In varied and sophisticated ways, then, Wyatt achieves the distinctive and individualized "voice" of his poetry by creating lyric speakers whose subjectivity comes to be both subject and strategy in the poetry. Wyatt treats conventions of love poetry as occasions for the lyric expression of states of mind. Analytical or narrative development is usually curtailed, or even excluded, in order to evoke inwardness in its full power. In this his poetry differs from the anonymity of the medieval love lyric as much as it does from the polished rhetorical investigations of late-Elizabethan Petrarchan poetry. Yet even here, let us consider, differences may be matters of degree rather than kind. The medieval and Tudor love lyric may not be as "anonymous" as it is commonly thought to be, nor may the later Renaissance lyric, perhaps, be so characteristically "impersonal." The nature of Wyatt's achievement may illuminate the need to redefine, or at least reopen, the problem of the speaker in the Renaissance lyric.

Twentieth-century literary scholarship has enabled us to see the intimate relations of music and poetry in the Renaissance, and the influence of rhetoric on poetry in the development of the medieval and Renaissance lyric styles. Yet the exploration of these contexts of Renaissance poetry, and the description of the developing styles of "plain" and "eloquent," or "drab" and "golden" poets, have made us wary of assuming or seeking an individualized voice in the poetry of the Renaissance. In a typical recent statement, G. K. Hunter asserts an "absence of personality in the Elizabethan lyric," due to its shaping contexts of rhetoric and music, which means that Renaissance lyrics do not give a sense of a speaker inside the poem.[15] Yet surely the lyrics of Wyatt do, and surely a reader familiar with Renaissance poetry can distinguish the speaker of a Sidney sonnet from one in Spenser, Shakespeare, or Donne. Why, then, do we often describe these distinctive "voices" shaped by the poetry in terms of somewhat vague qualities of tone and effect, like "dramatic," "psychological," or "polished"? Because, I suggest, our historical sense makes us cautious about conflating Renaissance poetry with post-Romantic kinds of lyric—wary, given the analogy between the fictive speaker who expresses particular attitudes and the poet who shapes them, of conflating the two.

This caution perpetuates a basic confusion. It is not necessary to understand the voice of a poetic speaker in terms of sincerity, of a real person pouring out his real feelings. But the *fiction* of an engaged speaker, created by the control of poetic form, is perfectly possible, and perhaps even necessary for a poet in sure control of a range of attitude and experience. It is this illusion of an engaged speaker that creates, as it specifies, the individualized voice for any given poet. The individual voice of a poet is the characteristic fiction of his typical speaker. The poetry of Wyatt shows in particularly clear form that such a fiction can be created within the traditions and contexts of Renaissance poetry, and so points to further exploration of the problem of the speaker in the Renaissance lyric.

NOTES

[1] *Tottel's Miscellany,* ed. Hyder E. Rollins (Cambridge, Mass., 1928), I, 2.

[2] E. M. W. Tillyard, *The Poetry of Sir Thomas Wyatt: A Selection and a Study* (London, 1929), pp. 31-36. On Wyatt's individuality, see also Kenneth Muir, *Life and Letters of Sir Thomas Wyatt* (Liverpool, 1963), whose defense of Wyatt against the charge of conventionality observes his "individual voice," though without exploring it (pp. 239-240); E. D.

Mackerness, "The Transitional Nature of Wyatt's Poetry," *English,* VII (1948), 120-124, who connects it with "the formation of attitudes within the framework of the poem itself" (123); D. W. Harding, "The Rhythmical Intention in Wyatt's Poetry," *Scrutiny,* XIV (Dec. 1946), 90-112, who provides an essential account of the relation of rhythm and meaning in Wyatt.

[3] Hallett Smith, "The Art of Sir Thomas Wyatt," *HLQ* IX (1946), 323-355; Patricia Thomson, *Sir Thomas Wyatt and His Background* (Stanford, 1964), esp. pp. 115ff; Douglas L. Peterson, *The English Lyric from Wyatt to Donne* (Princeton, 1967), pp. 87-119; Kenneth Muir's introduction to his *Collected Poems of Sir Thomas Wyatt,* the Muses Library (1949; Cambridge, Mass., 1950, rpt. 1963), pp. ix-xxx.

[4] For the assumption that Wyatt's distinctive "voice" is identified with the plain style of a central medieval lyric tradition, see Thomson, especially pp. 130-132. Raymond Southall views the poetry, and Wyatt's voice, as the expression of the insecurity and instability of the Tudor court; see his *The Courtly Maker: An Essay on the Poetry of Wyatt and His Contemporaries* (New York, 1964). Douglas Peterson's chapter on Wyatt, cited above, defines the aesthetic voice of Wyatt in terms of a plain style conditioned by rhetoric's influence on poetry, and the thematic concerns of that voice the "anticourtly" attitudes in which Wyatt anticipates the work of such poets as Gascoigne, Ralegh. Donne, and Herbert. Finally, Sergio Baldi's *Sir Thomas Wyatt,* trans. F. T. Prince (London. 1961), does comment on the "self-pity" and "naïveté" of Wyatt's voice, but in a way limited by an identification of the poet with his lyric speakers and by a view of Wyatt as a naïve Peterarch (pp. 21-26).

[5] The extent of this focus on the speaker may be suggested in a sample of the first 50 poems in Kenneth Muir's Muses Library edition. Of these 50 poems 43 involve an "I," and 4 others involve a "me" or "my." Further, in 41 of the 50 poems first person singular terms appear more than 4 times, although this is not to claim that every use of such pronouns represents a major attempt by Wyatt to shape a major voice.

[6] Muir, *Life,* p. 243.

[7] Thomson, p. 190; she cites A. K. Foxwell as the first to make this point.

[8] Thomson notes the "exclusion of the mythological paraphernalia of Love" as a sign of Wyatt's alignment with the plain lyric tradition (p. 131). The perceptive description of the handling of Fortune in Wyatt's poetry is Hallett Smith's (p. 351).

[9] Cf. Southall's comment on the "psychological" quality of the poetry: "unkindness, cruelty, and sin are made to appear simply as precipitants of various states of consciousness" (p. 68). Leigh Winser has suggested an analogous progression inward in "They flee from me," whose threefold progress, from initial image through open disclosure of the speaker's mind to final request for judgment, resembles the method of proposing *dubbi* or *questioni* in courtly amusements of the Renaissance; see "The Question of Love Tradition in Wyatt's 'They Flee from Me,'" *Essays in Literature,* II (Spring 1975), 3-9.

[10] The poem is No. 58 in Kenneth Muir's *Collected Poems* (1949; rpt. 1963), cited above; all the poems will be quoted from this edition and identified by the numbers it assigns to them. The poems mentioned in my essay are chiefly drawn from those identified by Richard Harrier, *The Canon of Sir Thomas Wyatt's Poetry* (Cambridge, Mass., 1975), as unquestionably Wyatt's; for the single exception, see n. 14. Likewise, H. A. Mason's study, *Editing Wyatt* (Cambridge, Eng., 1972), does not significantly affect the texts considered here.

[11] Perhaps this might explain an effect described by G. K. Hunter: "Wyatt can seem intensely personal and completely conventional at one and the same time"; see "Drab and Golden Lyrics of the Renaissance," in *Forms of Lyric,* ed. Reuben A. Brower (New York, 1970), p. 8.

[12] Wyatt's limitation of development in lyric is described by Peterson as a negative consequence of the techniques of repetition and dilation which are characteristic of the didactic medieval lyric in the plain style (pp. 9-19). Peterson's main concern, however, is not to describe specific techniques but to argue for a general development in Wyatt's poetic career toward logical and intellectual analysis, though this argument regrettably accepts Foxwell's assumptions about chronology, now generally questioned; on Foxwell, see, for example, Harrier, pp. 29ff.

[13] While other kinds of Wyatt poems clearly involve narrative elements, in this type of poem the narrative organization is central to its means of curtailing development; other examples of the type include "Helpe me to seke" (17), "My hope, Alas, hath my abused" (62), and "I have sought long with stedfastnes" (69).

[14] "Hate whome ye list" appears in both the Devonshire and Blage manuscripts, a fact which Muir takes to support its ascription to Wyatt; but Harrier calls the group of poems in which it appears "doubtful" in both cases. The matter is obviously uncertain, and Harrier concludes that ascriptions of Wyatt's authorship for these poems must depend on style (pp. 52-54, 62-64). On that basis, I am willing to risk the ascription of "Hate whome ye list" to Wyatt, since the poem seems so strikingly characteristic of him in language and structure.

[15] "Drab and Golden Lyrics of the Renaissance," pp. 3-5.

Del Chessell (review date 1978)

SOURCE: "Wyatt's 'Owen Thing,'" in *The Critical Review,* No. 20, 1978, pp. 42-54.

[*In the following essay, Wyatt's entire oevre is appraised highly as springing from the poetic centre of a man in the midst of turmoil.*]

> Fle fro the pres and dwelle with sothefastnesse,
> Suffise thine owen thing, thei it be smal. . . .
>
> (Chaucer)

Wyatt has by now pretty much consolidated his position as a "great minor poet". The greatness of a few poems, at any rate, is beyond dispute, and since H. A. Mason's account (*Humanism and Poetry in the Early Tudor Period*) there is no longer any excuse for praising him as a graceful court singer (a lesser Surrey) or congratulating him for having introduced the Petrarchan Sonnet into English. Yet for all that, Wyatt has the perhaps good fortune to be more read and talked about than written of. For twentieth-century readers he is very much a living poet, but he seems to many people the author of a few isolated brilliant poems rather than of an oeuvre of any intelligible shape. I think this is to do him less than justice. The great, even the very good, poems are certainly only a fraction of all he wrote, but the very qualities that distinguish them also link them together in such a way that we can see them as a quite distinctive and coherent poetic oeuvre, a life's work.

It is not easy to define these qualities, however. Wyatt's congeniality for the twentieth century seems to me to lie in the keenness with which he feels and articulates the destructive restlessness, instability, and lack of commitment of life in Henry VIII's Court. Something like that underlies all his best poems, so that love lyrics, satires and Penitential Psalms can all be seen to spring from the one poetic centre, as Raymond Southall argues in *The Courtly Maker.* But it takes more than social representation, however accurate and penetrating, to make a great poet. For me, the greatness of the poetry lies in its being, in itself, Wyatt's effort to be his own man in the midst of such a life. Its central impulse is to define and hold on to a sense of personal integrity, a basis for assurance and decisive moral action. This in part accounts for the poems' unity-indiversity: each one is its own separate effort. For Wyatt to achieve a real conviction of integrity is difficult enough; to hold on to it for the length of a poem is a triumph. Each new discovery of himself must be worked for in itself, whatever has been achieved elsewhere.

This claim might seem to lead straight to the usual dichotomy: the satires, Penitential Psalms and "court poems" on one side, as against the "love lyrics" on the other. While I think there is a line to be drawn between Wyatt at his best and Wyatt with that best not showing at all, this leaves a large grey area in between; at any rate, I think these distinctions are only blurred by shuffling the poems into genre-categories, with "lyrics" set off against the others.

> Who so list to hounte I knowe where is an hynde;
>   But as for me, helas, I may no more:
>   The vayne travaill hath weried me so sore,
>   I ame of theim that forthest cometh behinde;
> Yet may I by no meanes my weried mynde
>   Drawe from the Diere: but as she fleeth afore
>   Faynting I folowe; I leve of therefore,
>   Sithens in a nett I seke to hold the wynde.
> Who list her hount I put him owte of dowbte,
>   As well as I may spend his tyme in vain:
>   And graven with Diamondes in letters plain
> There is written her faier neck rounde abowte:
>   'Noli me tangere for Cesars I ame,
>   And wylde for to hold though I seme tame'.

(Text of all poems taken from *The Collected Poems of Sir Thomas Wyatt* ed. Kenneth Muir and Patricia Thomson, Liverpool University Press, 1969, incorporating corrections made by H. A. Mason in *Editing Wyatt,* Cambridge Quarterly Publications, 1972.)

This poem, one of Wyatt's best-known, may seem to be so patently about events in Wyatt's known history as to afford a very unpromising beginning to an inquiry into so inward a matter as a search for personal integrity. And yet, though the mimetic quality of those rhythms has often been noted, it is not the outward, physical motions of

hunting that they mime, but something much more intimate. The poem begins with a gesture that one comes to recognize as so characteristic of Wyatt as to be almost a trademark, the "who so list" that sets the speaker in isolation, over against what other men are seeking, and immediately calls the value of their activity into question. Here, having begun with that seemingly decisive gesture of dissociation and relinquishing, even as he points for others the way from which he has turned back, his mind is drawn irresistibly onward after that fleeing figure. The rhythms are at once delicate and subtle—the natural surges and checks of spontaneous feeling—and utterly irresistible; the pull over those line-breaks has the physical force of a strong magnet. The poem is almost half over before the speaker pulls up sharply and makes a first attempt to withdraw; but though "I leve of therefore" has the appearance of decisivness, the rhythms are still helplessly enmeshed and onward-pulling. Like a mocking echo, they return that consummate image of futility: "Sithens in a nett I seke to hold the wynde". The second recourse to the "who so list" gesture does finally produce a decisive withdrawal, but at the cost of the voice's coarsening into strident knowingness: "I put him owte of dowbte / As well as I may spend his tyme in vain". And, paradoxically, having extricated himself by so harshly snapping the sensitive thread of his feelings, it is only then that the speaker (drawn on again by that insidious "And. . . .") is confronted by the most arresting image in the poem: "graven with Diamondes in letters plain / There is written her faier neck rounde abowte . . .". The speaker is no longer in cavalier fashion directing others to a quarry he has long ago abandoned; he is confronting the inscription of those diamonds in all its naked, present import for himself.

But however much the movement of the poem is the movement of Wyatt's feeling, it does of course reach beyond the merely private. Indeed it is one of the comparatively few poems that positively gain from an awareness of their "context". If it is not about Anne Boleyn and Henry, it loses a good deal of its sharpness. Certainly it would blur the process by which Petrarch's diamonds and topazes (symbols of chastity, we are told) and the plea of his hind, "leave me free to go to my Caesar" (surely a heavenly emperor, that), are turned by Wyatt's parallels into an ironic dimension of his own poem. To call Wyatt's poem "a radical criticism of Petrarch's attitude to women", as Mason does, is to get the emphasis quite wrong. Wyatt's poem is not about Petrarch, it is "about" the experience of following that "diere", and he enlists Petrarch to that end, to provide a further ironic aspect to his final realization of her situation. For the immediate impact of those many-faceted diamonds is much starker. While the image has a simple kind of double suggestion, of a costly necklace flaunted as a badge of kingly possession, and of a collar that, however costly, is a token of enslavement, the bare, physically-explicit "graven . . . in letters plain" insists on the letters actually marked out in diamonds in her flesh. And as Vincent Buckley notes (*Poetry and the Sacred,* chap. 4) that "faier neck" is unmistakably human. The shock of the image registers the cost, for such a creature, of belonging to "Cesar".

Only by the unnatural harshness of a diamond embedded in flesh can such a wild thing be tamed. The challenge of the inscription, almost insolently explicit, seems to bring the speaker's pursuit to a full stop against the authority of Cesar. Which makes it no less surprising than wonderful that what reasserts itself in the last line is the *deer's* seductive, spell-binding elusiveness: "wylde for to hold though I seme tame". All the mysterious otherness of her animal energies leaps to life again here, so that one realizes, with a shock of exultation, that for anyone to try to hold that creature is truly to seek to hold the wind in a net. If we exult in the deer's final ungraspability, so does Wyatt. There is a ring of triumph in that last line, which makes us suddenly realize that the speaker has shed the weariness of "theim that forthest cometh behinde" and finds himself celebrating the deer's elusive vitality, celebrating it at the expense of Cesar. It may then be at this point that, returning to the poem, we suddenly see that "who list her hount" . . . , with its scornful ring, can be addressed to Cesar at least as well as to the undefined crowd of hunters invited at the beginning to join the chase. The lines—"Who list her hount I put him owte of dowbte, / As well as I may spend his tyme in vain"—become an unsympathetic warning from one who brutally insists on his knowledge; indeed it's not far from a taunt. That unobtrusive "And" is the link by which the ironic point is made: who list her hunt . . . may spend his time in vain, *and* it is Cesar's brand she is wearing!

I've spent a long time laboriously spelling out the quite un-laboured subtleties of this poem, to indicate the extent to which its central impulse is the effort of a mind to re-live a painful personal experience and establish its bearings within it. Despite the appearance of pulling back, the feeling is released into the poem in that opening gesture, and the curve of its rise and fall is the shape of the poem. Nothing could be further from taking a foreign form and pouring one's own feelings into that rigid mould, doing violence to them in order to make them fit. That, as a matter of fact, is why it happens to be one of the few most successful sonnets ever written in English—I certainly don't know another where form and feeling so organically coincide, where the couplet is both the natural close and set off against the rest in a continually fruitful tension. Wyatt's image of seeking to hold the wind in a net is suggestive beyond its immediate context in this poem, suggestive of the perilous difficulty of trying to catch and hold something as intangible as feeling in pre-determined patterns. The poet who produced it is unlikely to deserve, or to need, much praise as a "metrical experimenter".

Evaluating Wyatt's achievement is largely a matter of trying to piece together those moments when the poet flashes forth from inside the languid courtier. The nature of those moments, and the nature of the failures that surround them, are very instructive about the conditions of Wyatt's greatness. A poem like **"What no, perdy, ye may be sure! . . ."** is a case in point. The bravado of its opening:

> Thinck not to make me to your lure,
> With wordes and chere so contrarieng,

Swete and sowre contrewaing;
To much it were still to endure . . .

is transmuted by the delicately restless rhythms of the last few lines into something more bewildered and tentative:

> Within my hert shall still that thing,
> Vnstable, vnsure and wavering,
> Be in my mynde withoute recure?
>   What no, perdye!

Clearly this is a poem that fits Southall's account of Wyatt's activity, registering the fatal restlessness at the very heart of court life and love, without any further move towards mastery or understanding. Yet it is significant that the bravado doesn't follow the perception of instability, but precedes it. Even in so slight a poem Wyatt is sensitive enough to perceive that such a pose leads only to emotional stalemate, and so to drop it and allow the natural rhythms of his response to life to make themselves felt. Again, there is another kind of clue in a lyric like **"Madame, withouten many wordes"**. There is a good deal of impudence and bravado about this poem too—an irresistible urge to stick a pin in the balloon of courtly love. It's impossibly, if likeably, cut-and-dried. But when we come to the last stanza—

> Yf it be yea, I shalbe fayne;
> If it be nay, frendes as before;
> Ye shall an othre man obtain,
> And I myn owne and yours no more—

there's an edge to that word "obtain" (and the dictionary suggests there already was in the sixteenth century): it carries a hint of mercenary efficiency that makes its comment on the kind of values that lie behind this no-nonsense attitude to love and commitment. The poem remains very light, but it's a lightness with a considerable edge to it.

The much-anthologized **"My lute awake"** offers another angle on the charade of "courtly love". It begins with all the expected graceful platitudes—

> As to be herd where ere is none,
> As lede to grave in marbill stone,
> My song may perse her hert as sone . . .

and it seems set to continue its unremarkable course for several more stanzas when Wyatt takes the unprecedented step of shifting his attention from the lover's miserable destiny to the question of the lady's. Quite suddenly, versifying becomes poetry:

> Perchaunce the lye wethered and old,
> The wynter nyghtes that are so cold,
> Playnyng in vain vnto the mone;
> Thy wisshes then dare not be told;
> Care then who lyst, for I have done.

What begins as a vindictive, you'll-get-yours attitude quickly becomes penetrating insight and compassion, as

Wyatt perceives this desolation as the inevitable end-point of the conventional pose of disdain. After the elegance of the earlier parallels, the image of the woman's ageing body exposed by the moonlight in loveless cold is harsh and elemental. Her desires are elemental too—there's something of the animal howl in "playning in vain vnto the mone". The bareness of the last lines is terrible—it stretches over an abyss of dark frustrations and desires that Wyatt is poet enough to leave in shadow, as if, indeed, they are too unspeakable to bring to articulation.

Intensity of this kind might well have broken such a frail poem apart, and it's significant I think that it's at this point that Wyatt makes that characteristic gesture of dissociation: "Care then who lyst, for I have done". It's a more brutal, and a more defensive, repudiation than usual. Breaking through the endlessly-reflecting self-concern of the lover's stance has led Wyatt to this moment of insight, though this is not a poem in which to sustain it or press it further. But under its influence the generalizing tone of the next stanza is rescued from platitude by a subdued bareness and a muted echo of the deep feeling: "Then shalt thou knowe beaultie but lent / And wisshe and want as I have done." For a poet who could toss off love-laments with such facility, to give that kind of strength to "wisshe and want" is no mean feat. His capacity to grasp the emotional logic of these attitudes, the reality he uncovers behind the pose, and the lack of self-centredness that allows him to see the implications for the lady as well as for himself, are among the conditions that make for the exceptional fineness of **"They fle from me"**.

In that poem they run together with another important quality that distinguishes the poet from the poeticizer in Wyatt—the ability to examine his own bitterness, and so to press through to a range of feelings less destructively closed-off than that. "Bitter", in fact, is a word that is very seldom the right one for Wyatt at his best. It often fits him well enough, of course, **"Where shall I have at myn owne will"**:

> But syns that I for you, my dere,
> Have lost that thing that was my best,
> A right small losse it must appere
> To lese thes wordes and all the rest.
>
> But tho they sparkill in the wynde,
> Yet shall they shew your falsed faith
> Which is retorned vnto his kynde,
> For like to like the proverbe saieth.

It's this kind of thing that has led many a critic to praise Wyatt as "masculine"; but refreshing as it is, I think it lies at least as close to his weakness as to his strength. These lines are splendid in their tersely colloquial bite, and the image of the wasted words "sparkilling" in the wind, like some beautiful useless bauble that has slipped out of his grasp, is as piercingly suggestive as those in **"Who so list to hounte"**. But for all that, I think "bitterness" is a fair enough characterization of the feeling here, which is cut off from the kind of openness of response

Wyatt shows himself capable of at his very best. He's all too inclined, under the stress of painful feelings, to resort to that off-hand, "masculine" tone to shut off or at least mask the pain. The opening of **"What no, perdy"** is a case in point. But the off-handedness of these lines from "Where shall I have . . ." is so patently false that Wyatt seems at least partially aware of what he's doing. All the same, one can't claim a large measure of self-awareness for the poet who could leave the lines surrounded on both sides with such vapid courtly cliché.

Self-awareness is however the central virtue of **"It may be good"**, a tough, awkward poem quite lacking in Wyatt's usual grace. Its awkwardness is testimony to the difficulty of the moral struggle in which it shows him engaged, and a measure both of his failure in this poem to resolve it and of the tenacious honesty with which he keeps at it.

> It may be good, like it who list,
> But I do dowbt: who can me blame?
> For oft assured yet have I myst,
> And now again I fere the same:
> The wyndy wordes, the Ies quaynt game,
> Of soden chaunge maketh me agast:
> For dred to fall I stond not fast.
>
> Alas! I tred an endles maze
> That seketh to accorde two contraries;
> And hope still, and nothing hase,
> Imprisoned in libertes,
> As oon vnhard and still that cries;
> Alwaies thursty and yet nothing I tast:
> For dred to fall I stond not fast.
>
> Assured, I dowbt I be not sure;
> And should I trust to suche suretie
> That oft hath put the prouff in vre
> And never hath founde it trusty?
> Nay, sir, In faith it were great foly.
> And yet my liff thus I do wast:
> For dred to fall I stond not fast.

The poem announces its self-scrutiny with that now-familiar gesture of dissociation which calls into question the worth of the activity and those "who list" to engage in it. The first stanza see-saws uneasily between doubt and self-justification, creating the effect almost of a dialogue between one voice that talks a lot, with great force and vigorous emphasis, and a still small voice that, without actually being allowed to say anything, is continually present to be argued against. Both voices are Wyatt's. The poem is deeply self-divided, and the division is encapsulated in the refrain. It's easy to read it carelessly, as if it said "I dread to fall for I stond not fast", the fear, as we might expect, being the result of the unsteady footing. Actually, it's the other way round—"For dred to fall I stond not fast". The unsteady footing, the insecurity, is the result of the fear. Inability to trust is a fatal foundation for any kind of stable relationship. The rest of the poem goes on to examine that dilemma in greater depth.

The language of the poem is itself seeking "to accorde two contraries" in a way that could be called metaphysical if that were not taken to mean that Wyatt is in some way anticipating Donne. This is often said, but the two are enormously different, and perhaps the only thing Wyatt has in common with him is the fact of being a better poet than nearly all who come in between. But having said that, I would concede that "Imprisoned in libertes" is his most Donne-like line. The implications of "libertes" ramify almost to infinity as they do in Donne's "Whoever gives, takes libertie" from the "Hymn to Christ". And in the "endles maze" of those ambiguities lies Wyatt's dilemma, both here and in **"They fle from me"**. The "libertes" of courtly good-form, the easy-come-easy-go of **"Madame, withouten many wordes"**, the "libertes" that are all too easy to take where no one has any real privacy—such liberties are emotional shackles, within which the liberty of real commitment ("To enter in these bonds is to be free") becomes impossible.

This poem articulates the dilemma with self-lacerating honesty: unable to give, Wyatt acknowledges the impossibility of his receiving the open lasting commitment he so deeply needs. But having looked those facts squarely in the face, the poem does no more. The last stanza becomes increasingly strident as Wyatt tries to bluster his way out of the impasse. The hearty tone of "masculine Wyatt" rides roughshod over the scrupulous and intimate self-searching. Here, as before, he appears to recognize this, and drops it, but it has already closed off the possibility of proceeding further. The poem's last couplet is flat and defeated, circling wearily round to the impasse of the refrain.

Beside this poem, **"They fle from me"** seems extraordinarily serene and self-reconciled, though an awareness of the emotional dilemma that Wyatt has articulated with such honesty here helps us see how and why. Indeed, the isolated distinctions of many of his poems seem to come together to produce the unique fineness of **"They fle from me"**. At the beginning of it, the voice speaks as quietly and directly as in **"Who so list to hounte"**, and although there is no explicit gesture of dissociation, it is defining a sense of isolation. The rhythms of the first stanza with their delicate, irregular runs and pauses (especially the line-break, "raunge / Besely seking") catch the mysterious random restlessness of wild things in a way that recalls the evocation of the "diere" in that poem. The creatures are at once timid and stealthily purposive, "stalking" with leggy dignity on their naked feet: the reassuring domesticity of their taking bread at his hand modulates into the insatiable ranging of hungry animals. The human parallel has been evident from the beginning, but its implications in these lines still come with something of a shock, as one sees the sexuality "they" have satisfied, with the thoughtless expediency of wild things taking bread, becoming obsessive, predatory, insatiable.

The move from there has the simultaneous rightness and complete surprise that one finds only in the greatest poetry. The certainty and joy with which the speaker recollects his "ons in speciall" seem to come from nowhere.

By the end of the poem we realize that they well up from the depths of a personality whose delicacy and humaneness make it fundamentally, qualitatively different from the nature of those "besely seking" creatures. The lady's sensuality is forcefully dramatized, but it is not just sensuality. The unerringly-timed gesture of letting fall her seductive "lose gowne", the exuberance with which she "caught" him in her arms, and the enigmatically tender intimacy of her question, all combine to evoke a living presence in the poetry that leaves us no room to wonder at the speaker's complete captivation. Even though it is all in the past, he responds to his memories with an open-hearted joy and gratitude.

There's not much poetry of such openly joyful sexuality in English, yet the poem's fineness is in no way lost as the speaker moves on to brood on his present forsaken state. If possible, it is increased. The gently purposive rhythms are now those of the reflecting mind, and almost every word is double-edged—"gentilnes", "straunge fasshion", "goodenes", "kyndely". None is simply the sarcasm it is often taken for. Together, they create a tissue of interrelated ambiguities as the speaker reflects on the relationship and the forces in both the lovers and their world that brought it to nothing. The ironies of "I have leve to goo of her goodenes, / And she also . . ." recall those "liberties" that are paradoxically "imprisoning". Here those "liberties" (like the cliché we all know so well about being "free to live our own life") have made it impossible for him to take her forsaking as anything but the graciously-conferred permission to go while extorting from him, however unwilling he may be, her freedom in return. But here, Wyatt goes further. He turns his attention on himself, to scrutinize the passivity he has shown throughout, as the wild creatures, one among them "in speciall", first sought him out, then fled from him. "All is torned thorough my gentilnes": "gentilnes" implies both nobleness, generosity, and so an unwillingness to suspect or coerce her, and softness, pliancy, incapacity for decisive action that has perhaps "deserued" to be forsaken. All of this feeds into the bewildered, wondering last couplet. He has been served "kyndely", according to his kind (also perhaps, according to "the law of kind", animal nature): that he can see. But if his "kind" has brought him this, "I would fain knowe what she hath deserued". For all his vivid memories of their loving, he finds her ultimately unknowable, and reaches out almost fearfully for understanding in a spirit that is worlds away from the "bitterness" of which these lines are often accused. Of course there's a flicker of sarcasm in those double-meanings that gives the lines the sharpness of real hurt, but his attitude could hardly be further from the complacently insulated self-assurance that is necessary to nourish bitterness.

The whole enterprise of translating the Penitential Psalms obviously fits in with such an account as this of the central impulse in Wyatt's writing. So well, in fact, that it would seem perhaps begging the question to argue it from them. However, the fact that their liveliest passages are generally acknowledged to be those that stress the integrity of the private man, the need for "Inward Syon, the

Syon of the ghost", may perhaps be allowed to lend the case a little support. Likewise, I suppose, it seems obvious that the search for integrity is the central impulse of the Satires and of **"Stond who so list"**, yet it has been far from obvious to many of Wyatt's critics that in this they are continuous with the best of the love poems. It is that continuity, the recognizable sameness of the voice and of its values, on which I would base my claim that Wyatt has left us a genuine poetic oeuvre.

"Stond who so list" is perhaps the poem of Wyatt's that has had most nearly the treatment it deserves, at least from H. A. Mason and Vincent Buckley. Indeed the power of its conviction, the authority that produced "brackishe ioyes", "right hard by the croppe", and "dazed, with dreadfull face" seem inescapable. Less often remarked, but no less impressive, seems to me the understated dignity of its rendering of the alternative life, which marks it as no easily-invoked cliché but a deeply-felt personal aspiration:

> That when my yeares be done, withouten noyse,
> I may dye aged after the common trace.

The end of Satire I has also been much praised, but usually with a sense of amazed gratitude that it should come out of anything as "rough" as the rest of the poem. (There are some exceptions to this account). It is qualitatively different from the earlier part of the poem, and that earlier part is undeniably rough; nevertheless, the joyous freedom of the end grows organically out of the process of meditation on court life that the poem dramatizes in the form of a letter to John Poins. Nor has the roughness much to do with counting syllables. It's more often a matter of syntactic awkwardness, of Wyatt not quite being up to the simultaneous demands of idiomatic ease and the intricacies of *terza rima*, but more often than not it's the colloquial force that wins out:

> This is the cause that I could never yet
> Hang on their slevis that way as thou maist se
> A chipp of chaunce more than a pownde of witt.

Although the poem is an Englishing of Alamanni, this does not mean that Wyatt's account of the court cannot also be deeply, movingly personal:

> I am not he that can alow the state
> Off highe Cesar and dam Cato to dye,
> That with his dethe dyd skape owt off the gate
> From Cesares handes, if Lyvye do not lye,
> And wolld not lyve whar lyberty was lost. . . .

And what at first seems a rather inconsequential inability, to "Praysse Syr Thopas for a noble tale, / And skorne the story that the knyght tolld," is surely a moving testimony to what is everywhere apparent in Wyatt's work: the importance to him of Chaucer's generous, deeply humane vision of life. But the ending of the poem, in **"Kent and Christendome"**, is indeed wonderful, free and joyful as nothing else in Wyatt, except stanza two of **"They fle from me"**:

> This maketh me at home to hounte and hawke
>   And in fowle weder at my booke to sitt.
> In frost and snowe then with my bow to stawke;
>   No man doeth marke where so I ride or goo;
>   In lusty lees at libertie I walke,
> And of these newes I fele nor wele nor woo,
>   Sauf that a clogg doeth hang yet at my hele:
>   No force for that it is ordered so,
> That I may lepe boeth hedge and dike full well.

Even here, in the admission of the "clogg" that still hangs at his heel, Wyatt acknowledges his implication in the court world. Yet he has come to terms with that side of himself so that it no longer impedes his freedom—"it is ordered so, / That I may lepe boeth hedge and dike full well". The whole of Satire I has really been a "Who so list" poem, and it's no accident that Wyatt is most happily and fully himself at the end of such a sustained effort to assert his dissociation from the everday compromises and distortions of the courtier's life.

Vincent Buckley prefers Satire I, Mason Satire II; my own preference, as a complete poem, is for Satire III. Satire II, while pleasant enough in its retelling of **"The City-Mouse and the Country-Mouse"**, seems to me only at the end, where Wyatt sheets home the moral in his address to Poins, to achieve the passionate conviction of the other two:

> Then seke no more owte of thy self to fynde
>   The thing that thou haist sought so long before,
>   For thou shalt fele it sitting in thy mynde.

> And if Satire III has nothing to stand up against the
>   exhilaration of the end of Satire I, it seems to me
>   a more sustained and coherent achievement, and a
>   more radically original one.

It is addressed to another of Wyatt's friends, the diplomat Sir Francis Bryan, but unlike the others, it's not merely a letter but a dialogue. (There are editions that don't make this clear—perhaps there are editors that haven't perceived it?) Wyatt, or rather "Wyatt", begins with familiar ease, offering Bryan a series of well-worn proverbs to persuade him of the foolishness of his earnest service of the king:

> A spending hand that alway powreth owte
>   Had nede to have a bringer in as fast,
>   And on the stone that still doeth tourne abowte
> There groweth no mosse:

and why not "waste not want not" we might well ask? "Wyatt's" attitude to Bryan is a mixture of mockery with a real respect for the man's selfsacrifice:

> To the, therefore, that trottes still vp and downe,
>   And never restes: but runnyng day and nyght
> From Reaulme to Reaulme, from cite, strete and
>   towne;
>   Why doest thou were thy body to the bones,

And myghtst at home slepe in thy bed of downe
And drynck goode ale so nappy for the noyns. . . .

Bryan's first indignant reply, with its king-and-country rhetoric, provokes a little mock-admiration, and then the insinuating ease of the friend who is settling down at last to what he really means to say:

By god, well sayde, but what and if thou wist
  How to bryng in as fast as thou doest spend?

Bryan's obedient "That would I lerne" unleashes the "lesson" before the line has reached its end. Wyatt has learnt from Chaucer the comic possibilities of a hopelessly one-sided dialogue (see, for example, Geffrey and the Eagle in *The Hous of Fame*.) The catalogue of advice on How to Succeed in the World is openly sarcastic, and so the account of courtly hypocrisy is both more straightforward and more savage than in Satire I.

Sumtyme also riche age begynneth to dote:
Se thou when there thy gain may be the more.
  Stay him by the arme where so he walke or goo;
  Be nere alway: and if he koggh to sore,
When he hath spit, tred owte and please him so.

. . . . .

But if so chaunce you get nought of the man,
The wedow may for all thy charge deburse.
A ryveld skyn, a stynking breth, what than?
A tothles mowth shall do thy lips no harme:
The gold is good, and tho she curse or ban,
Yet where the list thou maist ly good and warme;
Let the old mule byte vpon the bridill,
Whilst there do ly a swetter in thyn arme.
In this also se you be not Idell:
  Thy nece, thy cosyn, thy sister or thy doghter,
  If she be faire, if handsom be her myddell,
Yf thy better hath her love besoght her,
  Avaunce his cause and he shall help thy nede.
  It is but love, turne it to a lawghter.

That, I would say, leaves Tourneur very little to discover! The distaste of "brackishe ioyes" has come pretty close to actual nausea.

It has been said that Wyatt is out of control, over-wrought, or worse still revelling in the nastiness he evokes. I don't think this is so, and it's here that the importance of Bryan comes in. As "Wyatt's" voice rises, becoming more and more stridently sarcastic, Bryan is allowed to interrupt by laughing at him:

Laughst thou at me? Why, do I speke in vayne?
  'No, not at the, but at thy thrifty gest.
  Wouldest thou I should for any losse or gayne
Chaunge that for gold that I have tan for best,
  Next godly thinges, to have an honest name?
  Should I leve that then take me for a best.'

(I have altered Muir's punctuation of this passage which seems to me patently wrong.)

The cadence of forthright, self-possessed integrity is unmistakable—and unmistakably affirmed. What Wyatt is doing is something it was left for Pope to re-discover: using the dialogue form to invoke the support of an apparently dissenting, but actually sympathetic friend, whose attitude thereby gives substance to the values in which the satirist's own attitude is grounded. Bryan functions something like the figure of Arbuthnot; and if this claim seems fanciful, notice the change in "Wyatt's" voice when he responds:

Nay, then, farewell, and if you care for shame
  Content the then with honest pouertie
  With fre tong what the myslikes to blame
And for thy truth sumtyme aduersitie:
  And therewithall this thing I shall the gyve—
  In this worould now litle prosperite,
And coyne to kepe as water in a syve.

It's a rueful, relaxed, affectionate benediction on his unworldly friend, that makes clear Wyatt's affirmation of all he stands for. Invoking Bryan's presence has liberated Wyatt, as Arbuthnot's does Pope—enabled him to affirm what he values, deeply and strongly, without self-righteousness or insistence. This is the same Wyatt we must take seriously all through his work: not the court entertainer, but the man for whom poetry was a necessity, a way of finding—indeed of being—himself in a world where "Ful nere that wynd goeth trouth in great misese".

Jerry Mermel (essay date 1978)

SOURCE: "Sir Thomas Wyatt's Satires and the Humanist Debate Over Court Service," in *Studies in the Literary Imagination*, Vol. XI, No. 1, Spring, 1978, pp. 69-79.

[*In the following essay, Wyatt's satires are seen as disparate portraits of courtly life.*]

Critical studies of Sir Thomas Wyatt's three verse epistles or satires have customarily found in them both a deeply felt indictment of the Tudor court and an equally strong vindication of the quiet, retired life. Typically, all three are said to have been "written in a mood of disillusionment with the life of the court and with the worldly arts necessary for success."[1] For Patricia Thomson, these poems need to be examined against the background of Wyatt's own somewhat turbulent career at court, for they "reflect not only the shock of the courtier's disillusion, but the studied criticism of an experienced Tudor 'governor.'"[2] Raymond Southall, who similarly feels that all the satires "issue from a disillusionment that is brought to comment directly upon the quality of court life," contends that "unlike the love poems, which are completely immersed in the conditions of court life, [the satires] are controlled by the awareness of a preferable way of life, that of the country squire."[3] Although no one who has read the satires will wish to deny the strong anti-courtly elements that they contain, these and other similar critical assessments seem to me to assume a greater uniformity in the tone and argument of the poems than actually exists. They tend, in fact, to conflate the argument of the first satire, which does present a strong case for abandoning the court, with those of the second and third satires, where the attitude toward court service is at once more complex and more sympathetic. This is a tendency that needs, I think, to be resisted.

If recent studies of the satires have usefully reminded us of the extent to which they are rooted in Wyatt's personal experience, it is equally helpful to recall that the miseries of courtly life and the joys of a quiet rural life were standard literary topics among Renaissance courtiers, most of whom had little intention of ever quitting the court. Luigi Alamanni, the Florentine poet who supplied Wyatt with a literary model for the first satire, sued successfully for the patronage of Francis I and had his court satires as well as other of his works published under the French king's auspices. A more extreme example is provided by Francis Brian, the courtier to whom Wyatt addressed the third satire. In translating Antonio de Guevara's *Menosprecio de Corte* (1539) as *A Dispraise of the Life of the Courtier* (1548), Brian managed the feat of denouncing in print most of the courtly vices which he was notorious for committing in practice.

Admittedly, Wyatt's career at court may have furnished him with legitimate grounds for complaint against the courtier's uncertain lot. He made enemies with several powerful men, most especially the Duke of Suffolk, and was twice summarily arrested and confined to the Tower. Both of Wyatt's arrests, however, were followed by speedy pardons and an immediate resumption of his sovereign's favor. Instead of abandoning public life in order to live out his days as a country squire in Kent, he continued to rise in the royal service, earning for himself a reputation as a polished courtier and a hardworking diplomat. If in such poems as **"In court to serve,"** he lashes out against the empty splendor of the court, its duplicity and treachery, in another of his poems he can with equal fervor proclaim himself a dedicated servant of the crown and the commonwealth:

Tagus, fare well, that westward with thy stremes
Torns up the grayns off gold already tryd:
With spurr and sayle for I go seke the Tems

. . . . .

My kyng, my Contry alone for whom I lyve
Of myghty love the winges for this me gyve.[4]

The satires, I believe, speak to both of these aspects of Wyatt's as well as other Renaissance writers' experiences at court: even as they level a powerful attack against courtly injustices, they point also to the attractions that court service could hold out for patriotic men of learning and ability. This essay, therefore, will examine the satires as poems which dramatize and delineate the problem of the learned man's role at court, rather than conclusively resolving it. Since it is my belief that the satires should be treated as separate, if closely related, poems instead of as a monolithic unit, I shall also attempt to indicate how in each of them Wyatt examines courtly life

from a distinctive point of view and so manages to create over the course of these works a complex, multifaceted portrait of the court, not simply an unrelievedly hostile picture of its darker side.

In *The Quyete of Mynde*, an essay that Wyatt translated into English in 1527, Plutarch advises the courtier who has suffered through the treachery of others that the "best remedy is with the muses / or in som place of lernyng to suffre over."[5] Wyatt's first satire, **"Myne owne John Poynz,"** describes a similar situation and advocates a similar "remedy."[6] The rhetorical stance that Wyatt adopts here is essentially forensic; he presents himself as a courtier who has decided to retire to his country home in Kent and who wishes to defend this course of action by demonstrating both its justifiability and its necessity. More specifically, Wyatt's is the complaint of a cultured Renaissance gentleman, nourished on the humanist hope for a reconciliation of the active and the studious life, but serving in a court where one must "Hang on their sleves that way as thou maist se / A chippe of chaunce more then a pownde of witt" (11.78-9). While his study of classical antiquity may have once furnished him with ample precedent to justify his active participation in political affairs, it now lends support to the contrary view that in some circumstances the refusal to serve in government is the best means of fulfilling one's duty to serve the commonwealth:

I am not he that can alow the state
  Off highe Cesar and dam Cato to dye,
  That with his deth dyd skape owt off the gate
From Cesares hands (if Lyve do not lye)
  And would not lyve whar liberty was lost:
  So did his hert the common wele aplye.
                                    (11. 37-42, my emphasis)

Wyatt's withdrawal from the court is thus portrayed as a principled response to royal and courtly wrongdoing by a man for whom a contemplative rural existence offers not only the leisure to "rede and ryme" (1.101), but also, and more importantly, the opportunity to preserve his liberty and integrity intact.

Of Wyatt's three satires the first presents the sharpest critique of what one modern scholar has aptly called the humanist "myth of the political effectiveness of learning."[7] But even here, I would argue, the criticism of the court and the preference expressed for country life may be more qualified than is usually acknowledged. To begin with, in its own way the first satire upholds rather than rejects the classical ideal of the learned man of affairs. Wyatt's chief grievance is with a court where virtue and learning are hindrances instead of assets. But he is hardly saying that the scholar or poet's calling is such that, ideally, he must seclude himself with the muses, refusing to play an active role in the governance or administration of the commonwealth. On the contrary, his complaint against the court is predicated on the assumption that the eloquent and the learned are precisely those who ought to be given positions of power in government. Wyatt, moreover, does not deny that some virtuous and able courtiers continue to serve though they are fully aware of the abuses that exist at court. The first satire is itself addressed to a courtier whom he quite obviously respects and who he believes is fair-minded enough to give his argument a sympathetic hearing. John Poins clearly does not belong to the company of sycophantic courtiers who are so vehemently denounced in the first satire, nor is he one of the "common sort" who see only the outward magnificence of courtly life "Without regarde what dothe inward resort" (1. 13). Yet Poins still remains at court, determined to pursue a career in public life. Certainly Wyatt, at least as he represents himself in this poem, has chosen a different course for himself. Nevertheless, even while explaining his decision, he indicates one of the reasons that court service might appeal to men like Poins or, indeed, himself.

Though Wyatt writes the first satire in order to justify his withdrawal to the country, early in the poem he concedes that even in Kent he still feels the desire for glory which first drew him to court:

> I grawnt sumtime that of glorye the fyar
> Dothe touche my hart; me lyst not to report
> Blame by honowr and honour to desyar.
>
> (11. 14-16)

These lines not only stress Wyatt's refusal to be hypocritical about his desire for glory but also suggest the need to distinguish between two constasting types of ambition, one which Wyatt strongly condemns, the other which he both approves of and shares. The same distinction is clearly in Wyatt's mind when, while writing to his son in April 1537, he again speaks of glory as a fire and insists that the quest for glory is compatible with a virtuous and honorable life:

> And here I call not honestye that men comenly call honestye, as reputation for riches, for authoritie, or some like thing, but that honestye that I dare well say your Grandfather (whos soule god pardon) had rather left to me then all the lands he did leave me—that was wisedome, gentlenes, sobrenes, disire to do good, frendlines to get the love of manye, and troughth above all the rest. A great part to have all thes things is to desire to have them: and altho Glorye and honest name are not the verye endes wherfor thes things are to be folowed, yet surely they must nedes folowe them as light folowth fire, though it wer kindled for warmth.[8]

Wyatt, I believe, is as concerned in the first satire with carefully distinguishing between an honorable and dishonorable quest for glory as he is in the letter to his son; he will not let Poins or his other readers confuse his own proper desire for honor with the unscrupulous ambition of the courtiers whom he attacks.

If the "fire of glory" still touches and moves Wyatt in Kent, he has obviously looked first to the court not the country as the place to realize his ambition. In the first satire, it is true, he describes the frustration of his hopes. Rather than winning honor through the performance of glorious deeds, he has found that as a courtier he must engage in a petty, though ruthless, striving for place with men who think nothing of resorting to deceit and flattery in order to secure preferment for themselves or deny it to others. Yet, at the same time, he understands that his exile from the court involves the loss of something that is important to him. In the first satire, then, one can sense the tension between a revulsion at the widespread corruption at court and the sense of the opportunities for glorious and honorable achievement that the court, at least potentially, offers. Thus even as Wyatt insists that his refusal to sacrifice his honesty for court favor has forced him to withdraw to Kent, he suggests, too, that for him country life is a second choice, an alternative compelled by the reality of a court where guile rather than merit is rewarded.

For his second satire Wyatt again chooses the form of a verse letter addressed to his fellow courtier John Poins. But the tone of this epistle is considerably more restrained and moderate than that of **"Myne owne John Poynz"**; the indignant protest of the first satire has given way here to detached philosophic reflection and observation. The shift in tone is accompanied by a corresponding shift in Wyatt's argument. No longer do we find him insisting upon the necessity of leaving the court. On the contrary, he now goes on to make the case that true inner contentment is available to all who rightly seek it, whether they live in the country, at court, or in town.

The procedure that Wyatt follows in the second satire is somewhat reminiscent of Chaucer's in *The Nun's Priest's Tale*. He begins by relating a fable about a town and a country mouse, draws a moral from it, and then applies this to Poins's and his own situation. While he speaks of this fable as a spinning song that he had learned from his mother's maids (1. 1), Horace as well as several earlier writers had provided renditions of the same story, and Wyatt probably made use of one or more of these for the second satire. It has been suggested that he "uses the fable of the town and country mice (as many had before him) to point the moral that a peaceful private life was preferable to the pursuit of ambition at court."[9] Yet rather than praising the retired rural life and contrasting it to the viciousness of court politics, as he had done in the first satire, in this poem Wyatt is able to conclude quite explicitly that "Eche kynd of lyff hath with hym his disease" (1. 80). The entire focus of his argument is, in fact, not upon a particular kind of life—urban, courtly, or rural—but rather upon a certain disposition of mind and the means to attain it.

Interestingly, in the fable that opens the second satire it is the city mouse who has learned to make the best of her situation. As alive to the dangers of urban life as her country sister is oblivious to them (11. 36-41), she is not caught off guard by the sudden arrival of a "traytour Catt" who interrupts her and her sister's meal. "The towney mouse fled," Wyatt observes, "she knew wither to goo" (1. 59). The country mouse, on the other hand, finds no peace in her rural home and quickly comes to grief in town, for the roots of her problem lie not in her surroundings but in herself, in a mind ruled by desire and torn by discontent. Jealous of her sister's imagined good fortune, she deludes herself into forsaking "her poure suretie and rest / For semyng welth wherein she thought to rayne" (11. 68-9).

In the *moralitas* of the second satire, Wyatt analyzes the broader implications of his fable. All men, he tells Poins, yearn for inner tranquillity, but many, like the country mouse of the fable, pursue it in the wrong way:

> Alas, my Poynz, how men do seke the best,
> And fynde the wourst by error as they stray!
> And no marvaill: when sight is so opprest,
> And blynde the gyde, anon owte of the way
> Goeth gyde and all in seking quyete liff.
> O wretched myndes, there is no gold that may
> Graunt that ye seke! No warr, no peace, no stryff,
> No, no all tho thy hed were howpt with gold,
> Sergeaunt with mace, hawbert, sword nor knyff
> Cannot repulse the care that folowe should.
>
> (11. 70-9)

The synecdoche, "O wretched myndes," functions particularly well in this context, for it emphasizes very pointedly Wyatt's insistence throughout the second satire that the source of iner peace is a disciplined mind—not a courtly or rural environment, both of which are equally powerless either to bring tranquillity of mind or, just as importantly, to take it away.

The argument that Wyatt makes to Poins in the second satire bears, I think, a marked similarity to the one which he had occasion to set forth a decade before when translating Plutarch's *The Quyete of Mynde* (1527). Here, as in the satires, there is sharp criticism of the court; the essay contains, as Patricia Thomson notes, "the core of the 'classic' case against courtly life—a case which the Renaissance was not slow to accept as its own."[10] At the very outset of the work, however, Plutarch challenges the view that those who desire tranquillity of mind cannot be actively engaged in public affairs. Such an attitude, he feels, mistakes idleness for inner peace:

> It will make unto us / qyuetnesse of mynde of a dere price / as to be bought/with sluggardy and slouthfullnesse / and as tho he were sicke / they warne every man / as it were with this worde / lye still wretch in thy bed. Trewly where as it is an hurtful medecin to the body that deedly sluggardy / nerawhit better phisicien for the sickenesse and trouble of the mynde / is slouth and tendernesse / & faynt hert forsaker of frendes / kyn / and countrey.
>
> (p. 442)

Plutarch also rejects as foolishly misguided the notion that inner peace can be won simply by exchanging one kind of life for another. "But them also," he writes, "that have chosen one maner of life to be void from trouble / as some do the life of these husbandmen/som of syngle men / and some of kynges, Menander warneth . . . that they err far (as they say) out of the way" (p. 443). The courtier turned husbandman or country squire will not, in

Plutarch's view, free himself from discontent merely because he has changed his occupation and address. For Plutarch, as for Wyatt, "the well of surete of minde" can be found only by those of us who have learned to look for it "springing in our self" (p. 445).

At one point in his essay Plutarch warns that quiet of mind will never be attained by those who ignore their natural limitations, seeking always for what is beyond their capacities:

> For of trouth it breketh marveylously the constant & quyet state of mynde / with hyer entent to stryve above the power to get any thing as to sayle with gretter sayles than proporcion/as when hope shyneth never so lytell / promysing our selfes unmesurable and great thynges/& than when chaunce foloweth nat / we accuse wicked fortune and our desteny / whan rather we shulde damn our selfes of foly / as it were to be angry with fortune / that thou canst nat shote an arowe with a plou / or hunt an hare with an oxe / and that some cruell god shulde be agaynst them / that with vayn indevour / hunt an hart with a dragge net / and nat that they attempt to do those impossibilytes by their owne madnesse and folysshnesse.
>
> (p. 452)

One can catch verbal as well as thematic echoes of Wyatt's 1527 translation in the following lines of the second satire:

> Non of ye all there is that is so madde
>   To seke grapes upon brambles or breers,
>   Nor none I trow that hath his wit so badd
> To set his hay for Conys over Ryvers,
>   Ne ye set not a dragg net for an hare.
>   And yet the thing that moost is your desire
> Ye do mysseke with more Travaill and care.
>   Make playn thyn hert that it be not knotted
>   With hope or dred and se thy will be bare
> From al affectes whom vice hath ever spotted;
>   Thy self content with that is the assigned
>   And use it well that is to the alloted.
>
> (11. 85-96)

In Wyatt's view, as in Plutarch's, men seek in vain for happiness unless they are willing to rest content with their natural lot, accepting with equanimity the duties as well as the rewards assigned to them by virtue of the position in society to which they were born.

Among the most marked differences between the first and second satires is the new vantage point from which Wyatt assesses city or court life in each. In the first satire, as we have noted, he speaks as a dignified country gentleman, incensed at both the general depravity of the court and the mistreatment that he has suffered there. In the second, he has his readers view town and country life from the perspective of an indigent and rather overworked rustic. The country mouse of the second satire does not enjoy the *otium litteratum* which is extolled by the landed aristocrat of **"Myne owne John Poynz"**; for her a rural existence is one of deprivation and hard labor:

She thought herself endured to much puin,
  the stormy blasts her cave so sore did sowse,
That when the forowse swymmed with the rain
  she must lie cold and whete in sorry plight;
  And wours then that bare meet did then remain
To comfort her when she her house did dight,
  sometyme a barley corne, sometyme a bene
  For which she laboured hard boeth daye and nyght.

(11. 5-12)

Obviously the country mouse has neither the means nor the time for the life of reading, writing, hunting, and hawking to which Wyatt retires in the first satire. While her life may be simpler and more secure than her "townyssh" sister's, it is one which is filled with exhausting, poorly rewarded toil rather than learning and contemplation.

The altered perspective from which Wyatt depicts the country and the city in the second satire allows him to reconsider the problem that he had posed in **"Myne owne John Poynz"** and to provide an alternative means of resolving it. Country life no longer serves as a touchstone to measure courtly depravity. Rather than advising Poins to flee the court, here Wyatt admonishes him to

  seke no more owte of thy self to fynde
  The thing that thou haist sought so long before,
  For thou shalt fele it sitting in thy mynde.
  Madde, if ye list to continue your sore,
    Let present passe and gape on tyme to come
  And diepe your self in travaill more and more.

(11. 97-102)

The loss or gain of court favor can now be accepted with equanimity; neither can touch the inviolable core of stability and contentment that, as Wyatt indicates to Poins, the mind can create and maintain within itself.[11]

Raymond Southall, whose reading of the second satire is quite different from the one presented here, stresses the thematic continuity between it and the third satire, which is addressed to another of Wyatt's colleagues at court, Sir Francis Brian:

Country life commends itself in the satires not because it is idyllic but because it is honest. The unidyllic rigors of such an honesty . . . are those of the life of country mouse in the second epistle to Poynz. . . . And it is to such a manner of living that Brian is recommended in the third satire after he has refused to adopt the standard of the successful courtier:

Nay then farewell! And if you care for shame

Content the then with honest povertie.

The criterion of inwardness, digested and consciously formulated, is brought in the satires to the juxtaposition of two ways of life and to the establishment of a preference for that which embraces naturalness even in poverty over that of courtly hypocrisy.[12]

Although in the third satire Brian is indeed made to reject such corrupt courtly practices as Wyatt had earlier denounced in **"Myne owne John Poynz,"** Professor Southall fails to point out that the "honest povertie" which Brian embraces is identified in this poem not with a retired country life but with a life of active political service. Here, as in the first satire, Wyatt is centrally concerned with the question of whether an adherence to high ethical standards is compatible with the pursuit of a courtly career. But he chooses now to examine the court from a fresh point of view, taking for himself a fictional or poetic voice that is strikingly different from those which he assumed in his two other satires. As a result, he can present here a vigorous critique of courtly abuses while at the same time lavishing as much praise on the life of the dedicated public servant as he had previously on the life of contemplative study.

The third satire is constructed as an informal dialogue in which two sharply opposed attitudes toward court service are presented. Brian's role in the discussion is reminiscent of Wyatt's in the first satire; his is the voice of outraged honesty which protests any suggestion that one must lie and flatter simply to get ahead in the world. Yet Brian is presented as a hard-working courtier and diplomat, not a country squire who has fled the court or a rural laborer who has been lured to town in the hopes of finding a more affluent and leisurely existence. For his part, Wyatt is no longer the high-minded aristocrat of **"Myne owne John Poynz"** or the calm, earnest moralist who discourses to Poins in the second satire. Instead he adopts the guise of a worldly-wise debauchee who advocates virtually the same course of action that is so emphatically denounced in the first epistle to Poins.

The satiric persona that Wyatt assumes in the third satire provides him with the opportunity to discuss the question of court service in a different way, or at least from a different angle, than he did in the letters to Poins. Once again, as in the first satire, he advocates retirement, arguing that Brian must come home rather than continue to pursue the taxing and poorly rewarded career of a royal diplomat. But the quiet life at home that he urges upon his courtier friend bears no resemblance to the attractive life of study and physical exercise enjoyed by the country squire of **"Myne owne John Poynz"** or the hard rural existence described in the fable of the second satire. In this poem the alternative to service at court is a life of idleness and self-indulgence:

  To the [Brian], therefore, that trottes still up and downe,
    And never restes: but running day and nyght
  Ffrom Reaulme to Reaulme, from cite, strete, and towne;
    Why doest thou were thy body to the bones,
    And myghtst at home slepe in thy bed of downe
  And drynk goode ale so nappy for the noyns,
    Fede thy self fat and hepe up pownd by pownd?

(11. 11-17)

Brian's response can serve as a measure of the distance travelled between the first and the third satire:

Tho I seme lene and dry withoute moyster,
Yet woll I serve my prynce, my lord and thyn,
and let theim lyve to fede the panche that list,
So I may fede to lyve both me and myn.

(11. 18-27)

If in the first satire Wyatt's withdrawal from the court is defended as morally imperative, in the third satire it is similarly high-minded principles rather than expedience that determine Brian's resolution to pursue a career in the royal service. He remains at court, for it is there, in his view, that he will find the most opportunity to be of service to his king and country.

Despite the fervor with which Brian defends his decision to remain in public life and the obvious appeal of his argument, the dialogue of the third satire ends without a firm resolution of the central problem that it raises. So radically divergent, in fact, are each of its speakers' views of court service that the reader is continually pulled in two directions: one can see the truth in the brutal assessment on how to get ahead at court that Wyatt's persona makes even as one is equally compelled to admire the idealism and self-sacrifice that underlie Brian's determination to try to be an honest courtier. It can be argued that the criticism of the court that Wyatt presents in the third satire is, if less direct, no less severe than it is in **"Myne owne John Poynz."** Certainly the advice that Brian is given regarding the various means he can use to grow rich as a courtier points to a courtly environment in which, as in the first satire, deceit and sycophancy still seem the surest vehicles to preferment. At the same time, however, such dispraise of the court coexists in an uneasy balance with an insistence upon the duty of the learned man to serve the state. Indeed, in Brian, Wyatt portrays a virtuous and able public servant who knows at first hand the injustices of court life and yet still regards political service to the commonwealth as the most suitable and necessary endeavor for men of virtue and learning.

To find in Wyatt's satires only the angry protest of a disheartened and disillusioned courtly maker is, I am convinced, to misread them fundamentally. Like the dialogue in the first book of More's *Utopia* or the discussion of the court in Spenser's *Colin Clouts Come Home Againe,* Wyatt's satires speak to the conflicting attitudes and feelings that the problem of court service generated among the humanistically trained readers and writers of Tudor England. In them we find no single or definitive solution to the question of whether the learned ought to pursue political careers at court. Instead, by skillfully shifting his point of view and assuming a new fictional voice in each satire, Wyatt is able to explore the arguments that might be heard on both sides of the humanist debate over court service. His satires are important to us, I would submit, not because they put an end to this debate but because they bring it alive.

NOTES

[1] Kenneth Muir, *Life and Letters of Sir Thomas Wyatt* (Liverpool: Liverpool Univ. Press, 1963), p. 251.

[2] *Sir Thomas Wyatt and His Background* (Stanford: Stanford Univ. Press, 1964), p. 44.

[3] *The Courtly Maker: An Essay on the Poetry of Wyatt and His Contemporaries* (New York: Barnes & Noble, 1964), pp. 92; 96.

[4] All citations in my text to Wyatt's poems are to the *Collected Poems of Sir Thomas Wyatt,* ed. Kenneth Muir and Patricia Thomson (Liverpool: Liverpool Univ. Press, 1969).

[5] Plutarch, *The Quyete of Mynde,* trans. Thomas Wyatt, in *Collected Poems of Sir Thomas Wyatt,* p. 446. Future citations to *The Quyete of Mynde* will be to the text of the essay reprinted in the *Collected Poems,* pp. 440-63.

[6] Wyatt's poem is written in imitation of Luigi Alamanni's tenth Provençal satire *"Io vi diro che d'udir vi cale."* It is a close imitation, but Wyatt anglicizes and personalizes his Italian model, and occasionally departs from it or reshapes it. For a detailed description of the relationship between the two poems, see Donald L. Guss, "Wyatt, Alamanni, and Literary Imitation," *Journal of the Rutgers University Library,* 26 (1962), 6-13. Patricia Thomson provides a most useful discussion of the sources for this as well as the other satires in *Sir Thomas Wyatt and His Background,* pp. 238-70.

[7] G. K. Hunter, *John Lyly: The Humanist as Courtier* (Cambridge: Harvard Univ. Press, 1962), p. 15.

[8] Muir, *Life and Letters,* p. 38.

[9] *Ibid.,* p. 253.

[10] *Sir Thomas Wyatt and His Background,* p. 84.

[11] Donald Friedman discusses the prevalence of this concept in Wyatt's verse in "The Thing in Wyatt's Mind," *Essays in Criticism,* 16 (1966), 375-81.

[12] *The Courtly Maker,* pp. 97-8.

Jonanthan Z. Kamholtz (essay date 1978)

SOURCE: "Thomas Wyatt's Poetry: The Politics of Love," in *Criticism,* Vol. XX, No. 4, Fall, 1978, pp. 349-65.

[In the following essay, Kamholtz argues that the interplay between politics and love in Wyatt's poetry expresses the limits of Henry VIII's court.]

Wyatt's **"He is not ded that sometyme hath a fall"** examines various natural consolations for political disgrace.

HE is not ded that sometyme hath a fall.
The Sonne retorneth that was vnder the clowd
And when fortune hath spitt oute all her gall
I trust good luck to me shalbe allowd.
For I have sene a shippe into haven fall
After the storme hath broke boeth mast and shrowd;

And eke the willowe that stowpeth with the wynde
Doeth ryse again, and greater wode doeth bynd.[1]

Wyatt, closely following his source in Serafino, search-es for a satisfactory metaphorical model: by grace of what force can the fallen one be restored?[2] In consider-ing these various alternatives, the speaker tries to find a way to exert some influence over circumstances that have bereft him of control of his life. As long as the speaker continues to propose comparisons, he stresses the ways that falls are unlike deaths. Activity of the imagination is itself a kind of consolation for political frustration. The speaker's imagination is the most *active* force in the poem. The images he chooses depict survival as a passive activity: the sun's reemergence depends upon the passing of the clouds, the ship must have luck befall it, and the willow "stowpeth." Yet only the willow, the speaker assures us, "doeth ryse"—al-though possibly in a different form, lending its strength to those who are greater: but it alone has specifically solved the problem of falling. Presumably by its very nature, it cannot help but be flexible. It is a worthy model for the courtier: it knows when to give.

Wyatt's political poetry is filled with ambiguity about the nature and identity of its heroes. The lyric begins "He is not ded," but by line four, it asserts "I trust good luck to me shalbe allowed." Muir-Thomson note that in the best manuscript, the Egerton, "I am not ded" has been altered in Wyatt's own hand to "He" (p. 312). Though Wyatt's alteration might be the rather obvious subterfuge of politically prudent disguise, the resulting confusion typifies larger problems in Wyatt's court poetry.[3] Is Wyatt more concerned with the fall of Henry's great men, con-tent to see himself as poet and observer while men like Cromwell and Wolsey pay for the risks they have taken, or is Wyatt concerned with his own political ups and downs, with himself as actor-victim? In choosing to re-treat to the pose of an outsider ("For I have sene a shippe . . ."), Wyatt suggests that he prefers to be re-membered as an observer, a mind that has visited the court and learned its lessons. In altering the manuscript's stoic—and possibly self-pitying—"I am not ded all though I had a fall" to "HE," Wyatt may also be obliquely trans-forming court politics into another phenomenon from which a shrewd observer—the speaker—can learn, as he did from observing the clouded sun, the battered ship and the bending willow. By alluding to the court but stepping back from it, Wyatt continues to pursue his quest for the still spot in the turning world where he might find quiet of mind.

The editor of Tottel's *Miscellany* printed the revised version ("He"), but adds a puzzling title: **"The lover hopeth of better chance."** The editor—the poem's ear-liest published interpreter and critic—has read the verse as a love lyric. But where is the erotic content?

We know that Tottel's editor altered and possibly warped many poems he printed (the regularization of the rhythm of **"They fle from me"** is the infamous example). Fur-thermore, the titles that Tottel's editor assigned the lyr-ics virtually created the persona of "the lover" through whose complaining lips we hear an enormous number of the anthologized lyrics. The very act of titling—asserting the presence of a speaker and frequently proposing moral *sententiae*—imposes some distortion on the courtly lyr-ics, as does the change from manuscript to printed word. The printed poem belongs to a different political context and a different literary tradition.[4] Perhaps Tottel's editor hoped to infuse bourgeois married love with the high-mindedness and sexual sublimation of the courtly love ethos.

Nevertheless, the title suggests that to the sixteenth cen-tury ear, **"He is not ded"** *could* sound like an amatory poem. Though we should not preclude the possibility that the imagery of rising and falling refers indirectly to the flux of male sexual energy, it seems more likely that the political-amatory correspondence takes place on a more general level: the problems of political flux were seen as being applicable to the flux of love's fortunes as well. The poet then seeks safe harbor from the storms of love as well as those of political controversy and disgrace.

The evidence in Tottel suggests that the poem has a fun-damentally dual significance. Courtly love achieves the status of a natural force—and of political forces. Per-haps "the lover" hopes that love places him beyond pol-itics—or that he will fare at least as well as disgraced courtiers, hoping that the same consolations are available to the heartbroken as to the crestfallen. This reading would add new poignance to the female personification of for-tune, and to the speaker's humbly passive suit when he deals with his own plight most directly: "I trust good luck to me shalbe allowed." Love and politics may be seen as complementary despotisms. Seeing both the political and erotic implications of the poem suggests the multiplicity of social obligations imposed upon the courtier poet: he can be distant from the fall of others, and yet is destined to love and have to sue politely to a force as powerful and potentially hostile as *fortuna*.

Raymond Southall, in *The Courtly Maker,* insists that Wyatt's reader not overlook "the political aspect of the amorous complaint," and notes that the conventions of the courtly love lyric could "express the real character of courtly existence," where, he notes, "the pattern of per-sonal relationships could be kaleidoscoped at any mo-ment by the exigencies of national and international pol-itics" (pp. 49, 25, 8). A review of the situation at court in the opening decades of the sixteenth century will help us understand the political world which Wyatt's love lyr-ics reflect and express.

Some of the anxieties of Wyatt's poetry may well reflect the political ambiguities that accompanied what has been called the Henrican revolution.[5] During the Tudor years, England underwent a basic transition from a medieval state, held together by the static, contractual interperson-al relationships of feudal ties, towards a modern state, governed by more impersonal, bureaucratic and fluid bonds. Court attitudes and courtly art forms reflect the transition between these two systems.

The medieval, feudal court depended upon mutual, reciprocal agreements between king and aristocracy; each offered protection to the other. The key term in medieval government, notes G. R. Elton, is the "household," and service to the state centered around the court—which was the royal household—and service to the king's person (p. 19). Security, the goal of the feudal state servant, was attained by being granted a court office, affording the courtier a literal as well as a metaphorical place at court.

Around the turn of the sixteenth century, however, new constituencies sought and found ways to serve the king. Louis B. Wright has called the Tudor monarchy a "bourgeois dynasty" and historians generally agree that members of the increasingly influential middle class rose into positions of greater public importance than ever before—men like Wolsey, Cromwell, More and even Wyatt himself.[6] Their loyalty was measured not merely by service to the king's person, but by serving the increasingly far-flung national and international network of laws and interests associated with the needs of a strong, centralized state.[7] Authority was increasingly delegated, and managerial and administrative talents became vital. But with avenues of success open to larger numbers of people, the terrors that accompany competition become of greater concern: fallings follow risings, successful men displace the less successful, factionalism disrupts unity of purpose.

Henry VIII combined the personal authority of the king's medieval role with the legal authority of the modern state. The feudal system had been weakened by years of war and the rise of new sources of economic strength and influence. Thomson notes the increasing fictiveness of traditional medieval roles: "The master-servant link had, in fact, lost much of its feudal strength. At most, the master represented an intermediate loyalty between servant and state" (p. 52). In this context, decisions to perpetuate feudal roles become stronger statements about the need for archaic political ideals. Henry was fascinated by medieval culture and kept alive its formal network of symbolic actions, including jousts and state pageants which were a form of public courtly romance. G. R. Elton notes that Henry's own talents and interests were more towards the older system. Henry seems to have rebelled against the bureaucratic state he had helped to create, preferring to exercise personal pleasure over legal needs (pp. 67-71). England's Reformation was itself a curious mixture of assertion of feudal prerogatives and the consolidation of a modern, independent national state.

The transitional nature of the state is reflected in changes, anxieties and pressures on courtly art as well. Even the system of unpublishing courtly amateurs whose poetry circulates in manuscript form is breaking down; nearly a century intervenes between Chaucer's death and the exposure of his poetry to a non-courtly audience, while Wyatt's poetry appears in print within fifteen years of his death.

C. S. Lewis asks us to see Wyatt as a feudal court poet; he notes that a song by Wyatt

was not intended to be read. It has little meaning until it is sung in a room with many ladies present. The whole scene comes before us. The poet did not write for those who would sit down to *The Poetical Works of Wyatt.* We are having a little music after supper. In that atmosphere all the confessional or autobiographical tone of the songs falls away. . . . . [8]

Lewis reminds us that the ceremonial conversations of the courtly love lyric can be envisioned within the feudal context of household service. But Lewis treats rather unambiguously a role in which Wyatt often seems to feel uncomfortable. The artificer as medieval court servant is perhaps a fading ideal, a nostalgic indulgence, against which to measure the true tone of Wyatt's poetry. The bitterness of Wyatt's songs may not merely be a pose adopted towards ungracious ladies. Songs like **"My lute, awake!"** (M-T LXVI) and **"My pen, take payn"** (M-T CLXXIX) hint at an artistic mode on the verge of collapse, for they are lyrics which end symbolically in the silence of the court artist. Wyatt's poetry moves beyond the conventions of court satire and amatory complaint to examine the difficulty he feels in transmitting his words in the sort of context Lewis describes.

Wyatt's love poetry reflects the ambiguity of functioning in a transitional state. Wyatt writes about both the courtly love situation, which depends upon a system of lovers with clear if frustrating hierarchical places, and the Petrarchan love situation, which depicts the lover without an authentic, natural place, thrown back upon, and within, himself. Wyatt complains about the oppressive rigidity of the courtly love setting with its accretion of traditional and restrictive understandings. Yet he equally fears the "newfanglenes" of the second, where lovers serve no system but themselves and their egos. Love is subjected to an unprecedented series of rises and falls. Wyatt sees himself as caught between the oppressions of stasis and the oppressions of change. Through it all, Wyatt seems to be searching for a harbor—for a place at court and a place in the heart, where a truce can be called to the warring competitions between individuals set free from the traditional feudal and courtly roles. In doing so, he wants to be part of a system that he can see is becoming weaker and weaker. Wyatt suggests that contemporary politician and contemporary lover share a common frame of mind: both lack, but need, a place.

The domestication of the Petrarchan paradox offered the early Renaissance poet a shorthand way of describing states of mind to which no known natural state corresponded. Love's freezing fires and burning rains can only be felt by men out of harmony with their world. Nature cannot cure the lover, or suggest a way for him to express himself, so he turns within. Only internally can the lover regain control over his situation, for the imagination, as Sidney was to argue, does not disdain to be bound by the limits of fallen nature's laws.

Wyatt's adaptation of Petrarch's *Rime* cii, **"Caesar, when that the traytour of Egipt"** (M-T III), explores the relationship between the paradoxical states of mind of the politician and the lover. We do not expect great men or political heroes to express themselves plainly:

> CAESAR, when that the traytour of Egipt
>   With th'onourale hed did him present
>   Covering his gladness did represent
>   Playnt with his teeres owteward, as it is writt:
> And Hannyball eke, when fortune him shitt
>   Clene from his reign and from all his intent,
>   Laught to his folke whome sorrowe did torment,
>   His cruell dispite for to disgorge and qwit.

Men who have a political role to play may have to divorce, for reasons of policy, their public selves from their private ones. They either hide or redirect the passions that demand expression.

Tottel's editor entitles the poem **"Of others fained sorrow, and the lovers fained mirth."** While Muir-Thomson warn that the poem does not need to be read as a love poem (p. 264), the sonnet's sestet seems to focus on amatory, not political, experiences:

> So chaunceth it oft that every passion
>   The mynde hideth by colour contrary
>   With fayned visage, now sad, now mery:
> Whereby, if I laught, any tyme, or season
>   It is for bicause I have nother way
>   To cloke my care but vnder spoort and play.[9]

In the public world, all passions are masked, but the poet's concern focuses only on the falseness of his expressions of joy. The sonnet is richest when read in a dual context. The sestet shows the poet anchoring the paradoxical style of his love in history, as well as in his emotions; the poet appropriates the unchanging exemplars of history to his argument about love. He has found models in the political world for love's "disdaynfull dowblenes" (M-T V). In so doing, he changes the status of the lover, giving the lover a new, if only partial, heroism: the lover is like a fragmented public hero—more like the conquered Hannibal, however, than the conquering Caesar in that his misery, rather than his mirth is being concealed.

The *Miscellany* title also suggests that this alliance with the past is accompanied by alienation from the present: "others" feel one way, the lover feels another. The title helps call to mind the competitive stance Wyatt so often adopts toward his fellow courtiers: the audience Wyatt tends to address remains an undifferentiated mass of male consciousness from whom he has detached himself (rather than, say, his friends at court). The alienation also suggests the continuing English Renaissance lyric drama between public calling and private pain. This receives expression in a line of courtier poems that extends from Wyatt's **"Ffarewel, Love, and all thy lawes for ever"** (M-T XIII) to Sidney's "Your words my friend" or "Having this day my horse" (*Astrophil and Stella* XXI and XLI). The conflict between the courtier's ambition to be absorbed into the public world and the lover's inability to express himself in publicly useful ways finds form in the deflected feudal imagery of such poems as **"The longe love"** (M-T IV).

These poems also reflect changes in the traditional expectations of the courtier. Under a feudal system, a young man's public duty was primarily military in nature. But as David Bevington notes:

> In its battle against maintenance and feudal autonomy, the Tudor monarchy introduced new criteria for political success in England. No longer supreme was the military warlord with his chivalrous pursuits. . . . [10]

The courtier's new duties were more literate—and even literary. These poems thus complain against a betrayal of political expectations in a transitional state. **"The furyous gonne"** (M-T LXI)—another poem which Tottel's editor takes to be a drama about "the lover"—can be read in terms of the courtier's fear that love has caused him to betray his calling as a public warrior.

> The furyous gonne in his rajing yre,
> When that the bowle is rammed in to sore,
> And that the flame cannot part from the fire,
> Cracketh in sonder, and in the ayre doeth rore
> The shevered peces; right so doeth my desire
> Whose flame encreseth from more to more,
> Wych to let owt I dare not loke nor speke:
> So now hard force my hert doeth all to breke.

Love is blocking the traditional public avenues of young men towards success. The lover is left only with self-destructive inner warfare as a way to release the latent violence of his ambitions—and the violence locked in the experience and language of love.

Wyatt sees both love and politics as a constant process of slipping and falling. He seeks a common goal in both: the desire to stand, to find independent footing. Raymond Southall notes that "experience for Wyatt is a continual search for stability within instability, for a point of rest within a restless world . . ." (p. 77). This stability is frequently pictured in terms of flexibility, mask and pretense, as well as stoic self-assertion and rigidity; the resolution of **"He is not ded,"** after all, was that a man can do worse that to be like the willow and rise with others, binding the "greater wode" which could not bend.

A similar image of the poet seeking a way to stand appears in M-T CCXXXVI:

> The piller pearisht is whearto I Lent
>   The strongest staye of myne vnquyet mynde;
>   The lyke of it no man agayne can fynde
>   From East to west still seking though he went. . . .

Muir-Thomson note that "modern scholars have not followed T[ottel] in labelling this a love poem" (p. 430). They stress the biographical nature of the poem as a response to the falls that threaten public life, especially Wyatt's emotional reaction to the execution of his patron Cromwell and Wyatt's own subsequent incarcerations.[11] And clearly the poem *is* occasional, but like most occasional poems, it reveals more about the speaker than about his subject. In entitling the sonnet **"The lover la-**

mentes the death of his love," Tottel's editor may have been reading the poem against the background of its Petrarchan original, which doubly lamented the losses of both patron and lover (Laura). Moreover, the reading implied in Tottel may suggest the intensity of the bond between courtier and patron; some public ties *are* private ties as well, just as some forms of public favor—especially those associated with the personal ties of feudalism—can be expressions of love.

While the poem's primary concern with grim political reality seems to have absorbed the amatory aspects of the lyric, Tottel's editor may also have responded to the general similarity of the terms of political and erotic mourning. In both types of poem, Wyatt is torn between dependence and independence—between leaning and standing. In both, the weakness of the individual is compensated for by union with others. Both types of poem depict the restless "unquyet mynde" seeking stability; both types depict the intangible spirit questing for something tangible to rest on.

Muir-Thomson points out that Wyatt has altered the Petrarchan original by focusing the last six lines upon his self-hatred and possible guilt. Perhaps Wyatt has replaced his mourning for a lost love with mourning for himself:

> But syns that thus it is by destenye
>   What can I more but have a wofull hart,
>   My penne in playnt, my voyce in wofull crye,
> My mynde in woe, my bodye full of smart,
>   And I my self my self alwayes to hate
>   Till dreadfull death do ease my dolefull state?

Both love and mourning turn the mind inward. Wyatt depicts the kind of self-conscious, divided self that produces the world of paradox: "I my self my self alwayes to hate." The themes of love and politics both produce a sense of doubleness, of dual selves; the unstable mind is the result of the unstable self, shaken by the fear that all around it is falling.[12]

The political form of Wyatt's fear of slipping and falling is expressed in Wyatt's adaptation of Seneca, "Stond who so list upon the Slipper toppe / Of courtes estates . . ." (M-T CCXL). The speaker sees himself looking on while others await their imminent fall.[13] (The fear of falling probably held a special poignance for Wyatt who, as a courtier with middle-class roots, had gotten where he was by rising. Surrey, who was to the manner born, looked upon his misfortunes differently.) Tottel's editor prints an altered version, locating the courtiers on Fortune's "slipper whele." The text of the Arundel manuscript suggests that the place itself, not the machinery of fate, is slippery. Wyatt poses frequently as one who is literally out of place: he is removed, looking out, withdrawn to find some place stabler and more quiet, as he does in **"Myne owne John Poyntz"** (M-T CV)—even though the place is an exile or prison as often as it is a true harbor.

The language of falling pervades Wyatt's love poetry as well as his political poetry. When Wyatt bids **"Fare-**

well, Love, and all thy lawes for ever" (M-T XIII), it is because he "lusteth no lenger rotten boughes to clyme." Love's laws create an insecure place from which the poet might someday fall. One can fall from love despite the faithfulness of one's service, as in **"My pen, take payn"** (M-T CLXXIX), where the poet asks "Wherefore / To hold so fast and yet to ffall?" In **"It may be good, like it who list"** (M-T XXI), the poet argues that the paradoxical state of mind itself creates an inherently unstable floor through which to fall:

> Alas! I tred an endles maze
> That seketh to accorde two contraries;
> And hope still, and nothing hase,
> Imprisoned in libertes,
> As oon unhard and still that cries;
> Alwaies thursty and yet nothing I tast:
> For dred to fall I stond not fast.

The need to stand and the fear to fall: the poet's private life and public life are brought together by a common language. Wyatt seeks the secure place but finds only pitfalls.

Love and the state both try to subject the courtier to authority. While Wyatt might be willing to be bound by court hierarchy and by "lovers laws" (M-T CCXIV), the laws of neither are plain or immutable. Both offer ways to ascend into favor, but the avenues are insecure and the perches gained are brittle. Wyatt seeks what Shakespeare's Ulysses, in his speech on order in *Troilus and Cressida,* called an "authentic place"—a place he may securely occupy in both a woman's heart and the world of court service. Wyatt pictures himself as being helpless in the face of political and sexual authority, but those authorities are in turn helpless to create stable order in their world. They are unable to serve those who serve them. Wyatt aspires to both types of preferment because they promise stability; but both are themselves unstable, constantly evolving new rules and creating new favorites. Both authorities are strong because of the intangible (or paradoxical) obligations they impose upon the speaker; both are weak because they can provide no tangible place or harbor for him. In consequence, Wyatt's standing in court and in love feels intangible, while his ensuing fall seems quite tangible.

Wyatt chooses to see himself as a reasoning man in an unreasonable world. Several of his lyrics counterpoint the stalemate of illogic with a brief climactic note of logic:

> I fynde no peace and all my warr is done;
>   I fere and hope I burne and freise like yse;
>   I fley above the wynde yet can I not arrise;
>   And noght I have and all the worold I seson. . . .
> Withoute Iyen, I se; and withoute tong I plain;
>   I desire to perisshe and yet I aske helthe;
>   I love an othre and thus I hate my self;
> I fede me in sorrowe and laugh in all my pain;
>   Likewise displeaseth me boeth deth and lyffe;
>   And my delite is causer of this stryff.
>
>   (M-T XXVI)

With "thus," the poet imposes momentary control over his situation, without of course resolving the internalized paradoxes from which many Petrarchan lyrics derive their energy. In **"What worde is this"** (M-T L), Wyatt tries to solve the problem of the illogic and instability of love by finding a word that will not slide:

> What wourde is that that chaungeth not,
> Though it be tourned and made in twain?
> It is myn aunswer, god it wot,
> And eke the causer of my payn.
> A love rewardeth with disdain,
> Yet is it loved. What would ye more?
> It is my helth eke and my sore.

The poem's energy comes from its mixture of stability and paradox. Wyatt's riddle creates a world of paradox for which he hopes to find an "aunswer" in a word that cannot be changed, no matter how it is assaulted by experience and intellectual ingenuity.

The "aunswer," of course, has traditionally been given as "Anna," and the poem is probably correctly read as one of Wyatt's poems to Anne Boleyn.[14] Tottel's editor, who characteristically prefers reason to paradox, agrees; he prints the third line as "It is mine Anna" and entitles the poem **"Of his love called Anna"**—thus overemphasizing the solution to the experiential and linguistic riddle. The editor is unable to abide Wyatt's question: "What would ye more?" Wyatt's interest is in *posing* the riddle; unresolvable paradoxes have more weight than their elusive resolutions. He searches for the plain word, and the plain love, but falls short of finding them.

There is a political dimension to love's paradoxes and ciphers in this case as well. In so far as the poem is addressed to Anne Boleyn, Wyatt's love is literally as unutterable as it is unfulfillable. The poet's choice of partial articulateness reflects political pressures. Numerous opaque legends have survived about Henry's jealousy of Wyatt; competition for this love was unthinkable. In noting that love could be "a form of social rebellion," and hence dangerous, Southall notes that "impolitic love, therefore, may be defined as real affection when opposed to the political order of degrees and estates" (p. 24). Prudence in dangerous situations could force the courtier-lover to speak in ciphers.[15] Part of the drama of the poem resides in Wyatt's quest for a forbidden word to express a still more forbidden experience. This complicates our reading of Wyatt's intentions and themes. As both courtly and Petrarchan lover, Wyatt would be expected to transform his attachment to others into internal stress. Tottel's emendation is thus considerably less perceptive than Wyatt's own vision of his situation: the correct answer is not the plain word but the paradox, not "Anna" but "It is my helth eke and my sore."

In **"Who so list to hounte"** (M-T VII), the speaker seeks to create stability and plainness for himself in a world that offers him only instability, paradox, uncertainty, exhaustion and danger. The poem depicts a moment at which the poet's sense of alienation from both court and love first becomes self-conscious and receives articulation. It revolves around an episode of political and sexual self-discovery. The sonnet suggests the kinds of burdens that the courtier's life places upon citizens of Henry's court, reminding the speaker that the fictions of neither courtly love nor Petrarchan love are experienced in a political vacuum.

The sonnet is another of Wyatt's "whoso" poems: one man at court is speaking to a faceless group of others. The poem is filled with reminders that love is a public, not a private, pursuit; the "I" and "thou" of the love unit is cluttered with the presence of others—those "who" are addressed, the group "of theim" with whom the poet shares his plight, and, of course, the implied presence of Caesar.

> Who so list to hounte I know where is an hynde;
>   But as for me, helas, I may no more:
>   The vayne travaill hath weried me so sore,
>   I ame of theim that farthest cometh behinde. . . .

In the second quatrain, he hints at his paradoxical situation: his mind, as well as his body, has become involved in love, for his mind becomes the wounding arrow. Yet it is the hunter who staggers as if wounded; the experience that seeks to go outward rebounds inwardly.

> Yet may I by no meanes my weried mynde
>   Drawe from the Diere: but as she fleeth afore
>   Faynting I folowe; I leve of therefore,
>   Sithens in a nett I seke to hold the wynde.

The resolution proposed is related to that of **"I fynde no peace"**—the speaker wishes to impose logic on his situation and presumably reassert his mind's control over his life (with the strong "therefore"). The speaker seeks to harness the resolving power of received, traditional language, and offers a proverbial explanation: "In a nett I seke to hold the wynde." Having extricated himself from vain seeking (another characteristic pose), and having found a verbal and even a natural excuse (the image of the wind) to leave off, the poem's personal drama ought to end here.

But the speaker remains haunted by his experience. Petrarch's dream is Wyatt's nightmare. He is dissatisfied with his proverbial solution; as in **"Satire III,"** Wyatt finds the plainness of commonplace to be inconclusive. The sestet reopens the case with almost the same formulation as the octet: "Who list her hount."

> Who list her hount I put him owte of dowbte,
>   As well as I may spend his tyme in vain;
>   And graven with Diamondes in letters plain
> There is written her faier neck rounde abowte:
>   'Noli me tangere for Cesars I ame,
>   And wylde for to hold though I seme tame'.

The sestet proposes an alternate explanation, one that will put its audience "owte of dowbte" and whose meaning is "plain."

The message he finds is, of course, not at all plain. In Petrarch's version, the collar explained that certain deer were still protected by Caesar even though they had been set free: Caesar's I was, not "for Cesars I ame." The message around her neck describes the complex interplay between obedience due to wordly and otherworldly rulers. The motto is composed of a conflation of the Gospels: John's touch me not, for I have not yet ascended, and Mark's and Luke's render unto Caesar what is Caesar's. The final two lines thus offer three possibly distinct reasons for the speaker's failure to hold his love: this beauty is other-wordly and belongs to no one (as in Petrarch's vision); this beauty has already been claimed by Caesar, one who is far more powerful than the speaker; this beauty is a wild thing of nature which no one captures. Stay back, stay back, stay back.

Critical interest has focused upon the middle message, the warning from wordly Caesar, who is usually seen as Henry pursuing his deer, Anne Boleyn, a reading I accept.[16] The poem thus fulfills our dual expectations of Henry's court, filled with hints of wondrous love and despotic terror. The pun on "graven" suggests both the glories of courtly artistic wealth and the morbidity of the tomb. The passive construction ("There is written"), of course, enables us to read the message as having been written by Anne as well. She warns the speaker to note the distinction between appearance and being, exposing the gap between "I ame" and "I seme." This gap was not an issue in the Petrarchan original, where the hind was a vision from start to finish.[17]

If, however, we choose to read the message as coming from Henry, the poem becomes more revealing about the relationship between Tudor love and politics. Lovers keep their physical distance because they sublimate their courtly passions, but also because of their obedience to King and state. The lover's alienation affirms the traditional social order and defuses his potential competition and rebellion. He must show reverence for Caesar as well as for the lady. Courtly love engenders a variety of conflicting and overlapping loyalties. The graven collar announces that the woman is the true servant of Caesar; the lover's alienation testifies that he too must primarily be Caesar's servant rather than Anne's.

The poem is about physical space as well as a frame of mind. The poem literally presents a speaker addressing his audience about a place ("I know where is an hynde") where they may see what he has seen. The poem depicts love that has left the ordered confines of the court for the forest wilderness, and in doing so, has lost its bearings. Wandering exhaustedly, the poet discovers that he has no authentic place. His search for a safe harbor has failed and he becomes like Wyatt's friend, Bryan, restless and rootless. The speaker's dreadful experience in the woods is augmented by the horror of court life, which has followed him into the forest: he both seeks endlessly and endlessly falls (**"Faynting I folowe"**).

In the sestet, the message on the collar modifies the images that might explain the speaker's failure. While he wanted to think in terms of having sought "to hold the wynde," the collar reminds him that he cannot touch her because she is "wylde for to hold though I seme tame." Wind is always wild and belongs to no one. But animals that are wild can be made tame, and tame animals can revert back to their wild state (as they do in **"They fle from me"**). In seeing Anne not as the "wynde" but as something "wylde," Wyatt reminds us that the human order can influence the natural order. This manipulation is the essence of societies, political systems and the arts. As we have seen in **"He is not ded,"** poets use metaphors to imaginatively manipulate nature. So do kings.

This interference in the natural order is a crucial element in considering the relationship between politics and love in Wyatt's lyrics. The Tudor court enclosed a world of symbol makers. **"Who so list to hounte"** describes the speaker's experience of coming across a symbol that he did not himself create: he has encountered another's metaphor. Part of the poem's impact comes from the speaker's implied discovery that love poetry is not the only means to impose symbolic values on events. Political power creates symbols as well.

Wyatt searches to find through love acceptable images to express his mind's quest for quiet and stability. Sometimes he finds other seekers—other courtly makers—instead. Perhaps Wyatt uses the example of the political powers of King and court to illustrate a general problem of the sixteenth century love poet: there are limits to the extent to which the artist can impose his reason and imagination upon another. There are rival quests to offer explanations for the human mystery. The poet's may be more haunting and even more persuasive, but the King's has more power and takes precedence. The interplay between love and politics in Wyatt's poetry demonstrates some limits to the poet's power to define his world. It is part of Wyatt's continuing struggle to try to see things in a stable way in a world where no one will let him do so.

NOTES

[1] Kenneth Muir and Patricia Thomson, eds., *Collected Poems of Sir Thomas Wyatt* (Liverpool: Liverpool Univ. Press, 1969), poem LX, p. 45. The text of all Wyatt poems is from the Muir-Thomson edition; subsequent references in the text will identify the poem by edition and roman numeral, e. g., M-T LX. The titles from Tottel are from Hyder Edward Rollins, ed., *Tottel's Miscellany (1557-1587)* (Cambridge: Harvard Univ. Press, 1928-9).

[2] Wyatt may have been drawn to Serafino's multiple alternatives, as in "Venemus Thorns" (M-T LXXVI)-part of the logical and rhetorical force Patricia Thomson sees as Wyatt's debt to Serafino. This essay—and any serious work on Wyatt—is much indebted to the full-length studies by Patricia Thomson, *Sir Thomas Wyatt and his Background* (Stanford: Stanford Univ. Press, 1964) and Raymond Southall, *The Courtly Maker* (Oxford: Basil Blackwell, 1964).

[3] Thomas A. Hannen notes that Wyatt's political verse is frequently "about the difficulty of achieving self-knowledge" in public situations. "The Humanism of Sir Thomas Wyatt" in *The Rhetoric of Renaissance Poetry from Wyatt to Milton*, Thomas O. Sloan and Raymond B. Waddington, eds. (Berkeley: Univ. of California Press, 1974), p. 39.

4 Significant discussions of this can be found in J. W. Saunders, *The Profession of English Letters* (London: Routledge and Kegan Paul, 1964), pp. 31-67, and Edwin H. Miller, *The Professional Writer in Elizabethan England* (Cambridge: Harvard Univ. Press, 1959). More theoretical accounts are given in Marshall MacLuhan, *The Gutenberg Galaxy: The Making of Typographic Man* (Toronto: Univ. of Toronto Press, 1962), and Walter Benjamin, "The Work of Art in the Age of Mechanical Reproduction" in *Illuminations,* ed. Hannah Arendt (New York: Schocken, 1968), pp. 217-51.

5 A good general discussion of the policies and ideals of Henry's court may be found in G. R. Elton, *The Tudor Revolution in Government* (Cambridge: Cambridge Univ. Press, 1953). Also valuable is Wallace T. MacCaffrey, "Place and Patronage in Elizabethan Politics" in *Elizabethan Government and Society: Essays Presented to Sir John Neale,* S. T. Bindoff et al., eds. (London: Univ. of London Press, 1961), p. 104.

6 Wright, *Middle-Class Culture in Elizabethan England* (1935; Ithaca: Cornell University Press, 1958), p. 5. An important dissenting view may be found in Jack H. Hexter, *Reappraisals in History* (London: Longmans, 1961), pp. 71-116.

7 See Lawrence Stone, *The Crisis of the Aristocracy: 1558-1641* (*Abridged Edition*) (New York: Oxford University Press, 1967), pp. 5-36.

8 Lewis, *English Literature in the Sixteenth Century Excluding Drama* (Oxford: Clarendon Press, 1954), p. 230. There is an interesting related discussion in H. A. Mason, *Humanism and Poetry in the Early Tudor Period: An Essay* (London: Routledge and Kegan Paul, 1959), pp. 164-65, 172-73.

9 While M-T argue for the occasional nature of the poem, Wyatt has explicitly denied the particularity of the occasion: "if I laught, *any* tyme, or season."

10 Bevington, *Tudor Drama and Politics* (Cambridge: Harvard Univ. Press, 1968), p. 42.

11 There is a detailed account of this episode in Wyatt's life in Mason, pp. 195-98.

12 Recent articles by Donald M. Friedman have focused upon the mental world of Wyatt's poems; note especially his "The Mind in the Poem: Wyatt's 'They Fle From Me,'" *SEL* 7 (1967), 1-13.

13 Strong readings of this poem can be found in Hannen, p. 39, and Mason, pp. 182-85.

14 Thomson discusses the relationship between Wyatt and Anne on pp. 18-45, and mentions the possibility of Anne's having written a riddling reply to this poem. Tottel printed a number of other riddling name poems, including "Of his love named White" and "Deserts of Nymphs," an acrostic.

15 Hannen notes that Henry's court "was a place of deadly serious intrigue where each faction plotted against every other for royal favor. Behind the artificial frivolity and the macabre mask of charm, every work or deed was weighed for the information it could yield . . ." (p. 43).

16 M-T summarize the scholarly positions on p. 267.

17 In concluding his remarks on this poem, Mason argues that "Pe-

trarch's moral world is mediaeval while Wyatt's is Humanist and modern" (p. 190).

David Matthew Rosen (essay date 1981)

SOURCE: "Time, Indentity, and Context in Wyatt's Verse," in *Studies in English Literature,* Vol. XXI, No. 1, Winter, 1981, pp. 5-20.

[*In the following essay, Rosen commentds Wyatt's use of narrative time as an artistic reflection of the features of sixteenth-century England.*]

In the last fifteen years critics have tended to find in Wyatt's verse an expression of his personality.[1] Wyatt has been perceived as working in a tradition or group of traditions—from *amour courtois* to *contemptu mundi*—which he gathered and transformed in ways that suggested an original thought, original voice, original personality.[2] What that personality contained precisely, what mixture of cynicism, stoicism, and naïveté, is more difficult to assess. Nonetheless, in Wyatt's best verse the reader feels an intimate contact with the poet, a sense of the poet's personality that seeps through what at first may appear conventional and almost faceless poetry.

There are many means by which Wyatt makes his presence felt in his verse. Among them, hitherto unmentioned, is his use of what could be called narrative time. By narrative time I mean the time that elapses in reading the poem and the order in which events and pieces of information are deployed in relation to the importance of those pieces of information and the chronological order of events. We will find that in his poetry Wyatt creates layers of time to thicken experience, thus suggesting the complexity of things and events. Revelation of this complexity is part of reading the poem. Our understanding of what we are being told and the author's understanding of what he is telling both change as new aspects of the matter are revealed and new contexts created by building up these layers of time. Wyatt's use of narrative time is an artistic decision that reflects his views generally of time, identity, and context as important features of his world.

To make clearer what I mean by narrative time in Wyatt's verse, compare his **"Who so list to hounte"** with the sonnet by Petrarch on which it is partly modeled:[3]

Who so list to hounte I know where is an hynde,
But as for me, helas, I may no more:
The vayne travaill hath weried me so sore,
I ame of theim that farthest cometh behinde;
Yet may I by no meanes my weried mynde
Drawe from the Diere: but as she fleeth afore,
Faynting I folowe; I leve of therefore,
Sithens in a nett I seke to hold the wynde.
Who list her hount I put him owte of dowbte,
As well as I may spend his tyme in vain:
And graven with Diamondes in letters plain
There is written her faier neck rounde abowte:
    'Noli me tangere, for Cesars I ame,

And wylde for to hold though I seme tame.'

Una candida cerva sopra l'erba
Verde m'apparve, con duo corna d'oro,
Fra due riviere, all'ombra d'un alloro,
Levando 'l sole, a la stagione acerba.

Era sua vista sí dolce superba,
Ch'i' lasciai per seguirla ogni lavoro;
Come l'avaro, che 'n cercar tesoro,
Con diletto l'affanno disacerba.

Petrarch's landscape is more visual and vivid than Wyatt's. His story is also more straightforward and crisper. Yet I believe that we respond to Wyatt's poem more complexly because the order in which it is told creates a tangle of qualifications, a tangle of viewpoints. While Petrarch's words suggest a sharply focused world of symbolic significance, Wyatt's verse creates significance by thickening qualifications to what is at best an ambiguous experience.

Basically, Wyatt's poem is broken into three parts: the present in which the hunter sits and waits, the past in which he had hopelessly pursued, and a more general time in which he is cognizant of the inscription on the deer's collar. Each part tends to modify our understanding of the present scene, subjecting it to a context of recollection. There is another present too. While the hunter sits forlorn in the woods, static, presenting an illusion of timelessness, other hunters approach for his advice and he imagines the continuing hunt, thus bringing into play a present that flits by without him. The hunter seems entrapped by the way in which his past has determined his present. Yet like a moving object that has come to rest, the hunter finds his past to be one from which he is irrevocably separated, except as a memory. The deer, fleeing before the hunter, attractive yet unattainable, captures the essence of those moments the hunter recalls. The sense of distance and regret is so pressing that our awareness of his lost time extends to an appreciation of the time he loses as he recounts his experience. In contrast, Petrarch's story follows a single line, theme, and time. Within his poem the reader does not leave the remembered present to observe the contexts which conditioned that moment.

Wyatt's world appears perceptibly more complex than Petrarch's, and the narrative time of the verse does service to this complexity. Unlike the time in Petrarch's poem, time in Wyatt's responds to the mind of the teller who enmeshes himself in qualifications as he tells his story. The story presents a process of penetration and analysis as well as narration. The hunter digs deeper and deeper into the sources of his frustration until he comes to the collar. The most important part of his warning, the collar is the last thing about which he tells, as if it were also the most painful. The progress of the poem in this way is the progress of thought as it engages more and more of the world, modifying the speaker's as well as the reader's reaction to that world.

The complexity of the hunter's frustrations, the complexity of the object he contemplates, is revealed in the inscription on the collar itself, an inscription that is also less straightforward than the one on Petrarch's doe. The pointed use of the familiar biblical phrase in the line "Noli me tangere, for Cesars I ame" juxtaposes the spiritual and political.[4] Although this marks a change from Petrarch, it is not particularly difficult to accomodate ideas of religious and temporal authority. More difficult to accomodate is the collar's further claim that this religious and political object is also wild. It may be suggested that Wyatt merely amalgamates every power that could make the object impossible to attain. In fact, Wyatt does not try to organize the information. The inscription, like the story, builds contexts and qualifications that baffle, frustrate, sadden, anger, but never satisfy. This juxtaposition of qualities reflects the complex nature of thing and circumstance that the hunter's narration attempts, unsuccessfully, to unravel.

Wyatt's poems seem to use time in two ways. First, the poems record the process of the poet's thoughts modifying and being modified by what he has just said, so that the end of a poem is rarely the same as the beginning though connected with it. This sense of connection and disconnection seems to correspond to Wyatt's sense of time, and the process of reading or thinking or speaking becomes a reflection of that sense. Second, by juxtaposing past and present and different aspects of the same time, the poet causes intricacies of identity to emerge. Because the poetry does service to the complexity of Wyatt's world and to the poet's attempts to come to grips with that world, it is useful to gain a fuller notion of that complexity.

Sometimes it may appear that Wyatt's sense of the complex extends no further than the "lover's paradox" in which the lover sweats and freezes, lives and dies, finds restless rest, loveless love, and fruitless fruit. This conventional paradox takes on unconventional emphasis, however, in much of Wyatt. Wyatt's riddle is perhaps paradigmatic:

What wourde is that that chaungeth not,
Though it be tourned and made in twain?
It is myn aunswer, god it wot,
And eke the causer of my payn.
A love rewardeth with disdain,
Yet is it loved. What would ye more?
It is my helth eke and my sore.

The answer to the poem, **"Anna,"** reflects Wyatt's view of complexity. One can turn the word so that it becomes two different words, each with its own meaning, each with the same spelling. One Anna is balm; one is gall; both are in fact the same person. By this turning and looking at the object from two different points of view it would appear to be two different objects. And yet it is one object seen complexly. The paradox is stated in such a way that it expands into a question about identity.

The process by which the poet considers his own riddle corresponds in its playful turning over of the matter to the turning of the name. In the first lines Wyatt proposes the riddle and in the third seems about to solve it: "It is myn aunswer." It becomes apparent, however, that he already knows the answer and that "aunswer" here means that the poem's answer will answer his needs (or maybe not). Instead of depending on the answer to the riddle, as in the riddle on the gun "Vulcane bygat me," cleverness depends on the way in which Wyatt increases the reader's information. Finally when he asks "What would ye more?" we are aware of how complex some simple questions can be. For here he means not only what further clues do you need but also what more do you want me to confess and how much worse could you possibly expect it to be? The poet is revealed digging further and further into his riddle. At the end what was merely playful seems personal. He reveals more than he intended: how deeply the riddle is felt, how closely its literary ambiguities resemble the ambiguities of life.

With the growing sense of complex identities and complex problems in Wyatt's poetry, there is also a growing despair over the adequacy of previous responses and structures. This is no longer an Edenic world in which each thing has a single word and nature, though there is often the feeling in Wyatt's poetry that things in nature are purer and simpler. The problem cannot simply be reduced to matters of steadfastness and mutability. The hunter resting in the woods poses no such antithesis. Although such categories and structures may still be convenient for expressing Wyatt's concerns, the concerns ultimately overpower conventional images.

We can see this happening in the simple poem **"Nature, that gave the bee so feet a grace"**:

> Nature, that gave the bee so feet a grace
> To fynd hony of so wondrous fashion
> Hath taught the spider owte of the same place
> To fetche poyson, by straynge alteration.
> Tho this be straynge, it is a straynger case
> With oon kysse by secret operation
> Boeth these at ons, in those your lippes to fynde,
> In chaunge wherof, I leve my hert behinde.

There seems nothing quite so conventional as this rhyme. And yet there are some interesting touches. The flower, depending on what approaches it, changes. It is ambiguous. But perhaps most striking, its ambiguity is not simply a matter of perception. It is also objective, as the kiss, which contains both honey and poison, shows. The two perceptions reveal competing aspects of the object. At the same time one will notice that the "secret operation" of the kiss is more like the honey-making of a bee or the bite of a spider than like the passive flower to which it is compared. Wyatt, in other words, is having a hard time finding the proper image to carry his experience. But the lack of correspondence adds to the subtle, mysterious flavor of the poem. The beloved becomes active/passive, bee/spider/flower. At the same time the initial image of beauty and ambiguity, regardless of its inexactness, conditions our response to the experience. This ploy of setting a general atmosphere in this manner

is a favorite of Wyatt's. The beauty of Wyatt's poetry in part lies, as others have pointed out, in the way he uses the tools that are at hand.

Perhaps the most highly structured expression of Wyatt's sense of complexity occurs in the three-part **"Lo what it is to love!"** In this poem, two lovers debate the nature of love. Final proof of love's nature boils down to a question of which debater has truly experienced love. The first states:

> Suche are the dyvers throws,
> Suche that no man knows
> That hath not profd
> And ons have lofd.
>
> (25-28)

But the second lover makes the same claim:

> Suche be the plaisaunt daies,
> Suche be the honest wayes;
> There is no man
> That fully can
> Knowe it but he that sayes
> Loving to ban
> Were folly then.
>
> (66-73)

When the first speaker is given a chance to rebut the allegations of the second, he produces some brilliant analyses, twitting, for instance, his opponent's use of "snare" to describe something pleasant. For the most part, however, the first speaker's charges of a jaded viewpoint only heighten the reader's awareness of the first speaker's own limited views. His chance to refute his adversary fails, therefore, to dispose of the matter. Not only does the reader bring the speaker's past performance to bear on his present, but we find that the first speaker is also affected by what has just passed, by his adversary's charges:

> Of all suche pleasaunt dayes,
> Of all suche pleasaunt playes,
> Without deserft
> You have your part,
> And all the worould so sayes;
> Save that poure hert
> That for more smert
> Feleth yet suche pleasaunt dayes.
>
> (106-113)

The first part of the first speaker's reply is merely an attack on his opponent's character and requires no expertise to be judged as accurate. But what is most interesting is the first speaker's attempt, having just dismissed his opponent, to shift his ground in order to accommodate his adversary's position. The lover may experience some pleasant days, but if he is a true lover such pleasant days only increase later pain. The first speaker, in shifting his position, acknowledges one that is more complex. Things shift in time, take on new meaning. And so shift the attitudes of both the first speaker and the reader.

The dialogue seems to be an interplay of personalities and views which develop as the poem progresses, develop for both the reader and the speakers. Contexts are created which qualify assertions and even experiences. Things are not so simple as they first appeared. Starting from dogmatic set-pieces, the speakers' responses, contingent on the arguments put forward at the moment, evolve from moment to moment as new information comes to light. In addition, the inherent complexities of identity are emphasized by the identical structure of all three parts, which appear to be three possible versions of the same poem, the same thing seen in different ways, like the word "Anna." They reveal the diversity of viewpoints and attributes in any question about nature and dramatize how, therefore, understanding must evolve through time.

We will easily see how Wyatt's ideas about identity, context, and time produce some remarkable effects when we turn our attention to some of Wyatt's greater works. In the often analyzed **"They fle from me,"** narrative time plays an important role in producing the powerful effects that make this one of the age's most beautiful lyrics.[5]

In the opening stanza of **"They fle from me,"** the poet relates his experience with some ambiguous creatures by juxtaposing their former tameness with their present return to a wilder state. The fragility of that momentary tameness is heightened by our awareness of its extraordinary character. The preciousness of this experience and the poignancy of its loss serve as the context for our understanding of what follows.

The second stanza recreates a more particular time when unexpectedly the beloved kissed her lover. When the woman catches the poet in her arms, it is a sweet moment because it is both unexpected and desired. Yet we are aware that, although longed for, the moment is disconnected from what appears to be the natural flow of things. Like the creatures' tameness, it is the possibility of reversion to a wilder state, the sense of wildness that is brought to the moment, in fact, that makes the moment precious. The woman and the creatures are so desirable because, as has been suggested by another critic in a different sense, they are "other" in such a way that they can never be fully possessed.[6] They are, in other words, like all Wyatt's creatures, too complex to be contained.

The moment of the kiss, nonetheless, remains a sacred moment, fixed and transcendent, as the poet exclaims at the beginning of the second stanza. But this transcendent past, this luminous moment that in religion would begin a new order different from the temporal, remains unfulfilled expectation. Still it is juxtaposed with events as they actually turn out. Like the past changing to a present with which it is both connected and disconnected, the woman changes. Like time, she recognizes her relationship with her lover, but like time, she invites "new fangilnes." Although the context created for the final stanza makes the woman's actions seem cruel and unexpected, they are no more cruel and unexpected than the creatures' actions in the first stanza with which they are linked. Only the static position of the poet makes them seem

unexpected. In terms of the general lesson of the creatures and the logic that makes the moment precious, the poet should have anticipated what would happen.

Here is the crux of the poem. The poet, unlike the changing and complex world about him, remains rigid in his view of things, not steadfast but rigid. Things, as a result, seem to happen to him, out of his control. His sense of his own helplessness and our sense of it as well is heightened by the awareness that we develop as the poem develops, the awareness that time moves, that past and present do not form a pattern, that the world is complex and therefore its moments of simplicity are precious. The sense of the distance of moments in a continuous time is intensified by the lover's static position, layering the final question with real emotion. Like the question "What would ye more," the artificial becomes real and personal: "I would fain knowe what she hath deserued." It is useless to answer, useless to ask. One might as properly inquire what "they" which flee deserve. There is no way for the speaker to ask for judgment, no way for him to assume control. By recourse to what system of rules? The question is heavy with emotion, vibrating sadness, cynicism, argumentativeness, and more.

Once again examination of the events leads to complications that result in despair. We find a similar structure to that in **"Nature, that gave the bee so feet a grace,"** where a general descriptive scene evoked contextual ambiguities and emotions that held even as the terms of the metaphorical equations were shifting. For instance, as a critic has pointed out, the woman alone does not resemble the creatures. The poet also resembles them.[7] When he is taken in the woman's arms, he imitates the creatures who fed at his hand. But when the woman gives him leave to fly, unlike the creatures and unlike her, he cannot. In spite of, or because of his various poses, the lover exposes his own complexity, a complexity he shares with all creatures. Although the speaker tries to maintain a steadfast position, his view continually evolves as it copes with the contexts of past actions. This forced complexity of the lover's view grinds against his static faith and only serves to isolate him further in a world he cannot account for, control, or accept. In this way time past becomes more precious and more hopelessly lost. In the end, his final words are rather unconvincing as a call for justice, unconvincing to himself as well, it seems. Yet they are convincing as an expression of mixed and authentic emotions. Our appreciation of the emotions that shape these words attests to the thickening of experience that the progress of the poem and Wyatt's handling of narrative time have achieved.

We now see that the past acts like an after-image of a continuous action. The after-image continues to affect our view of the present moment from which it is now disjoined and which it can only partly explain. The progress of the poem is a process of accumulating detail, of accumulating these images that create a context for a present in which it becomes clear how time works and how complex identity is. Reading becomes a process of changing or modifying our viewpoint so that reading resembles the time which it often contemplates and in which it takes place.

Poems like **"They fle from me"** or **"Who so list to hounte"** take a static present moment for their subject and in trying to account for it modify and complicate our view of it. The static nature of the moment seems to permit other moments to accumulate. Because the lover takes part in the process of accumulation and yet remains static, he eventually feels further isolated.

In another group of poems, however, the speaker remains active. Here the strategy changes slightly, for the speaker engages in a process of sorting rather than accumulating. That is, as new aspects of his situation emerge, he casts aside what he finds an inappropriate response and tries a new one, so that while his world may be in constant flux, he rarely appears to hold more than one view of it at a time. We will find here too, however, that old positions are rarely dropped completely. They remain to modify and complicate the new position. There is a compelling quality to these poems that is different from the more luxurious and mysterious qualities of **"They fle from me"** or **"Who so list to hounte."** Although this group of poems often appears to say nothing of particular importance or interest, it may be that very fact that accounts for their power. Beneath their surface the poems display a subtle modulation that makes them as complex as the world they examine. Moreover, the speaker's mental shiftings, his re-examinations, make him seem alive and present. The line of his words seems as fragile and illusive as the evanescent and precious moments of life he perceives. In short, these poems seem to recreate or dramatize the poet's world.

Such a poem is **"Where shall I have at myn owne will"**:

> Where shall I have at myn owne will
> Teres to complain? Where shall I fett
> Suche sighes that I may sigh my fill
> And then again my plaintes repete?
> For tho my plaint shall have none end,
> My teres cannot suffice my woo.
>
> (1-6)

The poem begins on an artificial and conventional note, through which there is nonetheless conveyed a sense of the speaker's frustration. The speaker, grieving his loss, feels as though he did not have tears or sighs enough to pour out all he feels. The speaker feels he wastes away as he wastes his breath. As the poem progresses we will find that the speaker's evolving understanding of his complaint turns his conventional and artificial words into something complex and real. This happens through the speaker's shifting attitude towards his words, his breath.

In the first stanzas the poet states that he wastes his words in the wind, speaking merely to release some of his grief because his beloved refuses to hear him. Yet as he pretends to sigh out his misery for himself alone, he addresses her:

> I speke not now to move your hert
> That you should rue vpon my pain;
> The sentence geven may not revert:
> I know such labour were but vayn.
>
> But syns that I for you, my dere,
> Have lost that thing. . . .
>
> (13-18)

As the poet's attitude towards his words shifts in line 17, as he begins addressing the lady directly to move her heart, the value of his words begins to shift as well and they become precious containers of meaning. Simultaneously as he begins to feel that his words require explanation, explanation begins to reawaken past hurts. The process of cogitation, developing as the poet speaks, necessarily shapes the poem and changes our knowledge and the poet's view. We are aware, for instance, of a building tone of cynicism. At the same time the theme of loss is carried forward as a more mournful countervailing force. Words become the focus of this sense of loss. "A right small losse it must appere / To lese these wordes and all the rest" (19-20) combines perfectly the tones of mourning and cynicism. Weighing the present with the past shows not only how much the speaker has lost, but how much he will lose. This knowledge becomes real and pointed when he observes how his words "sparkill in the wynde" (21), conjuring for the listener their evanescent brilliance, their spirit lost in the instant of revelation. The present moment, like the past ones, like the words, contains something valuable. The gathering sense of impending dissolution goes beyond the opening tropes.

The final lines give full weight to the sense of loss: "Farewell also with you my breth! / For I ame gone for evermore" (43-44). In these lines, soft, measured, and full of breath, the speaker conveys to his beloved's safekeeping the breath from which he is evermore separated. Although there is a partial sense of cynicism in these words, there is also a pressing sense of loss that has emerged in considering the words themselves. The fragile concatenation of words, all the beloved and the reader can know, once broken, the speaker is gone. It is hard to say precisely what the last lines mean. But somehow it does not matter. The speaker disappears with the last of his breath, as we keenly feel, having become aware of the fragility of the speaking voice, of the fragility of all temporal things. Once the moment is interrupted, there is an irremediable gap. Only memory, to which the poet consigns his breath, can preserve. But even then we are aware of something lost.

From the poem we learn that understanding the present and the future evolves by weighing past with present and by observing, by turning things over. There are no flashes of insight, just the constant gathering of information. Once again the handling of time reveals the complexity of life and of time itself in a way that can only heighten the poet's frustration, cynicism, and sadness. Although not very complex in diction nor much distinguished by image, the process of unfolding the scene and thought makes the poem impressive. Its modulations, subtle and changing with time, are appropriate to the speaking voice with which the poem is preoccupied. Such modulations complicate and intensify the speaker's presence so that at the end there is a real sense of loss when he ceases to speak.

In **"My lute, awake!"** the speaker again turns over in his mind former mistreatment and present condition, changing his viewpoint as the poem progresses. Significantly, the last stanza of the poem is the same as the first. Like the word "Anna," this stanza has been turned and changed, changed by the new contexts which develop with the poem. It is important to keep in mind that the poems generally begin with a fixed point of view which the poet seems intent on keeping but which he is ultimately unable to maintain in light of the discoveries made while accounting for his condition. The same information, put into new contexts, is exposed as more complex than at first appeared. The poet's frequent rage at the end of the poems is explained by his constant frustration and is simply the other side of his longing for a simpler time, one precluded by the very processes of time that allow him to reconsider every situation. This is certainly the case in **"My lute, awake!"**

The opening stanza has a beautiful love-lies-dying tone, not unlike **"Where shall I have at myn owne will"**:

> My lute, awake! perfourme the last
> Labour that thou and I shall wast
> And end that I have now begon;
> For when this song is sung and past,
> My lute be still, for I have done.
>
> (1-5)

The weary lover seems to revive for a single weary moment. The metaphors which follow in describing his cruel mistress reinforce the graveyard mood in which he views his condition:

> As to be herd where ere is none,
> As lede to grave in marbill stone,
> My song may perse her hert as sone;
>   . . . . .
> The Rokkes do not so cruelly
> Repulse the waves continuelly
> As she my suyte and affection.
>
> (6-8, 11-13)

Images of fultility and death are employed to evoke the lover's melancholic resignation to his fate. Yet as he continues, these images of cruelty, which seem purely rhetorical and which cloud his view of the situation, slowly are disengaged from the thought of the cruelty. Images are left behind, weariness retreats and contempt and anger rise.

Yet as in the other poems, images and original views do not part quietly. The tone of the opening situation continues to operate in the poem. More particularly, as in the other poems, the viewpoint expressed in the images finds another application elsewhere—here in the beloved. This is a startling new idea. The beloved might be subject to the same conditions as the speaker. This is a singular moment in Wyatt's poetry:

> Perchaunce the lye wethered and old,
> The wynter nyghtes that are so cold,
> Playnyng in vain unto the mone;
> Thy wisshes then dare not be told;
> Care then who lyst, for I have done.
>
> And then may chaunce the to repent
> The tyme that thou hast lost and spent
> To cause thy lovers sigh and swoune;
> Then shalt thou knowe beaultie but lent
> And wisshe and want as I have done.
>
> (26-35)

Here the images of remorseless time, irreversible time, irretrievable time are transferred to the beloved who now cries with none to hear her. The emphasis, somewhere between *contemptu mundi* and *carpe diem* and on neither, falls not on old age and ugliness, but on time. The lover is not merely "withered," but as the spelling emphasizes, she is "weathered." She has undergone a seasonal change. Like the speaker, she too is now aware of the "tyme thou hast lost and spent." By the end the singer no longer calls for justice in the courts of love. His retribution will come from the same remorseless movement of time that all beings suffer. The beloved is no longer a wild, natural force, more like a nymph than a fleshly being; she is no longer the goddess Fortune.

In this context, the first stanza takes on new meaning. When the singer puts down his lute, it is not because he has breathed his last, but because he has finally successfully dealt with and done with his beloved. His solution, however, is fraught with an underlying sadness that even finds its way into the bitter lines about his beloved as it had into the bitter lines about himself. There is something at points almost solicitous about the way the singer lectures his beloved. In fact, the situation and the words gain a power that the singer does not always have under control. In spite of the final tone of revenge, we feel a new emphasis in lines like "Now is this song boeth sung and past" (39), for "past" has become something complex and terrifying. The poet may have merely exchanged one pose for another, but one cannot escape the feeling that this time when he lays down his lute, the pose is not final, that the poet is itching to take it in his hands once more. There is the note of despair in the triumph.

In **"My lute, awake!"** the poses, changing as they do, seem to solidify as clearly rhetorical attitudes—attempts to grasp and control a situation. One pose failing, the speaker moves to another. Yet each pose also seems to represent one accurate aspect of the real situation. The shifting makes us aware of the complexity of the world and the difficulties of trying to cope with it in its complex state.

One final example of Wyatt's technique of evolving thought during the process of his verse is **"Hevyn and** erth," a lively poem, full of wit and well constructed. Like the others it begins with speaker assuming the pose of the weary lover: "Mercy, madame, alas, I dy, I dy!" (4). Tenderly the poet urges his sleeping mistress to wake and hear his last lament:

> Yf that you slepe, I humbly you require
> Forbere a while and let your rigour slake,
> Syns that by you I burne thus in this fire:
> To here my plaint, dere hert, awake, awake!
>
> Syns that so oft ye have made me to wake
> In plaint and teres and in right pitious case. . . .
>
> (5-10)

As he pleads, humbly touching his beloved's sleeve and excusing himself, the lover begins to realize that what he asks should be done out of justice. After all, he has often lost sleep because of her. Awakening memories cause a shift in his view of the present. Wyatt does not move quickly at these points. The speaker is apologetic. Having gained her attention, he slips back into his original pose:

> It is the last trouble that ye shall have
> Of me, madame, to here my last complaint:
> Pitie at lest your poure vnhappy slave,
> For in dispere, alas, I faint, I faint!
>
> (13-16)

Now begins a conventionally melancholy rendition of the lover's past: how happy he had been, how faithful he had remained when he was not happy, how his present condition is not really her fault since justice does not enter into considerations of love. On the other hand, as he points out a little disconcertingly, her "grace," if not her justice, might have saved him. But once again he quickly slips back to his rhetorical position, speaking of "my liff, / That fleith as fast as clowd afore the wynde" (21-22). Even though this shifting might bring doubts about the speaker's sincerity, the image of his life seems an apt figure of what has been recounted. The image seems weighted with real feeling and carries conviction to the reader.

It would not be surprising if it were because the image reveals to the speaker more clearly the hopelessness of his situation that at this point his emotions burst forth, shattering all pose. Suddenly he seems to touch a deeper sense of despair, a deeper sense of present powerlessness:

> Yf I had suffered this to you vnware,
> Myn were the fawte and you nothing to blame;
> But syns you know my woo and all my care
> Why do I dy? Alas, for shame, for shame!
>
> I know right well my face, my lowke, my teeres,
> Myn Iyes, my Wordes, and eke my drery chiere
> Have cryd my deth full oft vnto your eres;
> Herd of belefe it doeth appere, appere!

> A better prouff I se that ye would have
> How I ame dede; therefore when ye here tell
> Beleve it not all tho ye se my grave.
>
> (25-35)

The lines begin to accelerate as the speaker becomes increasingly incensed about his former treatment and present situation. His protests may at first appear simply contrived to convince her of his desperation. But the sense is more complex. It seems that his actions have been partially art and partially truth just as his new stance seems the same mixture, both an attempt to dramatize his plight and an accurate expression of that plight. The poetry is brilliant in its movement between these two views as the speaker shifts his stance, deepening the expressions of his disbelief, arousing his beloved's suspicions, and aggravating his frustration.

The development of the lover's argument must ring true to most readers: It is not as if you were unaware that I suffered. All you had to do was look at me. In fact, it is incredible that you did not believe that I suffered. You don't even believe it now! I suppose you won't be satisfied until I'm dead and then you won't believe it! Instead of describing life, the speaker's words dramatize life. The scene appears spontaneous and fully realized. The poem evokes vivid impressions of the lover's increasingly frenetic actions and the beloved's amused and unmoved response. Before the myriad views of the situation, the attempts to control it in some fashion, the original postures and structures collapse. We are left with a sense of the speaker's frustration and with the sense that precious time is being lost in exactly the way that the cloud-wind metaphor suggests. The lover's death may not be imminent as the first and last lines claim, but we have become aware that the drama takes place in a stream-like movement of time that severs connections in a way that suggests death. Not inappropriately the beloved is a sleeper who fails to wake fully to the moment. The elements of connection and disconnection, essential to Wyatt's view of time, become staple elements of the drama as well.

As in all the poems, there is a thickening of experience, a turning over of matters that is directly related to the handling of time. The present moment takes on meaning from its context of past moments that lead to it and from the emerging sense of what a moment of time is. Time also enters the poetry as a process that is simultaneous with reading or speaking the lines. In the course of the poem matters are turned over and changed. The resulting reflections give scope to the accumulating qualifications and press home the ambiguity of things, events, and circumstances. The passage of time exposes the mutiple facets and viewpoints that constitute identity. The passage of time force the observer to attempt to accomodate these views and facets.

If Wyatt maintains a faith that time could bring things right, it is a faith, like everything else, qualified and complex, tinged with experiences that question it. In his poetry Wyatt may speak of time as patterned like Fortune's wheel or as random moments of hap and mishap, but time rarely stays within these conceptions. There are no moments that can be taken in isolation. There are no transcendental moments that might start the reign of a new dispensation with its own sacred time. There are no complete returns to a favored past. Once time has passed, it cannot be caled back, although it must be accounted for. There are always scars from deep wounds and memories that one carries into the present and that, as the speaker becomes aware of as he speaks, help to shape the present and also help to make it unlike the past. In Wyatt's verse time "flits" (flows) and "flees" (flies), moving in a way that suggests continuity and hopeless discontinuity. The stream of time suggests Wyatt's possible incipient sense of causality, his fuller sense of building and destroying contexts that allow new aspects of old objects to emerge. The new makes old structures and solutions impossible to return to even though new ones have not been erected and seem impossible to conceive. Even as new awareness dawns, making the flat round, the simple complex, the poet, doing the best he can to understand, holds onto the old, stable points as long as possible—his beloved, his lute, his pen.

NOTES

[1] Raymond Southall claimed that the theme of Wyatt's personality was an old one when he published what seem to be seminal works on the subject: "The Personality of Sir Thomas Wyatt," *EIC* 14, no. 1 (Jan. 1964):43-64; *The Courtly Maker* (New York: Barnes & Noble, 1964).

[2] Again, there has been general discussion about the way in which personality and convention interact. Among the more particular treatments: J. D. Hainsworth, "Sir Thomas Wyatt's Use of the Love Convention," *EIC* 7, no. 1 (Jan. 1957):90-95; Leonard E. Nathan, "Tradition and Newfangleness in Wyatt's 'They Fle from Me'," *ELH* 32, no. 1 (March 1965):1-16; Michael McCanles, "Love and Power in the Poetry of Sir Thomas Wyatt," *MLQ* 29, no. 2 (June 1968):145-60.

[3] All citations are from *Collected Poems of Sir Thomas Wyatt,* ed. Kenneth Muir and Patricia Thomson (Liverpool: Liverpool University Press, 1969).

The text for the Petrarch sonnet (CXC) comes from *Sonnet & Songs,* trans. Anna Maria Armi (New York: Pantheon, 1946), p. 282. The translation is on the facing page:

A pure white doe in an emerald glade
Appeared to me, with two antlers of gold,
Between two streams, under a laurel's shade,
At sunrise, in the season's bitter cold.

Her sight was so suavely merciless
That I left work to follow her at leisure,
Like the miser who looking for his treasure
Sweetens with that delight his bitterness.

Around her lovely neck "Do not touch me"
Was written with topaz and diamond stone,
"My Ceasar's will has been to make me free."

Already toward noon had climbed the sun,
My weary eyes were not sated to see,

When I fell in the stream and she was gone.

"Nessun mi tócchi—al bel collo d'intorno
Scritto avea di diamanti e di topazî—
Libera farmi al mio Cesare parve".

Et era 'l sol giá vòlto al mezzo giorno;
Gli occhi miei stanchi di mirar non sazî,
Quand'io caddi ne l'acqua, et ella sparve.

[4] The modifications of the inscription on the doe's collar have been traced to the Petrarchan commentators by Patricia Thomson, "Wyatt and the Petrarchan Commentators," *RES* 10, no. 39 (Fall 1959):231. According to most commentators, Petrarch's phrase "was a well-known Latin motto. It had been inscribed on the collars of Caesar's hinds, which were then set free but which no man ever presumed to touch or harm" (p. 231). Although Professor Thomson sees "Una candida cerva" as "an unearthly vision of a sublime lady whose Lord and Master claimed her for Heaven" (p. 233)—although she sees it, in other words, as a dream-vision of the dead Laura, she does not comment on the echo of John 20:17, which Wyatt has discovered and emphasized. The scene during the resurrection when Jesus turns away Mary Magdalene seems appropriate to the confusion of earthly love and ideal expressed in both poems. Professor Thomson probably disregards the echo because she refuses to see the confusion as being part of Wyatt's dilemma. However, she does include the reference in the commentary to *The Collected Poems,* p. 267.

[5] For an amusingly jaundiced review of critical background see Richard L. Greene, "Wyatt's 'They Fle from Me' and the Busily Seeking Critics," *Bucknell Review* 12, no. 3 (Fall 1964): 17-30. Some have not been intimidated: Nathan, "Tradition"; Leigh Winser, "The Question of Love Tradition in Wyatt's 'They Fle from Me'," *ELWIU* 2, no. 1 (Spring 1975): 3-9; Carolyn Chiappelli, "A Late Gothic Vein in Wyatt's 'They Fle from Me'," *Ren & Ref,* 1 (New series), no. 2 (1977): 95-102.

[6] McCanles, "Love," pp. 147 ff.

[7] McCanles, "Love," p. 153.

C. F. Williamson (essay date 1982)

SOURCE: "Wyatt's Use of Repetitions and Refrains," in *English Literary Renaissance* Vol. XII, No. 3, Autumn, 1982, pp. 291-300.

[*The following essay points to the complex and subtle patterns of repetition and refrain in Wyatt's poetry as proof of his lyrical mastery.*]

It is no longer necessary to be defensive in writing about Wyatt. His subordination to Surrey is a thing of the past. The controversies about his competence as a metrist, his dependence on sources, or his lack of specifically poetic interest have all been settled in his favor, and he is now firmly established as one of the first and finest writers of love lyrics in the language. Recently the tendency has been to approach his poetry in the light of its social and courtly background to reveal how its tensions and stresses, once assumed to be exclusively those of the lover, are as much, perhaps even more, those of the courtier at a time when losing one's head was a matter of more concern than losing one's heart. But there are problems in this approach. As Alastair Fowler has suggested,[1] it is impossible for the modern reader to recapture all the complexities of the social context of Wyatt's day, and the critic is reduced to speculation and ultimately defeat in trying to recreate the exact impression these poems made on their original audience. Fortunately there are aspects of Wyatt's verse still unexplored where positive pronouncements remain a possibility, and it is to one of these that I want to address myself.

Anyone glancing rapidly through an edition of Wyatt's poems, and even more through his most anthologized pieces, will at once be struck by his use of refrains—"Is it possible?", "What meaneth this?", "Blame not my lute"—and repeated phrases that are not strictly refrains—"What vaileth truth?", "Help me to seek."[2] In this of course there is nothing novel. These features are common enough in English verse of the preceding hundred years, and in many cases Wyatt's use of them is attributable to his sources; but a careful examination of his practice will show that he sometimes used them with a skill and finesse of a very high order, so that, far from being merely formal decorations, they became organic and highly expressive elements in his verse.

That Wyatt used them in an unquestionably deliberate way is happily demonstrable from one poem, **"Such hap as I,"** in which he virtually draws attention to what he is doing. The first stanza makes two assertions:

> Such hap as I am happed in
> Had never man of truth I ween.
> At my fortune list to begin
> To show that never hath been seen,
> A new kind of unhappiness.
> Nor I cannot the thing I mean
>   Myself express
>
> (ll. 1-7)

He claims, first, that his is a new experience, and not only for himself; and, second, that he has difficulty in expressing it, presumably because of its novelty. The poet, that is to say, has a communication problem which he suggests is insoluble but which the structure of the poem attempts to solve through a verbal and formal notation appropriate to his feelings. As we read on to discover how the poet goes about finding a solution, what first strikes us is the formal device of linking the stanzas by repeating the final short line of one as the opening phrase of the next, with the last line of all, "Such hap as I," circling back to the beginning of the poem, suggesting, perhaps, an endless round of cogitation from which there is no escape. This is not the only occasion when Wyatt uses this device,[3] but the exact manner of its employment here is crucial. In the first stanza the last line has a negative sense—"I cannot . . . express"—whereas in the following stanza it is affirmative: "Myself express . . . that can I well." The last line of the second stanza has an affirmative sense, but this is effectively contradicted by the interrogative opening of the third, "To do me good what may prevail?" A similar reversal occurs in the link-

age between stanzas three and four: the unequivocal negative "It helpeth not" gives way to the effectively affirmative "It helpeth not but to increase." Again, the phrase "Refrain I must" which begins the final stanza, repeated from a clear affirmative in stanza four, is negated by being shown to be inapplicable to the poet—"in my case layeth no such clause." In each case, then, we have not mere repetition but repetition with a reversal of sense, the poet constantly going back on or contradicting what he has just said. Such consistent reversals can hardly be accidental. In a poem which proclaims itself as an attempt to communicate an enigmatic experience, whose difficulty, judging from the imagery of cold and fire, and hunger amidst food, lies in its paradoxical and self-contradictory nature, can there be any doubt that Wyatt was using these repetitions with reversal to build into the very structure of his poem the quality of the experience with which it is concerned?

Exactly what this experience was remains obscure. The poem nowhere mentions love, let alone a lady; but the imagery points in that direction.

> still of cold I me bewail,
> And raked am in burning fire;
> For though I have, such is my lot,
> In hand to help that I require,
>   It helpeth not.
>
> (ll. 17-21)

> What wonder is this greedy lust,
> To ask and have! And yet therefore
>   Refrain I must.
>
> (ll. 26-28)

Daalder's suggestion that "satisfaction of sexual appetite . . . leads to further 'hunger'" does not account for the apparent simultaneity of the opposing sensations. Clearly the hypothetical lady was not showing her traditional reluctance, and it may be that the poet, deprived of the guidelines of the familiar situation, was being forced to redefine his own role. Love intensifies desire and so pricks the poet on, but at the same time involves a respect for its object which holds him back. The recognition that he was in a situation not provided for by existing convention and established patterns of behavior could well account for Wyatt's claim to "a new kind of unhappiness."

Be that as it may. What is beyond doubt is that the poem shows the formal device of stanza linkage used to articulate meaning in a way that is certainly deliberate, and on this basis we are surely justified in seeing design in other instances where such formal devices appear to be not merely decorative but functional.

A simple case is **"Go burning sighs,"** based on Petrarch's *Rime* cliii, "Ite, caldi sospiri," or possibly on a French version of the Italian. Here we have the opening phrase repeated without alteration but taking on new meanings in different contexts and so serving to define the progressive changes of feeling in the poem. Initially the phrase bids the sighs go as messengers to the lady to melt with their heat her frozen heart and to win mercy for the poet or, failing that, death—which is precisely their function in Petrarch. By the time the phrase reappears in line 9, however, the mood has subtly changed.

> Take with thee pain whereof I have my part,
> And eke the flame from which I cannot start,
> And leave me then in rest, I you require:
>   Go, burning sighs!
>
> (ll. 6-9)

The sighs are now part of a syndrome of discomforts from which the poet wishes to be free. His plea to be left at rest points to less extreme feelings than those which could see mercy or death as the only alternative. The poet simply wants to escape the intensities of the lover. This relinquishment of the sighs (sighs which we may see as a kind of synecdoche for the whole pattern of behavior of the Petrarchan lover), appears to effect a radical change of feeling. Line 10, "I must go work I see by craft and art," sounds like the practical voice of Chaucer's "hende" Nicolas suddenly replacing the high-pitched plaints of his rival Absolon. The recognition of the lady's falseness leads the poet to abandon as ineffectual the proprieties of the by now moribund convention and to counter like with like. The "Go burning sighs" which concludes the poem, then, amounts to a total rejection of the Petrarchanism to which the poet had appeared to subscribe. The mere desire for a quiet life which the phrase had denoted in line 9 is no longer enough; it now proclaims a new pragmatism and a spirit of active opposition, thus defining the final stage of the poet's progressive alienation from Petrarch.

More complex are instances where Wyatt uses a change of word or a slight shift of expression to effect a re-definition of a situation or even to provide the solution to a problem. An instance is **"Since ye delight to know."** Initially this appears to be a slightly lugubrious poem in which the lover masochistically invites his own death in order to please his lady, with the refrain "For to content your cruelness."

> Since ye delight to know
> That my torment and woe
> Should still increase
> Without release,
> I shall enforce me so
> That life and all shall go,
> For to content your cruelness.
>
> (ll. 1-7)

This readiness to submit himself to the acknowledged cruelty of the mistress reaches its climax in the fourth stanza where the poet wishes for immediate decisive action from the lady "To do your heart such good / To see me bathe in blood," a degree of self-surrender with which the reader may well feel some impatience. But the change of a single word, indeed almost a single syllable, in the refrain effects a marked change of temper in the final stanza: "And you should evermore / Defamed be therefore, / For to repent your cruelness" (ll. 33-35).

The poet's apparent eagerness that the lady should make his quietus is revealed as a good deal less than the supreme demonstration of his devotion and subordination of his interests to hers. Now the poem suggests that he has been trying to provoke a final act of cruelty which will be its own revenge in the obloquy it will attract. Here the substitution of a single word brings us much nearer to the world of Donne's "The Apparition" than to that of a Palamon or a Troylus.

"Is it possible?" provides a good instance of modulations of tone and feeling largely created and certainly signalled by slight changes in the refrain. The first four stanzas are framed by the repeated question "Is it possible?", conveying the poet's astonished incredulity at the inconstancy he has encountered. In the fifth stanza there is a shift from question to statement:

> It is possible
> For to turn so oft,
> To bring that lowest that was most aloft,
> And to full highest yet to light soft:
> It is possible.
>
> (ll. 21-25)

The residual resistance to an unpalatable truth denoted by the repeated interrogatives has now collapsed and given way to a weary resignation and acceptance. But the change does not stop there. In the final stanza "It" gives way to "All"—"All is possible"; and this change (the central lines of the stanza mark little development) suddenly opens up the perspective of the poem from the narrow, almost obsessive world of the unhappy lover to something all-inclusive. The contemplation of the fickleness of his mistress has in effect carried the poet along a path, plotted with marvellous economy by "Is it?", "It is," and "All is," which parallels in miniature the progress of Lear from amazed incredulity through anguished recognition of his personal betrayal to a vision of an unredeemed and perhaps unredeemable universe.

Verbal variation is used again in **"Most wretched heart,"** but in this case to clinch rather than develop the debate which constitutes the poem, a kind of "Two Voices" in which the voice of despair suggests that the poet would be better off dead, while the poet's heart resolutely insists that whatever Fortune brings, one's attitude to it is or should be within one's own control.

> Most wretched heart, most miserable,
> Since thy comfort is from thee fled,
> Since all thy truth is turned to fable,
> Most wretched heart, why art thou not dead?
>
> "No, no, I live, and must do still,
> Whereof I thank God, and no mo.
> For I myself have all my will,
> And he is wretched that weens him so."
>
> (ll. 1-8)

The alternating viewpoints are summarized in the alternate refrains, "Most wretched heart, why art thou not dead?" and "he is wretched that weens him so." In the penultimate stanza, however, the voice of despair, succumbing to the fatal Cleopatra of a play on words, varies the pattern and thereby unwittingly sets a semantic trap for itself: "Thy great unhap thou canst not hide: / Unhappy then, why art thou not dead?" (ll. 43-44) The shift from "wretched" to "Unhappy" exploits the figure polyptoton, using the common root "hap" to imply that there is an inescapable link between "unhap" as *misfortune* and "Unhappy" as *wretched,* but it is a shift which gives the heart precisely the opening it needs finally to nail the insufficiency of the opposing argument. The shift to "unhap" in effect concedes the heart's position by recognizing that the forces ranged against it are essentially external circumstances. "Unhappy" can refer both to a subjective state, *wretched,* and an objective situation, *unfortunate;* "unhap" can refer only to the objective situation. The heart is not slow to seize the advantage thus given him by pointing precisely to this distinction:

> "Unhappy, but no wretch therefore!
> For hap doth come again and go,
> For which I keep myself in store,
> Since unhap cannot kill me so."
>
> (ll. 45-48)

It is a brilliant conclusion, vastly more satisfying than Tennyson's Victorian family on its way to church, but achieved with an economy possible only to a poet with a sharp sense of the significance of individual words and the semantic gaps between them.

This sense is again apparent in one of Wyatt's finest poems, **"And if an eye may save or slay."** We understand from the poem that the poet's mistress has been giving encouraging looks to other men and, when taxed with this by the poet, claims "that look all sole . . . of right to have,"[4] the lady has defended herself by claiming that her glances were given "unwittingly" and express only general sociability. Although the poet at length agrees to accept the lady's explanation, he is uneasy about it because not only he but also "men expert" take the view that such looks do reveal secret inclinations; in the words of the refrain, "the eye is traitor of the heart." Behind this particular disquiet lies Wyatt's general hostility, expressed most clearly in Satire I, ll. 19 *et. seq.,* to the role-playing demanded of the courtier, particularly in the courtly game of love, in which one's true feelings have always to be disguised in favor of what is prudent or expedient. In the penultimate stanza of this poem Wyatt declares his inability to participate in this courtly game of dissembling: "for my part / My eye must still betray my heart" (ll. 34-35). The poet recognizes that to accept the lady's explanation that society has forced her behavior on her is no more than an uneasy compromise, and in the concluding stanza he adumbrates a situation in which such play-acting will no longer be necessary, where he and his mistress take truth as their standard. The significance of the change is pinpointed by the introduction of the single word "show" in the last line: "Then fear not the eye to show the heart." On the surface it may appear to be a slight change, but recalling the key expressions it

replaces—"traitor of the heart" and "betray my heart"—its implications become weighty. What is betrayed or revealed by a traitor can only be something that should ideally remain secret because its revelation will be dangerous, damaging, or discreditable. To live in a state of complete openness renders betrayal impossible; what one has no wish to hide cannot be betrayed. In this context the force of "fear not the eye to show the heart" becomes clear. The poet contemplates a state where there is no discrepancy between what one seems and what one is, where by virtue of one's own absolute truth or integrity one becomes invulnerable to betrayal. Typically, in his conclusion Wyatt has opened up his poem to affirm a criterion for personal conduct that goes beyond the experience of love and embraces the whole range of human activity. The argument has of course been developed through the two closing stanzas, but it is finally crystallized by the introduction of the simple monosyllable "show" in the concluding line.

One of the best examples of Wyatt's skill in using slight but telling variations in a refrain is **"Deem as ye list, upon good cause."** Here the poet is revolving in his mind not so much the possibility of his mistress's infidelity (although that ultimately is his concern) as the way in which he is affected by his suspicions.

> Deem as ye list, upon good cause
> I may and think of this or that.
> But what or why my self best knows,
> Whereby I think and fear not;
> But thereunto I may well think
> The doubtful sentence of this clause:
> I would it were not as I think,
> I would I thought it were not.
>
> (ll. 1-8)

In the refrain of the first three stanzas he suggests two alternative states of affairs, either of which would be an improvement on his present uncertainty: "I would it were not as I think, / I would I thought it were not." To quote Daalder's paraphrase, "'I would like my suspicion to be unjustified, or that I had no suspicion—for if I could free my mind from that (even if it were correct) I would not suffer.'" Wyatt proceeds to make these alternatives the structural basis of his poem. The second stanza elaborates the idea that total ignorance would be preferable to grounds for suspicion which cannot be ignored—"I would I thought it were not"—and the third stanza considers the alternative possibility, that his suspicions are in fact groundless:

> Lo how my thought might make me free
> Of that perchance it needeth not!
> Perchance none doubt the dread I see,
> I shrink at that I bear not.
>
> (ll. 17-20)

But these are only half-solutions, ultimately unsatisfactory, and the final stanza makes a plea similar to that expressed in "And if an eye"—"If you are not in fact false, don't behave in a way that makes me suspect you are": "If it be not, show no cause why / I should so think, then care I not" (ll. 25-26). Again the ideal solution is defined by the slight variation in the refrain: "And if it be not as I think, / Likewise to think it is not" (ll. 31-32). In the first three stanzas the two lines of the refrain were linked by an implicit "or." This is now replaced by "likewise," which is tantamount to, although rather more emphatic than, "and." Thus, instead of two alternatives, neither very satisfactory, Wyatt offers a solution in which belief corresponds to fact, because, once again, appearance and reality coincide; and the shift from imperfect compromise to total clarification is elegantly registered by the replacement of the subjunctives—"it were not" and "if it be not"—which express the poet's uncertainty by the simple finality of the indicative "it is not." Once more Wyatt achieves his effect with supreme economy, using a slight modification of his refrain to achieve a solution at once verbal, syntactic, and emotional.

Wyatt was clearly aware that refrains and repetitions could be valuable not only decoratively but expressively because they throw into high relief small changes of phrasing or even of single words. The technique obviously works best at or toward the end of a poem; that Wyatt valued it highly is demonstrated by the fact that in several of the poems I have discussed he makes it the very basis of his conclusion. It seems characteristic of the man to be attracted by this device. On the whole he fights shy of hyperbole and verbal extravagance; irony and understatement seem more congenial—one thinks of the conclusion of **"They flee from me,"** or the last line of **"The long love,"** compared with Surrey's version or Petrarch's original; and one may suppose that to achieve an impact with a minimum of fuss would have appealed to him. But that is mere speculation. What is certain is that his practice in this respect reveals a degree of verbal artistry and sensitivity to the fine detail of language that must alert the reader to the probability of conscious design throughout his work and help to confirm his standing as the foremost lyric poet of the early Tudor period.

NOTES

[1] *Conceitful Thought* (Edinburgh, 1975), chapter I *passim.*

[2] All quotations are from *Collected Poems,* ed. J. Daalder (Oxford, 1975). Individual poems are referred to by first line so that they may be located in any edition. Not all editors agree that all the poems I discuss are by Wyatt (Daalder prints "Deem as ye list" among unascribed poems, and Rebholz [Penquin ed., 1978] includes it and "And if an eye" among poems not attributed to Wyatt until after the sixteenth century). I have not touched on the question of authorship however, and certainly would not wish to argue that the features I discuss constitute evidence one way or the other. But if these poems are not by Wyatt, we must assume the existence of at least one contemporary poet not only as good as Wyatt but good in very much the same way.

[3] See, e.g., "It was my choice, it was no chance."

[4] Daalder prints "soul"; but the manuscript spelling "sowle" and the rhyme with "school" permit "sole," and the sense demands it.

Joe Glaser (essay date 1984)

SOURCE: "Wyatt, Petrarch, and the Uses of Mistranslation," in *College Literature*, Vol. XI, No. 3, 1984, pp. 214-22.

[*In the following essay, Glaser argues that Wyatt's choice of Petrarchan sonnets realistically reflects the moral beliefs of the late Renaissance period.*]

Every student of English literature knows one thing about Sir Thomas Wyatt—he introduced the sonnet into England. Informed of this service, most of us nod approval and move on—but it does not do to move on too quickly. Serious problems surround Wyatt's sonnets, especially in light of their Italian originals. It is hard not to wonder why it was the sonnet Wyatt chose to introduce and why he chose to deal mainly with the sonnets of Petrarch. The answer to such questions are not simple. The more one thinks about Wyatt's sonnets, the more they open the way to considerations of what translation meant to Wyatt and how he felt to be an Englishman amid the first stirrings of the modern world, gazing back at the apparently serene heart of the Renaissance.

As Wyatt looked about for a way of inaugurating "Modern English Verse," he made some unexceptional choices, but also one that is still surprising. The natural choices were to imitate the classical and medieval, as well as the French and Italian forms that account for his more accessible work—riddles, epigrams, "ballets," songs, and satires. Wyatt seems quite at home in each of these traditions, writing with natural, charming rhythms in diction that is unstrained and clear.

The surprising choice produced more ambiguous results. In deciding to "English" the sonnet and assume what Sidney later called "poor Petrarch's long deceased woes," Wyatt seems to have gone against the grain of his own experience and personality. Not only did he not have a sonneteering sort of mind—his imagination is more adapted to linear development and reiteration than to the reversals and wit of sonnet organization—but his life and times were far different from Petrarch's. Instead of a bookish career in minor orders, Wyatt pursued an active and dangerous life. He was a politician in troubled times, serving a savagely unpredictable king in the slippery world of international diplomacy. His head was in the lion's mouth.[1]

It is not strange, then, that Wyatt is often at odds with the spirituality and endless cycles of hope and rejection that characterize the *Canzoniere*. He is, after all, the sort of man who can describe faithless friends as lice deserting a corpse or talk of swine chewing the turds in their sties.[2] The wonder instead is that he turned to the sonnet tradition at all. The rigor of his language and imagination makes the most conspicuous thing about his sonnet translations the degree to which they are *unlike* their originals, especially the majority of them that are based on Petrarch.

The most familiar example of Wyatt's transformation of Petrarch is **"Whoso list to hunt,"** the English poem he made of *Rime* 190, *"Una candida cerva."* Petrarch's sonnet is a dream vision with subtle comic possibilities. The speaker encounters a supernatural being—a pure white, golden-antlered doe, which appears against the dark green shade of a laurel between two streams at sunrise. Though her collar proclaims her Caesar's and beyond the reach of ordinary men, this speaker has no choice but to follow her, like a miser following his treasure. So follow he does—until he falls into a stream and she disappears.

Wyatt's poem could not be more different and still qualify even loosely as a translation. He hardens the tone into a hopeless cynicism, strips away almost all the visual elements, extends the encounter into an exhausting chase, transforms the dream-doe into the object of a general hunt, and identifies her with the quite real and all-too-vulnerable Anne Boleyn:

> Whoso list to hunt: I know where is an hind.
> But as for me, alas, I may no more:
> The vain travail hath wearied me so sore,
> I am of them that farthest cometh behind.
> Yet may I by no means my wearied mind
> Draw from the deer, but as she fleeth afore
> Fainting I follow. I leave off therefore,
> Sithens in a net I seek to hold the wind.
> Who list her hunt, I put him out of doubt,
> As well as I may spend his time in vain,
> And graven with diamonds in letters plain
> There is written her fair neck round about:
> *"Noli me tangere,* for Caesar's I am,
> And wild for to hold, though I seem tame."[3]

Calling this poem unlike Petrarch's falls far short of the mark. It is an aggressive act of deconstruction, swallowing up Petrarch's ironies in a spasm of bitterness. Notice the feeling of betrayal in Wyatt. Petrarch's speaker had not been disappointed. He was lucky to have received his vision; just seeing the deer was enough. But Wyatt's speaker feels abused. He will never get the girl, but he is equally troubled by the unfairness of his world. He has persevered. He has been faithful. But instead of being rewarded, he has only grown old empty-handed. And he is still being cheated. It does no good to realize the chase is hopeless or resolve to leave off: his mind is caught by the deer. No mere act of will can save him.

Implicit violence is another thing Wyatt superimposes on Petrarch. His poem is full of threats. Wyatt's hind does not wander freely. She is hunted. Just now she is far enough ahead to be almost unaware of her pursuers, but they are still there. And while her collar protects her, it does so at a price. In Petrarch the collar proclaims the dream-deer's freedom: "My Caesar's will has been to make me free."[4] But this collar asserts ownership: "Caesar's I am." Wyatt almost certainly wrote **"Whoso list to hunt"** while Anne Boleyn was still alive, but his decision to make her an owned and hunted creature already looks forward to the "bloody days" when he witnessed her beheading from his own cell in the Tower of London.[5]

What Wyatt did to *"Una candida cerva"* is typical. Each poem of Petrarch's he touched emerged coarser, heavier, more brutal. Stripping away the delicate imagery of the original sonnets is one way of achieving this effect, and so is curdling the speaker's attitude into a sense of injured merit. Even the rhythms of Wyatt's sonnets and the frequent awkwardness of their language may reflect an impatience with Petrarch's ease and melodiousness. Wyatt could handle pentameter lines quite gracefully when he wanted to; his satires are a case in point. But the sonnets bristle with "broken-backed" lines that seem to have been put there intentionally. There is manuscript evidence that Wyatt sometimes deliberately roughened the meter of his poems.[6] Even if that were not the case, however, he could hardly have been unconscious of how flat some of his writing was:

> Was I never yet of your love grieved,
> Nor never shall, while that my life doth last,
> But of hating myself that date is past,
> And tears continual sore have me wearied.
> I will not yet in my grave be buried,
> Nor on my tomb your name yfixed fast,
> As cruel cause that did the spirit soon haste
> From the unhappy bones, by great sighs stirred.
> Then if an heart of amorous faith and will
> May content you, without doing grief,
> Please it you so to this to do relief.
> If other wise ye seek for to fulfil
> Your disdain, ye err, and shall not as ye ween:
> And ye yourself the cause thereof hath been.
>
> (Daalder, pp. 13-14)

This sonnet is in the authoritative Egerton Manuscript and in the Wyatt section of *Tottel's Miscellany*. It is as surely Wyatt's as are any of the poems attributed to him. But it is a very bad poem, more a travesty than a variation on Petrarch. The combination of lead-footed pentameters ("As cruel cause that did the spirit soon haste") and clunking rhymes is overpowering, making the poem as painful to read as we can only hope it was to write.

It is important to realize that Wyatt can write better than he does in **"Was I never yet."** Though the poem does not succeed, in all probability he knew what he was doing. His decision to make the poem aggressively awkward is entirely consistent with his decision to replace the problematic, almost playful attitude of Petrarch's *"Io non fu d'amar"* with a relentless self-righteousness. In the original the speaker looks forward to having Laura's name, not his own, carved on his tomb. He hopes she will find him posthumously worthy of the recognition she denied him in life. But he has doubts. Maybe her contempt will dog him to his grave. He has lost his own identity in her service, yet she may never claim him. It is likely that his tombstone will remain forever blank. But no one promised him anything else; he has only himself and Love to thank. Wyatt changed not just the sound but the whole point of the poem. In his sonnet it is the *speaker* who refuses to have the lady's name on his marker. She hasn't killed him yet, he claims. Still, he has had about enough. He has not yet renounced his love for her, but he may. And *she* will have only her heartlessness to blame if he does.

There are many other changes Wyatt rings on Petrarch's sonnets, but the basic point remains the same. Wyatt's "translations" are often harsh and resentful poems, conspicuously untrue to their originals. It is not easy to know exactly how we should regard the discrepancies or how they might have struck Wyatt's friends, but it is impossible to ignore them. Some critics (the same ones in the main who see Wyatt's roughness as unconscious bumbling) consider his departures from Petrarch evidence of cultural backwardness. "The inward significance of Petrarch's poetry eludes him; and even when he describes the same emotions in similar terms, his poem obstinately takes on a different meaning."[7] According to this view, Wyatt was simply out of his depth in the Petrarch translations. The poems he produced are not only sterile exercises, but sterile exercises badly carried out: "For ten people who honestly enjoy the Petrarch translations . . . there must be a thousand who take unforced pleasure in **'They flee from me,' 'My lute awake,' 'Forget not yet'** and a number of other poems."[8] A more fashionable idea just now is that it was the semiotic universe, the *mundus significans,* of Wyatt's culture that caused the violence he did to Petrarch. For Wyatt, the argument goes, the idealism and subtlety of Petrarch were literally inexpressible. Wyatt no more spoke Petrarch's language than Tagalog. Tudor England was moved by power, not contemplation or love, so with no particular effort on Wyatt's part in his sonnets "The speaker's relations with women are charged with that will to power, that dialectic of domination and submission" whose presence effectively excludes Petrarch.[9]

Wyatt has not been overly fortunate in his critics. The common theme in both these ways of accounting for the stubborn individuality of his sonnets is the idea that it somehow shows his limitations as a poet. Either he was too dim to catch the "inward significance" of Petrarch, or he was too unconsciously a man of his times to be able to critique the world of his immediate experience. Neither view does Wyatt much credit or explains why he has so long and so consistently been considered a great writer. A more fundamental problem is that neither view explains why Wyatt turned to the sonnet and to Petrarch in the first place.

Did Wyatt misread Petrarch? Did he think the speaker in the *Rime* was simply as sullen and vengeful as the speaker in a typical Wyatt sonnet? I do not see how anyone could convince himself that this was the case. Even if he had not known the Petrarch-influenced literature of ideal love, widely read commentaries and how-to books like Bembo's and Castiglione's, Wyatt would surely have known Petrarch's reputation as a thinker. Chaucer's references to Petrarch alone would have taught him that the poems to Laura were full of hidden depths. He might still have misunderstood the sonnets in some way, but he could hardly have thought them simple.

And it is equally difficult to think that Wyatt's poems were shaped by his culture and not by himself. Readings that strip Wyatt of a clear consciousness of his times and deny his ability to judge them may be heavy with the terms of semiotic historical criticism, but they lack a convincing historicity of their own. Tudor England was hardly monolithic. Thomas More found a way to see his world from the outside, and he and the other humanists would have given Wyatt one system of values to pose against those of Henry VIII. Horace, the Psalmist, Serafino, Sannazaro, Plutarch, and Alamanni—all of whom Wyatt read—contributed other viewpoints. And so did Petrarch.

Besides, the twists Wyatt gives to his readings of Petrarch rarely *feel* unexamined. They are too systematic. Some of his changes are unmistakably intentional, as when Petrarch's Scylla and Charybdis become "'Tween rock and rock" in **"My galley charged with forgetfulness,"** or when the Tigris and Euphrates are transformed into the Thames in **"Ever mine hap is slack."** These details are part of the same "Englishing" tendency that caused Wyatt to change Petrarch's deer into Anne Boleyn or Giovanni Colonna into Thomas Cromwell in **"The pillar perished is."** Wyatt is always finding ways to recast the delicate abstractions of Petrarch into the harder realities of his own day. *Rime* 258 is a typical Petrarch poem. The speaker cannot enjoy Laura's favor or shrug off her anger because of his lively memory. When she looks kindly on him, he cannot forget past rebukes. When she is angry, he takes it more to heart because of her earlier melting looks. Petrarch, as always, is interested in the lover's psychology. He fills the poem with sighs, eloquent looks, remembrance, flagging spirits, the power of set habits, illness, and vacillation. Wyatt, by contrast, is topical and realistic in **"The lively sparks that issue from those eyes,"** his version of the same poem. His lady's eyes are more blinding than anything that could be rigged with mirrors or burning glasses:

> Was never man could anything devise
> The sunbeams to turn with so great vehemence
> To daze man's sight as by their bright presence. . . .

And Wyatt's sonnet climaxes with a good Kentish thunderstorm, which he invented out of whole cloth. He abandons Petrarch's psychological insight for the sheer disorientation of a man caught up in a consuming passion, one who finds his lady's favors every bit as explosive as her inevitable changes of heart:

> Dazed am I, much like unto the guise
> Of one ystricken with dint of lightning.
> Blinded by the stroke, erring here and there,
> So call I for help, I not when ne where,
> The pain of my fall patiently bearing:
> For after the blaze, as is no wonder,
> Of deadly 'Nay!' hear I the fearful thunder.
>
> (Daalder, p. 40)

In small things as in large, Wyatt is ready to give Petrarch a new, generally unsentimental turn. One element of Wyatt's art is the profound phrase, usually original with him, that places the lover's feelings in the harsh light of an unforgiving morality. The best example may be **"The long love that in my thought doth harbour,"** where it is Wyatt, not Petrarch, who sees love harboring like a thief in the speaker's mind, and speaks of "lust's negligence" and "the heart's forest." Petrarch was no stranger to St. Augustine, but in Wyatt the radical imperfection of human nature is a constant theme. It poisons every promising experience from the beginning.

This sort of disillusioned pessimism appears throughout Wyatt's Petrarchan poems. When Petrarch misses seeing Laura's eyes ("my two sweet accustomed signs") in *Rime* 189 and doubts reason and "art" will take their place, he *begins* to despair. Wyatt turns the ending of his version, **"My galley charged with forgetfulness,"** into a bleak comment on human knowledge and hope:

> The stars be hid that led me to this pain,
> Drowned is reason that should me comfort,
> And I remain despairing to the port.
>
> (Daalder, p. 26)

While in *Rime* 102 Petrarch has fortune become an enemy to Hannibal's *empire*, Wyatt refocuses the image on personal frustration. In his "Caesar when that the traitor of Egypt," he keeps Hannibal but speaks of the time "when fortune *him* shut /Clean from his reign, and from all his intent" (Daalder, 4, emphasis mine). The Italian is clear; the change of focus intentionally mirrors Wyatt's own history of personal disappointments.

And Wyatt is political. **"Whoso list to hunt"** is relevant here, and also **"The pillar perished is."** In this poem Wyatt changes *Rime* 269, commemorating Petrarch's dual loss of Laura and Giovanni Colonna, into a powerful reminder of the life-or-death nature of patronage in Henry VIII's court. Patrons competed for Petrarch's attention. There was no great urgency in his lament, which was sufficiently detached to include stylish references to the Indian and Moorish seas, gold, and oriental gems, and which concluded with magisterial generality, discussing life's beautiful prospects and how in one morning we can lose that which took years to acquire. But Wyatt's case was desperate. Cromwell was the only bulwark between him and his many enemies. Wyatt's poem reflects real fear and self-loathing. The failure of one of his diplomatic missions had helped bring on his patron's fall; he had made a wrong choice in backing Cromwell in the first place. The sonnet is haunted by visions of his own death. It ends with a forecast of his future, an outcast's life of supplication and danger:

> What can I more but have a woeful heart,
> My pen in plaint, my voice in woeful cry,
> My mind in woe, my body full of smart,
> And I myself myself always to hate
> Till dreadful death do cease my doleful state?
>
> (Daalder, p. 203)

Courtiers who guessed wrong about politics or even love affairs in Henry's court regularly found themselves in prison or on the scaffold. Wyatt was imprisoned at least three times, and no one knows yet how he escaped being beheaded along with the rest of Anne Boleyn's "lovers." These grim political realities are also reflected in **"I find no peace, and all my war is done,"** where the speaker abruptly departs from Petrarch's abstract complaints against love ("[Love] neither wants me to live nor draws me from my troubles") to add a very practical consideration: "And yet of death [love] giveth me occasion" (Daalder, p. 24).

It does not seem possible that Wyatt acted blindly in his reshaping of Petrarch. He too consistently toughens, sours, and politicizes his originals, making them reflect his own insecure and violent world. But the question of his ultimate intentions remains unanswered. If Petrarch needed so much manipulation before he would serve Wyatt's purposes, why meddle with him at all? Petrarch was a colossus, not just in literature but in the world of ideas. He was identified with a particularly hopeful philosophy—a way of reading love and reality ultimately based on the idealism of Plato. Wyatt knew this, and just as surely he knew how little Petrarch's sonnets had in common with the England of his own day. Why not go to another source?

The best answer seems to be that Wyatt wanted Petrarch as a context for his own grim vision. His translations do not so much bring Petrarch up to date as consciously force a confrontation between the early and late Renaissance. On one side is a universe of ideal promise that in the *Canzoniere* has the freshness of a Botticelli Madonna. On the other is Wyatt's present, as Machiavellian and dark as the world of the Revenge Plays. What emerges from this comparison is less easily defined, but it is an important component of our understanding of Wyatt. In general it is an informed and unsentimental presentation of what life had become in his times. And it is shaped by that blend of toughminded realism and moral seriousness that makes Wyatt a great poet.

NOTES

[1] See "The Public World of Courtly Love" in Raymond Southall, *The Courtly Maker: An Essay on the Poetry of Wyatt and His Contemporaries* (Oxford: Blackwell, 1964), pp. 39-53.

[2] The lice are in "Lux, my fair falcon" and the swine in the epistle to Sir Francis Brian.

[3] Quotations from Wyatt are from *Sir Thomas Wyatt: Collected Poems,* ed. Joost Daalder (London: Oxford University Press, 1975). "Whose list to hunt," p. 7.

[4] *Petrarch: Sonnets and Songs,* trans. Anna Maria Armi (New York: Grosset and Dunlap, 1968), p. 283.

[5] Wyatt commemorates the execution in "Who list his wealth and ease retain," Daalder, pp. 185-86.

[6] For a discussion of Wyatt's meters and revisions, see *Sir Thomas Wyatt: The Complete Poems,* ed. R. A. Rebholz (New Haven and London: Yale University Press, 1978), pp. 44-55.

[7] Sergio Baldi, *Sir Thomas Wyatt* (London: Longman, 1971), p. 31.

[8] Kenneth Muir, *Life and Times of Sir Thomas Wyatt* (Liverpool: Liverpool University Press, 1963), pp. 259-60.

[9] Stephen Greenblatt, *Renaissance Self-Fashioning: From More to Shakespeare* (Chicago and London: University of Chicago Press, 1980), p. 151.

W. S. Merwin (essay date 1989)

SOURCE: "Listening to Wyatt," in *The American Poetry Review*, Vol. XVIII, No. 2, pp. 51-54.

[*In the following essay, Merwin reevaluates Wyatt's work and life, bestowing credit where he believes it has been lacking.*]

What we hear when we read the poems of Sir Thomas Wyatt, some four and a half centuries after he wrote them, is a fair example of the ways of that elusive but inescapable figure who haunts the imagination of the Renaissance: Fortuna, that "torne as doeth a ball." There is no way of knowing now what Wyatt's poems sounded like to his contemporaries. His lyrics for the lute must have circulated as songs, and his other poems were read in manuscript, but their reception, their readers, their fate are, with very few exceptions, unknown to us. We do not really know, either, where Wyatt acquired his sense of what was available and desirable in poetry in his time. Nor do we know with whom he might have discussed such matters and talked over his free translations from the Italian, and his sonnets, which are said to be the first written in English. We know of a few of his contemporaries with whom he shared interests in such things. The Earl of Surrey, for one. But Wyatt and Surrey were separated by station and by political and religious differences as well as age (Wyatt was Surrey's elder by fourteen years). Nevertheless, Surrey wrote three poems in praise of Wyatt's gifts and character, and it is worth noting that the first of them, a sonnet in honor of Wyatt's **"Translations of the Psalms"**—clearly Wyatt's "Penitential Psalms"—was composed with a prosodic freedom more characteristic of Wyatt's poems than of Surrey's. For most of Surrey's poems—in such marked contrast to Wyatt's that the comparison became an academic cliché—are remarkably regular, and their "smoothness" has found its advocates in every age. It seems to be the main quality that led a line of editors and critics from Tottel's day to the twentieth century to consider Surrey the more gifted of the two poets. The fact that the poems of Wyatt and Surrey both were first published in *Tottel's Miscellany* in 1557 invited the comparison to begin with, even though Tottel had gone to the trouble of tampering extensively with Wyatt's lines to get them to scan to his satisfaction.

His metrical meddling emphasizes our ignorance of how Wyatt's readers in his own age received his poems. By the time *Tottel's Miscellany* was published, Wyatt had been dead for fifteen years. During that time the literate

fashion had been moving in favor of metrical regularity. No doubt there is always a taste for it, more pronounced and encouraged in some ages and circles, and in some readers, than in others, and perhaps there are always exceptions, too. The poets of Wyatt's generation had been just that much closer not only to Chaucer but also to the relatively free prosody of Middle English poetry, and to the archaic versions of the ballads; it is hard for us to imagine how those influenced the way they heard and conceived of iambic pentameter, and the way they wrote altogether. Obviously some of their writing suffers from lack of talent, of care, of skill, of sophistication, but it seems sweeping to suppose—as some editors have done—that all their departures from the imported iambic meter were the result of pure ineptitude, and that Wyatt's own metrical variations were nothing but his clumsy failures to conform to a regular pattern. If it seemed that way to the editor of *Tottel's Miscellany,* the opinion could not have been unanimous or it is unlikely that Wyatt's poems would have acquired the reputation that led to their publication and indeed to their occupying more of the *Miscellany* than the poems of anyone else including Surrey. It is hard to imagine that all of Wyatt's metrical roughnesses could have struck every reader at the time as entirely successful, but the beauty of many of them must have been evident to some readers from the beginning. And the taste for such prosodic syncopations clearly did not die out completely with Wyatt's generation. Others have commented on the affinity between the metrical complexities of Wyatt's poems and the still more pronounced prosodic inversions deliberately wrought, half a century later, by John Donne.

But the prevailing fashion, the conventions, the tradition of poetry in English, swept in a different direction as though it were the only one, and both Wyatt and Donne were all but ignored for most of three centuries. It was not until there were readers who could grasp and love the originality (in the sense of its relation to its source) and achievement of Hopkins that something at least of the power and beauty of Donne's poems and of Wyatt's could be rediscovered and heard again. Until then, Wyatt's reputation suffered from the opinions of editors and critics who could not hear as poetry any verse that departed from regular scansion, and for whom all such variations were the consequences—as Hyder Edward Rollins put it, in writing on *Tottel's Miscellany* in 1929—of the fact that Wyatt "was the pioneer who fumbled in the linguistic difficulties that beset him and prepared the way for Surrey's smoother lines and more pleasing accentuation." It was E.K. Chambers, focusing his attention upon Wyatt himself in the twenties and early thirties of this century (*Sir Thomas Wyatt and Some Collected Studies* was published in 1933), who rescued Wyatt at once from the improvements of previous editors and the metrical prissiness of former critics, and in so doing made some clear and important—and, it now seems, rather obvious—distinctions.

There are the poems that were written either to be sung or as though they were intended to be sung. The notion that Wyatt was a metrical clod might have been shaken by an examination—and above all by a reading aloud—of these poems. "The range of metrical variation," Chambers noted, "is very wide; more than seventy distinct stanza forms are to be found in the hundred and twenty examples. The basis is nearly always iambic." The forms, as he says, "are those known in the neo-Latin poetry of the *vagantes* and analysed in medieval treatises on poetics. Many of them also appear in earlier vernacular poetry. Here Wyatt is at the end rather than the beginning of a tradition. He handles it as a master, with a facility of rhythmical accomplishment to which his Elizabethan successors, although they had many qualities which he had not, rarely attained."

In speaking of the other poems, particularly the love poems, Chambers compares Wyatt with Petrarch, whom Wyatt translated. Wyatt, Chambers says, unlike Petrarch, "does not dwell upon the physical beauty of his lady. . . . He does not couple her in proud compare of everything that is in heaven and earth; there is but one perfunctory allusion to lilies and roses. Nor of course does he, like Petrarch, veil her in that circumambient penumbra of spirituality. He makes little use of visual imagery. His range of metaphor is restricted and rather conventional. For the most part he is content with the plainest of words, and relies for his effect upon his rhythmical accomplishment. This economy of speech gives him at times a singular plangency. In appeal or reproach every line tells like a hammer-stroke. . . .

"Nor does Wyatt," Chambers continues, "at all foreshadow the Elizabethans, with their lavishness, their passion for visible things, their ready flow of coloured utterance." It is in this comparison that Chambers suggests that "Wyatt's real affinities, if with any, are with John Donne. He has not Donne's depth of fiery and often turbid thought. His is a soul of lighter make. But there is something of the same characteristic poise."

Chambers, of course, intended no detraction from Wyatt in comparing him to Donne. He was suggesting a sympathy. But as we have seen, Wyatt's posthumous reputation has been afflicted repeatedly by comparisons, many of which were quite unjust; he has been blamed for not having another's talent and writing like someone else, and I have no wish to continue the practice, in suggesting yet another comparison from outside the course of English poetry altogether. For years Wyatt has seemed to me one of the very few figures in the language whose writing bore some relation, however distant and slight, to the great poems of François Villon. The differences are immediately obvious—differences of scale, of range, of volume and audacity, and of tragic power. As Chambers notes in comparing Wyatt with Donne, Wyatt does not have Villon's "depth of fiery and often turbid thought" either, and his "soul [is] of lighter make," I suppose. But I have not suggested the kinship in order to minimize Wyatt. The affinity with Villon, I think, is there in some of Wyatt's great songs, in which like Villon he uses—and masterfully—the exquisite delicacy of the late medieval lyric to articulate a harshness and irony of subject and feeling that can be startlingly at odds with the form, and

the result is the creation of a peculiar tension and power. Wyatt accomplishes it with his characteristic lightness of touch, usually. But not always, and the passages closest to Villon are those in which the lyric conveys irony, frustration, and in a few places rage:

> Perchaunce the lye wethered and old,
> The wynter nyghtes that are so cold,
>   Playnyng in vain unto the mone;
> Thy wisshes then dare not be told;
>   Care then who lyst, for I have done.

> And then may chaunce the to repent
> The tyme that thou hast lost and spent
>   To cause thy lovers sigh and swoune;
> Then shalt thou knowe beaultie but lent,
>   And wisshe and want as I have done.

It was writing like this, which includes of course some of his best-known poems, that first attracted me to Wyatt when I was a student, and it was the cranky artistry not just of his prosody but of his language as a whole, its mixture of bluntness and grace, directness and song, that first drew me to his poetry. Among the poems in this vein is the famous sonnet **"Who so list to hount, I knowe where is an hynde"**—number 7 in *The Egerton Ms.* I mention it not only because of its extraordinary beauty and life but also as an example of Wyatt's real originality.

The poem has been taken to refer, along with several others, to Wyatt's love affair with Anne Boleyn before Henry VIII laid claim to her. There is no way of knowing with certainty whether Wyatt and Anne Boleyn were ever actually lovers, and the sonnet itself is a translation from Petrarch. But whether the writing in English alludes to Anne Boleyn or not, it comes to us with the mysterious force of an intensely personal poem. The enigmatic nature of it is compounded by the fact that the line that seems most germane to the Anne Boleyn legend, *"Noli me tangere,* for Caesars I ame," is already there, at least in part, in the Italian. But the imperative phrase there is in Italian, not in Wyatt's dramatic Latin. *"Nessun mi tocchi"* are Petrarch's words, and the writing on the doe's collar, in his poem, says that "my Caesar's will is to make me free." Wyatt turns that to something far more intimate, tense, and conflicting: his "for Caesars I ame / And wylde for to hold, though I seme tame." The possession has been turned round, it may be noted. It is no longer "my Caesar," but "Caesars I ame." And incidentally, it would be hard to find a line in Wyatt that is a better example of his mastery of metrical variation and roughness for charging a line with dramatic intensity.

A close comparison of Wyatt's poem with the Petrarch original reveals this kind of dramatic shift again and again. The Italian sonnet seems to be a relatively conventional medieval dream poem: a vision of an enticing and haughty *white* doe *appears* to the speaker, who abandons all his labors to follow her, as the miser pursues the allurement of wealth. Wyatt turns this around too, and it is the "vayne travaille" of the pursuit itself that has wearied him until he has fallen back and given up the chase. "I leve of therefore, / Sins in a nett I seke to hold the wynde." The image, like much else in the English, is wholly Wyatt's, as are the tone, the pace, the whole presence of the sonnet, including its warning, in the voice of experience: "Who list her hount, I put him owte of dowbte, / As well as I may spend his tyme in vain." Whatever their root in his life and his reading, the lines are clearly his own, and close to the central theme and imagery of his poetry. And while he may have been less concerned with describing the object of his passion than was Petrarch, this poem is laden with a heat and sensuality and a convincing erotic bitterness nowhere to be found in the Italian sonnet on which it was based. Wyatt's poem, I think, is an exception to Kenneth Muir's assertion that Wyatt's sonnets were not among his best poems. In this sonnet the force and beauty, the authority and originality are evident whether or not we think of the poem as a translation, and whether or not we know to whom it refers or indeed whether it refers to any single affair or person. The feelings that made it and give it its urgency and authenticity obviously had their source in something real in Wyatt's life, but we are unlikely to find out more about them anywhere except in the poems.

Wyatt's biography, in fact, is one more of those Tudor and Elizabethan *vitae* that tell us tantalizingly little of which we can be sure, but we know more about Wyatt than we do of many other poets of the age, including perhaps Shakespeare. And we do have a portrait painted by Holbein. Wyatt was born in 1503 at Allington Castle on the river Medway. The castle had not been a family estate for very long, but had been given to Wyatt's father, Sir Henry, as a recompense for services and sufferings on behalf of the house of Tudor. Wyatt was present at court when he was still a child. He attended the christening of Princess Mary when he was twelve or thirteen, and he went to St. John's College, Cambridge, soon afterward. He married in 1520, when he was seventeen. His wife was Lord Cobham's daughter Elizabeth. They had children, Thomas and Bess, but Elizabeth was unfaithful to him, and they separated.

Wyatt embarked on a diplomatic career when he was twenty-two, accompanying the English ambassador to France in 1525, returning to England with official dispatches, then accompanying Sir John Russell, the English emissary to the pope, in 1526. In Italy he was captured by the Spanish, and managed to escape while his release was being negotiated. Other missions followed in the next few years and he took his father's place as chief ewer at the coronation of Anne Boleyn.

Their relation has been the subject of more romantic speculation than anything else in his life. There is circumstantial evidence to suggest that Wyatt's life and fate were for a while associated with hers, and there are several contemporary stories that are quite specific about what the relationship was, and what became of it. A contemporary of Wyatt's named Nicholas Sanders declared Anne and Wyatt had been lovers and that when Wyatt learned Henry VIII planned to marry her he told the Privy Council she was not a fit wife for the king. According to the story, Henry refused to believe what he was told and banished Wyatt from the court. Other writers told variants of the story, but it has been noted that they were biased—as Catholics these critics were happy to find or invent scurrilous or damaging stories about Anne at the time of her trial. Kenneth Muir (whose lucid summary of the probabilities forms part of his introduction to the Muses' Library edition of Wyatt, which I have used for this selection) is inclined to believe that there had been an affair, no doubt a rather dark and vexed one, between Wyatt and Anne Boleyn, and that the lines

> *sins I did refrayne*
> *Her that did set our country in a rore*

refer to Anne. Wyatt, for whatever reasons, was imprisoned and then banished to his castle in 1536, shortly before Anne's exposure, but was released in the summer of that year and given new official posts. He was appointed ambassador to Spain in the following year.

But his troubles were far from over. Besides his affairs of the heart, whatever they may have been, Wyatt had enemies at court, and we do not know how many of his tribulations they contrived. His finances, by now, were "chaotic," in Kenneth Muir's word, and were rescued from that state by the good offices of a friend and patron, Cromwell. In his late thirties Wyatt suffered the death of his father and the execution of this same friend Cromwell. Several of Wyatt's most personal poems—a few of them, again, evolved from translations—allude to this second appalling loss. The execution of Cromwell in the summer of 1540 was one event in a chain of intrigues that threatened Wyatt as well. At the beginning of the following year he was arrested and all his possessions seized. He was accused by the bishop of London of a list of offenses that included treason and immorality.

Wyatt defended himself vigorously and cogently, not only parrying the charges against him but also taking the initiative and attacking his accuser. "I know no man that did you dishonour," ran his reply to the bishop, "but your unmannerly behaviour, that made ye a laughing stock to all men that came in your company, and me sometime sweat for shame to see you." And he pressed the charge of immorality too upon its author:

> Come on now, my Lord of London, what is my abominable and vicious living? Do ye know it, or have ye heard it? I grant I do not profess chastity; but yet I use not abomination. If ye know it, tell it here, with whom and when. If ye heard it, who is your author? Have ye seen me have any harlot in my house whilst ye were in my company? Did you ever see woman so much as dine, or sup, at my table? None, but for your pleasure, the woman that was in the galley; which I assure you may well be seen; for, before you came, neither she nor any other came above the mast. But because the gentlemen took pleasure to see you entertain her, therefore they made her dine and sup with you; and they liked well your looks, your carving to Madonna, your drinking to her, and your playing under the table.

Ask Mason, ask Blage—Bowes is dead—ask Wolf, that
was my steward; they can tell how the gentlemen marked
it, and talked of it. It was a play to them, the keeping
of your bottles, that no man might drink of but yourself;
and "that the little fat priest were a jolly morsel for the
Signora." This was their talk; it is not my devise: ask
other, whether I do lie.

Wyatt was cleared of the accusations against him, and
released with a full pardon. He was given further diplomatic missions, was elected to Parliament, was made a
vice admiral of the fleet. In 1542, when he was thirty-
nine, he set out for Falmouth, to meet a Spanish emissary
to the court. He was stricken with a fever on the way
there, died at Sherborne, and is buried there.

What we know of his character comes partly from such
bare facts, partly from the testimony of a few of those
who knew him, and for the rest, from his poems. The
milieu in which he lived gave rise to intense loyalties and
ruthless defamation, and he had his share of both. In those
poems where his voice is clearest, we hear someone who
is forthright, independent, sensual, and dignified. He was
under few illusions concerning the life at court and its
deceptions, and some of his sharpest and most vigorous
writing arises from his sense of the falsity of many of
the assumptions and circumstances that claimed the greater
part of his life.

> Stond who so list upon the Slipper toppe
>   Of courtes estates, and lett me heare reioyce;
> And vse me quyet without lett or stoppe,
>   Vnknowen in courte, that hath suche brackishe
> ioyes:
>   In hidden place, so lett my dayes forthe passe,
>   That when my yeares be done, withouten
> noyse,
>   I may dye aged after the common trace.
> For hym death greep'the right hard by the croppe
>   That is moche knowen of other; and of him
> self alas,
>   Doth dye unknowen, dazed with dreadful face.

The poem, according to Kenneth Muir, is one of those
written after the execution of Cromwell, and it is full of
intimate and bitter urgency. Yet it is also true that it, too,
like the love poems, has its place in a broad and ancient
tradition—a convention, indeed—of decrying worldly life
and asserting a preference for rustic simplicity and seclusion. There is no reason to suppose, because of this
alone, or because Wyatt did not spend the remainder of
his life in rural seclusion and voluntary poverty, that the
impulse and feelings behind his poems in this vein are
not genuine, any more than we should dismiss the love
poems as mere conventions simply because a convention
lends them form and style.

Indeed, the play of contraries in Wyatt—convention and
directness, craving and withdrawal—makes him more interesting, personal, intimate than his contemporaries.
He has been criticized for the narrowness of his range,
and it is true that the basic attitudes he articulates, the
underlying dramatic positions and images, are relatively
few. His was not, we should remember, a life wholly
dedicated to poetry, as were Chaucer's or Shakespeare's,
Milton's or Wordsworth's. He was an aristocratic amateur and poetry, for him, was perforce an avocation—
one to which he was clearly born, nevertheless, and
which he must have practiced on occasion, to judge from
the poems alone, with a compelling passion. One of the
central attitudes (in the theatrical sense) in his poetry is
the lover's reproach to the unfeeling beloved, either for
ignoring his passion or for betraying it at some later
time. The theme is one of the most familiar of all the
conventions of European poetry from the age of chivalry to the seventeenth century. But in Wyatt's best poems it takes on a singular complexity of immediate and
conflicting feeling. Such poems as **"They fle from me"**
or **"My lute awake!"** or **"Who so list to hount"** vibrate with mixed feelings—desire, anger, mortification,
mockery, bitterness, even tenderness. And some of the
same complexity of feeling is present when the beloved
is the worldly life itself of fortune and favor and fickle
or loyal friends, and the poet speaks of his enforced or
voluntary distance from it, scorning it, rejecting it, and
at certain turns still fascinated and attracted by it. The
tension serves to increase the intimacy and force of the
language, and to fill it with that complex continuo, a
haunting, dissonant, disabused yet sensual song that is
Wyatt's alone. Once truly heard it is unlikely to be
forgotten.

Or so it seems, speaking only from my own experience.
The wry beauty of Wyatt's poems hung in my ear when I
was a student, and then and since exercised some indefin-
able influence upon what I heard and relished and listened
for in other poetry. He has been indifferently served by
anthologists, even in modern times. A number of his finest poems appear again and again, but others remarkable
for the beauty and life of their language have never been
anthologized at all, and some of them, such as **"Stond
who so list"** or **"Ye old mule,"** reveal facets of Wyatt's
talent and sensibility that are generally overlooked, so
that the range of his gift seems more limited than it really is.

But he is—as many poets seem, after four centuries—an
uneven poet, and I have indulged my fondness for him by
including here and there poems which, while they certainly do not strike me as wholly successful, contain
passages which have given me pleasure for so long that I
have been reluctant to pass up a chance to call attention
to them. **"Passe forth, my wonted cryes"** is simply one
more lyric in a much wonted vein until one comes to the
strength and freshness of

> For though hard rockes among
>   She semes to haue bene bred,
> And of the Tigre long
>   Bene nourished and fed:
> Yet shall that nature change,
>   If pitie once win place,
> Whom as unknowen and strange
>   She now away doth chase

And as the water soft,
    Without forcyng or strength,
Where that it falleth oft,
    Hard stones doth perse at length:
So in her stony hart
    My plaintes at last shall graue,
And, rygour set apart,
    Winne grant of that I craue.

Perez Zagorin (essay date 1993)

SOURCE: "Sir Thomas Wyatt and the Court of Henry VIII: The Courtier's Ambivalence," in *The Journal of Medieval and Renaissance Studies,* Vol. XXIII, No. 1, Winter, 1993, pp. 113-41.

[*In the following essay, Wyatt's conflicting attitudes toward the court are examined as a key to understanding his work.*]

In 1548, six years after Sir Thomas Wyatt's death, his good friend, Sir Francis Bryan, published an English translation of the Spaniard Antonio de Guevara's *Menosprecio de Corte y Alabanza de Aldea.*[1] As in the case of Wyatt, so also the most important fact about Bryan is that he spent his life as a courtier in the service of Henry VIII.[2] Like Wyatt, moreover, his contemporaries at Henry VIII's court knew him also as a poet. Those of his poems that may remain, however, are shrouded in anonymity, whereas Wyatt left a considerable body of identifiable work that has given him a secure reputation as perhaps the best English poet between Chaucer and Spenser.[3] That Bryan should have chosen to translate Guevara's *Menosprecio* is an ironic comment on his own vocation as a courtier, for this work is one of the foremost specimens of the anticourtier literature of Renaissance Europe.[4] Three verse satires by Wyatt belong to the same genre of criticism of courts and courtiers, while many of his other poems are strongly marked by the negative feelings court existence evoked in him. For this reason, Bryan's translation of Guevara's treatise offers a valuable point of entry to a fresh consideration of the relationship between Wyatt's experience as a courtier and the attitudes expressed in his work.

A Franciscan monk, court preacher and royal servant, official historiographer of Emperor Charles V, bishop successively of Guadix and Mondoñedo, and for many years a courtier himself, Antonio de Guevara (c. 1480-1545) was the most famous Spanish author of his time. He wrote chiefly as a moralist, filling his works with stories and quotations from classical sources that delighted his readers and gained him a wide European audience through the numerous translations of his writings.[5] The first of these to appear in English was *The Golden Boke of Marcus Aurelius,* published in 1535, which was made from a French version by Sir Francis Bryan's uncle, Lord Berners, best known as the translator of Froissart, who undertook the task at Bryan's request.[6] Bryan's translation of the *Menosprecio,* also based on a French version, was entitled *A Dispraise of the Life of the Courtier, and a Commenda-*

tion of the Life of the Labouring Man.[7] Like the posthumous edition in 1549 of Wyatt's paraphrase of the penitential psalms, it was dedicated to William Parr, marquis of Northampton, a considerable court personage and brother of Henry VIII's last queen, Catherine Parr.[8]

Guevara's treatise stands at the opposite pole from the idealization of courtiership in Castiglione's celebrated *Book of the Courtier,* published about a decade earlier.[9] There is no evidence, however, that he was acquainted with this Italian work, which was first translated into Spanish in 1534, although he had probably met and talked with Castiglione when the latter was papal nuncio in Spain between 1525 and 1529.[10] Even though its purpose was to delineate the virtues of the perfect courtier, Castiglione's portrayal was hardly free of ambiguities. Never alluded to, yet presupposed in the art of conduct it prescribed, was the political context of a princely despotism, and hence of the unfettered will of an absolute ruler such as existed in the author's own ducal state of Urbino, to which the courtier had to adapt himself. Moreover, in order to gain the prince's favor and the admiration of the court, the successful courtier, as Castiglione depicted him, needed to be an adept at dissimulation, cultivating by means of such qualities as *sprezzatura* faculties of artifice, flexibility, and role-playing scarcely distinguishable from duplicity and falsehood.[11] Despite the equivocal features implicit in Castiglione's conception, however, it nevertheless remains true that his intention was to glorify the court as the setting for a genuine type of human excellence incarnated in the ideal courtier.

For Guevara, on the other hand, the court was a noxious society whose manner of life doomed its members to moral and spiritual corruption. Heavily influenced by Marcus Aurelius and Plutarch (whom he read in Latin translations), he wrote from both a Stoic and a Christian perspective, urging the wisdom of attaching no value to the goods of this world.[12] The twenty chapters of his treatise were an outright condemnation of the court and courtiership, which he contrasted unfavorably with the healthy physical, moral, and spiritual condition of existence in the rural village. While careful to acknowledge that not everyone at court was vicious, the general impression of the courtier he conveyed was one of wretchedness, insecurity, and evil.[13] The courtier knows that the life he lives is a kind of death, yet he cannot bring himself to leave it. Lacking all honest liberty because of the constant demands upon him, in his pursuit of wealth and favor he ceases to be a Christian.[14] Amid the immorality that flourishes in the court, virtue is hard to find and dangerous to keep. Dissimulation and spying, malice and displeasure, abound. Court fortune, moreover, is always changeable, some men rising and others falling, unknown persons advanced and faithful servants forgotten, fools believed and wise men disregarded, opinion followed and reason ignored.[15] Courtiers forever complain that the king gives them nothing, while those in power "are ever in feare to be put doune from their auctoritie" and thus "in continuall drede and torment."[16] Observing that "in the courts of princes all say we will do it, but none do it," ("en las cortes de los principes todos dizen 'haremos' y ninguno dize 'hagamos'"), Guevara likened the court to "a perpetuall dreame, a botomelesse whorlepole, an inchaunted phantasy, and a mase."[17] Courtiers, he held, were incapable of either amity or fidelity, and "many there be that do of their bonette to you, that gladly would se your heades of by the shoulders" ("porque allí a muchos quitan la gorra que les querrían más quitar la cabeça").[18] These somber reflections were the product of his own experience, for before retiring to his bishopric, he had known the court and its disappointments at first hand, and he tells the reader how much he lamented the loss of his years there and the evil customs he had learned in its midst.[19] Hence, in a fitting conclusion, he expressed his renunciation of the world with its deceits and betrayals, avowing that he had given up worldly cares and bidden farewell to hope and fortune.[20]

In his unsparing verdict, Guevara could find nothing good to say about the court or courtiers. His observations, however, were entirely of a moral character, containing not the slightest hint of criticism of princes or their policies. By its moral commentary on the vices of courtiers, moreover, elaborated with many classical examples and sayings, his book served, as his French translator stated, as "a persuasion to virtue."[21] This explains why it was possible for Guevara to dedicate the *Menosprecio* to King John III of Portugal, and why Bryan said in his translation that it contained pleasant and fruitful matter.[22] One of its recurrent themes was the ambivalence of courtiers, who, though they knew the drawbacks of the court, felt its pull so strongly that they lacked the power to give it up. This theme may also have had considerable appeal to Bryan, and it is likewise prominent in the life and career of his fellow courtier Sir Thomas Wyatt.

Although Wyatt's relationship to the court has naturally been much discussed by students of his poetry, the note of ambivalence that marked this relationship has been largely overlooked. In this essay, accordingly, my aim is to explore the significance of ambivalence as a key to Wyatt's work. In doing so, I wish also to correct certain misconceptions concerning the effect on Wyatt of his court experience that have been advanced by Kenneth Muir, his distinguished editor and biographer, and even more misleadingly by Alistair Fox in his recent study of literature and politics in the reign of Henry VIII.[23]

Born in 1503, Wyatt belonged to a family of Yorkshire origin that was part of the Tudor service aristocracy and profited substantially by its association with the dynasty. His father, Sir Henry Wyatt, distinguished himself by his loyalty to the Tudor claimant, the future Henry VII, while the latter was still in exile during the usurpation of Richard III. With Henry VII's ascension to the throne, Sir Henry rose in the royal service, acquiring offices and increasing wealth. He became a member of Henry VII's council and was one of the executors of his will. In 1492 he purchased Allington Castle in Kent, henceforth the principal family residence, to which he made extensive improvements and where he and his son entertained Henry VII, Cardinal Wolsey, and Henry VIII. He continued in favor as a valued royal servant under Henry VIII, at whose

coronation he was made a Knight of the Bath and from whom he received grants of land, annuities, and offices. Among the latter were important positions in the royal household as Treasurer of the King's Jewels and Treasurer of the Chamber.[24]

Sir Thomas Wyatt was reared by his father for the service of the crown. Sent at the early age of twelve to the University of Cambridge, he was first introduced to the court in 1516, when his name appears on a list of officers and servants sworn to attend in the King's Chamber, which mentions him as one of the "sewers extraordinary," an office involving intermittent presence and service at meals.[25] In 1520 he married Elizabeth Cobham, a daughter of Lord Brooke, with whom his relationship became so unhappy that they separated soon after she bore him a son. During subsequently years he was the recipient of various posts from the king, such as Esquire of the Royal Body, Clerk of the King's Jewels, and Marshal of Calais. Most instrumental to his advancement, probably, was his appointment as a Gentleman of the King's Privy Chamber. Recent research has rescued the Privy Chamber from its previous obscurity and revealed its importance in the politics of Henry VIII's reign.[26] The office of Gentleman of the Privy Chamber may have been established in 1518 in imitation of a similar position in the household of the king of France, Francis I. Those who occupied this office were Henry VIII's "minions," his intimate companions and servants and the only persons at court permitted access to his private apartments in which he slept and lived. Consisting of young men chosen for their birth, charm, intelligence, and virile athleticism, the gentlemen looked after the king's personal and physical needs and accompanied him on the hunt, royal progresses, and other social occasions. Beside the domestic functions that brought them into continual contact with the monarch, they were also frequently employed in a political capacity as his agents in diplomacy, military matters, and local government. Sir Francis Bryan made his notable court career as a Gentleman of the Privy Chamber, achieving a relationship of extraordinary freedom with Henry VIII, who allowed him, according to report, to "boldly speak to the king's Grace the plainness of his mind and . . . his Grace doth well accept the same."[27] It was also as a Gentleman of the Privy Chamber that Wyatt rose to his highest official responsibility when, in 1537, he was made resident ambassador in Spain to Emperor Charles V, and when two years later he was appointed ambassador first to France and then to Emperor Charles V in the Netherlands.[28]

Wyatt cut a brilliant figure at the court. His exceptional good looks are apparent from Hans Holbein's beautiful and sensitive portrait drawing of him, which must have been done when he was in his late twenties or early thirties.[29] His poetic gifts, eloquence, wit, and intellectual versatility added to the attractiveness of his personality. The anonymous Spanish chronicler of Henry VIII's reign, who was probably a resident of London with some knowledge of the contemporary scene, described him as "a very gallant gentleman," the handsomest man at court, and noted his prowess in jousting.[30] His younger friend, the earl of Surrey, in a poem mourning Wyatt's death, praised his manhood and beauty and extolled his virtue and integrity in a life spent

> Amyd great stormes, whome grace assurid soo
> To lyve upright and smyle at fortunes choyse.

Wyatt possessed a heart, he wrote,

> . . . wheare drede yet neuer so opprest
> To hyde the thought that myght the trouthe
> avaunce;
> In nether fortune lost nor so represt,
> To swell at welthe, nor yelde unto myschaunce.[31]

In another elegy on his death, the antiquarian scholar John Leland, who had known him over many years, commemorated his nobility of mind, observing that

> Despite the ample gifts that Fortune brought,
>   He never swelled with pride, nor set the heart
> Upon the dazzling splendour of the Court,
>   Nor on the noise of the great world, nor sought
> A great man's favour—he chose the better part.[32]

Surrey's and Leland's tributes not only praise Wyatt's talents but also intimate the perils and ambiguities he encountered at court. He himself, in a solemn letter of advice written in 1537 to his fifteen-year-old son, spoke of the "thousand dangers and hazardes, enmyties, hatrids, prisonments, despits and indignations" he had incurred on account of his folly and extravagance.[33] This was a reflection on his life in Henry VIII's court, a perilously unstable world in which power and honors were always at risk. Never was this more true than in the years after 1529, when the king's quarrel with the pope over his divorce from Catherine of Aragon, followed by his marriage to Anne Boleyn and repudiation of papal authority, created enormous tensions at home and abroad. Not just personal ambitions and rivalries, but differences over religion and the question of the break with Rome, fears both of treason from within and of invasion from without by a Catholic coalition on the Continent, drove the factional politics of the court. This period was studded with the fall and destruction of such great ministers as Cardinal Wolsey, Sir Thomas More, and Thomas Cromwell, of such noble families as the Boleyns, Poles, and Howards, and of personal favorites whom the king suspected of disloyalty. In 1536 Sir Henry Norris, Henry's closest friend and Chief Gentleman of the Privy Chamber, was beheaded for adultery with Queen Anne Boleyn and conspiring with her to procure the king's death, charges of which the two were in all probability innocent. Along with him to execution beside the queen herself and her brother George Boleyn, Lord Rochford, went Sir William Brereton, also a Gentleman of the Privy Chamber, and several other members of the royal household.[34] In 1539 Sir Nicholas Carew, Sir Francis Bryan's brother-in-law, likewise a Gentleman of the Privy Chamber and long-time intimate of the king, was executed as a traitor for his sympathy and association with the faction of religious conservatives at court.[35] Every shift of royal policy in these years was attended with factional intrigue and

the possibility of disgrace and death for those on the wrong side. The insecurity of courtiers and political men was heightened by the king's growing suspiciousness and bloodthirstiness as he aged. At times the court appeared to live in an atmosphere of terror. The French ambassador Marillac reported in 1541 that many noblemen felt themselves "always under suspicion," believing "that lightly and for the most trifling matter they can be most grievously punished." In a subsequent dispatch he commented that "here they condemn men without hearing them" and that once someone was in the Tower, "there is no one living that dare intermeddle in his affairs, nor dare ope his mouth save to speak ill of him, for dread that he himself may come under suspicion of the same crime as that of which he is accused."[36] Sir Thomas Wyatt was to experience this terror in full force when he faced death twice as a prisoner in the Tower, the first time in 1536 because of the fall of Anne Boleyn, the second time in 1541 as a result of the fall of Thomas Cromwell.

Apart from the dangers incident to a stressful period of religious instability and relentless Tudor statebuilding, the court was the scene of a ceaseless competition for the rewards of favor and power. In this contest, conducted in a monarchical regime dominated by Henry VIII's autocratic will and in which politics and personal relationships were inextricably entangled, craft, sycophancy, and hypocrisy were indispensable to success and even to survival. In contrast to an ideal image of courtiership, a common opinion considered the name of courtier synonomous with dissimulation and falsehood. The wellknown aphorism, "Nescit dissimulare qui nescit vivere," was often seen as the courtier's maxim.[37] Courtiers and officials aiming at advancement and private persons pursuing suits at court found it essential to obtain the support of patrons, friends, and intermediaries if they were to have any hope of success. John Husee, the servant and London agent of Lord Lisle, the king's deputy or governor of Calais, who was entrusted with his master's varied business at the court, frequently reported on the deceit he encountered there. He had to reassure both Lord and Lady Lisle against the threat of "back-friends," the false friends who would hinder the progress of their suits.[38] Another of Lisle's agents, his receiver general Sir Antony Windsor, warned him of his "secret Enemies" at court, adding that "insomuch as your lordship is not at hand yourself, it is very necessary . . . to have a friend about the King so that I and others that be your officers may resort to have redress when case shall require."[39] Husee wrote Lisle that some at court "beareth your lordship fair face and a double dissembling heart."[40] To Lady Lisle he commented in another letter, "Your ladyship knoweth the Court is full of pride, envy, . . . mocking, scorning and derision."[41]

As the fount of honors, offices, and innumerable other benefits, the supreme patron was the king, to whom everyone at court looked for favor. Beneath him stood his ministers, councillors, officers of state, and prominent members of the royal household, who usually had their own followers and dependents and were also channels for the flow of royal bounty. Wyatt's chief patron and friend in the court was Thomas Cromwell, a great administrator and politician who had gathered a multiplicity of offices and as principal minister controlled the operation of the king's government from around 1532 until his fall eight years later. How and when Wyatt became associated with Cromwell remains unrecorded, but while he retained power, Wyatt enjoyed his constant support. It was no doubt through his influence that Wyatt was appointed in 1537 as ambassador to Spain. The minister's letters to him on his embassy contained frequent assurances that he was looking after Wyatt's interests and of his own and the king's good will. "The Kinges Maieste is your good and gratious lorde," he wrote on one occasion, and "I shall be suche a Freende unto you if nede require as your enemyes if you have any shall wynne litle at your hande in your absence."[42] In June 1540, less than two months after promoting him to the earldom of Essex, the king abruptly discarded Cromwell, and the court faction that opposed him finally had its revenge. He was promptly condemned and executed for heresy and treason by an act of attainder, without even the form of a legal trial.[43] His sudden overthrow was one of the greatest shocks to Wyatt's career. The loss of the minister's protection brought him into serious danger, and he voiced his grief over Cromwell's death in a sonnet whose opening lines betray its depth of feeling:

> The pillar perished is whereto I leant,
> The strongest stay of mine unquiet mind;
> The like of it no man again can find—
> From east to west still seeking though he went. . . . [44]

Wyatt's poetic originality lay partly in his being the first English poet to introduce the Petrarchan sonnet, that favorite verse form of the Elizabethans, and other foreign forms such as the French rondeau into English poetry.[45] By whatever means he acquired his knowledge of French and Italian, whether primarily through earlier study or as the result of his first journeys to the Continent in 1526 and 1527, he was apparently acquainted with the literature of both languages.[46] Foreign models inspired many of his own poems, which included numerous translations of Petrarch and other poets that are much more like free adaptations or, in their best specimens, inspired imitations than literal versions of the originals. Since he did not write for any public, none of his poetry was printed during his lifetime. His audience consisted entirely of members of the court, an exclusive group of men and women who read his and the work of other courtier poets in manuscript copies passed hand to hand and sometimes preserved in albums.[47]

The majority of his poems are lyrics in various forms that deal with the relationship between a man and a woman in accord with the conventions of courtly love observed by Petrarch and many other late medieval poets. But as C. S. Lewis remarked, the attitude they express is very different from Petrarch's "devout *Frauendienst*."[48] Concerned with love and desire, their main theme is the lover's resentment, unhappiness, and despair at his rejection by the woman he has vainly pursued or perhaps temporarily possessed, whom he discovers to be faithless, indifferent, and cruel. Typical are the following lines from one of his rondeaus:

> Behold, Love, thy power how she despiseth,
> My great pain how little she regardeth.
> The holy oath whereof she taketh no cure
> Broken she hath, and yet she bideth sure
> Right at her ease and little she dreadeth.
> Weaponed thou art, and she unarmed sitteth.
> To thee disdainful her life she leadeth,
> To me spiteful without cause or measure.[49]

Another example, but in a lighter vein, comes from one of his songs:

> With serving still
> This have I won:
> For my good will
> To be undone.
>
> And for redress
> Of all my pain
> Disdainfulness
> I have again.
>
> And for reward
> Of all my smart,
> Lo, thus unheard,
> I must depart.[50]

Even though Wyatt's lyrics so often deal with such subjects as the pain of love and frustrated desire, it is striking how easy it is to discern in them a direct echo and transposition of his perception of the nature of court life. The deceit and falsity, the capriciousness of power and mutability of fortune that the courtier learns to expect in the court, are also what he discovers in love, and a concern for truth and sincerity against craft and dissimulation recurs in such poems. **"What vaileth truth,"** for example, although a plaint about falsity in love, could apply equally to the court, as its first stanza makes clear:

> What vaileth truth or by it to take pain,
> To strive by steadfastness for to attain
> To be just and true and flee from doubleness,
> Sithens all alike, where ruleth craftiness,
> Rewarded is both false and plain?
> Soonest he speedeth that most can feign;
> True meaning heart is had in disdain.
> Against deceit and doubleness
>   What vaileth truth?[51]

In these lines, the duplicity, craftiness, and deceit that the lover associates with his mistress's cruelty are likewise essential tropes in the anticourtier literature of the sixteenth century and also figure prominently in Wyatt's satires on the court.

In other poems the lover reflects on "the falsehood love can frame," and on its guile and cunning;[52] or he sees through his mistress's deceit and takes his leave of her with the conclusion,

> For he that believeth bearing in hand,
> Plougheth in water and soweth in the sand.[53]

Dissimulation and doubleness are a constant preoccupation of the lover. He accuses his mistress of "coloured doubleness,"[54] and says of himself:

> And if ye find that I do feign,
> With just judgement myself I damn
>   To have disdain.
>   . . . . .
>
> If in my love there be one spot
> Of false deceit or doubleness
>   . . . . .
>
>   Esteem me not.[55]

Another striking feature of these poems is the need they express for trust and their lament for its lack. The lover is persuaded that "where I trust I am deceived,"[56] and that "he that seeks as I have sought / Shall find most trust oft-times untrue,"[57] because "they whom you trust most / Soonest deceive you shall."[58] He feels himself too a victim of fortune, the "depriver of all my comfort,"[59] and complains that

> Fortune doth frown.
> What remedy?
> I am down
> By destiny.[60]

A close correspondence exists between the states of mind these poems reveal and those the courtier experiences in the court, as displayed in such anticourt works as Guevara's *Dispraise of the Court*. In a number of other lyrics, Wyatt alluded very directly to the world of the court. The epigram, "Stand whoso list upon the slipper top / Of court's estates," rejects the court's "brackish joys" in favor of the peace and obscurity of private life. Its conclusion pictures the horrifying death of the courtier, a man who, while "much known of other," dies without ever knowing himself, "dazed, with dreadful face."[61] Other poems emphasize the danger of false friends[62] or expatiate on the prevalence of duplicity in speech:

> . . . well to say and so to mean—
> That sweet accord is seldom seen.[63]

Among the epigrams, "Lucks, my fair falcon and your fellows all," voices a longing for the falcons' liberty and contrasts the bird's fidelity to the poet with his betrayal by friends.[64] Another, "In court to serve," a comment on the court's supposed pleasures, asserts that the courtier's life

> Hath with it joined oft-times such bitter taste
> That whoso joys such kind of life to hold,
> In prison joys, fettered with chains of gold.[65]

The first big crisis in Wyatt's career as a courtier ensued in consequence of his relationship with Anne Boleyn. Since her marriage, Anne had failed to give Henry VIII a male heir; and even before he cast her off, he had begun his pursuit of Jane Seymour, her successor as queen. Her downfall occurred when, after a secret investigation by Cromwell, the king became convinced that she had committed adultery with several men of the court and incest with her brother. In the first week of May 1536 she and the others accused with her were sent to the Tower. Wyatt himself was committed to the Tower on 5 May. Although summoned immediately for questioning, his friend, Sir Francis Bryan, was not arrested. Within the next two weeks, Anne and five others were tried, convicted, and executed. Wyatt remained in prison without any formal charges preferred against him. There was speculation that he would suffer death with the others; but soon after his detention, Cromwell wrote his father that he was in no danger. On 14 June he was finally released.[66]

Both Ives and Warnicke, Anne Boleyn's latest biographers, concur that although she behaved indiscreetly, she was falsely accused and that no proof was produced of her alleged adultery, incest, or conspiracy to procure the king's death. Ives in particular has pictured her as the victim of a court faction, to which Cromwell was an accessory, that succeeded in destroying her once the king tired of her presence. In the most recent review of the evidence, another scholar has argued that faction did not cause her fall and that she may in fact have committed adultery.[67] As regards Wyatt, however, the most probable reason for his arrest is that he was suspected of being one of Anne's lovers.[68] Very likely he maintained his innocence to Cromwell, as the anonymous Spanish chronicler reported, and since none of the witnesses against Anne named him, he was not tried and his life was spared.[69]

This conclusion still leaves open, nonetheless, the question of the exact nature of his relationship to Anne. Of course, he must have known her quite well at court and possibly before then. The Boleyns and Wyatts belonged to the same inner court circle and were also neighbors in Kent, the Boleyn family seat at Hever lying not far distant from the Wyatts' at Allington Castle. In June 1533 Wyatt acted as chief server at Anne's coronation banquet in Westminster Hall. During her last days in the Tower, she mentioned his reputation as a writer of ballads.[70] Statements made many years later by English Catholic writers hostile to Anne speak of Wyatt's sexual intimacy with her and further relate that he warned Henry VIII against marrying her because she was a loose woman. Wyatt's grandson recorded a family tale that he had paid suit to Anne, who rejected his advances because he was married but remained his friend.[71] In the absence of reliable corroborative testimony, however, it is impossible to determine how much credence to give these stories. Warnicke strongly denies that Wyatt and Anne were ever lovers, while Ives believes that he may once have been in love with her but ceased his attentions after the king became attracted to her.[72]

The only strictly contemporary evidence that the two were romantically involved is contained in Wyatt's poetry. Although he never mentions her by name, some of his poems contain clues suggesting that she is their subject. The one that seems to point to her most clearly is the sonnet **"Whoso list to hunt, I know where is an hind,"** adapted from a poem by Petrarch. In it the lover envisages as a deer the woman he is wearily pursuing, and he realizes he must give up the chase because she is reserved for Caesar:

> And graven with diamonds in letters plain
> There is written her fair neck round about:
> 'Noli me tangere for Caesar's I am,
> And wild for to hold though I seem tame.'[73]

Another poem, a riddle in the form of an epigram beginning,

> What word is that that changeth not
> Though it be turned and made in twain?

may have "Anna" as its answer.[74] The sonnet **"If waker care, if sudden pale colour"** probably expresses a renunciation of Anne, who is twice referred to as "Brunet" and is replaced by "Phyllis" in the lover's affection. Wyatt altered the eighth line, "Her that did set our country in a roar," to "Brunet that set my wealth in such a roar," presumably to disguise Anne's identity.[75] Still another poem possibly associated with her is **"Sometimes I fled the fire that me brent,"** likewise an expression of renunciation and perhaps written on the occasion when he accompanied the king and Anne on a journey to Calais.[76]

While we may never learn the full truth about Wyatt's relationship to Anne Boleyn, it appears more than likely that at the very least he had once desired and sought to possess her. Apart from this, it is certain that the execution of the queen and her accused lovers affected him profoundly. The proof lies in the poem **"Who list his wealth and ease retain,"** which he may have composed in the Tower. In this work, which implies that he witnessed his friends' death, grief and horror mingle with ambivalence regarding court ambition and its dangers. Even more than grief, this ambivalence stands out as the pervasive theme and is underscored by the refrain imitated from Seneca, "circa Regna tonat," which concludes each of its five verses and calls to mind the menacing presence of the king's power throughout his kingdom. The thought that obscurity may be preferable to greatness is sounded in the opening lines,

> Who list his wealth and ease retain,
> Himself let him unknown contain

and, as the following stanzas illustrate, persists through the rest of the poem:

> The high mountains are blasted oft
> When the low valley is mild and soft.
> Fortune with Health stands at debate.
> The fall is grievous from aloft.
> And sure, circa Regna tonat.

> These bloody days have broken my heart.
> My lust, my youth did them depart,
> And blind desire of estate.
> Who hastes to climb seeks to revert.
> Of truth, circa Regna tonat.

> The bell tower showed me such sight
> That in my head sticks day and night.
> There did I learn out of a grate,
> For all favour, glory, or might,
> That yet, circa Regna tonat.[77]

With this poem in mind, Wyatt's biographer Kenneth Muir concluded that he was a "changed man" after his imprisonment and Anne Boleyn's calamitous end. More recently, Alistair Fox had argued similarly that the shock of Anne's fall made his self-identity precarious and destroyed his belief in conventional values by disclosing to him the contradiction between the moral principles preached by his society and the actual practice of Henry VIII's court.[78] These judgments seem to me to be greatly exaggerated. As a highly intelligent, perceptive observer, Wyatt would have been aware from an early time of the gulf between the ideal and the reality of the court and courtiership. His poems are undated, but there is no reason why some of those critical of the court should not have been written before 1536. As we shall see, moreover, his three anti-court satires, which were composed after his prison experience in 1536, belie the claim that Anne Boleyn's death and his own danger had left him with a shattered, decentered self.

Even with his mixed feelings about the court, however, Wyatt was too closely tied to it by personal and family interest to leave it. Nor could he have done so in any case as long as the king desired his service. Upon his release he returned to Allington, whence his father wrote Cromwell that he had ordered his son to amend his conduct and obey the king's pleasure and minister's commandments in all things.[79] His imprisonment did not cost him the king's favor. In the autumn of 1536 he was named sheriff of Kent and granted several offices belonging to his father, who had died in November. In the following March (1537), he was knighted and appointed ambassador to Spain.[80]

For the next three years he served intermittently as ambassador to Emperor Charles V and King Francis I, spending time in Spain, France, and the Low Countries. He had a number of meetings with these monarchs and their ministers, and his dispatches to Cromwell and Henry VIII constitute a valuable record of the ability and effort he devoted to collecting intelligence for his government and deciphering the intentions of the two sovereigns with a view to the danger of their combining against England.[81] In the spring of 1538, Edmund Bonner, a churchman soon to become bishop of London, was sent out with a colleague to join Wyatt in his negotiations with the emperor, who was then at Nice conferring with Francis I and Pope Paul III. Having little esteem for his fellow envoys, Wyatt treated them with scant consideration. In retaliation, Bonner wrote Cromwell some months later accusing Wyatt of serious misconduct. Among his charges was that Wyatt could not forget his earlier imprisonment and complained of it frequently. Another was that he had had suspicious dealings with Cardinal Reginald Pole, Henry VIII's cousin, whom the king had denounced as a traitor for opposing his repudiation of papal authority.[82] Not doubting his loyalty, Cromwell apparently suppressed these letters and continued to give Wyatt his confidence.[83]

The matter surfaced again following his return to England in May 1540 on the conclusion of his last diplomatic mission. A few weeks afterward Cromwell suddenly fell from power and was executed at the end of July. In the subsequent examination of Cromwell's papers, Bonner's charges were found and suspicion thrown on Wyatt. Especially grave was the accusation of correspondence with Cardinal Pole, whom the king hated as a personal enemy. In January 1541 Wyatt was arrested and thrown in the Tower. Several of his associates were also arrested. The French ambassador considered him a dead man, reporting that he had "earned the malevolence of all those who leagued against Cromwell, whose favorite he was." Several days later the Privy Council ordered the removal from Allington Castle for the king's use of plate, household goods, arms, and horses, and the dismissal of the servants and other persons living there.[84]

This was the second great crisis in Wyatt's courtier life, and he met it with exceptional courage, as is shown by the two statements pleading his case he drew up in the Tower. One was a short *Declaration* to the Privy Council insisting on his innocence, the other a detailed *Defence* refuting the charges and evidence against him, apparently intended as an address to his judges after his indictment. The second of these in particular was a remarkable document in several respects. It demonstrated great presence of mind, firmness of purpose, and force of expression, while also offering a revealing glimpse of his political beliefs. Of its many striking remarks, which with their political implications have been largely overlooked by historians of Henry VIII's reign, only a few can be mentioned here.[85]

Throughout his *Defence*, Wyatt refused to acknowledge any guilt or wrongdoing. In a vigorous rebuttal of the charge of treasonable correspondence with Pole, he explained that he had established contact with him through an intermediary in order to spy on him to obtain intelligence. "To sett spies ouer traytors," he asserted, "ys I thynke no newe practys of Imbassadours."[86] Against the accusation that he "grudged" his earlier imprisonment and sought out Pole from malice and desire to see the king's affairs miscarry, he admitted that while he felt grief and may have complained about his imprisonment, "I never so grudged." It was not in his nature, he said, "to studie to revenge" or injure those who injured him. Besides, he added, he did not impute his imprisonment to the king but to his court enemy the duke of Suffolk.[87] Citing the many signs of the king's confidence he had received after his release, he declared that if not for his zeal for the king's service he would never have wanted to be an ambassador, an office of great cares and burdens, since he was given "to a more pleasant kynde of life."[88]

His interrogators had put to him the dangerous question of whether a man could be a good subject who disliked or repugned his prince's proceedings. To this provocative query he replied that one could dislike something without harm to one's allegiance. He had also been charged with criticizing "the lawe of wordes," an allusion to the novel treason statute of 1534, which made not only certain actions but words as well a treasonable offense. Although denying that he had spoken critically of this law, he nevertheless maintained that even if he had done so it would not be treason or illegal. He was further alleged to have stated that while it was a good act to make the king supreme head of the church because of his virtue and wisdom, the same authority would be a "sore roode" if it fell to an evil prince. This, a possible impugning of the royal supremacy in religion, was perilous ground; yet Wyatt answered that he had not misspoken, "for all powers . . . absolute ar sore roodes when theie fall into evell mens handes and yet I say theie ar to be obeied by expres lawe of god."[89] He ended by urging his clearance of all charges, contending that it dishonored the king to suppose that he would be angry if a man accused of treason were acquitted. "God be thanked," he said, the king "is no tyrant" and willed only his laws, which he tempered with mercy. He even went so far as to bring up the recent trial of Lord Dacre, the sole case in Henry VIII's reign of a defendant ever acquitted of a charge of treason. Wyatt told his judges that the king took no displeasure from Dacre's acquittal and would feel none toward them for following their conscience in respect to himself.[90]

Wyatt probably never delivered this extraordinary statement, since there is no evidence that he was put on trial. Instead, according to a letter of the Privy Council, the queen, Catherine Howard, interceded for him and he was pardoned after confessing his offenses and suing for the king's mercy. The Spanish ambassador reported that he gained his pardon on condition that he acknowledged his guilt and resumed conjugal relations with his long-separated wife. The French ambassador, on the other hand, indicated only that he was pardoned for his great wit and his services past and to come.[91]

It is possible to interpret Wyatt's submission, as Alistair Fox does, as an abject collapse that deprived him of his last vestiges of self-respect and left him altogether broken in spirit.[92] A much likelier explanation, though, is that he went through the motions of confession and petitioning for mercy in order to save his life and regain his freedom. Only by appeasing the king in this way did he have any chance of survival.[93] On another occasion when Henry VIII spared a royal servant suspected of treasonable association after he admitted his wrongdoing and promised to reform, the king said, "Wot you what, you know what my nature and custom hath been in such matters, evermore to pardon them that will not dissemble but confess their faults."[94] The short poem to Sir Francis Bryan, **"Sighs are my food, drink are my tears,"** which Wyatt probably wrote while in prison at the time, makes it plain that he preserved his conviction of innocence. Moreover, in spite of its complaint of "fetters" and that "Stink and close air away my life wears," its conclusion is not devoid of hope: "Sure I am, Brian, this wound shall heal again / But yet, alas, the scar shall still remain."[95]

Wyatt resumed his career at court after his release, receiving fresh indications in the succeeding months that he had not fallen out of favor. It was on a hurried journey at the king's command to meet and escort a Spanish envoy to London that he contracted the fever of which he died suddenly in October 1542.[96] Among the poems dating from his last years is **"Mine own John Poyntz,"** the strongest of his anticourt satires.[97] Editors have agreed in assigning this work to the period after one or the other of his imprisonments in 1536 and 1541. The latter year is perhaps the more likely, however, in light of lines 89-96, which speak of France, Spain, and Flanders as countries the author has known in the past and may thus imply a date subsequent to the completion of his embassies.[98]

Cast in the form of a verse epistle to his friend and fellow courtier John Poyntz,[99] the satire was a translation and adaptation of an Italian original, an attack on the corruption of courts by Luigi Alamanni, a Florentine republican exile.[100] That Wyatt chose Alamanni's work as the model for one of his finest compositions shows how compelling its subject must have been to him. His own version is spirited and outspoken, and whether dating from 1541 or four or five years before, it could not possibly have been written by a man demoralized and stripped of self-confidence and self-respect.

The satire's subject is the difference between the evils of the court and the goodness of a private life in the country. At the outset the poet explains to Poyntz that he has fled the court to live at home, where he need no longer be in thralldom (ll. 1-6). He continues that he cannot esteem the great and powerful as the common people do, who judge only by outward show; and although confessing that he sometimes desires glory, he asks how he can attain it when he cannot lie and praise those steeped in vice (7-21). The main body of the poem is an indictment of the court's corruptions in which the poet proclaims his refusal to comply with them. "I cannot," he repeats again and again. Thus, he cannot crouch or kneel "To worship them like God on earth alone / That are like wolves these silly lambs among" (26-28). He cannot "speak and look like a saint," "Use wiles for wit and make deceit a pleasure / And call craft counsel," nor "wrest the law to fill the coffer, / With innocent blood to fee myself fat / And do most hurt where most help I offer" (31-36). He cannot "On other's lust . . . hang both night and day"; call vice virtue, drunkenness good fellowship, cruelty zeal of justice, or the lecher a lover (55-74).

Amidst this catalog of vices, the poet also touches a directly political note when he states that he cannot call "tyranny . . . the right of a prince's reign" (74-75). Although this line follows Alamanni's original ("Ne che'l tyranneggiar sia giusto impero"), it could be an allusion to Henry VIII. It should be compared, however, with the statement in Wyatt's *Defence* thanking God that the king is no tyrant. In an earlier passage the poet declares his unwillingness to condemn Cato to death, who escaped from Caesar's hands by suicide because he "would not live where liberty was lost" (37-41). Alamanni had written that he could not honor Caesar and Sulla with immor-

tal praise while wrongly condemning Brutus ("Non di loda honorar chiara immortale / Caesar & Sylla, condannando à torto Bruto"). For Brutus Wyatt substituted Cato, perhaps considering it unsafe to celebrate a monarch's assassin.

The satire reaches its resolution after a final, emphatic, "I cannot, I! No, no, it will not be!", as the poet announces that he will remain at home

> to hunt and to hawk
> And in foul weather at my book to sit;
> In frost and snow then with my bow to stalk.
> No man doth mark whereso I ride or go;
> In lusty leas in liberty I walk.
>
> (76-84)

The closing verse invited Poyntz to join him in his cheerful rural freedom:

> But here I am in Kent and Christendom
> Among the muses where I read and rhyme,
> Where if you list, my Poyntz, for to come,
> Thou shalt be judge how I do spend my time.
>
> (100-104)

"Mine own John Poyntz" stands out as one of the most forcible statements of the anticourt theme in sixteenth-century English literature. A moral condemnation of the court and courtiership with strong political overtones, its power lies in its penetrating exposure of the evil practices that courtiers cover under false and flattering names and in the contrast it presents between the court's servitude and the liberty and innocence of country living. Ambivalence, nevertheless, is implicit in the poem. For while it represents the poet's strongest expression of alienation and resolve to quit the court, the reader knows that this resolution cannot last, that the poet's fortune is still linked to the court, and that he must return to it when the king requires his service.

The two remaining satires by Wyatt, likewise in the form of verse epistles, were also probably written in the aftermath of his imprisonment in 1536 or 1541. One of them, **"My mother's maids when they did sew and spin,"** was again addressed to John Poyntz,[101] the other, **"A spending hand that alway poureth out,"** to Sir Francis Bryan.[102]

The first of these satires centers on the folly of a misguided life, including the misguided aims and ambition of the courtier. It relates a witty variation on Aesop's fable of the town and country mouse, which the poet's mother's maids used to sing as they spun. The country mouse, cold and hungry in her rural hole, goes to see her sister in town, hoping to live and feed better there. She is warmly welcomed and given good food and drink, when suddenly the cat appears. The town mouse flees, but the country mouse is caught, and though we are not told the end, it looks as if the cat will kill her. Her mistake was to forget "her poor surety and rest / For seeming wealth wherein she thought to reign" (68-69). The fable illustrates how men that seek the best "find the worst by error as they stray" (70-71). Its moral is that men should cease their foolish travail and striving for wealth and power, which bring only cares and burdens, and live content with what God has assigned them (95-96). Good does not lie in external things; therefore, "seek no more out of thyself to find / The thing that thou hast sought so long before, For thou shalt feel it sitting in thy mind." As for himself, the poet tells Poyntz, "these wretched fools shall have naught else of me," and he prays God that in their lust and departure from the right they may suffer the inward pain of knowing they have lost their virtue (104-12).

This satire reads like the courtier's consolation against the woes he has endured from the "wretched fools" in court. He finds a classic Stoic solution for these woes by vowing to renounce the futile competition for worldly goods and turning for refuge to an inner tranquillity of mind. In connection with this poem, it is of considerable significance that the only work Wyatt published during his lifetime was an English translation in 1528 of Plutarch's *De Tranquillitate et securitate animi,* made from Guillaume Budé's Latin rendering of the Greek original and dedicated to Catherine of Aragon.[103] Plutarch's treatise explores some of the same moral problems as **"My mother's maids"** and also asks in passing what use there is in the appearance of glory among courtiers.[104] There is no doubt that the idea of an inner stability and peace of mind against the blows of fortune through mastery of the affections had a strong and lasting appeal for Wyatt and was a reflection of his ambivalence toward court life and its demands.

The other satire, **"A spending hand that alway poureth out,"** had its principal source in a satire by Horace against various Roman types of parasites and flatterers. Tottel's miscellany, in which Wyatt's poem was first printed, entitled it, "How to use the court and himself therein, to Sir Francis Brian."[105] The author appears in it as the witty devil's advocate turning old proverbial sayings to his bad purpose, while his friend Bryan stands as the spokesman for a moral idea of public service. The poet both writes to Bryan and engages in dialogue with him, as he chides him for his extravagant expenditure and incessant "running day and night / From realm to realm, from city, street, and town," in disregard of the wise old proverbs that a spending hand must bring in as fast as it pours out and a rolling stone gathers no moss. Why, he asks, does Bryan wear his body to the bones rather than take his rest at home, drinking good ale and feeding himself fat (1-18)? His friend replies that the latter kind of life is fit only for swine, and that he will serve his prince, "my lord and thine, / And let them live to feed the paunch that list, / So I may feed to live, both me and mine" (18-27). The poet proceeds to counsel Bryan by offering him some ironical advice on how "to bring in as fast as thou dost spend." He should flee truth and gain friends by flattery; "use virtue as it goeth now-a-days," in words but not deeds; play the sycophant to rich men, marry a wealthy old widow, or prostitute a sister or daughter "if she be fair, if handsome be her middle"; think only of himself, "for friendship bears no prize" (33-78). Bryan laughingly

spurns this "thrifty jest"; he would not for any amount of wealth lose his honest name, which next to "godly things" he values most. If that is the case, responds the poet in conclusion, then Bryan will have to be content with "honest poverty" and with adversity on account of his "free tongue" and attachment to truth (80-91).

This last of Wyatt's satires once again stigmatizes the vices of the court, notably falsity and unscrupulous pursuit of gain. It has been claimed that Wyatt wrote it as a direct comment on Castiglione's *Book of the Courtier,* in which he confronted the ideal of the courtier with the reality.[106] There is nothing in it, however, nor in any of Wyatt's other writings, to indicate that he was acquainted with Castiglione's work or could have had it in mind. It is a further irony in the poem that he presents his friend Bryan as an emblem of rectitude. This picture did not chime with the latter's reputation, for while known for his free speaking, he was also noted for dissoluteness, so much so that Cromwell spoke of him as "the vicar of hell."[107] As a lifelong courtier and intimate of Henry VIII, Bryan knew better than most how to survive and prosper amidst the vicissitudes of the court. In making him the recipient of his epistle, Wyatt perhaps intensified the satire, since it is he, the poet, who would most wish to reject the immoral counsel he gives his friend.

In striking contrast to the three epistolary satires is Wyatt's *Paraphrase of the Penitential Psalms,* which constitutes a marked departure from his other poetry in its profoundly religious character. Although it is tempting to regard it as a very late if not his last composition, its contents offer no clue to its date. Like the satires, it could have been written in the period from 1536 to 1537 or any time thereafter.[108] The penitential psalms (Psalms 6, 31, 37, 50, 101, 129, and 142 in the Vulgate) were a common part of medieval devotion, used in connection with the sacrament of penance and in contemplation of death. Wyatt's paraphrase was a translation and imitation with considerable divergences of Pietro Aretino's Italian version of 1534. It took over Aretino's device of setting the seven psalms in a narrative context of the story of David and Bathsheba and expressed David's deep sorrow, fear and despair, remorse, and longing for God's forgiveness because of his adultery with Bathsheba and procurement of her husband Uriah's death (2 Samuel 11-12). Beside Aretino's original, the Vulgate, several Catholic authors, and a recent English translation of the Bible, Wyatt's sources included the Protestant Zwingli's Latin translation of the psalms and certain treatises and scriptual commentaries by the Protestant William Tyndale.[109]

We do not know why Wyatt turned from love poetry and secular themes to a traditional religious subject such as the psalms that resulted in the longest of all his poems. Perhaps the passionate outpouring that characterizes this work was a way of confessing his own sinfulness, repentance, and prayer for divine forgiveness. From the standpoint of his personal history, the most significant aspect of the paraphrase is its indication that he had come to hold the Protestant belief in justification by faith alone. A number of passages (e.g. ll. 217-24, 451-55, 520-24,

648-58) convey the distinct impression that salvation is in no way due to human merit, which "recompenseth not" (219), but only to faith in Christ, who clothes and justifies the sinner with his own righteousness.

Beside its essential religious message of a soul imploring mercy and pardon for the sins it has committed, the paraphrase may also harbor a latent political meaning, since its narrative centers on the sin, fear of God's punishment, and penitence of a great monarch. In a poem praising Wyatt's version of the penitential psalms, the earl of Surrey said that in its theme, "Rewlers may see in a myrrour clere / The bitter frewte of false concupicense," and he concluded with the wish that "In Prynces hartes goddes scourge yprynted depe / Might them awake out of their synfull slepe."[110] The lesson Surrey discerned might thus conceivably imply a veiled allusion to the transgressions of Henry VIII as part of the paraphrase's intentions. Considered still, however, in relation to Wyatt's personal history, his version of the penitential psalms may be read as evidence that in these heartfelt utterances of David he sought the inner strength and spiritual resources he needed to arm himself against the temptations and perils of the courtier's life from which he was never able to escape.

NOTES

[1] This work was first printed at Valladolid in 1539 in a volume with several of Guevara's other works entitled *Las Obras del Illustre Señor Don Antonio de Guevara*. I have used the Spanish text, *Menosprecio de Corte y Alabanza de Aldea*, ed. M. Martínez Burgos (Madrid: Espasa-Calpe, 1952). Bryan's translation was printed in London by Richard Grafton.

[2] Bryan, whose birth date is unrecorded, died in 1550. He is noticed in Leslie Stephen and Sidney Lee, eds., *Dictionary of National Biography*, 22 vols. (Oxford: Oxford University Press, 1963-64), s.v., and his name occurs frequently in J. S. Brewer et al., eds., *Letters and Papers, Foreign and Domestic, of the Reign of Henry VIII*, 21 vols. in 33 pts. (London: H. M. Stationery Office, 1862-1932), but no biography or study of his career exists. David Starkey writes about him in "The Court: Castiglione's Ideal and Tudor Reality: Being a Discussion of Sir Thomas Wyatt's Satire Adressed to Sir Francis Bryan," *Journal of the Warburg and Courtauld Institutes* 45 (1982), and in *The Reign of Henry VIII: Personalities and Politics* (New York: Franklin Watts, 1986), 69-70. Differing accounts of his role in the fall of Anne Boleyn are given by Eric Ives, *Anne Boleyn* (New York: Blackwell, 1988), 372 and Retha M. Warnicke, *The Rise and Fall of Anne Boleyn* (Cambridge: Cambridge University Press, 1989), 207, 299.

[3] Bryan was among the anonymous poets included in Richard Tottel's famous collection, *Songes and Sonnetes* (1557), but his work cannot be identified; see *Tottel's Miscellany 1557-1587*, ed. Hyder E. Rollins, 2 vols., rev. ed. (Cambridge: Harvard University Press, 1965), 2:82. Robert S. Kinsman has printed from a manuscript in the Huntington Library a poem that has been thought to be Bryan's; "'The Proverbes of Salmon Do Playnly Declare': A Sententious Poem Ascribed to Sir Francis Bryan," *Huntington Library Quarterly* 42 (1979): 279-312. A poor and awkward composition, if it is Bryan's it fails to justify his sixteenth-century reputation as a good poet, for which see p. 279 of Kinsman's article.

[4] Pauline Smith, *The Anti-Courtier Trend in Sixteenth-Century French Literature* (Geneva: Droz, 1966), and Claus Uhlig, *Hofkritik im England*

des Mittelalters und der Renaissance (Berlin: Walter de Gruyter, 1973), contain an account of the anticourt and anticourtier literature of the sixteenth century and its antecedents in antiquity, the Middle Ages, and the Italian Renaissance; see also the discussion in Perez Zagorin, *Rebels and Rulers 1500-1660*, 2 vols. (Cambridge: Cambridge University Press, 1982), 1:103-6.

[5] Augustin Redondo, *Antonio de Guevara (1480?-1545) et l'Espagne de son temps. De la carrière officielle aux oeuvres politico-morales* (Geneva: Droz, 1976), contains the fullest account of Guevara's life, career at court, and writings. Joseph R. Jones, *Antonio de Guevara* (Boston: Twayne, 1975), is a brief survey of his life and works.

[6] The colophon of Berner's translation of Guevara's *Libro Aureo de Marco Aurelio* states that it was done "at the instant desyre of his neuewe syr Francis Bryan"; cited in K. N. Colville's introduction to Sir Thomas North's translation of Guevara's *Relox de Principes, The Diall of Princes*, published in 1557 (London: Philip Allan, 1919), xv.

[7] The French version Bryan used was done by Antoine Alègre and published in 1542 by Dolet of Lyons under the title, *Du Mepris de la court et de la louange de la vie rusticque*. Bryan's translation was reprinted in 1575 as *A Looking Glasse for the Court*.

[8] *A Dispraise of the Life of a Courtier*, sig. aii; the dedication of Wyatt's paraphrase of the penitential psalms to the marquis of Northampton is mentioned in DNB, s.v. "Sir Thomas Wyatt," which gives the original title of this posthumously printed work as *Certayne Psalmes Chosen Out of the Psalter of David Commonly Called the VII Penytentiall Psalmes, Drawen into Englyshe Meter by Sir Thomas Wyatt Knight*.

[9] Baldassare Castiglione, *Il Libro del Cortegiano* (1528), in *Opere di Baldassare Castiglione, Giovanni della Casa, Benvenuto Cellini*, ed. Carlo Cordié (Milan: Ricciardi Editore, n.d.).

[10] Redondo, *Antonio de Guevara*, 390. Juan Boscán's translation of Castiglione's work appeared in Barcelona in 1534; see Redondo, 374.

[11] See the discussion and references in Perez Zagorin, *Ways of Lying: Dissimulation, Persecution, and Conformity* (Cambridge: Harvard University Press, 1990), 7-8, and the essays by David Javitch, "*Il Cortegiano* and the Constraints of Despotism," and Eduardo Saccone, "*Grazia, Sprezzatura, Affetazione*," in Robert W. Hanning and David Rosand, eds., *Castiglione: The Ideal and the Real in Renaissance Culture* (New Haven: Yale University Press, 1983).

[12] Redondo, *Guevara*, chap. 10; *Dispraise*, chap. 1.

[13] *Dispraise*, chaps. 11, 13.

[14] Ibid., chap. 3.

[15] Ibid., chaps. 8, 9, 11.

[16] Ibid., sigs. giiii, hi.

[17] Ibid., chap. 12, sig. IiiV.

[18] Ibid., chap. 15, sig. kviii.

[19] Ibid., chaps. 18-19; Redondo, *Antonio de Guevara*, chap. 7.

[20] *Dispraise,* chap. 20.

[21] See the French translator's epistle to Guillaume Duprat, bishop of Clermont, dated 1 May 1542, ibid., sig. avv.

[22] *Menosprecio,* 1; *Dispraise,* sig. aiiv.

[23] Muir discusses Wyatt's relationship and attitude to the court in his *Life and Letters of Sir Thomas Wyatt* (Liverpool: Liverpool University Press, 1963) and some of the notes in *Collected Poems of Sir Thomas Wyatt,* ed. Kenneth Muir and Patricia Thomson (Liverpool: Liverpool University Press, 1969); Fox does so in *Politics and Literature in the Reign of Henry VIII* (Oxford: Blackwell, 1989), chap. 14. Other works that deal with this subject include Raymond Southall, *The Courtly Maker* (Oxford: Basil Blackwell, 1964), one of the best accounts in its contextualization of Wyatt's poetry relative to the world of the court; Stephen Greenblatt, *Renaissance Self-Fashioning from More to Shakespeare* (Chicago: University of Chicago Press, 1980), chap. 3; H. A. Mason, *Sir Thomas Wyatt: A Literary Portrait* (Bristol: Bristol Classical Press, 1986); Stephen M. Foley, *Sir Thomas Wyatt* (Boston: Twayne, 1990).

[24] For the career of Sir Henry Wyatt and the life of Sir Thomas Wyatt, I have relied on the information and documents in Muir, *Life and Letters,* eked out by a few additional details I have culled from *Letters and Papers . . . of the Reign of Henry VIII,* Muir's principal source; for Sir Thomas Wyatt's early life and family background, see Muir, *Life and Letters,* chap. 1.

[25] Ibid., 4; *Letters and Papers . . . of the Reign of Henry VIII,* vol. 2, pt. 1, no. 2735.

[26] See David Starkey, "Intimacy and Innovation: The Rise of the Privy Chamber 1485-1547," in idem, ed., *The English Court from the Wars of the Roses to the Civil War* (New York: Longman, 1987).

[27] Cited in ibid., 102.

[28] Some of the letters from Thomas Cromwell, Henry VIII's chief minister, to Wyatt on his diplomatic mission were addressed to him not only as the king's ambassador, but as "gentilman of the Kinges Chambre" or "gentilman of the kinges prive chambre"; R. B. Merriman, *Life and Letters of Thomas Cromwell,* 2 vols. (Oxford: Clarendon, 1902; reprint 1968), 2: 158, 167, 179, 186, 211, 213.

[29] Holbein was in England during the years 1526-27 and for a considerable part of the period from 1532 until his death in 1543. K. T. Parker dates his drawing of Wyatt about 1537 or later; *The Drawings of Hans Holbein . . . at Windsor Castle* (Oxford: Oxford University Press, 1945), 53-54.

[30] *Chronicle of King Henry VIII of England,* ed. M. A. S. Hume (London: G. Bell and Sons, 1889), 63.

[31] Printed in Muir, *Life and Letters,* 218-19.

[32] The sentiment in these verses by Leland makes one think that he had read Wyatt's anticourt satire, "Mine Own John Poyntz," for which see below; they are part of a group of Latin funeral elegies for Wyatt and are printed in Muir, *Life and Letters,* 269.

[33] Printed in ibid., 40.

[34] For Sir Henry Norris, see DNB, s.v., and Ives, *Anne Boleyn,* chaps. 16-17.

[35] On Carew and his execution, see DNB, s.v.; G. R. Elton, *Reform and Reformation: England 1509-1558* (Cambridge: Harvard University Press, 1977), 280; Starkey, *The Reign of Henry VIII,* 118-19.

[36] Quoted in Muriel S. Byrne, ed., *The Lisle Letters,* 6 vols. (Chicago: University of Chicago Press, 1981), 6: 168-69.

[37] See Zagorin, *Ways of Lying,* 8.

[38] *Lisle Letters,* 5:115, 116, letter of 2 May 1538.

[39] Ibid., 50, letter of February 1538.

[40] Ibid., 2:92, letter of 1 April 1534.

[41] Ibid., 4:152, letter of 17 July 1537.

[42] Printed in Merriman, *Life and Letters of Thomas Cromwell,* 2:93.

[43] See the account of Cromwell's fall in Elton, *Reform and Reformation,* 288-93.

[44] *Sir Thomas Wyatt: The Complete Poems,* ed. Ronald Rebholz (Harmonds-worth: Penguin, 1978), XXIX, p. 86. I cite all of Wyatt's poems from this edition. Although this sonnet is an imitation of Petrarch's *Rime,* XXLXIX, "Rotta e l'alta colonna," it resounds with authentic personal feeling. For the likelihood that it refers to Cromwell, see the note in Wyatt, *Poems,* ed. Rebholz, 357.

[45] The critical appreciations of Wyatt's poetry all discuss his imitations and translations from Italian and French poets, in particular Petrarch's *Rime,* and his metrical innovations and experiments based on foreign models. *Wyatt: The Critical Heritage,* ed. Patricia Thomson (London: Routledge & Kegan Paul, 1974), contains a selection of important writings on Wyatt's work, including G. F. Nott's introduction to the earliest scholarly edition of the poems in 1816, and the noteworthy discussions by John M. Berdan in *Early Tudor Poetry* (1920), E. M. W. Tillyard in his introduction to *The Poetry of Sir Thomas Wyatt* (1929), and C. S. Lewis in his *English Literature in the Sixteenth Century* (1954). Muir, *Life and Letters,* chap. 8, presents a critical estimate of Wyatt's achievement as a poet. Rebholz, in his edition of Wyatt's poems, 59-67, provides a good bibliography of work relating to Wyatt, while Foley's discussion of the poetry also contains a brief review of the literature on Wyatt and a selective bibliography (pp. 106-12, 122-25) that includes both literary and historical studies. To the latter should be added H. A. Mason, ed., *Sir Thomas Wyatt: A Literary Portrait* (Bristol: Bristol Classical Press, 1986).

[46] See Muir, *Life and Letters,* 8.

[47] See H. A. Mason, *Humanism and Poetry in the Early Tudor Period* (London: Routledge & Kegan Paul, 1959), 146. Apart from his paraphrase of the penitential psalms, published in 1549, none of Wyatt's poems appeared in print until 1557, when Richard Tottel's miscellany, *Songes and Sonnetes,* included a selection. The several editors and scholars of Wyatt's work have discussed the various manuscripts of his poetry, the problem of determining the best text, and, in a number of instances, the problem of distinguishing his authorship from that of other poets of the court, which has made the establishment of a definitive canon an impossibility; on this subject, beside the editions of Rebholz and Muir and Thomson, see Southall, *The Courtly Maker,* chap. 2 and appendices A and B; *Sir Thomas Wyatt: Collected Poems,* ed. Joost Daalder (London: Oxford University Press, 1975); Richard Harrier, *The Canon of Sir Thomas Wyatt's Poetry* (Cambridge: Harvard University Press, 1975); and H.

A. Mason's critique of the edition of Muir and Thomson, *Editing Wyatt: An Examination of "Collected Poems of Sir Thomas Wyatt"* (Cambridge: Cambridge Quarterly Publications, 1972).

[48] C. S. Lewis, *English Literature in the Sixteenth Century* (Oxford: Clarendon, 1954), 229.

[49] *Poems,* ed. Rebholz, 1, p. 71.

[50] Ibid., CCXLI, pp. 296-97; Muir and Thomson include this poem, CLXXIV, p. 185, but Daalder omits it, presumably on the ground that it is not by Wyatt.

[51] *Poems,* ed. Rebholz, IV, p. 72. Greenblatt, *Renaissance Self-Fashioning,* 143, cites this poem as an illustration of the relationship between erotic disillusionment and Wyatt's experience of deception in his service as a diplomat. It relates much more directly, however, to the court milieu of which he was part.

[52] *Poems,* ed. Rebholz, CCXLIV, p. 300, ll. 18, 21, 25, 30.

[53] Ibid., XIV, p. 78, ll. 13-14; "bearing in hand" = pretending.

[54] Ibid., CCIV, p. 263, l. 18.

[55] Ibid., XCI, p. 126, ll. 5-7, 22-23, 28. This poem is omitted in Daalder.

[56] *Poems,* ed. Rebholz, CCVIII, p. 266, l. 9.

[57] Ibid., CLXXXVI, p. 245, ll. 10-11.

[58] Ibid., CCLIII, p. 312, ll. 33-34.

[59] Ibid., XXII, p. 82, ll. 5-6.

[60] Ibid., CCXLVI, p. 302. Daalder omits this poem.

[61] *Poems,* ed. Rebholz, XLIX, p. 94. This poem, a translation of some lines from Seneca's *Thyestes,* bore the title in Tottle's miscellany, where it was first printed, "Of the mean and sure estate."

[62] *Poems,* ed. Rebholz, LII, p. 95.

[63] Ibid., LXX, p. 101.

[64] Ibid., LXVIII, p. 101.

[65] Ibid., LXXI, p. 102. Mason, *Sir Thomas Wyatt,* 229-44, in an interesting commentary on four of the five poems I have cited in this paragraph, places them all under the heading, "Wyatt and the Court."

[66] Ives, *Anne Boleyn,* chaps. 16-17, and Warnicke, *The Rise and Fall of Anne Boleyn,* chap. 8, give details concerning Anne's fall, although they disagree sharply in their explanation of this event. Muir, *Life and Letters,* 28, discusses Wyatt's involvement. DNB, "Sir Thomas Wyatt," states the dates of Wyatt's arrest and release, but Ives, *Anne Boleyn,* 373, gives the day of his arrest as 8 May. For Bryan's summoning and interrogation, see *Letters and Papers . . . of the Reign of Henry VIII,* vol. 13, pt. 1, no. 981; for rumors that Wyatt would be executed, see *Lisle Letters,* 3:361. Cromwell's letter to Sir Henry Wyatt has not survived, but Muir, *Life and Letters,* 31, prints the latter's reply, expressing gratitude for the pains the minister had taken on his son's behalf.

[67] Ives, *Anne Boleyn,* chap. 17; Warnicke, *The Rise and Fall of Anne Boleyn,* chap. 8. G. W. Bernard, "The Fall of Anne Boleyn," *English Historical Review* 106, no. 420 (1991): 584-610.

[68] It is impossible to accept Warnicke's explanation (*The Rise and Fall of Anne Boleyn,* 230), that he was arrested because of "his reputation as a libertine." Bryan had an even worse reputation on this score, yet he was not detained.

[69] *Chronicle of Henry VIII,* 63-64.

[70] *Letters and Papers . . . of the Reign of Henry VIII,* vol. 6, no. 601; Muir, *Life and Letters,* 29-30.

[71] Muir, *Life and Letters,* chap. 2, quotes and summarizes these reports.

[72] Warnicke, *The Rise and Fall of Anne Boleyn,* 64-68 and Appendix C, and see also her article "The Eternal Triangle and Court Politics: Henry VIII, Anne Boleyn, and Sir Thomas Wyatt," *Albion* 18 (1986): 565-79; Ives, *Anne Boleyn,* 83-97.

[73] *Poems,* ed. Rebholz, XI, p. 77; see the commentary on this sonnet in *Poems,* ed. Muir and Thomson, 266-67.

[74] *Poems,* ed. Rebholz, LIV, p. 96.

[75] Ibid., XXVIII, p. 85; see the note of Muir and Thomson on l. 8, p. 335. Warnicke's argument in *The Rise and Fall of Anne Boleyn,* Appendix C, that this sonnet does not refer to Anne Boleyn is unpersuasive. She is probably mistaken in her supposition that "country" in the eighth line signified that the county of Kent, not England, was set in a roar, so that "Brunet" could have been Wyatt's wife or some other woman from Kent. Wyatt, however, used "country" to mean England, as in "Tagus farewell," written on his departure from Spain, where he speaks of "my king, my country." She is also mistaken in her belief that no one has yet speculated about the identity of "Phyllis" in this sonnet and in her own far-fetched conjecture on this subject. E. K. Chambers made the plausible suggestion that "Phyllis" is Elizabeth Darrell, who became Wyatt's mistress and whom he loved and remembered in his will; see the note in *Poems,* ed. Muir and Thomson, 335.

[76] *Poems,* ed. Rebholz, LV, p. 96, and note, p. 374.

[77] Ibid., CXXIII, p. 155, and note, p. 424. According to one report, the men accused with Anne Boleyn were beheaded on Tower Hill, she herself within the Tower; *Lisle Letters,* 3:365. It is not certain whether what Wyatt saw from his cell was their execution or hers.

[78] Muir, *Life and Letters,* 35; Fox, *Politics and Literature,* 265, 266-68. In disagreement with Muir, Mason, *Sir Thomas Wyatt,* 2-3, denies that Wyatt was a "burnt-out case" because of the death of Anne and his friends.

[79] Muir, *Life and Letters,* 35-36, prints this letter.

[80] Ibid., 26, 37; *Letters and Papers . . . of the Reign of Henry VIII,* vol. 11, no. 1217 (23). Even while still in the Tower, Wyatt seems to have tried to obtain the office of Marshal of Calais, which he had once held previously; *Lisle Letters,* 3:282.

[81] Muir, *Life and Letters,* chaps. 3-4, prints Wyatt's diplomatic correspondence with Cromwell and the king; Merriman, *Life and Letters of Thomas Cromwell,* vol. 2, passim, print's Cromwell's letters to Wyatt.

[82] For Bonner's letters, see Muir, *Life and Letters*, 64-69, 70, 83; *Letters and Papers . . . of the Reign of Henry VIII*, vol. 13, pt. 2, no. 615.

[83] Toward the end of his embassy to Spain, however, Wyatt believed he had fallen under suspicion. On 2 January 1539, in a letter to Cromwell not printed in Muir, he wrote, "Some tell me here I am in suspect with the King and you," and asked to be recalled; *Letters and Papers . . . of the Reign of Henry VIII*, vol. 14, pt. 1, no. 11. Cromwell nevertheless gave no sign of withdrawing his support, and Wyatt remained at his post for another six months before being permitted to come home.

[84] Muir, *Life and Letters*, 175-77.

[85] Both of Wyatt's statements are printed in ibid., 178-209.

[86] Ibid., 195. Later in the statement Wyatt said that Cromwell had probably instructed Bonner to spy on him, just as he had wanted Wyatt to spy on Bishop Gardiner, the king's ambassador to France (ibid., 207).

[87] Ibid., 200-201.

[88] Ibid., 202-3.

[89] Ibid., 204-5. See G. R. Elton, *The Tudor Constitution*, 2nd ed. (Cambridge: Cambridge University Press, 1982), 62-64, for the treason statute of 1534, 26 Henry VIII, c. 13.

[90] Muir, *Life and Letters*, 208. William Lord Dacre, fourth baron Dacre of Gilsland, was acquitted by his peers in 1534 of treasonable collusion with the Scots. The charge is said to have originated from his enemies with Cromwell's support, and Dacre was improbably reported to have spoken for seven hours in his own defense; see Penry Williams, *The Tudor Regime* (Oxford: Clarendon, 1979), 381, and Kenneth Pickthorn, *Early Tudor Government: Henry VIII* (Cambridge: Cambridge University Press, 1934), 243.

[91] Muir, *Life and Letters*, 209-10.

[92] Fox, *Politics and Literature*, 279-80. Fox cites as evidence the ballad, "Like as the bird in the cage enclosed" (*Poems*, ed. Rebholz, XC, p. 125), which he supposes to be a prison poem and assigns to this time as an expression of Wyatt's despair. He has failed to observe that this poem is addressed to "you lovers," as the last verse states, and that its subject, as editors have noted, is the lover's dilemma, for which death and prison are metaphors; see the editions of Rebholz, 406, and Daalder, 213. Moreover, the choice the lover in the poem must make is between death and prison, whereas Wyatt's choice in the Tower in 1541 was between death and freedom through confession and submission.

[93] This is the explanation proposed by Byrne, the editor of *The Lisle Letters*; see her acute discussion of Wyatt's case, 6:242, 244-45, 248-52.

[94] Cited in Lacey B. Smith, *Henry VIII: The Mask of Royalty* (Boston: Houghton Mifflin, 1971), 21. The king made this statement in 1544 with reference to Stephen Gardiner, bishop of Winchester, suspected of treason because of his association with his nephew, Germain Gardiner, who had denied royal supremacy in religion.

[95] *Poems*, ed. Rebholz, LXII, p. 99; see Rebholz's editorial note, p. 379, and that of Daalder, p. 209.

[96] Muir, *Life and Letters*, 211-12, 215-16.

[97] *Poems*, ed. Rebholz, CXLIX, pp. 186-89.

[98] For the poem's possible dates, see the comments in Muir, *Life and Letters*, 251; *Poems*, ed. Muir and Thomson, 349; *Poems*, ed. Rebholz, 437-38; Mason, *Sir Thomas Wyatt*, 266; *Poems*, ed. Daalder, 100.

[99] Poyntz was a member of the royal household. Among the drawings at Windsor Castle is a fine one of him that has been attributed to Holbein; see Parker, *The Drawings of Hans Holbein*, 50.

[100] On Luigi Alamanni, see Felix Gilbert, *Machiavelli and Guicciardini* (Princeton: Princeton University Press, 1965), 141, and J. G. Pocock, *The Machiavellian Moment* (Princeton: Princeton University Press, 1975), 151. Rudolf von Albertini, *Das florentinische Staatsbewusstsein im Übergang von der Republik zum Prinzipat* (Bern: Francke, 1955), contains many references to the political ideas of several members of the Alamanni family. The text of Luigi Alamanni's satire addressed to Tommaso Sertini, which served as Wyatt's model, was published in his *Opere Toscane* in 1532. It is printed in Wyatt, *Poems*, ed. Muir and Thomson, 347-49, and with an English prose translation in Mason, *Sir Thomas Wyatt*, 260-66.

[101] *Poems*, ed. Rebholz, CL, pp. 189-92.

[102] Ibid., CLI, pp. 192-94.

[103] *Tbo. Wyatis Translatyon of Plutarkes Boke of the Quyete of Mynde*, with its dedication to Catherine of Aragon dated 31 December 1527, is reprinted in *Poems*, ed. Muir and Thomson, 440-63.

[104] Ibid., 442.

[105] See the note in *Poems*, ed. Rebholz, 449.

[106] This is David Starkey's argument in his discussion of the poem in "The Court: Castiglione's Ideal and Tudor Reality."

[107] DNB, s.v. "Sir Francis Bryan"; Merriman, *Life and Letters of Thomas Cromwell*, 2:12.

[108] Editors have generally ascribed the work either to 1536 or 1541; see the discussion in *Poems*, ed. Rebholz, 455, which concludes that a precise dating is impossible.

[109] For the sources of Wyatt's paraphrase, see *Poems*, ed. Rebholz, 452-53, and the discussion and commentary by Mason, *Sir Thomas Wyatt*, 153-220.

[110] Printed in Wyatt, *Poems*, ed. Muir and Thomson, 98.

FURTHER READING

Bath, Michael. "Wyatt and 'Liberty,'" in *Essays in Criticism* XXIII, No. 3 (July 1973): 322-28.

Tries to resolve the "running discussion" of Wyatt's treatment of the concept of "liberty" as an issue raised by two prominent scholars of his work, Boyd and Daalder.

Boyd, John Douglas Boyd. "Literary Interpretation and the *Subjective* Correlative: An Illustration from Wyatt," in *Essays in Criticism* XXI, No. 4 (October 1971): 327-46.

Presents seven possible critical views of "There Was Never Nothing More Me Payned," illustrating the complex nature of Wyatt's poetry.

————. "The Subjective Correlative," in *Essays in Criticism* XXII, No. 3 (July 1972): 329-31.

In response to Daalder's assessment of Boyd's original article, Boyd clarifies his definition of objectivity within his argument.

Daalder, Joost. "'There Was Never Nothing More Me Payned': A Reply to John Douglas Boyd," in *Essays in Criticism* XXI, No. 4 (October 1971): 418-24.

Refutes the soundness of Boyd's arguments due to lack of textual evidence.

————. "Wyatt and 'Liberty,'" in *Essays in Criticism* XXIII, No. 1 (January 1973): 63-67.

"Liberty" as an attribute of peace of mind as expressed in several of Wyatt's poems.

————. "Wyatt and the Obstacles to Happiness," in *English* XXXII, No. 147 (Autumn 1984): 197-206.

Asserts that Wyatt as speaker of his poems believes his own psychological shortcomings cause his unhappiness.

————. "Wyatt's Prosody Revisited," in *Language and Style* X, No. 1 (Winter 1977): 3-15.

Identifies Wyatt's prosody as transitional, anticipating the iambic meter of his Renaissance successors.

Dasenbrock, Reed Way. "Understanding Renaissance Imitation: The Example of Wyatt." *Imitating the Italians: Wyatt, Spenser, Synge, Pound, Joyce* Baltimore: The John Hopkins University Press, 1991, pp. 19-31.

Asserts that understanding the positive aspects of the Italian poets must precede an evaluation of Wyatt's translations of their work.

Friedman, Donald M. "Wyatt's *Amoris Personae*," in *Modern Language Quarterly* XXVII, No. 2 (June 1966): 136-46.

Focuses on Wyatt's ballads and sonnets as expressions of the courtly "standards" within his time.

Greenblatt, Stephen. "Power, Sexuality, and Inwardness in Wyatt's Poetry," in *Renaissance Self-fashioning: From More to Shakespeare* Chicago: University of Chicago Press, 1980, 115-56.

A detailed analysis of the penitential psalms as indicative of an "intense inwardness" caused by the powers of the English high court.

Guss, Donald L. "Wyatt's Petrarchism: An Instance of Creative Imitation in the Renaissance," in *The Huntington Library Quarterly* XXIX, No. 1 (November 1965): 1-15.

Asserts that Wyatt's translations are humanistic, Neo-Stoic versions of Petrarchan rhetoric.

Healing, A. C. A review of *The Poetry of Sir Thomas Wyatt: A Selection and Study*, in *The Review of English Studies* VII, No. 25 (January 1931): 93-95.

Favorably reviews E. M. W. Tillyard's critical edition of Wyatt's poetry.

Heine, Ingeborg. "The Metrical Intentions of Wyatt's Sonnets: 'Who So List to Hount,' 'I Fynde No Peace,' and 'The Longe Love,'" in *Kwartalnik Neofilologiczny* XXV (April 1978): 407-20.

Defends Wyatt's use of a variety of metrical patterns.

Holahan, Michael. "Wyatt, the Heart's Forest, and the Ancient Savings," in *English Literary Renaissance* XXIII, No. 1 (Winter 1993): 46-80.

Commends Wyatt's use of the Petrarchan literary structure, especially in his "Rime 140."

Kerrigan, John. "Wyatt's Selfish Style." *Essays and Studies* XXIV (1981): 1-18.

A survey of Wyatt's verse focusing on his concern with the gambles of chance.

Low, Anthony. "Wyatt's 'What Word is That,'" in *English Language Notes* X, No. 2 (December 1972): 89-90.

Unravels the riddle in Wyatt's poem.

Luria, Maxwell S. "Wyatt's 'The Lover Compareth His State' and the Petrarchan Commentators," in *Texas Studies in Literature and Language* XII, No. 4 (Winter 1971): 531-35.

Suggests that Wyatt's translation of Petrarch reflects the humanist voice of his age.

Major, Virginia Banke. "Love and Legalisms in the Poetry of Sir Thomas Wyatt," in *Essays in Literature* XI, No. 2 (Fall 1984): 177-86.

Compares Wyatt's quest for a truly equal love in marriage compared with the strict moral codes imposed by the English court.

Maynard, Winifred. "The Lyrics of Wyatt: Poems or Songs?" in *The Review of English Studies* XVI, No. 61 (February 1965): 1-13.

Explores Wyatt's lyrics in song.

Muir, Kenneth and Patricia Thomson. A review of *Collected Poems of Sir Thomas Wyatt*, in *The Review of English Studies* XXII, No. 86 (May 1971): 187-89.

Praises the latest edition of Wyatt's *Collected Poems* that updates work from the Egerton and Blage manuscripts.

Richmond, Hugh M. "Wyatt and French 'Newfangledness.'" *Puritans and Libertines* Berkeley: University of California Press, 1981, pp. 149-78.

Centers on Wyatt's involvement with Anne Boleyn and its effect on the creative aspect of his work.

Sells, A. Lytton. "'Two Courtly Makers." *The Italian Influence in English Poetry*. London: George Allen & Unwin Ltd., 1955, pp. 68-81.

Attributes the revitalization of fifteenth-century English poetry to Wyatt as a student of the Italian tradition.

Winser, Leigh. "The Question of Love Tradition in Wyatt's 'They Flee From Me.'" *Essays in Literature* II, No. 1 (Spring 1975): 3-9.

Proposes that Wyatt's lyric follows the Renaissance tradition of posing and debating questions about love.

Additional coverage of Wyatt's life and career is contained in the following sources published by the Gale Group: *Dictionary of Literary Biography*, Vol. 132.

Adam Zagajewski
1945 -

Polish poet, novelist, and essayist

INTRODUCTION

Adam Zagajewski is considered the pre-eminent poet of the generation of Polish writers born after World War II. His literary career began with the protests that swept Poland in the late 1960s and early 1970s, and was primarily concerned with the political struggle to overturn totalitarianism. An exile since 1982, his later poetry addresses themes of both historical and metaphysical alienation. Balancing the concrete and the abstract, irony and mysticism, his poetry no longer advocates a single truth but chronicles the difficult and painful search for meaning in an unsettled world.

Biographical Information

Stanislaw Baranczak identifies Zagajewski as a member of "the generation whose birthdate coincides with the establishment of the Communist order and whose youth was spent rebelling against it." Zagajewski was born on June 21, 1945, in Lvov, in eastern Poland. When Eastern European borders were redrawn after World War II, Lvov became part of the Soviet Ukraine. By 1946 his family was living in Gliwice in western Poland. Zagajewski attended university in Cracow where he was also an editor of the journal *Student*. In March 1968 he participated in student protests against censorship, and this experience shaped his writing. A prominent voice of protest during the early 1970s, Zagajewski was eventually blacklisted by communist authorities. By 1975, he was editing an underground literary periodical called *Zapis* (*The Record*). He lived in Western Europe for several years, returning to Poland in 1981. Martial law was imposed soon after he arrived, and he did not manage to leave again for several months. He now divides his time between Paris and Houston, Texas, where he teaches at the University of Houston for part of each year.

Major Works

Zagajewski first came to prominence in Eastern European literary circles for attacking the generation of Polish poets that preceded him. As a member of a literary movement called the New Wave, he argued that poetry should address the social and political needs of the present day. In 1974 he and Julian Kornhauser published *Swiat nie przedstawiony* (*The World Not Represented*), a collection of essays criticizing older authors for endorsing an abstract, contemplative poetry that failed to do enough to change the totalitarian regime in Poland. Zagajewski maintained that poetry should remain focused on the "here and

now," and he advocated for a direct and unambiguous poetic language to represent the truth about current conditions in Poland. Straight talk would, he believed, undo or subvert the traditional "double-speak" of the communist party. This kind of language characterizes his first two collections of poetry, *Komunikat* (1972; *Bulletin*) and *Sklespy miesne* (1975; *Meat Market*).

Following the imposition of martial law and the beginning of his exile in Paris, Zagajewski began what Adam Kirsch called his "flight from history." He became increasingly concerned with defining a mission for poetry that encompassed, rather than served, politics. *Tremor: Selected Poems* (1985) includes the poems he wrote during his first few years in Paris. His first book translated into English, *Tremor* transcends the poetry of protest and confronts the multiplicity of individual experience. During the 1980s and 90s, his poetry became increasingly contemplative and metaphysical. In an essay published in *Solidarity, Solitude* (1990), Zagajewski writes "We have to conquer totalitarianism in passing, on our way to greater things . . ."; his focus shifted from the limitations of a communist regime to the psychological, moral, and spiritual restrictions on human existence. The poetry in *Canvas* (1991) displays a fascination with the mysterious or divine aspects of people. Here Zagajewski expresses his frustration with our conceptual development, rather than our political progress, as he writes of "dreams of imagination / homeless and mad." The theme of imaginative alienation continues in *Mysticism for Beginners* (1997). In these poems, Zagajewski attempts to restore mystery and ecstasy to modern poetry, as he expresses the conflict between his urge to accept the world and his impulse to flee from it.

Critical Reception

The arc of Zagajewski's career, from politics to mysticism, has shaped the critical debate about his poetry. In an introduction to *Tremor*, Czeslaw Milosz observed that protest poetry is "noble-minded, but often one-dimensional," and he praised Zagajewski for moving beyond political poetry. Most critics have echoed this praise, though all agree that history and politics retain an important role in his work. Scholar and poet Stanislaw Baranczak states that the historical context "cannot really be subtracted from Zagajewski's poems." Poet Robert Pinsky considers Zagajewski's view a recreation of the historical within the mundane, stating that it's "an immense, sometimes subtle force inhering in what people see and feel every day." Critic Adam Kirsch points to Zagajewski's interest in mysticism as "the natural consummation of the private, the ahistorical," emphasizing Zagajewski's synthesis of the concrete and factual with other, more personal opinions.

Zagajewski's poetry has frequently been compared to the work of English metaphysical poets such as John Donne, who often transformed sensual imagery into abstract metaphor. One critic, Eva Hoffman, admires his quest for transcendence that frequently begins with a concrete image: "The movement from a specificity of physical images to a moment of abstraction is characteristic of Mr. Zagajewski's poetry; it corresponds to his delight in the sensuous surfaces of things and his urge toward a disembodied, spiritual insight and for a breaking out of the self." Several critics have observed that Zagajewski's work celebrates the process of discovery, and the theme of transcendence may be what connects politics and metaphysics in his poetry. By contemplating people confined by the social and political constructs that evolved throughout history, he arrives at a deeper and more abstract understanding of the human experience. "Zagajewski may be looking at Eastern Europe," Steven Birkerts writes, "but his gaze wraps itself around the whole globe."

PRINCIPAL WORKS

Poetry

Komunikat 1972 [*Bulletin*]
Śklespy miesne 1975 [*Meat Market*]
List: Oda do wielo ci 1983
Jechać do Lwowa 1985
Tremor: Selected Poems 1985
Plótno 1990 [*Canvas*, 1991]
Mysticism for Beginners 1997

Other Works

Świat nie przedstawiony [with Julian Kornhauser] (essays) 1974 [*The World Not Represented*]
Cieplo, zimno (novel) 1975
Drugi oddech (essays) 1978
Cienka kreska (novel) 1983
Solidarność i samotność (essays) 1990 [*Solidarity, Solitude*, 1990]
Dwa miasta (essays) 1991 [*Two Cities: On Exile, History, and the Imagination* 1995]

CRITICISM

Czeslaw Milosz (essay date 1985)

SOURCE: Introduction to *Tremor: Selected Poems*, by Adam Zagajewski, Farrar Straus Giroux, 1985, pp. xi-xii.

[*In the following introduction to the first English translation of Zagajewski's poems, Milosz praises him for transcending protest poetry and admires "the steady increase of his creative powers."*]

What a joy to see a major poet emerging from a hardly differentiated mass of contemporaries and taking the lead in the poetry of my language, a living proof that Polish literature is energy incessantly renewed against all probabilities! Born in 1945, Zagajewski belonged to the angry "generation of 1968" and started by satirizing both in his verse and in his prose the surreal character of the totalitarian state. While mocking the official language, he gradually developed a taste for expressing the political opposition of his generation through a "naked" speech practically stripped of metaphors. I discovered him then and praised the freshness of his style, not expecting that it marked just a phase in his evolution. For soon he left behind that poetry of political commitment—noble-minded, but often one-dimensional—and embarked upon a new adventure, a search in a labyrinth where meditation on the flow of time brings together the historical and the metaphysical. His poems have been acquiring a more and more sumptuous texture, and now he appears to me as a skillful weaver whose work is not unlike Gobelin tapestries where trees, flowers, and human figures coexist in the same pattern. That rich and complex world re-created and transformed by art is for him not a place of escape. On the contrary, it is related in a peculiar way to the crude reality of our century, even if it is on the other side of "smooth water, an indifferent wave."

Zagajewski's poetry is a homage paid to our Central Europe and to the unity of Europe artificially divided into "the West" and "the East," much as is the prose of Milan Kundera, of George Konrad, or of Danilo Kiš. This unity is symbolized by the cities in which his life unfolded. He cultivates the legend of the city of his birth, Lvov, romantic and international; he grew up in Cracow and there

studied philosophy at the six-hundred-year-old university; he, like several generations of the intelligentsia, was
attracted by Vienna, a cultural center. Those places nourished his imagination and enabled him to converse with
mythic European figures, philosophers, painters, and com-
posers of the past. He is not disinherited, for he has
found his home in the common heritage ever present in
the very art and architecture that surrounded him in his
youth. Judging by the steady increase of his creative power
in the last years, his migration to Paris, where he has
been living since 1981, did not interrupt, but rather guar-
anteed, the continuity of his work by adding distance and
perspective. As I read him, I am inclined to apply his own
words to my feeling of wonder:

> Only in the beauty created
> by others is there consolation.

Stanislaw Baranczak (essay date 1986)

SOURCE: "Alone but Not Lonely," in *The New Republic*,
Vol. 194, No. 1-2, January 6 & 13, 1986, pp. 39-41.

[*In the following review of* Tremor: Selected Poems,
*Baranczak argues that Zagajewski's use of irony rais-
es his work beyond protest poetry.*]

The first of many things that make Adam Zagajewski's
poetry worthy of note is the author's birthdate: 1945. Thus
far, America's acquaintance with the most recent Polish
poetry (if we take only book-length selections of specific
authors into account) has been limited to a few aging giants, now in their 60s or 70s, such as Czeslaw Milosz,
Zbigniew Herbert, Tadeusz Rozewicz, or Wislawa Szymborska. *Tremor* is the first book of poems issued by a
major American publisher that presents one of the "children of People's Poland," the generation whose birthdates
coincide with the establishment of the Communist order
and whose youth was spent rebelling against it.

Of course, the multidimensional meaning of Zagajewski's
poetry can by no means be reduced to that of "a poetry of
protest" or a generational manifesto. The book can (and
should) be read also outside the framework of Poland's
recent history, and it will not lose much this way. After all,
it has something important to say about life, death, love,
loneliness, and other rather universal matters. And yet the
keen sense of history that pervades and distorts contemporary existence seems to be something that cannot really be
subtracted from Zagajewski's poems. While his work contains a wealth of sensuous imagination and philosophical
perspicacity, the reader here is not able to forget that he
is dealing with a poet born and raised in our age and in a
certain corner of Eastern Europe.

In fact, Zagajewski's literary beginnings were marked by
his and his generation's demand that Polish literature be
concerned with *hic et nunc* rather than with universal
issues and ahistorical settings. The poetic group he co-
founded in the late 1960s in Cracow was called *Teraz*
("Now"). His early poems owed a great deal to the experience of student protest in March 1968—a protest directed, on the surface, against the abuses of state censorship but also, in its deeper sense, against the omnipresent
ideological lie of the system—and its having been crushed
in due course by the police and slandered by the official
media. In 1974 he stirred up one of the greatest controversies in postwar Polish culture by co-authoring, with
Julian Kornhauser, a book of criticism titled *The World
Not Represented*—a sweeping assault on the noncommittal literature of the previous decades, with its thematic evasiveness and moral irresolution.

Under the circumstances of communism, even in its relatively mild Polish version of the early 1970s, voices
such as Zagajewski's must, as a rule, be silenced sooner
or later. The "1968 generation" of rebels and truth-seek-
ers had initially been allowed to speak out, but by mid-
decade all its leading representatives found themselves
blacklisted. This generation responded by creating an underground publishing network; Zagajewski, among others, served as co-editor of the first uncensored literary
periodical, the quarterly *Zapis* ("The Record"). After a
few years spent in Western Europe, he returned to Poland at the end of the fateful year 1981, only to witness
the imposition of martial law. It took him more than a
year to obtain another exit visa and leave for Paris, where
he has lived for the past three years and written his best
poems to date. Most of these are included in *Tremor*.

From such a biography, one might expect typically dissident poetry—vociferous protest, moralistic instruction,
and historiosophic generalization, all dutifully put in the
first person plural. Nothing like that takes place in Zagajewski's poems. By his personal inclination, but also by
a deliberate choice, his is a poetry of the first person
singular, the voice of an individual. It only so happens
that this individual's life coincides with that phase of
history when everything—from political systems and ideologies on the one hand to the dictates of one's conscience on the other—forces him to be social and makes
the very notion of individuality suspect. In other words,
if Zagajewski's poetry is a portrayal of an individual mind,
it is a mind torn asunder by opposite tendencies—by a
moral obligation to speak on behalf of others and by a
sense of the necessity of remaining one's unique self. In
the poem **"Fire,"** he says:

> I remember
> the blazing appeal of that fire which
>   parches
> the lips of the thirsty crowd and burns
> books and chars the skin of cities. I
>   used to sing
> those songs and I know how great it is
> to run with others; later, by myself,
> with the taste of ashes in my mouth, I
>   heard
> the lie's ironic voice and the choir
>   screaming
> and when I touched my head I could feel
> the arched skull of my country, its hard
>   edge.

The true "country," the authentic homeland of the individualist, is confined to the circumference of his skull. Whatever remains outside it is either uncertain or inauthentic, marred by banalities and dangerous collective illusions of unity. "The lie's ironic voice" is actually the voice of the poet's own ironic consciousness, which unmasks lies; which, moreover, never allows him to accept anything that is abstract, general, collectivist:

> Who has once met
> irony will burst into laughter
> during the prophet's lecture.
>
> **("Ode to Plurality")**

Irony, the device so characteristic of modern Polish poetry, serves a special purpose in the case of Zagajewski: it is used as a defensive weapon against a uniforming abstractness of ideologies and systems. In this capacity, ironic distance is necessary to take in the whole breathtaking *plurality* (the key philosophical concept in Zagajewski's recent poetry) of the concrete, tangible world. As a consequence, one could consider as ironic (in a positive sense of the word) such otherwise ecstatic hymns, compared by Milosz in his preface to Gobelin tapestries, as the above-quoted **"Ode to Plurality,"** or **"A View of Cracow,"** or the brilliant poem **"To Go to Lvov."**

But irony can also reveal its cutting edge—and it does so whenever Zagajewski writes of any attempt to supersede plurality with a false or shallow unity. **"A Polish Dictionary"** (the title of a poem), a dictionary of the common parlance of the collective imagination, must unavoidably consist of stereotypes: "Lances, banners, sabers, horses . . ." **"A Warsaw Gathering,"** even though it is a gathering of citizens sincerely concerned about their country's freedom (the poem thus titled was written in November 1981), cannot help but be a caricature of a group of people who fall prey to the tyranny of grand words and magnificent designs, whereas "In the last row . . . / The author of this little poem is sitting and dreaming of / music, music." The hero of Zagajewski's poems always sits "in the last row." He is a born dissident who (in the etymological sense of the Latin *dissidere*) always "sits apart"—apart not merely from the servants of the despotic system but, more generally, from any collectivity (even the collectivity of dissidents) that threatens his uniqueness and independence.

If Zagajewski stopped at this point, he would be nothing more than a post-Romantic individualist, a eulogist of self-imposed loneliness. His idea of "sitting apart" is, however, much more complicated. If I were to pinpoint the crucial sentence in *Tremor*, I would single out an almost casual statement that appears in the poem **"A Wanderer":** "I am alone but not lonely." The stance of the ironic individualist finds its counter-balance here in the idea of human solidarity: "Only others save us, / even though solitude tastes like / opium" (from another poem, **"In the Beauty Created by Others"**). If there is any discrepancy in this, it is the natural discrepancy between ontology and ethics. Reality makes us admire its existential plurality; at the same time, however, this plurality also encompasses evil and injustice, things to which we cannot reconcile ourselves because they affect or may affect, more or less directly, our own lives. This becomes particularly evident when we encounter evil masquerading as History. Zagajewski's poems about the reality of martial law in Poland are, naturally enough, no longer passionate hymns to the beauty of the visible world. Instead, they ask desperately:

> Why it has to be December.
> The dark doves of snow fly,
> falling on the slabs of the sidewalk.
>   What is
> talent against iron, what is
> thought against a uniform, what is music
> against a truncheon, what is joy against
> fear . . .
>
> **("Iron")**

Yet, in Zagajewski's world, even despair can be tempered by the ironic craft of poetry. True, those who "sit apart" are engulfed by the omnivorous jaws of History just as anyone else; but the individualist's distance at least gives him the chance to see everything more clearly and soberly. "On a hard dry substance / you have to engrave the truth"—this is the obligation that the poet faces. What truth? Which truth? Of course not the falsely assuring "truth" of an ideological dogma or a collective stereotype. "My masters are not infallible," says Zagajewski in yet another poem. In his vocabulary, "truth" is associated with probing the surrounding darkness rather than achieving any final clarity:

> Clear moments are so short.
> There is much more darkness. More
> ocean than firm land. More
> shadow than form.
>
> **("Moment")**

The poet's truth lies in his very search for the truth.

Eva Hoffman (essay date 1986)

SOURCE: "Remembering Poland," in *The New York Times Book Review*, February 16, 1986, pp. 14-15.

[*In the following excerpt, Hoffman examines Zagajewski's sensuous imagery and abstract insights in* Tremor: Selected Poems.]

. . . Adam Zagajewski, who has lived in Paris for the last few years and has emerged as one of the more noted poets of Poland's postwar generation, takes European culture as his native province, even as Mr. Herbert does. Many of his poems are reflections on actual figures—Beethoven, Schubert, Schopenhauer—or on moments in the past. And like Mr. Herbert he finds in civilization and art a solace for the ravages of history. Sometimes his poems seem written in dialogue with Mr. Herbert. The poem **"On the Escalator,"** for example, in which the speaker informs those who are riding up that "no one is waiting / up there," is surely a response to Mr. Herbert's

"From the Top of the Stairs," in which the poet wishes that "those who are standing at the top of the stairs" might come down and admit that "what the posters shout isn't true." But—and perhaps this is partly because he is further removed from the events that gave Mr. Herbert's poetry its original impetus—the balances in Mr. Zagajewski's writing are very different: power weighs less, and beauty, contemplative leisure or imaginative transcendence have at least as much significance as the stern lessons of history.

Also, where Mr. Herbert says that "the piano at the top of the Alps / played false concerts for him," Mr. Zagajewski's language cascades through sequences of metaphor and synesthetic, almost surreal juxtapositions of images—as in the lyrical opening poem, **"To Go to Lvov."**

> *and there was too much*
> *of Lvov, it brimmed the container,*
> *it burst glasses, overflowed*
> *each pond, lake, smoked through every*
> *chimney, turned into fire, storm,*
> *laughed with lightning, grew meek,*
> *returned home, read the New Testament,*
> *slept on a sofa beside the Carpathian rug,*
> *there was too much of Lvov, and now*
> *there isn't any.*

Although the tone of the poem is one of painful loss for the city that no longer exists in its former incarnation (and where Mr. Zagajewski, too, was born), in the end the loss is redeemed by this vision of extravagant plenitude, which re-creates the city in imaginative existence ("it exists, quiet and pure as / a peach. It is everywhere."

The movement from the specificity of physical images to a moment of abstraction is characteristic of Mr. Zagajewski's poetry; it corresponds to his delight in the sensuous surfaces of things and his urge toward a disembodied, spiritual insight and for a breaking out of the self. His poems repeatedly traverse the path from being arrested by appearances to making a leap outwards, or at least an intuition of such a leap:

> *We live in longing. In our dreams,*
> *locks and bolts open up. Who didn't find shelter*
> *in the huge looks to the small. God*
> *is the smallest poppy seed in the world,*
> *bursting with greatness.*

Such a quest for transcendence is essentially romantic in its impulse, but Mr. Zagajewski is a modern romantic, in whom an attraction to quietude and to interstitial, hidden spaces often coexists with mosaics of contemporary urban detail, a taste for incongruity and a sometimes ironic reflectiveness. Occasionally the gentleness of these poems' sensibility lapses into obvious sentiments, especially in the poems that come closest to explicit political commentary about Mr. Zagajewski's homeland ("A land of people so innocent that / they cannot be saved"). But on the whole, these are lovely evocations of mood and thought—and Renata Gorczynski has done a fine job of

conveying both the poems' striated textures and their calm lyricism. . . .

D. J. Enright (essay date 1987)

SOURCE: "Pure As a Peach," in *The Times Literary Supplement*, No. 4,382, March 27, 1987, p. 315.

[*In the following review of* Tremor: Selected Poems, *Enright praises the poetry for its clarity and simplicity as well as its distinctive humor.*]

Referring to the early writing of Adam Zagajewski (Polish, born in 1945, resident in Paris since 1981), Czeslaw Milosz remarks in his brief but weighty preface that the poetry of political commitment is "noble-minded, but often one-dimensional". The trouble with such poetry is that its message might as well be couched in prose, generally has been already, and, since the poetry soon vanishes out of the window, still is. However self-soothing for a while, protest poetry is rarely more productive than muttering into one's pillow in the dead of night. And yet, nothing should be alien to this most human of the arts, and it would be an odd poet, one of suspiciously iron control, who never touched on public events, on contemporary distresses and disgraces.

Zagajewski, Milosz continues, has abandoned the poetry of political engagement in favour of a meditation on the flow of time which brings together the historical and the metaphysical. The world thus created or recreated is not a place of escape, but "on the contrary, it is related in a peculiar way to the crude reality of our century". As inferred, Zagajewski's views on the world are unexceptional, and—in half of the world—unexceptionable. Once again, it is a case of what was fairly often thought but never expressed in quite this idiosyncratic way.

He proceeds by captivating indirection, by slipping in allusions and images which are apparently incidental and free of affect. An intermittently comic poem, **"Franz Schubert: A Press Conference"**, has the composer telling how he was chased "by the strangeness of style itself; no, not the police"; an address to Madam Death (a feminine noun in Polish) ends with a mention of "the sleepy complaints of the poor poets / whose passports you didn't renew"; a poem involving Cyprian Norwid, the nineteenth-century Polish poet and hater of jargon of any complexion, asks "is that the way / the new epoch begins, is this tank / with a long Gogolian nose its godfather . . . ?" And elsewhere, among character actors acting their characters, old people impersonating old people, the sick playing the sick, and so forth, the only example out of step is oppressors pretending they are oppressed.

Zagajewski was born in Lvov, now in the Soviet Ukraine. In **"To Go to Lvov"**, after memories or reconstructions of the city, the poet says, "There was too much of Lvov, and now / there isn't any"; it has been scissored out or pruned, as if by gardeners, tailors or censors. And yet you can go there every day, "after all / it exists, quiet and pure as / a peach. It is everywhere". We can see how the celebratory nature of the poetry, celebration against the odds, must recommend it to Milosz. **"Kierkegaard on Hegel"**—Zagajewski studied philosophy in Cracow—reflects that, since the glorious states (body politic? way of life?) we were promised have been shelved, for the time being we had better enjoy

> a cramped cell in the jailhouse, a prisoner's song,
> the good mood of a customs officer, the fist
> of a cop,

for those who don't find shelter in the huge will look to the small.

This sounds like resignation, but resignation of a positive and open kind, remote from giving up. Even honourable opinions can prove accursed. In time the rebels become barely distinguishable from what they were rebelling against, and humanity sickens under the frost of stalemate. What poets can do is show that, however detestable the régime, life must still have its attractions and the world retain its beauty, since if these have truly departed, what likelihood is there that they will reappear? If they are feeble enough to be nullified or repealed, are they worth having at all?

The poet as guardian is manifest in the richness of **"In the Trees"**, where so much is happening, including a woodpecker who "cables / an urgent report on the capture of / Carthage and on the Boston Tea Party"; and in **"Ode to Plurality"**, with its proliferating contradictions:

> Who once lived won't
> forget the changing delight of seasons,
> he will dream even of nettles and burdocks, and the
> spiders in his dream won't look any worse
> than swallows.

And most explicitly in a very Milszian piece, **"In the Past"**: the dawn and the mikman, running through the snow, make tiny pools of water—

> A small bird
> drinks that water and it sings and once more
> it saves the disorder of things and you and me
> and the singing.

The (first) impression here is commonly one of inconsequence. The verse is characterized by a jerky, disjointed procedure, as if a species of cataloguing were under way, and its rhythms are no more distinct than those present in well-written prose. I suspect that in this the translation reflects the original. For the seeming dislocations are offset by—in fact, are seen to be at one with—a singular presiding humour, both striking and anti-rhetorical. At times the humour lies in the situation itself—entering a station waiting-room, the wanderer is briefly uncertain which "suffering" he should join, the group of tramps and drunks, or the elderly, elegant couple staring upwards to heaven; finally he sits between them and opens a book of poems-but more commonly in the incidentals. In **"To Go to Lvov"**, joy hovers everywhere, in the thorns of roses, in coffee mills, in blue teapots, and in starch, "which was the first formalist". A poem about Schopenhauer, portending high seriousness, opens by announcing the philosopher's dates and the title of his chief work. By a similar incongruity or descent into "lowness", **"Without End"** declares that in the life after or in death the quest for perfection will casually bypass all obstacles "just as the Germans / learned how to bypass the Maginot Line". And elsewhere—among other things and other meanings, since "To survive means to be in storm"—a plane is "a waiting-room / in the act of displacement".

Zagajewski's poems are not markedly difficult, or perhaps are sufficiently simple and engaging in their parts to make us suppose we understand the whole. Description is inept, and the writer's qualities are better demonstrated by quoting one of his most readily accessible pieces, **"In the Beauty Created by Others"**, in its entirety.

> Only in the beauty created
> by others is there consolation,
> in the music of others and in others' poems.
> Only others save us,
> even though solitude tastes like
> opium. The others are not hell,
> if you see them early, with their
> foreheads pure, cleansed by dreams.
> That is why I wonder what
> word should be used, "he" or "you". Every "he"
> is a betrayal of a certain "you" but
> in return someone else's poem
> offers the fidelity of a sober dialogue.

Sven Birkerts (essay date 1989)

SOURCE: "Adam Zagajewski," in his *The Electric Life: Essays on Modern Poetry*, William Morrow and Company, 1989, pp. 423-31.

[*In the following essay, Birkerts argues that rather than writing poetry determined by history, Zagajewski has developed a metaphysical imagery that expresses "our common exile from a comprehensible reality."*]

A recent review of Adam Zagajewski's *Tremor* (Renata Gorczynski, translator) by his fellow Polish émigré, the poet Stanislaw Baranczak, points up to me just how much historical context conditions the interpretive act. Baranczak, as a member of Zagajewski's poetic generation—the so-called generation of 1968—and who surely knows the poems in their original cadences, writes as follows:

> . . . the multidimensional meaning of Zagajewski's poetry can by no means be reduced to that of "a poetry of protest" or a generational manifesto. The book can (and should) be read also outside the framework of Poland's recent history, and it will not lose much this way. After all, it has something important to say about life, death, love, loneliness, and other rather universal matters. And yet the keen sense of history that pervades

and distorts contemporary existence seems to be something that cannot really be subtracted from Zagajewski's poems. While his work contains a wealth of sensuous imagination and philosophical perspicacity, the reader here is not able to forget that he is dealing with a poet born and raised in our age and in a certain corner of Eastern Europe.

While I will not set myself up to dispute Baranczak—my position on the far side of the linguistic barricade precludes even the possibility of that—I will say that I registered a very different response in my reading of the poet. What I found was a metaphysics born from a deep sense of contradiction, a will that had as its impossible goal the destruction of the space/time axis. The question is one of emphasis. Where Baranczak states that *Tremor* "can (and should) be read also outside the framework of Poland's recent history," it seems to me that "Poland's recent history" has driven Zagajewski to a larger vision of history itself, and that the work is only in part concerned with the generational experience of the Poles. In other words, the effects, which are metaphysical, take precedence over the causes, which are historical.

I will be the first to admit that mine is a privileged, and American, reading. But the simple fact is that these poems, even in translation, captured with unnerving clarity my own feelings about life in our terrifying epoch—they reach past the surface lesions in order to search out the wounding source. Which is something more than ideology and state power. This poetry is quickened—now and then made feverish—by the tension between two orders of time, the meaningful and the meaningless: between time as it was lived, felt, *inhabited* before everything changed, and time as we know it now, an abstract series of dissociated moments, a conceptual grid. The application is universal; the digital instruments of the free, capitalist West mark the same empty intervals as the clocks of the state. What happened? Did historical developments accelerate and then destroy our collective sense of meaningful time, or did Chronos himself undergo some mutation, carrying history in his wake? The second possibility is more frightening, for it denies us the idea of freedom. And Zagajewski will, on occasion, incline this way. In **"Late Beethoven,"** for example, one of several meditations on the expiration of the nineteenth century, he writes: "Unending adagios. That's how tired freedom/breathes," as if to suggest the imminent collapse of human prerogative. So, too, in **"Schopenhauer's Crying"** we read:

> His vest. His starched collar.
> All these dispensables tremble,
> as if the bombs had already fallen
> on Frankfurt.

The implication, of course, is that there is a destiny inscribed on the fabric of history, and that the free acts of man are illusory. However—and this will become clear later—Zagajewski does not hold to any one position unequivocally.

Tremor begins with a breathless and image-haunted long poem entitled **"To Go to Lvov."** His trademark style is immediately obvious: the exploded syntax of his sentences, the prismatic juxtaposition of verb tenses, the massing of vivid threads of detail:

> To go to Lvov. Which station
> for Lvov, if not in a dream, at dawn, when dew
> gleams on a suitcase, when express
> trains and bullet trains are being born. To leave
> in haste for Lvov, night or day, in September
> or in March. But only if Lvov exists,
> if it is to be found within the frontiers and not just
> in my new passport, if lances of trees
> —of poplar and ash—still breathe aloud
> like Indians, and if streams mumble
> their dark Esperanto, and grass snakes like soft signs
> in the Russian language disappear
> into thickets.

The poem goes on for another seventy-odd lines, turning first into a catalogue of a vanished way of life, a dream picture of the European nineteenth century:

> . . . and joy hovered
> everywhere, in hallways and in coffee mills
> revolving by themselves, in blue
> teapots, in starch, which was the first
> formalist, in drops of rain and in the thorns
> of roses. Frozen forsythia yellowed by the window.
> The bells pealed and the air vibrated, the cornets
> of nuns sailed like schooners near
> the theater, there was so much of the world that
> it had to do encores over and over.

and then breaking its own reverie with this ominous metaphor:

> But scissors cut it, along the line and through
> the fiber, tailors, gardeners, censors
> cut the body and the wreaths, pruning shears
>   worked
> diligently, as in a child's cutout
> along the dotted line of a roe deer or a swan.
> Scissors, penknives, and razor blades scratched,
> cut, and shortened the voluptuous dresses
> of prelates, of squares and houses, and trees
> fell soundlessly, as in a jungle,
> and the cathedral trembled, people bade
>   goodbye.

Emotional narration finally gives way to a complex finale that mitigates its desperate cry with an unexpectedly consoling vision:

> . . . why must every city
> become Jerusalem and every man a Jew,
> and now in a hurry just
> pack, always, each day,
> and go breathless, go to Lvov, after all
> it exists, quiet and pure as
> a peach. It is everywhere.

I cite at length, both to show something of Zagajewski's manner, his idiosyncratic dovetailing of clauses, and to suggest the velocity—the gulped-air quality—that his longer poems often achieve. This, more than anything, establishes his stylistic distance from senior masters like Czeslaw Milosz and Zbigniew Herbert, both of whom sustain a certain intellectual/ironic fixity in their work; in Milosz particularly, the disruptive insanity of recent history is held up against a stable backdrop of natural order, childhood memories, and spiritual absolutes. Perhaps because Zagajewski is relatively young (he was born in 1945) and has had no direct experience of the prewar order, the past that he evokes is like a child's dream. But it is intention, not naïveté. In **"To Go to Lvov,"** this romanticized perception of the past is what allows the poem to attain its shuddering and all but self-negating climax. The image of a child's scissors cutting away the beautiful past paves the way for the chilling interrogative: "why must every city / become Jerusalem and every man a Jew." Two vastly different orders of experience are pushed together: Jerusalem is at once the mythic setting of the child's Bible story and the ultimate site of loss and redemption.

The problem of redemption is posed by the last three lines, which are baffling both logically and in terms of their suggestion. If Lvov is indeed "everywhere"—that is, if it exists unscarred in the collective memory of a people, or in some state of duration that cannot be assailed by sequent events—then there is, literally speaking, no reason to be packing and rushing to get there. Similarly, if the poem is intended to be an elegy for a lost world, why would Zagajewski alter its impact with a sudden swerve, an intimation of perfect restoration? The best answer I can devise is that the reversal results from an utterly irrational act of faith. It is a lightning stroke of pure paradox: So much life could not be destroyed so quickly; it must exist—like Jerusalem for the Jew—as a final destination; because it is nowhere, it must be everywhere. This is the soul's logic, not the mind's—it generates an affecting and unforgettable poetry.

There is often a kind of impossibility—or unattainability—in Zagajewski's work. As he writes in his **"Ode to Plurality"**: "a poem grows / on contradiction but it can't cover it." Historical truth and human desire move in opposite directions, the one telling us what *is,* the other telling us what we are and, therefore, what *could be.* Destiny versus freedom, reality versus art—the poet is the broker, the eternal victim and beneficiary of the double vision. The tension of this is sustained throughout the entire collection. If one poem declares a diminishing hope:

> He acts, in splendor and in darkness,
> in the roar of waterfalls and in the silence of sleep,
> but not as your well-protected shepherds
> would have it. He looks for the longest line,
> the road so circuitous
> it is barely visible, and fades away
> in suffering. Only blind men, only
> owls feel sometimes its dwindling trace
> under the eyelids.
>
> —"He Acts"

another, like **"Kierkegaard on Hegel,"** will seem to countermand it: "God / is the smallest poppy seed in the world, / bursting with greatness."

The reference of these quotations is deceptive, for Zagajewski is not a religious poet. God is, for him, more like an emblem of a vanishing spiritual heritage, a manifestation of the desire that flies in the face of the circumstantial fact. His own metaphysics is ultimately a good deal more impersonal. In **"Fire, Fire,"** for instance, he speaks of the force that "ravages and burns cities / made of wood, of stone" but also "comples Descartes / to overthrow philosophy." This Heraclitean sense of flux and opposition is everywhere in Zagajewski; a self-conflicted energy swirls at the core of creation:

> The force that grows
> in Napoleon's dreams
> and tells him to conquer Russia and snow
> is also in poems
> but it is very still.
>
> —from **"That Force"**

That stillness—which may represent the highest attainment of art, a surmounting of contradiction—is beautifully rendered in **"A View of Delft"**:

> Houses, waves, clouds, and shadows
> (deep-blue roofs, brownish bricks),
> all of you finally became a glance.
>
> The quiet pupil of things, unreined,
> glittering with blackness.
>
> You'll outlive our admiration, our tears,
> and our noisy, despicable wars.

But I cannot read this as a celebration of the final triumph of art.

Zagajewski writes comfortably in both compressed and extended forms. If the shorter lyrics at times resemble those of Milosz—direct, simplified statement enfolding a paradox or an irresoluble contradiction—the longer poems, *tours de force* many of them, announce his tonal distinctiveness. In these we feel most directly the impact of history upon sensibility, as much in the contents as in the syntactic cut and thrust. Indeed, the tremor in these pages issues from the active abrasion of clauses and image clusters; conclusions and meanings feel, at best, provisional.

Zagajewski's longer persona poems—like **"Late Beethoven"** and **"Franz Schubert: A Press Conference"**—warrant more discussion than I have space for. Each in its own way dissolves our imagining of the nineteenth century in the cataract of the twentieth. The measured movement of clock hands speeds up until there is nothing but a dizzying blur. But it is the penultimate long poem, **"A View of Cracow,"** that finds the words for the true terror.

> Before me, Cracow in a grayish dale.
> Swallows carry it on long braids

woven of air. Rooks in black
frock coats watch over it.

The poem begins with an easy mingling of perspectives. Glimpsed in its natural setting, the city exudes an enchanted timelessness. But before long, the past and present are delineated: "Of the more recent architecture, / the Palace of Police stands out" and "What was, what is, meticulously / separated." This troubling fact—that the extrusions of different epochs, different zones of being, can coexist in space—then triggers the first shift. We are moved from exterior, synoptic vantage to the human and inward:

> A lonely woman lived here
> and not long ago she died of old age
> or loneliness. Who remembers
> what pastry she used to bake
> or how much anger was stored in her eyes?

A commonplace reflection, but it yields immediately to a more strident indictment:

> Before me, character actors
> hidden in their apartments,
> hidden under their costumes. Oppressors
> pretend they are oppressed, women perform
> the roles of women, old people impersonate
> old people.

The litany goes on, builds, until at last the question is thrust under our noses: "Is it / a divine comedy or is it a divine / tragedy borrowed from the city library?" The poet does not answer. Instead, he slips a new panel into place:

> Through the park, through a dense tunnel,
> a young girl hurries, late for her lectures.
> Petals of peonies grow in her hair,
> the tenderness of time weaves a nest
> in her hair. She is running fast but
> she doesn't move, she is still
> in the same place, under the chestnut branches
> which fling off greenery
> and put on new greenery.

Zagajewski has summoned up the image of duration, that privileged mode of being that belongs to youth—and, in this poetry, to the historical past—and that is a form of timelessness. In the condition of duration, things are exactly themselves, seeming is banished, plunged in the plenitude of the moment, and meaning inheres in actions if only because they are unquestioned. The girl does not move because she is an anomaly in a world turned false. After a dozen more lines, Zagajewski concludes:

> Airy smoke drifts from the chimneys
> as if a conclave were still going on,
> as if the tenements wanted
> a turn to play at existence.
> Before me, Cracow, a gray planet,

the charcoal of bliss and expectation (life played the part of life, joy was joy, and suffering was suffering).

Difficult as it is to present a poem through episodic cuttings like these, the idea is central to the work and demands our attention. The final parenthetic statement—primerlike in its simplicity—sums up Zagajewski's vision of our posthistorical condition. We are no longer connected to meaningful time, to that sustaining taproot; every atom of our human cosmos is now merely impersonating itself. History has been succeeded by a stage act. To me, this is more than just an assessment of life under totalitarian rule—it is news about the collective life of our times. We do not have to be in Cracow, or in exile from it, to get the shudder of recognition. Our common exile from a comprehensible reality bound to tradition, natural process, and a living sense of the spiritual suffices. Zagajewski may be looking at Eastern Europe, but his gaze wraps itself around the whole globe.

Stanislaw Baranczak (essay date 1991)

SOURCE: Introduction to *Polish Poetry of the Last Two Decades of Communist Rule: Spoiling Cannibal's Fun*, Northwestern University Press, 1991, pp. 11-13.

[In the following excerpt from an introduction to a collection of Polish poetry, Baranczak argues that Zagajewski's reconciles individualism and moralism and calls this achievement "a unifying feature of whatever is most valuable in recent Polish poetry."]

. . . The question of how to reconcile poetry's natural individualism with human solidarity and respect for supraindividual values is, in fact, the single most pressing issue that Polish poetry faced during the last decades of Communist rule. It was fascinating to observe how this dilemma was approached by various poets of the younger generation, such as Ryszard Krynicki, Adam Zagajewski, Ewa Lipska, Julian Kornhauser, Piotr Sommer, Jan Polkowski, or Bronisław Maj. Born in the 1940s and 1950s, most of these poets entered literary life in the wake of the political protests of 1968, 1970, or 1976, and all of them contributed greatly to the "social awakening" of Polish poetry in the early 1970s and after. The recent poetry of Krynicki, for instance, is an extreme manifestation of the individual self's humility in the face of commonly shared values and compassion for human suffering. This essentially Christian attitude goes along with a heightened sense of responsibility for the word. Krynicki goes so far as to equate a poem with a slogan chalked on a wall or a demonstrator's cry: like these, the poem must be as brief as possible, cleansed of unnecessary words, reduced to its bare semantic essence. Accordingly, most of Krynicki's recent poems, sometimes consisting of just two or three lines, structurally resemble the genres of aphorism or parable.

By contrast, the recent poetry of Zagajewski, the other of the two most outstanding representatives of the so-called Generation of '68, appears to be headed in a diametrically opposed direction. Like Krynicki, Zagajewski began his literary career as a poet, novelist, and essayist protesting against the omnipresent ideological lie of the system. In particular, in 1974 he stirred up one of the greatest controversies in postwar Polish culture by coauthoring, with Kornhauser, a book of criticism titled *The World Not Represented,* a sweeping assault on the noncommittal literature of the preceding decades. Yet the poetry he has written since 1981, though concerned for a while with the reality of the "state of war," has been far from expressing any clear-cut political tendency. Rather, these poems form a portrayal of an individual mind torn asunder by contradictory tendencies—by the moral obligation to speak on behalf of others as opposed to the necessity of remaining one's unique self. The poet's ironic and self-ironic consciousness never allows him to accept anything that is abstract, general, collectivist; ironic distance is used here as a defensive weapon against the leveling abstractness of ideologies and systems. But it is, by the same token, also necessary to take in the whole breathtaking *plurality* of the concrete, tangible world. In poems where the concept of plurality becomes predominant, such as **"To Go to Lvov,"** Zagajewski moves in the opposite direction to Krynicki: while the latter's brief and concise utterances can be called poem-aphorisms, Zagajewski's rich, overflowing, almost baroque odes deserve the name of (to borrow a term from Milosz) poem-tapestries. But these poems are not merely outbursts of rapture and admiration for the fundamental plurality of the world. Zagajewski realizes that this plurality also encompasses evil and injustice. This becomes particularly evident when we encounter evil masquerading as History: witness Zagajewski's powerful poems about martial law in Poland, such as **"Iron."**

Yet even in such poems he remains an individualist whose ironic distance does not stand in opposition to his compassion and moralistic concern; on the contrary, it is exactly this ironic distance that gives him the chance to see reality's evil more clearly and soberly. And, in a sense, this paradoxical reconciliation between the extremes of individualism and moralism is, regardless of all the differences in approach and style, a unifying feature of whatever is most valuable in recent Polish poetry.

Donald Revell (essay date 1992)

SOURCE: "The Plural of Vision Remains Vision," in *Ohio Review,* Vol. 48, 1992, pp. 101-2, 108-11.

[*In the following review, Revell praises Zagajewski for his "poetry of witness," particularly for his ability to truthfully convey his vision.*]

Poetry survives ideology because poetry is the body, the act, and the desire of an entirely stateless radicalism. By "stateless" I mean a condition of constant dispossession on behalf of the freedom of the real. Eurydice travels ahead of Orpheus. And by "radicalism" I mean a dedication to root experience which, of necessity, requires the preliminary experience of uprootedness. The waking of a

poem uproots a dream from sleep. In the aftermath of ideologies and the unmasking of cynical reactionaries long disguised as reformers, only one radicalism, the Ur-radicalism, remains credible: vision, the gift to imagine without ownership or control. For poets, vision entails an unmethodical sequence of contacts and convulsions in the matters of language, identity, and community. It is vision that deprives poets of their original language and sends them out in search of new syllables which, when contacted in the moment of the poem, convulse and escape, requiring a further search. It is vision that erases the presumed identities of poets, their positive capabilities, and empowers them with the brief anonymity necessary to sympathy, the intensity of which results in the convulsion of many selves birthed out of one. Finally, it is vision that makes of these selves the community of the book, a community joined in the contact of reading and being read, of imagining an unquantified root-change together. When this community disperses at the end of reading, it either codifies or multiplies the vision it has shared. The former choice leads on to faction and ideology. The latter becomes the life of poetry. In making and in reading poems, what matters first is what matters most: the enlargement of verbal, personal, and communal possibility beyond the limited frontiers of a single poem. Vision is first *and* next. The interval is poetry. . . .

Sometimes, even the most fundamental acts of perception require great imagination, and in *Canvas*, the second of his collections to be translated into English, Polish-born Adam Zagajewski continues to exert the labor of vision upon much that, because it has disappeared into the mendacities of European history, demands an exemplary exercise of imagination merely to exist, merely to stray in and out of being. The wonder of these poems rests in their counter-balance of force and humility: the force to insist upon vision, and the humility to make no authorial demands upon what, with difficulty, with almost endless pathos and outrage, comes into view. Zagajewski understands the compulsory nature of human witness and how, under the strict conditions of exile (from homeland, from truthfulness), witness gradually becomes a universal. In **"Lava,"** he stages a confrontation between the laughing and the weeping circumstances of change, the Heraclitan and the Eleatic, discovering a new causticness of vision along the way.

> And what if Heraclitus and Parmenides
> are both right
> and two worlds exist side by side,
> one serene, the other insane; one arrow
> thoughtlessly hurtles, another, indulgent,
> looks on; the selfsame wave moves and stands still.
> Animals all at once come into the world
> and leave it, birch leaves dance in the wind
> as they fall apart in the cruel, rusty flame.
> Lava kills and preserves, the heart beats
> and is beaten; there was war, then there wasn't;
> Jews died, Jews stay alive, cities are razed,
> cities endure, love fades, the kiss everlasting,
> the wings of the hawk must be brown,
> you're still with me though we're no more,

ships sink, sand sings, clouds wander
like wedding veils in tatters.

The confrontation is elemental at the level of real earth.
As lava, the caustic overflow and release of interior pressure, creates a surface of the world, so does the vertigo
of opposing interpretations of time and change, equally
caustic, equally interior to the mind, eventually resolve
itself into a surface upon which the facts of change stand
outright, there to be seen divorced from interpretation
"like wedding veils in tatters" as the isolate complexities
they are and will remain. Such complexity needs endless
witness and is reconciled to the desires of vision only by
exhaustive fidelity:

> All's lost. So much brilliance. The hills
> gently descend with their long banners of woods.
> Moss inches up the stone tower of a church,
> its small mouth timidly praising the North.
> At dusk, the savage lamp of the jasmine is glowing,
> possessed by its own luminescence.
> Before a dark canvas in a museum,
> eyes narrow like a cat's. Everything's finished.
> Riders gallop black horses, a tyrant composes
> a sentence of death with grammatical errors.
> Youth dissolves
> in a day; girls' faces freeze
> into medallions, despair turns to rapture
> and the hard fruits of stars in the sky
> ripen like grapes, and beauty endures, shaken,
>   unperturbed,
> and God is and God dies; night returns to us
> in the evening, and the dawn is hoary with dew.

The sloth and revisionism of night yield again and again
to dawns of attention. The poem cannot transform loss
into "luminescence;" it can, however, by means of visionary witness, attest to the luminescence that loss *owns,*
something that a paraphrase of William Carlos Williams
might describe as the stark dignity of annihilation.

Having made contact with the first-principles of loss,
Zagajewski envisions its horrific proliferation, the Holocaust of European Jewry, in **"Watching *Shoah* in a
Hotel Room in America."** The title reifies an entire
poetic undeprived of any of the complexities or humility upon which historical vision depends. The poem
watches, and what it watches is a documentary of horrors spiraled first through aphasia and then through remembrance. The poem watches, witnessing in transience,
in exile, false pleas of innocence gathered into irrefutable guilt. The poem watches, poised in a very particular
nowhere in which only the undistracted can know the
unimaginable.

> There are nights as soft as fur on a foal
> but we prefer chess or card playing. Here,
> some hotel guests sing "Happy Birthday"
> as the one-eyed TV nonchalantly shuffles its images.
> The trees of my childhood have crossed an ocean
> to greet me cooly from the screen.
> Polish peasants engage with a Jesuitical zest

> in theological disputes: only the Jews are silent,
> exhausted by their long dying.
> The rivers of the voyages of my youth flow
> cautiously over the distant, unfamiliar continent.
> Hay wagons haul not hay, but hair,
> their axles squeaking under the feathery weight.
> We are innocent, the pines claim.
> The SS officers are haggard and old,
> doctors struggle to save them their hearts, lives,
>   consciences.
> It's late, the insinuations of drowsiness have me.
> I'd sleep but my neighbors
> choir "Happy Birthday" still louder:
> louder than the dying Jews.

The Old World and its old horrors insinuate themselves
into the New World's amnesiac nonchalance. Images of
measureless death compete with an audible but invisible
birthday. There is no limit to the depth of this poem's
"found" occasion, yet Zagajewski heroically maintains his
position at the surface where attention experiences the
harrowing extreme of vision. In this extremity, he learns
the dreadful equivalence of innocence and sleep, feeling
the exile's drift into homelessness and unconsciousness
as an unforgiveable collaboration with death. And the
furthest horror is that the unforgiveable may, under the
rubric of survival, be unavoidable:

> I grow more and more innocent, sleepy.
> The TV reassures me: both of us
> are beyond suspicion.
> The birthday is noisier.
> The shoes of Auschwitz, in pyramids
> high as the sky, groan faintly:
> Alas, we have outlived mankind, now
> let us sleep, sleep:
> we have nowhere to go.

Adorno questioned how poetry could be possible after
Auschwitz. Zagajewski poses the same question in a pyr-
amid of shoes. Who and where is the witness who has
outlived mankind? If he is an exile, he has nowhere to
go and no language in which to testify. If he is asleep,
his witness is a dream of denial that perpetuates a murderous reality. In **"Watching *Shoah* in a Hotel Room
in America,"** and throughout *Canvas,* Zagajewski responds to unanswerable questions of survival by maintaining a stillness which is the result of many tensions
focussed upon one place: the noplace where imagination entitles existence, where vision precedes, without
presuming, essence. . . .

Joachim T. Baer (essay date 1992)

SOURCE: A Review of *Canvas,* in *World Literature
Today,* Vol. 66, No. 4, Autumn, 1992, pp. 746-47.

[*In the following review of* Canvas, *Baer calls Zagajewski's metaphorical imagery "extraordinary" and suggests that he often writes his poetry as if in conversation with other poets and thinkers.*]

In his wonderful book of essays *Poetry and Experience* (1961) Archibald MacLeish quotes Yeats's lines on the "ultimate meaning of which poetry is capable": "What is the meaning of all song?" Yeats proceeded to answer the question himself: "Let all things pass away." It is this stance, this position toward the world, which projects from the slim collection of Adam Zagajewski's poetry titled *Canvas*, sensitively translated from the Polish originals, which had been published in a variety of Polish émigré publications.

One could use various epithets to describe Zagajewski's verse: reflective, metaphysical, atmospheric, impressionistic, pictorially vivid. Some of the longer poems are phrased as interrogative sentences: "Things, . . . have you loved, and died, at night, wind opening the windows, absorbing the cool heart? Have you tasted age, time, bereavement?" (**"From the Lives of Things"**). Others are brief statements of observations caught in the present (**"On a Side Street"**). All these exquisite poems, however, are cast in the context of the passage of things: "What was, endures in imagination. What is, waits for destruction" (**"Spider's Song"**). Zagajewski's themes are the night, dreams, history and time, infinity and eternity, silence and death. "Only the mysteries are immortal," he says in the poem **"Presence"**; elsewhere he speaks of the immortality of all things in life: "Windows open and close, trains ride leisurely through the hills, apples fall to the grass, heather breathes, all beings are busy with life and life lords it over the leaves; even the stones are immortal and full of themselves" (**"Stones"**).

In the poem **"Lullaby"** Zagajewski speaks of memory as a potent force of creative energy ("Memory will open, with a sudden hiss like a parachute's. Memory will open, you won't sleep, rocked slowly through clouds"), and then he evokes memories of his native Poland and of his youth in such poems as **"Wild Cherries"**: "Sunday morning a mother irons white shirts. The State is perfect, the weather fine." A certain irony is apparent in these paratactic statements. The most prominent themes are dreams, night, and silence ("Why do the incidental dreams vanish at dawn and the great ones keep growing?" [**"A Talk with Friedrich Nietzsche"**]; "You're only an image, a dream, you're made up wholly of yearning" [**"To Myself, in an Album"**]), the theme of silence being directly linked with the night, death, and darkness: "it's only the weary pilgrims come home, bearing the sugared bread of forgetfulness, exaltation, silence" (**"Vacation"**); "each drama unfolds in a different place, with a different ending; silence, tears, fright" (**"Islands and Towers"**); "Immediately that noted talent scout, Death, fawning all over him, signs him up. Sends invitations, one after another. . . . Fourteen years later he gives his first concert on the other side" (**"Seventeen,"** a poem on the adolescent Franz Schubert).

Zagajewski's style is marked by vivid metaphorical imagery, as in the quotation above on death, "that noted talent scout . . . fawning all over him." Elsewhere, in the poem **"At Daybreak"** he speaks of the "thick pelts of the parks" and the "shy light of morning, eternal débutante." His comparisons are equally extraordinary: "The living see

off their days that flee like negatives, exposed once but never developed." Some poems are written in haiku style (**"Soft air, wet leaves;—the scent was spring, the scent sorrow"** [**"Anecdote of Rain"**]); some are historical (**"Russia Comes into Poland"**), others metaphysical (**"A Talk with Friedrich Nietzsche"**).

Zagajewski likes to dedicate poems to other poets (e.g., Joseph Brodsky, Zbigniew Herbert, Czeslaw Milosz), critics (Constantin Jeleński), great twentieth-century thinkers (Mircea Eliade), and friends (Joseph Czapski). It is, in a sense, as if he were having a conversation with them, addressing issues with which they would be familiar. In this collection he is also conducting a conversation with his reader, and the reader's receptiveness is his response to the poet. Czapski, friend and painter, is the creator of the painting *The Yellow Cloud* which graces the jacket of this lovely volume.

Robert Pinsky (essay date 1993)

SOURCE: "Out of History," in *The New Republic*, Vol. 208, No. 4, January 25, 1993, pp. 43-45.

[*In the following review of* Canvas, *Pinsky finds Zagajewski's poetic expression of an individual persona within a larger, historical context provides a "revealing mirror of contrasts" for American readers.*]

Unlikely as it may seem, the poems of the Polish poet Adam Zagajewski, wonderful in themselves, may also suggest ways to think about American culture. Zagajewski's shrewd, clear, passionate poems have a distinctive way of touching the relation of historical reality to the lives of individuals, and to art. And because he writes in the language of a country that has seen itself as small, often-defeated, but innately noble and even aristocratic—a nation deeply unified by shared religion, art, historical knowledge—the contrast alone should interest us.

So Zagajewski deserves the attention of readers accustomed to swerve away from poetry. And moreover, he is good: the unmistakable quality of the real thing—a sun-like force that wilts clichés and bollixes the categories of expectation—manifests itself powerfully through able translation, both in Zagajewski's first book in English, *Tremor* (1985), and now in *Canvas*.

This book is about the presence of the past in ordinary life: history not as chronicle of the dead, or an *anima* to be illuminated by some doctrine, but as an immense, sometimes subtle force inhering in what people see and feel every day—and in the ways we see and feel. As an almost too-literal example of what I mean, here is the first two-thirds or so of the author's **"Electric Elegy"**:

Farewell, German radio with your green eye
and your bulky box,
together almost composing
a body and soul. (Your lamps glowed
with a pink, salmony light, like Bergson's

deep self.)
       Through the thick fabric
of the speaker (my ear glued to you as
to the lattice of a confessional), Mussolini
  once whispered,
Hitler shouted, Stalin calmly explained,
Beirut hissed, Gomulka held endlessly forth.
But no one, radio, will accuse you of treason;
no, your only sin was obedience: absolute,
tender faithfulness to the megahertz;
whoever came was welcomed, whoever was
  sent
was received.
       Of course I know only
the songs of Schubert brought you the jade
of true joy. To Chopin's waltzes
your electric heart was troubled delicately
and firmly and the cloth over the speaker
pulsated like the breasts of amorous girls
in old novels.

"History" in this poem is embodied not by the catalog of
dictators, but on the contrary by a whole web of forces
that have passed through the patient radio, and that the
poem acknowledges and resists. Such acknowledgment
and resistance generate a poise of emotional realities:
the affectionate irony toward Bergson's deep self; the
amused simile of the confessional lattice; the sensuous
loyalty to Chopin and Schubert; the way in which that
loyalty concedes its own schmaltziness with the "pulsat-
ing breasts"; and the corresponding way that the parade of
dictators is held back from mere rhetoric by the comically judicious precision of "Stalin calmly explained" and
"Gomulka held endlessly forth."

In the spirit of acknowledgment, the past of Europe cannot be separated from the life of the poet's own "body
and soul," tinted indelibly by history. But in the spirit of
resistance, the poem is written precisely to separate the
poet's body and soul from the history that pours through
him like a ferocious broadcast. Apart from the totality of
historical forces, as independent of that web as perceiving the web can make him, the poet is an animate version
of the humble radio: something a little different from
what passes through it and makes it tremble. This distinction is a potential bewilderment to us Americans, who
are sometimes ready to sentimentalize the presence of
history and politics in art.

Zagajewski is a prominent member of the generation of
Polish poets—a generation called "the '68 Generation"
in Tadeusz Nyczek's anthology *Humps and Wings*—who
took compulsory grade-school courses in dialectical materialism. Some of them were in the Marxist-Leninist
equivalent of the Boy Scouts. When they came of age,
they were active in the Solidarity movement and the student agitations that preceded it. As poets, Zagajewski and
such colleagues as Stanislaw Baranczak were drawn both
to the sharp, compressed ironies of Zbigniew Herbert
and to the deeply historical moral discrimination of the
exiled Czeslaw Milosz: poets of opposite kind who shared

the ability to immerse their work in the tidal force of
history without succumbing in those waters.

For these young poets, the great tower of pre-Marxist
European culture, officially minimized or rejected, held
the attraction of rich, forbidden territory. Thus, the American reader will find in Zagajewski's poems startlingly
many proper names of artists and thinkers: entires from
the great catalog of, in two words, Western Civilization.
Last year, in an essay in these pages called "History's
Children," Zagajewski evoked

> the incredible contempt with which the past was treated
> by communism when it still believed in itself. Antiquity,
> the Middle Ages and the Renaissance were depicted in
> school-books as epochs full of mistakes, ravings,
> misunderstandings, crimes. Perhaps this would not have
> been a bad description of history, if its goal and its
> premise were not the even more servile glorification of
> the existing system.

So knowledge of the proper names of European history—
knowledge that in the United States can seem curricular or
canonical in ways that might be associated with duty, or
even with oppression—for the Polish poet betokens liberty, and because it involves the forbidden garden of art,
liberty not only of the mind, but also of the senses.

Despite or because of this difference from the American
circumstance, Zagajewski's work has attracted the attention of young American poets, for whom I think he offers
a revealing mirror of contrasts. The Polish language binds
together a remarkably homogeneous people—nearly all
Catholics—for whom Polish poetry, both in its folk tradition and in its aristocratic tradition, is a readily available, sensory embodiment of national feeling. Poland's
student revolt of March 1968 began in response to the
banning of a work by the nineteenth-century Romantic
poet Adam Mickiewicz. Our own country, too diverse
and too raw to have a unifying folk tradition, with a problematic relation to the aristocratic, courtly origins of
English literature, has been held together by poetry only
in the enduring bardic dream of Whitman. And though
nothing reeks of history more than our diversity, our
national myth of an ahistorical present constitutes something like the opposite of the Polish myth of mystic
survival, in which such forces of memory as poetry and
religion overcome the temporary triumphs of tanks.

So for the American reader there may be something attractive, mysterious and alien in Zagajewski's buoyant,
even affectionate relation to the immense European car-
go of history, art and ideas. Such presence of history in
experience, for want of some other word, must be called
culture—a term whose solemnity does not fit the intimate, ironic, charitable voice of these poems. Here is
another example:

"SAILS"

There were evenings, as scarlet as
  Phoenician sails,

that soaked up the light and the air; I was
  suddenly nearly gasping
for breath, blinded by the slanted rays
of the somnolent sun. This is how epochs
  end, I thought,
how overloaded ships sink, how the eyelids
of old theaters droop, and what's left is
  dust, smoke,
sharp stones underfoot, and fear looking like
joy, and the end, which is tranquility.

Soon enough, though, it turns out to be
  only another
dress rehearsal, one more frantic
  improvisation:
the extras go home, swallows fall asleep
in precarious nests, the provincial
moon timidly slips into place,
robbers steal wigs, a priest writes to his
  mother.

How patiently you prepare and enure us,
what time you lavish on us,
what a teacher of history you are, Earth!

From its first bold simile, this brief meditation on the deceptive quality of historical time sees nature through human ideas and artifacts. The somnolent sun and the provincial moon are not the furniture of Romantic sentiment, however, but an acknowledgment of how one sees: an acknowledgment that the poet perceives all time as historical. To put such large propositions in terms that do not appear large, but fine-grained, tender and even domestic is Zagajewski's particular genius.

Thus, the scarlet sails of the evening, heroic and archaic, prepare the way for the less heroic moon, which sidles into place like a latecomer apologizing her way toward the appointed seat on a crowded theater aisle. The dramatic idea of epochs ending is amended by the image "how the eyelids of old theaters droop," a characteristic, brilliant image whose resonant wit combines architecture, the human body, moral time and the central concern of the poem. The compassionate theatricality of that drooping eyelid embodies the kind of history that earth teaches: a moral truth complexly epitomized by a physical process.

This is the reality of time: mere astonishment at such a reality is nostalgia, which like other naive forms of astonishment has no place in Zagajewski's art, precisely because his sense of time is historical. In such poetry, earthly time is perceived: as if the intervening color it places on perception could be described. The surface is frequently matter-of-fact and understated, emotion framed in an image, as in the German radio or in these lines from **"September Afternoon in the Abandoned Barracks,"** where it is a passing rooster that crystallizes feeling:

The overgrown grass in the yard
needs mowing.
Silence where blue-skulled

recruits sobbed.
In me, too, silence, no longer despair.
A black rooster, a hot black banner of blood
runs down a path.
Autumn fades,
war dims.

This is the way poetry can regard events: in the tone of someone who knows, not the answers or the facts or the truth, but exactly where he is in relation to what he sees.

From the firmness of this viewpoint, even Auschwitz can be invoked without excess or posturing. By viewpoint, I mean something more or less literal. Because the poet has thought through his place in time, and his relation to his locale, his voice can have a human sound, with neither complacency nor the borrowed thunder of atrocity-retailing. In **"Watching Shoah in a Hotel Room in America,"** fellow guests can be heard through the walls singing "Happy Birthday." The poet observes, "the trees of my childhood have crossed an ocean / to greet me coolly from the screen." The adverb "coolly" is precise, and laden with meaning that gives proportion to a later image: "only the aspen, as usual, trembles, / prepared to confess all its crimes." The poet grows sleepy, the singers of "Happy Birthday" persist, while on the screen "the Czech Jews sing the national anthem: 'Where is my home. . . . '" The words of the anthem are echoed in the lament of the remarkable final lines:

Alas, we outlived mankind, now
let us sleep, sleep:
we have nowhere to go.

In the essay "History's Children" Zagajewski offers a gloss on this notion of "outliving mankind." He tells of a lecture he heard when he was quite young, delivered by a poet, "talented, but not well known":

Have you noticed, ladies and gentlemen, he asked us, five people, three high school students, and two older women, one of whom fell asleep after a few minutes and slept as soundlessly as an Indian, have you noticed, ladies and gentlemen, that the poems, novels or screenplays being written now blame everything on history? Have you noticed that we no longer exist, we, that is, people who are the heart of will and thought, the lens of individual fate? Only history that fills, rents and destroys and exhaustively defines us is left. . . . But I will never agree to this. I would rather be mad than historical. I would rather be ridiculous than common. I would rather know nothing than understand everything.

This is not very different from the vision at the end of **"Watching Shoah in a Hotel Room in America"**: "alas, we have outlived mankind." Historical or cultural determinism, an idea that in some of its forms has seemed fresh and astringent to American academics of Zagajewski's generation, seems to the poet raised under state Marxism part of a dreary proposition—linked to atrocity and numbness. In his poems Zagajewski tests the contrary of that proposition by striving to perceive history from somewhere a little out of it, like a fish breaking water.

The achievement of these poems is partly in that act of rising above a lived-in element. In Zagajewski's work, the engulfing, ferocious historical reality appears as our habitat—not a well of horrors to be borrowed for rhetorical thunder, not an occasion for verse punditry, not a mere backdrop for sensibility. And the perception of that habitat has a mysterious, elating power.

In his poem, **"A Talk with Friedrich Nietzsche,"** Zagajewski touches on that mysterious power. "Most highly respected Professor Nietzsche," he begins. Then:

> Not tall, head like a bullet,
> You compose a new book
> and a strange energy hovers around you.
> Your thoughts parade
> like enormous armies.
>
> You know that Anne Frank died,
> and her classmates and friends, boys, girls,
> and friends of her friends, and cousins
> and friends of her cousins.
>
> What are words, I want to ask you, what
> is clarity and why do words keep burning
> a century later, though the earth
> weighs so much?

This daring blend of almost slapstick comedy and horror, the faux-naïf and the prophetic, makes its inventive way toward concluding lines that extend the series of questions still further:

> And from whence does joy come, and where
> does nothingness go? Where is forgiveness?
> Why do the incidental dreams vanish at
>   dawn
> and the great ones keep growing?

In their audacious humanity, these poems provide their own answer.

Bill Marx (essay date 1993)

SOURCE: "Gurus and Gadflies," in *Parnassus*, Vol. 18, No. 2, 1993, pp. 100-06.

[In the following excerpt, Marx claims that our expectations for poetry have changed since the end of the Cold War, and examines Zagajewski's poetry in relationship to this changing aesthetic.]

With freedom comes the inevitable trip back to prison for Central European poets. Not the boxes created by a class, a party, or a dictator, but the dusty cater-corners used moral exemplars are bundled into. For decades in the West, Central European poets were chiefly admired for their heroism and tenacity—they were embodiments of our guilty fantasy that persecution is not only good for the soul but essential for art. Aesthetics took a back seat to ethical, or political, admiration. Central European poets are still greeted with obligatory salutes to their civic gravity, but now the homage sounds like special pleading. With the Cold War over, critics and readers have a choice: either stow Central European poets in ethical limbo or throw them back into the boxing ring with all the rest, letting them slug it out for attention with Swedish, Japanese, and German versifiers. The Berlin Wall falls—dialectical materialism flies out, literary Darwinism flies in.

Though some admirers would like to preserve Central European poetry in righteous amber, a tumble into the contemporary slugfest would be salutary as well as revelatory. It would let us admire Central European poets as idiosyncratic artists as well as moral eminences. The truth is that many of these poets are stranger—and murkier—than we've been led to believe. Marina Tsvetaeva's insistence on poetry's irresponsibility also applies to the best of Central European verse: "Artistic creation is in some cases a sort of atrophy of conscience—more than that: a necessary atrophy of conscience, the moral flaw without which art cannot exist." These writers were never just mediums and victims of history, but poetic sinners. Writing eschatological ruminations and caustic anti-poems, satires of satire and ecstatic hymns to the everyday, they seize on history's barbarity for emblems of human indignation, on nature's sensuality for signs of human contentment.

Yet living in (or in the case of exiles, reacting to) an authoritarian state has also elicited certain set responses and mythologized certain dualities: the individual versus the state, tyranny versus freedom. The poet's reaction to a hostile reality sometimes settled into rote defensive postures, into metaphysical or nationalistic dogma. The tension between freedom of the imagination and loyalty to absolutes runs through the inner realms these poets built out of oppression, culture (high or folk), memory, intellect, and sensibility. These territories are craggy and contradictory: from the brusque introversions of Polish poet Tadeusz Rózewicz to the theological meditations of his compatriot Czeslaw Milosz, from the wry hypotheticals of Czechoslovakian immunologist Miroslav Holub to the shifting perspectives of Poles Adam Zagajewski and Piotr Sommer.

The unyielding ironic temper of the post-war Central European imagination reflected the rigidity of an authoritarian enemy. Today, it looks as if these poets eluded didacticism but stumbled, understandably, into philosophical intractability. In an effort to keep the mind above water, even the most complex poetry can lose its potential for flexibility and unpredictability. Thus the present conflicts in Central European poetry are partly generational: Those born after World War II find themselves dealing with the contradictory pressures of an evolving political situation and the hardened stances of poets such as Milosz and Rózewicz, who came out of the upheavals of the 1930's and 1940's. (Holub's attachment to the openness of the scientific method makes him a revealing exception.)

So history hasn't forsaken Central European poets; it's offering them fresh challenges with the advent of democracy and capitalism. The question is whether, after years of defying a ruthless ideology, Central European writers will change with the times or retreat into ethnic or nationalistic postures—the poetry of Zagajewski and Sommer is part of that self-conscious search to engage with (and mirror) cultural transformation. Their struggle is to determine which of the rigid values from the past need be (or can be) taken into the future. For the West, the end of Soviet domination is an opportunity to cast aside neat clichés, to appreciate the dark artistry of Central European poetry. This particular moment gives us a chance to reevaluate the old while the new is struggling to be born.

Poet Adam Zagajewski is one of the foremost advocates of artistic rejuvenation. Both in his superb essay collection *Solidarity, Solitude* and in his poetry, particularly his latest collection, *Canvas,* Zagajewski excavates the traditions of Central European poetry while keeping a wary eye on the future. He wants to accommodate, rather than repel, what the West offers, so he shifts literary ground from the political and moral to the perceptual and impressionistic. His concern is that the vision of Central European poetry should no longer be rooted in pervasive opposition, a certainty that precludes dissent. In Zagajewski's view, the resurgence of nationalism and the spread of commercialism behooves the Central European poets to become gadflies as well as gurus.

At a recent gathering of Central European writers sponsored by *Partisan Review* (Fall 1992), Zagajewski set what he calls the "Pre-Kantian" ontological tendency of Central European poetry ("Not how we perceive the world and ourselves but what the world is, what we are, what poetry is, and sometimes even what God is—those are dissidents' preoccupations") against the skepticism encouraged by democratic pluralism and its demand for "epistemological reflection." Zagajewski, who since 1981 has split his time between Paris and the University of Houston, doesn't feel entirely comfortable with the idea of relativity. Yet he doesn't want to continue what he sees as a tradition of absolutes, admirable as it may be:

> The problem with the ontological sensibility is that once your quest seems to be successful, you are ready to defend fanatically your position. Ontology makes us tolerate little or even be completely intolerant. The democratic sensibility, ridden by self-doubt and skepticism, has at least the wonderful capacity for leaving space for other thinkers, other beliefs, other doubts. Almost everything in Central and Eastern Europe looks like the fruit of ontological sensibility.

In his remarks, Zagajewski examines the seesaw of doubt and certainty in the thought of Poles Witold Gombrowicz and Milosz—comparing the former's mercurial disdain for any finality to the latter's "pendulum [which] swings between the two poles of the ontological planet, between fascination with the impetus of history and the joy of stillness. . . . "Zagajewski argues that these dependable extremes—defensive reactions against authoritarianism and modern Western culture—could become

traps for the Polish imagination. (Though Zagajewski thinks Milosz spikes his religious conservatism with "democratic, liberal, and very vocal anti-nationalistic political views.") In *Canvas*, these polarities are evoked and then confronted: Zagajewski writes epistemological/ontological verse, filled with comic bafflement, personal obsessions, and pervasive nostalgia for the big questions. A member of the rebellious generation of '68, Zagajewski isn't so much a mediator between the terse angst of a Rózewicz and the august dichotomies of Milosz as a wary freedom fighter trying to keep the self clear of the despotism of history and its counterpart, the poetry of extremes.

The most trenchant expression of Zagajewski's sense of words as a doleful site of liberation is the collection's title lyric, **"Canvas,"** which ends the book:

> I stood in silence before a dark picture,
> before a canvas that might have been
> coat, shirt, flag,
> but had turned instead into the world.
>
> I stood in silence before the dark canvas,
> charged with delight and revolt and I thought
> of the arts of painting and living,
> of so many blank, bitter days,
>
> of moments of helplessness
> and my chilly imagination
> that's the tongue of a bell,
> alive only when swaying,
>
> striking what it loves,
> loving what it strikes,
> and it came to me that this canvas
> could have become a winding sheet, too.

Zagajewski's imagination swings among countless end points: His "canvas" is the fabric of history, the tarpaulin of art, and the screen of consciousness. The poem is also a canvas, a shroud wound around the electric life of the soul, its flickers of incredulity and fear, inspiration and despair. **"Canvas"** covers the poet's usual bumpy territory; his persona recoils from a vaguely ominous external threat into a self-consciously romantic respite ("loving what it strikes"), ending in an inclusive conclusion. Avoiding endgames, *Canvas'* lyricism is tainted with political fact, its meditations on past horrors tinctured with divine indifference. Zagajewski's volatile poems remind me of how the Czech poet and scientist Miroslav Holub looks at his verse—it's "all about energy and steam, all about transformations of energy."

Zagajewski cogitates without settling on a Hegelian synthesis; he doubts without disappearing into his navel. His customary tone is one of jagged confrontation—his persona's quicksilver changes in tone (humorous, melancholic, sophisticated, innocent) disarm conclusion, as in **"Presence"**:

> Might only the absence of presence be perfect?
> Presence, after all, infected with the original

sin of existence, is excessive, savage,
Oriental, superb, while beauty, like a fruit knife,
snips its bit of plenitude off.

Yet castration—poetry as the nipped bud of life—serves as both an aggressive and defensive maneuver on Zagajewski's part. His poems give off a calculated air of bad faith, a determination to keep larger forces at bay. This need to play hooky, to tumble into feckless pleasure, accounts for his verse's shifty-eyed vulnerability, why his shaggy dog charm gambols with old-fashioned seriousness ("Most highly respected Professor Nietzsche, / sometimes I seem to see you / on a sanatorium terrace at dawn / with fog descending and song bursting / the throats of the birds."). It also links the poet's epistemological skepticism with a yearning for the dreamy realms of relaxation, the banishment of ego.

Zagajewski's poems evoke the ghosts of war and death, bow respectfully before Western and European intellectual traditions, swoon over the beauty of the earth. But underneath their ironic dialectics is a call for the end of talk, for the creation of a private dream space (Tsvetaeva's "atrophy of conscience"). Survival often comes down to a snooze, as in the poems **"Wind at Night"** ("We heard those voices with half / our attention, and, understanding little, / turned again to sleep") or the rock-a-bye revelation of **"The Sea Was Asleep"**:

> The sea was asleep, only occasionally
> did a whirlpool's sharp braid
> or a shimmer ripple
> its infinity-infatuated back.
> As dogs dream of running,
> we were thinking, that softly.
> We spoke little,
> walked warily
> on the wet sand, and animal sleep
> enveloped us like the future.

Once again, the external is transformed into a curtain upon which Zagajewski can project a moment of peace, of "animal" oblivion. But that momentary nothingness can turn into the big sleep. **"In Strange Cities"** directly links art and death ("The huge flags of the trees, though, / flutter as in places we know, / and the same lead is sewn in the hems / of winding-sheets, dreams, and the imagination, / homeless, and mad."). Zagajewski's verse is propelled by a fear of disappearing into the recesses of subjectivity as well as into history. His lively and melancholic mind swings in all directions, from the parodic strong-arming of political poems like **"Russia comes into Poland"** ("Russia comes in, marching / into a hamlet on the Pilica, / into the deep Mazovia forests, / rending posters and parliaments," to the wistful tenderness of nature poems like **"Fruit."** In the latter, Zagajewski pays tongue-in-cheek homage to Milosz's quest for stillness: "Intangible rainbows. Huge cliffs of clouds / flowing slowly through the sky. The sumptuous, / unattainable afternoon. My life, / swirling, unattainable, free." To Zagajewski, romantic extremity is another form of ego-denying captivity, which is why he describes his imagina-

tion as "chilly" rather than ecstatic. Irony no longer serves as the conservator of humanistic values, but as the cool guardian of the fragile self.

The future of Central European poetry lies in this kind of probing and wounded uncertainty—Zagajewski's homeland isn't the heroic nationalism of Polish history or the monomania of poetic resistance. The poet is the site of a succession of conflicts: "each drama unfolds in a different place, / with a different ending; silence, tears, fright, / joy, vision, success, a hymn; it ends in a church, / empty train, jail, lecture hall, mud." Ultimately, Zagajewski is surrounded by too much history and too much beauty. In **"Green Linnaeus,"** the classifier finds the plenitude of the world engulfing him: "the conductor of an orchestra that's grown beyond him, / grows still beyond him, infinitely, with all its roots, / leaves and buds." Ironically, the Linnaeus in Czeslaw Milosz's latest collection, *Provinces,* is "like Adam in the garden." His gift for naming is an ideal "in this bitter age deprived of harmony." And the author brings him a tribute: "A verse imitating the classical ode." Milosz stakes out his mental territory with an imaginative faith in the self that Zagajewski respects but can't match. . . .

Charles Simic (essay date 1994)

SOURCE: A Review of *Canvas*, in *Partisan Review*, Vol. 61, No. 4, Fall, 1994, pp. 704-8.

[*In the following review, Simic suggests that Zagajewski explores the philosophical and imaginative homelessness of modern men and women.*]

. . . When Adam Zagajewski's selected poems were first published in English in 1985, it was clear that he was a major poet. *Tremor* was a book that reminded one of other great contemporary Polish poets, Milosz, Herbert and Szymborska, especially in its preoccupation with history and its love of irony. It was equally clear, however, that Zagajewski is an original voice. This new, well-translated collection confirms it. His subject, if one could generalize about a poet so intellectually complex, is the epoch's end. Not solely the end of a long and murderous century, but the death of ideas that underwrote all our now failed utopian projects:

> dreams and imagination
> homeless and mad.

Philosophically and imaginatively we are once more homeless. We are once more jailbirds from every Garden of Eden of every lofty idea. Who could still be a follower of Hegel or Neitzsche in this age? Perhaps some professor, but not a poet. The ode is dead; long live the elegy! The past is like the tenement window in Zagajewski's poem called **"A Warm, Small Rain."**

> actors appeared,
> from your dreams and my dreams;
> I knew I was en route to the future, that lost
> epoch—a pilgrim trekking to Rome.

"Things, do you know suffering?" Zagajewski asks. . . . The mystery of the object is like the mystery of a closed door that we have no way of opening. We can only ask it questions. Zagajewski asks many difficult questions in his poems. For instance, how have evil and beauty lived side by side, and continue to do so even today? Here is how he begins his poem **"Lava"**:

> And what if Heraclitus and Parmenides
> are both right
> and two worlds exist side by side,
> one serene, the other insane; one arrow
> thoughtlessly hurtles, another, indulgent,
> look on; the selfsame wave moves and stands still.

"How unattainable life is," he says in a poem. For a poet for whom philosophy begins with the "simplest apple, inscrutable, round," each poetic image is the evidence of the unattainable, the place where the real and the imaginary collide, "nail scissors / three thousand years old." In his book of essays, *Solidarity Solitude* (published by Ecco Press), Zagajewski makes a point that is central to his work. He says: "Man's personality possesses something untamed, mysterious, divine, unhistorical, undomesticated, something that speaks quietly in art, in religion, in the search for truth, and it is exactly that delicate something that is the hunted animal, preyed upon by Political Systems and their countless conformities as well as by the conformities produced spontaneously by a collectivity." Listen to this fine poem:

> Evening, the edge of the city, a whole day
> of void, then all at once
> the late feast: the Sanskrit of dusk that speaks
> in a glowing tongue of joy.
> High overhead flow cigarette firelets
> no one is smoking.
> Sheets of blazing secrets aflame;
> what the serenely fading sky tells
> can't be remembered or even described.
> So what if Pharaoh's armies pursue you,
> when eternity is woven
> through the days of the week like moss
> in the chinks of a cabin?
>
> —"Late Feast"

Jarolsaw Anders (essay date 1998)

SOURCE: "Between Fire and Sleep," in *Los Angeles Times Book Review*, February 1, 1998, p. 6

[*In the following review, Anders suggests that in* Mysticism for Beginners *Zagajewski understands the contradictions intrinsic to modern mystical poetry but demonstrates that poetry can still transcend irony.*]

In the title poem of this remarkable volume by Polish poet Adam Zagajewski, the author takes us to an Italian town (Montepulciano in Tuscany) where, among the usual splendors of such places (the dusk "erasing the outlines of medieval houses," "olive trees on little hills," "stained-glass windows like butterfly wings"), he suddenly confesses his belief that the world given to our senses may not be all there is, that all this,

> and any journey, any kind of trip,
> are only mysticism for beginners,
> the elementary course, prelude
> to a test that's been
> postponed.

The phrase "mysticism for beginners," however, comes from the cover of a book spotted by the poet in the lap of a German tourist, possibly another New Age guide to higher spiritual awareness. The contrast between the serious, straightforward declaration of a mystical premise and the ironic, trivialized context in which the word "mysticism" appears points to the central question of Zagajewski's poetry: Can metaphysical inquiry still be a legitimate concern of poetry in a culture in which ideas of mystery and mysticism are most likely associated with "The X-Files" or "The Celestine Prophecy"? Or, to reverse the question: Can serious poetry survive without mystery and ecstasy; can it be sustained by irony alone, which the poet calls, in **"Long Afternoons,"** "the gaze / that sees but doesn't penetrate?"

Zagajewski, known to American readers from two earlier books of poetry (**Tremor** and **Canvas**), as well as two books of essays (*Solidarity, Solitude* and *Two Cities*), may seem an unlikely candidate to raise such questions. Born in 1945, the year of the Communist takeover in Poland, he belongs to what will always be known as the "Solidarity generation," that particular breed of tough, down-to-earth dreamers and pragmatic romantics who made ironic defiance their weapon of choice against totalitarian, ideological rant. In the '70s, he belonged to a small but vocal group of young writers who practiced literature that exposed the paradoxes and incongruities of "socialism" in an increasingly restless Poland. One of his early essays, *The Unrepresented World*, which called for a new version of "critical realism," was even adopted as the group's manifesto.

Yet Zagajewski soon parted ways—poetically, not politically—with most of his colleagues. As he explained later, cultural struggle against a collectivist idea tends to impose a rigidity of its own. "To be a Pole," he writes in one of his essays, "to participate in the work of Polish literature, is practically the same as becoming a member of a religious order with very strict rules. . . . Anyone who has an idea offers it to the others, immediately wants to change it into law or obligation—as if fearing his own tête-à-tête with originality." The best defense against collectivism, said the poet, was creative individualism and meditative solitude rather then forced solidarity and subservience to "the cause."

In the early '80s, Zagajewski, by that time living in Paris, responded to the imposition of martial law in Poland with the long poem **"Ode to Plurality"** contained in the volume **Tremor**. It is a paean to the pure ecstasy of life, the abundance of ideas, "a wild run of poetry," "the shock of love," "the changing delight of seasons," "the pleasure of hearing" and "the pleasure of seeing," the inexhaustible memory of civilizations and the "singular soul" that stands "before / this abundance. Two eyes, two hands, / ten inventive fingers, and / only one ego, the wedge of an orange, / the youngest of sisters." Although, characteristically, the poem does not mention any of the events that must have absorbed every Pole at that time—the crushing of the Solidarity movement, the apparent crushing of the dreams of the poet's own generation—one can clearly hear mighty laughter at a certain general who tried to plug the river of history with a couple of tanks and squads of riot police.

"**Ode to Plurality**" expresses a barely verbalized mystical longing that would mark Zagajewski's later poetry. In that particular poem, this longing takes the form of a rather cryptic and paradoxical image of "one of the colder stars" to whose power one wishes to give oneself yet is "mocking it / sometimes because it is slimy and cool / like a frog in a pond."

In *Mysticism for Beginners*, there are many similar litanies of sounds, sights, seemingly unconnected scenes and events, in which an almost childlike enchantment with life's multiplicity mixes with a longing to reach beyond the horizon of ordinary human experience. Sometimes plurality provides a lyrical framework for a simple emotion, as in the beautiful, nostalgic love poem "**For M.**" In other cases, it serves as a tool to recapture past experiences, as in the poem "**From Memory,**" in which a stream of remembered details transports the poet to the Silesian town of his childhood, still scarred by war "like a German student's cheek." In "**Elegy,**" within the space of 35 verses, the poet manages to reconstruct the whole monochrome, stillborn physical reality of Communist life ("houses small / as Tartar ponies," "Soviet gods with swollen eyelids," "sour smell of gas, sweet smell of tedium") and its moral climate ("endless winters, / in which there dwelled, as if in ancient lindens, / sparrows and knives and friendship and leaves of treason"), and then bid it farewell with a firm, conciliatory handshake ("but we lived there, and not as strangers").

Occasionally the richness becomes a thicket, an obstacle on the journey. In "**The Three Kings,**" the Magi come late for the Epiphany, and one of them, like a tardy employee, blurts out a litany of excuses ("Spring meadows detained us, cowslips, / the glances of country maidens"). There is also a constant mixing of "grief, despair, delight and pride" in the endless transformations of things as in "**The Blackbird,**" in which the bird, clearly identified with the poet himself, sings "a gentle, jazzy tune" of farewell to a "funeral cortege" of life that appears "the same each evening, there, on the horizon's thread."

More than a passing word of praise is due to Clare Cavanagh, who has rendered Zagajewski's difficult language in taut, limpid English. She has already distinguished herself as co-translator, with Stanislaw Baranczak, of two other important books: "Spoiling Cannibals' Fun" (1991), an anthology of Polish poetry from the last decades of Communism; and "View With a Grain of Sand" (1995) by Nobel laureate Wislawa Szymborska. She is a true asset to Polish poetry in America.

Plurality, in Zagajewski's poetry, can be exhilarating but also depressing: a road to ecstasy and an unfortunate distraction. Most of the poems in this volume seem to portray a state of foiled rapture or a journey that stops short of its goal. A trip into the past fails to recapture essential memories. A wanderer in "**September**" is unable to find the house of the Czech poet Vladimir Holan and the famous baroque churches of Prague appear to him as only "deluxe health clubs for athletic saints." Scraps of voices that follow the poet in "**Out Walking**" are drowned by the din of the city and never return. In the end, there is the ambiguous triumph of life that is mere repetition and accumulation of experience.

Only sometimes the cavalcade slows down, and plurality is replaced by a heightened experience of one particular moment that seems to expand into a small, self-contained, though fragile universe. In the beautiful short poem "**That's Sicily,**" the "three-cornered island" glimpsed during a night sea journey evokes in an instant an intensely sensual delight ("the huge leaves / of hills swayed like a giant's dreams"), the whole history of the world and a quiet contemplation of death. In "**On Swimming,**" a lonely swimmer converses with the sea while

> *Little village churches*
> *hold a fabric of silence so fine*
> *and old that even a breath*
> *could tear it.*

There are many such moments of sensual and cerebral ecstasy in Zagajewski's poems, but even they leave a residue of unfulfilled longing, a feeling that something very important has once again eluded our perceptions. Even the most exhilarating experiences in Zagajewski's verse are subdued and introspective. In "**Moment,**" the poet seems to suspend his own elation to make a melancholy comment:

> *This moment, mortal as you or I,*
> *was full of boundless, senseless,*
> *silly joy, as if it knew*
> *something we didn't*

The tension resulting from this elusiveness of ecstasy is more intellectual than emotional or spiritual. Only rarely does it result in moments of unmistakably religious disquiet, as in the poem "**Tierra del Fuego,**" in which the poet turns directly to the "Nameless, unseen, silent" God, asking Him to:

> *open the boxes full of song,*
> *open the blood that pulses in aortas*
> *of animals and stones,*
> *light lanterns in black gardens.*

For the most part, however, the poetic persona speaking in Zagajewski's verse seems to be in no great hurry to graduate beyond the "elementary course" of mystical initiation. He prefers to listen to the world, contemplate his "double-headed doubt" and bask in the light of small things, occasionally even mocking his own dreams. At the end, he is willing to concede, in **"Cicadas,"** that:

> We exist between the elements,
> between fire and sleep.
> Pain chases
> or outstrips us.

Zagajewski is clearly a very modern mystic, one who realizes that the mystical pursuit is essentially a contradictory one: Endless postponing of the "test," as the title poem suggests, is often a part of he course. It is his mixture of skepticism and passion that makes him one of the most interesting poets of his generation writing in any language.

Zagajewski speaks also to those of us who are not at all mystically inclined showing that poetry not resigned to irony but in which ecstasy and irony are more or less equal contenders, is capable of great unity of mind and feeling, the "sensuous apprehension of thought" that T. S. Eliot praised in his essay on the English Metaphysicals as the true measure of poetic achievement.

Adam Kirsch (essay date 1998)

SOURCE: "The Lucid Moment," in *The New Republic*, Vol. 218, No. 12, March 23, 1998, pp. 36-40.

[*In the following essay, Kirsch considers* Myticism for Beginners *in relation to Zagajewski's early work and compares his "philosophical wit" with the imagery of metaphysical poets such as John Donne.*]

A poetry of mysticism, now? For a mystic of the seventeenth century, for Vaughan or Traherne, the object of mysticism was the old one, the obvious one: God, or Christ. For a Romantic neo-Platonist such as Shelley, the object was less clear, but still plausible: the Idea, the great pattern hidden from human sight. But if Romanticism was spilt religion, today the spill has just about been sopped up; and the presumption, or even the suggestion, of a mystical dimension to life can seem anachronistic, an evasion of the real and secular responsibilities of the time. So how can a poet—an intelligent, serious poet—write mystical verse now? The poetry of Adam Zagajewski provides the beginning of an answer to this question.

Zagajewski is the preeminent Polish poet of his generation. He is a thoroughly contemporary man who aspires, without embarrassment, to a verse that is a concrete avenue to an invisible reality. And the peculiar forms into which this situation forces him, the poetic strategies and the poetic evasions that it requires, reveal a great deal about the possibilities of poetry today.

Zagajewski was born in Lvov, in eastern Poland, in 1945. Within the year his family was transplanted to the west-ern city of Gliwice, victims of the post-war redrawing of Poland's borders. As a student he moved to Cracow, and after several clashes with the authorities emigrated to Paris in 1982. Zagajewski emerged as a prominent poet and polemicist in 1974 with the publication of *The Unrepresented World*, a critical manifesto which, as Stanislaw Baranczak wrote in these pages, "stirred up one of the greatest controversies in postwar Polish culture [by attacking] the noncommittal literature of the previous decades." As Zagajewski ruefully wrote years later, "I took my place among the Catos of this world for a while, among those who know what literature should be and ruthlessly exact these standards from others." Of this phase of his career, English-readers have nothing—his first book published in English, *Tremor*, dates from 1985, well into his Paris period. Yet it is crucial for understanding his later development, since the poet whom we know from his five American books is in full flight from this politically engaged view of poetry. Indeed, the antinomy between politics and poetry—or between history and art, or between the collective and the private—is the main argument of his mature work.

This flight from history was a product of history, specifically the history of Communism in Poland. After the Solidarity movement rose to prominence in 1980, Zagajewski sensed that Communism in Poland was in retreat. Not defeated, of course—Solidarity was driven underground by the proclamation of martial law in 1981—but beginning its decline; within ten years it would be dead. Zagajewski's poems and essays of the 1980s—collected in *Tremor* and *Solidarity, Solitude*—look forward quite consciously to a life after totalitarianism, in which "antitotalitarianism" will no longer be a sufficient worldview. Zagajewski in this phase is preparing the ground for post-Communist Polish intellectual life. He points insistently to a world beyond the old definitions of good and evil, a world in which a truly private mental existence, unfettered but also unenergized by the struggle with communism, will have to find other reasons for being.

These concerns are announced in the title of *Solidarity, Solitude*, the remarkable collection of essays that appeared in 1990. As he writes in the preface to that book: "The word 'Solidarity' on the jacket of this book stands mostly for *the* Solidarity, a dynamic, robust, political and social movement in Poland. . . . Solitude stands for literature, art, meditation, for immobility." Zagajewski is not for solitude and against Solidarity, or solidarity; a concern for public justice is rather a kind of precondition, a given, for men of good will. But neither is he for solidarity at the expense of solitude, which gives access to another realm: the world of art, beauty, epiphanous experience. As he writes in the title essay of *Two Cities*:

> The piercing sense of community, intimacy, of possessing something elusive—that half-legendary country of Poland. . . . An even more important ingredient of this philosophy was a thesis I knew well . . . that all is social, common, and collective.

I did not know how to formulate my opposition, I did not have the appropriate arguments at my disposal; but I did feel that not everything belonged to everybody. We are different and we also experience things which social groups will never know.

Zagajewski's difficulty, as a poet in a time of national crisis, was that these two realms are, strictly speaking, incommensurable: art (that is, art which is truly and only art) does not get the tanks off the streets, and mass movements do not write poems.

The dilemma of solidarity and solitude is unfamiliar to an American, and it may be difficult for an American to enter into it fully. Here poetry is such a minor, sidelined pursuit that its practitioners by and large never even think of using their art to serve a larger cause. (The few writers who do make poems into polemics, such as Adrienne Rich or Audre Lorde, generally fail at both.) For some critics—George Steiner most egregiously—this amounts to a complacency that diminishes American art. On this view, the moral crisis of Eastern Europe gives poetry an urgency and a public stature that it can never have in the United States, where it is largely a hobby confined to writing workshops.

Zagajewski's work is important for its rejection of this view. His writing, in poetry and in prose, is in part an attempt to diagnose the deformities of a poetry under too much public pressure, a poetry that feels a duty to participate in politics. As a poet who feels poetry to be a calling in an older, more Romantic sense, Zagajewski knows well that there is a zone of solitude, of "immobility," which is necessary for writing perfectly achieved poetry. Indeed, Zagajewski parodies the Steiner view quite devastatingly in **"Central Europe,"** a short sketch from *Two Cities*:

He was an unremarkable, tiny man with dark greasy hair combed flat across his head who, without waiting for permission, joined my table. It was clear he was dying to talk. He would have exchanged half his life for a moment of conversation.

"Where are you from?" he asked.

"From Poland," I said.

"Ah, how lucky, how lucky you are!" he exclaimed, overcome by genuine Mediterranean enthusiasm. "Mourning! Long live mourning! . . . You are a lucky man."

"Why lucky?"

"Force. Force of conviction, Categorical feelings. Moral integrity. A literature that is not alienated from the polis. You have not experienced that alarming split. . . . I always felt in you the desire for unity, the Greek dream of combining emotion and courage. . . . "

This Westerner is using Poland just as generations of modern Westerners have used Greece, or the Renaissance, or the Middle Ages: as an imagined ideal, an instrument of vicarious living, a name for a condition of spiritual wholeness. He values the mournful country for its solidarity. He even envies it.

In Zagajewski's view, however, solidarity is not a mode in which the poet—or, indeed, any reflective person—can come to rest. Rather, he sees solidarity as the antithesis that arises in opposition to the thesis of totalitarianism: "Totalitarians have their own primitive seal, which they stamp onto the wax of reality. Antitotalitarians have fashioned their own seal. And it, too, shapes the wax. . . . Poor wax, lashed by seals!" Solidarity is something with which Zagajewski would like to dispense, in the way that one puts away a tool that has served its purpose. Scorn, hatred, loathing for totalitarianism is everywhere in his work; but so is a distrust of antitotalitarianism, the other seal that disfigures the wax of reality.

Solidarity, Solitude, then, is a manifesto, but not of the kind that Zagajewski produced in *The Unrepresented World.* It is a manifesto against manifestos, a warning against too much solidarity, written at a time when solidarity was both a necessary stance and a kind of moral intoxicant. Zagajewski reminds his countrymen that "we have to conquer totalitarianism in passing, on our way to greater things, in the direction of this or that reality, even though we may be unable to say exactly what reality is." When one considers how tempting solidarity can be, and how difficult and lonely a private definition of reality is, the real nobility of such a statement begins to emerge. At a time when collective thought and collective identity came under the seductive sign of liberation, Zagajewski was self-possessed enough to remain wary of history.

But once Zagajewski has made his choice for privacy, for the inner life, he is faced with a more difficult problem, and one which is less specific to Poland. To write against the public and historical life, and in favor of the private and individual life, is still to be conditioned by the public, even if one's response to it is a negative one. In *Solidarity, Solitude* Zagajewski turns his back on one definition of life and of its purpose, but it is not yet clear what he has turned toward. What *is* the inner life? And it is here that Zagajewski becomes, not only a Polish poet, but to a great extent a representative poet of our time.

When Zagajewski begins to write about things not conditioned by history—and, in his books, this is clearly the role set aside for poetry, as opposed to prose—we find him strangely inexplicit. Zagajewski is, in some sense, a mystic; the title of his new book is ***Mysticism for Beginners,*** and throughout his poetry we find a longing toward the mystical as the natural consummation of the private, the ahistorical. But he is certainly not a mystic in the sense that Yeats was a mystic. He doesn't have a doctrine or a system or a single truth; he remains at the point of hoping that perhaps there is such a truth, though he will probably never comprehend it.

In this paradoxical way, Zagajewski is representative: he is a mystical poet of the liberal imagination. He cannot abide oppression of the spirit, even when it comes wearing the friendly face of the Solidarity movement; he insists on solitude, on the freedom to go where his thoughts lead him. But then he finds that they lead him to no place in particular. One (admittedly narrow) definition of liberalism is neutrality; but what happens when the collective no longer cares to direct the spirit? The individual is thrown back on his own resources, which very often turn out to be inadequate. Zagajewski is the poet of this situation, which is responsible both for the universality of his appeal and for the important restrictions of his poetry.

One of those restrictions, of course, lies not in the poems, but in ourselves: almost no American reader will be able to read these poems in the original. How much is really lost in translation is a constant question; but it is likely to be closer to everything than to nothing. And the difficulty with Zagajewski's poetry is the greater because he is, in Schiller's sense, a sentimental poet: he writes about a feeling rather than from within a feeling, and writing about delicate emotions is perhaps the most difficult thing to do in poetry without sounding ridiculous. It is much easier successfully to write a clever line, or a sounding line, than a tender line. And the margin between the touching and the maudlin is inevitably blurred in translation.

Typically, Zagajewski reaches sentiment through the maze of irony, thus justifying the reward, by the difficulty of the quest. His characteristic voice is sophisticated and witty, with deep feeling lying just beneath the surface. But occasionally he will write a poem, usually a short one, that is pure sentiment:

"Anecdote of Rain"

I was strolling under
    the tents of trees
and raindrops occasion-
    ally reached me
as though asking:
Is your desire to suffer,
to sob?

Soft air,
wet leaves;
—the scent was spring,
    the scent sorrow.

This poem is like one of those sweet, sad lyrics of Eichendorff or Heine that Schumann set to music—not just because of the concision and the directness of the sentiment, but also because of the English speaker's sense that something is missing. It is a beautiful poem, but beautiful in a way that no one writing in English could manage without embarrassment. Reading Zagajewski is, in part, a continual negotiation with this embarrassment, an attempt to recognize that what's missing is just what could redeem the poems from excess of sentiment.

But this is a technical problem, which most likely arises from our ignorance of Polish. There is also a deeper

sentiment here, which is not accidental but essential. It is attached to the subject of mystical experience, which for Zagajewski is a constant, tantalizing possibility, if one which is seldom attained. In *Solidarity, Solitude*, the poet insisted that the most important events are private, not public; and in his poetry, we see that these important events are often mystical, which is privacy carried to the point of incommunicability.

In fact, they become more explicitly mystical as Zagajewski's work progresses. In *Tremor*, his first American book, we already see that what matters most to Zagajewski is the transitory feeling of completion, of clarity, which is the hallmark of mystical experience. This feeling comes up in poem after poem, sometimes tinged with wit, sometimes given directly:

Don't allow the lucid moment to dissolve
Let the radiant thought last in stillness
though the page is almost filled and
    the flame flickers . . .

At night, an invisible bonfire blazes,
the fire which, burning, doesn't destroy
but creates, as if it wanted to restore
in one moment all that was ravished
by flames on various continents . . .

    The quest for perfection
will find fulfillment casually, it will bypass
all obstacles just as the Germans
learned how to bypass the Maginot Line . . .

. . . . there was so much of the world that
it had to do encores over and over,
the audience was in frenzy and didn't want
to leave the house.

These are all descriptions of a single feeling, in various manifestations. And it is characteristic of this mystical feeling that it is transitory and incomplete:

The earth won't open up, a thunderbolt
won't burn fiery letters on
the sky's pelt. Did we deserve
a sign so distinct, we who
talk too loudly and can't
listen? A train pulls out
when the stationmaster raises his
arm, but a waterfall doesn't wait for a signal.
A leaf will sway, a drop of wate will glisten.

Or again:

Clear moments are so short.
There is much more darkness. More
ocean than firm land. More
shadow than form.

Such "clear moments" become more common in his later books of poetry, *Canvas* (1991) and now *Mysticism for Beginners*. In these later books, there is a growing sense that the instant of rapt attention to the world is the center of life, and the proper subject for poetry. These poems are shot through with intimations of immortality:

> So what if Pharaoh's armies pursue you,
> when eternity is woven
> through the days of the week like moss
> in the chinks of a cabin?
>
> Turn off the glaring sun,
> listen to the tale of the seed of a poppy.
> A fence, Chestnut trees. Bindweed. God.
>
> A moment of quiet covenant
> in the Egyptian museum
> in Turin . . .

Here the mysticism is reminiscent of Rilke, at a lower pitch. Zagajewski's litany ("A fence. Chestnut trees. Bindweed. God.") recalls the litany in the *Duino Elegies*:

> Maybe we're here only to
> say: house, bridge, well, gate, jug,
> olive tree, window—
> at most: pillar, tower. . . .

Like Rilke, Zagajewski is overcome at times by a powerful sense that the singular being of objects conceals some higher truth. For him, too, things are the sites of illumination.

But for Zagajewski these intimations remain intimations, not explanations or descriptions. And here we are faced with the central problem of his poetry, which is the problem of poetry in the face of the mystical: the mystical experience is not loquacious. The poet may seek "the still point of the turning world," but stillness writes no poetry. What yearns to be expressed, rather, is the experience of waiting for the sudden heightening of consciousness; waiting for it, or remembering it, or lacking it. These are situations of pathos; and the main colors in Zagajewski's palette are loss, longing, and awe, lightened from time to time with shades of wit.

And there is a further problem with mysticism as a subject for poetry: it does not admit of much variation. Poetry thrives on themes that are at the same time simple and fertile: thus Shakespeare can write 154 sonnets about love, and Tennyson can write hundreds of stanzas on mourning, because the subject is at the same time universal enough to compel our interest and general enough to admit of new situations, new shadings. But the mystic moment is indescribable, incommensurable: that is why it is so longed for. Thus Zagajewski, as a poet of the mystical, is condemned to a kind of eternal recurrence of the same poem. To look at the ends of the poems in *Mysticism for Beginners* is to see his predicament:

> I've taken long walks,
> craving one thing only:
> lightning,
> transformation,
> you.

> I don't know how—
> the palm trees opened up my greedy heart.

> . . . take me to Tierra del Fuego,
> take me where the rivers
> flow straight up, horizontal rivers
> flowing up and down.

> This moment, mortal as you or I,
> was full of boundless, senseless,
> silly joy, as if it knew
> something we didn't.

The destination of these poems is usually the same: the moment of opening out to the insensible object of the soul's yearning, whether it is described as "silly joy" or allegorized as **"Tierra del Fuego."** The poem wants to get to this point, and whatever it describes is a means to an end, not an end in itself.

Zagajewski himself describes this phenomenon in one of the aphoristic essays in *Two Cities*, "The Untold Cynicism of Poetry": "The inner world, which is the absolute kingdom of poetry, is characterized by its inexpressibility. . . . What then does this inner world accomplish if in spite of its inexpressibility it wants more than anything to express itself? It uses cunning. It pretends that it is interested, oh yes, very interested, in external reality. What we have here, perhaps, is the natural evolution of Zagajewski's praise of solitude. In his earlier work, solitude stood in opposition to the collective and the public; and it was good. But now solitude and inwardness are considered in themselves, and they are difficult things. They verge on inexpressibility. As Zagajewski writes in **"Lecture on Mystery"**:

> We do not know what poetry is. We do not know what suffering is. We do not know what death is.
>
> We do know what mystery is.

Even if we allow that this is true, it still leaves two possibilities for poetry. One is to make poetry describe its subject as attentively as possible: thus Shakespeare's sonnets do not tell us "what love is," but they bring us closer to such an understanding. The other possibility is to stand scrupulously back from the subject, honoring its inexpressibility. In this case, the ostensible subject of the poem—love, death, suffering—is no longer the real subject; rather, the subject is the author's consciousness in the face of this ultimate limiation. This is the kind of poetry Zagajewski writes. It is poetry that threatens to lead to silence.

But Zagajewski is in no danger of falling silent. He is not an otherworldly or ascetic mystic, who feels driven from this world by hints of another. His alienation is not radical, it is occasional. And in this, too, he is a poet of the liberal imagination: his vision of the mystical does not put everything at stake. Not for him wagers or leaps; he is content to see the lineaments of something higher peeking through the things of this world, without forcing it to reveal itself as a coherent structure.

The clearest sign of Zagajewski's attachment to the world is his wit. Mysticism and humor do not usually go together. But quick and memorable absurdities temper the darkness of much of Zagajewski's poetry:

> Practicing elocution like a timid
>   Demosthenes,
> the Danube flows over flat stones.
>
> What are baroque churches? Deluxe
> health clubs for athletic saints.
>
>   Now rain dictates
> a long, tedious lecture. . . .

Sometimes Zagajewski is simply funny, as in the title of one poem: **"Franz Schubert: A Press Conference."** ("No, I'm not familiar with Wagner's music.") But more often his wit is employed to intimate a darkness without stating it, as in this miniature theodicy:

>   At the Orthodox
> church in Paris, the last White
> gray-haired Russians pray to God, who
> is centuries younger than they and equally
> helpless.

Or this, about Stalinism:

> One day apes made their grab for power.
> Gold seal-rings,
> starched shirts,
> aromatic Havanas,
> feet squashed into patent feather.

Wit is even more evident in Zagajewski's prose. His most important achievement in prose is the development of a kind of very short essay, occasionally shrinking to aphorism, in which wit and irony can flourish. This is the style of **"The Little Larousse,"** from *Solidarity, Solitude*, and **"The New Little Larousse,"** from *Two Cities*. Here Zagajewski is very often brilliant:

> [The Poles] write books as if they were to be documents considered during a future peace conference that will decide the fate of Europe.
>
> Territorial conquests are not just changes in boundaries and the imposition of an unwanted government. They are also detectable when we cease to see the earth.
>
> The adjective is the indispensable guarantor of the individuality of people and things. I see a pile of melons at a fruit stand. For an opponent of adjectives, this matter presents no difficulty: "Melons are piled on the fruit stand." Meanwhile, one melon is as sallow as Talleyrand's complexion when he addressed the Congress of Vienna . . . another has sunken cheeks, and is lost in a deep, mournful silence, as if it could not bear to part with the fields of Provence.

This side of Zagajewski's sensibility seems far removed from the yearning mystic. Indeed, it is what can make him attractive even to those readers who have little patience for epiphany; it gives evidence of an unconstrained, undogmatic intelligence. With its rapid and unlikely juxtapositions, wit tends to undermine certainty. When you begin to see God as an old Russian exile, or commissars as cigar-smoking apes, you have stolen their old authority; a doubleness of perspective has set in.

In this respect, wit is intimately bound up with the liberal imagination, and with sentimental poetry. In *Solidarity, Solitude*, Zagajewski writes that "one must think against oneself . . . otherwise one is not free." But what is implied by this is that freedom of thought is more important than thinking rightly. Once the thinker becomes more devoted to his thinking than to his thought, dogma is impossible. And clearly the importance of thinking against oneself was brought home to Zagajewski living in a totalitarian state, where the stupidity and cruelty of the prevailing dogmas was plain.

What is left, then, is not correctness of thought, but nimbleness of thought. The Danube is not the Danube but Demosthenes; the rain is not the rain but a tedious professor. And the mystical is, perhaps, not the mystical at all, but merely a moment of contentment, a feeling, a shadow. This possibility hovers around the title poem of *Mysticism for Beginners*, itself a fine example of Zagajewski's philosophical wit:

> The day was mild, the light was generous.
> The German on the café terrace
> held a small book on his lap.
> I caught sight of the title:
> *Mysticism for Beginners*.
> Suddenly I understood that the swallows
> patrolling the streets of Montepulciano
> with their shrill whistles . . .
> and the dusk, slow and systematic,
> erasing the outlines of medieval houses,
> and olive trees on little hills . . .
> and any journey, any kind of trip,
> are only mysticism for beginners,
> the elementary course, prelude
> to a test that's been
> postponed.

Zagajewski does not disavow mysticism in this poem, but he makes it the subject of a melancholy lightness, and thus puts it at an immense remove from belief. It is the same thing that happens when Donne begins a poem about the Judgment Day with "At the round earth's imagined corners, blow / Your trumpets, angels": since we know that there are no corners, we start to question whether there are angels. Similarly, in Zagajewski, the unlikeliness of mysticism "for beginners," as if it were a hobby like woodworking, makes us wonder about mysticism itself. The test has been postponed. Or has it been cancelled? Perhaps the test was never scheduled at all.

And so the mystical for Zagajewski is never free from doubt. The last poem in his new book is a touching example of this:

> I walked through the medieval town
> in the evening or at dawn,
> I was very young or rather old.
> I didn't have a watch
> or a calendar, only my stubborn blood
> measured the endless expanse.
> I could begin life, mine
> or not mine, over,
> everything seemed easy,
> apartment windows were partway open,
> other fates ajar.
> It was spring or early summer,
> warm walls,
> air soft as an orange rind;
> I was very young or rather old,
> I could choose, I could live.

This is the emotional ground out of which mysticism grows; but here the poet sticks to what is empirical and indisputable, to the emotion itself. The ability of the man who aspires to certainty to stop short of certainty: this is the hallmark of the liberal intelligence. The "thinking against oneself" which gives rise to wit also gives rise to hesitancy in the face of the absolute and the infinite, even when they are devoutly desired. And for this reason, Zagajewski's verse is unsettled and unsettling. He puts the matter perfectly:

> Two contradictory elements meet in poetry: ecstasy and irony. The ecstatic element is tied to an unconditional acceptance of the world, including even what is cruel and absurd. Irony, in contrast, is the artistic representation of thought, criticism, doubt. Ecstasy is ready to accept the entire world; irony, following in the steps of thought, questions everything, asks tendentious questions, doubts the meaning of poetry and even of itself. Irony knows that the world is tragic and sad.
>
> That two such vastly different elements shape poetry is astounding and even compromising. No wonder almost no one reads poems.

John Haines (essay date 1998)

SOURCE: A Review of *Mysticism for Beginners*, in *The Hudson Review*, Vol. LI, No. 3, Autumn, 1998, pp. 609-11.

[*In the following excerpt, Haines praises the historical consciousness, and the concentrated imagery of the poems in* Mysticism for Beginners.]

. . . To turn from Stafford's poems to the Polish poet Adam Zagajewski[2] is to depart from a familiar terrain and enter another space altogether, strangely removed from our still coherent neighborhoods:

> Europe is already sleeping, Night's animals,
> mournful and rapacious

> move in for the kill.
> Soon America will be sleeping too.
>
> **"Houston, 6 p.m."**

I think I would know, without being told, that these lines were not written by an American. Indeed, it is hardly possible to find in this slim book a poem in which the history of our time is not in some way acknowledged. The events, the terrible absences, are there, even when not directly referred to.

> The train stopped at a little station
> and for a moment stood absolutely still.
> The doors slammed, gravel crunched underfoot,
> someone said goodbye forever,
>
> a glove dropped, the sun dimmed,
> the doors slammed again even louder,
> and the iron train set off slowly
> and vanished in the fog like the nineteenth century.
>
> **"Iron Train"**

If one has something to say, a few words will suffice. No thoughtful European writer today can entirely dismiss that inherited knowledge of camps and trains and exile—so lasting and searing an experience shared to a greater or lesser degree by every nation on the continent. And this fact alone will distinguish the writing from its American counterpart. The difference can be said to lie in that fact that, in the present case, Zagajewski has this knowledge as part of himself; he doesn't have to invent it: "You are my silent brethren, / the dead, / I won't forget you."

The one word, "refugees," calls up an image all too universal even now:

> and always that special slouch
>
> as if leaning toward another, better planet,
> with less ambitious generals,
> less snow, less wind, fewer cannons,
> less History (alas, there's no
> such planet, just that slouch).
>
> Shuffling their feet,
> they move slowly, very slowly,
> toward the country of nowhere
> and the city of no one
> on the river of never.
>
> **"Refugees"**

Even a consideration of Dutch painting, with its allusions to some of the famous works of a classical period, cannot be made entirely free of our modern history:

> Doors were wide open, the wind was friendly.
> Brooms rested after work well done.
> Homes bared all. The painting of a land
> without secret police.
> Only on young Rembrandt's face
> an early shadow fell. Why?

Tell us, Dutch painters, what will happen
when the apple is peeled, when the silk dims,
when all the colors grow cold.
Tell us what darkness is.

"Dutch Painters"

In an extended review of Zagajewski's work published in *The New Republic,* and in speaking of the often divided position of a writer in Poland today, the critic Adam Kirsch had this to say:

> The dilemma of solidarity and solitude is unfamiliar to an American, and it may be difficult for an American to enter into it fully. Here poetry is such a minor, sidelined pursuit that its practitioners by and large never even think of using their art to serve a larger cause . . . For some critics—George Steiner most egregiously—this amounts to a complacency that diminishes American Art. On this view, the moral crisis of Eastern Europe gives poetry an urgency and a public stature it can never have in the United States, where it is largely a hobby confined to writing workshops.[3]

Kirsch's remarks appear to me consistent with what I have found in reading through well over twnety books for this review.

A typical modern exile, Zagajewski lives in Paris and teaches for part of the year at the University of Houston in Texas. This is the third of his books to appear in English, and the first I have read. Of the translations, and with no knowledge of the Polish language, I can only say that they appear to be faithful to the originals and result in poems that are moving and instructive in their own right.

This is otherwise a book to be taught by, in which a single stanza may hold, concentrated in a few words, more knowledge than is likely to be found in a year's subscription to your favorite newspaper or literary journal.

Wisdom can't be found
in music or fine paintings,
in great deeds, courage,
even love,
but only in all these things,
in earth and air, in pain and silence.

"Shell"

NOTES

[2] *Mysticism for Beginners,* by Adam Zagajewski. Trans. by Clare Cavanagh. Farrar, Straus and Giroux.

[3] Adam Kirsch, "The Lucid Moment," *The New Republic,* March 23, 1998.

FURTHER READING

Criticism

Ascherson, Neal. "'How to Leave a House of Slavery.'" *The New York Review of Books* XXXVIII, No. 14 (August 15, 1991): 17-20.
    Considers Zagajewski's career in relation to changes in Poland and its intellectual culture since the end of the Cold War.

Gorczynski, Renata. "A Vindication of Being." *Parnassus* 14, No. 1 (1987), p. 77-78.
    Calls Zagajewski an able and original heir to Polish masters such as Czeslaw Milosz and Zbigniew Herbert.

Levine, Madeline G. A review of *Tremor: Selected Poems.* *The Partisan Review* 57, No. 1 (1990): pp. 145-50.
    Reviews Zagajewski's poetry along with books by Czeslaw Milosz and Anna Swir.

Maciuszko, Jerzy J. A review of *Tremor: Selected Poems.* *World Literature Today* 60, No. 3, (Summer, 1986): 489.
    Praises Zagajewski's originality and calls him a "major force in Polish poetry."

Parker, Michael. "Out of Suffering." *Times Literary Supplement* No. 4,723 (October 8, 1993): 33.
    Reviews *Canvas* along with two volumes of poetry by Zbigniew Herbert.

Witkowski, Tadeusz. "Between Poetry and Politics: Two Generations." *Periphery: Journal of Polish Affairs* 2, No. 1-2 (1996): 38-43.
    Explores the literary and philosophical conflicts that confront Zagajewski's early poetry.

Poetry Criticism
INDEXES

Literary Criticism Series
Cumulative Author Index

Cumulative Nationality Index

Cumulative Title Index

How to Use This Index

The main references

```
Calvino, Italo
    1923-1985 ....... CLC 5, 8, 11, 22, 33, 39,
                                    73; SSC 3
```

list all author entries in the following Gale Literary Criticism series:

BLC(S) = *Black Literature Criticism (Supplement)*
CLC = *Contemporary Literary Criticism*
CLR = *Children's Literature Review*
CMLC = *Classical and Medieval Literature Criticism*
DA = *DISCovering Authors*
DAB = *DISCovering Authors: British*
DAC = *DISCovering Authors: Canadian*
DAM = *DISCovering Authors: Modules*
    DRAM: *Dramatists Module*; *MST*: *Most-Studied Authors Module*;
    MULT: *Multicultural Authors Module*; *NOV*: *Novelists Module*;
    POET: *Poets Module*; *POP*: *Popular Fiction and Genre Authors Module*
DC = *Drama Criticism*
HLC(S) = *Hispanic Literature Criticism Supplement*
LC = *Literature Criticism from 1400 to 1800*
NCLC = *Nineteenth-Century Literature Criticism*
PC = *Poetry Criticism*
SSC = *Short Story Criticism*
TCLC = *Twentieth-Century Literary Criticism*
WLC = *World Literature Criticism, 1500 to the Present*

The cross-references

```
See also CANR 23; CA 85-88;
    obituary CA116
```

list all author entries in the following Gale biographical and literary sources:

AAYA = *Authors & Artists for Young Adults*
AITN = *Authors in the News*
BEST = *Bestsellers*
BW = *Black Writers*
CA = *Contemporary Authors*
CAAS = *Contemporary Authors Autobiography Series*
CABS = *Contemporary Authors Bibliographical Series*
CANR = *Contemporary Authors New Revision Series*
CAP = *Contemporary Authors Permanent Series*
CDALB = *Concise Dictionary of American Literary Biography*
CDBLB = *Concise Dictionary of British Literary Biography*
DLB = *Dictionary of Literary Biography*
DLBD = *Dictionary of Literary Biography Documentary Series*
DLBY = *Dictionary of Literary Biography Yearbook*
HW = *Hispanic Writers*
JRDA = *Junior DISCovering Authors*
MAICYA = *Major Authors and Illustrators for Children and Young Adults*
MTCW = *Major 20th-Century Writers*
NNAL = *Native North American Literature*
SAAS = *Something about the Author Autobiography Series*
SATA = *Something about the Author*
YABC = *Yesterday's Authors of Books for Children*

Literary Criticism Series
Cumulative Author Index

See also CA 85-88; CANR 81; DLB 108; HW 2

Albert the Great 1200(?)-1280 **CMLC 16**
See also DLB 115

Alcala-Galiano, Juan Valera y
See Valera y Alcala-Galiano, Juan

Alcott, Amos Bronson 1799-1888 **NCLC 1**
See also DLB 1

Alcott, Louisa May 1832-1888 **NCLC 6, 58; DA; DAB; DAC; DAM MST, NOV; SSC 27; WLC**
See also AAYA 20; CDALB 1865-1917; CLR 1, 38; DLB 1, 42, 79; DLBD 14; JRDA; MAICYA; SATA 100; YABC 1

Aldanov, M. A.
See Aldanov, Mark (Alexandrovich)

Aldanov, Mark (Alexandrovich) 1886(?)-1957 **TCLC 23**
See also CA 118

Aldington, Richard 1892-1962 **CLC 49**
See also CA 85-88; CANR 45; DLB 20, 36, 100, 149

Aldiss, Brian W(ilson) 1925- **CLC 5, 14, 40; DAM NOV**
See also CA 5-8R; CAAS 2; CANR 5, 28, 64; DLB 14; MTCW 1, 2; SATA 34

Alegria, Claribel 1924-**CLC 75; DAM MULT; HLCS 1; PC 26**
See also CA 131; CAAS 15; CANR 66; DLB 145; HW 1; MTCW 1

Alegria, Fernando 1918- **CLC 57**
See also CA 9-12R; CANR 5, 32, 72; HW 1, 2

Aleichem, Sholom **TCLC 1, 35; SSC 33**
See also Rabinovitch, Sholem

Aleixandre, Vicente 1898-1984
See also CANR 81; HLCS 1; HW 2

Alepoudelis, Odysseus
See Elytis, Odysseus

Aleshkovsky, Joseph 1929-
See Aleshkovsky, Yuz
See also CA 121; 128

Aleshkovsky, Yuz **CLC 44**
See also Aleshkovsky, Joseph

Alexander, Lloyd (Chudley) 1924- **CLC 35**
See also AAYA 1, 27; CA 1-4R; CANR 1, 24, 38, 55; CLR 1, 5, 48; DLB 52; JRDA; MAICYA; MTCW 1; SAAS 19; SATA 3, 49, 81

Alexander, Meena 1951- **CLC 121**
See also CA 115; CANR 38, 70

Alexander, Samuel 1859-1938 **TCLC 77**

Alexie, Sherman (Joseph, Jr.) 1966- **CLC 96; DAM MULT**
See also AAYA 28; CA 138; CANR 65; DLB 175, 206; MTCW 1; NNAL

Alfau, Felipe 1902- **CLC 66**
See also CA 137

Alger, Horatio, Jr. 1832-1899 **NCLC 8**
See also DLB 42; SATA 16

Algren, Nelson 1909-1981**CLC 4, 10, 33; SSC 33**
See also CA 13-16R; 103; CANR 20, 61; CDALB 1941-1968; DLB 9; DLBY 81, 82; MTCW 1, 2

Ali, Ahmed 1910- **CLC 69**
See also CA 25-28R; CANR 15, 34

Alighieri, Dante
See Dante

Allan, John B.
See Westlake, Donald E(dwin)

Allan, Sidney
See Hartmann, Sadakichi

Allan, Sydney
See Hartmann, Sadakichi

Allen, Edward 1948- **CLC 59**

Allen, Fred 1894-1956 **TCLC 87**

Allen, Paula Gunn 1939-**CLC 84;DAM MULT**
See also CA 112; 143; CANR 63; DLB 175; MTCW 1; NNAL

Allen, Roland
See Ayckbourn, Alan

Allen, Sarah A.
See Hopkins, Pauline Elizabeth

Allen, Sidney H.
See Hartmann, Sadakichi

Allen, Woody 1935- **CLC 16, 52; DAM POP**
See also AAYA 10; CA 33-36R; CANR 27, 38, 63; DLB 44; MTCW 1

Allende, Isabel 1942- **CLC 39, 57, 97; DAM MULT, NOV; HLC 1; WLCS**
See also AAYA 18; CA 125; 130; CANR 51, 74; DLB 145; HW 1, 2; INT 130; MTCW 1, 2

Alleyn, Ellen
See Rossetti, Christina (Georgina)

Allingham, Margery (Louise) 1904-1966**CLC 19**
See also CA 5-8R; 25-28R; CANR 4, 58; DLB 77; MTCW 1, 2

Allingham, William 1824-1889 **NCLC 25**
See also DLB 35

Allison, Dorothy E. 1949- **CLC 78**
See also CA 140; CANR 66; MTCW 1

Allston, Washington 1779-1843 **NCLC 2**
See also DLB 1

Almedingen, E. M. **CLC 12**
See also Almedingen, Martha Edith von
See also SATA 3

Almedingen, Martha Edith von 1898-1971
See Almedingen, E. M.
See also CA 1-4R; CANR 1

Almodovar, Pedro 1949(?)-**CLC 114; HLCS 1**
See also CA 133; CANR 72; HW 2

Almqvist, Carl Jonas Love 1793-1866 **NCLC 42**

Alonso, Damaso 1898-1990 **CLC 14**
See also CA 110; 131; 130; CANR 72; DLB 108; HW 1, 2

Alov
See Gogol, Nikolai (Vasilyevich)

Alta 1942- **CLC 19**
See also CA 57-60

Alter, Robert B(ernard) 1935- **CLC 34**
See also CA 49-52; CANR 1, 47

Alther, Lisa 1944- **CLC 7, 41**
See also CA 65-68; CAAS 30; CANR 12, 30, 51; MTCW 1

Althusser, L.
See Althusser, Louis

Althusser, Louis 1918-1990 **CLC 106**
See also CA 131; 132

Altman, Robert 1925- **CLC 16, 116**
See also CA 73-76; CANR 43

Alurista 1949-
See Urista, Alberto H.
See also DLB 82; HLCS 1

Alvarez, A(lfred) 1929- **CLC 5, 13**
See also CA 1-4R; CANR 3, 33, 63; DLB 14, 40

Alvarez, Alejandro Rodriguez 1903-1965
See Casona, Alejandro
See also CA 131; 93-96; HW 1

Alvarez, Julia 1950- **CLC 93;HLCS 1**
See also AAYA 25; CA 147; CANR 69; MTCW 1

Alvaro, Corrado 1896-1956 **TCLC 60**

See also CA 163

Amado, Jorge 1912- **CLC 13, 40, 106; DAM MULT, NOV; HLC 1**
See also CA 77-80; CANR 35, 74; DLB 113; HW 2; MTCW 1, 2

Ambler, Eric 1909-1998 **CLC 4, 6, 9**
See also CA 9-12R; 171; CANR 7, 38, 74; DLB 77; MTCW 1, 2

Amichai, Yehuda 1924- **CLC 9, 22, 57, 116**
See also CA 85-88; CANR 46, 60; MTCW 1

Amichai, Yehudah
See Amichai, Yehuda

Amiel, Henri Frederic 1821-1881 **NCLC 4**

Amis, Kingsley (William) 1922-1995**CLC 1, 2, 3, 5, 8, 13, 40, 44; DA; DAB; DAC; DAM MST, NOV**
See also AITN 2; CA 9-12R; 150; CANR 8, 28, 54; CDBLB 1945-1960; DLB 15, 27, 100, 139; DLBY 96; INT CANR-8; MTCW 1, 2

Amis, Martin (Louis) 1949- **CLC 4, 9, 38, 62, 101**
See also BEST 90:3; CA 65-68; CANR 8, 27, 54, 73; DLB 14, 194; INT CANR-27; MTCW 1

Ammons, A(rchie) R(andolph) 1926-**CLC 2, 3, 5, 8, 9, 25, 57, 108; DAM POET; PC 16**
See also AITN 1; CA 9-12R; CANR 6, 36, 51, 73; DLB 5, 165; MTCW 1, 2

Amo, Tauraatua i
See Adams, Henry (Brooks)

Amory, Thomas 1691(?)-1788 **LC 48**

Anand, Mulk Raj 1905- **CLC 23, 93;DAM NOV**
See also CA 65-68; CANR 32, 64; MTCW 1, 2

Anatol
See Schnitzler, Arthur

Anaximander c. 610B.C.-c. 546B.C.**CMLC 22**

Anaya, Rudolfo A(lfonso) 1937- **CLC 23; DAM MULT, NOV; HLC 1**
See also AAYA 20; CA 45-48; CAAS 4; CANR 1, 32, 51; DLB 82, 206; HW 1; MTCW 1, 2

Andersen, Hans Christian 1805-1875**NCLC 7, 79; DA; DAB; DAC; DAM MST, POP; SSC 6; WLC**
See also CLR 6; MAICYA; SATA 100; YABC 1

Anderson, C. Farley
See Mencken, H(enry) L(ouis); Nathan, George Jean

Anderson, Jessica (Margaret) Queale 1916- **CLC 37**
See also CA 9-12R; CANR 4, 62

Anderson, Jon (Victor) 1940- **CLC 9; DAM POET**
See also CA 25-28R; CANR 20

Anderson, Lindsay (Gordon) 1923-1994**CLC 20**
See also CA 125; 128; 146; CANR 77

Anderson, Maxwell 1888-1959**TCLC 2; DAM DRAM**
See also CA 105; 152; DLB 7; MTCW 2

Anderson, Poul (William) 1926- **CLC 15**
See also AAYA 5; CA 1-4R; CAAS 2; CANR 2, 15, 34, 64; CLR 58; DLB 8; INT CANR-15; MTCW 1, 2; SATA 90; SATA-Brief 39; SATA-Essay 106

Anderson, Robert (Woodruff) 1917-**CLC 23; DAM DRAM**
See also AITN 1; CA 21-24R; CANR 32; DLB 7

Anderson, Sherwood 1876-1941 **TCLC 1, 10, 24; DA; DAB; DAC; DAM MST, NOV; SSC 1; WLC**

See also AAYA 30; CA 104; 121; CANR 61; CDALB 1917-1929; DLB 4, 9, 86; DLBD 1; MTCW 1, 2

Andier, Pierre
See Desnos, Robert

Andouard
See Giraudoux, (Hippolyte) Jean

Andrade, Carlos Drummond de   **CLC 18**
See also Drummond de Andrade, Carlos

Andrade, Mario de 1893-1945   **TCLC 43**

Andreae, Johann V(alentin) 1586-1654 **LC 32**
See also DLB 164

Andreas-Salome, Lou 1861-1937   **TCLC 56**
See also CA 178; DLB 66

Andress, Lesley
See Sanders, Lawrence

Andrewes, Lancelot 1555-1626   **LC 5**
See also DLB 151, 172

Andrews, Cicily Fairfield
See West, Rebecca

Andrews, Elton V.
See Pohl, Frederik

Andreyev, Leonid (Nikolaevich) 1871-1919
    TCLC 3
See also CA 104

Andric, Ivo 1892-1975   **CLC 8**
See also CA 81-84; 57-60; CANR 43, 60; DLB 147; MTCW 1

Androvar
See Prado (Calvo), Pedro

Angelique, Pierre
See Bataille, Georges

Angell, Roger 1920-   **CLC 26**
See also CA 57-60; CANR 13, 44, 70; DLB 171, 185

Angelou, Maya 1928- CLC 12, 35, 64, 77; BLC 1; DA; DAB; DAC; DAM MST, MULT, POET, POP; WLCS
See also AAYA 7, 20; BW 2, 3; CA 65-68; CANR 19, 42, 65; CDALBS; CLR 53; DLB 38; MTCW 1, 2; SATA 49

Anna Comnena 1083-1153   **CMLC 25**

Annensky, Innokenty (Fyodorovich) 1856-1909
    TCLC 14
See also CA 110; 155

Annunzio, Gabriele d'
See D'Annunzio, Gabriele

Anodos
See Coleridge, Mary E(lizabeth)

Anon, Charles Robert
See Pessoa, Fernando (Antonio Nogueira)

Anouilh, Jean (Marie Lucien Pierre) 1910-1987
CLC 1, 3, 8, 13, 40, 50; DAM DRAM; DC 8
See also CA 17-20R; 123; CANR 32; MTCW 1, 2

Anthony, Florence
See Ai

Anthony, John
See Ciardi, John (Anthony)

Anthony, Peter
See Shaffer, Anthony (Joshua); Shaffer, Peter (Levin)

Anthony, Piers 1934-   **CLC 35; DAM POP**
See also AAYA 11; CA 21-24R; CANR 28, 56, 73; DLB 8; MTCW 1, 2; SAAS 22; SATA 84

Anthony, Susan B(rownell) 1916-1991 **TCLC 84**
See also CA 89-92; 134

Antoine, Marc
See Proust, (Valentin-Louis-George-Eugene-) Marcel

Antoninus, Brother

See Everson, William (Oliver)

Antonioni, Michelangelo 1912-   **CLC 20**
See also CA 73-76; CANR 45, 77

Antschel, Paul 1920-1970
See Celan, Paul
See also CA 85-88; CANR 33, 61; MTCW 1

Anwar, Chairil 1922-1949   **TCLC 22**
See also CA 121

Anzaldua, Gloria 1942-
See also CA 175; DLB 122; HLCS 1

Apess, William 1798-1839(?) NCLC 73; DAM MULT
See also DLB 175; NNAL

Apollinaire, Guillaume 1880-1918 TCLC 3, 8, 51; DAM POET; PC 7
See also Kostrowitzki, Wilhelm Apollinaris de
See also CA 152; MTCW 1

Appelfeld, Aharon 1932-   **CLC 23, 47**
See also CA 112; 133

Apple, Max (Isaac) 1941-   **CLC 9, 33**
See also CA 81-84; CANR 19, 54; DLB 130

Appleman, Philip (Dean) 1926-   **CLC 51**
See also CA 13-16R; CAAS 18; CANR 6, 29, 56

Appleton, Lawrence
See Lovecraft, H(oward) P(hillips)

Apteryx
See Eliot, T(homas) S(tearns)

Apuleius, (Lucius Madaurensis) 125(?)-175(?)
    CMLC 1
See also DLB 211

Aquin, Hubert 1929-1977   **CLC 15**
See also CA 105; DLB 53

Aquinas, Thomas 1224(?)-1274   **CMLC 33**
See also DLB 115

Aragon, Louis 1897-1982 CLC 3, 22; DAM NOV, POET
See also CA 69-72; 108; CANR 28, 71; DLB 72; MTCW 1, 2

Arany, Janos 1817-1882   **NCLC 34**

Aranyos, Kakay
See Mikszath, Kalman

Arbuthnot, John 1667-1735   **LC 1**
See also DLB 101

Archer, Herbert Winslow
See Mencken, H(enry) L(ouis)

Archer, Jeffrey (Howard) 1940-   CLC 28; DAM POP
See also AAYA 16; BEST 89:3; CA 77-80; CANR 22, 52; INT CANR-22

Archer, Jules 1915-   **CLC 12**
See also CA 9-12R; CANR 6, 69; SAAS 5; SATA 4, 85

Archer, Lee
See Ellison, Harlan (Jay)

Arden, John 1930- CLC 6, 13, 15; DAM DRAM
See also CA 13-16R; CAAS 4; CANR 31, 65, 67; DLB 13; MTCW 1

Arenas, Reinaldo 1943-1990 CLC 41; DAM MULT; HLC 1
See also CA 124; 128; 133; CANR 73; DLB 145; HW 1; MTCW 1

Arendt, Hannah 1906-1975   **CLC 66, 98**
See also CA 17-20R; 61-64; CANR 26, 60; MTCW 1, 2

Aretino, Pietro 1492-1556   **LC 12**

Arghezi, Tudor 1880-1967   **CLC 80**
See also Theodorescu, Ion N.
See also CA 167

Arguedas, Jose Maria 1911-1969 CLC 10, 18; HLCS 1
See also CA 89-92; CANR 73; DLB 113; HW 1

Argueta, Manlio 1936-   **CLC 31**

See also CA 131; CANR 73; DLB 145; HW 1

Arias, Ron(ald Francis) 1941-
See also CA 131; CANR 81; DAM MULT; DLB 82; HLC 1; HW 1, 2; MTCW 2

Ariosto, Ludovico 1474-1533   **LC 6**

Aristides
See Epstein, Joseph

Aristophanes 450B.C.-385B.C. CMLC 4; DA; DAB; DAC; DAM DRAM, MST; DC 2; WLCS
See also DLB 176

Aristotle 384B.C.-322B.C.   CMLC 31; DA; DAB; DAC; DAM MST; WLCS
See also DLB 176

Arlt, Roberto (Godofredo Christophersen) 1900-1942 TCLC 29; DAM MULT; HLC 1
See also CA 123; 131; CANR 67; HW 1, 2

Armah, Ayi Kwei 1939- CLC 5, 33; BLC 1; DAM MULT, POET
See also BW 1; CA 61-64; CANR 21, 64; DLB 117; MTCW 1

Armatrading, Joan 1950-   **CLC 17**
See also CA 114

Arnette, Robert
See Silverberg, Robert

Arnim, Achim von (Ludwig Joachim von Arnim) 1781-1831   **NCLC 5; SSC 29**
See also DLB 90

Arnim, Bettina von 1785-1859   **NCLC 38**
See also DLB 90

Arnold, Matthew 1822-1888 NCLC 6, 29; DA; DAB; DAC; DAM MST, POET; PC 5; WLC
See also CDBLB 1832-1890; DLB 32, 57

Arnold, Thomas 1795-1842   **NCLC 18**
See also DLB 55

Arnow, Harriette (Louisa) Simpson 1908-1986
    CLC 2, 7, 18
See also CA 9-12R; 118; CANR 14; DLB 6; MTCW 1, 2; SATA 42; SATA-Obit 47

Arouet, Francois-Marie
See Voltaire

Arp, Hans
See Arp, Jean

Arp, Jean 1887-1966   **CLC 5**
See also CA 81-84; 25-28R; CANR 42, 77

Arrabal
See Arrabal, Fernando

Arrabal, Fernando 1932-   CLC 2, 9, 18, 58
See also CA 9-12R; CANR 15

Arreola, Juan Jose 1918-
See also CA 113; 131; CANR 81; DAM MULT; DLB 113; HLC 1; HW 1, 2

Arrick, Fran   **CLC 30**
See also Gaberman, Judie Angell

Artaud, Antonin (Marie Joseph) 1896-1948
    TCLC 3, 36; DAM DRAM
See also CA 104; 149; MTCW 1

Arthur, Ruth M(abel) 1905-1979   **CLC 12**
See also CA 9-12R; 85-88; CANR 4; SATA 7, 26

Artsybashev, Mikhail (Petrovich) 1878-1927
    TCLC 31
See also CA 170

Arundel, Honor (Morfydd) 1919-1973 **CLC 17**
See also CA 21-22; 41-44R; CAP 2; CLR 35; SATA 4; SATA-Obit 24

Arzner, Dorothy 1897-1979   **CLC 98**

Asch, Sholem 1880-1957   **TCLC 3**
See also CA 105

Ash, Shalom
See Asch, Sholem

Ashbery, John (Lawrence) 1927- CLC 2, 3, 4,

See also AAYA 3; CA 5-8R; CANR 15, 39, 65; DLB 14, 207; MTCW 1, 2; SATA 93

Balmont, Konstantin (Dmitriyevich) 1867-1943 **TCLC 11**
See also CA 109; 155

Baltausis, Vincas
See Mikszath, Kalman

Balzac, Honore de 1799-1850**NCLC 5, 35, 53; DA; DAB; DAC; DAM MST, NOV; SSC 5; WLC**
See also DLB 119

Bambara, Toni Cade 1939-1995 **CLC 19, 88; BLC 1; DA; DAC; DAM MST, MULT; SSC 35; WLCS**
See also AAYA 5; BW 2, 3; CA 29-32R; 150; CANR 24, 49, 81; CDALBS; DLB 38; MTCW 1, 2

Bamdad, A.
See Shamlu, Ahmad

Banat, D. R.
See Bradbury, Ray (Douglas)

Bancroft, Laura
See Baum, L(yman) Frank

Banim, John 1798-1842 **NCLC 13**
See also DLB 116, 158, 159

Banim, Michael 1796-1874 **NCLC 13**
See also DLB 158, 159

Banjo, The
See Paterson, A(ndrew) B(arton)

Banks, Iain
See Banks, Iain M(enzies)

Banks, Iain M(enzies) 1954- **CLC 34**
See also CA 123; 128; CANR 61; DLB 194; INT 128

Banks, Lynne Reid **CLC 23**
See also Reid Banks, Lynne
See also AAYA 6

Banks, Russell 1940- **CLC 37, 72**
See also CA 65-68; CAAS 15; CANR 19, 52, 73; DLB 130

Banville, John 1945- **CLC 46, 118**
See also CA 117; 128; DLB 14; INT 128

Banville, Theodore (Faullain) de 1832-1891 **NCLC 9**

Baraka, Amiri 1934-**CLC 1, 2, 3, 5, 10, 14, 33, 115; BLC 1; DA; DAC; DAM MST, MULT, POET, POP; DC 6; PC 4; WLCS**
See also Jones, LeRoi
See also BW 2, 3; CA 21-24R; CABS 3; CANR 27, 38, 61; CDALB 1941-1968; DLB 5, 7, 16, 38; DLBD 8; MTCW 1, 2

Barbauld, Anna Laetitia 1743-1825**NCLC 50**
See also DLB 107, 109, 142, 158

Barbellion, W. N. P. **TCLC 24**
See also Cummings, Bruce F(rederick)

Barbera, Jack (Vincent) 1945- **CLC 44**
See also CA 110; CANR 45

Barbey d'Aurevilly, Jules Amedee 1808-1889 **NCLC 1; SSC 17**
See also DLB 119

Barbour, John c. 1316-1395 **CMLC 33**
See also DLB 146

Barbusse, Henri 1873-1935 **TCLC 5**
See also CA 105; 154; DLB 65

Barclay, Bill
See Moorcock, Michael (John)

Barclay, William Ewert
See Moorcock, Michael (John)

Barea, Arturo 1897-1957 **TCLC 14**
See also CA 111

Barfoot, Joan 1946- **CLC 18**
See also CA 105

Barham, Richard Harris 1788-1845**NCLC 77**

See also DLB 159

Baring, Maurice 1874-1945 **TCLC 8**
See also CA 105; 168; DLB 34

Baring-Gould, Sabine 1834-1924 **TCLC 88**
See also DLB 156, 190

Barker, Clive 1952- **CLC 52;DAM POP**
See also AAYA 10; BEST 90:3; CA 121; 129; CANR 71; INT 129; MTCW 1, 2

Barker, George Granville 1913-1991 **CLC 8, 48; DAM POET**
See also CA 9-12R; 135; CANR 7, 38; DLB 20; MTCW 1

Barker, Harley Granville
See Granville-Barker, Harley
See also DLB 10

Barker, Howard 1946- **CLC 37**
See also CA 102; DLB 13

Barker, Jane 1652-1732 **LC 42**

Barker, Pat(ricia) 1943- **CLC 32, 94**
See also CA 117; 122; CANR 50; INT 122

Barlach, Ernst 1870-1938 **TCLC 84**
See also CA 178; DLB 56, 118

Barlow, Joel 1754-1812 **NCLC 23**
See also DLB 37

Barnard, Mary (Ethel) 1909- **CLC 48**
See also CA 21-22; CAP 2

Barnes, Djuna 1892-1982**CLC 3, 4, 8, 11, 29; SSC 3**
See also CA 9-12R; 107; CANR 16, 55; DLB 4, 9, 45; MTCW 1, 2

Barnes, Julian (Patrick) 1946-**CLC 42; DAB**
See also CA 102; CANR 19, 54; DLB 194; DLBY 93; MTCW 1

Barnes, Peter 1931- **CLC 5, 56**
See also CA 65-68; CAAS 12; CANR 33, 34, 64; DLB 13; MTCW 1

Barnes, William 1801-1886 **NCLC 75**
See also DLB 32

Baroja (y Nessi), Pio 1872-1956**TCLC 8; HLC 1**
See also CA 104

Baron, David
See Pinter, Harold

Baron Corvo
See Rolfe, Frederick (William Serafino Austin Lewis Mary)

Barondess, Sue K(aufman) 1926-1977 **CLC 8**
See also Kaufman, Sue
See also CA 1-4R; 69-72; CANR 1

Baron de Teive
See Pessoa, Fernando (Antonio Nogueira)

Baroness Von S.
See Zangwill, Israel

Barres, (Auguste-) Maurice 1862-1923**T C L C 47**
See also CA 164; DLB 123

Barreto, Afonso Henrique de Lima
See Lima Barreto, Afonso Henrique de

Barrett, (Roger) Syd 1946- **CLC 35**

Barrett, William (Christopher) 1913-1992 **CLC 27**
See also CA 13-16R; 139; CANR 11, 67; INT CANR-11

Barrie, J(ames) M(atthew) 1860-1937 **T C L C 2; DAB; DAM DRAM**
See also CA 104; 136; CANR 77; CDBLB 1890-1914; CLR 16; DLB 10, 141, 156; MAICYA; MTCW 1; SATA 100; YABC 1

Barrington, Michael
See Moorcock, Michael (John)

Barrol, Grady
See Bograd, Larry

Barry, Mike

See Malzberg, Barry N(athaniel)

Barry, Philip 1896-1949 **TCLC 11**
See also CA 109; DLB 7

Bart, Andre Schwarz
See Schwarz-Bart, Andre

Barth, John (Simmons) 1930-**CLC 1, 2, 3, 5, 7, 9, 10, 14, 27, 51, 89; DAM NOV; SSC 10**
See also AITN 1, 2; CA 1-4R; CABS 1; CANR 5, 23, 49, 64; DLB 2; MTCW 1

Barthelme, Donald 1931-1989**CLC 1, 2, 3, 5, 6, 8, 13, 23, 46, 59, 115; DAM NOV; SSC 2**
See also CA 21-24R; 129; CANR 20, 58; DLB 2; DLBY 80, 89; MTCW 1, 2; SATA 7; SATA-Obit 62

Barthelme, Frederick 1943- **CLC 36, 117**
See also CA 114; 122; CANR 77; DLBY 85; INT 122

Barthes, Roland (Gerard) 1915-1980**CLC 24, 83**
See also CA 130; 97-100; CANR 66; MTCW 1, 2

Barzun, Jacques (Martin) 1907- **CLC 51**
See also CA 61-64; CANR 22

Bashevis, Isaac
See Singer, Isaac Bashevis

Bashkirtseff, Marie 1859-1884 **NCLC 27**

Basho
See Matsuo Basho

Basil of Caesaria c. 330-379 **CMLC 35**

Bass, Kingsley B., Jr.
See Bullins, Ed

Bass, Rick 1958- **CLC 79**
See also CA 126; CANR 53; DLB 212

Bassani, Giorgio 1916- **CLC 9**
See also CA 65-68; CANR 33; DLB 128, 177; MTCW 1

Bastos, Augusto (Antonio) Roa
See Roa Bastos, Augusto (Antonio)

Bataille, Georges 1897-1962 **CLC 29**
See also CA 101; 89-92

Bates, H(erbert) E(rnest) 1905-1974**CLC 46; DAB; DAM POP; SSC 10**
See also CA 93-96; 45-48; CANR 34; DLB 162, 191; MTCW 1, 2

Bauchart
See Camus, Albert

Baudelaire, Charles 1821-1867 **NCLC 6, 29, 55; DA; DAB; DAC; DAM MST, POET; PC 1; SSC 18; WLC**

Baudrillard, Jean 1929- **CLC 60**

Baum, L(yman) Frank 1856-1919 **TCLC 7**
See also CA 108; 133; CLR 15; DLB 22; JRDA; MAICYA; MTCW 1, 2; SATA 18, 100

Baum, Louis F.
See Baum, L(yman) Frank

Baumbach, Jonathan 1933- **CLC 6,23**
See also CA 13-16R; CAAS 5; CANR 12, 66; DLBY 80; INT CANR-12; MTCW 1

Bausch, Richard (Carl) 1945- **CLC 51**
See also CA 101; CAAS 14; CANR 43, 61; DLB 130

Baxter, Charles (Morley) 1947- **CLC 45, 78; DAM POP**
See also CA 57-60; CANR 40, 64; DLB 130; MTCW 2

Baxter, George Owen
See Faust, Frederick (Schiller)

Baxter, James K(eir) 1926-1972 **CLC 14**
See also CA 77-80

Baxter, John
See Hunt, E(verette) Howard, (Jr.)

Bayer, Sylvia
See Glassco, John

Benson, E(dward) F(rederic) 1867-1940
TCLC **27**
See also CA 114; 157; DLB 135, 153

Benson, Jackson J. 1930- CLC **34**
See also CA 25-28R; DLB 111

Benson, Sally 1900-1972 CLC **17**
See also CA 19-20; 37-40R; CAP 1; SATA 1,
35; SATA-Obit 27

Benson, Stella 1892-1933 TCLC **17**
See also CA 117; 155; DLB 36, 162

Bentham, Jeremy 1748-1832 NCLC **38**
See also DLB 107, 158

Bentley, E(dmund) C(lerihew) 1875-1956
TCLC **12**
See also CA 108; DLB 70

Bentley, Eric (Russell) 1916- CLC **24**
See also CA 5-8R; CANR 6, 67; INT CANR-6

Beranger, Pierre Jean de 1780-1857 NCLC' **34**

Berdyaev, Nicolas
See Berdyaev, Nikolai (Aleksandrovich)

Berdyaev, Nikolai (Aleksandrovich) 1874-1948
TCLC **67**
See also CA 120; 157

Berdyayev, Nikolai (Aleksandrovich)
See Berdyaev, Nikolai (Aleksandrovich)

Berendt, John (Lawrence) 1939- CLC **86**
See also CA 146; CANR 75; MTCW 1

Beresford, J(ohn) D(avys) 1873-1947 TCLC
81
See also CA 112; 155; DLB 162, 178, 197

Bergelson, David 1884-1952 TCLC **81**

Berger, Colonel
See Malraux, (Georges-)Andre

Berger, John (Peter) 1926- CLC **2, 19**
See also CA 81-84; CANR 51, 78; DLB 14, 207

Berger, Melvin H. 1927- CLC **12**
See also CA 5-8R; CANR 4; CLR 32; SAAS 2;
SATA 5, 88

Berger, Thomas (Louis) 1924-CLC **3, 5, 8, 11,
18, 38; DAM NOV**
See also CA 1-4R; CANR 5, 28, 51; DLB 2;
DLBY 80; INT CANR-28; MTCW 1, 2

Bergman, (Ernst) Ingmar 1918- CLC **16, 72**
See also CA 81-84; CANR 33, 70; MTCW 2

Bergson, Henri (-Louis) 1859-1941 TCLC **32**
See also CA 164

Bergstein, Eleanor 1938- CLC **4**
See also CA 53-56; CANR 5

Berkoff, Steven 1937- CLC **56**
See also CA 104; CANR 72

Bermant, Chaim (Icyk) 1929- CLC **40**
See also CA 57-60; CANR 6, 31, 57

Bern, Victoria
See Fisher, M(ary) F(rances) K(ennedy)

Bernanos, (Paul Louis) Georges 1888-1948
TCLC **3**
See also CA 104; 130; DLB 72

Bernard, April 1956- CLC **59**
See also CA 131

Berne, Victoria
See Fisher, M(ary) F(rances) K(ennedy)

Bernhard, Thomas 1931-1989 CLC **3, 32, 61**
See also CA 85-88; 127; CANR 32, 57; DLB
85, 124; MTCW 1

Bernhardt, Sarah (Henriette Rosine) 1844-1923
TCLC **75**
See also CA 157

Berriault, Gina 1926- CLC **54, 109; SSC 30**
See also CA 116; 129; CANR 66; DLB 130

Berrigan, Daniel 1921- CLC **4**
See also CA 33-36R; CAAS 1; CANR 11, 43,
78; DLB 5

Berrigan, Edmund Joseph Michael, Jr. 1934-
1983
See Berrigan, Ted
See also CA 61-64; 110; CANR 14

Berrigan, Ted CLC **37**
See also Berrigan, Edmund Joseph Michael, Jr.
See also DLB 5, 169

Berry, Charles Edward Anderson 1931-
See Berry, Chuck
See also CA 115

Berry, Chuck CLC **17**
See also Berry, Charles Edward Anderson

Berry, Jonas
See Ashbery, John (Lawrence)

Berry, Wendell (Erdman) 1934- CLC **4, 6, 8,
27, 46; DAM POET**
See also AITN 1; CA 73-76; CANR 50, 73; DLB
5, 6; MTCW 1

Berryman, John 1914-1972CLC **1, 2, 3, 4, 6, 8,
10, 13, 25, 62; DAM POET**
See also CA 13-16; 33-36R; CABS 2; CANR
35; CAP 1; CDALB 1941-1968; DLB 48;
MTCW 1, 2

Bertolucci, Bernardo 1940- CLC **16**
See also CA 106

Berton, Pierre (Francis Demarigny) 1920-
CLC **104**
See also CA 1-4R; CANR 2, 56; DLB 68; SATA
99

Bertrand, Aloysius 1807-1841 NCLC **31**

Bertran de Born c. 1140-1215 CMLC **5**

Besant, Annie (Wood) 1847-1933 TCLC **9**
See also CA 105

Bessie, Alvah 1904-1985 CLC **23**
See also CA 5-8R; 116; CANR 2, 80; DLB 26

Bethlen, T. D.
See Silverberg, Robert

Beti, Mongo CLC **27; BLC 1; DAM MULT**
See also Biyidi, Alexandre
See also CANR 79

Betjeman, John 1906-1984 CLC **2, 6, 10, 34,
43; DAB; DAM MST, POET**
See also CA 9-12R; 112; CANR 33, 56; CDBLB
1945-1960; DLB 20; DLBY 84; MTCW 1,
2

Bettelheim, Bruno 1903-1990 CLC **79**
See also CA 81-84; 131; CANR 23, 61; MTCW
1, 2

Betti, Ugo 1892-1953 TCLC **5**
See also CA 104; 155

Betts, Doris (Waugh) 1932- CLC **3, 6, 28**
See also CA 13-16R; CANR 9, 66, 77; DLBY
82; INT CANR-9

Bevan, Alistair
See Roberts, Keith (John Kingston)

Bey, Pilaff
See Douglas, (George) Norman

Bialik, Chaim Nachman 1873-1934 TCLC **25**
See also CA 170

Bickerstaff, Isaac
See Swift, Jonathan

Bidart, Frank 1939- CLC **33**
See also CA 140

Bienek, Horst 1930- CLC **7, 11**
See also CA 73-76; DLB 75

Bierce, Ambrose (Gwinett) 1842-1914(?)
TCLC **1, 7, 44; DA; DAC; DAM MST; SSC
9; WLC**
See also CA 104; 139; CANR 78; CDALB
1865-1917; DLB 11, 12, 23, 71, 74, 186

Biggers, Earl Derr 1884-1933 TCLC **65**
See also CA 108; 153

Billings, Josh
See Shaw, Henry Wheeler

Billington, (Lady) Rachel (Mary) 1942- C L C
43
See also AITN 2; CA 33-36R; CANR 44

Binyon, T(imothy) J(ohn) 1936- CLC **34**
See also CA 111; CANR 28

Bioy Casares, Adolfo 1914-1999CLC **4, 8, 13,
88; DAM MULT; HLC 1; SSC 17**
See also CA 29-32R; 177; CANR 19, 43, 66;
DLB 113; HW 1, 2; MTCW 1, 2

Bird, Cordwainer
See Ellison, Harlan (Jay)

Bird, Robert Montgomery 1806-1854NCLC **1**
See also DLB 202

Birkerts, Sven 1951- CLC **116**
See also CA 128; 133; 176; CAAS 29; INT 133

Birney, (Alfred) Earle 1904-1995CLC **1, 4, 6,
11; DAC; DAM MST, POET**
See also CA 1-4R; CANR 5, 20; DLB 88;
MTCW 1

Biruni, al 973-1048(?) CMLC **28**

Bishop, Elizabeth 1911-1979 CLC **1, 4, 9, 13,
15, 32; DA; DAC; DAM MST, POET; PC
3**
See also CA 5-8R; 89-92; CABS 2; CANR 26,
61; CDALB 1968-1988; DLB 5, 169;
MTCW 1, 2; SATA-Obit 24

Bishop, John 1935- CLC **10**
See also CA 105

Bissett, Bill 1939- CLC **18; PC 14**
See also CA 69-72; CAAS 19; CANR 15; DLB
53; MTCW 1

Bissoondath, Neil (Devindra) 1955-CLC **120;
DAC**
See also CA 136

Bitov, Andrei (Georgievich) 1937- CLC **57**
See also CA 142

Biyidi, Alexandre 1932-
See Beti, Mongo
See also BW 1, 3; CA 114; 124; CANR 81;
MTCW 1, 2

Bjarme, Brynjolf
See Ibsen, Henrik (Johan)

Bjoernson, Bjoernstjerne (Martinius) 1832-
1910 TCLC **7, 37**
See also CA 104

Black, Robert
See Holdstock, Robert P.

Blackburn, Paul 1926-1971 CLC **9, 43**
See also CA 81-84; 33-36R; CANR 34; DLB
16; DLBY 81

Black Elk 1863-1950 TCLC **33;DAM MULT**
See also CA 144; MTCW 1; NNAL

Black Hobart
See Sanders, (James) Ed(ward)

Blacklin, Malcolm
See Chambers, Aidan

Blackmore, R(ichard) D(oddridge) 1825-1900
TCLC **27**
See also CA 120; DLB 18

Blackmur, R(ichard) P(almer) 1904-1965
CLC **2, 24**
See also CA 11-12; 25-28R; CANR 71; CAP 1;
DLB 63

Black Tarantula
See Acker, Kathy

Blackwood, Algernon (Henry) 1869-1951
TCLC **5**
See also CA 105; 150; DLB 153, 156, 178

Blackwood, Caroline 1931-1996CLC **6, 9, 100**
See also CA 85-88; 151; CANR 32, 61, 65; DLB
14, 207; MTCW 1

Blade, Alexander
See Hamilton, Edmond; Silverberg, Robert

Bowers, Edgar 1924- **CLC 9**
See also CA 5-8R; CANR 24; DLB 5
Bowie, David **CLC 17**
See also Jones, David Robert
Bowles, Jane (Sydney) 1917-1973 **CLC 3, 68**
See also CA 19-20; 41-44R; CAP 2
Bowles, Paul (Frederick) 1910- CLC **1, 2, 19, 53; SSC 3**
See also CA 1-4R; CAAS 1; CANR 1, 19, 50, 75; DLB 5, 6; MTCW 1, 2
Box, Edgar
See Vidal, Gore
Boyd, Nancy
See Millay, Edna St. Vincent
Boyd, William 1952- **CLC 28, 53, 70**
See also CA 114; 120; CANR 51, 71
Boyle, Kay 1902-1992 CLC **1, 5, 19, 58, 121; SSC 5**
See also CA 13-16R; 140; CAAS 1; CANR 29, 61; DLB 4, 9, 48, 86; DLBY 93; MTCW 1, 2
Boyle, Mark
See Kienzle, William X(avier)
Boyle, Patrick 1905-1982 **CLC 19**
See also CA 127
Boyle, T. C. 1948-
See Boyle, T(homas) Coraghessan
Boyle, T(homas) Coraghessan 1948- CLC **36, 55, 90; DAM POP; SSC 16**
See also BEST 90:4; CA 120; CANR 44, 76; DLBY 86; MTCW 2
Boz
See Dickens, Charles (John Huffam)
Brackenridge, Hugh Henry 1748-1816 **NCLC 7**
See also DLB 11, 37
Bradbury, Edward P.
See Moorcock, Michael (John)
See also MTCW 2
Bradbury, Malcolm (Stanley) 1932- CLC **32, 61; DAM NOV**
See also CA 1-4R; CANR 1, 33; DLB 14, 207; MTCW 1, 2
Bradbury, Ray (Douglas) 1920- CLC **1, 3, 10, 15, 42, 98; DA; DAB; DAC; DAM MST, NOV, POP; SSC 29; WLC**
See also AAYA 15; AITN 1, 2; CA 1-4R; CANR 2, 30, 75; CDALB 1968-1988; DLB 2, 8; MTCW 1, 2; SATA 11, 64
Bradford, Gamaliel 1863-1932 **TCLC 36**
See also CA 160; DLB 17
Bradley, David (Henry), Jr. 1950- CLC **23, 118; BLC 1; DAM MULT**
See also BW 1, 3; CA 104; CANR 26, 81; DLB 33
Bradley, John Ed(mund, Jr.) 1958- **CLC 55**
See also CA 139
Bradley, Marion Zimmer 1930- CLC **30; DAM POP**
See also AAYA 9; CA 57-60; CAAS 10; CANR 7, 31, 51, 75; DLB 8; MTCW 1, 2; SATA 90
Bradstreet, Anne 1612(?)-1672 LC **4, 30; DA; DAC; DAM MST, POET; PC 10**
See also CDALB 1640-1865; DLB 24
Brady, Joan 1939- **CLC 86**
See also CA 141
Bragg, Melvyn 1939- **CLC 10**
See also BEST 89:3; CA 57-60; CANR 10, 48; DLB 14
Brahe, Tycho 1546-1601 **LC 45**
Braine, John (Gerard) 1922-1986 CLC **1, 3, 41**
See also CA 1-4R; 120; CANR 1, 33; CDBLB 1945-1960; DLB 15; DLBY 86; MTCW 1

Bramah, Ernest 1868-1942 **TCLC 72**
See also CA 156; DLB 70
Brammer, William 1930(?)-1978 **CLC 31**
See also CA 77-80
Brancati, Vitaliano 1907-1954 **TCLC 12**
See also CA 109
Brancato, Robin F(idler) 1936- **CLC 35**
See also AAYA 9; CA 69-72; CANR 11, 45; CLR 32; JRDA; SAAS 9; SATA 97
Brand, Max
See Faust, Frederick (Schiller)
Brand, Millen 1906-1980 **CLC 7**
See also CA 21-24R; 97-100; CANR 72
Branden, Barbara **CLC 44**
See also CA 148
Brandes, Georg (Morris Cohen) 1842-1927 **TCLC 10**
See also CA 105
Brandys, Kazimierz 1916- **CLC 62**
Branley, Franklyn M(ansfield) 1915- **CLC 21**
See also CA 33-36R; CANR 14, 39; CLR 13; MAICYA; SAAS 16; SATA 4, 68
Brathwaite, Edward (Kamau) 1930- **CLC 11; BLCS; DAM POET**
See also BW 2, 3; CA 25-28R; CANR 11, 26, 47; DLB 125
Brautigan, Richard (Gary) 1935-1984 **CLC 1, 3, 5, 9, 12, 34, 42; DAM NOV**
See also CA 53-56; 113; CANR 34; DLB 2, 5, 206; DLBY 80, 84; MTCW 1; SATA 56
Brave Bird, Mary 1953-
See Crow Dog, Mary (Ellen)
See also NNAL
Braverman, Kate 1950- **CLC 67**
See also CA 89-92
Brecht, (Eugen) Bertolt (Friedrich) 1898-1956 **TCLC 1, 6, 13, 35; DA; DAB; DAC; DAM DRAM, MST; DC 3; WLC**
See also CA 104; 133; CANR 62; DLB 56, 124; MTCW 1, 2
Brecht, Eugen Berthold Friedrich
See Brecht, (Eugen) Bertolt (Friedrich)
Bremer, Fredrika 1801-1865 **NCLC 11**
Brennan, Christopher John 1870-1932 **TCLC 17**
See also CA 117
Brennan, Maeve 1917-1993 **CLC 5**
See also CA 81-84; CANR 72
Brent, Linda
See Jacobs, Harriet A(nn)
Brentano, Clemens (Maria) 1778-1842 **NCLC 1**
See also DLB 90
Brent of Bin Bin
See Franklin, (Stella Maria Sarah) Miles (Lampe)
Brenton, Howard 1942- **CLC 31**
See also CA 69-72; CANR 33, 67; DLB 13; MTCW 1
Breslin, James 1930-1996
See Breslin, Jimmy
See also CA 73-76; CANR 31, 75; DAM NOV; MTCW 1, 2
Breslin, Jimmy **CLC 4, 43**
See also Breslin, James
See also AITN 1; DLB 185; MTCW 2
Bresson, Robert 1901- **CLC 16**
See also CA 110; CANR 49
Breton, Andre 1896-1966 **CLC 2, 9, 15, 54; PC 15**
See also CA 19-20; 25-28R; CANR 40, 60; CAP 2; DLB 65; MTCW 1, 2
Breytenbach, Breyten 1939(?)- **CLC 23, 37;**

DAM POET
See also CA 113; 129; CANR 61
Bridgers, Sue Ellen 1942- **CLC 26**
See also AAYA 8; CA 65-68; CANR 11, 36; CLR 18; DLB 52; JRDA; MAICYA; SAAS 1; SATA 22, 90; SATA-Essay 109
Bridges, Robert (Seymour) 1844-1930 **TCLC 1; DAM POET**
See also CA 104; 152; CDBLB 1890-1914; DLB 19, 98
Bridie, James **TCLC 3**
See also Mavor, Osborne Henry
See also DLB 10
Brin, David 1950- **CLC 34**
See also AAYA 21; CA 102; CANR 24, 70; INT CANR-24; SATA 65
Brink, Andre (Philippus) 1935- **CLC 18, 36, 106**
See also CA 104; CANR 39, 62; INT 103; MTCW 1, 2
Brinsmead, H(esba) F(ay) 1922- **CLC 21**
See also CA 21-24R; CANR 10; CLR 47; MAICYA; SAAS 5; SATA 18, 78
Brittain, Vera (Mary) 1893(?)-1970 **CLC 23**
See also CA 13-16; 25-28R; CANR 58; CAP 1; DLB 191; MTCW 1, 2
Broch, Hermann 1886-1951 **TCLC 20**
See also CA 117; DLB 85, 124
Brock, Rose
See Hansen, Joseph
Brodkey, Harold (Roy) 1930-1996 **CLC 56**
See also CA 111; 151; CANR 71; DLB 130
Brodskii, Iosif
See Brodsky, Joseph
Brodsky, Iosif Alexandrovich 1940-1996
See Brodsky, Joseph
See also AITN 1; CA 41-44R; 151; CANR 37; DAM POET; MTCW 1, 2
Brodsky, Joseph 1940-1996 CLC **4, 6, 13, 36, 100; PC 9**
See also Brodskii, Iosif; Brodsky, Iosif Alexandrovich
See also MTCW 1
Brodsky, Michael (Mark) 1948- **CLC 19**
See also CA 102; CANR 18, 41, 58
Bromell, Henry 1947- **CLC 5**
See also CA 53-56; CANR 9
Bromfield, Louis (Brucker) 1896-1956 **TCLC 11**
See also CA 107; 155; DLB 4, 9, 86
Broner, E(sther) M(asserman) 1930- **CLC 19**
See also CA 17-20R; CANR 8, 25, 72; DLB 28
Bronk, William (M.) 1918-1999 **CLC 10**
See also CA 89-92; 177; CANR 23; DLB 165
Bronstein, Lev Davidovich
See Trotsky, Leon
Bronte, Anne 1820-1849 **NCLC 71**
See also DLB 21, 199
Bronte, Charlotte 1816-1855 **NCLC 3, 8, 33, 58; DA; DAB; DAC; DAM MST, NOV; WLC**
See also AAYA 17; CDBLB 1832-1890; DLB 21, 159, 199
Bronte, Emily (Jane) 1818-1848 **NCLC 16, 35; DA; DAB; DAC; DAM MST, NOV, POET; PC 8; WLC**
See also AAYA 17; CDBLB 1832-1890; DLB 21, 32, 199
Brooke, Frances 1724-1789 **LC 6, 48**
See also DLB 39, 99
Brooke, Henry 1703(?)-1783 **LC 1**
See also DLB 39
Brooke, Rupert (Chawner) 1887-1915 **TCLC**

Cayrol, Jean 1911-   **CLC 11**
See also CA 89-92; DLB 83
Cela, Camilo Jose 1916- **CLC 4, 13, 59, 122;**
DAM MULT; HLC 1
See also BEST 90:2; CA 21-24R; CAAS 10;
CANR 21, 32, 76; DLBY 89; HW 1; MTCW
1, 2
Celan, Paul   **CLC 10, 19, 53, 82; PC 10**
See also Antschel, Paul
See also DLB 69
Celine, Louis-Ferdinand CLC **1, 3, 4, 7, 9, 15,**
47
See also Destouches, Louis-Ferdinand
See also DLB 72
Cellini, Benvenuto 1500-1571   **LC 7**
Cendrars, Blaise 1887-1961 **CLC 18, 106**
See also Sauser-Hall, Frederic
Cernuda (y Bidon), Luis 1902-1963 **CLC 54;**
DAM POET
See also CA 131; 89-92; DLB 134; HW 1
Cervantes, Lorna Dee 1954-
See also CA 131; CANR 80; DLB 82; HLCS 1;
HW 1
Cervantes (Saavedra), Miguel de 1547-1616
LC 6, 23; DA; DAB; DAC; DAM MST,
NOV; SSC 12; WLC
Cesaire, Aime (Fernand) 1913- **CLC 19, 32,**
112; BLC 1; DAM MULT, POET; PC 25
See also BW 2, 3; CA 65-68; CANR 24, 43,
81; MTCW 1, 2
Chabon, Michael 1963-   **CLC 55**
See also CA 139; CANR 57
Chabrol, Claude 1930-   **CLC 16**
See also CA 110
Challans, Mary 1905-1983
See Renault, Mary
See also CA 81-84; 111; CANR 74; MTCW 2;
SATA 23; SATA-Obit 36
Challis, George
See Faust, Frederick (Schiller)
Chambers, Aidan 1934-   **CLC 35**
See also AAYA 27; CA 25-28R; CANR 12, 31,
58; JRDA; MAICYA; SAAS 12; SATA 1, 69,
108
Chambers, James 1948-
See Cliff, Jimmy
See also CA 124
Chambers, Jessie
See Lawrence, D(avid) H(erbert Richards)
Chambers, Robert W(illiam) 1865-1933
TCLC 41
See also CA 165; DLB 202; SATA 107
Chandler, Raymond (Thornton) 1888-1959
TCLC 1, 7; SSC 23
See also AAYA 25; CA 104; 129; CANR
60;CDALB 1929-1941; DLBD 6; MTCW 1,
2
Chang, Eileen 1920-1995   **SSC 28**
See also CA 166
Chang, Jung 1952-   **CLC 71**
See also CA 142
Chang Ai-Ling
See Chang, Eileen
Channing, William Ellery 1780-1842 **NCLC**
17
See also DLB 1, 59
Chao, Patricia 1955-   **CLC 119**
See also CA 163
Chaplin, Charles Spencer 1889-1977 **CLC 16**
See also Chaplin, Charlie
See also CA 81-84; 73-76
Chaplin, Charlie
See Chaplin, Charles Spencer

See also DLB 44
Chapman, George 1559(?)-1634 **LC 22; DAM**
DRAM
See also DLB 62, 121
Chapman, Graham 1941-1989   **CLC 21**
See also Monty Python
See also CA 116; 129; CANR 35
Chapman, John Jay 1862-1933   **TCLC 7**
See also CA 104
Chapman, Lee
See Bradley, Marion Zimmer
Chapman, Walker
See Silverberg, Robert
Chappell, Fred (Davis) 1936-   **CLC 40, 78**
See also CA 5-8R; CAAS 4; CANR 8, 33, 67;
DLB 6, 105
Char, Rene(-Emile) 1907-1988 CLC **9, 11, 14,**
55; DAM POET
See also CA 13-16R; 124; CANR 32; MTCW
1, 2
Charby, Jay
See Ellison, Harlan (Jay)
Chardin, Pierre Teilhard de
See Teilhard de Chardin, (Marie Joseph) Pierre
Charles I 1600-1649   **LC 13**
Charriere, Isabelle de 1740-1805 **NCLC 66**
Charyn, Jerome 1937-   **CLC 5, 8, 18**
See also CA 5-8R; CAAS 1; CANR 7, 61;
DLBY 83; MTCW 1
Chase, Mary (Coyle) 1907-1981   **DC 1**
See also CA 77-80; 105; SATA 17; SATA-Obit
29
Chase, Mary Ellen 1887-1973   **CLC 2**
See also CA 13-16; 41-44R; CAP 1; SATA 10
Chase, Nicholas
See Hyde, Anthony
Chateaubriand, Francois Rene de 1768-1848
NCLC 3
See also DLB 119
Chatterje, Sarat Chandra 1876-1936(?)
See Chatterji, Saratchandra
See also CA 109
Chatterji, Bankim Chandra 1838-1894 **NCLC**
19
Chatterji, Saratchandra   **TCLC 13**
See also Chatterje, Sarat Chandra
Chatterton, Thomas 1752-1770 **LC 3; DAM**
POET
See also DLB 109
Chatwin, (Charles) Bruce 1940-1989 **CLC 28,**
57, 59; DAM POP
See also AAYA 4; BEST 90:1; CA 85-88; 127;
DLB 194, 204
Chaucer, Daniel
See Ford, Ford Madox
Chaucer, Geoffrey 1340(?)-1400 **LC 17; DA;**
DAB; DAC; DAM MST, POET; PC 19;
WLCS
See also CDBLB Before 1660; DLB 146
Chavez, Denise (Elia) 1948-
See also CA 131; CANR 56, 81; DAM MULT;
DLB 122; HLC 1; HW 1, 2; MTCW 2
Chaviaras, Strates 1935-
See Haviaras, Stratis
See also CA 105
Chayefsky, Paddy   **CLC 23**
See also Chayefsky, Sidney
See also DLB 7, 44; DLBY 81
Chayefsky, Sidney 1923-1981
See Chayefsky, Paddy
See also CA 9-12R; 104; CANR 18; DAM
DRAM
Chedid, Andree 1920-   **CLC 47**

See also CA 145
Cheever, John 1912-1982 CLC **3, 7, 8, 11, 15,**
25, 64; DA; DAB; DAC; DAM MST, NOV,
POP; SSC 1; WLC
See also CA 5-8R; 106; CABS 1; CANR 5, 27,
76; CDALB 1941-1968; DLB 2, 102; DLBY
80, 82; INT CANR-5; MTCW 1, 2
Cheever, Susan 1943-   **CLC 18, 48**
See also CA 103; CANR 27, 51; DLBY 82; INT
CANR-27
Chekhonte, Antosha
See Chekhov, Anton (Pavlovich)
Chekhov, Anton (Pavlovich) 1860-1904 **TCLC**
3, 10, 31, 55, 96; DA; DAB; DAC; DAM
DRAM, MST; DC 9; SSC 2, 28; WLC
See also CA 104; 124; SATA 90
Chernyshevsky, Nikolay Gavrilovich 1828-1889
NCLC 1
Cherry, Carolyn Janice 1942-
See Cherryh, C. J.
See also CA 65-68; CANR 10
Cherryh, C. J.   **CLC 35**
See also Cherry, Carolyn Janice
See also AAYA 24; DLBY 80; SATA 93
Chesnutt, Charles W(addell) 1858-1932
TCLC 5, 39; BLC 1; DAM MULT; SSC 7
See also BW 1, 3; CA 106; 125; CANR 76; DLB
12, 50, 78; MTCW 1, 2
Chester, Alfred 1929(?)-1971   **CLC 49**
See also CA 33-36R; DLB 130
Chesterton, G(ilbert) K(eith) 1874-1936
TCLC 1, 6, 64; DAM NOV, POET; SSC 1
See also CA 104; 132; CANR 73; CDBLB
1914-1945; DLB 10, 19, 34, 70, 98, 149,
178; MTCW 1, 2; SATA 27
Chiang, Pin-chin 1904-1986
See Ding Ling
See also CA 118
Ch'ien Chung-shu 1910-   **CLC 22**
See also CA 130; CANR 73; MTCW 1, 2
Child, L. Maria
See Child, Lydia Maria
Child, Lydia Maria 1802-1880 **NCLC 6, 73**
See also DLB 1, 74; SATA 67
Child, Mrs.
See Child, Lydia Maria
Child, Philip 1898-1978   **CLC 19, 68**
See also CA 13-14; CAP 1; SATA 47
Childers, (Robert) Erskine 1870-1922 **TCLC**
65
See also CA 113; 153; DLB 70
Childress, Alice 1920-1994 CLC **12, 15, 86, 96;**
BLC 1; DAM DRAM, MULT, NOV; DC 4
See also AAYA 8; BW 2, 3; CA 45-48; 146;
CANR 3, 27, 50, 74; CLR 14; DLB 7, 38;
JRDA; MAICYA; MTCW 1, 2; SATA 7, 48,
81
Chin, Frank (Chew, Jr.) 1940-   **DC 7**
See also CA 33-36R; CANR 71; DAM MULT;
DLB 206
Chislett, (Margaret) Anne 1943-   **CLC 34**
See also CA 151
Chitty, Thomas Willes 1926-   **CLC 11**
See also Hinde, Thomas
See also CA 5-8R
Chivers, Thomas Holley 1809-1858 **NCLC 49**
See also DLB 3
Choi, Susan   **CLC 119**
Chomette, Rene Lucien 1898-1981
See Clair, Rene
See also CA 103
Chopin, Kate TCLC **5, 14; DA; DAB; SSC 8;**
WLCS

See Reed, Ishmael

Coleridge, M. E.
See Coleridge, Mary E(lizabeth)

Coleridge, Mary E(lizabeth) 1861-1907**TCLC 73**
See also CA 116; 166; DLB 19, 98

Coleridge, Samuel Taylor 1772-1834**NCLC 9, 54; DA; DAB; DAC; DAM MST, POET; PC 11; WLC**
See also CDBLB 1789-1832; DLB 93, 107

Coleridge, Sara 1802-1852 **NCLC 31**
See also DLB 199

Coles, Don 1928- **CLC 46**
See also CA 115; CANR 38

Coles, Robert (Martin) 1929- **CLC 108**
See also CA 45-48; CANR 3, 32, 66, 70; INT CANR-32; SATA 23

Colette, (Sidonie-Gabrielle) 1873-1954**TCLC 1, 5, 16; DAM NOV; SSC 10**
See also CA 104; 131; DLB 65; MTCW 1, 2

Collett, (Jacobine) Camilla (Wergeland) 1813-1895 **NCLC 22**

Collier, Christopher 1930- **CLC 30**
See also AAYA 13; CA 33-36R; CANR 13, 33; JRDA; MAICYA; SATA 16, 70

Collier, James L(incoln) 1928-**CLC 30; DAM POP**
See also AAYA 13; CA 9-12R; CANR 4, 33, 60; CLR 3; JRDA; MAICYA; SAAS 21; SATA 8, 70

Collier, Jeremy 1650-1726 **LC 6**

Collier, John 1901-1980 **SSC 19**
See also CA 65-68; 97-100; CANR 10; DLB 77

Collingwood, R(obin) G(eorge) 1889(?)-1943 **TCLC 67**
See also CA 117; 155

Collins, Hunt
See Hunter, Evan

Collins, Linda 1931- **CLC 44**
See also CA 125

Collins, (William) Wilkie 1824-1889**NCLC 1, 18**
See also CDBLB 1832-1890; DLB 18, 70, 159

Collins, William 1721-1759 **LC 4, 40; DAM POET**
See also DLB 109

Collodi, Carlo 1826-1890 **NCLC 54**
See also Lorenzini, Carlo
See also CLR 5

Colman, George 1732-1794
See Glassco, John

Colt, Winchester Remington
See Hubbard, L(afayette) Ron(ald)

Colter, Cyrus 1910- **CLC 58**
See also BW 1; CA 65-68; CANR 10, 66; DLB 33

Colton, James
See Hansen, Joseph

Colum, Padraic 1881-1972 **CLC 28**
See also CA 73-76; 33-36R; CANR 35; CLR 36; MAICYA; MTCW 1; SATA 15

Colvin, James
See Moorcock, Michael (John)

Colwin, Laurie (E.) 1944-1992**CLC 5, 13, 23, 84**
See also CA 89-92; 139; CANR 20, 46; DLBY 80; MTCW 1

Comfort, Alex(ander) 1920-**CLC 7;DAM POP**
See also CA 1-4R; CANR 1, 45; MTCW 1

Comfort, Montgomery
See Campbell, (John) Ramsey

Compton-Burnett, I(vy) 1884(?)-1969**CLC 1,**

3, 10, 15, 34; DAM NOV
See also CA 1-4R; 25-28R; CANR 4; DLB 36; MTCW 1

Comstock, Anthony 1844-1915 **TCLC 13**
See also CA 110; 169

Comte, Auguste 1798-1857 **NCLC 54**

Conan Doyle, Arthur
See Doyle, Arthur Conan

Conde (Abellan), Carmen 1901-
See also CA 177; DLB 108; HLCS 1; HW 2

Conde, Maryse 1937- **CLC 52, 92; BLCS; DAM MULT**
See also Boucolon, Maryse
See also BW 2; MTCW 1

Condillac, Etienne Bonnot de 1714-1780 **LC 26**

Condon, Richard (Thomas) 1915-1996**CLC 4, 6, 8, 10, 45, 100; DAM NOV**
See also BEST 90:3; CA 1-4R; 151; CAAS 1; CANR 2, 23; INT CANR-23; MTCW 1, 2

Confucius 551B.C.-479B.C. **CMLC 19; DA; DAB; DAC; DAM MST; WLCS**

Congreve, William 1670-1729 **LC 5, 21; DA; DAB; DAC; DAM DRAM, MST, POET; DC 2; WLC**
See also CDBLB 1660-1789; DLB 39, 84

Connell, Evan S(helby), Jr. 1924-**CLC 4, 6, 45; DAM NOV**
See also AAYA 7; CA 1-4R; CAAS 2; CANR 2, 39, 76; DLB 2; DLBY 81; MTCW 1, 2

Connelly, Marc(us Cook) 1890-1980 **CLC 7**
See also CA 85-88; 102; CANR 30; DLB 7; DLBY 80; SATA-Obit 25

Connor, Ralph **TCLC 31**
See also Gordon, Charles William
See also DLB 92

Conrad, Joseph 1857-1924**TCLC 1, 6, 13, 25, 43, 57; DA; DAB; DAC; DAM MST, NOV; SSC 9; WLC**
See also AAYA 26; CA 104; 131; CANR 60; CDBLB 1890-1914; DLB 10, 34, 98, 156; MTCW 1, 2; SATA 27

Conrad, Robert Arnold
See Hart, Moss

Conroy, Pat
See Conroy, (Donald) Pat(rick)
See also MTCW 2

Conroy, (Donald) Pat(rick) 1945-**CLC 30, 74; DAM NOV, POP**
See also Conroy, Pat
See also AAYA 8; AITN 1; CA 85-88; CANR 24, 53; DLB 6; MTCW 1

Constant (de Rebecque), (Henri) Benjamin 1767-1830 **NCLC 6**
See also DLB 119

Conybeare, Charles Augustus
See Eliot, T(homas) S(tearns)

Cook, Michael 1933- **CLC 58**
See also CA 93-96; CANR 68; DLB 53

Cook, Robin 1940- **CLC 14;DAM POP**
See also BEST 90:2; CA 108; 111; CANR 41; INT 111

Cook, Roy
See Silverberg, Robert

Cooke, Elizabeth 1948- **CLC 55**
See also CA 129

Cooke, John Esten 1830-1886 **NCLC 5**
See also DLB 3

Cooke, John Estes
See Baum, L(yman) Frank

Cooke, M. E.
See Creasey, John

Cooke, Margaret

See Creasey, John

Cook-Lynn, Elizabeth 1930- **CLC 93;DAM MULT**
See also CA 133; DLB 175; NNAL

Cooney, Ray **CLC 62**

Cooper, Douglas 1960- **CLC 86**

Cooper, Henry St. John
See Creasey, John

Cooper, J(oan) California (?)-**CLC 56; DAM MULT**
See also AAYA 12; BW 1; CA 125; CANR 55; DLB 212

Cooper, James Fenimore 1789-1851**NCLC 1, 27, 54**
See also AAYA 22; CDALB 1640-1865; DLB 3; SATA 19

Coover, Robert (Lowell) 1932- **CLC 3, 7, 15, 32, 46, 87; DAM NOV; SSC 15**
See also CA 45-48; CANR 3, 37, 58; DLB 2; DLBY 81; MTCW 1, 2

Copeland, Stewart (Armstrong) 1952-**CLC 26**

Copernicus, Nicolaus 1473-1543 **LC 45**

Coppard, A(lfred) E(dgar) 1878-1957 **TCLC 5; SSC 21**
See also CA 114; 167; DLB 162; YABC 1

Coppee, Francois 1842-1908 **TCLC 25**
See also CA 170

Coppola, Francis Ford 1939- **CLC 16**
See also CA 77-80; CANR 40, 78; DLB 44

Corbiere, Tristan 1845-1875 **NCLC 43**

Corcoran, Barbara 1911- **CLC 17**
See also AAYA 14; CA 21-24R; CAAS 2; CANR 11, 28, 48; CLR 50; DLB 52; JRDA; SAAS 20; SATA 3, 77

Cordelier, Maurice
See Giraudoux, (Hippolyte) Jean

Corelli, Marie 1855-1924 **TCLC 51**
See also Mackay, Mary
See also DLB 34, 156

Corman, Cid 1924- **CLC 9**
See also Corman, Sidney
See also CAAS 2; DLB 5, 193

Corman, Sidney 1924-
See Corman, Cid
See also CA 85-88; CANR 44; DAM POET

Cormier, Robert (Edmund) 1925-**CLC 12, 30; DA; DAB; DAC; DAM MST, NOV**
See also AAYA 3, 19; CA 1-4R; CANR 5, 23, 76; CDALB 1968-1988; CLR 12, 55; DLB 52; INT CANR-23; JRDA; MAICYA; MTCW 1, 2; SATA 10, 45, 83

Corn, Alfred (DeWitt, III) 1943- **CLC 33**
See also CA 179; CAAE 179; CAAS 25; CANR 44; DLB 120; DLBY 80

Corneille, Pierre 1606-1684 **LC 28; DAB; DAM MST**

Cornwell, David (John Moore) 1931- **CLC 9, 15; DAM POP**
See also le Carre, John
See also CA 5-8R; CANR 13, 33, 59; MTCW 1, 2

Corso, (Nunzio) Gregory 1930- **CLC 1, 11**
See also CA 5-8R; CANR 41, 76; DLB 5, 16; MTCW 1, 2

Cortazar, Julio 1914-1984**CLC 2, 3, 5, 10, 13, 15, 33, 34, 92; DAM MULT, NOV; HLC 1; SSC 7**
See also CA 21-24R; CANR 12, 32, 81; DLB 113; HW 1, 2; MTCW 1, 2

Cortes, Hernan 1484-1547 **LC 31**

Corvinus, Jakob
See Raabe, Wilhelm (Karl)

Corwin, Cecil

Cunninghame Graham, R(obert) B(ontine)
1852-1936   **TCLC 19**
    See also Graham, R(obert) B(ontine)
        Cunninghame
    See also CA 119; DLB 98
Currie, Ellen 19(?)-   **CLC 44**
Curtin, Philip
    See Lowndes, Marie Adelaide (Belloc)
Curtis, Price
    See Ellison, Harlan (Jay)
Cutrate, Joe
    See Spiegelman, Art
Cynewulf c. 770-c. 840   **CMLC 23**
Czaczkes, Shmuel Yosef
    See Agnon, S(hmuel) Y(osef Halevi)
Dabrowska, Maria (Szumska) 1889-1965 **CLC 15**
    See also CA 106
Dabydeen, David 1955-   **CLC 34**
    See also BW 1; CA 125; CANR 56
Dacey, Philip 1939-   **CLC 51**
    See also CA 37-40R; CAAS 17; CANR 14, 32, 64; DLB 105
Dagerman, Stig (Halvard) 1923-1954 **TCLC 17**
    See also CA 117; 155
Dahl, Roald 1916-1990 **CLC 1, 6, 18, 79; DAB; DAC; DAM MST, NOV, POP**
    See also AAYA 15; CA 1-4R; 133; CANR 6, 32, 37, 62; CLR 1, 7, 41; DLB 139; JRDA; MAICYA; MTCW 1, 2; SATA 1, 26, 73; SATA-Obit 65
Dahlberg, Edward 1900-1977   **CLC 1, 7, 14**
    See also CA 9-12R; 69-72; CANR 31, 62; DLB 48; MTCW 1
Daitch, Susan 1954-   **CLC 103**
    See also CA 161
Dale, Colin   **TCLC 18**
    See also Lawrence, T(homas) E(dward)
Dale, George E.
    See Asimov, Isaac
Dalton, Roque 1935-1975
    See also HLCS 1; HW 2
Daly, Elizabeth 1878-1967   **CLC 52**
    See also CA 23-24; 25-28R; CANR 60; CAP 2
Daly, Maureen 1921-   **CLC 17**
    See also AAYA 5; CANR 37; JRDA; MAICYA; SAAS 1; SATA 2
Damas, Leon-Gontran 1912-1978   **CLC 84**
    See also BW 1; CA 125; 73-76
Dana, Richard Henry Sr. 1787-1879 **NCLC 53**
Daniel, Samuel 1562(?)-1619   **LC 24**
    See also DLB 62
Daniels, Brett
    See Adler, Renata
Dannay, Frederic 1905-1982   **CLC 11; DAM POP**
    See also Queen, Ellery
    See also CA 1-4R; 107; CANR 1, 39; DLB 137; MTCW 1
D'Annunzio, Gabriele 1863-1938 **TCLC 6, 40**
    See also CA 104; 155
Danois, N. le
    See Gourmont, Remy (-Marie-Charles) de
Dante 1265-1321   **CMLC 3, 18; DA; DAB; DAC; DAM MST, POET; PC 21; WLCS**
d'Antibes, Germain
    See Simenon, Georges (Jacques Christian)
Danticat, Edwidge 1969-   **CLC 94**
    See also AAYA 29; CA 152; CANR 73; MTCW 1
Danvers, Dennis 1947-   **CLC 70**
Danziger, Paula 1944-   **CLC 21**

    See also AAYA 4; CA 112; 115; CANR 37; CLR 20; JRDA; MAICYA; SATA 36, 63, 102; SATA-Brief 30
Da Ponte, Lorenzo 1749-1838   **NCLC 50**
Dario, Ruben 1867-1916   **TCLC 4; DAM MULT; HLC 1; PC 15**
    See also CA 131; CANR 81; HW 1, 2; MTCW 1, 2
Darley, George 1795-1846   **NCLC 2**
    See also DLB 96
Darrow, Clarence (Seward) 1857-1938 **TCLC 81**
    See also CA 164
Darwin, Charles 1809-1882   **NCLC 57**
    See also DLB 57, 166
Daryush, Elizabeth 1887-1977   **CLC 6, 19**
    See also CA 49-52; CANR 3, 81; DLB 20
Dasgupta, Surendranath 1887-1952 **TCLC 81**
    See also CA 157
Dashwood, Edmee Elizabeth Monica de la Pasture 1890-1943
    See Delafield, E. M.
    See also CA 119; 154
Daudet, (Louis Marie) Alphonse 1840-1897 **NCLC 1**
    See also DLB 123
Daumal, Rene 1908-1944   **TCLC 14**
    See also CA 114
Davenant, William 1606-1668   **LC 13**
    See also DLB 58, 126
Davenport, Guy (Mattison, Jr.) 1927- **CLC 6, 14, 38; SSC 16**
    See also CA 33-36R; CANR 23, 73; DLB 130
Davidson, Avram (James) 1923-1993
    See Queen, Ellery
    See also CA 101; 171; CANR 26; DLB 8
Davidson, Donald (Grady) 1893-1968 **CLC 2, 13, 19**
    See also CA 5-8R; 25-28R; CANR 4; DLB 45
Davidson, Hugh
    See Hamilton, Edmond
Davidson, John 1857-1909   **TCLC 24**
    See also CA 118; DLB 19
Davidson, Sara 1943-   **CLC 9**
    See also CA 81-84; CANR 44, 68; DLB 185
Davie, Donald (Alfred) 1922-1995   **CLC 5, 8, 10, 31**
    See also CA 1-4R; 149; CAAS 3; CANR 1, 44; DLB 27; MTCW 1
Davies, Ray(mond Douglas) 1944-   **CLC 21**
    See also CA 116; 146
Davies, Rhys 1901-1978   **CLC 23**
    See also CA 9-12R; 81-84; CANR 4; DLB 139, 191
Davies, (William) Robertson 1913-1995 **CLC 2, 7, 13, 25, 42, 75, 91; DA; DAB; DAC; DAM MST, NOV, POP; WLC**
    See also BEST 89:2; CA 33-36R; 150; CANR 17, 42; DLB 68; INT CANR-17; MTCW 1, 2
Davies, W(illiam) H(enry) 1871-1940 **TCLC 5**
    See also CA 104; 179; DLB 19, 174
Davies, Walter C.
    See Kornbluth, C(yril) M.
Davis, Angela (Yvonne) 1944- **CLC 77; DAM MULT**
    See also BW 2, 3; CA 57-60; CANR 10, 81
Davis, B. Lynch
    See Bioy Casares, Adolfo; Borges, Jorge Luis
Davis, B. Lynch
    See Bioy Casares, Adolfo
Davis, Harold Lenoir 1894-1960   **CLC 49**
    See also CA 178; 89-92; DLB 9, 206

Davis, Rebecca (Blaine) Harding 1831-1910 **TCLC 6**
    See also CA 104; 179; DLB 74
Davis, Richard Harding 1864-1916 **TCLC 24**
    See also CA 114; DLB 12, 23, 78, 79, 189; DLBD 13
Davison, Frank Dalby 1893-1970   **CLC 15**
    See also CA 116
Davison, Lawrence H.
    See Lawrence, D(avid) H(erbert Richards)
Davison, Peter (Hubert) 1928-   **CLC 28**
    See also CA 9-12R; CAAS 4; CANR 3, 43; DLB 5
Davys, Mary 1674-1732   **LC 1, 46**
    See also DLB 39
Dawson, Fielding 1930-   **CLC 6**
    See also CA 85-88; DLB 130
Dawson, Peter
    See Faust, Frederick (Schiller)
Day, Clarence (Shepard, Jr.) 1874-1935 **TCLC 25**
    See also CA 108; DLB 11
Day, Thomas 1748-1789   **LC 1**
    See also DLB 39; YABC 1
Day Lewis, C(ecil) 1904-1972   **CLC 1, 6, 10; DAM POET; PC 11**
    See also Blake, Nicholas
    See also CA 13-16; 33-36R; CANR 34; CAP 1; DLB 15, 20; MTCW 1, 2
Dazai Osamu 1909-1948   **TCLC 11**
    See also Tsushima, Shuji
    See also CA 164; DLB 182
de Andrade, Carlos Drummond 1892-1945
    See Drummond de Andrade, Carlos
Deane, Norman
    See Creasey, John
Deane, Seamus (Francis) 1940-   **CLC 122**
    See also CA 118; CANR 42
de Beauvoir, Simone (Lucie Ernestine Marie Bertrand)
    See Beauvoir, Simone (Lucie Ernestine Marie Bertrand) de
de Beer, P.
    See Bosman, Herman Charles
de Brissac, Malcolm
    See Dickinson, Peter (Malcolm)
de Chardin, Pierre Teilhard
    See Teilhard de Chardin, (Marie Joseph) Pierre
Dee, John 1527-1608   **LC 20**
Deer, Sandra 1940-   **CLC 45**
De Ferrari, Gabriella 1941-   **CLC 65**
    See also CA 146
Defoe, Daniel 1660(?)-1731   **LC 1, 42; DA; DAB; DAC; DAM MST, NOV; WLC**
    See also AAYA 27; CDBLB 1660-1789; DLB 39, 95, 101; JRDA; MAICYA; SATA 22
de Gourmont, Remy(-Marie-Charles)
    See Gourmont, Remy (-Marie-Charles) de
de Hartog, Jan 1914-   **CLC 19**
    See also CA 1-4R; CANR 1
de Hostos, E. M.
    See Hostos (y Bonilla), Eugenio Maria de
de Hostos, Eugenio M.
    See Hostos (y Bonilla), Eugenio Maria de
Deighton, Len   **CLC 4, 7, 22, 46**
    See also Deighton, Leonard Cyril
    See also AAYA 6; BEST 89:2; CDBLB 1960 to Present; DLB 87
Deighton, Leonard Cyril 1929-
    See Deighton, Len
    See also CA 9-12R; CANR 19, 33, 68; DAM NOV, POP; MTCW 1, 2
Dekker, Thomas 1572(?)-1632   **LC 22; DAM**

Difusa, Pati
See Almodovar, Pedro
Dillard, Annie 1945- **CLC 9, 60, 115; DAM NOV**
See also AAYA 6; CA 49-52; CANR 3, 43, 62; DLBY 80; MTCW 1, 2; SATA 10
Dillard, R(ichard) H(enry) W(ilde) 1937- **CLC 5**
See also CA 21-24R; CAAS 7; CANR 10; DLB 5
Dillon, Eilis 1920-1994 **CLC 17**
See also CA 9-12R; 147; CAAS 3; CANR 4, 38, 78; CLR 26; MAICYA; SATA 2, 74; SATA-Essay 105; SATA-Obit 83
Dimont, Penelope
See Mortimer, Penelope (Ruth)
Dinesen, Isak **CLC 10, 29, 95; SSC 7**
See also Blixen, Karen (Christentze Dinesen)
See also MTCW 1
Ding Ling **CLC 68**
See also Chiang, Pin-chin
Diphusa, Patty
See Almodovar, Pedro
Disch, Thomas M(ichael) 1940- **CLC 7, 36**
See also AAYA 17; CA 21-24R; CAAS 4; CANR 17, 36, 54; CLR 18; DLB 8; MAICYA; MTCW 1, 2; SAAS 15; SATA 92
Disch, Tom
See Disch, Thomas M(ichael)
d'Isly, Georges
See Simenon, Georges (Jacques Christian)
Disraeli, Benjamin 1804-1881 **NCLC 2, 39, 79**
See also DLB 21, 55
Ditcum, Steve
See Crumb, R(obert)
Dixon, Paige
See Corcoran, Barbara
Dixon, Stephen 1936- **CLC 52; SSC 16**
See also CA 89-92; CANR 17, 40, 54; DLB 130
Doak, Annie
See Dillard, Annie
Dobell, Sydney Thompson 1824-1874 **NCLC 43**
See also DLB 32
Doblin, Alfred **TCLC 13**
See also Doeblin, Alfred
Dobrolyubov, Nikolai Alexandrovich 1836-1861 **NCLC 5**
Dobson, Austin 1840-1921 **TCLC 79**
See also DLB 35; 144
Dobyns, Stephen 1941- **CLC 37**
See also CA 45-48; CANR 2, 18
Doctorow, E(dgar) L(aurence) 1931- **CLC 6, 11, 15, 18, 37, 44, 65, 113; DAM NOV, POP**
See also AAYA 22; AITN 2; BEST 89:3; CA 45-48; CANR 2, 33, 51, 76; CDALB 1968-1988; DLB 2, 28, 173; DLBY 80; MTCW 1, 2
Dodgson, Charles Lutwidge 1832-1898
See Carroll, Lewis
See also CLR 2; DA; DAB; DAC; DAM MST, NOV, POET; MAICYA; SATA 100; YABC 2
Dodson, Owen (Vincent) 1914-1983 **CLC 79; BLC 1; DAM MULT**
See also BW 1; CA 65-68; 110; CANR 24; DLB 76
Doeblin, Alfred 1878-1957 **TCLC 13**
See also Doblin, Alfred
See also CA 110; 141; DLB 66
Doerr, Harriet 1910- **CLC 34**
See also CA 117; 122; CANR 47; INT 122
Domecq, H(onorio Bustos)
See Bioy Casares, Adolfo

Domecq, H(onorio) Bustos
See Bioy Casares, Adolfo; Borges, Jorge Luis
Domini, Rey
See Lorde, Audre (Geraldine)
Dominique
See Proust, (Valentin-Louis-George-Eugene-) Marcel
Don, A
See Stephen, SirLeslie
Donaldson, Stephen R. 1947- **CLC 46; DAM POP**
See also CA 89-92; CANR 13, 55; INT CANR-13
Donleavy, J(ames) P(atrick) 1926- **CLC 1, 4, 6, 10, 45**
See also AITN 2; CA 9-12R; CANR 24, 49, 62, 80; DLB 6, 173; INT CANR-24; MTCW 1, 2
Donne, John 1572-1631 **LC 10, 24; DA; DAB; DAC; DAM MST, POET; PC 1; WLC**
See also CDBLB Before 1660; DLB 121, 151
Donnell, David 1939(?)- **CLC 34**
Donoghue, P. S.
See Hunt, E(verette) Howard, (Jr.)
Donoso (Yanez), Jose 1924-1996 **CLC 4, 8, 11, 32, 99; DAM MULT; HLC 1; SSC 34**
See also CA 81-84; 155; CANR 32, 73; DLB 113; HW 1, 2; MTCW 1, 2
Donovan, John 1928-1992 **CLC 35**
See also AAYA 20; CA 97-100; 137; CLR 3; MAICYA; SATA 72; SATA-Brief 29
Don Roberto
See Cunninghame Graham, R(obert) B(ontine)
Doolittle, Hilda 1886-1961 **CLC 3, 8, 14, 31, 34, 73; DA; DAC; DAM MST, POET; PC 5; WLC**
See also H. D.
See also CA 97-100; CANR 35; DLB 4, 45; MTCW 1, 2
Dorfman, Ariel 1942- **CLC 48, 77; DAM MULT; HLC 1**
See also CA 124; 130; CANR 67, 70; HW 1, 2; INT 130
Dorn, Edward (Merton) 1929- **CLC 10, 18**
See also CA 93-96; CANR 42, 79; DLB 5; INT 93-96
Dorris, Michael (Anthony) 1945-1997 **CLC 109; DAM MULT, NOV**
See also AAYA 20; BEST 90:1; CA 102; 157; CANR 19, 46, 75; CLR 58; DLB 175; MTCW 2; NNAL; SATA 75; SATA-Obit 94
Dorris, Michael A.
See Dorris, Michael (Anthony)
Dorsan, Luc
See Simenon, Georges (Jacques Christian)
Dorsange, Jean
See Simenon, Georges (Jacques Christian)
Dos Passos, John (Roderigo) 1896-1970 **CLC 1, 4, 8, 11, 15, 25, 34, 82; DA; DAB; DAC; DAM MST, NOV; WLC**
See also CA 1-4R; 29-32R; CANR 3; CDALB 1929-1941; DLB 4, 9; DLBD 1, 15; DLBY 96; MTCW 1, 2
Dossage, Jean
See Simenon, Georges (Jacques Christian)
Dostoevsky, Fedor Mikhailovich 1821-1881 **NCLC 2, 7, 21, 33, 43; DA; DAB; DAC; DAM MST, NOV; SSC 2, 33; WLC**
Doughty, Charles M(ontagu) 1843-1926 **TCLC 27**
See also CA 115; 178; DLB 19, 57, 174
Douglas, Ellen **CLC 73**
See also Haxton, Josephine Ayres; Williamson,

Ellen Douglas
Douglas, Gavin 1475(?)-1522 **LC 20**
See also DLB 132
Douglas, George
See Brown, George Douglas
Douglas, Keith (Castellain) 1920-1944 **TCLC 40**
See also CA 160; DLB 27
Douglas, Leonard
See Bradbury, Ray (Douglas)
Douglas, Michael
See Crichton, (John) Michael
Douglas, (George) Norman 1868-1952 **TCLC 68**
See also CA 119; 157; DLB 34, 195
Douglas, William
See Brown, George Douglas
Douglass, Frederick 1817(?)-1895 **NCLC 7, 55; BLC 1; DA; DAC; DAM MST, MULT; WLC**
See also CDALB 1640-1865; DLB 1, 43, 50, 79; SATA 29
Dourado, (Waldomiro Freitas) Autran 1926- **CLC 23, 60**
See also Autran Dourado, Waldomiro Freitas
See also CA 179; CANR 34, 81; DLB 145; HW 2
Dourado, Waldomiro Autran 1926-
See Dourado, (Waldomiro Freitas) Autran
See also CA 179
Dove, Rita (Frances) 1952- **CLC 50, 81; BLCS; DAM MULT, POET; PC 6**
See also BW 2; CA 109; CAAS 19; CANR 27, 42, 68, 76; CDALBS; DLB 120; MTCW 1
Doveglion
See Villa, Jose Garcia
Dowell, Coleman 1925-1985 **CLC 60**
See also CA 25-28R; 117; CANR 10; DLB 130
Dowson, Ernest (Christopher) 1867-1900 **TCLC 4**
See also CA 105; 150; DLB 19, 135
Doyle, A. Conan
See Doyle, Arthur Conan
Doyle, Arthur Conan 1859-1930 **TCLC 7; DA; DAB; DAC; DAM MST, NOV; SSC 12; WLC**
See also AAYA 14; CA 104; 122; CDBLB 1890-1914; DLB 18, 70, 156, 178; MTCW 1, 2; SATA 24
Doyle, Conan
See Doyle, Arthur Conan
Doyle, John
See Graves, Robert (von Ranke)
Doyle, Roddy 1958(?)- **CLC 81**
See also AAYA 14; CA 143; CANR 73; DLB 194
Doyle, Sir A. Conan
See Doyle, Arthur Conan
Doyle, Sir Arthur Conan
See Doyle, Arthur Conan
Dr. A
See Asimov, Isaac; Silverstein, Alvin
Drabble, Margaret 1939- **CLC 2, 3, 5, 8, 10, 22, 53; DAB; DAC; DAM MST, NOV, POP**
See also CA 13-16R; CANR 18, 35, 63; CDBLB 1960 to Present; DLB 14, 155; MTCW 1, 2; SATA 48
Drapier, M. B.
See Swift, Jonathan
Drayham, James
See Mencken, H(enry) L(ouis)
Drayton, Michael 1563-1631 **LC 8; DAM POET**

See also DLB 115

Eckmar, F. R.
See de Hartog, Jan

Eco, Umberto 1932- **CLC 28, 60; DAM NOV, POP**
See also BEST 90:1; CA 77-80; CANR 12, 33, 55; DLB 196; MTCW 1, 2

Eddison, E(ric) R(ucker) 1882-1945**TCLC 15**
See also CA 109; 156

Eddy, Mary (Ann Morse) Baker 1821-1910 **TCLC 71**
See also CA 113; 174

Edel, (Joseph) Leon 1907-1997 **CLC 29, 34**
See also CA 1-4R; 161; CANR 1, 22; DLB 103; INT CANR-22

Eden, Emily 1797-1869 **NCLC 10**

Edgar, David 1948- **CLC 42;DAM DRAM**
See also CA 57-60; CANR 12, 61; DLB 13; MTCW 1

Edgerton, Clyde (Carlyle) 1944- **CLC 39**
See also AAYA 17; CA 118; 134; CANR 64; INT 134

Edgeworth, Maria 1768-1849 **NCLC 1,51**
See also DLB 116, 159, 163; SATA 21

Edison, Thomas 1847-1931 **TCLC 96**

Edmonds, Paul
See Kuttner, Henry

Edmonds, Walter D(umaux) 1903-1998 **C L C 35**
See also CA 5-8R; CANR 2; DLB 9; MAICYA; SAAS 4; SATA 1, 27; SATA-Obit 99

Edmondson, Wallace
See Ellison, Harlan (Jay)

Edson, Russell **CLC 13**
See also CA 33-36R

Edwards, Bronwen Elizabeth
See Rose, Wendy

Edwards, G(erald) B(asil) 1899-1976**CLC 25**
See also CA 110

Edwards, Gus 1939- **CLC 43**
See also CA 108; INT 108

Edwards, Jonathan 1703-1758 **LC 7; DA; DAC; DAM MST**
See also DLB 24

Efron, Marina Ivanovna Tsvetaeva
See Tsvetaeva (Efron), Marina (Ivanovna)

Ehle, John (Marsden, Jr.) 1925- **CLC 27**
See also CA 9-12R

Ehrenbourg, Ilya (Grigoryevich)
See Ehrenburg, Ilya (Grigoryevich)

Ehrenburg, Ilya (Grigoryevich) 1891-1967 **CLC 18, 34, 62**
See also CA 102; 25-28R

Ehrenburg, Ilyo (Grigoryevich)
See Ehrenburg, Ilya (Grigoryevich)

Ehrenreich, Barbara 1941- **CLC 110**
See also BEST 90:4; CA 73-76; CANR 16, 37, 62; MTCW 1, 2

Eich, Guenter 1907-1972 **CLC 15**
See also CA 111; 93-96; DLB 69, 124

Eichendorff, Joseph Freiherrvon 1788-1857 **NCLC 8**
See also DLB 90

Eigner, Larry **CLC 9**
See also Eigner, Laurence (Joel)
See also CAAS 23; DLB 5

Eigner, Laurence (Joel) 1927-1996
See Eigner, Larry
See also CA 9-12R; 151; CANR 6; DLB 193

Einstein, Albert 1879-1955 **TCLC 65**
See also CA 121; 133; MTCW 1, 2

Eiseley, Loren Corey 1907-1977 **CLC 7**
See also AAYA 5; CA 1-4R; 73-76; CANR 6;

DLBD 17

Eisenstadt, Jill 1963- **CLC 50**
See also CA 140

Eisenstein, Sergei (Mikhailovich) 1898-1948 **TCLC 57**
See also CA 114; 149

Eisner, Simon
See Kornbluth, C(yril) M.

Ekeloef, (Bengt) Gunnar 1907-1968 **CLC 27; DAM POET; PC 23**
See also CA 123; 25-28R

Ekelof, (Bengt) Gunnar
See Ekeloef, (Bengt) Gunnar

Ekelund, Vilhelm 1880-1949 **TCLC 75**

Ekwensi, C. O. D.
See Ekwensi, Cyprian (Odiatu Duaka)

Ekwensi, Cyprian (Odiatu Duaka) 1921-**CLC 4; BLC 1; DAM MULT**
See also BW 2, 3; CA 29-32R; CANR 18, 42, 74; DLB 117; MTCW 1, 2; SATA 66

Elaine **TCLC 18**
See also Leverson, Ada

El Crummo
See Crumb, R(obert)

Elder, Lonne III 1931-1996 **DC 8**
See also BLC 1; BW 1, 3; CA 81-84; 152; CANR 25; DAM MULT; DLB 7, 38, 44

Elia
See Lamb, Charles

Eliade, Mircea 1907-1986 **CLC 19**
See also CA 65-68; 119; CANR 30, 62; MTCW 1

Eliot, A. D.
See Jewett, (Theodora) Sarah Orne

Eliot, Alice
See Jewett, (Theodora) Sarah Orne

Eliot, Dan
See Silverberg, Robert

Eliot, George 1819-1880 **NCLC 4, 13, 23, 41, 49; DA; DAB; DAC; DAM MST, NOV; PC 20; WLC**
See also CDBLB 1832-1890; DLB 21, 35, 55

Eliot, John 1604-1690 **LC 5**
See also DLB 24

Eliot, T(homas) S(tearns) 1888-1965**CLC 1, 2, 3, 6, 9, 10, 13, 15, 24, 34, 41, 55, 57, 113; DA; DAB; DAC; DAM DRAM, MST, POET; PC 5; WLC**
See also AAYA 28; CA 5-8R; 25-28R; CANR 41;CDALB 1929-1941; DLB 7, 10, 45, 63; DLBY 88; MTCW 1, 2

Elizabeth 1866-1941 **TCLC 41**

Elkin, Stanley L(awrence) 1930-1995 **CLC 4, 6, 9, 14, 27, 51, 91; DAM NOV, POP; SSC 12**
See also CA 9-12R; 148; CANR 8, 46; DLB 2, 28; DLBY 80; INT CANR-8; MTCW 1, 2

Elledge, Scott **CLC 34**

Elliot, Don
See Silverberg, Robert

Elliott, Don
See Silverberg, Robert

Elliott, George P(aul) 1918-1980 **CLC 2**
See also CA 1-4R; 97-100; CANR 2

Elliott, Janice 1931- **CLC 47**
See also CA 13-16R; CANR 8, 29; DLB 14

Elliott, Sumner Locke 1917-1991 **CLC 38**
See also CA 5-8R; 134; CANR 2, 21

Elliott, William
See Bradbury, Ray (Douglas)

Ellis, A. E. **CLC 7**

Ellis, Alice Thomas **CLC 40**
See also Haycraft, Anna

See also DLB 194; MTCW 1

Ellis, Bret Easton 1964-**CLC 39, 71, 117; DAM POP**
See also AAYA 2; CA 118; 123; CANR 51, 74; INT 123; MTCW 1

Ellis, (Henry) Havelock 1859-1939 **TCLC 14**
See also CA 109; 169; DLB 190

Ellis, Landon
See Ellison, Harlan (Jay)

Ellis, Trey 1962- **CLC 55**
See also CA 146

Ellison, Harlan (Jay) 1934- **CLC 1, 13, 42; DAM POP; SSC 14**
See also Jarvis, E. K.
See also AAYA 29; CA 5-8R; CANR 5, 46; DLB 8; INT CANR-5; MTCW 1, 2

Ellison, Ralph (Waldo) 1914-1994 **CLC 1, 3, 11, 54, 86, 114; BLC 1; DA; DAB; DAC; DAM MST, MULT, NOV; SSC 26;WLC**
See also AAYA 19; BW 1, 3; CA 9-12R; 145; CANR 24, 53; CDALB 1941-1968; DLB 2, 76; DLBY 94; MTCW 1, 2

Ellmann, Lucy (Elizabeth) 1956- **CLC 61**
See also CA 128

Ellmann, Richard (David) 1918-1987**CLC 50**
See also BEST 89:2; CA 1-4R; 122; CANR 2, 28, 61; DLB 103; DLBY 87; MTCW 1, 2

Elman, Richard (Martin) 1934-1997 **CLC 19**
See also CA 17-20R; 163; CAAS 3; CANR 47

Elron
See Hubbard, L(afayette) Ron(ald)

Eluard, Paul **TCLC 7, 41**
See also Grindel, Eugene

Elyot, Sir Thomas 1490(?)-1546 **LC 11**

Elytis, Odysseus 1911-1996 **CLC 15, 49, 100; DAM POET; PC 21**
See also CA 102; 151; MTCW 1, 2

Emecheta, (Florence Onye) Buchi 1944-**C L C 14, 48; BLC 2; DAM MULT**
See also BW 2, 3; CA 81-84; CANR 27, 81; DLB 117; MTCW 1, 2; SATA 66

Emerson, Mary Moody 1774-1863 **NCLC 66**

Emerson, Ralph Waldo 1803-1882 **NCLC 1, 38; DA; DAB; DAC; DAM MST, POET; PC 18; WLC**
See also CDALB 1640-1865; DLB 1, 59, 73

Eminescu, Mihail 1850-1889 **NCLC 33**

Empson, William 1906-1984**CLC 3, 8, 19, 33, 34**
See also CA 17-20R; 112; CANR 31, 61; DLB 20; MTCW 1, 2

Enchi, Fumiko (Ueda) 1905-1986 **CLC 31**
See also CA 129; 121; DLB 182

Ende, Michael (Andreas Helmuth) 1929-1995 **CLC 31**
See also CA 118; 124; 149; CANR 36; CLR 14; DLB 75; MAICYA; SATA 61; SATA-Brief 42; SATA-Obit 86

Endo, Shusaku 1923-1996 **CLC 7, 14, 19, 54, 99; DAM NOV**
See also CA 29-32R; 153; CANR 21, 54; DLB 182; MTCW 1, 2

Engel, Marian 1933-1985 **CLC 36**
See also CA 25-28R; CANR 12; DLB 53; INT CANR-12

Engelhardt, Frederick
See Hubbard, L(afayette) Ron(ald)

Enright, D(ennis) J(oseph) 1920-**CLC 4, 8, 31**
See also CA 1-4R; CANR 1, 42; DLB 27; SATA 25

Enzensberger, Hans Magnus 1929- **CLC 43**
See also CA 116; 119

Ephron, Nora 1941- **CLC 17, 31**

See also AITN 2; CA 65-68; CANR 12, 39
Epicurus 341B.C.-270B.C.   **CMLC 21**
  See also DLB 176
Epsilon
  See Betjeman, John
Epstein, Daniel Mark 1948-   **CLC 7**
  See also CA 49-52; CANR 2, 53
Epstein, Jacob 1956-   **CLC 19**
  See also CA 114
Epstein, Jean 1897-1953   **TCLC 92**
Epstein, Joseph 1937-   **CLC 39**
  See also CA 112; 119; CANR 50, 65
Epstein, Leslie 1938-   **CLC 27**
  See also CA 73-76; CAAS 12; CANR 23, 69
Equiano, Olaudah 1745(?)-1797 **LC 16; BLC 2; DAM MULT**
  See also DLB 37, 50
ER   **TCLC 33**
  See also CA 160; DLB 85
Erasmus, Desiderius 1469(?)-1536   **LC 16**
Erdman, Paul E(mil) 1932-   **CLC 25**
  See also AITN 1; CA 61-64; CANR 13, 43
Erdrich, Louise 1954-**CLC 39, 54, 120; DAM MULT, NOV, POP**
  See also AAYA 10; BEST 89:1; CA 114; CANR 41, 62; CDALBS; DLB 152, 175, 206; MTCW 1; NNAL; SATA 94
Erenburg, Ilya (Grigoryevich)
  See Ehrenburg, Ilya (Grigoryevich)
Erickson, Stephen Michael 1950-
  See Erickson, Steve
  See also CA 129
Erickson, Steve 1950-   **CLC 64**
  See also Erickson, Stephen Michael
  See also CANR 60, 68
Ericson, Walter
  See Fast, Howard (Melvin)
Eriksson, Buntel
  See Bergman, (Ernst) Ingmar
Ernaux, Annie 1940-   **CLC 88**
  See also CA 147
Erskine, John 1879-1951   **TCLC 84**
  See also CA 112; 159; DLB 9, 102
Eschenbach, Wolfram von
  See Wolfram von Eschenbach
Eseki, Bruno
  See Mphahlele, Ezekiel
Esenin, Sergei (Alexandrovich) 1895-1925 **TCLC 4**
  See also CA 104
Eshleman, Clayton 1935-   **CLC 7**
  See also CA 33-36R; CAAS 6; DLB 5
Espriella, Don Manuel Alvarez
  See Southey, Robert
Espriu, Salvador 1913-1985   **CLC 9**
  See also CA 154; 115; DLB 134
Espronceda, Jose de 1808-1842   **NCLC 39**
Esquivel, Laura 1951(?)-
  See also AAYA 29; CA 143; CANR 68; HLCS 1; MTCW 1
Esse, James
  See Stephens, James
Esterbrook, Tom
  See Hubbard, L(afayette) Ron(ald)
Estleman, Loren D. 1952-**CLC 48; DAM NOV, POP**
  See also AAYA 27; CA 85-88; CANR 27, 74; INT CANR-27; MTCW 1, 2
Euclid 306B.C.-283B.C.   **CMLC 25**
Eugenides, Jeffrey 1960(?)-   **CLC 81**
  See also CA 144
Euripides c. 485B.C.-406B.C.**CMLC 23; DA; DAB; DAC; DAM DRAM, MST; DC 4;**

WLCS
  See also DLB 176
Evan, Evin
  See Faust, Frederick (Schiller)
Evans, Caradoc 1878-1945   **TCLC 85**
Evans, Evan
  See Faust, Frederick (Schiller)
Evans, Marian
  See Eliot, George
Evans, Mary Ann
  See Eliot, George
Evarts, Esther
  See Benson, Sally
Everett, Percival L. 1956-   **CLC 57**
  See also BW 2; CA 129
Everson, R(onald) G(ilmour) 1903-   **CLC 27**
  See also CA 17-20R; DLB 88
Everson, William (Oliver) 1912-1994 **CLC 1, 5, 14**
  See also CA 9-12R; 145; CANR 20; DLB 212; MTCW 1
Evtushenko, Evgenii Aleksandrovich
  See Yevtushenko, Yevgeny (Alexandrovich)
Ewart, Gavin (Buchanan) 1916-1995**CLC 13, 46**
  See also CA 89-92; 150; CANR 17, 46; DLB 40; MTCW 1
Ewers, Hanns Heinz 1871-1943   **TCLC 12**
  See also CA 109; 149
Ewing, Frederick R.
  See Sturgeon, Theodore (Hamilton)
Exley, Frederick (Earl) 1929-1992 **CLC 6, 11**
  See also AITN 2; CA 81-84; 138; DLB 143; DLBY 81
Eynhardt, Guillermo
  See Quiroga, Horacio (Sylvestre)
Ezekiel, Nissim 1924-   **CLC 61**
  See also CA 61-64
Ezekiel, Tish O'Dowd 1943-   **CLC 34**
  See also CA 129
Fadeyev, A.
  See Bulgya, Alexander Alexandrovich
Fadeyev, Alexander   **TCLC 53**
  See also Bulgya, Alexander Alexandrovich
Fagen, Donald 1948-   **CLC 26**
Fainzilberg, Ilya Arnoldovich 1897-1937
  See Ilf, Ilya
  See also CA 120; 165
Fair, Ronald L. 1932-   **CLC 18**
  See also BW 1; CA 69-72; CANR 25; DLB 33
Fairbairn, Roger
  See Carr, John Dickson
Fairbairns, Zoe (Ann) 1948-   **CLC 32**
  See also CA 103; CANR 21
Falco, Gian
  See Papini, Giovanni
Falconer, James
  See Kirkup, James
Falconer, Kenneth
  See Kornbluth, C(yril) M.
Falkland, Samuel
  See Heijermans, Herman
Fallaci, Oriana 1930-   **CLC 11, 110**
  See also CA 77-80; CANR 15, 58; MTCW 1
Faludy, George 1913-   **CLC 42**
  See also CA 21-24R
Faludy, Gyoergy
  See Faludy, George
Fanon, Frantz 1925-1961   **CLC 74; BLC 2; DAM MULT**
  See also BW 1; CA 116; 89-92
Fanshawe, Ann 1625-1680   **LC 11**
Fante, John (Thomas) 1911-1983   **CLC 60**

See also CA 69-72; 109; CANR 23; DLB 130; DLBY 83
Farah, Nuruddin 1945-**CLC 53; BLC 2; DAM MULT**
  See also BW 2, 3; CA 106; CANR 81; DLB 125
Fargue, Leon-Paul 1876(?)-1947   **TCLC 11**
  See also CA 109
Farigoule, Louis
  See Romains, Jules
Farina, Richard 1936(?)-1966   **CLC 9**
  See also CA 81-84; 25-28R
Farley, Walter (Lorimer) 1915-1989 **CLC 17**
  See also CA 17-20R; CANR 8, 29; DLB 22; JRDA; MAICYA; SATA 2, 43
Farmer, Philip Jose 1918-   **CLC 1, 19**
  See also AAYA 28; CA 1-4R; CANR 4, 35; DLB 8; MTCW 1; SATA 93
Farquhar, George 1677-1707   **LC 21; DAM DRAM**
  See also DLB 84
Farrell, J(ames) G(ordon) 1935-1979   **CLC 6**
  See also CA 73-76; 89-92; CANR 36; DLB 14; MTCW 1
Farrell, James T(homas) 1904-1979**CLC 1, 4, 8, 11, 66; SSC 28**
  See also CA 5-8R; 89-92; CANR 9, 61; DLB 4, 9, 86; DLBD 2; MTCW 1, 2
Farren, Richard J.
  See Betjeman, John
Farren, Richard M.
  See Betjeman, John
Fassbinder, Rainer Werner 1946-1982**CLC 20**
  See also CA 93-96; 106; CANR 31
Fast, Howard (Melvin) 1914-   **CLC 23; DAM NOV**
  See also AAYA 16; CA 1-4R; CAAS 18; CANR 1, 33, 54, 75; DLB 9; INT CANR-33; MTCW 1; SATA 7; SATA-Essay 107
Faulcon, Robert
  See Holdstock, Robert P.
Faulkner, William (Cuthbert) 1897-1962**CLC 1, 3, 6, 8, 9, 11, 14, 18, 28, 52, 68; DA; DAB; DAC; DAM MST, NOV; SSC 1, 35; WLC**
  See also AAYA 7; CA 81-84; CANR 33; CDALB 1929-1941; DLB 9, 11, 44, 102; DLBD 2; DLBY 86, 97; MTCW 1, 2
Fauset, Jessie Redmon 1884(?)-1961 **CLC 19, 54; BLC 2; DAM MULT**
  See also BW 1; CA 109; DLB 51
Faust, Frederick (Schiller) 1892-1944(?) **TCLC 49; DAM POP**
  See also CA 108; 152
Faust, Irvin 1924-   **CLC 8**
  See also CA 33-36R; CANR 28, 67; DLB 2, 28; DLBY 80
Fawkes, Guy
  See Benchley, Robert (Charles)
Fearing, Kenneth (Flexner) 1902-1961   **CLC 51**
  See also CA 93-96; CANR 59; DLB 9
Fecamps, Elise
  See Creasey, John
Federman, Raymond 1928-   **CLC 6, 47**
  See also CA 17-20R; CAAS 8; CANR 10, 43; DLBY 80
Federspiel, J(uerg) F. 1931-   **CLC 42**
  See also CA 146
Feiffer, Jules (Ralph) 1929-   **CLC 2, 8, 64; DAM DRAM**
  See also AAYA 3; CA 17-20R; CANR 30, 59; DLB 7, 44; INT CANR-30; MTCW 1; SATA 8, 61

Feige, Hermann Albert Otto Maximilian
See Traven, B.

Feinberg, David B. 1956-1994   **CLC 59**
See also CA 135; 147

Feinstein, Elaine 1930-   **CLC 36**
See also CA 69-72; CAAS 1; CANR 31, 68;
DLB 14, 40; MTCW 1

Feldman, Irving (Mordecai) 1928-   **CLC 7**
See also CA 1-4R; CANR 1; DLB 169

Felix-Tchicaya, Gerald
See Tchicaya, Gerald Felix

Fellini, Federico 1920-1993   **CLC 16, 85**
See also CA 65-68; 143; CANR 33

Felsen, Henry Gregor 1916-   **CLC 17**
See also CA 1-4R; CANR 1; SAAS 2; SATA 1

Fenno, Jack
See Calisher, Hortense

Fenollosa, Ernest (Francisco) 1853-1908
TCLC 91

Fenton, James Martin 1949-   **CLC 32**
See also CA 102; DLB 40

Ferber, Edna 1887-1968   **CLC 18, 93**
See also AITN 1; CA 5-8R; 25-28R; CANR 68;
DLB 9, 28, 86; MTCW 1, 2; SATA 7

Ferguson, Helen
See Kavan, Anna

Ferguson, Samuel 1810-1886   **NCLC 33**
See also DLB 32

Fergusson, Robert 1750-1774   **LC 29**
See also DLB 109

Ferling, Lawrence
See Ferlinghetti, Lawrence (Monsanto)

Ferlinghetti, Lawrence (Monsanto) 1919(?)-
CLC 2, 6, 10, 27, 111; DAM POET; PC 1
See also CA 5-8R; CANR 3, 41, 73; CDALB
1941-1968; DLB 5, 16; MTCW 1, 2

Fernandez, Vicente Garcia Huidobro
See Huidobro Fernandez, Vicente Garcia

Ferre, Rosario 1942-
See also CA 131; CANR 55, 81; DLB 145;
HLCS 1; HW 1, 2; MTCW 1

Ferrer, Gabriel (Francisco Victor) Miro
See Miro (Ferrer), Gabriel (Francisco Victor)

Ferrier, Susan (Edmonstone) 1782-1854
NCLC 8
See also DLB 116

Ferrigno, Robert 1948(?)-   **CLC 65**
See also CA 140

Ferron, Jacques 1921-1985   **CLC 94; DAC**
See also CA 117; 129; DLB 60

Feuchtwanger, Lion 1884-1958   **TCLC 3**
See also CA 104; DLB 66

Feuillet, Octave 1821-1890   **NCLC 45**
See also DLB 192

Feydeau, Georges (Leon Jules Marie) 1862-
1921   **TCLC 22; DAM DRAM**
See also CA 113; 152; DLB 192

Fichte, Johann Gottlieb 1762-1814 **NCLC 62**
See also DLB 90

Ficino, Marsilio 1433-1499   **LC 12**

Fiedeler, Hans
See Doeblin, Alfred

Fiedler, Leslie A(aron) 1917-   **CLC 4, 13, 24**
See also CA 9-12R; CANR 7, 63; DLB 28, 67;
MTCW 1, 2

Field, Andrew 1938-   **CLC 44**
See also CA 97-100; CANR 25

Field, Eugene 1850-1895   **NCLC 3**
See also DLB 23, 42, 140; DLBD 13; MAICYA;
SATA 16

Field, Gans T.
See Wellman, Manly Wade

Field, Michael 1915-1971   **TCLC 43**

See also CA 29-32R

Field, Peter
See Hobson, Laura Z(ametkin)

Fielding, Henry 1707-1754   **LC 1, 46; DA;
DAB; DAC; DAM DRAM, MST, NOV;
WLC**
See also CDBLB 1660-1789; DLB 39, 84, 101

Fielding, Sarah 1710-1768   **LC 1, 44**
See also DLB 39

Fields, W. C. 1880-1946   **TCLC 80**
See also DLB 44

Fierstein, Harvey (Forbes) 1954-   **CLC 33;
DAM DRAM, POP**
See also CA 123; 129

Figes, Eva 1932-   **CLC 31**
See also CA 53-56; CANR 4, 44; DLB 14

Finch, Anne 1661-1720   **LC 3; PC 21**
See also DLB 95

Finch, Robert (Duer Claydon) 1900- **CLC 18**
See also CA 57-60; CANR 9, 24, 49; DLB 88

Findley, Timothy 1930-   **CLC 27, 102; DAC;
DAM MST**
See also CA 25-28R; CANR 12, 42, 69; DLB
53

Fink, William
See Mencken, H(enry) L(ouis)

Firbank, Louis 1942-
See Reed, Lou
See also CA 117

Firbank, (Arthur Annesley) Ronald 1886-1926
TCLC 1
See also CA 104; 177; DLB 36

Fisher, Dorothy (Frances) Canfield 1879-1958
TCLC 87
See also CA 114; 136; CANR 80; DLB 9, 102;
MAICYA; YABC 1

Fisher, M(ary) F(rances) K(ennedy) 1908-1992
CLC 76, 87
See also CA 77-80; 138; CANR 44; MTCW 1

Fisher, Roy 1930-   **CLC 25**
See also CA 81-84; CAAS 10; CANR 16; DLB
40

Fisher, Rudolph 1897-1934**TCLC 11; BLC 2;
DAM MULT; SSC 25**
See also BW 1, 3; CA 107; 124; CANR 80; DLB
51, 102

Fisher, Vardis (Alvero) 1895-1968   **CLC 7**
See also CA 5-8R; 25-28R; CANR 68; DLB 9,
206

Fiske, Tarleton 1917-1994
See Bloch, Robert (Albert)
See also CA 179; CAAE 179

Fitch, Clarke
See Sinclair, Upton (Beall)

Fitch, John IV
See Cormier, Robert (Edmund)

Fitzgerald, Captain Hugh
See Baum, L(yman) Frank

FitzGerald, Edward 1809-1883   **NCLC 9**
See also DLB 32

Fitzgerald, F(rancis) Scott (Key) 1896-1940
**TCLC 1, 6, 14, 28, 55; DA; DAB; DAC;
DAM MST, NOV; SSC 6, 31; WLC**
See also AAYA 24; AITN 1; CA 110; 123;
CDALB 1917-1929; DLB 4, 9, 86; DLBD 1,
15, 16; DLBY 81, 96; MTCW 1, 2

Fitzgerald, Penelope 1916-   **CLC 19, 51, 61**
See also CA 85-88; CAAS 10; CANR 56; DLB
14, 194; MTCW 2

Fitzgerald, Robert (Stuart) 1910-1985**CLC 39**
See also CA 1-4R; 114; CANR 1; DLBY 80

FitzGerald, Robert D(avid) 1902-1987**CLC 19**
See also CA 17-20R

Fitzgerald, Zelda (Sayre) 1900-1948**TCLC 52**
See also CA 117; 126; DLBY 84

Flanagan, Thomas (James Bonner) 1923-
CLC 25, 52
See also CA 108; CANR 55; DLBY 80; INT
108; MTCW 1

Flaubert, Gustave 1821-1880**NCLC 2, 10, 19,
62, 66; DA; DAB; DAC; DAM MST, NOV;
SSC 11; WLC**
See also DLB 119

Flecker, Herman Elroy
See Flecker, (Herman) James Elroy

Flecker, (Herman) James Elroy 1884-1915
TCLC 43
See also CA 109; 150; DLB 10, 19

Fleming, Ian (Lancaster) 1908-1964   **CLC 3,
30; DAM POP**
See also AAYA 26; CA 5-8R; CANR
59;CDBLB 1945-1960; DLB 87, 201;
MTCW 1, 2; SATA 9

Fleming, Thomas (James) 1927-   **CLC 37**
See also CA 5-8R; CANR 10; INT CANR-10;
SATA 8

Fletcher, John 1579-1625   **LC 33; DC 6**
See also CDBLB Before 1660; DLB 58

Fletcher, John Gould 1886-1950   **TCLC 35**
See also CA 107; 167; DLB 4, 45

Fleur, Paul
See Pohl, Frederik

Flooglebuckle, Al
See Spiegelman, Art

Flying Officer X
See Bates, H(erbert) E(rnest)

Fo, Dario 1926- **CLC 32, 109; DAM DRAM;
DC 10**
See also CA 116; 128; CANR 68; DLBY 97;
MTCW 1, 2

Fogarty, Jonathan Titulescu Esq.
See Farrell, James T(homas)

Folke, Will 1917-1994
See Bloch, Robert (Albert); Bloch, Robert
(Albert)
See also CA 179; CAAE 179

Follett, Ken(neth Martin) 1949-   **CLC 18;
DAM NOV, POP**
See also AAYA 6; BEST 89:4; CA 81-84; CANR
13, 33, 54; DLB 87; DLBY 81; INT CANR-
33; MTCW 1

Fontane, Theodor 1819-1898   **NCLC 26**
See also DLB 129

Foote, Horton 1916-**CLC 51, 91;DAM DRAM**
See also CA 73-76; CANR 34, 51; DLB 26; INT
CANR-34

Foote, Shelby 1916-**CLC 75; DAM NOV, POP**
See also CA 5-8R; CANR 3, 45, 74; DLB 2,
17; MTCW 2

Forbes, Esther 1891-1967   **CLC 12**
See also AAYA 17; CA 13-14; 25-28R; CAP 1;
CLR 27; DLB 22; JRDA; MAICYA; SATA
2, 100

Forche, Carolyn (Louise) 1950-   **CLC 25, 83,
86; DAM POET; PC 10**
See also CA 109; 117; CANR 50, 74; DLB 5,
193; INT 117; MTCW 1

Ford, Elbur
See Hibbert, Eleanor Alice Burford

Ford, Ford Madox 1873-1939**TCLC 1, 15, 39,
57; DAM NOV**
See also CA 104; 132; CANR 74; CDBLB
1914-1945; DLB 162; MTCW 1, 2

Ford, Henry 1863-1947   **TCLC 73**
See also CA 115; 148

Ford, John 1586-(?)   **DC 8**

See also CDBLB Before 1660; DAM DRAM; DLB 58

Ford, John 1895-1973   **CLC 16**
See also CA 45-48

Ford, Richard 1944-   **CLC 46, 99**
See also CA 69-72; CANR 11, 47; MTCW 1

Ford, Webster
See Masters, Edgar Lee

Foreman, Richard 1937-   **CLC 50**
See also CA 65-68; CANR 32, 63

Forester, C(ecil) S(cott) 1899-1966   **CLC 35**
See also CA 73-76; 25-28R; DLB 191; SATA 13

Forez
See Mauriac, Francois (Charles)

Forman, James Douglas 1932-   **CLC 21**
See also AAYA 17; CA 9-12R; CANR 4, 19, 42; JRDA; MAICYA; SATA 8, 70

Fornes, Maria Irene 1930- **CLC 39, 61; DC 10; HLCS 1**
See also CA 25-28R; CANR 28, 81; DLB 7; HW 1, 2; INT CANR-28; MTCW 1

Forrest, Leon (Richard) 1937-1997 **CLC 4; BLCS**
See also BW 2; CA 89-92; 162; CAAS 7; CANR 25, 52; DLB 33

Forster, E(dward) M(organ) 1879-1970 **C L C 1, 2, 3, 4, 9, 10, 13, 15, 22, 45, 77; DA; DAB; DAC; DAM MST, NOV; SSC 27; WLC**
See also AAYA 2; CA 13-14; 25-28R; CANR 45; CAP 1; CDBLB 1914-1945; DLB 34, 98, 162, 178, 195; DLBD 10; MTCW 1, 2; SATA 57

Forster, John 1812-1876   **NCLC 11**
See also DLB 144, 184

Forsyth, Frederick 1938- **CLC 2, 5, 36; DAM NOV, POP**
See also BEST 89:4; CA 85-88; CANR 38, 62; DLB 87; MTCW 1, 2

Forten, Charlotte L.   **TCLC 16; BLC 2**
See also Grimke, Charlotte L(ottie) Forten
See also DLB 50

Foscolo, Ugo 1778-1827   **NCLC 8**

Fosse, Bob   **CLC 20**
See also Fosse, Robert Louis

Fosse, Robert Louis 1927-1987
See Fosse, Bob
See also CA 110; 123

Foster, Stephen Collins 1826-1864 **NCLC 26**

Foucault, Michel 1926-1984 **CLC 31, 34, 69**
See also CA 105; 113; CANR 34; MTCW 1, 2

Fouque, Friedrich (Heinrich Karl) de la Motte 1777-1843   **NCLC 2**
See also DLB 90

Fourier, Charles 1772-1837   **NCLC 51**

Fournier, Henri Alban 1886-1914
See Alain-Fournier
See also CA 104

Fournier, Pierre 1916-   **CLC 11**
See also Gascar, Pierre
See also CA 89-92; CANR 16, 40

Fowles, John (Philip) 1926- **CLC 1, 2, 3, 4, 6, 9, 10, 15, 33, 87; DAB; DAC; DAM MST; SSC 33**
See also CA 5-8R; CANR 25, 71; CDBLB 1960 to Present; DLB 14, 139, 207; MTCW 1, 2; SATA 22

Fox, Paula 1923-   **CLC 2, 8, 121**
See also AAYA 3; CA 73-76; CANR 20, 36, 62; CLR 1, 44; DLB 52; JRDA; MAICYA; MTCW 1; SATA 17, 60

Fox, William Price (Jr.) 1926-   **CLC 22**
See also CA 17-20R; CAAS 19; CANR 11; DLB

2; DLBY 81

Foxe, John 1516(?)-1587   **LC 14**
See also DLB 132

Frame, Janet 1924- **CLC 2, 3, 6, 22, 66, 96; SSC 29**
See also Clutha, Janet Paterson Frame

France, Anatole   **TCLC 9**
See also Thibault, Jacques Anatole Francois
See also DLB 123; MTCW 1

Francis, Claude 19(?)-   **CLC 50**

Francis, Dick 1920- **CLC 2, 22, 42, 102; DAM POP**
See also AAYA 5, 21; BEST 89:3; CA 5-8R; CANR 9, 42, 68; CDBLB 1960 to Present; DLB 87; INT CANR-9; MTCW 1, 2

Francis, Robert (Churchill) 1901-1987 **C L C 15**
See also CA 1-4R; 123; CANR 1

Frank, Anne(lies Marie) 1929-1945 **TCLC 17; DA; DAB; DAC; DAM MST; WLC**
See also AAYA 12; CA 113; 133; CANR 68; MTCW 1, 2; SATA 87; SATA-Brief 42

Frank, Bruno 1887-1945   **TCLC 81**
See also DLB 118

Frank, Elizabeth 1945-   **CLC 39**
See also CA 121; 126; CANR 78; INT 126

Frankl, Viktor E(mil) 1905-1997   **CLC 93**
See also CA 65-68; 161

Franklin, Benjamin
See Hasek, Jaroslav (Matej Frantisek)

Franklin, Benjamin 1706-1790 **LC 25; DA; DAB; DAC; DAM MST; WLCS**
See also CDALB 1640-1865; DLB 24, 43, 73

Franklin, (Stella Maria Sarah) Miles (Lampe) 1879-1954   **TCLC 7**
See also CA 104; 164

Fraser, (Lady) Antonia (Pakenham) 1932- **CLC 32, 107**
See also CA 85-88; CANR 44, 65; MTCW 1, 2; SATA-Brief 32

Fraser, George MacDonald 1925-   **CLC 7**
See also CA 45-48; CANR 2, 48, 74; MTCW 1

Fraser, Sylvia 1935-   **CLC 64**
See also CA 45-48; CANR 1, 16, 60

Frayn, Michael 1933- **CLC 3, 7, 31, 47; DAM DRAM, NOV**
See also CA 5-8R; CANR 30, 69; DLB 13, 14, 194; MTCW 1, 2

Fraze, Candida (Merrill) 1945-   **CLC 50**
See also CA 126

Frazer, J(ames) G(eorge) 1854-1941 **TCLC 32**
See also CA 118

Frazer, Robert Caine
See Creasey, John

Frazer, Sir James George
See Frazer, J(ames) G(eorge)

Frazier, Charles 1950-   **CLC 109**
See also CA 161

Frazier, Ian 1951-   **CLC 46**
See also CA 130; CANR 54

Frederic, Harold 1856-1898   **NCLC 10**
See also DLB 12, 23; DLBD 13

Frederick, John
See Faust, Frederick (Schiller)

Frederick the Great 1712-1786   **LC 14**

Fredro, Aleksander 1793-1876   **NCLC 8**

Freeling, Nicolas 1927-   **CLC 38**
See also CA 49-52; CAAS 12; CANR 1, 17, 50; DLB 87

Freeman, Douglas Southall 1886-1953 **T C L C 11**
See also CA 109; DLB 17; DLBD 17

Freeman, Judith 1946-   **CLC 55**

See also CA 148

Freeman, Mary Eleanor Wilkins 1852-1930 **TCLC 9; SSC 1**
See also CA 106; 177; DLB 12, 78

Freeman, R(ichard) Austin 1862-1943 **T C L C 21**
See also CA 113; DLB 70

French, Albert 1943-   **CLC 86**
See also BW 3; CA 167

French, Marilyn 1929- **CLC 10, 18, 60; DAM DRAM, NOV, POP**
See also CA 69-72; CANR 3, 31; INT CANR-31; MTCW 1, 2

French, Paul
See Asimov, Isaac

Freneau, Philip Morin 1752-1832   **NCLC 1**
See also DLB 37, 43

Freud, Sigmund 1856-1939   **TCLC 52**
See also CA 115; 133; CANR 69; MTCW 1, 2

Friedan, Betty (Naomi) 1921-   **CLC 74**
See also CA 65-68; CANR 18, 45, 74; MTCW 1, 2

Friedlander, Saul 1932-   **CLC 90**
See also CA 117; 130; CANR 72

Friedman, B(ernard) H(arper) 1926- **CLC 7**
See also CA 1-4R; CANR 3, 48

Friedman, Bruce Jay 1930-   **CLC 3, 5, 56**
See also CA 9-12R; CANR 25, 52; DLB 2, 28; INT CANR-25

Friel, Brian 1929- **CLC 5, 42, 59, 115; DC 8**
See also CA 21-24R; CANR 33, 69; DLB 13; MTCW 1

Friis-Baastad, Babbis Ellinor 1921-1970 **C L C 12**
See also CA 17-20R; 134; SATA 7

Frisch, Max (Rudolf) 1911-1991 **CLC 3, 9, 14, 18, 32, 44; DAM DRAM, NOV**
See also CA 85-88; 134; CANR 32, 74; DLB 69, 124; MTCW 1, 2

Fromentin, Eugene (Samuel Auguste) 1820-1876   **NCLC 10**
See also DLB 123

Frost, Frederick
See Faust, Frederick (Schiller)

Frost, Robert (Lee) 1874-1963 **CLC 1, 3, 4, 9, 10, 13, 15, 26, 34, 44; DA; DAB; DAC; DAM MST, POET; PC 1; WLC**
See also AAYA 21; CA 89-92; CANR 33; CDALB 1917-1929; DLB 54; DLBD 7; MTCW 1, 2; SATA 14

Froude, James Anthony 1818-1894 **NCLC 43**
See also DLB 18, 57, 144

Froy, Herald
See Waterhouse, Keith (Spencer)

Fry, Christopher 1907- **CLC 2, 10, 14; DAM DRAM**
See also CA 17-20R; CAAS 23; CANR 9, 30, 74; DLB 13; MTCW 1, 2; SATA 66

Frye, (Herman) Northrop 1912-1991 **CLC 24, 70**
See also CA 5-8R; 133; CANR 8, 37; DLB 67, 68; MTCW 1, 2

Fuchs, Daniel 1909-1993   **CLC 8, 22**
See also CA 81-84; 142; CAAS 5; CANR 40; DLB 9, 26, 28; DLBY 93

Fuchs, Daniel 1934-   **CLC 34**
See also CA 37-40R; CANR 14, 48

Fuentes, Carlos 1928- **CLC 3, 8, 10, 13, 22, 41, 60, 113; DA; DAB; DAC; DAM MST, MULT, NOV; HLC 1; SSC 24; WLC**
See also AAYA 4; AITN 2; CA 69-72; CANR 10, 32, 68; DLB 113; HW 1, 2; MTCW 1, 2

Fuentes, Gregorio Lopez y

See Lopez y Fuentes, Gregorio

Fuertes, Gloria 1918- **PC 27**
See also CA 178; DLB 108; HW 2

Fugard, (Harold) Athol 1932-**CLC 5, 9, 14, 25,
40, 80; DAM DRAM; DC 3**
See also AAYA 17; CA 85-88; CANR 32, 54;
MTCW 1

Fugard, Sheila 1932- **CLC 48**
See also CA 125

Fuller, Charles (H., Jr.) 1939-**CLC 25; BLC 2;
DAM DRAM, MULT; DC 1**
See also BW 2; CA 108; 112; DLB 38; INT 112;
MTCW 1

Fuller, John (Leopold) 1937- **CLC 62**
See also CA 21-24R; CANR 9, 44; DLB 40

Fuller, Margaret **NCLC 5, 50**
See also Ossoli, Sarah Margaret (Fuller
marchesa d')

Fuller, Roy (Broadbent) 1912-1991**CLC 4, 28**
See also CA 5-8R; 135; CAAS 10; CANR 53;
DLB 15, 20; SATA 87

Fulton, Alice 1952- **CLC 52**
See also CA 116; CANR 57; DLB 193

Furphy, Joseph 1843-1912 **TCLC 25**
See also CA 163

Fussell, Paul 1924- **CLC 74**
See also BEST 90:1; CA 17-20R; CANR 8, 21,
35, 69; INT CANR-21; MTCW 1, 2

Futabatei, Shimei 1864-1909 **TCLC 44**
See also CA 162; DLB 180

Futrelle, Jacques 1875-1912 **TCLC 19**
See also CA 113; 155

Gaboriau, Emile 1835-1873 **NCLC 14**

Gadda, Carlo Emilio 1893-1973 **CLC 11**
See also CA 89-92; DLB 177

Gaddis, William 1922-1998**CLC 1, 3, 6, 8, 10,
19, 43, 86**
See also CA 17-20R; 172; CANR 21, 48; DLB
2; MTCW 1, 2

Gage, Walter
See Inge, William (Motter)

Gaines, Ernest J(ames) 1933- **CLC 3, 11, 18,
86; BLC 2; DAM MULT**
See also AAYA 18; AITN 1; BW 2, 3; CA 9-
12R; CANR 6, 24, 42, 75; CDALB 1968-
1988; DLB 2, 33, 152; DLBY 80; MTCW 1,
2; SATA 86

Gaitskill, Mary 1954- **CLC 69**
See also CA 128; CANR 61

Galdos, Benito Perez
See Perez Galdos, Benito

Gale, Zona 1874-1938 **TCLC 7;DAM DRAM**
See also CA 105; 153; DLB 9, 78

Galeano, Eduardo (Hughes) 1940- **CLC 72;
HLCS 1**
See also CA 29-32R; CANR 13, 32; HW 1

Galiano, Juan Valera y Alcala
See Valera y Alcala-Galiano, Juan

Galilei, Galileo 1546-1642 **LC 45**

Gallagher, Tess 1943- **CLC 18, 63; DAM
POET; PC 9**
See also CA 106; DLB 212

Gallant, Mavis 1922- **CLC 7, 18, 38; DAC;
DAM MST; SSC 5**
See also CA 69-72; CANR 29, 69; DLB 53;
MTCW 1, 2

Gallant, Roy A(rthur) 1924- **CLC 17**
See also CA 5-8R; CANR 4, 29, 54; CLR 30;
MAICYA; SATA 4, 68

Gallico, Paul (William) 1897-1976 **CLC 2**
See also AITN 1; CA 5-8R; 69-72; CANR 23;
DLB 9, 171; MAICYA; SATA 13

Gallo, Max Louis 1932- **CLC 95**

See also CA 85-88

Gallois, Lucien
See Desnos, Robert

Gallup, Ralph
See Whitemore, Hugh (John)

Galsworthy, John 1867-1933**TCLC 1, 45; DA;
DAB; DAC; DAM DRAM, MST, NOV;
SSC 22; WLC**
See also CA 104; 141; CANR 75; CDBLB
1890-1914; DLB 10, 34, 98, 162; DLBD 16;
MTCW 1

Galt, John 1779-1839 **NCLC 1**
See also DLB 99, 116, 159

Galvin, James 1951- **CLC 38**
See also CA 108; CANR 26

Gamboa, Federico 1864-1939 **TCLC 36**
See also CA 167; HW 2

Gandhi, M. K.
See Gandhi, Mohandas Karamchand

Gandhi, Mahatma
See Gandhi, Mohandas Karamchand

Gandhi, Mohandas Karamchand 1869-1948
TCLC 59; DAM MULT
See also CA 121; 132; MTCW 1, 2

Gann, Ernest Kellogg 1910-1991 **CLC 23**
See also AITN 1; CA 1-4R; 136; CANR 1

Garcia, Cristina 1958- **CLC 76**
See also CA 141; CANR 73; HW 2

Garcia Lorca, Federico 1898-1936**TCLC 1, 7,
49; DA; DAB; DAC; DAM DRAM, MST,
MULT, POET; DC 2; HLC 2; PC 3; WLC**
See also CA 104; 131; CANR 81; DLB 108;
HW 1, 2; MTCW 1, 2

Garcia Marquez, Gabriel (Jose) 1928-**CLC 2,
3, 8, 10, 15, 27, 47, 55, 68; DA; DAB; DAC;
DAM MST, MULT, NOV, POP; HLC 1;
SSC 8; WLC**
See also AAYA 3; BEST 89:1, 90:4; CA 33-
36R; CANR 10, 28, 50, 75, 82; DLB 113;
HW 1, 2; MTCW 1, 2

Garcilaso de la Vega, El Inca 1503-1536
See also HLCS 1

Gard, Janice
See Latham, Jean Lee

Gard, Roger Martin du
See Martin du Gard, Roger

Gardam, Jane 1928- **CLC 43**
See also CA 49-52; CANR 2, 18, 33, 54; CLR
12; DLB 14, 161; MAICYA; MTCW 1;
SAAS 9; SATA 39, 76; SATA-Brief 28

Gardner, Herb(ert) 1934- **CLC 44**
See also CA 149

Gardner, John (Champlin), Jr. 1933-1982
**CLC 2, 3, 5, 7, 8, 10, 18, 28, 34; DAM NOV,
POP; SSC 7**
See also AITN 1; CA 65-68; 107; CANR 33,
73; CDALBS; DLB 2; DLBY 82; MTCW 1;
SATA 40; SATA-Obit 31

Gardner, John (Edmund) 1926-**CLC 30; DAM
POP**
See also CA 103; CANR 15, 69; MTCW 1

Gardner, Miriam
See Bradley, Marion Zimmer

Gardner, Noel
See Kuttner, Henry

Gardons, S. S.
See Snodgrass, W(illiam) D(e Witt)

Garfield, Leon 1921-1996 **CLC 12**
See also AAYA 8; CA 17-20R; 152; CANR 38,
41, 78; CLR 21; DLB 161; JRDA; MAICYA;
SATA 1, 32, 76; SATA-Obit 90

Garland, (Hannibal) Hamlin 1860-1940
TCLC 3; SSC 18

See also CA 104; DLB 12, 71, 78, 186

Garneau, (Hector de) Saint-Denys 1912-1943
TCLC 13
See also CA 111; DLB 88

Garner, Alan 1934-**CLC 17; DAB;DAM POP**
See also AAYA 18; CA 73-76; 178; CAAE 178;
CANR 15, 64; CLR 20; DLB 161; MAICYA;
MTCW 1, 2; SATA 18, 69; SATA-Essay 108

Garner, Hugh 1913-1979 **CLC 13**
See also CA 69-72; CANR 31; DLB 68

Garnett, David 1892-1981 **CLC 3**
See also CA 5-8R; 103; CANR 17, 79; DLB
34; MTCW 2

Garos, Stephanie
See Katz, Steve

Garrett, George (Palmer) 1929-**CLC 3, 11, 51;
SSC 30**
See also CA 1-4R; CAAS 5; CANR 1, 42, 67;
DLB 2, 5, 130, 152; DLBY 83

Garrick, David 1717-1779**LC 15;DAM DRAM**
See also DLB 84

Garrigue, Jean 1914-1972 **CLC 2, 8**
See also CA 5-8R; 37-40R; CANR 20

Garrison, Frederick
See Sinclair, Upton (Beall)

Garro, Elena 1920(?)-1998
See also CA 131; 169; DLB 145; HLCS 1; HW
1

Garth, Will
See Hamilton, Edmond; Kuttner, Henry

Garvey, Marcus (Moziah, Jr.) 1887-1940
TCLC 41; BLC 2; DAM MULT
See also BW 1; CA 120; 124; CANR 79

Gary, Romain **CLC 25**
See also Kacew, Romain
See also DLB 83

Gascar, Pierre **CLC 11**
See also Fournier, Pierre

Gascoyne, David (Emery) 1916- **CLC 45**
See also CA 65-68; CANR 10, 28, 54; DLB 20;
MTCW 1

Gaskell, Elizabeth Cleghorn 1810-1865**NCLC
70; DAB; DAM MST; SSC 25**
See also CDBLB 1832-1890; DLB 21, 144, 159

Gass, William H(oward) 1924-**CLC 1, 2, 8, 11,
15, 39; SSC 12**
See also CA 17-20R; CANR 30, 71; DLB 2;
MTCW 1, 2

Gasset, Jose Ortega y
See Ortega y Gasset, Jose

Gates, Henry Louis, Jr. 1950-**CLC 65; BLCS;
DAM MULT**
See also BW 2, 3; CA 109; CANR 25, 53, 75;
DLB 67; MTCW 1

Gautier, Theophile 1811-1872 **NCLC 1, 59;
DAM POET; PC 18; SSC 20**
See also DLB 119

Gawsworth, John
See Bates, H(erbert) E(rnest)

Gay, John 1685-1732 **LC 49;DAM DRAM**
See also DLB 84, 95

Gay, Oliver
See Gogarty, Oliver St. John

Gaye, Marvin (Penze) 1939-1984 **CLC 26**
See also CA 112

Gebler, Carlo (Ernest) 1954- **CLC 39**
See also CA 119; 133

Gee, Maggie (Mary) 1948- **CLC 57**
See also CA 130; DLB 207

Gee, Maurice (Gough) 1931- **CLC 29**
See also CA 97-100; CANR 67; CLR 56; SATA
46, 101

Gelbart, Larry (Simon) 1923- **CLC 21, 61**

See also CA 73-76; CANR 45

Gelber, Jack 1932-   **CLC 1, 6, 14, 79**
See also CA 1-4R; CANR 2; DLB 7

Gellhorn, Martha (Ellis) 1908-1998 **CLC 14, 60**
See also CA 77-80; 164; CANR 44; DLBY 82, 98

Genet, Jean 1910-1986CLC **1, 2, 5, 10, 14, 44, 46; DAM DRAM**
See also CA 13-16R; CANR 18; DLB 72; DLBY 86; MTCW 1, 2

Gent, Peter 1942-   **CLC 29**
See also AITN 1; CA 89-92; DLBY 82

Gentile, Giovanni 1875-1944   **TCLC 96**
See also CA 119

Gentlewoman in New England, A
See Bradstreet, Anne

Gentlewoman in Those Parts, A
See Bradstreet, Anne

George, Jean Craighead 1919-   **CLC 35**
See also AAYA 8; CA 5-8R; CANR 25; CLR 1; DLB 52; JRDA; MAICYA; SATA 2, 68

George, Stefan (Anton) 1868-1933TCLC **2, 14**
See also CA 104

Georges, Georges Martin
See Simenon, Georges (Jacques Christian)

Gerhardi, William Alexander
See Gerhardie, William Alexander

Gerhardie, William Alexander 1895-1977 **CLC 5**
See also CA 25-28R; 73-76; CANR 18; DLB 36

Gerstler, Amy 1956-   **CLC 70**
See also CA 146

Gertler, T.   **CLC 34**
See also CA 116; 121; INT 121

Ghalib   **NCLC 39, 78**
See also Ghalib, Hsadullah Khan

Ghalib, Hsadullah Khan 1797-1869
See Ghalib
See also DAM POET

Ghelderode, Michel de 1898-1962CLC **6, 11; DAM DRAM**
See also CA 85-88; CANR 40, 77

Ghiselin, Brewster 1903-   **CLC 23**
See also CA 13-16R; CAAS 10; CANR 13

Ghose, Aurabinda 1872-1950   **TCLC 63**
See also CA 163

Ghose, Zulfikar 1935-   **CLC 42**
See also CA 65-68; CANR 67

Ghosh, Amitav 1956-   **CLC 44**
See also CA 147; CANR 80

Giacosa, Giuseppe 1847-1906   **TCLC 7**
See also CA 104

Gibb, Lee
See Waterhouse, Keith (Spencer)

Gibbon, Lewis Grassic   **TCLC 4**
See also Mitchell, James Leslie

Gibbons, Kaye 1960- **CLC 50, 88;DAM POP**
See also CA 151; CANR 75; MTCW 1

Gibran, Kahlil 1883-1931 **TCLC 1, 9; DAM POET, POP; PC 9**
See also CA 104; 150; MTCW 2

Gibran, Khalil
See Gibran, Kahlil

Gibson, William 1914- **CLC 23; DA; DAB; DAC; DAM DRAM, MST**
See also CA 9-12R; CANR 9, 42, 75; DLB 7; MTCW 1; SATA 66

Gibson, William (Ford) 1948-   **CLC 39, 63; DAM POP**
See also AAYA 12; CA 126; 133; CANR 52; MTCW 1

Gide, Andre (Paul Guillaume) 1869-1951 **TCLC 5, 12, 36; DA; DAB; DAC; DAM MST, NOV; SSC 13; WLC**
See also CA 104; 124; DLB 65; MTCW 1, 2

Gifford, Barry (Colby) 1946-   **CLC 34**
See also CA 65-68; CANR 9, 30, 40

Gilbert, Frank
See De Voto, Bernard (Augustine)

Gilbert, W(illiam) S(chwenck) 1836-1911 **TCLC 3; DAM DRAM, POET**
See also CA 104; 173; SATA 36

Gilbreth, Frank B., Jr. 1911-   **CLC 17**
See also CA 9-12R; SATA 2

Gilchrist, Ellen 1935-CLC **34, 48; DAM POP; SSC 14**
See also CA 113; 116; CANR 41, 61; DLB 130; MTCW 1, 2

Giles, Molly 1942-   **CLC 39**
See also CA 126

Gill, Eric 1882-1940   **TCLC 85**

Gill, Patrick
See Creasey, John

Gilliam, Terry (Vance) 1940-   **CLC 21**
See also Monty Python
See also AAYA 19; CA 108; 113; CANR 35; INT 113

Gillian, Jerry
See Gilliam, Terry (Vance)

Gilliatt, Penelope (Ann Douglass) 1932-1993 **CLC 2, 10, 13, 53**
See also AITN 2; CA 13-16R; 141; CANR 49; DLB 14

Gilman, Charlotte (Anna) Perkins (Stetson) 1860-1935   **TCLC 9, 37; SSC 13**
See also CA 106; 150; MTCW 1

Gilmour, David 1949-   **CLC 35**
See also CA 138, 147

Gilpin, William 1724-1804   **NCLC 30**

Gilray, J. D.
See Mencken, H(enry) L(ouis)

Gilroy, Frank D(aniel) 1925-   **CLC 2**
See also CA 81-84; CANR 32, 64; DLB 7

Gilstrap, John 1957(?)-   **CLC 99**
See also CA 160

Ginsberg, Allen 1926-1997CLC **1, 2, 3, 4, 6, 13, 36, 69, 109; DA; DAB; DAC; DAM MST, POET; PC 4; WLC**
See also AITN 1; CA 1-4R; 157; CANR 2, 41, 63; CDALB 1941-1968; DLB 5, 16, 169; MTCW 1, 2

Ginzburg, Natalia 1916-1991CLC **5, 11, 54, 70**
See also CA 85-88; 135; CANR 33; DLB 177; MTCW 1, 2

Giono, Jean 1895-1970   **CLC 4, 11**
See also CA 45-48; 29-32R; CANR 2, 35; DLB 72; MTCW 1

Giovanni, Nikki 1943- **CLC 2, 4, 19, 64, 117; BLC 2; DA; DAB; DAC; DAM MST, MULT, POET; PC 19; WLCS**
See also AAYA 22; AITN 1; BW 2, 3; CA 29-32R; CAAS 6; CANR 18, 41, 60; CDALBS; CLR 6; DLB 5, 41; INT CANR-18; MAICYA; MTCW 1, 2; SATA 24, 107

Giovene, Andrea 1904-   **CLC 7**
See also CA 85-88

Gippius, Zinaida (Nikolayevna) 1869-1945
See Hippius, Zinaida
See also CA 106

Giraudoux, (Hippolyte) Jean 1882-1944 **TCLC 2, 7; DAM DRAM**
See also CA 104; DLB 65

Gironella, Jose Maria 1917-   **CLC 11**
See also CA 101

Gissing, George (Robert) 1857-1903TCLC **3, 24, 47**
See also CA 105; 167; DLB 18, 135, 184

Giurlani, Aldo
See Palazzeschi, Aldo

Gladkov, Fyodor (Vasilyevich) 1883-1958 **TCLC 27**
See also CA 170

Glanville, Brian (Lester) 1931-   **CLC 6**
See also CA 5-8R; CAAS 9; CANR 3, 70; DLB 15, 139; SATA 42

Glasgow, Ellen (Anderson Gholson) 1873-1945 **TCLC 2, 7; SSC 34**
See also CA 104; 164; DLB 9, 12; MTCW 2

Glaspell, Susan 1882(?)-1948TCLC **55; DC 10**
See also CA 110; 154; DLB 7, 9, 78; YABC 2

Glassco, John 1909-1981   **CLC 9**
See also CA 13-16R; 102; CANR 15; DLB 68

Glasscock, Amnesia
See Steinbeck, John (Ernst)

Glasser, Ronald J. 1940(?)-   **CLC 37**

Glassman, Joyce
See Johnson, Joyce

Glendinning, Victoria 1937-   **CLC 50**
See also CA 120; 127; CANR 59; DLB 155

Glissant, Edouard 1928- **CLC 10, 68; DAM MULT**
See also CA 153

Gloag, Julian 1930-   **CLC 40**
See also AITN 1; CA 65-68; CANR 10, 70

Glowacki, Aleksander
See Prus, Boleslaw

Gluck, Louise (Elisabeth) 1943-CLC **7, 22, 44, 81; DAM POET; PC 16**
See also CA 33-36R; CANR 40, 69; DLB 5; MTCW 2

Glyn, Elinor 1864-1943   **TCLC 72**
See also DLB 153

Gobineau, Joseph Arthur (Comte) de 1816-1882   **NCLC 17**
See also DLB 123

Godard, Jean-Luc 1930-   **CLC 20**
See also CA 93-96

Godden, (Margaret) Rumer 1907-1998 **C L C 53**
See also AAYA 6; CA 5-8R; 172; CANR 4, 27, 36, 55, 80; CLR 20; DLB 161; MAICYA; SAAS 12; SATA 3, 36; SATA-Obit 109

Godoy Alcayaga, Lucila 1889-1957
See Mistral, Gabriela
See also BW 2; CA 104; 131; CANR 81; DAM MULT; HW 1, 2; MTCW 1, 2

Godwin, Gail (Kathleen) 1937- **CLC 5, 8, 22, 31, 69; DAM POP**
See also CA 29-32R; CANR 15, 43, 69; DLB 6; INT CANR-15; MTCW 1, 2

Godwin, William 1756-1836   **NCLC 14**
See also CDBLB 1789-1832; DLB 39, 104, 142, 158, 163

Goebbels, Josef
See Goebbels, (Paul) Joseph

Goebbels, (Paul) Joseph 1897-1945 **TCLC 68**
See also CA 115; 148

Goebbels, Joseph Paul
See Goebbels, (Paul) Joseph

Goethe, Johann Wolfgang von 1749-1832 **NCLC 4, 22, 34; DA; DAB; DAC; DAM DRAM, MST, POET; PC 5; WLC**
See also DLB 94

Gogarty, Oliver St. John 1878-1957TCLC **15**
See also CA 109; 150; DLB 15, 19

Gogol, Nikolai (Vasilyevich) 1809-1852NCLC **5, 15, 31; DA; DAB; DAC; DAM DRAM,**

MST; DC 1; SSC 4, 29; WLC
See also DLB 198

Goines, Donald 1937(?)-1974**CLC 80; BLC 2; DAM MULT, POP**
See also AITN 1; BW 1, 3; CA 124; 114; CANR 82; DLB 33

Gold, Herbert 1924- **CLC 4, 7, 14, 42**
See also CA 9-12R; CANR 17, 45; DLB 2; DLBY 81

Goldbarth, Albert 1948- **CLC 5, 38**
See also CA 53-56; CANR 6, 40; DLB 120

Goldberg, Anatol 1910-1982 **CLC 34**
See also CA 131; 117

Goldemberg, Isaac 1945- **CLC 52**
See also CA 69-72; CAAS 12; CANR 11, 32; HW 1

Golding, William (Gerald) 1911-1993**CLC 1, 2, 3, 8, 10, 17, 27, 58, 81; DA; DAB; DAC; DAM MST, NOV; WLC**
See also AAYA 5; CA 5-8R; 141; CANR 13, 33, 54; CDBLB 1945-1960; DLB 15, 100; MTCW 1, 2

Goldman, Emma 1869-1940 **TCLC 13**
See also CA 110; 150

Goldman, Francisco 1954- **CLC 76**
See also CA 162

Goldman, William (W.) 1931- **CLC 1,48**
See also CA 9-12R; CANR 29, 69; DLB 44

Goldmann, Lucien 1913-1970 **CLC 24**
See also CA 25-28; CAP 2

Goldoni, Carlo 1707-1793**LC 4; DAM DRAM**

Goldsberry, Steven 1949- **CLC 34**
See also CA 131

Goldsmith, Oliver 1728-1774 **LC 2, 48; DA; DAB; DAC; DAM DRAM, MST, NOV, POET; DC 8; WLC**
See also CDBLB 1660-1789; DLB 39, 89, 104, 109, 142; SATA 26

Goldsmith, Peter
See Priestley, J(ohn) B(oynton)

Gombrowicz, Witold 1904-1969**CLC 4, 7, 11, 49; DAM DRAM**
See also CA 19-20; 25-28R; CAP 2

Gomez de la Serna, Ramon 1888-1963**CLC 9**
See also CA 153; 116; CANR 79; HW 1, 2

Goncharov, Ivan Alexandrovich 1812-1891 **NCLC 1, 63**

Goncourt, Edmond (Louis Antoine Huot) de 1822-1896 **NCLC 7**
See also DLB 123

Goncourt, Jules (Alfred Huot) de 1830-1870 **NCLC 7**
See also DLB 123

Gontier, Fernande 19(?)- **CLC 50**

Gonzalez Martinez, Enrique 1871-1952 **TCLC 72**
See also CA 166; CANR 81; HW 1, 2

Goodman, Paul 1911-1972 **CLC 1, 2, 4, 7**
See also CA 19-20; 37-40R; CANR 34; CAP 2; DLB 130; MTCW 1

Gordimer, Nadine 1923-**CLC 3, 5, 7, 10, 18, 33, 51, 70; DA; DAB; DAC; DAM MST, NOV; SSC 17; WLCS**
See also CA 5-8R; CANR 3, 28, 56; INT CANR-28; MTCW 1, 2

Gordon, Adam Lindsay 1833-1870 **NCLC 21**

Gordon, Caroline 1895-1981**CLC 6, 13, 29, 83; SSC 15**
See also CA 11-12; 103; CANR 36; CAP 1; DLB 4, 9, 102; DLBD 17; DLBY 81; MTCW 1, 2

Gordon, Charles William 1860-1937
See Connor, Ralph

See also CA 109

Gordon, Mary (Catherine) 1949- **CLC 13, 22**
See also CA 102; CANR 44; DLB 6; DLBY 81; INT 102; MTCW 1

Gordon, N. J.
See Bosman, Herman Charles

Gordon, Sol 1923- **CLC 26**
See also CA 53-56; CANR 4; SATA 11

Gordone, Charles 1925-1995**CLC 1, 4; DAM DRAM; DC 8**
See also BW 1, 3; CA 93-96; 150; CANR 55; DLB 7; INT 93-96; MTCW 1

Gore, Catherine 1800-1861 **NCLC 65**
See also DLB 116

Gorenko, Anna Andreevna
See Akhmatova, Anna

Gorky, Maxim 1868-1936**TCLC 8; DAB; SSC 28; WLC**
See also Peshkov, Alexei Maximovich
See also MTCW 2

Goryan, Sirak
See Saroyan, William

Gosse, Edmund (William) 1849-1928**TCLC 28**
See also CA 117; DLB 57, 144, 184

Gotlieb, Phyllis Fay (Bloom) 1926- **CLC 18**
See also CA 13-16R; CANR 7; DLB 88

Gottesman, S. D.
See Kornbluth, C(yril) M.; Pohl, Frederik

Gottfried von Strassburg fl. c.1210-**CMLC 10**
See also DLB 138

Gould, Lois **CLC 4, 10**
See also CA 77-80; CANR 29; MTCW 1

Gourmont, Remy (-Marie-Charles) de 1858-1915 **TCLC 17**
See also CA 109; 150; MTCW 2

Govier, Katherine 1948- **CLC 51**
See also CA 101; CANR 18, 40

Goyen, (Charles) William 1915-1983**CLC 5, 8, 14, 40**
See also AITN 2; CA 5-8R; 110; CANR 6, 71; DLB 2; DLBY 83; INT CANR-6

Goytisolo, Juan 1931- **CLC 5, 10, 23; DAM MULT; HLC 1**
See also CA 85-88; CANR 32, 61; HW 1, 2; MTCW 1, 2

Gozzano, Guido 1883-1916 **PC 10**
See also CA 154; DLB 114

Gozzi, (Conte) Carlo 1720-1806 **NCLC 23**

Grabbe, Christian Dietrich 1801-1836**NCLC 2**
See also DLB 133

Grace, Patricia Frances 1937- **CLC 56**
See also CA 176

Gracian y Morales, Baltasar 1601-1658**LC 15**

Gracq, Julien **CLC 11, 48**
See also Poirier, Louis
See also DLB 83

Grade, Chaim 1910-1982 **CLC 10**
See also CA 93-96; 107

Graduate of Oxford, A
See Ruskin, John

Grafton, Garth
See Duncan, Sara Jeannette

Graham, John
See Phillips, David Graham

Graham, Jorie 1951- **CLC 48, 118**
See also CA 111; CANR 63; DLB 120

Graham, R(obert) B(ontine) Cunninghame
See Cunninghame Graham, R(obert) B(ontine)
See also DLB 98, 135, 174

Graham, Robert
See Haldeman, Joe (William)

Graham, Tom

See Lewis, (Harry) Sinclair

Graham, W(illiam) S(ydney) 1918-1986**C L C 29**
See also CA 73-76; 118; DLB 20

Graham, Winston (Mawdsley) 1910- **CLC 23**
See also CA 49-52; CANR 2, 22, 45, 66; DLB 77

Grahame, Kenneth 1859-1932**TCLC 64; DAB**
See also CA 108; 136; CANR 80; CLR 5; DLB 34, 141, 178; MAICYA; MTCW 2; SATA 100; YABC 1

Granovsky, Timofei Nikolaevich 1813-1855 **NCLC 75**
See also DLB 198

Grant, Skeeter
See Spiegelman, Art

Granville-Barker, Harley 1877-1946**TCLC 2; DAM DRAM**
See also Barker, Harley Granville
See also CA 104

Grass, Guenter (Wilhelm) 1927-**CLC 1, 2, 4, 6, 11, 15, 22, 32, 49, 88; DA; DAB; DAC; DAM MST, NOV; WLC**
See also CA 13-16R; CANR 20, 75; DLB 75, 124; MTCW 1, 2

Gratton, Thomas
See Hulme, T(homas) E(rnest)

Grau, Shirley Ann 1929- **CLC 4, 9;SSC 15**
See also CA 89-92; CANR 22, 69; DLB 2; INT CANR-22; MTCW 1

Gravel, Fern
See Hall, James Norman

Graver, Elizabeth 1964- **CLC 70**
See also CA 135; CANR 71

Graves, Richard Perceval 1945- **CLC 44**
See also CA 65-68; CANR 9, 26, 51

Graves, Robert (von Ranke) 1895-1985 **C L C 1, 2, 6, 11, 39, 44, 45; DAB; DAC; DAM MST, POET; PC 6**
See also CA 5-8R; 117; CANR 5, 36; CDBLB 1914-1945; DLB 20, 100, 191; DLBD 18; DLBY 85; MTCW 1, 2; SATA 45

Graves, Valerie
See Bradley, Marion Zimmer

Gray, Alasdair (James) 1934- **CLC 41**
See also CA 126; CANR 47, 69; DLB 194; INT 126; MTCW 1, 2

Gray, Amlin 1946- **CLC 29**
See also CA 138

Gray, Francine du Plessix 1930- **CLC 22; DAM NOV**
See also BEST 90:3; CA 61-64; CAAS 2; CANR 11, 33, 75, 81; INT CANR-11; MTCW 1, 2

Gray, John (Henry) 1866-1934 **TCLC 19**
See also CA 119; 162

Gray, Simon (James Holliday) 1936- **CLC 9, 14, 36**
See also AITN 1; CA 21-24R; CAAS 3; CANR 32, 69; DLB 13; MTCW 1

Gray, Spalding 1941-**CLC 49, 112; DAM POP; DC 7**
See also CA 128; CANR 74; MTCW 2

Gray, Thomas 1716-1771**LC 4, 40; DA; DAB; DAC; DAM MST; PC 2; WLC**
See also CDBLB 1660-1789; DLB 109

Grayson, David
See Baker, Ray Stannard

Grayson, Richard (A.) 1951- **CLC 38**
See also CA 85-88; CANR 14, 31, 57

Greeley, Andrew M(oran) 1928- **CLC 28; DAM POP**
See also CA 5-8R; CAAS 7; CANR 7, 43, 69;

MTCW 1, 2

Green, Anna Katharine 1846-1935 **TCLC 63**
See also CA 112; 159; DLB 202

Green, Brian
See Card, Orson Scott

Green, Hannah
See Greenberg, Joanne (Goldenberg)

Green, Hannah 1927(?)-1996 **CLC 3**
See also CA 73-76; CANR 59

Green, Henry 1905-1973 **CLC 2, 13, 97**
See also Yorke, Henry Vincent
See also CA 175; DLB 15

Green, Julian (Hartridge) 1900-1998
See Green, Julien
See also CA 21-24R; 169; CANR 33; DLB 4, 72; MTCW 1

Green, Julien **CLC 3, 11, 77**
See also Green, Julian (Hartridge)
See also MTCW 2

Green, Paul (Eliot) 1894-1981 **CLC 25; DAM DRAM**
See also AITN 1; CA 5-8R; 103; CANR 3; DLB 7, 9; DLBY 81

Greenberg, Ivan 1908-1973
See Rahv, Philip
See also CA 85-88

Greenberg, Joanne (Goldenberg) 1932- **C L C 7, 30**
See also AAYA 12; CA 5-8R; CANR 14, 32, 69; SATA 25

Greenberg, Richard 1959(?)- **CLC 57**
See also CA 138

Greene, Bette 1934- **CLC 30**
See also AAYA 7; CA 53-56; CANR 4; CLR 2; JRDA; MAICYA; SAAS 16; SATA 8, 102

Greene, Gael **CLC 8**
See also CA 13-16R; CANR 10

Greene, Graham (Henry) 1904-1991 **CLC 1, 3, 6, 9, 14, 18, 27, 37, 70, 72; DA; DAB; DAC; DAM MST, NOV; SSC 29; WLC**
See also AITN 2; CA 13-16R; 133; CANR 35, 61; CDBLB 1945-1960; DLB 13, 15, 77, 100, 162, 201, 204; DLBY 91; MTCW 1, 2; SATA 20

Greene, Robert 1558-1592 **LC 41**
See also DLB 62, 167

Greer, Richard
See Silverberg, Robert

Gregor, Arthur 1923- **CLC 9**
See also CA 25-28R; CAAS 10; CANR 11; SATA 36

Gregor, Lee
See Pohl, Frederik

Gregory, Isabella Augusta (Persse) 1852-1932 **TCLC 1**
See also CA 104; DLB 10

Gregory, J. Dennis
See Williams, John A(lfred)

Grendon, Stephen
See Derleth, August (William)

Grenville, Kate 1950- **CLC 61**
See also CA 118; CANR 53

Grenville, Pelham
See Wodehouse, P(elham) G(renville)

Greve, Felix Paul (Berthold Friedrich) 1879-1948
See Grove, Frederick Philip
See also CA 104; 141; 175; CANR 79; DAC; DAM MST

Grey, Zane 1872-1939 **TCLC 6; DAM POP**
See also CA 104; 132; DLB 212; MTCW 1, 2

Grieg, (Johan) Nordahl (Brun) 1902-1943 **TCLC 10**

See also CA 107

Grieve, C(hristopher) M(urray) 1892-1978 **CLC 11, 19; DAM POET**
See also MacDiarmid, Hugh; Pteleon
See also CA 5-8R; 85-88; CANR 33; MTCW 1

Griffin, Gerald 1803-1840 **NCLC 7**
See also DLB 159

Griffin, John Howard 1920-1980 **CLC 68**
See also AITN 1; CA 1-4R; 101; CANR 2

Griffin, Peter 1942- **CLC 39**
See also CA 136

Griffith, D(avid Lewelyn) W(ark) 1875(?)-1948 **TCLC 68**
See also CA 119; 150; CANR 80

Griffith, Lawrence
See Griffith, D(avid Lewelyn) W(ark)

Griffiths, Trevor 1935- **CLC 13, 52**
See also CA 97-100; CANR 45; DLB 13

Griggs, Sutton Elbert 1872-1930(?) **TCLC 77**
See also CA 123; DLB 50

Grigson, Geoffrey (Edward Harvey) 1905-1985 **CLC 7, 39**
See also CA 25-28R; 118; CANR 20, 33; DLB 27; MTCW 1, 2

Grillparzer, Franz 1791-1872 **NCLC 1**
See also DLB 133

Grimble, Reverend Charles James
See Eliot, T(homas) S(tearns)

Grimke, Charlotte L(ottie) Forten 1837(?)-1914
See Forten, Charlotte L.
See also BW 1; CA 117; 124; DAM MULT, POET

Grimm, Jacob Ludwig Karl 1785-1863 **NCLC 3, 77**
See also DLB 90; MAICYA; SATA 22

Grimm, Wilhelm Karl 1786-1859 **NCLC 3, 77**
See also DLB 90; MAICYA; SATA 22

Grimmelshausen, Johann Jakob Christoffel von 1621-1676 **LC 6**
See also DLB 168

Grindel, Eugene 1895-1952
See Eluard, Paul
See also CA 104

Grisham, John 1955- **CLC 84; DAM POP**
See also AAYA 14; CA 138; CANR 47, 69; MTCW 2

Grossman, David 1954- **CLC 67**
See also CA 138

Grossman, Vasily (Semenovich) 1905-1964 **CLC 41**
See also CA 124; 130; MTCW 1

Grove, Frederick Philip **TCLC 4**
See also Greve, Felix Paul (Berthold Friedrich)
See also DLB 92

Grubb
See Crumb, R(obert)

Grumbach, Doris (Isaac) 1918- **CLC 13, 22, 64**
See also CA 5-8R; CAAS 2; CANR 9, 42, 70; INT CANR-9; MTCW 2

Grundtvig, Nicolai Frederik Severin 1783-1872 **NCLC 1**

Grunge
See Crumb, R(obert)

Grunwald, Lisa 1959- **CLC 44**
See also CA 120

Guare, John 1938- **CLC 8, 14, 29, 67; DAM DRAM**
See also CA 73-76; CANR 21, 69; DLB 7; MTCW 1, 2

Gudjonsson, Halldor Kiljan 1902-1998
See Laxness, Halldor
See also CA 103; 164

Guenter, Erich

See Eich, Guenter

Guest, Barbara 1920- **CLC 34**
See also CA 25-28R; CANR 11, 44; DLB 5, 193

Guest, Edgar A(lbert) 1881-1959 **TCLC 95**
See also CA 112; 168

Guest, Judith (Ann) 1936- **CLC 8, 30; DAM NOV, POP**
See also AAYA 7; CA 77-80; CANR 15, 75; INT CANR-15; MTCW 1, 2

Guevara, Che **CLC 87; HLC 1**
See also Guevara (Serna), Ernesto

Guevara (Serna), Ernesto 1928-1967 **CLC 87; DAM MULT; HLC 1**
See also Guevara, Che
See also CA 127; 111; CANR 56; HW 1

Guicciardini, Francesco 1483-1540 **LC 49**

Guild, Nicholas M. 1944- **CLC 33**
See also CA 93-96

Guillemin, Jacques
See Sartre, Jean-Paul

Guillen, Jorge 1893-1984 **CLC 11; DAM MULT, POET; HLCS 1**
See also CA 89-92; 112; DLB 108; HW 1

Guillen, Nicolas (Cristobal) 1902-1989 **C L C 48, 79; BLC 2; DAM MST, MULT, POET; HLC 1; PC 23**
See also BW 2; CA 116; 125; 129; HW 1

Guillevic, (Eugene) 1907- **CLC 33**
See also CA 93-96

Guillois
See Desnos, Robert

Guillois, Valentin
See Desnos, Robert

Guimaraes Rosa, Joao 1908-1967
See also CA 175; HLCS 2

Guiney, Louise Imogen 1861-1920 **TCLC 41**
See also CA 160; DLB 54

Guiraldes, Ricardo (Guillermo) 1886-1927 **TCLC 39**
See also CA 131; HW 1; MTCW 1

Gumilev, Nikolai (Stepanovich) 1886-1921 **TCLC 60**
See also CA 165

Gunesekera, Romesh 1954- **CLC 91**
See also CA 159

Gunn, Bill **CLC 5**
See also Gunn, William Harrison
See also DLB 38

Gunn, Thom(son William) 1929- **CLC 3, 6, 18, 32, 81; DAM POET; PC 26**
See also CA 17-20R; CANR 9, 33; CDBLB 1960 to Present; DLB 27; INT CANR-33; MTCW 1

Gunn, William Harrison 1934(?)-1989
See Gunn, Bill
See also AITN 1; BW 1, 3; CA 13-16R; 128; CANR 12, 25, 76

Gunnars, Kristjana 1948- **CLC 69**
See also CA 113; DLB 60

Gurdjieff, G(eorgei) I(vanovich) 1877(?)-1949 **TCLC 71**
See also CA 157

Gurganus, Allan 1947- **CLC 70; DAM POP**
See also BEST 90:1; CA 135

Gurney, A(lbert) R(amsdell), Jr. 1930- **C L C 32, 50, 54; DAM DRAM**
See also CA 77-80; CANR 32, 64

Gurney, Ivor (Bertie) 1890-1937 **TCLC 33**
See also CA 167

Gurney, Peter
See Gurney, A(lbert) R(amsdell), Jr.

Guro, Elena 1877-1913 **TCLC 56**

Author Index

Gustafson, James M(oody) 1925-   CLC 100
    See also CA 25-28R; CANR 37
Gustafson, Ralph (Barker) 1909-   CLC 36
    See also CA 21-24R; CANR 8, 45; DLB 88
Gut, Gom
    See Simenon, Georges (Jacques Christian)
Guterson, David 1956-   CLC 91
    See also CA 132; CANR 73; MTCW 2
Guthrie, A(lfred) B(ertram), Jr. 1901-1991
    CLC 23
    See also CA 57-60; 134; CANR 24; DLB 212;
    SATA 62; SATA-Obit 67
Guthrie, Isobel
    See Grieve, C(hristopher) M(urray)
Guthrie, Woodrow Wilson 1912-1967
    See Guthrie, Woody
    See also CA 113; 93-96
Guthrie, Woody   CLC 35
    See also Guthrie, Woodrow Wilson
Gutierrez Najera, Manuel 1859-1895
    See also HLCS 2
Guy, Rosa (Cuthbert) 1928-   CLC 26
    See also AAYA 4; BW 2; CA 17-20R; CANR
    14, 34; CLR 13; DLB 33; JRDA; MAICYA;
    SATA 14, 62
Gwendolyn
    See Bennett, (Enoch) Arnold
H. D.   CLC 3, 8, 14, 31, 34, 73; PC 5
    See also Doolittle, Hilda
H. de V.
    See Buchan, John
Haavikko, Paavo Juhani 1931-   CLC 18, 34
    See also CA 106
Habbema, Koos
    See Heijermans, Herman
Habermas, Juergen 1929-   CLC 104
    See also CA 109
Habermas, Jurgen
    See Habermas, Juergen
Hacker, Marilyn 1942- CLC 5, 9, 23, 72, 91;
    DAM POET
    See also CA 77-80; CANR 68; DLB 120
Haeckel, Ernst Heinrich (Philipp August) 1834-
    1919   TCLC 83
    See also CA 157
Hafiz c. 1326-1389   CMLC 34
Hafiz c. 1326-1389(?)   CMLC 34
Haggard, H(enry) Rider 1856-1925TCLC 11
    See also CA 108; 148; DLB 70, 156, 174, 178;
    MTCW 2; SATA 16
Hagiosy, L.
    See Larbaud, Valery (Nicolas)
Hagiwara Sakutaro 1886-1942TCLC 60; PC
    18
Haig, Fenil
    See Ford, Ford Madox
Haig-Brown, Roderick (Langmere) 1908-1976
    CLC 21
    See also CA 5-8R; 69-72; CANR 4, 38; CLR
    31; DLB 88; MAICYA; SATA 12
Hailey, Arthur 1920-CLC 5; DAM NOV, POP
    See also AITN 2; BEST 90:3; CA 1-4R; CANR
    2, 36, 75; DLB 88; DLBY 82; MTCW 1, 2
Hailey, Elizabeth Forsythe 1938-   CLC 40
    See also CA 93-96; CAAS 1; CANR 15, 48;
    INT CANR-15
Haines, John (Meade) 1924-   CLC 58
    See also CA 17-20R; CANR 13, 34; DLB 212
Hakluyt, Richard 1552-1616   LC 31
Haldeman, Joe (William) 1943-   CLC 61
    See also CA 53-56; CAAS 25; CANR 6, 70,
    72; DLB 8; INT CANR-6
Hale, Sarah Josepha (Buell) 1788-1879NCLC

75
    See also DLB 1, 42, 73
Haley, Alex(ander Murray Palmer) 1921-1992
    CLC 8, 12, 76; BLC 2; DA; DAB; DAC;
    DAM MST, MULT, POP
    See also AAYA 26; BW 2, 3; CA 77-80; 136;
    CANR 61; CDALBS; DLB 38; MTCW 1, 2
Haliburton, Thomas Chandler 1796-1865
    NCLC 15
    See also DLB 11, 99
Hall, Donald (Andrew, Jr.) 1928- CLC 1, 13,
    37, 59; DAM POET
    See also CA 5-8R; CAAS 7; CANR 2, 44, 64;
    DLB 5; MTCW 1; SATA 23, 97
Hall, Frederic Sauser
    See Sauser-Hall, Frederic
Hall, James
    See Kuttner, Henry
Hall, James Norman 1887-1951   TCLC 23
    See also CA 123; 173; SATA 21
Hall, Radclyffe
    See Hall, (Marguerite) Radclyffe
    See also MTCW 2
Hall, (Marguerite) Radclyffe 1886-1943
    TCLC 12
    See also CA 110; 150; DLB 191
Hall, Rodney 1935-   CLC 51
    See also CA 109; CANR 69
Halleck, Fitz-Greene 1790-1867   NCLC 47
    See also DLB 3
Halliday, Michael
    See Creasey, John
Halpern, Daniel 1945-   CLC 14
    See also CA 33-36R
Hamburger, Michael (Peter Leopold) 1924-
    CLC 5, 14
    See also CA 5-8R; CAAS 4; CANR 2, 47; DLB
    27
Hamill, Pete 1935-   CLC 10
    See also CA 25-28R; CANR 18, 71
Hamilton, Alexander 1755(?)-1804 NCLC 49
    See also DLB 37
Hamilton, Clive
    See Lewis, C(live) S(taples)
Hamilton, Edmond 1904-1977   CLC 1
    See also CA 1-4R; CANR 3; DLB 8
Hamilton, Eugene (Jacob) Lee
    See Lee-Hamilton, Eugene (Jacob)
Hamilton, Franklin
    See Silverberg, Robert
Hamilton, Gail
    See Corcoran, Barbara
Hamilton, Mollie
    See Kaye, M(ary) M(argaret)
Hamilton, (Anthony Walter) Patrick 1904-1962
    CLC 51
    See also CA 176; 113; DLB 191
Hamilton, Virginia 1936-   CLC 26;DAM
    MULT
    See also AAYA 2, 21; BW 2, 3; CA 25-28R;
    CANR 20, 37, 73; CLR 1, 11, 40; DLB 33,
    52; INT CANR-20; JRDA; MAICYA;
    MTCW 1, 2; SATA 4, 56, 79
Hammett, (Samuel) Dashiell 1894-1961 C L C
    3, 5, 10, 19, 47; SSC 17
    See also AITN 1; CA 81-84; CANR 42; CDALB
    1929-1941; DLBD 6; DLBY 96; MTCW 1,
    2
Hammon, Jupiter 1711(?)-1800(?)   NCLC 5;
    BLC 2; DAM MULT, POET; PC 16
    See also DLB 31, 50
Hammond, Keith
    See Kuttner, Henry

Hamner, Earl (Henry), Jr. 1923-   CLC 12
    See also AITN 2; CA 73-76; DLB 6
Hampton, Christopher (James) 1946- CLC 4
    See also CA 25-28R; DLB 13; MTCW 1
Hamsun, Knut   TCLC 2, 14, 49
    See also Pedersen, Knut
Handke, Peter 1942-CLC 5, 8, 10, 15, 38; DAM
    DRAM, NOV
    See also CA 77-80; CANR 33, 75; DLB 85, 124;
    MTCW 1, 2
Hanley, James 1901-1985   CLC 3, 5, 8, 13
    See also CA 73-76; 117; CANR 36; DLB 191;
    MTCW 1
Hannah, Barry 1942-   CLC 23, 38, 90
    See also CA 108; 110; CANR 43, 68; DLB 6;
    INT 110; MTCW 1
Hannon, Ezra
    See Hunter, Evan
Hansberry, Lorraine (Vivian) 1930-1965CLC
    17, 62; BLC 2; DA; DAB; DAC; DAM
    DRAM, MST, MULT;DC 2
    See also AAYA 25; BW 1, 3; CA 109; 25-28R;
    CABS 3; CANR 58; CDALB 1941-1968;
    DLB 7, 38; MTCW 1, 2
Hansen, Joseph 1923-   CLC 38
    See also CA 29-32R; CAAS 17; CANR 16, 44,
    66; INT CANR-16
Hansen, Martin A(lfred) 1909-1955TCLC 32
    See also CA 167
Hanson, Kenneth O(stlin) 1922-   CLC 13
    See also CA 53-56; CANR 7
Hardwick, Elizabeth (Bruce) 1916- CLC 13;
    DAM NOV
    See also CA 5-8R; CANR 3, 32, 70; DLB 6;
    MTCW 1, 2
Hardy, Thomas 1840-1928TCLC 4, 10, 18, 32,
    48, 53, 72; DA; DAB; DAC; DAM MST,
    NOV, POET; PC 8; SSC 2;WLC
    See also CA 104; 123; CDBLB 1890-1914;
    DLB 18, 19, 135; MTCW 1, 2
Hare, David 1947-   CLC 29, 58
    See also CA 97-100; CANR 39; DLB 13;
    MTCW 1
Harewood, John
    See Van Druten, John (William)
Harford, Henry
    See Hudson, W(illiam) H(enry)
Hargrave, Leonie
    See Disch, Thomas M(ichael)
Harjo, Joy 1951-CLC 83; DAM MULT; PC 27
    See also CA 114; CANR 35, 67; DLB 120, 175;
    MTCW 2; NNAL
Harlan, Louis R(udolph) 1922-   CLC 34
    See also CA 21-24R; CANR 25, 55, 80
Harling, Robert 1951(?)-   CLC 53
    See also CA 147
Harmon, William (Ruth) 1938-   CLC 38
    See also CA 33-36R; CANR 14, 32, 35; SATA
    65
Harper, F. E. W.
    See Harper, Frances Ellen Watkins
Harper, Frances E. W.
    See Harper, Frances Ellen Watkins
Harper, Frances E. Watkins
    See Harper, Frances Ellen Watkins
Harper, Frances Ellen
    See Harper, Frances Ellen Watkins
Harper, Frances Ellen Watkins 1825-1911
    TCLC 14; BLC 2; DAM MULT, POET;
    PC 21
    See also BW 1, 3; CA 111; 125; CANR 79; DLB
    50
Harper, Michael S(teven) 1938-   CLC 7, 22

Heller, Joseph 1923-CLC 1, 3, 5, 8, 11, 36, 63; DA; DAB; DAC; DAM MST, NOV, POP; WLC
See also AAYA 24; AITN 1; CA 5-8R; CABS 1; CANR 8, 42, 66; DLB 2, 28; DLBY 80; INT CANR-8; MTCW 1, 2

Hellman, Lillian (Florence) 1906-1984CLC 2, 4, 8, 14, 18, 34, 44, 52; DAM DRAM; DC 1
See also AITN 1, 2; CA 13-16R; 112; CANR 33; DLB 7; DLBY 84; MTCW 1, 2

Helprin, Mark 1947-CLC 7, 10, 22, 32; DAM NOV, POP
See also CA 81-84; CANR 47, 64; CDALBS; DLBY 85; MTCW 1, 2

Helvetius, Claude-Adrien 1715-1771   LC 26

Helyar, Jane Penelope Josephine 1933-
See Poole, Josephine
See also CA 21-24R; CANR 10, 26; SATA 82

Hemans, Felicia 1793-1835   NCLC 71
See also DLB 96

Hemingway, Ernest (Miller) 1899-1961 C L C 1, 3, 6, 8, 10, 13, 19, 30, 34, 39, 41, 44, 50, 61, 80; DA; DAB; DAC; DAM MST, NOV; SSC 1, 25; WLC
See also AAYA 19; CA 77-80; CANR 34; CDALB 1917-1929; DLB 4, 9, 102, 210; DLBD 1, 15, 16; DLBY 81, 87, 96, 98; MTCW 1, 2

Hempel, Amy 1951-   CLC 39
See also CA 118; 137; CANR 70; MTCW 2

Henderson, F. C.
See Mencken, H(enry) L(ouis)

Henderson, Sylvia
See Ashton-Warner, Sylvia (Constance)

Henderson, Zenna (Chlarson) 1917-1983S S C 29
See also CA 1-4R; 133; CANR 1; DLB 8; SATA 5

Henkin, Joshua   CLC 119
See also CA 161

Henley, Beth   CLC 23; DC 6
See also Henley, Elizabeth Becker
See also CABS 3; DLBY 86

Henley, Elizabeth Becker 1952-
See Henley, Beth
See also CA 107; CANR 32, 73; DAM DRAM, MST; MTCW 1, 2

Henley, William Ernest 1849-1903   TCLC 8
See also CA 105; DLB 19

Hennissart, Martha
See Lathen, Emma
See also CA 85-88; CANR 64

Henry, O.   TCLC 1, 19; SSC 5; WLC
See also Porter, William Sydney

Henry, Patrick 1736-1799   LC 25

Henryson, Robert 1430(?)-1506(?)   LC 20
See also DLB 146

Henry VIII 1491-1547   LC 10
See also DLB 132

Henschke, Alfred
See Klabund

Hentoff, Nat(han Irving) 1925-   CLC 26
See also AAYA 4; CA 1-4R; CAAS 6; CANR 5, 25, 77; CLR 1, 52; INT CANR-25; JRDA; MAICYA; SATA 42, 69; SATA-Brief 27

Heppenstall, (John) Rayner 1911-1981 C L C 10
See also CA 1-4R; 103; CANR 29

Heraclitus c. 540B.C.-c.450B.C.   CMLC 22
See also DLB 176

Herbert, Frank (Patrick) 1920-1986 CLC 12, 23, 35, 44, 85; DAM POP
See also AAYA 21; CA 53-56; 118; CANR 5,

43; CDALBS; DLB 8; INT CANR-5; MTCW 1, 2; SATA 9, 37; SATA-Obit 47

Herbert, George 1593-1633   LC 24; DAB; DAM POET; PC 4
See also CDBLB Before 1660; DLB 126

Herbert, Zbigniew 1924-1998   CLC 9, 43; DAM POET
See also CA 89-92; 169; CANR 36, 74; MTCW 1

Herbst, Josephine (Frey) 1897-1969 CLC 34
See also CA 5-8R; 25-28R; DLB 9

Heredia, Jose Maria 1803-1839
See also HLCS 2

Hergesheimer, Joseph 1880-1954   TCLC 11
See also CA 109; DLB 102, 9

Herlihy, James Leo 1927-1993   CLC 6
See also CA 1-4R; 143; CANR 2

Hermogenes fl. c. 175-   CMLC 6

Hernandez, Jose 1834-1886   NCLC 17

Herodotus c.484B.C.-429B.C.   CMLC 17
See also DLB 176

Herrick, Robert 1591-1674LC 13; DA; DAB; DAC; DAM MST, POP; PC 9
See also DLB 126

Herring, Guilles
See Somerville, Edith

Herriot, James 1916-1995CLC 12;DAM POP
See also Wight, James Alfred
See also AAYA 1; CA 148; CANR 40; MTCW 2; SATA 86

Herrmann, Dorothy 1941-   CLC 44
See also CA 107

Herrmann, Taffy
See Herrmann, Dorothy

Hersey, John (Richard) 1914-1993CLC 1, 2, 7, 9, 40, 81, 97; DAM POP
See also AAYA 29; CA 17-20R; 140; CANR 33; CDALBS; DLB 6, 185; MTCW 1, 2; SATA 25; SATA-Obit 76

Herzen, Aleksandr Ivanovich 1812-1870 NCLC 10, 61

Herzl, Theodor 1860-1904   TCLC 36
See also CA 168

Herzog, Werner 1942-   CLC 16
See also CA 89-92

Hesiod c. 8th cent. B.C.-   CMLC 5
See also DLB 176

Hesse, Hermann 1877-1962CLC 1, 2, 3, 6, 11, 17, 25, 69; DA; DAB; DAC; DAM MST, NOV; SSC 9; WLC
See also CA 17-18; CAP 2; DLB 66; MTCW 1, 2; SATA 50

Hewes, Cady
See De Voto, Bernard (Augustine)

Heyen, William 1940-   CLC 13, 18
See also CA 33-36R; CAAS 9; DLB 5

Heyerdahl, Thor 1914-   CLC 26
See also CA 5-8R; CANR 5, 22, 66, 73; MTCW 1, 2; SATA 2, 52

Heym, Georg (Theodor Franz Arthur) 1887-1912   TCLC 9
See also CA 106

Heym, Stefan 1913-   CLC 41
See also CA 9-12R; CANR 4; DLB 69

Heyse, Paul (Johann Ludwig von) 1830-1914 TCLC 8
See also CA 104; DLB 129

Heyward, (Edwin) DuBose 1885-1940 T C L C 59
See also CA 108; 157; DLB 7, 9, 45; SATA 21

Hibbert, Eleanor Alice Burford 1906-1993 CLC 7; DAM POP
See also BEST 90:4; CA 17-20R; 140; CANR

9, 28, 59; MTCW 2; SATA 2; SATA-Obit 74

Hichens, Robert (Smythe) 1864-1950   T C L C 64
See also CA 162; DLB 153

Higgins, George V(incent) 1939-CLC 4, 7, 10, 18
See also CA 77-80; CAAS 5; CANR 17, 51; DLB 2; DLBY 81, 98; INT CANR-17; MTCW 1

Higginson, Thomas Wentworth 1823-1911 TCLC 36
See also CA 162; DLB 1, 64

Highet, Helen
See MacInnes, Helen (Clark)

Highsmith, (Mary) Patricia 1921-1995CLC 2, 4, 14, 42, 102; DAM NOV, POP
See also CA 1-4R; 147; CANR 1, 20, 48, 62; MTCW 1, 2

Highwater, Jamake (Mamake) 1942(?)- C L C 12
See also AAYA 7; CA 65-68; CAAS 7; CANR 10, 34; CLR 17; DLB 52; DLBY 85; JRDA; MAICYA; SATA 32, 69; SATA-Brief 30

Highway, Tomson 1951-CLC 92; DAC;DAM MULT
See also CA 151; CANR 75; MTCW 2; NNAL

Higuchi, Ichiyo 1872-1896   NCLC 49

Hijuelos, Oscar 1951- CLC 65; DAM MULT, POP; HLC 1
See also AAYA 25; BEST 90:1; CA 123; CANR 50, 75; DLB 145; HW 1, 2; MTCW 2

Hikmet, Nazim 1902(?)-1963   CLC 40
See also CA 141; 93-96

Hildegard von Bingen 1098-1179 CMLC 20
See also DLB 148

Hildesheimer, Wolfgang 1916-1991   CLC 49
See also CA 101; 135; DLB 69, 124

Hill, Geoffrey (William) 1932- CLC 5, 8, 18, 45; DAM POET
See also CA 81-84; CANR 21; CDBLB 1960 to Present; DLB 40; MTCW 1

Hill, George Roy 1921-   CLC 26
See also CA 110; 122

Hill, John
See Koontz, Dean R(ay)

Hill, Susan (Elizabeth) 1942-   CLC 4, 113; DAB; DAM MST, NOV
See also CA 33-36R; CANR 29, 69; DLB 14, 139; MTCW 1

Hillerman, Tony 1925-   CLC 62;DAM POP
See also AAYA 6; BEST 89:1; CA 29-32R; CANR 21, 42, 65; DLB 206; SATA 6

Hillesum, Etty 1914-1943   TCLC 49
See also CA 137

Hilliard, Noel (Harvey) 1929-   CLC 15
See also CA 9-12R; CANR 7, 69

Hillis, Rick 1956-   CLC 66
See also CA 134

Hilton, James 1900-1954   TCLC 21
See also CA 108; 169; DLB 34, 77; SATA 34

Himes, Chester (Bomar) 1909-1984CLC 2, 4, 7, 18, 58, 108; BLC 2; DAM MULT
See also BW 2; CA 25-28R; 114; CANR 22; DLB 2, 76, 143; MTCW 1, 2

Hinde, Thomas   CLC 6, 11
See also Chitty, Thomas Willes

Hindin, Nathan 1917-1994
See Bloch, Robert (Albert)
See also CA 179; CAAE 179

Hine, (William) Daryl 1936-   CLC 15
See also CA 1-4R; CAAS 15; CANR 1, 20; DLB 60

Hinkson, Katharine Tynan

See Tynan, Katharine

Hinojosa(-Smith), Rolando (R.) 1929-
See Hinojosa-Smith, Rolando
See also CA 131; CAAS 16; CANR 62; DAM
MULT; DLB 82; HLC 1; HW 1, 2; MTCW 2

Hinojosa-Smith, Rolando 1929-
See Hinojosa(-Smith), Rolando (R.)
See also CAAS 16; HLC 1; MTCW 2

Hinton, S(usan) E(loise) 1950- **CLC 30, 111;
DA; DAB; DAC; DAM MST, NOV**
See also AAYA 2; CA 81-84; CANR 32, 62;
CDALBS; CLR 3, 23; JRDA; MAICYA;
MTCW 1, 2; SATA 19, 58

Hippius, Zinaida **TCLC 9**
See also Gippius, Zinaida (Nikolayevna)

Hiraoka, Kimitake 1925-1970
See Mishima, Yukio
See also CA 97-100; 29-32R; DAM DRAM;
MTCW 1, 2

Hirsch, E(ric) D(onald),Jr. 1928- **CLC 79**
See also CA 25-28R; CANR 27, 51; DLB 67;
INT CANR-27; MTCW 1

Hirsch, Edward 1950- **CLC 31, 50**
See also CA 104; CANR 20, 42; DLB 120

Hitchcock, Alfred (Joseph) 1899-1980 **CLC 16**
See also AAYA 22; CA 159; 97-100; SATA 27;
SATA-Obit 24

Hitler, Adolf 1889-1945 **TCLC 53**
See also CA 117; 147

Hoagland, Edward 1932- **CLC 28**
See also CA 1-4R; CANR 2, 31, 57; DLB 6;
SATA 51

Hoban, Russell (Conwell) 1925- **CLC 7, 25;
DAM NOV**
See also CA 5-8R; CANR 23, 37, 66; CLR 3;
DLB 52; MAICYA; MTCW 1, 2; SATA 1,
40, 78

Hobbes, Thomas 1588-1679 **LC 36**
See also DLB 151

Hobbs, Perry
See Blackmur, R(ichard) P(almer)

Hobson, Laura Z(ametkin) 1900-1986 **CLC 7,
25**
See also CA 17-20R; 118; CANR 55; DLB 28;
SATA 52

Hochhuth, Rolf 1931- **CLC 4, 11, 18; DAM
DRAM**
See also CA 5-8R; CANR 33, 75; DLB 124;
MTCW 1, 2

Hochman, Sandra 1936- **CLC 3, 8**
See also CA 5-8R; DLB 5

Hochwaelder, Fritz 1911-1986 **CLC 36; DAM
DRAM**
See also CA 29-32R; 120; CANR 42; MTCW 1

Hochwalder, Fritz
See Hochwaelder, Fritz

Hocking, Mary (Eunice) 1921- **CLC 13**
See also CA 101; CANR 18, 40

Hodgins, Jack 1938- **CLC 23**
See also CA 93-96; DLB 60

Hodgson, William Hope 1877(?)-1918 **TCLC
13**
See also CA 111; 164; DLB 70, 153, 156, 178;
MTCW 2

Hoeg, Peter 1957- **CLC 95**
See also CA 151; CANR 75; MTCW 2

Hoffman, Alice 1952- **CLC 51;DAM NOV**
See also CA 77-80; CANR 34, 66; MTCW 1, 2

Hoffman, Daniel (Gerard) 1923- **CLC 6, 13, 23**
See also CA 1-4R; CANR 4; DLB 5

Hoffman, Stanley 1944- **CLC 5**
See also CA 77-80

Hoffman, William M(oses) 1939- **CLC 40**

See also CA 57-60; CANR 11, 71

Hoffmann, E(rnst) T(heodor) A(madeus) 1776-
1822 **NCLC 2; SSC 13**
See also DLB 90; SATA 27

Hofmann, Gert 1931- **CLC 54**
See also CA 128

Hofmannsthal, Hugo von 1874-1929 **TCLC 11;
DAM DRAM; DC 4**
See also CA 106; 153; DLB 81, 118

Hogan, Linda 1947- **CLC 73;DAM MULT**
See also CA 120; CANR 45, 73; DLB 175;
NNAL

Hogarth, Charles
See Creasey, John

Hogarth, Emmett
See Polonsky, Abraham (Lincoln)

Hogg, James 1770-1835 **NCLC 4**
See also DLB 93, 116, 159

Holbach, Paul Henri Thiry Baron 1723-1789
LC 14

Holberg, Ludvig 1684-1754 **LC 6**
See also CA 128

Holden, Ursula 1921- **CLC 18**
See also CA 101; CAAS 8; CANR 22

Holderlin, (Johann Christian) Friedrich 1770-
1843 **NCLC 16; PC 4**

Holdstock, Robert
See Holdstock, Robert P.

Holdstock, Robert P. 1948- **CLC 39**
See also CA 131; CANR 81

Holland, Isabelle 1920- **CLC 21**
See also AAYA 11; CA 21-24R; CANR 10, 25,
47; CLR 57; JRDA; MAICYA; SATA 8, 70;
SATA-Essay 103

Holland, Marcus
See Caldwell, (Janet Miriam) Taylor (Holland)

Hollander, John 1929- **CLC 2, 5, 8, 14**
See also CA 1-4R; CANR 1, 52; DLB 5; SATA
13

Hollander, Paul
See Silverberg, Robert

Holleran, Andrew 1943(?)- **CLC 38**
See also CA 144

Hollinghurst, Alan 1954- **CLC 55, 91**
See also CA 114; DLB 207

Hollis, Jim
See Summers, Hollis (Spurgeon, Jr.)

Holly, Buddy 1936-1959 **TCLC 65**

Holmes, Gordon
See Shiel, M(atthew) P(hipps)

Holmes, John
See Souster, (Holmes) Raymond

Holmes, John Clellon 1926-1988 **CLC 56**
See also CA 9-12R; 125; CANR 4; DLB 16

Holmes, Oliver Wendell, Jr. 1841-1935 **TCLC
77**
See also CA 114

Holmes, Oliver Wendell 1809-1894 **NCLC 14**
See also CDALB 1640-1865; DLB 1, 189;
SATA 34

Holmes, Raymond
See Souster, (Holmes) Raymond

Holt, Victoria
See Hibbert, Eleanor Alice Burford

Holub, Miroslav 1923-1998 **CLC 4**
See also CA 21-24R; 169; CANR 10

Homer c. 8th cent. B.C.- **CMLC 1, 16; DA;
DAB; DAC; DAM MST, POET; PC 23;
WLCS**
See also DLB 176

Hongo, Garrett Kaoru 1951- **PC 23**
See also CA 133; CAAS 22; DLB 120

Honig, Edwin 1919- **CLC 33**
See also CA 5-8R; CAAS 8; CANR 4, 45; DLB

5

Hood, Hugh (John Blagdon) 1928- **CLC 15, 28**
See also CA 49-52; CAAS 17; CANR 1, 33;
DLB 53

Hood, Thomas 1799-1845 **NCLC 16**
See also DLB 96

Hooker, (Peter) Jeremy 1941- **CLC 43**
See also CA 77-80; CANR 22; DLB 40

hooks, bell **CLC 94; BLCS**
See also Watkins, Gloria
See also MTCW 2

Hope, A(lec) D(erwent) 1907- **CLC 3, 51**
See also CA 21-24R; CANR 33, 74; MTCW 1,
2

Hope, Anthony 1863-1933 **TCLC 83**
See also CA 157; DLB 153, 156

Hope, Brian
See Creasey, John

Hope, Christopher (David Tully) 1944- **CLC
52**
See also CA 106; CANR 47; SATA 62

Hopkins, Gerard Manley 1844-1889 **NCLC
17; DA; DAB; DAC; DAM MST, POET;
PC 15; WLC**
See also CDBLB 1890-1914; DLB 35, 57

Hopkins, John (Richard) 1931-1998 **CLC 4**
See also CA 85-88; 169

Hopkins, Pauline Elizabeth 1859-1930 **TCLC
28; BLC 2; DAM MULT**
See also BW 2, 3; CA 141; CANR 82; DLB 50

Hopkinson, Francis 1737-1791 **LC 25**
See also DLB 31

Hopley-Woolrich, Cornell George 1903-1968
See Woolrich, Cornell
See also CA 13-14; CANR 58; CAP 1; MTCW
2

Horatio
See Proust, (Valentin-Louis-George-Eugene-)
Marcel

Horgan, Paul (George Vincent O'Shaughnessy)
1903-1995 **CLC 9, 53;DAM NOV**
See also CA 13-16R; 147; CANR 9, 35; DLB
212; DLBY 85; INT CANR-9; MTCW 1, 2;
SATA 13; SATA-Obit 84

Horn, Peter
See Kuttner, Henry

Hornem, Horace Esq.
See Byron, George Gordon (Noel)

**Horney, Karen (Clementine Theodore
Danielsen)** 1885-1952 **TCLC 71**
See also CA 114; 165

Hornung, E(rnest) W(illiam) 1866-1921
TCLC 59
See also CA 108; 160; DLB 70

Horovitz, Israel (Arthur) 1939- **CLC 56; DAM
DRAM**
See also CA 33-36R; CANR 46, 59; DLB 7

Horvath, Odon von
See Horvath, Oedoen von
See also DLB 85, 124

Horvath, Oedoen von 1901-1938 **TCLC 45**
See also Horvath, Odon von
See also CA 118

Horwitz, Julius 1920-1986 **CLC 14**
See also CA 9-12R; 119; CANR 12

Hospital, Janette Turner 1942- **CLC 42**
See also CA 108; CANR 48

Hostos, E. M. de
See Hostos (y Bonilla), Eugenio Maria de

Hostos, Eugenio M. de
See Hostos (y Bonilla), Eugenio Maria de

Hostos, Eugenio Maria
See Hostos (y Bonilla), Eugenio Maria de

Hostos (y Bonilla), Eugenio Mariade 1839-1903
  TCLC 24
  See also CA 123; 131; HW 1
Houdini
  See Lovecraft, H(oward) P(hillips)
Hougan, Carolyn 1943-   **CLC 34**
  See also CA 139
Household, Geoffrey (Edward West) 1900-1988
  CLC 11
  See also CA 77-80; 126; CANR 58; DLB 87;
  SATA 14; SATA-Obit 59
Housman, A(lfred) E(dward) 1859-1936
  **TCLC 1, 10; DA; DAB; DAC; DAM MST,
  POET; PC 2; WLCS**
  See also CA 104; 125; DLB 19; MTCW 1, 2
Housman, Laurence 1865-1959   **TCLC 7**
  See also CA 106; 155; DLB 10; SATA 25
Howard, Elizabeth Jane 1923-   **CLC 7, 29**
  See also CA 5-8R; CANR 8, 62
Howard, Maureen 1930-   **CLC 5, 14, 46**
  See also CA 53-56; CANR 31, 75; DLBY 83;
  INT CANR-31; MTCW 1, 2
Howard, Richard 1929-   **CLC 7, 10, 47**
  See also AITN 1; CA 85-88; CANR 25, 80; DLB
  5; INT CANR-25
Howard, Robert E(rvin) 1906-1936 **TCLC 8**
  See also CA 105; 157
Howard, Warren F.
  See Pohl, Frederik
Howe, Fanny (Quincy) 1940-   **CLC 47**
  See also CA 117; CAAS 27; CANR 70; SATA-
  Brief 52
Howe, Irving 1920-1993   **CLC 85**
  See also CA 9-12R; 141; CANR 21, 50; DLB
  67; MTCW 1, 2
Howe, Julia Ward 1819-1910   **TCLC 21**
  See also CA 117; DLB 1, 189
Howe, Susan 1937-   **CLC 72**
  See also CA 160; DLB 120
Howe, Tina 1937-   **CLC 48**
  See also CA 109
Howell, James 1594(?)-1666   **LC 13**
  See also DLB 151
Howells, W. D.
  See Howells, William Dean
Howells, William D.
  See Howells, William Dean
Howells, William Dean 1837-1920**TCLC 7, 17,
  41**
  See also CA 104; 134; CDALB 1865-1917;
  DLB 12, 64, 74, 79, 189; MTCW 2
Howes, Barbara 1914-1996   **CLC 15**
  See also CA 9-12R; 151; CAAS 3; CANR 53;
  SATA 5
Hrabal, Bohumil 1914-1997   **CLC 13, 67**
  See also CA 106; 156; CAAS 12; CANR 57
Hroswitha of Gandersheim c. 935-c.1002
  CMLC 29
  See also DLB 148
Hsun, Lu
  See Lu Hsun
Hubbard, L(afayette) Ron(ald) 1911-1986
  CLC 43; DAM POP
  See also CA 77-80; 118; CANR 52; MTCW 2
Huch, Ricarda (Octavia) 1864-1947**TCLC 13**
  See also CA 111; DLB 66
Huddle, David 1942-   **CLC 49**
  See also CA 57-60; CAAS 20; DLB 130
Hudson, Jeffrey
  See Crichton, (John) Michael
Hudson, W(illiam) H(enry) 1841-1922 **TCLC
  29**
  See also CA 115; DLB 98, 153, 174; SATA 35

Hueffer, Ford Madox
  See Ford, Ford Madox
Hughart, Barry 1934-   **CLC 39**
  See also CA 137
Hughes, Colin
  See Creasey, John
Hughes, David (John) 1930-   **CLC 48**
  See also CA 116; 129; DLB 14
Hughes, Edward James
  See Hughes, Ted
  See also DAM MST, POET
Hughes, (James) Langston 1902-1967**CLC 1,
  5, 10, 15, 35, 44, 108; BLC 2; DA; DAB;
  DAC; DAM DRAM, MST, MULT, POET;
  DC 3; PC 1; SSC 6; WLC**
  See also AAYA 12; BW 1, 3; CA 1-4R; 25-28R;
  CANR 1, 34, 82; CDALB 1929-1941; CLR
  17; DLB 4, 7, 48, 51, 86; JRDA; MAICYA;
  MTCW 1, 2; SATA 4, 33
Hughes, Richard (Arthur Warren) 1900-1976
  CLC 1, 11; DAM NOV
  See also CA 5-8R; 65-68; CANR 4; DLB 15,
  161; MTCW 1; SATA 8; SATA-Obit 25
Hughes, Ted 1930-1998   **CLC 2, 4, 9, 14, 37,
  119; DAB; DAC; PC 7**
  See also Hughes, Edward James
  See also CA 1-4R; 171; CANR 1, 33, 66; CLR
  3; DLB 40, 161; MAICYA; MTCW 1, 2;
  SATA 49; SATA-Brief 27; SATA-Obit 107
Hugo, Richard F(ranklin) 1923-1982 **CLC 6,
  18, 32; DAM POET**
  See also CA 49-52; 108; CANR 3; DLB 5, 206
Hugo, Victor (Marie) 1802-1885**NCLC 3, 10,
  21; DA; DAB; DAC; DAM DRAM, MST,
  NOV, POET; PC 17; WLC**
  See also AAYA 28; DLB 119, 192; SATA 47
Huidobro, Vicente
  See Huidobro Fernandez, Vicente Garcia
Huidobro Fernandez, Vicente Garcia 1893-
  1948   **TCLC 31**
  See also CA 131; HW 1
Hulme, Keri 1947-   **CLC 39**
  See also CA 125; CANR 69; INT 125
Hulme, T(homas) E(rnest) 1883-1917 **TCLC
  21**
  See also CA 117; DLB 19
Hume, David 1711-1776   **LC 7**
  See also DLB 104
Humphrey, William 1924-1997   **CLC 45**
  See also CA 77-80; 160; CANR 68; DLB 212
Humphreys, Emyr Owen 1919-   **CLC 47**
  See also CA 5-8R; CANR 3, 24; DLB 15
Humphreys, Josephine 1945-   **CLC 34, 57**
  See also CA 121; 127; INT 127
Huneker, James Gibbons 1857-1921**TCLC 65**
  See also DLB 71
Hungerford, Pixie
  See Brinsmead, H(esba) F(ay)
Hunt, E(verette) Howard, (Jr.) 1918- **CLC 3**
  See also AITN 1; CA 45-48; CANR 2, 47
Hunt, Kyle
  See Creasey, John
Hunt, (James Henry) Leigh 1784-1859**NCLC
  1, 70; DAM POET**
  See also DLB 96, 110, 144
Hunt, Marsha 1946-   **CLC 70**
  See also BW 2, 3; CA 143; CANR 79
Hunt, Violet 1866(?)-1942   **TCLC 53**
  See also DLB 162, 197
Hunter, E. Waldo
  See Sturgeon, Theodore (Hamilton)
Hunter, Evan 1926- **CLC 11, 31;DAM POP**
  See also CA 5-8R; CANR 5, 38, 62; DLBY 82;

  INT CANR-5; MTCW 1; SATA 25
Hunter, Kristin (Eggleston) 1931-   **CLC 35**
  See also AITN 1; BW 1; CA 13-16R; CANR
  13; CLR 3; DLB 33; INT CANR-13;
  MAICYA; SAAS 10; SATA 12
Hunter, Mary
  See Austin, Mary (Hunter)
Hunter, Mollie 1922-   **CLC 21**
  See also McIlwraith, Maureen Mollie Hunter
  See also AAYA 13; CANR 37, 78; CLR 25; DLB
  161; JRDA; MAICYA; SAAS 7; SATA 54,
  106
Hunter, Robert (?)-1734   **LC 7**
Hurston, Zora Neale 1903-1960**CLC 7, 30, 61;
  BLC 2; DA; DAC; DAM MST, MULT,
  NOV; SSC 4; WLCS**
  See also AAYA 15; BW 1, 3; CA 85-88; CANR
  61; CDALBS; DLB 51, 86; MTCW 1, 2
Huston, John (Marcellus) 1906-1987 **CLC 20**
  See also CA 73-76; 123; CANR 34; DLB 26
Hustvedt, Siri 1955-   **CLC 76**
  See also CA 137
Hutten, Ulrich von 1488-1523   **LC 16**
  See also DLB 179
Huxley, Aldous (Leonard) 1894-1963 **CLC 1,
  3, 4, 5, 8, 11, 18, 35, 79; DA; DAB; DAC;
  DAM MST, NOV; WLC**
  See also AAYA 11; CA 85-88; CANR 44;
  CDBLB 1914-1945; DLB 36, 100, 162, 195;
  MTCW 1, 2; SATA 63
Huxley, T(homas) H(enry) 1825-1895 **NCLC
  67**
  See also DLB 57
Huysmans, Joris-Karl 1848-1907**TCLC 7, 69**
  See also CA 104; 165; DLB 123
Hwang, David Henry 1957-   **CLC 55; DAM
  DRAM; DC 4**
  See also CA 127; 132; CANR 76; DLB 212;
  INT 132; MTCW 2
Hyde, Anthony 1946-   **CLC 42**
  See also CA 136
Hyde, Margaret O(ldroyd) 1917-   **CLC 21**
  See also CA 1-4R; CANR 1, 36; CLR 23; JRDA;
  MAICYA; SAAS 8; SATA 1, 42, 76
Hynes, James 1956(?)-   **CLC 65**
  See also CA 164
Hypatia c. 370-415   **CMLC 35**
Ian, Janis 1951-   **CLC 21**
  See also CA 105
Ibanez, Vicente Blasco
  See Blasco Ibanez, Vicente
Ibarbourou, Juana de 1895-1979
  See also HLCS 2; HW 1
Ibarguengoitia, Jorge 1928-1983   **CLC 37**
  See also CA 124; 113; HW 1
Ibsen, Henrik (Johan) 1828-1906 **TCLC 2, 8,
  16, 37, 52; DA; DAB; DAC; DAM DRAM,
  MST; DC 2; WLC**
  See also CA 104; 141
Ibuse, Masuji 1898-1993   **CLC 22**
  See also CA 127; 141; DLB 180
Ichikawa, Kon 1915-   **CLC 20**
  See also CA 121
Idle, Eric 1943-   **CLC 21**
  See also Monty Python
  See also CA 116; CANR 35
Ignatow, David 1914-1997 **CLC 4, 7, 14, 40**
  See also CA 9-12R; 162; CAAS 3; CANR 31,
  57; DLB 5
Ignotus
  See Strachey, (Giles) Lytton
Ihimaera, Witi 1944-   **CLC 46**
  See also CA 77-80

Ilf, Ilya   **TCLC 21**
See also Fainzilberg, Ilya Arnoldovich
Illyes, Gyula 1902-1983   **PC 16**
See also CA 114; 109
Immermann, Karl (Lebrecht) 1796-1840
     NCLC 4, 49
See also DLB 133
Ince, Thomas H. 1882-1924   **TCLC 89**
Inchbald, Elizabeth 1753-1821   **NCLC 62**
See also DLB 39, 89
Inclan, Ramon (Maria) del Valle
See Valle-Inclan, Ramon (Maria) del
Infante, G(uillermo) Cabrera
See Cabrera Infante, G(uillermo)
Ingalls, Rachel (Holmes) 1940-   **CLC 42**
See also CA 123; 127
Ingamells, Reginald Charles
See Ingamells, Rex
Ingamells, Rex 1913-1955   **TCLC 35**
See also CA 167
Inge, William (Motter) 1913-1973 **CLC 1, 8,**
19; DAM DRAM
See also CA 9-12R; CDALB 1941-1968; DLB
7; MTCW 1, 2
Ingelow, Jean 1820-1897   **NCLC 39**
See also DLB 35, 163; SATA 33
Ingram, Willis J.
See Harris, Mark
Innaurato, Albert (F.) 1948(?)-   **CLC 21, 60**
See also CA 115; 122; CANR 78; INT 122
Innes, Michael
See Stewart, J(ohn) I(nnes) M(ackintosh)
Innis, Harold Adams 1894-1952   **TCLC 77**
See also DLB 88
Ionesco, Eugene 1909-1994 **CLC 1, 4, 6, 9, 11,**
15, 41, 86; DA; DAB; DAC; DAM DRAM,
MST; WLC
See also CA 9-12R; 144; CANR 55; MTCW 1,
2; SATA 7; SATA-Obit 79
Iqbal, Muhammad 1873-1938   **TCLC 28**
Ireland, Patrick
See O'Doherty, Brian
Iron, Ralph
See Schreiner, Olive (Emilie Albertina)
Irving, John (Winslow) 1942- **CLC 13, 23, 38,**
112; DAM NOV, POP
See also AAYA 8; BEST 89:3; CA 25-28R;
CANR 28, 73; DLB 6; DLBY 82; MTCW 1,
2
Irving, Washington 1783-1859 **NCLC 2, 19;**
DA; DAB; DAC; DAM MST; SSC 2; WLC
See also CDALB 1640-1865; DLB 3, 11, 30,
59, 73, 74, 186; YABC 2
Irwin, P. K.
See Page, P(atricia) K(athleen)
Isaacs, Jorge Ricardo 1837-1895   **NCLC 70**
Isaacs, Susan 1943-   **CLC 32; DAM POP**
See also BEST 89:1; CA 89-92; CANR 20, 41,
65; INT CANR-20; MTCW 1, 2
Isherwood, Christopher (William Bradshaw)
1904-1986   **CLC 1, 9, 11, 14, 44; DAM**
DRAM, NOV
See also CA 13-16R; 117; CANR 35; DLB 15,
195; DLBY 86; MTCW 1, 2
Ishiguro, Kazuo 1954-   **CLC 27, 56, 59, 110;**
DAM NOV
See also BEST 90:2; CA 120; CANR 49; DLB
194; MTCW 1, 2
Ishikawa, Hakuhin
See Ishikawa, Takuboku
Ishikawa, Takuboku 1886(?)-1912 **TCLC 15;**
DAM POET; PC 10
See also CA 113; 153

Iskander, Fazil 1929-   **CLC 47**
See also CA 102
Isler, Alan (David) 1934-   **CLC 91**
See also CA 156
Ivan IV 1530-1584   **LC 17**
Ivanov, Vyacheslav Ivanovich 1866-1949
     TCLC 33
See also CA 122
Ivask, Ivar Vidrik 1927-1992   **CLC 14**
See also CA 37-40R; 139; CANR 24
Ives, Morgan
See Bradley, Marion Zimmer
Izumi Shikibu c. 973-c. 1034   **CMLC 33**
J. R. S.
See Gogarty, Oliver St. John
Jabran, Kahlil
See Gibran, Kahlil
Jabran, Khalil
See Gibran, Kahlil
Jackson, Daniel
See Wingrove, David (John)
Jackson, Jesse 1908-1983   **CLC 12**
See also BW 1; CA 25-28R; 109; CANR 27;
CLR 28; MAICYA; SATA 2, 29; SATA-Obit
48
Jackson, Laura (Riding) 1901-1991
See Riding, Laura
See also CA 65-68; 135; CANR 28; DLB 48
Jackson, Sam
See Trumbo, Dalton
Jackson, Sara
See Wingrove, David (John)
Jackson, Shirley 1919-1965 **CLC 11, 60, 87;**
DA; DAC; DAM MST; SSC 9; WLC
See also AAYA 9; CA 1-4R; 25-28R; CANR 4,
52; CDALB 1941-1968; DLB 6; MTCW 2;
SATA 2
Jacob, (Cyprien-)Max 1876-1944   **TCLC 6**
See also CA 104
Jacobs, Harriet A(nn) 1813(?)-1897 **NCLC 67**
Jacobs, Jim 1942-   **CLC 12**
See also CA 97-100; INT 97-100
Jacobs, W(illiam) W(ymark) 1863-1943
     TCLC 22
See also CA 121; 167; DLB 135
Jacobsen, Jens Peter 1847-1885   **NCLC 34**
Jacobsen, Josephine 1908-   **CLC 48, 102**
See also CA 33-36R; CAAS 18; CANR 23, 48
Jacobson, Dan 1929-   **CLC 4, 14**
See also CA 1-4R; CANR 2, 25, 66; DLB 14,
207; MTCW 1
Jacqueline
See Carpentier (y Valmont), Alejo
Jagger, Mick 1944-   **CLC 17**
Jahiz, al- c. 780-c. 869   **CMLC 25**
Jakes, John (William) 1932-   **CLC 29; DAM**
NOV, POP
See also BEST 89:4; CA 57-60; CANR 10, 43,
66; DLBY 83; INT CANR-10; MTCW 1, 2;
SATA 62
James, Andrew
See Kirkup, James
James, C(yril) L(ionel) R(obert) 1901-1989
     CLC 33; BLCS
See also BW 2; CA 117; 125; 128; CANR 62;
DLB 125; MTCW 1
James, Daniel (Lewis) 1911-1988
See Santiago, Danny
See also CA 174; 125
James, Dynely
See Mayne, William (James Carter)
James, Henry Sr. 1811-1882   **NCLC 53**
James, Henry 1843-1916 **TCLC 2, 11, 24, 40,**

47, 64; DA; DAB; DAC; DAM MST, NOV;
SSC 8, 32; WLC
See also CA 104; 132; CDALB 1865-1917;
DLB 12, 71, 74, 189; DLBD 13; MTCW 1,
2
James, M. R.
See James, Montague (Rhodes)
See also DLB 156
James, Montague (Rhodes) 1862-1936 **T C L C**
6; SSC 16
See also CA 104; DLB 201
James, P. D. 1920-   **CLC 18, 46, 122**
See also White, Phyllis Dorothy James
See also BEST 90:2; CDBLB 1960 to Present;
DLB 87; DLBD 17
James, Philip
See Moorcock, Michael (John)
James, William 1842-1910   **TCLC 15, 32**
See also CA 109
James I 1394-1437   **LC 20**
Jameson, Anna 1794-1860   **NCLC 43**
See also DLB 99, 166
Jami, Nur al-Din 'Abd al-Rahman 1414-1492
     LC 9
Jammes, Francis 1868-1938   **TCLC 75**
Jandl, Ernst 1925-   **CLC 34**
Janowitz, Tama 1957- **CLC 43; DAM POP**
See also CA 106; CANR 52
Japrisot, Sebastien 1931-   **CLC 90**
Jarrell, Randall 1914-1965 **CLC 1, 2, 6, 9, 13,**
49; DAM POET
See also CA 5-8R; 25-28R; CABS 2; CANR 6,
34; CDALB 1941-1968; CLR 6; DLB 48, 52;
MAICYA; MTCW 1, 2; SATA 7
Jarry, Alfred 1873-1907 **TCLC 2, 14; DAM**
DRAM; SSC 20
See also CA 104; 153; DLB 192
Jarvis, E. K. 1917-1994
See Bloch, Robert (Albert)
See also CA 179; CAAE 179
Jeake, Samuel, Jr.
See Aiken, Conrad (Potter)
Jean Paul 1763-1825   **NCLC 7**
Jefferies, (John) Richard 1848-1887 **NCLC 47**
See also DLB 98, 141; SATA 16
Jeffers, (John) Robinson 1887-1962 **CLC 2, 3,**
11, 15, 54; DA; DAC; DAM MST, POET;
PC 17; WLC
See also CA 85-88; CANR 35; CDALB 1917-
1929; DLB 45, 212; MTCW 1, 2
Jefferson, Janet
See Mencken, H(enry) L(ouis)
Jefferson, Thomas 1743-1826   **NCLC 11**
See also CDALB 1640-1865; DLB 31
Jeffrey, Francis 1773-1850   **NCLC 33**
See also DLB 107
Jelakowitch, Ivan
See Heijermans, Herman
Jellicoe, (Patricia) Ann 1927-   **CLC 27**
See also CA 85-88; DLB 13
Jen, Gish   **CLC 70**
See also Jen, Lillian
Jen, Lillian 1956(?)-
See Jen, Gish
See also CA 135
Jenkins, (John) Robin 1912-   **CLC 52**
See also CA 1-4R; CANR 1; DLB 14
Jennings, Elizabeth (Joan) 1926- **CLC 5, 14**
See also CA 61-64; CAAS 5; CANR 8, 39, 66;
DLB 27; MTCW 1; SATA 66
Jennings, Waylon 1937-   **CLC 21**
Jensen, Johannes V. 1873-1950   **TCLC 41**
See also CA 170

Jensen, Laura (Linnea) 1948-　　　　CLC 37
　See also CA 103
Jerome, Jerome K(lapka) 1859-1927 TCLC 23
　See also CA 119; 177; DLB 10, 34, 135
Jerrold, Douglas William 1803-1857 NCLC 2
　See also DLB 158, 159
Jewett, (Theodora) Sarah Orne 1849-1909
　　TCLC 1, 22; SSC 6
　See also CA 108; 127; CANR 71; DLB 12, 74;
　SATA 15
Jewsbury, Geraldine (Endsor) 1812-1880
　　NCLC 22
　See also DLB 21
Jhabvala, Ruth Prawer 1927-CLC 4, 8, 29, 94;
　　DAB; DAM NOV
　See also CA 1-4R; CANR 2, 29, 51, 74; DLB
　139, 194; INT CANR-29; MTCW 1, 2
Jibran, Kahlil
　See Gibran, Kahlil
Jibran, Khalil
　See Gibran, Kahlil
Jiles, Paulette 1943-　　　　　　CLC 13, 58
　See also CA 101; CANR 70
Jimenez (Mantecon), Juan Ramon 1881-1958
　　TCLC 4; DAM MULT, POET; HLC 1; PC
　　7
　See also CA 104; 131; CANR 74; DLB 134;
　HW 1; MTCW 1, 2
Jimenez, Ramon
　See Jimenez (Mantecon), Juan Ramon
Jimenez Mantecon, Juan
　See Jimenez (Mantecon), Juan Ramon
Jin, Ha 1956-　　　　　　　　　CLC 109
　See also CA 152
Joel, Billy　　　　　　　　　　CLC 26
　See also Joel, William Martin
Joel, William Martin 1949-
　See Joel, Billy
　See also CA 108
John, Saint 7th cent. -　　　　　CMLC 27
John of the Cross, St. 1542-1591　　LC 18
Johnson, B(ryan) S(tanley William) 1933-1973
　　CLC 6, 9
　See also CA 9-12R; 53-56; CANR 9; DLB 14,
　40
Johnson, Benj. F. of Boo
　See Riley, James Whitcomb
Johnson, Benjamin F. of Boo
　See Riley, James Whitcomb
Johnson, Charles (Richard) 1948-CLC 7, 51,
　　65; BLC 2; DAM MULT
　See also BW 2, 3; CA 116; CAAS 18; CANR
　42, 66, 82; DLB 33; MTCW 2
Johnson, Denis 1949-　　　　　　CLC 52
　See also CA 117; 121; CANR 71; DLB 120
Johnson, Diane 1934-　　　　　CLC 5, 13, 48
　See also CA 41-44R; CANR 17, 40, 62; DLBY
　80; INT CANR-17; MTCW 1
Johnson, Eyvind (Olof Verner) 1900-1976
　　CLC 14
　See also CA 73-76; 69-72; CANR 34
Johnson, J. R.
　See James, C(yril) L(ionel) R(obert)
Johnson, James Weldon 1871-1938 TCLC 3,
　　19; BLC 2; DAM MULT, POET; PC 24
　See also BW 1, 3; CA 104; 125; CANR 82;
　CDALB 1917-1929; CLR 32; DLB 51;
　MTCW 1, 2; SATA 31
Johnson, Joyce 1935-　　　　　　CLC 58
　See also CA 125; 129
Johnson, Judith (Emlyn) 1936-　CLC 7, 15
　See also CA 25-28R, 153; CANR 34
Johnson, Lionel (Pigot) 1867-1902 TCLC 19

　See also CA 117; DLB 19
Johnson, Marguerite (Annie)
　See Angelou, Maya
Johnson, Mel
　See Malzberg, Barry N(athaniel)
Johnson, Pamela Hansford 1912-1981 CLC 1,
　7, 27
　See also CA 1-4R; 104; CANR 2, 28; DLB 15;
　MTCW 1, 2
Johnson, Robert 1911(?)-1938　　TCLC 69
　See also BW 3; CA 174
Johnson, Samuel 1709-1784　LC 15, 52; DA;
　　DAB; DAC; DAM MST; WLC
　See also CDBLB 1660-1789; DLB 39, 95, 104,
　142
Johnson, Uwe 1934-1984　　CLC 5, 10, 15, 40
　See also CA 1-4R; 112; CANR 1, 39; DLB 75;
　MTCW 1
Johnston, George (Benson) 1913-　　CLC 51
　See also CA 1-4R; CANR 5, 20; DLB 88
Johnston, Jennifer 1930-　　　　　CLC 7
　See also CA 85-88; DLB 14
Jolley, (Monica) Elizabeth 1923-CLC 46; SSC
　19
　See also CA 127; CAAS 13; CANR 59
Jones, Arthur Llewellyn 1863-1947
　See Machen, Arthur
　See also CA 104
Jones, D(ouglas) G(ordon) 1929-　　CLC 10
　See also CA 29-32R; CANR 13; DLB 53
Jones, David (Michael) 1895-1974 CLC 2, 4, 7,
　13, 42
　See also CA 9-12R; 53-56; CANR 28; CDBLB
　1945-1960; DLB 20, 100; MTCW 1
Jones, David Robert 1947-
　See Bowie, David
　See also CA 103
Jones, Diana Wynne 1934-　　　　CLC 26
　See also AAYA 12; CA 49-52; CANR 4, 26,
　56; CLR 23; DLB 161; JRDA; MAICYA;
　SAAS 7; SATA 9, 70, 108
Jones, Edward P. 1950-　　　　　CLC 76
　See also BW 2, 3; CA 142; CANR 79
Jones, Gayl 1949-　CLC 6, 9; BLC 2; DAM
　　MULT
　See also BW 2, 3; CA 77-80; CANR 27, 66;
　DLB 33; MTCW 1, 2
Jones, James 1921-1977　　　CLC 1, 3, 10, 39
　See also AITN 1, 2; CA 1-4R; 69-72; CANR 6;
　DLB 2, 143; DLBD 17; DLBY 98; MTCW 1
Jones, John J.
　See Lovecraft, H(oward) P(hillips)
Jones, LeRoi　　　CLC 1, 2, 3, 5, 10, 14
　See also Baraka, Amiri
　See also MTCW 2
Jones, Louis B. 1953-　　　　　CLC 65
　See also CA 141; CANR 73
Jones, Madison (Percy, Jr.) 1925-　　CLC 4
　See also CA 13-16R; CAAS 11; CANR 7, 54;
　DLB 152
Jones, Mervyn 1922-　　　　CLC 10, 52
　See also CA 45-48; CAAS 5; CANR 1; MTCW
　1
Jones, Mick 1956(?)-　　　　　CLC 30
Jones, Nettie (Pearl) 1941-　　　CLC 34
　See also BW 2; CA 137; CAAS 20
Jones, Preston 1936-1979　　　　CLC 10
　See also CA 73-76; 89-92; DLB 7
Jones, Robert F(rancis) 1934-　　CLC 7
　See also CA 49-52; CANR 2, 61
Jones, Rod 1953-　　　　　　　CLC 50
　See also CA 128
Jones, Terence Graham Parry 1942- CLC 21

　See also Jones, Terry; Monty Python
　See also CA 112; 116; CANR 35; INT 116
Jones, Terry
　See Jones, Terence Graham Parry
　See also SATA 67; SATA-Brief 51
Jones, Thom 1945(?)-　　　　　　CLC 81
　See also CA 157
Jong, Erica 1942-　CLC 4, 6, 8, 18, 83; DAM
　　NOV, POP
　See also AITN 1; BEST 90:2; CA 73-76; CANR
　26, 52, 75; DLB 2, 5, 28, 152; INT CANR-
　26; MTCW 1, 2
Jonson, Ben(jamin) 1572(?)-1637　LC 6, 33;
　　DA; DAB; DAC; DAM DRAM, MST,
　　POET; DC 4; PC 17; WLC
　See also CDBLB Before 1660; DLB 62, 121
Jordan, June 1936-CLC 5, 11, 23, 114; BLCS;
　　DAM MULT, POET
　See also AAYA 2; BW 2, 3; CA 33-36R; CANR
　25, 70; CLR 10; DLB 38; MAICYA; MTCW
　1; SATA 4
Jordan, Neil (Patrick) 1950-　　　CLC 110
　See also CA 124; 130; CANR 54; INT 130
Jordan, Pat(rick M.) 1941-　　　CLC 37
　See also CA 33-36R
Jorgensen, Ivar
　See Ellison, Harlan (Jay)
Jorgenson, Ivar
　See Silverberg, Robert
Josephus, Flavius c. 37-100　　　CMLC 13
Josipovici, Gabriel 1940-　　　CLC 6, 43
　See also CA 37-40R; CAAS 8; CANR 47; DLB
　14
Joubert, Joseph 1754-1824　　　NCLC 9
Jouve, Pierre Jean 1887-1976　　CLC 47
　See also CA 65-68
Jovine, Francesco 1902-1950　　TCLC 79
Joyce, James (Augustine Aloysius) 1882-1941
　　TCLC 3, 8, 16, 35, 52; DA;DAB; DAC;
　　DAM MST, NOV, POET; PC 22; SSC 3,
　　26; WLC
　See also CA 104; 126; CDBLB 1914-1945;
　DLB 10, 19, 36, 162; MTCW 1, 2
Jozsef, Attila 1905-1937　　　　TCLC 22
　See also CA 116
Juana Ines de la Cruz 1651(?)-1695　　LC 5;
　　HLCS 1; PC 24
Judd, Cyril
　See Kornbluth, C(yril) M.; Pohl, Frederik
Julian of Norwich 1342(?)-1416(?)　LC 6, 52
　See also DLB 146
Junger, Sebastian 1962-　　　　CLC 109
　See also AAYA 28; CA 165
Juniper, Alex
　See Hospital, Janette Turner
Junius
　See Luxemburg, Rosa
Just, Ward (Swift) 1935-　　　　CLC 4, 27
　See also CA 25-28R; CANR 32; INT CANR-
　32
Justice, Donald (Rodney) 1925-　CLC 6, 19,
　　102; DAM POET
　See also CA 5-8R; CANR 26, 54, 74; DLBY
　83; INT CANR-26; MTCW 2
Juvenal c. 60-c. 13　　　　　　CMLC 8
　See also Juvenalis, Decimus Junius
　See also DLB 211
Juvenalis, Decimus Junius 55(?)-c. 127(?)
　See Juvenal
Juvenis
　See Bourne, Randolph S(illiman)
Kacew, Romain 1914-1980
　See Gary, Romain

Kesey, Ken (Elton) 1935- CLC 1, 3, 6, 11, 46, 64; DA; DAB; DAC; DAM MST, NOV, POP; WLC
See also AAYA 25; CA 1-4R; CANR 22, 38, 66; CDALB 1968-1988; DLB 2, 16, 206; MTCW 1, 2; SATA 66

Kesselring, Joseph (Otto) 1902-1967CLC 45; DAM DRAM, MST
See also CA 150

Kessler, Jascha (Frederick) 1929- CLC 4
See also CA 17-20R; CANR 8, 48

Kettelkamp, Larry (Dale) 1933- CLC 12
See also CA 29-32R; CANR 16; SAAS 3; SATA 2

Key, Ellen 1849-1926 TCLC 65

Keyber, Conny
See Fielding, Henry

Keyes, Daniel 1927-CLC 80; DA; DAC; DAM MST, NOV
See also AAYA 23; CA 17-20R; CANR 10, 26, 54, 74; MTCW 2; SATA 37

Keynes, John Maynard 1883-1946 TCLC 64
See also CA 114; 162, 163; DLBD 10; MTCW 2

Khanshendel, Chiron
See Rose, Wendy

Khayyam, Omar 1048-1131 CMLC 11; DAM POET; PC 8

Kherdian, David 1931- CLC 6, 9
See also CA 21-24R; CAAS 2; CANR 39, 78; CLR 24; JRDA; MAICYA; SATA 16, 74

Khlebnikov, Velimir TCLC 20
See also Khlebnikov, Viktor Vladimirovich

Khlebnikov, Viktor Vladimirovich 1885-1922
See Khlebnikov, Velimir
See also CA 117

Khodasevich, Vladislav (Felitsianovich) 1886-1939 TCLC 15
See also CA 115

Kielland, Alexander Lange 1849-1906 T C L C 5
See also CA 104

Kiely, Benedict 1919- CLC 23, 43
See also CA 1-4R; CANR 2; DLB 15

Kienzle, William X(avier) 1928- CLC 25; DAM POP
See also CA 93-96; CAAS 1; CANR 9, 31, 59; INT CANR-31; MTCW 1, 2

Kierkegaard, Soren 1813-1855 NCLC 34, 78

Kieslowski, Krzysztof 1941-1996 CLC 120
See also CA 147; 151

Killens, John Oliver 1916-1987 CLC 10
See also BW 2; CA 77-80; 123; CAAS 2; CANR 26; DLB 33

Killigrew, Anne 1660-1685 LC 4
See also DLB 131

Kim
See Simenon, Georges (Jacques Christian)

Kincaid, Jamaica 1949- CLC 43, 68; BLC 2; DAM MULT, NOV
See also AAYA 13; BW 2, 3; CA 125; CANR 47, 59; CDALBS; DLB 157; MTCW 2

King, Francis (Henry) 1923-CLC 8, 53; DAM NOV
See also CA 1-4R; CANR 1, 33; DLB 15, 139; MTCW 1

King, Kennedy
See Brown, George Douglas

King, Martin Luther, Jr. 1929-1968 CLC 83; BLC 2; DA; DAB; DAC; DAM MST, MULT; WLCS
See also BW 2, 3; CA 25-28; CANR 27, 44; CAP 2; MTCW 1, 2; SATA 14

King, Stephen (Edwin) 1947-CLC 12, 26, 37, 61, 113; DAM NOV, POP; SSC 17
See also AAYA 1, 17; BEST 90:1; CA 61-64; CANR 1, 30, 52, 76; DLB 143; DLBY 80; JRDA; MTCW 1, 2; SATA 9, 55

King, Steve
See King, Stephen (Edwin)

King, Thomas 1943- CLC 89; DAC;DAM MULT
See also CA 144; DLB 175; NNAL; SATA 96

Kingman, Lee CLC 17
See also Natti, (Mary) Lee
See also SAAS 3; SATA 1, 67

Kingsley, Charles 1819-1875 NCLC 35
See also DLB 21, 32, 163, 190; YABC 2

Kingsley, Sidney 1906-1995 CLC 44
See also CA 85-88; 147; DLB 7

Kingsolver, Barbara 1955-CLC 55, 81; DAM POP
See also AAYA 15; CA 129; 134; CANR 60; CDALBS; DLB 206; INT 134; MTCW 2

Kingston, Maxine (Ting Ting) Hong 1940- CLC 12, 19, 58, 121; DAM MULT, NOV; WLCS
See also AAYA 8; CA 69-72; CANR 13, 38, 74; CDALBS; DLB 173, 212; DLBY 80; INT CANR-13; MTCW 1, 2; SATA 53

Kinnell, Galway 1927- CLC 1, 2, 3, 5, 13, 29; PC 26
See also CA 9-12R; CANR 10, 34, 66; DLB 5; DLBY 87; INT CANR-34; MTCW 1, 2

Kinsella, Thomas 1928- CLC 4, 19
See also CA 17-20R; CANR 15; DLB 27; MTCW 1, 2

Kinsella, W(illiam) P(atrick) 1935- CLC 27, 43; DAC; DAM NOV, POP
See also AAYA 7; CA 97-100; CAAS 7; CANR 21, 35, 66, 75; INT CANR-21; MTCW 1, 2

Kinsey, Alfred C(harles) 1894-1956TCLC 91
See also CA 115; 170; MTCW 2

Kipling, (Joseph) Rudyard 1865-1936 T C L C 8, 17; DA; DAB; DAC; DAM MST, POET; PC 3; SSC 5; WLC
See also CA 105; 120; CANR 33; CDBLB 1890-1914; CLR 39; DLB 19, 34, 141, 156; MAICYA; MTCW 1, 2; SATA 100; YABC 2

Kirkup, James 1918- CLC 1
See also CA 1-4R; CAAS 4; CANR 2; DLB 27; SATA 12

Kirkwood, James 1930(?)-1989 CLC 9
See also AITN 2; CA 1-4R; 128; CANR 6, 40

Kirshner, Sidney
See Kingsley, Sidney

Kis, Danilo 1935-1989 CLC 57
See also CA 109; 118; 129; CANR 61; DLB 181; MTCW 1

Kivi, Aleksis 1834-1872 NCLC 30

Kizer, Carolyn (Ashley) 1925-CLC 15, 39, 80; DAM POET
See also CA 65-68; CAAS 5; CANR 24, 70; DLB 5, 169; MTCW 2

Klabund 1890-1928 TCLC 44
See also CA 162; DLB 66

Klappert, Peter 1942- CLC 57
See also CA 33-36R; DLB 5

Klein, A(braham) M(oses) 1909-1972CLC 19; DAB; DAC; DAM MST
See also CA 101; 37-40R; DLB 68

Klein, Norma 1938-1989 CLC 30
See also AAYA 2; CA 41-44R; 128; CANR 15, 37; CLR 2, 19; INT CANR-15; JRDA; MAICYA; SAAS 1; SATA 7, 57

Klein, T(heodore) E(ibon) D(onald) 1947-

CLC 34
See also CA 119; CANR 44, 75

Kleist, Heinrich von 1777-1811 NCLC 2, 37; DAM DRAM; SSC 22
See also DLB 90

Klima, Ivan 1931- CLC 56;DAM NOV
See also CA 25-28R; CANR 17, 50

Klimentov, Andrei Platonovich 1899-1951
See Platonov, Andrei
See also CA 108

Klinger, Friedrich Maximilianvon 1752-1831 NCLC 1
See also DLB 94

Klingsor the Magician
See Hartmann, Sadakichi

Klopstock, Friedrich Gottlieb 1724-1803 NCLC 11
See also DLB 97

Knapp, Caroline 1959- CLC 99
See also CA 154

Knebel, Fletcher 1911-1993 CLC 14
See also AITN 1; CA 1-4R; 140; CAAS 3; CANR 1, 36; SATA 36; SATA-Obit 75

Knickerbocker, Diedrich
See Irving, Washington

Knight, Etheridge 1931-1991CLC 40; BLC 2; DAM POET; PC 14
See also BW 1, 3; CA 21-24R; 133; CANR 23, 82; DLB 41; MTCW 2

Knight, Sarah Kemble 1666-1727 LC 7
See also DLB 24, 200

Knister, Raymond 1899-1932 TCLC 56
See also DLB 68

Knowles, John 1926- CLC 1, 4, 10, 26; DA; DAC; DAM MST, NOV
See also AAYA 10; CA 17-20R; CANR 40, 74, 76; CDALB 1968-1988; DLB 6; MTCW 1, 2; SATA 8, 89

Knox, Calvin M.
See Silverberg, Robert

Knox, John c. 1505-1572 LC 37
See also DLB 132

Knye, Cassandra
See Disch, Thomas M(ichael)

Koch, C(hristopher) J(ohn) 1932- CLC 42
See also CA 127

Koch, Christopher
See Koch, C(hristopher) J(ohn)

Koch, Kenneth 1925- CLC 5, 8, 44;DAM POET
See also CA 1-4R; CANR 6, 36, 57; DLB 5; INT CANR-36; MTCW 2; SATA 65

Kochanowski, Jan 1530-1584 LC 10

Kock, Charles Paul de 1794-1871 NCLC 16

Koda Shigeyuki 1867-1947
See Rohan, Koda
See also CA 121

Koestler, Arthur 1905-1983CLC 1, 3, 6, 8, 15, 33
See also CA 1-4R; 109; CANR 1, 33; CDBLB 1945-1960; DLBY 83; MTCW 1, 2

Kogawa, Joy Nozomi 1935- CLC 78; DAC; DAM MST, MULT
See also CA 101; CANR 19, 62; MTCW 2; SATA 99

Kohout, Pavel 1928- CLC 13
See also CA 45-48; CANR 3

Koizumi, Yakumo
See Hearn, (Patricio) Lafcadio (Tessima Carlos)

Kolmar, Gertrud 1894-1943 TCLC 40
See also CA 167

Komunyakaa, Yusef 1947-CLC 86, 94; BLCS
See also CA 147; DLB 120

9, 102; DLBD 1; MTCW 1, 2
Lewis, (Percy) Wyndham 1882(?)-1957**TCLC 2, 9; SSC 34**
See also CA 104; 157; DLB 15; MTCW 2
Lewisohn, Ludwig 1883-1955 **TCLC 19**
See also CA 107; DLB 4, 9, 28, 102
Lewton, Val 1904-1951 **TCLC 76**
Leyner, Mark 1956- **CLC 92**
See also CA 110; CANR 28, 53; MTCW 2
Lezama Lima, Jose 1910-1976**CLC 4, 10, 101; DAM MULT; HLCS 2**
See also CA 77-80; CANR 71; DLB 113; HW 1, 2
L'Heureux, John (Clarke) 1934- **CLC 52**
See also CA 13-16R; CANR 23, 45
Liddell, C. H.
See Kuttner, Henry
Lie, Jonas (Lauritz Idemil) 1833-1908(?) **TCLC 5**
See also CA 115
Lieber, Joel 1937-1971 **CLC 6**
See also CA 73-76; 29-32R
Lieber, Stanley Martin
See Lee, Stan
Lieberman, Laurence (James) 1935- **CLC 4, 36**
See also CA 17-20R; CANR 8, 36
Lieh Tzu fl. 7th cent. B.C.-5th cent. B.C. **CMLC 27**
Lieksman, Anders
See Haavikko, Paavo Juhani
Li Fei-kan 1904-
See Pa Chin
See also CA 105
Lifton, Robert Jay 1926- **CLC 67**
See also CA 17-20R; CANR 27, 78; INT CANR-27; SATA 66
Lightfoot, Gordon 1938- **CLC 26**
See also CA 109
Lightman, Alan P(aige) 1948- **CLC 81**
See also CA 141; CANR 63
Ligotti, Thomas (Robert) 1953-**CLC 44; SSC 16**
See also CA 123; CANR 49
Li Ho 791-817 **PC 13**
Liliencron, (Friedrich Adolf Axel) Detlevvon 1844-1909 **TCLC 18**
See also CA 117
Lilly, William 1602-1681 **LC 27**
Lima, Jose Lezama
See Lezama Lima, Jose
Lima Barreto, Afonso Henriquede 1881-1922 **TCLC 23**
See also CA 117
Limonov, Edward 1944- **CLC 67**
See also CA 137
Lin, Frank
See Atherton, Gertrude (Franklin Horn)
Lincoln, Abraham 1809-1865 **NCLC 18**
Lind, Jakov **CLC 1, 2, 4, 27, 82**
See also Landwirth, Heinz
See also CAAS 4
Lindbergh, Anne (Spencer) Morrow 1906- **CLC 82; DAM NOV**
See also CA 17-20R; CANR 16, 73; MTCW 1, 2; SATA 33
Lindsay, David 1878-1945 **TCLC 15**
See also CA 113
Lindsay, (Nicholas) Vachel 1879-1931 **TCLC 17; DA; DAC; DAM MST, POET; PC 23; WLC**
See also CA 114; 135; CANR 79; CDALB 1865-1917; DLB 54; SATA 40

Linke-Poot
See Doeblin, Alfred
Linney, Romulus 1930- **CLC 51**
See also CA 1-4R; CANR 40, 44, 79
Linton, Eliza Lynn 1822-1898 **NCLC 41**
See also DLB 18
Li Po 701-763 **CMLC 2**
Lipsius, Justus 1547-1606 **LC 16**
Lipsyte, Robert (Michael) 1938-**CLC 21; DA; DAC; DAM MST, NOV**
See also AAYA 7; CA 17-20R; CANR 8, 57; CLR 23; JRDA; MAICYA; SATA 5, 68
Lish, Gordon (Jay) 1934- **CLC 45;SSC 18**
See also CA 113; 117; CANR 79; DLB 130; INT 117
Lispector, Clarice 1925(?)-1977 **CLC 43; HLCS 2; SSC 34**
See also CA 139; 116; CANR 71; DLB 113; HW 2
Littell, Robert 1935(?)- **CLC 42**
See also CA 109; 112; CANR 64
Little, Malcolm 1925-1965
See Malcolm X
See also BW 1, 3; CA 125; 111; CANR 82; DA; DAB; DAC; DAM MST, MULT; MTCW 1, 2
Littlewit, Humphrey Gent.
See Lovecraft, H(oward) P(hillips)
Litwos
See Sienkiewicz, Henryk (Adam Alexander Pius)
Liu, E 1857-1909 **TCLC 15**
See also CA 115
Lively, Penelope (Margaret) 1933- **CLC 32, 50; DAM NOV**
See also CA 41-44R; CANR 29, 67, 79; CLR 7; DLB 14, 161, 207; JRDA; MAICYA; MTCW 1, 2; SATA 7, 60, 101
Livesay, Dorothy (Kathleen) 1909-**CLC 4, 15, 79; DAC; DAM MST, POET**
See also AITN 2; CA 25-28R; CAAS 8; CANR 36, 67; DLB 68; MTCW 1
Livy c. 59B.C.-c. 17 **CMLC 11**
See also DLB 211
Lizardi, Jose Joaquin Fernandez de 1776-1827 **NCLC 30**
Llewellyn, Richard
See Llewellyn Lloyd, Richard Dafydd Vivian
See also DLB 15
Llewellyn Lloyd, Richard Dafydd Vivian 1906-1983 **CLC 7, 80**
See also Llewellyn, Richard
See also CA 53-56; 111; CANR 7, 71; SATA 11; SATA-Obit 37
Llosa, (Jorge) Mario (Pedro) Vargas
See Vargas Llosa, (Jorge) Mario (Pedro)
Lloyd, Manda
See Mander, (Mary) Jane
Lloyd Webber, Andrew 1948-
See Webber, Andrew Lloyd
See also AAYA 1; CA 116; 149; DAM DRAM; SATA 56
Llull, Ramon c. 1235-c. 1316 **CMLC 12**
Lobb, Ebenezer
See Upward, Allen
Locke, Alain (Le Roy) 1886-1954 **TCLC 43; BLCS**
See also BW 1, 3; CA 106; 124; CANR 79; DLB 51
Locke, John 1632-1704 **LC 7, 35**
See also DLB 101
Locke-Elliott, Sumner
See Elliott, Sumner Locke

Lockhart, John Gibson 1794-1854 **NCLC 6**
See also DLB 110, 116, 144
Lodge, David (John) 1935-**CLC 36;DAM POP**
See also BEST 90:1; CA 17-20R; CANR 19, 53; DLB 14, 194; INT CANR-19; MTCW 1, 2
Lodge, Thomas 1558-1625 **LC 41**
Lodge, Thomas 1558-1625 **LC 41**
See also DLB 172
Loennbohm, Armas Eino Leopold 1878-1926
See Leino, Eino
See also CA 123
Loewinsohn, Ron(ald William) 1937-**CLC 52**
See also CA 25-28R; CANR 71
Logan, Jake
See Smith, Martin Cruz
Logan, John (Burton) 1923-1987 **CLC 5**
See also CA 77-80; 124; CANR 45; DLB 5
Lo Kuan-chung 1330(?)-1400(?) **LC 12**
Lombard, Nap
See Johnson, Pamela Hansford
London, Jack **TCLC 9, 15, 39; SSC 4; WLC**
See also London, John Griffith
See also AAYA 13; AITN 2; CDALB 1865-1917; DLB 8, 12, 78, 212; SATA 18
London, John Griffith 1876-1916
See London, Jack
See also CA 110; 119; CANR 73; DA; DAB; DAC; DAM MST, NOV; JRDA; MAICYA; MTCW 1, 2
Long, Emmett
See Leonard, Elmore (John, Jr.)
Longbaugh, Harry
See Goldman, William (W.)
Longfellow, Henry Wadsworth 1807-1882 **NCLC 2, 45; DA; DAB; DAC; DAM MST, POET; WLCS**
See also CDALB 1640-1865; DLB 1, 59; SATA 19
Longinus c. 1st cent. - **CMLC 27**
See also DLB 176
Longley, Michael 1939- **CLC 29**
See also CA 102; DLB 40
Longus fl. c. 2nd cent. - **CMLC 7**
Longway, A. Hugh
See Lang, Andrew
Lonnrot, Elias 1802-1884 **NCLC 53**
Lopate, Phillip 1943- **CLC 29**
See also CA 97-100; DLBY 80; INT 97-100
Lopez Portillo (y Pacheco), Jose 1920-**CLC 46**
See also CA 129; HW 1
Lopez y Fuentes, Gregorio 1897(?)-1966**CLC 32**
See also CA 131; HW 1
Lorca, Federico Garcia
See Garcia Lorca, Federico
Lord, Bette Bao 1938- **CLC 23**
See also BEST 90:3; CA 107; CANR 41, 79; INT 107; SATA 58
Lord Auch
See Bataille, Georges
Lord Byron
See Byron, George Gordon (Noel)
Lorde, Audre (Geraldine) 1934-1992**CLC 18, 71; BLC 2; DAM MULT, POET; PC 12**
See also BW 1, 3; CA 25-28R; 142; CANR 16, 26, 46, 82; DLB 41; MTCW 1, 2
Lord Houghton
See Milnes, Richard Monckton
Lord Jeffrey
See Jeffrey, Francis
Lorenzini, Carlo 1826-1890
See Collodi, Carlo

See also MAICYA; SATA 29, 100

Lorenzo, Heberto Padilla
See Padilla (Lorenzo), Heberto

Loris
See Hofmannsthal, Hugo von

Loti, Pierre   **TCLC 11**
See also Viaud, (Louis Marie) Julien
See also DLB 123

Lou, Henri
See Andreas-Salome, Lou

Louie, David Wong 1954-   **CLC 70**
See also CA 139

Louis, Father M.
See Merton, Thomas

Lovecraft, H(oward) P(hillips) 1890-1937
TCLC 4, 22; DAM POP; SSC 3
See also AAYA 14; CA 104; 133; MTCW 1, 2

Lovelace, Earl 1935-   **CLC 51**
See also BW 2; CA 77-80; CANR 41, 72; DLB
125; MTCW 1

Lovelace, Richard 1618-1657   **LC 24**
See also DLB 131

Lowell, Amy 1874-1925   **TCLC 1, 8; DAM**
POET; PC 13
See also CA 104; 151; DLB 54, 140; MTCW 2

Lowell, James Russell 1819-1891   **NCLC 2**
See also CDALB 1640-1865; DLB 1, 11, 64,
79, 189

Lowell, Robert (Traill Spence, Jr.) 1917-1977
CLC 1, 2, 3, 4, 5, 8, 9, 11, 15, 37; DA; DAB;
DAC; DAM MST, NOV; PC 3;WLC
See also CA 9-12R; 73-76; CABS 2; CANR 26,
60; CDALBS; DLB 5, 169;MTCW 1, 2

Lowenthal, Michael (Francis) 1969-**CLC 119**
See also CA 150

Lowndes, Marie Adelaide (Belloc) 1868-1947
TCLC 12
See also CA 107; DLB 70

Lowry, (Clarence) Malcolm 1909-1957**T C L C**
6, 40; SSC 31
See also CA 105; 131; CANR 62; CDBLB
1945-1960; DLB 15; MTCW 1, 2

Lowry, Mina Gertrude 1882-1966
See Loy, Mina
See also CA 113

Loxsmith, John
See Brunner, John (Kilian Houston)

Loy, Mina   **CLC 28; DAM POET; PC 16**
See also Lowry, Mina Gertrude
See also DLB 4, 54

Loyson-Bridet
See Schwob, Marcel (Mayer Andre)

Lucan 39-65   **CMLC 33**
See also DLB 211

Lucas, Craig 1951-   **CLC 64**
See also CA 137; CANR 71

Lucas, E(dward) V(errall) 1868-1938   **TCLC**
73
See also CA 176; DLB 98, 149, 153; SATA 20

Lucas, George 1944-   **CLC 16**
See also AAYA 1, 23; CA 77-80; CANR 30;
SATA 56

Lucas, Hans
See Godard, Jean-Luc

Lucas, Victoria
See Plath, Sylvia

Lucian c. 120-c. 180   **CMLC 32**
See also DLB 176

Ludlam, Charles 1943-1987   **CLC 46,50**
See also CA 85-88; 122; CANR 72

Ludlum, Robert 1927-**CLC 22, 43; DAM NOV,**
POP
See also AAYA 10; BEST 89:1, 90:3; CA 33-

36R; CANR 25, 41, 68; DLBY 82; MTCW
1, 2

Ludwig, Ken   **CLC 60**

Ludwig, Otto 1813-1865   **NCLC 4**
See also DLB 129

Lugones, Leopoldo 1874-1938   **TCLC 15;**
HLCS 2
See also CA 116; 131; HW 1

Lu Hsun 1881-1936   **TCLC 3; SSC 20**
See also Shu-Jen, Chou

Lukacs, George   **CLC 24**
See also Lukacs, Gyorgy (Szegeny von)

Lukacs, Gyorgy (Szegeny von) 1885-1971
See Lukacs, George
See also CA 101; 29-32R; CANR 62; MTCW 2

Luke, Peter (Ambrose Cyprian) 1919-1995
CLC 38
See also CA 81-84; 147; CANR 72; DLB 13

Lunar, Dennis
See Mungo, Raymond

Lurie, Alison 1926-   **CLC 4, 5, 18, 39**
See also CA 1-4R; CANR 2, 17, 50; DLB 2;
MTCW 1; SATA 46

Lustig, Arnost 1926-   **CLC 56**
See also AAYA 3; CA 69-72; CANR 47; SATA
56

Luther, Martin 1483-1546   **LC 9, 37**
See also DLB 179

Luxemburg, Rosa 1870(?)-1919   **TCLC 63**
See also CA 118

Luzi, Mario 1914-   **CLC 13**
See also CA 61-64; CANR 9, 70; DLB 128

Lyly, John 1554(?)-1606**LC 41; DAM DRAM;**
DC 7
See also DLB 62, 167

L'Ymagier
See Gourmont, Remy (-Marie-Charles) de

Lynch, B. Suarez
See Bioy Casares, Adolfo; Borges, Jorge Luis

Lynch, B. Suarez
See Bioy Casares, Adolfo

Lynch, David (K.) 1946-   **CLC 66**
See also CA 124; 129

Lynch, James
See Andreyev, Leonid (Nikolaevich)

Lynch Davis, B.
See Bioy Casares, Adolfo; Borges, Jorge Luis

Lyndsay, Sir David 1490-1555   **LC 20**

Lynn, Kenneth S(chuyler) 1923-   **CLC 50**
See also CA 1-4R; CANR 3, 27, 65

Lynx
See West, Rebecca

Lyons, Marcus
See Blish, James (Benjamin)

Lyre, Pinchbeck
See Sassoon, Siegfried (Lorraine)

Lytle, Andrew (Nelson) 1902-1995   **CLC 22**
See also CA 9-12R; 150; CANR 70; DLB 6;
DLBY 95

Lyttelton, George 1709-1773   **LC 10**

Maas, Peter 1929-   **CLC 29**
See also CA 93-96; INT 93-96; MTCW 2

Macaulay, Rose 1881-1958   **TCLC 7, 44**
See also CA 104; DLB 36

Macaulay, Thomas Babington 1800-1859
NCLC 42
See also CDBLB 1832-1890; DLB 32, 55

MacBeth, George (Mann) 1932-1992**CLC 2, 5,**
9
See also CA 25-28R; 136; CANR 61, 66; DLB
40; MTCW 1; SATA 4; SATA-Obit 70

MacCaig, Norman (Alexander) 1910-**CLC 36;**
DAB; DAM POET

See also CA 9-12R; CANR 3, 34; DLB 27

MacCarthy, Sir (Charles Otto) Desmond 1877-
1952   **TCLC 36**
See also CA 167

MacDiarmid, HughCLC 2, 4, 11, 19, 63; PC 9
See also Grieve, C(hristopher) M(urray)
See also CDBLB 1945-1960; DLB 20

MacDonald, Anson
See Heinlein, Robert A(nson)

Macdonald, Cynthia 1928-   **CLC 13, 19**
See also CA 49-52; CANR 4, 44; DLB 105

MacDonald, George 1824-1905   **TCLC 9**
See also CA 106; 137; CANR 80; DLB 18, 163,
178; MAICYA; SATA 33, 100

Macdonald, John
See Millar, Kenneth

MacDonald, John D(ann) 1916-1986 **CLC 3,**
27, 44; DAM NOV, POP
See also CA 1-4R; 121; CANR 1, 19, 60; DLB
8; DLBY 86; MTCW 1, 2

Macdonald, John Ross
See Millar, Kenneth

Macdonald, Ross   **CLC 1, 2, 3, 14, 34, 41**
See also Millar, Kenneth
See also DLBD 6

MacDougal, John
See Blish, James (Benjamin)

MacEwen, Gwendolyn (Margaret) 1941-1987
CLC 13, 55
See also CA 9-12R; 124; CANR 7, 22; DLB
53; SATA 50; SATA-Obit 55

Macha, Karel Hynek 1810-1846   **NCLC 46**

Machado (y Ruiz), Antonio 1875-1939**T C L C**
3
See also CA 104; 174; DLB 108; HW 2

Machado de Assis, Joaquim Maria 1839-1908
TCLC 10; BLC 2; HLCS 2; SSC 24
See also CA 107; 153

Machen, Arthur   **TCLC 4; SSC 20**
See also Jones, Arthur Llewellyn
See also DLB 36, 156, 178

Machiavelli, Niccolo 1469-1527**LC 8, 36; DA;**
DAB; DAC; DAM MST; WLCS

MacInnes, Colin 1914-1976   **CLC 4, 23**
See also CA 69-72; 65-68; CANR 21; DLB 14;
MTCW 1, 2

MacInnes, Helen (Clark) 1907-1985 **CLC 27,**
39; DAM POP
See also CA 1-4R; 117; CANR 1, 28, 58; DLB
87; MTCW 1, 2; SATA 22; SATA-Obit 44

Mackenzie, Compton (Edward Montague)
1883-1972   **CLC 18**
See also CA 21-22; 37-40R; CAP 2; DLB 34,
100

Mackenzie, Henry 1745-1831   **NCLC 41**
See also DLB 39

Mackintosh, Elizabeth 1896(?)-1952
See Tey, Josephine
See also CA 110

MacLaren, James
See Grieve, C(hristopher) M(urray)

Mac Laverty, Bernard 1942-   **CLC 31**
See also CA 116; 118; CANR 43; INT 118

MacLean, Alistair (Stuart) 1922(?)-1987**C L C**
3, 13, 50, 63; DAM POP
See also CA 57-60; 121; CANR 28, 61; MTCW
1; SATA 23; SATA-Obit 50

Maclean, Norman (Fitzroy) 1902-1990 **C L C**
78; DAM POP; SSC 13
See also CA 102; 132; CANR 49; DLB 206

MacLeish, Archibald 1892-1982**CLC 3, 8, 14,**
68; DAM POET
See also CA 9-12R; 106; CANR 33, 63;

CDALBS; DLB 4, 7, 45; DLBY 82; MTCW 1, 2

MacLennan, (John) Hugh 1907-1990 **CLC 2, 14, 92; DAC; DAM MST**
See also CA 5-8R; 142; CANR 33; DLB 68; MTCW 1, 2

MacLeod, Alistair 1936-**CLC 56; DAC; DAM MST**
See also CA 123; DLB 60; MTCW 2

Macleod, Fiona
See Sharp, William

MacNeice, (Frederick) Louis 1907-1963 **C L C 1, 4, 10, 53; DAB; DAM POET**
See also CA 85-88; CANR 61; DLB 10, 20; MTCW 1, 2

MacNeill, Dand
See Fraser, George MacDonald

Macpherson, James 1736-1796 **LC 29**
See also Ossian
See also DLB 109

Macpherson, (Jean) Jay 1931- **CLC 14**
See also CA 5-8R; DLB 53

MacShane, Frank 1927- **CLC 39**
See also CA 9-12R; CANR 3, 33; DLB 111

Macumber, Mari
See Sandoz, Mari(e Susette)

Madach, Imre 1823-1864 **NCLC 19**

Madden, (Jerry) David 1933- **CLC 5, 15**
See also CA 1-4R; CAAS 3; CANR 4, 45; DLB 6; MTCW 1

Maddern, Al(an)
See Ellison, Harlan (Jay)

Madhubuti, Haki R. 1942-**CLC 6, 73; BLC 2; DAM MULT; POET; PC 5**
See also Lee, Don L.
See also BW 2, 3; CA 73-76; CANR 24, 51, 73; DLB 5, 41; DLBD 8; MTCW 2

Maepenn, Hugh
See Kuttner, Henry

Maepenn, K. H.
See Kuttner, Henry

Maeterlinck, Maurice 1862-1949 **TCLC 3; DAM DRAM**
See also CA 104; 136; CANR 80; DLB 192; SATA 66

Maginn, William 1794-1842 **NCLC 8**
See also DLB 110, 159

Mahapatra, Jayanta 1928- **CLC 33;DAM MULT**
See also CA 73-76; CAAS 9; CANR 15, 33, 66

Mahfouz, Naguib (Abdel Aziz Al-Sabilgi) 1911(?)-
See Mahfuz, Najib
See also BEST 89:2; CA 128; CANR 55; DAM NOV; MTCW 1, 2

Mahfuz, Najib **CLC 52, 55**
See also Mahfouz, Naguib (Abdel Aziz Al-Sabilgi)
See also DLBY 88

Mahon, Derek 1941- **CLC 27**
See also CA 113; 128; DLB 40

Mailer, Norman 1923-**CLC 1, 2, 3, 4, 5, 8, 11, 14, 28, 39, 74, 111; DA; DAB; DAC; DAM MST, NOV, POP**
See also AITN 2; CA 9-12R; CABS 1; CANR 28, 74, 77; CDALB 1968-1988; DLB 2, 16, 28, 185; DLBD 3; DLBY 80, 83; MTCW 1, 2

Maillet, Antonine 1929- **CLC 54, 118; DAC**
See also CA 115; 120; CANR 46, 74, 77; DLB 60; INT 120; MTCW 2

Mais, Roger 1905-1955 **TCLC 8**
See also BW 1, 3; CA 105; 124; CANR 82; DLB

125; MTCW 1

Maistre, Joseph de 1753-1821 **NCLC 37**

Maitland, Frederic 1850-1906 **TCLC 65**

Maitland, Sara (Louise) 1950- **CLC 49**
See also CA 69-72; CANR 13, 59

Major, Clarence 1936-**CLC 3, 19, 48; BLC 2; DAM MULT**
See also BW 2, 3; CA 21-24R; CAAS 6; CANR 13, 25, 53, 82; DLB 33

Major, Kevin (Gerald) 1949- **CLC 26; DAC**
See also AAYA 16; CA 97-100; CANR 21, 38; CLR 11; DLB 60; INT CANR-21; JRDA; MAICYA; SATA 32, 82

Maki, James
See Ozu, Yasujiro

Malabaila, Damiano
See Levi, Primo

Malamud, Bernard 1914-1986**CLC 1, 2, 3, 5, 8, 9, 11, 18, 27, 44, 78, 85;DA; DAB; DAC; DAM MST, NOV, POP; SSC 15;WLC**
See also AAYA 16; CA 5-8R; 118; CABS 1; CANR 28, 62; CDALB 1941-1968; DLB 2, 28, 152; DLBY 80, 86; MTCW 1, 2

Malan, Herman
See Bosman, Herman Charles; Bosman, Herman Charles

Malaparte, Curzio 1898-1957 **TCLC 52**

Malcolm, Dan
See Silverberg, Robert

Malcolm X **CLC 82, 117; BLC 2; WLCS**
See also Little, Malcolm

Malherbe, Francois de 1555-1628 **LC 5**

Mallarme, Stephane 1842-1898 **NCLC 4, 41; DAM POET; PC 4**

Mallet-Joris, Francoise 1930- **CLC 11**
See also CA 65-68; CANR 17; DLB 83

Malley, Ern
See McAuley, James Phillip

Mallowan, Agatha Christie
See Christie, Agatha (Mary Clarissa)

Maloff, Saul 1922- **CLC 5**
See also CA 33-36R

Malone, Louis
See MacNeice, (Frederick) Louis

Malone, Michael (Christopher) 1942-**CLC 43**
See also CA 77-80; CANR 14, 32, 57

Malory, (Sir) Thomas 1410(?)-1471(?)**LC 11; DA; DAB; DAC; DAM MST; WLCS**
See also CDBLB Before 1660; DLB 146; SATA 59; SATA-Brief 33

Malouf, (George Joseph) David 1934-**CLC 28, 86**
See also CA 124; CANR 50, 76; MTCW 2

Malraux, (Georges-)Andre 1901-1976**CLC 1, 4, 9, 13, 15, 57; DAM NOV**
See also CA 21-22; 69-72; CANR 34, 58; CAP 2; DLB 72; MTCW 1, 2

Malzberg, Barry N(athaniel) 1939- **CLC 7**
See also CA 61-64; CAAS 4; CANR 16; DLB 8

Mamet, David (Alan) 1947-**CLC 9, 15, 34, 46, 91; DAM DRAM; DC 4**
See also AAYA 3; CA 81-84; CABS 3; CANR 15, 41, 67, 72; DLB 7; MTCW 1, 2

Mamoulian, Rouben (Zachary) 1897-1987 **CLC 16**
See also CA 25-28R; 124

Mandelstam, Osip (Emilievich) 1891(?)-1938(?) **TCLC 2, 6; PC 14**
See also CA 104; 150; MTCW 2

Mander, (Mary) Jane 1877-1949 **TCLC 31**
See also CA 162

Mandeville, John fl. 1350- **CMLC 19**
See also DLB 146

Mandiargues, Andre Pieyre de **CLC 41**
See also Pieyre de Mandiargues, Andre
See also DLB 83

Mandrake, Ethel Belle
See Thurman, Wallace (Henry)

Mangan, James Clarence 1803-1849**NCLC 27**

Maniere, J.-E.
See Giraudoux, (Hippolyte) Jean

Mankiewicz, Herman (Jacob) 1897-1953 **TCLC 85**
See also CA 120; 169; DLB 26

Manley, (Mary) Delariviere 1672(?)-1724 **L C 1, 42**
See also DLB 39, 80

Mann, Abel
See Creasey, John

Mann, Emily 1952- **DC 7**
See also CA 130; CANR 55

Mann, (Luiz) Heinrich 1871-1950 **TCLC 9**
See also CA 106; 164; DLB 66, 118

Mann, (Paul) Thomas 1875-1955 **TCLC 2, 8, 14, 21, 35, 44, 60; DA; DAB; DAC; DAM MST, NOV; SSC 5; WLC**
See also CA 104; 128; DLB 66; MTCW 1, 2

Mannheim, Karl 1893-1947 **TCLC 65**

Manning, David
See Faust, Frederick (Schiller)

Manning, Frederic 1887(?)-1935 **TCLC 25**
See also CA 124

Manning, Olivia 1915-1980 **CLC 5, 19**
See also CA 5-8R; 101; CANR 29; MTCW 1

Mano, D. Keith 1942- **CLC 2, 10**
See also CA 25-28R; CAAS 6; CANR 26, 57; DLB 6

Mansfield, KatherineTCLC 2, 8, 39; DAB; SSC 9, 23; WLC**
See also Beauchamp, Kathleen Mansfield
See also DLB 162

Manso, Peter 1940- **CLC 39**
See also CA 29-32R; CANR 44

Mantecon, Juan Jimenez
See Jimenez (Mantecon), Juan Ramon

Manton, Peter
See Creasey, John

Man Without a Spleen, A
See Chekhov, Anton (Pavlovich)

Manzoni, Alessandro 1785-1873 **NCLC 29**

Map, Walter 1140-1209 **CMLC 32**

Mapu, Abraham (ben Jekutiel) 1808-1867 **NCLC 18**

Mara, Sally
See Queneau, Raymond

Marat, Jean Paul 1743-1793 **LC 10**

Marcel, Gabriel Honore 1889-1973 **CLC 15**
See also CA 102; 45-48; MTCW 1, 2

March, William 1893-1954 **TCLC 96**

Marchbanks, Samuel
See Davies, (William) Robertson

Marchi, Giacomo
See Bassani, Giorgio

Margulies, Donald **CLC 76**

Marie de France c. 12th cent. - **CMLC 8; PC 22**
See also DLB 208

Marie de l'Incarnation 1599-1672 **LC 10**

Marier, Captain Victor
See Griffith, D(avid Lewelyn) W(ark)

Mariner, Scott
See Pohl, Frederik

Marinetti, Filippo Tommaso 1876-1944**TCLC 10**
See also CA 107; DLB 114

Marivaux, Pierre Carlet de Chamblain de 1688-

1763 **LC 4; DC 7**

Markandaya, Kamala **CLC 8, 38**
See also Taylor, Kamala (Purnaiya)

Markfield, Wallace 1926- **CLC 8**
See also CA 69-72; CAAS 3; DLB 2, 28

Markham, Edwin 1852-1940 **TCLC 47**
See also CA 160; DLB 54, 186

Markham, Robert
See Amis, Kingsley (William)

Marks, J
See Highwater, Jamake (Mamake)

Marks-Highwater, J
See Highwater, Jamake (Mamake)

Markson, David M(errill) 1927- **CLC 67**
See also CA 49-52; CANR 1

Marley, Bob **CLC 17**
See also Marley, Robert Nesta

Marley, Robert Nesta 1945-1981
See Marley, Bob
See also CA 107; 103

Marlowe, Christopher 1564-1593 **LC 22, 47;**
DA; DAB; DAC; DAM DRAM, MST; DC
1; WLC
See also CDBLB Before 1660; DLB 62

Marlowe, Stephen 1928-
See Queen, Ellery
See also CA 13-16R; CANR 6, 55

Marmontel, Jean-Francois 1723-1799 **LC 2**

Marquand, John P(hillips) 1893-1960 **CLC 2,**
10
See also CA 85-88; CANR 73; DLB 9, 102;
MTCW 2

Marques, Rene 1919-1979 **CLC 96; DAM**
MULT; HLC 2
See also CA 97-100; 85-88; CANR 78; DLB
113; HW 1, 2

Marquez, Gabriel (Jose) Garcia
See Garcia Marquez, Gabriel (Jose)

Marquis, Don(ald Robert Perry) 1878-1937
TCLC 7
See also CA 104; 166; DLB 11, 25

Marric, J. J.
See Creasey, John

Marryat, Frederick 1792-1848 **NCLC 3**
See also DLB 21, 163

Marsden, James
See Creasey, John

Marsh, (Edith) Ngaio 1899-1982 **CLC 7, 53;**
DAM POP
See also CA 9-12R; CANR 6, 58; DLB 77;
MTCW 1, 2

Marshall, Garry 1934- **CLC 17**
See also AAYA 3; CA 111; SATA 60

Marshall, Paule 1929- **CLC 27, 72; BLC 3;**
DAM MULT; SSC 3
See also BW 2, 3; CA 77-80; CANR 25, 73;
DLB 157; MTCW 1, 2

Marshallik
See Zangwill, Israel

Marsten, Richard
See Hunter, Evan

Marston, John 1576-1634 **LC 33; DAM DRAM**
See also DLB 58, 172

Martha, Henry
See Harris, Mark

Marti (y Perez), Jose (Julian) 1853-1895
NCLC 63; DAM MULT; HLC 2
See also HW 2

Martial c. 40-c. 104 **CMLC 35; PC 10**
See also DLB 211

Martin, Ken
See Hubbard, L(afayette) Ron(ald)

Martin, Richard

Martin, Steve 1945- **CLC 30**
See also CA 97-100; CANR 30; MTCW 1

Martin, Valerie 1948- **CLC 89**
See also BEST 90:2; CA 85-88; CANR 49

Martin, Violet Florence 1862-1915 **TCLC 51**

Martin, Webber
See Silverberg, Robert

Martindale, Patrick Victor
See White, Patrick (Victor Martindale)

Martin du Gard, Roger 1881-1958 **TCLC 24**
See also CA 118; DLB 65

Martineau, Harriet 1802-1876 **NCLC 26**
See also DLB 21, 55, 159, 163, 166, 190; YABC
2

Martines, Julia
See O'Faolain, Julia

Martinez, Enrique Gonzalez
See Gonzalez Martinez, Enrique

Martinez, Jacinto Benavente y
See Benavente (y Martinez), Jacinto

Martinez Ruiz, Jose 1873-1967
See Azorin; Ruiz, Jose Martinez
See also CA 93-96; HW 1

Martinez Sierra, Gregorio 1881-1947 **TCLC 6**
See also CA 115

Martinez Sierra, Maria (de la O'Le Jarraga)
1874-1974 **TCLC 6**
See also CA 115

Martinsen, Martin
See Follett, Ken(neth Martin)

Martinson, Harry (Edmund) 1904-1978 **C L C**
14
See also CA 77-80; CANR 34

Marut, Ret
See Traven, B.

Marut, Robert
See Traven, B.

Marvell, Andrew 1621-1678 **LC 4, 43; DA;**
DAB; DAC; DAM MST, POET; PC 10;
WLC
See also CDBLB 1660-1789; DLB 131

Marx, Karl (Heinrich) 1818-1883 **NCLC 17**
See also DLB 129

Masaoka Shiki **TCLC 18**
See also Masaoka Tsunenori

Masaoka Tsunenori 1867-1902
See Masaoka Shiki
See also CA 117

Masefield, John (Edward) 1878-1967 **CLC 11,**
47; DAM POET
See also CA 19-20; 25-28R; CANR 33; CAP 2;
CDBLB 1890-1914; DLB 10, 19, 153, 160;
MTCW 1, 2; SATA 19

Maso, Carole 19(?)- **CLC 44**
See also CA 170

Mason, Bobbie Ann 1940- **CLC 28, 43, 82; SSC**
4
See also AAYA 5; CA 53-56; CANR 11, 31,
58; CDALBS; DLB 173; DLBY 87; INT
CANR-31; MTCW 1, 2

Mason, Ernst
See Pohl, Frederik

Mason, Lee W.
See Malzberg, Barry N(athaniel)

Mason, Nick 1945- **CLC 35**

Mason, Tally
See Derleth, August (William)

Mass, William
See Gibson, William

Master Lao
See Lao Tzu

Masters, Edgar Lee 1868-1950 **TCLC 2, 25;**

DA; DAC; DAM MST, POET; PC 1;
WLCS
See also CA 104; 133; CDALB 1865-1917; DLB
54; MTCW 1, 2

Masters, Hilary 1928- **CLC 48**
See also CA 25-28R; CANR 13, 47

Mastrosimone, William 19(?)- **CLC 36**

Mathe, Albert
See Camus, Albert

Mather, Cotton 1663-1728 **LC 38**
See also CDALB 1640-1865; DLB 24, 30, 140

Mather, Increase 1639-1723 **LC 38**
See also DLB 24

Matheson, Richard Burton 1926- **CLC 37**
See also CA 97-100; DLB 8, 44; INT 97-100

Mathews, Harry 1930- **CLC 6, 52**
See also CA 21-24R; CAAS 6; CANR 18, 40

Mathews, John Joseph 1894-1979 **CLC 84;**
DAM MULT
See also CA 19-20; 142; CANR 45; CAP 2;
DLB 175; NNAL

Mathias, Roland (Glyn) 1915- **CLC 45**
See also CA 97-100; CANR 19, 41; DLB 27

Matsuo Basho 1644-1694 **PC 3**
See also DAM POET

Mattheson, Rodney
See Creasey, John

Matthews, Brander 1852-1929 **TCLC 95**
See also DLB 71, 78; DLBD 13

Matthews, Greg 1949- **CLC 45**
See also CA 135

Matthews, William (Procter, III) 1942-1997
CLC 40
See also CA 29-32R; 162; CAAS 18; CANR
12, 57; DLB 5

Matthias, John (Edward) 1941- **CLC 9**
See also CA 33-36R; CANR 56

Matthiessen, Peter 1927- **CLC 5, 7, 11, 32, 64;**
DAM NOV
See also AAYA 6; BEST 90:4; CA 9-12R;
CANR 21, 50, 73; DLB 6, 173; MTCW 1, 2;
SATA 27

Maturin, Charles Robert 1780(?)-1824 **N C L C**
6
See also DLB 178

Matute (Ausejo), Ana Maria 1925- **CLC 11**
See also CA 89-92; MTCW 1

Maugham, W. S.
See Maugham, W(illiam) Somerset

Maugham, W(illiam) Somerset 1874-1965
CLC 1, 11, 15, 67, 93; DA; DAB; DAC;
DAM DRAM, MST, NOV; SSC 8; WLC
See also CA 5-8R; 25-28R; CANR 40; CDBLB
1914-1945; DLB 10, 36, 77, 100, 162, 195;
MTCW 1, 2; SATA 54

Maugham, William Somerset
See Maugham, W(illiam) Somerset

Maupassant, (Henri Rene Albert) Guy de 1850-
1893 **NCLC 1, 42; DA; DAB; DAC; DAM**
MST; SSC 1; WLC
See also DLB 123

Maupin, Armistead 1944- **CLC 95; DAM POP**
See also CA 125; 130; CANR 58; INT 130;
MTCW 2

Maurhut, Richard
See Traven, B.

Mauriac, Claude 1914-1996 **CLC 9**
See also CA 89-92; 152; DLB 83

Mauriac, Francois (Charles) 1885-1970 **C L C**
4, 9, 56; SSC 24
See also CA 25-28; CAP 2; DLB 65; MTCW 1,
2

Mavor, Osborne Henry 1888-1951

See Bridie, James
See also CA 104

Maxwell, William (Keepers, Jr.) 1908-**CLC 19**
See also CA 93-96; CANR 54; DLBY 80; INT
93-96

May, Elaine 1932- **CLC 16**
See also CA 124; 142; DLB 44

Mayakovski, Vladimir (Vladimirovich) 1893-
1930 **TCLC 4, 18**
See also CA 104; 158; MTCW 2

Mayhew, Henry 1812-1887 **NCLC 31**
See also DLB 18, 55, 190

Mayle, Peter 1939(?)- **CLC 89**
See also CA 139; CANR 64

Maynard, Joyce 1953- **CLC 23**
See also CA 111; 129; CANR 64

Mayne, William (James Carter) 1928-**CLC 12**
See also AAYA 20; CA 9-12R; CANR 37, 80;
CLR 25; JRDA; MAICYA; SAAS 11; SATA
6, 68

Mayo, Jim
See L'Amour, Louis (Dearborn)

Maysles, Albert 1926- **CLC 16**
See also CA 29-32R

Maysles, David 1932- **CLC 16**

Mazer, Norma Fox 1931- **CLC 26**
See also AAYA 5; CA 69-72; CANR 12, 32,
66; CLR 23; JRDA; MAICYA; SAAS 1;
SATA 24, 67, 105

Mazzini, Guiseppe 1805-1872 **NCLC 34**

McAuley, James Phillip 1917-1976 **CLC 45**
See also CA 97-100

McBain, Ed
See Hunter, Evan

McBrien, William Augustine 1930- **CLC 44**
See also CA 107

McCaffrey, Anne (Inez) 1926- **CLC 17; DAM
NOV, POP**
See also AAYA 6; AITN 2; BEST 89:2; CA 25-
28R; CANR 15, 35, 55; CLR 49; DLB 8;
JRDA; MAICYA; MTCW 1, 2; SAAS 11;
SATA 8, 70

McCall, Nathan 1955(?)- **CLC 86**
See also BW 3; CA 146

McCann, Arthur
See Campbell, John W(ood, Jr.)

McCann, Edson
See Pohl, Frederik

McCarthy, Charles, Jr. 1933-
See McCarthy, Cormac
See also CANR 42, 69; DAM POP; MTCW 2

McCarthy, Cormac 1933- **CLC 4, 57, 59, 101**
See also McCarthy, Charles, Jr.
See also DLB 6, 143; MTCW 2

McCarthy, Mary (Therese) 1912-1989**CLC 1,
3, 5, 14, 24, 39, 59; SSC 24**
See also CA 5-8R; 129; CANR 16, 50, 64; DLB
2; DLBY 81; INT CANR-16; MTCW 1, 2

McCartney, (James) Paul 1942- **CLC 12, 35**
See also CA 146

McCauley, Stephen (D.) 1955- **CLC 50**
See also CA 141

McClure, Michael (Thomas) 1932-**CLC 6, 10**
See also CA 21-24R; CANR 17, 46, 77; DLB
16

McCorkle, Jill (Collins) 1958- **CLC 51**
See also CA 121; DLBY 87

McCourt, Frank 1930- **CLC 109**
See also CA 157

McCourt, James 1941- **CLC 5**
See also CA 57-60

McCourt, Malachy 1932- **CLC 119**

McCoy, Horace(Stanley) 1897-1955**TCLC 28**

See also CA 108; 155; DLB 9

McCrae, John 1872-1918 **TCLC 12**
See also CA 109; DLB 92

McCreigh, James
See Pohl, Frederik

McCullers, (Lula) Carson (Smith) 1917-1967
**CLC 1, 4, 10, 12, 48, 100; DA; DAB; DAC;
DAM MST, NOV; SSC 9, 24;WLC**
See also AAYA 21; CA 5-8R; 25-28R; CABS
1, 3; CANR 18; CDALB 1941-1968; DLB
2, 7, 173; MTCW 1, 2; SATA 27

McCulloch, John Tyler
See Burroughs, Edgar Rice

McCullough, Colleen 1938(?)- **CLC 27, 107;
DAM NOV, POP**
See also CA 81-84; CANR 17, 46, 67; MTCW
1, 2

McDermott, Alice 1953- **CLC 90**
See also CA 109; CANR 40

McElroy, Joseph 1930- **CLC 5, 47**
See also CA 17-20R

McEwan, Ian (Russell) 1948- **CLC 13, 66;
DAM NOV**
See also BEST 90:4; CA 61-64; CANR 14, 41,
69; DLB 14, 194; MTCW 1, 2

McFadden, David 1940- **CLC 48**
See also CA 104; DLB 60; INT 104

McFarland, Dennis 1950- **CLC 65**
See also CA 165

McGahern, John 1934- **CLC 5, 9, 48;SSC 17**
See also CA 17-20R; CANR 29, 68; DLB 14;
MTCW 1

McGinley, Patrick (Anthony) 1937- **CLC 41**
See also CA 120; 127; CANR 56; INT 127

McGinley, Phyllis 1905-1978 **CLC 14**
See also CA 9-12R; 77-80; CANR 19; DLB 11,
48; MTCW 2, 44; SATA-Obit 24

McGinniss, Joe 1942- **CLC 32**
See also AITN 2; BEST 89:2; CA 25-28R;
CANR 26, 70; DLB 185; INT CANR-26

McGivern, Maureen Daly
See Daly, Maureen

McGrath, Patrick 1950- **CLC 55**
See also CA 136; CANR 65

McGrath, Thomas (Matthew) 1916-1990**CLC
28, 59; DAM POET**
See also CA 9-12R; 132; CANR 6, 33; MTCW
1; SATA 41; SATA-Obit 66

McGuane, Thomas (Francis III) 1939-**CLC 3,
7, 18, 45**
See also AITN 2; CA 49-52; CANR 5, 24, 49;
DLB 2, 212; DLBY 80; INT CANR-24;
MTCW 1

McGuckian, Medbh 1950- **CLC 48; DAM
POET; PC 27**
See also CA 143; DLB 40

McHale, Tom 1942(?)-1982 **CLC 3, 5**
See also AITN 1; CA 77-80; 106

McIlvanney, William 1936- **CLC 42**
See also CA 25-28R; CANR 61; DLB 14, 207

McIlwraith, Maureen Mollie Hunter
See Hunter, Mollie
See also SATA 2

McInerney, Jay 1955-**CLC 34, 112;DAM POP**
See also AAYA 18; CA 116; 123; CANR 45,
68; INT 123; MTCW 2

McIntyre, Vonda N(eel) 1948- **CLC 18**
See also CA 81-84; CANR 17, 34, 69; MTCW
1

**McKay, ClaudeTCLC 7, 41; BLC 3; DAB;PC
2**
See also McKay, Festus Claudius
See also DLB 4, 45, 51, 117

McKay, Festus Claudius 1889-1948
See McKay, Claude
See also BW 1, 3; CA 104; 124; CANR 73; DA;
DAC; DAM MST, MULT, NOV, POET;
MTCW 1, 2; WLC

McKuen, Rod 1933- **CLC 1, 3**
See also AITN 1; CA 41-44R; CANR 40

McLoughlin, R. B.
See Mencken, H(enry) L(ouis)

McLuhan, (Herbert) Marshall 1911-1980
CLC 37, 83
See also CA 9-12R; 102; CANR 12, 34, 61;
DLB 88; INT CANR-12; MTCW 1, 2

McMillan, Terry (L.) 1951- **CLC 50, 61, 112;
BLCS; DAM MULT, NOV, POP**
See also AAYA 21; BW 2, 3; CA 140; CANR
60; MTCW 2

McMurtry, Larry (Jeff) 1936-**CLC 2, 3, 7, 11,
27, 44; DAM NOV, POP**
See also AAYA 15; AITN 2; BEST 89:2; CA 5-
8R; CANR 19, 43, 64; CDALB 1968-1988;
DLB 2, 143; DLBY 80, 87; MTCW 1, 2

McNally, T. M. 1961- **CLC 82**

McNally, Terrence 1939- **CLC 4, 7, 41, 91;
DAM DRAM**
See also CA 45-48; CANR 2, 56; DLB 7;
MTCW 2

McNamer, Deirdre 1950- **CLC 70**

McNeal, Tom **CLC 119**

McNeile, Herman Cyril 1888-1937
See Sapper
See also DLB 77

McNickle, (William) D'Arcy 1904-1977 **C L C
89; DAM MULT**
See also CA 9-12R; 85-88; CANR 5, 45; DLB
175, 212; NNAL; SATA-Obit 22

McPhee, John (Angus) 1931- **CLC 36**
See also BEST 90:1; CA 65-68; CANR 20, 46,
64, 69; DLB 185; MTCW 1, 2

McPherson, James Alan 1943- **CLC 19, 77;
BLCS**
See also BW 1, 3; CA 25-28R; CAAS 17;
CANR 24, 74; DLB 38; MTCW 1, 2

McPherson, William (Alexander) 1933- **C L C
34**
See also CA 69-72; CANR 28; INT CANR-28

Mead, George Herbert 1873-1958 **TCLC 89**

Mead, Margaret 1901-1978 **CLC 37**
See also AITN 1; CA 1-4R; 81-84; CANR 4;
MTCW 1, 2; SATA-Obit 20

Meaker, Marijane (Agnes) 1927-
See Kerr, M. E.
See also CA 107; CANR 37, 63; INT 107;
JRDA; MAICYA; MTCW 1; SATA 20,61, 99

Medoff, Mark (Howard) 1940- **CLC 6, 23;
DAM DRAM**
See also AITN 1; CA 53-56; CANR 5; DLB 7;
INT CANR-5

Medvedev, P. N.
See Bakhtin, Mikhail Mikhailovich

Meged, Aharon
See Megged, Aharon

Meged, Aron
See Megged, Aharon

Megged, Aharon 1920- **CLC 9**
See also CA 49-52; CAAS 13; CANR 1

Mehta, Ved (Parkash) 1934- **CLC 37**
See also CA 1-4R; CANR 2, 23, 69; MTCW 1

Melanter
See Blackmore, R(ichard) D(oddridge)

Melies, Georges 1861-1938 **TCLC 81**

Melikow, Loris
See Hofmannsthal, Hugo von

Melmoth, Sebastian
See Wilde, Oscar
Meltzer, Milton 1915- **CLC 26**
See also AAYA 8; CA 13-16R; CANR 38; CLR
13; DLB 61; JRDA; MAICYA; SAAS 1;
SATA 1, 50, 80
Melville, Herman 1819-1891 **NCLC 3, 12, 29,
45, 49; DA; DAB; DAC; DAM MST, NOV;
SSC 1, 17; WLC**
See also AAYA 25; CDALB 1640-1865; DLB
3, 74; SATA 59
Menander c. 342B.C.-c. 292B.C. **CMLC 9;
DAM DRAM; DC 3**
See also DLB 176
Menchu, Rigoberta 1959-
See also HLCS 2
Menchu, Rigoberta 1959-
See also CA 175; HLCS 2
Mencken, H(enry) L(ouis) 1880-1956 **TCLC
13**
See also CA 105; 125; CDALB 1917-1929;
DLB 11, 29, 63, 137; MTCW 1, 2
Mendelsohn, Jane 1965(?)- **CLC 99**
See also CA 154
Mercer, David 1928-1980 **CLC 5; DAM DRAM**
See also CA 9-12R; 102; CANR 23; DLB 13;
MTCW 1
Merchant, Paul
See Ellison, Harlan (Jay)
Meredith, George 1828-1909 **TCLC 17, 43;
DAM POET**
See also CA 117; 153; CANR 80; CDBLB 1832-
1890; DLB 18, 35, 57, 159
Meredith, William (Morris) 1919- **CLC 4, 13,
22, 55; DAM POET**
See also CA 9-12R; CAAS 14; CANR 6, 40;
DLB 5
Merezhkovsky, Dmitry Sergeyevich 1865-1941
TCLC 29
See also CA 169
Merimee, Prosper 1803-1870 **NCLC 6, 65; SSC
7**
See also DLB 119, 192
Merkin, Daphne 1954- **CLC 44**
See also CA 123
Merlin, Arthur
See Blish, James (Benjamin)
Merrill, James (Ingram) 1926-1995 **CLC 2, 3,
6, 8, 13, 18, 34, 91; DAM POET**
See also CA 13-16R; 147; CANR 10, 49, 63;
DLB 5, 165; DLBY 85; INT CANR-10;
MTCW 1, 2
Merriman, Alex
See Silverberg, Robert
Merriman, Brian 1747-1805 **NCLC 70**
Merritt, E. B.
See Waddington, Miriam
Merton, Thomas 1915-1968 **CLC 1, 3, 11, 34,
83; PC 10**
See also CA 5-8R; 25-28R; CANR 22, 53; DLB
48; DLBY 81; MTCW 1, 2
Merwin, W(illiam) S(tanley) 1927- **CLC 1, 2,
3, 5, 8, 13, 18, 45, 88; DAM POET**
See also CA 13-16R; CANR 15, 51; DLB 5,
169; INT CANR-15; MTCW 1, 2
Metcalf, John 1938- **CLC 37**
See also CA 113; DLB 60
Metcalf, Suzanne
See Baum, L(yman) Frank
Mew, Charlotte (Mary) 1870-1928 **TCLC 8**
See also CA 105; DLB 19, 135
Mewshaw, Michael 1943- **CLC 9**
See also CA 53-56; CANR 7, 47; DLBY 80

Meyer, June
See Jordan, June
Meyer, Lynn
See Slavitt, David R(ytman)
Meyer-Meyrink, Gustav 1868-1932
See Meyrink, Gustav
See also CA 117
Meyers, Jeffrey 1939- **CLC 39**
See also CA 73-76; CANR 54; DLB 111
Meynell, Alice (Christina Gertrude Thompson)
1847-1922 **TCLC 6**
See also CA 104; 177; DLB 19, 98
Meyrink, Gustav **TCLC 21**
See also Meyer-Meyrink, Gustav
See also DLB 81
Michaels, Leonard 1933- **CLC 6, 25; SSC 16**
See also CA 61-64; CANR 21, 62; DLB 130;
MTCW 1
Michaux, Henri 1899-1984 **CLC 8, 19**
See also CA 85-88; 114
Micheaux, Oscar (Devereaux) 1884-1951
TCLC 76
See also BW 3; CA 174; DLB 50
Michelangelo 1475-1564 **LC 12**
Michelet, Jules 1798-1874 **NCLC 31**
Michels, Robert 1876-1936 **TCLC 88**
Michener, James A(lbert) 1907(?)-1997 **C L C
1, 5, 11, 29, 60, 109; DAM NOV, POP**
See also AAYA 27; AITN 1; BEST 90:1; CA 5-
8R; 161; CANR 21, 45, 68; DLB 6; MTCW
1, 2
Mickiewicz, Adam 1798-1855 **NCLC 3**
Middleton, Christopher 1926- **CLC 13**
See also CA 13-16R; CANR 29, 54; DLB 40
Middleton, Richard (Barham) 1882-1911
TCLC 56
See also DLB 156
Middleton, Stanley 1919- **CLC 7, 38**
See also CA 25-28R; CAAS 23; CANR 21, 46,
81; DLB 14
Middleton, Thomas 1580-1627 **LC 33; DAM
DRAM, MST; DC 5**
See also DLB 58
Migueis, Jose Rodrigues 1901- **CLC 10**
Mikszath, Kalman 1847-1910 **TCLC 31**
See also CA 170
Miles, Jack **CLC 100**
Miles, Josephine (Louise) 1911-1985 **CLC 1, 2,
14, 34, 39; DAM POET**
See also CA 1-4R; 116; CANR 2, 55; DLB 48
Militant
See Sandburg, Carl (August)
Mill, John Stuart 1806-1873 **NCLC 11, 58**
See also CDBLB 1832-1890; DLB 55, 190
Millar, Kenneth 1915-1983 **CLC 14; DAM POP**
See also Macdonald, Ross
See also CA 9-12R; 110; CANR 16, 63; DLB
2; DLBD 6; DLBY 83; MTCW 1, 2
Millay, E. Vincent
See Millay, Edna St. Vincent
Millay, Edna St. Vincent 1892-1950 **TCLC 4,
49; DA; DAB; DAC; DAM MST, POET;
PC 6; WLCS**
See also CA 104; 130; CDALB 1917-1929;
DLB 45; MTCW 1, 2
Miller, Arthur 1915- **CLC 1, 2, 6, 10, 15, 26, 47,
78; DA; DAB; DAC; DAM DRAM, MST;
DC 1; WLC**
See also AAYA 15; AITN 1; CA 1-4R; CABS
3; CANR 2, 30, 54, 76; CDALB 1941-1968;
DLB 7; MTCW 1, 2
Miller, Henry (Valentine) 1891-1980 **CLC 1, 2,
4, 9, 14, 43, 84; DA; DAB; DAC; DAM

MST, NOV; WLC**
See also CA 9-12R; 97-100; CANR 33, 64;
CDALB 1929-1941; DLB 4, 9; DLBY 80;
MTCW 1, 2
Miller, Jason 1939(?)- **CLC 2**
See also AITN 1; CA 73-76; DLB 7
Miller, Sue 1943- **CLC 44; DAM POP**
See also BEST 90:3; CA 139; CANR 59; DLB
143
Miller, Walter M(ichael, Jr.) 1923- **CLC 4, 30**
See also CA 85-88; DLB 8
Millett, Kate 1934- **CLC 67**
See also AITN 1; CA 73-76; CANR 32, 53, 76;
MTCW 1, 2
Millhauser, Steven (Lewis) 1943- **CLC 21, 54,
109**
See also CA 110; 111; CANR 63; DLB 2; INT
111; MTCW 2
Millin, Sarah Gertrude 1889-1968 **CLC 49**
See also CA 102; 93-96
Milne, A(lan) A(lexander) 1882-1956 **TCLC 6,
88; DAB; DAC; DAM MST**
See also CA 104; 133; CLR 1, 26; DLB 10, 77,
100, 160; MAICYA; MTCW 1, 2; SATA 100;
YABC 1
Milner, Ron(ald) 1938- **CLC 56; BLC 3; DAM
MULT**
See also AITN 1; BW 1; CA 73-76; CANR 24,
81; DLB 38; MTCW 1
Milnes, Richard Monckton 1809-1885 **NCLC
61**
See also DLB 32, 184
Milosz, Czeslaw 1911- **CLC 5, 11, 22, 31, 56,
82; DAM MST, POET; PC 8; WLCS**
See also CA 81-84; CANR 23, 51; MTCW 1, 2
Milton, John 1608-1674 **LC 9, 43; DA; DAB;
DAC; DAM MST, POET; PC 19; WLC**
See also CDBLB 1660-1789; DLB 131, 151
Min, Anchee 1957- **CLC 86**
See also CA 146
Minehaha, Cornelius
See Wedekind, (Benjamin) Frank(lin)
Miner, Valerie 1947- **CLC 40**
See also CA 97-100; CANR 59
Minimo, Duca
See D'Annunzio, Gabriele
Minot, Susan 1956- **CLC 44**
See also CA 134
Minus, Ed 1938- **CLC 39**
Miranda, Javier
See Bioy Casares, Adolfo
Miranda, Javier
See Bioy Casares, Adolfo
Mirbeau, Octave 1848-1917 **TCLC 55**
See also DLB 123, 192
Miro (Ferrer), Gabriel (Francisco Victor) 1879-
1930 **TCLC 5**
See also CA 104
Mishima, Yukio 1925-1970 **CLC 2, 4, 6, 9, 27;
DC 1; SSC 4**
See also Hiraoka, Kimitake
See also DLB 182; MTCW 2
Mistral, Frederic 1830-1914 **TCLC 51**
See also CA 122
Mistral, Gabriela **TCLC 2; HLC 2**
See also Godoy Alcayaga, Lucila
See also MTCW 2
Mistry, Rohinton 1952- **CLC 71; DAC**
See also CA 141
Mitchell, Clyde
See Ellison, Harlan (Jay); Silverberg, Robert
Mitchell, James Leslie 1901-1935
See Gibbon, Lewis Grassic

See also CA 104; DLB 15

Mitchell, Joni 1943- **CLC 12**
See also CA 112

Mitchell, Joseph (Quincy) 1908-1996**CLC 98**
See also CA 77-80; 152; CANR 69; DLB 185;
DLBY 96

Mitchell, Margaret (Munnerlyn) 1900-1949
TCLC 11; DAM NOV, POP
See also AAYA 23; CA 109; 125; CANR 55;
CDALBS; DLB 9; MTCW 1, 2

Mitchell, Peggy
See Mitchell, Margaret (Munnerlyn)

Mitchell, S(ilas) Weir 1829-1914 **TCLC 36**
See also CA 165; DLB 202

Mitchell, W(illiam) O(rmond) 1914-1998**CLC
25; DAC; DAM MST**
See also CA 77-80; 165; CANR 15, 43; DLB
88

Mitchell, William 1879-1936 **TCLC 81**

Mitford, Mary Russell 1787-1855 **NCLC 4**
See also DLB 110, 116

Mitford, Nancy 1904-1973 **CLC 44**
See also CA 9-12R; DLB 191

Miyamoto, (Chujo) Yuriko 1899-1951 **T C L C
37**
See also CA 170, 174; DLB 180

Miyazawa, Kenji 1896-1933 **TCLC 76**
See also CA 157

Mizoguchi, Kenji 1898-1956 **TCLC 72**
See also CA 167

Mo, Timothy (Peter) 1950(?)- **CLC 46**
See also CA 117; DLB 194; MTCW 1

Modarressi, Taghi (M.) 1931- **CLC 44**
See also CA 121; 134; INT 134

Modiano, Patrick (Jean) 1945- **CLC 18**
See also CA 85-88; CANR 17, 40; DLB 83

Moerck, Paal
See Roelvaag, O(le) E(dvart)

Mofolo, Thomas (Mokopu) 1875(?)-1948
TCLC 22; BLC 3; DAM MULT
See also CA 121; 153; MTCW 2

Mohr, Nicholasa 1938-**CLC 12; DAM MULT;
HLC 2**
See also AAYA 8; CA 49-52; CANR 1, 32, 64;
CLR 22; DLB 145; HW 1, 2; JRDA; SAAS
8; SATA 8, 97

Mojtabai, A(nn) G(race) 1938- **CLC 5, 9, 15,
29**
See also CA 85-88

Moliere 1622-1673**LC 10, 28; DA; DAB; DAC;
DAM DRAM, MST; WLC**

Molin, Charles
See Mayne, William (James Carter)

Molnar, Ferenc 1878-1952 **TCLC 20;DAM
DRAM**
See also CA 109; 153

Momaday, N(avarre) Scott 1934- **CLC 2, 19,
85, 95; DA; DAB; DAC; DAM MST,
MULT, NOV, POP; PC 25; WLCS**
See also AAYA 11; CA 25-28R; CANR 14, 34,
68; CDALBS; DLB 143, 175; INT CANR-
14; MTCW 1, 2; NNAL; SATA 48; SATA-
Brief 30

Monette, Paul 1945-1995 **CLC 82**
See also CA 139; 147

Monroe, Harriet 1860-1936 **TCLC 12**
See also CA 109; DLB 54, 91

Monroe, Lyle
See Heinlein, Robert A(nson)

Montagu, Elizabeth 1720-1800 **NCLC 7**

Montagu, Mary (Pierrepont) Wortley 1689-
1762 **LC 9; PC 16**
See also DLB 95, 101

Montagu, W. H.
See Coleridge, Samuel Taylor

Montague, John (Patrick) 1929- **CLC 13, 46**
See also CA 9-12R; CANR 9, 69; DLB 40;
MTCW 1

Montaigne, Michel (Eyquem) de 1533-1592
LC 8; DA; DAB; DAC; DAM MST; WLC

Montale, Eugenio 1896-1981**CLC 7, 9, 18; PC
13**
See also CA 17-20R; 104; CANR 30; DLB 114;
MTCW 1

Montesquieu, Charles-Louis de Secondat 1689-
1755 **LC 7**

Montgomery, (Robert) Bruce 1921-1978
See Crispin, Edmund
See also CA 104

Montgomery, L(ucy) M(aud) 1874-1942
TCLC 51; DAC; DAM MST
See also AAYA 12; CA 108; 137; CLR 8; DLB
92; DLBD 14; JRDA; MAICYA; MTCW 2;
SATA 100; YABC 1

Montgomery, Marion H., Jr. 1925- **CLC 7**
See also AITN 1; CA 1-4R; CANR 3, 48; DLB
6

Montgomery, Max
See Davenport, Guy (Mattison, Jr.)

Montherlant, Henry (Milon) de 1896-1972
CLC 8, 19; DAM DRAM
See also CA 85-88; 37-40R; DLB 72; MTCW
1

Monty Python
See Chapman, Graham; Cleese, John
(Marwood); Gilliam, Terry (Vance); Idle,
Eric; Jones, Terence Graham Parry; Palin,
Michael (Edward)
See also AAYA 7

Moodie, Susanna (Strickland) 1803-1885
NCLC 14
See also DLB 99

Mooney, Edward 1951-
See Mooney, Ted
See also CA 130

Mooney, Ted **CLC 25**
See also Mooney, Edward

Moorcock, Michael (John) 1939-**CLC 5, 27, 58**
See also Bradbury, Edward P.
See also AAYA 26; CA 45-48; CAAS 5; CANR
2, 17, 38, 64; DLB 14; MTCW 1, 2; SATA
93

Moore, Brian 1921-1999**CLC 1, 3, 5, 7, 8, 19,
32, 90; DAB; DAC; DAM MST**
See also CA 1-4R; 174; CANR 1, 25, 42, 63;
MTCW 1, 2

Moore, Edward
See Muir, Edwin

Moore, G. E. 1873-1958 **TCLC 89**

Moore, George Augustus 1852-1933**TCLC 7;
SSC 19**
See also CA 104; 177; DLB 10, 18, 57, 135

Moore, Lorrie **CLC 39, 45, 68**
See also Moore, Marie Lorena

Moore, Marianne (Craig) 1887-1972**CLC 1, 2,
4, 8, 10, 13, 19, 47; DA; DAB; DAC; DAM
MST, POET; PC 4; WLCS**
See also CA 1-4R; 33-36R; CANR 3, 61;
CDALB 1929-1941; DLB 45; DLBD 7;
MTCW 1, 2; SATA 20

Moore, Marie Lorena 1957-
See Moore, Lorrie
See also CA 116; CANR 39

Moore, Thomas 1779-1852 **NCLC 6**
See also DLB 96, 144

Mora, Pat(ricia) 1942-

See also CA 129; CANR 57, 81; CLR 58; DAM
MULT; DLB 209; HLC 2; HW 1, 2; SATA
92

Morand, Paul 1888-1976 **CLC 41;SSC 22**
See also CA 69-72; DLB 65

Morante, Elsa 1918-1985 **CLC 8, 47**
See also CA 85-88; 117; CANR 35; DLB 177;
MTCW 1, 2

Moravia, Alberto 1907-1990**CLC 2, 7, 11, 27,
46; SSC 26**
See also Pincherle, Alberto
See also DLB 177; MTCW 2

More, Hannah 1745-1833 **NCLC 27**
See also DLB 107, 109, 116, 158

More, Henry 1614-1687 **LC 9**
See also DLB 126

More, Sir Thomas 1478-1535 **LC 10, 32**

Moreas, Jean **TCLC 18**
See also Papadiamantopoulos, Johannes

Morgan, Berry 1919- **CLC 6**
See also CA 49-52; DLB 6

Morgan, Claire
See Highsmith, (Mary) Patricia

Morgan, Edwin (George) 1920- **CLC 31**
See also CA 5-8R; CANR 3, 43; DLB 27

Morgan, (George) Frederick 1922- **CLC 23**
See also CA 17-20R; CANR 21

Morgan, Harriet
See Mencken, H(enry) L(ouis)

Morgan, Jane
See Cooper, James Fenimore

Morgan, Janet 1945- **CLC 39**
See also CA 65-68

Morgan, Lady 1776(?)-1859 **NCLC 29**
See also DLB 116, 158

Morgan, Robin (Evonne) 1941- **CLC 2**
See also CA 69-72; CANR 29, 68; MTCW 1;
SATA 80

Morgan, Scott
See Kuttner, Henry

Morgan, Seth 1949(?)-1990 **CLC 65**
See also CA 132

Morgenstern, Christian 1871-1914 **TCLC 8**
See also CA 105

Morgenstern, S.
See Goldman, William (W.)

Moricz, Zsigmond 1879-1942 **TCLC 33**
See also CA 165

Morike, Eduard (Friedrich) 1804-1875**NCLC
10**
See also DLB 133

Moritz, Karl Philipp 1756-1793 **LC 2**
See also DLB 94

Morland, Peter Henry
See Faust, Frederick (Schiller)

Morley, Christopher (Darlington) 1890-1957
TCLC 87
See also CA 112; DLB 9

Morren, Theophil
See Hofmannsthal, Hugo von

Morris, Bill 1952- **CLC 76**

Morris, Julian
See West, Morris L(anglo)

Morris, Steveland Judkins 1950(?)-
See Wonder, Stevie
See also CA 111

Morris, William 1834-1896 **NCLC 4**
See also CDBLB 1832-1890; DLB 18, 35, 57,
156, 178, 184

Morris, Wright 1910-1998**CLC 1, 3, 7, 18, 37**
See also CA 9-12R; 167; CANR 21, 81; DLB
2, 206; DLBY 81; MTCW 1, 2

Morrison, Arthur 1863-1945 **TCLC 72**

See also CA 120; 157; DLB 70, 135, 197

Morrison, Chloe Anthony Wofford
See Morrison, Toni

Morrison, James Douglas 1943-1971
See Morrison, Jim
See also CA 73-76; CANR 40

Morrison, Jim   **CLC 17**
See also Morrison, James Douglas

Morrison, Toni 1931-**CLC 4, 10, 22, 55, 81, 87;**
    BLC 3; DA; DAB; DAC; DAM MST,
    MULT, NOV, POP
See also AAYA 1, 22; BW 2, 3; CA 29-32R;
    CANR 27, 42, 67; CDALB 1968-1988; DLB
    6, 33, 143; DLBY 81; MTCW 1; SATA 57

Morrison, Van 1945-   **CLC 21**
See also CA 116; 168

Morrissy, Mary 1958-   **CLC 99**

Mortimer, John (Clifford) 1923- **CLC 28, 43;**
    DAM DRAM, POP
See also CA 13-16R; CANR 21, 69; CDBLB
    1960 to Present; DLB 13; INT CANR-21;
    MTCW 1, 2

Mortimer, Penelope (Ruth) 1918-   **CLC 5**
See also CA 57-60; CANR 45

Morton, Anthony
See Creasey, John

Mosca, Gaetano 1858-1941   **TCLC 75**

Mosher, Howard Frank 1943-   **CLC 62**
See also CA 139; CANR 65

Mosley, Nicholas 1923-   **CLC 43, 70**
See also CA 69-72; CANR 41, 60; DLB 14, 207

Mosley, Walter 1952- **CLC 97; BLCS; DAM**
    MULT, POP
See also AAYA 17; BW 2; CA 142; CANR 57;
    MTCW 2

Moss, Howard 1922-1987 **CLC 7, 14, 45, 50;**
    DAM POET
See also CA 1-4R; 123; CANR 1, 44; DLB 5

Mossgiel, Rab
See Burns, Robert

Motion, Andrew (Peter) 1952-   **CLC 47**
See also CA 146; DLB 40

Motley, Willard (Francis) 1909-1965 **CLC 18**
See also BW 1; CA 117; 106; DLB 76, 143

Motoori, Norinaga 1730-1801   **NCLC 45**

Mott, Michael (Charles Alston) 1930-**CLC 15,**
    34
See also CA 5-8R; CAAS 7; CANR 7, 29

Mountain Wolf Woman 1884-1960   **CLC 92**
See also CA 144; NNAL

Moure, Erin 1955-   **CLC 88**
See also CA 113; DLB 60

Mowat, Farley (McGill) 1921-**CLC 26; DAC;**
    DAM MST
See also AAYA 1; CA 1-4R; CANR 4, 24, 42,
    68; CLR 20; DLB 68; INT CANR-24; JRDA;
    MAICYA; MTCW 1, 2; SATA 3, 55

Mowatt, Anna Cora 1819-1870   **NCLC 74**

Moyers, Bill 1934-   **CLC 74**
See also AITN 2; CA 61-64; CANR 31, 52

Mphahlele, Es'kia
See Mphahlele, Ezekiel
See also DLB 125

Mphahlele, Ezekiel 1919-   **CLC 25; BLC 3;**
    DAM MULT
See also Mphahlele, Es'kia
See also BW 2, 3; CA 81-84; CANR 26, 76;
    MTCW 2

Mqhayi, S(amuel) E(dward) K(rune Loliwe)
    1875-1945TCLC 25; BLC 3;DAM MULT
See also CA 153

Mrozek, Slawomir 1930-   **CLC 3, 13**
See also CA 13-16R; CAAS 10; CANR 29;

MTCW 1

Mrs. Belloc-Lowndes
See Lowndes, Marie Adelaide (Belloc)

Mtwa, Percy (?)-   **CLC 47**

Mueller, Lisel 1924-   **CLC 13, 51**
See also CA 93-96; DLB 105

Muir, Edwin 1887-1959   **TCLC 2, 87**
See also CA 104; DLB 20, 100, 191

Muir, John 1838-1914   **TCLC 28**
See also CA 165; DLB 186

Mujica Lainez, Manuel 1910-1984   **CLC 31**
See also Lainez, Manuel Mujica
See also CA 81-84; 112; CANR 32; HW 1

Mukherjee, Bharati 1940-**CLC 53, 115; DAM**
    NOV
See also BEST 89:2; CA 107; CANR 45, 72;
    DLB 60; MTCW 1, 2

Muldoon, Paul 1951-**CLC 32, 72;DAM POET**
See also CA 113; 129; CANR 52; DLB 40; INT
    129

Mulisch, Harry 1927-   **CLC 42**
See also CA 9-12R; CANR 6, 26, 56

Mull, Martin 1943-   **CLC 17**
See also CA 105

Muller, Wilhelm   **NCLC 73**

Mulock, Dinah Maria
See Craik, Dinah Maria (Mulock)

Munford, Robert 1737(?)-1783   **LC 5**
See also DLB 31

Mungo, Raymond 1946-   **CLC 72**
See also CA 49-52; CANR 2

Munro, Alice 1931-   **CLC 6, 10, 19, 50, 95;**
    DAC; DAM MST, NOV; SSC 3; WLCS
See also AITN 2; CA 33-36R; CANR 33, 53,
    75; DLB 53; MTCW 1, 2; SATA 29

Munro, H(ector) H(ugh) 1870-1916
See Saki
See also CA 104; 130; CDBLB 1890-1914; DA;
    DAB; DAC; DAM MST, NOV; DLB 34, 162;
    MTCW 1, 2; WLC

Murdoch, (Jean) Iris 1919-**CLC 1, 2, 3, 4, 6, 8,**
    11, 15, 22, 31, 51; DAB; DAC; DAM MST,
    NOV
See also CA 13-16R; CANR 8, 43, 68; CDBLB
    1960 to Present; DLB 14, 194; INT CANR-
    8; MTCW 1, 2

Murfree, Mary Noailles 1850-1922   **SSC 22**
See also CA 122; 176; DLB 12, 74

Murnau, Friedrich Wilhelm
See Plumpe, Friedrich Wilhelm

Murphy, Richard 1927-   **CLC 41**
See also CA 29-32R; DLB 40

Murphy, Sylvia 1937-   **CLC 34**
See also CA 121

Murphy, Thomas (Bernard) 1935-   **CLC 51**
See also CA 101

Murray, Albert L. 1916-   **CLC 73**
See also BW 2; CA 49-52; CANR 26, 52, 78;
    DLB 38

Murray, Judith Sargent 1751-1820 **NCLC 63**
See also DLB 37, 200

Murray, Les(lie) A(llan) 1938-**CLC 40; DAM**
    POET
See also CA 21-24R; CANR 11, 27, 56

Murry, J. Middleton
See Murry, John Middleton

Murry, John Middleton 1889-1957 **TCLC 16**
See also CA 118; DLB 149

Musgrave, Susan 1951-   **CLC 13, 54**
See also CA 69-72; CANR 45

Musil, Robert (Edler von) 1880-1942 **T C L C**
    12, 68; SSC 18
See also CA 109; CANR 55; DLB 81, 124;

MTCW 2

Muske, Carol 1945-   **CLC 90**
See also Muske-Dukes, Carol (Anne)

Muske-Dukes, Carol (Anne) 1945-
See Muske, Carol
See also CA 65-68; CANR 32, 70

Musset, (Louis Charles) Alfred de 1810-1857
    NCLC 7
See also DLB 192

Mussolini, Benito (Amilcare Andrea) 1883-1945
    TCLC 96
See also CA 116

My Brother's Brother
See Chekhov, Anton (Pavlovich)

Myers, L(eopold) H(amilton) 1881-1944
    TCLC 59
See also CA 157; DLB 15

Myers, Walter Dean 1937-   **CLC 35; BLC 3;**
    DAM MULT, NOV
See also AAYA 4, 23; BW 2; CA 33-36R;
    CANR 20, 42, 67; CLR 4, 16, 35; DLB 33;
    INT CANR-20; JRDA; MAICYA; MTCW 2;
    SAAS 2; SATA 41, 71, 109; SATA-Brief 27

Myers, Walter M.
See Myers, Walter Dean

Myles, Symon
See Follett, Ken(neth Martin)

Nabokov, Vladimir (Vladimirovich) 1899-1977
    CLC 1, 2, 3, 6, 8, 11, 15, 23, 44, 46, 64;
    DA; DAB; DAC; DAM MST, NOV; SSC
    11; WLC
See also CA 5-8R; 69-72; CANR 20; CDALB
    1941-1968; DLB 2; DLBD 3; DLBY 80, 91;
    MTCW 1, 2

Nagai Kafu 1879-1959   **TCLC 51**
See also Nagai Sokichi
See also DLB 180

Nagai Sokichi 1879-1959
See Nagai Kafu
See also CA 117

Nagy, Laszlo 1925-1978   **CLC 7**
See also CA 129; 112

Naidu, Sarojini 1879-1943   **TCLC 80**

Naipaul, Shiva(dhar Srinivasa) 1945-1985
    CLC 32, 39; DAM NOV
See also CA 110; 112; 116; CANR 33; DLB
    157; DLBY 85; MTCW 1, 2

Naipaul, V(idiadhar) S(urajprasad) 1932-
    CLC 4, 7, 9, 13, 18, 37, 105; DAB; DAC;
    DAM MST, NOV
See also CA 1-4R; CANR 1, 33, 51; CDBLB
    1960 to Present; DLB 125, 204, 206; DLBY
    85; MTCW 1, 2

Nakos, Lilika 1899(?)-   **CLC 29**

Narayan, R(asipuram) K(rishnaswami) 1906-
    CLC 7, 28, 47, 121; DAM NOV; SSC 25
See also CA 81-84; CANR 33, 61; MTCW 1,
    2; SATA 62

Nash, (Frediric) Ogden 1902-1971   **CLC 23;**
    DAM POET; PC 21
See also CA 13-14; 29-32R; CANR 34, 61; CAP
    1; DLB 11; MAICYA; MTCW 1,2; SATA 2,
    46

Nashe, Thomas 1567-1601(?)   **LC 41**
See also DLB 167

Nashe, Thomas 1567-1601   **LC 41**

Nathan, Daniel
See Dannay, Frederic

Nathan, George Jean 1882-1958   **TCLC 18**
See also Hatteras, Owen
See also CA 114; 169; DLB 137

Natsume, Kinnosuke 1867-1916
See Natsume, Soseki

See also CA 104

Natsume, Soseki 1867-1916   **TCLC 2, 10**
See also Natsume, Kinnosuke
See also DLB 180

Natti, (Mary) Lee 1919-
See Kingman, Lee
See also CA 5-8R; CANR 2

Naylor, Gloria 1950-**CLC 28, 52; BLC 3; DA; DAC; DAM MST, MULT, NOV, POP; WLCS**
See also AAYA 6; BW 2, 3; CA 107; CANR 27, 51, 74; DLB 173; MTCW 1, 2

Neihardt, John Gneisenau 1881-1973**CLC 32**
See also CA 13-14; CANR 65; CAP 1; DLB 9, 54

Nekrasov, Nikolai Alekseevich 1821-1878 **NCLC 11**

Nelligan, Emile 1879-1941   **TCLC 14**
See also CA 114; DLB 92

Nelson, Willie 1933-   **CLC 17**
See also CA 107

Nemerov, Howard (Stanley) 1920-1991**CLC 2, 6, 9, 36; DAM POET; PC 24**
See also CA 1-4R; 134; CABS 2; CANR 1, 27, 53; DLB 5, 6; DLBY 83; INT CANR-27; MTCW 1, 2

Neruda, Pablo 1904-1973**CLC 1, 2, 5, 7, 9, 28, 62; DA; DAB; DAC; DAM MST, MULT, POET; HLC 2; PC 4; WLC**
See also CA 19-20; 45-48; CAP 2; HW 1; MTCW 1, 2

Nerval, Gerard de 1808-1855**NCLC 1, 67; PC 13; SSC 18**

Nervo, (Jose) Amado (Ruiz de) 1870-1919 **TCLC 11; HLCS 2**
See also CA 109; 131; HW 1

Nessi, Pio Baroja y
See Baroja (y Nessi), Pio

Nestroy, Johann 1801-1862   **NCLC 42**
See also DLB 133

Netterville, Luke
See O'Grady, Standish (James)

Neufeld, John (Arthur) 1938-   **CLC 17**
See also AAYA 11; CA 25-28R; CANR 11, 37, 56; CLR 52; MAICYA; SAAS 3; SATA 6, 81

Neville, Emily Cheney 1919-   **CLC 12**
See also CA 5-8R; CANR 3, 37; JRDA; MAICYA; SAAS 2; SATA 1

Newbound, Bernard Slade 1930-
See Slade, Bernard
See also CA 81-84; CANR 49; DAM DRAM

Newby, P(ercy) H(oward) 1918-1997 **CLC 2, 13; DAM NOV**
See also CA 5-8R; 161; CANR 32, 67; DLB 15; MTCW 1

Newlove, Donald 1928-   **CLC 6**
See also CA 29-32R; CANR 25

Newlove, John (Herbert) 1938-   **CLC 14**
See also CA 21-24R; CANR 9, 25

Newman, Charles 1938-   **CLC 2, 8**
See also CA 21-24R

Newman, Edwin (Harold) 1919-   **CLC 14**
See also AITN 1; CA 69-72; CANR 5

Newman, John Henry 1801-1890 **NCLC 38**
See also DLB 18, 32, 55

Newton, (Sir)Isaac 1642-1727   **LC 35, 52**

Newton, Suzanne 1936-   **CLC 35**
See also CA 41-44R; CANR 14; JRDA; SATA 5, 77

Nexo, Martin Andersen 1869-1954 **TCLC 43**

Nezval, Vitezslav 1900-1958   **TCLC 44**
See also CA 123

Ng, Fae Myenne 1957(?)-   **CLC 81**
See also CA 146

Ngema, Mbongeni 1955-   **CLC 57**
See also BW 2; CA 143

Ngugi, James T(hiong'o)   **CLC 3, 7, 13**
See also Ngugi wa Thiong'o

Ngugi wa Thiong'o 1938-   **CLC 36; BLC 3; DAM MULT, NOV**
See also Ngugi, James T(hiong'o)
See also BW 2; CA 81-84; CANR 27, 58; DLB 125; MTCW 1, 2

Nichol, B(arrie) P(hillip) 1944-1988 **CLC 18**
See also CA 53-56; DLB 53; SATA 66

Nichols, John (Treadwell) 1940-   **CLC 38**
See also CA 9-12R; CAAS 2; CANR 6, 70; DLBY 82

Nichols, Leigh
See Koontz, Dean R(ay)

Nichols, Peter (Richard) 1927- **CLC 5, 36, 65**
See also CA 104; CANR 33; DLB 13; MTCW 1

Nicolas, F. R. E.
See Freeling, Nicolas

Niedecker, Lorine 1903-1970   **CLC 10, 42; DAM POET**
See also CA 25-28; CAP 2; DLB 48

Nietzsche, Friedrich (Wilhelm) 1844-1900 **TCLC 10, 18, 55**
See also CA 107; 121; DLB 129

Nievo, Ippolito 1831-1861   **NCLC 22**

Nightingale, Anne Redmon 1943-
See Redmon, Anne
See also CA 103

Nightingale, Florence 1820-1910   **TCLC 85**
See also DLB 166

Nik. T. O.
See Annensky, Innokenty (Fyodorovich)

Nin, Anais 1903-1977 **CLC 1, 4, 8, 11, 14, 60; DAM NOV, POP; SSC 10**
See also AITN 2; CA 13-16R; 69-72; CANR 22, 53; DLB 2, 4, 152; MTCW 1, 2

Nishida, Kitaro 1870-1945   **TCLC 83**

Nishiwaki, Junzaburo 1894-1982   **PC 15**
See also CA 107

Nissenson, Hugh 1933-   **CLC 4, 9**
See also CA 17-20R; CANR 27; DLB 28

Niven, Larry   **CLC 8**
See also Niven, Laurence Van Cott
See also AAYA 27; DLB 8

Niven, Laurence Van Cott 1938-
See Niven, Larry
See also CA 21-24R; CAAS 12; CANR 14, 44, 66; DAM POP; MTCW 1, 2; SATA 95

Nixon, Agnes Eckhardt 1927-   **CLC 21**
See also CA 110

Nizan, Paul 1905-1940   **TCLC 40**
See also CA 161; DLB 72

Nkosi, Lewis 1936-   **CLC 45; BLC 3; DAM MULT**
See also BW 1, 3; CA 65-68; CANR 27, 81; DLB 157

Nodier, (Jean) Charles (Emmanuel) 1780-1844 **NCLC 19**
See also DLB 119

Noguchi, Yone 1875-1947   **TCLC 80**

Nolan, Christopher 1965-   **CLC 58**
See also CA 111

Noon, Jeff 1957-   **CLC 91**
See also CA 148

Norden, Charles
See Durrell, Lawrence (George)

Nordhoff, Charles (Bernard) 1887-1947 **TCLC 23**

See also CA 108; DLB 9; SATA 23

Norfolk, Lawrence 1963-   **CLC 76**
See also CA 144

Norman, Marsha 1947-**CLC 28; DAM DRAM; DC 8**
See also CA 105; CABS 3; CANR 41; DLBY 84

Normyx
See Douglas, (George) Norman

Norris, Frank 1870-1902   **SSC 28**
See also Norris, (Benjamin) Frank(lin, Jr.)
See also CDALB 1865-1917; DLB 12, 71, 186

Norris, (Benjamin) Frank(lin, Jr.) 1870-1902 **TCLC 24**
See also Norris, Frank
See also CA 110; 160

Norris, Leslie 1921-   **CLC 14**
See also CA 11-12; CANR 14; CAP 1; DLB 27

North, Andrew
See Norton, Andre

North, Anthony
See Koontz, Dean R(ay)

North, Captain George
See Stevenson, Robert Louis (Balfour)

North, Milou
See Erdrich, Louise

Northrup, B. A.
See Hubbard, L(afayette) Ron(ald)

North Staffs
See Hulme, T(homas) E(rnest)

Norton, Alice Mary
See Norton, Andre
See also MAICYA; SATA 1, 43

Norton, Andre 1912-   **CLC 12**
See also Norton, Alice Mary
See also AAYA 14; CA 1-4R; CANR 68; CLR 50; DLB 8, 52; JRDA; MTCW 1; SATA 91

Norton, Caroline 1808-1877   **NCLC 47**
See also DLB 21, 159, 199

Norway, Nevil Shute 1899-1960
See Shute, Nevil
See also CA 102; 93-96; MTCW 2

Norwid, Cyprian Kamil 1821-1883 **NCLC 17**

Nosille, Nabrah
See Ellison, Harlan (Jay)

Nossack, Hans Erich 1901-1978   **CLC 6**
See also CA 93-96; 85-88; DLB 69

Nostradamus 1503-1566   **LC 27**

Nosu, Chuji
See Ozu, Yasujiro

Notenburg, Eleanora (Genrikhovna) von
See Guro, Elena

Nova, Craig 1945-   **CLC 7, 31**
See also CA 45-48; CANR 2, 53

Novak, Joseph
See Kosinski, Jerzy (Nikodem)

Novalis 1772-1801   **NCLC 13**
See also DLB 90

Novis, Emile
See Weil, Simone (Adolphine)

Nowlan, Alden (Albert) 1933-1983 **CLC 15; DAC; DAM MST**
See also CA 9-12R; CANR 5; DLB 53

Noyes, Alfred 1880-1958   **TCLC 7;PC 27**
See also CA 104; DLB 20

Nunn, Kem   **CLC 34**
See also CA 159

Nye, Robert 1939-   **CLC 13, 42;DAM NOV**
See also CA 33-36R; CANR 29, 67; DLB 14; MTCW 1; SATA 6

Nyro, Laura 1947-   **CLC 17**

Oates, Joyce Carol 1938-**CLC 1, 2, 3, 6, 9, 11, 15, 19, 33, 52, 108; DA; DAB; DAC; DAM**

MST, NOV, POP; SSC 6;WLC
See also AAYA 15; AITN 1; BEST 89:2; CA 5-
8R; CANR 25, 45, 74; CDALB 1968-1988;
DLB 2, 5, 130; DLBY 81; INT CANR-25;
MTCW 1, 2

O'Brien, Darcy 1939-1998 **CLC 11**
See also CA 21-24R; 167; CANR 8, 59

O'Brien, E. G.
See Clarke, Arthur C(harles)

O'Brien, Edna 1936- **CLC 3, 5, 8, 13, 36, 65,**
116; DAM NOV; SSC 10
See also CA 1-4R; CANR 6, 41, 65; CDBLB
1960 to Present; DLB 14; MTCW 1, 2

O'Brien, Fitz-James 1828-1862 **NCLC 21**
See also DLB 74

O'Brien, Flann **CLC 1, 4, 5, 7, 10, 47**
See also O Nuallain, Brian

O'Brien, Richard 1942- **CLC 17**
See also CA 124

O'Brien, (William) Tim(othy) 1946- **CLC 7,**
19, 40, 103; DAM POP
See also AAYA 16; CA 85-88; CANR 40, 58;
CDALBS; DLB 152; DLBD 9; DLBY 80;
MTCW 2

Obstfelder, Sigbjoern 1866-1900 **TCLC 23**
See also CA 123

O'Casey, Sean 1880-1964 **CLC 1, 5, 9, 11, 15,**
88; DAB; DAC; DAM DRAM, MST;
WLCS
See also CA 89-92; CANR 62;CDBLB 1914-
1945; DLB 10; MTCW 1, 2

O'Cathasaigh, Sean
See O'Casey, Sean

Ochs, Phil 1940-1976 **CLC 17**
See also CA 65-68

O'Connor, Edwin (Greene) 1918-1968**CLC 14**
See also CA 93-96; 25-28R

O'Connor, (Mary) Flannery 1925-1964 **C L C**
1, 2, 3, 6, 10, 13, 15, 21, 66, 104; DA; DAB;
DAC; DAM MST, NOV; SSC 1, 23;WLC
See also AAYA 7; CA 1-4R; CANR 3, 41;
CDALB 1941-1968; DLB 2, 152; DLBD 12;
DLBY 80; MTCW 1, 2

O'Connor, Frank **CLC 23; SSC 5**
See also O'Donovan, Michael John
See also DLB 162

O'Dell, Scott 1898-1989 **CLC 30**
See also AAYA 3; CA 61-64; 129; CANR 12,
30; CLR 1, 16; DLB 52; JRDA; MAICYA;
SATA 12, 60

Odets, Clifford 1906-1963**CLC 2, 28, 98; DAM**
DRAM; DC 6
See also CA 85-88; CANR 62; DLB 7, 26;
MTCW 1, 2

O'Doherty, Brian 1934- **CLC 76**
See also CA 105

O'Donnell, K. M.
See Malzberg, Barry N(athaniel)

O'Donnell, Lawrence
See Kuttner, Henry

O'Donovan, Michael John 1903-1966**CLC 14**
See also O'Connor, Frank
See also CA 93-96

Oe, Kenzaburo 1935- **CLC 10, 36, 86; DAM**
NOV; SSC 20
See also CA 97-100; CANR 36, 50, 74; DLB
182; DLBY 94; MTCW 1, 2

O'Faolain, Julia 1932- **CLC 6, 19, 47, 108**
See also CA 81-84; CAAS 2; CANR 12, 61;
DLB 14; MTCW 1

O'Faolain, Sean 1900-1991 **CLC 1, 7, 14, 32,**
70; SSC 13
See also CA 61-64; 134; CANR 12, 66; DLB

15, 162; MTCW 1, 2

O'Flaherty, Liam 1896-1984**CLC 5, 34; SSC 6**
See also CA 101; 113; CANR 35; DLB 36, 162;
DLBY 84; MTCW 1, 2

Ogilvy, Gavin
See Barrie, J(ames) M(atthew)

O'Grady, Standish (James) 1846-1928 **T C L C**
5
See also CA 104; 157

O'Grady, Timothy 1951- **CLC 59**
See also CA 138

O'Hara, Frank 1926-1966 **CLC 2, 5, 13, 78;**
DAM POET
See also CA 9-12R; 25-28R; CANR 33; DLB
5, 16, 193; MTCW 1, 2

O'Hara, John (Henry) 1905-1970**CLC 1, 2, 3,**
6, 11, 42; DAM NOV; SSC 15
See also CA 5-8R; 25-28R; CANR 31, 60;
CDALB 1929-1941; DLB 9, 86; DLBD 2;
MTCW 1, 2

O Hehir, Diana 1922- **CLC 41**
See also CA 93-96

Ohiyesa 1858-1939
See Eastman, Charles A(lexander)
See also CA 179

Okigbo, Christopher (Ifenayichukwu) 1932-
1967 **CLC 25, 84; BLC 3; DAM MULT,**
POET; PC 7
See also BW 1, 3; CA 77-80; CANR 74; DLB
125; MTCW 1, 2

Okri, Ben 1959- **CLC 87**
See also BW 2, 3; CA 130; 138; CANR 65; DLB
157; INT 138; MTCW 2

Olds, Sharon 1942- **CLC 32, 39, 85; DAM**
POET; PC 22
See also CA 101; CANR 18, 41, 66; DLB 120;
MTCW 2

Oldstyle, Jonathan
See Irving, Washington

Olesha, Yuri (Karlovich) 1899-1960 **CLC 8**
See also CA 85-88

Oliphant, Laurence 1829(?)-1888 **NCLC 47**
See also DLB 18, 166

Oliphant, Margaret (Oliphant Wilson) 1828-
1897 **NCLC 11, 61; SSC 25**
See also DLB 18, 159, 190

Oliver, Mary 1935- **CLC 19, 34, 98**
See also CA 21-24R; CANR 9, 43; DLB 5, 193

Olivier, Laurence (Kerr) 1907-1989 **CLC 20**
See also CA 111; 150; 129

Olsen, Tillie 1912-**CLC 4, 13, 114; DA; DAB;**
DAC; DAM MST; SSC 11
See also CA 1-4R; CANR 1, 43, 74; CDALBS;
DLB 28, 206; DLBY 80; MTCW 1, 2

Olson, Charles (John) 1910-1970**CLC 1, 2, 5,**
6, 9, 11, 29; DAM POET; PC 19
See also CA 13-16; 25-28R; CABS 2; CANR
35, 61; CAP 1; DLB 5, 16, 193; MTCW 1, 2

Olson, Toby 1937- **CLC 28**
See also CA 65-68; CANR 9, 31

Olyesha, Yuri
See Olesha, Yuri (Karlovich)

Ondaatje, (Philip) Michael 1943-**CLC 14, 29,**
51, 76; DAB; DAC; DAM MST
See also CA 77-80; CANR 42, 74; DLB 60;
MTCW 2

Oneal, Elizabeth 1934-
See Oneal, Zibby
See also CA 106; CANR 28; MAICYA; SATA
30, 82

Oneal, Zibby **CLC 30**
See also Oneal, Elizabeth
See also AAYA 5; CLR 13; JRDA

O'Neill, Eugene (Gladstone) 1888-1953TCLC
1, 6, 27, 49; DA; DAB; DAC; DAM DRAM,
MST; WLC
See also AITN 1; CA 110; 132; CDALB 1929-
1941; DLB 7; MTCW 1, 2

Onetti, Juan Carlos 1909-1994 **CLC 7, 10;**
DAM MULT, NOV; HLCS 2;SSC 23
See also CA 85-88; 145; CANR 32, 63; DLB
113; HW 1, 2; MTCW 1, 2

O Nuallain, Brian 1911-1966
See O'Brien, Flann
See also CA 21-22; 25-28R; CAP 2

Ophuls, Max 1902-1957 **TCLC 79**
See also CA 113

Opie, Amelia 1769-1853 **NCLC 65**
See also DLB 116, 159

Oppen, George 1908-1984 **CLC 7, 13,34**
See also CA 13-16R; 113; CANR 8, 82; DLB
5, 165

Oppenheim, E(dward) Phillips 1866-1946
TCLC 45
See also CA 111; DLB 70

Opuls, Max
See Ophuls, Max

Origen c. 185-c. 254 **CMLC 19**

Orlovitz, Gil 1918-1973 **CLC 22**
See also CA 77-80; 45-48; DLB 2, 5

Orris
See Ingelow, Jean

Ortega y Gasset, Jose 1883-1955 **TCLC 9;**
DAM MULT; HLC 2
See also CA 106; 130; HW 1, 2; MTCW 1, 2

Ortese, Anna Maria 1914- **CLC 89**
See also DLB 177

Ortiz, Simon J(oseph) 1941- **CLC 45; DAM**
MULT, POET; PC 17
See also CA 134; CANR 69; DLB 120, 175;
NNAL

Orton, Joe **CLC 4, 13, 43; DC 3**
See also Orton, John Kingsley
See also CDBLB 1960 to Present; DLB 13;
MTCW 2

Orton, John Kingsley 1933-1967
See Orton, Joe
See also CA 85-88; CANR 35, 66; DAM
DRAM; MTCW 1, 2

Orwell, George **TCLC 2, 6, 15, 31, 51; DAB;**
WLC
See also Blair, Eric (Arthur)
See also CDBLB 1945-1960; DLB 15, 98, 195

Osborne, David
See Silverberg, Robert

Osborne, George
See Silverberg, Robert

Osborne, John (James) 1929-1994**CLC 1, 2, 5,**
11, 45; DA; DAB; DAC; DAM DRAM,
MST; WLC
See also CA 13-16R; 147; CANR 21, 56;
CDBLB 1945-1960; DLB 13; MTCW 1, 2

Osborne, Lawrence 1958- **CLC 50**

Osbourne, Lloyd 1868-1947 **TCLC 93**

Oshima, Nagisa 1932- **CLC 20**
See also CA 116; 121; CANR 78

Oskison, John Milton 1874-1947 **TCLC 35;**
DAM MULT
See also CA 144; DLB 175; NNAL

Ossian c. 3rd cent. - **CMLC 28**
See also Macpherson, James

Ossoli, Sarah Margaret (Fuller marchesa d')
1810-1850
See Fuller, Margaret
See also SATA 25

Ostrovsky, Alexander 1823-1886NCLC **30, 57**

Otero, Blas de 1916-1979 **CLC 11**
See also CA 89-92; DLB 134
Otto, Rudolf 1869-1937 **TCLC 85**
Otto, Whitney 1955- **CLC 70**
See also CA 140
Ouida **TCLC 43**
See also De La Ramee, (Marie) Louise
See also DLB 18, 156
Ousmane, Sembene 1923- **CLC 66; BLC 3**
See also BW 1, 3; CA 117; 125; CANR 81;
MTCW 1
Ovid 43B.C.-17 **CMLC 7; DAM POET; PC 2**
See also DLB 211
Owen, Hugh
See Faust, Frederick (Schiller)
Owen, Wilfred (Edward Salter) 1893-1918
**TCLC 5, 27; DA; DAB; DAC; DAM MST,
POET; PC 19; WLC**
See also CA 104; 141; CDBLB 1914-1945;
DLB 20; MTCW 2
Owens, Rochelle 1936- **CLC 8**
See also CA 17-20R; CAAS 2; CANR 39
Oz, Amos 1939- **CLC 5, 8, 11, 27, 33, 54; DAM
NOV**
See also CA 53-56; CANR 27, 47, 65; MTCW
1, 2
Ozick, Cynthia 1928- **CLC 3, 7, 28, 62; DAM
NOV, POP; SSC 15**
See also BEST 90:1; CA 17-20R; CANR 23,
58; DLB 28, 152; DLBY 82; INT CANR-
23; MTCW 1, 2
Ozu, Yasujiro 1903-1963 **CLC 16**
See also CA 112
Pacheco, C.
See Pessoa, Fernando (Antonio Nogueira)
Pacheco, Jose Emilio 1939-
See also CA 111; 131; CANR 65; DAM MULT;
HLC 2; HW 1, 2
Pa Chin **CLC 18**
See also Li Fei-kan
Pack, Robert 1929- **CLC 13**
See also CA 1-4R; CANR 3, 44, 82; DLB 5
Padgett, Lewis
See Kuttner, Henry
Padilla (Lorenzo), Heberto 1932- **CLC 38**
See also AITN 1; CA 123; 131; HW 1
Page, Jimmy 1944- **CLC 12**
Page, Louise 1955- **CLC 40**
See also CA 140; CANR 76
Page, P(atricia) K(athleen) 1916- **CLC 7, 18;
DAC; DAM MST; PC 12**
See also CA 53-56; CANR 4, 22, 65; DLB 68;
MTCW 1
Page, Thomas Nelson 1853-1922 **SSC 23**
See also CA 118; 177; DLB 12, 78; DLBD 13
Pagels, Elaine Hiesey 1943- **CLC 104**
See also CA 45-48; CANR 2, 24, 51
Paget, Violet 1856-1935
See Lee, Vernon
See also CA 104; 166
Paget-Lowe, Henry
See Lovecraft, H(oward) P(hillips)
Paglia, Camille (Anna) 1947- **CLC 68**
See also CA 140; CANR 72; MTCW 2
Paige, Richard
See Koontz, Dean R(ay)
Paine, Thomas 1737-1809 **NCLC 62**
See also CDALB 1640-1865; DLB 31, 43, 73,
158
Pakenham, Antonia
See Fraser, (Lady) Antonia (Pakenham)
Palamas, Kostes 1859-1943 **TCLC 5**
See also CA 105

Palazzeschi, Aldo 1885-1974 **CLC 11**
See also CA 89-92; 53-56; DLB 114
Pales Matos, Luis 1898-1959
See also HLCS 2; HW 1
Paley, Grace 1922- **CLC 4, 6, 37; DAM POP;
SSC 8**
See also CA 25-28R; CANR 13, 46, 74; DLB
28; INT CANR-13; MTCW 1, 2
Palin, Michael (Edward) 1943- **CLC 21**
See also Monty Python
See also CA 107; CANR 35; SATA 67
Palliser, Charles 1947- **CLC 65**
See also CA 136; CANR 76
Palma, Ricardo 1833-1919 **TCLC 29**
See also CA 168
Pancake, Breece Dexter 1952-1979
See Pancake, Breece D'J
See also CA 123; 109
Pancake, Breece D'J **CLC 29**
See also Pancake, Breece Dexter
See also DLB 130
Panko, Rudy
See Gogol, Nikolai (Vasilyevich)
Papadiamantis, Alexandros 1851-1911 **TCLC
29**
See also CA 168
Papadiamantopoulos, Johannes 1856-1910
See Moreas, Jean
See also CA 117
Papini, Giovanni 1881-1956 **TCLC 22**
See also CA 121
Paracelsus 1493-1541 **LC 14**
See also DLB 179
Parasol, Peter
See Stevens, Wallace
Pardo Bazan, Emilia 1851-1921 **SSC 30**
Pareto, Vilfredo 1848-1923 **TCLC 69**
See also CA 175
Parfenie, Maria
See Codrescu, Andrei
Parini, Jay (Lee) 1948- **CLC 54**
See also CA 97-100; CAAS 16; CANR 32
Park, Jordan
See Kornbluth, C(yril) M.; Pohl, Frederik
Park, Robert E(zra) 1864-1944 **TCLC 73**
See also CA 122; 165
Parker, Bert
See Ellison, Harlan (Jay)
Parker, Dorothy (Rothschild) 1893-1967 **CLC
15, 68; DAM POET; SSC 2**
See also CA 19-20; 25-28R; CAP 2; DLB 11,
45, 86; MTCW 1, 2
Parker, Robert B(rown) 1932- **CLC 27; DAM
NOV, POP**
See also AAYA 28; BEST 89:4; CA 49-52;
CANR 1, 26, 52; INT CANR-26; MTCW 1
Parkin, Frank 1940- **CLC 43**
See also CA 147
Parkman, Francis, Jr. 1823-1893 **NCLC 12**
See also DLB 1, 30, 186
Parks, Gordon (Alexander Buchanan) 1912-
CLC 1, 16; BLC 3; DAM MULT
See also AITN 2; BW 2, 3; CA 41-44R; CANR
26, 66; DLB 33; MTCW 2; SATA 8, 108
Parmenides c. 515B.C.-c.450B.C. **CMLC 22**
See also DLB 176
Parnell, Thomas 1679-1718 **LC 3**
See also DLB 94
Parra, Nicanor 1914- **CLC 2, 102; DAM
MULT; HLC 2**
See also CA 85-88; CANR 32; HW 1; MTCW
1
Parra Sanojo, Ana Teresa de la 1890-1936

See also HLCS 2
Parrish, Mary Frances
See Fisher, M(ary) F(rances) K(ennedy)
Parson
See Coleridge, Samuel Taylor
Parson Lot
See Kingsley, Charles
Partridge, Anthony
See Oppenheim, E(dward) Phillips
Pascal, Blaise 1623-1662 **LC 35**
Pascoli, Giovanni 1855-1912 **TCLC 45**
See also CA 170
Pasolini, Pier Paolo 1922-1975 **CLC 20, 37,
106; PC 17**
See also CA 93-96; 61-64; CANR 63; DLB 128,
177; MTCW 1
Pasquini
See Silone, Ignazio
Pastan, Linda (Olenik) 1932- **CLC 27; DAM
POET**
See also CA 61-64; CANR 18, 40, 61; DLB 5
Pasternak, Boris (Leonidovich) 1890-1960
**CLC 7, 10, 18, 63; DA; DAB; DAC; DAM
MST, NOV, POET; PC 6; SSC 31; WLC**
See also CA 127; 116; MTCW 1, 2
Patchen, Kenneth 1911-1972 **CLC 1, 2, 18;
DAM POET**
See also CA 1-4R; 33-36R; CANR 3, 35; DLB
16, 48; MTCW 1
Pater, Walter (Horatio) 1839-1894 **NCLC 7**
See also CDBLB 1832-1890; DLB 57, 156
Paterson, A(ndrew) B(arton) 1864-1941
TCLC 32
See also CA 155; SATA 97
Paterson, Katherine (Womeldorf) 1932- **CLC
12, 30**
See also AAYA 1; CA 21-24R; CANR 28, 59;
CLR 7, 50; DLB 52; JRDA; MAICYA;
MTCW 1; SATA 13, 53, 92
Patmore, Coventry Kersey Dighton 1823-1896
NCLC 9
See also DLB 35, 98
Paton, Alan (Stewart) 1903-1988 **CLC 4, 10,
25, 55, 106; DA; DAB; DAC; DAM MST,
NOV; WLC**
See also AAYA 26; CA 13-16; 125; CANR 22;
CAP 1; DLBD 17; MTCW 1, 2; SATA 11;
SATA-Obit 56
Paton Walsh, Gillian 1937-
See Walsh, Jill Paton
See also CANR 38; JRDA; MAICYA; SAAS 3;
SATA 4, 72, 109
Patton, George S. 1885-1945 **TCLC 79**
Paulding, James Kirke 1778-1860 **NCLC 2**
See also DLB 3, 59, 74
Paulin, Thomas Neilson 1949-
See Paulin, Tom
See also CA 123; 128
Paulin, Tom **CLC 37**
See also Paulin, Thomas Neilson
See also DLB 40
Paustovsky, Konstantin (Georgievich) 1892-
1968 **CLC 40**
See also CA 93-96; 25-28R
Pavese, Cesare 1908-1950 **TCLC 3; PC 13;
SSC 19**
See also CA 104; 169; DLB 128, 177
Pavic, Milorad 1929- **CLC 60**
See also CA 136; DLB 181
Pavlov, Ivan Petrovich 1849-1936 **TCLC 91**
See also CA 118
Payne, Alan
See Jakes, John (William)

Paz, Gil
See Lugones, Leopoldo
Paz, Octavio 1914-1998CLC **3, 4, 6, 10, 19, 51,
65, 119; DA; DAB; DAC; DAM MST,
MULT, POET; HLC 2; PC 1;WLC**
See also CA 73-76; 165; CANR 32, 65; DLBY
90, 98; HW 1, 2; MTCW 1, 2
p'Bitek, Okot 1931-1982 CLC **96; BLC 3;
DAM MULT**
See also BW 2, 3; CA 124; 107; CANR 82; DLB
125; MTCW 1, 2
Peacock, Molly 1947- CLC **60**
See also CA 103; CAAS 21; CANR 52; DLB
120
Peacock, Thomas Love 1785-1866 NCLC **22**
See also DLB 96, 116
Peake, Mervyn 1911-1968 CLC **7, 54**
See also CA 5-8R; 25-28R; CANR 3; DLB 15,
160; MTCW 1; SATA 23
Pearce, Philippa CLC **21**
See Christie, (Ann) Philippa
See also CLR 9; DLB 161; MAICYA; SATA 1,
67
Pearl, Eric
See Elman, Richard (Martin)
Pearson, T(homas) R(eid) 1956- CLC **39**
See also CA 120; 130; INT 130
Peck, Dale 1967- CLC **81**
See also CA 146; CANR 72
Peck, John 1941- CLC **3**
See also CA 49-52; CANR 3
Peck, Richard (Wayne) 1934- CLC **21**
See also AAYA 1, 24; CA 85-88; CANR 19,
38; CLR 15; INT CANR-19; JRDA;
MAICYA; SAAS 2; SATA 18, 55, 97
Peck, Robert Newton 1928- CLC **17; DA;
DAC; DAM MST**
See also AAYA 3; CA 81-84; CANR 31, 63;
CLR 45; JRDA; MAICYA; SAAS 1; SATA
21, 62; SATA-Essay 108
Peckinpah, (David) Sam(uel) 1925-1984 C L C
20
See also CA 109; 114; CANR 82
Pedersen, Knut 1859-1952
See Hamsun, Knut
See also CA 104; 119; CANR 63; MTCW 1, 2
Peeslake, Gaffer
See Durrell, Lawrence (George)
Peguy, Charles Pierre 1873-1914 TCLC **10**
See also CA 107
Peirce, Charles Sanders 1839-1914 TCLC **81**
Pellicer, Carlos 1900(?)-1977
See also CA 153; 69-72; HLCS 2; HW 1
Pena, Ramon del Valle y
See Valle-Inclan, Ramon (Maria) del
Pendennis, Arthur Esquir
See Thackeray, William Makepeace
Penn, William 1644-1718 LC **25**
See also DLB 24
PEPECE
See Prado (Calvo), Pedro
Pepys, Samuel 1633-1703 LC **11; DA; DAB;
DAC; DAM MST; WLC**
See also CDBLB 1660-1789; DLB 101
Percy, Walker 1916-1990CLC **2, 3, 6, 8, 14, 18,
47, 65; DAM NOV, POP**
See also CA 1-4R; 131; CANR 1, 23, 64; DLB
2; DLBY 80, 90; MTCW 1, 2
Percy, William Alexander 1885-1942TCLC **84**
See also CA 163; MTCW 2
Perec, Georges 1936-1982 CLC **56, 116**
See also CA 141; DLB 83
Pereda (y Sanchez de Porrua), Jose Mariade

1833-1906 TCLC **16**
See also CA 117
Pereda y Porrua, Jose Maria de
See Pereda (y Sanchez de Porrua), Jose Maria
de
Peregoy, George Weems
See Mencken, H(enry) L(ouis)
Perelman, S(idney) J(oseph) 1904-1979 C L C
**3, 5, 9, 15, 23, 44, 49; DAM DRAM; SSC
32**
See also AITN 1, 2; CA 73-76; 89-92; CANR
18; DLB 11, 44; MTCW 1, 2
Peret, Benjamin 1899-1959 TCLC **20**
See also CA 117
Peretz, Isaac Loeb 1851(?)-1915 TCLC **16;
SSC 26**
See also CA 109
Peretz, Yitzkhok Leibush
See Peretz, Isaac Loeb
Perez Galdos, Benito 1843-1920 TCLC **27;
HLCS 2**
See also CA 125; 153; HW 1
Peri Rossi, Cristina 1941-
See also CA 131; CANR 59, 81; DLB 145;
HLCS 2; HW 1, 2
Perrault, Charles 1628-1703 LC **3, 52**
See also MAICYA; SATA 25
Perry, Brighton
See Sherwood, Robert E(mmet)
Perse, St.-John
See Leger, (Marie-Rene Auguste) Alexis Saint-
Leger
Perutz, Leo(pold) 1882-1957 TCLC **60**
See also CA 147; DLB 81
Peseenz, Tulio F.
See Lopez y Fuentes, Gregorio
Pesetsky, Bette 1932- CLC **28**
See also CA 133; DLB 130
Peshkov, Alexei Maximovich 1868-1936
See Gorky, Maxim
See also CA 105; 141; DA; DAC; DAM DRAM,
MST, NOV; MTCW 2
Pessoa, Fernando (Antonio Nogueira) 1888-
1935TCLC **27; DAM MULT; HLC 2; PC
20**
See also CA 125
Peterkin, Julia Mood 1880-1961 CLC **31**
See also CA 102; DLB 9
Peters, Joan K(aren) 1945- CLC **39**
See also CA 158
Peters, Robert L(ouis) 1924- CLC **7**
See also CA 13-16R; CAAS 8; DLB 105
Petofi, Sandor 1823-1849 NCLC **21**
Petrakis, Harry Mark 1923- CLC **3**
See also CA 9-12R; CANR 4, 30
Petrarch 1304-1374 CMLC **20; DAM POET;
PC 8**
Petronius c. 20-66 CMLC **34**
See also DLB 211
Petrov, Evgeny TCLC **21**
See also Kataev, Evgeny Petrovich
Petry, Ann (Lane) 1908-1997 CLC **1, 7, 18**
See also BW 1, 3; CA 5-8R; 157; CAAS 6;
CANR 4, 46; CLR 12; DLB 76; JRDA;
MAICYA; MTCW 1; SATA 5; SATA-Obit 94
Petursson, Halligrimur 1614-1674 LC **8**
Peychinovich
See Vazov, Ivan (Minchov)
Phaedrus c. 18B.C.-c. 50 CMLC **25**
See also DLB 211
Philips, Katherine 1632-1664 LC **30**
See also DLB 131
Philipson, Morris H. 1926- CLC **53**

See also CA 1-4R; CANR 4
Phillips, Caryl 1958- CLC **96; BLCS; DAM
MULT**
See also BW 2; CA 141; CANR 63; DLB 157;
MTCW 2
Phillips, David Graham 1867-1911 TCLC **44**
See also CA 108; 176; DLB 9, 12
Phillips, Jack
See Sandburg, Carl (August)
Phillips, Jayne Anne 1952-CLC **15, 33; SSC 16**
See also CA 101; CANR 24, 50; DLBY 80; INT
CANR-24; MTCW 1, 2
Phillips, Richard
See Dick, Philip K(indred)
Phillips, Robert (Schaeffer) 1938- CLC **28**
See also CA 17-20R; CAAS 13; CANR 8; DLB
105
Phillips, Ward
See Lovecraft, H(oward) P(hillips)
Piccolo, Lucio 1901-1969 CLC **13**
See also CA 97-100; DLB 114
Pickthall, Marjorie L(owry) C(hristie) 1883-
1922 TCLC **21**
See also CA 107; DLB 92
Pico della Mirandola, Giovanni 1463-1494LC
15
Piercy, Marge 1936- CLC **3, 6, 14, 18, 27, 62**
See also CA 21-24R; CAAS 1; CANR 13, 43,
66; DLB 120; MTCW 1, 2
Piers, Robert
See Anthony, Piers
Pieyre de Mandiargues, Andre 1909-1991
See Mandiargues, Andre Pieyre de
See also CA 103; 136; CANR 22, 82
Pilnyak, Boris TCLC **23**
See also Vogau, Boris Andreyevich
Pincherle, Alberto 1907-1990 CLC **11, 18;
DAM NOV**
See also Moravia, Alberto
See also CA 25-28R; 132; CANR 33, 63;
MTCW 1
Pinckney, Darryl 1953- CLC **76**
See also BW 2, 3; CA 143; CANR 79
Pindar 518B.C.-446B.C. CMLC **12;PC 19**
See also DLB 176
Pineda, Cecile 1942- CLC **39**
See also CA 118
Pinero, Arthur Wing 1855-1934 TCLC **32;
DAM DRAM**
See also CA 110; 153; DLB 10
Pinero, Miguel (Antonio Gomez) 1946-1988
CLC **4, 55**
See also CA 61-64; 125; CANR 29; HW 1
Pinget, Robert 1919-1997 CLC **7, 13, 37**
See also CA 85-88; 160; DLB 83
Pink Floyd
See Barrett, (Roger) Syd; Gilmour, David; Ma-
son, Nick; Waters, Roger; Wright, Rick
Pinkney, Edward 1802-1828 NCLC **31**
Pinkwater, Daniel Manus 1941- CLC **35**
See Pinkwater, Manus
See also AAYA 1; CA 29-32R; CANR 12, 38;
CLR 4; JRDA; MAICYA; SAAS 3; SATA 46,
76
Pinkwater, Manus
See Pinkwater, Daniel Manus
See also SATA 8
Pinsky, Robert 1940- CLC **9, 19, 38, 94, 121;
DAM POET; PC 27**
See also CA 29-32R; CAAS 4; CANR 58;
DLBY 82, 98; MTCW 2
Pinta, Harold
See Pinter, Harold

Price, (Edward) Reynolds 1933-CLC **3, 6, 13, 43, 50, 63; DAM NOV; SSC 22**
See also CA 1-4R; CANR 1, 37, 57; DLB 2; INT CANR-37
Price, Richard 1949- **CLC 6, 12**
See also CA 49-52; CANR 3; DLBY 81
Prichard, Katharine Susannah 1883-1969
CLC 46
See also CA 11-12; CANR 33; CAP 1; MTCW 1; SATA 66
Priestley, J(ohn) B(oynton) 1894-1984CLC **2, 5, 9, 34; DAM DRAM, NOV**
See also CA 9-12R; 113; CANR 33;CDBLB 1914-1945; DLB 10, 34, 77, 100, 139; DLBY 84; MTCW 1, 2
Prince 1958(?)- **CLC 35**
Prince, F(rank) T(empleton) 1912- **CLC 22**
See also CA 101; CANR 43, 79; DLB 20
Prince Kropotkin
See Kropotkin, Peter (Aleksieevich)
Prior, Matthew 1664-1721 **LC 4**
See also DLB 95
Prishvin, Mikhail 1873-1954 **TCLC 75**
Pritchard, William H(arrison) 1932- CLC **34**
See also CA 65-68; CANR 23; DLB 111
Pritchett, V(ictor) S(awdon) 1900-1997 **C L C 5, 13, 15, 41; DAM NOV; SSC 14**
See also CA 61-64; 157; CANR 31, 63; DLB 15, 139; MTCW 1, 2
Private 19022
See Manning, Frederic
Probst, Mark 1925- **CLC 59**
See also CA 130
Prokosch, Frederic 1908-1989 **CLC 4, 48**
See also CA 73-76; 128; CANR 82; DLB 48; MTCW 2
Propertius, Sextus c. 50B.C.-c.16B.C. **C M L C 32**
See also DLB 211
Prophet, The
See Dreiser, Theodore (Herman Albert)
Prose, Francine 1947- **CLC 45**
See also CA 109; 112; CANR 46; SATA 101
Proudhon
See Cunha, Euclides (Rodrigues Pimenta) da
Proulx, Annie
See Proulx, E(dna) Annie
Proulx, E(dna) Annie 1935- **CLC 81;DAM POP**
See also CA 145; CANR 65; MTCW 2
Proust, (Valentin-Louis-George-Eugene-) Marcel 1871-1922 **TCLC 7, 13, 33; DA; DAB; DAC; DAM MST, NOV; WLC**
See also CA 104; 120; DLB 65; MTCW 1, 2
Prowler, Harley
See Masters, Edgar Lee
Prus, Boleslaw 1845-1912 **TCLC 48**
Pryor, Richard (Franklin Lenox Thomas) 1940-
CLC 26
See also CA 122; 152
Przybyszewski, Stanislaw 1868-1927TCLC **36**
See also CA 160; DLB 66
Pteleon
See Grieve, C(hristopher) M(urray)
See also DAM POET
Puckett, Lute
See Masters, Edgar Lee
Puig, Manuel 1932-1990CLC **3, 5, 10, 28, 65; DAM MULT; HLC 2**
See also CA 45-48; CANR 2, 32, 63; DLB 113; HW 1, 2; MTCW 1, 2
Pulitzer, Joseph 1847-1911 **TCLC 76**
See also CA 114; DLB 23

Purdy, A(lfred) W(ellington) 1918- CLC **3, 6, 14, 50; DAC; DAM MST, POET**
See also CA 81-84; CAAS 17; CANR 42, 66; DLB 88
Purdy, James (Amos) 1923- CLC **2, 4, 10, 28, 52**
See also CA 33-36R; CAAS 1; CANR 19, 51; DLB 2; INT CANR-19; MTCW 1
Pure, Simon
See Swinnerton, Frank Arthur
Pushkin, Alexander (Sergeyevich) 1799-1837
NCLC 3, 27; DA; DAB; DAC; DAM DRAM, MST, POET; PC 10; SSC 27;WLC
See also DLB 205; SATA 61
P'u Sung-ling 1640-1715 **LC 49; SSC 31**
Putnam, Arthur Lee
See Alger, Horatio, Jr.
Puzo, Mario 1920-1999 CLC **1, 2, 6, 36, 107; DAM NOV, POP**
See also CA 65-68; CANR 4, 42, 65; DLB 6; MTCW 1, 2
Pygge, Edward
See Barnes, Julian (Patrick)
Pyle, Ernest Taylor 1900-1945
See Pyle, Ernie
See also CA 115; 160
Pyle, Ernie 1900-1945 **TCLC 75**
See also Pyle, Ernest Taylor
See also DLB 29; MTCW 2
Pyle, Howard 1853-1911 **TCLC 81**
See also CA 109; 137; CLR 22; DLB 42, 188; DLBD 13; MAICYA; SATA 16, 100
Pym, Barbara (Mary Crampton) 1913-1980
CLC 13, 19, 37, 111
See also CA 13-14; 97-100; CANR 13, 34; CAP 1; DLB 14, 207; DLBY 87; MTCW 1, 2
Pynchon, Thomas (Ruggles, Jr.) 1937-CLC **2, 3, 6, 9, 11, 18, 33, 62, 72; DA; DAB; DAC; DAM MST, NOV, POP; SSC 14;WLC**
See also BEST 90:2; CA 17-20R; CANR 22, 46, 73; DLB 2, 173; MTCW 1, 2
Pythagoras c. 570B.C.-c.500B.C. **CMLC 22**
See also DLB 176
Q
See Quiller-Couch, SirArthur (Thomas)
Qian Zhongshu
See Ch'ien Chung-shu
Qroll
See Dagerman, Stig (Halvard)
Quarrington, Paul (Lewis) 1953- **CLC 65**
See also CA 129; CANR 62
Quasimodo, Salvatore 1901-1968 **CLC 10**
See also CA 13-16; 25-28R; CAP 1; DLB 114; MTCW 1
Quay, Stephen 1947- **CLC 95**
Quay, Timothy 1947- **CLC 95**
Queen, Ellery **CLC 3, 11**
See also Dannay, Frederic; Davidson, Avram (James); Lee, Manfred B(ennington); Marlowe, Stephen; Sturgeon, Theodore (Hamilton); Vance, John Holbrook
Queen, Ellery, Jr.
See Dannay, Frederic; Lee, Manfred B(ennington)
Queneau, Raymond 1903-1976 CLC **2, 5, 10, 42**
See also CA 77-80; 69-72; CANR 32; DLB 72; MTCW 1, 2
Quevedo, Francisco de 1580-1645 **LC 23**
Quiller-Couch, Sir Arthur(Thomas) 1863-1944
TCLC 53
See also CA 118; 166; DLB 135, 153, 190
Quin, Ann (Marie) 1936-1973 **CLC 6**

See also CA 9-12R; 45-48; DLB 14
Quinn, Martin
See Smith, Martin Cruz
Quinn, Peter 1947- **CLC 91**
Quinn, Simon
See Smith, Martin Cruz
Quintana, Leroy V. 1944-
See also CA 131; CANR 65; DAM MULT; DLB 82; HLC 2; HW 1, 2
Quiroga, Horacio (Sylvestre) 1878-1937
TCLC 20; DAM MULT; HLC 2
See also CA 117; 131; HW 1; MTCW 1
Quoirez, Francoise 1935- **CLC 9**
See also Sagan, Francoise
See also CA 49-52; CANR 6, 39, 73; MTCW 1, 2
Raabe, Wilhelm (Karl) 1831-1910 **TCLC 45**
See also CA 167; DLB 129
Rabe, David (William) 1940- CLC **4, 8, 33; DAM DRAM**
See also CA 85-88; CABS 3; CANR 59; DLB 7
Rabelais, Francois 1483-1553LC **5; DA; DAB; DAC; DAM MST; WLC**
Rabinovitch, Sholem 1859-1916
See Aleichem, Sholom
See also CA 104
Rabinyan, Dorit 1972- **CLC 119**
See also CA 170
Rachilde 1860-1953 **TCLC 67**
See also DLB 123, 192
Racine, Jean 1639-1699 LC **28; DAB; DAM MST**
Radcliffe, Ann (Ward) 1764-1823NCLC **6, 55**
See also DLB 39, 178
Radiguet, Raymond 1903-1923 **TCLC 29**
See also CA 162; DLB 65
Radnoti, Miklos 1909-1944 **TCLC 16**
See also CA 118
Rado, James 1939- **CLC 17**
See also CA 105
Radvanyi, Netty 1900-1983
See Seghers, Anna
See also CA 85-88; 110; CANR 82
Rae, Ben
See Griffiths, Trevor
Raeburn, John (Hay) 1941- **CLC 34**
See also CA 57-60
Ragni, Gerome 1942-1991 **CLC 17**
See also CA 105; 134
Rahv, Philip 1908-1973 **CLC 24**
See also Greenberg, Ivan
See also DLB 137
Raimund, Ferdinand Jakob 1790-1836NCLC **69**
See also DLB 90
Raine, Craig 1944- **CLC 32, 103**
See also CA 108; CANR 29, 51; DLB 40
Raine, Kathleen (Jessie) 1908- **CLC 7, 45**
See also CA 85-88; CANR 46; DLB 20; MTCW 1
Rainis, Janis 1865-1929 **TCLC 29**
See also CA 170
Rakosi, Carl 1903- **CLC 47**
See also Rawley, Callman
See also CAAS 5; DLB 193
Raleigh, Richard
See Lovecraft, H(oward) P(hillips)
Raleigh, Sir Walter 1554(?)-1618 **LC 31, 39**
See also CDBLB Before 1660; DLB 172
Rallentando, H. P.
See Sayers, Dorothy L(eigh)
Ramal, Walter
See de la Mare, Walter (John)

Ramana Maharshi 1879-1950 **TCLC 84**
Ramoacn y Cajal, Santiago 1852-1934**T C L C 93**
Ramon, Juan
See Jimenez (Mantecon), Juan Ramon
Ramos, Graciliano 1892-1953 **TCLC 32**
See also CA 167; HW 2
Rampersad, Arnold 1941- **CLC 44**
See also BW 2, 3; CA 127; 133; CANR 81; DLB 111; INT 133
Rampling, Anne
See Rice, Anne
Ramsay, Allan 1684(?)-1758 **LC 29**
See also DLB 95
Ramuz, Charles-Ferdinand 1878-1947**T C L C 33**
See also CA 165
Rand, Ayn 1905-1982 **CLC 3, 30, 44, 79; DA; DAC; DAM MST, NOV, POP; WLC**
See also AAYA 10; CA 13-16R; 105; CANR 27, 73; CDALBS; MTCW 1, 2
Randall, Dudley (Felker) 1914-**CLC 1; BLC 3; DAM MULT**
See also BW 1, 3; CA 25-28R; CANR 23, 82; DLB 41
Randall, Robert
See Silverberg, Robert
Ranger, Ken
See Creasey, John
Ransom, John Crowe 1888-1974**CLC 2, 4, 5, 11, 24; DAM POET**
See also CA 5-8R; 49-52; CANR 6, 34; CDALBS; DLB 45, 63; MTCW 1, 2
Rao, Raja 1909- **CLC 25, 56;DAM NOV**
See also CA 73-76; CANR 51; MTCW 1, 2
Raphael, Frederic (Michael) 1931-**CLC 2, 14**
See also CA 1-4R; CANR 1; DLB 14
Ratcliffe, James P.
See Mencken, H(enry) L(ouis)
Rathbone, Julian 1935- **CLC 41**
See also CA 101; CANR 34, 73
Rattigan, Terence (Mervyn) 1911-1977**CLC 7; DAM DRAM**
See also CA 85-88; 73-76; CDBLB 1945-1960; DLB 13; MTCW 1, 2
Ratushinskaya, Irina 1954- **CLC 54**
See also CA 129; CANR 68
Raven, Simon (Arthur Noel) 1927- **CLC 14**
See also CA 81-84
Ravenna, Michael
See Welty, Eudora
Rawley, Callman 1903-
See Rakosi, Carl
See also CA 21-24R; CANR 12, 32
Rawlings, Marjorie Kinnan 1896-1953**T C L C 4**
See also AAYA 20; CA 104; 137; CANR 74; DLB 9, 22, 102; DLBD 17; JRDA; MAICYA; MTCW 2; SATA 100; YABC 1
Ray, Satyajit 1921-1992 **CLC 16, 76; DAM MULT**
See also CA 114; 137
Read, Herbert Edward 1893-1968 **CLC 4**
See also CA 85-88; 25-28R; DLB 20, 149
Read, Piers Paul 1941- **CLC 4, 10, 25**
See also CA 21-24R; CANR 38; DLB 14; SATA 21
Reade, Charles 1814-1884 **NCLC 2, 74**
See also DLB 21
Reade, Hamish
See Gray, Simon (James Holliday)
Reading, Peter 1946- **CLC 47**
See also CA 103; CANR 46; DLB 40

Reaney, James 1926- **CLC 13; DAC;DAM MST**
See also CA 41-44R; CAAS 15; CANR 42; DLB 68; SATA 43
Rebreanu, Liviu 1885-1944 **TCLC 28**
See also CA 165
Rechy, John (Francisco) 1934- **CLC 1, 7, 14, 18, 107; DAM MULT; HLC 2**
See also CA 5-8R; CAAS 4; CANR 6, 32, 64; DLB 122; DLBY 82; HW 1, 2; INT CANR-6
Redcam, Tom 1870-1933 **TCLC 25**
Reddin, Keith **CLC 67**
Redgrove, Peter (William) 1932- **CLC 6, 41**
See also CA 1-4R; CANR 3, 39, 77; DLB 40
Redmon, Anne **CLC 22**
See also Nightingale, Anne Redmon
See also DLBY 86
Reed, Eliot
See Ambler, Eric
Reed, Ishmael 1938-**CLC 2, 3, 5, 6, 13, 32, 60; BLC 3; DAM MULT**
See also BW 2, 3; CA 21-24R; CANR 25, 48, 74; DLB 2, 5, 33, 169; DLBD 8; MTCW 1, 2
Reed, John (Silas) 1887-1920 **TCLC 9**
See also CA 106
Reed, Lou **CLC 21**
See also Firbank, Louis
Reeve, Clara 1729-1807 **NCLC 19**
See also DLB 39
Reich, Wilhelm 1897-1957 **TCLC 57**
Reid, Christopher (John) 1949- **CLC 33**
See also CA 140; DLB 40
Reid, Desmond
See Moorcock, Michael (John)
Reid Banks, Lynne 1929-
See Banks, Lynne Reid
See also CA 1-4R; CANR 6, 22, 38; CLR 24; JRDA; MAICYA; SATA 22, 75
Reilly, William K.
See Creasey, John
Reiner, Max
See Caldwell, (Janet Miriam) Taylor (Holland)
Reis, Ricardo
See Pessoa, Fernando (Antonio Nogueira)
Remarque, Erich Maria 1898-1970 **CLC 21; DA; DAB; DAC; DAM MST, NOV**
See also AAYA 27; CA 77-80; 29-32R; DLB 56; MTCW 1, 2
Remington, Frederic 1861-1909 **TCLC 89**
See also CA 108; 169; DLB 12, 186, 188; SATA 41
Remizov, A.
See Remizov, Aleksei (Mikhailovich)
Remizov, A. M.
See Remizov, Aleksei (Mikhailovich)
Remizov, Aleksei (Mikhailovich) 1877-1957 **TCLC 27**
See also CA 125; 133
Renan, Joseph Ernest 1823-1892 **NCLC 26**
Renard, Jules 1864-1910 **TCLC 17**
See also CA 117
Renault, Mary **CLC 3, 11, 17**
See also Challans, Mary
See also DLBY 83; MTCW 2
Rendell, Ruth (Barbara) 1930- **CLC 28, 48; DAM POP**
See also Vine, Barbara
See also CA 109; CANR 32, 52, 74; DLB 87; INT CANR-32; MTCW 1, 2
Renoir, Jean 1894-1979 **CLC 20**
See also CA 129; 85-88

Resnais, Alain 1922- **CLC 16**
Reverdy, Pierre 1889-1960 **CLC 53**
See also CA 97-100; 89-92
Rexroth, Kenneth 1905-1982 **CLC 1, 2, 6, 11, 22, 49, 112; DAM POET; PC 20**
See also CA 5-8R; 107; CANR 14, 34, 63; CDALB 1941-1968; DLB 16, 48, 165, 212; DLBY 82; INT CANR-14; MTCW 1, 2
Reyes, Alfonso 1889-1959 **TCLC 33;HLCS 2**
See also CA 131; HW 1
Reyes y Basoalto, Ricardo Eliecer Neftali
See Neruda, Pablo
Reymont, Wladyslaw (Stanislaw) 1868(?)-1925 **TCLC 5**
See also CA 104
Reynolds, Jonathan 1942- **CLC 6, 38**
See also CA 65-68; CANR 28
Reynolds, Joshua 1723-1792 **LC 15**
See also DLB 104
Reynolds, Michael Shane 1937- **CLC 44**
See also CA 65-68; CANR 9
Reznikoff, Charles 1894-1976 **CLC 9**
See also CA 33-36; 61-64; CAP 2; DLB 28, 45
Rezzori (d'Arezzo), Gregorvon 1914-1998 **CLC 25**
See also CA 122; 136; 167
Rhine, Richard
See Silverstein, Alvin
Rhodes, Eugene Manlove 1869-1934**TCLC 53**
Rhodius, Apollonius c. 3rd cent.B.C.- **C M L C 28**
See also DLB 176
R'hoone
See Balzac, Honore de
Rhys, Jean 1890(?)-1979 **CLC 2, 4, 6, 14, 19, 51; DAM NOV; SSC 21**
See also CA 25-28R; 85-88; CANR 35, 62; CDBLB 1945-1960; DLB 36, 117, 162; MTCW 1, 2
Ribeiro, Darcy 1922-1997 **CLC 34**
See also CA 33-36R; 156
Ribeiro, Joao Ubaldo (Osorio Pimentel) 1941- **CLC 10, 67**
See also CA 81-84
Ribman, Ronald (Burt) 1932- **CLC 7**
See also CA 21-24R; CANR 46, 80
Ricci, Nino 1959- **CLC 70**
See also CA 137
Rice, Anne 1941- **CLC 41;DAM POP**
See also AAYA 9; BEST 89:2; CA 65-68; CANR 12, 36, 53, 74; MTCW 2
Rice, Elmer (Leopold) 1892-1967 **CLC 7, 49; DAM DRAM**
See also CA 21-22; 25-28R; CAP 2; DLB 4, 7; MTCW 1, 2
Rice, Tim(othy Miles Bindon) 1944- **CLC 21**
See also CA 103; CANR 46
Rich, Adrienne (Cecile) 1929-**CLC 3, 6, 7, 11, 18, 36, 73, 76; DAM POET; PC 5**
See also CA 9-12R; CANR 20, 53, 74; CDALBS; DLB 5, 67; MTCW 1, 2
Rich, Barbara
See Graves, Robert (von Ranke)
Rich, Robert
See Trumbo, Dalton
Richard, Keith **CLC 17**
See also Richards, Keith
Richards, David Adams 1950- **CLC 59; DAC**
See also CA 93-96; CANR 60; DLB 53
Richards, I(vor) A(rmstrong) 1893-1979**C L C 14, 24**
See also CA 41-44R; 89-92; CANR 34, 74; DLB 27; MTCW 2

See also CA 85-88; CANR 34; DLB 65; MTCW
1

Romero, Jose Ruben 1890-1952 **TCLC 14**
See also CA 114; 131; HW 1

Ronsard, Pierre de 1524-1585 **LC 6; PC 11**

Rooke, Leon 1934- **CLC 25, 34;DAM POP**
See also CA 25-28R; CANR 23, 53

Roosevelt, Franklin Delano 1882-1945 **TCLC 93**
See also CA 116; 173

Roosevelt,Theodore 1858-1919 **TCLC 69**
See also CA 115; 170; DLB 47, 186

Roper, William 1498-1578 **LC 10**

Roquelaure, A. N.
See Rice, Anne

Rosa, Joao Guimaraes 1908-1967 **CLC 23; HLCS 1**
See also CA 89-92; DLB 113

Rose, Wendy 1948- **CLC 85; DAM MULT; PC 13**
See also CA 53-56; CANR 5, 51; DLB 175;
NNAL; SATA 12

Rosen, R. D.
See Rosen, Richard (Dean)

Rosen, Richard (Dean) 1949- **CLC 39**
See also CA 77-80; CANR 62; INT CANR-30

Rosenberg, Isaac 1890-1918 **TCLC 12**
See also CA 107; DLB 20

Rosenblatt, Joe **CLC 15**
See also Rosenblatt, Joseph

Rosenblatt, Joseph 1933-
See Rosenblatt, Joe
See also CA 89-92; INT 89-92

Rosenfeld, Samuel
See Tzara, Tristan

Rosenstock, Sami
See Tzara, Tristan

Rosenstock, Samuel
See Tzara, Tristan

Rosenthal, M(acha) L(ouis) 1917-1996 **CLC 28**
See also CA 1-4R; 152; CAAS 6; CANR 4, 51;
DLB 5; SATA 59

Ross, Barnaby
See Dannay, Frederic

Ross, Bernard L.
See Follett, Ken(neth Martin)

Ross, J. H.
See Lawrence, T(homas) E(dward)

Ross, John Hume
See Lawrence, T(homas) E(dward)

Ross, Martin
See Martin, Violet Florence
See also DLB 135

Ross, (James) Sinclair 1908-1996 **CLC 13; DAC; DAM MST; SSC 24**
See also CA 73-76; CANR 81; DLB 88

Rossetti, Christina (Georgina) 1830-1894 **NCLC 2, 50, 66; DA; DAB; DAC; DAM MST, POET; PC 7; WLC**
See also DLB 35, 163; MAICYA; SATA 20

Rossetti, Dante Gabriel 1828-1882 **NCLC 4, 77; DA; DAB; DAC; DAM MST, POET; WLC**
See also CDBLB 1832-1890; DLB 35

Rossner, Judith (Perelman) 1935-**CLC 6, 9, 29**
See also AITN 2; BEST 90:3; CA 17-20R;
CANR 18, 51, 73; DLB 6; INT CANR-18;
MTCW 1, 2

Rostand, Edmond (Eugene Alexis) 1868-1918 **TCLC 6, 37; DA; DAB; DAC; DAM DRAM, MST; DC 10**
See also CA 104; 126; DLB 192; MTCW 1

Roth, Henry 1906-1995 **CLC 2, 6, 11, 104**
See also CA 11-12; 149; CANR 38, 63; CAP 1;
DLB 28; MTCW 1, 2

Roth, Philip (Milton) 1933-**CLC 1, 2, 3, 4, 6, 9, 15, 22, 31, 47, 66, 86, 119; DA; DAB; DAC; DAM MST, NOV, POP; SSC 26; WLC**
See also BEST 90:3; CA 1-4R; CANR 1, 22,
36, 55; CDALB 1968-1988; DLB 2, 28, 173;
DLBY 82; MTCW 1, 2

Rothenberg, Jerome 1931- **CLC 6, 57**
See also CA 45-48; CANR 1; DLB 5, 193

Roumain, Jacques (Jean Baptiste) 1907-1944 **TCLC 19; BLC 3; DAM MULT**
See also BW 1; CA 117; 125

Rourke, Constance (Mayfield) 1885-1941 **TCLC 12**
See also CA 107; YABC 1

Rousseau, Jean-Baptiste 1671-1741 **LC 9**

Rousseau, Jean-Jacques 1712-1778**LC 14, 36; DA; DAB; DAC; DAM MST; WLC**

Roussel, Raymond 1877-1933 **TCLC 20**
See also CA 117

Rovit, Earl (Herbert) 1927- **CLC 7**
See also CA 5-8R; CANR 12

Rowe, Elizabeth Singer 1674-1737 **LC 44**
See also DLB 39, 95

Rowe, Nicholas 1674-1718 **LC 8**
See also DLB 84

Rowley, Ames Dorrance
See Lovecraft, H(oward) P(hillips)

Rowson, Susanna Haswell 1762(?)-1824 **NCLC 5, 69**
See also DLB 37, 200

Roy, Arundhati 1960(?)- **CLC 109**
See also CA 163; DLBY 97

Roy, Gabrielle 1909-1983 **CLC 10, 14; DAB; DAC; DAM MST**
See also CA 53-56; 110; CANR 5, 61; DLB 68;
MTCW 1; SATA 104

Royko, Mike 1932-1997 **CLC 109**
See also CA 89-92; 157; CANR 26

Rozewicz, Tadeusz 1921- **CLC 9, 23;DAM POET**
See also CA 108; CANR 36, 66; MTCW 1, 2

Ruark, Gibbons 1941- **CLC 3**
See also CA 33-36R; CAAS 23; CANR 14, 31,
57; DLB 120

Rubens, Bernice (Ruth) 1923- **CLC 19, 31**
See also CA 25-28R; CANR 33, 65; DLB 14,
207; MTCW 1

Rubin, Harold
See Robbins, Harold

Rudkin, (James) David 1936- **CLC 14**
See also CA 89-92; DLB 13

Rudnik, Raphael 1933- **CLC 7**
See also CA 29-32R

Ruffian, M.
See Hasek, Jaroslav (Matej Frantisek)

Ruiz, Jose Martinez **CLC 11**
See also Martinez Ruiz, Jose

Rukeyser, Muriel 1913-1980**CLC 6, 10, 15, 27; DAM POET; PC 12**
See also CA 5-8R; 93-96; CANR 26, 60; DLB
48; MTCW 1, 2; SATA-Obit 22

Rule, Jane (Vance) 1931- **CLC 27**
See also CA 25-28R; CAAS 18; CANR 12; DLB
60

Rulfo, Juan 1918-1986 **CLC 8, 80; DAM MULT; HLC 2; SSC 25**
See also CA 85-88; 118; CANR 26; DLB 113;
HW 1, 2; MTCW 1, 2

Rumi, Jalal al-Din 1297-1373 **CMLC 20**

Runeberg, Johan 1804-1877 **NCLC 41**

Runyon, (Alfred) Damon 1884(?)-1946**TCLC 10**
See also CA 107; 165; DLB 11, 86, 171; MTCW
2

Rush, Norman 1933- **CLC 44**
See also CA 121; 126; INT 126

Rushdie, (Ahmed) Salman 1947- **CLC 23, 31, 55, 100; DAB; DAC; DAM MST, NOV, POP; WLCS**
See also BEST 89:3; CA 108; 111; CANR 33,
56; DLB 194; INT 111; MTCW 1, 2

Rushforth, Peter (Scott) 1945- **CLC 19**
See also CA 101

Ruskin, John 1819-1900 **TCLC 63**
See also CA 114; 129; CDBLB 1832-1890;
DLB 55, 163, 190; SATA 24

Russ, Joanna 1937- **CLC 15**
See also CANR 11, 31, 65; DLB 8; MTCW 1

Russell, George William 1867-1935
See Baker, Jean H.
See also CA 104; 153; CDBLB 1890-1914;
DAM POET

Russell, (Henry) Ken(neth Alfred) 1927-**CLC 16**
See also CA 105

Russell, William Martin 1947- **CLC 60**
See also CA 164

Rutherford, Mark **TCLC 25**
See also White, William Hale
See also DLB 18

Ruyslinck, Ward 1929- **CLC 14**
See also Belser, Reimond Karel Maria de

Ryan, Cornelius (John) 1920-1974 **CLC 7**
See also CA 69-72; 53-56; CANR 38

Ryan, Michael 1946- **CLC 65**
See also CA 49-52; DLBY 82

Ryan, Tim
See Dent, Lester

Rybakov, Anatoli (Naumovich) 1911-1998 **CLC 23, 53**
See also CA 126; 135; 172; SATA 79; SATA-
Obit 108

Ryder, Jonathan
See Ludlum, Robert

Ryga, George 1932-1987**CLC 14; DAC; DAM MST**
See also CA 101; 124; CANR 43; DLB 60

S. H.
See Hartmann, Sadakichi

S. S.
See Sassoon, Siegfried (Lorraine)

Saba, Umberto 1883-1957 **TCLC 33**
See also CA 144; CANR 79; DLB 114

Sabatini, Rafael 1875-1950 **TCLC 47**
See also CA 162

Sabato, Ernesto (R.) 1911-**CLC 10, 23; DAM MULT; HLC 2**
See also CA 97-100; CANR 32, 65; DLB 145;
HW 1, 2; MTCW 1, 2

Sa-Carniero, Mario de 1890-1916 **TCLC 83**

Sacastru, Martin
See Bioy Casares, Adolfo

Sacastru, Martin
See Bioy Casares, Adolfo

Sacher-Masoch, Leopold von 1836(?)-1895 **NCLC 31**

Sachs, Marilyn (Stickle) 1927- **CLC 35**
See also AAYA 2; CA 17-20R; CANR 13, 47;
CLR 2; JRDA; MAICYA; SAAS 2; SATA 3,
68

Sachs, Nelly 1891-1970 **CLC 14, 98**
See also CA 17-18; 25-28R; CAP 2; MTCW 2

Sackler, Howard (Oliver) 1929-1982 **CLC 14**

See also CA 61-64; 108; CANR 30; DLB 7

Sacks, Oliver (Wolf) 1933-   **CLC 67**
See also CA 53-56; CANR 28, 50, 76; INT CANR-28; MTCW 1, 2

Sadakichi
See Hartmann, Sadakichi

Sade, Donatien Alphonse Francois, Comte de 1740-1814   **NCLC 47**

Sadoff, Ira 1945-   **CLC 9**
See also CA 53-56; CANR 5, 21; DLB 120

Saetone
See Camus, Albert

Safire, William 1929-   **CLC 10**
See also CA 17-20R; CANR 31, 54

Sagan, Carl (Edward) 1934-1996CLC **30, 112**
See also AAYA 2; CA 25-28R; 155; CANR 11, 36, 74; MTCW 1, 2; SATA 58; SATA-Obit 94

Sagan, Francoise   **CLC 3, 6, 9, 17, 36**
See also Quoirez, Francoise
See also DLB 83; MTCW 2

Sahgal, Nayantara (Pandit) 1927-   **CLC 41**
See also CA 9-12R; CANR 11

Saint, H(arry) F. 1941-   **CLC 50**
See also CA 127

St. Aubin de Teran, Lisa 1953-
See Teran, Lisa St. Aubin de
See also CA 118; 126; INT 126

Saint Birgitta of Sweden c. 1303-1373CMLC **24**

Sainte-Beuve, Charles Augustin 1804-1869 **NCLC 5**

Saint-Exupery, Antoine (Jean Baptiste Marie Roger) de 1900-1944 TCLC **2, 56; DAM NOV;WLC**
See also CA 108; 132; CLR 10; DLB 72; MAICYA; MTCW 1, 2; SATA 20

St. John, David
See Hunt, E(verette) Howard, (Jr.)

Saint-John Perse
See Leger, (Marie-Rene Auguste) Alexis Saint-Leger

Saintsbury, George (Edward Bateman) 1845-1933   **TCLC 31**
See also CA 160; DLB 57, 149

Sait Faik   **TCLC 23**
See also Abasiyanik, Sait Faik

Saki   **TCLC 3; SSC 12**
See also Munro, H(ector) H(ugh)
See also MTCW 2

Sala, George Augustus   **NCLC 46**

Salama, Hannu 1936-   **CLC 18**

Salamanca, J(ack) R(ichard) 1922-CLC **4, 15**
See also CA 25-28R

Salas, Floyd Francis 1931-
See also CA 119; CAAS 27; CANR 44, 75; DAM MULT; DLB 82; HLC 2; HW 1, 2; MTCW 2

Sale, J. Kirkpatrick
See Sale, Kirkpatrick

Sale, Kirkpatrick 1937-   **CLC 68**
See also CA 13-16R; CANR 10

Salinas, Luis Omar 1937-   **CLC 90; DAM MULT; HLC 2**
See also CA 131; CANR 81; DLB 82; HW 1, 2

Salinas (y Serrano), Pedro 1891(?)-1951 **TCLC 17**
See also CA 117; DLB 134

Salinger, J(erome) D(avid) 1919-CLC **1, 3, 8, 12, 55, 56; DA; DAB; DAC; DAM MST, NOV, POP; SSC 2, 28; WLC**
See also AAYA 2; CA 5-8R; CANR 39; CDALB 1941-1968; CLR 18; DLB 2, 102, 173;

MAICYA; MTCW 1, 2; SATA 67

Salisbury, John
See Caute, (John) David

Salter, James 1925-   **CLC 7, 52, 59**
See also CA 73-76; DLB 130

Saltus, Edgar (Everton) 1855-1921   **TCLC 8**
See also CA 105; DLB 202

Saltykov, Mikhail Evgrafovich 1826-1889 **NCLC 16**

Samarakis, Antonis 1919-   **CLC 5**
See also CA 25-28R; CAAS 16; CANR 36

Sanchez, Florencio 1875-1910   **TCLC 37**
See also CA 153; HW 1

Sanchez, Luis Rafael 1936-   **CLC 23**
See also CA 128; DLB 145; HW 1

Sanchez, Sonia 1934-   **CLC 5, 116; BLC 3; DAM MULT; PC 9**
See also BW 2, 3; CA 33-36R; CANR 24, 49, 74; CLR 18; DLB 41; DLBD 8;MAICYA; MTCW 1, 2; SATA 22

Sand, George 1804-1876NCLC **2, 42, 57; DA; DAB; DAC; DAM MST, NOV; WLC**
See also DLB 119, 192

Sandburg, Carl (August) 1878-1967CLC **1, 4, 10, 15, 35; DA; DAB; DAC; DAM MST, POET; PC 2; WLC**
See also AAYA 24; CA 5-8R; 25-28R; CANR 35; CDALB 1865-1917; DLB 17, 54; MAICYA; MTCW 1, 2; SATA 8

Sandburg, Charles
See Sandburg, Carl (August)

Sandburg, Charles A.
See Sandburg, Carl (August)

Sanders, (James) Ed(ward) 1939-   **CLC 53; DAM POET**
See also CA 13-16R; CAAS 21; CANR 13, 44, 78; DLB 16

Sanders, Lawrence 1920-1998CLC **41; DAM POP**
See also BEST 89:4; CA 81-84; 165; CANR 33, 62; MTCW 1

Sanders, Noah
See Blount, Roy (Alton), Jr.

Sanders, Winston P.
See Anderson, Poul (William)

Sandoz, Mari(e Susette) 1896-1966   **CLC 28**
See also CA 1-4R; 25-28R; CANR 17, 64; DLB 9, 212; MTCW 1, 2; SATA 5

Saner, Reg(inald Anthony) 1931-   **CLC 9**
See also CA 65-68

Sankara 788-820   **CMLC 32**

Sannazaro, Jacopo 1456(?)-1530   **LC 8**

Sansom, William 1912-1976 **CLC 2, 6; DAM NOV; SSC 21**
See also CA 5-8R; 65-68; CANR 42; DLB 139; MTCW 1

Santayana, George 1863-1952   **TCLC 40**
See also CA 115; DLB 54, 71; DLBD 13

Santiago, Danny   **CLC 33**
See also James, Daniel (Lewis)
See also DLB 122

Santmyer, Helen Hoover 1895-1986 **CLC 33**
See also CA 1-4R; 118; CANR 15, 33; DLBY 84; MTCW 1

Santoka, Taneda 1882-1940   **TCLC 72**

Santos, Bienvenido N(uqui) 1911-1996 **CLC 22; DAM MULT**
See also CA 101; 151; CANR 19, 46

Sapper   **TCLC 44**
See also McNeile, Herman Cyril

Sapphire
See Sapphire, Brenda

Sapphire, Brenda 1950-   **CLC 99**

Sappho fl. 6th cent. B.C.-   **CMLC 3; DAM POET; PC 5**
See also DLB 176

Saramago, Jose 1922-   **CLC 119;HLCS 1**
See also CA 153

Sarduy, Severo 1937-1993CLC **6, 97; HLCS 1**
See also CA 89-92; 142; CANR 58, 81; DLB 113; HW 1, 2

Sargeson, Frank 1903-1982   **CLC 31**
See also CA 25-28R; 106; CANR 38, 79

Sarmiento, Domingo Faustino 1811-1888
See also HLCS 2

Sarmiento, Felix Ruben Garcia
See Dario, Ruben

Saro-Wiwa, Ken(ule Beeson) 1941-1995 **C L C 114**
See also BW 2; CA 142; 150; CANR 60; DLB 157

Saroyan, William 1908-1981CLC **1, 8, 10, 29, 34, 56; DA; DAB; DAC; DAM DRAM, MST, NOV; SSC 21; WLC**
See also CA 5-8R; 103; CANR 30; CDALBS; DLB 7, 9, 86; DLBY 81; MTCW 1, 2; SATA 23; SATA-Obit 24

Sarraute, Nathalie 1900-CLC **1, 2, 4, 8, 10, 31, 80**
See also CA 9-12R; CANR 23, 66; DLB 83; MTCW 1, 2

Sarton, (Eleanor) May 1912-1995 CLC **4, 14, 49, 91; DAM POET**
See also CA 1-4R; 149; CANR 1, 34, 55; DLB 48; DLBY 81; INT CANR-34; MTCW 1, 2; SATA 36; SATA-Obit 86

Sartre, Jean-Paul 1905-1980CLC **1, 4, 7, 9, 13, 18, 24, 44, 50, 52; DA; DAB; DAC; DAM DRAM, MST, NOV; DC 3; SSC 32; WLC**
See also CA 9-12R; 97-100; CANR 21; DLB 72; MTCW 1, 2

Sassoon, Siegfried (Lorraine) 1886-1967C L C **36; DAB; DAM MST, NOV, POET; PC 12**
See also CA 104; 25-28R; CANR 36; DLB 20, 191; DLBD 18; MTCW 1, 2

Satterfield, Charles
See Pohl, Frederik

Saul, John (W. III) 1942-CLC **46; DAM NOV, POP**
See also AAYA 10; BEST 90:4; CA 81-84; CANR 16, 40, 81; SATA 98

Saunders, Caleb
See Heinlein, Robert A(nson)

Saura (Atares), Carlos 1932-   **CLC 20**
See also CA 114; 131; CANR 79; HW 1

Sauser-Hall, Frederic 1887-1961   **CLC 18**
See also Cendrars, Blaise
See also CA 102; 93-96; CANR 36, 62; MTCW 1

Saussure, Ferdinand de 1857-1913 TCLC **49**

Savage, Catharine
See Brosman, Catharine Savage

Savage, Thomas 1915-   **CLC 40**
See also CA 126; 132; CAAS 15; INT 132

Savan, Glenn 19(?)-   **CLC 50**

Sayers, Dorothy L(eigh) 1893-1957 TCLC **2, 15; DAM POP**
See also CA 104; 119; CANR 60; CDBLB 1914-1945; DLB 10, 36, 77, 100; MTCW 1, 2

Sayers, Valerie 1952-   **CLC 50, 122**
See also CA 134; CANR 61

Sayles, John (Thomas) 1950-   **CLC 7, 10, 14**
See also CA 57-60; CANR 41; DLB 44

Scammell, Michael 1935-   **CLC 34**
See also CA 156

Scannell, Vernon 1922-   **CLC 49**

See also CA 5-8R; CANR 8, 24, 57; DLB 27;
SATA 59

Scarlett, Susan
See Streatfeild, (Mary) Noel

Scarron
See Mikszath, Kalman

Schaeffer, Susan Fromberg 1941- **CLC 6, 11, 22**
See also CA 49-52; CANR 18, 65; DLB 28;
MTCW 1, 2; SATA 22

Schary, Jill
See Robinson, Jill

Schell, Jonathan 1943- **CLC 35**
See also CA 73-76; CANR 12

Schelling, Friedrich Wilhelm Josephvon 1775-1854 **NCLC 30**
See also DLB 90

Schendel, Arthur van 1874-1946 **TCLC 56**

Scherer, Jean-Marie Maurice 1920-
See Rohmer, Eric
See also CA 110

Schevill, James (Erwin) 1920- **CLC 7**
See also CA 5-8R; CAAS 12

Schiller, Friedrich 1759-1805 **NCLC 39, 69; DAM DRAM**
See also DLB 94

Schisgal, Murray (Joseph) 1926- **CLC 6**
See also CA 21-24R; CANR 48

Schlee, Ann 1934- **CLC 35**
See also CA 101; CANR 29; SATA 44; SATA-Brief 36

Schlegel, August Wilhelmvon 1767-1845 **NCLC 15**
See also DLB 94

Schlegel, Friedrich 1772-1829 **NCLC 45**
See also DLB 90

Schlegel, Johann Elias (von) 1719(?)-1749**LC 5**

Schlesinger, Arthur M(eier), Jr. 1917-**CLC 84**
See also AITN 1; CA 1-4R; CANR 1, 28, 58;
DLB 17; INT CANR-28; MTCW 1, 2; SATA 61

Schmidt, Arno (Otto) 1914-1979 **CLC 56**
See also CA 128; 109; DLB 69

Schmitz, Aron Hector 1861-1928
See Svevo, Italo
See also CA 104; 122; MTCW 1

Schnackenberg, Gjertrud 1953- **CLC 40**
See also CA 116; DLB 120

Schneider, Leonard Alfred 1925-1966
See Bruce, Lenny
See also CA 89-92

Schnitzler, Arthur 1862-1931**TCLC 4; SSC 15**
See also CA 104; DLB 81, 118

Schoenberg, Arnold 1874-1951 **TCLC 75**
See also CA 109

Schonberg, Arnold
See Schoenberg, Arnold

Schopenhauer, Arthur 1788-1860 **NCLC 51**
See also DLB 90

Schor, Sandra (M.) 1932(?)-1990 **CLC 65**
See also CA 132

Schorer, Mark 1908-1977 **CLC 9**
See also CA 5-8R; 73-76; CANR 7; DLB 103

Schrader, Paul (Joseph) 1946- **CLC 26**
See also CA 37-40R; CANR 41; DLB 44

Schreiner, Olive (Emilie Albertina) 1855-1920 **TCLC 9**
See also CA 105; 154; DLB 18, 156, 190

Schulberg, Budd (Wilson) 1914- **CLC 7, 48**
See also CA 25-28R; CANR 19; DLB 6, 26, 28; DLBY 81

Schulz, Bruno 1892-1942**TCLC 5, 51; SSC 13**

See also CA 115; 123; MTCW 2

Schulz, Charles M(onroe) 1922- **CLC 12**
See also CA 9-12R; CANR 6; INT CANR-6;
SATA 10

Schumacher, E(rnst) F(riedrich) 1911-1977 **CLC 80**
See also CA 81-84; 73-76; CANR 34

Schuyler, James Marcus 1923-1991**CLC 5, 23; DAM POET**
See also CA 101; 134; DLB 5, 169; INT 101

Schwartz, Delmore (David) 1913-1966**CLC 2, 4, 10, 45, 87; PC 8**
See also CA 17-18; 25-28R; CANR 35; CAP 2;
DLB 28, 48; MTCW 1, 2

Schwartz, Ernst
See Ozu, Yasujiro

Schwartz, John Burnham 1965- **CLC 59**
See also CA 132

Schwartz, Lynne Sharon 1939- **CLC 31**
See also CA 103; CANR 44; MTCW 2

Schwartz, Muriel A.
See Eliot, T(homas) S(tearns)

Schwarz-Bart, Andre 1928- **CLC 2, 4**
See also CA 89-92

Schwarz-Bart, Simone 1938- **CLC 7;BLCS**
See also BW 2; CA 97-100

Schwitters, Kurt (Hermann Edward Karl Julius) 1887-1948 **TCLC 95**
See also CA 158

Schwob, Marcel (Mayer Andre) 1867-1905 **TCLC 20**
See also CA 117; 168; DLB 123

Sciascia, Leonardo 1921-1989 **CLC 8, 9, 41**
See also CA 85-88; 130; CANR 35; DLB 177;
MTCW 1

Scoppettone, Sandra 1936- **CLC 26**
See also AAYA 11; CA 5-8R; CANR 41, 73;
SATA 9, 92

Scorsese, Martin 1942- **CLC 20, 89**
See also CA 110; 114; CANR 46

Scotland, Jay
See Jakes, John (William)

Scott, Duncan Campbell 1862-1947 **TCLC 6; DAC**
See also CA 104; 153; DLB 92

Scott, Evelyn 1893-1963 **CLC 43**
See also CA 104; 112; CANR 64; DLB 9, 48

Scott, F(rancis) R(eginald) 1899-1985**CLC 22**
See also CA 101; 114; DLB 88; INT 101

Scott, Frank
See Scott, F(rancis) R(eginald)

Scott, Joanna 1960- **CLC 50**
See also CA 126; CANR 53

Scott, Paul (Mark) 1920-1978 **CLC 9, 60**
See also CA 81-84; 77-80; CANR 33; DLB 14, 207; MTCW 1

Scott, Sarah 1723-1795 **LC 44**
See also DLB 39

Scott, Walter 1771-1832 **NCLC 15, 69; DA; DAB; DAC; DAM MST, NOV, POET; PC 13; SSC 32; WLC**
See also AAYA 22; CDBLB 1789-1832; DLB 93, 107, 116, 144, 159; YABC 2

Scribe, (Augustin) Eugene 1791-1861 **NCLC 16; DAM DRAM; DC 5**
See also DLB 192

Scrum, R.
See Crumb, R(obert)

Scudery, Madeleine de 1607-1701 **LC 2**

Scum
See Crumb, R(obert)

Scumbag, Little Bobby
See Crumb, R(obert)

Seabrook, John
See Hubbard, L(afayette) Ron(ald)

Sealy, I. Allan 1951- **CLC 55**

Search, Alexander
See Pessoa, Fernando (Antonio Nogueira)

Sebastian, Lee
See Silverberg, Robert

Sebastian Owl
See Thompson, Hunter S(tockton)

Secundus, H. Scriblerus
See Fielding, Henry

Sedges, John
See Buck, Pearl S(ydenstricker)

Sedgwick, Catharine Maria 1789-1867**NCLC 19**
See also DLB 1, 74

Seelye, John (Douglas) 1931- **CLC 7**
See also CA 97-100; CANR 70; INT 97-100

Seferiades, Giorgos Stylianou 1900-1971
See Seferis, George
See also CA 5-8R; 33-36R; CANR 5, 36;
MTCW 1

Seferis, George **CLC 5, 11**
See also Seferiades, Giorgos Stylianou

Segal, Erich (Wolf) 1937- **CLC 3, 10; DAM POP**
See also BEST 89:1; CA 25-28R; CANR 20, 36, 65; DLBY 86; INT CANR-20; MTCW 1

Seger, Bob 1945- **CLC 35**

Seghers, Anna **CLC 7**
See also Radvanyi, Netty
See also DLB 69

Seidel, Frederick (Lewis) 1936- **CLC 18**
See also CA 13-16R; CANR 8; DLBY 84

Seifert, Jaroslav 1901-1986 **CLC 34, 44, 93**
See also CA 127; MTCW 1, 2

Sei Shonagon c. 966-1017(?) **CMLC 6**

Sejour, Victor 1817-1874 **DC 10**
See also DLB 50

Sejour Marcou et Ferrand, Juan Victor
See Sejour, Victor

Selby, Hubert, Jr. 1928-**CLC 1, 2, 4, 8; SSC 20**
See also CA 13-16R; CANR 33; DLB 2

Selzer, Richard 1928- **CLC 74**
See also CA 65-68; CANR 14

Sembene, Ousmane
See Ousmane, Sembene

Senancour, Etienne Pivert de 1770-1846 **NCLC 16**
See also DLB 119

Sender, Ramon (Jose) 1902-1982**CLC 8; DAM MULT; HLC 2**
See also CA 5-8R; 105; CANR 8; HW 1;
MTCW 1

Seneca, Lucius Annaeus c. 1-c. 65 **CMLC 6; DAM DRAM; DC 5**
See also DLB 211

Senghor, Leopold Sedar 1906- **CLC 54; BLC 3; DAM MULT, POET; PC 25**
See also BW 2; CA 116; 125; CANR 47, 74;
MTCW 1, 2

Senna, Danzy 1970- **CLC 119**
See also CA 169

Serling, (Edward) Rod(man) 1924-1975 **CLC 30**
See also AAYA 14; AITN 1; CA 162; 57-60;
DLB 26

Serna, Ramon Gomez de la
See Gomez de la Serna, Ramon

Serpieres

See Guillevic, (Eugene)

Service, Robert
See Service, Robert W(illiam)
See also DAB; DLB 92

Service, Robert W(illiam) 1874(?)-1958 **TCLC 15; DA; DAC; DAM MST, POET; WLC**
See also Service, Robert
See also CA 115; 140; SATA 20

Seth, Vikram 1952- **CLC 43, 90;DAM MULT**
See also CA 121; 127; CANR 50, 74; DLB 120; INT 127; MTCW 2

Seton, Cynthia Propper 1926-1982 **CLC 27**
See also CA 5-8R; 108; CANR 7

Seton, Ernest (Evan) Thompson 1860-1946 **TCLC 31**
See also CA 109; CLR 59; DLB 92; DLBD 13; JRDA; SATA 18

Seton-Thompson, Ernest
See Seton, Ernest (Evan) Thompson

Settle, Mary Lee 1918- **CLC 19, 61**
See also CA 89-92; CAAS 1; CANR 44; DLB 6; INT 89-92

Seuphor, Michel
See Arp, Jean

Sevigne, Marie (de Rabutin-Chantal) Marquise de 1626-1696 **LC 11**

Sewall, Samuel 1652-1730 **LC 38**
See also DLB 24

Sexton, Anne (Harvey) 1928-1974 **CLC 2, 4, 6, 8, 10, 15, 53; DA; DAB; DAC; DAM MST, POET; PC 2; WLC**
See also CA 1-4R; 53-56; CABS 2; CANR 3, 36; CDALB 1941-1968; DLB 5, 169; MTCW 1, 2; SATA 10

Shaara, Jeff 1952- **CLC 119**
See also CA 163

Shaara, Michael (Joseph, Jr.) 1929-1988 **CLC 15; DAM POP**
See also AITN 1; CA 102; 125; CANR 52; DLBY 83

Shackleton, C. C.
See Aldiss, Brian W(ilson)

Shacochis, Bob **CLC 39**
See also Shacochis, Robert G.

Shacochis, Robert G. 1951-
See Shacochis, Bob
See also CA 119; 124; INT 124

Shaffer, Anthony (Joshua) 1926- **CLC 19; DAM DRAM**
See also CA 110; 116; DLB 13

Shaffer, Peter (Levin) 1926- **CLC 5, 14, 18, 37, 60; DAB; DAM DRAM, MST; DC 7**
See also CA 25-28R; CANR 25, 47, 74; CDBLB 1960 to Present; DLB 13; MTCW 1, 2

Shakey, Bernard
See Young, Neil

Shalamov, Varlam (Tikhonovich) 1907(?)-1982 **CLC 18**
See also CA 129; 105

Shamlu, Ahmad 1925- **CLC 10**

Shammas, Anton 1951- **CLC 55**

Shange, Ntozake 1948- **CLC 8, 25, 38, 74; BLC 3; DAM DRAM, MULT; DC 3**
See also AAYA 9; BW 2; CA 85-88; CABS 3; CANR 27, 48, 74; DLB 38; MTCW 1, 2

Shanley, John Patrick 1950- **CLC 75**
See also CA 128; 133

Shapcott, Thomas W(illiam) 1935- **CLC 38**
See also CA 69-72; CANR 49

Shapiro, Jane **CLC 76**

Shapiro, Karl (Jay) 1913- **CLC 4, 8, 15, 53; PC 25**
See also CA 1-4R; CAAS 6; CANR 1, 36, 66;

DLB 48; MTCW 1, 2

Sharp, William 1855-1905 **TCLC 39**
See also CA 160; DLB 156

Sharpe, Thomas Ridley 1928-
See Sharpe, Tom
See also CA 114; 122; INT 122

Sharpe, Tom **CLC 36**
See also Sharpe, Thomas Ridley
See also DLB 14

Shaw, Bernard **TCLC 45**
See also Shaw, George Bernard
See also BW 1; MTCW 2

Shaw, G. Bernard
See Shaw, George Bernard

Shaw, George Bernard 1856-1950 **TCLC 3, 9, 21; DA; DAB; DAC; DAM DRAM, MST; WLC**
See also Shaw, Bernard
See also CA 104; 128; CDBLB 1914-1945; DLB 10, 57, 190; MTCW 1, 2

Shaw, Henry Wheeler 1818-1885 **NCLC 15**
See also DLB 11

Shaw, Irwin 1913-1984 **CLC 7, 23, 34; DAM DRAM, POP**
See also AITN 1; CA 13-16R; 112; CANR 21; CDALB 1941-1968; DLB 6, 102; DLBY 84; MTCW 1, 21

Shaw, Robert 1927-1978 **CLC 5**
See also AITN 1; CA 1-4R; 81-84; CANR 4; DLB 13, 14

Shaw, T. E.
See Lawrence, T(homas) E(dward)

Shawn, Wallace 1943- **CLC 41**
See also CA 112

Shea, Lisa 1953- **CLC 86**
See also CA 147

Sheed, Wilfrid (John Joseph) 1930- **CLC 2, 4, 10, 53**
See also CA 65-68; CANR 30, 66; DLB 6; MTCW 1, 2

Sheldon, Alice Hastings Bradley 1915(?)-1987
See Tiptree, James, Jr.
See also CA 108; 122; CANR 34; INT 108; MTCW 1

Sheldon, John 1917-1994
See Bloch, Robert (Albert)
See also CA 179; CAAE 179

Shelley, Mary Wollstonecraft (Godwin) 1797-1851 **NCLC 14, 59; DA; DAB; DAC; DAM MST, NOV; WLC**
See also AAYA 20; CDBLB 1789-1832; DLB 110, 116, 159, 178; SATA 29

Shelley, Percy Bysshe 1792-1822 **NCLC 18; DA; DAB; DAC; DAM MST, POET; PC 14; WLC**
See also CDBLB 1789-1832; DLB 96, 110, 158

Shepard, Jim 1956- **CLC 36**
See also CA 137; CANR 59; SATA 90

Shepard, Lucius 1947- **CLC 34**
See also CA 128; 141; CANR 81

Shepard, Sam 1943- **CLC 4, 6, 17, 34, 41, 44; DAM DRAM; DC 5**
See also AAYA 1; CA 69-72; CABS 3; CANR 22; DLB 7, 212; MTCW 1, 2

Shepherd, Michael
See Ludlum, Robert

Sherburne, Zoa (Lillian Morin) 1912-1995 **CLC 30**
See also AAYA 13; CA 1-4R; 176; CANR 3, 37; MAICYA; SAAS 18; SATA 3

Sheridan, Frances 1724-1766 **LC 7**
See also DLB 39, 84

Sheridan, Richard Brinsley 1751-1816 **NCLC**

5; **DA; DAB; DAC; DAM DRAM, MST; DC 1; WLC**
See also CDBLB 1660-1789; DLB 89

Sherman, Jonathan Marc **CLC 55**

Sherman, Martin 1941(?)- **CLC 19**
See also CA 116; 123

Sherwin, Judith Johnson
See Johnson, Judith (Emlyn)

Sherwood, Frances 1940- **CLC 81**
See also CA 146

Sherwood, Robert E(mmet) 1896-1955 **TCLC 3; DAM DRAM**
See also CA 104; 153; DLB 7, 26

Shestov, Lev 1866-1938 **TCLC 56**

Shevchenko, Taras 1814-1861 **NCLC 54**

Shiel, M(atthew) P(hipps) 1865-1947 **TCLC 8**
See also Holmes, Gordon
See also CA 106; 160; DLB 153; MTCW 2

Shields, Carol 1935- **CLC 91, 113;DAC**
See also CA 81-84; CANR 51, 74; MTCW 2

Shields, David 1956- **CLC 97**
See also CA 124; CANR 48

Shiga, Naoya 1883-1971 **CLC 33;SSC 23**
See also CA 101; 33-36R; DLB 180

Shikibu, Murasaki c. 978-c. 1014 **CMLC 1**

Shilts, Randy 1951-1994 **CLC 85**
See also AAYA 19; CA 115; 127; 144; CANR 45; INT 127; MTCW 2

Shimazaki, Haruki 1872-1943
See Shimazaki Toson
See also CA 105; 134

Shimazaki Toson 1872-1943 **TCLC 5**
See also Shimazaki, Haruki
See also DLB 180

Sholokhov, Mikhail (Aleksandrovich) 1905-1984 **CLC 7, 15**
See also CA 101; 112; MTCW 1, 2; SATA-Obit 36

Shone, Patric
See Hanley, James

Shreve, Susan Richards 1939- **CLC 23**
See also CA 49-52; CAAS 5; CANR 5, 38, 69; MAICYA; SATA 46, 95; SATA-Brief 41

Shue, Larry 1946-1985 **CLC 52;DAM DRAM**
See also CA 145; 117

Shu-Jen, Chou 1881-1936
See Lu Hsun
See also CA 104

Shulman, Alix Kates 1932- **CLC 2,10**
See also CA 29-32R; CANR 43; SATA 7

Shuster, Joe 1914- **CLC 21**

Shute, Nevil **CLC 30**
See also Norway, Nevil Shute
See also MTCW 2

Shuttle, Penelope (Diane) 1947- **CLC 7**
See also CA 93-96; CANR 39; DLB 14, 40

Sidney, Mary 1561-1621 **LC 19, 39**

Sidney, Sir Philip 1554-1586 **LC 19, 39; DA; DAB; DAC; DAM MST, POET**
See also CDBLB Before 1660; DLB 167

Siegel, Jerome 1914-1996 **CLC 21**
See also CA 116; 169; 151

Siegel, Jerry
See Siegel, Jerome

Sienkiewicz, Henryk (Adam Alexander Pius) 1846-1916 **TCLC 3**
See also CA 104; 134

Sierra, Gregorio Martinez
See Martinez Sierra, Gregorio

Sierra, Maria (de la O'LeJarraga) Martinez
See Martinez Sierra, Maria (de la O'LeJarraga)

Sigal, Clancy 1926- **CLC 7**
See also CA 1-4R

Sigourney, Lydia Howard (Huntley) 1791-1865 **NCLC 21**
See also DLB 1, 42, 73

Siguenza y Gongora, Carlos de 1645-1700**L C 8; HLCS 2**

Sigurjonsson, Johann 1880-1919 **TCLC 27**
See also CA 170

Sikelianos, Angelos 1884-1951 **TCLC 39**

Silkin, Jon 1930- **CLC 2, 6, 43**
See also CA 5-8R; CAAS 5; DLB 27

Silko, Leslie (Marmon) 1948-**CLC 23, 74, 114; DA; DAC; DAM MST, MULT, POP; WLCS**
See also AAYA 14; CA 115; 122; CANR 45, 65; DLB 143, 175; MTCW 2; NNAL

Sillanpaa, Frans Eemil 1888-1964 **CLC 19**
See also CA 129; 93-96; MTCW 1

Sillitoe, Alan 1928- **CLC 1, 3, 6, 10, 19, 57**
See also AITN 1; CA 9-12R; CAAS 2; CANR 8, 26, 55; CDBLB 1960 to Present; DLB 14, 139; MTCW 1, 2; SATA 61

Silone, Ignazio 1900-1978 **CLC 4**
See also CA 25-28; 81-84; CANR 34; CAP 2; MTCW 1

Silver, Joan Micklin 1935- **CLC 20**
See also CA 114; 121; INT 121

Silver, Nicholas
See Faust, Frederick (Schiller)

Silverberg, Robert 1935- **CLC 7;DAM POP**
See also Jarvis, E. K.
See also AAYA 24; CA 1-4R; CAAS 3; CANR 1, 20, 36; CLR 59; DLB 8; INT CANR-20; MAICYA; MTCW 1, 2; SATA 13, 91; SATA-Essay 104

Silverstein, Alvin 1933- **CLC 17**
See also CA 49-52; CANR 2; CLR 25; JRDA; MAICYA; SATA 8, 69

Silverstein, Virginia B(arbara Opshelor) 1937-
CLC 17
See also CA 49-52; CANR 2; CLR 25; JRDA; MAICYA; SATA 8, 69

Sim, Georges
See Simenon, Georges (Jacques Christian)

Simak, Clifford D(onald) 1904-1988**CLC 1, 55**
See also CA 1-4R; 125; CANR 1, 35; DLB 8; MTCW 1; SATA-Obit 56

Simenon, Georges (Jacques Christian) 1903-1989 **CLC 1, 2, 3, 8, 18, 47; DAM POP**
See also CA 85-88; 129; CANR 35; DLB 72; DLBY 89; MTCW 1, 2

Simic, Charles 1938- **CLC 6, 9, 22, 49, 68; DAM POET**
See also CA 29-32R; CAAS 4; CANR 12, 33, 52, 61; DLB 105; MTCW 2

Simmel, Georg 1858-1918 **TCLC 64**
See also CA 157

Simmons, Charles (Paul) 1924- **CLC 57**
See also CA 89-92; INT 89-92

Simmons, Dan 1948- **CLC 44;DAM POP**
See also AAYA 16; CA 138; CANR 53, 81

Simmons, James (Stewart Alexander) 1933-
CLC 43
See also CA 105; CAAS 21; DLB 40

Simms, William Gilmore 1806-1870 **NCLC 3**
See also DLB 3, 30, 59, 73

Simon, Carly 1945- **CLC 26**
See also CA 105

Simon, Claude 1913-1984 **CLC 4, 9, 15, 39; DAM NOV**
See also CA 89-92; CANR 33; DLB 83; MTCW 1

Simon, (Marvin) Neil 1927-**CLC 6, 11, 31, 39, 70; DAM DRAM**

See also AITN 1; CA 21-24R; CANR 26, 54; DLB 7; MTCW 1, 2

Simon, Paul (Frederick) 1941(?)- **CLC 17**
See also CA 116; 153

Simonon, Paul 1956(?)- **CLC 30**

Simpson, Harriette
See Arnow, Harriette (Louisa) Simpson

Simpson, Louis (Aston Marantz) 1923-**CLC 4, 7, 9, 32; DAM POET**
See also CA 1-4R; CAAS 4; CANR 1, 61; DLB 5; MTCW 1, 2

Simpson, Mona (Elizabeth) 1957- **CLC 44**
See also CA 122; 135; CANR 68

Simpson, N(orman) F(rederick) 1919-**CLC 29**
See also CA 13-16R; DLB 13

Sinclair, Andrew (Annandale) 1935- **CLC 2, 14**
See also CA 9-12R; CAAS 5; CANR 14, 38; DLB 14; MTCW 1

Sinclair, Emil
See Hesse, Hermann

Sinclair, Iain 1943- **CLC 76**
See also CA 132; CANR 81

Sinclair, Iain MacGregor
See Sinclair, Iain

Sinclair, Irene
See Griffith, D(avid Lewelyn) W(ark)

Sinclair, Mary Amelia St. Clair 1865(?)-1946
See Sinclair, May
See also CA 104

Sinclair, May 1863-1946 **TCLC 3, 11**
See also Sinclair, Mary Amelia St. Clair
See also CA 166; DLB 36, 135

Sinclair, Roy
See Griffith, D(avid Lewelyn) W(ark)

Sinclair, Upton (Beall) 1878-1968 **CLC 1, 11, 15, 63; DA; DAB; DAC; DAM MST, NOV; WLC**
See also CA 5-8R; 25-28R; CANR 7; CDALB 1929-1941; DLB 9; INT CANR-7; MTCW 1, 2; SATA 9

Singer, Isaac
See Singer, Isaac Bashevis

Singer, Isaac Bashevis 1904-1991**CLC 1, 3, 6, 9, 11, 15, 23, 38, 69, 111; DA; DAB; DAC; DAM MST, NOV; SSC 3; WLC**
See also AITN 1, 2; CA 1-4R; 134; CANR 1, 39; CDALB 1941-1968; CLR 1; DLB 6, 28, 52; DLBY 91; JRDA; MAICYA; MTCW 1, 2; SATA 3, 27; SATA-Obit 68

Singer, Israel Joshua 1893-1944 **TCLC 33**
See also CA 169

Singh, Khushwant 1915- **CLC 11**
See also CA 9-12R; CAAS 9; CANR 6

Singleton, Ann
See Benedict, Ruth (Fulton)

Sinjohn, John
See Galsworthy, John

Sinyavsky, Andrei (Donatevich) 1925-1997
CLC 8
See also CA 85-88; 159

Sirin, V.
See Nabokov, Vladimir (Vladimirovich)

Sissman, L(ouis) E(dward) 1928-1976**CLC 9, 18**
See also CA 21-24R; 65-68; CANR 13; DLB 5

Sisson, C(harles) H(ubert) 1914- **CLC 8**
See also CA 1-4R; CAAS 3; CANR 3, 48; DLB 27

Sitwell, Dame Edith 1887-1964 **CLC 2, 9, 67; DAM POET; PC 3**
See also CA 9-12R; CANR 35; CDBLB 1945-1960; DLB 20; MTCW 1, 2

Siwaarmill, H. P.
See Sharp, William

Sjoewall, Maj 1935- **CLC 7**
See also CA 65-68; CANR 73

Sjowall, Maj
See Sjoewall, Maj

Skelton, John 1463-1529 **PC 25**

Skelton, Robin 1925-1997 **CLC 13**
See also AITN 2; CA 5-8R; 160; CAAS 5; CANR 28; DLB 27, 53

Skolimowski, Jerzy 1938- **CLC 20**
See also CA 128

Skram, Amalie (Bertha) 1847-1905 **TCLC 25**
See also CA 165

Skvorecky, Josef (Vaclav) 1924- **CLC 15, 39, 69; DAC; DAM NOV**
See also CA 61-64; CAAS 1; CANR 10, 34, 63; MTCW 1, 2

Slade, Bernard **CLC 11, 46**
See also Newbound, Bernard Slade
See also CAAS 9; DLB 53

Slaughter, Carolyn 1946- **CLC 56**
See also CA 85-88

Slaughter, Frank G(ill) 1908- **CLC 29**
See also AITN 2; CA 5-8R; CANR 5; INT CANR-5

Slavitt, David R(ytman) 1935- **CLC 5, 14**
See also CA 21-24R; CAAS 3; CANR 41; DLB 5, 6

Slesinger, Tess 1905-1945 **TCLC 10**
See also CA 107; DLB 102

Slessor, Kenneth 1901-1971 **CLC 14**
See also CA 102; 89-92

Slowacki, Juliusz 1809-1849 **NCLC 15**

Smart, Christopher 1722-1771 **LC 3; DAM POET; PC 13**
See also DLB 109

Smart, Elizabeth 1913-1986 **CLC 54**
See also CA 81-84; 118; DLB 88

Smiley, Jane (Graves) 1949-**CLC 53, 76; DAM POP**
See also CA 104; CANR 30, 50, 74; INT CANR-30

Smith, A(rthur) J(ames) M(arshall) 1902-1980
CLC 15; DAC
See also CA 1-4R; 102; CANR 4; DLB 88

Smith, Adam 1723-1790 **LC 36**
See also DLB 104

Smith, Alexander 1829-1867 **NCLC 59**
See also DLB 32, 55

Smith, Anna Deavere 1950- **CLC 86**
See also CA 133

Smith, Betty (Wehner) 1896-1972 **CLC 19**
See also CA 5-8R; 33-36R; DLBY 82; SATA 6

Smith, Charlotte (Turner) 1749-1806 **NCLC 23**
See also DLB 39, 109

Smith, Clark Ashton 1893-1961 **CLC 43**
See also CA 143; CANR 81; MTCW 2

Smith, Dave **CLC 22, 42**
See also Smith, David (Jeddie)
See also CAAS 7; DLB 5

Smith, David (Jeddie) 1942-
See Smith, Dave
See also CA 49-52; CANR 1, 59; DAM POET

Smith, Florence Margaret 1902-1971
See Smith, Stevie
See also CA 17-18; 29-32R; CANR 35; CAP 2; DAM POET; MTCW 1, 2

Smith, Iain Crichton 1928-1998 **CLC 64**
See also CA 21-24R; 171; DLB 40, 139

Smith, John 1580(?)-1631 **LC 9**
See also DLB 24, 30

See Stael-Holstein, Anne Louise Germaine
Necker Baronn
See also DLB 119

**Stael-Holstein, Anne Louise Germaine Necker
Baronn** 1766-1817   **NCLC 3**
See also Stael, Germaine de
See also DLB 192

Stafford, Jean 1915-1979**CLC 4, 7, 19, 68; SSC
26**
See also CA 1-4R; 85-88; CANR 3, 65; DLB 2,
173; MTCW 1, 2; SATA-Obit 22

Stafford, William (Edgar) 1914-1993 **CLC 4,
7, 29; DAM POET**
See also CA 5-8R; 142; CAAS 3; CANR 5, 22;
DLB 5, 206; INT CANR-22

Stagnelius, Eric Johan 1793-1823   **NCLC 61**

Staines, Trevor
See Brunner, John (Kilian Houston)

Stairs, Gordon
See Austin, Mary (Hunter)

Stairs, Gordon
See Austin, Mary (Hunter)

Stalin, Joseph 1879-1953   **TCLC 92**

Stannard, Martin 1947-   **CLC 44**
See also CA 142; DLB 155

Stanton, Elizabeth Cady 1815-1902**TCLC 73**
See also CA 171; DLB 79

Stanton, Maura 1946-   **CLC 9**
See also CA 89-92; CANR 15; DLB 120

Stanton, Schuyler
See Baum, L(yman) Frank

Stapledon, (William) Olaf 1886-1950 **TCLC
22**
See also CA 111; 162; DLB 15

Starbuck, George (Edwin) 1931-1996**CLC 53;
DAM POET**
See also CA 21-24R; 153; CANR 23

Stark, Richard
See Westlake, Donald E(dwin)

Staunton, Schuyler
See Baum, L(yman) Frank

Stead, Christina (Ellen) 1902-1983 **CLC 2, 5,
8, 32, 80**
See also CA 13-16R; 109; CANR 33, 40;
MTCW 1, 2

Stead, William Thomas 1849-1912 **TCLC 48**
See also CA 167

Steele, Richard 1672-1729   **LC 18**
See also CDBLB 1660-1789; DLB 84, 101

Steele, Timothy (Reid) 1948-   **CLC 45**
See also CA 93-96; CANR 16, 50; DLB 120

Steffens, (Joseph) Lincoln 1866-1936 **TCLC
20**
See also CA 117

Stegner, Wallace (Earle) 1909-1993**CLC 9, 49,
81; DAM NOV; SSC 27**
See also AITN 1; BEST 90:3; CA 1-4R; 141;
CAAS 9; CANR 1, 21, 46; DLB 9, 206;
DLBY 93; MTCW 1, 2

Stein, Gertrude 1874-1946**TCLC 1, 6, 28, 48;
DA; DAB; DAC; DAM MST, NOV, POET;
PC 18; WLC**
See also CA 104; 132; CDALB 1917-1929;
DLB 4, 54, 86; DLBD 15; MTCW 1, 2

Steinbeck, John (Ernst) 1902-1968**CLC 1, 5, 9,
13, 21, 34, 45, 75; DA; DAB; DAC; DAM
DRAM, MST, NOV; SSC 11;WLC**
See also AAYA 12; CA 1-4R; 25-28R; CANR
1, 35; CDALB 1929-1941; DLB 7, 9, 212;
DLBD 2; MTCW 1, 2; SATA 9

Steinem, Gloria 1934-   **CLC 63**
See also CA 53-56; CANR 28, 51; MTCW 1, 2

Steiner, George 1929-   **CLC 24;DAM NOV**

See also CA 73-76; CANR 31, 67; DLB 67;
MTCW 1, 2; SATA 62

Steiner, K. Leslie
See Delany, Samuel R(ay, Jr.)

Steiner, Rudolf 1861-1925   **TCLC 13**
See also CA 107

Stendhal 1783-1842**NCLC 23, 46; DA; DAB;
DAC; DAM MST, NOV; SSC 27; WLC**
See also DLB 119

Stephen, Adeline Virginia
See Woolf, (Adeline) Virginia

Stephen, Sir Leslie 1832-1904   **TCLC 23**
See also CA 123; DLB 57, 144, 190

Stephen, Sir Leslie
See Stephen, SirLeslie

Stephen, Virginia
See Woolf, (Adeline) Virginia

Stephens, James 1882(?)-1950   **TCLC 4**
See also CA 104; DLB 19, 153, 162

Stephens, Reed
See Donaldson, Stephen R.

Steptoe, Lydia
See Barnes, Djuna

Sterchi, Beat 1949-   **CLC 65**

Sterling, Brett
See Bradbury, Ray (Douglas); Hamilton,
Edmond

Sterling, Bruce 1954-   **CLC 72**
See also CA 119; CANR 44

Sterling, George 1869-1926   **TCLC 20**
See also CA 117; 165; DLB 54

Stern, Gerald 1925-   **CLC 40, 100**
See also CA 81-84; CANR 28; DLB 105

Stern, Richard (Gustave) 1928-   **CLC 4, 39**
See also CA 1-4R; CANR 1, 25, 52; DLBY 87;
INT CANR-25

Sternberg, Josefvon 1894-1969   **CLC 20**
See also CA 81-84

Sterne, Laurence 1713-1768   **LC 2, 48; DA;
DAB; DAC; DAM MST, NOV; WLC**
See also CDBLB 1660-1789; DLB 39

Sternheim, (William Adolf) Carl 1878-1942
TCLC 8
See also CA 105; DLB 56, 118

Stevens, Mark 1951-   **CLC 34**
See also CA 122

Stevens, Wallace 1879-1955 **TCLC 3, 12, 45;
DA; DAB; DAC; DAM MST, POET; PC
6; WLC**
See also CA 104; 124; CDALB 1929-1941;
DLB 54; MTCW 1, 2

Stevenson, Anne (Katharine) 1933-**CLC 7, 33**
See also CA 17-20R; CAAS 9; CANR 9, 33;
DLB 40; MTCW 1

Stevenson, Robert Louis (Balfour) 1850-1894
**NCLC 5, 14, 63; DA; DAB; DAC; DAM
MST, NOV; SSC 11; WLC**
See also AAYA 24; CDBLB 1890-1914; CLR
10, 11; DLB 18, 57, 141, 156, 174; DLBD
13; JRDA; MAICYA; SATA 100; YABC 2

Stewart, J(ohn) I(nnes) M(ackintosh) 1906-
1994   **CLC 7, 14, 32**
See also CA 85-88; 147; CAAS 3; CANR 47;
MTCW 1, 2

Stewart, Mary (Florence Elinor) 1916-**CLC 7,
35, 117; DAB**
See also AAYA 29; CA 1-4R; CANR 1, 59;
SATA 12

Stewart, Mary Rainbow
See Stewart, Mary (Florence Elinor)

Stifle, June
See Campbell, Maria

Stifter, Adalbert 1805-1868**NCLC 41; SSC 28**

See also DLB 133

Still, James 1906-   **CLC 49**
See also CA 65-68; CAAS 17; CANR 10, 26;
DLB 9; SATA 29

Sting 1951-
See Sumner, Gordon Matthew
See also CA 167

Stirling, Arthur
See Sinclair, Upton (Beall)

Stitt, Milan 1941-   **CLC 29**
See also CA 69-72

Stockton, Francis Richard 1834-1902
See Stockton, Frank R.
See also CA 108; 137; MAICYA; SATA 44

Stockton, Frank R.   **TCLC 47**
See also Stockton, Francis Richard
See also DLB 42, 74; DLBD 13; SATA-Brief
32

Stoddard, Charles
See Kuttner, Henry

Stoker, Abraham 1847-1912
See Stoker, Bram
See also CA 105; 150; DA; DAC; DAM MST,
NOV; SATA 29

Stoker, Bram 1847-1912**TCLC 8; DAB; WLC**
See also Stoker, Abraham
See also AAYA 23; CDBLB 1890-1914; DLB
36, 70, 178

Stolz, Mary (Slattery) 1920-   **CLC 12**
See also AAYA 8; AITN 1; CA 5-8R; CANR
13, 41; JRDA; MAICYA; SAAS 3; SATA 10,
71

Stone, Irving 1903-1989   **CLC 7;DAM POP**
See also AITN 1; CA 1-4R; 129; CAAS 3;
CANR 1, 23; INT CANR-23; MTCW 1, 2;
SATA 3; SATA-Obit 64

Stone, Oliver (William) 1946-   **CLC 73**
See also AAYA 15; CA 110; CANR 55

Stone, Robert (Anthony) 1937-**CLC 5, 23, 42**
See also CA 85-88; CANR 23, 66; DLB 152;
INT CANR-23; MTCW 1

Stone, Zachary
See Follett, Ken(neth Martin)

Stoppard, Tom 1937-**CLC 1, 3, 4, 5, 8, 15, 29,
34, 63, 91; DA; DAB; DAC; DAM DRAM,
MST; DC 6; WLC**
See also CA 81-84; CANR 39, 67; CDBLB
1960 to Present; DLB 13; DLBY 85; MTCW
1, 2

Storey, David (Malcolm) 1933-**CLC 2, 4, 5, 8;
DAM DRAM**
See also CA 81-84; CANR 36; DLB 13, 14, 207;
MTCW 1

Storm, Hyemeyohsts 1935-   **CLC 3;DAM
MULT**
See also CA 81-84; CANR 45; NNAL

Storm, Theodor 1817-1888   **SSC 27**

Storm, (Hans) Theodor (Woldsen) 1817-1888
NCLC 1; SSC 27
See also DLB 129

Storni, Alfonsina 1892-1938   **TCLC 5; DAM
MULT; HLC 2**
See also CA 104; 131; HW 1

Stoughton, William 1631-1701   **LC 38**
See also DLB 24

Stout, Rex (Todhunter) 1886-1975   **CLC 3**
See also AITN 2; CA 61-64; CANR 71

Stow, (Julian) Randolph 1935-   **CLC 23, 48**
See also CA 13-16R; CANR 33; MTCW 1

Stowe, Harriet (Elizabeth) Beecher 1811-1896
**NCLC 3, 50; DA; DAB; DAC; DAM MST,
NOV; WLC**
See also CDALB 1865-1917; DLB 1, 12, 42,

Tutuola, Amos 1920-1997 CLC 5, 14, 29; BLC 3; DAM MULT
See also BW 2, 3; CA 9-12R; 159; CANR 27, 66; DLB 125; MTCW 1, 2

Twain, Mark TCLC 6, 12, 19, 36, 48, 59; SSC 34; WLC
See also Clemens, Samuel Langhorne
See also AAYA 20; CLR 58; DLB 11, 12, 23, 64, 74

Tyler, Anne 1941- CLC 7, 11, 18, 28, 44, 59, 103; DAM NOV, POP
See also AAYA 18; BEST 89:1; CA 9-12R; CANR 11, 33, 53; CDALBS; DLB 6, 143; DLBY 82; MTCW 1, 2; SATA 7, 90

Tyler, Royall 1757-1826 NCLC 3
See also DLB 37

Tynan, Katharine 1861-1931 TCLC 3
See also CA 104; 167; DLB 153

Tyutchev, Fyodor 1803-1873 NCLC 34

Tzara, Tristan 1896-1963 CLC 47; DAM POET; PC 27
See also CA 153; 89-92; MTCW 2

Uhry, Alfred 1936- CLC 55; DAM DRAM, POP
See also CA 127; 133; INT 133

Ulf, Haerved
See Strindberg, (Johan) August

Ulf, Harved
See Strindberg, (Johan) August

Ulibarri, Sabine R(eyes) 1919- CLC 83; DAM MULT; HLCS 2
See also CA 131; CANR 81; DLB 82; HW 1, 2

Unamuno (y Jugo), Miguel de 1864-1936 TCLC 2, 9; DAM MULT, NOV; HLC 2; SSC 11
See also CA 104; 131; CANR 81; DLB 108; HW 1, 2; MTCW 1, 2

Undercliffe, Errol
See Campbell, (John) Ramsey

Underwood, Miles
See Glassco, John

Undset, Sigrid 1882-1949 TCLC 3; DA; DAB; DAC; DAM MST, NOV; WLC
See also CA 104; 129; MTCW 1, 2

Ungaretti, Giuseppe 1888-1970 CLC 7, 11, 15
See also CA 19-20; 25-28R; CAP 2; DLB 114

Unger, Douglas 1952- CLC 34
See also CA 130

Unsworth, Barry (Forster) 1930- CLC 76
See also CA 25-28R; CANR 30, 54; DLB 194

Updike, John (Hoyer) 1932- CLC 1, 2, 3, 5, 7, 9, 13, 15, 23, 34, 43, 70; DA; DAB; DAC; DAM MST, NOV, POET, POP; SSC 13, 27; WLC
See also CA 1-4R; CABS 1; CANR 4, 33, 51; CDALB 1968-1988; DLB 2, 5, 143; DLBD 3; DLBY 80, 82, 97; MTCW 1, 2

Upshaw, Margaret Mitchell
See Mitchell, Margaret (Munnerlyn)

Upton, Mark
See Sanders, Lawrence

Upward, Allen 1863-1926 TCLC 85
See also CA 117; DLB 36

Urdang, Constance (Henriette) 1922- CLC 47
See also CA 21-24R; CANR 9, 24

Uriel, Henry
See Faust, Frederick (Schiller)

Uris, Leon (Marcus) 1924- CLC 7, 32; DAM NOV, POP
See also AITN 1, 2; BEST 89:2; CA 1-4R; CANR 1, 40, 65; MTCW 1, 2; SATA 49

Urista, Alberto H. 1947-
See Alurista

See also CA 45-48; CANR 2, 32; HLCS 1; HW 1

Urmuz
See Codrescu, Andrei

Urquhart, Jane 1949- CLC 90; DAC
See also CA 113; CANR 32, 68

Usigli, Rodolfo 1905-1979
See also CA 131; HLCS 1; HW 1

Ustinov, Peter (Alexander) 1921- CLC 1
See also AITN 1; CA 13-16R; CANR 25, 51; DLB 13; MTCW 2

U Tam'si, Gerald Felix Tchicaya
See Tchicaya, Gerald Felix

U Tam'si, Tchicaya
See Tchicaya, Gerald Felix

Vachss, Andrew (Henry) 1942- CLC 106
See also CA 118; CANR 44

Vachss, Andrew H.
See Vachss, Andrew (Henry)

Vaculik, Ludvik 1926- CLC 7
See also CA 53-56; CANR 72

Vaihinger, Hans 1852-1933 TCLC 71
See also CA 116; 166

Valdez, Luis (Miguel) 1940- CLC 84; DAM MULT; DC 10; HLC 2
See also CA 101; CANR 32, 81; DLB 122; HW 1

Valenzuela, Luisa 1938- CLC 31, 104; DAM MULT; HLCS 2; SSC 14
See also CA 101; CANR 32, 65; DLB 113; HW 1, 2

Valera y Alcala-Galiano, Juan 1824-1905 TCLC 10
See also CA 106

Valery, (Ambroise) Paul (Toussaint Jules) 1871-1945 TCLC 4, 15; DAM POET; PC 9
See also CA 104; 122; MTCW 1, 2

Valle-Inclan, Ramon (Maria) del 1866-1936 TCLC 5; DAM MULT; HLC 2
See also CA 106; 153; CANR 80; DLB 134; HW 2

Vallejo, Antonio Buero
See Buero Vallejo, Antonio

Vallejo, Cesar (Abraham) 1892-1938 TCLC 3, 56; DAM MULT; HLC 2
See also CA 105; 153; HW 1

Valles, Jules 1832-1885 NCLC 71
See also DLB 123

Vallette, Marguerite Eymery
See Rachilde

Valle Y Pena, Ramon del
See Valle-Inclan, Ramon (Maria) del

Van Ash, Cay 1918- CLC 34

Vanbrugh, Sir John 1664-1726 LC 21; DAM DRAM
See also DLB 80

Van Campen, Karl
See Campbell, John W(ood, Jr.)

Vance, Gerald
See Silverberg, Robert

Vance, Jack CLC 35
See also Kuttner, Henry; Vance, John Holbrook
See also DLB 8

Vance, John Holbrook 1916-
See Queen, Ellery; Vance, Jack
See also CA 29-32R; CANR 17, 65; MTCW 1

Van Den Bogarde, Derek Jules Gaspard Ulric Niven 1921-1999
See Bogarde, Dirk
See also CA 77-80; 179

Vandenburgh, Jane CLC 59
See also CA 168

Vanderhaeghe, Guy 1951- CLC 41

See also CA 113; CANR 72

van der Post, Laurens (Jan) 1906-1996 CLC 5
See also CA 5-8R; 155; CANR 35; DLB 204

van de Wetering, Janwillem 1931- CLC 47
See also CA 49-52; CANR 4, 62

Van Dine, S. S. TCLC 23
See also Wright, Willard Huntington

Van Doren, Carl (Clinton) 1885-1950 TCLC 18
See also CA 111; 168

Van Doren, Mark 1894-1972 CLC 6, 10
See also CA 1-4R; 37-40R; CANR 3; DLB 45; MTCW 1, 2

Van Druten, John (William) 1901-1957 TCLC 2
See also CA 104; 161; DLB 10

Van Duyn, Mona (Jane) 1921- CLC 3, 7, 63, 116; DAM POET
See also CA 9-12R; CANR 7, 38, 60; DLB 5

Van Dyne, Edith
See Baum, L(yman) Frank

van Itallie, Jean-Claude 1936- CLC 3
See also CA 45-48; CAAS 2; CANR 1, 48; DLB 7

van Ostaijen, Paul 1896-1928 TCLC 33
See also CA 163

Van Peebles, Melvin 1932- CLC 2, 20; DAM MULT
See also BW 2, 3; CA 85-88; CANR 27, 67, 82

Vansittart, Peter 1920- CLC 42
See also CA 1-4R; CANR 3, 49

Van Vechten, Carl 1880-1964 CLC 33
See also CA 89-92; DLB 4, 9, 51

Van Vogt, A(lfred) E(lton) 1912- CLC 1
See also CA 21-24R; CANR 28; DLB 8; SATA 14

Varda, Agnes 1928- CLC 16
See also CA 116; 122

Vargas Llosa, (Jorge) Mario (Pedro) 1936- CLC 3, 6, 9, 10, 15, 31, 42, 85; DA; DAB; DAC; DAM MST, MULT, NOV; HLC 2
See also CA 73-76; CANR 18, 32, 42, 67; DLB 145; HW 1, 2; MTCW 1, 2

Vasiliu, Gheorghe 1881-1957
See Bacovia, George
See also CA 123

Vassa, Gustavus
See Equiano, Olaudah

Vassilikos, Vassilis 1933- CLC 4, 8
See also CA 81-84; CANR 75

Vaughan, Henry 1621-1695 LC 27
See also DLB 131

Vaughn, Stephanie CLC 62

Vazov, Ivan (Minchov) 1850-1921 TCLC 25
See also CA 121; 167; DLB 147

Veblen, Thorstein B(unde) 1857-1929 TCLC 31
See also CA 115; 165

Vega, Lope de 1562-1635 LC 23; HLCS 2

Venison, Alfred
See Pound, Ezra (Weston Loomis)

Verdi, Marie de
See Mencken, H(enry) L(ouis)

Verdu, Matilde
See Cela, Camilo Jose

Verga, Giovanni (Carmelo) 1840-1922 TCLC 3; SSC 21
See also CA 104; 123

Vergil 70B.C.-19B.C. CMLC 9; DA; DAB; DAC; DAM MST, POET; PC 12; WLCS
See also Virgil

Verhaeren, Emile (Adolphe Gustave) 1855-1916 TCLC 12

See also CA 109

Verlaine, Paul (Marie) 1844-1896**NCLC 2, 51; DAM POET; PC 2**

Verne, Jules (Gabriel) 1828-1905**TCLC 6, 52**
See also AAYA 16; CA 110; 131; DLB 123; JRDA; MAICYA; SATA 21

Very, Jones 1813-1880 **NCLC 9**
See also DLB 1

Vesaas, Tarjei 1897-1970 **CLC 48**
See also CA 29-32R

Vialis, Gaston
See Simenon, Georges (Jacques Christian)

Vian, Boris 1920-1959 **TCLC 9**
See also CA 106; 164; DLB 72; MTCW 2

Viaud, (Louis Marie) Julien 1850-1923
See Loti, Pierre
See also CA 107

Vicar, Henry
See Felsen, Henry Gregor

Vicker, Angus
See Felsen, Henry Gregor

Vidal, Gore 1925-**CLC 2, 4, 6, 8, 10, 22, 33, 72; DAM NOV, POP**
See also AITN 1; BEST 90:2; CA 5-8R; CANR 13, 45, 65; CDALBS; DLB 6, 152; INT CANR-13; MTCW 1, 2

Viereck, Peter (Robert Edwin) 1916- **CLC 4; PC 27**
See also CA 1-4R; CANR 1, 47; DLB 5

Vigny, Alfred (Victor) de 1797-1863**NCLC 7; DAM POET; PC 26**
See also DLB 119, 192

Vilakazi, Benedict Wallet 1906-1947**TCLC 37**
See also CA 168

Villa, Jose Garcia 1904-1997 **PC 22**
See also CA 25-28R; CANR 12

Villarreal, Jose Antonio 1924-
See also CA 133; DAM MULT; DLB 82; HLC 2; HW 1

Villaurrutia, Xavier 1903-1950 **TCLC 80**
See also HW 1

Villiers de l'Isle Adam, Jean Marie Mathias Philippe Auguste, Comte de 1838-1889 **NCLC 3; SSC 14**
See also DLB 123

Villon, Francois 1431-1463(?) **PC 13**
See also DLB 208

Vinci, Leonardo da 1452-1519 **LC 12**

Vine, Barbara **CLC 50**
See also Rendell, Ruth(Barbara)
See also BEST 90:4

Vinge, Joan (Carol) D(ennison) 1948-**CLC 30; SSC 24**
See also CA 93-96; CANR 72; SATA 36

Violis, G.
See Simenon, Georges (Jacques Christian)

Viramontes, Helena Maria 1954-
See also CA 159; DLB 122; HLCS 2; HW 2

Virgil 70B.C.-19B.C.
See Vergil
See also DLB 211

Visconti, Luchino 1906-1976 **CLC 16**
See also CA 81-84; 65-68; CANR 39

Vittorini, Elio 1908-1966 **CLC 6, 9, 14**
See also CA 133; 25-28R

Vivekananda, Swami 1863-1902 **TCLC 88**

Vizenor, Gerald Robert 1934-**CLC 103; DAM MULT**
See also CA 13-16R; CAAS 22; CANR 5, 21, 44, 67; DLB 175; MTCW 2; NNAL

Vizinczey, Stephen 1933- **CLC 40**
See also CA 128; INT 128

Vliet, R(ussell) G(ordon) 1929-1984 **CLC 22**

See also CA 37-40R; 112; CANR 18

Vogau, Boris Andreyevich 1894-1937(?)
See Pilnyak, Boris
See also CA 123

Vogel, Paula A(nne) 1951- **CLC 76**
See also CA 108

Voigt, Cynthia 1942- **CLC 30**
See also AAYA 3, 30; CA 106; CANR 18, 37, 40; CLR 13, 48; INT CANR-18; JRDA; MAICYA; SATA 48, 79; SATA-Brief 33

Voigt, Ellen Bryant 1943- **CLC 54**
See also CA 69-72; CANR 11, 29, 55; DLB 120

Voinovich, Vladimir (Nikolaevich) 1932-**CLC 10, 49**
See also CA 81-84; CAAS 12; CANR 33, 67; MTCW 1

Vollmann, William T. 1959- **CLC 89; DAM NOV, POP**
See also CA 134; CANR 67; MTCW 2

Voloshinov, V. N.
See Bakhtin, Mikhail Mikhailovich

Voltaire 1694-1778 **LC 14; DA; DAB; DAC; DAM DRAM, MST; SSC 12; WLC**

von Aschendrof, Baron Ignatz
See Ford, Ford Madox

von Daeniken, Erich 1935- **CLC 30**
See also AITN 1; CA 37-40R; CANR 17, 44

von Daniken, Erich
See von Daeniken, Erich

von Heidenstam, (Carl Gustaf) Verner
See Heidenstam, (Carl Gustaf) Verner von

von Heyse, Paul (Johann Ludwig)
See Heyse, Paul (Johann Ludwig von)

von Hofmannsthal, Hugo
See Hofmannsthal, Hugo von

von Horvath, Odon
See Horvath, Oedoen von

von Horvath, Oedoen
See Horvath, Oedoen von

von Liliencron, (Friedrich Adolf Axel) Detlev
See Liliencron, (Friedrich Adolf Axel) Detlev von

Vonnegut, Kurt, Jr. 1922-**CLC 1, 2, 3, 4, 5, 8, 12, 22, 40, 60, 111; DA; DAB; DAC; DAM MST, NOV, POP; SSC 8; WLC**
See also AAYA 6; AITN 1; BEST 90:4; CA 1-4R; CANR 1, 25, 49, 75; CDALB 1968-1988; DLB 2, 8, 152; DLBD 3; DLBY 80; MTCW 1, 2

Von Rachen, Kurt
See Hubbard, L(afayette) Ron(ald)

von Rezzori (d'Arezzo), Gregor
See Rezzori (d'Arezzo), Gregor von

von Sternberg, Josef
See Sternberg, Josef von

Vorster, Gordon 1924- **CLC 34**
See also CA 133

Vosce, Trudie
See Ozick, Cynthia

Voznesensky, Andrei (Andreievich) 1933-**CLC 1, 15, 57; DAM POET**
See also CA 89-92; CANR 37; MTCW 1

Waddington, Miriam 1917- **CLC 28**
See also CA 21-24R; CANR 12, 30; DLB 68

Wagman, Fredrica 1937- **CLC 7**
See also CA 97-100; INT 97-100

Wagner, Linda W.
See Wagner-Martin, Linda (C.)

Wagner, Linda Welshimer
See Wagner-Martin, Linda (C.)

Wagner, Richard 1813-1883 **NCLC 9**
See also DLB 129

Wagner-Martin, Linda (C.) 1936- **CLC 50**

See also CA 159

Wagoner, David (Russell) 1926- **CLC 3, 5, 15**
See also CA 1-4R; CAAS 3; CANR 2, 71; DLB 5; SATA 14

Wah, Fred(erick James) 1939- **CLC 44**
See also CA 107; 141; DLB 60

Wahloo, Per 1926-1975 **CLC 7**
See also CA 61-64; CANR 73

Wahloo, Peter
See Wahloo, Per

Wain, John (Barrington) 1925-1994 **CLC 2, 11, 15, 46**
See also CA 5-8R; 145; CAAS 4; CANR 23, 54; CDBLB 1960 to Present; DLB 15, 27, 139, 155; MTCW 1, 2

Wajda, Andrzej 1926- **CLC 16**
See also CA 102

Wakefield, Dan 1932- **CLC 7**
See also CA 21-24R; CAAS 7

Wakoski, Diane 1937- **CLC 2, 4, 7, 9, 11, 40; DAM POET; PC 15**
See also CA 13-16R; CAAS 1; CANR 9, 60; DLB 5; INT CANR-9; MTCW 2

Wakoski-Sherbell, Diane
See Wakoski, Diane

Walcott, Derek (Alton) 1930-**CLC 2, 4, 9, 14, 25, 42, 67, 76; BLC 3; DAB; DAC; DAM MST, MULT, POET; DC 7**
See also BW 2; CA 89-92; CANR 26, 47, 75, 80; DLB 117; DLBY 81; MTCW 1, 2

Waldman, Anne (Lesley) 1945- **CLC 7**
See also CA 37-40R; CAAS 17; CANR 34, 69; DLB 16

Waldo, E. Hunter
See Sturgeon, Theodore (Hamilton)

Waldo, Edward Hamilton
See Sturgeon, Theodore (Hamilton)

Walker, Alice (Malsenior) 1944- **CLC 5, 6, 9, 19, 27, 46, 58, 103; BLC 3; DA; DAB; DAC; DAM MST, MULT, NOV, POET, POP; SSC 5; WLCS**
See also AAYA 3; BEST 89:4; BW 2, 3; CA 37-40R; CANR 9, 27, 49, 66, 82; CDALB 1968-1988; DLB 6, 33, 143; INT CANR-27; MTCW 1, 2; SATA 31

Walker, David Harry 1911-1992 **CLC 14**
See also CA 1-4R; 137; CANR 1; SATA 8; SATA-Obit 71

Walker, Edward Joseph 1934-
See Walker, Ted
See also CA 21-24R; CANR 12, 28, 53

Walker, George F. 1947- **CLC 44, 61; DAB; DAC; DAM MST**
See also CA 103; CANR 21, 43, 59; DLB 60

Walker, Joseph A. 1935- **CLC 19; DAM DRAM, MST**
See also BW 1, 3; CA 89-92; CANR 26; DLB 38

Walker, Margaret (Abigail) 1915-1998**CLC 1, 6; BLC; DAM MULT; PC 20**
See also BW 2, 3; CA 73-76; 172; CANR 26, 54, 76; DLB 76, 152; MTCW 1, 2

Walker, Ted **CLC 13**
See also Walker, Edward Joseph
See also DLB 40

Wallace, David Foster 1962- **CLC 50, 114**
See also CA 132; CANR 59; MTCW 2

Wallace, Dexter
See Masters, Edgar Lee

Wallace, (Richard Horatio) Edgar 1875-1932 **TCLC 57**
See also CA 115; DLB 70

Wallace, Irving 1916-1990 **CLC 7, 13; DAM**

NOV, POP
See also AITN 1; CA 1-4R; 132; CAAS 1; CANR 1, 27; INT CANR-27; MTCW 1, 2
Wallant, Edward Lewis 1926-1962**CLC 5, 10**
See also CA 1-4R; CANR 22; DLB 2, 28, 143; MTCW 1, 2
Wallas, Graham 1858-1932   **TCLC 91**
Walley, Byron
See Card, Orson Scott
Walpole, Horace 1717-1797   **LC 49**
See also DLB 39, 104
Walpole, Hugh (Seymour) 1884-1941**TCLC 5**
See also CA 104; 165; DLB 34; MTCW 2
Walser, Martin 1927-   **CLC 27**
See also CA 57-60; CANR 8, 46; DLB 75, 124
Walser, Robert 1878-1956   **TCLC 18;SSC 20**
See also CA 118; 165; DLB 66
Walsh, Jill Paton   **CLC 35**
See also Paton Walsh, Gillian
See also AAYA 11; CLR 2; DLB 161; SAAS 3
Walter, Villiam Christian
See Andersen, Hans Christian
Wambaugh, Joseph (Aloysius, Jr.) 1937-**CLC 3, 18; DAM NOV, POP**
See also AITN 1; BEST 89:3; CA 33-36R; CANR 42, 65; DLB 6; DLBY 83; MTCW 1, 2
Wang Wei 699(?)-761(?)   **PC 18**
Ward, Arthur Henry Sarsfield 1883-1959
See Rohmer, Sax
See also CA 108; 173
Ward, Douglas Turner 1930-   **CLC 19**
See also BW 1; CA 81-84; CANR 27; DLB 7, 38
Ward, E. D.
See Lucas, E(dward) V(errall)
Ward, Mary Augusta
See Ward, Mrs. Humphry
Ward, Mrs. Humphry 1851-1920   **TCLC 55**
See also DLB 18
Ward, Peter
See Faust, Frederick (Schiller)
Warhol, Andy 1928(?)-1987   **CLC 20**
See also AAYA 12; BEST 89:4; CA 89-92; 121; CANR 34
Warner, Francis (Robert le Plastrier) 1937-
CLC 14
See also CA 53-56; CANR 11
Warner, Marina 1946-   **CLC 59**
See also CA 65-68; CANR 21, 55; DLB 194
Warner, Rex (Ernest) 1905-1986   **CLC 45**
See also CA 89-92; 119; DLB 15
Warner, Susan (Bogert) 1819-1885 **NCLC 31**
See also DLB 3, 42
Warner, Sylvia (Constance) Ashton
See Ashton-Warner, Sylvia (Constance)
Warner, Sylvia Townsend 1893-1978 **CLC 7, 19; SSC 23**
See also CA 61-64; 77-80; CANR 16, 60; DLB 34, 139; MTCW 1, 2
Warren, Mercy Otis 1728-1814   **NCLC 13**
See also DLB 31, 200
Warren, Robert Penn 1905-1989**CLC 1, 4, 6, 8, 10, 13, 18, 39, 53, 59; DA; DAB; DAC; DAM MST, NOV, POET; SSC 4;WLC**
See also AITN 1; CA 13-16R; 129; CANR 10, 47;CDALB 1968-1988; DLB 2, 48, 152; DLBY 80, 89; INT CANR-10; MTCW 1, 2; SATA 46; SATA-Obit 63
Warshofsky, Isaac
See Singer, Isaac Bashevis
Warton, Thomas 1728-1790   **LC 15;DAM POET**

See also DLB 104, 109
Waruk, Kona
See Harris, (Theodore) Wilson
Warung, Price 1855-1911   **TCLC 45**
Warwick, Jarvis
See Garner, Hugh
Washington, Alex
See Harris, Mark
Washington, Booker T(aliaferro) 1856-1915
TCLC 10; BLC 3; DAM MULT
See also BW 1; CA 114; 125; SATA 28
Washington, George 1732-1799   **LC 25**
See also DLB 31
Wassermann, (Karl) Jakob 1873-1934 **TCLC 6**
See also CA 104; 163; DLB 66
Wasserstein, Wendy 1950-   **CLC 32, 59, 90; DAM DRAM; DC 4**
See also CA 121; 129; CABS 3; CANR 53, 75; INT 129; MTCW 2; SATA 94
Waterhouse, Keith (Spencer) 1929-   **CLC 47**
See also CA 5-8R; CANR 38, 67; DLB 13, 15; MTCW 1, 2
Waters, Frank (Joseph) 1902-1995   **CLC 88**
See also CA 5-8R; 149; CAAS 13; CANR 3, 18, 63; DLB 212; DLBY 86
Waters, Roger 1944-   **CLC 35**
Watkins, Frances Ellen
See Harper, Frances Ellen Watkins
Watkins, Gerrold
See Malzberg, Barry N(athaniel)
Watkins, Gloria 1955(?)-
See hooks, bell
See also BW 2; CA 143; MTCW 2
Watkins, Paul 1964-   **CLC 55**
See also CA 132; CANR 62
Watkins, Vernon Phillips 1906-1967 **CLC 43**
See also CA 9-10; 25-28R; CAP 1; DLB 20
Watson, Irving S.
See Mencken, H(enry) L(ouis)
Watson, John H.
See Farmer, Philip Jose
Watson, Richard F.
See Silverberg, Robert
Waugh, Auberon (Alexander) 1939-   **CLC 7**
See also CA 45-48; CANR 6, 22; DLB 14, 194
Waugh, Evelyn (Arthur St. John) 1903-1966
CLC 1, 3, 8, 13, 19, 27, 44, 107; DA; DAB; DAC; DAM MST, NOV, POP; WLC
See also CA 85-88; 25-28R; CANR 22; CDBLB 1914-1945; DLB 15, 162, 195; MTCW 1, 2
Waugh, Harriet 1944-   **CLC 6**
See also CA 85-88; CANR 22
Ways, C. R.
See Blount, Roy (Alton), Jr.
Waystaff, Simon
See Swift, Jonathan
Webb, (Martha) Beatrice (Potter) 1858-1943
TCLC 22
See also Potter, (Helen) Beatrix
See also CA 117; DLB 190
Webb, Charles (Richard) 1939-   **CLC 7**
See also CA 25-28R
Webb, James H(enry), Jr. 1946-   **CLC 22**
See also CA 81-84
Webb, Mary (Gladys Meredith) 1881-1927
TCLC 24
See also CA 123; DLB 34
Webb, Mrs. Sidney
See Webb, (Martha) Beatrice (Potter)
Webb, Phyllis 1927-   **CLC 18**
See also CA 104; CANR 23; DLB 53
Webb, Sidney (James) 1859-1947   **TCLC 22**

See also CA 117; 163; DLB 190
Webber, Andrew Lloyd   **CLC 21**
See also Lloyd Webber, Andrew
Weber, Lenora Mattingly 1895-1971 **CLC 12**
See also CA 19-20; 29-32R; CAP 1; SATA 2; SATA-Obit 26
Weber, Max 1864-1920   **TCLC 69**
See also CA 109
Webster, John 1579(?)-1634(?)   **LC 33; DA; DAB; DAC; DAM DRAM, MST; DC 2; WLC**
See also CDBLB Before 1660; DLB 58
Webster, Noah 1758-1843   **NCLC 30**
See also DLB 1, 37, 42, 43, 73
Wedekind, (Benjamin) Frank(lin) 1864-1918
TCLC 7; DAM DRAM
See also CA 104; 153; DLB 118
Weidman, Jerome 1913-1998   **CLC 7**
See also AITN 2; CA 1-4R; 171; CANR 1; DLB 28
Weil, Simone (Adolphine) 1909-1943**TCLC 23**
See also CA 117; 159; MTCW 2
Weininger, Otto 1880-1903   **TCLC 84**
Weinstein, Nathan
See West, Nathanael
Weinstein, Nathan von Wallenstein
See West, Nathanael
Weir, Peter (Lindsay) 1944-   **CLC 20**
See also CA 113; 123
Weiss, Peter (Ulrich) 1916-1982**CLC 3, 15, 51; DAM DRAM**
See also CA 45-48; 106; CANR 3; DLB 69, 124
Weiss, Theodore (Russell) 1916-**CLC 3, 8, 14**
See also CA 9-12R; CAAS 2; CANR 46; DLB 5
Welch, (Maurice) Denton 1915-1948**TCLC 22**
See also CA 121; 148
Welch, James 1940-   **CLC 6, 14, 52; DAM MULT, POP**
See also CA 85-88; CANR 42, 66; DLB 175; NNAL
Weldon, Fay 1931-**CLC 6, 9, 11, 19, 36, 59, 122; DAM POP**
See also CA 21-24R; CANR 16, 46, 63; CDBLB 1960 to Present; DLB 14, 194; INT CANR-16; MTCW 1, 2
Wellek, Rene 1903-1995   **CLC 28**
See also CA 5-8R; 150; CAAS 7; CANR 8; DLB 63; INT CANR-8
Weller, Michael 1942-   **CLC 10, 53**
See also CA 85-88
Weller, Paul 1958-   **CLC 26**
Wellershoff, Dieter 1925-   **CLC 46**
See also CA 89-92; CANR 16, 37
Welles, (George) Orson 1915-1985**CLC 20, 80**
See also CA 93-96; 117
Wellman, John McDowell 1945-
See Wellman, Mac
See also CA 166
Wellman, Mac 1945-   **CLC 65**
See also Wellman, John McDowell; Wellman, John McDowell
Wellman, Manly Wade 1903-1986   **CLC 49**
See also CA 1-4R; 118; CANR 6, 16, 44; SATA 6; SATA-Obit 47
Wells, Carolyn 1869(?)-1942   **TCLC 35**
See also CA 113; DLB 11
Wells, H(erbert) G(eorge) 1866-1946**TCLC 6, 12, 19; DA; DAB; DAC; DAM MST, NOV; SSC 6; WLC**
See also AAYA 18; CA 110; 121; CDBLB 1914-1945; DLB 34, 70, 156, 178; MTCW 1, 2; SATA 20

Willard, Nancy 1936-   **CLC 7, 37**
  See also CA 89-92; CANR 10, 39, 68; CLR 5;
  DLB 5, 52; MAICYA; MTCW 1; SATA 37,
  71; SATA-Brief 30

William of Ockham 1285-1347 **CMLC 32**

Williams, Ben Ames 1889-1953 **TCLC 89**
  See also DLB 102

Williams, C(harles) K(enneth) 1936-**CLC 33,**
  56; DAM POET
  See also CA 37-40R; CAAS 26; CANR 57; DLB
  5

Williams, Charles
  See Collier, James L(incoln)

Williams, Charles (Walter Stansby) 1886-1945
  TCLC 1, 11
  See also CA 104; 163; DLB 100, 153

Williams, (George) Emlyn 1905-1987**CLC 15;**
  DAM DRAM
  See also CA 104; 123; CANR 36; DLB 10, 77;
  MTCW 1

Williams, Hank 1923-1953 **TCLC 81**

Williams, Hugo 1942- **CLC 42**
  See also CA 17-20R; CANR 45; DLB 40

Williams, J. Walker
  See Wodehouse, P(elham) G(renville)

Williams, John A(lfred) 1925-**CLC 5, 13; BLC**
  3; DAM MULT
  See also BW 2, 3; CA 53-56; CAAS 3; CANR
  6, 26, 51; DLB 2, 33; INT CANR-6

Williams, Jonathan (Chamberlain) 1929-
  CLC 13
  See also CA 9-12R; CAAS 12; CANR 8; DLB
  5

Williams, Joy 1944- **CLC 31**
  See also CA 41-44R; CANR 22, 48

Williams, Norman 1952- **CLC 39**
  See also CA 118

Williams, Sherley Anne 1944-**CLC 89; BLC 3;**
  DAM MULT, POET
  See also BW 2, 3; CA 73-76; CANR 25, 82;
  DLB 41; INT CANR-25; SATA 78

Williams, Shirley
  See Williams, Sherley Anne

Williams, Tennessee 1911-1983**CLC 1, 2, 5, 7,**
  8, 11, 15, 19, 30, 39, 45, 71, 111; DA; DAB;
  DAC; DAM DRAM, MST; DC 4;WLC
  See also AITN 1, 2; CA 5-8R; 108; CABS 3;
  CANR 31; CDALB 1941-1968; DLB7;
  DLBD 4; DLBY 83; MTCW 1, 2

Williams, Thomas (Alonzo) 1926-1990**CLC 14**
  See also CA 1-4R; 132; CANR 2

Williams, William C.
  See Williams, William Carlos

Williams, William Carlos 1883-1963**CLC 1, 2,**
  5, 9, 13, 22, 42, 67; DA; DAB; DAC; DAM
  MST, POET; PC 7; SSC 31
  See also CA 89-92; CANR 34; CDALB 1917-
  1929; DLB 4, 16, 54, 86; MTCW 1, 2

Williamson, David (Keith) 1942- **CLC 56**
  See also CA 103; CANR 41

Williamson, Ellen Douglas 1905-1984
  See Douglas, Ellen
  See also CA 17-20R; 114; CANR 39

Williamson, Jack **CLC 29**
  See also Williamson, John Stewart
  See also CAAS 8; DLB 8

Williamson, John Stewart 1908-
  See Williamson, Jack
  See also CA 17-20R; CANR 23, 70

Willie, Frederick
  See Lovecraft, H(oward) P(hillips)

Willingham, Calder (Baynard, Jr.) 1922-1995
  CLC 5, 51

See also CA 5-8R; 147; CANR 3; DLB 2, 44;
  MTCW 1

Willis, Charles
  See Clarke, Arthur C(harles)

Willis, Fingal O'Flahertie
  See Wilde, Oscar

Willy
  See Colette, (Sidonie-Gabrielle)

Willy, Colette
  See Colette, (Sidonie-Gabrielle)

Wilson, A(ndrew) N(orman) 1950- **CLC 33**
  See also CA 112; 122; DLB 14, 155, 194;
  MTCW 2

Wilson, Angus (Frank Johnstone) 1913-1991
  CLC 2, 3, 5, 25, 34; SSC 21
  See also CA 5-8R; 134; CANR 21; DLB 15,
  139, 155; MTCW 1, 2

Wilson, August 1945- **CLC 39, 50, 63, 118;**
  BLC 3; DA; DAB; DAC; DAM DRAM,
  MST, MULT; DC 2; WLCS
  See also AAYA 16; BW 2, 3; CA 115; 122;
  CANR 42, 54, 76; MTCW 1, 2

Wilson, Brian 1942- **CLC 12**

Wilson, Colin 1931- **CLC 3, 14**
  See also CA 1-4R; CAAS 5; CANR 1, 22, 33,
  77; DLB 14, 194; MTCW 1

Wilson, Dirk
  See Pohl, Frederik

Wilson, Edmund 1895-1972**CLC 1, 2, 3, 8, 24**
  See also CA 1-4R; 37-40R; CANR 1, 46; DLB
  63; MTCW 1, 2

Wilson, Ethel Davis (Bryant) 1888(?)-1980
  CLC 13; DAC; DAM POET
  See also CA 102; DLB 68; MTCW 1

Wilson, John 1785-1854 **NCLC 5**

Wilson, John (Anthony) Burgess 1917-1993
  See Burgess, Anthony
  See also CA 1-4R; 143; CANR 2, 46; DAC;
  DAM NOV; MTCW 1, 2

Wilson, Lanford 1937- **CLC 7, 14, 36; DAM**
  DRAM
  See also CA 17-20R; CABS 3; CANR 45; DLB
  7

Wilson, Robert M. 1944- **CLC 7, 9**
  See also CA 49-52; CANR 2, 41; MTCW 1

Wilson, Robert McLiam 1964- **CLC 59**
  See also CA 132

Wilson, Sloan 1920- **CLC 32**
  See also CA 1-4R; CANR 1, 44

Wilson, Snoo 1948- **CLC 33**
  See also CA 69-72

Wilson, William S(mith) 1932- **CLC 49**
  See also CA 81-84

Wilson, (Thomas) Woodrow 1856-1924**TCLC**
  79
  See also CA 166; DLB 47

Winchilsea, Anne (Kingsmill) Finch Counte
  1661-1720
  See Finch, Anne

Windham, Basil
  See Wodehouse, P(elham) G(renville)

Wingrove, David (John) 1954- **CLC 68**
  See also CA 133

Winnemucca, Sarah 1844-1891 **NCLC 79**

Winstanley, Gerrard 1609-1676 **LC 52**

Wintergreen, Jane
  See Duncan, Sara Jeannette

Winters, Janet Lewis **CLC 41**
  See also Lewis, Janet
  See also DLBY 87

Winters, (Arthur) Yvor 1900-1968 **CLC 4, 8,**
  32
  See also CA 11-12; 25-28R; CAP 1; DLB 48;

MTCW 1

Winterson, Jeanette 1959-**CLC 64; DAM POP**
  See also CA 136; CANR 58; DLB 207; MTCW
  2

Winthrop, John 1588-1649 **LC 31**
  See also DLB 24, 30

Wirth, Louis 1897-1952 **TCLC 92**

Wiseman, Frederick 1930- **CLC 20**
  See also CA 159

Wister, Owen 1860-1938 **TCLC 21**
  See also CA 108; 162; DLB 9, 78, 186; SATA
  62

Witkacy
  See Witkiewicz, Stanislaw Ignacy

Witkiewicz, Stanislaw Ignacy 1885-1939
  TCLC 8
  See also CA 105; 162

Wittgenstein, Ludwig (Josef Johann) 1889-1951
  TCLC 59
  See also CA 113; 164; MTCW 2

Wittig, Monique 1935(?)- **CLC 22**
  See also CA 116; 135; DLB 83

Wittlin, Jozef 1896-1976 **CLC 25**
  See also CA 49-52; 65-68; CANR 3

Wodehouse, P(elham) G(renville) 1881-1975
  CLC 1, 2, 5, 10, 22; DAB; DAC; DAM
  NOV; SSC 2
  See also AITN 2; CA 45-48; 57-60; CANR 3,
  33; CDBLB 1914-1945; DLB 34, 162;
  MTCW 1, 2; SATA 22

Woiwode, L.
  See Woiwode, Larry (Alfred)

Woiwode, Larry (Alfred) 1941- **CLC 6, 10**
  See also CA 73-76; CANR 16; DLB 6; INT
  CANR-16

Wojciechowska, Maia (Teresa) 1927-**CLC 26**
  See also AAYA 8; CA 9-12R; CANR 4, 41; CLR
  1; JRDA; MAICYA; SAAS 1; SATA 1, 28,
  83; SATA-Essay 104

Wolf, Christa 1929- **CLC 14, 29, 58**
  See also CA 85-88; CANR 45; DLB 75; MTCW
  1

Wolfe, Gene (Rodman) 1931- **CLC 25; DAM**
  POP
  See also CA 57-60; CAAS 9; CANR 6, 32, 60;
  DLB 8; MTCW 2

Wolfe, George C. 1954- **CLC 49; BLCS**
  See also CA 149

Wolfe, Thomas (Clayton) 1900-1938**TCLC 4,**
  13, 29, 61; DA; DAB; DAC; DAM MST,
  NOV; SSC 33; WLC
  See also CA 104; 132; CDALB 1929-1941;
  DLB 9, 102; DLBD 2, 16; DLBY 85, 97;
  MTCW 1, 2

Wolfe, Thomas Kennerly, Jr. 1930-
  See Wolfe, Tom
  See also CA 13-16R; CANR 9, 33, 70; DAM
  POP; DLB 185; INT CANR-9; MTCW 1, 2

Wolfe, Tom **CLC 1, 2, 9, 15, 35, 51**
  See also Wolfe, Thomas Kennerly, Jr.
  See also AAYA 8; AITN 2; BEST 89:1; DLB
  152

Wolff, Geoffrey (Ansell) 1937- **CLC 41**
  See also CA 29-32R; CANR 29, 43, 78

Wolff, Sonia
  See Levitin, Sonia (Wolff)

Wolff, Tobias (Jonathan Ansell) 1945- **C L C**
  39, 64
  See also AAYA 16; BEST 90:2; CA 114; 117;
  CAAS 22; CANR 54, 76; DLB 130; INT 117;
  MTCW 2

Wolfram von Eschenbach c. 1170-c. 1220
  CMLC 5

See also DLB 138

Wolitzer, Hilma 1930- **CLC 17**
See also CA 65-68; CANR 18, 40; INT CANR-18; SATA 31

Wollstonecraft, Mary 1759-1797 **LC 5, 50**
See also CDBLB 1789-1832; DLB 39, 104, 158

Wonder, Stevie **CLC 12**
See also Morris, Steveland Judkins

Wong, Jade Snow 1922- **CLC 17**
See also CA 109

Woodberry, George Edward 1855-1930
TCLC 73
See also CA 165; DLB 71, 103

Woodcott, Keith
See Brunner, John (Kilian Houston)

Woodruff, Robert W.
See Mencken, H(enry) L(ouis)

Woolf, (Adeline) Virginia 1882-1941**TCLC 1,
5, 20, 43, 56; DA; DAB; DAC; DAM MST,
NOV; SSC 7; WLC**
See also CA 104; 130; CANR 64; CDBLB
1914-1945; DLB 36, 100, 162; DLBD 10;
MTCW 1

Woolf, Virginia Adeline
See Woolf, (Adeline) Virginia
See also MTCW 2

Woollcott, Alexander (Humphreys) 1887-1943
TCLC 5
See also CA 105; 161; DLB 29

Woolrich, Cornell 1903-1968 **CLC 77**
See also Hopley-Woolrich, Cornell George

Wordsworth, Dorothy 1771-1855 **NCLC 25**
See also DLB 107

Wordsworth, William 1770-1850 **NCLC 12,
38; DA; DAB; DAC; DAM MST, POET;
PC 4; WLC**
See also CDBLB 1789-1832; DLB 93, 107

Wouk, Herman 1915-**CLC 1, 9, 38; DAM NOV,
POP**
See also CA 5-8R; CANR 6, 33, 67; CDALBS;
DLBY 82; INT CANR-6; MTCW 1, 2

Wright, Charles (Penzel, Jr.) 1935-**CLC 6, 13,
28, 119**
See also CA 29-32R; CAAS 7; CANR 23, 36,
62; DLB 165; DLBY 82; MTCW 1, 2

Wright, Charles Stevenson 1932- **CLC 49;
BLC 3; DAM MULT, POET**
See also BW 1; CA 9-12R; CANR 26; DLB 33

Wright, Frances 1795-1852 **NCLC 74**
See also DLB 73

Wright, Frank Lloyd 1867-1959 **TCLC 95**
See also CA 174

Wright, Jack R.
See Harris, Mark

Wright, James (Arlington) 1927-1980**CLC 3,
5, 10, 28; DAM POET**
See also AITN 2; CA 49-52; 97-100; CANR 4,
34, 64; CDALBS; DLB 5, 169; MTCW 1, 2

Wright, Judith (Arandell) 1915- **CLC 11, 53;
PC 14**
See also CA 13-16R; CANR 31, 76; MTCW 1,
2; SATA 14

Wright, L(aurali) R. 1939- **CLC 44**
See also CA 138

Wright, Richard (Nathaniel) 1908-1960 **C L C
1, 3, 4, 9, 14, 21, 48, 74; BLC 3; DA; DAB;
DAC; DAM MST, MULT, NOV; SSC 2;
WLC**
See also AAYA 5; BW 1; CA 108; CANR
64;CDALB 1929-1941; DLB 76, 102; DLBD
2; MTCW 1, 2

Wright, Richard B(ruce) 1937- **CLC 6**

See also CA 85-88; DLB 53

Wright, Rick 1945- **CLC 35**

Wright, Rowland
See Wells, Carolyn

Wright, Stephen 1946- **CLC 33**

Wright, Willard Huntington 1888-1939
See Van Dine, S. S.
See also CA 115; DLBD 16

Wright, William 1930- **CLC 44**
See also CA 53-56; CANR 7, 23

Wroth, Lady Mary 1587-1653(?) **LC 30**
See also DLB 121

Wu Ch'eng-en 1500(?)-1582(?) **LC 7**

Wu Ching-tzu 1701-1754 **LC 2**

Wurlitzer, Rudolph 1938(?)- **CLC 2, 4, 15**
See also CA 85-88; DLB 173

Wyatt, Thomas c. 1503-1542 **PC 27**
See also DLB 132

Wycherley, William 1641-1715**LC 8, 21; DAM
DRAM**
See also CDBLB 1660-1789; DLB 80

Wylie, Elinor (Morton Hoyt) 1885-1928
TCLC 8; PC 23
See also CA 105; 162; DLB 9, 45

Wylie, Philip (Gordon) 1902-1971 **CLC 43**
See also CA 21-22; 33-36R; CAP 2; DLB 9

Wyndham, John **CLC 19**
See also Harris, John (Wyndham Parkes Lucas)
Beynon

Wyss, Johann David Von 1743-1818**NCLC 10**
See also JRDA; MAICYA; SATA 29; SATA-
Brief 27

Xenophon c. 430B.C.-c.354B.C. **CMLC 17**
See also DLB 176

Yakumo Koizumi
See Hearn, (Patricio) Lafcadio (Tessima Carlos)

Yamamoto, Hisaye 1921-**SSC 34; DAM MULT**

Yanez, Jose Donoso
See Donoso (Yanez), Jose

Yanovsky, Basile S.
See Yanovsky, V(assily) S(emenovich)

Yanovsky, V(assily) S(emenovich) 1906-1989
CLC 2, 18
See also CA 97-100; 129

Yates, Richard 1926-1992 **CLC 7, 8, 23**
See also CA 5-8R; 139; CANR 10, 43; DLB 2;
DLBY 81, 92; INT CANR-10

Yeats, W. B.
See Yeats, William Butler

Yeats, William Butler 1865-1939**TCLC 1, 11,
18, 31, 93; DA; DAB; DAC; DAM DRAM,
MST, POET; PC 20; WLC**
See also CA 104; 127; CANR 45; CDBLB
1890-1914; DLB 10, 19, 98, 156; MTCW 1,
2

Yehoshua, A(braham) B. 1936- **CLC 13, 31**
See also CA 33-36R; CANR 43

Yep, Laurence Michael 1948- **CLC 35**
See also AAYA 5; CA 49-52; CANR 1, 46; CLR
3, 17, 54; DLB 52; JRDA; MAICYA; SATA
7, 69

Yerby, Frank G(arvin) 1916-1991 **CLC 1, 7,
22; BLC 3; DAM MULT**
See also BW 1, 3; CA 9-12R; 136; CANR 16,
52; DLB 76; INT CANR-16; MTCW 1

Yesenin, Sergei Alexandrovich
See Esenin, Sergei (Alexandrovich)

Yevtushenko, Yevgeny (Alexandrovich) 1933-
CLC 1, 3, 13, 26, 51; DAM POET
See also CA 81-84; CANR 33, 54; MTCW 1

Yezierska, Anzia 1885(?)-1970 **CLC 46**
See also CA 126; 89-92; DLB 28; MTCW 1

Yglesias, Helen 1915- **CLC 7, 22**

See also CA 37-40R; CAAS 20; CANR 15, 65;
INT CANR-15; MTCW 1

Yokomitsu Riichi 1898-1947 **TCLC 47**
See also CA 170

Yonge, Charlotte(Mary) 1823-1901 **TCLC 48**
See also CA 109; 163; DLB 18, 163; SATA 17

York, Jeremy
See Creasey, John

York, Simon
See Heinlein, Robert A(nson)

Yorke, Henry Vincent 1905-1974 **CLC 13**
See also Green, Henry
See also CA 85-88; 49-52

Yosano Akiko 1878-1942 **TCLC 59;PC 11**
See also CA 161

Yoshimoto, Banana **CLC 84**
See also Yoshimoto, Mahoko

Yoshimoto, Mahoko 1964-
See Yoshimoto, Banana
See also CA 144

Young, Al(bert James) 1939-**CLC 19; BLC 3;
DAM MULT**
See also BW 2, 3; CA 29-32R; CANR 26, 65;
DLB 33

Young, Andrew(John) 1885-1971 **CLC 5**
See also CA 5-8R; CANR 7, 29

Young, Collier 1917-1994
See Bloch, Robert (Albert)
See also CA 179; CAAE 179

Young, Edward 1683-1765 **LC 3, 40**
See also DLB 95

Young, Marguerite(Vivian) 1909-1995**CLC 82**
See also CA 13-16; 150; CAP 1

Young, Neil 1945- **CLC 17**
See also CA 110

Young Bear, Ray A. 1950- **CLC 94;DAM
MULT**
See also CA 146; DLB 175; NNAL

Yourcenar, Marguerite 1903-1987**CLC 19, 38,
50, 87; DAM NOV**
See also CA 69-72; CANR 23, 60; DLB 72;
DLBY 88; MTCW 1, 2

Yurick, Sol 1925- **CLC 6**
See also CA 13-16R; CANR 25

Zabolotsky, Nikolai Alekseevich 1903-1958
TCLC 52
See also CA 116; 164

Zagajewski, Adam **PC 27**

Zamiatin, Yevgenii
See Zamyatin, Evgeny Ivanovich

Zamora, Bernice (B. Ortiz) 1938- **CLC 89;
DAM MULT; HLC 2**
See also CA 151; CANR 80; DLB 82; HW 1, 2

Zamyatin, Evgeny Ivanovich 1884-1937
TCLC 8, 37
See also CA 105; 166

Zangwill, Israel 1864-1926 **TCLC 16**
See also CA 109; 167; DLB 10, 135, 197

Zappa, Francis Vincent, Jr. 1940-1993
See Zappa, Frank
See also CA 108; 143; CANR 57

Zappa, Frank **CLC 17**
See also Zappa, Francis Vincent, Jr.

Zaturenska, Marya 1902-1982 **CLC 6,11**
See also CA 13-16R; 105; CANR 22

Zeami 1363-1443 **DC 7**

Zelazny, Roger(Joseph) 1937-1995 **CLC 21**
See also AAYA 7; CA 21-24R; 148; CANR 26,
60; DLB 8; MTCW 1, 2; SATA57; SATA-
Brief 39

Zhdanov, Andrei Alexandrovich 1896-1948
TCLC 18
See also CA 117; 167

Zhukovsky, Vasily(Andreevich) 1783-1852
     NCLC 35
     See also DLB 205
Ziegenhagen, Eric   CLC 55
Zimmer, Jill Schary
     See Robinson, Jill
Zimmerman, Robert
     See Dylan, Bob
Zindel, Paul 1936-CLC 6, 26; DA; DAB; DAC;
     DAM DRAM, MST, NOV; DC 5
     See also AAYA 2; CA 73-76; CANR 31, 65;
          CDALBS; CLR 3, 45; DLB 7, 52; JRDA;
          MAICYA; MTCW 1, 2; SATA 16, 58, 102
Zinov'Ev, A. A.
     See Zinoviev, Alexander (Aleksandrovich)
Zinoviev, Alexander(Aleksandrovich) 1922-
     CLC 19
     See also CA 116; 133; CAAS 10
Zoilus
     See Lovecraft, H(oward) P(hillips)
Zola, Emile (Edouard Charles Antoine) 1840-
     1902TCLC 1, 6, 21, 41; DA; DAB; DAC;
     DAM MST, NOV; WLC
     See also CA 104; 138; DLB 123
Zoline, Pamela 1941-   CLC 62
     See also CA 161
Zorrilla y Moral, Jose 1817-1893   NCLC 6
Zoshchenko, Mikhail (Mikhailovich) 1895-1958
     TCLC 15; SSC 15
     See also CA 115; 160
Zuckmayer, Carl 1896-1977   CLC 18
     See also CA 69-72; DLB 56, 124
Zuk, Georges
     See Skelton, Robin
Zukofsky, Louis 1904-1978CLC 1, 2, 4, 7, 11,
     18; DAM POET; PC 11
     See also CA 9-12R; 77-80; CANR 39; DLB 5,
          165; MTCW 1
Zweig, Paul 1935-1984   CLC 34, 42
     See also CA 85-88; 113
Zweig, Stefan 1881-1942   TCLC 17
     See also CA 112; 170; DLB 81, 118
Zwingli, Huldreich 1484-1531   LC 37
     See also DLB 179

Poetry Criticism
Cumulative Nationality Index

481

Title Index

Title Index

Title Index

Title Index

Title Index

"Toward the Empty Earth" (Mandelstam)
  See "K pustoi zemle nevol'no pripadaia"
Toward the Gulf (Masters) 1:330, 332, 335, 342-44
"Toward the Piraeus" (H. D.) 5:268, 304
"Toward the Solstice" (Rich) 5:374
Towards a New Poetry (Wakoski) 15:359
"Towards a New Scotland" (MacDiarmid) 9:176
"Towards the Slave Quisqueya" (Guillen)
  See "Towards the Slave Quisqueya"
"The Tower" (Yeats) 20:310, 318, 320, 329, 334, 342
The Tower (Yeats) 20:307, 311, 333, 335
"The Tower beyond Tragedy" (Jeffers) 17:106,
  108, 110, 112, 135, 144-46
The Tower of Babel (Merton) 10:344, 349
"The Tower of Pisa" (Song) 21:344
"The Tower of Siloam" (Graves) 6:133
"The Town" (Pushkin)
  See "Gorodok"
"Town and Country" (Brooke) 24:56
The Town down the River (Robinson) 1:462-63,
  467, 474, 478, 490
"The Town Dump" (Nemerov) 24:257, 261, 291-92
"A Town Eclogue" (Swift) 9:278
Town Eclogues (Montagu)
  See *Court Poems*
"Towns in Colour" (Lowell) 13:79
"Tract" (Williams) 7:348, 362, 378
Tractatus (Marie de France) 22:
"Tractor" (Hughes) 7:166
"The Trade of an Irish Poet" (Heaney) 18:201
"Tradimento" (Pavese) 13:202, 226
"Traditions" (Heaney) 18:252
"Tragedy of Teeth" (Kipling) 3:194
"The Tragedy of the Leaves" (Bukowski) 18:6, 21
"Tragic Destiny" (Aleixandre) 15:10
"Traigo conmigo un cuidado" (Juana Ines de la
  Cruz) 24:188
"Train Time" (Bogan) 12:107
"Training" (Owen) 19:336
"Trainor the Druggist" (Masters) 1:347
"Trakat poetycki" (Milosz) 8:198-99, 204
"Tramontana" (Montale) 13:105, 126
"Tramontana at Lerici" (Tomlinson) 17:342
"The Tramp Transfigured" (Noyes) 27:121, 134
"Las Trampas USA" (Tomlinson) 17:353
"A Trampwoman's Tragedy" (Hardy) 8:99
"Trams" (Sitwell) 3:301
"Transaction" (Ammons) 16:22
"Transcedental Etude" (Rich) 5:381
The Transformation/Transformations (Ovid)
  See *Metamorphoses*
"Transformations" (Hardy) 8:113
"Transformations" (Wright) 14:339
Transformations (Sexton) 2:349, 354-55, 362, 364-
  65, 368
"The Transformed One" (Olds) 22:326
"Transgressing the Real" (Duncan) 2:104
"Transients and Residents" (Gunn) 26:220
"Transitional" (Williams) 7:392
Transitional Poem (Day Lewis) 11:123-25, 128-31,
  133-35, 137, 143-45, 148, 151
"Translating the Birds" (Tomlinson) 17:348, 350
*A Translation of the Psalms of David, Attempted in
  the Spirit of Christianity, and Adapted to the
  Divine Service* (Smart) 13:330-32, 341-42, 362
"Translations" (Rich) 5:397
Translations, 1915-1920 (H. D.) 5:304
The Translations of Ezra Pound (Pound) 4:331
"Translations of the Psalms" (Wyatt) 27:359
"Transparent Garments" (Hass) 16:199, 210
"Transplanting" (Roethke) 15:295
"The Transport of Slaves from Maryland to Mis-
  sissippi" (Dove) 6:108

Transport to Summer (Stevens) 6:301-03
"The Trap" (Wright) 14:356
"Trapped Dingo" (Wright) 14:345
"Le Trappist" (Vigny) 26:401-402, 404
"The Trappist Abbey: Matins" (Merton) 10:332
"The Trappist Cemetery, Gethsemani" (Merton)
  10:332-33, 342
"Trappists, Working" (Merton) 10:332-33
Trasumanar e organizzar (Pasolini) 17:273, 286
"Traum und Umnachtung" (Trakl) 20:239, 268
"Träumerei am Abend" (Trakl) 20:239
"Travel" (Brooke) 24:66
"The Traveler" (Apollinaire)
  See "Le voyageur"
"A Traveler at Night Writes His Thoughts" (Tu Fu)
  9:324
The Traveler Does Not Return (Nishiwaki)
  See *Tabibito Kaerazu*
"Traveling on an Amtrack Train Could Humanize
  You" (Sanchez) 9:234
"Traveling through Fog" (Hayden) 6:194
"The Traveller and the Angel" (Wright) 14:339,
  346
"Traveller's Curse after Misdirection" (Graves)
  6:137
"Traveller's Palm" (Page) 12:181
"Travelogue for Exiles" (Shapiro) 25:269, 279, 290
"Travels in the South" (Ortiz) 17:227, 231
"Tre donne intorno al cor mi son venute" (Dante)
  21:87
"The Treasure" (Brooke) 24:87-9
"The Treasure" (Jeffers) 17:117
"Treatise on Poetry" (Milosz)
  See "Trakat poetycki"
"Trébol" (Dario) 15:89
"The Tree" (Aleixandre) 15:22
"The Tree" (Finch) 21:149
"Tree" (Rukeyser) 12:224
"Tree at My Window" (Frost) 1:197, 205
"Tree Burial" (Bryant) 20:14, 17
"Tree Disease" (Hughes) 7:120
"Tree Planting" (Tagore)
  See "Vriksha-ropan"
"A Tree Telling of Orpheus" (Levertov) 11:177
The Tree Witch (Viereck) 27:275-76, 278-80, 282
"The Trees" (Carruth) 10:71
"Trees" (Hughes) 7:120
"Trees" (Nemerov) 24:266-67
"Trees" (Tsvetaeva)
  See "Derev'ya"
"Trees" (Williams) 7:351
"treez" (Bissett) 14:24, 33
"La Treizieme" (Nerval) 13:196; 67:360
"A Trellis for R." (Swenson) 14:267, 280
The Trembling of the Veil (Yeats) 20:330
"Tremor" (Zagajewski) 27:395
Tremor (Zagajewski) 27:380-81, 383-84, 389, 395,
  397, 399
"Trench Poems" (Owen) 19:350
"Trespass Into Spirit" (Baraka) 4:24
The Trespasser (Stryk) 27:191, 194, 197-98, 215-16,
  218
"Tri palmy" (Lermontov) 18:290-91
"A Triad" (Rossetti) 7:272-3, 275, 291
"The Trial" (Sassoon) 12:260
"Trial of a Poet" (Shapiro) 25:277-79
Trial of a Poet (Shapiro) 25:273-74, 285, 290, 296,
  319, 322, 324
"The Trial of Dead Cleopatra" (Lindsay) 23:280,
  286
"Trial-Pieces" (Heaney) 18:246
"Tribal Scenes" (Song) 21:345
"Tribe" (Song) 21:336, 343

Tribunals (Duncan) 2:106, 116, 127
"Tribute" (Brutus) 24:111
"The Tribute" (H. D.) 5:298, 304
Tribute to the Angels (H. D.) 5:272, 274-75, 283-84,
  286-87, 293-97, 308-09, 313, 315
"Trickle Drops" (Whitman) 3:406
"Tricks with Mirrors" (Atwood) 8:21-6
"Trickster 1977" (Rose) 13:232
"Trillium" (Gluck) 16:171
Trilogie der Leidenschaft (Goethe) 5:250
Trilogy (H. D.) 5:281, 283-86, 292-93, 2960-98, 304-
  07, 310-15
Trilogy (Wakoski) 15:365
"Trinchera" (Borges) 22:92
"Trinity Churchyard" (Rukeyser) 12:225
"Trinity Peace" (Sandburg) 2:304
"Trio for Two Cats and a Trombone" (Sitwell) 3:303,
  306
"Triolet" (Brooke) 24:54
Trionfi (Petrarch) 8:224-26, 238, 240, 243, 246, 252,
  254, 257, 260, 273-78
"The Triple Fool" (Donne) 1:125
"The Triple Fool" (Millay) 6:243
"Triple Time" (Larkin) 21:227, 236, 242
"Triptych" (Heaney) 18:246
"El triste" (Borges) 22:80
"Triste, triste" (Laforgue) 14:86, 88-9
"Tristesse" (Lamartine) 16:293
"Tristesse d'Olympio" (Hugo) 17:64, 76-77, 82, 97
"Tristesse d'un étoile" (Apollinaire) 7:3
"Les tristesses de la lune" (Baudelaire) 1:44-5
"Tristia" (Mandelstam) 14:106
Tristia (Mandelstam)
  See *Vtoraya kniga*
Tristia (Ovid) 2:233, 240-42, 244-45, 252-53, 255-59
Tristibus (Ovid)
  See *Tristia*
Tristram (Robinson) 1:470-72, 474-75, 481, 489
"Tristram and Iseult" (Arnold) 5:9, 12, 33-4, 42, 49,
  64
Tristram of Lyonesse (Swinburne) 24:307, 309, 310,
  313-14, 316, 319, 321-23, 348-50, 352, 355-57
"Tritiya" (Tagore) 8:415
The Triumph of Achilles (Gluck) 16:149, 151-52,
  155-57, 159, 163
"Triumph of Charis" (Jonson)
  See *A Celebration of Charis in Ten Lyric Pieces*
The Triumph of Life (Shelley) 14:174, 188, 193, 211
"The Triumph of Time" (Swinburne) 24:308, 322,
  325, 337-38, 342-43
Triumphal March (Eliot) 5:168, 185
Triumphs (Petrarch)
  See *Trionfi*
"The Triumphs of Bacchus" (Pushkin) 10:407
"Trivial Breath" (Wylie) 23:310
Trivial Breath (Wylie) 23:302, 307-309, 324-25
"Trofeo" (Borges) 22:93
Troilus (Chaucer)
  See *Troilus and Criseyde*
Troilus and Criseyde (Chaucer) 19:6-7, 11, 13, 15,
  23, 36-9, 42-3, 60-1, 63, 73-5
Troilus and Cryseide (Chaucer)
  See *Troilus and Criseyde*
"Trois Ans après" (Hugo) 17:83
Les trois livres du recueil des nouvelles poesies
  (Ronsard) 11:248
Troisime livre des odes (Ronsard) 11:283
"Trompeten" (Trakl) 20:250, 254-55
"Troop Train" (Shapiro) 25:263, 268, 288, 295, 297,
  324
"Tropical Birdland" (Alegria) 26:
"The Tropics in New York" (McKay) 2:228
"Trostnik" (Lermontov) 18:304

Title Index

MONTVILLE TWP. PUBLIC LIBRARY
90 Horseneck Road
Montville, N.J. 07045